A TREATISE

OF THE

WRIT OF HABEAS CORPUS

INCLUDING

JURISDICTION, FALSE IMPRISONMENT, WRIT
OF ERROR, EXTRADITION, MANDAMUS,
CERTIORARI, JUDGMENTS, ETC.

WITH

PRACTICE AND FORMS.

By WILLIAM S. CHURCH,
Of the California Bar.

THE LAWBOOK EXCHANGE, LTD.
Clark, New Jersey

ISBN 978-1-58477-277-4 (hardcover)
ISBN 978-1-61619-403-1 (paperback)

Lawbook Exchange edition 2003, 2013

The quality of this reprint is equivalent to the quality of the original work.

THE LAWBOOK EXCHANGE, LTD.
33 Terminal Avenue
Clark, New Jersey 07066-1321

*Please see our website for a selection of our other publications
and fine facsimile reprints of classic works of legal history:*
www.lawbookexchange.com

Library of Congress Cataloging-in-Publication Data

Church, William S. (William Smithers)
    A treatise on the writ of Habeas Corpus, including jurisdiction, false
imprisonment, writ of error, extradition, mandamus, certiorari, judgments, etc. :
with practice and forms / by William S. Church.
    p. cm.
    Originally published: San Francisco : Brancroft-Whitney Co., 1886.
    Includes bibliographical references and index.
    ISBN 1-58477-277-8 (cloth: acid-free paper)
    1. Habeas corpus—United States. I. Title.
KF9011 .C47 2002
345.73'056—dc21   2002073033

Printed in the United States of America on acid-free paper

A TREATISE

OF THE

WRIT OF HABEAS CORPUS

INCLUDING

JURISDICTION, FALSE IMPRISONMENT, WRIT
OF ERROR, EXTRADITION, MANDAMUS,
CERTIORARI, JUDGMENTS, ETC.

WITH

PRACTICE AND FORMS.

By WILLIAM S. CHURCH,
Of the California Bar.

SAN FRANCISCO:
BANCROFT-WHITNEY CO.
LAW PUBLISHERS AND LAW BOOKSELLERS.
1886.

Entered according to Act of Congress, in the year 1884,
By A. L. BANCROFT & COMPANY,
In the Office of the Librarian of Congress, at Washington.

THIS WORK

IS DEDICATED TO MY FRIEND,

COLONEL CREED HAYMOND,

Whose experience and success in the practice of criminal law in California has crowned him a leading member of the profession which he adorns. And this tribute of appreciation is made not only in acknowledgment of his rich mental endowments, his ability as a lawyer, and his eloquence as an advocate; but of his uniform courtesy and kindness to members of the legal fraternity.

PREFACE.

An apology for the appearance of a new work on any branch of the law is always a graceful performance when such a work is not needed by lawyers; but we feel that we are now doing nothing wrong or unjustifiable in offering to the bench and bar a new treatise upon the writ of habeas corpus. The number of decisions upon this branch of the law is surprising, and a classified collection of them, it seems to us, will be of at least some assistance to the members of a busy profession. There is now but one work, to our knowledge, upon the subject, and the first edition of that appeared in 1858, followed by a second in 1876. But even since the appearance of the last edition of Judge Hurd's treatise, this branch of the law has had many valuable additions, and we have attempted in the following pages to give a full and correct exposition of the entire law relating to proceedings on the writ of habeas corpus.

With the investigation required in our labors we have been pleased, for this is eminently the most celebrated writ known to the law, and is justly esteemed the great bulwark of personal liberty. We have indulged, however, in a very little laudation of this birthright of civil liberty handed down to us from the fathers of the law; but have preferred simply to present the law as found in judicial decision and legislation, and to leave the reader to his own reflections concerning the enhanced state of personal liberty now compared with what it was away back "in the night of English history." We have had no need to lavish praises upon this writ, "the glory of the English law." Rather let the united voice of a multitude of decisions show the fountain whence flows the law that makes man free when unjustly deprived of his personal liberty. It will be apparent to the reader that this law, which has been floating upon the tide of centuries, may need some repairs; but we have refrained from suggesting any needed legislation, as this was not included in the purpose of our writing, and might have caused us to transcend the limits of our work without improving it.

The mass of statutory law concerning the writ of habeas corpus would fill volumes, so we have been content to use that only which was necessary to our purpose in presenting the adjudications of the courts. It is intended that this work will be used as an auxiliary to the statutes of each respective state, as well as to those of the United States. Its object is to give the law as established by well-settled judicial decision, but not to give all legislation concerning the topics involved. A short review of the cases where principles of law have been established by the courts in habeas corpus proceedings, and where these principles have been discussed or ventilated, will serve to better elucidate the ground upon which they rest, and to show the circumstances in which they have been applied. But a mere reference to cases is not always satisfactory to either bench or bar, so we have been at some labor in quite fully presenting the substance of most of the adjudications referred to in the following pages, the better to illustrate the general meaning, signification, and extent of each doctrine; in other words, to give the reason of the law: for Coke has said, "He that knoweth not the reason of the law knoweth not the law." Some of these illustrations, however, are brief, but it is hoped they will not mislead the profession.

The chapter on extradition embodies the law as the author has found it, and no room has been therein denied to the decisions of the state courts. But the reader will observe that there is a serious conflict of decisions between the state and federal courts in extradition matters. And while we think the federal courts are right under the present legislation of congress in their views of extradition law, and while we recognize the perfect and complete panoply of federal jurisdiction in such cases, we are not one of those who rejoice that "the state courts are now lying at the feet of the federal judiciary;" for a conflict of jurisdiction between federal and state courts is a thing to be much deprecated in all federative governments.

Finally, the arrangement of this volume will show for itself, in the table of contents, head-lines, and index. We have sought to aid research by a clear arrangement, and have endeavored to make the citations absolutely correct. The result of our work we now give to the profession for their judgment; and if it tends to aid the active practitioner at the bar, or his honor on the bench, in dispensing good law from the arks of justice, the author's labor will not have been in vain.

SACRAMENTO, CAL., May 23, 1884.

TABLE OF CONTENTS.

CHAPTER I.
HISTORY OF THE WRIT.

PART I.—TRACES OF IT IN THE ROMAN LAW.

§ 1. The Roman Edict.

PART II.—ITS USE IN THE EARLIER COMMON LAW.

§ 2. Magna Charta.
§ 3 a. Ancient Writs.
§ 3 b. The Knights' Habeas Corpus Case.
§ 4. Idem—Arguments for the Prisoners.
§ 5. Idem—Arguments for the Crown.
§ 6. Idem—The Decision.
§ 7. Petition of Right.
§ 8. Contempt by Members of the House of Commons.
§ 9. Idem—Abolition of Star-Chamber and Other Arbitrary Courts.
§ 10. Cases of Streater, and Fox, the Quaker.
§ 11. The Celebrated Bushell and Shaftesbury Cases.
§ 12. Long Duration of Imprisonment.
§ 13. The Habeas Corpus Bill.
§ 14. Condition of the Prisoners.
§ 15. Removal of Prisoners.
§ 16. The Celebrated Jenkes Case.
§ 17. Issuance of the Writ in Vacation.
§ 18. Imperfections of the Writ.

PART III.—THE HABEAS CORPUS ACT, 31 CAR. II.

§ 19. Passage of the Famous Habeas Corpus Act.
§ 20. Why the Act is Famous.
§ 21. Auspicious Times of the Bill's Passage.
§ 22. Why the King Assented to the Act.
§ 23. Its Relation to Other Acts.
§ 24. To What the Act may be Assigned.

PART IV.—A BRIEF REVIEW OF THIS STATUTE

§ 25 a. It Introduced No New Principle.
§ 25 b. Enumeration of Abuses.
§ 26. Title—Copy of Warrant—Statement of Cause of Commitment—Expenses.

§ 27. Denied Copy—Bail.
§ 28. Exceptions.
§ 29. Treason and Felony.
§ 30. Courts—Places—Removals—Recommitments.
§ 31. Beyond the Seas.
§ 32. Operation of the Act—Bail.
§ 33. Bail, Continued—Amount thereof, etc.
§ 34. Detention without Warrant—Return, and Statute of George III.
§ 35. The Opinion of James II.
§ 36. Requirements to take Advantage of the Writ.
§ 37. Eulogies.

PART V.—IN THE COLONIES.

§ 38. Birthright to English Laws.
§ 39. The Opinion of Chalmers.
§ 40. Use of the Writ in Massachusetts.
§ 41. Its History in South Carolina.
§ 42. In the Province of Maryland.
§ 43. In New Jersey and Pennsylvania.
§ 44. Cases of the Presbyterian Ministers, New York.
§ 45. Habeas Corpus Act Extended to Virginia.
§ 46. Denial of Writ to Province of Quebec.

PART VI.—ITS GENERAL HISTORY IN THE UNITED STATES.

§ 47. Constitutional Provisions.
§ 48. Statutory Enactments.
§ 49. Conflict between State and Federal Governments.

PART VII.—SUSPENSION OF THE WRIT.

§ 50. What is Suspended.
§ 51. Power to Suspend.
§ 52. Act of Congress Authorizing its Suspension.
§ 53. Suspension of It under This Act.
§ 54. Validity of the Act.
§ 55. Expiration of Authority Conferred by Act.
§ 56. Writ Issued by State Court.
§ 57. In the Confederate States.

CHAPTER II.

HABEAS CORPUS ACT, 31 CAR. II., A. D. 1679.

CHAPTER III.

HABEAS CORPUS ACT OF THE UNITED STATES.

(R. S., 2D ED., SECS. 751-766.)

CHAPTER IV.

JURISDICTION OF THE WRIT IN ENGLAND.

§ 60. Common-law Jurisdiction.
§ 61. Statutory Jurisdiction.

CHAPTER V.

JURISDICTION OF THE FEDERAL COURTS.

PART I.—JURISDICTION OF THE UNITED STATES SUPREME COURT.

§ 62. Its Original Jurisdiction.
§ 63. Its Appellate Jurisdiction.
§ 64. When an Appeal may be Taken to the Supreme Court.

PART II.—JURISDICTION OF THE DISTRICT AND CIRCUIT COURTS.

§ 65. The District Courts.
§ 66. The Circuit Courts.

PART III.—JURISDICTION IN TERRITORIAL COURTS.

§ 67. Legislation.
§ 68. Writ of Error or Appeal.

PART IV.—POWERS OF THE FEDERAL COURTS GENERALLY.

§ 69. Limitations and Benefits of the Writ.
§ 70. Habeas Corpus a Civil Proceeding.
§ 71. Examination of the Facts.
§ 72. Substance of Inquiry on Judgments.
§ 73. Territorial Extension of Jurisdiction.
§ 74. The Proceedings are Governed by the Common Law.
§ 75. Jurisdiction must be Shown.
§ 76. *Habeas Corpus cum Causa.*

CHAPTER VI.

JURISDICTION OF THE STATE COURTS.

CHAPTER VII.

CONFLICT OF JURISDICTION BETWEEN STATE AND FEDERAL COURTS.

PART I.—CAUSES OF VARIOUS PROVISIONS OF SECTION 753, UNITED STATES REVISED STATUTES.

§ 78. Division into Classes.
§ 79. Cause of Class Second.
§ 80. Cause of Class Third.
§ 81. Cause of Fourth Class.

PART II.—CONCURRENT JURISDICTION.

§ 82. Views of State and Inferior Federal Courts.

PART III.—EFFECT OF JUSTICE TANEY'S DECISION.

§ 83. History of Booth's Case.
§ 84. Decision of the United States Supreme Court.
§ 85. "Authority of the United States."
§ 86. Tarble's Case.

CHAPTER VIII.

APPLICATION FOR THE WRIT.

§ 87. Circumstances under Which an Application can be Made.
§ 88. When the Application will be Entertained.
§ 89. Requisites of the Petition.
§ 90. Further Matters concerning the Petition.
§ 91. Who may Make an Application.
§ 92. Probable Cause must be Shown.
§ 93. When the Application must be Granted.
§ 94. When the Application ought to be Denied.
§ 95. Verification of the Petition.
§ 96. Penalty for Refusing the Writ.
§ 97. *Mandamus* to Compel the Writ to Issue.
§ 98. Injunction to Restrain Issuance of Writ.

CHAPTER IX.

THE WRIT.

§ 99. The Writ must be Grounded upon Affidavits.
§ 100. How Granted at Common Law.
§ 101. How Granted under Statute.
§ 102. Signature to the Writ, and Seal.
§ 103. How the Writ is Sometimes Marked.
§ 104. Noting the Allowance of the Writ.
§ 105. Notice of Allowance.
§ 106. How and to Whom Directed.
§ 107. Where It Runs at Common Law and under the English Statutes.
§ 108. On the Rule of Locality in the United States.
§ 109. Service of the Writ.
§ 110. Amendment of the Writ.
§ 111. Objections to the Writ.
§ 112. When the Prisoner may be Brought into Court.

CHAPTER X.

COSTS AND SECURITY AGAINST ESCAPE.

PART I.—ACCORDING TO THE COURSE OF THE COMMON LAW.

§ 113. Generally, and under Habeas Corpus Act.
§ 114. In Bankruptcy Proceedings.
§ 115. On *Habeas Corpus ad Testificandum*.
§ 116. In Particular Instances.

PART II.—IN THE FEDERAL COURTS.

§ 117. Legislation, Decisions, and Rules.

PART III.—IN THE STATE COURTS.

§ 118. Summary of Statutes.
§ 119. Judicial Constructions.

TABLE OF CONTENTS. xiii

CHAPTER XI.

THE RETURN.

PART I.—VARIOUS MATTERS OF LAW CLOSELY CONNECTED WITH THE RETURN.

- § 120. Definition and Observations.
- § 121. Form of the Return.
- § 122. Verification of the Return.
- § 123. When It will be Received.
- § 124. May be Enforced by Attachment.
- § 125. The Return should be Liberally Construed.
- § 126. Certainty Required in the Return.
- § 127. Warrant Need not Always be Returned.
- § 128. The Return may be Amended.
- § 129. Whether Return may be Fortified by Affidavit.
- § 130. When Petitioner can not be Held by Virtue of the Warrant.
- § 131. On What Return the Writ will be Dismissed.
- § 132. When Court will Immediately Discharge the Prisoner.
- § 133. Enlarging Time for Return of Writ.
- § 134. Full Answer to Return.
- § 135. Jailer may Substitute Return Prepared by Counsel for his Own.
- § 136. Objections to the Return.
- § 137. Failure, or to Make an Evasive or Insufficient Return, is a Contempt of Court.
- § 138. True Return could not be Enforced at Common Law.
- § 139. New Habeas Corpus not Required.
- § 140. Recommitment.
- § 141. Order of the Argument.
- § 142. Rule upon Process.
- § 143. Return of Substituted Warrant.
- § 144. Return must Show that Evidence was Given in Prisoner's Presence.
- § 145. Relying upon a Conviction where Commitment is Bad.
- § 146. Return must Remain in Court.
- § 147. Return Need not Specifically Set out Documents Referred to.
- § 148. When Warrant must Contain Certain Words.
- § 149. Questioning Jurisdiction on Defective Warrant.
- § 150. Examination into Cause on Rule *Nisi*.
- § 151. Discussing Validity of Warrant upon Rule to Show Cause.
- § 152. When Motion to Quash Writ, after Return Filed, will be Entertained.
- § 153. Making a Bad Return on Good Judgment.
- § 154. Judicial Notice.
- § 155. Reply to Return Denying Truth of the Matters Contained in Affidavit on Which *Capias* Issued.
- § 156. Return of Execution against the Person.
- § 157. When Demand should be Made for Child.
- § 158. Time when Errors should be Corrected.
- § 159. State Court can not Determine What is a Crime against the United States.
- § 160. What is Meant by the Term "Process."
- § 161. A Few Instances of a Bad Return.
- § 162. A Few Instances of a Good Return.

PART II.—PRODUCTION OF THE BODY, AND STATEMENTS OF THE CAUSE OF ARREST AND DETENTION.

§ 163. Sufficient Reasons for not Producing the Body.
§ 164. Statement of the Cause of Arrest.
§ 165. Statement of the Cause of Detention.

PART III.—ANSWERING THE RETURN.

§ 166. Return not Controvertible at Common Law.
§ 167. But Return may be Confessed and Avoided.
§ 168. Doctrine in the United States.

CHAPTER XII.

THE ISSUES, AND HOW TRIED—CUSTODY OF THE PRISONER.

PART I.—ISSUES OF LAW AND FACT.

§ 169. Issue of Law.
§ 170. Issues of Both Law and Fact.

PART II.—THE MODE OF TRIAL.

§ 171. At Common Law.
§ 172. Jury Trial.
§ 173. In the United States.
§ 174. Tom Tong, and the Indiana Cases—Change of Venue.

PART III.—CUSTODY OF PRISONER DURING THE TRIAL.

§ 175. At Common Law.
§ 176. In the United States.

CHAPTER XIII.

THE EVIDENCE.

PART I.—EVIDENCE IN GENERAL.

§ 177. Preliminary Observations.
§ 178. Oral Testimony, as Well as Written, will be Received.
§ 179. Sufficient Evidence to Authorize Commitment.
§ 180. Weighing Evidence Taken before Committing Magistrate.
§ 181. Weighing Evidence, Continued.
§ 182. Hearing Evidence *de Novo*.
§ 183. Evidence in Petition.
§ 184. Commitment without Testimony.
§ 185. Statement of Evidence in Judgment.
§ 186. Several Indictments Found on the Same Evidence.
§ 187. Case Once Heard upon Same Evidence.
§ 188. Second Application, Continued—Newly Discovered Evidence.
§ 189. Newly Discovered Testimony, Continued—Evidence upon Subsequently Occurring Events.
§ 190. Additional Proof.
§ 191. Postponement for Further Testimony.
§ 192. Proper Evidence.
§ 193. Competent Testimony.

TABLE OF CONTENTS. xv

§ 194. Hearing Evidence.
§ 195. Conversations.
§ 196. Correcting Errors in Evidence.
§ 197. Contradicting Return.
§ 198. Record Evidence.
§ 199 a. Evidence *Aliunde*.
§ 199 b. Defendant has a Right to be Confronted by Witnesses.
§ 200. Impeaching Witnesses.
§ 201. Subpœna for Witness.
§ 202. Fine against Defaulting Witness.
§ 203. Officers may be Examined as Witnesses.
§ 204. Examination of Witnesses, Continued.
§ 205. Evidence of Service.
§ 206. Commenting on Testimony.

PART II.—EVIDENCE BY AFFIDAVIT.

§ 207. Value of Such Evidence.
§ 208. Defects—Want of Notice, etc.
§ 209. Use of Affidavits in English Practice.
§ 210. In Applications for Habeas Corpus.
§ 211. Jurisdiction.
§ 212. Contradicting Return by Affidavit.
§ 213. Examination of Indictment.
§ 214. Enlarging Time.
§ 215. Fortifying Return.
§ 216. Denying Statement in Warrant.
§ 217. Cases of Bollman and Swartwout and Burr.
§ 218. Arrest on State Process.
§ 219. Affidavit should State Facts.
§ 220. Effect of No Objection to Irregular Evidence.

CHAPTER XIV.

WHAT MAY BE INQUIRED INTO ON THE RETURN.

PART I.—ORDINARY EXTENT OF INQUIRY IN THE FEDERAL COURTS.

§ 221. Recollections of Chapter on "The Return."
§ 222. General Review of the Subject.
§ 223. Distinction between Jurisdiction and its Exercise Pointed out.
§ 224. Appearance of Jurisdiction upon Face of Proceedings.
§ 225. Distinction between Void and Voidable Jurisdictional Proceedings.
§ 226. A Leading Principle.
§ 227. General Rules and their Application.
§ 228. Conflict of Jurisdiction.
§ 229. Inquiry where there is No Formal or Technical Commitment.
§ 230. Inquiry into and behind Commitment.
§ 231. Inquiry into and behind Commitment made by a United States Commissioner.
§ 232. When Order for Discharge may be Entered.

TABLE OF CONTENTS.

PART II.—EXTENT OF INQUIRY IN THE STATE COURTS BEFORE INDICTMENT.

§ 233. General Inquiries.
§ 234. Inquiry Extending Only to Jurisdiction into and behind Warrant of Committing Magistrate.
§ 235. Examination of Depositions, Evidence, and the Entire Proceedings before the Committing Magistrate.
§ 236. Effect of Statutes on These Two Rules.
§ 237. Guilt or Innocence of the Prisoner.
§ 238. Commitment by Court of General Jurisdiction.
§ 239. Cause for Detention after Failure to Indict.
§ 240. Convictions by Inferior Courts.
§ 241. Vacating Orders of Court.
§ 242. Habeas Corpus Pending Examination on Criminal Charge.
§ 243. Waiving Examination.

PART III.—INQUIRIES AFTER INDICTMENT AND BEFORE JUDGMENT OF CONVICTION.

§ 244. Reasons why the Courts Decline to Make Inquiry into a Commitment after Indictment Found.
§ 245. Inquiry may Go to whether Indictment Charges Any Offense.
§ 246. Defective Indictment.
§ 247. "Guilty or not Guilty."
§ 248. Continuing Indictment.
§ 249. Two Bills of Indictment—Death Penalty on One, No Trial on the Other.
§ 250. Existence of Indictment—Its Legality—Bench Warrant.
§ 251. Judgment on Sufficiency of the Indictment.
§ 252. Process without Warrant of Law.
§ 253. Effect of Order Arresting Judgment.
§ 254. New Trial—Delay in Bringing to Trial.
§ 255. Discharge of Jury in Absence of Defendant.

CHAPTER XV.

HABEAS CORPUS AS A QUO WARRANTO.

§ 256. Title to Office.
§ 257. Sentences by Officers *de Facto*.
§ 258. Mere Usurpers, etc.

CHAPTER XVI.

USE OF CERTIORARI.

PART I.—AS ANCILLARY TO THE HABEAS CORPUS.

§ 259. In the English Law.
§ 260. Doctrine in the Federal Courts.
§ 261. In the State Courts.

PART II.—WITH HABEAS CORPUS AS A WRIT OF ERROR.

§ 262. At Common Law.
§ 263. In the Federal Courts.
§ 264. In the State Courts.

CHAPTER XVII.
COMITY OF COURTS.

CHAPTER XVIII.
PRESUMPTIONS.

§ 266. Distinction between Superior and Inferior Courts.
§ 267. Presumptions of Jurisdiction Relating to Superior Courts.
§ 268. Presumptions of Jurisdiction Relating to Inferior Courts.

CHAPTER XIX.
FALSE IMPRISONMENT.

§ 269. What is an Imprisonment.
§ 270. Acts of Indemnity during the Suspension of the Habeas Corpus Act.
§ 271. Arrest, What Constitutes.
§ 272. Restraint and Detention.
§ 273. Matters concerning Bail.

CHAPTER XX.
WARRANTS.
PART I.—WARRANTS OF ARREST.

§ 274. General Warrants.
§ 275. The Direction.
§ 276. Name of the Offender.
§ 277. Statement of Offense in Magistrate's Warrant.
§ 278. Statement of Offense in Warrant of Superior Judge.
§ 279. Oath, Jurat, and Seal.

PART II.—WARRANTS TO ANSWER.

§ 280. Commitments for Treason.
§ 281. Cause and Certainty.
§ 282. Orders and Commitments by Superior Court.
§ 283. The Direction and Conclusion.
§ 284. Signature and Seal.
§ 285. What Face of Warrant should Show.

PART III.—REVIEW BY HABEAS CORPUS.

§ 286. The Warrant of Arrest.
§ 287. The Warrant of Commitment.

CHAPTER XXI.
POWER OF COURTS AT THE HEARING.
PART I.—MAY RECOMMIT IF WARRANT IS DEFECTIVE.

§ 288. Practice in the English Courts.
§ 289. Illustrations.
§ 290. Practice in our Courts.
§ 291. Illustrations.

PART II.—MAY DISCHARGE OR LET TO BAIL THOUGH WARRANT IS PERFECT.
§ 292. Practice at Common Law.
§ 293. Practice in the United States.

CHAPTER XXII.

ASSAILING JUDGMENTS OF SUMMARY CONVICTIONS BY HABEAS CORPUS.

§ 294. Definition and History.
§ 295. Constitutionality of These Statutes.
§ 296. How These Statutes are to be Construed.
§ 297. Errors, Irregularity, and Jurisdiction.
§ 298. Statement of Proceedings on Face of Commitment.
§ 299. Conviction without Authority of Law.
§ 300. Security to Keep the Peace.
§ 301. Commitment of Seaman.
§ 302. Commitment of Sheriff.
§ 303. Cumulative and Erroneous Sentences.
§ 304. Custody of Children.
§ 305. Commitment of Witness.

CHAPTER XXIII.

ASSAILING JUDGMENTS FOR CONTEMPT BY HABEAS CORPUS.

§ 306. Definitions.
§ 307. Power of Courts to Punish for Contempt.
§ 308. Punishment for Contempt.
§ 309. Punishment for Contempt, Continued.
§ 310. Attachment for Contempt.
§ 311. Attachment, Continued.
§ 312. Commitments by Notary Public.
§ 313. Modifying Judgments.
§ 314. Assailing Judgment of Court of Competent Jurisdiction.
§ 315. In the Supreme Court of the United States.
§ 316. Conflict of Federal and State Authority in the United States Circuit and in the State Courts.
§ 317. Jurisdiction—Two Questions Involved in a Commitment for Contempt.
§ 318. The General Rule.
§ 319. Answering Questions.
§ 320. Orders of Court to Pay over Money.
§ 321. Conditions Impossible of Performance.
§ 322. Neglect to Pay Tax.
§ 323. Disobedience of Orders, Judgments, and Decrees of Court.
§ 324. Disobedience of Orders, Judgments, and Decrees of Court, Continued.
§ 325. Notice and Service of Orders, etc.—Ability to Pay—Demand, etc.
§ 326. Suspending Attorney.
§ 327. Malpractice of Sheriff.
§ 328. Judgment for Contempt under Unconstitutional Law.
§ 329. Irony.
§ 330. Disobedience of Subpœna.

§ 331. Jurisdiction to Commit—*Mandamus.*
§ 332. Jurisdiction—No Offense.
§ 333. Jurisdiction—Refusal to Give Evidence.
§ 334. "Until Discharged by Due Course of Law"—Time Certain—English Courts.
§ 335. "Until Further Order of the Court," Continued—Time Certain in the United States.
§ 336. Commitments for Contempt in Parliamentary Bodies.
§ 337. Definite Time Fixed by Statute.
§ 338. Exemption from Jury Service.
§ 339. Publication during Trial.
§ 340. Statement of Facts Need not be Made unless Statute Requires It.
§ 341. Where the Warrant of Commitment Omits to State Facts, the Cause can not be Inquired into.
§ 342. Judgments of "Superior" and "Inferior" Courts.
§ 343. Jury Trial—Change of Venue.
§ 344. Error and Irregularities must be Cured by Motion.
§ 345. Pardon.
§ 346. Evidence.

CHAPTER XXIV.

ASSAILING JUDGMENTS OF COURTS OF SPECIAL OR LIMITED JURISDICTION IN CASES TRIABLE BY JURY.

Part I.—Criminal Cases.

§ 347. Explanatory Remarks.
§ 348. Error and Irregularities not Reviewable.
§ 349. Defective Complaint.
§ 350. Retrial of Issue of Fact.
§ 351. Sentences Unauthorized by Law.
§ 352. Unauthorized Sentences, Continued—Ordinances Violated.
§ 353. Erroneous Sentences.
§ 354. When Sentence for Misdemeanor Begins to Run.
§ 355. Commitment or *Mittimus.*
§ 356. Remarks on Jurisdiction.

Part II.—Civil Cases.

§ 357. Void Summons, Judgment, and Execution.
§ 358. Process and Judgments Running by Wrong Name—*Ca. Sa.*
§ 359. *Capias ad Satisfaciendum,* Continued.
§ 360. Staying, and Failure to Issue, Execution.
§ 361. Defective Execution.

CHAPTER XXV.

ASSAILING JUDGMENTS OF COURTS OF GENERAL JURISDICTION BY HABEAS CORPUS.

Part I.—In Criminal Cases.

§ 362. General Principles.
§ 363. Errors can not be Reviewed.
§ 364. Place of Imprisonment—Error.
§ 365. Irregularities can not be Reviewed.

§ 366. Reviewing Evidence and Retrying Issues of Fact.
§ 367. Pleadings—Insufficiency of the Indictment or Information.
§ 368. Jurisdiction of Person and Subject-matter.
§ 369. Sentence by Court or Judge *de Facto*.
§ 370. Unauthorized Convictions.
§ 371. Power to Render the Particular Judgment.
§ 372. Erroneous Sentences.
§ 373. Excessive Sentences—In English and Federal Courts.
§ 374. Excessive Sentences, Continued—In the State Courts.
§ 375. The *Mittimus*.
§ 376. Cumulative Sentences.
§ 377. Power of Courts to Modify their Own Judgments.
§ 378. Miscellaneous Matters.
§ 379. Conflict of Jurisdiction.
§ 380. Power of United States Supreme Court to Review the Judgments of the Inferior Courts of the United States.
§ 381. Sentences in Violation of the Constitution or of United States Laws, and Acts Done or Omitted in Pursuance thereof.
§ 382. Courts-martial.

PART II.—IN CIVIL CASES.

§ 383. Mere Errors and Irregularities will not be Reviewed.
§ 384. *Capias ad Satisfaciendum*.
§ 385. Other Matters.

CHAPTER XXVI.
RES ADJUDICATA.

§ 386. Writ of Error, etc.
§ 387. Cases Affecting Custody of Children.
§ 388. Statutory Provisions, Writs of Error, Appeals, etc.
§ 389. Second Applications.

CHAPTER XXVII.
THE RIGHT TO BAIL.

PART I.—POWER TO BAIL, BAILABLE OFFENSES, EVIDENCE, ETC.

§ 390. Doctrine of the Common Law.
§ 391. 31 Car. II. and Other English Statutes.
§ 392. The Power to Bail, and Bailable Offenses in the United States.
§ 393. Right to Bail, and for What Offenses.
§ 394. Legislative Powers.

PART II.—INQUIRY BEFORE INDICTMENT.

§ 395. Who may Bail.
§ 396. Application is Addressed to Sound Discretion of Court.
§ 397. Excessive Bail.
§ 398. To Reduce Bail.
§ 399. Examination and Reducing Offense to Bailable One.
§ 400. Examination of Evidence.

PART III.—INQUIRY AFTER INDICTMENT.

§ 401. Rules for Guidance of Court's Discretion.
§ 402. Meaning of "When Proof is Evident."

§ 403. Presumption Great.
§ 404. When Prisoner must Take Initiative.
§ 405. Evidence.
§ 406. Evidence, Continued.
§ 407. Special and Extraordinary Circumstances.
§ 408. Disagreement of Jury—New Trial, etc.
§ 409. Other Circumstances.
§ 410. Sickness of the Prisoner.
§ 411. Continuance—Term.
§ 412. Arrest on Bench-warrant.
§ 413. Excessive Bail.
§ 414. Insanity of Prisoner.
§ 415. Appeal from Judgment Refusing Bail.
§ 416. Appeal from Order Admitting to Bail.

PART IV.—INQUIRY AFTER CONVICTION.

§ 417. But before Final Judgment.
§ 418. Bail Pending Steps to Reverse Sentence.
§ 419. After Sentence or Commitment in Execution.

CHAPTER XXVIII.
HUSBAND AND WIFE.

§ 420. Remarks.
§ 421. Husband for Wife.
§ 422. Wife for or against Husband.

CHAPTER XXIX.
PARENT FOR HIS CHILD.

§ 423. Upon What Restraint the Writ is Based.
§ 424. Powers of Common-law Courts.
§ 425. Powers of Courts of Chancery.

CHAPTER XXX.
CUSTODY OF LEGITIMATE CHILDREN IN ENGLAND.

PART I.—DOCTRINES IN ENGLAND AT LAW.

§ 426. The Rights of the Father during his Life.
§ 427. Appointment of Testamentary Guardian.
§ 428. Surrender of Custody by Parent.
§ 429. How Far the Courts will Actively Interfere to Deliver the Custody of a Child.
§ 430. The Court's Discretion.
§ 431. Infant's Liberty of Choice.
§ 432. Infant's Age of Discretion.
§ 433. The Parent's Right of Access to Children, though not Entitled to their Custody.

PART II.—ENGLISH DOCTRINES IN EQUITY.

§ 434. Cause of the Talfourd Act.
§ 435. Provisions of the Talfourd Act, 2 & 3 Vict., c. 54.
§ 436. Effect of This Act.
§ 437. Modes of Procedure.

CHAPTER XXXI.
CUSTODY OF LEGITIMATE CHILDREN IN THE UNITED STATES.

§ 438. Application of English Cases.
§ 439. Scope of Habeas Corpus in Cases Affecting the Custody of Children.
§ 440. Authority to Apply for a Habeas Corpus.
§ 441. The Father's Rights to the Custody of his Children.
§ 442. The Same, Continued.
§ 443. The Mother's Rights.
§ 444. How Far a Parent may by Agreement Surrender the Custody of his Child.
§ 445. How Far the Courts will Actively Interfere to Deliver the Custody of a Child.
§ 446. Welfare of the Child to be Considered.
§ 447. Infant's Liberty of Choice.
§ 448. Test of Infant's Judgment.
§ 449. Parent's Right of Access, though not Entitled to Custody.
§ 450. *Supersedeas*, Appeal, Action, and Foreign Jurisdiction.
§ 451. In Divorce Matters.
§ 452. Doctrines in Chancery.

CHAPTER XXXII.
CUSTODY OF ILLEGITIMATE CHILDREN.

§ 453. Views of the English Courts.
§ 454. Doctrine in the United States.

CHAPTER XXXIII.
MASTER AND APPRENTICE.

§ 455. Which One may Obtain the Writ.
§ 456. Concerning the Indentures.

CHAPTER XXXIV.
GUARDIAN AND WARD.

§ 457. Guardian may have the Writ of Habeas Corpus to Bring up his Ward.

CHAPTER XXXV.
PARDONS.

§ 458. Nature and Acceptance of Pardons.

CHAPTER XXXVI.
FOREIGN EXTRADITION.

PART I.—EXTRADITION TO THE UNITED STATES.

§ 459. The Demand.
§ 460. Application for a Habeas Corpus.

TABLE OF CONTENTS.   xxiii

§ 461. Illegal Extradition.
§ 462. Can the Surrendered Fugitive be Tried for an Offense Other than the Extradition Crime?

PART II.—EXTRADITION FROM THE UNITED STATES.

§ 463. Executive Functions.
§ 464. Judicial Functions—Issuance of Habeas Corpus.
§ 465. Reviewing Decision of Commissioner on Habeas Corpus.
§ 466. Of the Complaint, Statement of Offense, Authentication of Documents, etc.
§ 467. Checks of Legal Functions upon Each Other.
§ 468. Conflict between State and Federal Authority.

CHAPTER XXXVII.
INTERSTATE EXTRADITION.

PART I.—CONSTITUTIONAL AND LEGISLATIVE PROVISIONS.

§ 469. Constitution of the United States.
§ 470. Statutory Enactment.
§ 471. State Authority.
§ 472. Authority in Absence of State Legislation.

PART II.—DUTY AND DISCRETION OF EXECUTIVE.

§ 473. The Demanding Discretion.
§ 474. The Delivering Discretion.

PART III.—JUDICIAL POWERS.

§ 475. Courts can not Control Discretion of Executive.
§ 476. The Affidavit.
§ 477. Concerning the Indictment.
§ 478. Person Charged must be Shown to be a Fugitive Criminal.
§ 479. Authentication of the Papers.
§ 480. Vacating Executive Warrant—Sufficiency of the Papers.
§ 481. Awaiting Requisition.
§ 482. Can Only be Tried for Extradition Crime.
§ 483. Illegal Extradition.
§ 484. Other Matters.

PART IV.—JURISDICTION OF THE FEDERAL COURTS.

§ 485. May Issue Habeas Corpus in Cases of Interstate Extradition.
§ 486. Scope of Inquiry.
§ 487. Conflict of Jurisdiction.

FORMS USED IN HABEAS CORPUS PROCEEDINGS.

PETITIONS.

FORM		PAGE
No. 1.	Petition for a Habeas Corpus...............................	631
1.	Petition for a Habeas Corpus...............................	632
2.	Another Form—Second Application.........................	633
3.	Usual Form of, by Party Confined..........................	634
4.	Application by a Third Party................................	635
5.	Petition under Extraordinary Circumstances.................	635
6.	For the Purpose of Being Bailed...........................	636
7.	In Case of Private Restraint, as That of Master or Other Person.	636
8.	By a Parent for a Child......................................	637
9.	Affidavit and Application for Writ to Testify................	637

WRITS.

No. 10.	Habeas Corpus *ad Subjiciendum*............................	638
11.	Another Writ of Habeas Corpus............................	639
12.	Habeas Corpus *ad Testificandum*...........................	639
13.	Another Form of Writ to Testify...........................	640

RETURNS.

No. 14.	Where Facts Correspond with Those in Petition............	641
15.	Where Petitioner is not in Custody..........................	641
16.	Where Custody of Prisoner has been Transferred...........	642
17.	Where Petitioner is in Custody.............................	642
18.	To Habeas Corpus or *Certiorari*............................	643
19.	To Habeas Corpus *ad Testificandum*........................	643
20.	Where Prisoner was Committed on Execution..............	643
21.	Where Prisoner was Committed for Contempt..............	644
22.	Where Prisoner was Committed on Warrant................	644
23.	Where Prisoner was Committed on Suspicion...............	644
24.	Where Prisoner was Committed on Indictment.............	645
25.	Additional Clauses for Several Causes of Detention...........	645
26.	Where Infants are in Custody...............................	645
27.	Where the Body Only is Brought...........................	646
28.	Where Body of Prisoner is too Infirm to be Brought.........	646
29.	Where Prisoner is under Sentence of Death.................	646

MISCELLANEOUS FORMS.

FORM		PAGE
No. 30.	Order Granting Writ	647
31.	Notice of Application to District Attorney	647
32.	Notice of Application to Other Interested Parties	648
33.	Commitment for Disobedience of Writ	648
34.	Attachment for Disobedience of Writ	649
35.	Certificate of Service of Writs of Habeas Corpus	649
36.	Bond in Serving the Writ	650
37.	Precept to Bring up Party Illegally Restrained	650
38.	Warrant under Form V	651
39.	Federal Writ of *Certiorari*	651
40.	State Writ of *Certiorari*	652
41.	Traverse to Return	652
42.	Recognizance on being Bailed	653
43.	Order of Discharge	654

TABLE OF CASES.

N. B.—The Figures Refer to the Pages.

A

Abbott v. Booth, 51 Barb. 546	354
Abeles, In the Matter of, 12 Kan. 451	393, 405
Ableman v. Booth, 21 How. 506	37, 56, 57, 73, 78, 79, 119, 126, 175, 176, 217, 218, 276, 332, 338, 519, 611, 626, 627, 628
Abranches v. Schell, 4 Blatch. 256	61, 333
Adams, Ex parte, 25 Miss. 883	394, 412, 419, 436
Adams, In the Matter of, 7 Law Rep. 386	617
Adams v. Vose, 1 Gray, 51	386
Adcock v. Fiske, 8 Scott, 138	202
Addington's Case, 2 Bailey, 516	598
Adriance et al. v. Lagrave, 59 N. Y. 110; S. C., 14 Abb. Pr., N. S., 333	603, 605
Ah Bau and Ah You, 10 Nev. 264	237, 314, 362
Ahitbol v. Beniditto, 2 Taunt. 401	355
Ah Sing, In re, 8 Pac. C. L. J. 213	148
Ainsworth, Ex parte, 27 Tex. 731	239, 521
Albany City Bank v. Schermerhorn, 9 Paige, 372	399, 452
Alexander, Ex parte, 2 Am. L. Reg. 44	394, 439, 441, 452, 519
Alexander, Ex parte, 14 Fed. Rep. 680	339, 551
Alexander, In the Matter of, 59 Mo. 598	544
Alfred v. McKay, 36 Ga. 440	590
Allen, Ex parte, 3 Nev. & M. 35	104
Allen, Ex parte, 12 Nev. 87	232, 249
Allen, In the Matter of, 13 Blatch. 271	59
Allis, Ex Parte, 12 Ark. 101	110
Allison, In re, 28 Eng. L. & Eq. 281	335
Allison, In re, 29 Eng. L. & Eq. 406	335
Almeida, Ex parte, 2 Wheeler's Cr. Cas. 576	78
Ambrose, In the Matter of, Phill. 91	220, 313
American Ex. Co. et al. v. Patterson, 73 Ind. 430	243
Anderson v. Dunn, 6 Wheat. 204	393, 409, 441
Anderson, Ex parte, 16 Iowa, 595	82
Andrews, Case of, L. R., 8 Q. B. 153	595
Andrews, In the Matter of, 4 Eng. Rep., Moak's Notes, 261	558, 560, 561, 562, 566, 569, 586
Androscoggin & Ken. R. R. v. And. R. R. Co., 49 Me. 392	390, 392
Angel v. Smith, 9 Ves. 335	338
Anon., 3 Cro. Car. 579	526, 552
Anon., Fortes. 242	362, 363
Anon., Fortes. 273	201
Anon., 1 Mod. 103	170
Anon., 6 Mod. *p. 180	180
Anon., 7 Mod. 118	489
Anon., 11 Mod. 45	552
Anon., 2 Stra. 83	525
Anon., Vent. 330	227

TABLE OF CASES.

Archer's Case, 6 Gratt. 705.. 546
Archer's Case, Fortes. 197.. 201
Archer's Case, 1 Ld. Raym. 673...................................... 559
Armstead, In re, v. Confederate States, 38 Ala., N. S., 458............ 110
Armstrong v. Lisle, 1 Salk. 60..........................526, 550, 551, 552
Armstrong v. Stone et Ux., 9 Gratt. 102................571, 576, 579, 585
Askew v. Hayton, 1 Dowl. 510.. 368
Atkinson v. Carty, 1 Jebb & S. 369................................... 384
Attorney General v. Cleave, 2 Dowl. 668.............................. 100
Attorney General v. Fadden, 1 Price, 403 100
Attorney General v. Fadden, 1 Price, 152............................. 137
Attorney General v. Hunt, 9 Price, 147............................... 104

B

Bacharach v. Lagrave, 1 Hun (N. Y.), 689.......................604, 605
Bagnall v. Ableman, 4 Wis. 163...............................624, 627
Bailey's and Collier's Case, 3 El. & Bl. 607; S. C., 25 Eng. L. & Eq. 240..259, 272
Baker v. Gordon et al., 23 Ind. 209................................... 225
Baker, In re, 29 How. Pr. 485.. 101
Baker, In re, 2 Hurl. & N. 239....................................... 260
Baker, In the Matter of, 11 How. Pr. 418...233, 247, 251, 328, 336, 474, 482
Balcom, In re, 12 Neb. 316; S. C., 11 N. W. Rep. 312.....92, 292, 236, 372
Ballenger v. McLain, 54 Ga. 159..................................593, 594
Banks, Ex parte, 28 Ala. 89.............................. 532, 536, 541
Bank of United States v. Jenkins, 18 Johns. 305...................... 515
Bank of Labitut, 1 Wood, 11... 406
Bank of United States v. Moss, 6 How. 31............................ 406
Barada v. The State, 13 Mo. 94...................................... 463
Barkham's Case, 3 Cro. Car. 507.................................149, 526
Barnes v. Barnes, L. R., 1 Prob. & Div. 463......................564, 569
Barnes, Ex parte, 1 Sprague, 133.................................... 63
Barrack v. Newton, 1 Ad. & El., Q. B., 525........................... 112
Barre, Matter of, 14 Abb. Pr., N. S., 426.........................593, 594
Barrett, In the Matter of, 42 Barb. 479............................... 82
Barrett v. Hopkins, 2 McCrary, 129; S. C., 7 Fed. Rep. 312........513, 514
Barry, Ex parte, 2 How. 65....................................57, 64, 279
Barry v. Mercein et al., 5 How. 103.................................. 279
Barth v. Clise, Sheriff, 12 Wall. 401................................. 227
Batchelder v. Moore, 42 Cal. 414..................................... 425
Baxter, Ex parte, Mont. & McA. 16.................................. 134
Bayley, Ex parte, 1 West Coast Rep. 485..........................622, 628
Beacom, Ex parte, 12 Tex. App. 318........................536, 541, 548
Bealls' Case, 39 Miss. 715.. 531
Beard, In the Matter of, 4 Ark. 9.................................... 91
Beatty, Ex parte, 12 Wend. 229..................................115, 517
Beebe, In re, 3 Prac. Rep. (U. C.) 270.............................148, 362
Beeching et al., Ex parte, 3 Appeals from Mag. to K. B. 174; S. C., 4 Barn. & Cress. 136.. 261
Beeching et al., Ex parte, 4 Barn. & Cress. 136; S. C., 6 Dow. & Ry. 209 ....213, 215, 260
Beekman v. Traver, 20 Wend. 67.................................... 360
Beers v. Beers, 4 Conn. 535.. 379
Bell v. State of Maryland, 4 Gill, 301.............................240, 467
Bell v. The State, 4 Gill, 301...................................381, 382, 519
Belligerent Asylum, 7 Opinions Atty. Gen. 123....................... 78
Bennac v. The People, 4 Barb. 31.............................233, 310, 383
Bennet v. Bennet, 2 Beas. 114...................................574, 583, 585
Bennett v. Bennett, 1 Deady, 299.................................59, 64
Bennett's Case, 2 Cranch C. Ct. 612................280, 332, 364, 372, 376
Benns v. Mosely, 2 Com. B. N. S. 116; S. C., 40 Eng. L. & Eq. 342.... 104
Bently v. Terry, 59 Ga. 555.. 580
Bernert, Ex parte, 7 Pac. C. L. J. 460........174, 462, 463, 494, 495, 497

TABLE OF CASES.   xxix

Bessett, Ex parte, 51 Eng. Com. L. 480............................... 368
Beswick, In the Matter of, 25 How. Pr. 149.... 82
Bethell's Case, 1 Salk. 347.......................362, 363, 367, 368, 369
Bethuram v. Black, 11 Bush, 628....................... 90, 532, 533
Bicknell et al. v. Newton, 1 Ad. & El., Q. B., 525................... 112
Bigelow v. Forrest, 9 Wall. 339...................................... 499
Bird, Ex parte, 19 Cal. 130....................................429, 457
Bird, In re, 2 Saw. 33...63, 338
Bissell, In the Matter of, 40 Mich. 63.............................. 429
Blair, In re, 4 Wis. 522....................240, 288, 420, 474, 485, 519
——— v. Cooper, 6 Mod. 90... 187
———, Ex parte, 3 Dowl. 161.. 257
Blisset's Case, Lofft. 748....................................559, 563
Blundell v. Blundell, 1 Dow. & Ry. 142.............................. 137
Boaz, Ex parte, 31 Ala. 425...................................575, 576
Bogart, In re, 2 Saw. 396............... 63, 274, 276, 481, 513, 514
Boland, Ex parte, 11 Tex. App. 159..................................
..............523, 342, 471, 472, 473, 474, 475, 476, 477, 479, 489, 521
Bollman and Swartwout's Case, 4 Cranch, 75; S. C., Marshall on the
  Federal Constitution, 33..
........56, 65, 87, 275, 278, 279, 280, 283, 332, 336, 340, 360, 376, 509
Bomar, Ex parte, 9 Tex. App. 610..............................538, 541
Bond, Ex parte, 30 Am. L. Rep. 20; S. C., 9 S. C. 80, and 11 Cent. L. J.
  59.. 495
Booth, Sherman M., In re, 3 Wis. 2.................................. 175
Booth's Case, 3 Wis. 1.. 78
Booth, Ex parte, 3 Wis. 145... 338
Booth, In re, 3 Wis. 1..................................1, 218, 288, 486
Boothroyd, 15 Mee & W. 1......................................335, 368
Bort, In re, 25 Kan. 308; S. C., 20 Am. Law Reg., N. S., 493......583, 587
Bosen v. Brandt, 2 King, 289.. 401
Botts v. Williams, 17 B. Mon. 687................................... 617
Boucher's Case, Cro. Jac. 81.. 360
Bourne's Case, 4 Cro. Jac. 543..................................118, 121
Boven's Case, 9 Ad. & El. 669....................................... 150
Bowen, Ex parte, 46 Cal. 112.. 105
Boyd v. Glass, 34 Ga. 253... 582
Boyce, In re, 22 Eng. L. & Eq. 131; S. C., 17 Jur. 715, and 2 El. & Bl.
  521... 189
Boyle, Re, 9 Wis. 264... 288
Boyleston v. Kerr, 2 Daly, 220...................................... 356
Bracy's Case, 1 Ld. Raym. 100....................................... 437
Bradstreet v. Ferguson, 23 Wend. 637 ....384, 385
Brady v. Davis, 9 Ga. 73.. 362
Branigan, Ex parte, 19 Cal. 133.....................354, 362, 372, 373, 374
Brenan and Galen's Case, 10 Ad. & El., Q. B., 492; 59 Eng. Com. L.
  492..162, 258, 260, 338, 498
Brenan and Gallan's Case, 2 Cox C. C. 193...........204, 488
Brewers' Case, The, Roll. 134....................................... 359
Brice's Case, 3 Cro. Car. 593....................................... 163
Bridewell, Ex parte, 57 Miss. 39.......531, 534, 535, 537, 541, 546, 548, 549
Bridge's Dock, Ex parte, 2 Wood, 428. ....75, 199, 276
Bridges, Ex parte, 2 Wood, 428; S. C., 2 Cent. L. J. 327.......472, 487
Brinster v. Compton, 68 Ala. 299.....................574, 576, 582, 583
Briscoe, Matter of, 51 How. Pr. 422...........................616, 617, 619
British Prisoners, 1 Woodb. & M. 66................................. 606
Brittain v. Kinnaird, 1 Brod. & B. 432.............................. 260
Britten, Matter of, Ex parte, 2 Mont. D. & De G. 335................ 135
Bromley's Case, 2 Jac. & W. 458..................................... 116
Broomhead v. Chisolm, 47 Ga. 390.............................91, 243, 465
Brown, Ex parte, 63 Ala. 187..................................246, 456
Brown, In re, 4 Col. 438.. 441
Brown v. The People, 19 Ill. 613.................................... 398
Brown's Case, 112 Mass. 409...................................615, 619, 622

Brown v. Rice, 57 Me. 55.. 507
Brown v. United States, 14 Am. Law Reg. N. S. 566; S. C., 2 Cent. Law
　J. 368..60, 75
Browne v. Gisborne, 2 A. & V. Dowl. N. S. 963...................... 91
Bryant, Ex parte, 34 Ala. 270.. 538
Bryant, In re, 1 Deady, 118... 59
Bryant, Ex parte, 2 Tyler, 269......................................205, 206
Buck v. Colbath, 3 Wall. 334.. 411
Buell, In re Augustus C., 3 Dill. 116.................................. 61
Bulger, Ex parte, 60 Cal. 438......................................471, 501
Bull, Ex parte, 42 Cal. 196....................................307, 361, 376
Bull, Ex parte, 1 Saund. & C. 141...............................188, 192
Bull & Turtle, In re, 4 Dill. 323.....................................75, 472
Bullen's Petition, 28 Kan. 781......................................572, 583
Burdett v. Abbott, 14 East, 1.............72, 390, 393, 438, 447, 449, 518
Burford, Ex parte, 3 Cranch, 448.......................................
　........................57, 65, 278, 279, 332, 336, 357, 359, 360, 372, 509
Burnett, Ex parte, 30 Ala. 461................................92, 462, 492
Burnham v. Morrissey, 14 Gray, 226...................390, 393, 441, 443
Burns, Ex parte, 7 Mo. App. 564, app................................. 468
Burns v. Erben, 40 N. Y. 463.. 356
Burritt v. Burritt, 29 Barb. 124... 587
Burr's Case, 1 Burr's Trial, 21; S. C., 4 Cranch, app...............262, 373
1 Burr's Trial, 97; S. C., Marshall on the Federal Constitution, 53..... 266
Burt v. Bryant, 5 Dowl. 726.. 132
Bush v. Bush, 37 Ind. 164.. 587
Bushell's Case, Freeman's K. B. & C. P. 1; S. C., T. Jones, 13; 1 Vaugh.
　135; 6 Howell's State Trial, 999...13, 19, 54, 86, 407, 445, 449, 490, 518
Bushell's Case, Freeman K. B. & C. P. 1............................ 447
Bushnell et al., Ex parte, 8 Ohio St. 599.............78, 79, 108, 338, 339
Bushnel et al., Ex parte, 9 Ohio St. 77................................. 78
Bustamento v. Analla, 1 N. M. 255....................583, 585, 590, 591
Butler v. Freeman, Amb. 302... 557
Byers & Davis v. Commonwealth, 42 Pa. St. 89..................379, 383
Byrd v. The State, 1 How. (Miss.) 163.................................. 345
Byrne v. Love et al., 14 Tex. 81....................................581, 591

C

Cable v. Cooper, 15 Johns. 152.. 84
Cabrera, Ex parte, 1 Wash. 232... 64
Cain, In the Matter of, 2 Winst. 141................................... 43
Caldwell's Case, 13 Abb. Pr. 405; S. C., 35 Barb. 444............. 515
Calder, In re, 6 Opin. Atty. Gen. 91................................... 606
Callicot, In re, 8 Blatch. 89......................................64, 493, 599
Call, jun., Ex parte, 2 Tex. App. 497..........................327, 342, 489
Camfield v. Patterson, 33 Ga. 561...................................... 218
Campbell, Ex parte, 20 Ala. N. S. 89.........................94, 108, 522
Canadian Prisoners' Case, 5 Mee. & W. 32; S. C., 9 Ad. & El. 731; 36
　Eng. Com. L. 254, and 7 Dowl. P. C. 208..72, 108, 161, 162, 178, 180, 371
Cancemi v. The People, 18 N. Y. 129.................................. 317
Cannon's Case, 47 Mich. 481; S. C., 11 N. W. Rep. 280.......620, 624, 627
Cannon v. Stuart, 3 Houst. 223.....................................593, 594
Carll, Ex parte, 1 Sup. Ct. Rep. 535................................70, 509
Carll, Ex parte, 1 Sup. Ct. Rep. 535; S. C., 106 U. S. 521.......276, 511
Carlton, In the Matter of, 7 Cow. 471.............................78, 124
Carlton, In re, 11 Neb. 99; S. C., 7 N. W. Rep. 755................ 244
Carpenter v. Simmons, 1 Robt. 360.................................... 469
Carpenter, Ex parte, 12 Pac. C. L. J. 274............................ 361
Carroll, In re, Chic. L. N., Sept. 28, 1878.......................617, 625
Cartlidge v. Cartlidge, 2 Sw. & Tr. 567; S. C., 31 L. J., N. S., P. M. &
　A. 85.. 569
Carty, Ex parte, Sup. Ct. Cal., Dec. 29, 1883........................ 551
Case of the Twelve Commitments, 19 Abb. Pr. 394...............336, 385
Caudle v. Seymour, 41 Eng. Com. L. 825; S. C., 1 Gale & Dav. 454.359, 364

TABLE OF CASES. xxxi

Chambers' Case, 3 Cro. Car. 133..................162, 170, 187, 526
Champion, Ex parte, 52 Ala. 311......90, 110, 234, 252, 298, 303, 535
Chaney, Ex parte, 8 Ala. 424..................................545, 549
Chapman v. Woodruff, 34 Ga. 91................................... 333
Chemung Canal Bank v. Judson, 8 Seld. 254......................... 344
Child, Ex parte, 29 Eng. L. & Eq. 259; S. C., 15 C. B. 238.........
....91, 93, 138, 257, 572
Childs v. Martin, 69 N. C. 126.................................... 337
Chow Goo Pooi, 1 W. C. Rep. 535................................... 528
City of Kansas v. Flanagan, 69 Mo. 22............................. 464
City of London's Case, 4 Fraser 8 Co. 121......................... 518
Cinn. House of Refuge v. Ryan, 37 Ohio St. 197..........575, 583, 588
Clark v. Bayer, 32 Ohio St. 299....................574, 577, 581, 583
Clark v. Commonwealth, 29 Pa. St. 129.............219, 325, 327, 490
Clark, Ex parte, 100 U. S. 399................70, 71, 87, 88, 472, 510
Clark v. Gautier, 8 Fla. 360...................................... 219
Clark, Matter of, 2 Ben. 540....................................... 62
Clark, Matter of, 9 Wend. 212............................615, 619, 622
Clark v. McComman, 7 Watts & S. 470............................... 342
Clark v. Smith, 3 Com. B. 984..................................... 100
Clark v. The People, etc., 1 Breese, 340..................392, 394, 446
Clark v. Wellington, 5 Hun, 640................................... 267
Clarke, In the Matter of, 2 Ad. & El., Q. B., 619; S. C., 2 Gale & Dav.
  780.....................................171, 172, 195, 212, 215, 258, 260
Clarke's Case, 12 Cush. 320....................................... 405
Clasby, In re, 1 W. C. Rep. 524................................... 522
Cleveland, Ex parte, 36 Ala. 306................................... 92
Cobbett, Ex parte, 53 Eng. Com. L. 185; S. C., 7 Ad. & El., Q. B., 187;
  14 Mee. & W. 175; 5 Com. B. 418, and 3 Hurl. & N. 155............
....104, 105, 131, 331, 448
Cobbett v. Hudson, 15 Ad. & El., Q. B., 988...................93, 554
Coffman v. Hampton, 2 Watts & S. 377.............................. 343
Cohen and Jones, 5 Cal. 495....................................... 432
Cohen, Ex parte, 6 Cal. 318....................................... 428
Cohn, Ex parte, 54 Cal. 193....................................... 421
Cole v. Cole, 23 Iowa, 433....................................573, 583
Cole v. Thayer, 8 Cow. 249.. 110
Coleman v. Tennessee, 97 U. S. 509................................. 75
Collier, Ex parte, 6 Ohio St. 55............................39, 43, 337
Collier's Case, 6 Opinions Attorney General...................71, 78
Comas v. Reddish, 35 Ga. 236...................................... 594
Commonwealth v. Addicks et Ux., 5 Binn. 520; S. C., 2 Serg. & R. 174.
....556, 575, 577, 582, 583, 595
Commonwealth v. Atkinson, 8 Phila. 375............................. 99
Commonwealth v. Barney, 4 Brewst. 408.................571, 583, 595, 596
Commonwealth v. Beck, 1 Browne, 277............................98, 593
Commonwealth v. Biddle, 6 Penn. L. J. 287, 4 Clark, 35............ 519
Commonwealth v. Briggs et al., 16 Pick. 203..............103, 575, 582
Commonwealth v. Burrell, 7 Pa. St. 34; S. C., 7 Barr, 34......327, 490
Commonwealth ex rel. Chew v. Carlisle, Bright. 36......288, 372, 375
Commonwealth ex rel. Chauncey v. Keeper, etc., 2 Ashm. 227........
....530, 531, 534, 536
Commonwealth v. Chandler, 11 Mass. 83........................174, 207
Commonwealth v. Crans, 2 Penn. L. J. 75........................... 372
Commonwealth v. Crans, 3 Penn. L. J. 459.......................... 375
Commonwealth v. Crotty et al., 10 Allen, 403...................... 355
Commonwealth v. Curby et al., 3 Brewst. 610; S. C., 8 Phil. 372.... 99
Commonwealth v. Cushing, 11 Mass. 66.............................. 78
Commonwealth v. Deacon, 10 Serg. & R. 125...................614, 615
Commonwealth v. Dean, 9 Gray, 283................................. 358
Commonwealth v. Downer, 24 Pick. 227.............................. 78
Commonwealth ex rel. Webster v. Fox, 7 Pa. St. 336............78, 82
Commonwealth v. Frink, 4 Am. Law Reg., N. S., 700................. 42
Commonwealth v. Gamble, 11 Serg. & R. 93.......................... 514

HAB. CORP.—c

TABLE OF CASES.

Commonwealth v. Gilkeson, 1 Phila. 194; S. C., 7 Leg. Int. 195....574, 580
Commonwealth v. Green, 17 Mass. 515.............................. 615
Commonwealth v. Hall, 9 Gray, 262................................. 622
Commonwealth v. Hamilton, 6 Mass. 272.......219, 555, 576, 585, 593, 594
Commonwealth v. Hammond, 10 Pick. 274......................584, 595
Commonwealth v. Harrison, 11 Mass. 63.........................78, 593
Commonwealth v. Hawes, 13 Ky. (Bush), 697; S. C., 17 Alb. L. J. 325,
   and Spear on Extradition, 138...............................604, 605
Commonwealth v. Hickey, 2 Pars. Sel. Cas. 317..................... 375
Commonwealth v. Hitchings, 5 Gray, 482............................ 529
Commonwealth v. Holloway, 5 Binn. 512; S. C., 42 Pa. St. 446, and 1
   Serg. & R. 390..78, 107, 386
Commonwealth v. Hoye, 9 Gray, 283................................. 358
Commonwealth v. Jailer of Alleghany Co., 7 Watts, 366.............. 105
Commonwealth v. Keeper, etc., 1 Ashm. 10.......................... 338
Commonwealth v. Keeper, etc., 1 Ashm. 183......................... 353
Commonwealth ex rel. Wilson v. Keeper, etc., 26 Pa. St. 279......... 474
Commonwealth v. Killacky, 3 Brewst. 565............................ 91
Commonwealth v. Kirkbride, 7 Phil. 1; S. C., 2 Brewst. 419...162, 206, 501
Commonwealth ex rel. Helmbold v. Kirkbride, Physician, etc., 11 Phila.
   427..220, 235
Commonwealth v. Leath, 1 Va. Cas. 151............................. 459
Commonwealth v. Lecky, 1 Watts, 66 ....108, 382, 453, 515
Commonwealth v. McBride, 2 Brewst. 545............................ 520
Commonwealth v. Moore, 19 Pick. 339................................ 92
Commonwealth v. Murray, 4 Binn. 487................................ 78
Commonwealth v. Murray, 2 Va. Cas. 504.......................364, 306
Commonwealth v. Newton, 1 Grant's Cas. 453.............399, 431, 453
Commonwealth v. Nutt, 1 Browne, 143................................ 582
Commonwealth ex rel. Lowry v. Reed, 59 Pa. St. 425....166, 210, 588, 597
Commonwealth v. Ridgway, 2 Ashm. 247.......................103, 117, 351
Commonwealth v. Robinson, 1 Serg. & R. 353.....................78, 219, 593
Commonwealth v. Rutherford, 5 Rand. 646 ....532, 540
Commonwealth v. Semmes, 11 Leigh, 665............................ 546
Commonwealth v. Sheriff, etc., 16 Serg. & R. 304................... 105
Commonwealth v. Smith, 1 Brews. 547........574, 575, 578, 582, 586, 595
Commonwealth ex rel. Herring v. Smith, 13 Rep. 124................ 324
Commonwealth v. Sumner, 5 Pick. 360............................... 102
Commonwealth v. Superintendent Philadelphia Co. Prison, 4 Brews. 320, 105
Commonwealth v. Taylor et al., 11 Phila. 386..................289, 305
Commonwealth v. Taylor, 3 Met. 72...........................555, 572, 585
Commonwealth v. Ward, 4 Mass. 496................................ 366
Commonwealth v. Waite, 2 Pick. 445................................ 105
Commonwealth v. Weymouth, 2 Allen, 144 ....505, 506
Commonwealth v. Whitney, 10 Pick. 434........................108, 516
Company of Vintners v. Clerke, 5 Mod. 156......................... 194
Conner v. Commonwealth, 3 Binn. 38............................359, 364
Connor, In re, 16 I. R. C. L. 112.................................. 564
Cook, Ex parte, 35 Cal. 107....................................320, 547
Cook v. Cook, 1 Barb. Ch. 639..................................... 580
Cooper, In re, 32 Vt. 253.. 434
Copeland v. The State, 60 Ind. 394................................. 590
Corbett v. The State, 24 Ga. 391................................... 551
Corbett's Petition, 9 Ben. 274..................................... 62
Corrie v. Corrie, 42 Mich. 509; S. C., 4 N. W. Rep. 213 ......333, 583, 584
Corryell, In the Matter of, 22 Cal. 178 ....293, 316, 323, 460, 486
Cotes v. Michill, 3 Lev. 20.. 359
Cottrell, Ex parte, 59 Cal. 417; S. C., 8 Pac. C. L. J. 875.....400, 417, 429
Coupland, Ex parte, 26 Tex. 386............................174, 207, 521
Cowell v. Patterson, 49 Iowa, 514..............................298, 363
Crandall, Petition of, 34 Wis. 177.................288, 471, 472, 485, 496
Crawford, Matter of, 13 Ad. & El., Q. B., 613..................118, 437
Crepps v. Durden et al., 1 Sm. L. C., part 2, 7th Am. ed., 1095 ......
   ....341, 345, 346, 358, 364

TABLE OF CASES. xxxiii

Crittenden, Ex parte, 7 Pac. C. L. J., 483.........................391, 395
Crook et al. v. People, 16 Ill. 534.. 453
Croom and May, Ex parte, 19 Ala. 561...................246, 530, 547, 549
Cropper v. The Commonwealth, 2 Rob. (Va.) 842................487, 489
Crosby's Case, 2 W. Black. 754 ....149, 154
Crosby's Case, 3 Wils. 188; S. C., 2 W. Black. 754 ....392, 407, 408
Cross, Ex parte, 2 Hurlst. & N. 354.................................188, 192, 526
Crowley's Case, 2 Swanst. 1..... 17, 18, 86, 110, 113, 151, 182, 191, 212, 556
Cubreth, Ex parte, 49 Cal. 435 623
Cuneen, In the Matter of, 17 How. Pr. 516.....................575, 583
Cunningham v. Thomas, 25 Ind. 171...................................... 218
Curley, In re, 34 Iowa, 184.. 519
Curtis v. Curtis, 5 Jur. N. S. 1147................................558, 559, 569
Curtis, Ex parte, 1 Sup. Ct. Rep. 381; S. C., 5 Mor. Trans. 469; and 106 U. S. 371 ....69, 70, 276, 509, 511

D

Dabbs, In the Matter of, 9 Am. Law Reg. 565; S. C., 12 Abb. Pr. 113.. 82
Dabzell v. Cullen, 1 Dow. & L. 448.. 132
Da Costa, In the Matter of, 1 Park. Cr. 129............................. 520
Dakin, Ex parte; In re Swann v. Dakins, 29 Eng. L. & Eq. 331; S. C., 16 Com. B. 77..215, 261, 272
Daley, 2 F. & F. 258.. 93
Dalton v. The State, 6 Blackf. 357... 590
D'Argent and Vivant, 1 East, 330... 199
Darnall v. Mullikin et al., 8 Tanner (Ind.), 152....................... 587
Darrah v. Westerlage, 44 Tex. 388................................342, 456, 457
Davies, Ex parte, 5 Scott, 241; S. C., 6 Dowl. 181................... 127
Davis' Case, 122 Mass. 324; S. C., 12 Am. L. Rev. 753, and 5 Cent. L. J. 273 ....619, 622
Davis, Ex parte, 18 Vt. 401..225, 516
Davis, Mary Ann, 5 T. R. 715... 179
Davis v. Clements, 2 N. H. 390... 359
Davis and Owen, 1 Bos. & Pul. 342....................................... 199
Davis v. The State, 6 How. (Miss.) 399................................. 550
Davison's Case, 13 Abb. Pr. 129.................................423, 448, 453
Day v. Micou, 18 Wall. 156.. 499
Deckard v. State of Maryland, 38 Md. 186.........................346, 488
De Lacy v. Antoine, 7 Leigh, 438.....................................109, 219
De La Montange's Case, 19 Abb. Pr. 413, n........................... 385
Denny v. Tyler, 3 Allen, 225.. 108
Deny, Ex parte, 10 Nev. 212.. 88
De Puy, Moses, In the Matter of, 3 Ben. 307......................... 62
Des Rochers, Ex parte, 1 McAll. 68..............................59, 64, 99
Devlin's Case, 5 Abb. Pr. 281..98, 329
Devoe, In re, 1 Lowell, 251... 63
Deybel's Case, 4 Barn & Ald. 243..................................163, 164
D'Hautville Case, cited in Hurd on Habeas Corpus, 2d ed., 479........ 577
Dimes, In the Matter of, 14 Ad. & El., Q. B., 554; S. C., 68 Eng. Com. L. 554, and 3 Mac. & G. 5............................192, 258, 272, 331
Dinckerlocker v. Marsh, 75 Ind. 548..................................... 507
Disinger, 12 Ohio St. 256... 78
Divine, In the Matter of, 21 How. Pr. 80............................... 310
Divine's Case, 11 Abb. Pr. 90; S. C., 5 Park. Cr. 62; and 21 How. Pr. 80. 466
Dixon, Ex parte, 1 Utah, 192.. 466
Dobson, Ex parte, 31 Cal. 407... 98
Dodds' Case, 2 De G. & J. 510.. 133
Dodge's Case, 6 Mart. (La.) 569.......................................84, 519
Doig, In re, 4 Fed. Rep. 193...69, 609
Donahue, Matter of, 1 Pac. C. L. Mag. 22.........................619, 620
Donnelly v. The State, 2 Dutch. 463...................................... 100
Donohue, Matter of, 1 Abb. N. C 1; S. C., 52 How. Pr. 251.......387, 594
Doo Woon, In re, 1 West Coast Rep. 333........................625, 627
Dorr, Ex parte, 3 How. 103.............................67, 75, 91, 120, 279

xxxiv   TABLE OF CASES.

Dougherty, In re, 27 Vt. 325..342, 481
Douglas, In the Matter of, 3 Ad. & El., Q. B., 825..................... 178
Dow's Case, 18 Pa. St. 37..208, 624
Doyle, Matter of, 1 Clarke Ch. 154..........   ....562, 564, 590
Doyle's, Ann, Case, 19 Abb. Pr. 269... 385
Drumb v. Keen et Ux., 47 Iowa, 435................................ 583
Drury v. The State, 25 Tex. 45..541, 548
Dudley, Ex parte, 38 Ala., N. S., 458.. 110
Duffy v. The People, 6 Hill (N. Y.), 75...................................... 379
Dumain and Wife v. Gwynne, 10 Allen, 270..............206, 573, 582, 583
Duncan, Ex parte, 53 Cal. 410 ....106, 547
Duncan, Ex parte, 54 Cal. 75 ....547, 548
Dunn, Ex parte, 5 Dow. & L. 345; S. C., 5 Com. B. 215, and 12 Jur. 99. 498
Du Puy, In the Matter of, 3 Ben. 307.. 599
Durming v. Ketle, 2 Cro. Eliz. 543.. 127
Dwire v. Saunders, 15 Ind. 306.. 196
Dynes v. Hoover, 20 How. 82.. 513
Dyson, Ex parte, 25 Miss. 356..532, 550

E

Eanes v. The State, 6 Humph. 53... 356
Earl of Ferrer's Case, 2 Hawk. P. C., Curwood's ed., c. 44, seç. 18, p. 585, note 1.. 106
Eaton, Matter of, 27 Mich. 1..474, 484
Eden's Case, 2 Mau. & Sel. 225..161, 170, 192
Edgington, Ex parte, 10 Nev. 215; S. C., 3 Cent. L. J. 618........... 488
Eggington, Ex parte, 24 Eng. L. & Eq. 146; S. C., 18 Jur. 224, and 2 El. & Bl. 717.. 214, 261
Elderton's Case, 2 Ld. Raym. 978; S. C., 6 Mod. 73...............363, 400
Eldred, In re, 46 Wis. 530.. 288
Electoral College of S. C., Case of the, 1 Hughes, 571; S. C., 4 Cent. L. J. 72..75, 276, 409
Ellis, Ex parte, 11 Cal. 222..............................88, 110, 126, 240, 519
Ellis v. Jesup et Ux., 11 Bush, 403.................574, 580, 583, 584, 585
Elliott v. Piersol, 1 Pet. 340.. 495
Elsee v. Smith, 1 Dow. & Ry. 97; S. C., 2 Chit., Q. B., 304............ 359
Emanuel & Giles v. The State, 36 Miss. 627..................323, 484, 522
Emerton's Case, Freem. K. B. & C. P. 389................................... 203
Erwin, Ex parte, 7 Tex. App. 288...549, 624
Esselborn, In re, 12 Rep. 454... 284
Evans v. Foster, 1 N. H. 374..529, 532, 533
Everts, Ex parte, 1 Bond, 197... 64
Exposition of Fugitive Slave Law, 1 Blatchf. 641–643.................. 78

F

Fagan, In re, 2 Sprague, 91...39, 42
Falvey, Re, 7 Wis. 630..288, 444
Farez, In re, 7 Blatchf. 34; S. C., Id. 345...........333, 606, 607, 608, 609
Farez' Case, 2 Abb. U. S. 346...609, 610
Farnham, Ex parte, 3 Col. 545...471, 474
Farrand, Matter of, 1 Abb. U. S. 140.....................................75, 78
Faust v. Judge, etc., 30 Mich. 266.. 111
Fazacherly v. Baldo, 1 Salk. 351; S. C., 6 Mod. 177..........187, 272, 330
Feeley's Case, 12 Cush. 598.. 458
Fell, In re, 3 Dow. & L. 373..202, 204
Fennessy, Ex parte, 4 Pac. C. L. J. 496...................................... 92
Ferguson v. Ferguson et al., 36 Mo. 197.....................219, 521, 595
Ferguson, Matter of, 9 Johns. 239...78, 110
Fernandez, Ex parte, 7 Jur., N. S., 529; S. C., 10 C. B., N. S., 3......
....394, 445, 448
Ferrens, In the Matter of, 3 Ben. 442.................................62, 93, 219
Fetter, Matter of, 3 Zab. 311..614, 615, 618
Field, Ex parte, 5 Blatchf. 63...153, 400

TABLE OF CASES. xxxv

Finch, Ex parte, 15 Fla. 630..................................521, 532, 549
Finch v. Florida, 15 Fla. 633.....................532, 539, 543, 544, 549
Fisher, Ex parte, 6 Neb. 309...493, 496
Fischer v. Hayes, 6 Fed. Rep. 63..............391, 392, 394, 399, 448, 453
Fitts v. Fitts, 21 Tex. 511... 219
Flavell's Case, 8 Watts & S. 197.. 598
Fleming v. Bradley, 1 Call (Va.), 203................................... 126
Fleming v. Clark, 12 Allen, 191... 76
Fletcher, Ex parte, 1 Dow. & L. 726; S. C., 8 Jur. 146, and 13 L. J., N. S. M. C., 16..202, 335, 361
Flower v. Bright, 2 Johns. & H. 590.................................... 422
Foot & Beebe v. Stevens, 17 Wend. 483............................... 343
Forbes' Case, 11 Abb. Pr. 52...310, 311
Forbes et al., Ex parte, 1 Dill. 363....................................... 75
Ford v. Graham, 10 Com. B. 369... 104
Ford v. Nassau, 9 Mee. & W. 792....................................... 104
Ford, In re, 46 Wis. 530.. 288
Foster et Ux. v. Alston, 6 How. (Miss.) 406................219, 571, 596
Foster, Ex parte, 5 Tex. App. 625............... 93, 240, 542, 548, 521, 536
Fowler v. Hollenbeck & Pillow, 9 Barb. 309.......................580, 593
Fowler, In re, 4 Fed. Rep. 303.......................................609, 610
Fox and Money, 1 Bos. & Pul. 250....................................... 199
Frankenstein's Case, 1 Crim. L. Mag. 498............................. 111
Frazer, In re, 7 Blatchf. 34... 69
Freeman v. Howe, 24 How. 450... 411
Freestone, In re, 36 Eng L. & Eq. 532................................. 335
French v. Lighty, 9 Ind. 475.. 225
Fugitive Slave Law, 1 Blatchf. 635, app.............................339, 503
Fynn, In re, 12 Jur. 713.........................556, 559, 560, 562, 569

G

Gano v. Hall, 42 N. Y. 67; S. C., 5 Park Cr. 651.................... 364
Garner v. Gordon, 41 Ind. 92...................225, 228, 245, 578, 583, 586
Garvin, In re, 3 Col. 67...89, 236
Geary, Ex parte, 2 Biss. 485.......................................62, 477, 478
Geissler, Ex parte, 4 Fed. Rep. 188.................................69, 609
Gener v. Sparks, 1 Salk. 79.. 348
Gerdemann v. Commonwealth, 11 Phila. 374.....................234, 252
Geter v. Commissioners of Tobacco Inspection, 1 Bay, 354........ 384
Geyger v. Stoy, 1 Dall. (Pa.) 146.....................................98, 366
Gibb v. King, a prisoner, 1 Com. B. 1; S. C., 2 Dow. & L. 806..... 127
Giboney v. Rogers, Judge etc., 32 Ark. 462........................... 111
Gibson, Ex parte, 31 Cal. 619.......................98, 471, 474, 477, 503
Gill, Ex parte, 7 East, 376.. 179
Gilliam v. McJunkin, 2 Rich. (S. C., N. S.) 442...................419, 445
Gishwiler et al. v. Dodez, 4 Ohio St. 615...........................583, 585
Gist et al. v. Bowman, 2 Bay, 182.. 401
Glynn et al. v. Hutchinson, 3 Dowl. 529............................... 127
Goff's Case, 3 Mau. & Sel. 202.. 437
Goldsmith, In the Matter of, 24 Kan. 757........................346, 465
Goldswain's Case, 2 W. Black. 1205.........................113, 212, 261
Good et al., Ex parte, 19 Ark. 410................................110, 549
Goodenough, In re, 19 Wis. 274.................................585, 593, 594
Goodhue, In the Matter of, 1 Wheel. Cr. Cas. 427................. 527
Goodin, Ex parte, 67 Mo. 637.......................................445, 451
Goodright v. Dring, 2 Dow. & Ry. 407...........................330, 367
Gorden v. The State, 35 Ala. 452... 373
Gorman, In re, 6 Cent. L. J. 366... 515
Gorsline, In the Matter of, 21 How. Pr. 85........................... 547
Gosline v. Place, 32 Pa. St. 520..........................221, 268, 333, 361
Gosset v. Howard, 10 Ad. & El. Q. B. 411............................ 358
Graham, Ex parte, 4 Wash. 211... 70
Graham v. Graham, 1 Serg. & R. 330..........................225, 593, 594

TABLE OF CASES.

Granice, Ex parte, 51 Cal. 375 .... 305, 365, 474
Gray's Case, 11 Abb. Pr. 56; S. C., 4 Park. Cr. 616 311
Greathouse, In re, 4 Saw. 487 .... 61, 507, 598, 599
Green v. Burke, 23 Wend. 490 489
Green v. The People, 3 Col. 619 474
Greenough, In re, 31 Vt. 270 619
Gregg, In re, 15 Wis. 479 .... 82, 94, 108
Gregg, In the Matter of, 5 N. Y. Leg. Obs. 265 575
Gregg v. Wynn, 22 Ind. 373 92
Gregory, Ex parte, 56 Miss. 164 .... 144, 599
Griffin's Case, Chase, 364 .... 61, 76, 328, 489
Griffin v. Hoskyns, 1 Hurl. & N. 94 136
Griffin v. The State, 5 Tex. App. 457 481
Griffin v. Wilcox, 21 Ind. 370 .... 39, 43
Griffith, Ex parte, 5 Barn. & Ald. 730 100
Grignon's Lessee v. Astor et al., 2 How. 338 .... 274, 275, 341
Griner, In re, 16 Wis. 423 .... 94, 108
Griswold v. Sedgwick, 6 Cow. 456; S. C., 1 Wend. 126 .... 353, 355
Grocot, Ex parte, 2 App. from Mag. to K. B. 594 593
Guilford v. Hicks, 36 Ala. 95 522
Guiteau's Case, 14 Rep. 1 511
Gurney v. Tufts, 37 Me. 130 .... 364, 384
Gurnsey & Knight v. Lovell, 9 Wend. 319 .... 353, 355

H

Hackett, In re, 53 Vt. 354 291
Hackley's Case, 21 How. Pr. 103; S. C., 24 N. Y. 74 445
Hagan v. Lucas, 10 Pet. 400 338
Hagan, Ex parte, 25 Ohio St. 426 502
Hahn v. Kelly, 34 Cal. 391 345
Hakewill, 12 Com. B. 223; S. C., 22 Eng. L. & Eq. 395 ....
 .... 126, 150, 151, 222, 553
Hall, In the Matter of, 10 Mich. 210 436
Halliday's Estate, In re, 17 Jur. 56 509
Halpine, Ex parte, 30 Ind. 254 .... 540, 549
Hamilton, In the Matter of, 1 Ben. 455 .... 59, 62, 220
Hamilton's Case, 3 Dall. 17 .... 57, 278, 332, 509
Hamilton v. Flowers, 57 Miss. 14 .... 240, 250, 522
Hamilton v. Hector, 2 Eng. Rep., Moak's Notes, 393; S. C., L. R., 13
  Eq. Cas. 511 562
Hammel, In the Matter of, 9 R. I. 248 440
Hammond v. Howell, 2 Mod. 219 367
Hammond, John, In the Matter of, 9 Ad. & El., Q. B., 92 . . 150, 189, 190, 335
Hammond v. The People, 32 Ill. 446 .... 145, 463, 467, 519
Hard v. Shipman, 6 Barb. 621 247
Hardy, Ex parte, 68 Ala. 315; S. C., 13 Cent. L. J. 50 .... 399, 433, 453
Harfourd, Ex parte, 16 Fla. 283; S. C., 13 Am. Law Rev. 543 ....
 .... 235, 299, 372, 532, 535, 539, 549
Harris v. Bridges, 57 Ga. 407 350
Harris, In the Matter of, 47 Mo. 164 .... 291, 464, 493
Harrison's Case, 1 Cranch C. Ct. 159 .... 87, 91
Harrison, Ex parte, 2 Smith, 409 152
Hart v. Seixas, 21 Wend. 45 343
Hartman, Ex parte, 44 Cal. 32 .... 324, 471, 474, 476
Harvey v. Huggins, 2 Bailey, 252 468
Hatch, Ex parte, 2 Aik. 28 115
Hathaway v. Holmes, 1 Vt. 417 291
Hansen, In re, 1 Edm. Sel. Cas. 9 .... 583, 584
Hauser v. The State of Wisconsin, 33 Wis. 678 485
Hautefeuille, des Droits et des Devoirs des Nations Neutres, tom. 1 78
Hayne et al., Ex parte, 1 Hughes, 571; S. C., 4 Cent. L. J. 72 .... 409, 487
Hayes, In re, 15 Rep. 259 82
Hazelett v. Ford, 10 Watts, 101 343
Hibler v. The State, 43 Tex. 197 .... 616, 619, 621, 622

TABLE OF CASES. xxxvii

Hickey, Ex parte, 4 Smed. & M. 751.................390, 396, 446, 453, 455
Hight v. United States, 1 Morr. 407..........................535, 537, 539
Hill, Ex parte, 38 Ala., N. S., 458.. 110
Hill, Ex parte, 5 Nev. 154...82, 148, 175, 195
Heath, Mary, Proceedings against, 18 Howell's State Trials, 14, 19..... 255
Heather Children, Matter of the, 50 Mich. 261.....................583, 597
Hebard, Ex parte, 4 Kenyon, 380... 71
Hebard, Ex parte, 4 Dill. 380... 508
Hecker v. Jarret, 3 Binn. 404...84, 116
Heilbonn, Matter of, 1 Park. Cr. 429..................................... 611
Heilbronn, In re, 12 N. Y. Leg. Obs. 65..........................333, 608
Henrich, In re, 5 Blatchf. 414......................333, 606, 607, 608
Henry Arthur, In the Matter of, 29 How. Pr. 187..................... 356
Hernandez v. The State, 4 Tex. App. 425.................................. 92
Herr v. Herr, 5 Pa. St. 428... 343
Herrick's Case, 1 Gray, 50... 102
Herrick v. Smith, 1 Gray, 1.............................365, 474, 491
Herring v. Tyler, 1 Johns. Cas 32... 399
Hetherington v. Reynolds, Fortes. 269.................................... 330
Hewitt, Ex parte, 11 Rich. 325..................................573, 574
Heyward, In the Matter of, 1 Sandf. 701............250, 618, 621, 623
Hobhouse's Case, 2 Chit. 207; S. C., 3 Barn. & Ald. 420.............
....95, 96, 97, 112, 113, 447
Hoffman v. Hoffman, 15 Ohio St. 427..................................... 587
Hoge, Ex parte, 48 Cal. 3... 551
Hoglan v. Carpenter, 4 Bush, 89... 489
Holcomb v. Cornish 8 Conn. 380.. 342
Holley v. The State 15 Fla. 683... 544
Holley v. Mix & Clute, 3 Wend. 350.................................354, 355
Hollingshead's Case, 1 Salk. 351.. 437
Hollingsworth v. Duane, Wall. 46..................................309, 446, 452
Hollis, Ex parte, 59 Cal. 405... 430
Hollman, Ex parte, 23 Iowa, 88..82, 411
Hollwedell, 74 Mo. 403.. 464
Holman v. Mayor of Austin, 34 Tex. 668...............413, 417, 445, 452
Holmes, In re, 19 How. Pr. 32... 579
Holmes v. Jennison, 14 Pet. 540......................................611, 616
Holsey v. Trevillo, 6 Watts, 403.. 101
Hope v. Hope, 8 De G. M. & G. 751... 562
Hopman v. Barber, 2 Stra. 801... 131
Hopson, In the Matter of, 40 Barb. 40..................82, 172, 175, 207
Ho Quan, 8 Pac. C. L. J. 51... 148
Horton v. Auchmoody, 7 Wend. 200.. 247
Hosley, In re, 22 Vt 363.. 291
Hottentot Venus, Case of, 13 East, 194...............................94, 108, 572
Houghton, Ex parte, 7 Fed. Rep. 657...................................60, 503
Houston v. Moore, 5 Wheat. 1.. 613
Hovey et Ux. v. Morris, 7 Blackf. 559.................................... 218
Howard v. People, 3 Mich. 207... 464
Howe v. The State, 9 Mo. 690.. 519
Hoye v. Bush, 1 Man. & G. 775... 355
Hubbard, Ex parte, 35 Ala. 479......................337, 343, 456, 462
Hughes, Matter of, Phill. L. 57....................................615, 618, 624
Hunt v. Hunt, 4 G. Greene, 216.....................................574, 580, 588
Hunter, Ex parte, 16 Fla. 575... 464
Hussey and Wilson, 5 T. R. 254.. 199
Husted's Case, 1 Johns. Cas. 133.. 78
Hutchins v. Player, 1 Bridg. 275...................163, 170, 172, 208
Hyde et al. v. Jenkins, 6 La. 436... 101

I

Inglee v. Coolidge, 2 Wheat. 363.. 139
Irwin, In the Matter of, 9 Cong. Rec. 615................................ 390
Isbell, Ex parte, 11 Nev. 295......................247, 308, 362, 535

xxxviii TABLE OF CASES.

J

Jackson, In re, 12 Am. Law Rev. 602......................618, 625, 626, 627
Jackson v. Boyd, 53 Iowa, 536; S. C., 5 N. W. Rep. 734.............. 463
Jackson, In re, 3 McArthur, 24...................................... 460
Jackson, In the Matter of, 15 Mich. 417.................120, 203, 587, 597
Jackson, Ex parte, 96 U. S. 727..........................332, 496, 510
Jameson v. Schonswar, 1 Dowl. 177................................... 331
Janes v. Cleghorn, 54 Ga. 9.. 580
Janes v. Cleghorn, 63 Ga. 335.. 583
J. C. H., Ex parte, 17 Fla. 362................................471, 494
Jenkes' Case, 6 Howell's State Trials, 1189......................86, 113
Jenkins, Ex parte, 2 Wall. jun. 521....75, 78, 176, 216, 231, 267, 280, 339, 411
Jilz, Ex parte, 64 Mo. 205... 520
Johns v. Emmert, 62 Ind. 533.. 591
Johnson v. Smith, 1 H. Black. 105................................... 132
Johnson v. Terry, 34 Conn. 259............................574, 580, 581
Johnson v. Tompkins et al., 1 Bald. 600............................. 348
Johnson v. United States, 3 McLean, 89......................64, 487, 488
Johnston v. Commonwealth, 1 Bibb, 598............................... 432
Johnston v. Riley, 13 Ga. 97.. 615
Johnstone v. Beattie, 10 Cl. & Fin. 42.............................. 557
Jones v. Danvers, 5 Mee. & W. 234................................... 104
Jones v. Kelly, 17 Mass. 116................................103, 529, 532
Jones v. Leonard, 50 Iowa, 106................................620, 622
Jones v. Spicer, 6 Cow. 391... 188
Jones v. Timberlake, 6 Rand. 678..............................248, 363
Jones, Ex parte, 4 Nev. & M. 340.................................... 104
Jones, Ex parte, 7 Tex. App. 365.................................... 548
Jones, Ex parte, 20 Ark. 9..................................532, 534, 549
Jordan, Peck & Hedges, In re, 2 Am. Law Reg., N. S., 749............ 82

K

Kahn's Case, 11 Abb. Pr. 147; S. C., 19 How. Pr. 475..........423, 448
Kaine, In re, 14 How. 103; S. C., 10 N. Y. Leg. Obs, 257, and 3 Blatchf. 1
    ....57, 66, 71, 72, 96, 227, 240, 279, 333, 509, 519, 606, 607, 608
Kaufman, Ex parte, 73 Mo. 588; S. C., 12 Cent. L. J. 574............ 482
Kearney, Ex parte, 7 Wheat. 38........65, 66, 70, 108, 276, 278, 392, 408
Kearney, Ex parte, 55 Cal. 212; S. C., 5 Pac. C. L. J. 549; 14 Am. Law
    Rev. 675.....................67, 295, 310, 323, 345, 471, 486, 494
Kearney's Case, 13 Abb. Pr. 459; S. C., 22 How. Pr. 309............. 424
Keating v. Spink, 3 Ohio St. 105.................................... 339
Keeler, In the Matter of, 1 Hempst. 306...................78, 82, 94, 195
Keeling, 50 Ala. 474.. 110
Keen v. McDonough, 8 La. 185.. 474
Kelley, 9 Am. Law Rev. 167.. 606
Kelley v. Thomas, 15 Gray, 192...................................... 372
Kellogg, Ex parte, 6 Vt. 509.......................291, 342, 514, 515, 517
Kelly and Dodge's Case, 37 Ala. 474.............................78, 82
Kelsey v. Parmelee, 15 Conn. 260.................................... 354
Kemp, In re, 16 Wis. 359.............................40, 78, 148, 153, 338
Kempe's Lessee v. Kennedy et al., 5 Cranch, 173..................... 340
Kendal et al., 5 Mod. 83.. 163
Kentucky v. Dennison, 24 How. 66.............................615, 616, 618
Kenyon, Ex parte, 5 Dill. 385........................61, 64, 70, 276, 512
Ker, Ex parte, 16 Rep. 580.. 602
Keyes v. The United States, 3 Sup. Ct. Rep. 202..................... 67
Kimball, Moore & Stone, 9 Law Rep. (Mass.) 500...................... 78
King v. Armiger, 1 Keb. 272....................................131, 133
King v. Barber, 2 Keny. 289... 401
King v. Bethel, 5 Mod. 21......................................149, 155, 227
King v. Bethuen, Andr. 281.. 203
King v. Bourne et al., 7 Ad. & El., 58........................498, 502
King v. Bowerbank, Skin. 676.. 202

TABLE OF CASES. xxxix

King v. Brooke, 2 T. R. 190... 524
King v. Bythell, 12 Mod. 75......... .... 194, 518
King v. Clerk, 1 Salk. 348............................. 149, 194, 209
King v. Crisp, 2 Stra. 271..... 525
King v. Dean and Chapter of Trinity Chapel, etc., 8 Mod. 27........ 518
King v. De Manneville, 5 East, 220......................... 558, 560, 562
King v. Despard, 7 T. R. 736. 360
King v. Dobbin, 4 Ad. & El. 644.................................... 555
King v. Earl Mountnorris, Reid et al., 1 Ridg. 460 200
King v. Earl of Orrery et al., 8 Mod. 98......................... 38, 39
King v. Edwards, 7 T. R. 745...................................107, 593
King v. Ellis, 5 Barn. & Cress. 395............................498, 502
King v. Fowler, Fortes. 243.. 117
King v. Greenway, 2 Show. 172...............................131, 151
King v. Gibson, Fortes. 272.. 201
King v. Hawkins, Fortes. 272....................................... 201
King v. Hobhouse, 2 Chit. 207; S. C., 3 Barn. & Ald. 420....257, 392, 393, 438
King v. Horner, Leach, 270... 376
King v. Inhabitants of Winwick, 8 T. R. 454....................... 355
King v. James, 1 Dow. & Ry. 559; S. C., 5 Barn. & Ald. 894.......... 437
King v. Jones, 1 Barn. & Ald. 209.................................. 367
King v. Judd, 2 T. R. 455.. 369
King v. Justices, 1 Mau. & Sel. 442................................ 505
King v. Kendal and Roe, 1 Salk. 346................................ 360
Ring v. Lyme Regis, 1 Doug. 158...............................160, 161
King v. Marks, 3 East, 157.........................283, 332, 525, 527
King v. Marsh, Bulst., part 3, p. 27............................... 96
King v. Massey, 6 Mau. & Sel. 108.................................. 367
King v. Mayor of Saltash, 2 Show. 96 ....550, 552
King v. Nagapen, 2 Notes of Cases at Madras, 253 589
King v. Penelope, 7 Mod. 235....................................... 262
King v. Reynolds, 6 T. R. 497 ....107, 593
King v. Rogers, 3 Dow. & Ry. 607................................... 261
King v. Rogers, 1 Dow. & Ry. 156................................... 335
King v. Smith, 7 Mod. 234; S. C., Ld. Hardwicke's Rep. 149, and 2 Stra.
  967.. 595
King v. Smith, 7 Mod. 235.. 172
King v. Soper, 5 T. R. 278... 589
King v. Suddis, 1 East, 306....................72, 96, 203, 204, 381, 518
King v. Taylor et al., 7 Dow. & Ry. 622............................ 335
King v. Walker, 1 Leach Cas. in Crown Law, 98...................... 527
King v. Weir et al., 1 Barn. & Cress. 288.......................... 354
King v. Wilkes, 2 Wils. 151....................................359, 360
King v. Wilson, 4 Ad. & El. 644................................555, 559
King v. Winton, 5 T. R. 89....................................151, 152, 182
Kingbury's Case, 106 Mass. 223.................................621, 622
Kinney, Ex parte, 3 Hughes, 9; S. C., 1 Crim. L. Mag. 268......64, 72, 509
Kinniston's Case, 9 Law. Rep. (Mass.) 548........................... 78
Kirby v. The State, 62 Ala. 51........337, 462, 471, 474, 478, 496, 507
Kirk's Case, 5 Mod. 455.. 546
Kite v. Commonwealth, 11 Met. 582.................................. 459
Kittrel, Ex parte, 20 Ark. 499................................92, 339, 546
Klepper, Ex parte, 26 Ill. 532.................................89, 236
Kline et al. v. Kline et al., 57 Iowa, 386.....................501, 583, 586
Knox, Ex parte, 1 Bos. & Pul. 148.................................. 589
Kottman, In the Matter of, 2 Hill (S. C.), 363..................... 582
Krans et al., Ex parte, 1 Barn. & Cress. 25; S. C., 2 Dow. & Ry. 411...
  ....178, 367, 368
Kreiger, Ex parte, 7 Mo. App. 337.....................393, 406, 452, 454

L

Ladow v. Groom, 1 Denio, 429....................................... 363
La Fonta, Ex parte, 2 Rob. (La.) 495............................... 519

TABLE OF CASES.

Lagrave, In the Matter of, 45 How. Pr. 301; S. C., 14 Abb. Pr., N. S., 333..603, 611
Lampon, Ex parte, 3 Deac. & Ch. 751...............................261, 272
Lampon, In the Matter of, 3 Deac. & Ch. 751.......................... 261
Lane, Ex parte, 18 Wall. 163....................57, 65, 67, 70, 276, 332
333, 336, 392, 406, 435, 462, 463, 471, 494, 495, 499, 500, 505, 506, 509
Langdon, Ex parte, 25 Vt. 680....................................430, 452
Langston, Ex parte, 8 Ohio St. 599.................................... 338
Laren v. Brown, 34 Ga. 583.. 333
Lark v. The State of Georgia, 55 Ga. 435.......................106, 497, 521
Larrabee v. Selby, 52 Id. 508.. 430
Lauge, Ex parte, 6 Fed. Rep. 34...................................609, 610
Lawes v. Hutchinson, 3 Dowl. P. C. 506................................ 526
Lawler, Ex parte, 28 Ind. 241.. 393
Lawrence, Ex parte, 5 Binn. 304...............................92, 238, 522
Lawson v. Buzines, 3 Harr. (Del.) 418.................................. 348
Lawson's Case, 3 Cro. Car. 507... 526
Lea v. White, 4 Sneed, 73......................................107, 219, 519, 593
Leach, In re, 51 Vt. 630, app.. 441
Leary's Case, 6 Abb. N. C. 43; S. C., 10 Ben. 197, and 1 Crim. L. Mag. 265....................................219, 220, 334, 622, 625, 626, 627, 629
Le Bur, Ex parte, 2 Cent. L. J. 122.................................... 78
Lees, Ex parte, El. Bl. & El. 828...............................336, 367, 552
Leland, Matter of, 7 Abb. Pr., N. S., 64........................618, 619, 623
Leverick v. Mercer, 14 Ad. & El. Q. B. 759............................ 354
Levy v. Shurman, 6 Ark. 182... 345
Lewis v. Brackenridge, 1 Blackf. 112................................... 268
Linda v. Hudson, 1 Cush. 385.......................................99, 572
Lindsey v. Lindsey, 14 Ga. 657... 586
Lippman, In the Matter of, 3 Ben. 95.................................. 62
Lister's Case, 8 Mod. 22... 554
Livingston v. Livingston, 24 Ga. 379................................... 333
Lloyd, In re, 3 Man. & G. 547; S. C., 4 Scott N. R. 200.......562, 563, 589
Lloyd, In re, 3 Man. & G. 547....................................562, 564
Lockhart v. John, 7 Pa. St. 137.. 343
Lockington's Case, Bright. 269... 78
Lockwood v. The State, 1 Ind. (Cart.) 161............................. 416
Loder v. Phelps, 13 Wend. 46.. 267
Logan v. The State, 3 Brev. 415....................................... 545
Logan's Case, 5 Gratt. 692... 463
Long, In the Matter of, 2 Winst. 150................................. 43
Longworth's Case, 7 La. Ann. 247..................................550, 551
Lord Mayor of London's Case, 3 Wils. 199............................. 524
Lord Mohun's Case, 1 Salk. 104.. 525
Lorraine, Ex parte, 16 Nev. 63... 623
Lough v. Millard, 2 R. I. 436.. 364
Lovejoy v. Webber, 10 Mass. 101..................................108, 516
Lumly v. Quarry, 7 Mod. 9... 489
Lumm v. The State, 3 Port. (Ind.) 293............90, 99, 115, 521, 538, 549
Lynch v. The State, 38 Ill. 494...................................545, 549
Lynde v. Noble, 20 Johns. 80.. 334
Lyon v. Lyon, 21 Conn. 185.. 421
Lyons v. Blenkin, Jac. 255..556, 557

M

Macready v. Wilcox, 33 Conn. 321...................................... 596
Magennis v. Parkhurst, 3 Green's Ch. 433.............................. 399
Mahone, Ex parte, 30 Ala. 49.................................110, 234, 298, 301
Manchester, In re, 5 Cal. 237..................................618, 619, 621, 622
Manneville v. Manneville, 10 Ves. 53.................................. 556
Maples v. Maples, 49 Miss. 393......................................91, 578
Marbury v. Madison, 1 Cranch, 137..................................... 278
Marbury v. Madison, 1 Cranch, 170..................................... 275
Maria v. Kirby, 12 B. Mon. 550.. 522

TABLE OF CASES. xli

Marks, Ex parte, Sup. Ct. Cal., Opin. filed July 24, 1883 598
Marks, Ex parte, 49 Cal. 680 551
Martin, In re, 5 Blatchf. 303 .... 281, 332
Martin, In re, 4 Dow. & L. 768 261
Martin, In the Matter of, 3 Prac. Rep. (U. C.) 298 362
Martin, Matter of, 45 Barb. 142 82
Martin's Case, 1 Bright. Dig. 1240 99
Martins, Ex parte, 9 Dowl. 194 131
Mash's Case, 2 W. Black. 804 151
Mason, Ex parte, 14 Rep. 193 67
Mason, Ex parte, 105 U. S. 696 514
Mason, In re, 8 Mich. 70 .... 107, 220, 245, 246, 372, 458
Mathews v. Wade et Ux., 2 W. Va. 464 .... 219, 595
Mathews, Contractor, v. Walker, Sheriff, 57 Miss. 337 144
Maulsby, Ex parte, 13 Md. 625 app. 392, 421, 441, 448, 450
May v. Shumway, 16 Gray, 86 103
Mayo v. Wilson, 1 N. H. 53 355
McCall v. McDowell, 1 Pac. L. Mag. 360; S. C., 1 Abb. U. S. Rep. 212.. 39
McCann, Ex parte, 5 Am. Law Reg., N. S., 158 63
McCardle, Ex parte, 6 Wall. 318; S. C., 7 Id. 506, and 1 Hughes, 598 ...
.... 57, 58, 278, 472, 509
McClellan, Ex parte, 1 Dow P. C. 81 555
McCoy v. The State, 25 Tex. 33 537
McConnell v. The State, 13 Tex. App. 390 .... 532, 536, 541, 548
McConologue's Case, 107 Mass. 154 .... 82, 520, 595
McCready, Ex parte, 1 Hughes, 598 512
McCready v. Virginia, 94 U. S 391 512
McCready v. Wilcox, 33 Conn. 321 521
McCullough, Ex parte, 35 Cal. 97 .... 84, 293, 305, 313
McCullough v. State of Maryland, 4 Wheat. 423 275
McCullough, Ex parte, 35 Cal. 88 474
McDonald, In the Matter of, 9 Am. Law Reg. 661 .... 59, 78, 279
McDonald, Emmett, In the Matter of, 9 Am. Law Reg. 692 278
McDonnell, In re, 11 Blatchf. 79; S. C., 11 Id. 170 ....
.... 69, 333, 606, 607, 609, 610, 611, 625, 628
McDowles, In the Matter of, 8 Johns. 328 .... 582, 593
McFarland v. Johnson, 27 Tex. 105 .... 519, 521
McGear v. Woodruff, 33 N. J. L. 213 379
McGill, Ex parte, 6 Tex. App. 498 .... 456, 471, 473, 474, 480, 521
McIntyre, In re, 5 Gilm. 422 236
McIver v. Wattles, 9 Wheat. 650 139
McKean, Ex parte, 3 Hughes, 23 .... 621, 625, 626
McKee, Ex parte, 18 Mo. 599 .... 393, 445
McKinney, 5 Tex. App. 500 .... 537, 549
McLaughlin, 41 Cal. 211 544
McLeod's Case, 1 Hill (N. Y.) 377; S. C., 25 Wend. 482; 37 Am. Dec.
  328; 26 Wend. 663, and 3 Hill (N. Y.), 635 .... 77, 102, 300, 316
McPherson v. Cunliff, 11 Serg. & R. 422 .... 275, 343
McRoberts, Ex parte, 16 Iowa, 600 82
McShan v. McShan, 56 Miss. 413 .... 578, 583
Mead v. Haws, 7 Cow. 332 355
Meade v. The Dept. Marshal, etc., 2 Wheel. Cr. Cas. 569 514
Melvin v. Fisher, 8 N. H. 406 353
Mercein v. The People, 25 Wend. 63 ...... 336, 520, 555, 566, 574, 577, 579
Merryman, Ex parte, 9 Am. Law Reg. 524; S. C., 1 Taney's Dec. 246.. 39
Merryman v. Morgan, 7 Or. 68 287
Mess, Ex parte, 12 Pac. C. L. J. 279 .... 471, 474, 475
Metzger, In the Matter of, 1 Barb. 248; S. C., 5 How. 176 ....
.... 57, 67, 279, 509, 606, 607, 608
Miles, In re, 52 Vt. 609 624
Milford v. Milford, L. R., 1 Prob. & Div. 715 569
Milburn, Ex parte, 9 Pet. 704 .... 66, 72, 606
Miller, Mary, In the Matter of, 1 Abb. N. C. 1, note 387
Miller v. Finkle, 1 Park. Cr. 374 .... 505, 506

TABLE OF CASES.

Miller v. Rosier, 31 Mich. 475... 365
Miller v. The State, 43 Tex. 579....................................533, 549
Miller v. Snyder, 6 Ind. (Port. 1)............471, 472, 473, 487, 488, 521
Millett v. Baker, 42 Barb. 215... 359
Millington, Ex parte, 24 Kan. 214....................................... 100
Milligan, Ex parte, 4 Wall. 2..39, 40, 42, 57, 65, 69, 72, 94, 97, 108, 109, 514
Milwaukee Industrial School v. Supervisors of Milwaukee Co., 40 Wis. 328... 349
Mitchell v. Mitcheson, 1 Barn. & Cress. 513............................. 367
Mitchell, In re, R. M. Charlt. 489........350, 555, 571, 572, 574, 582, 583
Mitchell, Ex parte, 1 La. Ann. 413...................................... 519
Money v. Leach, 3 Burr. 1742; S. C., 1 W. Black. 555, 563........352, 355
Moore, In re, 11 I. R. C. L. 1... 564
Moore, Ex parte, 62 Ala. 471... 479
Moore et al., Ex parte, 64 N. C. 815..................................... 106
Moore v. Christian, 56 Miss. 408......................578, 579, 585, 586
Moore v. Ewing & Bowen, 1 Coxe, 146..................................... 257
Moore v. The State, 36 Miss. 137............................531, 535, 549
Morris v. Marcy, 4 Ohio, 84.. 309
Morton, In the Matter of, 10 Mich. 208..........................358, 436
Munns v. Dupont de Nemours, 3 Wash. 31................................. 357
Murphy v. The People, 2 Cow. 815... 379
Murray, Ex parte, 43 Cal. 455.......................................345, 461, 465
Musgrove v. Kornegay et al., 7 Jones, 71.........................593, 594

N

Nash's Case, 4 Barn. & Ald. 295.. 164
Nash v. The People, 36 N. Y. 607... 110
Nauer v. Thomas, 13 Allen, 572... 76
Neel v. State, 9 Ark. 259.. 452
Nelson & Graydon v. Cutter & Tyrrell, 3 McLean, 326.........................
....61, 216, 268, 366, 516
Neill, In re, 8 Blatch. 156...............................151, 176, 207, 411
New Orleans v. Steamship Co., 20 Wall. 387........................301, 411
Newton, In re, 16 Com. B. 97; S. C., 30 Eng. L. & Eq. 432; 2 Smith, 617, and 24 L. J., N. S. C. P., 148..........................93, 488, 553
Nicholls v. The State, 5 N. J. L. 539..............................372, 374
Nichols v. Cornelius, 7 Port. 611.....................117, 218, 521, 622
Nickols v. Giles, 2 Root, 461......................................575, 583
Nixon, Ex parte, 2 S. C., N. S., 4....................................... 106
Noonan v. Bradley, 12 Wall. 129.. 505
Norris v. Newton et al., 5 McLean, 99.................................... 78
Nye, Ex parte, 8 Kan. 99...88, 465

O

O'Conner, In re, 6 Wis. 288.............................288, 465, 485
O'Conner, Matter of, 48 Barb. 258.. 82
Oldfield v. Cobbett, 22 Eng. Ch. Rep. 289; S. C., 2 Ph. 289............. 190
Oliver, In re, 17 Wis. 681... 42
Oliver, Ex parte, 2 Ves. & B. 244..................................180, 212
Olmstead's Case, Bright, 9... 78
Olmsted v. Hoyt, 4 Day, 436.. 474
O'Malia v. Wentworth, 65 Me. 129...................................383, 387, 474
O. & M. R. R. Co. v. Fitch, 20 Ind. 498................................. 82
O'Neal, Petitioner, 3 Am. Law Rev. 578.............................577, 581, 586
Onslow's and Whalley's Case, 9 L. R., Q. B., 229........................ 394
Ooton v. The State, 5 Ala. 464... 463
Opinions Att'y Gen. N. Y., 1796-1872, 518................................ 464

P

Page, Ex parte, 1 Barn. & Ald. 568.................................165, 208
Page, Ex parte, 49 Mo. 291.........................445, 451, 502, 507
Painter v. Henderson, 7 Pa. St. 48....................................... 343

Pardy, Ex parte, 1 Lownd. Max. & Pol. 26	108
Park v. Torre, 6 Moore, 260	135
Parker v. The State, 5 Tex. App. 579............484, 493,	538
Parker et al., 5 Mee. & W. 31; S. C., 7 Dowl. 208	93
Parker and Sawyer, Ex parte, 11 Neb. 309	292
Parks, Ex parte, 93 U. S. 18; S. C., 16 Am. L. Reg., N. S., 84, and 1 Hughes, 604...61, 65, 66, 67, 70, 75, 276, 332, 435, 471, 474, 475, 482,	511
Parrish v. The State 14 Md. 233	374
Parsons, Levi, Impeachment of, 1 Cal., app	446
Parsons v. Loyd, 3 Wils. 341	359
Partington, Ex parte, 51 Eng. Com. L. 648; S. C., 13 Mee. & W. 679, and 2 Dow. & L. 650...............72, 96, 240, 331,	518
Patterson v. United States, 2 Wheat. 221............332,	356
Patterson v. Pressley, 70 Ind. 94.................472, 473,	477
Pattison, Ex parte, 56 Miss. 161..........241, 522, 543, 544,	546
Paul v. Vankirk, 6 Binn. 123	354
Payne v. Payne, 39 Ga. 174	596
Payson, In re, 23 Kan. 757	492
Peacock v. Bell & Kendal, 1 Saund. 73............341, 342,	359
Pearson, Ex parte, 59 Ala. 654	465
Pease v. Shrimpton, Styles, 261	526
Peck v. Jenness, 7 How. 612	411
Pember's Case, 1 Whart. 439....................107,	459
Pender v. Herle, 3 Bro. P. C. 505	518
Pennoyer v. Neff, 95 U. S. 714	501
Penryce and Wynn's Case, 2 Mod. 306..............86,	113
People v. Alexander, 2 Am. Law Reg. 44	102
People ex rel. Trainer v. Baker, 80 N. Y. 460......92, 169, 173, 180, 209, 247, 269, 343, 475, 500,	503
People v. Ball, 5 Cow. 415	399
People v. Beigler, 3 Park. Cr. 316	533
People ex rel. Nickerson v. ———, 19 Wend. 16.......573, 577,	578
People v. Bowe, 58 How. Pr. 393	533
People ex rel. Cowley v. Bowe, 58 How. Pr. 393.........532,	551
People ex rel. Thayer v. Bowe, 20 Hun, 547; S. C., 21 Id. 614	460
People v. Brady, 56 N. Y. 182............519, 520, 615, 617, 618, 619,	622
People v. Bradley, 60 Ill. 390........110, 127, 252, 333, 401,	454
People v. Brooks, 35 Barb. 85	578
People v. Brown, 6 Cow. 41	399
People v. Burtnett, 13 Abb. Pr. 8; S. C., 5 Park. Cr. 113............88,	521
People ex rel. Waldron v. Carpenter, etc., 46 Barb. 619	246
People v. Cassels, 5 Hill, 164...........116, 186, 293, 418, 421,	448
People v. Carrique, 2 Hill (N. Y.), 93	489
People v. Cavanagh, 2 Park. Cr. 650; S. C., 2 Abb. Pr. 84......172, 180, 336, 343, 383, 471, 474, 475, 477,	521
People ex rel. Ordronaux v. Chegary, 18 Wend. 637...92, 128, 575, 579,	586
People v. Cole, 6 Park. Cr. 695..........532, 536, 539, 543, 544,	546
People v. Commissioners, etc., 9 Hun, 212	388
People ex rel. Walters v. Conner, 15 Abb. Pr., N. S., 430......106, 373,	422
People ex rel. Trainer v. Cooper, 8 How. Pr. 288........521, 571, 573,	590
People v. Cowles, 34 How. Pr. 481; S. C., 4 Keyes, 38, and 3 Abb. App. Dec. 507...........376, 427,	507
People ex rel. Rosenthal v. Cowles, 59 How. Pr. 287..............91,	572
People v. Cunningham, 3 Park. Cr. 531................336,	519
People v. Curtis, 50 N. Y. 321..........611,	616
People v. Divine, 21 How. Pr. 80; S. C., 11 Abb. Pr. 90, and 5 Park. Cr. 62............102,	248
People v. Dixon, 4 Park. Cr. 651........532, 535, 536, 537, 539,	542
People v. Donohue, 84 N. Y. 438	622
People v. Donohue, 14 Hun, 133	334
People ex rel. Johnson v. Erbert, 17 Abb. Pr. 395................574,	583
People ex rel. Eldridge et al. v. Fancher, 3 N. Y. Sup. Ct. 189; S. C., 1 Hun, 27...........516,	519
People v. Fiske, 45 How. Pr. 294..................625,	628

TABLE OF CASES.

People v. Forbes, 4 Park. Cr. 611................ ....379, 380, 383, 384
People ex rel. Davis v. Foster, 104 Ill. 156...................471, 474, 475
People v. Fullerton, 10 Hun, 63.. 336
People v. Gaul, 44 Barb. 98; S. C., 5 Am. Law Reg., N. S., 380 .....42, 82
People v. Gates, 39 How. Pr. 74.......................................593, 594
People v. Gilmore, 26 Hun, 1..426, 572
People v. Goodhue, 2 Johns. Ch. 198................................... 614
People v. Goodwin, 1 Wheel. Cr. Cas. 434............................ 527
People v. Gray, 4 Park. Cr. 616.....................................381, 383
People v. Hackley, 24 N. Y. 74........392, 406, 414, 416, 417, 445, 451, 454
People ex rel. Philmot v. Hessing, 28 Ill. 410.........245, 247, 463, 549
People v. Hicks, 15 Barb. 153.. 448
People v. Hoster, 14 Abb. Pr., N. S., 414.........................593, 594
People v. Humphreys, 24 Barb. 521..............................333, 573
People v. Hyler, 2 Park. Cr. 570..........................532, 537, 540
People ex rel. Woolf v. Jacobs, 66 N. Y. 8......................424, 500
People v. Kehl, 15 Mich. 33... 115
People v. Keeper etc., 37 How. Pr. 494................................ 458
People ex rel. Caldwell v. Kelly, 35 Barb. 444...................... 336
People ex rel. Hackley v. Kelly, 21 How. 54; S. C., 12 Abb. Pr. 150...
....414, 416, 445, 451
People v. Kling, 6 Barb. 366.............................336, 571, 583, 590
People v. Landt, 2 Johns. 374... 590
People v. Lincoln, 25 Hun, 306... 464
People ex rel. Tweed v. Liscomb, 60 N. Y. 559; S. C., 11 Alb. L. J. 396,
  and 19 Am. Rep. 211..344, 345, 387,
  ....388, 448, 451, 463, 471, 472, 474, 488, 494, 495, 500, 501, 521
People v. Lohman, 2 Barb. 450...533, 535, 551
People v. Lomax, 6 Abb. Pr. 139... 102
People v. Manley, 2 How. Pr. 61..................................92, 128, 129
People v. Markham, 7 Cal. 208.. 464
People v. Martin, 1 Park. Cr. 187....................283, 297, 300, 315
People v. Mason, 9 Wend. 505 101
People v. Mayer, 16 Barb. 362......................................334, 336
People v. McCarthy, 45 How. Pr. 97.................................... 379
People v. McCormack, 4 Park. Cr. 9.........................244, 295, 336
People v. McLeod, 1 Hill (N. Y.), 377; S. C., 26 Wend. 697...........
  ....248, 300, 315, 357, 474, 527, 535, 539, 542
People v. McLeod, 3 Hill (N. Y.), 647; S. C., 26 Wend. 697..........
  ....110, 116, 180, 186, 197, 293, 522
People ex rel. Barry v. Mercein, 3 Hill (N. Y.) 399; S. C., 8 Paige, 47..
  ......101, 117, 145, 219, 520, 556, 557, 572, 573, 578, 579, 585, 588, 595
People v. Mitchell et al., 44 Barb. 245.................. 590
People v. Mitchell, Sheriff etc., 29 Barb. 622........................ 337
People v. Moore et al., 3 Park. Cr. 465..........................311, 383
People v. Nash, 5 Park. Cr. 473; S. C., 25 How. Pr. 307, and 16 Abb.
  Pr. 281... 110
People v. Neilson, 16 Hun, 214...237, 465
People v. Nevins, 1 Hill (N. Y.), 154........................154, 155, 156,
  ......195, 200, 200, 355, 362, 400, 430, 448, 449, 450, 451, 453, 474, 475
People v. Olmstead, 27 Barb. 1.................................573, 577, 588
People ex rel. Hinckley v. Pirfenbrink, 96 Ill. 68.................... 440
People v. Pelham, 14 Wend. 48.. 115
People v. Perry, 8 Abb. Pr., N. S., 27.................................... 544
People v. Phillips, 1 Park. Cr. 95................................379, 380, 383, 384
People v. Pillow, 1 Sand. 672... 593
People v. Pinkerton, 17 Hun, 199; S. C., 77 N. Y. 245............620, 622
People v. Porter, 1 Duer, 709.............................555, 571, 585, 588
People v. Potter, 1 Park. Cr. 47.. 598
Pearson and Rawlings, 1 East, 77...
People v. Rhoner, 4 Park. Cr. 166..................................372, 374
People v. Richardson, 4 Park. Cr. 656; S. C., 18 How. Pr. 92........
  ....242, 297, 298, 317, 365
People ex rel. Roddy v. N. Y. Juv. Asylum, 12 Abb. Pr. 92............ 575

TABLE OF CASES. xlv

People v. Roff, 3 Park. Cr. 216................................... 493
People v. Rulloff, 5 Park. Cr. 77..............314, 317, 318, 319, 325
People v. Schenck, 2 Johns. 478.................................. 614
People v. Schuster, 40 Cal. 627..............................522, 532
People ex rel. Utley v. Seaton & White, 25 Hun, 305; S. C., Gould's
   Ann. Dig. N. Y. 181 (1881).................................469, 515
People v. Sennott, 20 Alb. L. J. 230; S. C., 1 Crim. L. Mag. 265....... 620
People v. Shea, 3 Park. Cr. 562.................................. 175
People v. Sheriff, 7 Abb. Pr. 96; S. C., 29 Barb. 622..........417, 445, 448
People ex rel. Hewlett v. Sheriff Brennan, 61 Barb. 540.............. 115
People v. Smith, 1 Cal. 1............181, 195, 357, 362, 365, 372, 535, 543
People v. Stanley & Stewart, 18 How. Pr. 179...................... 297
People v. Stephens, 5 Hill (N. Y.) 616.........................327, 489
People v. Stilwell, 10 N. Y. 531.................................. 334
People v. Supervisors of Queens, 1 Hill (N. Y.) 195................. 334
People v. Supt. House of Refuge, 8 Abb. Pr. N. S. 112.............. 220
People ex rel. McCabe v. Supt. etc., 8 Abb. Pr., N. S., 112.......... 294
People v. Tefft, 3 Cow. 340...................................... 399
People v. Tinder, 19 Cal. 187, 539..........530, 532, 537, 539, 540, 543, 545
People v. Tompkins, 1 Park. Cr. 224.............294, 295, 297, 298, 366
People v. Town, 3 Scam. 19...................................... 533
People v. Turley, 50 Cal. 469..................................... 463
People ex rel. Stokes v. Warden, etc., 66 N. Y. 342................. 464
People v. Van Horne, 8 Barb. 158......................532, 537, 542, 544
People v. Warner, 45 How. Pr. 97................................ 379
People v. Weissenbach et al., 60 N. Y. 385...................584, 593, 594
People v. White, 24 Wend. 520................................... 489
People v. Wilcox, 22 Barb. 178.....219, 570, 571, 576, 583, 585, 588, 596
People v. Willett, 6 Abb. Pr. 37; S. C., 26 Barb. 78; S. C., 15 How.
   Pr. 210..85, 466, 535
People v. Wright, 2 Cai. 212...................................... 614
People v. Ybarra, 17 Cal. 171..................................... 463
Peoples, In the Matter of, 47 Mich. 626; S. C., 15 Rep. 828........314, 545
Percy, In the Matter of, 2 Daly, 530.......372, 411, 430, 445, 451, 453, 552
Perham, In re, 5 Hurl. & N. 30................................... 361
Perkins v. Fairfield, 11 Mass. 227................................. 275
Perkins, In the Matter of, 2 Cal. 424..........................240, 519
Perkins, Ex parte, 18 Cal. 60.........................416, 421, 428, 445
Perry, Re, 30 Wis. 268... 288
Perry v. The State, 41 Tex. 488.................................. 238
Perrin v. West, 3 Ad. & El. 405..............................256, 272
Perry, In re, 30 Wis. 268... 485
Perry et al. v. McLendon, Sheriff, 62 Ga. 598...................... 519
Perry v. The State, 41 Tex. 488.................................. 481
Peter v. The State, 3 How. (Miss.) 433.......................372, 374
Peters, Ex parte, 12 Fed. Rep. 461; S. C., 4 Dill. 169............... 504
Petrie v. Fitzgerald, 1 Daly, 401.................................. 604
Pettier v. Pennington et al., 14 N. J. L. 312...................292, 515
Petty's Case, 22 Kan. 477; S. C., 9 Cent. L. J. 135..........471, 474, 479
Pfitzer, Ex parte, 28 Ind. 450..................................... 622
Phelan's Case, 9 Abb. Pr. 286..................................... 82
Pike v. Hanson, 9 N. H. 493..................................... 348
Pitman, Matter of, 1 Curt. 186.................................... 400
Place, In the Matter of, 34 How. Pr. 259......................... 522
Platt v. Harrison, 6 Iowa, 79................................344, 493, 496
Pleasant's Case, 11 Am. Jur. 257................................. 78
Poole, In re, 2 MacArthur, 583..............572, 583, 584, 585, 587, 595
Pong Ah Lung, In re, 16 Fed. Rep. 577........................... 64
Pong Ah Lung, 12 Pac. C. L. J. 67................................ 228
Potts v. Chumasero, 92 U. S. 358................................ 519
Power, In the Matter of, 2 Russ. 583............................. 209
Power and Jackson, In the Matter of, 2 Russ. 583...............170, 172
Powers, In re, 25 Vt. 261.. 291
Pray, In the Matter of, 60 How. Pr. 194....................577, 578, 583

xlvi TABLE OF CASES.

President of Orphans' Court v. Groff, 14 Serg. & R. 181 .... **343**
Preston, In re, 5 Dow. & L. 247 564
Price, In re, 2 F. & F. 263 554
Price v. Graham et al., 3 Jones, 545 358
Prigg v. Commonwealth of Pennsylvania, 16 Pet. 539 ....
....613, 614, 616, 625, 628
Prime, In the Matter of, 1 Barb. 340 ....181, 233, 234, 304, 365
Prince v. The State, 37 Tex. 477 342
Prohibitory Amendment Cases, 24 Kan. 700 456
Providence Bank v. Billings & Pittman, 4 Pet. 563 275
Pulbrook, In re, 11 Jur. 185 ....558, 559, 562

Q

Queen v. Baines, 12 Ad. & El. 210 ....187, 272
Queen v. Batchelder, 1 Per. & Dav. 516; S. C., 9 Ad. & El. 731, and 36 Eng. Com. L. 285 ....172, 262
Queen v. Boyle, 3 Prac. Rep. (U. C.) 270; S. C., 4 Prac. Rep. (U. C.) 256 ....148, 214, 364
Queen v. Chantrell, 10 L. R., Q. B., 38 Vict. 587 383
Queen v. Clarke, In the Matter of Race, 7 El. & Bl. 186; S. C., 26 L. J., N. S., Q. B., 169, and 40 Eng. L. & Eq., 109 ....561, 562, 563, 564
Queen v. Gossett, 3 Per. & Dav. 349 448
Queen v. Lefroy, 8 L. R. Q. B. 134 ....393, 394
Queen v. Leggatt, 18 Ad. & El. Q. B. 781 554
Queen v. Mickal, 11 Mod. 261 525
Queen v. Mount & Morris, 12 Eng. Rep., Moak's notes, 181 ....205, 371
Queen v. Paty et al., 2 Salk. 503; S. C., 2 Ld. Raym. 1105 518
Queen v. Richards, Bird, et al., 5 Ad. & El. Q. B. 926; S. C., 48 Eng. Com. L. 926 ....188, 208
Queen v. Smith, In re Boreham, 22 L. J., N. S., Q. B., 116; S. C., 17 Jur. 24, and 16 Eng. L. & Eq. 221 ....561, 568
Queen v. Tordoft, 5 Ad. & El. Q. B. 933 ....189, 190
Quong Woo, In the Matter of, 9 Pac. C. L. J. 815 60

R

Rafter, In the Matter of, 2 Winst. 153 43
Ralston, Ex parte, R. M. Charlt. 119 ....584, 595, 596
Randall v. Bridge, 2 Mass. 549 ....209, 210
Randolph, Ex parte, 2 Brock. 447 ....59, 72, 85, 519
Randon, Ex parte, 12 Tex. App. 145 ....538, 542, 548
Ratcliff's Case, 3 Co. Rep. 37, note 13 564
Rea, Re, 14 Cox C. C. 256 202
Reardon's Case, 2 Cranch C. Ct. 639 59
Reddill's Case, 1 Whart. 445 ....107, 459
Redfield v. Cabell et al., Willes, 411 359
Reed, Ex parte, 100 U. S. 13 ....67, 381, 382, 474, 513
Reeves v. Reeves, 75 Ind. 342 577
Regina v. Andrews, 2 Dow. & L. 10 ....525, 545
Regina v. Bartlett, 7 Jur. 649; S. C., 12 L. J., N. S., M. C. 127 361
Regina v. Clark, 40 Eng. L. & Eq. 114 349
Regina v. Chaney, 6 Dowl. P. C. 281 ....335, 368, 382
Regina v. Day, 3 F. & F. 526 104
Regina v. Douglas, 7 Jur. 39; S. C., 12 Law Jour. Rep. (N. S.) 49..215, 261
Regina v. Gavin, 15 Jur. 329 401
Regina v. Harris, 4 Cox C. C. 21 550
Regina v. Inhabitants of Cartworth, 1 Dow. & L. 837 368
Regina v. Martin, 2 Ad. & El. Q. B. 1037 335
Regina v. Mayor of Derby, 2 Salk. 436 435
Regina v. Nesbitt, 2 Dow. & L. 529 ....194, 354
Regina v. Newton et al., 1 Jur., N. S., Q. B. 591 488
Regina v. Nugent, 11 Cox C. C. 64 39
Regina v. Paty, 2 Ld. Raym. 1105; S. C., 2 Salk. 504 ....407, 438, 449
Regina v. Roberts and Mary Carthy, 2 F. & F. 272 ....165, 172, 261, 262

TABLE OF CASES.

Regina v. Weil, 15 Rep. 412 603
Reilly, In re, 10 L. T., N. S., 853 138
Republic of Texas v. Bynum, Dallam, 376 98
Republic v. Wingate, cited in 2 Tex. 523 538
Respublica v. Arnold et al., 3 Yeates, 263 350
Respublica v. Keeper of the Jail, 2 Yeates, 349 108
Respublica v. Jailer of Philadelphia, 2 Yeates, 258 .... 101, 108, 175, 224
Rex v. Acton, 2 Stra. 851; S. C., 1 Barn. K. B. 250 525
Rex v. Ailsbury, Comb. 422 546
Rex v. Barber, 1 Stra. 444 410
Rex v. Bishop, 1 Stra. 9 .... 546, 550
Rex v. Carlisle, 4 Car. & P. 415 .... 474, 480
Rex v. Clarke, 1 Burr. 603 .... 94, 123
Rex v. Clarke, 3 Burr. 1362 .... 177, 206, 262, 572
Rex v. Clarkson, 1 Stra. 445 .... 219, 554
Rex v. Collyer and Capon, Say, 44 497
Rex v. Cowle, 2 Burr. 834 118
Rex v. Croker, 2 Chit. Q. B. 138 .... 360, 361
Rex v. Dalton, 2 Stra. 911 .... 283, 525
Rex v. Davison, 4 Barn. & Ald. 336; S. C., 1 Raym. 603 .... 407, 526
Rex v. Delaval et al., 3 Burr. 1434 .... 219, 556, 559, 562, 582
Rex v. Delamere, Comb. 6 545
Rex v. De Manneville, 1 Smith, 358 558
Rex v. Drew, 1 Stra. 408 200
Rex v. Elkins, 4 Burr. 2129 400
Rex v. Evered, Cald. 26 361
Rex v. Fenwick, 3 Smith, 369 .... 272, 593
Rex v. Flower, 8 T. R. 325 .... 95, 407
Rex v. Fowler, 1 Salk. 293, 350; S. C., 1 Raym. 586 .... 117, 193
Rex v. Goodall, Sayer, 129; S. C., 1 Ken. 122 .... 361, 363, 364
Rex v. Greenhill, 4 Ad. & El. 624 ..... 555, 558, 559, 562, 563, 564, 565, 566
Rex v. Greenwood, 2 Stra. 1138 .... 375, 376, 525
Rex v. Gregory, 4 Burr. 1991 94
Rex v. Grieffenburgh, 4 Burr. 2179 524
Rex v. Hall, 3 Burr. 1636 437
Rex v. Hobhouse, 2 Ch. Q. B. 207 .... 407, 449
Rex v. Hood, 1 Moo. C. C. 281 355
Rex v. Horne, 2 Cowp. 682 160
Rex v. Isley, 5 Ad. & El. 441 .... 556, 562
Rex v. James, 5 Barn. & Ald. 894 437
Rex v. Jones, 1 Barn. & Ald. 209 526
Rex v. Johnson, 1 Stra. 579; S. C., 2 Ld. Raym. 1333 .... 219, 562, 564
Rex v. Justices, etc., 1 Dowl. 484 368
Rex v. Justices of Somersetshire, 5 Barn. & Cress. 816 260
Rex v. Magrath, 2 Stra. 1242 525
Rex v. Marks, 3 East, 157 .... 367, 368, 369, 370, 371, 375
Rex v. Massey, 6 Maa. & Sel. 108 526
Rex v. Mead, 1 Burr. 542 554
Rex v. Mosely, 5 East, 223 589
Rex v. Pain, Holt, 294; S. C., Comberbach, 359 359
Rex v. Parkyns, 3 Barn. & Ald. 679 104
Rex v. Parnam, Cunn. 96 525
Rex v. Remnant, 2 Leach, 583; S. C., 5 T. R. 169, and Nolan, 205 361
Rex v. Roddam, 2 Cowp. 672 114
Rex v. Rogers, 1 Dow. & Ry. 156 382
Rex v. Rudd, 1 Cow. 331 524
Rex v. Salisbury, 1 Stra. 547 525
Rex v. Sheriff of Middlesex, 1 H. Black. 544; S. C., 11 Ad. & El. 273.. 432
Rex v. Smith, 2 Stra. 982; S. C., Ridg. Rep. 200 219
Rex v. Swallow, 8 T. R. 284 380
Rex v. Taylor, 7 Dow. & Ry. 622 382
Rex v. Thompson, 2 T. R. 18 380
Rex v. Turlington, 2 Burr. 1115 206
Rex v. Turner, 5 Maa. & Sel. 206 380

TABLE OF CASES.

Rex v. Waddington, 1 East, 159.................................... 524
Rex v. Wilkes, 4 Burr. 2539....................................459, 524
Rex v. Wright, 2 Stra. 901........................151, 152, 203, 207
Rex v. Wright, Voss et al., 2 Burr. 1099.......................... 206
Rex v. Wyndham, 1 Stra. 3....................................359, 360
Reynolds, Ex parte, 3 Hughes, 559; S. C., 1 Crim. L. Mag. 268 ....75, 509
Reynolds, Ex parte, 6 Park. Cr. 276............................... 519
Reynolds et al., In re, 1 Dow. & L. 846........................189, 335
Reynolds v. Orvis, 7 Cow. 269..................................... 488
Rhodes, Ex parte, 2 Wheeler's Cr. Cas. 559; S. C., Niles' Reg. 264, June 21, 1817.. 78
Ricord, Ex parte, 11 Nev. 287...............................372, 373, 374
Riley's Case, 2 Pick. 172.. 491
Ring, In the Matter of, 28 Cal. 247............................... 519
Rising v. Dodge, 2 Duer, 42....................................... 586
Rivers v. Mitchell, 57 Iowa, 193; S. C., 13 Rep. 106; and 10 N. W. Rep. 626.. 587
Robalina v. Armstrong, 15 Barb. 247............................... 590
Robb, In re, 1 W. C. Rep. 439; S. C., Id. 255.................625, 628
Robb v. McDonald, 29 Iowa, 330; S. C., 6 Am. Law Rev. 320......292, 434
Roberts, Ex parte, 9 Nev. 44...................................... 507
Roberts' Case, 2 Am. Law J. 192................................... 78
Robinson v. Flanders, 29 Ind. 10.................................. 622
Robinson, Ex parte, 6 McLean, 355.....................75, 96, 176, 243, 338
Robinson's Case, cited in People v. Tinder, 19 Cal. 539........... 543
Robinson, Ex parte, 1 Bond, 39................................75, 78
Robinson v. Hall, Taylor (U. C.), 482............................. 132
Robinson, Ex parte, 19 Wall. 505.................................. 446
Robinson, Ex parte, 6 McLean, 355; S. C., 4 Am. Law Reg. 617...... 411
Rogers v. Bradshaw, 20 Johns. 739................................. 275
Rohan v. Sawin, 5 Cush. 281....................................... 355
Romaine, Matter of, 23 Cal. 585...............................613, 614
Romanes, Ex parte, 1 Utah, 23..................................... 623
Rosenblat, 51 Cal. 285.. 614
Ross, In re, 3 Pr. Rep. (U. C.) 301............................... 193
Ross, Ex parte, 2 Bond, 252....................................... 606
Roth & Boyle v. House of Refuge, 31 Md. 329..................219, 522
Rothschild, Ex parte, 2 Tex. App. 560........................541, 548
Rowe v. Rowe, 28 Mich. 353...................................334, 583
Rowe, Ex parte, 7 Cal. 175; S. C., Id. 184...................415, 416
Rowland et al., Ex parte, 3 Mor. Trans. 608....................... 435
Roy v. Overton, Siderfin, 386..................................... 19
Royster, Ex parte, 6 Ark. 28..................................91, 108
Rucker & Quisenberry, Ex parte, 6 Tex. App. 81.................... 549
Ruddle's Executors v. Ben, 10 Leigh, 468.......................... 219
Rush, Ex parte, 60 Cal. 5... 427
Russell v. Whiting, 1 Winst. 465.............................219, 327
Russen v. Lucas, 1 Car. & P. 153.................................. 348
Rust v. Van Vacter, 9 W. Va. 600.......................372, 571, 573, 585
Rutter, Matter of, 7 Abb. Pr. N. S. 67....................618, 619, 623
Ryan, Ex parte, 44 Cal. 555..................................533, 547

S

Sam, Ex parte, 51 Ala. 34..................................456, 466, 474
Sanborn v. Carleton, 15 Gray, 399............................103, 354
Sanders v. Rodway, 13 Eng. L. & Eq. 463; S. C., 16 Jur. 1005...... 554
Sandilands, Ex parte, 12 Eng. L. & Eq. 463; S. C., 21 L. J. Rep. N. S., Q. B., 342..554, 555
Sanford v. Nichols, 13 Mass. 286.................................. 359
Sargeant, Ex parte, 17 Vt. 425.................................... 510
Satterlee v. Matthewson, 2 Pet. 412............................... 275
Schenck, In re, 74 N. C. 607.................................337, 474, 502
Schmeid, Ex parte, 1 Dill. 587................................61, 82
Schofield v. Root, 12 Phila. 333.............................290, 297

TABLE OF CASES.

Schumpert, Ex parte, 6 Rich. 344..................571, 574, 582, 583, 585
Scoggin, Ex parte, 6 Tex. App. 546..........................538, 541, 542
Scott v. Ely, 4 Wend. 556....................................353, 355
Scott, Ex parte, 9 Barn. & Cress. 446................................. 178
Scwartz, Ex parte, 2 Tex App. 74.....342, 456, 471, 472, 473, 474, 476, 551
Sears v. Dessar, 28 Ind. 472.........................203, 582, 587
Seavey et al. v. Seymour, 3 Cliff. 439..................59, 82, 92, 149, 231
Seeles et al., 3 Cro. Car. 557....................................... 163
Semler, Petition of, 41 Wis. 517; S. C., 16 Alb. L. J. 119.............
..................................288, 471, 474, 486, 496, 539
Shadgett v. Clipson, 8 East, 329...................................... 355
Shafer & Wife v. Mumma, 17 Md. 331.................................. 379
Shaffenburg, Ex parte, 4 Dill. 271............................61, 276, 475
Shaftsbury's Case, Earl of, 5 Howell's State Trials, 1269; S. C., 1 Mod. 144..407, 524
Shand v. Henderson, 2 Dow. (H. of L. R.) 521......................... 275
Shanks' Case, 15 Abb. Pr. N. S 38..............................407, 445
Sharpe, Ex parte, 9 Dowl. 513.. 178
Shaw, Ex parte, 7 Ohio St. 81...................................463, 495
Shaw, Ex parte, 61 Cal. 58... 388
Shaw v. McHenry, Judge, etc. 2 N. W. Rep. 1096...................... 587
Shaw ex rel. v. Nacthwey, 43 Iowa, 653..................581, 583, 584
Shaw v. Smith, 8 Tanner (Ind.), 485......................203, 597
Sheehan's Case, 122 Mass. 445; S. C., 4 Cent. L. J. 524............328, 490
Sheldon, 34 Ohio St. 319...............................618, 619, 620, 621
Shelley v. Westbrooke, Jac. 266....................................... 569
Shepherd v. Dean, 13 How. Pr. 173.................................... 423
Sheriff of Middlesex, Case of, 1 Ad. & El. 273.......................
..................................273, 407, 438, 447, 448, 449
Shirk's Case, 5 Phila. 333... 82
Shortz v. Quigley, 1 Binn. 222.. 230
Shue v. Turk, 15 Gratt. 256.. 219
Shuttleworth, In the Matter of, 9 Ad. & El., Q. B., 651............... 369
Siebold, Ex parte, 100 U. S. 371..................56, 57, 58, 65, 67, 70,
       276, 332, 336, 387, 435, 471, 473, 474, 487, 490, 491, 493, 494, 495, 510
Sifford, Ex parte, 5 Am. L. Reg. 659..................75, 176, 207, 216, 339
Sims's Case, 7 Cush. 285..78, 94, 96, 97
Simmons, Ex parte, 62 Ala. 416....................462, 464, 471, 474, 496
Simpson v. Hill, 1 Esp. 431.. 348
Skeen v. Monkeimer, 21 Ind. 1... 82
Skinner, Ex parte, 9 Moore, 278..........................556, 558, 559, 560
Slater and Wells, In re, 9 U. C. Law Jour. O. S. 21.................. 148
Sloan, Ex parte, 4 Saw. 330... 71
Smallman et al., Ex parte, 54 Cal. 35................................ 551
Smethurst, In the Matter of, 2 Sandf. 724........................396, 400
Smith, In re, 4 Col. 532... 372
Smith, In re, 3 Hurl. & N. 225................................188, 259
Smith, In re, 1 Cal. 1... 374
Smith, Ex parte, 5 Cow. 273.. 372
Smith, Ex parte, 2 Nev. 338......................231, 471, 474, 475, 481
Smith, Ex parte, 3 McLean, 121; S. C., 6 L. R. 57....................
..................................216, 606, 609, 618, 625, 628
Smith v. McIver, 9 Wheat. 532.. 339
Smith v. McLendon, 59 Ga. 523.........................396, 400, 405, 454
Smith v. Randall, 3 Hill (N. Y.), 495................................ 360
Smith v. Rhoades, 1 Day, 168... 343
Snowden et al. v. The State, 8 Mo. 483............................... 286
Snyder, In re, 17 Kan. 542...........................92, 235, 236, 244, 298
Somervell v. Hunt, 3 Har. & McH. 113................................. 364
Souden's Case, 4 Barn. & Ald. 294.................................... 164
Spalding v. The People, 7 Hill, 301.................................. 521
Spangler, In the Matter of, 11 Mich. 298............................. 82
Speaker and Styant, Comb. 127.. 201
Speer v. Davis, 38 Ind. 271.........................198, 219, 521, 572

TABLE OF CASES.

Case	Page
Spivey, In the Matter of, 2 Winst. 156	43
Spradlend, In the Matter of, 38 Mo. 547	545
Springer, Ex parte, 1 Utah, 214	320, 538
Squires' Case, 12 Abb. Pr. 38	297
Stacy, In the Matter of, 10 Johns. 328	78, 153
Staples v. Fairchilds, 3 Comst. 41	344
Starr v. Barton, 34 Ga. 99	481
State v. Asselin, T. U. P. Charlt. 184	287, 376, 533
State v. Baird & Torrey, 18 N. J. Eq. 194	571, 573, 583, 585, 586
State v. Baird, 21 N. J. Eq. 384	584, 586, 588
State v. Baldwin, 5 N. J. Eq. 454	555, 572, 579
State v. Bandy, 2 Ga. Dec. 40	362
State v. Banks, 25 Ind. 495	219, 571, 575, 585
State ex rel. Jewett v. Barrett et Ux. 45 N. H. 15	580
State v. Beaver, 1 Coxe, 80	224
State v. Best et al., 7 Blackf. 611	372, 532, 533
State v. Bloom, 17 Wis. 521	219, 287, 328, 372, 481
State v. Blundell, 39 N. J. L. 612	516
State of Illinois v. Bradley, 60 Ill. 390	155
State ex rel. Lynch v. Bratton, 15 Am. Law Reg., N. S., 359	574, 577, 581, 582, 584, 585
State v. Brearly and Berryman, 2 South. 555	78, 522, 503
State ex rel. Lynch v. Bridges, Jailer, et al., 64 Ga. 146	90, 252
State ex rel. Thomas v. Bruslé, 14 Rep. 114	320
State v. Buckham, 29 Minn. 462	521
State v. Buyck, 2 Bay, 563	527
State v. Buzine, 4 Harr. (Del.) 572	364, 375, 614, 615
State v. Chancellor, 1 Strobh. 347	598
State v. Cheeseman, 2 South. 445	595
State v. Clover, 1 Harr. (N. J.) 419	595
State v. Collins et al., 54 Iowa, 441; S. C., 6 N. W. Rep. 274	145
State v. Conlin, 27 Vt. 318	379
State v. Connor, 2 Bay, 34	550
State v. Dimick, 12 N. H. 194	78
State of Maine v. Drake, 36 Me. 366	364
State v. Ensign, 13 Neb. 250	88, 92, 236
State v. Everett, Dudley (S. C.), 295	357, 360, 362, 521, 527, 529
State v. Farlee, 1 Coxe, 41, 82	224
State of Louisiana v. Fenderson, 28 La. Ann. 82	471, 474, 480, 488, 490
State v. Fraser, Dudley (Ga.), 42	219
State v. Galloway & Rhea, 5 Coldw. 326	394, 396, 446, 454, 522
State v. Glenn, 54 Md. 572	336, 378, 379, 381, 382
State v. Green, 3 Green (15 N. J.), 88	363
State v. Harrison, 10 Yerg. (Tenn.) 541	505
State v. Heathman, Wright (Ohio), 690	362
State v. Hill, 3 Brev. 89	538, 540
State v. Howell, R. M. Charlt. 120	614
State v. Hufford, 28 Iowa, 391	621, 623
State v. J. H., 1 Tyler, 444	359, 364
State v. Killett, 2 Bailey, 289	359, 360
State v. King, 1 and 2 Ga. Dec. 93	583, 588
State v. Kirkpatrick, 54 Iowa, 373	521, 573, 583
State of Iowa v. Klingman, 14 Iowa, 404	531
State v. Lamos, 26 Me. 258	359
State ex rel. Hodgdon v. Libbey, 44 N. H. 321	579
State v. Loper, Ga. Dec., pt. 2, p. 33	613, 614, 615
State v. Lyon, 1 Coxe, 403	143, 231, 242, 256
State v. Malone, 3 Sneed, 413	521
State v. Manley, 1 Overt. 428	363, 364
State v. Matthews, 37 N. H. 451	392, 399, 400, 401, 452
State v. Maurignos, T. U. P. Charlt. 24	527
State v. Maxcy, 1 McMull. 501	379
State v. McKnight, cited in State v. Farlee, 1 Coxe, 41	224
State v. McLeod, 1 Hill (N. Y.), 377	529

TABLE OF CASES. li

State v. McNally, 34 Me. 210.................................. 359
State v. Mills, 2 Dev 420................................537, 539
State v. Munson, Hurd on Habeas Corpus, 2d ed. 385, citing 2 Hall's
    Jour. Jur. 257...110, 360
State v. Paine, 4 Humph., sec. 523......................523, 573, 583
State of Louisiana ex rel. Williams v. Persdorf, 13 Rep. 47............ 490
State v. Philpot, Dudley (Ga.), 46....................9, 166, 183, 198
State v. Plime and Vessel, T. U. P. Charlt. 142....................... 78
State v. Potter, Dudley (S. C.), 295; S. C., note to People v. McLeod, 1
    Hill (N. Y.), 377......................................357, 360, 521
State v. Raborg, 2 South. 545...................................... 153
State v. Randolph, 26 Mo. 213..................................... 366
State ex rel. Herrick v. Richardson, 40 N. H. 272.............575, 585
State v. Roger, 7 La. Ann. 382..................................... 545
State of Louisiana v. Sauvinet, 24 La. Ann. 119............390, 392, 454
State v. Schlemn, 4 Harr. 577.................................619, 622
State v. Schuster, 40 Cal. 627...................................... 550
State v. Scott et Ux., 30 N. H. 274...........................576, 585
State v. Shattuck, 45 N. H. 205.................................... 387
State v. Sheriff of Hennepin Co., 24 Minn. 87.................326, 489
State v. Smith, 54 Me. 33... 359
State v. Smith, 1 Bailey, 283; S. C., 19 Am. Dec. 679................ 598
State v. Smith, 6 Greenl. 400......................574, 577, 580, 583
State v. Sparks, 27 Tex. 705.. 43
State v. Staples, 37 Me. 228....................................... 364
State v. Statnaker, 2 Brev. 44...................................... 319
State of Ohio v. Summons, 19 Ohio, 139.......................537, 543
State v. Stigall, 2 Zab. 286.................574, 577, 582, 583, 584
State v. Stinson, 17 Me. 154....................................... 387
State v. Tipton, 1 Blackf. 166..................................... 432
State ex rel. Welsh v. Towle, 42 N. H. 540................393, 418, 445
State v. Vaughn, Harp. 313...................................359, 364
State v. Van Horne, cited in State v. Farlee, 1 Coxe, 41.............. 224
State v. Ward, 3 Halst. 120....................................101, 466
State v. Ward, 2 Hawk. 443....................................... 551
State v. Wederstrandt, T. U. P. Charlt. 213.......................... 78
State v. White, T. U. P. Charlt. 136............................... 432
State v. Wiley, 64 N. C. 823....................................... 92
State v. Wolcott, 21 Conn. 272.................................... 266
State v. Woodfin, 5 Ired. 199..............................394, 432, 452
State v. Worley, 11 Ired. 242.................................359, 360
State v. Zulich, 5 Dutch. 409...................................... 82
Stephen, In the Matter of, 1 Wheel. Cr. Cas. 323.............78, 297, 519
Stephens, In re, Dudley (Ga.), 42................................. 582
Stevenson v. Danvers, 2 Bos. & Pul. 210........................... 199
Stevens v. Clark, 2 Moo. & R. 435; S. C., 1 Car. & M. 509............ 361
Stewart's Case, 1 Abb. Pr. 210.................................311, 336
Stickney v. Davis, 17 Pick. 169.................................... 505
Stockdale v. Hansard, 9 Ad. & El. 1; S. C., 3 Per. & Dav. 349; 9 Ad. &
    El. 228; 8 Dowl. 174, and 11 Ad. & El. 253......152, 390, 407, 447, 449
Stockwin, In re, 5 Ad. & El. 266................................... 135
Stoner v. State of Missouri, 4 Mo. 614.........................314, 457
Strahle, Ex parte, 16 Iowa, 369.............................219, 327, 328
Strange, Ex parte, 59 Cal. 416..................................... 538
Strangeways v. Robinson, 4 Taunt. 497............................ 589
Street v. The State, 43 Miss. 1.....................................
    .... 245, 243, 252, 527, 531, 537, 538, 540, 541, 546, 549
Striplin v. Ware, 36 Ala. 87....................................... 588
Stuart v. The People, 3 Scam. 395................390, 392, 393, 398, 446
Stupp, In re, 12 Blatchf. 501; S C., 11 Id. 124.......69, 332, 333, 606, 609
Suggate v. Suggate, 1 Sw. & Tr. 492............................... 564
Summers, Ex parte, 5 Ired. 149............394, 396, 432, 445, 447, 450, 454
Suttor, In re, 2 F. & F. 267.. 104
Swann, In re, v. Dakins, 29 Eng. Law & Eq. 331; S. C., 16 Com. B. 77. 261
Sweatman, In the Matter of, 1 Cow. 144......................91, 459, 500

T

Tackett v. The State, 3 Yerg. 393 359
Taff v. Hosmer, 14 Mich. 249 120
Talbot v. Shrewsbury, 4 Jur. 380 569
Tarble's Case, 13 Wall. 397 ....
.... 37, 73, 82, 125, 175, 176, 207, 276, 519, 626, 627, 628
Tarble, In re, 25 Wis. 390; S. C., 13 Wall. 397, and 6 Am. Law Rev. 314 .... 82, 288, 338
Tatem, Ex parte, 1 Hughes, 588 .... 75, 339
Tayloe, Ex parte, 5 Cow. 39 ....
.... 283, 372, 527, 529, 532, 533, 535, 536, 537, 539, 542
Taylor, In re, 1 Crim. L. Mag. 126; S. C., 12 Chic. L. N., Oct. 4, p. 17, 1880 .... 63, 508
Taylor, In re, L. R., 4 Ch. Div. 157 .... 219, 565, 569
Taylor v. Reignolds, 12 Mod. 666 201
Taylor v. Taintor, 16 Wall. 366 .... 615, 616, 622
Templer, Ex parte, 2 Saund. & C. 169 555
Territory v. Benoit, 1 Mart. (La.), 142 .... 537, 539
Ter. of Kan. v. Cutler, 1 McCahon, 152 .... 84, 106, 174
Thatcher, Ex parte, 2 Gilm. 167 398
Thomas, In re, 12 Blatchf. 370 606
Thomas v. Crossin et al., 3 Am. Law Reg. 207 .... 76, 78
Thomas v. The State, 40 Tex. 6 239
Thomlinson's Case, 6 Co. 340 201
Thompson, Ex parte, 3 Cent. Law J. 729; S. C., 15 Am. Law. Reg., N. S., 522, and 1 Flipp. 507 .... 75, 76
Thompson, Ex parte, 30 L. J., N. S., M. C., 19 (Exch.) 93
Thompson, Ex parte, 93 Ill. 89 .... 462, 463, 519
Thompson v. Fellows, 1 Fost. 425 359
Thompson's Case, 122 Mass. 428 103
Thompson v. Oglesby, 42 Iowa, 598 90
Thompson v. Tolmie, 2 Pet. 168 275
Thornton v. Lane, 11 Ga. 460 402
Tims v. The State, 26 Ala. 165 379
Timson, Re, L. R., 5 Exch. 257 171
Titus, In the Matter of, 8 Ben. 411 .... 60, 625
Tomlin v. Fisher, 27 Mich. 524 336
Tom Tong, 2 Sup. Ct. Rep. 871 69
Toney, Ex parte, 11 Mo. 661 .... 445, 451, 464, 474, 489
Touchman, Ex parte, 1 Hughes, 601 64
Townsend v. Kendall, 4 Minn. 412 597
Tracy, Ex parte, 25 Vt. 93 .... 291, 342
Treton v. Squire, Sty. 230 136
Troia, In the Matter of, Opin. Sup. Ct. Cal., filed Sept. 17, 1883 534
Troutman's Case, 4 Zab. 634 625
Truman, In re, 44 Mo. 181 .... 464, 471, 474, 484
Tung Yeong, In the Matter of, 1 W. C. Rep. 647 528
Turner v. Felgate, 1 Lev. 95 359
Turner and Mayer, Ex parte, 3 Wood, 603 .... 75, 411
Tweed v. Liscomb, 60 N. Y. 559; S. C., 11 Alb. L. J. 396 .... 326, 506
Twohig v. Fitzgerald, 13 Nev. 302 .... 320, 480, 489

U

Underwood, Matter of, 30 Mich. 502 493
United States v. Aaron Burr, 4 Cranch, app., 470–507; S. C., Marshall on the Federal Constitution, 53 360
United States v. Almeida, 2 Wheel. 577 249
United States v. Arrendondo et al., 6 Pet. 709 .... 274, 275
United States v. Bainbridge, 1 Mason, 71 82
United States v. Barker, 2 Wheat. 395 138
United States v. Benner, 1 Bald. 239 348
United States v. Bollman and Swartwout, 1 Cranch C. Ct. 376 152
United States v. Boyd, 5 How. 30 138
United States v. Burr, 1 Burr's Trial, 312 .... 537, 539

TABLE OF CASES.

United States v. Booth, 21 How. 506..........................73, 79, 218
United States v. Brawner, 7 Fed. Rep. 86......................528, 532
United States v. Caldwell, 8 Blatchf. 131...........................604, 605
United States v. Collier, 6 Ohio St. 61................................. 78
United States v. Crook, 5 Dill. 453.................................... 60
United States v. Davis, 5 Cranch C. Ct. 622.................120, 121, 123
United States v. Doss, 11 Am. Law Reg., N. S., 320................. 78
United States v. French, 1 Gal. 1...................................... 61
United States v. Green, 3 Mason, 482.................................
.....................64, 154, 166, 186, 210, 216, 555, 556, 574, 583
United States v. Hamilton, 3 Dall. 17................................65, 528
United States v. Holmes, 1 Wall. jun. 1.............................. 446
United States v. Hooe, 3 Cranch, 73................................... 138
United States v. Jailer, 2 Abb. U. S. 265.............................. 75
United States ex rel. Roberts v. Jailer of Fayette Co., 2 Abb. U. S. 267. 277
United States v. Johns, 4 Dall. 382; S. C., 1 Wash. 363.........372, 374
United States v. Jones et al., 3 Wash. 224....................537, 539, 546
United States v. Lawrence, 13 Blatchf. 295......................604, 605
United States v. Lawrence, 4 Cranch C. Ct. 518...........94, 532, 536, 548
United States v. McClay, 4 Cent. L. J. 255..................619, 625, 626
United States v. McLemore, 4 How. 286............................. 138
United States v. Morris, 2 Am. Law Reg. 348...............75, 338, 339
United States v. Rector, 5 McLean, 174............................64, 78
United States v. R. R. Co., 105 U. S. 263............................. 64
United States v. Smith, 2 Cranch C. Ct. 111......................... 373
United States v. Travers, 2 Wheel. 509................................ 63
United States v. Van Fossen, 1 Dill. 406.............................. 78
United States v. Watts, 8 Saw. 370.................................... 605
United States v. Williamson, 3 Am. Law Reg. 729; S. C., 4 Id. 5, and 5
 Pa. Law Jour. Rep. 365............59, 76, 186, 193, 216, 219, 220, 231
United States v. Wilson, 7 Pet. 150.................................... 598
United States v. Wyngall, 5 Hill, 16................................... 78

V

Van Aernam, Ex parte, 3 Blatchf. 160.......................333, 607, 608
Van Boven's Case, 9 Ad. & El., Q. B., 669.................190, 283, 332
Van Campen, In the Matter of, 2 Ben. 419....................332, 608
Vandervelpen, In re 14 Blatchf. 137.................................. 609
Vanderbilt, Matter of, 4 Johns. Ch. 57................................ 399
Van Hagan, Ex parte, 25 Ohio St. 432................................ 463
Van Hoven, Ex parte, 4 Dill. 411; S. C., Id. 415..............607, 609
Van Orden, Ex parte, 3 Blatchf. 167.................................. 332
Van Sandau, Ex parte, 1 Ph. 445, 605................................. 359
Vaughan, Ex parte, 44 Ala. 417...................................... 538
Veremaitré, Matter of, 10 N. Y. Leg. Obs. 137...................... 608
Vermaitre, In re, 9 N. Y. Leg. Obs. 137............................... 333
Viele, Matter of, 44 How. Pr. 14....................................... 588
Village of Chorley, Case of the, 1 Salk. 176......................... 353
Villareal v. Mellish, 2 Swans. 538..................................... 595
Viner's Case, Freem. K. B. & C. P..........................389, 401, 522
Virginia, Ex parte, 100 U. S. 339; S. C., 19 Am. Law Reg., N. S., 256,
 and 14 Am. Law Rev. 320......65, 70, 332, 336, 435, 471, 472, 474, 509
Voll, Ex parte, 41 Cal. 29.. 551
Voorhees, 32 N. J. L 141.....................................615, 619, 620

W

Wade v. Judge, 5 Ala., N. S., 130.....................110, 366, 516, 519
Wahl, In re, 15 Blatchf. 334... 609
Wakely v. Hart et al., 6 Binn. 316..................................... 355
Wakely, Law Jour., 1845; Com. L. Mag. Cas., 188.................. 105
Wakker, In the Matter of, 3 Barb. 162..........................219, 327
Walbridge v. Hall, 3 Vt. 114... 474
Waldron, Matter of, 13 Johns. 417.....................186, 556, 582, 583

TABLE OF CASES.

Walker and Black, 3 Tex. App. 668 .... 541, 547, 548
Walker, In re, 3 Am. Jur. 281 63
Walker, Ex parte, 53 Miss. 366 .... 249, 550
Walker v. Cruikshank, 2 Hill (N. Y.), 296 359
Wall, In re, 12 Rep. 322 82
Walrond v. Walrond, John. 18 562
Walton, Ex parte, 2 Whart. 501 105
Wand v. Wand, 14 Cal. 512 .... 577, 583, 586
Ward v. Roper, 7 Humph. 80 596
Warde v. Warde, 2 Ph. 786 568
Ware v. The State, 33 Ga. 338 143
Warman's Case, 2 W. Black. 1203 208
Warren v. Paul, 22 Ind. 276 40
Watkins, Ex parte, 3 Pet. 193; S. C., 7 Id. 568 .... 56, 57, 58, 65, 66,
   72, 94, 95, 274, 276, 278, 279, 280, 381, 382, 460, 474, 483, 498, 509, 519
Watson, Leonard, et al., 9 Ad. & El. 731; S. C., Queen & Batcheldor, 1
   Per. & Dav. 516; S. C., Watson et al., 36 Eng. Com. L. 254..18, 54,
   72, 85, 86, 150, 162, 171, 177, 187, 190, 209, 213, 215, 218, 222, 260, 261
Watson, Ex parte, 2 Cal. 59 621
Watson, In the Matter of, 5 Lans. 466 .... 400, 451, 466
Watson, In the Matter of, 3 Lans. 408 427
Watson v. Clerke, Holt, 428 201
Watson v. Williams, 36 Miss. 331 .... 392, 400, 425
Way v. Wright, 5 Met. 380 103
Webb's Case, 24 How. Pr. 247 82
Weddington v. Sloan, 15 B. Mon. 147 519
Welch v. Scott, 5 Ired. 72 .... 359, 366
Welch v. Nash, 8 East, 403 452
Wellesley v. Wellesley, 2 Bligh, N. S., 124 .... 556, 557
Wellesley v. Duke of Beaufort, 2 Russ. 1; S. C., 3 Eng. Ch. R. 10..557, 569
Wells, Ex parte, 18 How. 307 .... 56, 57, 65, 67, 70, 332, 509, 598, 599
Wells v. Sisson, 14 Hun, 267 268
Wheeler v. Raymond, 8 Cow. 311 343
Wheeler v. Thomas, 57 Ga. 161 403
Whitaker, Ex parte, 43 Ala. 323 .... 317, 484
White v. State of Mississippi, 1 Smed. & M. 156 113
White, Ex parte, 49 Cal. 433 .... 614, 618
Whitehouse, In re, 1 Lowell, 429 63
Whiting, In the Matter of, 2 Barb. 513 327
Whitney v. Shufelt, 1 Denio, 592 267
Wicker v. Dresser, 13 How. Pr. 331 423
Wickes v. Clutterbuck, 2 Bing. 483 335
Wiegand, Matter of, 14 Blatchf. 370 609
Wilcox v. Nolze, 34 Ohio St. 520 .... 620, 621
Wilcox v. Wilcox, 14 N. Y. 575 596
Wiles v. Brown, 3 Barb. 37 515
Williams, Ex parte, 1 Wash. T. 240 .... 471, 474, 508
Williams, Ex parte, 11 Rich. 452 .... 573, 574, 582, 583, 586
Williams v. Bacon, 10 Wend. 636 604
Williamson v. Lewis, 39 Pa. St. 9 .... 85, 110, 290
Williamson's Case, 19 Abb. Pr. 394 385
Williamson's Case, 26 Pa. St. 9; S. C., 4 Am. L. Reg. 27; 3 Am. L. Reg.
   741, and 7 Opin. Att. Gen. 482 .... 76, 78, 94, 108, 399, 411, 474, 611
Willoughby, Ex parte, 14 Nev. 451 .... 233, 362
Wilson's Case, 7 Ad. & El. Q. B. 984 .... 114, 118, 178, 187, 518
Wilson's Case, 6 Cranch, 52 .... 65, 66, 84
Wilson's, Jane, Case, 4 City Hall Rec. 47 78
Wilson v. Rastall, 4 T. R. 757 524
Winder, In the Matter of, 2 Cliff. 89 .... 59, 61, 94, 104
Winnington's Case, 1 Keb. 566 .... 131, 133
Winston, Ex parte, 9 Nev. 71 .... 456, 466, 474, 493
Wise v. Withers, 3 Cranch, 331 513
Wishard v. Medaris, 34 Ind. 168 581
Witte, Ex parte, 13 Com. B. 680 555

TABLE OF CASES. lv

Wolff, Ex parte, 57 Cal. 94... 542
Wollstonecraft, Matter of, 4 Johns. Ch. 79..........556, 571, 584, 588, 595
Wong Yung Qui, 9 Rep. 366; S. C., 4 Pac. C. L. J. 564.......276, 472, 508
Wong Yung Quy, Ex parte, 2 Fed. Rep. 624, and 6 Saw. 237.......61, 75
Wood v. Neale, 5 Gray, 538.. 102
Woodcraft v. Kinaston, 2 Atk. 316....... ....330, 331, 368
Work v. Corrington, 34 Ohio St. 64; S. C., 6 Cent. L. J. 377.......... 617
Wray, Ex parte, 30 Miss. 673 ....531, 532, 540
Wright et al. v. Cogswell, 1 McLean, 471.............................. 268
Wright v. Hazen, 24 Vt. 143 342
Wright v. Johnson, 5 Ark. 687 110
Wright v. The State, 5 Ind. 290.... 326
Wyatt, Ex parte, Will., Woll. & Dav. 76; S. C., 5 Dowl. P. C. 389.... 402
Wyeth v. Richardson, 10 Gray, 240............................. .....372, 519
Wyndham's Case, 1 Stra. 3.. 364

Y

Yarbrough v. The State of Texas, 2 Tex. 519............842, 527, 538, 548
Yates, Case of, 4 Johns. 314; S. C., 6 Id. 337 ....210, 439, 452
Yates v. Lansing, 9 Johns. 395 ....400, 412, 439, 452
Yates v. Lansing, 5 Johns. 282.. 110
Yates v. The People 6 Johns. 335.........187, 200, 391, 400, 412, 452, 519
Yerger, Ex parte, 8 Wall. 85...
..................56, 57, 58, 65, 67, 276, 278, 332, 336, 471, 474, 509
Young v. The State, 15 Ind. 480........ ....221, 581

Z

Zembrod v. The State, 25 Tex. 519............................. ..538, 548

REFERENCE TO OTHER AUTHORITIES CITED IN THIS VOLUME.

TREATIES.
Treaty of 1843.. 6
Treaty of 1845... 60

CONSTITUTIONS.
Constitution of Massachusetts.. 442
Constitution of Mississippi.. 454
Constitution of New York... 141
Constitution of the United States..
.... 56, 64, 119, 278, 352, 441, 452, 508, 529, 607, 612, 625
Constitutions of the States.. 453
Constitution of Texas, 1845.. 537
Constitution of Texas, 1876...529, 537
Constitution of Wisconsin.. 198

ENGLISH STATUTES.
Car. I., 16.. 85
Car. II., 31....4, 13, 14, 15, 16, 18, 20, 23, 28, 29, 34, 35, 37, 44, 54, 55, 85,
   86, 95, 97, 108, 112, 113, 114, 126, 130, 147, 151, 152, 210, 211, 212,
   215, 220, 221, 222, 223, 257, 260, 261, 262, 271, 368, 369, 375, 526, 571
Geo. II., 5... 165
Geo. II., 20... 179
Geo. III., 24.. 164
Geo. III., 42.. 164
Geo. III., 44.. 194
Geo. III., 45.. 164
Geo. III., 56...85,
   118, 163, 212, 213, 215, 218, 221, 222, 261, 262, 271, 272, 273, 401, 448
Geo. III., 57.. 213
Geo. III., 58.. 348
Geo. IV., 3.. 178
Geo. IV., 4.. 188
Geo. IV., 5.. 377
Geo. IV., 9.. 189
Geo. IV., 11... 422
Habeas Corpus Act, 31 Car. II... 44
Hen. III., 9... 378
Infants' Custody Act, 8 L. R., 36 and 37 Vict...................557, 567, 569
Ph. & M. 1 and 2.. 114
Summary Jurisdiction Act of 1879.........................378, 379, 382, 386
Supreme Court of Judicature Act, 1873.. 87
Suspension Act of 1866.. 38
Talfourd's Act, 2 and 3 Vict.........................557, 558, 565, 567, 568
Vict. 1 and 2.. 377
Vict. 5 and 6.. 177
Vict. 6 and 7.. 368
Vict. 8 and 9...150, 190, 202, 204, 283
Vict. 9 and 10.. 188
Vict. 11 and 12...377, 380

OTHER AUTHORITIES CITED. lvii

Vict. 12 and 13... 383
Vict. 16 and 17... 205
Vict. 31... 364
Vict. 31 and 32..377, 380
Vict. 32 and 33..377, 380
Vict. 33 and 34... 605
Vict. 36 and 37... 87
Vict. 42 and 43..243, 377, 379, 380, 383
Wm. IV., 1... 422
Wm. IV., 2 and 3... 204

FEDERAL STATUTES.

Chinese Prohibitory Act...64, 228
Confiscation Act of July 17, 1862... 498
Habeas Corpus Act United States.. 51
Statutes at Large, 1..................57, 58, 59, 64, 75, 216, 273, 279, 332
Statutes at Large, 4............................65, 76, 121, 216, 273, 446
Statutes at Large, 5...............................65, 77, 78, 216, 273, 316
Statutes at Large, 9... 79
Statutes at Large, 12..30, 41, 42, 63
Statutes at Large, 14.......................................65, 216, 273
Statutes at Large, 19.. 610
Statutes at Large, 19, c. 287.. 510
Statutes of March 27, 1860... 58
Statutes of February 5, 1867... 77
U. S. R. S., sec. 641.. 508
U. S. R. S., secs. 641-643... 72
U. S. R. S., sec. 650.. 67
U. S. R. S., secs. 651, 652.. 68
U. S. R. S., sec. 711.. 60
U. S. R. S., sec. 716.. 332
U. S. R. S., sec. 725..391, 392, 395, 446
U. S. R. S., secs. 751, 752...284, 607
U. S. R. S., secs. 751-753... 65
U. S. R. S., sec. 754.. 87
U. S. R. S., sec. 753..................................74, 273, 410, 471, 512
U. S. R. S., sec. 755.. 138
U. S. R. S., sec. 760.. 273
U. S. R. S., sec. 761.. 376
U. S. R. S., sec. 763...58, 59
U. S. R. S., sec. 764.. 58
U. S. R. S., sec. 1014... 532
U. S. R. S., secs. 1014, 1015, 1016.. 527
U. S. R. S., sec. 1017... 551
U. S. R. S., sec. 1024... 504
U. S. R. S., sec. 1028... 503
U. S. R. S., sec. 1909... 62
U. S. R. S., secs. 2016, 2017, 2021, 2022, tit. 26......................... 510
U. S. R. S., sec. 3894... 510
U. S. R. S., sec. 5271... 610
U. S. R. S., secs. 5273, 5279...613, 625, 628
U. S. R. S., sec. 5339... 511
U. S. R. S., secs. 5515, 5522.. 510
U. S. R. S., tit. 66... 605

STATE STATUTES.

Alabama, 2 Brick. Dig.. 91
Alabama, Code of.......................................139, 301, 302, 376, 462, 478
Arkansas, Digest... 139
California, Civil Code...429, 579
California, Code of Civil Procedure..................................427, 428, 429
California, Criminal Practice Act....................................324, 537, 545
California, Hittell's Codes.. 150
California, Political Code... 139

lviii   OTHER AUTHORITIES CITED.

California, Penal Code.......223, 303, 305, 376, 388, 472, 475, 540, 551, 624
California, Statutes of 1867-8... 312
California, Statutes of 1855... 416
Delaware, Revised Code... 139
District of Columbia, Revised Statutes................................... 511
Georgia, Code of...89, 139, 402
Illinois, Revised Statutes of.. 453
Indiana, Acts of 1881, p. 560.. 507
Indiana, Bill of Rights, sec. 20... 225
Indiana, 2 Gavin & Hord, 154... 225
Indiana, 2 Laws of, 1870... 150
Indiana, 2 Revised Statutes.. 197
Indiana, 2 Revised Statutes, 1852.. 196
Iowa, Revision of 1860... 434
Kansas, Compiled Laws of, 1879......................................139, 465
Kansas, General Statutes of, 1868...................................235, 298
Kansas, Laws of, 1866 and 1872......................................479, 480
Kentucky, General Statutes of, 1873...................................... 140
Maine, Revised Statutes of, 1857... 140
Maine, Statutes of, 1852... 386
Massachusetts, Pub. Stats. of, 1882.................................140, 616
Michigan, Compiled Laws of, 1871... 140
Michigan, General Statutes of.. 326
Mississippi, Code of, 1871.....................................240, 482, 578
Missouri, Habeas Corpus Act.. 286
Missouri, Revised Statutes of, 1879.................................140, 472
Nebraska, Comp. Statutes of, 1881.. 140
New Hampshire, Gen. Laws of, 1878.. 140
New Jersey, Revision of Laws..142, 143
New York, Code of...423, 424
New York, Code of Civil Procedure.. 426
New York, Extradition Act of 1822.. 611
New York, 2 Fay's Digest............... 141, 150, 298, 303, 376, 472, 579
New York, Laws of 1874... 387
New York, Laws of 1876... 387
New York, Laws of 1881... 516
New York, 2 R. S., Edm. ed... 572
New York, 2 R. S......................... 293, 376, 388, 417, 472, 501, 504
New York, 1 R. S., Laws of 1833.. 310
New York, 2 R. S., 1829.. 451
New York, 2 R. S. 1836...424, 427, 444, 445
New York, 3 R. S., 5th Banks' ed....................................444, 445
New York, 2 R. S., 4th Banks' ed... 318
New York, 3 R. S., 6th Banks' ed..........90, 115, 116, 333, 334, 521
New York, Session Laws of 1853... 380
North Carolina, Battle's Revisal... 141
Ohio, 2 R. S. 1880..141, 150
Oregon, Gen. Laws of Oregon, 1843-1872................................... 142
Pennsylvania, Act of Assembly, May 1, 1861............................... 106
Pennsylvania, 1 Brightly's Purdon's Digest............................... 142
Tennessee, Code of... 396
Texas, Code of Criminal Procedure.. 536
Texas, Paschal's Digest..238, 240, 303, 376
Tennessee, 2 Statutes of 1871.......................................142, 143
Vermont, Revised Laws of... 142
Wisconsin, Revised Statutes of 287, 396, 397, 398

MISCELLANEOUS WORKS.

Albany Law Journal, vol. 18.. 617
Amos' English Constitution
..............4, 6, 8, 12, 13, 14, 15, 16, 17, 20, 24, 27, 28, 29, 30, 54
American Archives, 4th ed.. 36
Archbold's Criminal Practice and Pleading, Pomeroy's Notes, vol. 1..363, 593

OTHER AUTHORITIES CITED.

Bacon's Abridgment..
 19, 20, 54, 113, 114, 117, 119, 131, 147, 151, 187, 206, 209, 210, 212,
 221, 227, 230, 330, 334, 335, 348, 360, 362, 486, 524, 525, 530, 550, 598
Bentham's Works, vol. 3..20, 38
Bishop's Criminal Procedure.......................................
 ....354, 355, 356, 357, 359, 360, 363, 372, 374, 531, 550, 552
Blackstone's Commentaries.........................86, 359, 363, 562, 598
Bouv. Law Dict., vol. 1.. 135
British Constitution... 22
British Liberties.. 23
Broom & Hadley's Com., vol. 2.. 377
Bryant's Popular History of the United States, vol. 3................ 35
Burn's Justice..359, 363, 364, 379
Casey's Justices' Manual... 355
Central Law Journal.......................64, 558, 559, 560, 562, 563
Chalmers' Annals...31, 35
Charters and Constitutions of the United States...........31, 528, 529, 530
Chicago Legal News.. 111
Chitty's Blackstone's Commentaries, vol. 2..................353, 355, 453
Chitty's Criminal Law, vol. 1.......................................
 85, 87, 94, 113, 117, 147, 208, 331, 332, 353, 355, 359, 360, 363, 375, 524, 526
Chitty's General Practice..............................349, 380, 474
Cobbett's State Trials......................................7, 8, 14, 17, 22
Cobbett's Parliamentary History of England......7, 8, 9, 10, 12, 14, 15, 21
Coke's Institutes..200, 356, 598
Coke upon Littleton..160, 564, 598
Colonial Laws of Pennsylvania, vol. 1................................ 34
Colonial Records, vol. 1... 34
Comyn's Digest...........................149, 151, 154, 202, 208, 359, 524
Congressional Globe.. 315
Conkling's Pleas..63, 71
Cooley's Constitutional Limitations, 5th ed...............189, 344, 345
Criminal Law Magazine, vol. 1........................63, 92, 111, 262
Dalton's Sheriff..203, 206
Dane's Abridgment, vol. 5.. 103
Daniell's Chancery Pleading and Practice............................. 399
East's Pleas of the Crown, vol. 1...........................354, 355, 361
Fields' Colonial Courts, N. J.. 34
Force's Collection of Historical Tracts, in Account of Revolution in New
 England, vol. 4..33, 35
Forsythe's Custody of Infants, found in 52 Law Lib., N. S............
 ....556, 558, 559, 560, 561, 562, 564, 566, 569
Freeman on Judgments, 3d ed..............................486, 505, 520
Godbolt's Reports.. 117
Great Opinions of Great Judges....................................... 23
Green's History of England.......................................21, 38, 39
Hale's Pleas of the Crown...
 ....18, 85, 86, 354, 355, 357, 359, 360, 363, 486, 524, 526
Hallam's Constitutional History of England, vol. 4...................
 ....3, 6, 7, 8, 19, 20, 21, 22, 23, 29
Hand's Practice.. 126
Hawkins' Pleas of the Crown...
 ....210, 214, 261, 359, 360, 363, 375, 524, 525, 526, 550, 598
Hewitt's History of South Carolina................................... 34
Howell's State Trials.. 212
Hume's History of England, vol. 2.................................... 21
Hurd on Habeas Corpus, 2d ed..................31, 34, 36, 99, 115, 126,
 127, 147, 172, 207, 218, 253, 356, 375, 445, 456, 462, 529, 555, 562, 563, 570
Kent's Commentaries....................................37, 110, 590
Kerr's Blackstone's Commentaries............85, 86, 87, 347, 349, 401, 453
Lilly's Register...................126, 136, 163, 169, 201, 272, 330, 554
Magna Charta..54, 378
Nasmith's Institutes Public Law...................................... 17
North American Review, vol. 99....................................... 40

OTHER AUTHORITIES CITED.

Opinions Attorney General..................513, 600, 603, 606, 609, 625, 628
Parliamentary Debates.. 566
Phillip's Evidence, Cowen and Hill's Notes................................ 364
President's Proclamation of December 8, 1863............................. 598
Rapalje and Lawrence's Law Dictionary...........................353, 454
Reeves' History of the English Law, 195.................................. 524
Robinson's Elementary Law................................ 353, 354, 363
Russell on Crimes, vol. 1... 355
Schouler's Dom. Rel., 3d ed.. 554
Smith's Leading Cases, 4th ed., vol. 1..................................... 259
Spear on Extradition.600, 601, 604, 605, 610, 611, 613, 614, 615, 616, 617, 621
Spear on the Law of the Federal Judiciary........................72, 77
Starkie's Evidence, vol. 3.. 348
Story's Constitution, vol. 1.. 31
Story's Equity Jurisprudence, vol. 2....................................... 557
Summary of the Roman Civil Law.. 3
Thatcher's Practice.. 72
Thatcher's Digest U. S. Courts.. 139
Thompson's Essay on Magna Charta.. 3
Tidd's Practice, vol. 1, 3d Am. ed............94, 198, 260, 330, 367, 456, 474
Tremaine's Pleas of the Crown.. 85
Viner's Abridgment..201, 360
Wait's Annotated Code of Civil Procedure, N. Y.......................... 515
Washburn's Judicial History of Massachusetts....................32, 33
Wharton's Criminal Pleading and Practice, 8th ed....................... 379
Wharton's Law Lexicon, 7th ed... 390
Wilmot's Opinions and Judgments.......................95, 217, 221, 253
Wyatt's Register...113, 126, 151, 181

A TREATISE

ON THE

WRIT OF HABEAS CORPUS.

THE WRIT OF HABEAS CORPUS.

CHAPTER I.

HISTORY OF THE WRIT.

PART I.—TRACES OF IT IN THE ROMAN LAW.

- § 1. The Roman Edict.

PART II.—ITS USE IN THE EARLIER COMMON LAW.

- § 2. Magna Charta.
- § 3 a. Ancient Writs.
- § 3 b. The Knights' Habeas Corpus Case.
- § 4. Idem—Arguments for the Prisoners.
- § 5. Idem—Arguments for the Crown.
- § 6. Idem—The Decision.
- § 7. Petition of Right.
- § 8. Contempt by Members of the House of Commons.
- § 9. Idem—Abolition of Star-Chamber and Other Arbitrary Courts.
- § 10. Cases of Streater, and Fox, the Quaker.
- § 11. The Celebrated Bushell and Shaftesbury Cases.
- § 12. Long Duration of Imprisonment.
- § 13. The Habeas Corpus Bill.
- § 14. Condition of the Prisons.
- § 15. Removal of Prisoners.
- § 16. The Celebrated Jenkes Case.
- § 17. Issuance of the Writ in Vacation.
- § 18. Imperfections of the Writ.

PART III —THE HABEAS CORPUS ACT, 31 CAR. II.

- § 19. Passage of the Famous Habeas Corpus Act.
- § 20. Why the Act is Famous.
- § 21. Auspicious Times of the Bill's Passage.
- § 22. Why the King Assented to the Act.
- § 23. Its Relation to Other Acts.
- § 24. To What the Act may be Assigned.

PART IV.—A BRIEF REVIEW OF THIS STATUTE.

§ 25 a. It Introduced No New Principle.
§ 25 b. Enumeration of Abuses.
§ 26.   Title—Copy of Warrant—Statement of Cause of Commitment—Expenses.
§ 27.   Denied Copy—Bail.
§ 28.   Exceptions.
§ 29.   Treason and Felony.
§ 30.   Courts—Places—Removals—Recommitments.
§ 31.   Beyond the Seas.
§ 32.   Operation of the Act—Bail.
§ 33.   Bail, Continued—Amount thereof, etc.
§ 34.   Detention without Warrant—Return, and Statute of George III.
§ 35.   The Opinion of James II.
§ 36.   Requirements to take Advantage of the Writ.
§ 37.   Eulogies.

PART V.—IN THE COLONIES.

§ 38.   Birthright to English Laws.
§ 39.   The Opinion of Chalmers.
§ 40.   Use of the Writ in Massachusetts.
§ 41.   Its History in South Carolina.
§ 42.   In the Province of Maryland.
§ 43.   In New Jersey and Pennsylvania.
§ 44.   Cases of the Presbyterian Ministers, New York.
§ 45.   Habeas Corpus Act Extended to Virginia.
§ 46.   Denial of Writ to Province of Quebec.

PART VI.—ITS GENERAL HISTORY IN THE UNITED STATES.

§ 47.   Constitutional Provisions.
§ 48.   Statutory Enactments.
§ 49.   Conflict between State and Federal Governments.

PART VII.—SUSPENSION OF THE WRIT.

§ 50.   What is Suspended.
§ 51.   Power to Suspend.
§ 52.   Act of Congress Authorizing its Suspension.
§ 53.   Suspension of It under This Act.
§ 54.   Validity of the Act.
§ 55.   Expiration of Authority Conferred by Act.
§ 56.   Writ Issued by State Court.
§ 57.   In the Confederate States.

PART I.—TRACES OF IT IN THE ROMAN LAW.

§ 1. **The Roman Edict.**—Patrick MacChombaich de Colquhoun says that "in the interdict, *De libero homine exhibendo*, the origin of the English habeas corpus may be traced." And as to the edict, *Quem liberum hominem dolo malo retines, exhibeas*, he lays down the Roman law as follows: "The individual object of this edict can not repudiate its benefits, nor does it derogate from the *Lex Favia*. It extends to all ages and to both sexes, where the party is not *sub potestate paterno*, because there can be no fraud in such case, *quis dolo malo non videtur habere qui suo jure utitur;* nor to him who retains a free man without fraud—as, for instance, his own child, freedman, or the like, or a willing person. If the party be clearly not a free man, this interdict has no place, because the *status civilis* can not be tried by this edict, but must be referred to a præjudicial action. The individual must be publicly exhibited, that is to say, produced; and as any one may make application for this interdict, it is for the prætor to choose the more fitting person to whom to grant it; and, like all public judgments, it can not be twice tried, except, indeed, some perfidy be proved; or if the defendant, being condemned, prefers submitting to the *litis æstimatic*, to producing the man. The interdict may be prayed against an absentee, and if he do not appear, his goods may be distrained to compel appearance. It will not lie by a creditor for the production of the debtor. The interdict is perpetual." [1]

PART II.—ITS USE IN THE EARLIER COMMON LAW.

§ 2. **Magna Charta.**—The twenty-ninth section of Magna Charta reads like this: "No freeman shall be seized, or imprisoned, or dispossessed, or outlawed, or in any way destroyed; nor will we condemn him, nor will we commit him to prison, excepting by the legal judgment of his peers, or by the laws of the land." [2] King John, on the fifteenth day of June, 1215, met the barons at Runnymede, "which is still a pleasant meadow by the Thames, where rushes grow in the clear water of the winding river, and its banks are green with grass and trees." There he smilingly, though reluctantly, signed the charter which is sometimes called by his name. And though he broke the charter immediately afterwards, it formed a basis for hundreds of years on which prisoners unlawfully confined could ground their demand for liberty.[3]

§ 3 *a*. **Ancient Writs.**—Prior to the signing of the charter of King John, however, other writs for liberating persons from prison on certain criminal charges were in existence. Glanville, the earliest English law-writer, who composed his treatise in the reign of Henry II., 1154–1189, details the particulars of a writ called *De odio et atia* which was used for this purpose. Other ancient writs were devised for securing personal liberty,

---
[1] 3 Summary of the Roman Civil Law, 551, sec. 2274.
[2] Thompson's Essay on Magna Charta, etc., 63.
[3] 4 Hallam's Constitutional History of England, 220.

as particularly those called *De homine replegiando* and *De manucaptione capienda*. Subsequently to the signing of the great charter, all these gradually gave place to the more summary and efficacious writ of habeas corpus. This last-named writ, requiring a return of the body of the person imprisoned, and the cause of his detention, and hence anciently called *Corpus cum causa*, was in familiar use between subject and subject in the reign of Henry VI., 1422-1461. It was apparently used as a means of relief from private restraint, and at that period it seems to have been familiar to and well understood by the judges. But its use by the subject against the crown has not been traced during the time of the Plantagenet dynasty; the earliest precedents known commencing with the reign of the Tudors, in the times of Henry VII., 1485-1509. From this time on, the use of the habeas corpus became more frequent, and before the act of 31 Car. II. it had become an admitted constitutional remedy—probably as early as the reign of Charles I., 1625-1649.[1]

§ 3 *b*. **The Knights' Habeas Corpus Case.**—During the reign of Charles I., five knights were committed to prison for refusing to contribute to an arbitrary loan demanded by the king. They sued the court of king's bench for their writ of habeas corpus, which was granted. The exigency of the writ in this case was fully recognized, but a discussion arose concerning the validity of the return, in which no other cause was assigned for the imprisonment than the special command of the king. "This," says Hallam, "gave rise to a most important question, whether such a return was sufficient in law to justify the court in remitting the parties to custody. The fundamental immunity of English subjects from arbitrary detention had never before been so fully canvassed; and it is to the discussion which arose out of the case of these five gentlemen that we owe its continued assertion by parliament, and its ultimate establishment in full practical efficiency by the statute of Charles II."

§ 4. **Idem—Arguments for the prisoners** were made with great ability by Noy, Selden, and other eminent lawyers. These arguments were based on Magna Charta, above referred to, and embraced the principle alluded to in that memorable instrument. "This principle," says Hallam, "having been frequently transgressed by the king's privy council in earlier times, statutes had been repeatedly enacted, independently of the general confirmations of the charter, to redress this material grievance. Thus, in the statute of 25 Edw. III., it is provided, that

[1] Amos' English Constitution, 170, and authorities cited.

'no one shall be taken by petition or suggestion to the king or his council, unless it be [*i. e.*, but only] by indictment or presentment, or by writ original at the common law.' And this is again enacted three years afterward, with little variation, and once again in the course of the same reign. It was never understood, whatever the loose language of these old statutes might suggest, that a man could be kept in custody upon a criminal charge before indictment, which would have afforded too great security to offenders; but it was the regular practice that every warrant of commitment, and every return by a jailer to the writ of habeas corpus, must express the nature of the charge, so that it might appear whether it were no legal offense, in which case the party must be instantly set at liberty, or one for which bail ought to be taken, or one for which he must be remanded to prison. It appears, also, to have been admitted without controversy, though not perhaps according to the strict letter of law, that the privy council might commit to prison on a criminal charge, since it seemed preposterous to deny that power to those intrusted with the care of the commonwealth, which every petty magistrate enjoyed. But it was contended that they were as much bound as every petty magistrate to assign such a cause for their commitments as might enable the court of king's bench to determine whether it should release or remand the prisoner brought before them by habeas corpus.

"The advocates for this principle alleged several precedents, from the reign of Henry VII. (1485-1509) to that of James (1603-1625), where persons committed by the council generally, or even by the special command of the king, had been admitted to bail on their habeas corpus. 'But I conceive,' said one of these, 'that our case will not stand upon precedent, but upon the fundamental laws and statutes of this realm; and though the precedents look one way or the other, they are to be brought back unto the laws by which the kingdom is governed.' He was aware that a pretext might be found to elude most of his precedents. The warrant had commonly declared the party to be charged on suspicion of treason or of felony, in which case he would, of course, be bailed by the court; yet in some of these instances the words 'by the king's special command' were inserted in the commitment, so that they served to repel the pretension of an arbitrary right to supersede the law by his personal authority. Ample proof was brought from the old lawbooks that the king's command could not excuse an illegal act. 'If the king command me,' said one of the judges under

Henry VI. (1422–1461), 'to arrest a man, and I arrest him, he shall have an action of false imprisonment against me, though it were done in the king's presence.' 'The king,' said Chief Justice Markham to Edward IV. (1461–1483), 'can not arrest a man upon suspicion of felony or treason, as any of his subjects may, because if he should wrong a man by such arrest, he can have no remedy against him.' No verbal order of the king, nor any under his sign-manual or privy signet, was a command, it was contended by Selden, which the law would recognize as sufficient to arrest or detain any of his subjects; a writ duly issued under the seal of a court being the only language in which he could signify his will. They urged further, that even if the first commitment[1] by the king's command were lawful, yet when a party had continued in prison for a reasonable time he should be brought to answer, and not be indefinitely detained; liberty being a thing so favored by the law that it will not suffer any man to remain in confinement for any longer time than of necessity it must."[2]

§ 5. **Idem—Argument for the Crown.**—"To these pleadings for liberty, Heath, the attorney general, replied in a speech of considerable ability, full of those high principles of prerogative which, trampling as it were on all statute and precedent, seemed to tell the judges that they were placed there to obey rather than to determine. 'This commitment,' he says, 'is not in a legal and ordinary way, but by the special command of our lord the king, which implies not only the fact done, but so extraordinarily done that it is notoriously his majesty's immediate act and will that it should be so.' He alludes afterward, though somewhat obscurely, to the king's absolute power, as contradistinguished from that according to law—a favorite distinction, as I have already observed, with the supporters of despotism. 'Shall we make inquiries,' he says, 'whether his commands are lawful? Who shall call in question the justice of the king's actions, who is not to give account for them?' He argues from the legal maxim, that the king can do no wrong, that a cause must be presumed to exist for the commitment,

---

[1] Amos, in his English Constitution, says that the writ was not returned on the day specified for its return, a breach of duty which the attorney general admitted was owing to commandment; and that a motion was made in court and granted for postponing the return till another day, but that upon the second day the body was not forthcoming; and that afterwards, not the prisoner, but the attorney general, applied *ex officio* for an *alias* writ, stating that such was the wish of the king, in consequence of a prevalent clamor that his majesty was delaying justice: P. 171.

[2] 4 Hallam's Constitutional History of England, 220.

though it be not set forth. He adverts with more success to the number of papists and other state prisoners detained for years in custody for mere political jealousy. 'Some there were,' he says, 'in the tower, who were put in when very young; should they bring a habeas corpus, would the court deliver them?' Passing next to the precedents of the other side, and condescending to admit their validity, however contrary to the tenor of his former argument, he evades their application by such distinctions as I have already mentioned."[1]

§ 6. **Idem--The Decision.**—"The judges," continues Hallam, "behaved during this great cause with apparent moderation and sense of its importance to the subject's freedom. Their decision, however, was in favor of the crown, and the offenders were remanded to custody. In pronouncing this judgment, the chief justice, Sir Nicholas Hyde, avoiding the more extravagant tenets of absolute monarchy, took the narrower line of denying the application of those precedents which had been alleged to show the practice of the court in bailing persons committed by the king's special command. He endeavored also to prove that where no cause had been expressed in the warrant, except such command as in the present instance, the judges had always remanded the parties, but with so little success that I can not perceive more than one case mentioned by him, and that above a hundred years old, which supports this doctrine. The best authority on which he had to rely was the resolution of the judges in the statute of 34 Elizabeth, published in Anderson's Reports;[2] for, though this is not grammatically worded, it seems impossible to doubt that it acknowledges the special command of the king, or the authority of the privy council as a body, to be such sufficient warrant for a commitment as to require no further cause to be expressed, and to prevent the judges from discharging the party from custody, either absolutely or upon bail; yet it was evidently the consequence of this decision, that every statute from the time of Magna Charta designed to protect the personal liberties of Englishmen, became a dead letter, since the insertion of four words in a warrant (*per speciale mandatum regis*), which might become

---

[1] 4 Hallam's Constitutional History of England, 221.

[2] In a note to the text the author says: "Coke himself, while chief justice, had held that one committed by the privy council was not bailable by any court in England:" 2 Cobbett's Parliamentary History of England, 310. He had nothing to say when pressed with this in the next parliament, but that he had misgrounded his opinion upon a certain precedent, which being nothing to the purpose, he was now assured his opinion was as little to the purpose: Id. 325; 3 Cobbett's State Trials, 81.

matter of form, would control their remedial efficacy; and this wound was the more deadly, in that the notorious cause of these gentlemen's imprisonment was their withstanding an illegal exaction of money. Everything that distinguished our constitutional laws, all that rendered the name of England valuable, was at stake in this issue. If the judgment in the case of ship-money[1] was more flagrantly iniquitous, it was not so extensively destructive as the present."[2]

§ 7. **Petition of Right.**—These measures, however, of illegal severity toward the uncompliant, "backed as they were by a timid court of justice," did not divert the nation from its cardinal point of faith in its own prescriptive franchises; and a few months after this adjudication upon the law of commitments, a parliament was summoned by the king, and their earliest proceedings were directed to the forced loan and the imprisonment of the persons who had refused to contribute toward it. "The discussion," says Amos[3]—"in the course of which reliance was placed on the precedent of Festus' opinion in the case of Paul, 'It seemeth to me unreasonable to send a prisoner, and not withal to signify the crimes laid against him'—resulted in the famous Petition of Right, 3 Car. I., c. 1. This act, after reciting among other things Magna Charta and the statute of 28 Edw. III., c. 3, states that 'nevertheless, against the tenor of the said statutes, divers of your subjects have of late been imprisoned without any cause shown; and when for their deliverance they were brought before your justices by your majesty's writs of habeas corpus, there to undergo and receive as the court should order, and their keepers commanded to certify the causes of their detainer, no cause was certified, but that they were detained by your majesty's special command, signified by the lords of your privy council; and yet were returned back to several prisons, without being charged with anything to which they might make answer according to law.' The act then provides, among other enactments, that 'no freeman in any such manner as is before mentioned be imprisoned or detained.'"

§ 8. **Contempt by Members of the House of Commons.**—Another memorable example of habeas corpus occurred in 1628, during the reign of Charles I. It arose from the imprisonment of members of the house of commons for their speeches and conduct in parliament. The speaker had delivered

---

[1] 3 Cobbett's State Trials, 1–234; 2 Cobbett's Parliamentary History of England, 246, 259 et seq. (Rushworth.)
[2] 4 Hallam's Constitutional History of England, 221, 222.
[3] Amos' English Constitution, 172.

the king's message, commanding him to adjourn the house, and put no question. This power of adjournment the house claimed to be inherent in themselves, and several members said that "after they had settled some things convenient to be spoken of, they would satisfy the king." Sir John Elliott then offered a remonstrance concerning tonnage and poundage. When this was offered to be put to the question, the speaker refused, on account of the king's command, to rise after his message had been delivered. He rose and left the chair, but was drawn to it again by Mr. Hollis, Valentine, and other members. Mr. Hollis—notwithstanding Sir Thomas Edmunds and other privy councilors endeavored to free the speaker—swore, "God's wounds!" "he should sit still till it pleased them to rise." The articles of protestation were read and allowed with a loud voice by the house.[1] Warrants were issued by the council, commanding the personal appearance of Elliott—who, we are informed, afterwards died, a victim of imprisonment in this affair—the learned and patriotic Selden, and other members of the parliament. The members summoned by the council refused to answer for what was done in parliament, and were committed to the marshal of the king's bench. The members were brought before the king's bench on habeas corpus in Easter term of the year of their commitment, 1629. The returns showed, first, that they were committed by virtue of a warrant under the hands of twelve privy councilors, without any cause shown, and which was contrary to the Petition of Right; secondly, that they were also detained by virtue of a warrant under his majesty's hand, and commanding the marshal to take notice that the previous commitment was "for notable contempt, committed against ourself and our government, and for stirring up sedition against us."[2]

Easter term was lost; but on the first day of Trinity term, when the court was ready to have delivered its opinion upon these writs of habeas corpus, the prisoners were not brought to the bar, according to the rule of the court. The marshal of the king's bench, however, appeared and informed the court that his prisoners had been removed the day before, and put in the tower of London by the king's own warrant. On the evening before the day for judgment, the king had written several letters to the judges, informing them why the prisoners were not suffered to come at the day appointed. The king was at first inclined to

---

[1] 2 Cobbett's Parliamentary History of England, 487–491.
[2] Id. 513, 514.

favor that great lawyer, Selden, one of the prisoners, and Valentine, and let them go before the court at the appointed time. This was intimated in one of his letters; but he immediately changed his mind, countermanded his instructions to that effect, and resolved that they all should receive the same treatment, and that none of them should go before the court "until we have cause given us to believe they will make a better demonstration of their modesty and civility, both towards us and your lordships, than at their last appearance they did." So the court delivered no opinion this term, and the imprisoned gentlemen continued in restraint all the long vacation. Towards the latter end of this term, on Michaelmas day, the chief justice and judge Whitlock of the king's bench, and the king himself, at Hampton, talked over the matter of the gentlemen's imprisonment in the tower. The king was willing, notwithstanding the prisoners' obstinacy, to let them be bailed, provided they would express "that they were sorry he was offended with them." He manifested his intention to proceed against them by the common law in the king's bench, and to have his proceeding in the star-chamber. But the judges said that the offenses were not capital, and that by law the prisoners ought to be bailed, giving security for their good behavior. At the conclusion of the good offices which these judges did to cause a healing of the breach, the king said "that he would never be offended with his judges so they dealt plainly with him, and did not answer him by oracles and riddles." So a motion was made to bail the prisoners. This was unanimously granted by the court, provided the prisoners would find sureties for their good behavior. But with this condition the prisoners refused to comply,[1] "therein acting up to the motto which Selden chose for one of his prison lucubrations at this juncture, *Sordes arcta inter vincla recusat.*" These arbitrary and high-handed proceedings were at the instance of a king who, we are informed, inscribed upon his coins, "*Relig. Prot. Leg. Ang. Liber. Parl.*"[2] What became of the prisoners will be made known in the next section.

§ 9. **Idem—Abolition of Star-Chamber and Other Arbitrary Courts.**—In Hilary term following, Walter Long, mentioned in note to the preceding section, had his case tried, on

---

[1] Mr. Long, though he had found sureties in the chief justice's chamber for good behavior, refused to continue his sureties any longer, inasmuch as they were bound in a great sum of two thousand pounds, and the good behavior was a ticklish point. So he was remanded to the tower with the other prisoners.

[2] 2 Cobbett's Parliamentary History of England, 513-516.

an information exhibited against him, in the star-chamber. He was sentenced to stand committed to the prison of the tower, there to remain during his majesty's pleasure, and to pay a fine of two thousand marks to his majesty's use; and further, to make his humble submission and acknowledgment of his offense, both in the court of star-chamber and to his majesty, before his enlargement. Proceedings were had in the same term, in the court of king's bench, against Sir John Elliott and others, on an information filed against them. The defendants refused to plead, and judgment was given against them upon a *nihil dicit*. It was to this effect: "1. That every of the defendants shall be imprisoned during the king's pleasure; Sir John Elliott to be imprisoned in the tower of London, and the other defendants in other prisons. 2. That none of them shall be delivered out of prison until he gives security in this court for his good behavior, and have made submission and acknowledgment of his offense. 3. Sir John Elliott [who offered the remonstrance mentioned in the preceding section], inasmuch as we think him the greatest offender and the ringleader, shall pay to the king a fine of two thousand pounds; and Mr. Hollis [who drew the speaker back to his chair], a fine of one thousand marks; and Mr. Valentine [who assisted Mr. Hollis in the interesting scene in parliament], because he is of less ability than the rest, shall pay a fine of five hundred pounds." "To all this the justices with one voice accorded. Some of these died in prison because they would not pay the fine; others, not able to pay it, on their petitions, submissions, and condition not to come nearer the court than ten miles, and give a bond of two thousand pounds for their good behavior, were released."

This parliament was dissolved, and it was not until 1640 that a new one was called. This was the "long parliament," lasting from 1640 to the forcible dissolution thereof by Cromwell, in 1653. It was during this period, in 1640, that the memorable statute of 16 Car. I., c. 10, was passed. This act regulated the privy council and dissolved the star-chamber. It contained a clause providing that any person imprisoned by order of the abolished star-chamber and other arbitrary courts, or by command or warrant of the king's majesty in his own person, or by command or warrant of the council board, or of the lords or others of his majesty's privy council, should be entitled to a writ of habeas corpus from the courts of king's bench or common pleas, without delay upon any pretense whatsoever; that the officer having the prisoner in custody should produce him and certify the cause of his detention; and that the court before which the prisoner was produced should either remand, bail, or deliver him within three court days after the writ's return. A violation of this section was punishable by treble damages.[1] During this parliament many of the star-chamber proceedings were annihilated, and the house of commons severely censured the speaker of the late parliament for his conduct. It further resolved that the proceedings had against the members for their speeches and conduct in parliament were a breach of privilege, and that there had been a delay of justice in not bailing them in the Easter and Trinity terms mentioned; and that the securities for good behavior, etc., demanded in the ensuing Michaelmas term, were without authority of law. "To each of the sufferers," we are informed by Mr. Amos, in his English Constitution, page 175, "five thousand pounds was awarded as a compensation for the unjust denial of that liberty which they had demanded, and to which they had been entitled by the writ of habeas corpus."[2]

§ 10. **Cases of Streater, and Fox, the Quaker.**—Mr. Amos tells us that during the commonwealth, the writ of habeas corpus was fully recognized as available against the government when Cromwell was on the point of assuming the title of protector. And that to a writ obtained by one Streater there was a return of two commitments: one by the council of state, for publishing seditious pamphlets against the state, signed by the president and three members, etc.; the other was a commitment by order of parliament, and signed by the speaker of that body. The first was dated September 12, 1653; the other, November 21, 1653. The judge hearing the habeas corpus remanded the prisoner, on the warrant by order of parliament. The parliament, however, was dissolved between the next Michaelmas and Hilary terms. So on the twenty-third of January, in the next Hilary term, Streater moved for and obtained a new writ of habeas corpus, made returnable the twenty-sixth of January. On the eleventh of February following, Chief Justice

---

[1] 4 Statutes at Large, 810.
[2] 2 Cobbett's Parliamentary History of England, 518, 520, 524, 854, 876, 877. This parliament also found the former speaker guilty of a breach of parliament, and ordered him to be committed to the tower "during the pleasure of this house." The speaker, on bended knees, received his sentence. He received permission from the house to speak for himself. He denied not the fact, but endeavored to extenuate it by the confusion of the times; the period which had elapsed since the crime was committed being thirteen years; and the command that lay upon him being commanded by the king and twenty-three councilors. But this was of no avail, and he was sent to the tower: Id. 877.

Rolle ruled that "the first part of the return was too general; it mentioneth not what books, whose books, or where they were, or when published. The second part is grounded on an order of parliament, which is reversed by the parliament being dissolved." The prisoner was accordingly discharged, and liberty was vindicated.[1]

He also informs us that throughout the reign of Charles II., before the passing of the habeas corpus act, the writ of habeas corpus continued to be used. He narrates that Fox the Quaker, in his remarkable diary, mentions his having availed himself of three writs of habeas corpus. One of them was issued in the year of the restoration, 1660, by the express direction of the king, who was moved thereto by two Quakeresses that had a personal interview with him; it may mitigate scandal to add, that the father of one of them had been hanged at his own door during the commonwealth for favoring the royal cause. Fox gives a description of being taken before a cross-grained, ill-tempered judge, Twisden of the king's bench, who spoke "angry words." A lord of the bed-chamber interposed, and his case was referred to the king in council. The king ordered Judge Mallett, knight and justice of the king's bench, to release Fox, which he did. This was simply because of his majesty's pleasure—an unprecedented proceeding. This was in 1660. In 1673 Fox obtained another writ, when he was released on bail, to appear at the Worcester sessions. In 1674 he obtained a third, after commitment upon a judgment of *præmunire* by the Worcestershire court of quarter sessions, when he was discharged by the court of king's bench, under the presidency of Sir Matthew Hale.[2]

§ 11. **The Celebrated Bushell and Shaftesbury Cases.**— On the ninth day of November, in the twenty-second year of the reign of Charles II., 1670, the writ of habeas corpus was issued by the king's bench in the celebrated Bushell case, which is so often cited as a leading authority in both England and the United States, as settling the immunity of juries for their verdicts. It was at the hearing on the return to this writ that Chief Justice Vaughan displayed so much judicial eloquence.[3]

Lord Ashley, soon afterward known by the name of earl of Shaftesbury, and one of the most remarkable characters of the age, had been committed to the tower during the king's pleasure, and that of the house of lords, for a contempt, by moving that a prorogation of parliament for fifteen months was

[1] Amos' English Constitution, 175.   [2] Id. 176, 177.
[3] Bushell's Case, 1 Vaugh. 135.

equivalent to a dissolution. He was brought up under an *alias* writ of habeas corpus, but was remanded, on inspection of the return of the constable of the tower, from which it appeared that he had been committed for a contempt of the house of lords.[1] The lords, however, soon after got the king to discharge him.

§ 12. **Long Duration of Imprisonment.**—In those olden times of Charles II., when for publishing pamphlets against the king and church a man could be censured, fined for all he was worth, sentenced to lose the remainder of his ears in the pillory, branded on both cheeks with an "S" for schismatic, and doomed to perpetual imprisonment, the duration of confinement before he could have his rights finally determined became an interesting question to the offender.[2] There is little doubt that many subjects were sent out of the kingdom to various places to put it out of their power to apply for and obtain a writ of habeas corpus. Lord Clarendon, that brilliant and talented earl, once lord high chancellor of England, and chancellor of the University of Oxford, who raised such a gust of envy and suspicion whirling round his head by building an extravagantly expensive house, costing fifty thousand pounds, on the site near St. James, granted him by the king, that he was obliged to flee the kingdom under an impeachment for high treason, and for which he was banished, was charged in the fourth article of impeachment agreed upon with having advised and procured many of his majesty's subjects to be imprisoned against law in remote islands, garrisons, and other places, to prevent them from the benefit of the law, and to produce a precedent for imprisoning other of his majesty's subjects in like manner. This charge, however, was never proved.[3] Yet Sir R. Temple said, in a debate in the house of commons, in a proposed habeas corpus act, in 1674, that since the king was restored, "several had been sent to Tangier and the islands."[4] At this day, no matter how or where the chains of his captivity may be forged, the power of the judiciary is adequate to crumble them to dust, if an individual is deprived of his liberty contrary to the law of the land; but it was obvious then, that the writ of habeas corpus "which could unbar all the prisons of England, was powerless at the dungeon-gates of Tangier."

[1] 4 Cobbett's Parliamentary History of England, 451; Amos' English Constitution, 177, 178. For full proceedings concerning Shaftesbury's trial, see 6 Cobbett's State Trials, 1270.

[2] 2 Cobbett's Parliamentary History of England, 732.

[3] 4 Cobbett's Parliamentary History of England, 379. For Clarendon's trial, see 6 Cobbett's State Trials, 291.

[4] 4 Cobbett's Parliamentary History of England, 661.

Mr. Amos writes, that notwithstanding the writ of habeas corpus, Sir Harry Vane, to the eternal opprobrium of Charles II., and Clarendon, the unscrupulous minister of a very bad king, complained, before trial, that he had been imprisoned two full years before an indictment was preferred against him. And that Colonel Hutchinson was imprisoned, under the administration of Lord Clarendon, for eleven months, without being brought to trial, in the castle of Sandoway Down—one of the castles built for the protection of the Kentish coast by orders of Henry VIII.—then in a very dilapidated condition. Colonel Hutchinson died, apparently in consequence of the severity of his punishment.[1]

§ 13. **The Habeas Corpus Bill**, entitled "An act to prevent the illegal imprisonment of the subject," was read a third time and passed the house of commons in 1674. "This," says Cobbett, quoting Ralph, " gave rise to the famous habeas corpus bill, which was calculated to set bounds to the arbitrary proceedings of ministers, and preserve to those who fell under their displeasure from being sent into banishment, or otherwise imprisoned, without cause, measure, or relief. But though this invaluable bill was now perfected by the commons and sent up to the lords, it did not receive the royal assent till some years after."[2]

§ 14. **Condition of the Prisons.**—In order to fully understand the terms of imprisonment in the reign of "The Merry Monarch," and why subjects were so eager to protect their liberty, we may be pardoned for giving a short description of the condition of the prisons at that time. We can present it in no better light than to quote the words of Mr. Amos: "With respect to rigor of imprisonment in the pre-Howard reign of Charles II., the punishment was aggravated by the state of the jails to an extent which can scarcely now be conceived. The circumstances of Colonel Hutchinson's imprisonment are particularly related by his widow in one of the most interesting of English memoirs. During the last eleven months of her husband's life, Mrs. Hutchinson remained at Deal, the nearest habitable place to the castle. She describes Sandoway castle as washed by the sea, of which the unwholesome damp moldered every article, and incrusted the dungeons with saltpeter, a peck of which might have been swept from the walls every day.

"Fox the Quaker has given most revolting descriptions of the state of the prisons in which he was incarcerated; that of

---

[1] Amos' English Constitution, 178.
[2] 4 Cobbett's Parliamentary History of England, 665.

Doomsdale, as Sir J. Mackintosh observes, 'surpassing all imagination.' Of the jail at Scarborough, Fox writes, 'there was no chimney nor fire-hearth in winter; the prison lying to the seaside, the wind drove in the rain, and the water came over my bed and flooded the room, so that I skimmed it up with a platter; when my clothes were wet, there was no fire to dry them; my fingers swelled, and one grew as big as two.' Elwood the Quaker complained that in Newgate he saw the heads of men executed for treason tossed about in sport by the hangman and the more hardened malefactors."[1]

These things make an honest American's blood boil. Could it have had less effect on the liberty-loving Englishman? The more so, when it is reflected that the end of those cruel imprisonments might be a revival of those horrible scenes described in the graphic words of Dickens, and which Cromwell had abandoned. "The hearts of the sufferers were torn out of their living bodies; their bowels were burned before their faces; the executioner cut jokes to the next victim, as he rubbed his filthy hands together that were reeking with the blood of the last; and the heads of the dead were drawn on sledges with the living to the place of suffering." Let us now call the writ of habeas corpus a general jail-deliverer, if we will; but remember, that "in the merry days, when this merry gentleman sat upon his merry throne, in merry England," it meant something to the unfortunate subject who needed its use.

§ 15. **Removal of Prisoners.**—A statute of Charles II., 18 & 19 Car. II., c. 9, recites that "sometimes by occasion of the plague, and other whiles by the great number of prisoners, great and infectious diseases have happened among the prisoners, whereby it hath come to pass sometimes that the judges, justices, and jurors have, upon the occasion of their attendance at the trials of prisoners, been infected, and many of them have died thereof, and sometimes such infection hath spread through the country." Instead of conforming to the dictates of humanity and mercy by improving the dismal condition of the foul dens in which the unfortunate beings were confined, the statute then provided for the removal of "sick prisoners," apparently not out of compassion for the prisoners, but concern for the health of judges, justices, and jurors. Later, in 1750, a jail fever was brought into the court of the Old Bailey in the clothes of the prisoners for trial. This caused the death of two judges, a lord mayor, and forty by-standers.

[1] Amos' English Constitution, 179.

§ 16. **The Celebrated Jenkes Case.**—This man, a linen-draper of London, on the popular or factious side, having been committed by the king in council for a so-called seditious and mutinous speech in Guildhall, demanded a copy of the warrant. This was delayed a few days, but finally given, with an excuse by the keeper that "before there was an order to deny it, now to give it." This manner of delaying a copy of the warrant, to acquaint the prisoner of the cause of his imprisonment, was subsequently remedied by the habeas corpus act, 31 Car. II. Jenkes' offense was simply making arrangements whereby a petition might be made for a new parliament to remedy the mischiefs and grievances the people were groaning under. Jenkes, in his highly dramatic examination before the king and council, among whom was Lord Shaftesbury,[1] above mentioned, made no attempt to deny or extenuate his offense, but in rather a presumptuous and arrogant manner endeavored to justify the same. He applied to Chief Justice Raynsford, of the king's bench, on the twenty-ninth of June, 1676, the next day after his commitment, for a habeas corpus, but it was refused, on the ground that it was vacation time. On the next day the like application was made, at a general seal, to Lord Chancellor Nottingham, who ordered the matter to stand over till the next seal, which he put off from the fourth to the sixth of July. The motion being renewed, Lord Coke's authority in his Institutes was pointed out, wherein he calls the court of chancery an *officina justitiæ*, that is ever opened and never adjourned. But Lord Nottingham replied that "Lord Coke was not infallible," and refused to grant the writ because it was the long vacation. Jenkes made other unsuccessful attempts to regain his liberty, and endeavored to get tried at the Westminster quarter sessions, but was told that it was not the usage to calendar prisoners committed by the council. After being in prison for over four months, Michaelmas term drew nigh. For some unaccountable reason, the approach of term seemed to have a subduing and awe-inspiring effect upon king, council, and judges, and as the writ of habeas corpus could be no longer delayed, the prisoner was bailed *sub silentio*.[2]

---

[1] During the inquisition a lord asked the prisoner, "Do you think any one may petition for a parliament?" Jenkes answered, "I believe they may." To this the king said, "I know whose scholar you are [probably glancing at Lord Shaftesbury, Mr. Amos imagines, and very properly too], and I will take care that none such as you shall have to do with the government:" See Amos' English Constitution, 184; 6 Cobbett's State Trials, 1194.

[2] Crowley's Case, 2 Swans. 5-20, 43-47; 6 Cobbett's State Trials, 1193; Nasmith's Inst. Pub. Law, 180.

§ 17. **Issuance of the Writ in Vacation.**—Although Chief Justice Raynsford denied the writ in Jenkes' Case, on the ground that it was the time of vacation, this is not the present law even in cases not affected by the habeas corpus act, either in England or the United States, as we shall hereafter see.[1] It has been questioned whether the decision arrived at in the Canadian Prisoners' Case would have been arrived at if unaided by the analogy of the statute. Mr. Amos attributes Lord Nottingham's refusal of the writ to an obviously "willful and corrupt denial of justice, a heartless want of sympathy for the personal liberty of the subject, aggravated by the circumstance that he had been himself one of Jenkes' inquisitors" in the dramatic examination above referred to, and which is given in full in 6 Cobbett's State Trials, 1193. Lord Nottingham was undoubtedly one of the ablest judges who ever sat in any court of England, but notwithstanding his high reputation, his decision in Jenkes' Case was said by Lord Eldon to be unsupported by either principle or authority. Coke's powerful authority did not stand alone. Sir Matthew Hale, Nottingham's contemporary, wrote: "By virtue of the statute of Magna Charta, and by the very common law, a habeas corpus in criminal cases may issue out of the chancery; but it seems regularly this should issue out of this court in the vacation time, and out of the king's bench in the term time."[2] The decision of Nottingham has been called "a wicked judgment; a judgment which evinced the necessity of some new provision for enforcing the writ of habeas corpus in the time of vacation." In conclusion, it may be said that before the statute of 31 Car. II., many difficulties were often experienced in obtaining a writ of habeas corpus in the times of vacation, and that irregular and arbitrary practices sprang up "during such partial eclipses of justice."

§ 18. **Imperfections of the Writ.**—We have seen that there were good times and bad times in the common law—a system to which has been attributed the peculiar merit of having a flexible character, enabling it to be accommodated to the condition, exigencies, and conveniences of the people. But personal liberty was subject to these fluctuations and changes, and it was in the bad times that this right was violated. This called for improvements in the remedy by writ of habeas corpus. The imperfections attached to relief by means of this writ would probably have not stood in need of a remedy, had they not been

---

[1] See Leonard Watson's Case, 9 Ad. & El. 731.
[2] 2 Hale's P. C , 147; Crowley's Case, 2 Swans. 7.

incident to this unwritten and flexible law. For instance, had the common law in regard to the granting of the writ of habeas corpus in vacation, as declared by Coke and Hale, been "stereotyped"—a process to which common-law lawyers on both continents express a positive and intemperate aversion—in a statutory form, it is said that Lord Nottingham would not have ventured to make that declaration of the common law which tarnishes his bright fame. It was this peculiar nature of the common law—its flexibility, we may say—that caused the two conflicting currents of authority, in the profligate reign of Charles II., as to the power of the court of common pleas to grant writs of habeas corpus.[1] It appears that the speedy trial of prisoners was sometimes evaded by colorably assigning a treasonable or felonious cause for their commitments; but as to this, Chief Justice Vaughan, in Bushell's Case,[2] stated that upon a commitment for treason or felony the prisoner may "press for his trial, which ought not to be denied or delayed." It was declared in the house of commons, by North, when attorney general, that at common law "no man can be imprisoned but in a legal prison, nor sent abroad but in order to trial." And as to the place where the writ would run, the court of king's bench, in 1668, had issued a writ of habeas corpus at common law to the governor of Jersey.[3] Andrew Amos, Esq., in treating of this topic, makes a very beautiful allusion to mythology. "The common law was doubtless, in some respects, chargeable with inadequacy; but personal liberty was chiefly compromised by means of its uncertainty and flexibility, and of its springing, in a great measure, from the heads of judges, not always with the like happy result as when Minerva sprung from the head of Jupiter." He further says: "Sagaciously did Lord Nottingham insert in his MS. treatise, called *Prolegomena*, a separate chapter, which, if continued to the present day, would fill a large book, entitled *L'où les juges del common ley ont agreed to alter it sans act de parlement, et l'où nemy.*"

PART III.—THE HABEAS CORPUS ACT, 31 CAR. II.

§ 19. **Passage of the Famous Habeas Corpus Act.**—By reference to the fourth volume of Cobbett's Parliamentary History of England, it will be seen that several times between 1668 and 1679 were bills for the amendment of the law of habeas

---

[1] For authorities pro and con, see 4 Bac. Abr., B, sec. 1, tit. Habeas Corpus; 4 Hallam's Constitutional History of England, 500.
[2] 1 Vaugh. 135. [3] See Siderfin, 386.

corpus debated in parliament, but none passed until the latter date. We left the bill of 1674 at the house of lords. On May 26, 1679, while Sir Robert Clayton was giving an account of members who had pensions, etc., and just before the parliament was prorogued and dissolved by proclamation, the black rod knocked at the door and commanded the house to attend the king in the house of lords, where his majesty passed the habeas corpus bill. This was the crowning act of this parliament, the great, essential, and inestimable service done to the people of England.

The familiar story of Rome's being saved by the cackling of geese seems to have a parallel in the manner in which this act is related to have been passed. Burnet is reported to have said that the act was passed by an odd artifice in the house of lords; and in these words he tells the substance of the story: "Lord Grey and Lord Norris were named to be the tellers. Lord Norris, being a man subject to vapors, was not at all attentive to what he was doing; so a very fat lord coming in, Lord Grey counted him for ten, as a jest at first; but seeing Lord Norris had not observed it, he went on with the misreckoning of ten. So it was reported to the house, and declared that they who were for the bill were the majority, though it indeed went on the other side; and by this means the bill was passed."[1] This almost incredible story, however, seems to be borne out by the minute-book of the lords, which, it is said, shows that there were only one hundred and seven peers in the house, while Lord Campbell is credited with mentioning that the numbers declared were fifty-seven and fifty-five.[2]

§ 20. **Why the Act is Famous.**—Although Magna Charta provided immunity from arbitrary imprisonment, this great privilege was impaired seriously by abuses of power. Ministers were guilty of this. And what renders it famous is, that the ministers, who act by order of the king, are subject to it as well as others. Under the statute, no minister would venture to exercise a sort of oppression so dangerous to himself.[3]

§ 21. **Auspicious Times of the Bill's Passage.**—The habeas corpus act of 31 Car. II. was passed amidst a political storm, which the ministry had to face; and great as was its value, it passed almost unnoticed, and with little debate. The nation was frenzied with suspicion and panic. The elections to the new parliament had taken place amidst a whirl of excite-

---

[1] 4 Bac. Abr., 600, sec. 13, tit. Habeas Corpus, B.
[2] Amos' English Constitution, 190.
[3] See 4 Hallam's Constitutional History of England, 501; 3 Bentham's Works, 204, note.

ment which left no place for candidates of the court. At this time, also, the statute for the regulation of printing expired, and the temper of the parliament at once put an end to any attempt at re-establishing the censorship. To the new freedom of the press the habeas corpus act added new security for the personal freedom of every Englishman.[1] In the short speech he made just before proroguing parliament, his majesty adverted to the differences between the two houses, and expressed his fears of their ill effects.[2] The kingdom was regularly and openly divided into two zealous parties, and it was not difficult for the king to know that the majority of the new house of commons was engaged in interests opposite to the court. This compelled him to leave no expedient untried to compose the unhappy differences among his subjects.[3] Not only this, but that bold measure, the bill of exclusion, had been read the first time. It was too bold for the spirit of the country, and the rock on which English liberty was nearly shipwrecked. While the exclusion bill was passing the commons, the king took the pains to speak himself to almost every lord, to dissuade them from assenting to it when it should come up; telling them, at the same time, let what would happen, he would never suffer such a villainous bill to pass.[4] The singularly propitious aspect of public affairs at the time will further be seen by spending a few hours in the company of the English historians. It may be remarked that the lords opposed the bill as first drafted. No agreement was reached until the last hour of the session. The commons then gladly admitted the lords' amendments, that they might have the merit and their fellow-subjects the benefit of so useful a law.[5]

§ 22. "**Why did the King Assent to the Act?**" has probably been asked. This, of course, is a matter for speculation. Macaulay's is this: "The king would gladly have refused his assent to that measure, but he was about to appeal from his parliament to his people on the question of the succession; and he could not venture, at so critical a moment, to reject a bill which was in the highest degree popular." Bolingbroke, in his dissertation on parties, thus refers to the spirit of concession in King Charles which manifested itself on this occasion, as it had at other times during his reign: " Charles could not have divided and led

---

[1] 3 Green's History of the English People, 428, 429.
[2] 4 Cobbett's Parliamentary History of England, 1149.
[3] 2 Hume's History of England, 576.
[4] 4 Hallam's Constitutional History of England, 473, and note (from Life of James, 553), 474.
[5] 4 Cobbett's Parliamentary History of England, 1149 (from Ralph).

the people if he had wanted any of the qualities he possessed, or had held another conduct than he held. He observed their temper, and he complied with it. He yielded to them in points from which he had determined, and declared too, that he would never depart. To know when to yield in government is at least as necessary as to know when to lose in trade, and he who can not do the first is so little likely to govern a kingdom well that it is more than probable he would govern a shop ill."

§ 23. **Its Relation to Other Acts.**—A perusal of the first four volumes of Cobbett's Parliamentary History of England reveals the fact that in the three parliaments of Charles' reign, immediately following the dissolution of the long parliament, there were only five public and three private acts passed. The public acts were, in the third parliament, an act for a supply to enable the king to disband his forces, the habeas corpus act, and an act for re-engrossing the records of fines burned in a fire at the temple; in the fourth parliament, an additional act for burying in woolen, and an act for prohibiting the importation of cattle from Ireland. Under this condition of parliamentary enactments, the learned Amos makes the following beautiful simile: "The habeas corpus act may thus be regarded as an oasis in English legislation, seeing that three parliaments in succession have left no lasting memorial of their existence save this evergreen vestige in the midst of a legislative desert."

§ 24. **To What the Act may be Assigned.**—Cobbett thinks it probable that Jenkes' Case contributed to the passage of the habeas corpus act,[1] and Blackstone attributes it to the same source. Lord John Russell[2] adduces this case as an example of a "sense of justice" in the nation, which, on this occasion, as on two others which he mentions, vindicated the cause of a private individual when oppressed by the power of the executive government. But Hallam controverts these statements, and says the arbitrary proceedings of Lord Clarendon were real ve rise to it.[3] The occasion for the habeas corpus act may have been contributed to by both Jenkes and Clarendon; some of its clauses appear to point to the one and some to the other cause, and some to neither of the two. Mr. Andrew Amos says: "The principal author of the habeas corpus act was doubtless Lord Shaftesbury, and it was for a number of years called 'Lord Shaftesbury's act;'" and considering the ability of this lord, his irrepressible energy, his own imprison-

---

[1] 6 Cobbett's State Trials, 1208. [2] British Constitution.
[3] 4 Hallam's Constitutional History of England, 499.

ment, and his wonderful influence in the third and fourth parliaments, we are strongly inclined to lend our adherence to the latter view. Fox observes: "It is to one of those parliaments [the third] which so disgraced themselves and the nation by the countenance given to Oates and Bedloe, and by the prosecution of so many innocent victims, that we are indebted for the habeas corpus act."[1]

PART IV.—A BRIEF REVIEW OF THIS STATUTE.

§ 25 *a*. **It Introduced No New Principle.**—"It is a very common mistake," says Hallam, "and that not only among foreigners, but many from whom some knowledge of our constitutional laws might be expected, to suppose that this statute of Charles II. enlarged in a great degree our liberties, and forms a sort of epoch in their history; but though a very beneficent enactment, and eminently remedial in many cases of illegal imprisonment, it introduced no new principle, nor conferred any right upon the subject. From the earliest records of the English law, no freeman could be detained in prison except upon a criminal charge or conviction, or for a civil debt. In the former case, it was always in his power to demand of the court of king's bench a writ of *habeas corpus ad subjiciendum*, directed to the person detaining him in custody, by which he was enjoined to bring up the body of the prisoner, with the warrant of commitment, that the court might judge of its sufficiency, and remand the party, admit him to bail, or discharge him, according to the nature of the charge. This writ issued of right, and could not be refused by the court. It was not to bestow an immunity from arbitrary imprisonment, which is abundantly provided for in Magna Charta—if, indeed, it were not much more ancient—that the statute of Charles II. was enacted; but to cut off the abuses by which the government's lust of power, and the servile subtlety of crown lawyers, had impaired so fundamental a privilege."[2]

§ 25 *b*. **Enumeration of Abuses.**—Although the habeas corpus act was not what it ought to have been, it was highly remedial in regard to the evasions of the writ which it obviates. In what follows, continual reference must be made to the copy of the act, which will be found in another portion of this work.[3]

---

[1] Sir Edward Coke is credited with having drawn the resolution which was the basis of the habeas corpus act, declaring that no man could be detained in prison unless the cause of his commitment was shown, and proclaiming that the writ of habeas corpus was a writ of right, and could not be denied to any man: See Great Opinions of Great Judges, 3.

[2] 4 Hallam's Constitutional History of England, 500; same principle, see British Liberties, printed in London, 1706.

[3] See *post*, sec. 58.

We have already adverted to some of these abuses, among which are: 1. Denial of the copy of commitment; 2. Neglect in returning the writ; 3. Cavils as to the authority granting the writ; 4. Scruples as to the time of granting it; 5. Delay of adjudication; 6. Reach of the writ; 7. Imprisonment beyond seas; 8. Removals; 9 and 10. Colorable commitments for treason or felony. Another abuse provided for by the statute is that of recommitment for the same offense. A reference to the preamble will show that the enacting clauses of the statute are far more comprehensive than it is. The preamble refers only to subterfuges employed in delaying a return of the writ—an abuse of which jailers were sometimes guilty, though probably in consequence of commands. This striking difference between the preamble and enacting clauses of the act has been attributed to a hasty copying of the act from one of the previous abortive bills.[1]

§ 26. **Title—Copy of Warrant—Statement of Cause of Commitment—Expenses.**—The title shows the consolidation of two bills, and reads: "An act for the better securing the liberty of the subject, and for prevention of imprisonments beyond the seas." Section 5 shows that the prisoner, or a person on his behalf, may demand a copy of the warrant of his commitment in the prescribed manner, and that it is to be delivered to him within six hours, under a penalty of one hundred pounds to the prisoner. Section 2 provides that every writ of habeas corpus is to be returned to the authority whence it issued the periods of time therein mentioned, varying according to distance. A statement of the true causes of his detention was to be carried up with the body of the prisoner, within the varying periods and times therein mentioned, under a penalty of five hundred pounds to the prisoner. The prisoner had to pay the charges of his being carried up, and also those of his return to jail in case he was remanded. The first were estimated by the judge allowing the writ, indorsed on it, and paid at once; the amount, however, was not to exceed twelvepence a mile. The second were provided for by the prisoner's bond in case he was remanded. No fee could be demanded for the copy of the *mittimus;* and the turnkey had to deliver it at his peril.

§ 27. **Denied Copy—Bail.**—Sections 7 and 10. Any person, as seen by these sections, could carry a true copy of the commitment to the officers therein mentioned, and upon view of it, or upon oath made that a copy was demanded and denied, they

[1] Amos' English Constitution, 194.

would issue a writ of habeas corpus returnable immediately; and within two days of its return discharge the prisoner from his imprisonment, "taking his or their recognizance, with one or more surety or sureties in any sum, according to their discretions, having regard to the quality of the prisoner and nature of the offense, for his appearance before the king's bench, or at the assizes or sessions." The judge had to grant the writ or forfeit five hundred pounds to the prisoner. But it must be noted that the request had to be in writing, and attested by two witnesses. Section 7 permits bail, except where by law the offense is not bailable. It must be observed that the provisions of this section and of the preceding one are confined to imprisonments for criminal or supposed criminal matters, and do not apply where the commitment is for "treason or felony, plainly and specially expressed in the warrant of commitment."

§ 28. **Exceptions.**—The provisions of the habeas corpus act are subject to exceptions; they are not to apply if it appear to the authority issuing the writ that the prisoner is detained by legal process, order, or warrant out of some court that hath jurisdiction in criminal matters, or by legal warrant for such matters or offenses for which, by the law, the prisoner is not bailable; or if he be committed for treason or felony, plainly expressed in the warrant of commitment, or if he be convict or in execution by legal process, or if he be charged with process in any civil suit. The exceptions will be found straggling along through the act. The implied exception of commitment for contempt of the houses of parliament has been previously considered. This rests on the ground that every court is the sole judge of its own contempts, that an adjudication of contempt or breach of privilege is a conviction, and that a commitment in consequence is an execution.

§ 29. **Treason and Felony.**—If high treason or felony is plainly and specially expressed, that is, not only generally for treason or felony, but treason in conspiring to kill the king, or in counterfeiting the king's coin, or felony for stealing the goods of such a one to such a value, etc., then the prisoner can not have his habeas corpus till he has, in the first week of the term, or on the first day of sessions of oyer and terminer, or general jail-delivery, petitioned in open court to be brought to his trial; and then if he is not brought to trial, he shall be bailed on the last day of the next term or sessions; and if not indicted at the second term or sessions, he shall be discharged: Sec. 7.

§ 30. **Courts—Places—Removals—Recommitments.—**
The writ of habeas corpus could be sued for out of the court of chancery, court of exchequer, king's bench, or common pleas in term time, and the lord chancellor, any judge of the king's bench, common pleas, or exchequer, was required to issue the writ in vacation, as provided in section 10. Hallam informs us that at common law the court of exchequer seems never to have issued the writ; but an exception seems to have been made in case of its own officers. At common law, Hale asserted the power of the common pleas to issue the writ, and Vaughn denied it. The places to which the writ may run are enumerated in section 11. Sections 9 and 21 specify the circumstances in which prisoners can only be removed out of their original custody. Section 6 prohibits prisoners set at large by habeas corpus from being recommitted for the same offense, "any colorable pretense or variation in the warrant of commitment notwithstanding," under a penalty of five hundred pounds to the prisoner.

§ 31. **Beyond the Seas.—**Section 12 provides that no subject of the realm shall be sent a prisoner into Scotland, Ireland, Jersey, Guernsey, Tangier, or into parts, garrisons, islands, or places beyond the seas. This is strongly prohibited by placing any person concerned in commitments beyond the seas under a penalty of treble damages and costs, and the damages not to be less than five hundred pounds; besides which, upon his conviction he shall be incapacitated from holding any office of trust or profit, and shall undergo the punishment of *præmunire*—involving forfeiture of goods and chattels, and imprisonment during the pleasure of the king—and shall be "incapable of any pardon from the king of the said forfeitures, losses, or disabilities, or any of them." Amos says that the penalties for this last offense "were meant to terrify ministers like Clarendon, who might otherwise feel secure from popular gales, whilst basking under the favor of the sovereign whose pardon, as in the case of Danby, might have blunted the sword of justice."

§ 32. **Operation of the Act—Bail.—**"The immediate operation of the habeas corpus act," says Amos, "was not to dispel, as with a magic wand, all delays of trial for state offenses, and all illegal imprisonments. A few days before the passing of the habeas corpus act, Pepys had been committed to the tower, under a warrant of the speaker of the house of commons, upon a treasonable charge of being a Roman Catholic and concerned in the popish plot. On the second of June, a week after the passing of the act, he was brought to the bar of the king's bench, under a writ of habeas corpus, when he applied to be bailed, but was denied, probably on the ground that treason was expressed on the face of the warrant. He then demanded to be tried within the time specified by the act. This application was refused, on the suggestion of the attorney general that he expected further evidence of treasonable correspondence with France. Pepys was thereupon remanded to the tower, and after being brought to the bar a second and a third time, was bailed in the excessive sum of thirty thousand pounds. To save his securities, he was obliged to appear before the court of king's bench four times more, on each of which occasions the trial was postponed on the same plea. Afterwards, upon a statement of the attorney general that the solitary witness, Scott, had refused to adhere to his original accusation, Pepys was relieved from bail in Easter term, 1680, about a year after his commitment.

"Narcissus Luttrell, indeed, writes in his diary, in November, 1683: 'The first week of this term, several persons committed on account of the plot—the Rye-house plot—made their prayers to the court of king's bench to be either tried or bailed according to the habeas corpus act, which prayers were accordingly recorded.' But Algernon Sidney was sent to the tower on the twenty-sixth of May, 1683, and was not tried till the twenty-first of November in that year. Narcissus Luttrell mentions, that on the seventh of November, 1683, Speke—who had been indicted for spreading rumors concerning the earl of Essex's death—was bailed, 'but in going home was arrested in an action of *scandalum magnatum*, for one hundred thousand pounds, at the suit of the duke of York, and carried to prison for want of bail.' From the same authority we learn that St. Nicholas island, at Plymouth, was kept up as a state prison, supposed to be out of the reach of the writ of habeas corpus; and that Colonel Rumsey, after the contradictions in his evidence at the trials of Lord Russell and Cornish had rendered him too infamous to be used any longer as a king's evidence, ended his days in that place of confinement."[1]

§ 33. **Bail, Continued—Amount thereof, etc.**—We have adverted to the provision in section 7 of the act, affording security against any protracted detention of an innocent man, though some matter of treason or felony be expressed against him in the warrant, by way of evading the remedial provisions of the act, the judges not being empowered to inquire into the truth of the

[1] Amos' English Constitution, 198.

facts contained in it. Another evasion might have been found in the bailing of prisoners. The act is silent upon the subject of the amount of bail; "and it might easily have been made a dead letter," says Mr. Amos, "by an abuse of the discretionary power by it of bailing; the party imprisoned, when brought before a judge, being entitled to be set free only on condition of being bailed, the amount being left to the judge's discretion, who might have none." Since the reign of Charles II., however, an important security for liberty has been gained in the declaration of the bill of rights, that "excessive bail ought not to be required."

The same learned author mentioned above says: "Considering the ferment of politics in which the habeas corpus act was passed, it will not be surprising, if, after the lapse of nearly two centuries, that act may appear open to some criticisms, and may have been somewhat dilapidated by time. The provisions of the act turn very much on the distinction between felonies and misdemeanors, which, in the reign of Charles II., was a clear and sensible distinction; for, in that reign, felonies were almost synonymous with capital offenses, and the expressions "felonies" and "capital offenses" are often used indiscriminately by Sir Matthew Hale. Felonies were generally not bailable, at least by justices of the peace; misdemeanors were almost universally so. In the present day (1857), felonies are generally bailable by justices, and a series of misdemeanors is not bailable of right, but only at discretion. What occasion, then, is there for summary and extraordinary relief in the case of those misdemeanors the perpetrators of which are not now, as of common right, entitled to be set free upon bail? And on the other hand, what provision does the act contain for forcing on trials of persons committed for such misdemeanors as are bailable only at discretion? Perhaps, in this respect, the habeas corpus act partakes, in some measure, of the crust of antiquity."[1]

§ 34. **Detention without Warrant—Return, and Statute of George III.**—The statute of 31 Car. II. was only applicable to cases of commitment on a criminal charge, every other species of restraint on personal liberty being left to the ordinary remedy as it subsisted before this enactment. An obvious defect was in not providing for cases of imprisonment without warrant. In such a case the party detained had to sue out his remedy at common law. But after the statute the judges of king's bench adopted the practice of issuing the writ in vacation in all cases

[1] Amos' English Constitution, 200.

§ 35.   HISTORY OF THE WRIT.   29

whatsoever. A sensible difficulty was sometimes felt, from the officer's incompetency to judge of the truth of a return made to the writ: for though, in cases within the statute, the prisoner might always look to his legal discharge at the next sessions of jail-delivery, the same redress might not always be obtained when he was not in the custody of a common jailer. If the person, therefore, who detained any one in custody should think fit to make a return to the writ of habeas corpus, alleging matter sufficient to justify the party's restraint, yet false in fact, there would be no means, at least by this summary process, of obtaining relief. The subsequent statute of George III., however, not only extended the power of issuing the writ during the vacation, in cases not within the act of Charles II., to all the judges, but enabled the judge before whom the writ was returned to inquire into the truth of the facts alleged therein, and to dispose of the prisoner as justice might demand.[1]

Several useful provisions in this statute are made applicable to the act of Charles II., and may be regarded as expedient modifications of that act. Amos says: "It may be questioned whether most of the discrepancies remaining between the two statutes are not to be attributed to the alteration of times rather than to diversity in their subject-matters. The curtailment of the power of pardoning, for instance, and the penalty of five hundred pounds on judges, would probably not have been inserted in a habeas corpus act made in the present reign" (Victoria's). Further: "That it seems to deserve the attention of the legislature whether, as in several codes of America, all extant provisions touching illegal imprisonment might, to nearly their whole extent, be advantageously consolidated, thus methodizing many rambling enactments, avoiding unnecessary diversities and repetitions, and making the English law concerning the personal liberty of the subject simple, accessible, and uniform; rendering it in form, as well as substance, a just cause of national pride."[2]

§ 35. The Opinion of James II. has been reported as follows: "James II. evidently considered the act as, if not introductory of a new element of the constitution, eminently conducive to the people's safety, or as he deemed it, their licentiousness. Among the Stuart papers is a document dated A. D. 1692—shortly before James' death—and headed 'For my son, the prince of Wales,' containing these words: ''Twas a great

[1] See 4 Hallam's Constitutional History of England, 501.
[2] Amos' English Constitution, 202.

misfortune to the people as well as to the crown, the passing of the habeas corpus act; since it obliged the crown to keep a greater force on foot than it needed otherwise to preserve the government, and encouraged disaffected, turbulent, and unquiet spirits to contrive and carry with more security to themselves their wicked designs. 'Twas contrived and carried by the earl of Shaftesbury to that intent.'"[1]

§ 36. **Requirements to Take Advantage of the Writ.**—The same learned author cited in the preceding section, and whose words we can not forbear to quote in this, discourses on this point as follows: "Beneficial as is the remedy by writ of habeas corpus, it is necessary, in order to take advantage of it, to possess some knowledge of law, some friends, some money; and to prisoners who want these *desiderata*, the habeas corpus act affords a remedy beyond reach. Chief Justice Scroggs, when printers of libels were brought before him, refused to bail them, but left them to sue out writs of habeas corpus, well knowing that to some of them this prospect afforded only a bare imagination of liberty. The leaders of a party and their friends, whose safety was probably the immediate inducement for passing the habeas corpus act, might have experienced no difficulty in availing themselves of the relief it presented; but there are many persons to whom, even in the present days of schooling, the habeas corpus act would be a remediless remedy. More universally obtainable relief than by the habeas corpus act is now secured to the subject by the visitations of prisons, the regular order of judicature, the improvements of the constitution in respect of the tenure of judges, and the frequent holding of parliament; but more than all, by the omnipotent voice of public opinion."

§ 37. **Eulogies.**—We have adverted to the words of Hallam relative to the rights which the statute of Charles II. conferred. It is common to find in both English and American works—in both historical and legal literature—extravagant and undue praises of this act, when, as Mr. Hallam suggests, they more properly belong to the writ of habeas corpus devised by our more remote ancestors, and which, before the creation of that act, had been in existence for centuries. An elegant writer has attributed the cause of this to ignorance occasionally, "but more frequently, perhaps, to that admiration which follows the crowning operation of any noble fabric."

[1] Amos' English Constitution, 203.

PART V.—IN THE COLONIES.

§ 38. **Birthright to English Laws.**—A birthright in the laws has always been a favorite idea in England, and the American colonies always claimed this inheritance—to possess "all the rights, liberties, and immunities of free and natural-born subjects within the realm of England."[1] Indeed, it was expressly declared in all the charters under which the colonies were settled, except that to William Penn, that all subjects and their children inhabiting the colonies should be deemed natural-born subjects, and entitled to all the liberties and immunities thereof.[2] But even this omission in the charter to Penn was never supposed to deprive the Pennsylvania colonist of his rights as an Englishman. On the contrary, it was considered that the clause was wholly unnecessary, as the allegiance to the crown was reserved; and the common law thence inferred that all the inhabitants were subjects, and of course were entitled to all the privileges of Englishmen.[3] In almost all of the early legislation of the colonies, their respective assemblies insisted upon a declaratory act, acknowledging and confirming these rights, liberties, and immunities of British subjects. As the approach of the revolution threatened these rights and privileges, they were reasserted from time to time by the colonies, both severally and collectively.[4] These assertions may be seen in the proceedings of the congress of the nine colonies, in 1765, and the continental congress of 1774. These views were not unindorsed in parliament, where it was said that the Americans "were the sons, not the bastards, of England."

§ 39. **The Opinion of Chalmers** was, that there was no circumstance in the history of colonial jurisprudence better established than the fact that the habeas corpus act was not extended to the plantations till the reign of Anne. "The colonists," said he, "had a right to possess every immunity which Englishmen within a distant and subordinate territory of the empire could possibly enjoy. They were entitled to personal security, to private property, and what was of most importance of all, to personal liberty." He endeavors to show that before the reign of Anne they enjoyed the two first, but did not possess the last at all, because the effectual remedy, the writ of habeas corpus, was unknown to them.[5] Whatever may have

---

[1] 1 Story's Constitution, sec. 165.
[2] Charters and Constitutions of the United States.
[3] 1 Story's Constitution, sec. 122.
[4] Id., sec. 165.
[5] Hurd's Habeas Corpus, 2d ed., 95, citing Chalmer's Annals, 677.

been the opinion in England as to whether the privilege of the writ of habeas corpus extended to the plantations until it was expressly extended in the reign of Anne, and however much less efficient the writ may have been in the colonies than it was in England, it is certain that it was not unknown or undervalued, or considered by the colonists as inapplicable prior to that time, as a few subsequent scraps of colonial history will show.

§ 40. **Use of the Writ in Massachusetts.**—In this province we are informed that among other writs in use during the period of the province charter was that of habeas corpus. Washburn says: "It seems to have been adopted at first as a common-law remedy. In 1689, application for such a writ was made to Judge Dudley by Mr. Wise, but the application was arbitrarily refused. In 1706, an application was made to Chief Justice Sewall for a writ of habeas corpus, and, although it was refused for satisfactory reasons, there is nothing to indicate that the court regarded it as a novel application. I have, however, found no one of a similar kind made at any earlier period of the provincial government. A writer in the Historical Collections suggests a query, if this was not the first instance of an application for this writ in Massachusetts. The instance of the Rev. Mr. Wise, in 1689, has already been noticed, and the refusal of Judge Dudley to grant it was made the ground of a suit for damages, after the revolution in New England—1688-9—which shows that the right to this writ was regarded as one of the existing privileges of the colonists."[1]

Mr. Wise's offense was this: Among other towns which were ordered to raise money for the government was Ipswich, over which the Rev. Mr. Wise was settled as minister. A town meeting was called to act upon this requisition, and as they doubted the authority of the governor and council to raise money in that way, they declined making the grant. Whereupon Mr. Wise and five others of the principal inhabitants of the town were arrested. The *mittimus* charged them with contempts and high misdemeanors. They demanded a habeas corpus, which was denied.[2] "After a tedious and harassing delay the prisoners were put upon their trial. They claimed the privileges secured to them as Englishmen by the magna charta and the laws of England. The chief justice, however, informed them that they must not expect that the laws of England would follow them to

---

[1] Washburn's Judicial History of Massachusetts, 195.
[2] Id., 105.

the ends of the earth, and concluded by telling them that they had no more privileges left them than not to be sold as slaves. He charged the jury, and stated that the court 'expected a good verdict from them, seeing the matter had been so sufficiently proved against the criminals.' A verdict was accordingly rendered against them, and a severe punishment thereupon inflicted, because the town in which they resided declined yielding to an arbitrary and illegal act."[1]

This doctrine of the English laws not following the New Englanders to the ends of the world was adverted to in a pamphlet, containing a statement of the grievances of the people, published April 18, 1689, and entitled "The Declaration of the Gentlemen, Merchants, and Inhabitants of Boston and the Country Adjacent." The denial of the writ of habeas corpus was alleged as one of those grievances.[2] In 1692 the power of granting writs of habeas corpus was conferred by act of assembly of Massachusetts upon the justices of the superior court, but on the arrival of Lord Bellamont, three years later, he officially announced the disallowance of the act of 1692.[3]

§ 41. **Its History in South Carolina** is thus told by Dr. Hewitt: "About the year 1692, forty men arrived in a privateer, called the Royal Jamaica, who had been engaged in a course of piracy, and brought into the country treasures of Spanish gold and silver. These men were allowed to enter into recognizances for their peaceable and good behavior for one year, with securities, till the governor should hear whether the proprietors would grant them a general indemnity. At another time a vessel was shipwrecked on the coast, the crew of which openly and boldly confessed they had been on the Red sea plundering the dominions of the Great Mogul. The proprietors instructed Governor Ludwell to change the form of electing juries, and required that all pirates should be tried and punished by the laws of England made for the suppression of piracy. Before such instructions reached Carolina the pirates, by their money, and by their freedom of intercourse with the people, had so ingratiated themselves into the public favor that it was become no easy matter to bring them to trial, and dangerous to punish them as they deserved. The courts of law became scenes of altercation, discord, and confusion. Bold and seditious speeches were made from the bar, in contempt of the proprietors and their govern-

---

[1] Washburn's Judicial History of Massachusetts, 116.
[2] 4 Force's Collection of Historical Tracts, in Account of Revolution in New England.
[3] Washburn's Judicial History of Massachusetts, 152.

ment. Since no pardons could be obtained but such as they had authorized the governor to grant, the assembly took the matter under deliberation, and fell into hot debates among themselves about a bill of indemnity. When they found the governor disposed to refuse his assent to such a bill, they made a law empowering magistrates and judges to put in force the habeas corpus act, 31 Car. II., made in England. Hence it happened that several of these pirates escaped, purchased lands from the colonists, and took up their residence in the country. While money flowed into the colony in this channel, the authority of government was a barrier too feeble to stem the tide and prevent such illegal practices. At length the proprietors, to gratify the people, granted an indemnity to all the pirates, excepting those who had been plundering the Great Mogul, most of whom also found means of making their escape out of the country."[1] This law adopting the habeas corpus act was, Hurd says on page 98, repealed in 1712, and another passed, which existed many years.

§ 42. **In the Province of Maryland,** the people did not believe that the statutes of England did not extend to them; or believe in the expressed opinions of some of the best lawyers of England that they did not; or that the habeas corpus act did not extend to the plantations. There was no provincial act upon the subject; yet the act was recognized and practically adopted.[2]

§ 43. **In New Jersey and Pennsylvania.**—In New Jersey, in 1710, the assembly denounced one of the judges, William Pinhorne, for having corruptly refused the writ of habeas corpus to Thomas Gordon, which they said was "the undoubted right and great privilege of the subject."[3] In Pennsylvania, while the council exercised the power of discharging from illegal imprisonment upon petition, they sometimes referred such applications to the county courts as the proper tribunals to afford relief.[4] "A court," says Hurd,[5] "possessing common-law powers, invoked to protect an admitted common-law right, may reasonably be supposed to have employed the well-known common-law remedy."

§ 44. **Cases of the Presbyterian Ministers of New York.**—In New York, in January, 1707, Makemie and Hamp-

---

[1] Dr. Hewitt's History of South Carolina, 115.
[2] Hurd's Habeas Corpus, 2d ed., 100.
[3] Field's Colonial Courts, N. J., 76.
[4] 1 Colonial Records, 24 (1683); 1 Colonial Laws of Pennsylvania, 327.
[5] Hurd's Habeas Corpus, 2d ed., 101.

ton, two ministers of the designated denomination, were arrested on the warrant of the governor, Cornbury, for preaching without a license. They refused to give bond and security that they would preach no more in that government; so they were committed to prison under the governor's warrant, which simply directed the prisoners to be safely kept until further orders, and did not even attempt to designate any offense. Chief Justice Mompesson allowed the prisoners writs of habeas corpus on the eighth of March of the same year. His honor was considered the finest lawyer in America, and was the warm personal friend of the governor. The *mittimus* was fatally defective in not specifying any offense. The sheriff received the writ of habeas corpus on Saturday, and deferred its service until Monday. In the mean time the sheriff was furnished with another *mittimus* containing a statement of the offense. On this the prisoners were admitted to bail. Makemie only was indicted. He was tried and acquitted.[1]

§ 45. **Habeas Corpus Act Extended to Virginia.**—In March, 1700, Edward Randolph, the surveyor general of the plantations during the reign of William, represented their lamentable condition to the board of trade, and recommended that, as the governors had been in the habit of imprisoning subjects without bail, the habeas corpus act should be extended as fully to the colonies as it was in England. This resulted in the extension of the privilege of the writ of habeas corpus 'to Virginia in 1710 by Queen Anne. That was the year when Virginia's bright young governor, Colonel Alexander Spottswood, came over, and it was he who was ordered to confer this benefit. It was accepted as a happy augury of his rule.[2]

It is thus seen that while the statute of Charles II. was not expressly adopted by all the provincial assemblies, or expressly extended to all of them by parliament or royal authority, it was not therefore held to be wholly inoperative in the colonies. In some there was a practical adoption of it, and long usage, by which it was held to have acquired the force of law. This was peculiarly so, at least, as to the mode of procedure. Many more cases may doubtless be discovered by searching the early judicial records of the colonies, in which the writ of habeas corpus was employed as a familiar remedy; but a further enumeration of instances will serve no useful purpose in this work.

---

[1] A particular narrative of this long and interesting trial will be found in 4 Force's Collection of Historical Tracts.

[2] Chalmer's Annals, 74; 3 Bryant's Popular History of the United States, 72.

§ 46. **Denial of Writ to Province of Quebec.**—The bill entitled "An act making more effectual provision for the government of the province of Quebec in North America," was presented to the house of lords on May 2, 1774. It passed that house on the 17th, and was read the first time on the next day in the house of commons, where it was opposed because it left the inhabitants under the civil law of France, denying them the right of trial by jury, the writ of habeas corpus; and also left them exposed to the French process, *lettre de cachet*, more odious than general search warrants. The opposition was ruin. The proposition to extend to the inhabitants the benefit of the English law of habeas corpus was defeated by a vote of seventy-six to twenty-one; and the bill was soon passed by a large majority. The passage of the bill was an augury of misgovernment to the other colonies. The writ of habeas corpus was regarded as one of the "dearest birthrights of Britons." They called the habeas corpus act the "great bulwark and palladium of English liberty;" and the denial of the benefit of it to a sister colony indicated to them the sure approach of tyranny towards the rest. The act was immediately denounced in the journals of the colonies, and was made a special ground of complaint by the continental congress which assembled in September, 1774. And it was finally regarded as manifesting so clearly the general spirit of tyranny of the British government towards the colonies that it was included in that short catalogue of insupportable wrongs which was embodied in the declaration of independence.[1]

PART VI.—ITS GENERAL HISTORY IN THE UNITED STATES.

§ 47. **Constitutional Provisions.**—In the articles of confederation there was no provision relating to the writ of habeas corpus. The only provision in the constitution of the United States is, that "the privilege of the writ of habeas corpus shall not be suspended, unless when in cases of rebellion or invasion the public safety may require it."[2] This, it will be seen, assumes the existence of the privilege, and provides against its infringement, even by the highest power in the state. Most of the state constitutions contain similar provisions. In some of them it is provided that the writ shall in no case be suspended, and in others the suspension can not exceed a specified time. These constitutional provisions do not, in any case, confer the right

---

[1] Hurd's Habeas Corpus, 2d ed., 104, citing American Archives, 4th ser., 170; 1 American Archives, 4th ed., 920, 931.
[2] Sec. 9, art. 1.

nor do they operate as grants of jurisdiction over the writ of habeas corpus. They simply recognize the existence of the right, and declare that the benfit of it shall not be taken away, except under the specified circumstances. These provisions, embodied as they are in the constitutions, operate as a limitation upon legislative power, and afford a complete security against the abuses of the writ's suspension.

§ 48. **Statutory Enactments.**— Congress prescribed the jurisdiction of the federal courts and justices under the writ of habeas corpus by the judiciary act of September 24, 1789, so that this great constitutional privilege "might receive life and activity." But even before this, some of the states had passed acts for the same purpose, and in 1787 New York adopted almost literally the statute of Charles II. This, of course, has since been materially changed. This same statute was re-enacted in New Jersey in 1795, and was adopted in South Carolina and Georgia before the revolution. The new states have generally passed laws defining the jurisdiction and regulating the practice under this writ. It is a valuable testimonial to the constitutional importance of the habeas corpus act of Charles II., that in our government, besides the adoption of the common law of habeas corpus which was in force prior to the revolution, the statute of Charles II. has been made the basis of laws enacted with the same object, both in the general constitution of the Union and in those of most of its separate states. There are some differences in the mode of procedure, but no such material departures in the statutes of any of the states from the established principles by which the practice at common law was governed as to render the general rules of the common procedure wholly inapplicable. Chancellor Kent expresses a deserved eulogium on the practical merits of the statute of Charles II. He says that "nothing similar to it can be found in any of the free commonwealths of antiquity. Its excellence consists in the easy, prompt, and efficient remedy afforded for all unlawful imprisonment, not leaving personal liberty to rest for its security upon general and abstract declarations of right."[1]

§ 49. **Conflict between State and Federal Governments.**—Prior to the decisions in the case of Ableman v. Booth,[2] 1858, and Tarble's Case,[3] 1371, there had grown up in the United States a most interesting question concerning the concurrent jurisdiction of the state courts to issue the writ of habeas corpus in cases of commitment or detention under the authority

---

[1] 1 Kent's Com., 9th ed., 646.   [2] 21 How. 506.   [3] 13 Wall. 397.

of the United States. Before the decision in these cases the weight of authority was most unquestionably in favor of the concurrent jurisdiction of the state courts. These cases settled the question—that they have no jurisdiction in such cases whatever—and may be said to have consigned the immense body of decisions concerning the question to the field of history; yet we shall give this interesting matter of history attention in a subsequent chapter.

Part VII.—Suspension of the Writ.

§ 50. **What is Suspended.**—In England it appears to be the habeas corpus act itself which is suspended. Thus by the statute of 9 Geo. I., c. 1, the habeas corpus act was suspended for a time, and in Green's History of England[1] will be found other instances of suspensions of the act. Where the judges can neither bail the prisoners nor try them, they will not issue the writ of habeas corpus if the act at the time be suspended, as it is to no purpose.[2] The intention of the legislature must be considered in interpreting an act of suspension, and this need not be by express words, if the intention to suspend the act is plainly indicated.[3] Jeremy Bentham gives a good view of the English suspensions of the act in this language: "As for the habeas corpus act, better the statute book were rid of it. Standing or lying as it does, up one day, down another, it serves but to swell the list of sham securities, with which, to keep up the delusion, the pages of our law books are defiled. When no man has need of it, then it is that it stands; comes a time when it might be of use, and then it is suspended."[4]

But in the United States it is not the habeas corpus act, or the writ of habeas corpus, which is suspended. It is the privilege of the writ which is suspended. This is the express language of the constitution, which accurately expresses the restriction imposed and the power which it necessarily implies; viz., the power to suspend the privilege of the writ, when in cases of rebellion or invasion the public safety may require it— and then only. So where a writ of habeas corpus had been actually issued before a proclamation of the president directing its suspension, and the return of the respondent had been made before the fact of the proclamation was known, and perhaps before it issued, all relief under such writ was denied after the

---

[1] Vol. 4, pp. 130, 315, 320.
[2] King v. Earl of Orrery et al., 8 Mod. 98.
[3] Id. As to habeas corpus suspension act (Ireland), 1866, see 11 Cox C. C. 64; and 1 Stats. 1866, c. 119, Eng. L. Reps.
[4] 3 Bentham's Works, 435.

proclamation was made known. It will be seen that the writ here issued, but the privilege under it was denied.[1] The suspension of the privilege of the writ does not suspend the writ itself. The writ issues as a matter of course; and the court decides, upon the return, whether the party applying is denied the right of proceeding any further with it.[2] A wrongful arrest and imprisonment, however, can not be legalized by the suspension of the privilege of the writ. The suspension of the privilege of the writ only deprives an individual wrongfully arrested of the means of procuring his liberty; it does not exempt the one making an arrest illegally from liability to damages in a civil action for such arrest. Neither does it exempt him from punishment in a criminal prosecution.[3]

§ 51. **Power to Suspend.**—The history of the writ of habeas corpus in England shows that parliament alone can suspend or authorize the suspension of the habeas corpus act, and that body has exercised this power more than once.[4] This was at one time a debatable question in the United States, and it arose in the case of Ex parte Merryman,[5] in 1861, in the state of Maryland, and was heard in the United States circuit court of that state, before Taney, chief justice. His honor said the case was simply: "A military officer residing in Pennsylvania, issues an order to arrest a citizen of Maryland upon vague and indefinite charges, without any proof so far as appears under this order; his house is entered in the night; he is seized as a prisoner and conveyed to Fort McHenry, and there kept in close confinement; and when a habeas corpus is served on the commanding officer, requiring him to produce the prisoner before a justice of the supreme court in order that he may examine into the legality of the imprisonment, the answer of the officer is that he is authorized by the president to suspend the writ of habeas corpus at his discretion, and in the exercise of that discretion suspends it in this case, and on that ground refuses obedience to the writ." The question was then considered, whether the president had the power to suspend the privilege of the writ, and his honor

---

[1] In re Fagan, 2 Sprague, 91.
[2] Ex parte Milligan, 4 Wall. 130; In the Matter of Collier, 6 Ohio St. 55.
[3] Griffin v. Wilcox, 21 Ind. 372; contra: McCall v. McDowell, 1 Pac. L. Mag. 360, decided in the circuit court of the United States, district of California. In the first case the act of congress of March 3, 1863, assuming to indemnify officers for arrests of questionable legality, was pronounced unconstitutional; but in the second case these indemnity laws were said to be constitutional: S. C., 1 Abb. U. S. Rep. 212.
[4] King v. Earl of Orrery et al., 8 Mod. 98; 11 Cox C. C. 64; 4 Green's History of England, 130, 315, 320.
[5] 9 Am. Law Reg. 524; S. C., 1 Taney's Dec. 246.

decided that, under the constitution of the United States, congress only possesses that power.

Shortly after this, and without any act of congress upon the subject, President Lincoln issued a proclamation, in which he attempted to suspend the writ "in respect to all persons arrested, or who are now or hereafter during the rebellion shall be imprisoned in any fort, camp, arsenal, military prison, or other place of confinement, by any military authority, or by the sentence of any court-martial or military commission." In December, 1862, the supreme court of Wisconsin ordered General Elliott, commanding the department of the north-west, to bring Nicholas Kemp before them, etc. The prisoner had been arrested for being present at a riot at Port Washington, in Wisconsin. The respondent returned to the habeas corpus that Kemp was in his custody by order of the president of the United States, and that the president had on the twenty-fourth day of September, 1862, suspended the writ of habeas corpus for persons held in custody as the prisoner was. Here again came up the question of the president's power to suspend the writ, and the court held that he has no such power; that the power of suspending the writ of habeas corpus under the constitution of the United States is a legislative power, and is vested in congress.[1]

§ 52. **Act of Congress Authorizing its Suspension.**—The public safety during the great rebellion no doubt required the privilege of the writ of habeas corpus to be suspended. This we have seen the president had practically done, and had detained suspected persons in custody without trial. We have seen, too, that his authority to do this was seriously questioned. The privilege of this great writ had never before been withheld from the citizen; and as the exigencies of the times demanded immediate action, it was of the utmost importance that the lawfulness of the suspension should be fully established. It was

---

[1] In Kemp's Case, 16 Wis. 359, the case of Merryman was cited and approved. See, for same doctrine, Warren v. Paul, 22 Ind. 276; that the president had the right to suspend the writ in case of military arrests, see Ex parte Anson Field, 5 Blatchf. 63. For an able exposition and maintenance of the doctrine that the president has power as commander in chief of the army and navy to establish martial law, and in consequence thereof to suspend the writ of habeas corpus without an act of congress, read an article entitled "Habeas Corpus and Martial Law," printed in the North American Review, of October, 1861, vol. 93, being an article supposed to be from the distinguished pen of Professor Parker of Cambridge, on the opinon of Chief Justice Taney, in the case of John Merryman, applicant for a habeas corpus, and cited *supra*. See Ex parte Milligan, 4 Wall. 127, for the law in an extreme case in which the civil courts might be actually closed. Also read opinion of Chief Justice Dixon, 16 Wis. 365.

under these circumstances, right in the midst of the rebellion, and such as to arrest the attention of the whole country, that congress passed the act of March 3, 1863,[1] authorizing the president to suspend the writ of habeas corpus during the rebellion, throughout the United States.

§ 53. **A Suspension of It under This Act** was ordered by the president on September 15, 1863, "throughout the United States, in the cases where, by the authority of the president of the United States, military, naval, and civil officers of the United States, or any of them, hold persons under their command or in their custody, either as prisoners of war, spies, or aiders or abettors of the enemy, or officers, soldiers, or seamen enrolled, or drafted, or mustered, or enlisted in or belonging to the land or naval forces of the United States, or as deserters therefrom, or otherwise amenable to military law or the rules or articles of war, or the rules or regulations prescribed for the military or naval services by authority of the president of the United States, or for resisting a draft, or for any other offense against the military or naval service."

§ 54. **Validity of the Act.**—One of the effects of this proclamation was to raise the objection that the act of congress, instead of suspending the writ, only attempted to confer upon the president the power to do so, and that this was void, as an attempt to delegate legislative power to the executive. And this point seems to have been undecided in subsequent decisions respecting the suspension of the writ, with the exception of one so far as we have seen. It was directly presented before the supreme court of Wisconsin in 1864. After stating that there is perhaps no class of questions ever presented for judicial consideration which involve more real difficulty, or leave greater room for the mind to remain in doubt, than those which involve the boundaries between that legislative power which can not be delegated and those discretionary powers which the legislature may intrust to other departments or persons in the execution of the laws, Justice Paine, for the court, said: "I have finally come to the conclusion that although this act professes to confer on the president authority to suspend the privilege of the writ whenever in his judgment the public safety should require it during the present rebellion, yet that it is itself an expression of the legislative judgment that the time has already arrived when the public safety requires the legislature to provide for a suspension, and that it does provide for a suspension,

[1] 12 Stats. at Large, 755.

not absolute, but to take effect according to the judgment of the president, whether the authority conferred should be exercised in particular cases or not. * * * The law itself suspends the right in these cases when the president, in the exercise of the discretion conferred upon him, elects to have it suspended."[1] This objection was not answered in considering the effect of the proclamation in the case of In re Fagan,[2] or in the well-considered case of Ex parte Milligan,[3] discussed by the supreme court of the United States. In the latter case the court seemed to proceed upon the assumption that the president was invested by that act with power to suspend the privilege of the writ.

The privilege of the writ was held to be suspended, under this proclamation and act of congress, as to minors who had been unlawfully enlisted without the consent of their parents.[4] The language of the act was also held broad enough to include the case of a recruit, though not a prisoner, in its technical sense, charged with a criminal offense.[5]

§ 55. **Expiration of Authority Conferred by Act.**—The suspension of the privilege of the writ was only to continue during the rebellion. When that ceased, the right of the president to continue the suspension also ceased, and the courts were bound to give to the citizen his rights under the privilege. There was nothing prescribed as to what should be the evidence of it. This was then to be ascertained, like any other fact, by evidence appropriate to such a fact: the abundant evidence in the current history of the times that the rebellion no longer continued; that its organization was destroyed, its armies captured or surrendered, and its officers imprisoned or paroled; that the Union armies were being rapidly mustered out, the returning soldiers daily crowding the streets; that there were no battles, no single known body of men in arms anywhere under the once well-known organization called the "Confederate States of America," etc.—all were received as sufficient evidence that war had ceased everywhere in the land. This being so, the authority of the president under the act of March 3, 1863, section 1, to suspend the privilege of the writ of habeas corpus had expired. So the relator, having been arrested, sued out a habeas corpus. The return was detention by authority of the president. The prisoner was discharged.[6]

[1] In re Oliver, 17 Wis. 681.
[2] 2 Sprague, 91.
[3] 4 Wall. 1.
[4] In re Fagan, 2 Sprague, 91; *contra:* People v. Gaul, 44 Barb. 98; S. C., 5 Am. Law Reg., N. S., 380.
[5] In re Oliver, 17 Wis. 687.
[6] Commonwealth v. Frink, 4 Am. Law Reg. 700, N. S., decided by Justice Thompson of the supreme court of Pennsylvania, at *nisi prius*, July 5, 1865.

§ 56. **Writ Issued by State Court.**—In Indiana, in 1863, it was decided by the supreme court of Indiana, in Griffin v. Wilcox,[1] and in which much learning was displayed, that neither the president nor the congress of the United States could suspend the privilege of a writ of habeas corpus issued by a state court. State courts, it was said, have the undoubted right to issue writs of habeas corpus in all cases, till a suspension of the right by the state legislature; but all authority of the state courts to interfere with the jurisdiction of the United States or her courts was clearly disclaimed.

§ 57. **In the Confederate States.**—The privilege of the writ of habeas corpus was also suspended during the civil war. For the views of the courts as to the power to suspend, and the effect of the suspension, see cases cited in foot-note.[2]

[1] 21 Ind. 370. As to withholding writ, see In the Matter of Collier, 6 Ohio St. 55.

[2] In the Matter of Cain, 2 Winst. 141; In the Matter of Long, Id. 150; In the Matter of Rafter, Id. 153; In the Matter of Spivey, Id. 156; State v. Sparks, 27 Tex. 705.

CHAPTER II.
HABEAS CORPUS ACT, 31 CAR. II., A. D. 1679.

§ 58. **Copy of the Act.**—As frequent allusions will be made to this act hereafter, and as it will be convenient for reference, a transcript of the act is here given. It reads as follows:

AN ACT FOR THE BETTER SECURING THE LIBERTY OF THE SUBJECT, AND FOR PREVENTION OF IMPRISONMENT BEYOND THE SEAS.

WHEREAS, great delays have been used by sheriffs, jailers, and other officers, to whose custody any of the king's subjects have been committed for criminal or supposed criminal matters, in making the returns of writs of habeas corpus, to them directed, by standing out on *alias* or *pluries* habeas corpus, and sometimes more, and by other shifts to avoid their yielding obedience to such writs, contrary to their duty and the known laws of the land, whereby many of the king's subjects have been and hereafter may be long detained in prison, in such cases where by law they are bailable, to their great charges and vexation:

II. **Writs of Habeas Corpus within Three Days after Service to be Returned, and the Body Brought, if within Twenty Miles, etc.** For the prevention whereof, and the more speedy relief of all persons imprisoned for any such criminal matters, or supposed criminal matters, *Be it enacted by the king's most excellent majesty, by and with the advice and consent of the lords, spiritual and temporal, and commons in this present parliament assembled, and by the authority thereof*, that whensoever any person or persons shall bring any habeas corpus directed unto any sheriff or sheriffs, jailer, minister, or other person whatsoever, for any person in his or their custody, and the said writ shall be served upon the said officer, or left at the jail or prison with any of the under-officers, under-keepers, or deputy of the said officers or keepers, that the said officer or officers, his or their under-officers, under-keepers, or deputies, shall within three days after the service thereof, as aforesaid (unless the commitment aforesaid were for treason or felony, plainly and especially expressed in the warrant of commitment), upon payment or tender of the charges of bringing the said prisoner, to be ascertained by the judge or court that awarded the same, and indorsed upon the said writ, not exceeding twelvepence per mile, and upon security given by his own bond to pay the charges of carrying back the prisoner if he shall be remanded by the court or judge to which he shall be brought, according to the true intent of this present act, and that he will not make any escape by the way, make return of such writ; and bring or cause to be brought the body of the party so committed or restrained, unto or before the lord chancellor or lord keeper of the great seal of England for the time being, or the judges or barons of the said court from whence the said writ shall issue, or unto and before such other person or persons before whom the said writ is made returnable, according to the command thereof; and shall then likewise certify the true causes of his detainer or imprisonment, unless the commitment of the said party be in any place beyond the distance of twenty miles from the place or places where such court or person is or shall be residing; and if beyond the distance of twenty miles, and not above one hundred miles, then within the space of ten days, and if beyond the distance of one hundred miles, then within the space of twenty days, after such delivery aforesaid, and not longer.

III. *Such Writs, how to be Marked — Writs of Habeas Corpus, and the Proceedings Thereon in Vacation Time.*—And to the intent that no sheriff, jailer, or other officer may pretend ignorance of the import of any such writ: *Be it enacted by the authority aforesaid,* that all such writs shall be marked in this manner, *Per statutum tricesimo primo Caroli secundi regis,* and shall be signed by the person that awards the same; and if any person or persons shall be or stand committed or detained as aforesaid, for any crime, unless for felony or treason, plainly expressed in the warrant of commitment, in the vacation time and out of term, it shall and may be lawful to and for the person or persons so committed or detained (other than persons convict or in execution by legal process), or any one in his or their behalf, to appeal or complain to the lord chancellor or lord keeper, or any one of his majesty's justices, either of the one bench or of the other, or the barons of the exchequer of the degree of the coif; and the said lord chancellor, lord keeper, justices, or barons, or any of them, upon view of the copy or copies of the warrant or warrants of commitment and detainer, or otherwise upon oath made that such copy or copies were denied to be given by such person or persons in whose custody the prisoner or prisoners is or are detained, are hereby authorized and required, upon request, made in writing, by such person or persons, or any on his, her, or their behalf, attested and subscribed by two witnesses who were present at the delivery of the same, to award and grant a habeas corpus, under the seal of such court whereof he shall then be one of the judges, to be directed to the officer or officers in whose custody the party so committed or detained shall be, returnable immediate before the said lord chancellor or lord keeper, or such justice, baron, or any other justice or baron of the degree of the coif, of any of the said courts; and upon service thereof as aforesaid, the officer or officers, his or their under-officer or under-officers, under-keeper or under-keepers, or their deputy, in whose custody the party is so committed or detained, shall, within the times respectively before limited, bring such prisoner or prisoners before the said lord chancellor or lord keeper, or such justices, barons, or one of them, before whom the said writ is made returnable, and in case of his absence, before any other of them, with the return of such writ and the true causes of the commitment and detainer; and thereupon, within two days after the party shall be brought before them, the said lord chancellor or lord keeper, or such justice or baron before whom the prisoner shall be brought as aforesaid, shall discharge the said prisoner from his imprisonment, taking his or their recognizance, with one or more surety or sureties, in any sum, according to their discretions, having regard to the quality of the prisoner and the nature of the offense, for his or their appearance in the court of king's bench the term following, or at the next assizes, sessions, or general jail-delivery of and for such county, city, or place where the commitment was, or where the offense was committed, or in such other court where the said offense is properly cognizable, as the case shall require, and then shall certify the said writ, with the return thereof, and the said recognizance or recognizances, into the said court where such appearance is to be made; unless it shall appear unto the said lord chancellor or lord keeper, or justice or justices, or baron or barons, that the party so committed is detained upon a legal process, order, or warrant out of some court that hath jurisdiction of criminal matters, or by some warrant signed and sealed with the hand and seal of any of the said justices or barons, or some justice or justices of the peace, for such matters or offenses for the which, by the law, the prisoner is not bailable.

IV. **Persons Neglecting Two Terms to Pray a Habeas Corpus.**—*Provided always, and be it enacted*, that if any person shall have willfully neglected, by the space of two whole terms after his imprisonment, to pray a habeas corpus for his enlargement, such person so willfully neglecting shall not have any habeas corpus to be granted in vacation time, in pursuance of this act.

V. **Officers not Obeying Such Writs—Second Offense.**—*And be it further enacted by the authority aforesaid*, that if any officer or officers, his or their under-officer or under-officers, under-keeper or under-keepers, or deputy, shall neglect or refuse to make the returns aforesaid, or to bring the body or bodies of the prisoner or prisoners according to the command of said writ, within the respective times aforesaid, or upon demand made by the prisoner or person in his behalf, shall refuse to deliver, or within the space of six hours after demand shall not deliver, to the person so demanding a true copy of the warrant or warrants of commitment and detainer of such prisoner, which he and they are hereby required to deliver accordingly, all and every the head jailers and keepers of such prisons, and such other person in whose custody the prisoner shall be detained, shall for the first offense forfeit to the prisoner or party grieved the sum of one hundred pounds; and for the second offense the sum of two hundred pounds, and shall and is hereby made incapable to hold or execute his said office; the said penalties to be recovered by the prisoner or party grieved, his executors or administrators, against such offender, his executors or administrators, by any action of debt, suit, bill, plaint, or information, in any of the king's courts at Westminster, wherein no essoin, protection, privilege, injunction, wager of law, or stay of prosecution by *non vult ulterius prosequi*, or otherwise, shall be admitted or allowed, or any more than one imparlance; and any recovery or judgment at the suit of any party grieved shall be a sufficient conviction for the first offense; and any after recovery or judgment at the suit of a party grieved, for any offense after the first judgment, shall be a sufficient conviction to bring the officers or person within the said penalty for the second offense.

VI. **Persons Set at Large not to be Recommitted but by Order of Court—Penalty.**—And for the prevention of unjust vexation by reiterated commitments for the same offense: *Be it enacted by the authority aforesaid*, that no person or persons, which shall be delivered or set at large upon any habeas corpus, shall at any time hereafter be again imprisoned, or committed for the same offense, by any person or persons whatsoever, other than by the

§ 58.　　ENGLISH HABEAS CORPUS ACT.　　　　47

legal order and process of such court wherein he or they shall be bound by recognizance to appear, or other court having jurisdiction of the cause; and if any person or persons shall knowingly, contrary to this act, recommit or imprison, or knowingly procure or cause to be recommitted or imprisoned, for the same offense or pretended offense, any person or persons delivered or set at large as aforesaid, or be knowingly aiding or assisting therein, then he or they shall forfeit to the prisoner or party grieved the sum of five hundred pounds, any colorable pretense or variation in the warrant or warrants of commitment notwithstanding, to be recovered as aforesaid.

VII. **Persons Committed for Treason or Felony shall be Indicted the Next Term, or Let to Bail and Tried the Term, etc., after, or Discharged.**—*Provided always, and be it further enacted*, that if any person or persons shall be committed for high treason or felony, plainly and specially expressed in the warrant of commitment, upon his prayer or petition in open court, the first week of the term, or first day of the sessions of oyer and terminer or general jail-delivery, to be brought to his trial, shall not be indicted some time in the next term, sessions of oyer and terminer or general jail-delivery, after such commitment, it shall and may be lawful to and for the judges of the court of king's bench, and justices of oyer and terminer or general jail-delivery, and they are hereby required, upon motion to them made in open court the last day of the term, sessions, or jail-delivery, either by the prisoner or any one in his behalf, to set at liberty the prisoner upon bail, unless it appear to the judges and justices upon oath made, that the witnesses for the king could not be produced the same term, sessions, or general jail-delivery; and if any person or persons committed as aforesaid, upon his prayer or petition in open court the first week of the term or the first day of the sessions of oyer and terminer and general jail-delivery, to be brought to his trial, shall not be indicted and tried the second term, sessions of oyer and terminer, or general jail-delivery after his commitment, or upon his trial shall be acquitted, he shall be discharged from his imprisonment.

VIII. **Pending Civil Suit No Ground for Discharge.**—*Provided always*, that nothing in this act shall extend to discharge out of prison any person charged in debt, or other action, or with process in any civil cause, but that after he shall be discharged of his imprisonment for such his criminal offense, he shall be kept in custody according to the law for such other suit.

IX. **Persons Committed for Criminal Matter—Warrant Unduly Countersigned—Penalty.**—*Provided always, and be it further enacted by the authority aforesaid*, that if any person or persons, subjects of this realm, shall be committed to any prison, or in custody of any officer or officers whatsoever, for any criminal or supposed criminal matter, that the said person shall not be removed from the said prison and custody into the custody of any other officer or officers; unless it be by habeas corpus or some other legal writ; or where the prisoner is delivered to the constable or other inferior officer, to carry such prisoner to some common jail; or where any person is sent by order of any judge of assize or justice of the peace to any common work-house or house of correction; or where the prisoner is removed from one prison or place to another within the same county in order to his or her trial or discharge in due course of law; or in case of sudden fire or infection, or other necessity; and if any person or persons shall, after such commitment aforesaid, make out and sign or countersign any warrant or warrants for such removal aforesaid, contrary to this act, as well he that makes or signs or countersigns such warrant or warrants as the officer or officers that obey or execute the same, shall suffer and incur the pains and forfeitures in this act before mentioned, both for the first and second offense respectively, to be recovered in manner aforesaid by the party grieved.

X. **Lord Chancellor, Lord Keeper, or Judge Denying Habeas Corpus—Penalty.**—*Provided also, and be it further enacted by the authority aforesaid,* that it shall and may be lawful to and for any prisoner and prisoners as aforesaid to move and obtain his or their habeas corpus, as well out of the high court of chancery or court of exchequer as out of the courts of king's bench or common pleas, or either of them; and if the said lord chancellor or lord keeper, or any judge or judges, baron or barons, for the time being, of the degree of the coif, of any of the courts aforesaid in the vacation time, upon view of the copy or copies of the warrant or warrants of commitment or detainer, upon oath made that such copy or copies were denied as aforesaid, shall deny any writ of habeas corpus by this act required to be granted, being moved for as aforesaid, they shall severally forfeit to the prisoner or party grieved the sum of five hundred pounds, to be recovered in manner aforesaid.

XI. **Where Habeas Corpus shall Run.**—*And be it declared and enacted by the authority aforesaid,* that a habeas corpus, according to the true intent and meaning of this act, may be directed and run into any county palatine, the Cinque Ports, or other privileged places within the kingdom of England, dominion of Wales, or town of Berwick-upon-Tweed, and the islands of Jersey or Guernsey; any law or usage to the contrary notwithstanding.

XII. **No Subjects shall be Sent to Foreign Prisons—Action of False Imprisonment—Costs and Damages—Person Sealing Warrant, etc.—Penalty.**—And for preventing illegal imprisonment in prisons beyond the seas: *Be it further enacted by the authority aforesaid,* that no subject of this realm, that now is or hereafter shall be an inhabitant or resident of this kingdom of England, dominion of Wales, or town of Berwick-upon-Tweed, shall or may be sent prisoner into Scotland, Ireland, Jersey, Guernsey, Tangier, or into parts, garrisons, islands, or places beyond the seas, which are or at any time hereafter shall be within or without the dominions of his majesty, his heirs or successors; and that every such imprisonment is hereby enacted and adjudged to be illegal; and that if any of the said subjects now is or hereafter shall be so imprisoned, every such person and persons so imprisoned shall and may, for every such imprisonment, maintain, by virtue of this act, an action or actions of false imprisonment in any of his majesty's courts of record, against the person or persons by whom he or she shall be so committed, detained, imprisoned, sent prisoner, or transported contrary to the true meaning of this act, and against all or any person or persons that shall frame, contrive, write, seal, or countersign any warrant or writing for such commitment, detainer, imprisonment, or transportation, or shall be advising, aiding, or assisting in the same, or any of them; and the plaintiff in every such action shall have judgment to recover his treble costs, besides damages, which damages so to be given shall not be less than five hundred pounds; in which action no delay, stay, or stop of proceedings by rule, order, or command, nor no injunction, protection, or privilege whatsoever, nor any other than one imparlance shall be allowed, excepting such rule of the court wherein such action shall depend, made in open court, as shall be thought in justice necessary for special cause to be expressed in the said rule; and the person or persons who shall knowingly frame, contrive, write, seal, or countersign any warrant for such commitment, detainer, or transportation, or shall so commit, detain, imprison, or transport any person or persons, contrary to this act, or be anyways advising, aiding, or assisting therein, being lawfully convicted thereof, shall be disabled from thenceforth to bear any office of trust or profit within the said realm of England, dominion of Wales, or town of Berwick-upon-Tweed, or any of the islands, territories, or dominions thereunto belonging; and shall incur and sustain the pains, penalties, and forfeitures limited, ordained, and provided in and by statute of provision and *præmunire*, made in the sixteenth year of King Richard II.; and be incapable of any pardon from the king, his heirs or successors, of the said forfeitures, losses, or disabilities, or any of them.

XIII. **Exception.**—*Provided always*, that nothing in this act shall extend to give benefit to any person who shall, by contract in writing, agree with any merchant or owner of any plantation, or other person whatsoever, to be transported to any parts beyond the seas, and receive earnest upon such agreement, although that afterwards such person shall renounce such contract.

XIV. **Exception.**—*Provided always, and be it enacted*, that if any person or persons, lawfully convicted of any felony, shall, in open court, pray to be transported beyond the seas, and the court shall think fit to leave him or them in prison for that purpose, such person or persons may be transported into any parts beyond the seas; this act, or anything herein contained, to the contrary notwithstanding.

XV. **Exception.**—Imprisonments before the first of June, one thousand six hundred and seventy-nine, excepted.

XVI. **Where Offenders may be Sent to be Tried.**—*Provided also*, that if any person or persons, at any time resident in this realm, shall have committed any capital offense in Scotland or in Ireland, or any of the islands or foreign plantations of the king, his heirs or successors, where he or she ought to be tried for such offense, such person or persons may be sent to such place, there to receive such trial in such manner as the same might have been used before the making of this act; anything herein contained to the contrary notwithstanding.

XVII. **Prosecutions for Offenses, within What Time to be Made** *Provided also, and be it enacted*, that no person or persons shall be sued, impleaded, molested, or troubled for any offense against this act, unless the party offending be sued or impleaded for the same within two years, at the most, after such time wherein the offense shall be committed, in case the party grieved shall not be then in prison; and if he shall be in prison, then within the space of two years after the decease of the person imprisoned, or his or her delivery out of prison, which shall first happen.

XVIII. **After the Assizes Proclaimed, No Prisoner to be Removed but before the Judge of Assize.**—And to the intent no person may avoid his trial at the assizes or general jail delivery, by procuring his removal before the assizes, at such time as he can not be brought back to receive his trial there: *Be it enacted*, that after the assizes proclaimed for that county where the prisoner is detained, no person shall be removed from the common jail upon any habeas corpus granted in pursuance of this act, but upon any such habeas corpus shall be brought before the judge of assize in open court, who is thereupon to do what to justice shall appertain.

XIX. **Habeas Corpus after Assizes are Ended.**—*Provided nevertheless*, that after the assizes are ended, any person or persons detained may have his or her habeas corpus according to the direction or intention of this act.

XX. **In Suits for Offense against This Law, the Defendant may Plead the General Issue, etc.**—*And be it also enacted by the authority aforesaid*, that if any information, suit, or action shall be brought or exhibited against any person or persons for any offense committed or to be committed against the form of this law, it shall be lawful for such defendants to plead the general issue, that they are not guilty, or that they owe nothing, and to give such special matter in evidence to the jury that shall try the same, which matter being pleaded had been good and sufficient matter in law to have discharged the said defendant or defendants against the said information, suit, or action, and the said matter shall be then as available to him or them, to all intents and purposes, as if he or they had sufficiently pleaded, set forth, or alleged the same matter in bar, or discharge of such information, suit, or action.

XXI. **Accessaries before the Fact to Petty Treason or Felony.**— And because many times persons charged with petty treason or felony, or accessaries thereunto, are committed upon suspicion only, whereupon they are bailable or not according as the circumstances making out that suspicion are more or less weighty, which are best known to the justices of the peace that committed the persons and have the examinations before them, or to other justices of the peace in the county: *Be it therefore enacted*, that where any person shall appear to be committed by any judge or justice of the peace and charged as accessary before the fact to any petty treason or felony, or upon suspicion thereof, or with suspicion of petty treason or felony, which petty treason or felony shall be plainly and specially expressed in the warrant of commitment, that such person shall not be removed or bailed by virtue of this act, or in any other manner than they might have been before the making of this act.

CHAPTER III.

HABEAS CORPUS ACT OF THE UNITED STATES.

(R. S., 2D ED., SECS. 751-766.)

§ 59. **Transcript of the Act.**—The following is a copy of the act mentioned. Frequent allusions are made to it, and a convenient reference is here afforded.

SEC. 751. **Courts have Power to Issue.**—The supreme court and the circuit and district courts shall have power to issue writs of habeas corpus.

SEC. 752. **For What Purpose Justices and Judges may Issue.**—The several justices and judges of the said courts within their respective jurisdictions shall have power to grant writs of habeas corpus for the purpose of an inquiry into the cause of restraint of liberty.

SEC. 753. **Shall not Extend to Prisoner in Jail, unless, etc.**—The writ of habeas corpus shall in no case extend to a prisoner in jail, unless where he is in custody under or by color of the authority of the United States, or is committed for trial before some court thereof; or is in custody for an act done or omitted in pursuance of a law of the United States, or of an order, process, or decree of a court or judge thereof; or is in custody in violation of the constitution or of a law or treaty of the United States, or being a subject or citizen of a foreign state and domiciled therein; or is in custody for an act done or omitted under any alleged right, title, authority, privilege, protection, or exemption claimed under the commission or order or sanction of any foreign state, or under color thereof, the validity and effect whereof depend upon the law of nations; or unless it is necessary to bring the prisoner into court to testify.

SEC. 754. **How Application shall be Made.**—Application for a writ of habeas corpus shall be made to the court or justice or judge authorized to issue the same, by complaint in writing, signed by the person for whose relief it is intended, setting forth the facts concerning the detention of the party restrained, in whose custody he is detained, and by virtue of what claim or authority, if known. The facts set forth in the complaint shall be verified by the oath of the person making the application.

SEC. 755. **Duty of Court or Officer.**—The court or justice or judge to whom such application is made shall forthwith award a writ of habeas corpus, unless it appears from the petition itself that the party is not entitled thereto. The writ shall be directed to the person in whose custody the party is detained.

SEC. 756. **The Return.**—Any person to whom such writ is directed shall make due return thereof within three days thereafter, unless the party be detained beyond the distance of twenty miles; and if beyond that distance, and not beyond a distance of a hundred miles, within ten days; and if beyond the distance of a hundred miles, within twenty days.

SEC. 757. **Return and Cause of Detention.**—The person to whom the writ is directed shall certify to the court or justice or judge before whom it is returnable the true cause of the detention of such party.

SEC. 758. **Return and Body.**—The person making the return shall at the same time bring the body of the party before the judge who granted the writ.

SEC. 759. **Return and Day of Hearing.**—When the writ is returned, a day shall be set for the hearing of the cause, not exceeding five days thereafter, unless the party petitioning requests a longer time.

SEC. 760. **Denial or Allegation of Facts—Amending Return.**—The petitioner or the party imprisoned or restrained may deny any of the facts set forth in the return, or may allege any other facts that may be material in the case. Said denials or allegations shall be under oath. The return and all suggestions made against it may be amended, by leave of the court or justice or judge, before or after the same are filed, so that the material facts may be ascertained.

SEC. 761. **Determination of the Case.**—The court or justice or judge shall proceed in a summary way to determine the facts of the case, by hearing the testimony and arguments, and thereupon to dispose of the party as law and justice require.

SEC. 762. **Proceedings in Case of the Issue of the Writ to Custodian of Foreign Subject, etc.**—When a writ of habeas corpus is issued in the case of any prisoner who, being a subject or citizen of a foreign state and domiciled therein, is committed or confined or in custody by or under the authority or law of any one of the United States, or process founded thereon, on account of any act done or omitted under any alleged right, title, authority, privilege, protection, or exemption, claimed under the commission or order or sanction of any foreign state, or under control thereof, the validity and effect whereof depend upon the law of nations, notice of the said proceeding, to be prescribed by the court or justice or judge at the time of granting said writ, shall be served on the attorney general or other officer prosecuting the pleas of said state, and due proof of such service shall be made to the court or justice or judge before the hearing.

SEC. 763. **Cases of Appeal to Circuit Court.**—From the final decision of any court justice or judge inferior to the circuit court, upon an application for a writ of habeas corpus, or upon such writ when issued, an appeal may be taken to the circuit court for the district in which the cause is heard: 1. In the case of any person alleged to be restrained of his liberty in violation of the constitution, or of any law or treaty of the United States; 2. In the case of any prisoner who, being a subject or citizen of a foreign state and domiciled therein, is committed or confined or in custody by or under the authority or law of the United States, or of any state or process founded thereon, for or on account of any act done or omitted under any alleged right, title, authority, privilege, protection, or exemption, set up or claimed under the commission, order, or sanction of any foreign state or sovereignty, the validity and effect whereof depend upon the law of nations, or under the color thereof.

SEC. 764. **Appeal to the Supreme Court of the United States.**—From the final decision of such circuit court, an appeal may be taken to the supreme court in the cases described in the last clause of the preceding section.

SEC. 765. **Conditions of Appeal for Two Preceding Sections.**—The appeals allowed by the two preceding sections shall be taken on such terms and under such regulations and orders, as well for the custody and appearance of the person alleged to be in prison or confined, or restrained of his liberty, as for sending up to the appellate tribunal a transcript of the petition, writ of habeas corpus, return thereto, and other proceedings as may be prescribed by the supreme court, or in default thereof, by the court or judge hearing the cause.

SEC. 766. **Certain Pending Proceedings to be Deemed Null and Void.**—Pending the proceedings on appeal in the cases mentioned in the three preceding sections, and until final judgment therein, and after final judgment or discharge, any proceeding against the person so imprisoned or confined, or restrained of his liberty, in any state court, or by or under the authority of any state, for any matter so heard and determined, or in process of being heard and determined under such writ of habeas corpus, shall be deemed null and void.

CHAPTER IV.

JURISDICTION OF THE WRIT IN ENGLAND.

§ 60. Common-law Jurisdiction.
§ 61. Statutory Jurisdiction.

§ 60. **The Common-law Jurisdiction.**—The origin of this jurisdiction over the writ of habeas corpus is lost in antiquity. It was, we have seen from the history of the writ, undoubtedly exercised before Magna Charta,[1] and it extends to all cases of illegal imprisonment, whether claimed under public or private authority. It was exercised by the courts of chancery, king's bench, common pleas, and exchequer, though the last-named court only issued it in a case of privilege, as in the case of its own officers,[2] and at one time it was a moot question between Hale and Vaughan whether the common pleas could issue the writ at common law, where no privilege was involved.[3] Bushell's Case, however, decided this in the affirmative.[4] The writ was issued out of the court of chancery, either in term time or vacation.[5] At one period it was thought that it could issue out of the king's bench only in term time;[6] but Watson's Case has settled it that the king's bench may grant the writ, at common law, in vacation, and returnable immediate at chambers.[7]

§ 61. **Statutory Jurisdiction.**—By referring to section 3 of the statute of 31 Car. II.,[8] it will be seen that the court of exchequer, in cases of imprisonment for "criminal or supposed criminal matters," was authorized to grant the writ in term time, as well as the courts of chancery, king's bench, and common pleas; and upon a proper application, it was made the duty of the "lord chancellor, lord keeper, or any of his majesty's justices, either of the one bench or of the other, or the barons of the exchequer of the degree of the coif," to grant the writ in in vacation.

[1] See c. 1.
[2] Bac. Abr., Habeas Corpus, B, sec. 1.
[3] Amos' English Constitution, 197.
[4] Vaugh. 155.
[5] Bac. Abr., Habeas Corpus, B, sec. 1.
[6] Id., and cases cited.
[7] Case of Leonard Watson et al., 36 Eng. Com. L. 254; S. C., 9 Ad. & El. 731.
[8] *Ante*, sec. 58.

Similar jurisdiction was conferred by the act of 56 Geo. III., c. 100, in cases of imprisonment or restraint of liberty, other than those provided for by the statute of Charles II., upon any baron of the exchequer or any judge of either bench in England or Ireland, in vacation time.

By the statute of 25 Vict., c. 20, passed in 1862, it was provided that no writ of habeas corpus should issue out of England into any colony or foreign dominion of the crown where there was a lawfully established court of justice having authority to grant and issue the writ, and to insure the due execution thereof throughout such colony or dominion.[1]

[1] 80 Stats. at Large, 25 & 26 Vict.

CHAPTER V.

JURISDICTION OF THE FEDERAL COURTS.

PART I.—JURISDICTION OF THE UNITED STATES SUPREME COURT.
  § 62. Its Original Jurisdiction.
  § 63. Its Appellate Jurisdiction.
  § 64. When an Appeal may be Taken to the Supreme Court.

PART II.—JURISDICTION OF THE DISTRICT AND CIRCUIT COURTS.
  § 65. The District Courts.
  § 66. The Circuit Courts.

  PART III.—JURISDICTION IN TERRITORIAL COURTS.
  § 67. Legislation.
  § 68. Writ of Error or Appeal.

PART IV.—POWERS OF THE FEDERAL COURTS GENERALLY.
  § 69. Limitations and Benefits of the Writ.
  § 70. Habeas Corpus a Civil Proceeding.
  § 71. Examination of the Facts.
  § 72. Substance of Inquiry on Judgments.
  § 73. Territorial Extension of Jurisdiction.
  § 74. The Proceedings are Governed by the Common Law
  § 75. Jurisdiction must be Shown.
  § 76. *Habeas Corpus cum Causa.*

PART I.—JURISDICTION OF THE UNITED STATES SUPREME COURT.

§ 62. **Its Original Jurisdiction.**—To issue the writ of habeas corpus has been conferred by the constitution of the United States, but a limitation is therein contained, that it can only exercise original jurisdiction in cases affecting ambassadors, public ministers, consuls, and those in which a state shall be a party, and the original jurisdiction of this court can not be extended by congress to any other cases than those expressly defined by the constitution. Having this general power to issue the writ, the court may issue it in the exercise of original jurisdiction, where it has original jurisdiction.[1]

[1] U. S. Const., art. 3, sec. 6, subd. 2; Ex parte Yerger, 8 Wall. 85; Ex parte Bollman and Swartwout, 4 Cranch, 100, 101; Ex parte Watkins, 3 Pet. 202; S. C., 7 Id. 568; Ex parte Wells, 18 How. 307, 328; Ableman v. Booth, 21 Id. 506; Ex parte Siebold, 100 U. S. 371. See Hamilton's

§ 63. **Its Appellate Jurisdiction,** however, extends to all other cases of federal cognizance, with such exceptions and under such regulations as congress, in the exercise of its discretion, has made or may see fit to make. And the court may, in the exercise of this appellate jurisdiction, issue the writ of habeas corpus in cases where it has such jurisdiction, which is in all cases not prohibited by law, except those in which it has original jurisdiction. This appellate jurisdiction extends both to the law and fact.[1] "The intent of the constitution in respect to the suit of habeas corpus is manifest," said Chief Justice Chase, in Ex parte Yerger.[2] "It is that every citizen may be protected by judicial action from unlawful imprisonment. To this end, the act of 1789[3] provided that every court of the United States should have power to issue the writ. The jurisdiction thus given in law to the circuit and district courts is original; that given by the constitution and the law to this court is appellate. Given in general terms, its must necessarily extend to all cases to which the judicial power of the United States extends, other than those expressly excepted from it." Congress has never excepted writs of habeas corpus and *mandamus* from this appellate jurisdiction, but on the contrary, has expressly provided for the exercise of this jurisdiction by means of these writs.[4]

§ 64. **When an Appeal may be Taken to the Supreme Court.**—An appeal may be taken to the supreme court of the United States in all cases where the circuit court has exercised original jurisdiction. If a person deems himself illegally restrained of his liberty, he may take out a writ of habeas corpus from the circuit court, and if that court refuses to discharge him, and remands him into custody, he may thereupon apply to the supreme court, which will issue a writ of habeas corpus, accompanied by a writ of *certiorari*, to bring up the record of the

---

Case, 3 Dall. 17; Burford's Case, 3 Cranch, 448. An application to bring up the body of petitioner's infant daughter, alleged to be unlawfully detained from him, was denied by the United States supreme court, in Ex parte Barry, 2 How. 65, as it called for a naked exercise of original jurisdiction by that court, and did not concern an ambassador or other public minister, consul, or case in which a state was a party.

[1] Ex parte Barry, 2 How. 65; Ex parte Yerger, 8 Wall. 85; Ex parte Siebold, 100 U. S. 371.

[2] 8 Wall. 85.
[3] 1 Stats. at Large, 81.
[4] See generally, on this section, Ex parte Burford, 3 Cranch, 446; Ex parte Bollman and Swartwout, 4 Id. 100, 101; Ex parte Watkins, 3 Pet. 202; S. C., 7 Id. 568; Ex parte Wells, 18 How. 307, 328; Ableman v. Booth, 21 Id. 506; Hamilton's Case, 3 Dall. 17; Ex parte Metzger, 5 How. 176; Ex parte Kaine, 14 Id. 103; Ex parte Milligan, 4 Wall. 2; Ex parte McCardle, 6 Id. 318; S. C., 7 Id. 506; Ex parte Lange, 18 Id. 163.

proceedings below, and they will take jurisdiction of the case under these two writs. If they find that the circuit court erred, they will discharge the prisoner; otherwise they will remand him.[1]

In those cases mentioned in the United States revised statutes, section 763, clause 2,[2] the petitioner for the writ may have the advantage of at least two hearings. But it is the only case in which an appeal can be taken from the judgment of the circuit court, acting in the exercise of its appellate jurisdiction, to the United States supreme court, as the limitation made by section 764 of the United States revised statutes[3] cuts off any right of appeal of cases described in the first clause of section 763, United States revised statutes, relating to appeals from inferior courts to the circuit court.[4]

PART II.—JURISDICTION OF THE DISTRICT AND CIRCUIT COURTS.

§ 65. **The District Courts**, as we have seen above, have only an original jurisdiction. This was conferred by the judiciary act of 1789, and their power thus given to issue writs of habeas corpus, when necessary for the exercise of their jurisdiction, still remains.[5]

§ 66. **The Circuit Courts** also had this same original jurisdiction to issue the writ of habeas corpus, in cases necessary to the exercise of their respective jurisdictions, conferred upon them by the same act.[6] But under the judiciary act of 1789, the circuit court had no appellate jurisdiction from the decision of the district courts in habeas corpus cases. The act of 1867,[7] however, after conferring upon the several justices and judges of the courts of the United States power to grant writs of habeas corpus, in addition to their authority in that behalf under prior laws, in all cases where any one was restrained of

---

[1] Ex parte Yerger, 8 Wall. 85; see also cases cited in preceding note; Ex parte Siebold, 100 U. S. 371.

[2] See *ante*, sec. 59.

[3] Id.

[4] For a history of appeals from district to circuit courts, and from the circuit court to the United States supreme court, as established by the act of February 5, 1867, 14 Stat. at Large, 385; and the statute of March 27, 1860, repealing so much of the statute of 1867 as granted appellate power to the supreme court in all cases in which the writ might be issued under the act of 1867, see Ex parte McCardle, 6 Wall. 318; S. C., 7 Id. 509; and Ex parte Yerger, 8 Id. 85. This repealing act of 1868 did not take away or affect the appellate jurisdiction under the United States supreme court under the constitution and acts of congress prior to 1867. It reached no act except the act of 1867.

[5] Judiciary act, sec. 14, 1 Stat. at Large, 81; Ex parte Watkins, 3 Pet. 193; Ex parte Yerger, 8 Wall. 85. For cases in which these courts and the circuit courts have refused and issued the writ of habeas corpus, see note 2 in next section.

[6] 1 Stat. at Large, 81; Ex parte Yerger, 8 Wall. 85.

[7] Restored May 31, 1884.

§ 66   JURISDICTION OF THE FEDERAL COURTS.   59

his or her liberty, in violation of the constitution, or of any treaty or law of the United States, provided for an appeal in all such cases, where the petition is commenced in the district court, and to lie from the final decision of that court in the case to the circuit court of the United States for the district in which the case is heard. An appeal in the same way also lies from the district to the circuit court in the cases mentioned in the United States revised statutes, section 763, clause 2. Except in the cases provided for in this section of said statute, however, no appeal lies to a circuit court from a decision of the district court on an application for a habeas corpus.[1]

---

[1] Seavey v. Seymour, 3 Cliff. 439.

(a) *Instances in Which Circuit and District Courts have Granted the Writ of Habeas Corpus.*—It applies to civil as well as criminal process: Ex parte Randolph, 2 Brock. 447. Where the detention is of a civil nature, it will be granted where the applicant and respondent are citizens of different states: U. S. v. Williamson, 3 Am. Law Reg. 729; reaffirmed in same case, 4 Id. 5. That it might issue in all cases, where it would issue at common law, provided it was not to any person in jail, unless confined under or by color of the authority of the United States, see Ex parte Des Rochers, 1 McAll. 68. An insolvent debtor will be discharged who has been arrested upon a *capias ad satisfaciendum* issued by a justice of the peace for a debt accruing before his discharge under the insolvent act of the District of Columbia: Reardon's Case, 2 Cranch C. Ct. 639. So long as the case is exclusively within the jurisdiction of the courts of the United States, there need not necessarily be a formal or technical commitment, as one illegally restrained may have the matter heard without any formal or technical commitment: In the Matter of McDonald, 9 Am. Law Reg. 661—a case valuable for its references. To one in custody under or by color of the authority of the United States, or who is imprisoned without just cause, the habeas corpus is a writ of right, and should not be denied: In the Matter of W. H. Winder, 2 Cliff. 89. The term "state," as used in section 1 of the act for the government of seamen in the merchant service, 1 Stat. at Large, 131, is used rather as a geographical expression than a political one, and includes a territory of the United States. And a shipping master, who is the agent of the master, should not act as the agent of the seaman, and should not be allowed to sign the seaman's name to the shipping articles. In such a case, the arrest of a seaman for desertion is without authority of law, and wrongful, and he will be discharged on habeas corpus: In re Bryant, 1 Deady, 118. If a deputy marshal arrest one, ordered by the court to be committed for a contempt, without the jurisdiction of the court, and beyond his own precincts, and bring the offender back to that jurisdiction by the wrongful act of arrest, the writ will issue and the party be discharged: In the Matter of Allen, 13 Blatchf. 271. Where one is brought up from a state court for the purpose of testifying, he is under the control of the court requiring his testimony, and should be sent back to the place from which he was brought for the purpose of testifying. And though the prisoner has been discharged by another court on habeas corpus in the state where he is wanted to testify, because no commitment papers are produced, and no valid reason appears for detaining the prisoner, yet the court issuing the writ of *habeas corpus ad testificandum* will not allow such an action on the part of another court to affect its rights, and will order a marshal to return the prisoner whence he was brought: In the Matter of Hamilton, 1 Ben. 455. Conflicting claims of parents for the custody of infant children is a question of which these courts have jurisdiction, where the petitioner is a citizen of one state and the respondent a citizen of another: Bennett v. Bennett, 1 Deady, 299. Any person arrested for an act done in the discharge of an obligation to the United States,

PART III.—JURISDICTION IN TERRITORIAL COURTS.

§ 67. Legislation.—Most, if not all, of the territorial courts have passed habeas corpus acts, and provided therein for the security of personal liberty. But it does not come within the

and arising under the constitution and laws of the United States, is entitled to the writ: In the Matter of Titus, 8 Ben. 411. An Indian is a person within the meaning of the laws of the United States, and has therefore the right to sue out a writ of habeas corpus in a federal court, or before a federal judge, in all cases where he may be confined or in custody under color of authority of the United States, or where he is restrained of liberty in violation of the constitution or laws of the United States. "Indians possess the inherent right of expatriation as well as the more fortunate white race, and have the inalienable right to 'life, liberty, and the pursuit of happiness,' so long as they obey the laws and do not trespass on forbidden ground." Persons found in the Indian country may be dealt with under such regulations as the president may direct, and in their removal be proceeded against in due course of law; but in time of peace no military or civil authority exists to authorize the transportation of Indians from one part of the country to another, nor to confine them to any particular reservation. Where a commissioner or officer of the government attempts to do this, and arrest and hold Indians who are at peace with the government, for the purpose of removing them to and confining them in a reservation in the Indian territory, they will be released on writs of habeas corpus: United States v. Crook, 5 Dill. 453. A state court has no jurisdiction over the offense of passing counterfeited national bank notes or bills; and one imprisoned for such an offense by a state court will be released by a federal court on habeas corpus: Ex parte Houghton, District Court of Vermont, 7 Fed. Rep. 657; Brown v. United States, 14 Am. Law Reg., N. S., 566, and cases cited in each; also U. S. R. S., sec. 711. This, however, does not relieve the criminal from punishment according to the laws of the United States: Ex parte Houghton, 7 Fed. Rep. 657. No restriction can be placed upon the pursuit of a lawful and inoffensive occupation, by a legislative body—particularly by a board of supervisors—and in violation of a common right. Such a restriction is void. And the business of a laundry has been held to be such an unobjectionable occupation. An alien has the right to pursue any lawful business here, when there is a treaty stipulation between his country and the United States that the citizens or subjects of his country shall have all the rights, privileges, and immunities of the most favored nation with which the United States has a treaty. And he can not be prevented from the pursuit of such legitimate and lawful business by an invalid act of a board of supervisors. One arrested and imprisoned for the violation of such an act will be released by a federal court on habeas corpus: In the Matter of Quong Woo, 9 Pac. C. L. J. 815. Mr. Justice Dillon, circuit judge for the eastern district of Missouri, has held, "that in the District of Columbia, it appears that for a libel composed and published there the petitioner may be indicted and punished as for an offense against the laws of the United States. And if found beyond the district, the petitioner may be removed to the district for trial for a criminal offense committed within the said district. But when the judge of a national court is called upon to issue his warrant for the removal of an alleged offender to the district where the offense was committed, he may look into the indictment, and if it is so fatally defective in its essential averments as not to show an offense triable in the district in which the indictment was found, he may refuse to issue the warrant for the prisoner's removal." This was said on an appeal—from an order of the Hon. Samuel Treat, district judge of the United States district court for the eastern district of Missouri, discharging on habeas corpus A. C. Buell from an arrest and custody in Missouri, for a criminal libel composed and written in the District of Columbia, and printed in the Detroit Free Press, Michigan, and refusing, upon motion of the district attorney, to order his transfer for trial to the District of

scope of this work to view the various statutory provisions in the territories relative to the writ of habeas corpus, and the reader must be referred to their various legislative enactments for information on the subject.

Columbia—to the circuit court for the eastern district of Missouri. In the District of Columbia, a new indictment was found against Buell. He was again arrested in St Louis, but was discharged by Justice Treat of the United States circuit court, on the ground that the indictment was found by a grand jury of a court having no jurisdiction of the offense: In re Augustus C. Buell 3 Dill. 116, and note thereto. In one case where the service of the writ was prevented by force, the writ was ordered to be placed on the files of the court, to be served when and where its service might become practicable: Matter of Winder, 2 Cliff. 89. On habeas corpus, the court will inquire whether the *capias* was rightfully issued. This involves the sufficiency of the affidavit: Nelson v. Cutter, 3 McLean, 326. A United States judge will, on habeas corpus, inquire into the validity of the enlistment of a person into the military service of the United States: Ex parte Schmeid, 1 Dill. 587. Where the prisoner is held in violation of the constitution, laws, or treaties of the United States, it matters not by whom he is held, the courts of the United States, within their respective territorial divisions, have power to, and on application will, issue the writ of habeas corpus to inquire into the cause of his imprisonment; and though he be so held by virtue of the judgment of a court of another jurisdiction, they will examine the case on this writ so far as to ascertain that fact: Ex parte Kenyon, 5 Id. 385. A circuit court has power on habeas corpus to inquire into the validity of the imprisonment of a person held under its own sentence: In re Greathouse, 4 Saw. 487. An alien is in execution of a judgment rendered by a state court, convicting him of an offense created by the state statute. He alleges in his petition for a habeas corpus, that the statute under which he is convicted was passed in violation of the constitution of the United States, and of the provisions of a treaty of the United States with the nation of which he is a subject. In such a case a Federal court has jurisdiction to inquire into the validity of the statute and judgment, and if found to be in violation of the constitution and such treaty, may discharge the prisoner from custody: In re Wong Yong Quy, 6 Saw. 237.

(b) *Instances in Which Circuit and District Courts have Refused to Discharge a Prisoner on the Writ of Habeas Corpus.*—The writ will not be issued to bring up the body of the defendant to surrender him in court in discharge of bail, though in an affidavit that defendant is confined in jail on mesne civil process under the authority of a state court. The writ does not extend to cases where the process is from a state court, and the object is to surrender the party in discharge of bail. Neither will a motion to discharge the bail from their recognizance, on the ground that as it has become impossible to bring the defendant into court, without any default on his or their part, they ought not to be sufferers, be entertained. The defendant will not be allowed, by granting such a motion, to escape from punishment under the law. U. S. v. French, 1 Gall. 1. Where jurisdiction of the subject-matter and of the person exists, a decision simply erroneous, but not void, can not be corrected in habeas corpus. Ex parte Shaffenberg, 4 Dill. 271; Ex parte Parks, 93 U. S. 18. Where the petitioner is duly committed for felony or treason plainly expressed in the warrant of commitment, a court may refuse to grant the writ: In the Matter of Winder, 2 Cliff. 89. After conviction by a jury, sentence in court by a judge *de facto*, acting under color of office, though not *de jure*, and detention in custody in pursuance of his sentence, the prisoner can not be properly discharged upon habeas corpus: Cæsar Griffin's Case, Chase, 364, and numerous cases cited by counsel. Neither the habeas corpus nor the *certiorari* is required to remove a cause from a state court: Abranches v. Schell, 4 Blatchf. 256. Article of War 70 applies solely to confinement before trial. So after trial by a court-martial, the prisoner can

§ 68. **Writ of Error or Appeal.**—Section 1909 of the revised statutes of the United States provides that a writ of error or appeal shall be allowed to the supreme court of the United

not avail himself of habeas corpus, because more than eight days have elapsed since he was placed in confinement. The words of limitation are, "eight days, or until a court-martial can be assembled." The assembling of a court-martial for the trial of an offender was not intended to entitle such offender to his release. The right to confine a soldier during a trial and while awaiting sentence is conferred by Article of War 66: Corbett's Petition, 9 Ben. 274. On the return of a habeas corpus where the question was raised as to the identity of a military deserter, the court, on finding him the person regularly enlisted, remanded him: In the Matter of Hamilton, 1 Id. 455. On a habeas corpus and *certiorari*, the question whether an indictment sufficiently avers an offense in another district, should not be prejudiced, and the indictment must be considered sufficient unless it be so defective in the material averments that it is the manifest duty of a court before which it may be presented by the grand jury to decline to take action upon it. Where one has been committed by a United States commissioner, he will not be released on habeas corpus where the indictment is not of this character. *Quære:* On an examination before the commissioner prior to commitment, is he at liberty to examine the indictment, and pass upon the sufficiency of its averments? In the Matter of Clark, 2 Id. 540. Where there has been no delivery of a pardon to a petitioner, nor to any one for him, nor to the warden of the prison, who by law has exclusive control and custody of the petitioner, the prisoner can not be released on habeas corpus: In the Matter of Moses De Puy, 3 Id. 307. The wife of an enlisted married man may prosecute the writ; but where the evidence shows that he is regularly and lawfully enlisted, the recruit will be remanded to service under his proper officer: In the Matter of Ferrens, Id. 442. Though it appear in the return to a habeas corpus that a criminal prosecution has been commenced against the prisoner for making false returns to an assessor, and that he can not produce certain books, or give information desired without criminating himself, and where it appears that he has been previously committed by a United States commissioner, under the provisions of the internal revenue act, for not producing account books, etc., relating to his business, he can not be released unless he comply with certain conditions. He must bring his books, but the entries, and not the books, are the things sought for by the law. The party is protected from exhibiting an entry which will criminate him, or furnish a link in a chain of evidence which might do so. He is also protected from giving testimony in reply to any particular question put to him. He is protected in withholding and concealing all entries as to which he does claim protection, in disclosing entries to which he does not claim protection. But for the full practice, see In the Matter of Lippman, 3 Ben. 95. A court may sentence a prisoner to jail for a definite period, and upon its expiration to confinement in a penitentiary, and fine him, etc. The prisoner can not object that the state legislature has given no authority to have persons convicted and sentenced in the courts of the United States confined in the state penitentiary. This objection can come from the state only. Neither is there anything in the laws of congress that restricts the authority of a court to the place of imprisonment. Where the defendant is already imprisoned in the jail of a county, the marshal may have a given time in which to remove the prisoner to the penitentiary of the state. None of these facts will authorize a release on habeas corpus, and an application for it will be refused: Ex parte Geary, 2 Diss. 485. A court will not try the merits of an action by habeas corpus, and determine whether the petitioner happens to be a bankrupt or not, where he has been arrested on mesne process, in an action for fraud, either by a state or federal court. The truth of such a case set up against the petitioner is not to be established on habeas corpus, but only the legality of his imprisonment, so far as the laws of the United States are concerned. When a prisoner in such a case is entitled to be released, under

§ 68.   JURISDICTION OF THE FEDERAL COURTS.   63

States from any decision of the supreme courts created by this title, "the territories," or of any judge thereof, or of the district courts created by this title, or of any judge thereof,

the terms of a bankrupt law, the court will release him on habeas corpus, otherwise it will not: In re Devoe, 1 Lowell, 251. An arrest on execution in an action similar to that just mentioned, or issued on a judgment in an action for deceit, comes within the same rule, and in such a case the civil action upon which a petitioner is arrested being distinctly and solely founded upon fraud, he will not be released upon habeas corpus: In re Whitehouse, Id. 429. Mr. Justice Deady, of the district court for Oregon, in Bird's Case, held, that when a soldier is discharged from the military service by the sentence of a court-martial before the expiration of his term of enlistment, and such sentence is afterwards set aside as null and void, the standing of such soldier is not affected in any degree by such sentence, and he is considered to have been in the service during all of the time between the sentence and the order setting it aside. That under Article of War 88 it appeared that a soldier might be arrested and tried after the expiration of his term of service, for a military offense committed during such term of service, provided the order for the court-martial is issued, within the military statute of limitations in such case, within two years from the commission of the offense; and that a soldier may be held for trial after the term of his enlistment, by military authority, if arrested for the offense before the expiration of his term of service. The soldier's petition was dismissed: In re Bird, 2 Saw. 33; see In re Walker, 3 Am. Jur. 281; United States v. Travers, 2 Wheel. 509. A court-martial is a lawful tribunal, and where the navy department is proceeding, in all essential particulars, regularly in the exercise of its jurisdiction before such a tribunal, against an offender, a federal court will not interfere on habeas corpus, and enter into an examination of the merits of the charges. An offender against the naval service, committing a crime while in actual service may be tried by a naval court-martial after his connection with the service has ceased. A paymaster's clerk is clearly a person in the naval forces and service within the meaning of the act of congress of March 2, 1863, 12 Stat. at Large, 696, sec. 1. An alleged former conviction and the bar of the statute of limitations, as for embezzlement, are matters of defense, and are questions for the determination of the tribunal having jurisdiction to try the charge. They arise in the exercise of jurisdiction, and must be pleaded as a defense. They will not be examined on a petition for a discharge on habeas corpus: In re Bogart, 2 Saw. 396. The authority of a United States commissioner to issue a writ of habeas corpus, to take from jail a person committed by authority of the United States, and to bring him before him for the purpose of giving his deposition, to be used in a district court, has been denied: Ex parte Barnes, 1 Sprague, 133. And even the power of a judge or a justice of a court of the United States, to issue a writ of *habeas corpus ad testificandum*, in vacation, for the purpose of bringing witnesses into court at the approaching session, has been questioned: Conkling's Pl. 247; Ex parte Barnes, 1 Sprague, 133; but see *post*, sec. 73. "Where a petition for a habeas corpus shows on its face that the petitioner is confined upon a regular charge and commitment for a criminal offense, after examination had by a court of competent jurisdiction; that the offense is exclusively cognizable by the laws of the state; and that the petitioner is not restrained of his liberty without due process of law and contrary to the constitution of the United States, the federal courts have not jurisdiction to grant the prayer of the petition:" 1 Crim. Law Mag. 126, citing In re Taylor, 12 Chic. Leg. News, Oct. 4, 1880, p. 17, U. S. Dist. Ct., Minn.; See Ex parte McCann, 5 Am. Law Reg., N. S., 158. Where a person residing in a state violates the marriage laws thereof, and is prosecuted and imprisoned for such violation, and sues out a writ of habeas corpus from a court of the United States for his release, on the ground that such a law violates the constitution or a law of the United States, the court will dismiss the petition and refuse to dis-

upon writs of habeas corpus involving the question of personal freedom.[1]

PART IV.—POWERS OF THE FEDERAL COURTS GENERALLY.

§ 69. **Limitations and Benefits of the Writ.**—The supreme court, and the circuit and district courts and the several justices and judges thereof within their respective jurisdictions, have power to grant writs of habeas corpus for the purpose of

charge the prisoner: Ex parte Kinney, 3 Hughes, 9. Where the circuit court has passed judgment, a circuit judge, it has been held, can not, on habeas corpus, review the judgment of the circuit court, on an allegation that the statute under which such sentence was imposed had been repealed before the sentence was passed. And where it appears that the prisoner upon whom such sentence was passed has been pardoned unconditionally, has had notice of the pardon, and is not restrained of his liberty, a habeas corpus will be refused on such allegation, even though it fails to appear that he has accepted the pardon: In re Callicot, 8 Blatchf. 89. A circuit court can not quash proceedings against a public minister depending in a state court, as it can not in any way interfere with the jurisdiction of the courts of a state: Ex parte Cabrera, 1 Wash. 232. The judge of a federal court will not release a prisoner, on habeas corpus, who is a non-resident of a state in which he is under arrest for an act which would subject a resident to persecution, though committed in violation of a law which, in some of its provisions in regard to non-residents, is in violation of the constitution of the United States: Ex parte Touchman, 1 Hughes, 601. Under the first clause of section 14 of the judiciary act of 1789, it was held that the federal courts could not issue a habeas corpus, unless it was necessary in aid of jurisdiction in a case or proceeding there pending. So it was refused a father to recover the custody of his infant child, because not ancillary to the court's jurisdiction. And it was also said that a circuit court could not take jurisdiction under section 11 of the act, although the father was a citizen of another state, as the matter in dispute had no pecuniary value, and could not be estimated in money: Ex parte Everts, 1 Bond, 197 (1858). The cases of United States v. Green, 3 Mason, 482; Barry's Case, 2 How. 65; and Judge Betts' decision in Barry's Case, were referred to and commented upon. But under the revised statutes this is not now the law. "Where one person claims the legal right to have the custody of an infant child, and that right is denied, and the custody of such child is withheld by another, this constitutes a controversy within the purview of the constitution of the United States: Art. 3, sec. 2; and if the parties thereto be citizens of different states, it is a controversy within the judicial power of the United States to hear and determine by the proceeding known as the writ of habeas corpus:" Bennett v. Bennett, 1 Deady, 299, and cases alluded to; see also Ex parte Des Rochers, 1 McAll 68. The sentence of a court will not be examined on habeas corpus, where the court rendering it had jurisdiction: Johnson v. United States, 3 McLean, 89. Neither will the writ issue to bring up a person in custody under state authority, except to testify, etc.: United States v. Rector, 5 Id. 174. Under the treaty with China and the act of congress of May 6, 1882, known as the "Chinese Prohibitory Act," a "laborer" who is Chinese by race, though born a subject of Great Britain, has been held to be within the provisions of said act excluding Chinese laborers from the United States, and has been refused the writ of habeas corpus: In re Pong Ah Lung, 16 Fed. Rep. 577. But a conflict of opinion has arisen between federal courts regarding the proper interpretation to be given to the treaty and to the act; and a conclusion diametrically opposed to the construction given has been reached by a circuit court of the United States sitting at Boston, and in a case apparently exactly similar to the above in the facts and questions presented: Art. in 17 Cent. L. J. 261.

[1] United States v. R. R. Co., 105 U. S. 263; Ex parte Kenyon, 5 Dill. 385.

§ 69. JURISDICTION OF THE FEDERAL COURTS.

inquiry into the cause of restraint of liberty; but they will not issue it for such a purpose where the party for whose benefit it is invoked is a prisoner in jail, unless " he is in custody," etc.[1] "As limited by the judiciary act of 1789, this power did not extend to cases of imprisonment after conviction, under sentences of competent tribunals; nor to prisoners in jail, unless in custody under or by color of the authority of the United States, or committed for trial before some court of the United States, or required to be brought into court to testify. But this limitation has been gradually narrowed, and the benefits of the writ have been extended, first in 1833,[2] to prisoners confined under any authority, whether state or national, for any act done or omitted in pursuance of a law of the United States, or of any order, process, or decree of any judge or court of the United States; then in 1842,[3] to prisoners, being citizens or subjects of foreign states, in custody under national or state authority for acts done or omitted by or under color of foreign authority, and alleged to be valid under the law of nations; and finally in 1867,[4] to all cases where any person may be restrained of liberty in violation of the constitution or of any treaty or law of the United States. This brief statement shows how the general spirit and genius of our institutions have tended to the widening and enlarging of the habeas corpus jurisdiction of the courts and judges of the United States."[5]

---

[1] See U. S. R. S., secs. 751-753, ante, sec. 59.
[2] 4 Stat. at Large, 634.
[3] 5 Id. 539.
[4] 14 Id. 385.
[5] Ex parte Yerger, 8 Wall. 85.

Instances in Which the United States Supreme Court have Granted the Writ. They have issued the writ to review the proceedings of an illegal commitment made by the circuit court of the District of Columbia: Ex parte Burford, 3 Cranch, 448. Where the evidence is not direct, certain, and convincing, a prisoner who has been committed by a district judge on a charge of treason will be admitted to bail by the supreme court on habeas corpus: United States v. Hamilton, 3 Dall. 17. A cause of commitment made by the circuit court for the District of Columbia was examined into, found insufficient, and the prisoners discharged: Ex parte Bollman and Swartwout, 4 Cranch, 75. The writ was issued to inquire into the legality of defendant's imprisonment under process of a ca. sa. awarded against him by the circuit court of the District of Columbia, it being a case of appellate jurisdiction: Ex parte Watkins, 7 Pet. 568, effectually removing the doubt in Wilson's Case, 6 Cranch, 52, *infra*. The writ will be issued to review the judgment of a military commission, where such commission has no authority for its existence: Ex parte Milligan, 4 Wall. 2. Whenever the supreme court finds that the court below has transcended its jurisdiction, and the proceedings are entirely void, from either a want of jurisdiction in the court below or any other cause, it will grant a writ of habeas corpus, and discharge the prisoner even after judgment: Ex parte Lange, 18 Id. 163; Ex parte Parks, 93 U. S. 18; Ex parte Kearney, 7 Wheat. 38; Ex parte Wells, 18 How. 307. So where the prisoner is held by unlawful authority: Ex parte Virginia, 100 U. S. 339. And, too, where the imprisonment is under an unconstitutional law: Ex parte Siebold, Id. 371. Mere errors in the court

§ 70. A Proceeding by Habeas Corpus is a Civil Proceeding.

—On a certificate of division of opinion between the judges of the circuit court of the United States for the district of California, the following opinion was delivered by Chief Justice Waite of the United States supreme court, on May 7, 1883·
"This is a writ of habeas corpus sued out of the circuit court of the United States for the district of California, by the prisoner, Tom Tong, a subject of the emperor of China, for the purpose of an inquiry into the legality of his detention by the chief of police of the city and county of San Francisco, for an alleged violation of an order or ordinance of the board of supervisors of such city and county, regulating the licensing, etc., of public laundries, and the case comes here before judgment below can not be corrected on habeas corpus. In such cases, the ordinary methods of review are by appeal or writ of error. But where the proceedings are absolutely void, where the court below is without jurisdiction of the person or cause, and a party is made to suffer illegal imprisonment through the usurpation of such assumed jurisdiction, a superior court, or one having the prerogative to issue a habeas corpus, will review the proceedings by that writ and discharge the prisoner from illegal imprisonment. This, however, is a special mode of exercising supervisory power over inferior courts and tribunals, and is confined to a limited class of cases. So where an inferior court has jurisdiction of the cause and person in a criminal suit, the supreme court will not review the legality of the proceedings on habeas corpus, unless a writ of error lies to that court. Such relief, however, will be given where the proceedings below are entirely void, from either a want of jurisdiction or any other cause: Mr. Justice Bradley, in Ex parte Parks, 93 U. S. 18; see 16 Am. Law Reg., N. S., 84. It may here be said that the judgments of the courts of the United States are not void, because the record does not show jurisdiction. They are only voidable by writ of error: Ex parte Watkins, 3 Pet. 193.

Instances in Which the United States Supreme Court have Refused a Discharge on the Writ.—This court at one time doubted whether a habeas corpus was the proper remedy in a case of arrest under a civil process, as where one was confined upon a *ca. sa.* issued in a civil suit, and refused the writ: Ex parte Wilson, 6 Cranch, 52. But this doubt was afterwards effectually removed, and the writ issued in such a case: Ex parte Watkins, 7 Pet. 568, *supra*. The writ was refused in 1830 for the purpose of inquiring into and revising the proceedings of the circuit court for the District of Columbia, under an indictment and conviction of the prisoner. But this must be examined in connection with recent decisions of the court: See chapter on Judgments; Ex parte Watkins, 3 Id. 193. The writ was refused to bring up the body of a person committed for a contempt by the circuit court for the District of Columbia: See chapter on Contempts; Ex parte Kearney, 7 Wheat. 38. The prisoner's discharge on habeas corpus, from the process under which he is imprisoned, discharges him from any further confinement under such process; but not under any other process which may be issued against him under the same indictment: Ex parte Milburn, 9 Pet. 704. Where an alleged fugitive was held for extradition, under the treaty between the United States and Great Britain, by a United States commissioner, a circuit court remanded him on habeas corpus. And on an application to the United States supreme court, that court was divided in opinion as to the decision of the circuit court. The jurisdiction of the circuit court was considered doubtful. The matter ended in dismissing the petition: In re Kaine, 14 How. 103. And where a district judge at chambers decided in 1847 that there was sufficient cause for the surrender of a person claimed

§ 70.   JURISDICTION OF THE FEDERAL COURTS.   67

below, on a certificate of division of opinion between the judges holding the court as to certain questions which arose at the hearing. The allegation in the petition is, that the order, for the violation of which the petitioner is held, is in contravention of the constitution of the United States and of a treaty between the United States and the emperor of China. A question which meets us at the outset is whether we have jurisdiction, and that depends on whether the proceeding is to be treated as civil or criminal. Section 650 of the revised statutes provides that whenever, in any civil suit or proceeding in a circuit court, there occurs a difference of opinion between the judges holding the court as to any matter to be decided, ruled, or ordered, the opinion of the presiding judge shall prevail and be considered the opinion of the court for the time being; and

by the French government under the treaty of 1843, and committed him to custody to await the order of the president of the United States, the United States supreme court denied an application for a habeas corpus to revise that decision. Justice McLean said: "There is no form in which an appellate power can be exercised by this court over the proceedings of a district judge at his chambers. He exercises a special authority, and the law has made no provision for the revision of his judgment. It can not be brought before the district or circuit court; consequently it can not, in the nature of an appeal, be brought before this court. The exercise of an original jurisdiction only could reach such a proceeding, and this has not been given by congress, if they have the power to confer it:" Ex parte Metzger, 5 Id. 176. But the general doctrine which now seems to be established by the recent decisions of the supreme court is, that if a party is imprisoned under the authority or the color of the authority of the United States, the supreme court may by writ of habeas corpus inquire into the lawfulness of that imprisonment, and afford relief if such imprisonment be without due legal authority: Ex parte Yerger, 8 Wall. 85. No court of the United States or judge thereof can issue a writ of habeas corpus to bring up a prisoner who is in custody under sentence or execution of a state court for any other purpose than to use him as a witness, whether the imprisonment be under civil or criminal process: Ex parte Dorr, 3 How. 103. One under sentence of death can not accept a pardon upon condition of suffering imprisonment for life; and afterwards, on habeas corpus, claim the pardon to be absolute and the condition void, and plead constraint of duress of imprisonment, and duress *per minas* in subscribing an acceptance of the pardon with the condition annexed: Ex parte Wells, 18 Id. 307. In cases where the inferior court has jurisdiction, the supreme court will not review the proceedings on habeas corpus: Ex parte Parks, 93 U. S. 18; Ex parte Yerger, 8 Wall. 85; Ex parte Lange, 18 Id. 163; Ex parte Siebold, 100 U. S. 371. Neither will the decision by a district court or circuit court that a fact is a crime be reviewed by the supreme court on habeas corpus: Ex parte Parks, 93 Id. 18. Read state case of Kearney's, 55 Cal. 212. See also chapter on Judgments. A paymaster's clerk in the navy was, by a court-martial, found guilty of certain charges and specifications of malfeasance in the discharge of his official duties. Sentence was passed upon him, and after its revision by a superior officer, another and a severer one was passed upon him. His application for a habeas corpus was refused. But see chapter on Assailing Judgments; Ex parte Reed, 100 U. S. 13. The writ will be refused where a general military court-martial has jurisdiction to try the offender for the crime with which he is charged, and the sentence is one which the court can lawfully pronounce: Ex parte Mason, 14 Rep. 193; Keyes v. The United States, 3 Sup. Ct. Rep. 202.

section 652, that when final judgment or decree is rendered, the points of disagreement shall be certified and entered of record under the direction of the judges. That being done, the judgment or decree may, under the provisions of section 693, be brought here for review by writ of error or appeal, as the case may be. By section 651 it is provided that whenever any question occurs on the trial or hearing of any criminal proceeding before a circuit court, and the judges are divided in opinion, the point on which they disagree shall, during the same term, upon the request of either party, or of their counsel, be stated under the direction of the judges, and certified under the seal of the court to this court at its next session. It follows, from these provisions of the statutes, that if this is a civil suit or proceeding, we have no jurisdiction, as there has been no final judgment in the circuit court; but if it is a criminal proceeding, we have.

"The writ of habeas corpus is the remedy which the law gives for the enforcement of the civil right of personal liberty. Resort to it sometimes becomes necessary, because of what is done to enforce laws for the punishment of crimes; but the judicial proceeding under it is not to inquire into the criminal act which is complained of, but into the right to liberty, notwithstanding the act. Proceedings to enforce civil rights are civil proceedings, and proceedings for the punishment of crimes are criminal proceedings. In the present case, the petitioner is held under criminal process. The prosecution against him is a criminal prosecution, but the writ of habeas corpus which he has obtained is not a proceeding in that prosecution. On the contrary, it is a new suit brought by him to enforce a civil right, which he claims, as against those who are holding him in custody, under the criminal process. If he fails to establish his right to his liberty, he may be detained for trial for the offense; but if he succeeds, he must be discharged from custody. The proceeding is one instituted by himself for his liberty, not by the government to punish him for his crime.

"This petitioner claims that the constitution and a treaty of the United States give him the right to his liberty, notwithstanding the charge that has been made against him, and he has obtained judicial process to enforce that right. Such a proceeding on his part is, in our opinion, a civil proceeding, notwithstanding his object is, by means of it, to get released from custody under a criminal prosecution. It was said by Chief Justice Marshall, speaking for the court, as long ago as Ex parte Bollman: 'The question whether the individual shall be imprisoned is always distinct from the question whether he shall be convicted or acquitted of the charge on which he is to be tried, and therefore these questions are separated, and may be decided in different courts.'

"The questions that may be certified to us on a division of opinion before judgment are those which occur on the trial or hearing of a criminal proceeding before a circuit court. It follows that we can not take jurisdiction of the case in its present form, and it is consequently remanded to the circuit court for further proceedings according to law."[1]

§ 71. **Examination of the Facts.**—In reviewing a decision, the weight and sufficiency of the evidence on which it was based will not be considered where the court or officer having jurisdiction of the case had before him legal and competent evidence of criminality. "When the various sections of the revised statutes speak of denying the 'facts' set forth in the return," says Mr. Justice Blatchford, in a recent case, "and of alleging any other material 'fact,' and of ascertaining the material 'facts,' and of determining the 'facts' of the case, they have no reference to the merits of the evidence which was put in before the commissioner, as tending to the conclusion of criminality. Where a person is held on process on a final judgment, after conviction, on a trial of an indictment, and a habeas corpus is issued, the return to the writ states, as the cause of his detention, the process, and either on such return alone or by the aid of a *certiorari*, the final judgment, the conviction, the fact of a trial, and the indictment are brought before the court. These are the 'facts' of the case on the habeas corpus. The particulars of the evidence which led to the conviction are no part of such facts. In determining, on habeas corpus, the 'facts' of the case, the court does not determine what were the facts of the transaction which constituted the crime of which the party was convicted. It only determines whether there was an indictment, a trial, a conviction, a final judgment, a sentence and process of execution, and jurisdiction of such proceedings. It does not retry the case."[2] Questions of this character have most frequently been presented in the execution of judicial duties under extradition treaties, where the person is held in custody under a

---

[1] Ex parte Tom Tong, 2 Sup. Ct. Rep. 871; see Ex parte Milligan, 4 Wall. 2.

[2] Justice Blatchford, in In re Stupp, 12 Blatchf. 501 (1875); see In re Frazer, 7 Id. 34; In re McDonnell, 11 Id. 170; In re Stupp, Id. 124; Ex parte Geissler, 4 Fed. Rep. 188; In re Doig, Id. 193; Ex parte Curtis, 5 Morrison's Transcript, 469.

commitment by a commissioner. These questions, however, will be examined in a future chapter devoted to that subject.

§ 72. **Substance of Inquiry on Judgments.**—The supreme court of the United States has no general power to review the judgments of the inferior courts of the United States in criminal cases by habeas corpus, or otherwise. Their jurisdiction is limited to the single question of the power of the court to commit the prisoner for the act of which he has been convicted. When the court below has jurisdiction of the cause, and the matter charged is indictable under a constitutional law, any errors committed by the inferior court can only be reviewed by writ of error, and can not be reviewed at all if no writ of error lies. But the supreme court will exercise its appellate jurisdiction on habeas corpus, in a case of imprisonment upon conviction and sentence of a party by an inferior court of the United States, under and by virtue of an unconstitutional act of congress, whether it has jurisdiction to review the judgment of conviction by writ of error or not, as the jurisdiction of this court, by habeas corpus, when not restrained by some special law, extends generally to imprisonment under the judgment of an inferior tribunal of the United States which has no jurisdiction of the cause, or whose proceedings are otherwise void and not merely erroneous. Such a case occurs when the proceedings are had under an unconstitutional law. "Personal liberty is of so great moment in the eye of the law that the judgment of an inferior court affecting it is not deemed so conclusive but that, as we have seen, the question of the court's authority to try and imprison the party may be reviewed on habeas corpus by a superior court or judge having authority to award the writ." This matter, however, will subsequently be more fully considered in a chapter on Assailing Judgments by Means of Habeas Corpus.[1]

§ 73. **Territorial Extension of Jurisdiction.**—The jurisdiction of the circuit and district courts is limited to their respective geographical divisions. The reason of this is evident. Were it otherwise, the court of one district could send compulsory process into another, so as to draw to itself a jurisdiction over persons without the limits of its district, and there would result a clashing of jurisdiction between the different courts not easily adjusted, and an oppression upon suitors too intolerable to be endured.[2]

---

[1] Ex parte Parks, 93 U. S. 18; Ex parte Kearney, 7 Wheat. 38; Ex parte Wells, 18 How. 307; Ex parte Lange, 18 Wall. 163; Ex parte Virginia, 100 U. S. 339; Ex parte Siebold, Id. 371; Ex parte Clark, Id. 399; Ex parte Carll, 1 Sup. Ct. Rep. 535; Ex parte Curtis, Id. 381.

[2] U. S. R. S., s. 752, *ante*, s. 59; Ex parte Graham, 4 Wash. 211. Writ runs into Indian territory, Ex parte Kenyon, 5 Dill. 385; as to jurisdiction over mil-

But any justice of the supreme court may, in vacation, issue a writ of habeas corpus in any case in which the supreme court can do so. And where the object is to revise the action of an inferior court or officer, the justice issuing the writ may dispose of the case himself, or refer it to the whole court for determination. That a justice of the supreme court who issues the writ may exercise all the powers of the court in disposing of the case, seems to be implied by the provisions of the statute regulating proceedings under the writ of habeas corpus.[1] We quote from Mr. Justice Bradley:

"This appellate character of the proceeding attaches to a large portion of the cases on habeas corpus, whether issued by a single judge or by a court. The presence of this feature in the case was no objection to the issue of the writ by the associate justice, and is essential to the jurisdiction of this court. The justice who issued it could undoubtedly have disposed of the case himself, though not, at the time, within his own circuit. A justice of this court can exercise the power of issuing the writ of habeas corpus in any part of the United States where he happens to be. But as the case is one of which this court also has jurisdiction, if the justice who issued the writ found the questions involved to be of great moment and difficulty, and could postpone the case here for the consideration of the whole court without injury to the petitioner, we see no good reason why he should not have taken this course as he did. It had merely the effect of making the application for a discharge one addressed to the court, instead of making one addressed to a single justice. This has always been the practice of English judges in cases of great consequence and difficulty, and we do not see why it may not be done here."[2]

§ 74. **The Proceedings Governed by the Common Law.** Proceedings upon the writ of habeas corpus are governed, in

itary reservation: Ex parte Hebard, 4 Id. 380; as to jurisdiction of murder on an Indian reservation, after a state has been admitted into the Union: Ex parte Sloan, 4 Saw. 330; as to crime committed in divided judicial district, and release on habeas corpus, etc., see Collier's Case, 6 Opinions Att. Gen. 103.

[1] Ex parte Clarke 100 U. S. 399; In re Guiteau, 14 Rep. 1, where it was held to be the duty of a justice of the United States supreme court to decide upon an application when he was reasonably certain of his own conclusion. Kaine's Case, in 14 How. 103. is referred to and explained in 100 U. S. 399. Note the opinion in Conkling's

Pl. 247, referred to *ante*, sec. 66, note (b).

[2] Ex parte Clarke, 100 U. S. 399. The writ of habeas corpus in this case was granted by Mr. Justice Strong, who admitted the petitioner to bail, and made an order for the hearing of the case before the whole court. This raised the question whether the supreme court could proceed upon a writ of habeas corpus which was originally issued by a justice thereof, and was postponed and referred by him to the whole court for determination. This was decided in the affirmative, as shown by the first two citations in the preceding note.

the federal courts, by the common law of England as it existed at the time of the adoption of the constitution, except where changes have been made by acts of congress.[1] According to the doctrines of the common law, the decision of one court or magistrate, refusing to discharge a prisoner, was no bar to the issuing of other writs by other courts or magistrates having jurisdiction of the case. So a court or magistrate could discharge a prisoner, in the exercise of an independent power, upon a second or a third application or inquiry into the cause of his detention, although his discharge had been refused by other courts or magistrates on other writs.[2] This is a question of *res adjudicata*, however, and will be examined hereafter. The manner in which appeals are taken and the rules governing them are prescribed by the United States revised statutes. They also provide for notice to be given where a writ of habeas corpus is issued in cases involving the law of nations.[3]

§ 75. **Jurisdiction must be Shown**, as the writ does not issue as a matter of course. "It is true," said Mr. Justice Davis in Ex parte Milligan, "that it is usual for a court, on application for a writ of habeas corpus, to issue the writ, and on the return, to dispose of the case; but the court can elect to waive the issuing of the writ, and consider whether, upon the facts presented in the petition, the prisoner, if brought before it, could be discharged." So where the cause of imprisonment is shown as fully by the petitioner as it could appear on the return of the writ, the writ ought not to be awarded if the court is satisfied that the prisoner would be remanded to prison.[4]

§ 76. **Habeas Corpus cum Causa.**—In suits and criminal prosecutions against persons denied any civil right, etc., and in suits and criminal prosecutions against revenue officers and officers acting under registration and election laws, a *habeas corpus cum causa* is authorized to be issued, when the defendant has properly petitioned for a removal of the cause from the state to a United States circuit court, to bring the body of the defendant into the circuit court where any civil suit or criminal prosecution has been commenced in any state court in the above-named causes. But as we have no room in which to quote these statutes, a reference simply must be made to them.[5]

[1] Ex parte Randolph, 2 Brock. 447; Ex parte Watkins, 3 Pet. 193.
[2] King v. Suddis, 1 East, 306; Canadian Prisoners' Case, 5 Mee. & W. 32; Ex parte Partington, 13 Id. 679; Burdett v. Abbott, 14 East, 91; Watson's Case, 9 Ad. & El. 731; Ex parte Kaine, 3 Blatchf. 1.
[3] *Ante*, sec. 59.
[4] 4 Wall. 2; Ex parte Milburn, 9 Pet. 704; Ex parte Watkins, 3 Id. 192; Ex parte Kinney, 3 Hughes, 9.
[5] U. S. R. S., secs. 641-643; see Spear on the Law of the Federal Judiciary, 475, 480; Thatcher's Practice, 283.

CHAPTER VI.

JURISDICTION OF THE STATE COURTS.

§ 77. Inherent Powers of the States.—It is gathered from the preceding chapter that the states have granted certain powers to the federal government; but with this exception, they possess, in their character "of sovereign political communities," all the judicial power of independent nations. The state constitutions recognize the writ of habeas corpus as an existing remedy in the cases to which it properly applies, and designate the courts or officers which may issue it. They do not, however, point out the cases in which it may be employed. But the statutes have done this to some extent, although their specific provision for particular cases falls far short of the scope of the writ. Then both to the common law and the statutes must we look for our guide upon this subject. The tendency of modern decisions and modern legislation has been to extend the scope of the writ, rather than to restrict the remedy. The aim has been to make it at least as broad and effectual as it was at common law. This tendency has been uniform, and shows the general spirit and genius of our institutions. But there are two distinct and separate forms of government in this country, each conducted by distinct and separate agencies, legislative, executive, and judicial; and the theory of the constitution is that neither shall interfere with the legitimate operations of the other. In both these systems of government the writ of habeas corpus is a well-recognized and established legal process, resting, as we have said, upon and regulated by constitutional and statutory provisions. In the preceding chapter we saw the nature of the federal writ of habeas corpus, issued under the authority of the United States. In this chapter we see the nature of the state writ of habeas corpus, issued under state authority. Both these writs are essentially the same in their general characteristics, purpose, and scope.[1]

[1] Ableman v. Booth, and United States v. Booth, 21 How. 506; Tarble's Case, 13 Wall. 397.

CHAPTER VII.

CONFLICT OF JURISDICTION BETWEEN STATE AND FEDERAL COURTS.

PART I.—CAUSES OF VARIOUS PROVISIONS OF SECTION 753, UNITED STATES REVISED STATUTES.

§ 78. Division into Classes.
§ 79. Cause of Class Second.
§ 80. Cause of Class Third.
§ 81. Cause of Fourth Class.

PART II.—CONCURRENT JURISDICTION.

§ 82. Views of State and Inferior Federal Courts.

PART III.—EFFECT OF JUSTICE TANEY'S DECISION.

§ 83. History of Booth's Case.
§ 84. Decision of the United States Supreme Court.
§ 85. "Authority of the United States."
§ 86. Tarble's Case.

PART I.—CAUSES OF VARIOUS PROVISIONS OF SECTION 753, UNITED STATES REVISED STATUTES.

§ 78. **Division into Classes.**—Section 753 of the revised statutes[1] of the United States specifies five classes of cases, in any one of which the writ of habeas corpus may be issued. And in each of these classes the writ may extend to a prisoner in jail provided his case comes within one of these classes, but in no other case does it extend to a prisoner in jail. *Class first* embraces the cases in which the prisoner "is in custody under or by color of the authority of the United States, or is committed for trial before some court thereof." This has nothing to do with custody under state authority. *Class second* embraces cases in which the prisoner "is in custody for an act done or omitted in pursuance of a law of the United States, or of an order, process, or decree of a court or judge thereof." *Class third* embraces any case in which the prisoner "is in custody in violation of the constitution or a law or treaty of the United States." *Class fourth* embraces any case in which the

[1] *Ante*, sec. 59.

§ 78. CONFLICT OF JURISDICTION. 75

prisoner, "being a subject or citizen of a foreign state and domiciled therein, is in custody for an act done or omitted under any alleged right, title, authority, privilege, protection, or exemption claimed under the commission, or order, or sanction of any foreign state, or under color thereof, the validity and effect whereof depend upon the law of nations." *And class fifth* embraces the cases in which "it is necessary to bring the prisoner into court to testify." This provision is also found in the fourteenth section of the judiciary act of 1789. It raises no question as to the lawfulness of the custody, as the object of the writ in such cases is simply to obtain the testimony of the prisoner in a case pending before the court which brings him up.[1]

---

[1] See, generally, Electoral College of South Carolina, 1 Hughes, 571, where writ issued in favor of petitioners imprisoned for contempt by a state court, where they were acting under United States laws; Ex parte Reynolds, 3 Id. 559, where two colored persons were brought before a federal court, because they had been tried before a state court, for a capital crime, by a jury exclusively white; Ex parte Turner, 3 Woods, 603, where two United States officers were imprisoned, for a contempt, by a state court for disobeying a *subpœna duces tecum*, and released by a federal court on habeas corpus; Ex parte McCready, 1 Hughes, 598, released from imprisonment under an unconstitutional state law; In re Neill, 8 Blatchf. 156, federal officer released for contempt in disobeying an order of a state court to produce the body of an enlisted soldier and make a sworn return of the cause of his detention; Ex parte Waddy Thompson, 15 Am. Law Reg., N. S., 522, where it is said that federal authority should only be exercised in arresting the arm of state authorities when it clearly appears that justice demands it; In re Bull, 4 Dill. 323, and the case must come within one of the clauses specified by congress, in which the writ may issue; United States v. Jailer, 2 Abb. U. S. 265, one indicted for murder, under a state law, committed while executing federal process, released on this writ. See also United States v. Morris, 2 Am. Law Reg. 348. See Ex parte Robinson, 1 Bond, 39; In re Farrand, Abb. U. S. 140; In re Neill, 8 Blatchf. 156; Ex parte Jenkins, 2 Wall. jun. 521; Ex parte Robinson, 6 McLean, 355; Ex parte Sifford, 5 Am. Law Reg. 659; that a federal officer, imprisoned under process issued by a state court for an act done in pursuance of a law of the United States, may be released on habeas corpus; Ex parte Parks, 1 Hughes, 604, release from judgment refused, though indictment charged the forgery of an officer's name, who was not required to make and sign the document; Coleman v. Tennessee, 97 U. S. 509, one convicted in a state court for an act done in the military service of the United States, while in a rebellious territory, released on habeas corpus; Ex parte Dock Bridges, 2 Woods, 428, and Brown v. United States, 2 Cent. Law J., 368, that the federal courts may release one convicted in a state court for perjury before a United States officer; In re Wong Yung Quy, 2 Fed. Rep. 624, release on habeas corpus, from judgment under void state law; Ex parte Tatem, 1 Hughes, 588, one imprisoned by a state court for a crime committed in a place under the exclusive jurisdiction of the United States may be released by this writ; Ex parte Dorr, 3 How. 103, this writ can not be used by the prisoner for the purpose of being brought up to sue out a writ of error; Ex parte Jenkins, 2 Wall. jun. 521, and Ex parte Sifford, 5 Am. Law Reg. 659, that a federal court may go behind process of a state court and inquire into the cause of commitment on this writ; Ex parte Forbes et al., 1 Dill. 363, where a federal court refused to discharge one committed by a state court for contempt, committed in the course of a suit, though such state court had no jurisdiction of the sub-

§ 79. **The Cause of Class Second** was the nullification troubles in South Carolina. Under the judiciary act of 1789 no court of the United States nor a judge thereof could issue a habeas corpus to bring up a prisoner in custody under a sentence or execution of a state court for any other purpose than to be used as a witness; and this, whether the imprisonment was under civil or criminal process.[1] This defect of federal jurisdiction in respect to the writ became apparent during the rebellious attitude of South Carolina, and another act was passed having for its object, among other things, the protection of persons who might be prosecuted under assumed state authority for acts done or omitted in pursuance of the laws of the United States, or of the orders or processes of any court or judge thereof.[2] This was the act of March 2, 1833, the seventh section of which is the basis of the class of cases in the revised statutes now being considered. This provision amply protects a person held in custody under state authority, or under color thereof, for any of the causes mentioned. The authority of the United States in such cases is evidently supreme, and the federal courts and federal judges will always grant relief in such cases by habeas corpus, as "the general government surely has the right to protect its own officers and citizens against imprisonment by state authority for obedience to its laws."[3]

§ 80. **The Cause of Class Third** grew out of circumstances connected with the war of the rebellion. It makes no difference whether the custody in such a case is under color of state or federal authority: it is not only unlawful, but is so in violation of "the supreme law of the land." The original act was

---

ject-matter. But this case was not provided for by federal legislation: See cases cited. In Fleming v. Clark, 12 Allen, 191, and Nauer v. Thomas, 13 Id. 572, the supreme court of Massachusetts refused to discharge a prisoner who had been sentenced for a violation of a state law, though a writ of error had been issued in the case by a justice of the United States supreme court, the court being of the opinion that the United States supreme court had no jurisdiction to revise the judgment, and assuming that the writ had been improvidently issued, and would be dismissed: Ex parte Thompson, 3 Cent. Law J. 729; S. C., 15 Am. Law Reg., N. S., 522; 1 Flipp. 507, where a party is in the custody of a state officer under an indictment for larceny, he can not set up a writ of replevin issued from a United States court, if fraudulent. The federal court will inquire whether the writ was obtained for the purpose of carrying off the property. If found to be so, it will remand the prisoner to the custody of the state officer. Ex parte Passmore Williamson, 3 Am. Law Reg. 741, and United States v. Williamson, 4 Id. 5, where it was said that a state court would not issue the writ to inquire into a contempt before a federal court, though it might not have jurisdiction of the subject-matter of the original proceeding.

[1] 1 Stat. at Large, 81.
[2] 4 Id., 634.
[3] See Thomas v. Crossin et al., 3 Am. Law Reg. 214, 215, for discussion of the nullification acts. For brief statement of "force bill," read Griffin's Case, Chase, 393.

§ 81. CONFLICT OF JURISDICTION. 77

that of February 5, 1867, and declared in such cases that such state authority "shall be deemed null and void." "This provision," says Spear, in his Law of the Federal Judiciary, page 619, "is applicable to any case that comes within its terms. If, for example, the government of the United States should, under the stipulations of a treaty, demand and receive a fugitive criminal from a foreign state, on the charge that he had violated a law of one of the states, and should then deliver the accused to the authorities of that state, and if these authorities, having obtained the custody, were to maintain and continue it in violation of the treaty under which the delivery was made by the foreign state, then, upon a proper application setting forth the facts, a federal court would be authorized to grant a writ of habeas corpus, and if upon the hearing of the case it appeared that the custody was in violation of the treaty, to discharge the prisoner therefrom. The provision clearly covers such a case should it be found to exist; and it is equally clear that there should be some way in which the general government, having obtained from a foreign government the custody of fugitive criminals against state authority, and having delivered them to such authority for trial and punishment, may secure to them all the rights guaranteed to them by the treaty, whether expressly or by implication. It is the duty of the general government to see to it that the treaty is in no respect violated."

§ 81. **The Fourth Class** was provided for by the legislation of 1842.[1] This then seemed to be a necessity, in order to give to the federal courts authority, upon the writ of habeas corpus, over cases involving questions of international law, and which of course could only be disposed of by "a jurisdiction to which international concerns were by the constitution committed." This legislation was suggested by the McLeod Case,[2] which arose in the state of New York, and at one time threatened to involve the United States in serious complications with Great Britain; because McLeod was a subject of Great Britain, and the New York authorities arrested, indicted, and tried him for an act—murder—which his government avowed and took the responsibility of, and which was the subject of diplomatic correspondence between the two nations. At that time there was no United States law giving any federal court the power to

[1] 5 Stat. at Large, 539.
[2] 1 Hill (N. Y.) 377; S. C., 25 Wend. 482; S. C., 37 Am. Dec. 328; see 26 Wend. 663; 3 Hill (N. Y.) 635.

exercise any jurisdiction in such cases. McLeod was acquitted, but congress passed a law making the writ of habeas corpus applicable to such cases in the future. These questions are passed upon exclusively by the federal courts. The act also provided that during the hearing of the prisoner's case on habeas corpus, proceedings against him must be suspended. So after his discharge on this writ, any further proceedings against him were made unlawful.[1]

PART II.—CONCURRENT JURISDICTION.

§ 82. **Views of State and Inferior Federal Courts.**— Prior to the decision of the United States supreme court in Ableman v. Booth, in 1858, many of the state courts claimed and exercised the right to inquire into the lawfulness of restraint under national authority.[2] In other states, the courts disclaimed this concurrent jurisdiction, and refused to exercise it.[3] Most of the decisions of the inferior federal courts, however, denied any such concurrent power in the state courts.[4] This exercise of power, in passing upon the validity of the commitment or detention under the authority of the United States, and sometimes deciding against the validity thereof, naturally led to a conflict of decisions. This conflict of authority led to the decision mentioned in the next section.

---

[1] 5 Stat. at Large, 539.

[2] State v. Wederstrandt, T. U. P. Charlt. 213; Olmstead's Case, Bright. 9; Commonwealth v. Murray, 4 Binn. 487; Ferguson's Case, 9 Johns. 239; Matter of Stacy, 10 Id. 328; Commonwealth v. Holloway, 5 Binn. 512; Lockington's Case, Bright. 269; Ex parte Almeida, 2 Wheeler's Cr. Cas. 576; Com. v. Cushing, 11 Mass. 66; Com. v. Harrison, Id. 63; Com. v. Robinson, 1 Serg. & R. 353; State v. Brearly and Berryman, 2 South. 555; Jane Wilson's Case, 4 City H. Rec. 47; In the Matter of Carlton, 7 Cow. 471; Pleasant's Case, 11 Am. Jur. 257; Com. v. Downes, 24 Pick. 227; State v. Dimick, 12 N. H. 194; Kimball, Moore & Stone, 9 Law Rep. (Mass.) 500; Kinniston's Case, Id. 548; Com. ex rel. Webster v. Fox, 7 Pa. St. 336; Petition of Thomas Sims, 7 Cush. 285; Thomas v. Crossin et al., 3 Am. Law Reg. 216, 217; Booth's Case, 3 Wis. 1; U. S. v. Collier, 6 Ohio St. 61; Ex parte Bushnell et al., 8 Id. 599; Com. v. Fox, 7 Pa. St. 336.

[3] Husted's Case, 1 Johns. Cas. 136; State v. Plime and Vessel, T. U. P. Charlt. 142; Roberts' Case, 2 Am. Law J. 192; see Matter of Ferguson, 9 Johns. 239; Matter of Stephen, 1 Wheeler's Cr. Cas. 323; Ex parte Rhodes, 2 Id. 559; S. C., Niles' Reg. 264, June 21, 1817; United States v. Wyngall, 5 Hill, 16; Ex parte Le Bur, 2 Cent. L. J. 122; Ex parte Bushnell et al., 9 Ohio St. 77; In the Matter of Disinger, 12 Id. 256; Ex parte Kelly, 37 Ala. 474; In re Kemp, 16 Wis. 359.

[4] Norris v. Newton et al., 5 McLean, 99; U. S. v. Rector and Ellis, Id. 174; Justice Nelson's Exposition of the Fugitive Slave Law, 1 Blatchf. 641–643; Ex parte Jenkins, 2 Wall. jun. 521; see Thomas v. Crossin et al., 3 Am. Law Reg. 207, note; Collier's Case, 6 Opinions Atty. Gen. 103; Belligerent Asylum, 7 Id. 123, citing Hautefeuille, des Droits et des Devoirs des Nations Neutres, tom. 1, 475, 476; Passmore Williamson's Case, 7 Opinions Att. Gen. 482; U. S. v. Van Fossen, 1 Dill. 406; Matter of Farrand, 1 Abb. U. S. 140; U. S. v. Doss, 11 Am. Law Reg., N. S., 320; Ex parte Robinson, 1 Bond, 39; In re McDonald, 9 Am. Law Reg. 661; In re Keeler, 1 Hempst. 306.

PART III.—EFFECT OF ABLEMAN v. BOOTH, AND THE UNITED STATES v. BOOTH, 21 How. 506.

§ 83. **History of Booth's Case.**—Booth had been arrested on warrants granted by a United States commissioner, for aiding in the escape of a fugitive slave from service, contrary to the law of 1850.[1] A justice of the supreme court of Wisconsin, upon habeas corpus, discharged Booth from the custody of the marshal, on the ground that the fugitive-slave law of 1850 was unconstitutional. This judgment was affirmed by the supreme court of that state on *certiorari*. Booth was subsequently indicted in the United States district court for Wisconsin for the same offense, and arrested by the marshal on a warrant issued thereon. Booth thereupon applied to the same supreme court, then in session, for a habeas corpus to be delivered from the custody of the marshal; but the writ was unanimously refused, on the ground that it appeared from the application that he was under arrest upon an indictment of a court having jurisdiction of alleged offenses against the United States, and that the case was still pending and undetermined. That court decided that they had no legal right to interfere in his behalf while the prosecution was pending, even though the law of congress under which he was indicted was unconstitutional and void; thus sustaining, in its fullest extent, the principle and practice of judicial comity adverted to by Mr. Justice Peck, in the supreme court of Ohio in 1858.[2] The Wisconsin court conceded the privilege and right of the district court to determine first and for itself the question of its own jurisdiction; and in reply to the claim that the law was unconstitutional and void, and that therefore the district court could not have any jurisdiction, very aptly remarked that that fact, if true, amounted, after all, to a question of jurisdiction, which they, in the first place, must decide for themselves. Subsequently, the prosecution having terminated by a conviction and sentence of imprisonment, the same court allowed a habeas corpus, and discharged Booth for alleged defects in the indictment, which did not bring the counts upon which he was convicted within the purview of the act of congress of September 18, 1850.[3]

In the first case, after Booth's discharge and affirmance of the judgment by the supreme court of Wisconsin, the marshal, Ableman, sued out a writ of error, returnable to the supreme court of Wisconsin, thereby bringing the case before that court for a review of the judgment of the supreme

---

[1] 9 Stats. at Large, 462.   [2] Ex parte Bushnell et al., 8 Ohio St. 602.
[3] Mr. Justice Peck, 8 Ohio St. 599.

court of Wisconsin. In the second case, the attorney general of the United States, by a proper proceeding, brought the judgment of the supreme court of Wisconsin before the United States supreme court for review. These cases were heard together.

§ 84. **Decision of the United States Supreme Court.**— These two cases arose out of the same transaction, and depended, to some extent, upon the same principles, and were purposely heard together. The opinion of the court was rendered by Chief Justice Taney. "A judge of the supreme court of the state of Wisconsin," said he, "in the first of these cases claimed and exercised the right to supervise and annul the proceedings of a commissioner of the United States, and to discharge a prisoner who had been committed by the commissioner for an offense against the laws of this government, and that this exercise of power by the judge was afterwards sanctioned and affirmed by the supreme court of the state. In the second case, the state court has gone a step further, and claimed and exercised jurisdiction over the proceedings and judgment of the district court of the United States, and upon a summary and collateral proceeding by habeas corpus has set aside and annulled its judgment, and discharged a prisoner who had been tried and found guilty of an offense against the laws of the United States, and sentenced to imprisonment by the district court." The question in these cases was whether a state court or a state judge could by writ of habeas corpus discharge a prisoner held in custody under the authority of the United States, as exercised by an officer thereof, and was answered in the negative.

"We do not," said the learned justice, "question the authority of state court or judge who is authorized by the laws of the state to issue the writ of habeas corpus, to issue it in any case where the party is imprisoned within its territorial limits, provided it does not appear, when the application is made, that the person imprisoned is in custody under the authority of the United States. The court or judge has a right to inquire, in this mode of proceeding, for what cause and by what authority the prisoner is confined within the territorial limits of the state sovereignty. And it is the duty of the marshal, or other person having the custody of the prisoner, to make known to the judge or court, by a proper return, the authority by which he holds him in custody. This right to inquire by process of habeas corpus, and the duty of the officer to make a return, grows, necessarily, out of the complex character of our government, and the existence of two distinct and separate sovereignties within the same territorial space, each of them restricted in its powers, and each within its sphere of action prescribed by the constitution of the United States, independent of the other. But after the return is made, and the state judge or court judicially apprised that the party is in custody under the authority of the United States, they can proceed no further. They then know that the prisoner is within the dominion and jurisdiction of another government, and that neither the writ of habeas corpus nor any other process issued under state authority can pass over the line of division between the two sovereignties. He is then within the dominion and exclusive jurisdiction of the United States. If he has committed an offense against their laws, their tribunals alone can punish him. If he is wrongfully imprisoned, their judicial tribunals can release him and afford him redress. And although, as we have said, it is the duty of the marshal or other person holding him to make known, by a proper return, the authority under which he detains him, it is at the same time imperatively his duty to obey the process of the United States, to hold the prisoner in custody under it, and to refuse obedience to the mandate or process of any other government. And consequently it is his duty not to take the prisoner, nor suffer him to be taken before a state judge or court upon a habeas corpus issued under state authority. No state judge or court, after they are judicially informed that the party is imprisoned under the authority of the United States, has any right to interfere with him, or to require him to be brought before them. And if the authority of a state, in the form of judicial process or otherwise, should attempt to control the marshal or other authorized officer or agent of the United States, in any respect, in the custody of his prisoner, it would be his duty to resist it, and to call to his aid any force that might be necessary to maintain the authority of law against illegal interference. No judicial process, whatever form it may assume, can have any lawful authority outside of the limits of the jurisdiction of the court or judge by whom it is issued, and an attempt to enforce it beyond these boundaries is nothing less than lawless violence."

§ 85. **"Authority of the United States."**—These words, found in the above decision, were variously construed by the state courts: some holding that they applied only to those cases in which the prisoner was held under undisputed lawful authority of the United States; and others, that they applied to any case in which the prisoner was held in the custody of a federal officer under claim and color of the authority of the United States. A distinction was made between cases where the imprisonment was under federal authority judicial, and where it was not judicial. By some it was thought that it was merely intended that a prisoner could not be taken out of the custody of the judicial department of the federal government by a habeas corpus issued by a state court. In short, the various constructions put upon these words by the state courts caused conflicts of jurisdiction, which were unsettled until the rendering of the decision mentioned in the next section.[1]

§ 86. **Tarble's Case, 13 Wall. 397.**—Tarble was an enlisted soldier, and in the custody of a recruiting officer of the United States. He sued out a habeas corpus, and was discharged by a court commissioner of Wisconsin, who, under the laws of that state, was authorized to issue the writ. The commissioner's order was subsequently affirmed by the supreme court of the state, and that judgment was carried, by writ of error, to the supreme court of the United States for review. This class of cases, it will be perceived by reading the cases cited in the preceding section, are the particular ones which caused such a diversity of opinion in the state courts respecting the meaning of the words of Justice Taney. Mr. Justice Field, in delivering the opinion of a majority of the court, said:

" The decision of this court in the two cases which grew out

---

[1] Phelan's Case, 9 Abb. Pr. 286, enlistment of minor; O. & M. R. R. Co. v. Fitch, 20 Ind. 498, and authorities collected; Skeen v. Monkeimer, 21 Id. 1; In the Matter of Dabbs, 9 Am. Law Reg. 565; S. C., 12 Abb. Pr. 113, enlistment; Kelly & Dodge's Case, 37 Ala. 474; State v. Zulich, 5 Dutch. 409; In re Gregg, 15 Wis. 479, enlistment case; In re Hopson, 40 Barb. 34; In the Matter of Beswick, 25 How. Pr. 149; Webb's Case, 24 Id. 247; In the Matter of Barrett, 42 Barb. 479, an enlistment case; In the Matter of Jordan et al., In re Jordan, Peck & Hedges, 2 Am. Law Reg., N. S., 749 Sup. Ct. N. Y., enlistment cases; In the Matter of Spangler, 11 Mich. 298; Shirk's Case, 5 Phila. 333, overruling a number of Pennsylvania decisions, holding that a state court had no jurisdiction to discharge an enlisted minor from the United States service: Ex parte McRoberts, 16 Iowa, 600; Ex parte Anderson, Id. 595, enlistment case; Ex parte Holman, 28 Id. 89, a valuable case; People ex rel. Starkweather v. Gaul, 44 Barb. 98, enlistment case; Matter of Martin, 45 Id. 142; In the Matter of O'Conner, 48 Id. 258, enlistment case; Ex parte Hill, 5 Nev. 154; McConologue's Case, 107 Mass. 154, enlisted minor; Tarble's Case, 25 Wis. 390; S. C., 6 Am. Law Rev. 314, the enlistment case which eventually went to the United States supreme court on a writ of error, and which led to Justice Field's decision. Under the present federal law, the enlistment of a person under age without the consent of his parents is invalid, and they may procure his discharge on habeas corpus proceedings, upon the advance made at the time of enlistment being refunded: In re Hayes, U. S. C. C. District of Massachusetts, 1883, 15 Rep. 259. But the enlistment contract of a minor who is old enough to understand it is voidable only and not void, particularly where he was accepted in good faith as of full age. So for desertion, he can not be released on habeas corpus from the custody of a court-martial about to try him for his offense: In re Wall, 12 Id. 322; see Seavey v. Seymour, 3 Cliff. 439. As to discharge from fraudulent enlistment, see Ex parte Schmeid, 1 Dill. 587; see In re Keeler, 1 Hempst. 307; United States v. Bainbridge, 1 Mason, 71; Com. v. Fox, 7 Pa. St. 336.

§ 86. CONFLICT OF JURISDICTION. 83

of the arrest of Booth, that of Ableman v. Booth and that of the United States v. Booth, disposes alike of the claim of jurisdiction by a state court, or by a state judge, to interfere with the authority of the United States, whether that authority be exercised by a federal officer or be exercised by a federal tribunal. * * * Such being the distinct and independent character of the two governments within their respective spheres of action, it follows that neither can intrude with its judicial process into the domain of the other, except so far as such intrusion may be necessary on the part of the national government to preserve its rightful supremacy in cases of conflict of authority. In their laws and mode of enforcement, neither is responsible to the other. How their respective laws shall be enacted; how they shall be carried into execution; and in what tribunals or by what officers; and how much discretion, or whether any at all, shall be vested in their officers, are matters subject to their own control, and in the regulation of which neither can interfere with the other. * * * Some attempt has been made in adjudications, to which our attention has been called, to limit the decision of this court in Ableman v. Booth, and the United States v. Booth, to cases where a prisoner is held in custody under undisputed lawful authority of the United States, as distinguished from his imprisonment under claim and color of such authority. But it is evident that the decision does not admit of any such limitation. It would have been unnecessary to enforce, by any extended reasoning, such as the chief justice uses, the position that when it appeared to the judge or officer issuing the writ that the prisoner was held under undisputed lawful authority he should proceed no further. No federal judge even could, in such case, release the party from imprisonment, except upon bail when that was allowable. The detention being by admitted lawful authority, no judge could set the prisoner at liberty, except in that way, at any stage of the proceeding. All that is meant by the language used is, that the state judge or state court should proceed no further when it appears from the application of the party, or the return made, that the prisoner is held by an officer of the United States under what in truth purports to be the authority of the United States; that is, an authority the validity of which is to be determined by the constitution and laws of the United States. If a party thus held be illegally imprisoned, it is for the courts or judicial officers of the United States, and those courts or officers alone, to grant him release."

CHAPTER VIII.

APPLICATION FOR THE WRIT.

§ 87. Circumstances under Which an Application can be Made.
§ 88. When the Application will be Entertained.
§ 89. Requisites of the Petition.
§ 90. Further Matters concerning the Petition.
§ 91. Who may Make an Application.
§ 92. Probable Cause must be Shown.
§ 93. When the Application must be Granted.
§ 94. When the Application ought to be Denied.
§ 95. Verification of the Petition.
§ 96. Penalty for Refusing the Writ.
§ 97. *Mandamus* to Compel the Writ to Issue.
§ 98. Injunction to Restrain Issuance of Writ.

§ 87. **Circumstances under Which an Application may be Made.**—An application for a writ of habeas corpus may be made before the proper court or judge, whenever a party is restrained of his liberty, or is unlawfully detained or confined.[1] A mere moral restraint, however, can not be an illegal one; and if a person is under no physical restraint, and there is no necessity to recur to a court or judge, as in trying to cause a moral restraint to cease, the writ of habeas corpus is improperly resorted to. A person who has been committed on an execution from a court, and admitted to the bounds of the prison, after having given bond and security according to law, is under only a moral restraint, and can not prosecute the writ.[2] It matters not whether the imprisonment is under criminal or civil process; if it be contrary to law, the one so imprisoned is entitled to the benefit of the writ of habeas corpus,[3] although in our earlier jurisprudence the supreme court of the United States was not satisfied that a writ of habeas corpus was the proper remedy in a case of arrest under a civil process;[4] but this doubt probably arose from the fact that only the celebrated habeas corpus act of 31

---

[1] Territory of Kansas v. Cutler, McCahon, 153.
[2] Dodge's Case, 6 Mart. (La.) 569.
[3] Hecker v. Jarret, 3 Binn. 404; Ex parte McCullough, 35 Cal. 97.
[4] Ex parte Wilson, 6 Cranch, 52; see also Cable v. Cooper, 15 Johns. 152.

Car. II. was viewed in the consideration of the question, which had been held in England to be confined to criminal cases. But when the common-law jurisdiction of the English courts, as well as of our own, was looked to, the doubt was removed.[1] The common-law writ has a broader signification than the form of it secured by the habeas corpus act, for there it may issue in all sorts of cases where it is shown to the court that there is probable cause for believing that a person is restrained of his liberty unlawfully or against the due course of law. By an examination of the act, it will be seen that the statutory remedy falls far short of this.[2]

§ 88. **When the Application will be Entertained.**—Under the older common law, the writ could be obtained in term time only from the court of king's bench—which was one of the grievances the habeas corpus act was intended to remedy[3]— and in vacation by a fiat from the chief justice or any of the other justices; though it seems it might even then have been awarded by the court of chancery, which was always open.[4] If it issued in vacation it was usually made returnable before the judge himself who awarded the writ, and he proceeded thereon unless the term should intervene, when it could be returned in court.[5] The judge might also grant a writ returnable immediately before himself at chambers.[6] Under the statute of 16 Car. I., c. 10, it was held that every subject of the kingdom was equally entitled to the benefit of the common-law writ in either the king's bench or common pleas, at his option.[7] And afterwards, under the statute of 56 Geo. III., c. 100, sec. 2, it could be sued out as well in the exchequer.[8] "Lords Coke, Hale, and Comyns, as text-writers upon this subject, appear to confine to chancery, which was always open, the *officina justitiæ*, the power of issuing a habeas corpus in vacation time. But Tremaine's Pleas of the Crown contains four precedents of writs, in the exact form of that now before us, earlier than 31 Car. II., one as early as 43 Eliz. Wilmot, in his answer to the house of lords, refers to others anterior to the habeas corpus act, and observes that the great men who framed it would never have left so obvious a defect without a remedy. In 1758 he and the judges consulted by the house of lords affirmed this power; and the reforming bill which

---

[1] Ex parte Randolph, 2 Brock. 476, 477; see also People v. Willett, 15 How. Pr. 210.
[2] Williamson v. Lewis, 39 Pa. St. 29.
[3] 1 Ch. Crim. L. 124.
[4] 3 Kerr's Bla. Com. 124; 1 Ch. Crim. L. 124; 2 Hale's P. C. 147.
[5] 3 Kerr's Bla. Com. 124.
[6] Leonard Watson's Case, 36 Eng. Com. L. 278; State v. Hill, 10 Minn. 66.
[7] 3 Kerr's Bla. Com. 124.
[8] See statute.

had been introduced would scarcely have been suffered to fall, had it not been, in that respect, deemed unnecessary."[1]

The writ of *habeas corpus ad subjiciendum*, which was only for matters of crime, was not regularly to issue, nor be returnable, except out of chancery in vacation, only in the term time, in king's bench;[2] but by the statute of 31 Car. II., such writ might issue in vacation on behalf of any person, except, etc.[3] The application by this act was made by a request, in writing, by the imprisoned person, or any one on his behalf, attested and subscribed by two witnesses who were present at the delivery of the same.[4] At the very common law the practice was to apply for this writ by motion to a court or to a judge at chambers, as in the case of all other prerogative writs, *certiorari*, prohibition, *mandamus*, etc.[5] Lord Chief Justice Vaughan[6] argued: "It is granted on motion, because it can not be had of course; and there is, therefore, no necessity to grant it; for the court ought to be satisfied that the party hath a probable cause to be delivered." One important reason was, that when once granted, the person to whom it was directed could then return no satisfactory excuse for not bringing up the body of the prisoner. But under the statute of Charles II., any one of the judges in vacation, and any of the courts in term time, are authorized to grant this writ, upon due cause being shown them. By one of the pro-

---

[1] Leonard Watson's Case, 36 Eng. Com. L. 278. Denman, C. J., in the course of his delivery of the judgment of the court, said: "In 1765, then, Blackstone's statement, 3 Com. 131, is a valuable testimony of the general opinion at that time; and the practice from that period has been uniform. It is also true that, in deciding Crowley's Case, 2 Swans. 1, Lord Eldon doubted the power of a judge in vacation to issue a habeas corpus, saying there is much good principle for it, but very little practice. That doubt assisted this argument in favor of overruling the solemn decision of Lord Nottingham in Jenkes' Case, 6 Howell's State Trials, 1189, and in Crowley's Case, 2 Swans. 12, 83; but the passages in his judgment, which occur at page 65 and page 68, 2 Swans., distinctly prove that he formed his opinion partly on the inconvenience and oppression which might have accrued to the subject if deprived of the means of obtaining a release from imprisonment in time of vacation by a writ sued out in the court of chancery. Now the same ill consequences would follow in criminal cases, notwithstanding the power of issuing these writs in vacation by chancery, unless the judges of the court of king's bench have power to decide immediately on the right to restrain a subject of his personal freedom. In favor of this practice, we have the authority of Lord Nottingham himself, who, in his judgment, preserved by Mr. Swanston, mentions that precedents of such writs being issued by Kelyng, C. J., were brought before him. He says, indeed, that Rainsford, then chief justice, had refused a habeas corpus to Jenkes, but not because he doubted his power to do so. It is far more likely he did not choose to enter into a controversy with the privy council, by whom Jenkes had been committed."

[2] 2 Hale's P. C. 147.

[3] See statute, *ante*, sec. 58; and 2 Hale's P. C. 145.

[4] 31 Car. II.; see *ante*, sec. 58.

[5] 3 Kerr's Bla. Com. 124; Penrice and Wynn's Case, 2 Mod. 306, citing authorities.

[6] Bushell's Case, Vaugh. 135.

§ 88. APPLICATION FOR THE WRIT. 87

visions of that act, however, a prisoner who has for two whole terms after his imprisonment willfully neglected to apply for a habeas corpus is precluded from obtaining it in vacation, and must wait till the term ensuing.[1] "In term time the application, grounded upon affidavits, is made by the prisoner's counsel; and in vacation his solicitor lays them before a judge at chambers, accompanied in both cases with a copy of the warrant, or of an affidavit that it has been denied. When the motion is made to the court, upon just cause being shown, a rule is granted for the writ to issue; and when an application is made to a judge in chambers, he grants his fiat; whereupon the clerk in court makes out the habeas corpus, and delivers it to the solicitor of the applicant. The writ will not, it is said, be granted on the mere affidavit of the prisoner; but the application must be supported by other evidence."[2]

The statute of 56 Geo. III., c. 100, simplified proceedings under this writ very much. It was enacted that a judge of any of the courts shall award a writ of habeas corpus in vacation, returnable immediately before himself or any other judge of the same court, if it shall appear by affidavit or information that there is probable and reasonable cause. Willful disobedience of the writ shall be deemed a contempt of court, and the judge before whom it is returnable may bind the offender to appear in court in the ensuing term to answer the contempt, or, on his refusal to give security, may commit him to prison. A writ awarded late in vacation time might be made returnable in term time, and one awarded in term time might be made returnable before a judge in vacation; but the supreme court of judicature act, 1873, section 26, abolished terms.[3]

The prevailing practice of the federal courts of the United States is much the same as that under the modern common law.[4] In one of the United States circuit courts, as early as 1804, the court required a petition in writing, and a production of the warrant of commitment, or a copy, or an affidavit of refusal of the jailer to give a copy.[5] Section 754 of the United States revised statutes, found on a preceding page, now designates the manner in which the application shall be made in those courts.[6] And it may be made to the courts either in term time or to any justice or judge of the district or circuit courts within their respec-

[1] 31 Car. II.; see *ante*, sec. 53.
[2] 1 Ch. Crim. L. 124, and authorities cited.
[3] 3 Kerr's Bla. Com. 129; 8 Law Rep., 36 & 37 Vict. 321, sec. 26.
[4] Ex parte Bollman and Swartwout, 4 Cranch, 75.
[5] Harrison's Case, 1 Cranch C. Ct. 159.
[6] Ex parte Clarke, 100 U. S. 399.

tive jurisdictions, or to any justice of the supreme court of the United States, at any time, wherever he may be within the United States.[1] In the state courts, application may be made to officers authorized to issue the writ, or probably to the courts generally in term time; but the prisoner's constitutional right "must be exercised in a reasonable manner," and the writ's allowance in term time rests in the sound discretion of the court.[2]

§ 89. **Requisites of the Petition.**—One of the fundamental rules of pleading should be followed in drawing a petition for a writ of habeas corpus; and that is, to state facts. Put before the court or judge facts enough in the petition to allow an intelligent judgment to be formed on the case.[3] Conclusions of law should be avoided. A general statement that the warrant of the justice is illegal, null, and void, and that it was issued without authority of law, is a mere conclusion of law, and not a statement of any fact.[4] The petition should show in what the illegality of the imprisonment consists, and this should be done by stating the facts showing it.[5] The prisoner should state in his petition for what offense he was arrested, if any, and a copy of the warrant of the committing magistrate should be set out in the petition, and Chief Justice Hawley, of the supreme court of Nevada, held, that even where a proper showing was otherwise made, it was questionable whether he would make a writ returnable before that court in the first instance, where it was sought to bring the petitioner from a distant county, without a showing of the absence, disability, or refusal of the district judge of the county to act, or other good cause why it should be heard by the supreme court, or a justice thereof, and cited authorities: Ex parte Nye, 8 Kan. 99; Ex parte Ellis, 11 Cal. 223.[6] A petitioner can not be in the custody of two different officers at the same time; and when he alleges that he is in the custody of a sheriff, but suggests to the court that if he be released from his charge that the sheriff will deliver him to another officer upon the receipt of a governor's requisition waiting for him, the court will not anticipate such an arrest in order to determine the validity of the governor's warrant.[7] A peti-

---

[1] Justice Bradley in Ex parte Clarke, 100 U. S. 403.
[2] Ex parte Ellis, 11 Cal. 222.
[3] Ex parte Nye, 8 Kan. 99; State v. Ensign, 13 Neb. 250.
[4] Ex parte Deny, 10 Nev. 212.
[5] Id.
[6] Ex parte Deny, 10 Nev. 212; see also People v. Burtnett, 13 Abb. Pr. 8; S. C., 5 Park. Cr. 113, where it said that if petitioner makes application in an adjoining county, he must explicitly show that there is no officer in his own county authorized to grant the writ. It is insufficient to state that he could find none; and his affidavit will be objectionable if made several days prior to the time when it is used.
[7] Ex parte Deny, 10 Nev. 212.

§ 89.   APPLICATION FOR THE WRIT.   89

tion should set forth the evidence given before the committing magistrate, where any has been adduced, in order that the court may act advisedly. Where this is not done, the court will presume in favor of the conduct of the committing officer.[1] This rule was also followed in the state of Colorado, when it was a territory.[2]

In Georgia, in 1879, it was held by the supreme court that when the wife of a prisoner sues out a habeas corpus, she can bring a writ of error upon the final decision made on the hearing of the habeas corpus, and Justice Bleckley said: "There was an action or trover, and the court had jurisdiction both of the person and the subject-matter. There was such an affidavit as the statute prescribes. The declaration sets forth a cause of action; there was regular process and due service. The property had not been seized, because the officer could not find it, and the requisite bond and security were not given by the defendant. These facts made a case for imprisonment: Code, sec. 3420. To go beneath them, and inquire into the truth of the matters alleged in the declaration and affidavit, would be to engage the habeas corpus court in a work of subsoiling which can be fitly done only by the court in which the main action is pending, and upon a regular trial in the due course of proceedings. Imprisonment until a trial can be had does not depend upon whether the plaintiff has a good case for a recovery, but upon whether he puts a good case upon paper, and locates it in the proper forum. In what he alleges there may not be one word of truth, but his alleging it in the manner prescribed, and upon the sanctions which the law ordains, entitles him to have the property produced or the defendant imprisoned, if the latter will not give bond and security. What is needed to justify imprisonment is only due process of law, and it is obvious that there may be the same legality of process in behalf of an unjust suitor as of a just one. The time for discriminating between cases of merit and those without merit is at the trial. Indeed, the sole object of a trial is to find out whether the complaint is well or ill founded. Where imprisonment takes place on mesne process, the range of inquiry upon habeas corpus is simply whether the plaintiff has brought a proper suit in the proper court, and has taken all the steps in procedure which the law lays down as conditions precedent; these things appearing, the lawfulness of the custody follows necessarily. The

[1] Ex parte Klepper, 26 Ill. 532.   [2] In re Garvin, 3 Col. 67.

investigation relates to what has been done, not to whether it ought to have been done."[1]

In a state where prevails a statute "that application for the writ [of habeas corpus] must be made to the court or judge most convenient in point of distance to the applicant, and the more remote court or judge may refuse the same unless a sufficient reason be stated in the petition for not making the application to the more convenient court or judge thereof," it has been held that the person restrained was the applicant, within the meaning of the statute, and that the application should have been made to the court or judge nearest her, where the mother, residing in one judicial district, made application to the judge of that district for a habeas corpus to release from custody her daughter, a minor, alleged to be restrained of her liberty in another judicial district. It was also observed that the proper court or judge to whom the application should be made is not the one nearest the residence of the applicant, but the one nearest the applicant.[2] Where a statute prescribed that the writ of habeas corpus should be issued by a judge of a circuit court, or any chancery court, in term time or in vacation, or where there was no such judge in the county at the time, then by any police judge or judge of the county court, or in their absence from the county, by a justice of the peace, a justice of the peace issued the writ upon the application of a prisoner, and in which he stated that the circuit judge was absent from the county, and that the county judge was so prejudiced against him that he refused to grant the writ and was incapacitated to act in the matter, it was held that the statement of this fact in the application did not confer jurisdiction upon a justice of the peace to issue it, and that the writ was void.[3] A petition which contains a statement of facts as prescribed by statute, and properly verified, is not demurrable because it fails to allege that the petitioner is illegally restrained of his liberty.[4]

The restriction in the habeas corpus act of New York,[5] that application for a writ must be to a judge or officer within the county where the prisoner is detained, or in an adjoining county, does not apply to the supreme court or one of its justices. An application may be made to the supreme court, or to one of its

---

[1] State ex rel. Lynch v. Bridges, Jailer, et al., 64 Ga. 146. In Indiana, too, a writ of error lies from an order refusing bail on habeas corpus for that purpose: Lumm v. State. 3 Port. (Ind.) 293.

[2] Thompson v. Oglesby, 42 Iowa, 598.

[3] Bethuram v. Black, 11 Bush, 628.

[4] Ex parte Champion, 52 Ala. 311.

[5] 3 R. S., 6th ed., 875 et seq.

justices anywhere within the state, but when it is made "to any officer who may be authorized to perform the duties of a justice of the supreme court at chambers," that officer must be or reside "within the county where the prisoner is detained," unless there "be no such officer within such county, or if he be absent, or for any cause be incapable of acting, or have refused to grant such writ."[1] A petition is defective which fails to aver the locality of the confinement. This averment should be made in order that the discretion of the court or judge, as to the place of the return of the writ, may be properly exercised.[2] Where a statute exempts certain persons from the benefit of the habeas corpus act, the petition must show that the party detained is without the exception. A detention for a cause specified in a statute should be negatived affirmatively in the petition.[3]

§ 90. **Further Matters concerning the Petition.**—The English practice in obtaining a *habeas corpus ad testificandum* is to apply for it to a judge at chambers, and not in court.[4] One making an application for the writ of *habeas corpus ad subjiciendum* must, if he apply for or on behalf of another, make an affidavit of authority, or show that there is such a restraint that it can not be given.[5] But the affidavit is not of the essence of the writ, and in cases of urgent necessity, the writ will be allowed to issue without affidavit—in fact to allow the prisoner to make it.[6] The omission of the name of the person imprisoned is not an irregularity, if enough appear to indicate the person intended.[7] Upon his petition for a habeas corpus, the relator must produce a sworn copy of the warrant of commitment, or an affidavit that the jailer refused to give him a copy.[8] The same with any order or process under which he may be imprisoned, or a legal excuse be shown for the omission.[9] On a mere copy of the indictment being shown, where the prisoner is indicted for murder, accompanied by a statement that there has been a mistrial, the application will be refused.[10] When an application for bail is pending, it is irregular for another court of concurrent jurisdiction to grant a habeas

---

[1] People ex rel. Rosenthal v. Cowles, 59 How. Pr. 287.
[2] Id.
[3] Id.
[4] Browne v. Gisborne, 2 A. & V. Dowl., N. S., 963.
[5] Ex parte Child, 29 Eng. L. & Eq. 259; Broomhead v. Chisolm, 47 Ga. 390; 2 Brick. Dig. 63; Com. v. Killacky, 3 Brewst. 565; Maples v. Maples, 49 Miss. 393; see Ex parte Dorr, 3 How. 103; but this decision is to be considered in connection with the United States revised statutes of 1867.
[6] State v. Philpot, Dudley (Ga.), 46.
[7] Id.
[8] In the Matter of Sweatman, 1 Cow. 144; Harrison's Case, 1 Cranch C. Ct. 159.
[9] In the Matter of Beard, 4 Ark. 9; Ex parte Royster, 6 Id. 28.
[10] In the Matter of Beard, 4 Ark. 9.

corpus to admit a prisoner to bail.[1] To obtain a reduction of bail, by means of habeas corpus, the petition should be especially framed to that purpose. It should allege that the bail is excessive.[2] An application on the ground that the prisoner has not had a speedy trial, must first be made in the trial court.[3] One refused a habeas corpus by one of the inferior courts may then apply directly to the supreme court in many of the states, but the grounds of the lower court's refusal ought to be shown.[4] A guardian petitioning for a habeas corpus to obtain the custody of his ward must make his letters of guardianship a part of his petition.[5]

Where statute confers power upon officers to issue the writ in certain specified cases, it ought to appear on the face of the writ, or else on the face of the petition, such petition being annexed to the writ and referred to therein, that the case exists in which authority has been given to such officer or magistrate to issue the writ. It tends to uniformity of practice, but does not affect the validity of the writ.[6] Where the case has been already heard by another court upon the same evidence, it has been held in Pennsylvania that the application may be refused.[7] A petition for the transfer of children is addressed to the sound discretion of the court, which will require a full disclosure of all essential facts before awarding a habeas corpus.[8] In the federal courts it has been said that the petitioner's proper course is to make his answer on the writ's return, and not make his allegations in full in the petition.[9] Where a petition is presented for alleged want of probable cause it should set forth all the testimony taken before the examining magistrate.[10] Where it is not alleged that the relator is detained without a proper warrant of commitment, and the writ does not require the keeper to return it, the certified minutes of the court showing judgment and sentence imposed sufficiently answer the writ, without a return of the warrant of commitment.[11] Where applicant grounds his right to a second writ of habeas corpus upon newly discovered evidence the application must set it forth, and if it be that of a witness, the affidavit of the witness must ac-

---

[1] Ex parte Kittrel, 20 Ark. 499.
[2] Hernandez v. The State, 4 Tex. App. 425.
[3] Ex parte Fennessy, 4 Pac. C. L. J. 496, cited in 1 Crim. Law Mag. 532.
[4] Ex parte Cleveland, 36 Ala. 306; Ex parte Burnett, 30 Id. 461.
[5] Gregg v. Wynn, 22 Ind. 373.
[6] Com. v. Moore, 19 Pick. 339.
[7] Ex parte Lawrence, 5 Binn. 304.
[8] People v. Chegary, 18 Wend. 637; People v. Mauley, 2 How. Pr. 61.
[9] Seavey v. Seymour, 3 Cliff. 439.
[10] In re Snyder, 17 Kan. 553; In re Balcom, 12 Neb. 316; State v. Ensign, 13 Id. 250; State v. Wiley, 64 N. C. 823.
[11] People v. Baker, 89 N. Y. 460.

company the petition. The same with evidence which it was out of the power of the witness to produce on the first hearing.[1]

§ 91. **Who may Make an Application.**—While the prisoner has an unquestionable right to make an application, it may sometimes happen that circumstances will not permit him to do so. He may be so restrained or coerced that it is impossible for him to act; and to discourage any such undue trespasses upon personal liberty, it has been held by the courts that an application need not proceed directly from the prisoner. Under the English practice, as well as our own, an affidavit is absolutely necessary; and it should be made by the party who claims the writ, or by some other person, so as to satisfy the court that he is so coerced as to be unable to make it. Unless this is done, a habeas corpus will not issue to bring up a prisoner.[2] A wife may move for the writ on behalf of her husband.[3] The sister of an orphan girl under fourteen may apply for a habeas corpus to remove the orphan from an asylum where the applicant was denied access to her.[4] A rule having been obtained for a habeas corpus to bring up a lunatic confined in an English asylum under Irish medical certificates, the court discharged it with costs, there being no affidavit to show that the party promoting the application was duly authorized by the lunatic. Jervis, C. J.: "A mere stranger has no right to come to the court and ask that a party who makes no affidavit, and who is not suggested to be so coerced as to be incapable of making one, may be brought up on habeas corpus to be discharged from restraint. For anything that appears, Captain Child may be very well content to remain where he is."[5] The court declined to allow the motion for a habeas corpus to be made by the father of the prisoner, and required it to be made by counsel.[6] Where a father wished to see his son, imprisoned in jail, and was denied access to him by the jailer, upon the application of the father the court granted a rule *nisi* for a habeas corpus to bring up the prisoner.[7]

The court, upon affidavit laid before them suggesting probable cause to believe that a helpless and ignorant foreigner, taken from the cape of Good Hope into England and exhibited there for money, against her consent, by those in whose keeping she was, granted a rule upon her keepers to show cause why a writ

---

[1] Ex parte Foster, 5 Tex. App. 625.
[2] Parker et al., 5 Mee. & W. 31; S. C., 7 Dowl. 208.
[3] Cobbett v. Hudson, 15 Ad. & El. 988, and Matter of Ferrens, 3 Ben. 442.
[4] In re Daley, 2 F. & F. 258 (Wilde).
[5] Ex parte Child, 15 C. B. 238.
[6] In re Newton, 16 C. B. 97; S. C., 24 L. J., N. S., C. P. 148 (1855).
[7] Ex parte Thompson, 30 L. J., N. S., M. C. 19 (Exch.)

of habeas corpus should not issue to bring her before the court, and directed an examination to be taken of her in the mean time before the coroner and attorney of the court, in the presence of proper persons, representing the persons applying for the writ as well as those against whom it was prayed.[1] The bail of a prisoner who has been taken upon a criminal accusation may have a writ of *habeas corpus cum causa* in the court of king's bench, in order to render him in their own discharge.[2] The prisoner may also be rendered, upon the same process, in discharge of his bail, when he is in custody on civil process.[3] The writ has issued on the application of the husband to bring up his wife in the custody of her mother and uncle;[4] and on the application of the father to bring up his daughter in the custody of third persons.[5]

§ 92. **Must Show Probable Cause.**—It is sometimes said that the habeas corpus is a writ of right, but not a writ of course, since cause must be shown. It is a high and imperative writ, and issues, it is true, as a matter of peremptory right, but it can only issue to one entitled to it either at common law or under statutes. Neither should it be granted without inquiry. To confine the issuing of the writ to this narrow and technical sense would make it a mere ministerial act, and it might be issued by the clerk of a court or other ministerial officer as any ordinary writ in such cases. But "it is a right in a larger and more liberal sense; a right to be delivered from all unlawful imprisonment."[6] There seems to have obtained in England, prior to the year 1820, an erroneous opinion that the court was bound in the first instance to issue a habeas corpus at all events, without exercising its discretion as to the grounds upon which the writ was moved.[7] But the direct course of all the later decisions with which we are acquainted, both English and American, is to establish the rule that probable cause must first be shown to obtain the writ, whether it be granted at common law or under the statute. This rule has been uniformly followed in the United States in both the state and federal courts, and is maintained by a multitude of authorities.[8]

This question came before the court of king's bench in Rex

[1] Hottentot Venus, 13 East, 194.
[2] 1 Ch. Crim. L. 132.
[3] 1 Tidd's Pr. 286.
[4] Rex v. Gregory, 4 Burr. 1991.
[5] Rex v. Clarke, 1 Burr. 606.
[6] Sim's Case, 7 Cush. 285.
[7] Rex v. Hobhouse, 2 Chit., Q. B., 211.
[8] Ex parte Tobias Watkins, 3 Pet. 201; United States v. Lawrence, 4 Cranch C. C. 521; Ex parte Winder, 2 Cliff. 89; Matter of Keeler, Hempst. 311; In re Gregg, 15 Wis. 479; In re Griner, 16 Id. 423; Ex parte Milligan, 4 Wall. 3; Ex parte Passmore Williamson, 4 Am. Law Reg. 27; Ex parte Campbell, 20 Ala., N. S., 89; Sim's Case, 7 Cush. 285.

§ 92.   APPLICATION FOR THE WRIT.   95

v. Hobhouse, and was well considered. It was there decided that whether the court granted a habeas corpus under the common-law jurisdiction or under the statute there ought always to be a proper ground laid before the court as justification in granting it. "It is not to be granted as a matter of course and at all events, but the party seeking to be brought up by habeas corpus must lay such a case on affidavit before the court as will be sufficient to regulate the discretion of the court in that respect. The court will not in the first instance grant a habeas corpus, when they see that in the result they must inevitably remand the party."[1] The principle of practice involved in the last sentence is found in many American authorities.[2] The court, in that case, which was a commitment by the house of commons, had ordered the writ to issue, upon a suggestion that the court was bound at all events to grant it, and the citation of a most respectable authority to sustain the proposition. The court, in favor of personal liberty, and in deference to the authority of Lord Kenyon in Rex v. Flower, 8 T. R. 314, granted the writ, but settled the question on its return.

Chief Justice Abbott, in commenting upon the propriety of granting the writ in this case, referred to an elaborate opinion, delivered by Lord Chief Justice Wilmot in 1758, in the house of lords, in answer to a question put by that house, whether, in cases not within the statute of 31 Car. II., c. 2, writs of *habeas corpus ad subjiciendum*, by the law then ought to issue of course, or upon probable cause verified by affidavit.[3] He there states it to be his opinion, that those writs ought not to issue of course; adding, that a writ which issues on a probable cause, verified by affidavit, is as much a writ of right as a writ which issues of course. And again, page 87, he says: "There is no such thing in the law as writs of grace and favor issuing from the judges. They are all writs of right, but then they are not all writs of course." And on page 88: "Writs of habeas corpus upon imprisonment, for criminal matters, were never writs of course; they always issued upon a motion, grafted on a copy of the commitment."[4] In spreading the cause upon the petition for the edification of the judge, if the prisoner is held upon legal process, or color or pretense of legal process, a copy of the process

---

[1] Hobhouse's Case, 2 Chit. 211.

[2] Chief Justice Marshall, in Ex parte Tobias Watkins, 3 Pet. 201, said: "The cause of imprisonment is shown as fully by the petitioner as it could appear on the return of the writ; consequently, the writ ought not to be awarded, if the court is satisfied that the prisoner would be remanded to prison."

[3] Citing Wilmot's Opinions and Judgments, 81.

[4] Hobhouse's Case, 3 Barn. & Ald. 420.

should be set forth in full; and if the prisoner has applied to his detainer for a copy of such process, and it has been refused, that fact should be shown by affidavit, the same as other facts where a party is not imprisoned on legal process. A copy of the warrant or process is to enable the court or judge to form an opinion as to the validity of the commitment. The judge must pass upon the warrant or process after the writ is issued; why not do so before, and avoid the doing of an act nugatory in itself?[1] Where insufficient cause is shown, the writ will be withheld; but the ordinary course is for the court to grant a rule *nisi*, in the first instance, to show cause why the writ should not issue. "When it appears upon the party's own showing that there is no sufficient ground *prima facie* for his discharge, the court will not issue the writ."[2]

Over two hundred years ago, in the suit of the King v. Marsh, a motion was made by counsel to the court of king's bench for a habeas corpus on the part of defendant, who was indicted in the admiralty prison for piracy. The facts were somewhat compromising to defendant, and Chief Justice Coke said: "If you had not opened the matter as you have done, then peradventure, upon the *ignoramus* found, we would have granted you a habeas corpus; but as you have now opened the verity of the matter (in which you have done well), we will not now grant you a habeas corpus, for upon your own showing, we have very great cause now to suspect him for piracy, and that he had his hand in this."[3] The idea seems to be that, if the writ was granted as a matter of course, without showing to the court or judge some reasonable ground for awarding it, criminals of every grade, from the malefactor under sentence of death to the one who has committed a simple misdemeanor, and even lunatics, children, and soldiers in the service, could obtain a temporary enlargement by suing out a habeas corpus, though sure to be remanded after hearing. The sentence of the law might be suspended and oftentimes eluded by them.[4] Abuses of discretion by the judge or court in deciding upon the question of probable cause can hardly be a subject of complaint by criminals, when they have such unlimited power to choose from the judiciary in making numerous applications, which they have in both England and America.[5]

In Ex parte Milligan it was held that a petition for a habeas

[1] Hobhouse's Case, 3 Barn. & Ald. 420.
[2] Sim's Case, 7 Cush. 292.
[3] King v. Marsh, Bulst., part 3, p. 27.
[4] Hobhouse's Case, 3 Barn. & Ald. 420.
[5] Ex parte Partington, 13 Mee. & W. 682; King v. Suddis, 1 East, 314; Ex parte Kaine, 14 How. 117; Ex parte Robinson, 6 McLean, 360.

corpus, properly presented to a court of competent jurisdiction, is the institution of a "cause" on petitioner's behalf, and the allowance or refusal of the process is matter of law, and not of discretion. According to that decision, "when the petition is filed and the writ prayed for, it is a suit—the suit of the party making the application."[1] We apprehend that when a petitioner, having a legal cause of complaint, has put his application in proper form, and prosecuted his "suit" in every way known to the law without error, the writ must be issued; but short of this, the domain of the judge's discretion begins and increases in inverse ratio with the correctness and validity of the process, and the truth of the affidavit or complaint filed. Chief Justice Shaw says, that requiring probable cause to be shown "does not restrain the full and beneficial operation of this writ, so essential to the protection of personal liberty. The same court must decide whether the imprisonment complained of is illegal; and whether the inquiry is had in the first instance on the application or subsequently on the return of the writ, or partly on one and partly on the other, it must depend upon the same facts and principles and be governed by the same rule of law."[2]

Unless a statute prescribes some penalty for refusing the writ, it is probably granted by judges in vacation upon the same foundation as is enunciated above. The statute of 31 Car. II., c. 2, made no alteration in the practice of the courts in granting the writs of habeas corpus, and when a single judge in vacation time grants them under this statute in criminal cases, a copy of the commitment, or an affidavit of the refusal of it, must be laid before him. The practice of the court of king's bench and of the judges of that court has been, that the foundation upon which the writ is prayed should be laid before the court or judge who awards it.[3] The same principle of practice is established in the courts of the United States, both state and federal.[4]

§ 93. **When the Application must be Granted.**—Upon probable cause being shown, the writ of habeas corpus can not be denied to the relator, for it then becomes a constitutional right; neither can it be denied where the granting of it is made an imperative duty by statute. The United States habeas corpus act, and that of most of the states, provides that it shall be granted without delay, upon the proper showing. The existence

---

[1] 4 Wall. 112, 113.
[2] Sim's Case, 7 Cush. 293.
[3] Hobhouse's Case, 3 Barn. & Ald. 422, 423.
[4] See United States habeas corpus act, *ante*, sec. 59, and the habeas corpus acts of the various states—the common law prevailing where no statutory provisions are found.

of probable cause may be illustrated by the following instances in which courts have allowed the writ:

A convict may be released upon habeas corpus, where he has been committed to the state prison on conviction and sentence for a felony, if the commitment fails to contain a certified copy of the judgment as entered in the minutes of the court, and consists only of a history of the proceedings against the prisoner; provided that no certified copy of a valid judgment of imprisonment against the prisoner can be obtained from a court of competent jurisdiction sentencing him.[1] The words importing an offense should be definite and certain, and the words "or other articles of value" are not of that nature, and do not import any offense. A prisoner committed and detained under a commitment so defective in this particular, may apply for the writ.[2]

One who has been committed under an execution by a justice of the peace for a sum exceeding his jurisdiction may be discharged upon a habeas corpus.[3] The master may file a petition for the body of his apprentice, and a court will refuse to quash the habeas corpus.[4] Under the revised statutes of New York, page 115, section 61, a party committed to prison for default in delivering up books and papers appertaining to a public office, pursuant to an order of a judge under the statute, is entitled to his discharge on habeas corpus if there is any doubt of the jurisdiction of the judge to make the order for the delivery of the books, etc.[5] In 1856, in the United States circuit court for California, an alien, a subject of Napoleon III., emperor of the French, applied for a writ of habeas corpus to relieve the Hon. David S. Terry, then one of the judges of the supreme court of California, from the unlawful custody of certain persons who it was thought were about to transfer and convey the said justice beyond the limits of the state and of the United States, illegally and against his will. The alien was plaintiff in an action at law pending in the supreme court of the state, involving the sum of sixteen thousand dollars, and delay in the decision thereof was greatly injuring him. He alleged that the court was composed of three judges; that the presence of two was necessary for the transaction of business; and that one was absent from the state. He wished his business attended to, and prayed the court to relieve the restrained judge from imprisonment. The writ was issued

---

[1] Ex parte Dobson, 31 Cal. 497; Ex parte Gibson, Id. 619.
[2] Republic of Texas v. Bynum, Dallam, 376.
[3] Geyger v. Stoy, 1 Dall. (Pa.) 146.
[4] Com. v. Beek, 1 Browne, 277.
[5] Devlin's Case, 5 Abb. Pr. 281.

§ 93. APPLICATION FOR THE WRIT. 99

but not served, as Judge Terry was released prior to the service of the writ.[1]

A defendant in arrest on a civil process void for want of jurisdiction may be relieved by habeas corpus.[2] A daughter may take out a habeas corpus to relieve her aged mother taken from her residence by force, against her remonstrance and without authority of law, from her restraint.[3] A minor may apply for discharge upon habeas corpus, where his indenture of apprenticeship is void upon its face.[4] If a person imprisoned gives authority or makes a request that a complaint and petition for a writ of habeas corpus be filed, and the prisoner is brought up on the writ upon the strength of this authority, he can not recover in an action on the case; otherwise he may maintain such an action.[5] "It is not, however, required as a condition, without which the writ will be withheld, that a party suffering the imprisonment expressly authorized the application; for that would be in many cases to furnish a spur to a closer and more rigorous confinement. It is enough that the application, by whomsoever presented, shows probable ground to suspect that the person on whose behalf it is made is suffering an involuntary and wrongful restraint or imprisonment."[6] It may be said that there are two kinds of applications for an ordinary habeas corpus — one entirely for illegal arrest and detention, the other for bail. Prosecuting attorneys, it has been said, in Indiana, sometimes, as a matter of policy, draw their indictments covering the highest offense, "thus including the inferior, rather than for either of the lower, which does not include the superior. The indictment, therefore, should not be taken as conclusive of the grade of the offense in determining the question of bail." Where this practice, then, prevails, a prisoner indicted for murder in the first degree may sue out a habeas corpus to be bailed, and upon proof that he is guilty of a bailable homicide, he should be allowed to give bail.[7]

An order was entered in the district court of Cowley county, Kansas, on the thirteenth day of May, 1880, adjourning that court until Monday, May 17th, which was the day fixed by law for the commencement of the term of the Sedgwick county district court, Sedgwick county being in the same judicial district. The term commenced on that day, according to law, and the

---

[1] Ex parte Des Rochers, 1 McAll. 68.
[2] Martin's Case, 1 Bright. Dig. 1240.
[3] Com. v. Curby et al., 3 Brewst. 610; S. C., 8 Phila. 372.
[4] Com. v. Atkinson, 8 Phila. 375.
[5] Linda v. Hudson, 1 Cush. 385.
[6] Hurd on Habeas Corpus, 2d ed., 204.
[7] Lumm v. The State, 3 Port. (Ind.) 293.

regular judge being absent, a judge *pro tem.* was elected, who held court on both the seventeenth and eighteenth. The regular judge was present in Cowley county, assuming to hold court pursuant to adjournment on the seventeenth and eighteenth, and at the same time the district court of Sedgwick county was in session. The supreme court held, "that such order of adjournment was void, and the proceedings on the seventeenth and eighteenth in the circuit of Cowley county were extrajudicial and void. There was no court then in session in that county. There is but one district court and one district judge in a district. The officer is not to be duplicated, and when a term commences in one county, the court everywhere else in the district is closed or suspended. A judge *pro tem.* is only a substitute and never a duplicate." A defendant who had been tried and sentenced in Cowley county on the above-mentioned dates was held to be entitled to his discharge on habeas corpus.[1]

A prisoner who wishes to be brought up on habeas corpus to conduct his defense in person should apply to the court in which the proceedings are pending. Even after conviction, if he is not represented by counsel, he has a right to appear personally in court to have counsel assigned him, or to assign errors, and conduct his cause in person.[2] In England the writ of habeas corpus has been issued to the prisoner, who was charged with selling unstamped papers, for the purpose of enabling him to conduct his defense in person.[3] So in case of a question of identity of the person of a defendant to an information, and who is in prison, the court will grant a habeas corpus to bring him up to be present at the trial, the prisoner paying his own expenses both ways. The form of such a writ is rather that of a *habeas corpus ad testificandum.*[4] In England it has been held, too, that the writ may issue to bring up the body of a prisoner confined for debt, before a magistrate to be examined from day to day respecting a charge of felony or misdemeanor.[5] To entitle a prisoner to this writ, however, to be brought up to be present on the argument of a rule in which he is interested, he must satisfy the court that substantial justice can not be done without his presence.[6]

The writ of habeas corpus may be used in civil as well as in criminal and political cases. A tutor deprived of the custody

---

[1] Ex parte Millington, 24 Kan. 214.
[2] Donnelly v. The State, 2 Dutch. 463.
[3] Attorney General v. Cleave, 2 Dowl. 668.
[4] Attorney General v. Fadden, 1 Price, 403.
[5] Ex parte Griffith, 5 Barn. & Ald. 730.
[6] Clark v. Smith, 3 Com. B. 984.

§ 93.   APPLICATION FOR THE WRIT.   101

of his ward, or a husband of the company of his wife, may seek a restoration to their rights by a recourse to the writ of habeas corpus; and so may a debtor illegally confined in a civil case.[1] A wife may leave her husband, with or without justifiable cause, and no court, upon his application, has any power to compel her to return to matrimonial relations and to the performance of her conjugal duties.[2] No contract, even in writing, which deprives a man of his liberty, can be specifically enforced by the judgment or order of a court; and where force is attempted to be used to compel any person to perform such contract, he may find relief in an application for habeas corpus.[3] Where it appears that the wrong person has been arrested and deprived of his liberty, the court will, on an application for a habeas corpus, interpose immediately for his relief, but where the identity is doubtful, a jury must decide the question.[4] If a person, while he is applying for the benefit of the insolvent laws in New Jersey, and previous to his liberation, has a judgment rendered against him for a debt contracted previous to his confinement, and after his discharge as an insolvent debtor is arrested by virtue of an execution issued upon that judgment and committed to jail, his arrest and imprisonment are unlawful, and he may apply for and be released upon habeas corpus.[5]

Upon the principle that public justice requires the punishment of offenders, and in the absence of legislative provisions pertaining to such a case, the public prosecutor of a county in which property has been stolen may apply for a habeas corpus to bring up a prisoner—who has stolen property in that county and is apprehended and committed for such offense to the jail of another county, if he is indicted in the county where the property was stolen—so that he may be delivered to the sheriff of the county within which the property was stolen, and there tried.[6] Any party who has the right to the custody of another may sue out this writ, as in special bail. In civil cases this is matter of course; but in criminal cases, it must be on motion. In either case, it is not a matter of favor, but *ex debito justitiæ*. The power of special bail over the principal is very great: they may arrest in the night, on Sunday, may force the doors, and in case of resistance, use any force necessary to overcome the resistance.[7] A prisoner may apply for and be discharged upon

---

[1] Hyde et al. v. Jenkins, 6 La. 436.
[2] People ex rel. Barry v. Mercein, 8 Paige, 54.
[3] In re Baker, 29 How. Pr. 485.
[4] Respublica v. Jailer of Philadelphia, 2 Yeates, 258.
[5] State v. Ward, 3 Halst. 120.
[6] People v. Mason, 9 Wend. 505.
[7] Holsey v. Trevillo, 6 Watts, 403.

a writ of habeas corpus, where he has been committed by a magistrate whose want of jurisdiction appears upon the face of the proceedings. In such a case, the proceedings are wholly void, and the commitment is without authority. He has a right to impeach the commitment, and offer proofs *aliunde* the commitment or return to sustain his allegation of illegal commitment, or that the court sentencing him was not legally constituted. Here a reversal of the judgment is not necessary for the enlargement of the prisoner.[1]

Sometimes a statute requires certain conditions precedent to be established to maintain a case. Thus, to constitute the crime of seduction, if the legislature require that it must be effected under the promise of marriage, that the female should be of previous chaste character, and that no conviction shall take place on the testimony of the seduced unsupported by other evidence, these propositions must all be established, or a defendant committed to answer to a prosecution for this crime may be discharged on habeas corpus, and in some cases upon *certiorari*, where that remedy is applicable.[2] Where one is arrested upon process in the form of a writ of attachment or *capias*, in which is inserted a bill in equity setting forth a copartnership, demand for an accounting, etc., the question is raised whether the party against whom a suit in equity is instituted can lawfully be arrested and held to bail, or be imprisoned for failing to give bail. And it has been held that he can not. He will be discharged on habeas corpus.[3] A resident of New Hampshire went to Boston, Massachusetts, for the purpose of attending a hearing before commissioners appointed by the judge of probate to examine claims against the estate of a deceased person, he being an interested party, and while there he was arrested on mesne process in an action of contract. On habeas corpus it was decided that he was privileged from arrest on civil process in this case, upon the principle that the law extended its protection " to all legal tribunals of a judicial character, whether strictly courts of record or not, recognized by the laws of the state, and having power to pass upon the rights of persons attending them," and he was discharged.[4] So where an inhabitant of New Hampshire went into Massachusetts solely for the purpose of voluntarily appearing before a joint committee of the legislature to present

---

[1] Herrick's Case, 1 Gray, 50; People v. Alexander, 2 Am. Law Reg. 44; McLeod's Case, 1 Hill (N. Y.) 377; People v. Divine, 21 How. Pr. 80; S. C., 11 Abb. Pr. 90; 5 Park. Cr. 62.

[2] People v. Lomax, 6 Abb. Pr. 139.

[3] Com. v. Sumner, 5 Pick. 360.

[4] Wood v. Neale, 5 Gray, 538.

and testify to a claim of his against that commonwealth, and intended to return without unnecessary delay, it was held that he was privileged from arrest on civil process, while so attending and returning, and that upon such an arrest, based upon an execution issuing from the supreme court of that state, the prisoner might be discharged upon habeas corpus.[1]

Where a witness was cited to appear before a committee of the United States senate, and he disobeyed the summons, it was held in Massachusetts, upon habeas corpus, that a warrant issued by order of the United States senate, for his arrest for such contempt, and addressed only to the sergeant-at-arms of the senate, could not be served by deputy in that commonwealth, and the prisoner was discharged.[2] It is a good defense to a writ of *scire facias* against bail that the principal, after they became his bail, was convicted of a crime, and is imprisoned under sentence. In such a case, the bail need not bring the principal into court on habeas corpus to be surrendered, but they will be discharged on motion. The principle of law applicable is: "Where, by the act of God, or the act of the government, or by sentence of the law, the principal is removed or taken from the custody or control of the bail, before they are fixed, so that they can not surrender him, to enable the creditor to charge him in execution, and that without any fault on their part, then the bail are entitled to their discharge," as is well expressed by Mr. Dane, in his Abridgment, vol. 5, p. 290.[3] A defendant had been bound over, in Philadelphia, to answer the charge of a "conspiracy with Dr. Dyott to defraud the community." He refused to give bail to the mayor, who committed him, and was turned over to the custody of a high constable, whereupon he sued out a habeas corpus. Held, that in cases where the committing magistrate has no authority to take bail, the writ may issue to the constable or other officer having the defendant in charge.[4] In Massachusetts, where excessive bail was required, the prisoner was ordered, on habeas corpus, to be released, upon giving sureties in a reasonable sum—one thousand dollars on an action for false imprisonment, where three thousand dollars was required in the court below.[5] The writ may issue against a wife, on the application of the husband to obtain the custody of their child.[6] A sister may have the writ to relieve her sister from re-

---

[1] Thompson's Case, 122 Mass. 428; May v. Shumway, 16 Gray, 86.
[2] Sanborn v. Carleton, 15 Gray, 399.
Way v. Wright, 5 Met. 380.
[4] Commonwealth v. Ridgway, 2 Ashm. 247.
[5] Jones v. Kelly, 17 Mass. 116.
[6] Commonwealth v. Briggs, 16 Pick. 203.

straint.[1] If a prisoner's evidence is necessary at his own trial, he is as much entitled to a *habeas corpus ad testificandum* for himself as for any other witness.[2]

§ 94. **When the Application Ought to be Denied.**—Courts of justice may refuse to grant the writ of habeas corpus where no probable ground for relief is shown in the petition, or where it appears that the petitioner is duly committed for felony or treason expressed in the warrant of commitment.[3] To grant or refuse a habeas corpus to enable a prisoner to attend to show cause against a summons is entirely within the discretion of the court or judge.[4] The courts will not issue the writ for the purpose of bringing up a prisoner to move for or to show cause against rules, as there is no writ known to the law applicable to such a purpose;[5] as to move to set aside an attachment;[6] or to move for a new trial in an action in which he is a party;[7] or to show cause in person against a rule for a criminal information, where the defendant is under sentence of imprisonment for a misdemeanor.[8] Neither will it be granted to bring up a debtor in military custody for the purpose of charging him in execution;[9] or to bring up a prisoner in a county jail for the purpose of voting for a member of parliament;[10] or to bring up a party who had been admitted to bail, and afterwards committed to jail upon additional evidence.[11] The court of exchequer has refused the application of a defendant confined in a county jail for libel, under sentence of another court, to attend at Westminster to conduct his defense in person, as the application for the habeas corpus should have been made to the court by whom the defendant was sentenced.[12] Where the plaintiff in an action is in lawful custody for debt, he is not entitled, as a matter of right, to a habeas corpus to have himself brought up to conduct his own cause at the trial, though a court would doubtless grant it in a proper case.[13] It will not be granted to bring up a prisoner from jail, where he is undergoing sentence, in order that he may be taken before a magistrate in another county to have another charge preferred against him.[14] Nor will the queen's

---

[1] In re Suttor, 2 F. & F. 267, 272.
[2] Ex parte Cobbett, 3 Hurl. & N. 155.
[3] In the Matter of Winder, 2 Cliff. 89.
[4] Ford v. Graham, 10 Com. B. 369.
[5] Benns v. Mosely & Cobbett, 40 Eng. L. & Eq. 342.
[6] Ford v. Nassau, 9 Mee. & W. 792.
[7] Benns v. Mosely, 2 Com. B., N. S., 116.
[8] Rex v. Parkyns, 3 Barn. & Ald. 679, note.
[9] Jones v. Danvers, 5 Mee. & W. 234.
[10] Ex parte Jones, 4 Nev. & M. 340.
[11] Ex parte Allen, 3 Nev. & M. 35.
[12] Att. Gen. v. Hunt, 9 Price, 147.
[13] Ex parte Cobbett, 3 Hurl. & N. 155.
[14] Reg. v. Day, 3 F. & F. 526.

§ 94.   APPLICATION FOR THE WRIT.   105

bench, on the mere instance of the coroner, and where no urgent necessity is shown, issue the writ to bring before a coroner's jury, who are holding an inquest upon the murdered body, a prisoner committed for trial on a charge of murder.[1] Neither will the writ issue to bring up a prisoner in custody under process out of the court of chancery, on the ground that the keeper of the queen's prison had improperly removed him to a part of the prison provided for criminals of a particular class.[2]

In Pennsylvania a prisoner stood indicted for aiding and abetting another to commit murder. He was not tried at the second term, and where the principal had absconded, and proceedings to outlawry against him were commenced without delay, but insufficient time having elapsed in which to finish them before a writ of habeas corpus was applied for by the prisoner, the writ was refused.[3] When the judgment of a county court for a felony is reversed by the supreme court, after the prisoner has been sent to the state prison in pursuance of his sentence, the refusal of the county court to order the prisoner to be brought back to the county for a new trial is no ground for his discharge on habeas corpus. The action of the county court can not be reviewed upon an application for this writ, and the fact determined whether there were or were not sufficient reasons for denying the order, under the circumstances, made to that court. If there were no sufficient reasons for denying it, that may afford ground for some appropriate proceeding to compel the court to correct the error and proceed with the trial, "but it is clearly no reason why the accused should be discharged from custody."[4]

The supreme court of California has also held that it will not, on an application for this writ, interfere with the amount of bail demanded in the court below, unless it is "*per se* unreasonably great and clearly disproportionate to the offense involved,

---

[1] Ex parte Wakely, Law Jour., 1845; Com. L. Mag. Cas. 188.
[2] Ex parte Cobbett, 5 Com. B. 418.
[3] Com. v. Sheriff etc., 16 Serg. & R. 304; Ex parte Walton, 2 Whart. 501; Com. v. Sup't of Phila. Co. Prison, 4 Brews. 320; and Com. v. Jailer of Alleghany Co., 7 Watts, 366, where a prisoner having an infectious disease, small-pox, was denied a trial at the second term, and it was held that he was not entitled to it as a matter of right, upon a motion made for his discharge upon habeas corpus. Where, upon the commitment of a debtor on an execution then in force, a copy was left with the jailer, from which the execution seemed not to be in force, and upon a habeas corpus the jailer returned this copy as the cause of detention, but immediately afterwards a correct copy was left with him, and he then returned this last copy, the court refused to discharge the debtor. It is not bad practice for a copy of the execution to be left with the jailer upon such a commitment: Com. v. Waite, 2 Pick. 445.
[4] Ex parte Bowen, 46 Cal. 112.

or so great as to shock the common sense."[1] A prisoner who has been convicted of murder, and sentenced to be executed, can not be relieved upon habeas corpus, where the sheriff has permitted the day assigned for the execution to elapse. A new day will be assigned.[2] A prisoner out on bail is not considered as so restrained of his liberty as to entitle him to the writ of habeas corpus, directed to his bail.[3] A commitment for a contempt in not delivering possession of property, pursuant to order of court, must show on its face that the person committed had possession or control of the property, and if it does not do so, the court can not supply the defect by resorting to the papers on which the original order to give possession was made, where the prisoner seeks his discharge on habeas corpus.[4] In North Carolina it has been held that the chief justice of the supreme court of that state has no power under the habeas corpus act to order the arrest of the governor of the state.[5]

Under the code of Georgia it has been held, that where a prisoner has been sentenced, for simple larceny, "to work in the chain-gang on the streets of Augusta, for twelve months," and where a habeas corpus and writ of error thereon have been brought to free the party from such sentence alleged to be illegal, the writ of error will not be dismissed, when reached for argument in the supreme court, on the ground that the period of time covered by the sentence has expired. "An illegal imprisonment is not to be supposed to terminate in a voluntary discharge." The sentence was considered legal, and Judge Bleckley thought it was not one of which the convict should complain by petition for habeas corpus, and that the streets of the city were part and parcel of the public works, and the sentence within the law, though more narrow than the law would have sanctioned. His honor considered it no deprivation of any right of personal liberty not to be constrained to labor on all of the public works instead of a part only. Under that code convicts may be hired out as well to the city as to other hirers, and a convict under such a state of law and facts can not obtain his release from custody under habeas corpus.[6] The Pennsylvania supreme court, in 1862, declared the act of assembly of May 1, 1861, providing for a graduated "deduction from the term of sentence" which a prisoner might be serving out in the

---

[1] Ex parte Duncan, 53 Cal. 410.
[2] Ex parte Nixon, 2 S. C., N. S., 4; Earl of Ferrer's Case, 2 Hawk. P. C., Curwood's ed., c. 44, sec. 18, p. 585, note 1.
[3] T. of Kan. v. Cutler, McCahon, 152.
[4] People ex rel. Walters v. Conner, 15 Abb. Pr., N. S., 430.
[5] Ex parte Moore et al., 64 N. C. 815.
[6] Lark v. State, 55 Ga. 435.

state penitentiary, as a reward for good conduct, to be an interference with the judgment of the court sentencing the criminal, and therefore unconstitutional. Under this act two prisoners sought their discharge upon habeas corpus, and the court held that the legislature evidently meant to leave to the boards of inspectors of the penitentiaries a measure of discretion in carrying out the provisions of the act, and in the execution of that discretion, where the boards declined to discharge the prisoners, or to execute the act, on the ground that public justice would not be promoted thereby, it would not control that discretion, if the reasons assigned by the inspectors were such as to justify their course.[1] A person convicted of crime and sentenced to imprisonment at hard labor is not entitled to relief on habeas corpus upon the ground that he has not been removed to the penitentiary nor put to hard labor.[2]

It has been held in Michigan that a boy committed to the reform school can not have his age inquired into on habeas corpus, and that if the recorder of Detroit, who sentenced him, made a mistake in his age, it does not vitiate the sentence. It was further held that the recorder had no authority to issue a habeas corpus to take him from the school after having been lawfully sentenced there, unless to testify as a witness.[3] The English rule does not permit a master to sue out a habeas corpus to bring up his apprentice, of the age of eighteen, voluntarily enlisted into the sea service, or from the service of any other master. As the master is entitled to the wages of his apprentice, he can bring his action for wages in the former case, and action for seduction of his apprentice in the latter; but habeas corpus is an improper remedy. Lord Kenyon was of the opinion that the writ should only be issued at the instance of a party who is in custody, or at least with his consent.[4] In cases of this kind Lord Mansfield frequently exercised the power of granting warrants under an old English statute, for the purpose of bringing up apprentices in this situation (impressed into the sea service) to be released.[5] This view of the functions of habeas corpus has been taken in the United States, and the doctrine followed.[3]

Where a writ of *ne exeat* has not been improvidently issued, and is based upon a proper showing, a petitioner can not be released upon habeas corpus until he makes satisfaction of the

---

[1] Com. ex rel. Johnson v. Halloway, 42 Pa. St. 446.
[2] Pember's Case, 1 Whart. 439; see Reddill's Case, Id. 445.
[3] In re Mason, 8 Mich. 70.
[4] King v. Reynolds, 3 T. R. 407.
[5] King v. Edwards, 7 T. R. 745.
[6] Lea v. White, 4 Sneed, 73.

debt or the matter is finally determined.¹ In the state of Kansas a defendant was refused the writ where an information had been filed in a court having jurisdiction, and where the defendant had been put upon his trial and a jury sworn, but where a juror was withdrawn before the introduction of any testimony, the jury discharged, the case continued, and the defendant committed for trial at the next term.² A habeas corpus will not be allowed for a married woman upon the petition of her brother, where she is confined in an insane asylum which is well managed, and where she is properly treated and cared for by the officers thereof and liberally provided for by her husband.³ A party arrested on regular process out of another court can not be discharged on a writ of habeas corpus.⁴ So the Pennsylvania supreme court refused to discharge a prisoner from a commitment upon a *capias ad satisfaciendum* issued out of the court of common pleas.⁵ The application may be denied in the cases excepted in the habeas corpus acts of the various states; but as we have said, it can not be denied where the granting of it is made an imperative duty by statute, and, we repeat, it ought not to be granted where the party is not entitled to it on his own showing.⁶

§ 95. **Verification of the Petition.**—We have seen that at common law and under the statute of 31 Car. II., an affidavit of the circumstances under which the relator was imprisoned was usually required.⁷ The habeas corpus act of the United States requires the complaint to be verified, and in most of the states there are statutory provisions requiring that the petition shall be verified. And it seems that the writ may be verified by an

---

¹ Ex parte Royster, 6 Ark. 29. An interesting question was presented many years ago in Massachusetts to the supreme court. A judgment was recovered, and an execution issued thereon before the death of the plaintiff; and the defendant was committed on the execution after the death of the plaintiff. The court refused to discharge the prisoner upon the summary process of habeas corpus, because they were not prepared to say that the imprisonment was unlawful, so as to entitle the prisoner to his discharge forthwith as a matter of right, but if it was, he had his remedy by writ of *audita querela*, in which the facts could be put in issue and the rights of the parties more regularly settled; Commonwealth v. Whitney, 10 Pick. 434; citing Lovejoy v. Webber, 10 Mass. 101.
² Ex parte Phillips, 7 Kan. 48.
³ Denny v. Tyler, 3 Allen, 225.
⁴ Respublica v. Keeper of the Jail, 2 Yeates, 349.
⁵ Com. v. Lecky, 1 Watts, 66.
⁶ Ex parte Milligan, 4 Wall. 2; Ex parte Williamson, 4 Am. Law Reg. 27; Ex parte Campbell, 20 Ala. 89; Ex parte Kearney, 7 Wheat. 38; Com. v. Robinson, 1 Serg. & R. 353; Ex parte Pardy, 1 Lownd. Max. & Pol. 20; In re Griner, 16 Wis. 447; Ex parte Bushnell, 8 Ohio St. 599; In re Gregg, 15 Wis. 479.
⁷ In re Canadian Prisoners, 7 Dowl. P. C. 208; but where the party is under coercion, see Hottentot Venus, 13 East, 195.

incompetent witness, as the writ will stand, not as a matter of evidence, but as a foundation for future proceedings.[1]

§ 96. **Penalty for Refusing the Writ.**—It will be seen by the statute of Charles, given on a preceding page, that the officers authorized to grant the writ were subjected to a penalty for refusing it where it should have been granted. There is no pecuniary penalty of this kind provided for in the habeas corpus act of the United States, but there is in the acts of most of the individual states. In some of them[2] the statutes are silent as to any penalty in case of a refusal of the writ. In some,[3] the penalty applies only to a refusal of the writ by a judge in vacation or at chambers; while in others,[4] the courts, as well as the judges in vacation, are not only subject to a penalty for refusing a habeas corpus, but also for unnecessarily delaying to issue it.

At common law, we have seen that the writ of habeas corpus was a prerogative writ, not issued as a matter of course, or ministerially; yet that it was a writ of right on a proper foundation being made out by proof. Judicial tribunals, having acquired jurisdiction of the writ, had power to decide, right or wrong, but they were governed by the rules of law collectible from principle and precedent. In the federal courts of the United States it has been held, that the petition for the writ, duly presented, is the institution of a cause on behalf of the petitioner, and that the allowance or refusal of the process, as well as the subsequent disposition of the prisoner, is matter of law, and not of discretion.[5] But in our state courts it has been said that no power is judicial that does not imply discretion—the right to grant or refuse, according to what the officer deems right or just, and in conformity with the laws of the land. And in those states where a penalty is attached for the refusal of the writ, upon proper application, by a judge in vacation or at chambers, the tendency seems to be to regard the act of issuing it as a merely ministerial one. So it was said by Chief Justice Kent, in New York, prior to the revision of laws of 1830, that it was only when the chancellor or judges refused the writ in a mere ministerial capacity that they were responsible for the penalty. The allowance of the writ in vacation, said he, was not a judicial act. The chancellor and judges might refuse such

---

[1] De Lacy v. Antoine, 7 Leigh, 438.

[2] Texas, Virginia, Connecticut, Ohio, New Hampshire, Rhode Island, Kansas, Vermont, Maine, Oregon, Alabama, Florida, and West Virginia.

[3] Michigan, Tennessee, Delaware, New York, Iowa, Arkansas, Missouri.

[4] California, Pennsylvania, Georgia, Kentucky, South Carolina, New Jersey, North Carolina, Nebraska, Nevada, Minnesota, Mississippi, Illinois, and Wisconsin.

[5] Ex parte Milligan, 4 Wall. 2.

a writ, at their discretion, if applied for in term time, and the penalty would not attach.¹ This is now the law in California,² but under the present law of New York, and it is apprehended in other states, where the statutory obligation rests upon the courts in term time, as well as upon the judges in vacation and at chambers, to grant the habeas corpus upon a legal application, the issuing of the writ is a ministerial act, and not a judicial one.³ Under such statutes, it can not be expected that courts or judges will refuse the writ where there is the least color for asking it, as the penalty would attach where the denial proceeds on the most honest doubt; although whether an act is a judicial or ministerial one would seem to depend fairly and squarely upon the nature of the act itself.⁴ In a case where the statute does not require the writ to issue, a judge is not liable to the penalty for refusing it.⁵

§ 97. **Mandamus to Compel the Writ to Issue.**—In Arkansas it has been held that where one entitled to the writ makes a proper application for it to one of the inferior courts, conforming to all the statutory requirements, and that court refuses to issue it, the supreme court, by *mandamus*, will compel the writ to issue.⁶ This also appears to be true in Alabama, where the prisoner has the right, when brought before a proper officer on habeas corpus, to demand that all the evidence which he offers touching his guilt shall be heard and decided, and to any judicial officer denying the prisoner this right, *mandamus* will lie to enforce it and compel a hearing.⁷ In this state a *mandamus* will lie to set aside an order of prohibition, improperly granted by a circuit judge to restrain a probate judge from acting on an application for bail which is within his jurisdiction.⁸ In Arkansas the writ of *mandamus* has been refused to compel a circuit court to admit to bail, unless all the facts upon which such court based its decision were legally certified to the court whence the writ would emanate.⁹ In a purely discretion-

---

¹ Yates v. Lansing, 5 Johns. 282. See Matter of Ferguson, 9 Id. 239.
² Ex parte Ellis, 11 Cal. 222.
³ People v. Nash, 5 Park. Cr. 473; S. C., 25 How. Pr. 307; 16 Abb. Pr. 281; Nash v. The People, 36 N. Y. 607.
⁴ Read Crowley's Case, 2 Swans. 12; notes in appendix to 3 Hill (N Y.), 647; Cole v. Thayer, 8 Cow. 249; 1 Kent's Com. 634; State v. Munson, Hall's Jour. Jur. 257; People v. Bradley, 60 Ill. 390.
⁵ Williamson v. Lewis, 39 Pa. St. 9.

⁶ Wright v. Johnson, 5 Ark. 687; Ex parte Allis, 12 Ark. 101; Ex parte Good et al., 19 Ark. 410.
⁷ Ex parte Mahone, 30 Ala. 49; Wade v. Judge, 5 Ala., N. S., 130; Ex parte Champion, 52 Ala. 311.
⁸ Ex parte Keeling, 50 Ala. 474; see Ex parte Hill, and In re Armstead v. Confederate States, as to application for prohibition to probate judge, and Ex parte Dudley, as to application for *mandamus* in matter of habeas corpus, 38 Ala., N. S., 458.
⁹ Ex parte Good et al., 19 Ark. 410.

ary matter, as whether a prisoner confined in jail shall be brought up on habeas corpus to testify on behalf of the defendant in a criminal case, or whether his deposition shall be taken, the discretion of the lower court will not be controlled by *mandamus*.[1] In Michigan the supreme court refused an application for *mandamus* to require a circuit judge to sign a bill of exceptions to bring up for review, on writ of error, proceedings on habeas corpus had before him at chambers, as such proceedings were not according to the course of the common law, in the sense in which that expression is applied to proceedings reviewable on writ of error. The proper remedy, they said, was by *certiorari*, or by habeas corpus in the supreme court, and neither of them would be available where the imprisonment had expired.[2]

§ 98. **Injunction to Restrain Issuance of Writ.**—From the Criminal Law Magazine, vol. 1, p. 498 (1880), we learn that the supreme court of Louisiana is reported to have rendered a curious decision. "In the case of one Frankenstein, who was sentenced to twenty days' imprisonment and one hundred dollars' fine for selling lottery tickets other than those of the Louisiana state lottery, application was made to one of the district judges for a writ of habeas corpus. The state applied to the supreme court for an injunction restraining the district judge from issuing the writ, and an injunction was granted." We quite fully agree with the remark that "such a decision is a virtual suspension of the writ of habeas corpus in that state, and can not but be regarded as a most dangerous application of the remedy by injunction." But it is suggested that, "from the unusual character of the decision as reported, some doubt may be expressed as to whether the case in all its points has been correctly stated in the meager report given."[3]

---

[1] Giboney v. Rogers, Judge etc., 32 Ark. 462.
[2] Faust v. Judge etc., 30 Mich. 266.
[3] From the Chicago Legal News.

CHAPTER IX.
THE WRIT.

§ 99. The Writ must be Grounded upon Affidavits.
§ 100. How Granted at Common Law.
§ 101. How Granted under Statute.
§ 102. Signature to the Writ, and Seal.
§ 103. How the Writ is Sometimes Marked.
§ 104. Noting the Allowance of the Writ.
§ 105. Notice of Allowance.
§ 106. How and to Whom Directed.
§ 107. Where It Runs at Common Law and under the English Statutes.
§ 108. On the Rule of Locality in the United States.
§ 109. Service of the Writ.
§ 110. Amendment of the Writ.
§ 111. Objections to the Writ.
§ 112. When the Prisoner may be Brought into Court.

§ 99. **Writ to be Grounded upon Affidavit.**—Before a court or judge grants a habeas corpus, whether at common law or under the statute of 31 Car. II., there should always be laid a proper ground therefor by affidavit, in order to justify the granting of the writ. It is a writ of right, but not granted as a matter of course, and the party seeking its benefit must lay such a case on affidavit before the court or judge as will be sufficient to regulate his discretion in granting it. The court will not grant the writ where the party will, after hearing, be inevitably remanded. And when a single judge in vacation time grants the writ under the statute of 31 Car. II., in criminal cases, a copy of the commitment or an affidavit of the refusal of it must be laid before him. He must judge, even in that case, whether felony or treason is specially expressed in the warrant of commitment.[1] In a *habeas corpus cum causa*, upon a single affidavit entitled in several causes, a rule may be moved for making the same order in all the causes.[2] If one is illegally detained in custody, it is sufficient for him to make an affidavit to that effect, and he is entitled as a matter of right to the issu-

---

[1] Hobhouse's Case, 2 Chit. 207; S. C., 3 Barn. & Ald. 420.
[2] Barrack v. Newton, and Bicknell et al. v. Newton, 1 Ad. & El., Q. B., 525.

ance of a writ of habeas corpus, whatever immaterial averments the affidavit may contain.[1]

§ 100. **How Granted at Common Law.**— Before the habeas corpus act of 31 Car. II., suitors could only obtain a writ of habeas corpus from the king's bench, and the court of chancery, which is always open. From the court of king's bench it could be obtained in term time only, and it was one of the objects of the act to remedy this evil.[2] The court of chancery, however, could grant the writ in vacation as well as term time.[3] It was had upon petition or motion stating probable cause for the application, and, as said before, verified by affidavit. It always did issue, and still issues, upon a motion, grafted on a copy of the commitment where the detention is under legal process. The statute of 31 Car. II. made no alteration in the practice of the courts in granting the writ.[4] The question as to the power of the court of chancery to issue a habeas corpus in vacation at the common law was at first, in Jenke's Case,[5] decided in the negative; but afterwards Lord Eldon, after an elaborate examination, overruled this doctrine, and announced the law to be as above stated—following the previous *dicta* of the illustrious Lords Coke and Hale.[6]

§ 101. **How Issued under Statutes.**—The statute of 31 Car. II. provides that one committed or detained for a crime, felony or treason plainly expressed in the warrant of commitment excepted, may make application to the lord chancellor or lord keeper, or any one of his majesty's justices, either of one bench or of the other, either in the vacation or term time, for a habeas corpus; and, upon view of a copy of the warrant of commitment or detainer, or upon affidavit showing that such a copy has been denied to be given to one in custody, if the application has been made in writing by the prisoner, or any one on his behalf, and attested and subscribed by two witnesses who were present at the delivery of the same, it becomes the duty of the officers named to award the writ.[7]

In the courts of the United States and of the several states of the Union the same general principle is adopted. The application is made to a court, or justice, or judge authorized to issue the same, in writing, setting forth the facts concerning the de-

---

[1] White v. State of Mississippi, 1 Smed. & M. 156.
[2] 1 Ch. Crim. L. 124.
[3] Goldswain's Case, 2 W. Black. 1207, note b; Crowley's Case, 2 Swans. 1; Wyatt's Reg. 215; Penrice and Wynn's Case, 2 Mod. 307;
[4] Bac. Abr., tit. Habeas Corpus, B, sec. 1.
[4] Hobhouse's Case, 3 Barn. & Ald. 420.
[5] 6 Howell's State Trials, 1189.
[6] Crowley's Case, 2 Swans. 1.
[7] See Stat. 31 Car. II., sec. 58.

tention of the party restrained, in whose custody he is detained, and, if known, by virtue of what claim or authority. The complaint containing the facts set forth must be verified by the oath of the person making the application.[1]

§ 102. **Signature to the Writ, and Seal.**—By referring to the statute of 31 Car. II., it will be seen that a particular provision requires that the writ shall be signed by the person that awards the same, and shall be under the seal of the court whereof he shall then be one of the judges.[2] By the statute of 1 & 2 Ph. & M., c. 13, sec. 7, "no writ of habeas corpus or *certiorari* shall be granted to remove any person out of any jail, or to remove any recognizance, except the same writ be signed with the proper hands of the chief justice, or, in his absence, of one of the justices of the court out of which the same writ shall be awarded or made, upon pain that he that writeth any such writs, not being signed as is aforesaid, to forfeit to our said sovereign lord, the king and the queen, for every such writ and writs five pounds."[3] In Rex v. Roddam, Lord Mansfield refused to sign the writ directed to defendant, who was not called upon to obey the same.[4] We imagine the same result would follow in the United States were the writ to issue, without being signed, by any court, justice, judge, or other officer authorized to grant it.

§ 103. **How the Writ is Sometimes Marked.**—In order that no sheriff, jailer, or other officer may pretend ignorance of the import of any writ of habeas corpus, it is enacted by the statute 31 Car. II., that all such writs shall be marked *"Per statutum tricesimo primo Caroli secundi regis."*[5] But while the statute required a writ issued under it to be marked in this manner, it must be observed that the regularity of a writ could not be attacked because it did not purport to be issued under the statute of 31 Car. II., c. 3, if it could be supported at common law.[6] The statute did not take away any rights to the writ under the common law, but was passed to the more effectually protect the liberty of the subject.

§ 104. **Noting the Allowance.** —"Where the writ is awarded by the court in term, the fact is shown by an order under his hand, indorsed usually upon the petition." The indorsement, however, need not necessarily be made upon the peti-

---

[1] See habeas corpus act of United States, *ante*, sec. 59, and state statutes.
[2] See Stat. 31 Car. II., sec. 58.
[3] Bac. Abr., tit. Habeas Corpus, B, sec. 5.
[4] 2 Cowp. 672.
[5] See Stat. 31 Car. II., sec. 58.
[6] Wilson's Case, 7 Ad. & El., Q. B., 984.

tion, but may be made upon a detached piece of paper—the better practice, as stated by Mr. Hurd, because it preserves neatness, order, and uniformity among the papers on file, a *desideratum* greatly to be desired in all court papers.

§ 105. **Notice of Allowance.**—" While it is a matter of great moment to the prisoner to be speedily released from illegal imprisonment, it is also a matter of concern to the state that public offenders should not escape merited punishment, and one of interest to the citizen that he should not be wrongfully deprived of any remedy, however severe, which the law may afford him. Hence it has been customary for the court, in cases of habeas corpus, to require notice of the application for or pendency of the writ to be served upon the public prosecutor, where the imprisonment is under criminal process, and upon the creditor, or party interested in continuing the imprisonment, where it is under civil process."[1] In a habeas corpus proceeding in the state of Michigan, before a commissioner of the circuit court, and in behalf of one held under an execution against his body, the plaintiff is entitled to four days' notice before an order of discharge can be made.[2] In Indiana their statute has been construed as authorizing notice to be given to the party interested in resisting the application for a habeas corpus, or his attorney, by direction of the court or judge hearing the application.[3] So has it been suggested in Vermont, that where an execution is between party and party, it is proper to give some sort of notice to the creditor.[4] The statutes of New York seem to require notice of the proceeding, in case of custody on civil process, to be given to the party interested in continuing the imprisonment or restraint;[5] but while notice of the time and place of the return of the writ should be given to apprise a party of proceedings pending, it is not necessary to serve with such notice a copy of the petition or other paper upon which the writ was granted, or of any other paper whatever.[6] It has been held that even eight days' notice must, in such a case, be given to the party or his attorney, and without it the court had no power to grant a discharge.[7] In the same state, when it appears from the return that the party is detained upon any criminal accusation, the court or officer can make no order for his discharge

---

[1] Hurd on Habeas Corpus, 2d ed., 227.
[2] People v. Kehl, 15 Mich. 330.
[3] Lumm v. The State, 3 Port. (Ind.) 293.
[4] Ex parte Hatch, 2 Aik. 28.
[5] 3 R. S., 6th ed., 879, sec. 61; see People v. Pelham, 14 Wend. 48.
[6] Ex parte Beatty, 12 Wend. 229.
[7] People ex rel Hewlett v. Sheriff Brennan, 61 Barb. 540.

until proper notice has been given to the district attorney of the county in which the court or officer may be, or in which the prisoner is detained.[1] We believe this notice should be given without regard to the residence of the parties. Process is not the only means of imprisonment sometimes used, and notice is doubtless as important in many other cases as it is when the detention or restraint is under legal process, and should be required to be given.[2] Should the order of discharge abovementioned be made without the statutory notice being given, it will be reversed on *certiorari*.[3]

In one of his opinions, that great judge, Chief Justice Tilghman, held the want of notice to the creditor sufficient to vitiate the discharge on habeas corpus of a debtor in execution by a single judge of the common pleas. "I am of opinion, however, that, granting his right to discharge, his proceedings were void for want of notice to the plaintiff in the execution. It is contrary to the first principles of justice to deprive a man of his rights without a hearing or an opportunity of a hearing. * * * The impropriety of the proceeding on the first habeas corpus was manifest to the judge himself. The consequence was what might be expected—he was imposed on by one party because he did not hear the other. Of this he was afterwards sensible, when he remanded the prisoner on the second habeas corpus"—issued by the judge after the plaintiff had been retaken under the same execution from which he had been discharged.[4] In England, where a bankrupt was brought up the next Monday after the Saturday on which his assignees were served with notice, the lord chancellor disposed of the matter in this wise: "I apprehend that it is the constant course in the courts of law, when a person is brought up by habeas corpus, to hear the parties, who have a right to contend that the commitment was proper; and therefore there must be some notice, though I will not go so far as to say that there may not be cases where the right to the discharge may be so clear that it may be done at once. If the assignees were not served till past ten on Saturday, that is good for nothing." It afterwards appeared that the notice had been given on Saturday, at 4:30 P. M.; but the lord chancellor thought it insufficient, and directed the bankrupt to be brought up again the day following.[5]

§ 106. **How and to Whom Directed.**—It was early holden by the English courts that the habeas corpus should be directed

---

[1] 3 R. S., 6th ed., 879, sec. 62.
[2] People v. McLeod, 3 Hill (N. Y.), 657, sec. 22.
[3] People v. Cassels, 5 Hill (N.Y.), 165.
[4] Hecker v. Jarret, 3 Binn. 404.
[5] Bromley's Case, 2 Jac. & W. 453.

to him who had the custody of the body, and it was declared that in London the writ should be directed, "Majori & Vicecomit, London," because they have the custody, and not to the whole corporation;[1] and Chief Justice Holt decided that where a man is committed to the keeper of the jail, there the habeas corpus must be directed; but when he was committed by process, it must be directed to the sheriff.[2] Neither should the writ be directed in the disjunctive, "to the sheriff or the jailer," for this is wrong. Where a man is taken on the warrant of the sheriff, in pursuance of a writ to the sheriff, the habeas corpus ought to be directed to the sheriff, for the party is in his custody, and the writ itself must be returned; but where one is committed immediately to the jailer, it is otherwise, as in criminal cases.[3] The prisoner's solicitor then delivers the writ to the person to whom it is properly directed.[4] It is not only to those who are concerned in the administration of justice that the writ may be directed, but it is properly addressed to such as a doctor of physic, who confines a person under the pretense of curing him of madness, etc.[5]

These doctrines prevail in the American courts; and it has been decided in the state of Indiana, that an officer claiming a right to imprison by virtue of process is properly a party for the purpose of testing the legality of the commitment upon a proceeding by habeas corpus.[6] It is also admitted in Pennsylvania, that in cases where the committing magistrate has no authority to take bail, a writ of habeas corpus may issue to the constable or any other officer having the defendant in charge. The writ should be directed to the person or persons having the defendant in custody.[7] If this can not readily be determined, it may be addressed to any one countenancing or consenting to the illegal detention or restraint; as when a wife voluntarily deserts her husband and goes to live with her father, and with the father's knowledge and permission withholds from her husband the custody of one of their children, the writ of habeas corpus sued out by the husband to recover the child may properly be directed to the father, he being a party in the wrong.[8]

§ 107. **Where It Runs at Common Law and under the English Statutes.**—By the common law, the writ of habeas

---

[1] Godb. 44.
[2] King v. Fowler, Fortes. 243.
[3] Dom. Rex v. Fowler, 1 Salk. 350; S. C., 1 Raym. 586.
[4] 1 Ch. Crim. L. 126.
[5] 4 Bac. Abr., tit. Habeas Corpus, B, sec. 6, p. 581.
[6] Nichols v. Cornelius, 7 Ind. 611.
[7] Commonwealth v. Ridgway, 2 Ashm. 247.
[8] People ex rel. Barry v. Mercein, 3 Hill (N. Y.), 399.

corpus lies to any part of the king's dominions, for it is a prerogative writ, and the king ought to know why any of his subjects are imprisoned. Therefore no answer will satisfy the writ, but to return the cause with *paratum habeo corpus*, etc. Prerogative writs, which issue on the part of the king, such as *mandamus*, prohibition, habeas corpus, and *certiorari*, are not ministerially issued, and are not restrained by any clause[1] in the constitution of England given to Berwick from extending there. Hence it has been held that all prerogative writs run to the Cinque Ports. The privilege of the Cinque Ports, that the king's writ runs not there, has been construed to be intended as between party and party. The writ has been awarded to all places within the kingdom; and it has been said that "to dispute it is not to dispute the jurisdiction, but the power of the king and his court, which is not to be disputed."[2]

The writ has gone to Calais,[3] and the writ of *habeas corpus ad subjiciendum* has also run to Jersey,[4] and to the Isle of Man.[5] There is no power in any of the English courts to send a writ of any kind to foreign dominions which belong to a prince who succeeds to the throne of England. They can not send a habeas corpus to Scotland, or to the Electorate, but they can to Ireland, to Guernsey, and Jersey, in addition to the places above named. The general principle is, that the writ of habeas corpus may issue to every dominion of the crown of England, upon a proper cause being shown. There is no doubt of the court's power to issue the writ to any place under the subjection of the crown of England; but where a court can not judge of the cause, or give relief upon it, they will exercise their discretion as to the propriety of granting the writ.[6] Under the statute of 31 Car. II., the writ runs into any county palatine, the Cinque Ports, or other privileged places within the kingdom of England, dominion of Wales, or town of Berwick-upon-Tweed, and the islands of Jersey or Guernsey.[7] Another statute extended the language to include the Isle of Man, and "any port, harbor, road, creek, or bay upon the coast of England or Wales, although the same should be out of the body of any county; and if such writ shall issue in Ireland, the same may be directed and run into any port, harbor, road, creek, or bay, although the same should not be in the body of any county," etc.[8] These statutes are but

---

[1] Rex v. Cowle, 2 Burr. 834.
[2] Bourne's Case, 4 Cro. Jac. 543.
[3] Id.
[4] Wilson's Case, 7 Ad. & El., Q. B., 984.
[5] Matter of Crawford, 13 Ad. & El. 613.
[6] Rex v. Cowle, 2 Burr. 834, by Lord Mansfield.
[7] See Stat. Car. II., sec. 58.
[8] 56 Geo. III., c. 100, sec. 5.

affirmatory of the principles of common law above stated. The writ of *habeas corpus ad faciendum et recipiendum*, however, does not lie to the Cinque Ports.[1]

§ 108. **On the Rule of Locality in the United States.**— In the United States the supreme court and the circuit and district courts, and the several justices and judges thereof, have power to grant writs of habeas corpus " within their respective jurisdictions."[2] The supreme court having original jurisdiction in all cases affecting ambassadors, other public ministers, and consuls, and those in which a state shall be a party,[3] it is apprehended that this court, in the exercise of that jurisdiction, can issue the writ of habeas corpus to any part of the United States; but the jurisdiction of this court in all other cases having been declared to be appellate, this question will seldom be raised. The circuit and district courts and the judges thereof are also confined within the territorial limits of their respective jurisdictions, and the writ of each should not be sent across the line into the jurisdiction of the other. Such irregularities are calculated to produce irritation, and to disturb the harmony of federal jurisprudence. The duplex nature of our government has another factor which enters into the question as to the locality into which the writ will run, and that is the sphere of the state individually. There is no question of the authority of a state court, or judge who is authorized by the laws of the state to issue the writ of habeas corpus, to issue it in any case where the party is imprisoned within its territorial limits; but it must be remembered that within the sphere of the state government is another distinct and separate sovereignty, acting within the same territorial space—the dominion of the federal government; and it having been decided in Ableman v. Booth[4] that no judicial process, whatever form it may assume, can have any lawful authority outside of the limits of the jurisdiction of the court or judge by whom it is issued, neither can intrude with its judicial process into the domain of the other, except so far as to maintain its rightful supremacy of jurisdiction. If a prisoner has committed an offense against the laws of the United States within the bounds of that government, yet within the same territorial space over which a state exercises its sovereignty, the federal tribunals alone can punish him; and on habeas corpus, if the state court or judge is judicially apprised

[1] 4 Bac. Abr., B, 570.
[2] See habeas corpus act of the United States, secs. 751, 752, *ante*, sec. 59.
[3] Const. U. S., art. 3, sec. 6.
[4] 21 How. 524.

that the party is in custody under the authority of the United States, they can proceed no further. If one has committed a crime in violation of state law, the state has full, complete, and exclusive jurisdiction, and the federal tribunals will not interfere, and neither the supreme court nor any other court of the United States, or a judge thereof, can issue a habeas corpus to bring up a prisoner who is in custody under a sentence or execution of a state court for any other purpose than to be used as a witness.[1]

The only case brought to our notice in which the writ has been made a foundation for reaching persons restrained of their freedom beyond the jurisdiction of the court or judge issuing the writ is that of United States v. Davis.[2] This was a habeas corpus directed to defendant, and commanding him to produce three colored persons before the circuit court of the District of Columbia, with the cause of their detention. Davis' return showed, on oath, that he had purchased the negroes in the city of Washington as his slaves; that they were removed, as he believed, beyond the district before the service of the writ, and before he heard even of the existence of such process; and that they were out of his custody and beyond his control, and were, he believed, beyond the District of Columbia. The evidence tended to show that Davis had removed the negroes, because he suspected they would apply for a writ of habeas corpus. The court considered the return evasive and insufficient, and ordered Davis to produce the negroes, and ordered him to be committed until he should do so, or be otherwise discharged in due course of law. The court further ordered that when two of the negroes were surrendered by defendant, the marshal should discharge him from jail. The other negro had run away, and had been arrested and lodged in jail in Maryland. On the last day of the term Davis produced the two negroes.

This same principle, however, afterwards arose in the supreme court of Michigan,[3] but it was not decided; Chief Justice Martin and Justice Campbell, who rendered an opinion, not looking upon it as sound law, and Justices Cooley and Christiancy recognizing the precedent in Davis' case as warranting such a proposition. The respondent in this case, it was alleged, had caused an infant, Samuel W. Jackson, to be removed from Michigan, with the design of keeping him from his guardian's custody,[4] and had, since that time, been instrumental in having

---

[1] Ex parte Dorr, 3 How. 103.
[2] 5 Cranch C. Ct. 622.
[3] In the Matter of Jackson, 15 Mich. 417.
[4] For the full history of the case relative to the guardianship, see Taff v. Hosmer, 14 Mich. 249.

§ 108. THE WRIT. 121

him detained beyond the state, but remained himself within the state. The question before the court was, whether it had any authority by the writ of habeas corpus to compel the child, who had all this time been in a foreign jurisdiction,[1] to be brought back to Michigan, the respondent meanwhile being within the jurisdiction of the court.[2]

[1] Canada.

[2] Justice Campbell, after thoroughly ventilating the common law and English statutes concerning the places to which the writ would run, declared it to be universally admitted that it can in no case run beyond the dominions of what is technically the crown of England, and asserted that the only disputes have been as to what countries were crown dominions. "The question, then," he says, "arises, whether the running of this writ is determined by the situation of the person to be relieved, or by that of the persons concerned in the unlawful detention. Among all the precedents, ancient and modern, which I have been able to find, there is none which does not show the question as to whether the writ would run into the privileged places to have arisen concerning an imprisonment there. No point was ever made upon the service of the writ upon the wrong-doer outside of the place of imprisonment as making any difference. And there can be no doubt that the legal purpose of the writ is to relieve from the illegal restraint on the ground of its illegality, and on no other ground. It is not a private remedy in favor of the parent or guardian, or even, except indirectly, of the prisoner himself. It is a prerogative writ, issued on behalf of the king, who is entitled to 'have an account why any of his subjects are imprisoned, and therefore no answer will satisfy the writ but to return the cause with *paratum habeo corpus*.' Bourne's Case, Cro. Jac. 543. The exigency of the writ is to bring up the body, and there is no instance in the law where a writ requires any act to be done beyond the jurisdiction which issues it. If there are attachments and penalties, they all refer to some refusal or neglect to do an act lawfully prescribed; and no one can maintain that if a person to whom such a writ is directed should do anything abroad towards complying with it he could thereby justify himself against conflicting claims asserted in the foreign jurisdiction. A writ must spend itself in the jurisdiction which issues it; and there is no principle which can give one state a right to consider an act done in another to an individual as an offense against itself. If a person is unlawfully held in New York, and a person in Michigan is implicated at all, it is as an offender against New York, and not against Michigan. It is a principle of universal application in the criminal law, that the place of the wrong done, and not the place of the wrongdoer, is the *locus delicti*. The kidnaper completes his offense against the state when he removes the victim from its borders. He can no more be responsible to that state for detention abroad than for murder abroad. The private grievance is the subject of a private action. The habeas corpus, while practically aiding the prisoner, is professedly for the public grievance." This accomplished justice further on severely criticised Davis' Case, cited above, in this wise: "There it does not appear that the application for the writ disclosed the absence of the parties. But it appearing, after the writ issued, that Davis had sent them out of the District of Columbia, he was attached until he produced two of them, the third being under arrest in Maryland. This case is entirely bald of reasons, and the most that can be said in its favor is that the judges probably decided the matter in haste, and looked more to the demerits of the respondent than to any rules of law. The present statutes regulating the power of the courts of the United States to punish contempts could not be legitimately construed to authorize such a proceeding: Referring to 4 U. S. Stat. at Large, Act of March 2, 1831, p. 487. The facts were such as to make it very desirable to deal with the wrong-doer; and if courts were allowed to devise remedies at their option, there could be no objection to

In New York, in 1827, it was decided that a habeas corpus under the authority of the state run to West Point. To take following the precedent. But it seems difficult to maintain it upon any sound principle." Whether the case does not come within the jurisdiction of equity, his honor thought might be worthy of consideration; but if the writ of habeas corpus did not lie, the court were precluded from any further inquiry. "I have arrived at these conclusions with regret. A criminal complaint does not afford the redress needed. It is true that the obstinacy of a party might prevent any means of obtaining an infant who has been concealed elsewhere. But coercive measures would, in most cases, be effectual, and I should be glad to believe we could inquire into the merits of this matter. But for the reasons given, I think the writ must be quashed."

On the other hand, the graceful Justice Cooley very elaborately presented his reasons why the writ should issue. "I have not yet seen sufficient reason to doubt the power of this court to issue the present writ on the petition which was laid before us. The subject of the petition was a minor of tender years, incapable of judging and acting for himself, whose custody was sought by his legal guardians, and who, according to the petition, had been removed from this state, where his residence was, apparently to avoid the process of this court, by a person who was a party to litigation before us respecting the guardianship, and who was still within the jurisdiction. The writ, if issued, would not be for the purpose of releasing the child from custody, but to subject him to the custody of those who had been adjudged by our decision to be lawfully entitled to it; but the case stood upon no different ground than if a citizen *sui juris* had been kidnaped and removed, or enticed beyond the limits of the state, and was now confined abroad by a person resident here, and within reach of our process. The question, nakedly presented, therefore, was whether we had any jurisdiction to relieve from unlawful imprisonment a person contined beyond the limits of the state, but who was one of our citizens, removed wrongfully, to evade process, and for the purpose of the unlawful confinement, and whose jailer was here, and might be compelled to open his prison doors by our order, if we have power to make one. It appeared to me at the outset that we were able to give the proper relief; and examination and reflection have only tended to confirm my first impressions. * * * Bounded, as we are, on two sides by a foreign nation, with whom we are liable at any time to have such relations as will not permit us to rely upon the cordial enforcement of the usual rules of interstate comity, we are peculiarly interested in knowing whether our laws are so defective that one of our own citizens may imprison his fellow across the border, and own the act with impunity in our courts, while the person thus deprived of his birthright of liberty has no resource but to appeal to the justice of the foreign power, which may or may not feel an interest in his release and protection."

It was argued at the bar that the act of removing the child in the manner charged was a criminal offense, and the person guilty thereof could only be proceeded against for the crime. "The sole question, then," said the justice, "on this branch of the case, is, whether the fact that respondent may be liable criminally for what he has done precludes our compelling the delivery of the child to his guardians on this writ. Clearly it does not." It was also argued at the bar that the statutory provisions respecting the writ were applicable by their express terms only to the case of confinements within the state; but his honor thought this proposition based upon a misconception as to the source of the court's jurisdiction. He exhaustively reviewed the English authorities, and showed that the court of king's bench, to which the jurisdiction of the supreme court of Michigan in this case must be likened, never derived its jurisdiction to issue and enforce the writ from the statute of 31 Car. II., but that it existed long before; that the statute was not passed to give the right, but to compel the observance of rights which already existed; that the act itself was much less broad than the remedy had been before. As the statute does not give the writ, but

away the jurisdiction of the state courts on a habeas corpus, within state territory ceded to the United States, such jurisdiction shall have been expressly surrendered by the state. This prin-

renders it more effectively and actively remedial, "I therefore attach no special importance to the particular wording of the statute where it speaks of the cases in which the writ is to be issued; though I should not concede that, within the words employed, the actual presence of the body of the petitioner within the state was a controlling circumstance. * * * The common-law jurisdiction is ample. As it came from no statute, it is not confined in its scope to any prescribed limits, but is co-extensive with the cases to which its principles can be applied, and in which it can afford a remedy. I am aware of nothing which limits the power of the court upon this writ, but its capacity to give relief in the particular case in accordance with the settled rules which govern this mode of proceeding. I know of no other test that can have determined its jurisdiction at the common law; and while the law holds the right to personal liberty in the same high regard as now, the same test will probably continue to be applied. The important fact to be observed in regard to the mode of procedure upon this writ is, that it is directed to and served upon, not the person confined, but his jailer. It does not reach the former except through the latter. The officer or person who serves it does not unbar the prison doors and set the prisoner free, but the court relieves him by compelling the oppressor to release his constraint. The whole force of the writ is spent upon the respondent; and if he fails to obey it, the means to be resorted to for the purposes of compulsion are fine and imprisonment. This is the ordinary mode of affording relief; and if any other means are resorted to, they are only auxiliary to those which are usual. The place of confinement is therefore not important to the relief, if the guilty party is within reach of process, so that by the power of the court he can be compelled to release his grasp. The difficulty of affording redress is not increased by the confinement being beyond the limits of the state, except as greater distance may affect it. The important question is, Where is the power of control exercised? And I am aware of no other remedy. * * * What I say on this subject is carefully restricted to the case of a citizen of our own state unlawfully held in custody elsewhere by another person, who is himself within the jurisdiction of this court. If he is here, the wrong is being done here; for the wrong is done wherever the power of control is exercised. There is no inherent difficulty in the case; and the court of chancery, in the exercise of its power to compel specific performance, frequently exerts an authority over a subject-matter in a foreign jurisdiction similar to that which is sought for here. I think the case presented by the petition is one in which we can give relief, and the decision in United States v. Davis, 5 Cranch C. Ct. 622, is in point, and will warrant it. There are no conflicting decisions. The incidental remarks which have been made in some cases about the remedy applying where the imprisonment is within the state seem to me of no significance. In none of those cases was attention directed to this particular point; and I have already indicated my opinion that imprisonment, within the meaning of the law, may be held to be wherever the person is who imprisons. This writ is based upon no technical reasons, but its scope is as broad as its power to give redress."

We are rather inclined to lend our adherence to the views of Mr. Justice Cooley on the questions in this case thus far involved, so long as the imprisonment in the foreign jurisdiction is under the control of the one within the jurisdiction of the court endeavoring to exercise its power. But immediately after the unlawful act of removing an infant from the state, circumstances may place it beyond the control of the one who spirited it away. In this case, will the court punish its "jailer" as for a contempt? or keep the kidnaper in custody until he produces the infant? Such a course might lead to perpetual imprisonment, and this would be tyranny. In Davis' Case why did not the court compel him to produce the negro who had run away, who had been arrested, and who was put in

ciple was applied In the Matter of Carlton,[1] an enlisted minor, and who was discharged from the service of the United States jail in Baltimore? And had it been satisfactorily shown to the court that the other two negroes were in a like condition, would it have compelled Davis to produce them? We think not. But this view is fully elucidated by the learned justice in his closing words In the Matter of Jackson, in examining the case as affected by the subsequent pleadings, the nature of which will sufficiently appear from the opinion:

"The motion to dismiss, when renewed, was in the nature of a demurrer to the traverse of respondent's answer. The answer denied, with considerable particularity, the principal facts set out in the petition; averred the child to be in Canada, in the custody of respondent's wife, who refused to submit to respondent's control, and declared her purpose of remaining abroad, with a view to retaining the child's custody. The answer also averred, that on application to a court of competent jurisdiction in Canada the wife had been appointed the child's guardian, and now held and controlled it under that appointment; and that the child was in no degree under the power, custody, or control of the respondent. This last averment of the answer, as well as the respondent's denial that the child was originally removed from the state by his means, are put in issue by the answer. I am constrained to say that, in my opinion, the traverse does not cover the ground of the answer. It is not denied that the wife has procured herself to be appointed guardian of the child abroad, and that she now assumes to hold it under that appointment. This fact is an element in the case which can not be overlooked, and which quite distinguishes it from the simple case of a detention by a person here by means of an agent abroad. Leaving out of view all those delicate questions which might arise as to compelling the delivery up of the child by the wife against her will, through the coercion of the husband, and coming directly to the point which alone we must consider now, whether the coercion can be applied when it already appears that the wife is acting as guardian under an appointment which we must assume to be good in form, and recognized there as valid, I am unable to see upon what ground we could base our justification in issuing compulsory process against the husband. The fact that he originally connived at and assisted in removing the child, is not important now, unless it is still within his control. This is not the proper proceeding in which to punish him for that act, except by way of compelling him to deliver the child to the proper custody, if he now has the power to do so. If the child is held in a foreign jurisdiction by one appointed his guardian there, the respondent has legally no such power as is claimed, even though the person having the custody may have been his agent, and as such procured the appointment. The agency does not enter into the guardianship. The law then will know nothing of such an agency, and will refuse to recognize it. The custody has ceased to be that of the individual, and has become that of the agent of the law. That law is the foreign law; and we must come directly in conflict with it if we exercise jurisdiction on the facts here shown. The case, as it would stand in Canada, would be that of a guardian appointed by its courts over a minor within its jurisdiction, coerced indirectly by a foreign court, to remove the child abroad, and there deliver it to custodians whose authority would not be recognized in Canada while the present appointment stands. It would be an indirect assumption of jurisdiction by the court in Michigan over the appointment made in Canada, even to the extent of reversing that action. I know of no precedent for such a course, and a due regard to interstate comity should incline us to forbear. It is quite probable that the appointment in Canada was made in ignorance of the real facts of the case. I can not doubt, if these were fully presented, the court there would revoke its action, and cause the child to be delivered to the testamentary guardians. In my opinion, that court is the tribunal to appeal to under the facts disclosed by the pleadings."

The justices all concurring that the proceedings should be dismissed, it was ordered accordingly.

[1] 7 Cow. 471.

by a court, who, at that time, held the enlistment of a minor, without consent of his parent or guardian, into such service to be void, and that he might be discharged by state authority.[1]

In an early California case the supreme court denied a petition for a habeas corpus to one who had not previously made an application to the local judge or court. The statute then read: "The writ of habeas corpus may be granted by the supreme court or any judge thereof, or any district or county court in term time, or by any judge of such at any time, whether in term or vacation." It also provided that the writ should issue, and be served without delay, and that it should be heard immediately after the return, etc. Chief Justice Terry, in rendering the decision of the court, used this language: "The legislature can never have intended that a party imprisoned under sentence of conviction for a misdemeanor should have the privilege of selecting from the judiciary of the whole state the individual to whom he prefers to make his application, however distant from the place of his detention, and compel the officer having him in charge to convey him, at the expense of the county, it may be from San Diego to Klamath, in order that he might avail himself of a remedy which the local judge of his county was equally authorized to grant. Nor need he stop here; the refusal to discharge by one judge is not a bar to another application before a different judge. After failing in his first application, the party may sue out another writ before a different officer, and thus the term of his imprisonment may be passed in traveling from one part of the state to another, at the expense of the county in which he was convicted, to the entire subversion of justice. Such a construction would lead to manifest absurdity. The mere caprice of the prisoner ought not to prevail against the interests of the people and the public convenience." Mr. Justice Field added: "It is true, the writ of habeas corpus is one of right, to which every person unlawfully restrained of his liberty is entitled *ex merito justitiæ*. It is true the privilege of the writ is an express constitutional right at all times, except in cases of rebellion or invasion, when the public safety may require its suspension; but, like any other constitutional right, its privilege is to be exercised in a reasonable manner. Local judges of the county and district are as fully competent to inquire into the causes of an alleged restraint as this court, and ought to be applied to in the first instance. Although this court may issue the writ, its allowance in term time is not obligatory.

[1] See Ableman v. Booth, 21 How. 506; Tarble's Case, 13 Wall. 397.

That must rest in the sound legal discretion of the court. To allow it may be obligatory upon the judges in their individual capacity, but no such obligation lies upon the court. * * * In the present case, no reason being assigned in the petition for the exercise of the discretion of the court which may not be urged in every instance, I am of opinion that the writ should be disallowed."[1]

§ 109. **Service of the Writ.**—The writ at common law and under the statute of 31 Car. II. was not required to be served by an officer. The solicitor of the prisoner, or any person in his behalf, might deliver it to the person to whom it was directed.[2] Under the statute, it might be delivered to the officer to whom it was directed, or left at the jail or prison with any of the under-officers, under-keepers, or deputy of the said officers or keepers.[3] Under both the common law and the act of 31 Car. II., the better practice was, after delivering the writ to the keeper, or other person in whose custody the party was, to keep a copy thereof.[4] In the United States there are statutes treating of service, and in some of the states there are special provisions relating to the action to be taken when evasion of service is attempted. When the officer or person to whom the writ is directed refuses to receive it, there is but one thing for the party serving the writ to do, and that is to state the contents to the one upon whom it is to be served, which will be recognized as a sufficient and valid service. If the party conceal himself to avoid service, or refuse admittance to one endeavoring to serve the writ, it may be posted up on his residence, or on the prison where the prisoner is confined.[5] Service of the writ by leaving it with the "brother and agent" of the party called upon, at his place of abode, has been held sufficient.[6] At the common law, no writ of habeas corpus, or other writ to remove a cause out of an inferior court, could be allowed, unless the same were delivered to the judge of the court before the jury who were to try the cause had appeared and one of them had been sworn to try the said cause.[7] In the United States a writ for this purpose must, at least, be shown to the inferior court or delivered to the sheriff, or there can be no removal of the cause.[8] Where a writ of habeas corpus is applied

---

[1] Ex parte Ellis, 11 Cal. 222.
[2] Hurd on Habeas Corpus, 2d ed., 233, citing Hand's Pr. 73.
[3] See habeas corpus act, *ante*, sec. 58.
[4] Wyatt's Reg. 215.
[5] This is the substance of the statutes in California, New York, and Indiana.
[6] In the Matter of Hakewill, 12 Com. B. 223; S. C., 22 Eng. L. & Eq. 395.
[7] 2 Lilly's Reg. 4.
[8] Fleming v. Bradley, 1 Call (Va.), 203.

for and issued in open court, in the presence of the one to whom it is directed, and who has the custody of the prisoner, and the fact is known to him, and the writ can be handed to him if he desires it, that he may make his return, it amounts to an acceptance of the service, and a waiver of the delivery of the writ to him.[1] For any particular or peculiar provisions relating to the service of the writ, the practitioner must be referred to the statutes of his own state, as the plan of this work will not permit a reference to them all; and this section will be closed by saying that the certified return of an officer who is authorized to serve the writ will be sufficient evidence of service; and if served by any other person, it may be proved by the oath of the party making it.[2]

§ 110. **Amendment of the Writ.**—There is no doubt that a writ of habeas corpus may be amended like any other judicial process. The principle that a judicial writ may be amended was decided in Durming v. Ketle,[3] and afterwards Justice Tindal allowed a writ to be amended which had been erroneously tested as "of the last day of Trinity term, 1 Victoriæ," instead "of 7 Will. 4." He called it "a mere mistake, which ought, particularly when the application has been made on behalf of the prisoner, to be set right. We take judicial notice that her present majesty's accession did not take place until after the last day of Trinity term in 1837."[4]

§ 111. **Objections.**—It is no objection to the writ of *habeas corpus cum causa* that the attorney suing it out was not on the roll. The objection is not tenable, because the party ought not to be affected by the omission of the attorney.[5] Neither can the objection, that a writ of *habeas corpus ad satisfaciendum* to bring up a prisoner to charge him in execution, issued without the leave of the court or a judge, be sustained, if the writ bears the indorsement of one of the judges, for that is the only mode in which authority for issuing the writ is given.[6]

§ 112. **When the Prisoner may be Brought into Court.** Although the general direction of the writ is to produce the body at a given time and place, etc., it is not always so, and the court will exercise its discretion in the matter. Over one hundred and twenty years ago, James Mervin inveigled James

---

[1] People v. Bradley, 60 Ill. 390.
[2] Hurd on Habeas Corpus, 2d ed., 233, 234.
[3] 2 Cro. Eliz., 543.
[4] Ex parte Davies, 5 Scott, 241; S. C., 6 Dowl. 181.
[5] Glynn et al. v. Hutchinson, 3 Dowl. 529.
[6] Gibb v. King, a prisoner, 1 Com. B. 1; S. C., 2 Dow. & L. 806.

Clarke's daughter away from him with the design of marrying her to a minor holding a station in life much inferior to that of the young woman. The father secured her return home, and fully impressed upon her the necessity and want and disgrace and shame which would follow her falling into the contemplated marriage. He treated her kindly and with parental care, and she continued to live and reside with him of her own accord and under no restraint whatever. She was twenty-two years of age. Mervin filed a false affidavit, making a plausible case, fully sufficient, if true, to obtain a habeas corpus. It alleged that the young woman had been hardly used by her father, and that he held her in confinement. However, Mervin obtained his writ. It came up immediately, and the writ being directed to the father, he asked for time to consult counsel. The young woman at this time declared that she had no objection to remaining with her father, and that he was kind to her. Mervin was waiting to take her away should she be released. Lord Mansfield judged it proper to adjourn the hearing, and directed her to be brought into court at a future time. He did this that she, in the mean time, might reflect, and be better advised, for if she had been then taken from her father, it was plain she would have pursued her improvident design. She was afterward brought into court by virtue of the same writ. His lordship asked her whether she desired to continue with her father, or to go elsewhere. She answered: "To continue with my father." The court told her she was at liberty to go, which she did.[1]

So, too, in the United States, a motion for a writ of habeas corpus for the purpose of awarding the custody and care of children to one parent is addressed to the discretion of the court,[2] and a motion for the writ on the part of the mother, who is living in a state of separation from her husband without being divorced, to issue against the father directing him to bring their infant children into court, that matters may be examined, and that the care and custody of the children may be awarded to her, the father being an immoral person and keeping the children constantly exposed to injury from the examples of vice constantly before them, will be denied unless the case be more fully stated. Mr. Justice Bronson said: "We ought to know something about the ability of the mother to provide for the

---

[1] Rex v. Clarke, 1 Burr. 606. Mr. Norton moved that Mervin's affidavits might be filed, together with the return, as Mr. Clarke was determined to prosecute him for perjury. The court ordered it to be done, and recommended the prosecution very strongly to Mr. Clarke.

[2] People v. Chegaray, 18 Wend. 637; People v. Manley, 2 How. Pr. 61.

children; and also about the pecuniary condition of the father. It is quite possible that the father would not be able to obey the writ, by bringing the children into court, should the motion be granted; and it is also possible that the mother could not provide for the maintenance and education of the children should they be committed to her charge. We must have a more full statement of facts."[1]

[1] People v. Manley, 2 How. Pr. 61.

CHAPTER X.

COSTS, AND SECURITY AGAINST ESCAPE.

PART I.—ACCORDING TO THE COURSE OF THE COMMON LAW.
  § 113. Generally, and under Habeas Corpus Act.
  § 114. In Bankruptcy Proceedings.
  § 115. On *Habeas Corpus ad Testificandum.*
  § 116. In Particular Instances.

  PART II.—IN THE FEDERAL COURTS.
  § 117. Legislation, Decisions, and Rules.

  PART III.—IN THE STATE COURTS.
  § 118. Summary of Statutes.
  § 119. Judicial Constructions.

PART I.—ACCORDING TO THE COURSE OF THE COMMON LAW.

§ 113. **Generally, and under Habeas Corpus Act.**—The famous habeas corpus act of 31 Car. II. contemplated that the question of a person's right to liberty, when unlawfully detained or imprisoned, should be determined without fee and without price. One of the paramount objects of the act was to correct abuses which had previously grown up in administering the law of the writ of habeas corpus. It will readily be seen that if one imprisoned could not obtain the writ without being subjected to the payment of costs and fees, that it might operate as a barrier to his freedom. By the provisions of the act mentioned, the officer to whom the writ was directed was required to make a return of it within three days after the service thereof, " upon payment or tender of the charges of bringing the said prisoner, to be ascertained by the judge or court that awarded the same, and indorsed upon the said writ, not exceeding twelvepence per mile, and upon security given by his own bond to pay the charges of carrying back the prisoner, if he shall be remanded by the court or judge to which he shall be brought, according to the true intent of this present act, and that he will not make any escape by the way."[1] It was resolved, however, by the court,

[1] See habeas corpus act, 31 Car. II., *ante,* sec. 58.

§ 113.   COSTS, AND SECURITY AGAINST ESCAPE.   131

that the jailer was bound to bring the body, although he was not tendered his charges. But it was held that the sheriff might move the court, and a rule would be granted that he have his charges first.[1] On the return to a *habeas corpus ad faciendum et recipiendum*, the sheriff may suggest to the court that the party will not pay his charges, for this writ issues at the suit of the party; but this he can not do on the return of a *habeas corpus ad subjiciendum*, because this writ is at the suit of the king, and the sheriff must return at his peril. Both writs must be obeyed, but if the prisoner is brought up by virtue of the former writ, he will not be turned over by the court until the jailer be paid all his fees.[2]

In civil cases the general rule is, that whoever procures a writ of habeas corpus shall tender reasonable fees to the jailer, and if the jailer demand unreasonable fees, the court will, when the matter is properly brought before it, do what right and justice require.[3] But in criminal cases, where the validity of a commitment is to be discussed, the practice is for the prisoner to appear before the court, and though he be poor and unable to bear the expense of a habeas corpus without greatly distressing himself, the practice of the court will not be altered for his benefit.[4] Where the court has directed a writ of *habeas corpus ad subjiciendum* to issue, with notice to the party interested in opposing the prisoner's discharge, and the prisoner is remanded to his former custody, the court will not allow the costs of the opposition.[5] Nearly one hundred years ago the warden of the Fleet charged a prisoner two guineas for making at his request an expeditious return to a habeas corpus. The prisoner, it appears, knew the usual fee, and was informed of the additional one to be paid for expedition. The warden asserted that he had only followed the example of his predecessors in office in exacting the additional compensation for this purpose. The court took the view, however, that whatever might be the effect of the prisoner's consent to make the extra payment, as between the parties themselves, this was a question between the warden and the public. The duty of an officer requires him to make an expeditious return, and he has no authority to demand an additional fee for expedition. His honor said that advantages of this kind should not be taken of the distress of persons under confinement, and that they would not be endured. The motion

[1] King v. Greenway, 2 Show. *172; Hopman v. Barber, 2 Stra. 801
[2] King v. Armiger, 1 Keb. 272; 4 Bac. Abr., sec. 8, p. 583, B.
[3] Winnington's Case, 1 Keb. 566 (11).
[4] Ex parte Martins, 9 Dowl. 194.
[5] In re Cobbett, 3 Dow. & L. 79; S. C., 14 Mee. & W. 175.

to refer the charge made by the warden to a prothonotary for examination was refused, and at the warden's costs.[1] It has been held that a charge of sixpence per mile, in both going and returning with a prisoner under a writ of habeas corpus, is not an unreasonable charge for the jailer to make.[2]

On an application by a defendant who was imprisoned in the Fleet, and removed therefrom by habeas corpus, at his own request, to the king's bench, and who paid the commitment fee to the warden of the Fleet—a charge which should have been paid by the plaintiff, but which for some reason was not done—to compel the plaintiff to reimburse him, the rule was discharged, without costs; the judge remarking that it would have been better for the parties to have proceeded in the straightforward and usual way, and that it was the plaintiff's duty to pay the fee. "If it was the plaintiff's duty to pay it, what right had the warden to ask the defendant for it? and why did the latter pay it? He ought not to have paid it, but should have called upon the warden to obey the order of the court, which it would have compelled him to do, and would not have allowed as an excuse for disobedience to that order that some other person had not paid a fee, which it was his duty to have paid, on some previous occasion. It would have been much better for him to have applied to the court for a rule calling on the warden to obey the writ than to have paid the fee first, and then have come to the court to endeavor to make the plaintiff reimburse him."[3] Where a defendant was brought into court under a writ of *habeas corpus ad satisfaciendum* for the purpose of being charged in execution, the court fees on the writ having previously been, in the defendant's presence, paid by the plaintiff's attorney, the court held that, as the prisoner was ready to pay the debt and taxed costs, he was by law entitled to his discharge on payment of them, there being no statute requiring him to pay the costs or fees on the writ.[4]

In a comparatively late case, Lord Chancellor Chelmsford gave the subject of costs his careful consideration. The prisoner had been brought up from her majesty's jail in the island of Jersey on a habeas corpus in a civil suit; it being alleged in the committing order of the justice, on the one hand, that he was detained in the Jersey prison for debt, and on the other, by the prisoner himself, that he was illegally detained there upon

---

[1] Johnson v. Smith, 1 H. Black. 105.
[2] Robinson v. Hall, Taylor (U. C.), 482.
[3] Burt v. Bryant, 5 Dowl. 726.
[4] Dabzell v. Cullen, 1 Dow. & L. 448.

mesne process and had been remanded. Upon the remanding order being made, counsel for the jailer asked for costs of them directed to produce the prisoner, and their expenses of bringing him up. His lordship thought that a jailer might require payment of the expenses before bringing up a prisoner on habeas corpus, on the principle that he is to lose nothing by bringing him up, and in making his award used these words: "I have looked very carefully into the authorities in this case, in which it appeared to me that I ought, if I could do so, to award the costs against Mr. Dodd. I think that there is a distinction between what may be called the expenses and the costs. I certainly have great difficulty in saying that I have any jurisdiction to award the costs generally, which would include the costs of the hearing against Mr. Dodd, the prisoner; but with regard to the expenses, I have a strong impression, after considering the cases and the act of parliament, which (although this is not an application under it) may not be wholly immaterial. The result of my opinion upon the whole matter is, that so far as the expenses are concerned—that is, the expenses of bringing Mr. Dodd from Jersey—I ought to make an order for the payment of them by him.

"It appears that prior to the passing of the habeas corpus act (in which provision is made for the payment of the expenses for the conveyance of the prisoner), there are authorities to show that the jailer or sheriff had a right to demand from the prisoner what are called in one case[1] the charges, and in another the fees.[2] I think that this must be understood to embrace the expenses of bringing him before the court. And when I find that under the second section of the habeas corpus act, which applies to criminal cases, there is a provision made even for the criminal prisoner paying or tendering the charges of bringing him before the court, it strengthens the opinion which I have formed upon authorities, that in a habeas corpus at common law and in a civil suit, as this is, the sheriff or viscount is entitled to his expenses.

"Under these circumstances, I consider that though I have no jurisdiction to award the costs generally, I have power to award the expenses as distinguished from the general costs, and that under the circumstances of this case it is my duty to do so."[3]

§ 114. **In Bankruptcy.**—Although the control of a creditor over the person of his debtor has been very nearly abolished in

[1] King v. Armiger, 1 Keb. 272.   [2] Winnington's Case, 1 Keb. 566.
[3] Dodd's Case, 2 De G. & J. 510.

the United States, as well as in England, by various constitutional and statutory provisions, some cases involving the question of costs in bankruptcy proceedings have arisen in the latter country. One of these is in relation to properly answering questions before the commissioners in bankruptcy when a witness is brought before them for the purpose of testifying. Where a party, the brother of the bankrupt, having been examined under this commission and committed to prison on two different occasions for not satisfactorily answering the questions put to him by the commissioners, presented a petition before Lord Chancellor Lyndhurst that the commissioners should be directed to meet forthwith for the purpose of taking his further examination, and that the expense of the meeting should be paid out of the bankrupt's estate, an order was made that upon the witness tendering to the solicitor under the commission the costs of the proposed meeting and of being brought up, the petitioner be again examined. His lordship wished to protect the estate against the consequences of the prisoner's obstinacy, as he would have been entitled to discharge had he answered satisfactorily in the first instance.[1]

Again, a defendant had been arrested at the suit of the plaintiff in an action on debt, and afterwards committed to the custody of the warden of the Fleet. Final judgment having been obtained by plaintiff, he caused a writ of habeas corpus *ad satisfaciendum* to be issued against defendant to satisfy him for the damages and costs recovered against defendant on the judgment. There being no return, a motion for an attachment against the warden was made. The warden during this time had given his prisoner the benefit of the rules of the prison, and upon service of the writ he was unable to find him or produce him in obedience to its mandate. An officer of the prison filed an affidavit that he sent a turnkey repeatedly to the defendant's lodgings for the purpose of obeying the writ, and notwithstanding every possible exertion he was not able to see the defendant until late in the afternoon of the last day of the last term, when it was too late to bring him before the court; that he was immediately deprived of the benefit of the rules and confined within the walls of the prison, where he continued a prisoner at the suit of the plaintiff until he was discharged under an order of the insolvent debtor's court, as well from the above-named action as all other debts on which he was detained in custody. The turnkey, however, made no affidavit as

Ex parte Baxter, Mont. & McA. 16.

§ 115. COSTS, AND SECURITY AGAINST ESCAPE. 135

to the diligence he used on those occasions. Dallas, J., could surmise no intentional contempt on the part of the warden, but said he was bound to obey the writ, and that the cause assigned for his not bringing the defendant into court did not amount to a sufficient excuse. The plaintiff, in point of fact, sustained no injury from such neglect, but the court would impose on the warden the payment of the costs attending the application for the attachment; and on those terms the rule was discharged.[1]

A party committed to prison by the commissioners forming a subdivision court of bankruptcy, for refusing to answer questions to their satisfaction, may obtain a habeas corpus to be again brought before the court upon giving notice that he is ready to answer, but he is not entitled to a meeting for the particular purpose of hearing his answers without paying the costs of the sitting. He must do this or wait until a meeting is held for any other purpose, although he file an affidavit of his inability to pay the costs of the meeting to be held for his own benefit.[2]

A bankrupt was a prisoner in the custody of the marshal of the queen's bench, and the question was how far the detention of the bankrupt could be insured by the court of review so as to compel the payment of certain costs of a petition which had been presented to annul the fiat, and which had been twice dismissed at his cost. The court granted an order for bringing up the bankrupt from the queen's bench for the purpose of recommitting him to that prison under an order of detention until the costs should be paid, but were inclined to the opinion that they had, in such a case, no authority to issue a writ of *habeas corpus cum causa* to bring up the party in order to charge him with the warrant of commitment of the court itself for non-payment of the costs.[3]

These cases may illustrate principles which may arise in some form in the future, although the bankrupt laws are now, and for some time past have been, regarded as a connected system of civil legislation, having the object of both enforcing a complete discovery and equitable distribution of the property of an insolvent debtor, and of conferring upon him the reciprocal advantage of security of person and a discharge from all claims of his creditors.[4]

§ 115. **On Habeas Corpus ad Testificandum.**—It is sometimes desirable and even necessary that a prisoner be brought

---

[1] Park v. Torre, 6 Moore, 260.
[2] In re Stockwin, 5 Ad. & El. 266.
[3] Ex parte and Matter of Britten, 2 Mont. D. & De G. 335.
[4] 1 Bouv. Law Dict. 188.

up to testify in a cause. This fact has been recognized for centuries, and over two hundred years the court granted a habeas corpus to have a prisoner, who was not in execution, out of prison to be a witness for one at a trial; but at the charge of him that desired the habeas corpus, and at his peril to take care that the prisoner do not make an escape.[1] So in another early case the court was moved that a prisoner in the Marshalsea might have liberty by rule of court to be at a trial to give his testimony as a witness in a cause. Justice Ierman answered: "Bring him thither by a habeas corpus, but take a good guard with him, for it shall be at your peril if he escape; and he shall be brought thither and carried back again at your own charge."[2]

If the plaintiff has two actions pending against a defendant at the same time, and for some cause is imprisoned himself, and is brought up on a *habeas corpus ad testificandum* to attend the trial of one of the actions as a witness, and though present at that particular trial is not called upon to give evidence, but is called and gives evidence in the trial of the other action, which is tried on the same day, and succeeds in the first cause and fails in the second, on taxation of the costs of the first cause he will be entitled to only one moiety of the costs of the habeas corpus. Pollock, C. B., decided that "a party who fails in a cause must bear the expense of his failure. The rule is, if a witness attends in one cause only, he will be entitled to the full allowance. If he attend in more than one cause, he will be entitled to a proportionate part in each cause only. If the expense of bringing up this party as a witness was ten pounds, a proportion, one half, must be allowed."[3]

§ 116. **In Particular Instances.**—The court will compel an attorney to pay the costs occasioned by his vexatious conduct in giving repeated notices of bail who do not attend and justify at the judge's chambers, according to appointment, during the vacation. A defendant had removed himself by habeas corpus from Lincoln castle into the king's bench prison, and the plaintiff had been put to the expense of inquiring after six sets of bail. It appeared that one of the bail was a discharged insolvent, and that a false description had been given of the residence of the other bail, which circumstances were calculated to deceive the plaintiff, and as they must certainly have been known to the defendant's attorney, it was a sufficient ground for the exercise of the discretion of the court in com-

---

[1] 2 Lilly's Reg. 3, E. [2] Treton v. Squire, Sty. 230.
[3] Griffin v. Hoskyns, 1 Hurl. & N. 94.

pelling him, as one of its officers, to pay the costs of these vexatious proceedings, although it was sworn that he had no personal knowledge of the insufficiency or misdescription of the bail. Chief Justice Abbott thought, the rest of the court concurring, "that it would operate as a wholesome lesson to attorneys to order the attorney in this case to pay the costs of the different notices which had been given. It is his duty to make himself acquainted with the condition and circumstances of the persons who propose to become bail, and he ought not to tender them, unless he is satisfied of their sufficiency. Negligence of their duty in this respect leads to great expense, and frequently ends in fraud upon the party who is interested in the justification of the bail."[1]

Where the defendant, against whom an information had been filed for importing prohibited goods, was apprehended by *capias* and committed to prison, and remained there for want of bail, instructed his solicitor that the person who actually committed the offense imputed to him had assumed his name and that the question would be one of mere identity, and caused an affidavit to that effect to be prepared for the purpose of grounding an application to the court for a habeas corpus, under which he might be brought up to be present at the trial of the cause and avail himself of that point in his case, averring that he could not otherwise safely proceed in his defense, the court granted the application, on condition of the defendant being brought up on a day certain and paying the costs of being brought up and remanded, intimating that the writ should be in form of the *habeas corpus ad testificandum*.[2]

A mere stranger has no right to come to the court and ask that a party who makes no affidavit, and who is not suggested to be so coerced as to be incapable of making one, may be brought up by habeas corpus to be discharged from restraint. So where a rule was obtained for a habeas corpus to bring up a lunatic confined in an asylum in England under Irish medical certificates, the court under these circumstances discharged it with costs, saying: "For anything that appears, Captain Child [the lunatic] may be very well content to remain where he is. The rule must be discharged; and as Mr. Lord [the keeper of the asylum in which Captain Child was detained] has been put to the expense of coming here fruitlessly and unnecessarily, it must be with costs." The opposing counsel asked

---

[1] Blundell v. Blundell, 1 Dow. & Ry. 142.
[2] Attorney General v. Fadden, 1 Price, 152.

that the costs of the rule might be ordered to be paid by the attorney, but the court said: "We can not do that."[1]

In one case, on the crown side of the court of queen's bench in Ireland, a writ of habeas corpus had issued directing the defendant to bring up the body of a child named Reilly, in defendant's custody. The writ had been allowed to go, and had been obeyed without any argument, and the child handed over to his mother, who had obtained the writ. The prosecutor of the writ applied for costs; but the court disclaimed any jurisdiction to grant costs under the circumstances.[2]

PART II.—IN THE FEDERAL COURTS.

§ 117. **Legislation, Decisions, and Rules.**—There seems to have been little or no legislation concerning costs on habeas corpus proceedings in the courts of the United States, and the decisions of the United States courts upon the subject appear to be very meager. Section 755 of the revised statutes of the United States has provided that the justice or judge to whom a proper and sufficient application has been made shall forthwith award a writ of habeas corpus, etc.; and having provided this means of speedy inquiry into the cause for which a citizen may be detained or imprisoned, congress has not seen fit to interpose obstructions in the way of assessing costs, which it was the very policy of the common law to forbid. The effect of taxing costs would sometimes be to entirely prevent the relief intended to be afforded by the writ of habeas corpus, unless the unfortunate prisoner could himself procure the means of defraying this preliminary expense; and his situation, already sufficiently distressing, would be seriously exasperated, and that liberty which it is the object of the government to protect, and of its laws to promote, would be oppressed and destroyed.

Costs are not to be awarded against the United States,[3] nor can a decree or judgment be entered against the government for costs;[4] and if a judgment for costs be given against the United States by the court below, it must be reversed, as the United States are not liable for costs.[5] The various statutes and laws of the United States regarding costs and fees in other cases probably contain regulations respecting costs and fees in proceedings in habeas corpus in the event of the prisoner's dis-

[1] Ex parte Child, 29 Eng. L. & Eq. 259; S. C., 15 Com. B. 238.
[2] In re Reilly, 10 L. T., N. S., 853.
[3] United States v. Hooe, 3 Cranch,
73; United States v. Barker, 2 Wheat. 395.
[4] United States v. McLemore, 4 How. 286.
[5] United States v. Boyd, 5 How. 30.

§ 118.   COSTS, AND SECURITY AGAINST ESCAPE.   139

charge; and if he be remanded, we see no reason why judgment should not be given against him for costs.

The first section of rule 10 of the United States supreme court reads: "In all cases the plaintiff in error, or appellant, on docketing the cause and filing the record shall enter into an undertaking to the clerk, with surety to his satisfaction, for the payment of his fees, or otherwise satisfy him in that behalf."[1] Under rule 24, the court awards costs in certain cases, in its own judgment, as may seem right and proper between the parties. Under section 4 of rule 24, no costs are allowed in the United States supreme court for or against the United States in cases where it is a party.[2] And when a cause is dismissed for want of jurisdiction, no costs are allowed;[3] in fact, in such case the court can not give a judgment for costs.[4]

PART III.—IN THE STATE COURTS.

§ 118. **Statutes.**—By an examination of the various constitutional and statutory provisions of the several states, it will be seen that the subject of costs and security against escape has, in some of them, been regulated by law; but in others, their statutes are silent upon the matter.[5] In some of the states an

[1] Thatcher's Dig., U. S. Courts 352.
[2] Id., 383.
[3] Inglee v. Coolidge, 2 Wheat. 368.
[4] McIver v. Wattles, 9 Wheat. 650.
[5] *Alabama* has a provision in her code that the court, judge, or chancellor may impose costs on either party. Costs may be taxed by the clerk of the circuit or city court, and may be collected by execution: Code of Ala. 1876, sec. 4972. The same law also gives the officer a fixed fee for serving the writ—the mileage being proved by his own affidavit—and for issuing and serving subpœnas there is a fixed compensation. These fees are collected in certain cases by execution: Id., sec. 4973.
Arkansas has a law that the officer granting the writ may previously require bond with surety in sufficient penalty, payable to the state or to the person against whom the writ is directed, conditioned that the person so detained shall not escape by the way, and for the payment of such costs and charges as may be awarded against him. The bond shall be filed with the other proceedings in the court, and may be sued on by the state for the benefit of any person injured by the breach of it: Ark. Dig. 1874 sec. 3110.

California.—No fee or compensation of any kind must be charged or received by any officer for duties performed or services rendered in proceedings upon habeas corpus: Pol. Code, sec. 4333.
Delaware's laws provide that the costs in any proceeding under the chapter relating to habeas corpus may be ordered to be paid by the county or otherwise; but if the commitment be insufficient, the justice or officer who made it shall have no compensation for attendance: Rev. Code of Del. 1874, p. 699, sec. 15.
Georgia has a code which gives the judge hearing the return to a writ of habeas corpus power, in his discretion, to award the costs of the proceedings against either party, and to order execution to issue therefor by the clerk: Code of Ga. 1873, sec. 4028.
Kansas requires no deposit or security for costs of an applicant for the writ: Laws of Kan. 1879, sec. 4224.
Kentucky has general statutes empowering the judge or court before whom a cause in proceedings by habeas corpus shall be returned to award costs to be paid, and including pay for transportation of the prisoner

appeal may be taken in different forms from the order or judgment of the inferior court, or judge thereof, or a judge of the supreme court, against an application in a habeas corpus proceeding, to the supreme court; and we apprehend that the gen-

as shall seem right: Gen. Stat. of Ky. 1873, p. 208, sec. 30.

Maine has a law that when the writ is offered to the officer to whom it is directed he shall receive it, and on payment or tender of such sum as the court or justice thereof directs, shall make due return, etc. Such officer must, on demand, deliver to the applicant a copy of the precept by which he is restrained, etc., and if he refuse or neglect to do so, he shall be bound to obey the writ without payment or tender of expenses: Rev. Stat. of Me. 1857, p. 595, sec. 12.

Massachusetts.—If the party is confined in a common jail, or in the custody of a civil officer, the court or magistrate granting the writ shall certify thereon the sum to be paid for the expense of bringing such party from the place of imprisonment, and the officer shall not be bound to obey the writ unless that sum is paid or tendered to him: Pub. Stat. of Mass. 1882, p. 1068, sec. 10.

Michigan.—Every officer allowing a writ of habeas corpus directed to any person other than a sheriff, coroner, constable, or marshal may, in his discretion, require as a duty to be performed, in order to render the service thereof effectual, that the charges of bringing up such prisoner shall be paid by the petitioner; and in such case he shall, in the allowance of the writ, specify the amount of such charges so to be paid, which shall not exceed the fees allowed by law to sheriffs for similar services: Comp. Laws of Mich. 1871, vol. 2, p. 1956, sec. 67.

Missouri.—The courts and magistrates allowing a writ of habeas corpus may, in their discretion, require, as a duty to be performed in order to render the service thereof effectual, that the charges of bringing up the prisoner, and conveying him back if remanded, shall be paid by the petitioner; and, in such case, the court or magistrate shall, on the allowance of the writ, specify the amount, which shall not exceed ten cents per mile; and the amount so to be paid shall be stated in writing on the writ, signed by the clerk if in term, or by the officer by whom the writ is awarded: 1 Rev. Stat. of Mo. 1879, p. 441. In all cases where charges are allowed by the court or officer awarding the writ, the person serving the same shall pay or tender to the officer, or other person having custody of the prisoner, the amount of the charges for bringing up such prisoner; and shall also give bond, with security if required, to the officer or person having custody of the party to be relieved, conditioned for the payment of the charges of conveying back the prisoner if remanded; otherwise the service shall not be deemed complete: Id., p. 442.

Nebraska.—In this state, upon the final disposition of any case arising upon a writ of habeas corpus, the court or judge determining the same shall make such order as to costs as the case may require: Comp. Stat. of Neb. 1881, p. 722, sec. 373.

New Hampshire.—Here the court or justice may require and take security by recognizance, with sufficient sureties if necessary, for the appearance of any party at the time and place of hearing on a writ of habeas corpus, and to abide the order of court thereon; and may make all decrees necessary to insure the attainment of the object of such writ, and enforce the same upon the principles of equity: Gen. Laws of N. H. (1878), 561, sec. 20.

New York.—The party serving a writ of habeas corpus in this state shall tender to the person in whose custody the prisoner may be, if such person be a sheriff, coroner, constable, or marshal, the fees allowed by law for bringing up such prisoner, and shall also give a bond to such sheriff, coroner, constable, or marshal, as the case may be, in a penalty double the amount of the sum for which such prisoner may be detained, if he be detained for any specific sum of money, and if not, then in the penalty of one thousand dollars, conditioned that such person will pay the charges of carrying back such prisoner, if he shall be remanded, and that such prisoner will not escape by the way, either in going to or returning from the place to which he is to be taken:

§ 118.   COSTS, AND SECURITY AGAINST ESCAPE.   141

eral rule governing the appellate courts in such appeals in awarding costs is the general principle that the prevailing party in suits in all courts of law is entitled to costs. The discretion of the court, however, is an element in the matter, and

2 Fay's Dig. 129, sec. 5. This section, however, does not apply to any case where the writ is sued out by the attorney general, or by any district attorney: Id., sec. 6. It shall be the duty of every sheriff, coroner, constable, or marshal upon whom a writ of habeas corpus shall be served, whether such writ be directed to him or not, upon payment or tender of the charges allowed by law, and the delivery or tender of the bond herein prescribed, to obey and return such writ according to the exigency thereof; and it shall be the duty of every other person upon whom such writ shall be served, having the custody of the individual for whose benefit the writ shall be issued, to obey and execute such writ, according to the command thereof, without requiring any bond or the payment of any charges, unless the payment of such charges shall have been required by the officer issuing such writ: Id., sec. 9. The writ of *certiorari* shall in like manner be obeyed and returned, according to the exigency thereof, by the person upon whom it is served, upon payment or tender of the fees allowed by law for making a return to such writ, and for copying the warrant or other process to be annexed thereto: Id., sec. 10. Every officer allowing a writ of habeas corpus, directed to any other than a sheriff, coroner, constable, or marshal, may in his discretion require as a duty to be performed, in order to render the service thereof effectual, that the charges of bringing up such prisoner shall be paid by the petitioner; and in such case he shall, in the allowance of the writ, specify the amount of such charges so to be paid, which shall not exceed the fees allowed by law to sheriffs for similar services: Id., 130, sec. 11. This provision shall be construed to apply, so far as it may be applicable, and except where otherwise provided, to every writ of habeas corpus authorized to be issued by any statute of the state: Id., sec. 13. In the city and county of New York there shall be no costs or fees charged or received upon any proceedings upon writs of habeas corpus, either by the judge or commissioner granting them, or by the officer serving them, or the jailer obeying their orders: Id., sec. 14. All judicial fees, except to justices of the peace, have been abolished by the constitution: Amendments to the Constitution of 1846, ratified 1869, sec. 21.

North Carolina.—The costs on a writ of habeas corpus may be awarded at the discretion of the court or judge who shall hear the same; and he may direct what officer shall tax the costs, and execution may issue therefor as in other cases: Battle's Revisal, 465, sec. 38. The service of the writ, however, shall not be complete unless the applicant for the same shall tender to the person in whose custody the prisoner may be, if such person be a sheriff, constable, coroner, or marshal, the fees and expenses allowed by law for bringing such prisoner, nor unless he shall also give bond, with sufficient security, to such sheriff, coroner, constable, or marshal, as the case may be, conditioned that such applicant will pay the charges of carrying back such prisoner: Id. 466, sec. 44.

Ohio.—The fees of officers and witnesses shall be taxed by the judge, on his return of his proceedings on the writ, and shall be collected as part of the original costs in the case; and when the prisoner is discharged, the costs shall be taxed to the state and paid out of the county treasury, upon the warrant of the county auditor; but no officer or person shall have the right to demand payment in advance of any fees which he is entitled to by virtue of the proceedings, when the writ is demanded or issued for the discharge from custody of a person confined under color of proceedings in any criminal case. When a person in custody by virtue or under color of proceedings in any civil case is discharged, costs shall be taxed against the party at whose instance he was so in custody; and if he be remanded to custody, costs shall be taxed against him: 2 Rev. Stat. of Ohio, 1880, sec. 5753. When a writ of habeas corpus is issued for any person removed from one county and confined in the jail of another, to inquire into the cause of his capture and detention, the county

they will make such order relative to the costs as may seem right.[1] And in New Jersey, "if any suit commenced in any circuit court or court of common pleas shall be removed by writ of habeas corpus into the supreme court by the defendant, and the plaintiff shall recover in the supreme court, he shall recover full costs, in case he would have been entitled to recover costs had the suit remained and been tried in the circuit court or court of common pleas."[2] A statement of the fees allowed officers for services in habeas corpus proceedings, as shown in the two following instances, will illustrate, at least in part, the

from which such person was sent shall pay all the costs of such proceeding; and upon the presentation of the certificate of the clerk of the proper court, showing the amount of such costs, to the auditor of the county from which such person was sent, he shall draw his order therefor on the treasurer, in favor of the clerk or such person as he shall order, and the clerk shall pay the same to the persons entitled thereto: Id., sec. 7387. Section 7384 provides for fees to be paid to the sheriff or jailer of a county to which a prisoner has been removed.

Oregon.—The civil code of Oregon also requires a tender of fees and the execution of an undertaking to complete the service of a writ: Gen. Laws of Or. 1843-1872, Deady & Lane, 239, sec. 631.

Pennsylvania.—The officer serving the process and the witness in attendance shall be entitled to the same mileage, fees, and allowances as for similar service and attendance before a justice of the peace; and the costs of service and attendance on the part of the commonwealth shall be paid by the proper county and taxed as costs in the case: 1 Bright. Pur. Dig., 758, sec. 21. It shall be lawful for the court of common pleas, or any judge thereof before whom any writ of habeas corpus shall be heard, upon the petition of any person or persons charged with any criminal or supposed criminal matter, to make an order for the payment by the proper county, or by the prosecutor or prosecutors in the case, as the said court or the judge hearing the case may determine, of the costs and fees of the witnesses subpœnaed by the district attorney on the part of the commonwealth, provided that the fees of witnesses shall be the same as are allowed by law in civil cases: Id., 758, sec. 22.

Tennessee.—Here the judge or court, except when otherwise expressly provided, awards the costs as may be right, and they are taxed and collected as in other cases: 2 Stat. of Tenn. 1871, sec. 3762. Where the defendant in a criminal prosecution is brought before any circuit or criminal judge on a writ of habeas corpus, and discharged by the judge, the costs shall be paid as in other state cases when the defendant is tried and acquitted by a jury: Id., sec. 3763. When the defendant, in the cases provided for in the preceding section, is charged with a felony, the judge shall make out and certify the bill of costs, and deliver the same to the clerk of the circuit court before which the defendant is bound to appear, by whom the costs shall be collected and paid out as in other cases: Id., sec. 3764. If the defendant is charged with a misdemeanor, the judge shall deliver the bill of costs, made out and certified as before, to the county clerk of the county in which the defendant was charged with committing the offense, by whom the same shall be allowed, as in the other cases: Id., sec. 3765.

Vermont.—If the prisoner is confined in a common jail, or in the custody of a civil officer, the court or judge granting the same shall certify thereon the sum to be paid for bringing him from the place of imprisonment; and the officer to whom the writ is directed shall not be bound to obey it, unless that sum is paid or tendered to him: Rev. Laws of Vt. 1880, sec. 1353.

[1] Texas, New York, Indiana, Mississippi, and New Jersey, we believe, are among the number.

[2] Revision of New Jersey, 891, sec. 270.

rule in some of the other states. In New Jersey the sheriff or other officer gets for making the return two dollars, and mileage for himself and prisoner, going and returning, at the rate of four cents a mile for each. The fee of the court of justice for granting the writ is two dollars, and for taking a recognizance, one dollar. The justice taking examination of witnesses on return of writ gets three dollars per diem; but if the same be taken before a commissioner, the same fees are allowed as in like cases. If writ be granted by court or justice on their own motion, no fees shall be allowed.[1]

In Tennessee the sheriff's fee for conveying a prisoner before a judge on a writ of habeas corpus, per mile going and returning, ten cents; and for guards, not exceeding two for each prisoner, each per mile, going and returning, five cents.[2]

§ 119. **Judicial Constructions.**—In a very early case in our judicial history it was determined that the court would not require the prosecutor to enter security for costs in a habeas corpus proceeding.[3] But in a later case, in a state where fees are allowed by statutory law, it has been held that where there are different hearings upon a writ of habeas corpus, the officers are entitled to their fees for each.[4] In another late case the question presented to a Mississippi court was: "Whether a pardoned convict can be held in confinement in order to compel payment of the costs adjudged against him." It was decided in the negative. Justice Chalmers, in rendering the opinion of the court, enunciated and sustained the following propositions by authorities: "Where the pardon is granted before conviction, no judgment for costs can be rendered against the party. Where it is granted after conviction, and after rendition of judgment for costs, the pardon does not extinguish the civil liability for the costs; because it is uniformly held, both in England and America, that the pardoning power does not extend to the remission, after judgment, of any pecuniary penalty which has inured to private persons or public officers, and hence that execution may be levied on the property of the party, notwithstanding the pardon. But there can be no right in the officers or other persons to hold the party in confinement, because this would amount substantially to imprisonment for debt. The imprisonment is a part of the punishment, and is remitted by the pardon; but the judgment for costs is a debt which, while it can not be extinguished by the governor, must

---

[1] Revision of New Jersey, 476, sec. 57.
[2] 2 Stat. of Tenn. 1871, sec. 4564 a.
[3] The State v. Lyon, 1 N. J. L. 403.
[4] Ware v. The State, 33 Ga. 338.

be collected like other judgments, after the term of imprisonment has expired, or been abrogated by executive clemency." In this case the prisoner had been sentenced to twelve months' imprisonment in the county jail and to pay the costs.[1]

In a state where prevails a statute that certain persons convicted and committed to the jail of a county are to be delivered to a contractor to be kept and worked under the provisions of the act, and which directs that "whenever said convict shall be sentenced to jail as a part of his punishment, he shall first serve out said term, and shall then commence to work to pay said fine and costs," it has very lately been held that the sheriff who keeps the prisoner in jail after the contractor has made a demand for him, and not the county or the prisoner, is chargeable with the jail fees, as well as the costs of a writ of habeas corpus sued out by the contractor to obtain the custody of the prisoner. The object of the language in quotation-marks above, said Chief Justice George, "is meant to fix the date for the commencement of the labor of the prisoner, which is to be applied to the payment of the fine and costs, in cases where imprisonment is made a part of the punishment. This construction is also in accordance with the spirit and object of the act, which are to reduce costs and expenses. The contrary view must require the prisoner or the county to pay his jail fees during the time for which he was imprisoned as a punishment. It would operate hardly upon the public and the prisoner. For the guidance of the contractor, we state that the imprisonment for the costs and fine imposed by this act was intended solely to secure their payment; and whenever these are paid, the prisoner is entitled to be discharged, provided the term for which he has been imprisoned as a part of his punishment has expired." So in this case, which was an appeal from a decision denying the appellant's (the contractor's) application by habeas corpus for the custody of a convict, and remanding him to the custody of the appellee, the sheriff, the court made the following order: "The costs of the proceeding, both before the chancellor and in this court, will be taxed against the appellee. The cost of keeping the prisoner in jail, after the demand for him made by Mathews, is a just charge against the sheriff, who unlawfully refused to deliver him to the contractor, and can not be charged against either the prisoner or the county."[2]

[1] Ex parte Gregory, 56 Miss. 164.
[2] Mathews, Contractor, v. Walker, Sheriff, 57 Miss. 337.

§ 119.   COSTS, AND SECURITY AGAINST ESCAPE.   145

In a proceeding instituted in the name of the state, and for the purpose of restoring to liberty a person entitled to the protection of the state, on habeas corpus for the custody of an infant, in which the applicant fails and the child is allowed to remain with the defendant, the costs can not be taxed to the county where such action is brought and tried and the applicant resides. Such a proceeding is not criminal in its nature; and where no statute expressly provides that costs in a habeas corpus proceeding can be taxed to the county, there is nothing to justify it in the nature of the case. Under these circumstances, Chief Justice Adams of Iowa, for the court, said: "We are not called upon to determine how the costs in question should be taxed. It is evident that they could not be taxed to the defendants, because they were successful. They ought not to be taxed to the child, because while the petition was filed ostensibly in her behalf, it appears that it was not by her consent. The evidence shows that she desired to remain with the defendants, and that the claims of the petitioners should be denied. Possibly the costs should have been taxed to the petitioners, and possibly there is a defect of legislation in this respect. However that may be, we are agreed that they can not properly be taxed to the county."[1]

Where a relator's claim has been examined in different aspects, and decided on several previous writs before different courts—the proceedings on one of which resulted in a writ of *certiorari* to the supreme court of New York, followed by a writ of error— and costs were awarded against the relator, and a preliminary objection was taken in a subsequent proceeding by him on *habeas corpus ad subjiciendum* that he was not entitled to be again heard till these costs were paid, it was ruled that the legislature had prescribed certain limitations for the course of both commissioners and the court, and that neither, if the habeas corpus act of New York was intended for the government of the latter, had the power to order such a stay; and that this was equally the case whether the objection were taken under the common law or the statute.[2] Where the prisoner has been arrested by an officer under valid process, and has been committed to jail under such arrest, the officer is not liable for costs upon the prisoner being discharged from his custody upon habeas corpus.[3]

---

[1] State v. Collins et al., 54 Iowa, 441; S. C., 6 N. W. Rep. 274.
[2] People v. Mercein, 3 Hill (N. Y.), 399.
[3] Hammond v. The People, 32 Ill. 446.

CHAPTER XI.

THE RETURN.

PART I.—VARIOUS MATTERS OF LAW CLOSELY CONNECTED WITH THE RETURN.

§ 120. Definition and Observations.
§ 121. Form of the Return.
§ 122. Verification of the Return.
§ 123. When It will be Received.
§ 124. May be Enforced by Attachment.
§ 125. The Return should be Liberally Construed.
§ 126. Certainty Required in the Return.
§ 127. Warrant Need not Always be Returned.
§ 128. The Return may be Amended.
§ 129. Whether Return may be Fortified by Affidavit.
§ 130. When Petitioner can not be Held by Virtue of the Warrant.
§ 131. On What Return the Writ will be Dismissed.
§ 132. When Court will Immediately Discharge the Prisoner.
§ 133. Enlarging Time for Return of Writ.
§ 134. Full Answer to Return.
§ 135. Jailer may Substitute Return Prepared by Counsel for his Own.
§ 136. Objections to the Return.
§ 137. Failure, or to Make an Evasive or Insufficient Return, is a Contempt of Court.
§ 138. True Return could not be Enforced at Common Law.
§ 139. New Habeas Corpus not Required.
§ 140. Recommitment.
§ 141. Order of the Argument.
§ 142. Rule upon Process.
§ 143. Return of Substituted Warrant.
§ 144. Return must Show that Evidence was Given in Prisoner's Presence.
§ 145. Relying upon a Conviction where Commitment is Bad.
§ 146. Return must Remain in Court.
§ 147. Return Need not Specifically Set out Documents Referred to.
§ 148. When Warrant must Contain Words.
§ 149. Questioning Jurisdiction on Defective Warrant.
§ 150. Examination into Cause on Rule *Nisi.*
§ 151. Discussing Validity of Warrant upon Rule to Show Cause.
§ 152. When Motion to Quash Writ, after Return Filed, will be Entertained.
§ 153. Making a Bad Return on Good Judgment.

§ 154. Judicial Notice.
§ 155. Reply to Return Denying Truth of the Matters Contained in Affidavit on Which *Capias* Issued.
§ 156. Return of Execution against the Person.
§ 157. When Demand should be Made for Child.
§ 158. Time when Errors should be Corrected.
§ 159. State Court can not Determine What is a Crime against the United States.
§ 160. What is Meant by the Term "Process."
§ 161. A Few Instances of a Bad Return.
§ 162. A Few Instances of a Good Return.

PART II.—PRODUCTION OF THE BODY, AND STATEMENTS OF THE CAUSE OF ARREST AND DETENTION.

§ 163. Sufficient Reasons for not Producing the Body.
§ 164. Statement of the Cause of Arrest.
§ 165. Statement of the Cause of Detention.

PART III.—ANSWERING THE RETURN.

§ 166. Return not Controvertible at Common Law.
§ 167. But Return may be Confessed and Avoided.
§ 168. Doctrine in the United States.

PART I.—VARIOUS MATTERS OF LAW CLOSELY CONNECTED WITH THE RETURN.

§ 120. **Definition and Observations.**—"The answer in writing, signed by the party to whom the writ is addressed, stating the time and cause of the caption and detention of the prisoner and his production before the court or judge, or if the prisoner be not produced, then the reasons for not producing him, constitutes the return."[1] The writ of habeas corpus must also be returned by the very same person to whom it is addressed or directed; and if this writ has been awarded to the sheriff of a certain county, who goes out of office before returning it, and a new sheriff is elected as his successor, who returns *languidus*, it is not good. The writ ought to be returned by both of them: the first that he had the body, and had delivered it to the new sheriff; the second one or new sheriff may then properly return *languidus*.[2] When the return is made, the evidence or depositions upon which the commitment was founded should be sent up to the court or judge who is to pass upon it, in order that the means may be furnished of judging in what way they should dispose of the prisoner.[3] The return should be made without the delay which caused so much hardship on prisoners prior to the act of 31 Car. II. To correct dilatory returns was

---

[1] Hurd on Habeas Corpus, 2d ed., 235.
[2] 4 Bac. Abr. 581.   [3] 1 Ch. Crim. L. 127.

in fact one of the objects of the passage of the act. Events often occur, however, over which there is no control, that will excuse and permit delay, as we shall see in subsequent sections regarding lunatics, disability from sickness, etc. The officer or person to whom the writ is directed must, upon due service thereof, make a return thereto, and upon his failure to do so, such return will be enforced by means hereafter described, and this duty applies to a United States marshal in response to a writ from a state court or judge.[1] But in times of war a military commander may sometimes declare and enforce martial law, and may justifiably disregard a writ of habeas corpus when obedience to it would necessarily interrupt and hinder him in the discharge of important military duties, yet this kind of justifiable disregard of the writ, growing out of the existence of martial law, or the local and temporary necessities of military duty, does not amount to the suspension of the writ referred to by the constitution.[2] It is the duty of a judge or court hearing an application for a discharge under a writ of habeas corpus, when a prisoner is restrained of his liberty, to discharge him if there appear to be no reasonable grounds for his detention, or if the imprisonment be illegal. Where the detention or imprisonment is under a statute, the court or judge should discharge the prisoner, unless satisfied by unequivocal words in the statute that the statute warrants the imprisonment.[3] So is it also the duty of the court or judge to discharge when the sufficiency of the warrant of commitment is doubtful,[4] in which cases the court will always incline in favor of liberty.[5] On the other hand, where the return shows that the petitioner is regularly in custody, and no reasons are assigned why he should be discharged, the writ will be dismissed, and the prisoner remanded.[6]

§ 121. **Form of the Return.**—The return must be in writing and signed by the party making it, and it should be addressed to the court or officer before whom it is returnable. The general form is, "That the party has not the person in his possession, custody, or power," when the detention is denied. Irregularities which will justify the quashing of the return, or for which it may be amended, will be considered hereafter. The return must show by whom and for what cause the pris-

---

[1] Ex parte Hill, 5 Nev. 154.
[2] In re Kemp, 16 Wis. 382.
[3] In re Slater and Wells, 9 U. C. Law Jour., O. S., 21.
[4] In re Beebe, 3 Prac. Rep. (U. C.) 270.
[5] Queen v. Boyle, 4 Prac. Rep. (U. C.) 264.
[6] In re Ho Quan, 8 Pac. C. L. J. 51; Ah Sing, Id. 213.

§ 121. THE RETURN.

oner was committed,[1] although a return alleging him to have been committed on suspicion of treason has been held sufficient.[2] A mere want of form will not render it invalid if the return discloses a good cause of detainer.[3] Sometimes a commitment is made in court to a proper officer there present. In such cases there is no warrant of commitment; and therefore, when such officer is called upon, he can not return a warrant *in hæc verba* to a writ of habeas corpus, but he must return the truth of the whole matter under peril of an action. When one is committed in open court to a person not an officer, there must be a warrant of commitment in writing; and where there is one, it must be returned, otherwise it would be in the power of the jailer to alter the case of the prisoner and make it either better or worse than it is upon the warrant. Furthermore, if he take upon himself the liberty to return what he will, he makes himself judge, and usurps the power and duty of the court to pass upon the warrant itself.[4] A mistake in the address or direction of a return will not vitiate it, and such error will not be deemed material. A direction to the chief justice only, and not to the other judges of the court, has been held to be good.[5] In fact, it has been conceded that the return may have no direction at all and still be valid—the direction being mere surplusage. The return must be signed by the person to whom the writ is directed, or some explanation made why it is not done. A failure to do this is error.[6]

Where a return to a habeas corpus made by a keeper of a house of correction stated that the prisoner was in custody under a commitment, the tenor of which was as follows—and here set out a document addressed to all the constables, etc., and to the keeper, reciting that a complaint had been made to a justice, on oath, that the prisoner had made and violated a certain contract of apprenticeship; that the justices duly examined the proofs and allegations of the parties; that they found the complaint to be true, and that they therefore convicted the prisoner of the offense, in pursuance of the statute, etc.; and commanded the prisoner to be taken to the house of correction, and delivered to the keeper, together with this warrant—the said keeper being required to hold him to hard labor, etc.—" and for so doing this shall be your sufficient warrant"—it was held, no other document being before the court, that this document

---

[1] Barkham's Case, 3 Cro. Car. 507.
[2] 4 Com. Dig. 562.
[3] King v. Bethel, 5 Mod. 21.
[4] King v. Clerk, 1 Salk. 348.
[5] Crosby's Case, 2 W. Black. 754.
[6] Seavey et al. v. Seymour, 3 Cliff. 455.

was, by its very terms, both a conviction and a commitment in respect of such conviction, under a statute which did not use the word "convict," but merely enacted that if it should appear to the justice that the defendant was guilty, it should be lawful to commit, and abate the wages or discharge from the service; and that as it did not set out the evidence, or in form adjudge any imprisonment, it was bad in the character of a conviction. There being no warrant of commitment before the court, the prisoner was discharged.[1] It seems, too, that in England, where a statute imposes a penalty for an act indifferent in its own nature, and which is by the statute itself not an offense if done under circumstances therein specified, the informer must show enough to give it the character of an offense, and in order to make it criminal, must furthermore negative the circumstances under which criminality does not attach, whether they be embodied in the penal clause or not, notwithstanding the general rule that where an offense is created by one section of a statute and an exemption given by another, it is unnecessary to negative the exemption.[2] An English statute[3] also prescribes that every warrant of commitment under any act relating to the customs shall be deemed valid if it set forth an offense in the words of the act; and no such warrant shall be held void for any defect therein if it allege a conviction of such offense, and if it appear to the court before which the warrant is returned that the conviction proceeded on good and valid grounds; and it seems that it lies upon the party supporting the conviction to prove those grounds, upon a return of such warrant to a writ of habeas corpus, if they are relied upon in answer to an allegation of defect in the warrant, and to do this he must bring up the depositions by *certiorari*.[4]

§ 122. **Verification of the Return.**—At common law no verification of the return was necessary; neither was it the practice to verify it. The return to a habeas corpus *prima facie* imported verity, and other securities were provided by law, and which were generally sufficient, against false returns.[5] The revised statutes of the United States require the person to whom the writ is directed to certify to the court or justice or judge before whom it is returnable the true cause of the detention of such party. In some of the states[6] it is required that the return

---

[1] In the Matter of John Hammond, 9 Ad. & El., Q. B., 92.
[2] Boven's Case, 9 Ad. & El. 669.
[3] Smuggling Act, 63 Stat. at Large, 8 & 9 Vict. 688, sec. 103.
[4] Boven's Case, 9 Ad. & El. 669.
[5] Watson's Case, 9 Ad. & El. 794; In re Hakewill, 22 Eng. L. & Eq. 399.
[6] Ohio, 2 R. S., sec. 5739; Indiana, 2 Laws of Indiana (1870), 318; New York, 2 Fay's Dig. 122; California, 2 Hittell's Codes, sec. 14,480.

or statement shall be signed by the person making it, and shall be sworn to by him, unless he is a sworn public officer and makes the return in his official capacity. A return to a writ of habeas corpus issued by a state judge need not be verified by oath when it is made by an officer of the United States army.[1]

§ 123. **When It will be Received.**—While the writ must be returned by the same person to whom it is directed, it is not absolutely necessary that the party to whom the writ is addressed should appear before the court or judge in all cases unless so required by statute. If the prisoner be produced, the hearing may be had in the respondent's absence, and the return will be received and acted upon.[2] If a writ of habeas corpus is returnable at a certain day, the court will not receive the return until return day; but if it be returnable immediately, the court will not refuse to file it when it comes in.[3]

§ 124. **May be Enforced by Attachment.**—According to the course of the common law, the method to compel a return to a habeas corpus was by first taking out an *alias* habeas corpus, and then a *pluries*, and if no return was made to that, an attachment issued as of course.[4] The court might also make a rule on the officer to return his writ, and if disobeyed, the court might proceed against such disobedience in the same manner as they usually did against the disobedience of any other rule.[5] But subsequently to the passage of the act of 31 Car. II. the practice was materially changed, and the former methods are now seldom employed, because an attachment may immediately issue upon the first refusal.[6] By that act the party to whom the writ of habeas corpus is directed is bound to return the body within three days if within twenty miles; ten days if within a hundred miles; and within twenty days for any greater distance. If he refuse to do so he is liable, for the first offense, to a penalty of one hundred pounds, and for the second, two hundred pounds.[7] It is no excuse for not complying with the writ, as we have elsewhere seen,[3] that the prisoner has not paid to the jailer the charges allowed by the act for his conveyance, as the court will allow them on the return. The question of personal liberty has long been held to be the subject of so much concern that upon disobedience to a writ of habeas corpus courts and judges

---

[1] In re Neill, 8 Blatchf. 165.
[2] In re Hakewell, 22 Eng. L. & Eq. 395; S. C., 12 Com. B. 223.
[3] Mash's Case, 2 W. Black. 804.
[4] Wyatt's Reg. 215.
[5] 4 Bac. Abr., Habeas Corpus, B, sec. 8.
[6] King v. Winton, 5 T. R. 89; Com. Dig., Habeas Corpus, E; Rex v. Wright, 2 Stra. 901.
[7] See act of 31 Car. II., *ante*, sec. 58.
[8] King v. Greenway, 2 Show. 183; Crowley's Case, 2 Swans. 73.

will not first grant the indulgence of a rule to return the writ, but will require all the expedition possible.[1] They will, however, sometimes grant an attachment *nisi*,[2] etc. In one case it appeared that under the practice the party should search the crown-office for a return to the writ, and if no return was filed he should apply for an attachment upon affidavit of that fact.[3]

"The liberty of the subject essentially depends on a ready compliance with the requisitions of the writ, and the courts are jealous whenever any attempt is made to deviate from the usual form of the return."[4] But one should not be too hasty in making an application for an attachment. A reasonable time should be allowed for the preparation of a return, and the court will not suppose that one will not be made where the writ of habeas corpus is served upon a respondent one day, and no return has been made on the succeeding one, even where the writ is returnable immediately.[5] In the United States the judges (*nem. con.*) of the circuit court of the District of Columbia were of opinion, "that although the practice at common law before the statute of 31 Car. II. was that an *alias* and *pluries* should issue before an attachment, yet that the practice since the statute has been to issue an attachment without an *alias* and *pluries*, in cases not within the statute. That this practice has been founded upon the statute, the judges having considered it as furnishing a good rule of proceeding in all cases; and that in adopting the statute as a guide in one respect, viz., in dispensing with the *alias* and *pluries*, they also adopted it as a rule in regard to the time of the return, viz., in allowing three days to make it; and that therefore in the present case an attachment ought not to be issued until the expiration of three days after the service of the writ."[6]

The court must be satisfied that there has been a willful disobedience or a contempt of its process before it will award an attachment. During the dark hours of our own country's history, circumstances arose in Wisconsin, under which the supreme court of that state in their reasonable discretion and wise judgment refused a motion for a rule requiring a military officer, who had been required to surrender a citizen held in custody under military authority, and who had made a return alleging that he held the prisoner by order of the president of the United

---

[1] Rex v. Wright, 2 Stra. 901.
[2] Id.
[3] Ex parte Harrison, 2 Smith, 409.
[4] Justice Grose in King v. Winton, 5 T. R. 89.
[5] Stockdale v. Hansard, 8 Dowl. 474.
[6] United States v. Bollman and Swartwout, 1 Cranch C. Ct. 376.

States, but declining to produce the body, and which was held to be insufficient, to bring the body of the petitioner into court by a certain hour of a certain day—or in default thereof to have an attachment issued against him. The court said that the respondent, General Elliott, was undoubtedly acting under the orders of his superior officers; and that he would doubtless refuse to produce the petitioner, Kemp, in court. "If an attachment issues, it must necessarily bring on a conflict between the state and federal governments. This is to be avoided if possible."[1] It is different with a respondent who does not show by what authority he has arrested the petitioner in the first instance, and with this fatal return declines to produce the body. In such a case a respondent, a United States marshal, was adjudged guilty of contempt of court and fined, although the court held that it would have remanded the petitioner if he had been before it when this decision was made (nearly a month after the order of the court was made for him to produce the petitioner), as the president of the United States had in the interim between the date of the return and of the decision suspended the writ of habeas corpus.[2]

In the state of New Jersey a writ of habeas corpus was directed to the defendant to bring up several colored persons. The sheriff of Somerset sent up a copy of the writ, with a certificate of service indorsed upon it. The defendant did not appear or return the writ, and it was suggested that he intended to depart the state, taking with him the persons named in said writ. It was therefore moved that an attachment issue; but it was refused, because the return and evidence were insufficient. At a subsequent day the affidavit of William Hoagland was read, proving the service of the habeas corpus; and it appearing that the said writ had not been returned by the defendant, it was on motion ordered that an attachment forthwith issue against him for contempt of the court in disobeying the said writ of habeas corpus.[3]

Where the court is satisfied that a return has been intentionally eluded and disregarded, it will order an attachment to immediately issue against the delinquent respondent for his contempt. This was done in Stacy's Case,[4] in New York. Morgan Lewis, general of division in the army of the United States, on being commanded to produce the body, etc., returned, "that

---

[1] In re Kemp, 16 Wis. 379. [2] Ex parte Field, 5 Blatchf. 83.
[3] State v. Raborg, 2 South. 545.
[4] In the Matter of Samuel Stacy, jun., 10 Johns. 327.

the within-named Samuel Stacy, jun., is not in my custody." This was held to be an evasive and insufficient return, and that the officer, to excuse himself for not producing the body of the prisoner, ought to have returned, "that he was not in his custody, possession, or power;" and it appearing from affidavits that the party was in fact in the custody of one of General Lewis' subordinate officers, the court ordered an attachment to issue against the general. Chief Justice Kent said: "Nor can we hesitate in promptly enforcing a due return to the writ when we recollect that in this country the law knows no superior, and that in England their courts have taught us, by a series of instructive examples, to exact the strictest obedience to whatever extent the persons to whom the writ is directed may be clothed with power or exalted in rank.[1] On ordinary occasions the attachment does not issue until after a rule to show cause; but whether it shall or shall not issue in the first instance must depend upon the sound discretion of the court under the circumstances of each particular case. It may, and it often does, issue in the first instance without a rule to show cause, if the case be urgent or the contempt flagrant."

If a person be in court after his failure to make a good and sufficient return, the process of attachment is not necessary, for the only object of such process is to bring the prisoner before the court, and when he is there the court may pass an order directing him immediately to answer interrogatories.[2] Where a defendant has committed a contempt, his presence in court, either voluntarily or by compulsion under process of attachment, gives the court jurisdiction of his person, and an arrest under this process confers a jurisdiction which continues while his case is in course of examination, whether he be actually in court, or ordered to stand committed, or let out on bail.[3] Writs of attachment and commitments for contempt need express no particulars of the contempts, for if they were expressed, they could not be examined.[4]

It may be conceded that, if a court has no authority to issue a writ of *habeas corpus ad subjiciendum* in a given case, the writ would be void, and the person to whom it is directed would not be bound to obey it, and would not be in contempt for re-

---

[1] If a habeas corpus is not obeyed, the court will grant attachment even against a peer, for he has no privilege against the process of Westminster hall to compel obedience to habeas corpus: Com. Dig., Habeas Corpus, E, 1.

[2] United States v. Green, 3 Mason, 482.

[3] People v. Nevins, 1 Hill (N. Y.), 159, 160.

[4] Brass Crosby's Case, 2 W. Black. 756.

fusing to do so; but where a court of first instance has jurisdiction of both the habeas corpus and an attachment issued for disobeying it, and has heard evidence as to the service of the writ of habeas corpus and disobedience of its command, its determination upon these matters is conclusive; and where the evidence heard below can not be properly brought before a higher or superior court in such a case, it will be presumed by the higher court, in its absence, that it showed a service of the writ, and such a willful disobedience or evasion of it as amounted to a contempt of the authority of the court.[1]

§ 125. **The Return should be Liberally Construed.**—This is the general doctrine now, and has long been, in the courts both of England and America. In Rex v. Bethel,[2] the court of king's bench were asked on habeas corpus to construe a return of the sheriff very strictly; but they would not. They read it liberally and intended much, to make good the commitment, which appeared to be insufficient in every respect, but which contained enough to justify the court in remanding the defendant. Justice Eyre said: "It might rid all the jails in England, if the jailer's return should be taken so strictly." This case was cited and approved by Mr. Justice Cowen, of the supreme court of New York, in The People ex rel. Ebenezer Johnson v. Thomas J. Nevins.[3] Nevins was an attorney, and had received a sum of money for his client, the plaintiff in a suit. The said plaintiff had assigned the amount to the relator, who sought the assistance of the court to compel defendant Nevins to pay the money over to him. Interrogatories and defendant's answer thereto were filed, upon which the court ordered the matter to be referred to the clerk at Albany, with directions to forthwith tax and assess the amount of the costs and expenses of the proceedings of the relator in the matter, and of the amount directed to be paid by the defendant under the order of the court, a copy of which was annexed to the interrogatories in the cause. On the filing of the report of said taxation and assessment, the court ordered and adjudged that a fine be imposed upon said Nevins, to the amount of the sum reported by the said clerk as aforesaid, to indemnify the said relator, to whom the same was ordered to be paid; and that Nevins be committed to the custody of the sheriff of the county of Erie until the sum above mentioned, and the costs and expenses of the said commitment, be paid. The clerk reported the whole

---

[1] State of Illinois v. Bradley, 60 Ill. 390.
[2] King v. Bethel, 5 Mod. 19.
[3] 1 Hill, 154.

amount due to be eight hundred and sixty dollars and sixty cents.[1]

" On this report being filed, January 11, 1839, and the above rules and report being certified by the clerk, with this caption— 'In supreme court, tenth of January, 1839'—under his hand, and delivered to the sheriff of Erie, he, the sheriff, arrested Nevins January 11th, in a public street in Albany, and committed him to the jail of Erie county. Thence he was brought before a commissioner of that county on habeas corpus; to which the sheriff returned the above-mentioned certified copies as his authority. The commissioner made an order discharging Nevins from custody; to reverse which order the relater sued out a *certiorari*, to which the commissioner returned the above proceedings before him." Justice Cowen said: " The counsel for the defendant justifies his discharge, not because this court had not jurisdiction in fact, but because it did not appear on the papers in the hands of the sheriff that it had been duly exercised; in short, because the authority or warrant to arrest and commit was formally defective. The objections are: 1. That the defendant, being out of court, could not be arrested without writ; or, if he could be arrested by rule, this was defective in not reciting and showing jurisdiction; and, 2. That the rule was irregular on its face in not being for a sum certain, nor showing a demand of the money previous to the conviction. The objections as to jurisdiction of the person, and regularity, are all answerable by general arguments showing that both must be intended; though I think that both sufficiently appear on the return. * * * The rule in this case was, in substance, that the defendant Nevins be committed to the custody of the sheriff of Erie, till he paid a fine of eight hundred and sixty dollars and sixty cents, imposed upon him by that rule. The sum for the non-payment of which a man is committed for contempt should no doubt be specified by the rule, but that may be either directly or by reference to a proceeding taken to ascertain the amount through the proper officer, whose report, on its being filed and confirmed, or not objected to, becomes the act of the court, and is then to be read as part of the rule. *Id certum est quod certum reddi potest.* Here was a return by the sheriff of the commitment and cause, which was plain enough; and even more full and certain than appears in common process, such as a *capias*. The least liberality of intendment by the commissioner would have made the case equivalent to a full re-

---

[1] Hill, 157.

cital of all the proceedings. * * * That this court has jurisdiction of the person must be intended, and this court has the power to fine, and to imprison till the fine be paid. That is ordinarily done on the defendant's answer to interrogatories and other proofs touching the matter in question. But it is not necessary to the validity of the rule that all these things should be recited on its face. Such a thing is never thought of. The rule is commonly very brief; and if it be such as this court is authorized to make under any given concourse of circumstances, all jurisdictional steps and matters of regularity are to be presumed. If there be any defect in the latter, the only course is to raise the question by motion. * * *

"Take, for instance, the little slip called a bail-piece, on which a man may be arrested, and, under a short *committitur* indorsed by a judge, incarcerated either before or after judgment, at the pleasure of his manucaptors. Would a commissioner have power, on a sheriff returning these upon a habeas corpus, to look behind them, and inquire whether the court in which the bail-piece was taken had acquired jurisdiction, or proceeded regularly? This will not be pretended. If there should be anything so irregular that the arrest and commitment were irregular and unwarranted, the course of every intelligent lawyer would be an application to the court. Who ever thought it necessary that jurisdictional steps should appear on such a piece of paper? And yet it is the most authoritative warrant for an arrest and commitment of any instrument known to the law. * * *

"Under a non-bailable attachment it is the business of the sheriff to hold the defendant in custody till he is discharged in due and ordinary course of law, bringing him before the court on the return of the writ. The defendant is sometimes, in such case, an attorney, who, as in the instance before us, is proceeded against for neglect to pay over moneys collected for his client. His name is on the roll, and so long as it is there he is legally and customarily denominated a gentleman; and because a confiding sheriff happens to treat him as such, by allowing him to go into the street, does it follow that this shall oust the court of its jurisdiction? If that be so, there is a good deal of difficulty to see how any court can sustain its jurisdiction through the course of a protracted examination. Should it adjourn to another day, the prisoner must, in the mean time, be personally removed from its presence, and peradventure be part of the time in the street. This would be fatal to jurisdiction, should he refuse voluntarily to return! The difficulty could hardly be obviated by ordering the prisoner into close custody with the sheriff or into the jail of the immediate county. And surely, on the principle in question, our right to imprison on a bail-piece would be absolutely subverted. Yet it has been supposed to continue, even though the defendant depart from the state."

After showing that attorneys are always, in term time, as much within the jurisdiction of the courts in which they are licensed, as a prisoner in custody of the sheriff or marshal; that no process was, in strictness, necessary to bring him into court; that a rule peremptory may be made against him to pay such sum as shall be taxed by the clerk, even before attachment; and that the course is first to make a rule to answer the complaint, and afterwards such ultimate rule thereon as the justice of the case may require, his honor continued: "In practice, a rule is deemed sufficiently certain in the sum to be paid, where it refers to it as yet to be ascertained by the clerk. It can not be denied that we might have ordered Mr. Nevins to be committed till he should pay a certain sum, for instance one thousand dollars, he to be discharged on paying a less sum, to be ascertained by the clerk. But it is objected, that we made the amount depend on a report subsequent. Any substantial difference is not perceived, however. In either case, the committing officer must be furnished with a copy of the report, to show on what returns he may allow the prisoner to go at large. In the case at bar, were we to lay aside all intendment, and take the rule strictly, it shows that the defendant had answered interrogatories, was heard by counsel, whereupon the reference was made, on filing the report upon which the amount of the fine was fixed, and the defendant ordered to pay accordingly, or in default thereof to be committed to the sheriff. It seems a forced and unnatural construction, to suppose that he was not all the time, during which these proceedings and orders were passing, actually within the jurisdiction of the court, receiving its directions in person or through his counsel, according to the usual course when a man is brought in on attachment."

After an elaborate review of the authorities it was shown that at common law courts of general jurisdiction had the power to commit by order, without writ, on conviction for a contempt; that the revised statutes had in no instance required courts to pursue a different practice from the common law, at least not in the institution and pursuit of the prosecution to conviction, particularly of proceedings for a contempt to enforce civil remedies, and protect the rights of parties in civil actions; that at common law the rule need not contain any recital of the proceedings; nor, indeed, set forth any specific ground of commitment, although the revised statutes certainly do require that the ground should appear; that where a cause was assigned in substance, even if it were without technical words, the commissioner in this case had no power whatever to interfere for a mere defect of form; that if disobedience to an order of court was a contempt, here was one plainly expressed, the rule mentioning a previous order to pay, which had not been complied with; that the court had raised no new principle of contempt, unwarranted by precedent, principle, or statute, which would justify the commission in pronouncing the order of the court to be a nullity; and that the commissioner was mistaken in supposing that the commitment in this case was without process. "We were told loudly," he said, "that we had violated the revised statutes, in committing by rule, and not by writ. Perhaps, if the statute has unequivocally ousted us of all authority to commit by rule, we must then, *quoad hoc*, be considered a court of inferior jurisdiction, which, it is conceded, has no power to commit, even for a contempt, without a regular warrant in writing." The learned justice then dwelt upon the revised statutes, and showed that "contempts in presence of the courts are made subjects of conviction, without previous process, and all other contempts may be pursued as at common law; that is, by rule to show cause, followed by attachment, or by attachment absolute in the first instance;" that with regard to the form of conviction, as whether by rule or not, the statute has in no way interposed, nor pretended to interpose, though it certainly had in respect to the commitment, both in civil and criminal cases; that the statute says, to enforce the performance of a duty, the order and process of commitment shall specify the act or duty to be performed, and in other cases the order and process of commitment shall specify the duration of the imprisonment; that in the case at bar the duty to be performed and the duration of the imprisonment were both specified in the rule; and that the word "process," taken even in its strictest sense, did not necessarily mean a warrant or a writ, but that it meant a good deal more—that it meant "all the proceedings in a cause after the first step;" and that it comprehended a rule or order to commit.

The court maintained the position, that whenever a commissioner sees that a prisoner is properly detained, it is his duty to remand; that is, whenever he is properly committed and held by authority of law, unless in a bailable case where bail is offered and receivable; and this whether there be a warrant in deed, that is, a formal warrant under hand and seal, or warrant in law, which means any legal authority; and that the words legal commitment mean any act of committing justifiable by the law of the land. On the whole, the court were clear that the commissioner acted in the case before them entirely without jurisdiction; and even had there been no entry at the time of the arrest, it might have been made, according to the truth of the case; and that if the imprisonment were not warrantable, they would have discharged the prisoner on motion; that proceedings like this should, in point of form, be finally judged of by the tribunal where they originate; and that the proceedings of the commissioner should be reversed, which was ordered accordingly. We do not believe that a liberal construction given to the return will come in conflict with what Lord Mansfield said in King v. Lyme Regis:[1] "It is not true that you are to presume everything against a return. You are not to presume for or against it." The peculiar facts and circumstances of a case may at times give rise to an apparent conflict, but we conceive that after close examination it will be found more imaginary than real.

§ 126. **Certainty Required in the Return.**—Though we have seen that the return should be liberally construed, the element of certainty must not be overlooked. The law requires certainty in the return; yet this is a term difficult to define. Lord Chief Justice De Gray once said: "We have no precise idea of the signification of the word, which is as indefinite in itself as any word that can be used." His lordship quoted Lord Coke as speaking of it thus: "There are three kinds of certainties: certainty to a certain intent in general; certainty to a common intent; and certainty to a certain intent in every particular." "This last is rejected in all cases as partaking of too much subtlety; the second is sufficient in defense; and the first is required in a charge or accusation."[2] Lord Coke also says that the first applies in indictments, and in counts, replications, and other pleadings of the plaintiff to convince the defendant; that the second is sufficient in a law which is to defend the party and to excuse him; and that the third applies in estoppels.[3] Justice Butler in speaking of returns to *mandamus* acknowledged that they required the same certainty as indictments, or returns to

---

[1] 1 Doug. 158.   [2] Rex v. Horne, 2 Cowp. 682.   [3] 2 Co. Lit. 303 a.

writs of habeas corpus, and that "certainty to a common intent in general" was the requirement; and he understood it to mean "what, upon a fair and reasonable construction, may be called certain, without recurring to possible facts which do not appear."[1]

One of the first principles of good pleading is to state the facts. This must be done for the purpose of informing the court whose duty it is to pass upon the law arising from a given state of facts, and apprise the opposite party of what is meant to be proved, in order to give him an opportunity to answer or traverse it. So should facts be stated clearly and tersely in an application for a writ of habeas corpus, and in the return thereto.[2] Verbosity, profuseness, and a general muddle should be avoided. This will lessen the labor of the court as well as of counsel, and enable the matter to be settled with facility. All material matters should be made the subject of distinct and positive allegation, and although minute correctness is not required, the substance of the facts necessary to justify the detention must be stated, and not left to intendment. A return to a habeas corpus, brought for the discharge of an apprentice above the age of twenty-one, stating the custom of London by which apprentices who were bound by indenture above the age of fourteen and under twenty-one were compelled to serve a full term of seven years or more, though that might extend beyond their age of twenty-one, was held insufficient; and that it must show that the apprentice was within those ages when he bound himself apprentice, for the court will not intend that from matter *dehors* the return.[3] In the Canadian Prisoners' Case,[4] Lord Chief Justice Denman thought "the court ought to be extremely careful that the facts should be truly stated to them," but he would not enter into the question as to how far the warrant was material. "I think that no such minute inquiry ought to be made upon such a subject."[5]

It is not necessary that the return set out documents which are immaterial to the validity of the imprisonment; but if such documents are set out, and have been intentionally misstated by the respondent, neither their immateriality nor the fact that the prisoner has not been injured by the falsehood will protect him

---

[1] King v. Regis, 1 Doug. 156.
[2] Id.
[3] Eden's Case, 2 Mau. & Sel. 225.
[4] 9 Ad. & El. 731; S. C., 36 Eng. Com. L. 254.
[5] 9 Ad. & El. 731; S. C., 36 Eng. Com. L. 285. The "warrant" was one set out in the return. What the learned justice said in that case, however, must be applied with caution in dealing with the defects of warrants generally; and particularly so, where these very defects are the main questions before the court.

from an attachment for contempt.[1] Where the relator is held as an insane patient, the doctor's certificate upon which he was originally received, need not be attached to the return of a habeas corpus issued in the matter.[2] So where a court of first instance has competent jurisdiction to try and punish an offense, the higher court will not assume that the sentence is invalid or unwarranted by law so long as it remains unreversed. Neither will the court require the authority of the court of first instance to pass sentence, to be set out in the return to a writ of habeas corpus. It is bound to assume, *prima facie*, that the unreversed sentence of a court of competent jurisdiction is correct.[3] A return stating a capital conviction for high treason and felony and a commutation of the sentence is sufficient without specifying the treason or felony.[4]

In an early English case where a prisoner was committed to the King's Bench prison upon a warrant which read *verbatim et literatim* that he was "committed for insolent behavior and words spoken at the council table," and which was subscribed by the lord keeper and twelve others of the council, the return was held to be insufficient and uncertain because the court to whom an application for a writ of habeas corpus was made could not tell what the words were, and could not give judgment upon them. So they advised the marshal to amend his return. The words, however, were not subsequently given, and he was bailed by the court, that an indictment or information might be drawn against him.[5] The evidence and matter of law ought to be returned; but how can such a return, made by a sheriff or marshal, who in some special cases may not be acquainted with the minute details of the cause of commitment, contain all particulars of the proceedings? One who detains another by written authority can return only that authority; and if it be insufficient, we believe the general practice and law now to be that the prisoner is, as to that special commitment, entitled to his discharge; but the court or judge hearing the application need not finally discharge him if there is reasonable cause to believe that a crime has been committed. Another return showing that prisoners were committed by virtue of an order from the lords of the council was held utterly insufficient and uncertain because it did not state what the order

---

[1] 9 Ad. & El. 731; S. C., 36 Eng. Com. L. 255.

[2] Commonwealth v. Kirkbride, 7 Phil. 1.

[3] Lord Chief Justice Denman in Brennan & Galen's Case, 10 Ad. & El., Q. B., 502.

[4] Leonard Watson's Case, 9 Ad. & El. 731; S. C., 36 Eng. Com. L. 254.

[5] Chambers' Case, 3 Cro. Car. 133.

was.¹ This return was furthermore utterly uncertain because it showed an award to prison "to remain there until further order taken."² The return in Brice's Case was held to be too general, and that it showed no special cause of commitment; for the earl of Denbigh committed him to the Oxon jail, "to remain there without bail or mainprise until he were delivered by the justices in eyre." It was pronounced absolutely void; and the court said that unless the return were amended by a certain day, they would absolutely dismiss the matter.³

The statement of the exact day when the prisoner was taken is seldom material, so it be *ante adventum brevis* and within the statute of limitations. If it be conceived material, the return may be amended; but such an uncertainty is no cause to discharge a party, if the cause of the imprisonment sufficiently appears to enable the court to declare whether the prisoner should be remanded or discharged.⁴ Under a statute where the question of distance is material in a return to a writ of habeas corpus, it should be averred with certainty,⁵ and in setting forth

---

¹ Seeles et al., 3 Cro. Car. 557. In some of the earlier cases the courts made a distinction between a commitment made by one of the privy council and one made by the whole council. In the first instance the return had to express the cause; but in the second, it was not necessary: 2 Lilly's Reg. 3, I; *vide* Case of Kendal et al., 5 Mod., p. 83.

² Seeles et al., 3 Cro. Car. 557.

³ Brice's Case, 3 Cro. Car. 593.

⁴ Hutchins v. Player, 1 Bridg. 275.

⁵ Deybel's Case, 4 Barn. & Ald. 243. The act of 59 Geo. III., c. 121, sec. 1, provided that if any foreign smuggling vessel or boat, in which there should be one or more subjects of his majesty, whether mariners or persons pretending to be passengers, should be found or discovered to have been within four leagues of that part of the coast of Great Britain which is between the North Foreland, on the coast of Kent, and Beachy-Head, on the coast of Sussex, or within eight leagues of any other part of the coast of Great Britain or Ireland, having on board any foreign brandy, etc., such vessel should be forfeited; and every such subject of his majesty who should be found on board of such vessel should be liable to all the pains and penalties, etc., in like manner as persons, being subjects of his majesty, found on board vessels liable to forfeiture, belonging wholly or in part to his majesty's subjects, are by the previous laws liable. The prisoner, an impressed seaman, was brought up by virtue of a habeas corpus, directed to the admiral of the fleet at Chatham. The return to the writ stated that on the twenty-eighth of November, 1820, a certain smuggling vessel, called the George of Flushing, on board of which were divers persons, to wit, six subjects of his majesty, being mariners, was found and discovered by the commander and crew of his majesty's revenue cruiser called the Griper, to have been and to be within eight leagues of that part of the coast of Great Britain called Suffolk, that is to say, within eight leagues of Orfordness, in the county of Suffolk, having then and there on board thereof divers large quantities of foreign spirits, etc. The return was considered insufficient by the court. They held the allegation of the return, taken altogether, to be positive that the vessel was found within eight leagues of a part of the county of Suffolk, and that while a part of the allegation was under a *videlicet*, it was nevertheless sufficiently certain. But assuming it to be so, still they could not take judicial notice of the local situation of Orfordness, and that it was necessary to have stated that

an offense it should be sufficiently stated.[1] Where a magistrate commits a party "upon due proof," etc., under a statute made and provided in a certain case, it is necessary, to insure certainty, to state distinctly what proof was given, in order that the court hearing the application for a habeas corpus may see whether it is the due proof required by the statute.[2]

Orfordness was not between the North Foreland and Beachy-Head. They would not take notice judicially, either that Orfordness may not be an isolated part of the county of Suffolk, or even if it were part of the body of that county, that it is not within eight leagues of Beachy-Head. The objections to the writ were sustained, and the prisoner discharged.

[1] Souden's Case, 4 Barn. & Ald. 294. In the return to a habeas corpus it was stated that the prisoner, who was a subject of the king of Great Britain, was duly convicted on the eleventh of September, 1820, for being found on board a certain ship or vessel, to wit, a passage vessel called The Rose in June; the said vessel being liable to forfeiture under the provisions of two acts of parliament, viz., 24 Geo. III., sess. 2, c. 46, sec. 1, and 42 Geo. III., c. 82, sec. 1, for having after the passing of those acts and of the 45 Geo. III., c. 121, been found at the fish market within the limits of the ancient town of Rye, in the county of Sussex, having on board divers large quantities of East India silk handkerchiefs, etc. The prisoner was adjudged to forfeit the sum of one hundred pounds in consequence thereof; and in default of payment he was committed to jail. The statute of 24 Geo. III., sess. 2, c. 47, enacted that if any ship or vessel should be found at anchor or hovering within the limits of any of the ports of the kingdom, or within four leagues of the coast itself, having on board any goods liable to forfeiture, such ship should be liable to forfeiture. But in this case it was only stated that the ship was found at the fish market within the limits of the ancient town of Rye, and Sergeant Lawes made the point that unless the ship were liable to forfeiture, the defendant had not incurred any penalty. The court looked upon the objection as well founded, the *corpus delicti* not being sufficiently stated, inasmuch as it was quite consistent with the return that the vessel might be in the fish market in the ancient town of Rye, but drawn up on the land, which would clearly not be a case within the statute, and discharged the prisoner.

[2] Nash's Case, 4 Barn. & Ald. 295. The return in this case stated that the prisoner was found on board a smuggling vessel liable to forfeiture, and that he was a seaman, etc. It further stated that he, being a subject of the king of Great Britain and a seafaring man, and not being only a passenger on board the vessel at the time she became liable to forfeiture, was afterwards carried before a justice, and upon due proof as by the statute in that case made and provided is required, was committed to answer such information and abide such judgment as might be given. It then proceeded to set forth an impressment and detainer as in Deybel's Case, above, to which this case was quite similar. Sargeant Lawes, for the prisoner, admitted it sufficiently stated that the vessel was liable to forfeiture under the statute, but made the point that "it is only stated that the prisoner was committed upon due proof as required by the statute; but whether such proof be or be not within the statute is a question of law. The return ought, therefore, to have stated what proof was given before the magistrate, in order that it may be ascertained whether his judgment was correct." The court held the averment to be one of a conclusion of law; because it stated that upon due proof the party was committed. "Now, whether this was so or not, this return does not enable us to judge; for unless we know what the proof was which was given, it is impossible for us to tell whether it was the proof required by the act of parliament. The circumstances stated in the introductory part of this return seem to me to be quite sufficient to warrant this commitment; and if it had been stated, that upon due proof of the matters

§ 126. THE RETURN. 165

Where a warrant of commitment by commissioners in bankruptcy, after setting out the issuing of the commission, the adjudication of bankruptcy, etc., stated, as the ground of commitment, that the bankrupt being brought before them, and they having proposed to administer an oath to him, and he refused to be sworn, or to give an account of his property, it was held that such warrant was legal; and that it was not necessary in it to set out any particular question in such a case; for a refusal to be sworn is a refusal to answer all lawful questions which the commissioners might put to him; that after the issuing of the writ of habeas corpus, and before the return to it, the commissioners might have made a fresh warrant, if necessary, stating more fully the cause for detaining the bankrupt in custody; and that such warrant might by words of inference incorporate the formal parts of the first warrant; and that even if both warrants were defective in form the court would, *ex officio*, if a substantial cause of commitment appeared, recommit the bankrupt *de novo* under the eighteenth section of the act of 5 Geo. II., c. 30.[1] A return to a writ of habeas corpus that a child under fourteen years of age was not "at the time either of the issuing or of the serving of the said writ, nor has she been at any time since, nor is she now, in any manner detained by or in their custody, power, or possession, or under the care, control, or authority of defendants, or either of them, or of any person employed by them or either of them, or acting under the control or authority of them or either of them," was held bad in an English case, and the defendants declared in contempt.[2]

The general rule in the United States is that a return to be full should deny the custody, power, possession, or control of

before mentioned, the prisoner was committed, I should have thought it sufficient." Another of the justices said: "The power of the magistrate to commit depends on the proof before him; and the rule is, that where a limited authority is given it must be shown to have been strictly pursued. Here it is only stated, that on due proof the justice committed; but he may suppose that to be due proof which is not the proof required by the statute. He ought, therefore, to state what it was, and then the court will be enabled to form a judgment whether he has judged right." The prisoner was discharged.

[1] Ex parte Page, a Bankrupt, 1 Barn. & Ald. 568.
[2] Regina v. Roberts and Mary McCarthy, 2 F. & F. 272. The defendant, Roberts, was the superintendent of the Roman Catholic School where the child was last seen, and Mary McCarthy was a school-mistress in said school. In a note to this case the reporter says of the return: "This word [detained] overrides the entire sentence, and merely denies a compulsory detention, which would be sufficient in the case of an adult, but not in the case of a child, who is not *sui juris*." He cites a case, which, however, we have been unable to find; and as the decision of the court fails further to ventilate this remarkably fine point, the reader is left to his own reflections as to why it is not a good return.

the one alleged to be detained, not only at the time of the return, but also at the service of the writ. For the court to receive any return short of this, would be to enable all who might choose to evade the writ to easily do so by simply transferring the person confined to another between its service and return; yet a full return in form will not always satisfy the conscience of the court, and fill their minds with an abiding consciousness of the certainty of all the material facts which should be disclosed.[1] The returns to the writ of habeas corpus will be watched with jealous scrutiny by the courts, particularly those referring to the custody of infants. If the conscience of the court is not satisfied, in these cases, that all the material facts are disclosed, or if there be any attempt at evasion, the return will be declared insufficient.[2]

Where imprisonment takes place on *mesne* process, the range of inquiry upon habeas corpus is simply whether the plaintiff has brought a proper suit in the proper court, and has taken all the steps in procedure which the law lays down as conditions precedent; these things appearing, the lawfulness of the custody necessarily follows, as the investigation relates to what has been done, and not to what ought to have been done; as where there was an action of trover, and the court had jurisdiction both of the person and the subject-matter, there being such an affidavit as prescribed by statute. The declaration set forth a cause of action; there was regular process and due service. The property had not been seized because the officer could not find it, and the requisite bond and security were not given by the defendant—these facts making a case of imprisonment under statute. In such case the legality of the imprisonment does not depend upon the truth of the plaintiff's affidavits, but upon the sufficiency and due verification of the material facts alleged therein, together with the substance of the declaration, the jurisdiction of the court, and the sheriff's return. Upon habeas corpus issued in behalf of one so imprisoned, the party ought to be remanded. It can not be urged that the tort complained of amounts to a felony in law, and that therefore the action of trover can not be maintained without an averment in the declaration that the wrong-doer had been prosecuted, etc., unless the commission of a larceny after trust appears with full certainty, from either the affidavit or the declaration, or from both together.[3]

---

[1] State v. Philpot, Dudley (Ga.), 58.
[2] U. S. v. Green, 3 Mason, 482; Com. ex rel. Lowry v. Reed, 59 Pa. St. 425.
[3] The State ex rel. Lynch v. Bridges, Jailer, et al., 64 Ga. 146. In this case a declaration in trover at common law was filed on the eighteenth of No-

§ 127. Warrant Need not Always be Returned.

A statute may require that after a criminal has been sentenced to confinement in a penitentiary, a warrant of commitment shall be signed by the judge, justice, or magistrate giving the sen-

vember, 1878, by a corporation, the Southern Express Company, charging the relator, Lynch, with converting and disposing of, to his own use, certain personal property, consisting of a certain package done up in buff paper, and having written thereon "$25,000, Reeves, Nicholson & Co., Athens, Ga.," the same being sealed with wax, having the initials " G. W. W. & Co." stamped thereon, measuring about ten inches in length by seven and a half inches in width and about six and a half inches in depth, and shipped by George W. Williams & Co., of Charleston, South Carolina. An original affidavit in the case made by Hugh Dempsey, the superintendent and agent of, and acting in behalf of, the corporation, showed that the said personal property had been delivered to the relator, Lynch, on the fifth day of November, 1878, as a messenger between Port Royal and Augusta, to be brought by him to Augusta, Georgia, for transmission to Athens, Georgia, and that the same had not been, prior to the filing of the declaration in trover, transmitted by him or delivered to the Southern Express Company, and that the same was still in the possession and under the control of the said Walter S. Lynch. Bail was put at fifty thousand dollars. An original declaration and copy were placed in the sheriff's hands, whose action was set forth in the original writ as follows: "Served a copy of the within petition and process and copy of the affidavit on the defendant, Walter S. Lynch; arrested him at the same time, and not being able to give bond and not producing the property, I put him in jail this eighteenth day of November, 1878, in the custody of Theodore C. Bridges, jailer. Charles H. Sibley, Sheriff Richmond Co." The original papers were first lodged with the jailer, but withdrawn, and the following paper deposited with the jailer when the originals were returned to court: "The Southern Express Company v. Walter S. Lynch. Trover and bail. April term, 1879, Richmond superior court. Sum sworn to, $25,000. The defendant, having been this day served with a copy of the petition, process, and bail affidavit in the above-stated case, was arrested by me, and on failure to enter into recognizance for the forthcoming of the property sued for, and being unable to find that property myself, or to seize and take possession thereof, I now, pursuant to the requirements of the law, commit him to jail, to be kept in safe and close custody until the property sued for is produced, or until he shall enter into bond, with good security, for the eventual condemnation money. Charles H. Sibley, Sheriff Richmond Co., November 18, 1878." On February 10, 1879, Mrs. Elizabeth M. Lynch, as wife of Walter S. Lynch, petitioned Judge Snead of the superior court at chambers, for a writ of habeas corpus, alleging a number of grounds to show that the arrest and confinement was illegal. The jailer returned, as the cause of commitment, the paper lodged by the sheriff, and justified his confinement of relator solely under the act of December 13, 1820. He prayed that the city council of Augusta, or the sheriff of Richmond county, and the Southern Express Company, be made parties, for various reasons; and upon the filing of the return the court ordered that the sheriff, Charles H. Sibley, and the Southern Express Company be made parties, but the request to have the city council also made a party was refused. The sheriff then answered, adopting the return of the jailer, and that he also, on the eighteenth day of November, 1878, personally served the defendant, Walter S. Lynch, with a copy of the petition and process and bail affidavit in the case, and that his return upon the original papers to April term, 1879, of Richmond superior court, was correct and true. The Southern Express Company also adopted the answer of the jailer. The petitioner's attorneys then filed a traverse to the answers of the jailer and express company, but accepted the answer of the sheriff as true, and contested the sufficiency of the causes set forth in the answer of the said Bridges, the jailer, on the grounds that "the affidavit for bail in said action was not

tence, or by the clerk of the court; and, on habeas corpus to inquire into the cause of detention of one confined in a penitentiary, it may be claimed that no such warrant was signed in his case or held by the keeper of the penitentiary, and that the

filed in the clerk's office of the court to which said petition was returnable, to wit, the superior court of said county, and a copy thereof affixed to the original petition and the copy thereof; and because the copy of the original petition, affidavit, and process was not served upon Walter S. Lynch by the sheriff or other lawful officer, but was served upon him (if such an act can be called a service) by being handed to him by Hugh Dempsey, who was neither the sheriff nor other lawful officer." Prior to the commencement of the suit the express company, through Hugh Dempsey, its superintendent, made a proper and formal demand upon said Lynch for the money. The bill of exceptions in the case recited some of the facts already mentioned. Upon the issue joined by the traverse to the jailer's return, the petitioner offered evidence to disprove the statement made in the original affidavit of the superintendent of the express company, Hugh Dempsey, for bail, or bond and security, "that the same [the personal property sued for] is in the possession and under the control of the said Walter S. Lynch," and to show that the same was lost or stolen from the possession, custody, or control of the said Walter S. Lynch while in the employ of the Southern Express Company, November 5, 1878, evidence of which was in the possession of the maker of said affidavit, prior to and at the time of the making of said affidavit, and that said property had not been in the possession, custody, or control of the said Walter S. Lynch since that time. Petitioner offered also to prove that the failure to deliver said personal property to the plaintiff on demand, or surrender or point out the same for seizure by the sheriff, was due alone to the inability of the said Walter S. Lynch to comply therewith on account of the loss or theft as aforesaid. That he did not enter into there-cognizance provided for by law, solely because that by reason of his poverty he was unable to give such a bond. This was all repelled by the court, which announced that it would only receive evidence as to whether or not the Southern Express Company, as plaintiff in said action, had prosecuted the defendant under section 2970 of the code, or alleged a good excuse for its failure to prosecute. The petitioner thereupon put in evidence the admission of the plaintiff, that it had not prosecuted the defendant, the original declaration with affidavit attached, and accepted in lieu of said original affidavit, and the demand made by plaintiff upon the defendant prior to the filing of said suit, to be found in the brief of the evidence. The respondent Bridges and the Southern Express Company offered the commitment from the sheriff, under which the defendant was held after the withdrawal of the declaration, etc. The judge refused to discharge the prisoner, whereupon a bill of exceptions was sued out by Elizabeth M. Lynch, and error was assigned on several grounds, among which was the following: "3. Because the court erred in deciding that section 2970 of the code was limited to physical injuries, and did not apply to torts to property, although such torts amounted to a felony, as defined by the code of this state, and that therefore, although the record in said case made out a *prima facie* case of larceny after trust, which was a felony as defined by the code of Georgia, it was not incumbent upon the said Southern Express Company, as plaintiff in said action, to prosecute for the same, or to allege a good excuse for the failure to so prosecute, and that plaintiff could maintain said civil action without being 'either simultaneously, or concurrently, or previously' prosecuted for the same, or alleging a good excuse for the failure so to prosecute." When this case was called a motion to dismiss the writ of error was submitted, upon the ground that the wife of the prisoner was not herself entitled to a review of the decision by bill of exceptions, the prisoner not complaining. And because the acknowledgment of service was simply signed by "Frank H. Miller and J. S. & W. T. Davidson, attorneys for respondents," not showing that all of

prisoner is entitled to his discharge. But if the petition for the writ contain no allegation that the relator is detained without a proper warrant of commitment, and the writ does not command the keeper to return the warrant or other instrument under or by virtue of which he detains the relator, but simply commands him to return the cause of his imprisonment and detention, the certified minutes of the court, showing the sentence imposed, will be a sufficient answer to the writ, and sufficiently show the cause of the detention. Even under such a statute the relator is not detained or required to be detained by virtue of any warrant. In the language of Mr. Justice Earl, of the court of appeals of New York, with reference to such a case: "He was detained by virtue of the judgment of the court, and that judgment was a sufficient authority for his detention. The warrant of commitment is simply an authority and direction to the sheriff or other officer to convey the prisoner to the penitentiary. That need not necessarily be left with the keeper. If he has no other evidence of his authority to detain the prisoner, he should have that. But if the officer who brings a prisoner to the penitentiary furnishes the keeper with a certified copy of the judgment of the court, then that is sufficient evidence of the keeper's authority, and he need have no other. A prisoner who has been properly and legally sentenced can not be released simply because there is an imperfection in what is commonly called the *mittimus*. A proper *mittimus* can, if needed, be supplied at any time, and if the prisoner is safely in the proper custody, there is no office for a *mittimus* to perform." This was concurred in by the full court.[1]

§ 128. **The Return may be Amended.**—Under the earlier practice in England this was the rule, but it was applied to the return before the filing thereof. After it was read and filed, it could not be amended, for it had then become a record of the court.[2] Any defect in form, or averment in fact, or the want

the parties respondent were represented in such acknowledgment. The record failed to disclose that any of such respondents had been represented by other and different counsel in the court below. The motion was overruled, the court holding that "when the wife of a prisoner sues out a habeas corpus she can bring a writ of error upon the final decision made on the hearing of the habeas corpus," and that "an acknowledgment of service on a bill of exceptions, by counsel signing as attorneys for 'respondents,' will be construed as evidence of service on all the respondents, where the record fails to show that any of the respondents were represented by different counsel in the court below." The supreme court decided that the motion to dismiss the writ of error was not well taken on either of the grounds, and affirmed the judgment of the lower court.

[1] The People ex rel. Trainor, Appellant, v. Samuel Baker, Keeper etc., Respondent, 89 N. Y. 460.

[2] 2 Lilly's Reg. 2, D.

thereof, could be so amended, but it was at the peril of the officer making the amendment, in the same manner as if the return were originally what it was after amendment.[1] The warrant omitting the words for which one was committed for contempt was a subject of amendment.[2] So with the return of the day on which the prisoner was taken. Were the exact day conceived to be material, a party might move for an amendment of the return.[3] Where a return which should have shown that an apprentice was between fourteen and twenty-one years of age when he bound himself failed to do so, the court, after hearing, would neither intend it to be so nor allow the return to be amended, saying, they "had never known an instance of amending a return of this sort."[4] In the return to a writ of habeas corpus sued out by a bankrupt committed by commissioners in bankruptcy for not giving satisfactory answers on his examination, the questions put to the bankrupt and the full warrant should be set out. And in a case where the omission of a part of the commissioners' warrant and all of the questions was made in a return, Lord Chancellor Eldon said: "There was no doubt that if the committal corresponded with the return, it is as bad as any committal can be; and unquestionably the jailer ought to set forth in this return the whole of the questions put to the bankrupt, and the bankrupt's answers, as they appear in the warrant of the commissioners. But it would be a strong thing to say, that the merits of a committal are to be tried merely by the return to the writ, however erroneous that return may be. If such were the rule, then the person who makes the return to the writ would, in fact, by making a return short of the truth, assume to himself the power of discharging a prisoner who may have been properly committed. On the other hand, there is this inconvenience, that a prisoner may be improperly detained while time is spent in amending the return, or in calling for further information."[5] In this case, his lordship stated that he had consulted with the lord chief justice of the king's bench; and the opinion of the lord chief justice was: "That the chancellor could and should order the jailer to amend his return, by annexing thereto a copy of the warrant of the commissioners or the warrant itself; that it seemed very manifest, in this case, that the whole of the warrant was not set forth in the return; and that the question might be put to the jailer in court, 'Whether it was or was not fully set forth?'"

[1] Anon., 1 Mod. 103.
[2] Chambers' Case, 3 Cro. Car. 133.
[3] Hutchins v. Player, 1 Bridg. 275.
[4] Ex parte Eden, 2 Mau. & Sel. 229.
[5] In the Matter of Power and Jackson, 2 Russ. 583.

The rigor of the old English rule was, however, relaxed in Leonard Watson's case.[1] There a prayer for an amendment of the return was granted after the return was filed—not as varying the nature of the case, but because it was not fit or decent that a false statement should remain on the files of the court. The court could not see that the amendment prejudiced the prisoner, but thought that it rather tended to aid him. They left it open to Watson to state any fact upon affidavit which would show that the amendment ought not to be made, but this not being done, the amendment was ordered.[2] A return to a *habeas corpus cum causa*, made by the warden of the Fleet, stating that a prisoner was committed to his custody " upon the following order," and then setting out an order purporting to be made by the master of the rolls, was held insufficient, as not directly averring by whom the order was made. It was simply a written paper, without stating from what quarter it came; and although there was no question whence it really came in fact, the court held that the return ought to be good in itself, and allowed it to be amended after the filing thereof, and without the consent of the prisoner.[3]

But even where the power exists to allow returns to be amended, the court will not always allow it to be done. Where a prisoner is brought up on a writ of habeas corpus, and the return shows a commitment bad upon the face of it, the court will not, on the suggestion that the conviction is good, adjourn the case for the purpose of having the conviction brought and amending the commitment by it. Under these circumstances, where all the parties are before the court, and the committing magistrate, though served with notice, appears by counsel, but fails to produce the conviction before the court, it will discharge the prisoner.[4]

The practice in this country is to allow an amendment of the return at any time before the case is finally disposed of, when

---

[1] 9 Ad. & El. 731; S. C., 38 Eng. Com. L. 285; 1 Per. & Dav. 516.

[2] The complaint was that the jailer stated that Watson was named in the warrant in one of the steps of the transaction, when, in fact, his name did not appear in the operative part at all, and it appeared by affidavit that the omission of the name was unknown to the jailer. The prisoner's name was omitted in the mandatory part of the letters patent addressed to the master of the bark, though it stood in the recital. The court considered the jailer blamable for negligence, but refused an attachment against him. It would not say that he was free from blame in receiving, under what he treated as a warrant, the body of a man which the warrant did not instruct him to receive, but from the facts in the case it appeared that he had no intention of imposing upon the court.

[3] In re Clarke, 2 A. & El., Q. B., 619; S. C., 2 Gale & Dav. 786.

[4] Re Timson, L. R., 5 Exch., 257.

it is deemed by the court to be subservient to the ends of justice.[1] The liberality of our courts in allowing pleadings in civil actions to be amended before judgment is also found in the summary proceedings under habeas corpus, and we apprehend that any defect in the return which may be amended or remedied by further motion may be so cured, upon application to the court.[2] The matter has doubtless been settled by statute in many of the states; and the reader is left for further information to the statutes of his own individual state.

§ 129. **Whether Return may be Fortified by Affidavit.** It was early held in England, that the return to a habeas corpus of privilege should not be taken so strictly as other pleadings were, and that the court ought not to be tied up wholly to the matter appearing upon the record, but that the return might be supplied and supported by evidence of fact, record, custom, or the like. If it appeared to the court *in rei veritate*, either implicitly upon the return, or otherwise per matter *dehors*, that there was cause to proceed below, it might grant a *procedendo*.[3] Chief Justice Hardwicke objected to the practice, as irregular, of supplying by affidavits what ought to appear on the face of the return, but the court of king's bench, over which he presided, allowed a general *paratum habeo* returned to a habeas corpus issued to bring up an infant between thirteen and fourteen years of age, who was in the custody of his aunt, but which did not specify any reason in the return for keeping him from his father, to be supplied by affidavits.[4] The later English practice admits the fortification of the return by affidavits. On the return which sets forth a warrant of committal imperfectly, the whole warrant may be shown on affidavit by those opposed to the prisoner's discharge.[5] The return to the writ, however, imports verity, and it is not necessary to prove it, and it need not be supported by affidavit or otherwise until it is impeached.[6] The return will be held evasive and bad if it is ambiguous upon its face, unless it is fortified by affidavit.[7]

In the courts of the United States there is great freedom allowed in the use of affidavits—probably more than this particular class of evidence deserves. In a late case the court, upon

---

[1] In the Matter of Hopson, 40 Barb. 40; Hurd on Habeas Corpus, 2d ed., 257, 258.
[2] People v. Cavanagh, 2 Park. Cr. 658.
[3] Hutchins v. Player, 1 Bridg. 285.
[4] King v. Smith, 7 Mod. 235.
[5] In the Matter of Power and Jackson, 2 Russ. 583; Ex parte Clarke, 2 Gale & Dav. 780; S. C., 2 Ad. & El., Q. B., 619.
[6] Queen v. Batchelder, 1 Per. & Dav. 516; S. C., 9 Ad. & El. 731; 36 Eng. Com. L. 285.
[7] Regina v. Roberts et al., 2 F. & F. 272.

appeal from a judgment on habeas corpus, went so far as to allow a district attorney to show, by his affidavit, that the relator had been convicted and sentenced under a particular statute, where the minutes of the court below, furnished to the keeper, imperfectly described the crime of which the relator was convicted. They held that the keeper could, upon the return to the writ, show by the records of the court what the precise crime was, and thus that the sentence was regular and legal, and the detention thereby authorized; that it is the judgment of the court which authorizes the detention, and which may always be shown in justification of it, but that it can not be shown by parol evidence, and must be proved by the records of the court; and that if the records are imperfect, they may be amended so as to conform to the actual facts. They said it would have been most proper, upon the hearing of the return to the writ, to have produced or proved the records of the court by a certified copy thereof, and indeed, it was required if insisted upon by the relator; but, so long as the form of proof offered by the district attorney was not objected to, and it did not appear to have been objected to, the court was authorized to hold it sufficient and to act upon it.[1]

§ 130. **When Petitioner can not be Held by Virtue of the Warrant.**—Where the return shows that the petitioner has been confined under a void judgment of a court of competent jurisdiction, he can not be legally restrained of his liberty under the warrant issued at the commencement of the proceedings against him. The reasons for this, as expressed by Mr. Justice McKinstry of California, in a very recent case, are that, after judgment, "the sheriff has the body of petitioner as jailer, not in his capacity as arresting officer. This is not a case in which a party is held under illegal restraint, and another person, or the same in a distinct capacity, is legally entitled to his custody. Here the warrant, if any was issued, has discharged its function. Its office was to give to the court, by its officer, unless bail was given, the control of the defendent arrested, that he might be tried and be present for judgment and execution. When a judgment was pronounced, the court took the defendant from the sureties or sheriff, as the case might be, and placed him in jail. As the sureties on a bail bond would be discharged when a judgment was rendered—although not such a judgment as would authorize the jailer to keep the defendant in prison, because the

---

[1] People ex rel. Trainor, Appellant, v. Baker, Keeper etc., Respondent, 89 N. Y. 460.

law does not intend that the liabilities of the sureties shall depend upon the validity or invalidity of the judgment—so the arresting officer, as arresting officer, is fully protected by a judgment of the court of which he is the minister, whether the court regularly pursues its jurisdiction in rendering the judgment or not, from the time that he surrenders the person of his prisoner in accordance with the terms of the judgment."[1]

§ 131. **On What Return the Writ will be Dismissed.**—On the return of an officer to a writ of habeas corpus, showing that, at the time of the service of the writ, he had not the body of the petitioner in his custody, or under his power or restraint; and that the petitioner, by his own voluntary act, had answered the demands of the commitment by virtue of which he had been in custody, by giving a bail bond as required by law, to appear and answer to any indictment which might be found against him at the next term of the district court of the proper county, the writ will be dismissed.[2] This rests on the principle that, to entitle one to release on habeas corpus, there must be more than a mere moral restraint, and that there must be a duress or restraint, whereby he is prevented from exercising the liberty of going when and where he pleases, whether it be by an officer of the law or a private individual; from which it follows that persons discharged on bail will not be considered so restrained of their liberty as to entitle them to the writ directed to their bail. If a party has been entirely released from custody previous to the service of the writ, its object and purpose have been accomplished, and the court will take no order on the subject. The only object of the writ is to relieve the party detained from the illegal restraint; and if this has been accomplished before the jurisdiction of the court attaches by the service of the writ, there is nothing upon which it can attach. It is not the object of the writ, or its intention, to punish the respondent, or afford the party redress for his illegal detention.[3]

If it appears by a return to a writ of habeas corpus that the prisoner in whose behalf it is issued is detained by virtue of the final judgment or decree of a court of competent jurisdiction, either civil or criminal, the general rule is that the officer or judge or court before whom the writ is returnable will forthwith remand him, and dismiss the writ. We do not know that this rule is always infallible, and we shall have more to say of it

---

[1] Ex parte Bernert, 7 Pac. C. L. J. 460.
[2] Ter. of Kan. ex rel. Goss, Agt., v. Cutler, 1 McCahon, 152.
[3] Ex parte Coupland, 26 Tex. 386; Com. v. Chandler, 11 Mass. 83.

in treating of the impeachment of judgments on habeas corpus.[1] In every case where process regular upon its face has been issued from a United States court having power to issue process of such a nature, the officer, while acting thereunder, is fully protected against any interference from state authorities while so acting; and a state court, when judicially informed of the existence of the process, can not go behind the same to make any further inquiry. The state court can not continue the proceedings; and it will remand the prisoner, or direct him to remain in the charge of the United States officer, and discharge the writ of habeas corpus.[2] The remanding of the prisoner, however, does not depend upon any principles of "comity," as expressed by the Wisconsin court in Booth's Case, but because the prisoner is within the exclusive domain of another jurisdiction—that of the government of the United States. He being held under what in truth purports to be the authority of the United States, its validity must be determined by the constitution and laws of the United States. It is for the courts or judicial officers of the federal government alone to grant him release.[3] This being law, the prisoner's remedy is direct and plain. He may apply to a judge or court of the United States to ascertain the lawfulness of his imprisonment and the authority by which he is held, whether the officer is really acting under the authority of the United States, etc. They have unquestionable power to afford him adequate relief in a proper case.[4]

§ 132. **When Court will Immediately Discharge the Prisoner.**—If it clearly appears upon the return that the wrong person has been arrested and deprived of his liberty, the court will immediately interpose for his relief, and in doing what "appertains to justice" they will order the party to be discharged from imprisonment.[5] So a state judge has no jurisdiction to issue a writ of habeas corpus for a prisoner in custody of an officer of the United States, if the fact of such custody is known to him before issuing the writ. It is well settled, that if upon the return of the writ it appears that the prisoner is in custody under the authority of the United States, the jurisdiction of the state judge is at an end, and all further proceedings by him are

---

[1] People v. Mary Shea, 3 Park. Cr. 562.
[2] Ableman v. Booth, 21 How. 506; Ex parte Hill, 5 Nev. 154; In the Matter of Hopson, 40 Barb. 34; In re Sherman M. Booth, 3 Wis. 2; Tarble's Case, 13 Wall. 397.
[3] Tarble's Case, 13 Wall. 397.
[4] In the Matter of Hopson, 40 Barb. 34.
[5] Respublica v. Jailer of the City and County of Philadelphia, 2 Yeates, 258.

void. Therefore a federal judge or court, upon the return of a habeas corpus, setting up an imprisonment under state process regular on its face, may receive evidence as to the facts connected with such imprisonment; and if it appear that the prisoner is, in fact, held for an act done or omitted in the performance of official duty, under the constitution or a law of the United States, or a treaty, etc., the court will order his discharge immediately. Where the sheriff admits in his oral evidence, if not in his affidavit, that he was notified when a writ of habeas corpus was placed in his hands that the persons having the custody of the prisoners were deputy marshals, and held the prisoners under the authority of the United States, the power of the sheriff ends with a knowledge of such fact, and though the writ be valid, he does wrong in attempting the service thereof. As an officer sworn to support the constitution of the United States, he is under no legal obligation to serve it, and can incur no liability for refusing to do so. His return of the fact that the prisoners are held by the paramount authority of the United States is a complete justification for not even serving the writ.[1]

§ 133. **Enlarging Time for Return of Writ.**—Under certain circumstances the court will extend the time for returning the writ. One of them may be illustrated by the following example: A habeas corpus was directed to Mr. Clarke, who was the keeper of a private mad-house at Clapton, in England, commanding him to bring up the body of Mrs. Anne Hunt, who was kept confined in his house. At the proper time for considering the matter the solicitor general moved to return the writ, at the same time offering an affidavit from Dr. Monro, importing "that about nine months ago he was applied to by Mrs. Threlkeld, Mrs. Hunt's daughter, for his advice and assistance concerning Mrs. Hunt, as a person disordered in her senses; and that thereupon he recommended her to the care of the said William Clarke, who keeps a private mad-house, and is accustomed to have the care of such unfortunate persons; and that she is still in the custody of the said William Clarke, upon the same occasion; that from the time of her being so placed under the care of the said William Clarke to this time, the said Anne Hunt hath appeared and is yet, in his judgment, a lunatic, and is now in so disordered a state of mind, that she is not fit to be brought into this court; that he is informed, and verily believes, that a

---

[1] Ex parte Sifford, Marshal, et al., 5 Am. Law Reg. 659; Ableman v. Booth, 21 How. 506, 523; Ex parte Robinson, 6 McLean, 355; Ex parte Jenkins, 2 Wall. jun. 521; In re Neill, 8 Blatchf. 156; Tarble's Case, 13 Wall. 397.

commission of lunacy will shortly be issued against the said Anne Hunt; and that the same hath been deferred on no other account but because of the late minority of Anne Bowen, the granddaughter and one of the next akin of the said Anne Hunt; which said Anne Hunt is now come of age, as the doctor hath been informed and believes." Lord Mansfield proposed "to put this matter into another method, viz., to use this affidavit of Dr. Monro as a reason for enlarging the time to return the writ," instead of actually filing it then. So the solicitor took back the writ and return, and the court enlarged the time for making the return until the next term, conceiving that the contemplated proceedings were for Mrs. Hunt's benefit and advantage.[1]

§ 134. **Full Answer to Return.**—Where express authority is given by a statutory act to a petitioner to deny, under oath, any of the material facts set forth in the return, and to allege any fact to show that the detention is in contravention of the constitution or any law of the United States, it should properly be done after the return is made and in the court of first instance. But instead of waiting until the return is made, and then making answer to it, if petitioner anticipates the return and sets forth a response to it in his petition, an objection on this account will not prevail in the appellate court, especially where it is not made in the court of first instance, or in the appellate court until the attention of counsel subsequent to the hearing is called to it by the appellate court—if the allegations of the petition are full and explicit to the point, and are also made under oath.[2]

§ 135. **Jailer may Substitute Return Prepared by Counsel for his Own**, where his own is defective, where peculiar skill is required in the making thereof, and where the jailer is ready to assent to any statement consistent with what he deems to be true, and which will amount to a sufficient return in law.[3]

§ 136. **Objections to the Return.**—It has been held in England that on the return to a habeas corpus alleging that the prisoner is detained as a deserter under the statute of 5 & 6 Vict., c. 12, sec. 22, it must be expressly shown that the party is a soldier, and ought to be with his corps. This objection is fatal to the return unless these matters appear upon the face of

---

[1] Rex v. Clarke, 3 Burr. 1362.
[2] Seavey et al. v. Seymour, 3 Cliff. 455.
[3] Leonard Watson's Case, 9 Ad. & El. 731; S. C., 36 Eng. Com. L. 254; 1 Per. & Dav. 516.

it, and if they fail to appear, the party must be discharged.[1] The return on a commitment for contempt is not objectionable because it fails to show a warrant for the caption or detainer.[2] A warrant under the statute of 3 Geo. IV., c. 88, sec. 3, was issued for the apprehension of a defaulter, by commissioners of taxes of Cambridge district. Upon a habeas corpus, it was returned as the cause of detainer by the keeper of the jail at Cambridgeshire. It was backed by two justices of the peace outside of Cambridge district, and the objection was raised that the party was arrested outside of Cambridge district, illegally detained by virtue of a warrant executed out of the jurisdiction of the persons who had issued it. The court would not sustain the objection, however; for although it was conceded that the two indorsements were not proper, because it was not a warrant of a justice of the peace, there was nothing to show that he was not taken within the borough of Cambridge, within which the commissioners had power to act, as appeared on the face of their own proceeding, which was not controverted. No objection was made to the form of the warrant, and no affidavits were filed. It was assumed that this warrant was issued by persons competent to issue it within the borough of Cambridge, and that the person in whose hands it was put to execute had authority to do so in Cambridge, to which their jurisdiction extended. Nothing appearing to show the contrary of his being so taken, the prisoner was remanded.[3]

An application was made to bring up Mary Ann Davis on habeas corpus, that she might be discharged from certain indentures of apprenticeship, entered into between herself and Edward Whitehouse, by which she bound herself to him as an apprentice for seven years. She was described therein as of the age of fourteen, but was in fact over seventeen years old at the time of the binding; and was at the time of the application over twenty-one—the indenture still subsisting. The application was grounded upon the principle that infants could not be

---

[1] In the Matter of Douglas, 3 Ad. & El., Q. B., 825. Section 22 of said act contains the term "soldier," by which is clearly meant a common soldier. That the party is a soldier, and that he ought to be with his corps, are facts the statement of which are necessary to give the justice jurisdiction.

[2] Wilson's Case, 7 Ad. & El., Q. B., 984.

[3] Ex parte Sharpe, 9 Dowl. 513.

The counsel in this case opposed to the application cited the following authorities to show that a prisoner should not be discharged because the original taking was outside of the jurisdiction of the court hearing the matter: Ex parte Scott, 9 Barn. & Cress. 446; Canadian Prisoners' Case, 5 Mee. & W. 32; S. C., Queen v. Batchelder, 1 Per. & Dav. 516; Ex parte Krans, 1 Barn. & Cress. 258; which will be found as cited.

bound by indentures of apprenticeship beyond twenty-one; but that they might dissent from them after they arrived at that age. As reported, Chief Justice Kenyon, the other judges concurring, rendered the opinion of the court in this language: "It is clear that the apprentice must be discharged. Every indenture of an infant is voidable at his election; and in such cases the master must trust to the covenant of those who engage for the infant. But where the binding is under the authority of an act of parliament, that takes away the power of electing to vacate the indentures. But I know of no act which prohibits the party in a case like the present to make such election upon her coming of age. According to the argument of the counsel against the rule, an infant who improvidently bound himself until the age of fifty and upwards would be bound to serve till that time; but it is impossible to support such a proposition. This apprentice ought not to have been bound longer than till she was twenty-one; and we ought now to discharge her."[1] The criticism of the report of Mary Davis' case does not commend itself to our understanding. What force and effect would the judgment of the court have in simply discharging the party out of the custody of her master, if he were immediately allowed to compel her to comply with her indentures, and keep her under his control until she was twenty-four years old? The law will do no idle acts, and this would appear to us to be

---

[1] Ex parte Mary Ann Davis. 5 T. R. 715. The principle that the court of king's bench could, on habeas corpus, discharge an apprentice from his indentures was not approved by that court in a decision rendered some twelve years subsequently to the one in the case under consideration. This disavowal of such power is found in Ex parte Gill, 7 East, 376; where it is said by the court that there was a mistake respecting this principle, in the report of Davis' case; "the judgment of the court there being that the apprentice should be discharged out of the custody of her master, in whose custody she was then brought up before the court." Gill's case was this: An apprentice had bound himself at the age of eighteen to serve until he was twenty-five. After he was twenty-one years of age he was committed to a house of correction upon a conviction before two magistrates founded on the statute of 20 Geo. II., c. 19, at the suit of his master for a misdemeanor in absenting himself from his service. On habeas corpus brought, the body and conviction were returned; and the objection was raised to the return by prisoner's counsel that the indentures which had been been executed by him when an infant were not binding upon him after he came of age, but that he might elect to avoid them, as he had done before the offense alleged. The court overruled the objection, saying in substance, that, if well founded, the circumstances laid before the court by affidavit would be matter of defense against the charge before the magistrates, but the court could not examine them; that if the defense had been properly made before the magistrates, and they had disregarded it, the party had a remedy against them; but that the court had no authority to direct that the apprentice should be discharged from his indentures; and were bound, by the return of a regular conviction, where no objection appears upon the face of the return, to remand the party.

one. Lord Kenyon's decision appears plain, and we believe is good law. The action in Gill's case, so far as concerned the return of a regular conviction, was correct enough; but it must have appeared to the court that the infant could avoid his indentures after reaching the age of twenty-one; and if so, why was not the conviction void? And if void, the apprentice was restrained without authority of law. And being held without authority of law, why could not the court, as in Davis' case, release him from imprisonment? The impeachment of judgments, however, will be treated in another chapter, where we shall give the matter extended consideration.[1]

In bankrupt proceedings, the bankrupt is not bound to answer a question that has a tendency to accuse him of a criminal act, but he must submit to the consequence of the refusal being unsatisfactory to his examiners. He can not object to answering a question which tends to criminate another.[2] In the Canadian Prisoners' Case, it was held that the return was not bad for any of the following objections: "That the prisoner was not a convict, and therefore could not be transported; that there was no judgment of transportation; that the colonial legislature could not authorize transportation *intra fines* of another territory; that the condition of the pardon being transportation for fourteen years, to commence from the prisoner's arrival at Van Dieman's land was bad for uncertainty; that the transportation had miscarried for want of a continued authority from the governor of Upper Canada throughout the intermediate places between that province and Liverpool; or that the various documents referred to, and especially the letters-patent, under which the prisoner was detained by the party making the return, were not set out."[3]

In the courts of the United States the general doctrine is, that "when the imprisonment is under process, valid on its face, it will be deemed *prima facie* legal, and the prisoner must assume the burden of impeaching it by showing a want of jurisdiction in the magistrate or court whence it emanated." If he fail in thus impeaching it, his body is to be remanded to custody. Error, irregularity, or want of form is no objection. Nor is any defect which may be amended by further entry or motion.[4] An affidavit in pursuance of which a warrant of arrest is issued is

---

[1] See chapter on Assailing Judgments by Habeas Corpus.
[2] Ex parte Oliver, 2 Ves. & B. 244.
[3] Queen v. Batchelder, 1 Per. & Dav. 516; S. C., 9 Ad. & El. 731; 36 Eng. Com. L. 285.
[4] 3 Hill, 661, note 31; People v. Cavanagh, 2 Park Cr. 650; People ex rel. Trainor, Appellant, v. Samuel N. Baker, Keeper, etc., Respondent, 89 N. Y. 460.

of but little value, if it is alleged to be upon information merely. It should state facts within the knowledge of the party making it. But on an application for a writ of habeas corpus it is too late to raise this objection to an affidavit, or warrant of arrest on a criminal charge, after the prisoner has been examined and an order of commitment has been made by the committing magistrate, if it appear upon the examination that there is probable cause to suppose that the prisoner has been guilty of a felony. The only period at which the defendant can avail himself of any defect in such an affidavit, is previous to the examination and final order of commitment.[1] After commitment, a court, on habeas corpus, will merely look into the sheriff's return, which contains the warrant by virtue of which a relator is held; and also into the affidavits contained in the traverse, and upon which the judge issued the warrant, so far as to see that the judge had colorable jurisdiction. If the warrant upon which the relator is imprisoned is regular upon its face, and *prima facie* sufficient to justify the imprisonment, and if the affidavits upon which the warrant was issued have a tendency to show to the court that there was at least colorable proof upon which the judge or justice in awarding the process might exercise his judgment, it will remand the prisoner.[2] No objection to additional clauses in an order of commitment, and which neither enlarge nor diminish the powers of the trial court to which the prisoners have been committed, can be taken and sustained, if the order be sufficient in substance. The unnecessary matter will be regarded as mere surplusage.[3]

§ 137. **Failure, or to Make an Evasive, False, or Insufficient Return, is a Contempt of Court.**—Over two hundred years ago Chief Justice Lord Hale said that an indictment would lie against a man for a false return upon a habeas corpus.[4] The rule is not so strict at present, however, and the summary process of commitment for contempt in later times has proved to be fully adequate to the efficacy of the great writ of habeas corpus. In the earlier English practice the courts would also punish for a contempt in not yielding obedience to the writ; but they would do nothing of the kind until an *alias* and a *pluries* had been issued. Commitments under the present practice, in both England and America, may be made after refusal and attachment to comply with the first writ.[5] The English

[1] People v. Smith, 1 Cal. 1.
[2] In the Matter of Prime, 1 Barb. 340.
[3] People v. Smith et al., 1 Cal. 9.
[4] Sir Robert Viner's Case, Freem. K. B. & C. P. 389, 401, 522.
[5] Wyatt's Reg. 215.

court of chancery issued the process of contempt for the purpose of enforcing obedience to writs of habeas corpus, and applied the process in the same manner in which it was applied in other cases. The legal principle upon which the processes of attachment and contempt rest is: "That disobeying the king's writ is a contempt, and equally a contempt to disobey the first as the last."[1] Even in the thirty-third year of George III. an attachment could be granted for making an insufficient return to the first writ of habeas corpus, without the issuing of an *alias* or *pluries* writ.[2]

This was done in Rex v. Winton,[3] on a rule to show cause why an attachment should not issue against defendant for making such a return. The affidavit of J. Greygoose on which the writ in that case issued, stated that his wife was in June, 1790, seduced by the defendant, with whom she continued to live until the month of May last, when she returned to her husband; that about three days afterwards, in consequence of a letter written by the defendant, threatening to publish her conduct in case of a refusal to go back again to him, she was induced to go back to the defendant, who, as the deponent believed, detained her by threats, and with whom she was now living in a state of adultery, but that she was desirous of returning to her husband. The words of the return were: "I had not at the time of receiving this writ, nor have I since, had the body of the within named M. Greygoose detained in my custody, so that I could not have her before the within-named W. H. Ashurst, as within I am commanded." The opinions of the judges in this important case are worthy of perusal. Justice Buller said: "I will first dispose of the last objection against the attachment (that an attachment should not issue immediately, but an *alias* habeas corpus awarded), because it is of more general consequence than the two others. Notwithstanding what is to be found in some of the old books on this subject, it has been long settled that the court will require a return to be made to the first writ of habeas corpus; and it is of infinite importance to every individual in the kingdom that we should insist on a return being made to that writ, without issuing an *alias* and a *pluries*. If the first writ be not obeyed, an attachment must issue immediately. Then it was argued on the authority of a case in 2 Lev. that this is a sufficient return; but I am of opinion that that case is by no means an authority to support this return.

---

[1] Crowley's Case, 2 Swans. 73.   [2] King v. Winton, 5 T. R. 89.
[3] 5 T. R. 89.

There the words were widely different from those used in this case. There Sir R. Viner returned that 'he had no such person in his custody, nor had he on the day of issuing that [*pluries*] writ, or afterwards.' But here the return is: 'I had not at the time of receiving this writ, etc., detained in my custody,' etc. This is an equivocal return; the defendant does not deny having the party, he only denies the detaining of her; but we must inquire when she is brought up whether or not she be detained."

Justice Grose followed with: "The courts always look with a watchful eye at the returns to writs of habeas corpus. The liberty of the subject so essentially depends on a ready compliance with the requisitions of this writ, that we are jealous whenever an attempt is made to deviate from the usual form of the return. The general form is: 'that the party has not the person in his possession, custody, or power;' that has not been adopted in this case, but another, and that an equivocal one, substituted in its place, 'detained,' etc., omitting the words 'power and possession.' What the defendant means by the word 'detained' I know not; but it does not satisfy me that the woman is not under the defendant's control." The rule was made absolute.

What constituted a return for which no attachment would issue for contempt was discussed in the case of The State v. Philpot.[1] The defendant had been imprisoned for contempt in making an evasive return. The order of imprisonment was objected to on the grounds that it was impossible for the defendant to produce the body of the boy, and that the court was not authorized to require his production as a condition to the purging of his contempt, if any were committed. The court replied: "As has been repeatedly said, the attachment was for an evasion and disobedience of the writ, and the only condition imposed on him was obedience. His imprisonment was not made to depend upon the arbitrary will of the judge, but upon his own will, if that should lead to action. That such an order is not illegal, must be manifest to any one who considers the order and allows to the court the power of enforcing its own process. Such orders are of common occurrence, and are absolutely necessary for the attainment of justice. They are issued and enforced against sheriffs, justices of the peace, and constables, who collect money and neglect or refuse to pay it over when ordered to do so; to compel the production of personal chattels under a warrant for restitution, and in a variety of instances of small

[1] Dudley (Ga.), 46.

importance compared with personal liberty; and it would be a very singular defect of power in the court not to possess the same means of enforcing the writ of habeas corpus. If the court has a right to issue the writ, it has the right to compel the production of the boy, and to use the only means adequate to attainment of that end. The indefinite use of the means beyond the attainment of the end would be illegal and improper; up to that period it is both legal and proper." The court was of the opinion that Philpot ought to remain attached until he produced the boy, James, or showed that it was impossible for him to produce him. The evidence showed that after the service of the habeas corpus Philpot had had possession of James, and sold him, and that he had been taken away to the western country. This was shown by voluntary affidavits of persons not subject to the process of the court, or bound to state more than in the opinion of Philpot might suit his purpose, and were prepared under his direction and to effect his enlargement, after he had been attached. "If Philpot's return had shown that neither at the service of the writ, nor at any time since, had the boy been in his possession, custody, power, or control, it would have been full and perfect; but he evades a part, and will not swear that at the service of the writ the boy was not in his power or control. Had Philpot, however, sworn that the boy was not in his possession, power, or custody, still, if upon looking at the facts stated in the return, the conscience of the court should not be satisfied that all the material facts were disclosed, it was not bound to discharge him."

The truthfulness of the return, however, will not always be made to depend upon the affidavit of the one making it; although it be perfect in form, and, so far as the eye can reach, unobjectionable. The court will allow the relator to traverse the return, and if a preponderance of testimony shows it to be false, the one who makes it will be in contempt. Thus: "Colonel John H. Wheeler, of North Carolina, the United States Minister to Nicaragua, was on board a steamboat at one of the Delaware wharves, on his way from Washington to embark at New York for his post of duty. Three slaves belonging to him were sitting at his side on the upper deck. Just as the last signal bell was ringing, Passmore Williamson came up to the party, declared to the slaves that they were free, and forcibly pressing Mr. Wheeler aside, urged them to go ashore. He was followed by some dozen or twenty negroes, who by muscular strength carried the slaves to the adjoining pier; two of the slaves at least, if not all

§ 137. THE RETURN. 185

three, struggling to release themselves, and protesting their wish to remain with their master; two of the negro mob in the mean time grasping Colonel Wheeler by the collar, and threatening to cut his throat if he made any resistance. The slaves were borne along to a hackney-coach that was in waiting, and were conveyed to some place of concealment, Mr. Williamson following, and urging the mob forward, and giving his name and address to Colonel Wheeler, with the declaration that he held himself responsible towards him for whatever might be his legal rights; but taking no personally active part in the abduction after he had left the dock." Mr. Williamson returned to a habeas corpus that the persons named in the writ, "nor either of them, are not now, nor was at the time of the issuing of the writ, or the original writ, or at any other time, in the custody, power, or possession of the respondent, nor by him confined or restrained; wherefore he can not have the bodies," etc. The evidence showed this return to be false; and Mr. Justice Kane, of the district court of the United States for the eastern district of Pennsylvania, said: "I can not look upon this return otherwise than as illusory, in legal phrase, as evasive, if not false. It sets out that the alleged prisoners are not now, and have not been since the issue of the habeas corpus, in the custody, power, or possession of the respondent; and in so far, it uses legally appropriate language for such a return.

"But it goes further, and by added words gives an interpretation to that language essentially variant from its legal import. It denies that the prisoners were within his power, custody, or possession at any time whatever. Now the evidence of respectable uncontradicted witnesses, and the admission of the respondent himself, establish the fact beyond controversy, that the prisoners were at one time within his power and control. He was the person by whose counsel the so-called rescue was devised. He gave the directions, and hastened to the pier to stimulate and supervise its execution. He was the spokesman, and first actor after arriving there. * * * It is clear, then, as it seems to us, that in legal acceptance the parties whom this writ called on Mr. Williamson to produce, were at one time within his power and control; and his answer, so far as it relates to his power over them, makes no distinction between that time and the present. I can not give a different interpretation to his language from that which he has practically given himself, and can not regard him as denying his power over the prisoners now, when he does not aver that he has lost the power which he formerly had. He has thus refused, or at least he has failed, to answer to the command of the law. He has chosen to decide for himself upon the lawfulness as well as the moral propriety of his act, and to withhold the ascertainment and vindication of the rights of others from that same form of arbitrament on which all his own rights repose. In a word, he has put himself in contempt of the process of this court and challenges its action. * * * It is enough that I find, as the case stands now, the plain and simple grounds of adjudication, that Mr. Williamson has not returned truthfully and fully to the writ of habeas corpus. He must, therefore, stand committed for a contempt of the legal process of the court. * * * Let him be committed to the custody of the marshal without bail or mainprise, as for a contempt of the court in refusing to answer to the writ of habeas corpus heretofore awarded against him at the relation of Mr. Wheeler." [1]

In cases where the party is restrained of his liberty without the authority of legal process, and where the return is usually made by a person having an interest in the question, and who has exercised the restraint upon his own personal responsibility, such as a parent, husband, master, or guardian of the person imprisoned, it is very proper that the facts which they state in the return should be open to investigation, and the court will not discharge one against whom an attachment has been issued for contempt, unless the conscience of the court is satisfied that all the material facts have been disclosed, notwithstanding the return declares that the party is not in the "possession, power, or control" of defendant.[2] The question as to how far the facts constituting a contempt may be inquired into on habeas corpus will be considered in another chapter, for they are rather an exception to the general rule allowing a free investigation into all the facts where the party is restrained without the authority of legal process and allowing a traverse to the return showing its falsity. All that we have said above must be considered in the light that at common law the return could not be controverted, but that now the rule is otherwise.

§ 138. **True Return could not be Enforced at Common Law.**—The easy and efficacious remedy which now exists for enforcing a true return to a habeas corpus has not always been in vogue. At common law, there was regularly no remedy

---

[1] United States ex rel. John H. Wheeler v. Passmore Williamson, 5 Pa. Law Jour. Rep. 365; S. C., 3 Am. Law Reg. 729.

[2] 3 Hill (N. Y.), 660; People v. Cassels, 5 Id. 168; United States v. Green, 3 Mason, 482; In the Matter of Waldron, 13 Johns. 417.

against an officer for a false return but an action on the case at the suit of the party grieved, and an information or indictment at the suit of the king.[1] The return had to be filed, however, before any proceedings were had. Otherwise a party could have no remedy if the return was false.[2] The return to a habeas corpus in this respect was put upon the same footing as returns to writs of *certiorari*, on which the court would sometimes hear affidavits contradictory of the return, but simply for the purpose of proving corruption on the part of the magistrate, and to lay a foundation for an information to be filed against him for the abuse. To these returns, if false, the party had his action of false return.[3]

§ 139. **New Habeas Corpus not Required.**—Whenever any reason exists for a temporary adjournment of the court, or a postponement of the hearing, or any event occurs which will prevent the matter from being debated on the day set for treating of the matter, the prisoner may be remanded and brought up again by order of the court, without the issuing of a new writ of habeas corpus.[4]

§ 140. **Recommitment.**—A person who has been regularly committed and then set at large can not be recommitted by an order grounded upon and reciting the original warrant of commitment or writ of attachment for a contempt.[5]

§ 141. **Order of the Argument.**—In the case of the Canadian Prisoners, Leonard Watson's Case,[6] the course pursued by counsel and sanctioned by the court was, that the counsel for the prisoner should first be heard, then the counsel for the crown; and then the counsel for the prisoner to reply generally. This has become the established rule in both England and the United States. Particularly is this the practice where an objection is raised to the return. The respondent answers the objections raised by the relator, and the relator is entitled to reply to the answer. This practice was followed in Carus Wilson's Case,[7] and also in The Queen v. Baines.[8]

§ 142. **Rule upon Process.**—Where a cause has been removed by habeas corpus, returnable at a day certain, and the writ is returned and filed on a preceding day, and before the return day; and the plaintiff takes the usual rule to appear, and gives notice; and the defendant not appearing pursuant to the

---

[1] Bac. Abr., Habeas Corpus, B. sec. 8.
[2] Fazacharly v. Baldo, 1 Salk. 351.
[3] —— v. Cowper a Justice of the Peace, 6 Mod. 90.
[4] Chambers' Case, 3 Cro. Car. 133.
[5] Yates v. The People, 6 Johns. 507.
[6] 9 Ad. & El. 731; S. C., 36 Eng. Com. L. 285.
[7] 7 Ad. & El., Q. B., 984.
[8] 12 Ad. & El. 210.

rule; and the plaintiff enters a rule for a *procedendo ;* his proceeding is irregular, for a rule can not be taken upon process until the return day. This is true of rules to bring in the body on writs of *capias,* as well as on writs of habeas corpus.[1]

§ 143. **Return of Substituted Warrant.**—Can the court, upon seeing a good warrant of commitment returned to a writ of habeas corpus, discharge the prisoner? The general rule gives a negative answer to this question. Where the jailer has, at the time of the return, a good warrant from the committing justice, it is immaterial how many bad ones he has. They are merely waste paper. This has been decided in the queen's bench. A return to a writ of habeas corpus stated that the prisoner was committed for the period of three months by warrant of a justice, set forth in the return, and recited a conviction by the justice, on which the warrant was based, for an offense under the statute of 4 Geo. IV., c. 34, sec. 3. The recited conviction was upon the face of it bad. The return then stated, that a week after such commitment, the prisoner being still in custody, the same justice delivered to the jailer another warrant of commitment, which recited and was grounded upon a conviction of the same date as the first, made by the same justice, and setting forth the same offense and imposing the same punishment. There being no material defect in this conviction, the court held that the prisoner was not entitled to be discharged, the return showing a good warrant, under which he was in custody.[2] It was also held in the exchequer of pleas that a defect in the first warrant might be cured by the second, where it appeared by the return that the second warrant was substituted by the same magistrate as an amendment of the first.[3] The same principle was determined in the bail court, and it would pay no attention to objections raised to the validity of the first warrant, as its judgment turned upon the validity of the second. Where no sufficient ground of objection appeared to the second warrant, the court discharged the rule to show cause why a writ of habeas corpus should not issue to bring up the body of the bankrupt.[4]

[1] Jones v. Spicer, 6 Cow. 391.
[2] Queen v. Richards, Bird et al., 5 Ad. & El., Q. B., 926; S. C., 48 Eng. Com. L. 926; Ex parte Cross, 2 Hurl. & N. 354.
[3] In re Smith, 3 Hurl. & N. 225.
[4] Ex parte Bull, 1 Saund. & C. 141. *Successive Warrants of Commitment.* Before the abolition of arrest on *mesne* process, and of imprisonment for debt in England, the judge of a county court upon a judgment summons, under the statute of 9 & 10 Vict., c. 95, sec. 103, had power to commit as often as a new default rendering the judgment debtor liable to imprisonment was made, though each default was of the same kind; and where the return to a writ of habeas corpus for the discharge of a judgment debtor

§ 144. **Return must Show that Evidence was Given in Prisoner's Presence.**—A summary conviction which does not show that evidence against the prisoner on his examination was given in his presence is bad; and the rule applies as well to warrants of commitment, which operate in themselves as convictions. On the return of a warrant to a writ of *habeas corpus ad subjiciendum*, and which fails to show that the evidence heard before the committing magistrate was given in the presence of the party to be charged, the court will release the prisoner from custody.[1]

§ 145. **Relying upon a Conviction where Commitment is Bad.**—Where the warrant of commitment returned to a writ of habeas corpus recites a conviction, the recital should be made correctly; although in England, by the seventh section of the statute of 9 Geo. IV., c. 69, sec. 1, the night poaching act, the *certiorari* was taken away, in cases arising under that act, and it was also enacted that "no warrant of commitment shall be held void by reason of any defect therein, provided it be therein alleged that the party has been convicted, and there be a good and valid conviction to sustain the same." But it was held by the courts that where the conviction was *prima facie* bad, as it appeared on the face of the warrant of commitment, it was for those who asserted it to be in a different form to bring it before the court. Unless this was done, the prisoner would be discharged.[2] Section 103 of the smuggling

set out two warrants of commitment, of different dates, made by the judge of a county court; where the warrants in precisely the same terms recited the judgment recovered in the county court, a subsequent order to pay by installments and default made, and that a judgment summons had been issued; where they then stated that the defendant had appeared and been examined; and where it appeared to the satisfaction of the court that the defendant had, since the judgment recovered against him, and still had sufficient means to satisfy the said judgment, but refused and neglected to pay the same, and it was ordered that he be imprisoned for forty days; the court justified the detention under the last warrant, and presumed that a new default in non-payment had been made, upon which the last warrant was granted, and that the imprisonment was, therefore, legal: In re Boyce, 22 Eng. L. & Eq. 131; S. C., 17 Jur. 715; and 2 El. & Bl. 521. The control of the creditor over the person of his debtor, through the process which the law gives for the enforcement of his demand, now being very nearly abolished throughout the United States, with the exception of torts and the fraudulent contraction of debts, or where there is an attempt at a fraudulent disposition of property with intent to delay the creditor or to deprive him of payment, the above class of decisions mentioned in this note establishes principles now seldom applied: Cooley on Const. Lim., 5th ed., 417.

[1] Queen v. Tordoft, 5 Ad. & El., Q. B., 933; In re Hammond, 9 Id. 92. A warrant of commitment which has the double character of a conviction and commitment should set out the evidence, and adjudge a form of imprisonment, or it will be bad in the character of a conviction: Id.

[2] In re Reynolds and Another, 1 Dow. & L. 846.

act, 8 & 9 Vict., c. 87, sec. 2, contained a similar provision concerning defective warrants, so long as it appeared to the court before which the warrant was returned that the conviction proceeded on good and valid grounds. In a case arising under this act, it was thought, where the party disputing the commitment wished to show the want of grounds, by bringing up the depositions, that the proper course would have been to have them brought up by *certiorari*.[1] If there is a conviction, it ought to be shown up in proper form; and where it is neither returned nor recited in a warrant of commitment, the court will not look upon the commitment and conviction as two distinct acts, and presume the conviction to be good.[2]

§ 146. **Return must Remain in Court.** — Chief Justice Holt, in Queen Anne's reign, established a rule for the future, that, when one was brought up by habeas corpus, the return must remain in court, and a copy of it only given to the marshal.[3] In 1847, Lord Chancellor Cottenham also mentioned the matter, and decided that returns to writs of habeas corpus, when disposed of, were to be sent to the record office, and not redelivered to the officer who made them. It appears that Justice Holt's rule had not been strictly complied with, and that the returns were too frequently delivered back to the officer who made them. The lord chancellor reprobated such practice, and referred particularly to the inconvenience which such a practice was calculated to produce in certain cases where the correctness of the return was afterwards questioned.[4]

§ 147. **Return Need not Specially Set out Documents Referred to.**—In the leading English case of Leonard Watson,[5] the return was challenged for the want of every one of the numerous documents whence the right to imprison was inferred. The indictment for treason, it was contended, ought to have been recited, if not set forth in terms; the petition, the confession, the pardon, and the assent, though that was not required by the act. "We were told," said Chief Justice Lord Denman, "that it was our duty to inspect these papers, and not receive a merely general description from the party imprisoning, that we might judge for ourselves whether the description was correct, and whether they really conferred the authority ascribed to them. To this manifold objection one answer must

---

[1] Van Boven's Case, 9 Ad. & El., Q. B., 669; In the Matter of John Hammond, Id. 92, note a.
[2] Queen v. Tordoft, 5 Ad. & El., Q. B., 933; In re Hammond, 9 Id. 99, note a.
[3] Anon., 6 Mod. *p. 180.
[4] Oldfield v. Cobbett, 22 Eng. Ch. Rep. 289; S. C., 2 Ph. 289.
[5] 9 Ad. & El. 731.

serve. The fact is stated to the court upon the return; and we are bound to receive it as true. The party who makes the return has probably never seen the documents, but, at his peril, places his confidence in the captain who brought the prisoners from Canada, or in some other person; but he is bound by the assertion which he makes on their credit; and their truth may be questioned in any ulterior proceeding which it may be competent to the party to adopt." We do not believe that our practice—where the return may be controverted, and where statute often requires it to be verified—will materially affect the substance of this rule. The return, whether at common law, or under statute, generally imports verity until it is impeached, and when one has returned all the facts within his knowledge, and they constitute a sufficient return in law, the court will so consider it, until its verity is assailed.

§ 148. **When Warrant must Contain Certain Words.**—In proceedings in bankruptcy, Lord Chancellor Eldon said, in a leading case:[1] "The distinction established by all the cases is this, that if the commissioners say to the bankrupt, 'On your former examination you answered to this effect,' and he does not qualify that statement, the court must take it to be true—a hard rule, but now clearly settled. But if the commissioners state that they have derived information from other persons, and the bankrupt does not qualify that statement, I am not bound to take it to be true, because he has no means of knowing whether or how far it is true. When the commissioners receive facts on the deposition of persons other than the bankrupt, they ought to set out in the warrant the deposition *in hæc verba;* for if they state only what they consider to be the effect of the deposition, the court before which the writ is brought is to judge whether the effect of the deposition is such as the commissioners represent, without the means of forming that judgment."

§ 149. **Questioning Jurisdiction on Defective Warrant.** W. Dimes, the principal defendant in the suit of The Grand Junction Canal Company v. Dimes, had been committed to the queen's prison, under the order of the vice-chancellor of England, for breach of the injunction granted in the cause. The warrant returned on habeas corpus had the letters " C. C." attached to it, the prisoner's counsel claiming that they showed that the order for commitment was made by the lord chancellor, Lord Cottenham; and that his lordship being interested in the subject-matter of the suit as a holder of shares in the Grand

---
[1] Crowley's Case, 2 Swans. 81.

Junction Canal Company, the order of committal was illegal. Lord Chancellor Truro, in his decision upon the matter, said: "The vice-chancellor has authority, under the statute, to decide on a question of commitment; and this being so, his decision on that point can not be reviewed on the present occasion, and in the form now attempted. This is quite a distinct matter from the power of the lord chancellor to review all decrees, orders, and acts of the vice-chancellor. The return to the writ shows that the vice-chancellor has exercised the authority given to him by the statute, and has made an order for the committal of Mr. Dimes. It does not cease to be the order of the vice-chancellor merely because the letters "C. C." are attached to the warrant. I have only on the present occasion to see that Mr. Dimes is in custody under the order of some court having authority to commit, and I am satisfied that this is the case."[1]

§ 150. **Examination into Cause on Rule Nisi.**—Upon the argument of a rule *nisi* for a writ of habeas corpus, the case will be treated as if a habeas corpus had already been issued, and the prisoner brought up as in the first instance. The court will consequently look to the whole cause appearing upon the return to the rule.[2]

§ 151. **Discussing Validity of Warrant upon Rule to Show Cause.**—The court of exchequer of pleas, in England, has exercised the power of granting a rule calling on a committing magistrate to show cause why a writ of habeas corpus should not issue to bring up a prisoner, in order that the validity of the warrant of commitment may be discussed on showing cause.[3]

§ 152. **When Motion to Quash Writ after Return Filed will be Entertained.**—Should a case arise in which the court will not permit the return to be amended, or allow time for it, a motion to quash the return will of course be in order.[4] A writ of habeas corpus may be itself quashed if directed to the sheriff *or* jailer in the disjunctive. And where a sheriff took a party upon a writ of *excommunicato capiendo* for subtraction of tithes and other ecclesiastical duties, and returned to a habeas corpus the warrant simply, the return was held insufficient by the court, who said the writ of *excommunicato capiendo* itself ought to have been returned, "because the warrant may be wrong when the

---

[1] In re Dimes, 3 Mac. & G. 5. Mr. Dimes was, on the lord chancellor's suggestion, released with the consent of the company, on his giving an undertaking not further to infringe the injunction. (Note.)

[2] Ex parte Bull, 1 Saund. & C. 141.

[3] Ex parte Cross, 2 Hurl. & N. 354.

[4] Eden's Case, 2 Mau. & Sel. 229.

writ is right; and though the warrant may be wrong, yet if the writ is right, the party is rightfully in the custody of the sheriff." So they quashed the writ of *excommunicato capiendo*. Prior to the statute of 5 Elizabeth there were no discharges on *excommunicato capiendos*, except where a man was excommunicated pending a prohibition. But after that the court of king's bench could quash the writ of *excommunicato capiendo*, or award a *supersedeas*, because the court were judges of the cause, and had it before them, and the party could not go into chancery for a *supersedeas*, because the writ was returnable in king's bench. So where a return was made that the party was taken and in custody by this writ, and the writ did not set forth the cause of excommunication, the return was held uncertain and the party was discharged because the writ of *de excommunicato capiendo* was quashed.[1]

Where a judge at chambers made an order upon which a writ of habeas corpus was issued, where it afterwards appeared to have been issued improvidently, and where the return was immediately made and heard in chambers by the judge making the order, it was considered doubtful by Justice Wilson of queen's bench, in Canada, whether he had the power to quash the writ, or rescind his order upon which it issued; "and," said he, "even if it were clear to me that I have the power, I do not know that I would exercise it now that the writ has been returned and filed, and the prisoner is here awaiting my judgment." So, instead of quashing the writ on motion made for that purpose, he discharged the prisoner on defects in the warrant returned.[2]

Judge Kane, of the United States district court for the eastern district of Pennsylvania, said: "Of course, if it appears to the court at any time that the writ was asked for by an intermeddling stranger, one who had no authority to intervene, and whose intervention is repudiated, the writ will be quashed. But it is for the defendant, to whom the writ is addressed, to allege a want of authority in the relator. The motion to quash can not be the act of a volunteer. Still less can it come to us by written suggestion, from without our jurisdiction, in the name of the party who is alleged to be under constraint, and whose very denial that she is so may be only a proof that the restraint is effectual."[3]

---

[1] Dominus Rex v. Fowler, 1 Salk. 293, 350.
[2] In re Ross, 3 Prac. Rep.(U. C.) 301.
[3] United States v. Williamson, 5 Pa. Law Jour. Rep. 398. The last sentence refers to "the suggestion and petition of Jane Johnson," a negro woman then in Massachusetts, and who was one of the three parties named in the writ of habeas corpus.

§ 153. **Making a Bad Return on Good Judgment.**—If a good judgment be returned, although the return be otherwise informal and defective, the prisoner will be remanded. Said Justice Earl, of king's bench, "If we should discharge him, we should at that rate rid all the jails in England," and he cited a case where a habeas corpus was directed to the porter of Ludlow, upon which it appeared that damages were given beyond the instructions of the council of the Marches, by whom judgment was given; yet because a fine was set on them to the king, and that remained unpaid, the court remanded them. So here, said he, a fine being set, the king would lose by his discharge.[1]

§ 154. **Judicial Notice.**—On the return to a writ of habeas corpus, it appeared that the prisoner was detained by virtue of a warrant purporting to be issued by a court of quarter sessions in Ireland. It was backed by the indorsement of a metropolitan police magistrate, under the statute of 44 Geo. III., c. 92, sec. 3. It stated that the prisoner "stood indicted in the peace-office of the county of Tipperary" for a "rescue" and for "a riot," and directed "the police of the county of Tipperary" to apprehend him, etc. Justice Patterson, in rendering his decision, said: "I rather think I am bound to take judicial notice that the common law of England prevails in Ireland; and if so, whatever doubt I may entertain as to the word 'rescue,' the term 'riot' clearly enough designates an offense known and punishable by the common law of England; and consequently must be taken to be an offense against the laws of Ireland." But he could not understand that the word "peace-office" had any distinct and definite meaning; and was therefore unable to see that the proper steps had been taken to bring the offender within the jurisdiction of the court of quarter sessions. On this and another defect in the warrant, he discharged the prisoner.[2]

The English court of king's bench have also held that they would take notice of a livery-man, and the nature of his office, and that he who comes into a company agrees to incident charges and duties; but that they could not take notice that the keeper of Newgate was an officer of the city of London.[3] A non-conformist was discharged for coming within five miles of a town that sent members to parliament; because it did not appear that London sent burgesses to parliament, though as Chief Justice Holt said, "all the world knows they do."[4] The

---

[1] King v. Bythell, 12 Mod. 75.
[2] Regina v. Nesbitt, 2 Dow. & L. 529.
[3] King v. Clerk, 1 Salk. 348.
[4] The Company of Vintners v. Clerke, 5 Mod. 156.

queen's bench has also taken judical notice that the master of the rolls is a judge of the court of chancery.¹

In California, in the first case before the supreme court of that state, Mr. Justice Bennett, for the court, said, on petition for a release on a writ of habeas corpus previously issued by that court, "that courts take judicial notice of the territorial extent of the jurisdiction and sovereignty exercised *de facto* by their own government; and of the local divisions of their country, as into states, provinces, counties, cities, towns, or the like, so far as political government is concerned or affected: Greenl. Ev. 8. And we recognize judicially that Napa valley is embraced within the territorial limits of this state, the same as we should that San Francisco is included within its boundaries if an offense were charged to have been committed there."² It has also been held on proceedings on habeas corpus that state courts will take judicial cognizance of the laws of the United States. In the words of Justice Whitman of Nevada: "All citizens of the United States are bound to know the laws thereof, and state courts take judicial cognizance of such, without formal proof, and are 'bound thereby;' but to decide whether any particular statute of the United States is or is not existent—or, if existent, valid or invalid—requires an investigation and determination, the exercise of which, in a proceeding like the present, as against the process of a court of the United States, is not only uncalled for, but unwarranted; for the reason that such action is an absorption *in limine* of the very question of the power, the right to decide which underlies and supports the entire jurisdiction of the courts of the United States, which would be rendered powerless if unable to decide this preliminary point without interference from state tribunals."³ So will a court take judicial notice that a man brought before it on habeas corpus is an attorney, when, in fact, such is the case. Sheriffs and commissioners, under like circumstances, may and should do the same thing.⁴ But judicial notice can not be taken of a justice of the peace of a sister state. The certificate of the justice simply will not be received as evidence of this authority, because he is not an officer of such grade and rank as to make his official acts prove themselves. He is unlike a notary public, whose acts prove themselves in all commercial countries of the world, when verified by his official seal.⁵

¹ Ex parte Clarke, 2 Gale & Dav. 780.
² People v. Smith et al., 1 Cal. 13.
³ Ex parte Hill, 5 Nev. 159.
⁴ People v. Nevins, 1 Hill (N. Y.), 161.
⁵ In the Matter of Kesler, 1 Hempst. 312.

§ 155. **Reply to Return Denying Truth of the Matters Contained in Affidavit on Which Capias Issued.**—In an Indiana case the appellant had sued out a writ of habeas corpus against Saunders, who returned that he held Dwire by virtue of a writ of *capias ad respondendum*, issued to him, as constable, by a justice of the peace, at the suit of William McFall. Dwire replied, denying the truth of the matters contained in the affidavit on which the *capias* issued. The *capias* was issued in accordance with the provisions of the statute.[1] No objection was made, in the appellate court, as to the sufficiency of the writ of *capias*, or the affidavit on which it issued. It appeared, on the hearing of the habeas corpus to the judge of the court below, Fountain common pleas, that twenty-four hours, the time within which a defendant was entitled under statute to be tried, had not elapsed from the time of Dwire's arrest until the writ of habeas corpus issued. So the judge remanded the prisoner to the custody of the constable. No proof being given or offered of the truth of the matters stated in the affidavit, Dwire appealed and made the point that he should have been discharged, unless the matters charged in the affidavit on which the *capias* issued were proven. The supreme court said: "The appellant being arrested immediately seeks to be discharged on habeas corpus. This, of course, could not be done without notice to McFall, the plaintiff in the suit: 2 R. S. 1852, sec. 728, p. 196. We think it clear, that under these statutory provisions, the plaintiff in a suit can not be required, on a writ of habeas corpus thus issued, to appear and prove the truth of his affidavit. Were the writ on which the appellant was held void for the want of a sufficient affidavit to support it, or for any other cause, a different question would be presented; but here it seems to have been valid. It was an ample protection to the officer, and it rendered the custody and detention of the appellant legal." The judgment below was affirmed.[2]

§ 156. **Return of Execution against the Person.**—"The keeper of the jail returned that he detained the petitioner by virtue of the execution against his person, which he produced. To this return the petitioner demurred, on the ground that it did not deny that the action was one in which he could not be arrested, and that he had turned out unincumbered real estate upon the execution against his property, on which the sheriff had refused to levy. If the petitioner desired an inquiry into the nature of the action between himself and Wood, and the

---

[1] 2 R. S. 1852, p. 454, sec. 24.   [2] Dwire v. Saunders, 15 Ind. 306.

facts touching the service and return of the first execution, as he evidently did, this was an entire mistake of practice. The jailer was only required to return the authority and true cause of imprisonment, as they had come to his knowledge, and it being an execution, he was to annex a copy to his return and produce the original: R. S., c. 155, sec. 18. This he did, and the execution being valid on its face, constituted, as to him, a good cause for the detention, which the demurrer admitted: 3 Hill, 658, note 28, app. The causes assigned for the demurrer were not matters of fact, which the officer, in his return, was bound to admit or deny. They were strictly matters in avoidance of the return, which the petitioner should have alleged and proved by way of answer to show that the imprisonment, apparently lawful, was nevertheless not so, and that he was entitled to his discharge. This is the practice clearly indicated by the statute: R. S., c. 158, sec. 26."[1]

[1] Dixon, C. J., for the supreme court of Wisconsin, In the Matter of the Petition of Luke Mowry for a Writ of Habeas Corpus, 12 Wis. 52. The supreme court had issued a writ of *certiorari* to the judge of the ninth circuit, to bring up proceedings had before him on an application for a writ of habeas corpus, and for the discharge of a petitioner from imprisonment. The judge's return showed that the petitioner, Luke Mowry, was brought before him on a habeas corpus, the petition showing that he was confined upon an execution issued on a judgment rendered in the circuit court for that county, in favor of Algernon S. Wood, and against the petitioner, for a debt arising out of an express contract, and that he had offered to turn out property upon execution against it, but which in reality was so worthless that the sheriff refused to levy upon it. The sheriff returned the execution unsatisfied. A copy of the sheriff's return was annexed to the petition. Execution then against the person was issued. "The circuit judge," said the supreme court, "overlooked the mistake of the counsel for the petitioner, and proceeded to investigate the merits of his imprisonment, so far as they were made to appear, and we will do the same thing. The record in the case of Wood v. Mowry, was produced, but no other proof was offered. A copy of the record is returned by the judge, from which it appears that the action was for damages alleged to have been sustained by Wood on account of the wrongful and fraudulent misapplication and conversion, by the petitioner, of certain school-land certificates, the property of Wood. The complaint alleged that Wood had borrowed from the petitioner a sum of money, and to secure the payment of the note, deposited with him the certificates, a description of which was given; that the petitioner had transferred the note to third parties, who had obtained a judgment thereon; that the plaintiff was ready and willing and had offered to pay the judgment to the owners or to the petitioner, provided the certificates were delivered up to him; but that the owners of the judgment could not do so, as they had never had them in their possession, and the petitioner refused, falsely and fraudulently pretending he had sold them as a pledge, when, in truth and in fact, he had wrongfully and fraudulently misapplied and converted them to his own use. The value of the certificates was alleged to have largely exceeded the amount of the note. The petitioner, by his answer, denied the wrongful and fraudulent misapplication and conversion of the certificates, and insisted that he had made sale of them whilst the note was still in his possession, and applied the proceeds in part payment, as it was lawful for him to do. The jury, under the instructions of the court, found him

§ 157. **When Demand should be Made for Child.**—The return to a writ of habeas corpus showing that the petitioner has left a child in the custody of respondent will operate against the applicant for the writ. Before the respondent can be placed in the wrong and subjected to legal proceedings by the petitioner on account of the custody of the child, it must appear upon the return that he has demanded the custody of the child, and that the respondent, having the power to do so, has refused to restore the child to him.[1]

§ 158. **Time when Errors should be Corrected.**—The rule in the courts with reference to mere irregularity alone is, that they must be taken advantage of in due time, or the party affected by them will lose his opportunity of doing it entirely. The court, in The State v. Philpot,[2] laid down this doctrine very clearly, and supported it by reliable English authorities. "In Tidd's Practice, 513, 514, the rule of law on this subject is stated to be 'that whenever proceedings are irregular, the court on motion will set them aside, provided the application for that purpose be made in the first instance; for in all cases of irregularity the party should apply to the court as early as possible; and if he proceed himself after discovering the irregularity, or lie by and suffer the other party to proceed, the court will not assist him.' The language of the court in the case of Pearson and Rawlings, 1 East, 77, is clear and very strong: 'It is the universal practice of the court, that where there has been an irreg-

'guilty as charged in the complaint,' and assessed the plaintiff's damages, for which the judgment was entered. Two questions were considered by the judge: 1. Whether the judgment was for a debt arising out of a contract; and, 2. Whether the return of the sheriff to the execution against the property of the petitioner was sufficient to authorize the issuing of an execution against his person. He decided both against the petitioner, and we think he was unquestionably right." The constitution of Wisconsin, section 16, article 1, provides that "no person shall be imprisoned for debt arising out of or founded on a contract, expressed or implied," and it was held that the defendant in this case was not entitled to exemption from imprisonment under this section. The court argued, with reference to the sufficiency of the return of the execution against the property: "The sheriff may not have a very wide discretion in determining the value of the property upon which he is to levy, but when he honestly thinks it will not pay the expense of sale, and will therefore increase instead of diminishing the amount of the judgment, we think it clear that he may, at his peril, refuse to levy, and stating the facts, return the execution unsatisfied (which was here done). If it should turn out that he is mistaken, or if he acts in bad faith, he undoubtedly becomes liable to the injured party. Such a case would present a very different question from that now before us. No attempt was made to impeach the return by showing that the sheriff was mistaken, nor that he acted unfairly, and until that is done, the presumption is in favor of its correctness. For these reasons, the order of the circuit judge remanding the petitioner is affirmed with costs."

[1] Speer v. Davis, 38 Ind. 271.
[2] Dudley (Ga.), 46.

ularity, if the party overlook it and take subsequent steps in the cause, he can not afterwards revert back to their regularity and object to it. Justice requires that that rule should be general in its operation, having in view the advancement of right. And however we may be inclined to favor persons in the situation of the defendant, yet we must not go to the length of breaking in upon the general practice of the court.' The same doctrine is held in the case of D'Argent and Vivant, 1 Id. 330: 'A defendant may waive irregularity, and is considered as having done so, by submitting to the process, instead of taking steps to avail himself of the irregularity, which ought always to be done in the first instance.' See also Fox and Money, 1 Bos. & Pul. 250; Davis and Owen, Id. 342. This rule is applicable, however, only to cases of mere irregularity. It is different where there is a complete defect in the proceedings. The former may be waived, but not the latter: Goodwin and Parry, 4 T. R. 577; Hussey and Wilson, 5 Id. 254; Stevenson and Danvers, 2 Bos. & Pul. 110. The distinction is then plainly this, that where that is wanting without which the whole proceedings are void, no subsequent steps will cure the defects. It is radical, but if that be wanting which will merely render the proceedings voidable, it may be waived by subsequent steps."

§ 159. **State Court can not Determine What is a Crime against the United States.**—A person who has been convicted in a state court for the offense of committing perjury in the course of a judicial investigation conducted under authority of acts of congress, and is suffering imprisonment in the penitentiary therefor, will be discharged upon the return to a writ of habeas corpus showing this fact. Such an offense is one against the public justice and laws of the United States, and is exclusively cognizable in her courts. This is rather an exception to the general rule of the common law, that when it appears by the return to a writ of habeas corpus that the prisoner is confined upon a regular charge and commitment for a criminal offense, particularly if he be confined in execution after conviction, he will be immediately returned to custody.[1]

§ 160. **What is Meant by the Term "Process."**—Mr. Justice Cowen, in defining the meaning of the word "process" as used in the New York habeas corpus act, spoke thus: "There is no doubt that a rule or order to commit as plainly comes within the meaning of the word 'process' as a precept under the fourth section, or a *capias ad respondendum*, or an execution.

---
[1] Ex parte Dock Bridges, 2 Woods, 428.

The definition of 'process' given by Lord Coke comprehends any lawful warrant, authority, or proceeding by which a man may be arrested. He says: 'Process of law is twofold, viz., by the king's writ, or by due proceeding and warrant, either in deed or in law, without warrant:' 2 Inst. 51, 52. By 'warrant of law' he comprehends any authority of law, as is plain by the instances which he gives. He adds: 'If treason or felony be done, and one hath just cause of suspicion, this is a good cause and warrant in law to arrest any man.' Again: 'A watchman may arrest a night-walker by warrant in law.' And he concludes by saying that 'a commitment by lawful warrant, either in deed or in law, is accounted in law due process or proceeding in law:' *Vide* also 6 Johns. 478, and the books there cited by Lansing, chancellor, in Yates v. The People. The constitution says that no person shall be deprived of his liberty without due process of law. Yet who ever supposed that this took away the right to arrest on a bail-piece, or for an escape without a sealed warrant, and so of many cases. We have already seen that a rule to stand committed has always been a very common warrant for the sheriff to commit.[1] It is, therefore, process; and the statute saying 'order and process of commitment' is either no more than a repetition, or, which is more probable, the statute is to be understood distributively, viz., that when a precept issues, which would more commonly be called process, it should fix the time, etc.; and when the proceeding is by rule or order, this should also do the same thing. It can not be that this accidental dropping in of an equivocal word was intended to deprive all courts of their known and acknowledged power to commit, except in a new form never before required. Had any such thing been intended, it seems to me the provision would have been direct and explicit."[2]

§ 161. **A Few Instances of a Bad Return.**—A return that the prisoner is detained in custody, being charged upon oath with being a deserter from the Royal Leinster Regiment, held insufficient; it ought to have appeared that he was committed by some person having authority to commit.[3] A return that the African company had retained the defendant in their service, and sent him to the Savoy to be provided with necessaries, till he should embark for Africa, held so insufficient that defendant was discharged, and an information ordered against the colonel who lifted the men, and the keepers of the Savoy.[4]

---

[1] Speaking of commitments for contempt.
[2] People v. Nevins, 1 Hill (N.Y.), 170.
[3] King v. Earl Mountnorris, Reid et al., 1 Ridg. 460.
[4] Dominus Rex v. Drew, 1 Stra. 408.

§ 161. THE RETURN.

On a *habeas corpus cum causa* to remove a plaint in trespass into the court of king's bench, and before a declaration has been delivered to defendant, the return should contain a copy of the declaration or, at least, show what the cause of action was: held insufficient, but amendment allowed.[1] *Nullum habeo talem in custodia mea, nec habui die impetrationis*, was adjudged an insufficient return to a habeas corpus.[2] Where the custodian of the prisoner returns "that he has him ready to be delivered to the court, but states no cause for the detention," it is bad; and the prisoner will be released if he wishes to be.[3] A return that the defendant was committed for back-bearing and carrying away a deer, without using the words "unlawfully taken away," held bad before conviction; but after conviction, good. The deer might have been taken with the owner's consent. After conviction, the court is not so particular. The words may be in the conviction; and the court will sometimes adjourn to have it returned.[4] A return that defendant was committed by two justices of the peace, that he being overseer of the poor did not account as by the statute directed, and that he had not accounted before them, held bad. He might have accounted before two other justices.[5] A court will be very strict with a return which tends to oust it of its jurisdiction, and will not allow it to be amended in such a way as to still leave the court in the dark as to what the merits of the cause are, where it originally failed to do so.[6] A return not specifying for what cause or matter a party was examined is too general and insufficient.[7] Conusance of pleas, or exempt jurisdiction, should never be returned to a habeas corpus; for then they might return a falsity to support their jurisdiction, which would not be traversable, and so a subject would be ousted of the privilege of suing, or being sued, in the king's superior court, without an opportunity of controverting the matter.[8]

On a habeas corpus it was returned that issue was joined before the writ was served upon the respondent, but it did not say that issue was not joined within six weeks, etc., as it ought to have been by the statute, and it was pronounced ill. And where a cause arose in an inferior court, the return is bad unless it shows that the cause of action arose within its jurisdiction.[9]

[1] Watson v. Clerke, Holt, 423.
[2] 2 Lilly's Reg. 3, H.
[3] Mr. Archer's Case, Fortes. 197. Case of infancy.
[4] King v. Hawkins, Fortes. 272.
[5] King v. Gibson, Fortes. 272.
[6] Anonymous, Fortes. 273.
[7] Thomlinson's Case, 6 Co. (Fraser), 340; 14 Vin. Abr. 218.
[8] Taylor v. Reignolds, 12 Mod. 666.
[9] Speaker and Styant, Comb. 127.

A return *pro mala praxi* is uncertain.[1] Where a man has been committed for any crime, either at common law or by act of parliament, for which he is punishable by indictment, a return that he was committed until discharged by due course of law is good. But if the commitment be in pursuance of a special authority, the terms of the commitment must be special, and exactly pursue that authority; and therefore, if it do not appear on the return to have been according to that authority, the return will be bad; as, showing that the commitment was for a contempt of the court of chancery, without showing where the contempt was; or for giving a verdict contrary to law, to the oath, or the evidence, without saying what the evidence was; or for a contempt of a command; or for a contempt contrary to an order or decree of the court, or contrary to an order between A. and B.; or for refusal of an answer to articles before the high commissioners, without saying what articles, as they might not be within their jurisdiction; or by a precept of the secretary of state, etc., or of the privy council; or by command of the commisioners in causes ecclesiastical. A return that one is committed for aiding the escape of one in custody for high treason, without saying what species of treason, is bad. So, that one was committed for refusing sureties for his good behavior, without saying in what sense; the same for refusal to account for toll, and until the defendant does account, without saying for what sum.[2] Where a return simply recites the fact of the defendant having been outlawed, without stating it as a ground of detention, there is nothing upon which the defendant can be charged in execution. The return is insufficient.[3] On a return to a writ of habeas corpus, the court will not, at the desire of the committing magistrate, direct or advise the jailer to substitute another return for the one proffered to be made.[4] It seems that a medical certificate under the statute of 8 & 9 Vict., c. 100, sec. 46, should state specific facts on which the opinion of insanity has been formed; and that, therefore, the statement that the patient has "a general suspicion of the motives of every person" is insufficient.[5] A return that defendant was committed upon complaint for such an offense, and there being cause upon examination to suspect him, without an express charge of any offense, held bad.[6] Where *alias*

---

[1] The King and Bowerbank, Skin. 676.
[2] Com. Dig., tit. Habeas Corpus, E, 3, and authorities there cited.
[3] Adcock v. Fiske, 8 Scott, 138.
[4] In re Fletcher, 1 Dow. & L. 726.
[5] In re Fell, 3 Dow. & L. 373.
[6] Com. Dig., tit. Habeas Corpus, E, 3, 564.

and *pluries* writs were issued at common law, a return to a *pluries* habeas corpus denying the detention at the time of or since the service of the *pluries* writ was bad.[1]

In the United States a return to a writ of habeas corpus setting up a will as the written authority for the restraint, but which contains no copy of the will, is bad on exception, and clearly insufficient.[2] A return which discloses that immediately prior to the issuing of the writ the custody of the child in controversy had been transferred to another, is bad, if it fails to disclose the reasons for such change. "Had the return complied with this requirement, it might have disclosed that the object had been to avoid the expected process of the court, and called for the exercise of a power which would perhaps bring the child again within the jurisdiction of the court."[3] Sometimes a return is insufficient even though it be in the general form of return and denial prescribed by statute; and the court will direct the respondent to specifically answer the matters alleged in the petition.[4]

§ 162. **A Few Instances of a Good Return.**—"That before the delivery of the writ he had delivered the woman to her husband, and knows not where she is," held a good return.[5] A return that the person was discharged out of custody by an order of sessions, held a good return for filing the writ.[6] Strange, in argument, said "that at the coming of the writ defendant was not in the keeper of the prison's custody" was a good return.[7] A return by an officer that a party is in his custody under the sentence of a court of competent jurisdiction to inquire into the offense for which he is imprisoned, and having power to pass such a sentence, seems to be sufficient, without setting forth the particular circumstances necessary to warrant the sentence.[8] Upon a habeas corpus or *corpus cum causa* it is a good return that the party is dead.[9] A return stating that upon a certain charge exhibited against the defend-

[1] Emerton's Case, Freem. K. B. & C. P., 389.
[2] Shaw v. Smith, Guardian, 8 Ind. 485. This habeas corpus was to obtain the possession of an infant. Respondent set forth in his return that Mary Shaw, the mother of said infant, in her last sickness, and who was then dead, by her will appointed him as the guardian of the child, his father being dead long before the mother. The court below had awarded the child to its legally appointed guardian, Smith, and the appellate court affirmed the judgment, saying it would not go beyond the statute to hold courts intrusted with the interests of minors to a strict regularity, and would not interfere unless a strong case were made.
[3] Sears v. Dessar, 28 Ind. 472.
[4] In the Matter of Jackson, 15 Mich. 418.
[5] Dom. Rex v. Wright, 2 Stra. 901.
[6] King v. Bethuen, Andr. 281.
[7] Id.
[8] King v. Suddis, 1 East, 306.
[9] Dalton's Sheriff, 251.

ant before a court-martial, for certain offenses alleged to have been committed by him at Gibraltar, and that such proceedings were had that the court-martial, after hearing the charge and the defense, found the defendant guilty of receiving certain goods named from the warehouse of W. at Gibraltar, knowing them to be stolen, in breach of the articles of war, whereupon they sentenced him to transportation for fourteen years; held to be good under the mutiny act whereby the king might make articles of war and constitute courts-martial with power to try and punish, as well in Great Britain, etc., as in Gibraltar, etc.[1] Where a return stated that the prisoners had been convicted of burglary by the royal court of Jersey, which was a court competent to try and punish that offense; and had been sentenced by that court to transportation, and were in custody under such sentence; it was held sufficient without stating that the court had jurisdiction to pass the particular sentence, for the court of queen's bench would presume that in such a case the sentence was one which the court had authority to pass.[2]

The return to a writ of habeas corpus to bring up the body of an alleged lunatic, stated that "on, etc., under the authority and in pursuance of the act of parliament," etc., 2 & 3 Wm. IV., c. 107, Robert Fell, "in the said writ named, was committed under our custody, and was received into and détained in the Newcastle-upon-Tyne Lunatic Asylum, etc., and that on the day and year aforesaid," an order and medical certificates were received, which were as follows. Here were set out the order for the lunatic's reception; having the signature of the patient himself at the foot of it, instead of his wife's, she being the party named in it as giving the order, and who had also signed the order in a different place; and also medical certificates. A subsequent order under the 8 & 9 Vict., c. 100, and medical certificates, were also set out, and the detention of the lunatic was justified under the latter order. Held, that it sufficiently appeared upon the face of the return, that the first order and medical certificates were received with the lunatic; that under the statute of 2 & 3 Wm. IV., c. 107, the first order was a sufficient cause of detention; that obtaining an order for his detention under the statute of 8 & 9 Vict., c. 100, was unnecessary, and that the return need not show who delivered the first order.[3] Two persons, convicted at the sessions of the supreme criminal court of Victoria, of the crime of manslaughter, com-

---

[1] King v. Suddis, 1 East, 306.
[2] Re Brenan and Gallan, 2 Cox C. C. 193.
[3] In re Fell, 3 Dow. & L. 373.

mitted on board a British ship on the high seas, were sentenced to penal servitude for fifteen years, and were subsequently detained in a public jail, within the meaning of the colonial act, the "Statute of Jails," 1864. The return to a writ of habeas corpus showed that they were detained "for the cause and to the end that they may undergo the sentence aforesaid," and the court ordered that the prisoners be discharged, for the reason that, by the statute of 16 & 17 Vict., c. 99, sec. 6, a sentence of penal servitude, whether passed in the United Kingdom or in a colony, could not be executed in the colony without the intervention of the secretary of state. But on appeal to the privy council the return was held to be sufficient, and that the prisoners ought not to have been set at large during the term of their sentence, until it was clear that no lawful means of executing it could be found.[1]

In the United States it has been held, that it is a sufficient return to a *habeas corpus ad prosequendum*, directed to a sheriff as chief keeper of the prison, to bring the prisoner into court, "that the prisoner is sick and languishing, so that he can not be removed without endangering his life." But such a return ought always to be accompanied with affidavits of visiting physicians.[2]

PART II.—PRODUCTION OF THE BODY AND STATEMENTS OF THE CAUSE OF ARREST AND DETENTION.

§ 163. **Sufficient Reasons for not Producing the Body.**— The writ of habeas corpus is so worded as to require both the production of the body and a statement of the cause of arrest and detention; but while the production of the body is one of the most essential elements of the summary proceeding by habeas corpus, it is not always indispensably necessary that the body be produced in order to administer justice. This exception applies sometimes in cases concerning the custody of infant children. Where a married woman has been compelled to live separate from her husband on account of his intemperance and crime; and where she is unable to support their children, and for this reason voluntarily gives them up to a charitable institution established for the purpose of furnishing homes to destitute children, under a written contract by which the children are to be placed out or adopted in a good family, and she is not to seek to discover them or to deprive such family of

[1] Queen, Appellant, v. Mount and Morris, Respondents, 12 Eng. Rep., Moak's Notes, 181.
[2] Ex parte Bryant, 2 Tyler, 269.

them; such a contract has been held in Massachusetts to be valid; but the court, on a writ of habeas corpus subsequently brought by the parents for the recovery of their children, will inquire into such children's welfare without being restricted by the ordinary modes of trial. Neither will it require the children to be brought into open court, nor their residence disclosed to their parents.[1] But where there is a contest between rival claimants for the custody of a child, nothing short of the production of the body will satisfy the exigency of the writ.[2]

The discharge of an insane man by his keeper, who is satisfied of his restoration to reason, and before the return day of the writ, will also excuse the non-production of the body. "If the relator were detained 'for any criminal or supposed criminal matter,' it would be worse than a contempt, after service of the writ, for the respondent to discharge the relator. In such a case the jailer would be liable for an escape; but if mental disease is a cause of detention, restoration to health is *ipso facto*, and *eo instanti*, a clamorous reason for discharge."[3] That the prisoner is a lunatic on the return day of the writ will excuse his non-production.[4] In such cases, however, the court will sometimes have the matter investigated, and act upon the truth of the matters shown by such inspection.[5] Sickness is also another exception to the general rule. In early English practice, it was held that if a jailer return one *languidas*, when the party himself brought his habeas corpus, and was in good health, an attachment should be issued against him; otherwise if the habeas corpus was brought by another.[6] In cases of illness the court will frequently make a rule that at all proper times and seasonable hours relatives and others shall be admitted to consult with, advise, and assist a distressed prisoner;[7] but a request for such purposes will be denied to those who have not the least pretension to demand it.[8] In the United States it has been held that a return to the writ that the party is sick and languishing, so that his production would imperil and endanger his life, will excuse the non-production of the body.[9] Neither can the body be produced if the prisoner be dead.[10] That before the service of the writ the prisoner was discharged out of respondent's custody by competent legal

[1] Dumain and Wife v. Anne L. Gwynne, 10 Allen, 271.
[2] Commonwealth v. Kirkbride, 7 Phila. 1.
[3] Id.
[4] Rex v. Clarke, 3 Burr. 1363.
[5] Rex v. Turlington, 2 Burr. 1115.
[6] Bac. Abr., Habeas Corpus, sec. 8.
[7] Rex v. Wright, Voss, et al., 2 Burr. 1099.
[8] Rex v. Clarke, 3 Burr. 1363.
[9] Ex parte Bryant, 2 Tyler, 269.
[10] Dalton's Sheriff, 251.

authority, is also a valid excuse.[1] Where the defendant is a physician, and has been treating a woman for lunacy, and returned "that before the delivery of the writ he had delivered the woman to her husband, and that he does not know where she is, nor can he produce her," the non-production of the body will be excused;[2] so will it be where it is returned "that before the coming of the writ the party had, by force and arms, broke the said prison, and out of my custody, without any leave and against my will, escaped and fled to places to me unknown, and is not yet brought back or retaken."[3]

Another very important exception to the general rule is found in the practice in this country, viz.: where it appears on the return to the writ of habeas corpus before a state court or judge that the imprisoned party is "held by an officer of the United States under what in truth purports to be the authority of the United States." On such a return to the writ the respondent is not bound to produce the body of the prisoner.[4]

A return not accompanied by the production of the body will be scanned with great caution;[5] and upon the return to a habeas corpus that the party was not in respondent's custody, nor within his control, the court refused to hear evidence that the prisoner was a minor, and had enlisted in the army; where it was desired that an order should be passed upon such evidence, declaring the restraint to be unlawful.[6] Section 758 of the habeas corpus act of the United States[7] requires the person making the return to bring the body of the party detained before the judge who granted the writ at the same time the return is made. This seems to admit of no exceptions; at least, none are expressed. But there is an express exception in the statute of 31 Car. II.,[8] that the one to whom the writ is directed is not obliged to bring up one who is charged with treason or felony plainly expressed in the warrant of commitment. The practice under this statute seems to have been that the reasons simply of the prisoner's detention, without the production of his body, could be returned where he was in execution upon process after judgment from any court of competent jurisdiction; and also where the party detained was imprisoned for any civil cause of action, but this was changed by the statute of 56 Geo. III., c. 100. In these cases

[1] King v. Bethuen Andr. 281.
[2] Rex v. Wright, 2 Stra. 901.
[3] Hurd on Habeas Corpus, 2d ed., 249.
[4] Ableman v. Booth, 21 How. 506; Tarble's Case, 13 Wall. 397; Ex parte Sifford, Marshal, et al., 5 Am. Law Reg. 659; In re Neill, 8 Blatchf. 156; In the Matter of Hopson, 40 Barb. 34.
[5] Ex parte Coupland, 26 Tex. 386.
[6] Commonwealth v. Chandler, 11 Mass. 83.
[7] See sec. 59.
[8] Id., 58.

it was required that the return distinctly show by whom and for what cause the prisoner was committed.[1] It is obvious to the reader that such a practice gave to the jailer, or one who detained another, the power to put his own construction upon the warrant of commitment; and just how far this indulgence would be allowed to them can only be mentioned as a matter of curiosity.

§ 164. **Statement of the Cause of Arrest.**—As upon the return of the writ the court is to judge whether the cause of the commitment and detainer be according to law or against it, so the officer, or party in whose custody the prisoner is, must, according to the command of the writ, certify on the return thereof the day, and cause of caption and detainer.[2] The object of the proceeding in habeas corpus is to set the prisoner free from present illegal restraint, and he is entitled to it although the original taking was unlawful;[3] and if on return day the respondent shows a legal cause for the detention of the prisoner, the relator will be remanded or bailed, notwithstanding the original taking was unlawful.[4] And, as we have already seen,[5] the original warrant of commitment may be irregular, but if a regular warrant of detention for the same offense, issued subsequently to the writ of habeas corpus, be returned, the prisoner will not be discharged.[6] We have also seen[7] that the day of taking is seldom material, so it be *ante adventum brevis;*[8] but a return "that he did not detain and never had detained her" is no answer to the taking, and as the court will require this, the return may be so amended as to include it.[9]

§ 165. **Statement of the Cause of Detention.**—The return should show an express and certain cause of commitment;[10] and it is said in general that upon the return to the writ of habeas corpus the cause of imprisonment ought to appear as specifically and certainly to the judges before whom it is returned as it did to the court or person authorized to commit; for if the commitment be against law, as being made by one who had no jurisdiction of the cause, or for a matter for which by law no man ought to be punished, the court are to discharge him, and therefore the certainty of the commitment ought to appear; and the commitment is liable to the same objection, where the cause

---

[1] 1 Ch. Crim. L. 128.
[2] Bac. Abr., Habeas Corpus, sec. 9.
[3] Hurd on Habeas Corpus, 2d ed., 251.
[4] Dows' Case, 18 Pa. St. 37.
[5] See sec. 143.
[6] Ex parte Cross, 2 Hurl. & N. 354; Queen v. Richards Bird et al., 5 Ad. & El. Q. B. 926; S. C., 48 Eng. Com. L. 926; Ex parte Page, 1 Barn. & Ald. 568.
[7] See sec. 126.
[8] Hutchins v. Player, Bridg. 275.
[9] Warman's Case, 2 W. Black. 1203.
[10] Com. Dig., Habeas Corpus, E, 3.

is so loosely set forth that the court can not adjudge whether it were a reasonable ground of imprisonment or not.[1]

The authority which will justify the detention may be either that which purports to be by legal process or that which is founded upon private relations. Detention under legal process may be by a commitment in writing, or by an order of court or authority of law. And, as before observed,[2] Chief Justice Holt has said: "Where there is a warrant in writing, it must be returned, for otherwise it would be in the power of the jailer to alter the case of the prisoner, and make it either better or worse than it is upon the warrant, and if he may take it upon himself to return what he will, he makes himself judge; whereas the court ought to judge, and that upon the warrant itself."[3] In fact, the whole commitment must be set out.[4] The return need not be confined to the officer's warrant. If that contains recitals or references to other papers, documents, or proceedings relating to the authority to commit, they may be embodied in the return; but it is not necessary that the return should specially set out the document referred to.[5] "Where the commitment is in court to a proper officer there present, there is no warrant of commitment, and therefore he can not return a warrant *in hæc verba*, but must return the truth of the whole matter under peril of an action," said Lord Hale.[6] Chief Justice Parsons, of the supreme judicial court of Massachusetts, long ago decided that "a commitment for legal cause of any man present in court by an order of a competent court, entered of record, is still a legal commitment, and the sheriff is bound to obey the order. The prisoner knows for what cause and by whom he is committed, and he may at any time have a copy of the record; and the sheriff, if called upon to justify the imprisonment, or to certify the cause of it, may have access to the same record, a copy of which the clerk will give him *ex officio*."[7] And when the officer is called upon to justify a detention upon such a commitment, he should return a copy of the record of the commitment as the cause. So where the minutes of the court below furnished to a keeper imperfectly describe the crime of which a relator has been convicted, he should resort to the records of the court to show what the precise crime was when called upon to make return, etc.[8]

[1] Bac. Abr., Habeas Corpus, sec. 10.
[2] See sec. 121.
[3] King v. Clerk, 1 Salk. 349.
[4] In the Matter of Power, 2 Russ. 583.
[5] Leonard Watson's Case, 9 Ad. & El. 731.
[6] King v. Clerk, 1 Salk. 349.
[7] Randall v. Bridge, 2 Mass. 549; People v. Nevins, 1 Hill (N. Y.), 154.
[8] People v. Baker, 89 N. Y. 460.

Where a prisoner charged with an offense comes into court on a recognizance, and after conviction is sentenced to imprisonment, the sheriff is obliged to obey the order of court, and to commit the prisoner in execution. Here, too, on application to the clerk, he may have a copy after sentence.[1] That the return need not be confined to the simple copy of the order of commitment, but may include copies of any other orders or proceedings referred to in the order of commitment, and showing the grounds of commitment, was shown in the celebrated case of Yates.[2] The sheriff returned that he held the prisoner by order of the court of chancery, which order referred to a former attachment, setting forth the grounds of commitment, and from which the prisoner had been discharged by a judge of the supreme court in vacation, on another habeas corpus, and he also returned the attachment and proceedings prior to the last order of commitment. It was ruled that the sheriff could not return the true cause of the caption without also stating the original attachment and subsequent orders; and that the whole might be received and examined into by the court.[3]

Detention which is not by legal process, or that which purports to be, is generally exercised by private authority, and is founded upon some right, or supposed right, arising or growing out of the domestic or civil relations, and when the restraint or detention is exercised by this power, the return must set forth all the facts which are relied on to justify the detention or restraint.[4]

PART III.—ANSWERING THE RETURN.

§ 166. **Return not Controvertible at Common Law.**—The general English doctrine, both under the common law and the statute of 31 Car. II., is that the truth of the return can not be controverted with a view to the discharge of the prisoner; but with a view to determine whether it be reasonable to bail the prisoner or not, the court will sometimes examine by affidavit the circumstances of a fact on which a prisoner brought before them by habeas corpus has been indicted, in order to inform themselves, on examination of the whole matter.[5] There

---

[1] Randall v. Bridge, 2 Mass. 549.
[2] Case of Yates, 4 Johns. 314.
[3] Id.; see also Bac. Abr., Habeas Corpus, sec. 9.
[4] U. S. v. Green, 3 Mason, 482; Com. v. Reed, 59 Pa. St. 425.
[5] 2 Hawk. P. C., c. 15, sec. 79. In 1758, while a bill concerning the writ of habeas corpus was before the house of lords, several questions were proposed to the judges, and among them this one: "Whether, in all cases whatsoever, the judges are so bound by the facts set forth in the return to the writ of habeas corpus, that they can not discharge the person brought up before them, although it should appear most manifestly to the judges,

§ 166. THE RETURN. 211

are some exceptions to this rule occasionally to be met with, but they can not be noted or classified without transcending the limits of this work. To keep in mind that one of the paramount objects of the statute of 31 Car. II. was and is to allow prisoners committed for criminal or supposed criminal matters to be speedily let to bail, where by law they are bailable, will afford a sufficient general guide and rule in all cases. It will by the clearest and most undoubted proof, that such return is false in fact, and that the person so brought up is restrained of his liberty by the most unwarrantable means, and in direct violation of law and justice." Lord Chief Justice Willes, and Justices Noel, Bathurst, Clive, and Baron Legge, answered briefly in the negative: Bac. Abr., Habeas corpus, sec. 13. Mr. Justice Foster, who was prevented from attending the house on account of the illness and death of Lady Foster, subsequently concurred with them, having previously written in the margin of his manuscript, "God forbid that they should." Chief Baron Parker's answer ran thus: "That in no cases whatsoever the judges are so bound by the facts set forth in the returns to the writ of habeas corpus that they can not discharge the person brought up before them, if it should appear most manifestly to the judges, by the clearest and most undoubted proof, that such return is false in fact, and that the person so brought up is restrained of his liberty by the most unwarrantable means, and in direct violation of law and justice; but by the clearest and most undoubted proof." But by "the clearest and most undoubted proof" he understood the verdict of a jury, or judgment on demurrer, or otherwise, in an action for a false return; and in case the facts returned to a writ of habeas corpus showed a sufficient ground in point of law for such restraint, he was of opinion that the court or judge before whom such writ was returnable could not try the facts contained in such return by affidavits. The question was answered in nearly the same way by Messrs. Barons Smythe and Adams and Messrs. Justices Wilmot and Dennison. Mr. Justice Foster observed, that if the opinions of these judges were agreeable to law, the greatest injury might be done to a man without a possibility of redress. And as is shown in a copy of a letter which this learned justice wrote to Mr. Solicitor General Yorke, early in 1758, he appears to have used this language: "As I always considered the case of a barely wrongful detention as not within the habeas corpus act, but merely at common law, I thought a legal sound discretion ought to be used, and generally expected an affidavit, on behalf of the party applying for the writ, setting forth some probable ground for relief upon the merits of his case. This method I constantly observed in the case of men pressed into the service; and that the public service might not suffer by an abuse of the writ, I ordered notice to be given to the proper officers of the crown, of the time at which the party was to be brought before me, with copies of the affidavits. * * * From the few notes which I have relating to that matter, I find that the court hath not granted the writ as of course, and within the habeas corpus act, but hath required affidavits on the behalf of the party applying for it, setting forth the merits of his case; and on the other hand, though proper returns in point of form may have been made, the court hath not given entire credit to them, and put the party complaining to his remedy by action for a false imprisonment; but hath constantly entered into the merits of the case upon affidavits, and either discharged or remanded the party, as the case hath appeared."

On May 24, 1758, he also wrote to Lord Chief Baron Parker as follows: "I agree with your lordship in the truth of the general doctrine, that a return to a writ of habeas corpus is conclusive in point of fact. It can not be traversed; the court is bound by it, and the injured party is driven to his action. This, I admit, is the general rule; but I think that it is not universally true. Cases may be put which are exceptions to it; and exceptions do not, as your lordship well knows, destroy, but rather establish, a general rule. The case of persons

be perceived that the provisions of the statute of 31 Car. II. extend only to cases of commitment or detainer for criminal or supposed criminal matters, and excepted even out of that class all who were convict or in execution by legal process, or who were committed for felony or treason, plainly expressed in the warrant of commitment;[1] so the statute of 56 Geo. III. was passed in 1816 for more effectually securing the liberty of the subject, and which enacted that the truth of the facts set forth in the return to a writ of habeas corpus isued in favor of any

pressed into service is, I conceive, one of them, for this plain reason, that if the party can not controvert the truth of the facts set forth in the return, he is absolutely without remedy. An inadequate, ineffectual remedy is no remedy; it is a rope thrown out to a drowning man which can not reach him or will not bear his weight. It is the offering of baubles to the children of one's family when they are crying for bread. In common cases, in every case where the general rule is laid down, the injured party must wait with patience till he can falsify the return in a proper action. This, it must be confessed, is a great misfortune; but till the day of his deliverance comes, he continues at home in the custody of the law, and under its protection. This your lordship knows is not the case of a man pressed into the service by land or sea, supposing him to be no object of the law. * * * The principle, as I take it, is, that though in common cases the return is conclusive in point of fact, yet these special cases, as they come not within the general reason of the law, are not within the general rule. The parties are without remedy if they are not to controvert the truth of the return in a summary way; and therefore they shall do it:" 20 Howell's State Trials, 1375, 1380. No other exceptions were mentioned by the learned justice, and the unimportance at this day of the practice regarding them will not justify the almost interminable task of searching them out and setting them forth in these pages. The exception of impressment, however, seems to have been clearly established, and it may be assumed safely that the controlling principle governing the discretion of the courts in all exceptions to cases of imprisonment or restraint, other than for criminal or supposed criminal matters, is to allow the truth of the facts set forth in the return to be controverted where the prisoner has no other effectual remedy.

Yet, notwithstanding all this, no notice was taken in the following session of the bill which the judges had prepared, nor was the subject in any, the slightest, manner touched upon. All that had passed seemed to have at once sunk into oblivion; and the law as it stood was acquiesced in, as fully adequate to the public security: Bac. Abr., Habeas Corpus, sec. 13. The views entertained by the courts since this matter was stirred in the house of lords may be only briefly illustrated by a few examples for want of space.

Goldswain's Case.—Here the court took into consideration the affidavits on which the writ was issued, but the facts of which were not noticed on the return. Justice Gould said: "I do not conceive that either the court or the party are concluded by the return of a habeas corpus, but may plead to it any special matter necessary to regain his liberty." This was the case of an impressed seaman, and who was liable to be sent immediately to America: 2 W. Black. 1205.

Ex parte Clarke.—Here there was an adjudication by the court of first instance that it was sitting, and that a contempt had been committed at the bar of the court; but the court of queen's bench would not allow affidavits to be received to contradict that adjudication: 2 Gale & Dav. 788; S. C., 2 Ad. & El. 619.

Crowley's Case.—In this celebrated and leading case in bankruptcy the lord chancellor said that a court before which the writ is brought can not travel out of the return: 2 Swans. 82. The same thing was said in Ex parte Oliver, 2 Ves. & B. 244, a similar case.

[1] See habeas corpus act, 31 Car. II., *ante*, sec. 58.

§ 166.   THE RETURN.   213

one " confined or restrained of his or her liberty (otherwise than for some criminal or supposed criminal matter, and except persons imprisoned for debt, or by process in any civil suit) within that part of Great Britain," etc., could be inquired into either by the judges or court authorized to issue the writ.[1] This statute somewhat abated the rigor of the rule that the return could not be controverted, at least in a certain class of cases to which it applies in its limited application. The effect of this statute, with the doubt expressed by Lord Chief Justice Denman in Leonard Watson's Case, in 1839, would seem to indicate that

---

[1] 56 Geo. III., c. 100, secs. 1, 3, 4. Probably the first decision made upon this statute as to inquiry into the return was nearly ten years after its passage. It was given in Ex parte Beeching, 6 Dow. & Ry. 209. Writs of habeas corpus were issued to bring up several persons who had been taken into custody at sea under the provisions of the customs acts, and carried to the city of Rochester and detained an unreasonable length of time, for the purpose of being examined before a justice of that city, contrary to the provisions of the statute of 57 Geo. III., c. 87, sec. 6, which enacts that persons arrested under the authority of that statute shall be conveyed before one or more justices of the peace residing near the place where such persons shall be so taken or arrested. The return alleged, among other matters, that the prisoners had been carried to Rochester with their own consent, and there detained for the purpose of being examined on a charge of smuggling; whereupon affidavits were tendered on behalf of the prisoners, for the purpose of contradicting the facts so stated in the return, but the court, at first doubting its authority to inquire into the truth of the return, called upon Barrister Platt to show that the court had such authority, which he did; and after argument to the contrary, Chief Justice Abbott said: "If no decision has taken place upon this statute, it is probable that the point was never made before. The object of the habeas corpus act of 31 Car. II., c. 2, was to provide against delays in bringing to trial such subjects of the king as are committed to custody for criminal or supposed criminal matters. The person making this return is not an officer to whose custody these persons have been committed, but he is a person who, by the authority given him, has taken them into custody. It seems to me, therefore, that the writs of habeas corpus in this instance are not to be considered as writs issuing under the statute of 31 Car. II., but as writs issuing at common law under the general authority of the court, and consequently that the discussion of the truth of the return is left open by virtue of the statute of 56 Geo. III., c. 100, sec. 4. This is not the case of a committal to a jailer or an officer of the court for an offense known as a crime, and the only question is whether this is a criminal matter. The object of the statute of 56 Geo. III. was to give the party a summary remedy by controverting the truth of a return, instead of putting him to bring an action for a false return. There is very good reason for not permitting the truth of a return to be traversed where the party is charged with a crime, for that would be trying him upon affidavits; but here we are not called upon to try whether these persons have committed an offense, or that which may be called an offense. The objection to the proceeding against these persons is, that they have been carried a distance of one hundred and forty miles from the place where they were originally arrested. Part of the allegation in the return is, that they were taken to Rochester with their own consent. Now I think the truth of the return in that respect may be controverted. The statute of 56 Geo. III. was passed in furtherance of the liberty of the subject, and therefore ought not to receive a restrained construction." Justices Bayley, Holroyd, and Littledale concurred. The merits of the case were then discussed on affidavits, resulting in the prisoners being remanded.

there is a tendency in England to mollify the strict rule of the incontrovertibility of the return in all cases of habeas corpus. It is true his lordship left the question undecided in Watson's Case, but he said: "As to the question how far the truth of this return might be canvassed, I neither assent to nor dissent from the propositions which have been laid down. I am not prepared to say that if Watson (the prisoner) had pledged his oath (he had not verified the return) to the falsity of any statement of fact on the return, we might or might not make that the foundation of a proceeding to quash the return. If we could, there is no foundation for the complaint that the remedy by habeas corpus is illusory. Nor, indeed, in so singular and anomalous a case, could it be inferred, from the absence of precedent, that those who framed or have administered the law on this subject were imposing anything like a fraud on the country, or that those provisions can therefore be said to be ineffectual which for so long a time have bestowed upon the liberty of the subject a protection unknown in other countries."

In Canada it has been held that the prisoner may contradict the return to the writ of habeas corpus by showing that one of the persons who signed the warrant was not a legally qualified justice of the peace.[1]

§ 167. **But Return may be Confessed and Avoided.**— At common law the return to a writ of habeas corpus can be confessed and avoided by admitting the truth of the matters contained in it, and suggesting others, not repugnant, which take off the effect of them.[2] Swallow, a citizen of London, was committed for refusing to accept the office of an alderman of the said city, to which he had been elected. The custom of the city justifying a commitment for such a refusal, and the election and refusal, were set forth in the return to the habeas corpus. He filed a suggestion in the crown office, that he was an officer of the king's mint, and that all such officers were exempted from all city offices, both by prescription and by the king's charter. Thereupon, the patent of the grant of his office, and also the patent of the exemption, being enrolled in the court, he was discharged.[3]

Where a return to a writ of habeas corpus shows that a prisoner is detained under civil process, it is competent for him to show by affidavit that he was originally arrested on a privileged day, as on Sunday,[4] where there is a statute which enacts

---

[1] The Queen v. Patrick Boyle, 4 Prac. Rep. (U. C.) 256.
[2] Hawk. P. C., c. 15, sec. 78.   [3] Id.
[4] Ex parte Eggington, 24 Eng. L. & Eq. 146; S. C., 18 Jur. 224; 2 El. & Bl. 717.

that no person upon the Lord's day shall serve or execute any writ, process, warrant, order, judgment, or decree (except in cases of treason felony, or breach of peace), and that it shall be void, etc.; or that he is privileged against arrest in execution for debt where he is entitled by law to be discharged from a commitment in execution for debt.[1]

It will be observed that in the three instances given above, the arrests were not made on criminal process—or rather, that the detention was not "for any criminal or supposed criminal matters," and therefore not within the statute of 31 Car. II. In 1843, on motion to discharge a party who had been charged with being a deserter, and committed therefor, and who had been brought up by a writ of habeas corpus, affidavits suggesting matters which, though not repugnant to the return, showed the custody to be illegal, would not be admitted or noticed.[2] This detention was "for a criminal matter or supposed criminal matter," and consequently within the statute of 31 Car. II. And while the court would not notice affidavits here, and while the court in Leonard Watson's Case,[3] which was also for "a criminal matter or supposed criminal matter," considered it questionable whether the return could be traversed in pleading, or merely confessed and avoided, there are doubtless cases under the statute of 31 Car. II. where the return may be confessed and avoided, although it makes no direct allusion to the subject, but the courts and judges have not been free to enumerate the instances in which "confession and avoidance" applies under this statute.[4] The statute of 56 Geo. III. has already been referred to, and while under it the return can be controverted in certain enumerated cases, there is no question but what the plea of confession and avoidance can be used.[5] Under this statute the return may be controverted, or confessed and avoided, even where the prisoner is brought up under a habeas corpus issued at common law.[6]

§ 168. **Doctrine in the United States.**—Except as otherwise provided by the habeas corpus act of the United States, the federal courts are governed, in proceedings on habeas corpus, by the rules of the common law, and what that law is has been, in some measure the result of our investigation. The subject under consideration seems to be fully provided for by section

---

[1] Ex parte Dakin; In re Swann v. Dakins, 29 Eng. L. & Eq. 331.
[2] Reg. v. Douglas, 7 Jur. 59; 12 Law Jour. Rep., N. S., 49.
[3] 9 Ad. & El. 731; S. C., 1 Per. & Dav. 516.
[4] In the Matter of Clarke, 2 Ad. & El. 619.
[5] See sec. 166.
[6] Ex parte Beeching et al., 4 Barn. & Cress. 136.

760 of said act, which reads: "The petitioner, or the party imprisoned or restrained, may deny any of the facts set forth in the return, or may allege any other facts that may be material in the case. Said denials or allegations shall be under oath. The return and all suggestions made against it may be amended, by leave of the court or justice or judge, before or after the same are filed, so that thereby the material facts may be ascertained."[1]

Statutory enactments have, in most of the states, illuminated this vexed question which seems so dark in the common law. They have conferred upon the courts power to hear allegations and evidence controverting the return, or that the truth of the facts set forth in the return may be confessed and avoided. These provisions are so numerous, however, that we must refer the searcher for information concerning them to the laws of each respective state.

---

[1] See habeas corpus act of the United States, *ante*, sec. 59. The current of the decisions of the federal courts under various acts of congress laid a broad and solid foundation for this statute. It was conceded in Ex parte Jenkins et al., 2 Wall. jun. 521, and Ex parte Sifford, Marshal et al., 5 Am. Law Reg. 659, that upon a habeas corpus issued under the judiciary act of 1789, the return of the warrant of commitment, under the proviso to the fourteenth section, would be conclusive. It ran thus: "That all the before-mentioned courts [the supreme court, the circuit courts, and the district courts of the United States] shall have power to issue writs of *scire facias*, habeas corpus, and all other writs not especially provided for by statute, which may be necessary for the exercise of their respective jurisdictions, and agreeable to the principles and usages of law, and that either of the justices of the supreme court, as well as judges of the district courts, shall have power to grant writs of habeas corpus for the purpose of an inquiry into the cause of commitment; provided, that writs of habeas corpus shall in no case extend to prisoners in jail unless they are in custody under or by order of the authority of the United States, or are committed for trial before some court of the same, or are necessary to be brought into court to testify:" 1 U. S. Stat. at Large, 81. But this act was extended in 1833 by statute, 4 Stat. at Large, 634, "to prisoners confined under any authority, whether state or national, for any act done or omitted in pursuance of a law of the United States, or of any order, process, or decree of any judge or court of the United States;" and by act of 1842, 5 Stat. at Large, 539, "to prisoners being subjects or citizens of foreign states, in custody under national or state authority for acts done or omitted by or under color of foreign authority, and alleged to be valid under the law of nations;" and by act of 1867, 14 Stat. at Large, 385, it was still further provided "that the several courts of the United States, and the several justices and judges of such courts, within their respective jurisdictions, in addition to the authority already conferred by law, shall have power to grant writs of habeas corpus in all cases where any person may be restained of his or her liberty, in violation of the constitution, or of any treaty or law of the United States," etc.

Since the act of 1833 was passed, the federal courts have not denied that the return may be controverted; that it may be traversed and proved false on the hearing; and, in short, that all facts material in the case may be shown on the hearing. For authority, see United States ex rel. Wheeler v. Passmore Williamson, 3 Am. Law Reg. 729; S. C., 5 Pa. Law Jour. Rep. 365; Ex parte Jenkins, 2 Wall. jun. 521; Nelson & Graydon v. Cutter & Tyrrell, 3 McLean, 326; Ex parte Smith, 3 Id. 121; United States v. Green, 3 Mason, 482.

CHAPTER XII.

THE ISSUES, AND HOW TRIED—CUSTODY OF THE PRISONER.

PART I.—ISSUES OF LAW AND FACT.

§ 169. Issue of Law.
§ 170. Issues of Both Law and Fact.

PART II.—THE MODE OF TRIAL.

§ 171. At Common Law.
§ 172. Jury Trial.
§ 173. In the United States.
§ 174. Tom Tong, and the Indiana Cases—Change of Venue.

PART III.—CUSTODY OF PRISONER DURING THE TRIAL.

§ 175. At Common Law.
§ 176. In the United States.

PART I.—ISSUES OF LAW AND FACT.

§ 169. **Issues of Law.**—The issue raised on the hearing of a habeas corpus may be one of law simply. This is the issue raised where the facts stated in the return are not controverted. That is, when the detention of the prisoner is claimed to be illegal, and he claims a legal exemption from it. "The writ of habeas corpus," said Mr. Justice Wilmot, "is not framed or adapted to litigating facts; it is a summary, short way of taking the opinion of the court upon a matter of law, where the facts are disclosed and admitted; it puts the case exactly in the same situation as if an action of false imprisonment had been brought, and the defendant had set forth the facts to justify the imprisonment, and the plaintiff had demurred to the plea."[1] In this country the issue has been thus defined: "In habeas corpus, where the petitioner alleges imprisonment by the respondent, under a specific claim of authority, and an exemption in law by reason of certain stated facts, and the respondent asserts the authority, and admitting the facts stated, denies the legal exemption set up, there arises a simple issue of law, which must be

[1] Wilmot's Opinions, 106.

tried by the case made, and no fact *dehors* the record can be legally considered."[1]

A motion to discharge will raise all the issues in the case. If the petition is considered defective, the respondent should move to quash the writ of habeas corpus on the ground of the alleged insufficiency of the petition, which objection would come in the form of a reply to the petition. A demurrer to the petition is not good practice, though it has been allowed.[2] But the question raised by either course is the same, viz.: Was sufficient cause shown to authorize the issuing of the writ? The sufficiency of the return in law may be tested on a motion to discharge the prisoner. And this motion has the effect of a demurrer. On demurrer, either to the petition or on a motion to discharge, the facts stated in the petition or in the return are conceded to be true. On a motion to discharge the prisoner, the sufficiency of the return alone is examined.[3]

§ 170. **Issues of Both Law and Fact.**—But the prisoner may not wish to admit certain facts set forth in the return, and in this country he has power, in most of the states and in the federal courts, and also under the English statute of 56 Geo. III., c. 100, sec. 4, to deny or controvert any material allegations of fact set up in the return; or he may wish to confess and avoid them. This will raise a question of fact, which must first be determined; and then, if a question of law remain, it will be disposed of. What facts may properly be put in issue covers a wide field of inquiry, and must depend upon each particular case. But the rule expressive of the general doctrine is, that only those matters which have a necessary connection with the question of the validity of the detention or imprisonment will be considered, and other matters will be uniformly rejected. Only such questions as are necessarily involved will be determined. "When the commitment is under express legal process," says Hurd,[4] "those facts may be put in issue which, on a question arising only collaterally, are necessary to warrant the imprisonment; and where the restraint is claimed under private authority, those facts may be put in issue which are legally

---

[1] Camfield v. Patterson, 33 Ga. 561.
[2] Hovey et ux. v. Morris, 7 Blackf. 559. In Wisconsin a demurrer to the return has been allowed: In re Booth, 3 Wis. 12; see Ableman v. Booth, and United States v. Booth, 21 How. 506. But in Indiana it has been said that this is not the proper method of testing the sufficiency of the return: Cunningham v. Thomas, 25 Ind. 171. And exceptions will not lie to the return. It should be met by reply or answer: Nichols v. Cornelius, 7 Port. 611.
[3] Watson's Case, 36 Eng. Com. L. 254.
[4] Habeas Corpus, 2d ed., 291.

necessary to justify the detention." In determining the delicate and embarrassing questions which sometimes arise on the return to a writ of habeas corpus, the true nature of the writ, to free from unlawful restraint, should be constantly kept in view. We shall hereafter see that in cases affecting the custody of infants, lunatics, etc., it is sometimes necessary for the courts to dispose of the prisoner under certain circumstances, and this involves additional inquiries; but in ordinary cases the only question is, whether the complaining party is illegally deprived of his liberty.[1]

The right of guardianship will not be tried on habeas corpus.[1] It is true that if a ward obtains the writ to be released from his guardian's control, the court will determine whether the guardian has the right to the ward's custody; and if it finds that he has, the court has *eo instanti* determined that the ward is under no unlawful restraint; no judgment is given in favor of the guardian, and he is left to take charge of his ward. And where the guardian sues out the writ to recover his ward from the custody of another, or intervenes on the hearing of a writ concerning the custody of his ward, his right of guardianship, if controverted in good faith, will not, as a general thing, be adjudicated; for it is not the office of the writ to recover wards or infants, or to determine questions not necessarily involved under it.

The prisoner may raise an issue of fact on the return by a clear and definite statement, in the form of a reply to the return, of any fact which he relies upon to show the illegality of his imprisonment.[2] An issue of fact may also be formed upon the return by a denial of its averments; or by alleging new facts, legally admissible, to avoid the effect of such averments.[3] The issues raised in contests affecting the custody of persons under private authority will hereafter be seen in chapters devoted to that subject.[4] The writ will not be used to try the rights of property,[5] nor as a writ of *quo warranto*.[6] When the return to

---

[1] People v. Mercein, 5 Paige, 47; Ferguson v. Ferguson, 36 Mo. 197; Commonwealth v. Hamilton, 6 Mass. 273; Fitts v. Fitts, 21 Tex. 511; Mathews v. Wade, 2 W. Va. 464; People v. Wilcox, 22 Barb. 186; State v. Banks, 25 Ind. 495; Rex v. Smith, 2 Stra. 982; S. C., Ridgw. Rep. 200; Rex v. Johnson, 1 Stra. 579; S. C., 2 Ld. Raym. 1333; Rex v. Delaval, 3 Burr. 1436; In re Taylor, an infant, L. R., 4 Ch. Div., 157.

[2] In the Matter of Ferrens, 3 Ben. 442.

[3] Speer v. Davis, 38 Ind. 271; Leary's Case, 6 Abb. N. C. 43; United States v. Williamson, 3 Am. Law Reg. 729; Roth v. House of Refuge, 31 Md. 329.

[4] See Rex v. Clarkson, 1 Stra. 447; Commonwealth v. Robinson, 1 Serg. & R. 353; Lea v. White, 4 Sneed, 73.

[5] State v. Fraser, Dudley (Ga.), 42; Foster et ux. v. Alston, 6 How. (Miss.) 406; Clark v. Gautier, 8 Fla. 360; De Lacy v. Antoine, 7 Leigh, 438; Ruddle's Executors v. Ben, 10 Id. 468; Shue v. Turk, 15 Gratt. 256.

[6] In the Matter of Wakker, 3 Barb. 162; Ex parte Strahl, 16 Iowa, 369; State v. Bloom, 17 Wis. 521; Clark v. Com., 29 Pa. St. 129; Russell v. Whiting, 1 Winst. 465.

a habeas corpus is traversed, no further pleading is required to put its affirmance in issue, as the averments of the answer are to be taken as denied by the respondent.[1] If the return contain an averment of insanity, and the relator traverses this averment in due form, the issue is directly raised, whether the relator is of unsound mind or not.[2] The question of identity is always an open one in habeas corpus proceedings—the mandate must be served on the party named therein, in extradition matters.[3] So the question of identity must be raised in determining whether the petitioner is the person enlisted or not.[4] So in a case where an apprentice sues out the writ, and the respondent, his master, sets out an order of a court binding the petitioner to him; the apprentice may reply that the order is void, and show this by proving that he is not such person as the court had power to bind out at all; or that he had no notice of the proceedings against him, and therefore no opportunity of being heard.[5] A mistake in age is not one which a court will investigate on habeas corpus, particularly after commitment—as to house of refuge, etc.[6]

PART II.—THE MODE OF TRIAL.

§ 171. **At Common Law.**—When the bill entitled "An act for giving a more speedy remedy to the subject upon the writ of habeas corpus" was before the house of lords in 1758, the second of a series of questions proposed to the judges was, whether, in cases not within the act of 31 Car. II., writs of *habeas corpus ad subjiciendum*, by the law as it then stood, might issue in vacation by fiat from a judge of the court of king's bench, returnable before himself. To this question Lord Chief Justice Willes, Lord Chief Baron Parker, Messrs. Justices Wilmot and Dennison, and Messrs. Barons Adams, Smythe, and Legge answered: "That in cases not within the act of 31 Car. II., writ of *habeas corpus subjiciendum*, by the law as it now stands, may issue in the vacation by fiat from a judge of the court of king's bench, returnable before himself." Messrs. Justices Noel, Bathurst, and Clive went one step further, and said "that at the common law, before the statute of 31 Car. II., no judge could regularly issue writ of habeas *corpus ad subjiciendum* in vacation; but

---

[1] Leary's Case, 6 Abb. N. C. 43; United States v. Williamson, 3 Am. Law Reg. 729. See U. S. R. S., sec. 760, *ante*, sec. 59.
[2] Commonwealth ex rel. Helmbold v. Kirkbride, Physician etc., 11 Phila. 427.
[3] Leary's Case, 6 Abb. N. C. 43.
As to identity of infant, see Young v. The State, 15 Ind. 480.
[4] In the Matter of Hamilton, 1 Ben. 455.
[5] In the Matter of Ambrose, Phill. 91.
[6] People v. Superintendent House of Refuge, 8 Abb. Pr., N. S., 112; In the Matter of Mason, 8 Mich. 70.

by the law as it now stands, upon the practice of the courts of king's bench ever since the said statute, such writs may issue in the vacation by a fiat from a judge of the court of king's bench, returnable before himself, in cases not within the said act."[1] It would seem, however, from the inquiries made by Mr. Justice Wilmot into the question that writs of habeas corpus, in criminal cases, were awarded by the chief justice of the king's bench, and the judges of that court, long before the passage of the statute of 31 Car. II.[2] By reference to the statutes of 56 Geo. III. and 31 Car. II., it will be seen that writs of habeas corpus, in both civil and criminal cases, may be issued by a judge in vacation and made returnable before himself, or probably before another officer designated by the one issuing the writ. The trial or hearing then is had before the officer or officers sitting on the return to the writ. But at common law, before the statute of 31 Car. II., when no judge could regularly issue a writ of *habeas corpus ad subjiciendum*, returnable before himself in vacation, the hearing or trial was had before the court in bank.[3]

§ 172. **Jury Trial.**—A very important question is whether the issues in habeas corpus proceedings are to be tried by a judge or jury. The trial of questions of fact by the court seems to be the prevailing practice in both England and the United States. Lord Chief Justice Wilmot, in his opinion cited above, said: "The nature and quality of the fact with which the party is charged, and the jurisdiction which has taken cognizance of it, are to be considered on the return; but the existence of the fact, that is, whether such a fact was committed, or whether there is such a warrant of commitment as the jailer has returned, is a matter which belongs *ad aliud examen*. The court says, 'Tell the reason why you confine him.' The court will determine whether it is a good or bad reason, but not whether it is a true or a false one. The judges are not competent to this inquiry; it is not their province, but the province of a jury, to determine it; *ad questionem juris, non facti, judices respondent*. The writ is not framed or adapted to litigating facts; it is a summary, short way of taking the opinion of the court upon a matter of law, where the facts are disclosed and admitted; it puts the case exactly in the same situation as if an action of false imprisonment had been brought, and the defendant had set forth a series of facts to justify the imprisonment, and the

---

[1] 4 Bac. Abr., Habeas Corpus, 593, B. For Wilmot's opinion, see Wilmot's Opinions, 94.
[2] Wilmot's Opinions, 94.
[3] See Gosline v. Place, 32 Pa. St. 523.

plaintiff had demurred to the plea. A return is the same as the justification demurred to; but in both cases, if the facts are controverted, they must go to a jury; and when the return to a habeas corpus is made and filed, there is an end of the whole proceeding, and the parties have 'no day' in court; and therefore it is impossible that a proceeding, by way of trial, should be grafted upon it. * * * There is no difference between facts in a return and any other facts averred upon record. Suppose an action brought upon a bond for any given sum of money, and the party is arrested upon it and he pleads that he never executed the bond; suppose he could show by affidavits ever so clearly that he did not execute the bond, or, by a copy of the register, that he was not born when it is dated: the court could not interpose. Why? Because the law says the fact must be tried by a jury; the judges have no more cognizance or power to try it than if they were not judges. If they were to do it where there was the clearest and most undoubted proof, they must do it in every case; for the degree of proof can not alter or vary the mode of trial, and translate the examination of the fact from the jury to the judge."

It must be remembered, however, that this was said when the return could not be controverted. Since this pronounced language by his lordship, statutory enactment, 56 Geo. III., has permitted the facts set forth in the return to a habeas corpus proceeding, other than for a criminal or supposed criminal matter, under the statute of 31 Car. II., to be controverted by the party interested in doing so. This necessitates a trial of the facts in many cases, and while the courts have the undoubted power to have their truth determined by a jury, they have appropriated this province themselves; and the decisions of the courts have settled the law, at least so far as the practice goes, in favor of having all issues of fact raised on the return tried by the judge or court. The matter was alluded to in In re Hakewill.[1] This was a case under the statute of 56 Geo. III., which allowed the truth of the facts set forth in the return to be examined into, and the officer hearing the return to do justice in the matter; and was a habeas corpus brought by the mother of some children to have them removed from the custody of their father, who was living separate and apart from his wife. Chief Justice Jervis referred to Lord Denman's doubt expressed in Leonard Watson's Case,[2] as to whether there was

---

[1] 22 Eng. L. & Eq. 395.
[2] 1 Per. & Dav. 516; S. C., 9 Ad. & El. 731; 36 Eng. Com. L. 254.

any mode (other than by action) of impeaching the truth of the return, or of introducing new matter; and added: "I must confess I should have thought that it was competent to the party at whose suit the writ is obtained, to impeach the return upon affidavit, or to traverse it and go to a jury, or to argue upon the return that it does not justify the detention." We must again recollect, in this connection, that the writ in Leonard Watson's Case was for a criminal or supposed criminal matter, and was issued under the statute of 31 Car. II., as all such writs are issued, and where the return is generally looked upon as conclusive.

§ 173. **In the United States.**—The hearing or trial is had before the court or judge before whom the writ is made returnable. By statute it is frequently provided that the writ may be issued by one court or judge, and be made returnable before another judge or court.[1] By the habeas corpus acts of the United States, and of many of the several states, the truth of the facts set forth in the return to a writ of habeas corpus may be inquired into, but this trial of the facts will generally be conducted by the judges or courts. This has become a well-established rule of procedure, and is found to be conducive to the best interests of the prisoner. It affords him the invaluable right to have the question of his personal liberty determined at once. Whatever objections may have ever been raised to thus leaving all the issues of facts involved in habeas corpus proceedings to be determined by the court, they have been silenced by the long and well settled practice in both England and the United States; and if "the course of a court makes a law," and "the practice is a decisive evidence of the law," then is the law well founded, that the issues of fact in such proceedings should be left to the determination of the court. The practice of the courts, however, is not to be understood as affecting their powers. A trial by jury can not be demanded by a prisoner or respondent in a habeas corpus proceeding as a matter of right. Might as well a trial in a preliminary examination, or in chancery, by jury be demanded. There is no provision in the constitution of the United States, neither is there in any of the state constitutions, which gives the right to have these issues of fact tried by a jury in such proceedings. The constitutions, federal and state, provide, substantially, that the right of jury trial shall not be violated, but it is no violation of this inestimable privilege to deny it in chancery proceedings, preliminary examina-

[1] Penal Code of California, sec. 1475.

tions, and proceedings by habeas corpus. But the court or judge sitting on the return to a writ of habeas corpus may, in its discretion, order any controverted fact in the matter to be tried by a jury. This power may be exercised, but it is not the practice to do so, and it has met with little favor.

In New Jersey, applications to the court to impanel a jury to ascertain the facts in habeas corpus proceedings were, in some very early cases, refused,[1] the court expressing itself to the following effect: "We have no power in such a case to order a jury. This is not directly a case of property—it is one of personal liberty—it is a writ of right, intended for the protection of individuals against arbitrary or illegal detentions, and we are to decide upon it in our constitutional capacity, sitting here to superintend the liberty of the citizen, and to protect it from violation."[2] But in Pennsylvania the court said: "We are called on to examine into the facts relating to the case, and must, in some instances, necessarily determine contested facts. If we had any doubt whether the true person was arrested, we should hold ourselves bound to submit the matter to a decision by a jury;"[3] and in 1815, on a habeas corpus depending before the court of common pleas of Philadelphia county, the court ordered an issue to try whether a certain Edward Simmons had a right to hold Shepherd Graham by virtue of an indenture of apprenticeship, whereby the said Shepherd was bound to the said Simmons until he attained the age of fifteen years, to be instructed in the art of a chimney-sweep. A verdict was given in favor of Simmons, which was set aside by the court and a new trial ordered. On the second trial the jury found against Simmons, but a bill of exceptions was taken to the charge of the president of the court.

Chief Justice Tilghman, in rendering the decision of the supreme court in error, observed: "The habeas corpus act authorizes the court to decide both fact and law; but it has been the practice in the common pleas to direct an issue for trial of facts in doubtful cases. The right to order an issue is not denied, but it is said that when an issue is ordered the court have parted with all their power over the facts. It is true they have so far parted with their power that they can not themselves decide the fact. But they still retain the superin-

---

[1] See State v. Farlee, 1 Coxe, 41, 82; and where counsel cites State v. McKnight, in Nov. term, 1782, and State v. Vanhorne, in May, 1785, as cases in which the same application was refused; State v. Beaver, Id. 80.

[2] State v. Farlee, 1 Coxe, 41.

[3] Respublica v. Jailer, 2 Yeates, 258 (1797).

§ 174. THE ISSUES, AND HOW TRIED. 225

tending authority over the verdict. This authority is incident to the trial by jury, by the principles of the common law, where the trial is in a court of record of general jurisdiction, such as the court of common pleas."[1]

In Vermont it was objected, in behalf of the creditors, that a case was not a proper one for the writ of habeas corpus, but that the complainant should be put to his *audita querela*. "This objection," said the court, "would have much force, and probably be decisive, did the party ground this claim to be discharged upon any matter *in pais*, upon which an issue suitable for a jury trial might be expected to arise. But when all is made to depend upon certain papers or documents prescribed by statute, the objection does not hold."[2]

§ 174. **Tom Tong, and the Indiana Cases—Change of Venue.**—In Indiana, in 1864, it was contended that the petitioner[3] for a writ of habeas corpus had the right to a trial by jury. Section 20 of the bill of rights in the constitution of that state then read as follows: "In all civil cases the right of trial by jury shall remain inviolate." The court said in rendering its opinion: "It has been the practice in this state, as well before as since the adoption of our constitution, to try the issues of fact in habeas corpus cases by the court or judge, without a jury. Such a proceeding is not a civil case within the meaning of section 20 of the bill of rights. * * * The habeas corpus act, which is substantially the same as all previous acts on this subject, by providing for a hearing before a judge in vacation, shows that it is a proceeding not embraced in this clause of the bill of rights; that it is not a civil case, and the hearing not a trial; but, like a contested election, it is just what it is called, 'the writ of habeas corpus.'"[4] Again, in 1872, the supreme court of that state in Garner v. Gordon, 41 Ind. 92, adhered to this ruling, and also held that a proceeding by habeas corpus was not a civil action within the meaning of the section of the code giving the right to a change of venue. In arriving at this opinion, the solution of the question by the court as to whether the appellant was entitled to a change of venue was made to depend upon whether the proceeding by habeas corpus was a civil action within the meaning of section 207, 2 G. & H. 154, which gave a right to a change "of venue of any civil action."

[1] Graham v. Graham, 1 Serg. & R. 330.
[2] Ex parte Davis, 18 Vt. 401.
[3] In Baker v. Gordon et al., 23 Ind. 209.
[4] See also French v. Lighty, 9 Ind. 475.

It is clearly understood from the Indiana decisions that a proceeding by habeas corpus is not a civil action; but it is equally well understood from the decision of the supreme court of the United States of May, 1883, in Tom Tong's case, that such a proceeding is a civil proceeding. The latter decision has been made by the highest tribunal known to our law, and has settled a long existing doubt respecting the nature of the writ of habeas corpus. It has been generally regarded by the profession, we believe, as a sort of *quasi* criminal proceeding. But what is the effect of the latter decision? It affects these questions at least: 1. The United States supreme court will have no jurisdiction to review by writ of error or appeal, as the case may be, any judgment or decree of a circuit court of the United States, in proceedings by habeas corpus, until there has been a final judgment or decree rendered in the circuit court. 2. An order or judgment on a habeas corpus proceeding may be rendered in a state court, and where no statute prohibits an appeal to be taken from such order or judgment of the lower court to a higher court, and the statute does allow an appeal from an order or judgment of the lower court in civil actions, why may not an appeal be taken from an adverse decision in a habeas corpus proceeding? Where the whole judiciary of the state may be exhausted by the prisoner in his applications for writs of habeas corpus, there would be little use in taking an appeal, but otherwise, the right of appeal might be of inestimable value to the one against whom the judgment is rendered in the lower court. 3. Again, if it is a civil proceeding, and the statute allows a change of venue in such proceedings upon certain grounds—as, where the judge before whom such a cause may be pending is and will be a material witness for the defendant on the trial of said cause; or where such judge has a bias and prejudice in favor of the plaintiff and against the defendant in said cause, etc.—has not the defendant the right to insist upon his motion for a change of venue where he sets up the required statutory grounds? 4. In states where jury trial is secured to all, and shall remain inviolate, and the prisoner demands a jury trial to pass upon his civil right to personal liberty, how can there be any escape from his demand?

PART III.—CUSTODY OF PRISONER DURING THE TRIAL.

§ 175. **At Common Law.**—It was ruled at common law that the court of king's bench might, after the return to the habeas corpus was filed, remand the prisoner to the same jail

§ 176.   THE ISSUES, AND HOW TRIED.   227

whence he came, and order him to be brought up from time to time, till they should have determined whether it was proper to bail, discharge or remand him absolutely.¹ It seems that it was not necessary for the prisoner to be kept in the Marshalsea, where that court would have complete power over him, but that pending the hearing he might be sent from time to time to the same prison whence he came, and be brought up by rule of court until he was either bailed, discharged, or remanded.² And he might be committed to the sheriff or to the gate-house.³ It was also said, that if the court was in doubt whether to discharge, bail, or remand the prisoner, he might be bailed to appear *de die in diem* till the matter was determined.⁴ In bailing and afterwards remanding the prisoner, it was no escape, for the entry was "*remittitur*," and that was a commitment grounded on the old one.⁵ In short, the efficacy of the original commitment was considered to be superseded by the writ of habeas corpus while the proceedings under it were pending, and the safe keeping of the prisoner was entirely under the authority and direction of the court issuing it, or to which the return was made.

§ 176. **In the United States**, the same principles and practice apply. "Pending the examination or hearing, the prisoner, in all cases, on the return of the writ, is detained, not on the original warrant, but under the authority of the writ of habeas corpus. He may be bailed on the return *de die in diem*, or be remanded to the same jail whence he came, or to any other place of safe keeping under the control of the court or officer issuing the writ, and by its order brought up from time to time, till the court or officer determines whether it is proper to discharge or remand him absolutely." ⁶ This language was substantially repeated in Barth v. Clise, Sheriff.⁷ In this case, where the body of the prisoner was committed by a judge to the custody of a sheriff, it was held that he was not responsible for the escape of the prisoner. Clise, the sheriff, had complied with the order of the court to produce the prisoner on a writ of habeas corpus. While the argument upon the writ was in progress, Clise put Brinkman, the prisoner, in the charge of Judge Dunn, one of his counsel, and absented himself. Before the argument was concluded Brinkman fled to Canada, and failed to return. An action against

---

¹ Bac. Abr., Habeas Corpus, B, sec. 13.
² Anon., Vent. 330; King v. Bethel, 5 Mod. 22.
³ King v. Bethel, 5 Mod. 22.
⁴ Bac. Abr., Habeas Corpus, B, sec. 13.
⁵ King v. Bethel, 5 Mod. 22.
⁶ Mr. Justice Curtis, in In re Kaine, 14 How. 133.
⁷ 12 Wall. 401.

Clise for the escape of Brinkman followed. Verdict and judgment were rendered for defendant Clise. Plaintiff sued out a writ of error from the United States supreme court to the circuit court for the district of Wisconsin, in which state the following statute was in force.[1] The decision of the supreme court was that the entire responsibility for the safe keeping of the prisoner rested with the officer before whom the prisoner was brought pursuant to the writ. It said: "When Clise produced the body of Brinkman before Judge Mills, Clise's duties as the custodian of Brinkman ceased, and this cesser could be terminated only by an order of the judge clothing him with new duties and responsibilities. No such order was made. The flight of Brinkman was, therefore, in no sense an escape from the custody of Clise. His custody by Clise, in the absence of an order from the judge, would have been false imprisonment. The act of Clise in putting Brinkman in the charge of Dunn was simply a nullity. He had no authority at that time to do any act or to give any direction touching the subject." The judgment for the defendant in error was accordingly affirmed.

A Chinese petitioner for a writ of habeas corpus set forth that he was unlawfully restrained of his liberty, and detained on the steamship Oceanic by its captain, in the harbor of San Francisco; and that the alleged ground of his detention was that he came within the act of congress of May 6, 1882, "to execute certain treaty stipulations relating to the Chinese," but Circuit Justices Field and Sawyer, for the district of California, refused to release the prisoner, and ordered him to be returned to the ship from which he was taken.[2]

Where a mother has sued out a writ of habeas corpus which is directed to a guardian to obtain the custody and control of her children, and there is a finding in her favor, it is error for the judge, after an appeal is prayed for and bond given by the guardian, to change the custody of the children from the guardian to the mother pending the appeal.[3]

---

[1] "Until judgment be given upon the return, the officer before whom such party shall be brought may either commit such party to the custody of the sheriff of the county in which such officer shall be, or place him in such care or under such custody as his age and other circumstances may require."

[2] In the Matter of Pong Ah Lung, 12 Pac. C. L. J. 67.

[3] Garner v. Gordon, 41 Ind. 93.

CHAPTER XIII.

THE EVIDENCE.

Part I.—Evidence in General.

§ 177. Preliminary Observations.
§ 178. Oral Testimony, as Well as Written, will be Received.
§ 179. Sufficient Evidence to Authorize Commitment.
§ 180. Weighing Evidence Taken before Committing Magistrate.
§ 181. Weighing Evidence, Continued.
§ 182. Hearing Evidence *de Novo*.
§ 183. Evidence in Petition.
§ 184. Commitment without Testimony.
§ 185. Statement of Evidence in Judgment.
§ 186. Several Indictments Found on the Same Evidence.
§ 187. Case Once Heard upon Same Evidence.
§ 188. Second Application, Continued—Newly Discovered Evidence.
§ 189. Newly Discovered Testimony, Continued—Evidence upon Subsequently Occurring Events.
§ 190. Additional Proof.
§ 191. Postponement for Further Testimony.
§ 192. Proper Evidence.
§ 193. Competent Testimony.
§ 194. Hearing Evidence.
§ 195. Conversations.
§ 196. Correcting Errors in Evidence.
§ 197. Contradicting Return.
§ 198. Record Evidence.
§ 199 *a*. Evidence *Aliunde*.
§ 199 *b*. Defendant has a Right to be Confronted by Witnesses.
§ 200. Impeaching Witnesses.
§ 201. Subpœna for Witness.
§ 202. Fine against Defaulting Witness.
§ 203. Officers may be Examined as Witnesses.
§ 204. Examination of Witnesses, Continued.
§ 205. Evidence of Service.
§ 206. Commenting on Testimony.

Part II.—Evidence by Affidavit.

§ 207. Value of Such Evidence.
§ 208. Defects—Want of Notice, etc.
§ 209. Use of Affidavits in English Practice.
§ 210. In Applications for Habeas Corpus.

§ 211. Jurisdiction.
§ 212. Contradicting Return by Affidavit.
§ 213. Examination of Indictment.
§ 214. Enlarging Time.
§ 215. Fortifying Return.
§ 216. Denying Statement in Warrant.
§ 217. Cases of Bollman and Swartwout and Burr.
§ 218. Arrest on State Process.
§ 219. Affidavit should State Facts.
§ 220. Effect of No Objection to Irregular Evidence.

PART I.—EVIDENCE IN GENERAL.

§ 177. **Preliminary Observations.**—The subject of evidence by affidavit will be treated in a subsequent division, and will be excluded from the present one. It has been heretofore observed that proceedings by habeas corpus are summary in their character, and that great discretion is given to and exercised by courts and judges in such proceedings. Where the statute provides that courts and judges may ventilate the whole matter brought before them by habeas corpus, the general principles of evidence are doubtless their rule and guide, but they are not bound to so strict an adherence to them as govern them in trials by jury; because, in the words of that great judge, Tilghman, "it is presumed that their knowledge of the law prevents their being carried away by the weight of testimony not strictly legal."[1] And, upon reflection, this will be found to be a wise provision of the law; for courts and judges, in the exercise of a sound discretion, may compel an offender against the laws of the commonwealth to stand his trial for an offense for which he has been committed or indicted; while, on the other hand, an imprisoned individual, innocent of any crime, may, by this safeguard to liberty, speedily make his way to freedom without being exposed to the delay, expense, and humiliation of a trial. This result might be averted in either case by a rigid and strict adherence to all the technical rules of evidence. We have seen what may be inquired into, and we shall now attempt to illustrate the means by which this inquiry is made, reserving the consideration of some particular provisions of evidence connected with the subject of bail, extradition, *certiorari*, custody of children, etc., until those respective subjects are treated.

§ 178. **Oral Testimony, as Well as Written, will be Heard.**—Parol evidence is of a higher grade than that by affidavit, and as these are the two species of evidence generally

[1] Shortz v. Quigley, 1 Binn. 222.

§ 179.   THE EVIDENCE.   231

used in habeas corpus proceedings, it will generally be heard where any evidence at all is admissible. A claim to freedom has been supported by such evidence. Its introduction was objected to, but the evidence was allowed by the court and accompanied with the following language: "It has been the constant practice of the court in cases of this kind to hear *viva voce* testimony when offered. The general principle in the admission of evidence is, not that courts are restricted by narrower rules in receiving testimony than juries are, but that they, being able to discriminate between that which ought to be listened to and that which should be disregarded, are not prohibited from hearing any evidence which they may think calculated to illustrate the subject before them."[1] But oral testimony can not be introduced for the purpose of attacking a judgment of a court of first instance. The proposition to introduce oral evidence to show error in the proceedings of the court below was considered by the supreme court of Nevada to be a "novel one, to say the least of it;" but say they: "Oral evidence is sometimes introduced in connection with the judgment record to show what was litigated by the parties; to show the facts more fully than they would be shown by the record. But oral evidence is never admitted to contradict the record or to show error in the court rendering a judgment."[2]

The federal courts and judges also receive this kind of evidence,[3] and where no objection on the part of the respondent is made, will allow a return to be traversed orally.[4] Parol evidence is also admissible in enlistment cases into the service of the United States to show the age of the recruit, upon proceedings by habeas corpus, and where he is a person under eighteen years of age, and enlisted without the consent of parent or guardian. Proof of that fact seems to have always been admissible in evidence, except for the period of three months from the organization of the judicial system of the United States.[5]

§ 179. **Sufficient Evidence to Authorize Commitment.**— Statutes sometimes provide that the writ of habeas corpus shall

---

[1] State v. Lyon, 1 Coxe, 403.
[2] Ex parte Smith, 2 Nev. 338.
[3] Ex parte Jenkins, 2 Wall. jun. 546.
[4] U. S. v. Williamson, 3 Am. Law Reg. 730.
[5] Seavey et al. v. Seymour, 3 Cliff. 445. The three months' time referred to existed between the tenth day of December, 1814, and the third day of March, 1815. The new act fixing the military peace establishment of the third of March, 1815, repealed that part of section 1 of the act of the tenth of December, 1814, which made the enlistment absolute and binding upon all persons under the age of twenty-one years, as well as upon persons of full age.

issue "where a party has been committed on a criminal charge without reasonable or probable cause." These words have been held to apply only to cases where the evidence given upon the examination was insufficient to warrant the committing magistrate in holding the prisoner to answer; and that they do not authorize a retrial on proceedings by habeas corpus of the matters then in issue; that the prisoner is not entitled to be discharged upon habeas corpus unless his imprisonment was unlawful; that his imprisonment is not unlawful, no matter how innocent he may be able to prove himself, if the evidence taken on his examination was sufficient to warrant the belief that he was guilty; and that in such a case he must wait until the charge against him has been ignored by the grand jury, or until he has been tried and acquitted.[1]

We shall hereafter see[2] that the rule concerning inquiry into commitments made by magistrates is not uniform, sometimes even in the same state. In some of the states such commitments will be reviewed; in others, they will not. Then in states where nothing beyond the jurisdiction of the committing magistrate is inquired into, the above observations are doubtless good law, particularly after indictment found; but in those states where the commitment of the magistrate is subject to review, the evidence should be weighed by the judge or court on habeas corpus, for the committing magistrate may have come to a wrong conclusion. Even here, however, the evidence is thus weighed generally before indictment found. After such an event, the judges or courts are not free to weigh the testimony given before the committing magistrate where he had jurisdiction of the person and the subject-matter.

William Willoughby, a petitioner for a writ of habeas corpus, had been held to answer the charge of murder by being an accessary before the fact to the killing of P. L. Traver, at Metallic City, Esmeralda county, state of Nevada, on or about the fifth day of January, 1880. On his preliminary examination testimony was given to the effect that Traver was shot and killed in the street by one Owen, who came out of petitioner's saloon, and who had been, three days previously, told by petitioner that he would give him a month's whisky, and that another man then present would give him a month's board, if he would whip or kill old Traver. This was held to make out a *prima facie* case of a willful, deliberate, and premeditated killing of Traver by Owen, without justification, excuse, or provocation, and that

---

[1] Ex parte Allen, 12 Nev. 87.   [2] See p. 286.

the petitioner counseled, advised, and encouraged it. The action of the committing magistrate was sustained, and the habeas corpus court would not go into the question of the credibility of the witnesses, saying that that was a question for the justice of the peace to decide, and that its power in reviewing his action extended no further than to determine whether the testimony, assuming its truth, was sufficient in law to warrant the finding of the magistrate. There was, in other words, reasonable or probable cause for the commitment.[1]

§ 180. **Weighing Evidence Taken before Committing Magistrate.**—As observed in the preceding section, where the inquiry does not extend beyond the jurisdiction of the committing magistrate, it is not allowable on habeas corpus to inquire into the sufficiency of the evidence before him, or accuracy of the decision rendered by him in commitment proceedings. This has been held in New York.[2] And it is said that if the justice convicts upon insufficient evidence, the remedy of the party injured is not by habeas corpus, but that he must resort to a direct proceeding, such as a writ of error, *certiorari*, motion to quash, etc., according to the nature of the case.[3] And so in a civil case, in the same state, has it been held that if the court found that the committing magistrate had jurisdiction of the process, and assumed to take proof upon the issuing of the same, and which proof he had adjudged to be sufficient, they would not, upon the writ of habeas corpus, review his adjudication upon that question, nor undertake to say whether he erred in adjudging the proof to be sufficient.[4] This commitment was made, however, by the judge of a court of general jurisdiction.

In Nebraska, Justice Maxwell of the supreme court, in a very late case (1882), used these words: "An examination before a magistrate can only be instituted by filing a complaint under oath, alleging positively the commission of an offense, and also that there is reason to believe that the accused committed the same. The finding of the justice that there is or is not probable cause that the accused committed the offense charged may be entirely disregarded by the grand jury, as it is in no sense a judgment. On such an examination, the rules of evidence as to the presumption of innocence in favor of the accused until he is found guilty should be given full weight, and the magistrate should be satisfied, not only that a crime has actually been committed as charged, but that ' there is probable cause to believe

---

[1] Ex parte Willoughby, 14 Nev. 451.
[2] In the Matter of Baker, 11 How. Pr. 418.
[3] Bennac v. The People, 4 Barb. 35.
[4] In the Matter of Prime, 1 Barb. 340.

the prisoner guilty.' A writ of habeas corpus is not a proceeding to correct errors; and where it appears that the court whose action is sought to be reviewed had jurisdiction, that an offense has been committed, and there is testimony tending to show that the accused committed the offense, this court in this proceeding will not weigh evidence to see whether it is sufficient to hold the accused. Should it do so, the administration of justice would be obstructed, and the court would be usurping the duties of the grand jury."[1]

§ 181. **Weighing Evidence, Continued.**—But in those states or in those courts where not only the jurisdiction of the committing magistrate but the entire proceedings before him may be reviewed by a court on habeas corpus, the prisoner may require of the latter that it shall hear and pass upon the evidence in regard to his guilt, and ask to be discharged if it shall appear that no offense has been committed, or that there is no probable cause for charging him therewith.[2] This he can insist upon before indictment, but not afterwards. And where the court will examine not only the proceedings, but the evidence, the commonwealth is not required to show the offense by proof beyond a reasonable doubt. It is enough if the evidence be sufficient to warrant the court in saying that a verdict founded thereon would not be without evidence to sustain it. Consequently, wherever a court would be compelled to set aside the verdict of a jury for want of evidence, it will discharge a relator. As Mr. Justice Finletter, of the quarter sessions of Philadelphia, says: "It is not necessary that the specific complaint upon which the defendant has been arrested should be made out. If any violation of the criminal code appear, he will be remanded to answer such bills of indictment as the grand jury may present."[3] In the same court, in 1876, Justice Briggs did not think that, under the evidence in the cause, the relator, who was detained in an insane asylum, should be discharged on habeas corpus. Said he: "If I believe the testimony on the side of the respondent, the relator is assuredly insane; if I believe that on the part of the relator, he is as assuredly sane. The legal presumption is in favor of sanity, and to overcome this the evidence should preponderate for the respondent. And if withal a doubt exist, that, too, goes in favor of sanity, as it does in a criminal accusation in favor of

---

[1] In re Balcom, 12 Neb. 316; S. C., 11 N. W. Rep. 312.
[2] Ex parte Mahone, 30 Ala. 49; Ex parte Champion, 52 Id. 311.
[3] Gerdemann v. Commonwealth, 11 Phila. 374.

innocence and liberty. In marshaling evidence, greater weight should be given to the judgment of medical experts, and those closely allied and associated with the relator, whose opportunities in consequence the better qualify them to speak with accuracy. Next to these, great respect should be accorded to those lay witnesses whose intercourse and public relations with men enable them, from experience and observation, to form an opinion of men's motives from their speech and action."[1]

§ 182. **Hearing Evidence de Novo.** — In those states where the entire proceedings before the justice of the peace in making a commitment for a criminal offense may be reviewed on proceedings by habeas corpus, the court or judge on the return to the writ will hear evidence anew if justice require it, and for that purpose may summon the prosecuting witnesses, investigate the criminal charge, and discharge, let to bail, or recommit the prisoner, as may be just and legal. And it appears that under a statute of Kansas,[2] this may be done there even where there is no defect in the charge or process, upon the petition of one complaining that the person in whose behalf the writ is applied for is restrained of his liberty without probable cause. Sometimes the justice of the peace before whom a prisoner is examined fails to reduce the testimony to writing; examination of evidence *de novo* is then absolutely necessary, and the court will summon witnesses and receive their evidence orally.[3] The statutes in Florida relating to habeas corpus give ample power to the judges and courts to examine into the cause of an imprisonment, notwithstanding a previous commitment, and to discharge, admit to bail, or remand to custody, as the law and evidence shall require.[4]

In Illinois, John McIntyre was accused of the crime of the murder of Thomas Cunningham, was duly examined before Warren Brown, a justice of the peace of La Salle county, and was admitted to bail to answer to a charge of manslaughter. Subsequently the accused was again arrested on a warrant issued by M. E. Hollingsworth, another justice of the peace of the same county, to answer to the same charge. The case was removed from said justice to be heard before Joseph H. Morrill, the next nearest justice. The accused exhibited to the latter the proceedings before the said Brown, when he was immediately discharged from arrest. A third arrest was made upon a warrant issued by Nicholas Keating, founded upon the same charge, and the ac-

---

[1] Commonwealth ex rel. Dr. H. T. Helmbold v. Dr. F. S. Kirkbride, Physician, etc., 11 Phila. 427.
[2] Gen. Stat. 1868, p. 763.
[3] In re Snyder, 17 Kan. 542.
[4] Ex parte Harford, 16 Fla. 287.

cused was brought before him for examination, when, before any testimony was heard, the accused stated the proceedings before the said Brown and the said Morrill, and offered to prove the same if required. The said Keating, however, refused to allow any proof of such prior proceedings, and proceeded to hear a part of the testimony heard before the said Brown, and also the testimony of one of the people's witnesses who was present at the examination before said Brown, and who was not then examined by either party, but heard no further evidence. The application for the writ of habeas corpus set forth that the last-mentioned witness testified to nothing more than the other witnesses had, in substance, stated on the examination before said Brown.

It further appeared from the application for the writ, that the said Brown, after the examination of the witnesses, asked the witness last referred to whether he was present at the commission of the homicide, and on his replying in the affirmative, the said Brown further inquired of him whether the facts had been fully and truly stated by the other witnesses, four of whom had been examined on behalf of the people and six on behalf of the accused, to which he replied that they had so far as he knew, and that he had heard their testimony. Keating held McIntyre to answer the charge of murder in killing the aforesaid Thomas Cunningham, and he was committed accordingly. The supreme court said they were inclined to hold that the justice had jurisdiction, and that it was their duty to hear the witnesses, and then determine whether the prisoner be remanded, held to bail, or discharged from custody. The reporter of this case says, in a note, that the witnesses were subsequently examined before the justices of the supreme court, and the accused bailed in the sum of three thousand dollars to answer to an indictment for murder or manslaughter in killing the said Thomas Cunningham. He failed to procure bail, and was committed.[1]

§ 183. **Evidence in Petition.**—A petition for habeas corpus should set forth the evidence before the examining officer, so that the court may act advisedly before the writ is granted.[2] Particularly should this be done where the petition for the writ is presented for alleged want of probable cause.[3]

§ 184. **Commitment without Testimony.**—It has been held in the state of Nevada that, in all cases where a party has been arrested, charged with a crime, and brought before a com-

---

[1] In re McIntyre, 5 Gilm. 422.
[2] Ex parte Klepper, 26 Ill. 532; In re Garvin, 3 Col. 67.
[3] In re Snyder, 17 Kan. 553; In re Balcom, 12 Neb. 316; State v. Ensign, 13 Id. 250.

mitting magistrate, an examination should take place; but where the preliminary examination is waived by the defendant, the fact that the justice of the peace issues his commitment without the introduction of any testimony, although erroneous, furnishes no ground for his discharge upon proceedings by habeas corpus.[1]

§ 185. **Statement of Evidence in Judgment.**—On the return to a writ of habeas corpus, if it be shown that the relator is held under a commitment issued by a court of special and limited jurisdiction, after a trial and conviction by it, the only question presented for the consideration of the court is, whether or not such inferior court had jurisdiction to try the relator, convict him, and issue the commitment. If so, the commitment is sufficient if it contain a brief statement of the offense charged, and the conviction and judgment thereon. It is not necessary that the commitment should contain a recital of the names of the witnesses examined, or of the testimony given by them.[2]

§ 186. **Several Indictments Found on the Same Evidence.**—From a judgment refusing to discharge a prisoner, an appeal was taken to the supreme court of Texas. The facts, as stated by Associate Justice Moore of that court, were in this form: "It appears from the record that appellant is held in custody by the sheriff of Kaufman county to answer five several indictments for theft, returned into the district court of said county, wherein they are still pending and undetermined. It further appears that the writ of habeas corpus for which appellant prayed was not sought, that he might be enlarged on bail. But it is claimed by him that he is entitled to an absolute and unconditional discharge from custody. The right to a discharge is based upon the fact of appellant's having been previously convicted in said court on another indictment for theft of a steer, found at the same term of the court as the indictments under which he is now held in custody. All of said indictments, it is insisted, having been found on the same evidence, and on account of the same transaction, are therefore claimed to be for one and the same supposed offense."

Said his honor: "An application for a habeas corpus for the purpose and under the circumstances for which this was made is certainly novel, and without precedent in the courts of this state. It would seem to have been long since much too well established by the common law, as well as our statutes, that an indictment not void upon its face, regularly returned to and

---

[1] Ex parte Ah Bau and Ah You, 10 Nev. 264.
[2] The People of the State of New York ex rel. Catlin v. Neilson, Chief Judge City Court of Brooklyn, Respondent, 16 Hun, 214.

pending in a court having jurisdiction thereof, could only be disposed of by some appropriate proceeding in such court, for an experiment such as the present. * * * There is no error in the judgment, and it is affirmed."[1]

§ 187. **Case Once Heard upon Same Evidence.**—Where a case has already been once heard upon a habeas corpus, and the prisoner has been remanded, another court will not always deem it expedient to grant another writ and hear the case again upon the same evidence, particularly where the party is not without another remedy; as, where he may resort to a *homine replegiando*. This is not to be understood, however, as saying that a court or judge has no power to issue the writ in such a case should they deem it expedient to do so.[2]

§ 188. **Second Application Continued — Newly Discovered Evidence.**—In Texas an appeal was taken, in 1879, to the supreme court, or court of appeals, from a judgment rendered upon a second application for habeas corpus, refusing bail to the applicant. The first application was made and heard before indictment found, and the second application after indictment. Applicant's right to a second writ was based upon the ground of newly discovered evidence. The judgment of the district judge, rendered at chambers, ran as follows: "It appearing to the court that the evidence introduced by the applicant alleged to be newly discovered was not in fact such evidence, and accordingly not sufficient to authorize the court to change the former judgment of the court refusing bail, and for other and sufficient reasons, it is ordered and adjudged," etc. The following statute[3] regarding second applications for the writ of habeas corpus was then in force; and Mr. Justice White made the following observations:

"A casual reading of the language of this statute might lead to the inference that such second applications would be limited exclusively to evidence which was newly discovered. Such, however, is not our interpretation, based upon a proper construction of the whole article, and, as we think, in perfect consonance with the broad principles of justice and human liberty upon which the writ is founded, and for the better protection and security of which its privileges were intended mostly to subserve.

---

[1] Perry v. The State, 41 Tex. 488.
[2] Ex parte Lawrence, 5 Binn. 304.
[3] "A party may obtain the writ of habeas corpus a second time by stating in the application therefor that since the hearing in his first application important testimony has been obtained, which it was not in his power to produce at the former hearing. He shall also set forth the testimony so newly discovered; and if it be that of a witness, the affidavit of the witness shall also accompany such application:" Paschal's Dig., art. 2642.

We are of opinion that the statute intended to confer the right in two classes of cases: first, where important testimony has been obtained, which, though not newly discovered, or which, though known to him, it was not in his power to produce at the former hearing; second, where the evidence was newly discovered.

"In either case his application, if it be on account of the testimony of a witness, should not only be accompanied by the affidavit of the witness, but the reasons why the testimony was not adduced should be fully stated, in order that the judge or court to whom the application was addressed might know, in the one case, why it was out of his power to produce it at the former hearing; and in the other, such facts stated as would satisfy the court that the failure to discover the testimony was not attributable to any lack of proper diligence on his part; in other words, the application should be so full and complete as to apprise the court of all the facts necessary to be known, that it might act advisedly in granting or refusing the application.

"We can not better, perhaps, illustrate our idea than by the facts presented in the case at bar. As we have seen, the application was based upon the ground of newly discovered evidence. In such a case, we take it, all the recognized rules with reference to newly discovered testimony on motions for new trials would obtain and govern. The showing should be the same. If the showing itself discloses, we will say, want of diligence, or that the evidence is cumulative, or that it was intended to impeach a witness, or any other fact which would render it insufficient or invalid on a motion for new trial, then the judge or court would be fully authorized in refusing the writ, and his refusal would be conclusive; for an appeal does not lie from the refusal of a district judge to grant a writ of habeas corpus: Ex parte Ainsworth, 27 Tex. 731; Thomas v. The State, 40 Id. 6.

"In this case, however, the judge granted the writ; and then, upon the hearing, determined that the evidence was not newly discovered. A question is here presented which has never before arisen in this state, and that is, What should be the practice in this court on appeal, even supposing the court should concur in the view of the district court that the evidence was not newly discovered? Will we affirm the judgment because the party was not primarily entitled to the writ? Clearly not. Having granted the writ and heard the testimony, the evidence thus heard becomes part of the facts of the record. The rule of practice as prescribed by the statute applies.[1] The case, then, must be determined by us, not upon the question as to whether the evidence is newly discovered, but upon the evidence as we find it adduced on the hearing and presented in the record. Taking the record as an entirety, and considering all the testimony as it here appears, is the prisoner entitled to bail?" The court believed that the applicant was entitled to bail, and granted it.[2]

§ 189. **Newly Discovered Testimony, Continued—Evidence upon Subsequently Occurring Events.**—We have seen that at common law an adverse decision on one writ of habeas corpus does not prevent the issuance of a second one, and that the petitioner is entitled to the judgment of every court upon the question of his personal liberty, when he is deprived of it. The matter may have been before another court, yet still, in favor of liberty, the prisoner is entitled to the opinion of each court. Every judge in the realm may, each in turn, pass upon the question until all have refused to grant the application, or until one is found who does grant it.[3] Such is the rule in many of the states in the American Union,[4] and in the federal courts.[5] Statutes, however, in some of the states change the rule that the refusal of one writ is no bar to another application for it. This is the case in Mississippi.[6]

In that state, in 1878, the relator, being under indictment for murder, was denied bail on habeas corpus. He was afterwards tried in a circuit court. The jury failed to agree, a mistrial was entered, and he was remanded to jail. He then sued out a second writ before a circuit court, but upon the hearing it was dismissed, upon the ground that the decision upon the first writ, remaining unreversed and unappealed from, operated as a bar to the new proceeding.

Mr. Justice Chalmers rendered the opinion of the supreme

---

[1] "The supreme court [court of appeals] shall hear the appeal upon the facts and law arising upon the record, and shall enter such judgment and make such orders as the law and the nature of the case may require:" Paschal's Dig., art. 3221. "The opinion of a district or supreme judge shall not be revised as to any incidental question which may have arisen on the hearing of the application for habeas corpus, the only design of the appeal being to do substantial justice to the party appealing:" Id., art. 3222.

[2] Ex parte Foster, 5 Tex. App. 643.

[3] Ex parte Partington, 2 Dow. & L. 653.

[4] In the Matter of Perkins, 2 Cal. 424; Ex parte Ellis, 11 Id. 222; Bell v. State of Maryland, 4 Gill, 301; In re Blair, 4 Wis. 522.

[5] Ex parte Kaine, 3 Blatchf. 1.

[6] Section 1418 of the code of 1871 declares that "the judgment rendered on the first trial of any writ of habeas corpus shall be conclusive until reversed, as hereinafter provided, and whilst so in force shall be a bar to any other proceedings to bring the same matter again in question, except by appeal," etc.

court, and considered the statute alluded to. Said he: "The object and effect of this is to make the decision on a writ of habeas corpus *res adjudicata*, and conclusive as to all matters which were or might properly have been investigated upon the hearing thereof. We do not think, however, that it will preclude the issuance and maintenance of a second writ based upon subsequently occurring events. So to construe the statute might work the greatest injustice and hardship, and is not demanded by its language. But the new writ must be based upon facts which have actually occurred since the hearing of the original writ, and not upon a claim of newly discovered testimony as to old facts; for otherwise the prisoner could make out his claim by piecemeal, and thus, by repeated applications upon successive claims of newly discovered testimony, defeat the element of finality and conclusiveness which the statute gives to the proceeding.

"In the case at bar, the newly occurring facts set forth in the second petition were the mistrial before the petit jury, and the serious impairment of the relator's health, caused by his imprisonment. The first petition had expressed fears that his health would suffer from confinement, and the second averred that those fears had been realized, and that a longer imprisonment would prove fatal, or at least inflict permanent and irreparable injury. We think these allegations were sufficient to give jurisdiction to entertain the new writ. While neither necessarily entitled the party to bail, either sufficed to give jurisdiction and to demand investigation.

"The failure of the petit jury to find a verdict is held by some authorities as of itself sufficient to entitle to bail. We do not so regard it, but only as giving jurisdiction for a new hearing, and justifying the introduction of additional testimony, not considered on the first trial. While the former adjudication must be considered as conclusive in the testimony then adduced, the subsequent mistrial before the petit jury, in connection with newly developed exculpatory evidence, may authorize the admission to bail. The mistrial gives the jurisdiction, and justifies the production of the new testimony. Together they may suffice for the enlargement on bond."

The judgment of the circuit court judge was reversed, and the cause remanded, with directions that the matter be heard and determined, in accordance with the principles above announced, before Judge Chrisman, or any other authorized judge or chancellor.[1]

[1] Ex parte Pattison, 56 Miss. 161.

§ 190. **Additional Proof.**—The fifty-eighth section of the habeas corpus act in force in New York in 1860 provided, "that if the prisoner appear to have been legally committed for the offense, or if he appear, by the testimony offered with the return or on the hearing, to be guilty, the court should remand him." This, it was held, contemplated an examination of the evidence returned by the magistrate, or of the evidence offered on the hearing, and allowed such evidence then to be received before indictment. This was applied in a case of embezzlement. The prisoner had been committed by a magistrate, but had not been indicted. The prisoner had proposed to one Little to retain the money of his employer, which he was sent to obtain from the bank, and knowing the money to be the property of Winslow, Lanier & Co., he took the money from Little and concealed it. The prisoner asked his discharge, on the ground that the clerk, Little, was under eighteen years of age when the embezzlement was committed. The money was the property of the firm, although in the possession of their servant, and if taken from the servant without his consent it would clearly have been a larceny. But if Little was under eighteen years of age, assuming the crime to be nothing more than embezzlement, that crime could not be charged upon him, and the prisoner would not, of course, be liable under that charge. The district attorney offered additional evidence to show that Little was mistaken as to his age, and that he was over nineteen years of age. Justice Ingraham said he would receive the evidence, and that if the correct age of Little was proved to be over eighteen years, the prisoner must be remanded.[1]

§ 191. **Postponement for Further Testimony.**—While the parties concerned in a hearing upon habeas corpus should always be prepared for the trial of issues of fact therein, cases no doubt will occasionally occur in which time should be allowed to produce new testimony, as where a party is surprised by the case proved, or where there is reason to believe that witnesses may have given incorrect testimony. The practice is not to be commended, however, as a rule, and great care will be taken by the courts and judges to provide against its dangers. To illustrate the first instance, it may be considered advisable to allow time for a will to be produced under the peculiar circumstances of a case to prove a certain fact otherwise unsupported;[2] and the second may be illustrated by quoting the words of Mr.

---

[1] People v. Richardson, 4 Park. Cr. 656; S. C., 18 How. Pr. 92.
[2] State v. Lyon, 1 Coxe, 403.

Justice McLean of the United States circuit court: "Some years ago I was consulted by a commissioner on the propriety, after a hearing, of giving time to obtain new evidence. Several unimpeached witnesses swore positively to the identity of the fugitive. I advised that time should be given, and eventually it was satisfactorily shown that the first witnesses were mistaken, and that the fugitive was living in Canada. This discharged him from custody."[1]

§ 192. **Proper Evidence.**—All testimony received on the hearing of a writ of habeas corpus should be competent, material, relevant, and pertinent to all the issues of fact involved. We shall not attempt to illustrate all these various attributes of evidence to any extent, for any satisfactory elucidation of them would lead us too far into the realms of the general subject of evidence, and with which, too, it is supposed the reader is already familiar. The judge before whom a prisoner is convicted, should fix some reasonable time within which a fine must be paid, where he passes an alternative sentence of fine or imprisonment; and if he fails to do so, the convict has at least a reasonable time within which to pay the fine. Where the imprisonment was for four months, commencing March 12th, and the fine of fifty dollars was paid on the second of April following, the time was held to be not unreasonable; and on the hearing of such a case, the official receipt of the clerk of the convicting court, acknowledging the payment of the fine and costs, was held to be proper evidence to be considered by the judge, and if not rebutted, entitled the prisoner to his discharge.[2]

§ 193. **Competent Testimony.**—In an action for false imprisonment, evidence of the proceedings on a writ of habeas corpus, by which the plaintiff was discharged from custody, is competent and pertinent.[3] On the hearing and determination of a cause arising upon a writ of habeas corpus, before a judge or court investigating a criminal charge against a person committed by an examining magistrate for the offense of having obtained money or property by false pretenses, the prosecutor, when examined as a witness, may testify that he believed the pretenses, and confiding in their truth, was induced thereby to part with his money or property. The objection to such testimony on the ground of its incompetency is not well taken, because in such an action the inducement to part with the money or property is a

---

[1] Ex parte Robinson, Mar. of U. S., 6 McLean, 360 (1855).
[2] Broomhead v. Chisolm, 47 Ga. 390.
[3] American Ex. Co. et al. v. Patterson, 73 Ind. 430.

material fact to be established. If the representations of the one charged have no influence at all upon the one induced to part with money or property, the prosecution must fail. It is the fact sought after, and not the opinion of the witness. While such evidence may not be the best, nor the most reliable, it is admissible. It is not necessary, however, for the prosecutor to state that he believed and relied upon the pretense: this may be inferred.[1] So, too, on a complaint against a defendant as a disorderly person, for neglecting to support his wife, evidence showing that the parties had for many years lived as husband and wife is competent to prove the marriage.[2] Except in a few of the states, the interest of the witness no longer renders him incompetent to testify; and this rule applies, of course, as well to testimony given on proceedings by habeas corpus as it does to evidence given in general actions.

§ 194. **Hearsay Evidence.**—It has been held that in a prosecution for bastardy by a woman claiming to be unmarried because of her husband's having a wife living at the time of her marriage to him, hearsay evidence of such former marriage of her husband having been admitted without objection, it tended to prove that she was unmarried and would be sufficient, when the offense was clearly proved, to prevent the court from discharging the accused on a writ of habeas corpus.[3]

§ 195. **Conversations.**—Upon proceedings under the writ of habeas corpus concerning the custody of an infant child, it is error for the court to permit the petitioner to testify to a conversation between her and the wife of the defendant, which occurred at the house of the defendant when he was not present. Where the wife of the defendant has not been made a party to the proceedings, her declarations are no more binding upon her husband than those of an entire stranger; particularly where it is not shown that she is in any sense the agent of her husband.[4]

§ 196. **Correcting Errors in Evidence.**—The writ of habeas corpus was not intended to operate as a writ of review or *certiorari*, and where a relator has been sentenced to imprisonment by a court of competent jurisdiction, a mistake made in the prisoner's age, even where that is a material fact, will not entitle him to have the testimony reviewed by a higher court upon this writ. Errors of evidence, no more than any other

---

[1] In re Snyder, 17 Kan. 542.
[2] People v. McCormack, 4 Park. Cr. 9.
[3] In re Carlton, 11 Neb. 99; S. C., 7 N. W. Rep. 755.
[4] Garner v. Gordon, 41 Ind. 92.

errors or irregularities, can be cured by it after indictment found or judgment rendered against the prisoner—so long as they do not affect the question of the jurisdiction of the acting officer or court. A court acting within the sphere of its jurisdiction is conclusively presumed, so far as all collateral inquiries are concerned, to have performed its duty, and the question whether other than legal evidence was admitted in its proceedings will not be considered by a higher court.[1]

So, too, in the decisions of courts of last resort in the several states, a distinction must be made between original applications for the writ of habeas corpus and those in which the high or supreme court exercises purely a revisory and correctionary jurisdiction. In the first class of cases the court will hear evidence *de novo* and give a full hearing; but in the second, the judgment of the court of first instance is presumably correct. For example, where statute provides for the granting, by the supreme court, of a writ of error for the reversal of the judgment of the lower court. Here the supreme court exercises purely a revisory or correctionary jurisdiction, and it will not disturb the decision of the lower court until error is shown, and it will pause long before it will disturb the decision of the lower court where the weight of the evidence depends on the credibility of witnesses. So where the evidence is conflicting or contradictory, and which necessarily raises the question of credibility, the primary court has a better opportunity and is more favorably situated to come to a safe, reliable, and just opinion than the court of error. Much depends upon the manner of witnesses and their seeming bias or fairness, that can not be brought before the higher court, and which should yet have a material bearing on the weight of evidence. In such cases the testimony of the false, biased, prevaricating witness is properly weighed by the primary court, and its decision will be regarded as conclusive, particularly where the application is for bail, and where the supreme court has no larger jurisdiction or discretion to bail than the court whose judgment is before them on a writ of error. Error must be shown, or the judgment of the court of first instance will be regarded as presumptively right.[2]

Another example may be shown by a decision under a statute in Alabama, which gives to the supreme court of that state power "to issue writs of injunction, habeas corpus, and such

---

[1] Matter of Mason, 8 Mich. 70.
[2] Street v. The State, 43 Miss. 1. See People ex rel. Philmot v. Hessing, 28 Ill. 410.

other remedial and original writs as are necessary to give it a general superintendence and control of inferior jurisdictions." A prisoner who, by some court or judge competent to act in the premises, has on a proper application been denied relief on habeas corpus may renew his application in the supreme court of that state; but the jurisdiction of that court is revisory and appellate, not original; and facts which were not before the court or judge hearing the application originally can not there be introduced, and that court will not, therefore, look into the papers attached to the petition to that court which were not before the judge of the primary court.[1]

§ 197. **Contradicting Return.**—It is hardly necessary to say that, where the statutes of a state allow a prisoner to deny the truth of the return, or establish his discharge by proof of certain facts, until he introduces testimony to that end, the return, thus being admitted to be true, will prevail, if it shows a sufficient cause of detention.[2] But where the return to a writ of habeas corpus shows a regular execution issued upon the judgment of a court of competent jurisdiction, and it is not traversed or denied in the manner required by law, evidence to contradict it is, nevertheless, admissible if no objection is made that no traverse has been interposed at the proper time.[3]

§ 198. **Record Evidence.**—A petition was filed in court by one Peck, praying for an order to be directed to another, one Baker, to show cause why he should not be compelled to deliver certain records, books, papers, etc., belonging to said Peck. The order to show cause was made, and returnable on the fourteenth of April. On the hearing Baker did not show that he had delivered the said records, etc., to Peck or any one else, and it appeared to the judge that they were improperly withheld, but the order of commitment for contempt was not made until the thirtieth of April following. In the mean time Baker understood that the proceedings were ended and returned home, and stated, under oath, that he had heard no more of them until he was arrested on the first of May following. Upon habeas corpus the jurisdiction of the warrant was assailed, on the ground that there was no continuance or adjournment of the proceedings before the county judge, from the fourteenth of April, when the order to show cause, granted upon the petition, was returnable. On the face of the warrant issued on the

---

[1] Ex parte Brown, 63 Ala. 187 (1879); see also Ex parte Croom and May, 19 Id. 561.
[2] Street v. State, 43 Miss. 1; Matter of Mason, 8 Mich. 70.
[3] People ex rel. Waldron v. Carpenter etc., 46 Barb. 619.

thirtieth of April, it did not appear that there was any continuance or adjournment from the fourteenth of April; and it was insisted that, without a continuance or adjournment, the proceedings terminated on the fourteenth; that as the warrant did not show a continuance or adjournment, none could be intended; and that parol proof could not be received to establish that there was one in fact, and supply the omission. The judge sitting on the habeas corpus was, however, not able to assent to the position that jurisdiction was disproved by the absence of a recital in the warrant of a continuance of the proceedings. On the contrary, he was satisfied that without such a recital, and without any parol testimony on the subject, no want of jurisdiction thereby appeared; and that it was not necessary that all the facts requisite to the jurisdiction of the officer should be disclosed by the warrant.[1]

Upon error brought from the decision of the primary court upon habeas corpus, all the evidence heard in the court below should be incorporated in the record, or the revisory court will not review the decision, as the presumptions are all in favor of the rulings of the court of first instance.[2]

Where an order has been made by the court submitting the case to another grand jury, and it is recited in the record that the order resubmitting the case to the next grand jury was made because "sufficient cause" was shown, the presumption is, in the absence of any cause showing to the contrary, that the court did not act arbitrarily in the premises.[3]

The keeper of a prison may have been furnished with a certified copy of the minutes of the court, and which gives an imperfect description of the crime of which the prisoner was convicted. In such a case the keeper can, upon the return to a writ of habeas corpus, show by the records of the court what the precise crime was—and thus that the sentence was legal, and the detention authorized; but this must be done by the records and not by parol evidence. If, however, these facts are shown by affidavit without objection, the court will hold the proof sufficient to act upon.[4]

§ 199 a. **Evidence Aliunde.**—The statute of New York, running in these words, "The party brought before such court or officer, on the return of any writ of habeas corpus, may deny

---

[1] In the Matter of Baker, 11 How. Pr. 418; vide post, sec. 203; see also the authorities cited by his honor; Horton v. Auchmoody, 7 Wend. 200; Hard v. Shipman, 6 Barb. 621.

[2] People ex rel. Philmot v. Hessing, 28 Ill. 410.

[3] Ex parte Isbell, 11 Nev. 295.

[4] People ex rel. Trainor v. Baker, 89 N. Y. 460.

any of the material facts set forth in the return, or allege any fact to show either that his imprisonment or detention is unlawful, or that he is entitled to his discharge, which allegations or denials shall be on oath," etc., was construed by Mr. Justice Cowen, in the well-known McLeod Case, as not intended to give the prisoner the right of a summary trial as to the question of his guilt or innocence; but merely to enable him by evidence *aliunde* the return to dispute the fact of his being detained on the process or proceeding set forth, to impeach it for lack of jurisdiction, or to show that it has ceased to be a lawful cause of detention, from the effect of some subsequent act or event; such as, if he be committed till he pay a fine, which he has paid accordingly, and the return states the commitment only; or the allegation of a pardon after conviction; or that the judgment under which he was imprisoned has been reversed, etc.[1]

Where the law required that there must be three police justices to hold a competent court of special sessions in the city of New York, and upon the return to a writ of habeas corpus the imprisonment was justified under a commitment in due form, showing that the prisoner had been regularly tried and convicted of petit larceny before a court of special sessions held by three police justices, evidence *aliunde* that only two of the police justices were in fact present when the prisoner was arraigned and pleaded, and when he was tried and sentenced, was held to be competent for the prisoner to show that the proceedings before the court of special sessions were *coram non judice* and void.[2] It will readily be seen that the effect of the evidence in this instance was to prove the want of jurisdiction, thus rendering the proceedings void.

In the general court of Virginia it has been said that an escape warrant ought regularly to show upon its face that the person who issues it, a justice of the peace, is a justice of the peace; but that upon habeas corpus sued out by the person arrested under it, if it is proved by evidence *aliunde* that he is a justice, the prisoner ought not to be discharged. This was before indictment, and even before a preliminary examination, and immediately after arrest. It was also said that the want of a jail repelled any presumption arising from the lapse of time.[3]

§ 199 *b*. **Defendant has a Right to be Confronted by Witnesses.**—In many of the states it is held that "every free-

---
[1] People v. McLeod, 1 Hill (N. Y.), 377.
[2] People v. Divine, 5 Park Cr. 62; S. C., 21 How. Pr. 80.
[3] Jones v. Timberlake, 6 Rand. 678.

man has a right to be confronted with the witnesses against him in all stages of his accusation; the privilege is inherent, and the right to demand the enjoyment of proving his innocence simultaneous with the first step of the prosecution. Before, therefore, any commitment can be lawfully made, the accused is entitled to an opportunity of showing either that the act he is charged with is no crime in the eye of the law—that if any wrong has been done he is not the perpetrator of it; or that however strong the evidence may be against him, the offense is of a class justifying the discharge of his person, upon the production of such bail as may be legally required of him. If the condition of society were otherwise, the time would have arrived ere now when the occasion and the disposition would have presented themselves of deciding all such questions in a very summary manner."[1] The right in habeas corpus to prove his innocence, however, is not allowed after indictment found.[2]

§ 200. **Impeaching Witnesses.**—The petitioner for a habeas corpus can not claim the issuance of the writ for the sole purpose of impeaching the witnesses who testified against him at his examination.[3]

§ 201. **Subpœna for Witness.**—In Mississippi it has been held, that if a convict who sues out a writ of habeas corpus to obtain his release from the penitentiary escapes before the hearing thereof, the proceeding should be dismissed;[4] and that where the writ of habeas corpus was issued by the clerk under the fiat of the chancellor, and a subpœna for a witness was issued by the circuit clerk at the court-house of whose county the writ was made returnable, but without the chancellor's order, it was sufficient to support a fine for non-attendance, because the clerk was authorized to issue subpœnas for witnesses, as in other cases pending in his court.[5]

§ 202. **Fine against Defaulting Witness.**—"But," said George, C. J., of the supreme court, "we do not regard the fine imposed as within the rules which govern ordinary fines imposed by courts as punishments for contempts against their authority and dignity. The statute directs the imposition of fines against defaulting witnesses summoned for the relator, in the shape of judgments in his favor. A proceeding of that character we regard rather as a means of assessing damages to the relator for his failure to get the evidence of a defaulting witness, than

---

[1] U. S. v. Almeida, 2 Wheel. 577; but see note to sec. 307, *post*.
[2] See part iii, c. xiv.
[3] Ex parte Allen, 12 Nev. 87.
[4] Ex parte Walker, 53 Miss. 366; Hamilton v. Flowers, 57 Id. 14.
[5] Hamilton v. Flowers, 57 Miss. 14.

as an exertion of power by the chancellor to protect his authority and to enforce obedience to lawful process. The fine imposed is the private property of the relator, who may remit it if he sees proper. Regarding it in this light, we must consider the right of the relator to the money, as well as the default of the witness. As the prisoner had escaped, and was not present by his own free will, and as it was impossible for him to avail himself while absent of the witness's evidence, we can not see how he has been damnified by the failure of the witness to attend, nor how he can demand the punishment for a default which worked no possible injury to him. The relator having sued out a writ of habeas corpus when he had escaped, or having escaped afterwards, so that he could not be produced, whereby the proceedings must necessarily come to an end without a trial on the merits, we can not see the propriety of allowing them to be continued for the sole purpose of securing to him a pecuniary benefit which he does not deserve. He must be treated as having released the witness from his obligation to attend and testify." The judgments rendered in the lower court were reversed, and the proceedings dismissed.[1]

§ 203. **Officers may be Examined as Witnesses.**—In the Matter of Heyward,[2] the validity of the process under which the prisoner was detained by the police justice was called in question. It appeared to be sufficent in form, and the burden of proving a want of jurisdiction or other defect to avoid its force was thrown upon the prisoner. The justice and the police clerk, who happened to be present, were called as witnesses by the prisoner, to prove upon what complaint or other papers the prisoner was arrested and committed. It happened that the clerk had with him the original complaint, which the counsel called upon him to produce to the judge. To this the opposing counsel objected *in toto*. He said the complaint was a record of the police court, which was deemed in law on file there, and which could not be thus produced and carried about the city. And as to the police justice, it was entirely improper to call him as a witness to prove his judicial acts or omissions.

Justice Sanford observed: "The inquiry before me is, On what documents did the justice issue his warrant against the prisoner? This inquiry is by the statute made summary; and if these gentlemen were not present, or if they were here without the complaint, I should feel bound to receive the best evidence that was at hand, or which a prisoner with reasonable diligence.

---

[1] Hamilton v. Flowers, 57 Miss. 14.   [2] 1 Sandf. 701.

might procure, both as to what writings were the ground of the proceeding against him, and what those writings contained, without regard to the ordinary rules of evidence. The clerk is here, and, as he states, has the complaint. I think he should produce it. It will not go out of his custody, and it is but proper that all the light should be afforded that is possible to a correct ascertainment of the facts. As to the justice, he is not to be asked about his reasons or his judgment in the matter. It is simply this, On what affidavits and papers did this warrant issue? Neither the justice nor the clerk interposes any objection to being sworn, and can have no feeling on the subject. It is in no respect *infra dignitatum* for the judge to appear as a witness in this mode. In the habeas corpus case of Prime, Ward & Co., in which I sat with the chief justice at his request last December, Judge Edmonds, of the supreme court, whose warrant was under review, came voluntarily, and was examined as a witness. And Judge Betts, of the United States district court, as I am informed, appeared in the same manner before Judge Edmonds, in the extradition case of Metzger." This rule is not applicable to cases of extradition or fugitives from justice alone; it applies generally in all proceedings under habeas corpus. Judge Folger, of New York, who had issued the warrant of commitment in the matter of D. S. Baker, above mentioned,[1] was, at the hearing on the habeas corpus, examined as a witness on the part of the sheriff, and testified in substance, under an objection by the counsel of the said Baker to any evidence conflicting with what appeared on the face of the warrant of commitment, "that the issue was joined at Geneva (on the fourteenth of April); that the matter was adjourned to the twentieth of April, at Canandaigua; that at the close of the argument before him he stated he would take a few days to consider the case, if no objection was made; that none was made; that one of the counsel for the relator asked if it was best to adjourn to any particular day; the witness stated, just as they saw fit; that it was not necessary, as he could inform the prevailing party by letter when he had made his decision; that no objection was taken to that course; that before issuing the warrant he wrote to the counsel of the relator, stating the decision and ground of it, and requested him to inform the counsel of the other party."

§ 204. **Examination of Witnesses Continued.**—"As the proceedings upon habeas corpus in criminal matters are only to ascertain whether or not the charge is sustained, it can never

---

[1] 11 How. Pr. 425.

be proper to permit the accused to introduce his defense by witnesses. He may, however, upon cross-examination, bring out his whole explanation. To permit him to call witnesses to explain or refute the evidence against him would be to try the cause; and that is solely the province of a jury."[1]

If an individual has been committed, after a prior investigation by an officer authorized by law to make it, the prisoner ought not to be discharged until all the witnesses who have previously been examined against him, if still living and attainable, have been produced and examined. In the absence of any material witness who previously testified in the examination against him, the question should relate only to the amount of the bail, if the case be bailable, and if it be not, the prisoner should be remanded by the judge into custody, to be safely kept until discharged by due course of law.[2]

§ 205. **Evidence of Service.**—Where the primary court has jurisdiction of both the writ of habeas corpus and an attachment for its disobedience, and has heard evidence both as to the service of the writ of habeas corpus and disobedience of its command, the determination of the court of first instance on those matters is conclusive. That evidence can not be properly brought to a higher court on proceedings by habeas corpus, and in its absence it will be presumed to have shown a service of the writ, and such a willful disobedience or evasion of the writ as amounted to a contempt of the authority of the court.[3]

An acknowledgment of service on a bill of exceptions by counsel signing as "attorneys for respondents" will be construed as evidence of service on all of the respondents, where the record fails to show that any of the respondents were represented by different counsel in the primary court.[4]

§ 206. **Commenting on Testimony.**—In the supreme court of Mississippi and in the Texas court of appeals a highly commendable rule has been established and followed, viz., to abstain from commenting upon the evidence in habeas corpus cases, lest their comment should influence the final trial, it being a delicate matter to argue on the testimony in advance of the jury trial as to its criminating or exculpatory effect. This is a uniform rule in the last-named court.[5]

---

[1] Gerdemann v. Com., 11 Phila. 374.
[2] Ex parte Champion, 52 Ala. 311.
[3] People v. Bradley, 60 Ill. 390. See in connection with this, the chapter on contempts.
[4] State ex rel. Lynch v. Bridges, 64 Ga. 146.
[5] Street v. The State, 43 Miss. 30; Ex parte Foster, 5 Tex. App. 648.

PART II.—EVIDENCE BY AFFIDAVIT.

§ 207. **Value of Such Evidence.**—This species of evidence is of very low order, and it is with reluctance that judges and courts will receive it in many cases. It is received with caution and closely scrutinzed. Affidavits are highly objectionable if not taken before competent authority and properly authenticated; but when they are so taken, though without notice to the adverse party, they may be offered and received in evidence, but their reception is addressed to the sound discretion of the court, and which must be regulated by the circumstances of each particular case. Affidavits should not be used where the attendance of witnesses can be obtained with reasonable diligence, and when this can be done the attendance of witnesses will be required in examinations in criminal proceedings. That it is *ex parte* is a very strong objection to this species of evidence. "It does not," says Mr. Hurd, in his very valuable work on habeas corpus, "admit of the application of that invaluable test of truthfulness, a cross-examination."[1] In his opinion on the writ of habeas corpus, before the house of lords, in 1758, Lord Chief Justice Wilmot used this language: "To enter into a disquisition of this sort upon affidavits would be confounding the offices of judge and jury, and introducing a mode of trial where no issue is or can be joined. The parties in such a summary way of trial must lose the benefit of a *viva voce* examination, where the looks, the manner, and the deportment of the witness are extremely material to confirm or discredit his testimony; it is found by the experience of ages, that nothing does so effectually explore the truth as a cross-examination, which strikes so suddenly that fiction can never endure it. Another decisive reason against this mode of trial is, that there is no compulsory method of forcing men to swear affidavits; so that if a person were obliged to prove the truth of his return by affidavit, he is totally destitute of any means of obliging men to make affidavits to prove it."[2]

The weakness and abuse of this kind of evidence are shown in the proceedings against Mary Heath. The propriety of prompt action on the part of the court is also shown by it when fraud and imposition are suspected. During the several proceedings had upon an indictment against the said Mary Heath for perjury, previous to her trial, a motion was made for a writ of habeas corpus to be directed to Colonel John Blakeney, re-

[1] 2d ed., p. 305.   [2] Wilmot's Opinions, 108

quiring him to bring up the body of Sarah Weedon. The motion was grounded upon two affidavits, made respectively by her two sons, and stating positively that their mother was detained against her will, etc. Mr. Thomas Blakeney, attorney, offered to falsify their affidavits by affidavits, and the court put off the motion until the next day, when two affidavits were produced and read, tending to show that Mrs. Weedon was not detained against her will. At this juncture, the court said, "Call John Weedon;" and upon Mr. Harward offering to speak, continued: "Here is affidavit against affidavit. We must hear which of these affidavits is true. We are imposed on by one affidavit or the other; the honor of the court is concerned, and therefore, before we do anything, we will hear what John Weedon has to say." Mr. Harward objected, that "if this person is to be examined, I do apprehend it must be on the foot of some supposed transgression that he hath committed." Court: "No, sir; it is to discover the truth. We will have no concealing of the truth in this court. Swear him." The two sons were then examined, and it appeared from the examination that their mother was not really detained by Blakeney against her will. The judges rendered their decisions as follows:

Lord Chief Justice Marlay: "We are of opinion, in the first place, that no habeas corpus can be granted in this case. A habeas corpus for the liberty of the subject is a writ of right, and may be applied for without an affidavit of the party, as was done in the cases of my Lord Leigh, Sir Robert Viner, and Sir Robert Howard. In the case of Sir Robert Viner a habeas corpus was sued for to obtain the liberty of a woman confined in his house; the woman said she was not confined by him, but chose to stay with him. But this does not appear to us at all to be the case here, that there is the least restraint upon Sarah Weedon, but on the contrary, that she is at her full liberty; for notwithstanding these affidavits of these men, it does appear so. Edward Weedon, of the Gravelly Hill, in the county of Carlow, maketh oath that Sarah Weedon is now detained (sworn the eighth of November) by Colonel John Blakeney at Abbort, near Castle Blakeney, in the county of Galway. John Weedon, of the city of Dublin, maketh oath that Sarah Weedon is now detained at the house of John Blakeney, Esq., at Abbort in the county of Galway; *in terminis terminantibus*, the same; both illiterate persons, and yet both make these positive affidavits of her being under restraint, when it appears that she was at her full liberty, not only before but after these affidavits were made. These affidavits were made by marksmen, and therefore the court sent for the person that drew the affidavits, to know why he drew them in the manner they appear to us; for upon the table, these men have declared that they do not know, nay, they can not say they believe, that she is restrained of her liberty. Can we then, when they have declared that their affidavits are not true, grant the habeas corpus? By no means. * * *

"The next point to be considered is, whether these men could be attached for falsifying their affidavits. I am amazed to hear it said there are no precedents of persons being attached for prevarication and imposing on the court. May be not in this case, but in most great causes that have been long depending such things have happened. Suppose a man in an affidavit to put off a trial should swear that such a bond was perfected, and he explains himself when he comes to be examined that he heard such a one say so; is not he guilty in conscience of perjury? and ought he not to be punished for prevarication and for the imposition? I can give instances where persons have endeavored by artful affidavits to extort exorbitant bail, for which they have been committed by the court. Now, as to these two persons, they have sworn in the most express terms, in their affidavits, everything which is necessary to induce the court to grant a habeas corpus. * * * Therefore, as they have endeavored to impose upon the court, and injure an innocent person, Mr. Blakeney, I think they ought to be committed."

Mr. Justice Ward: "The only thing to excuse them is their ignorance. But as the matter now stands, it is plain that the person who drew the affidavits knew they were false, knew that these men swore to a fact they did not know to be true. Really, a man of business must know the practice in drawing affidavits, and what kind of affidavits will serve the end proposed by them; but these men swear further, and say that they told him the same story they do now. If that be true, he drew these affidavits most falsely; he led them into perjury, and is as guilty as they are, and should as certainly be punished if we had him; but I find on inquiry he is not here; therefore, as we have nobody else to punish, we must punish these men, who have thus prevaricated and imposed upon the court."

Lord Chief Justice Marlay: "It is a most wicked, profligate thing in an agent to make an illiterate man swear an affidavit he knows to be false. Whether that be Goosetry's case or no, I will not say, because he is not here to clear himself; but it looks very much like it."[1]

[1] 18 Howell's State Trials, 14, 19.

§ 208.—Defects—**Want of Notice, etc.**—In our perusal of the English reports, we have found nothing explicit upon the practice in the taking and admission of affidavits in habeas corpus proceedings, so far as their being taken upon notice is concerned. The general practice in England seems to be to receive affidavits as evidence in these matters, but the cases, so far as we have examined them, do not state whether they should be taken upon notice or not, or state anything concerning cross-examinations in connection with them. From what is said in many of the opinions concerning the use of affidavits in English practice, it is to be easily inferred, however, that affidavits have frequently been taken under circumstances which preclude the idea of any notice or opportunity to cross-examine. But the English practice of examining cases of habeas corpus upon affidavits prevails to a less extent in the United States than it does in England, and the English cases cited on this subject are not always applicable to our situation and our laws. Here it is the constant practice of courts in cases of this kind to hear *viva voce* testimony when offered. In the habeas corpus case of The State v. Lyon,[1] where the only evidence offered by the defendant was an affidavit, taken *ex parte*, without notice to any one interested for the prosecution, and without being entitled as of any cause in court, it was objected to on those grounds and excluded by the court, who said: "The party adducing it is bound to show that the testimony is legal, and taken in a mode conformable to law. The fact which constitutes the ground of objection has not been denied, and as we are not satisfied that there exist any reasons to take it out of the general rule, the evidence must be overruled."

But see Perrin v. West,[2] where Lord Chief Justice Denman said, with respect to an objection taken to the titles of affidavits, that it appeared to him that when a party is before the court by habeas corpus, the cause is there for all purposes. Justice Littledale also thought that the affidavits might properly be entitled in the cause in that court.[3] The manner in which affidavits are

---

[1] 1 Coxe, 409.
[2] 3 Ad. & El. 405.
[3] This was said in king's bench, to which a defendant in actual custody had been removed by *habeas corpus cum causa*, directed to the sheriff and issued by a judge of the court of king's bench, and had been committed by said judge to the custody of the marshal. It was claimed that such a proceeding did not remove the cause, but only the body; that to remove the cause the writ should have been directed to the judge of the inferior court; that the judge of the lower court had no notice of the proceedings; and that the affidavits were improperly entitled, as if the cause were in the court of king's bench, instead of in the court of first instance.

taken will sometimes meet with the disapprobation of the court. Each witness should be examined as to the facts which have come under his cognizance, and he should tell them in his own way, and not merely swear to what has been sworn by another. When several affidavits are used in one matter or action, they should never appear to be exact copies of each other as to material parts of the testimony. If they do appear to be so, this circumstance will render them objectionable, and tend to have them regarded with suspicion.[1]

§ 209. **Use of Affidavits in English Practice.**—The following are instances of some of the uses to which affidavits have been put in the courts of England:

§ 210. **Applications** for the writ were, as we have seen,[2] verified by affidavit whether the writ was to be issued either at common law or under the statute of 31 Car. II. The courts exercised their discretion upon the affidavit on which the application was grounded, and determined whether the writ should or should not issue. It did not issue as a matter of course in the first instance upon application.[3] Where a habeas corpus was applied for to bring up a person confined in a lunatic asylum for the purpose of producing him as a witness; and on an affidavit that he was rational the court said the writ might be had by applying to a judge at chambers, upon an affidavit that the lunatic was in a fit state to be removed, and was not dangerous.[4] One prosecuting the writ in behalf of a lunatic must make an affidavit or show that the lunatic is so coerced as to be incapable of making one, and that he is duly authorized by the lunatic to promote the application.[5]

§ 211. **Jurisdiction.**—William Dimes had been committed by order of the vice-chancellor of England, for a contempt or the violation of an injunction ordered by the lord chancellor, as shown by the return to a habeas corpus. The prisoner made a motion for time to file affidavits to show that the lord chancellor had a personal interest in the cause, and that in consequence thereof his injunction was void; but the court of queen's bench refused it, as the order of committal was that of the vice-chancellor, who had jurisdiction to decide whether there was proper ground for a commitment, and they could not review his decision. The court said they would not grant time to file affidavits for the purpose of disclosing matters not apparent on

---

[1] Moore v. Ewing & Bowen, 1 Coxe, 146.
[2] See sec. 95.
[3] King v. Hobhouse, 2 Chit. 207; S. C., 3 Barn. & Ald. 420.
[4] Ex parte ——, 3 Dowl. 161.   [5] Ex parte Child, 15 Com. B. 238.

the face of the return, unless the nature of those facts to be sworn to was suggested, and it appeared that such affidavits might be available. The vice-chancellor in this case was acting as a superior court. The return showed a commitment by a court of general or competent jurisdiction, acting within its jurisdiction, and the adjudication of that court would not be reviewed by the queen's bench.[1] So a commitment for a contempt "by an order of the court of chancery, made by H. Lord L., master of the rolls," was held to be made in the due exercise of his jurisdiction, and the court of queen's bench would not receive affidavits to show that the prisoner had not been brought to the bar of the court as was stated in the order —thereby being entitled to his discharge by statute—or that the order was made in a private room and not in court, for the master of the rolls had a jurisdiction not confined to any particular place, and had competent authority to decide on facts necessary to give him jurisdiction, which was sufficient. The matter would be different, said the court, if the affidavits tended to show that the magistrate's order was obtained by fraud, or that he was not really exercising the functions which he professed to exercise.[2]

Neither would the court of queen's bench allow affidavits to be used to disturb the sentence of transportation by the court of Jersey, one of competent criminal jurisdiction, where it was alleged in the return that that court had jurisdiction to try and punish the offense, so long as the sentence remained unreversed. The court said: "We can not assume that it is invalid or not warranted by law, or require the authority of the court to pass the sentence to be set out on the return. We are bound to assume, *prima facie*, that the unreversed sentence of a court of competent jurisdiction is correct; otherwise we should, in effect, be constituting ourselves a court of appeal without power to reverse the judgment."[3] It will be observed that the three judgments in the three respective cases above mentioned were made by courts of competent or general jurisdiction, and which the court of queen's bench could not set aside or reverse on habeas corpus; but where a prisoner had been convicted before a justice of the peace, the queen's bench held that it might be shown by affidavits that there was no evidence of such subject-matter as to give the justice jurisdiction—or, in other

---

[1] Dimes' Case, 14 Ad. & El., Q. B., 554.
[2] In the Matter of Clarke, 2 Ad. & El., Q. B., 619; S. C., 2 Gale & Dav. 780.
[3] Brenan and Galen's Case, 10 Ad. & El., Q. B., 492.

words, that they might be used to show a want of jurisdiction; yet, if there was any evidence to justify the finding of the justice, the court would not interfere.[1] The exchequer of pleas would not receive an affidavit to show that an offense was not committed within the jurisdiction of a justice of the peace. They thought the finding of that fact by him should be final so far as their jurisdiction to inquire where the offense was committed was concerned.[2]

Again: a prisoner had been convicted by a justice of the peace, and in the exchequer of pleas, Bramwell, B., said: "I think that the prisoner ought to be discharged. Upon the question whether we can look at the affidavits in order to ascertain whether the magistrate had jurisdiction, I own the inclination of my opinion is, that we are not at liberty to look at them. Perhaps what I am now saying may be extrajudicial, because it is not the point on which the prisoner is to be discharged; but I wish to state shortly the grounds on which I think the affidavits ought not to be received. I am inclined to adopt the rule laid down by the learned editors of Smith's Leading Cases, vol. 1, p. 591, 4th ed. 'Possibly the distinction may be between cases in which the conviction or order is made by persons who are admitted to constitute a legal court, and who have stated facts which, on information being laid or a case coming before them, would be matter to be proved and adjudicated upon by them, and cases in which the objection is that they are not a court at all, because not in fact magistrates, or because interested, because they sat out of the limit of their jurisdiction, or for some other reason striking at their existence as a court, so that the objection is not that the statement of a court is erroneous, but that the source of the statement is not a court at all.' I do not otherwise see why a person might not contest the jurisdiction of the magistrate either by an action against him or in any other way; for the principle on which we examine the propriety of these convictions must be equally applicable whether personal liberty or property is concerned; and the inconvenience of revoking the adjudication of magistrates in matters of this kind is so great, that I think the rule which I have referred to ought to be adopted. But, assuming that we have power to examine into the jurisdiction, as it is called, or into the existing facts necessary to give jurisdiction, it ought not to be more extensive than this, viz., we may inquire into the truth of every-

[1] Bailey's and Collier's Case, 3 El. & Bl. 607; S. C., 25 Eng. L. & Eq. 240.
[2] In re Smith, 3 Hurl. & N. 234.

thing except the subject-matter of the complaint. Therefore, all that we are at liberty to inquire into is, whether the person convicting was a magistrate, whether a complaint was made, whether the prisoner was a potter, and whether there had been an entry into the service; those facts existing, it was for the magistrate to adjudicate on the complaint. On these grounds, I think that we ought not to look at the affidavits."[1]

§ 212. **Contradicting Return by Affidavit.**—We have seen that the return is to be taken as *prima facie* true.[2] Independently of the statutes, the rule at common law seems to have been, not to allow the return to be contradicted, but to leave the party to bring an action for a false return.[3] In modern times, however, the return may be quashed, on showing its falsity by affidavit, on application for an attachment.[4] Prior to the passage of the statute of 56 Geo. III., c. 100, sec. 3, it was not the regular practice to allow the truth of the facts set forth in the return in cases other than commitments for criminal or supposed criminal matters, to be examined into by affidavit, yet it was sometimes done.[5] Under the statute of 31 Car. II., affidavits in answer to the return are not expressly authorized, and are not allowed, when the application for the writ is made under that statute;[6] but by the statute of 56 Geo. III., c. 100, affidavits are allowed.[7] Thus it will be seen that the competency or incompetency to contradict the return depends on whether the writ is issued under the statute of 31 Car. II., or not. If it is not, then affidavits to contradict the return are allowed.[8]

It will be seen[9] that the act of 31 Car. II. provides for cases of commitment for criminal or supposed criminal matters. Affidavits were refused in Brenan and Galen's Case, cited above,[10] and also refused to contradict the return in The Matter of Clarke, heretofore referred to.[11] In Brittain v. Kinnaird it was shown that a fact directly stated on a conviction could not be controverted.[12] In Rex v. The Justices of Somersetshire, and other cases of the same class, no attempt was made to raise an objection on the proceedings themselves; but facts collateral to them were added, to show want of jurisdiction.[13] The court

[1] In re Baker, 2 Hurl. & N. 239.
[2] Leonard Watson's Case, 9 Ad. & El. 731; S. C., 1 Per. & Dav. 516.
[3] See sec. 138.
[4] Leonard Watson's Case, 9 Ad. & El. 731; S. C., 1 Per. & Dav. 516.
[5] See sec. 129.
[6] See *ante*, sec. 58.
[7] 1 Tidd's Prac. 347.
[8] Ex parte Beeching, 4 Barn. & Cress. 136.
[9] See *ante*, sec. 58.
[10] 10 Ad. & El., Q. B., 492.
[11] 2 Ad. & El., Q. B., 619; S. C., 2 Gale & Dav. 780.
[12] 1 Brod. & B. 432.
[13] 5 Barn. & Cress. 816.

would not allow the validity of the return in The King v. Rogers to be impeached on affidavit—where the prisoner sought to be relieved from a charge of desertion.[1] In Leonard Watson's Case,[2] involving a criminal matter, as well as those mentioned above, it was a *quære*, however, with the court as to what mode of precedure should be used to impeach the return and inquire into its truth. It seems to be intimated that, if the return could have been controverted, affidavits might be used. Lord Denman, C. J., said there: "And even in this case, where there is before us a statement, to which I, for one, give entire credence, of legal proceedings which authorize Watson's imprisonment, I am not prepared to say that, if any part of such proceedings could be impeached by him as untrue, there should not be full inquiry, and the means afforded him of making the truth appear." So affidavits suggesting matters which, though not repugnant to the return, show the custody to be illegal will not be received.[3] But where the commitment is not under the statute of 31 Car. II., affidavits, as said, may be used; as, on an application for a bankrupt's discharge, to show circumstances not set forth in the warrant of the commissioners,[4] or to show facts which do not appear upon the face of the return.[5] A prisoner on the charge of smuggling, and brought up by habeas corpus at common law, may controvert the truth of the return by affidavit under the statute of 56 Geo. III., c. 100, sec. 4.[6] Privilege from arrest may thus be shown on affidavit where one is detained for debt,[7] or where he was arrested on Sunday, making the arrest void.[8] A case of cruelty should be raised on the return, and not brought in by affidavit merely to uphold a bad and evasive return.[9]

§ 213. **Examination of Indictment.**—Under the statute of 31 Car. II. the court will sometimes examine by affidavit the circumstances of a fact on which a prisoner brought before them by habeas corpus has been indicted, in order to inform themselves, on examination of the whole matter, whether it is reasonable to bail him or not.[10]

---

[1] 3 Dow. & Ry. 607.
[2] 1 Per. & Dav. 567; S. C., 9 Ad. & El. 731.
[3] Reg. v. Douglas, 7 Jur., part i, 39; and see 2 Hawk. P. C. c. 15, sec. 78.
[4] Ex parte Lampon, and in the Matter of Lampon, 3 Deac. & Ch. 751.
[5] In re Martin, 4 Dow. & L. 768.
[6] Ex parte Beeching et al., 3 Appeals from Mag. to K. B. 174; S. C., 4 Barn. & Cress. 136.
[7] Ex parte Dakins; In re Swann v. Dakins, 29 Eng. L. & Eq. 331; S. C., 16 Com. B. 77.
[8] Eggington's Case, 2 El. & Bl. 717.
[9] Regina v. Roberts et al., 2 F. & F. 272.
[10] 2 Hawk. P. C., c. 15, sec. 79; see 2 W. Black. 1208, note.

§ 214. **Enlarging Time.**—An affidavit may be used as a reason for enlarging the time to return the writ.[1]

§ 215. **Fortifying Return.**—In an early case, Lord Hardwicke thought it a bad practice to supply by affidavits what ought to have appeared on the return;[2] but in later times it has been said, even in cases under the statute of 31 Car. II., that the return need not be supported by affidavits or otherwise until it is impeached, and that it is not necessary to support a return to a writ of habeas corpus by affidavit, as the law provides means to secure its truth;[3] and on the hearing of a writ issued pursuant to the statute of 56 Geo. III., the court went so far as to say that they would hold an ambiguous return, unless it was fortified by affidavit clearing up all doubt, to be evasive and bad.[4] The tendency of the English courts under these decisions is evident.

§ 216. **Denying Statement in Warrant.**—In a very late case, where a commitment stated that a solicitor who had been committed for a contempt had been offered an opportunity of showing cause why he should not be committed for contempt, but that instead of doing so he proceeded to interrupt the proceedings of the court, it was held on habeas corpus that affidavits could not be read to show that this statement in the warrant of commitment was untrue.[5]

§ 217. **In Colonel Aaron Burr's Case, and in Bollman and Swartwout's Case,**[6] the supreme court of the United States considered some very important questions concerning the admissibility and value of affidavits as evidence under proceedings by habeas corpus.[7] It appears from this case that the

---

[1] Rex v. Clarke, 3 Burr. 1363.
[2] King v. Penelope, 7 Mod. 235.
[3] Queen v. Batchelder, 1 Per. & Dav. 510; S. C., 9 Ad. & El. 731.
[4] Regina v. Roberts et al., 2 F. & F. 272.
[5] 1 Crim. Law Mag. 410; citing high court of justice, Q. B. D.; Re Rea, 14 Cox C. C. 256.
[6] 4 Cranch, 75; S. C., 1 Burr's Trial, 21; Marshall on the Federal Constitution, 33, 53.
[7] Bollman and Swartwout had been committed by the circuit court for the District of Columbia, on a charge of treason. On habeas corpus and *certiorari* the supreme court examined the evidence on which the commitment of the primary court was grounded, in order "to do that which the court below ought to have done." Bollman and Swartwout had been brought by a military force from New Orleans, and detained in the city of Washington under a military guard. The motion for a bench warrant to issue for their arrest was founded upon the affidavit of General Wilkinson, made in New Orleans, and a printed copy of the president's message to congress, on the twenty-second of January, 1807: See 4 Cranch, 75, and 4 Cranch App., note a. , This affidavit was offered in evidence and objected to. The chief justice stated that the court had difficulty upon two points, viz.: 1. Whether the affidavit of General Wilkinson was evidence admissible in that stage of the prosecution; and, 2. Whether, if admissible, his statement of the contents of the substance of a letter, when the original was in his possession, was such evidence as the court ought to notice. The first point involved the question whether an affidavit made

§ 217.   THE EVIDENCE.   263

provision in the constitution of the United States (and which is found in the constitutions of most of the states in the same terms), that "in all criminal prosecutions the accused shall enjoy the right to be confronted with the witnesses against

before a magistrate to obtain a warrant of arrest could be used as evidence on the motion to commit, after the accused was taken, and also whether the accused was not entitled to demand that he should be confronted with his accuser, and that the evidence against him should be given *viva voce*, in order that by that means circumstances which at first view might criminate him could be explained. To this Chief Justice Marshall observed: "The objection that the affidavit is extrajudicial resolves itself into the question whether one magistrate may commit on an affidavit taken before another magistrate. For if he may, an affidavit made as the foundation of a commitment ceases to be extrajudicial, and the person who makes it would be as liable to a prosecution for perjury as if the warrant of commitment had been issued by the magistrate before whom the affidavit was made. To decide that an affidavit made before one magistrate would not justify a commitment by another, might in many cases be productive of great inconvenience, and does not appear susceptible of abuse if the verity of the certificate be established. Such an affidavit seems admissible on the principle that before the accused is put upon his trial all the proceedings are *ex parte*. The court therefore overrule this objection." On the second point a division of the court took place. Said the chief justice: "Two judges are of opinion that as such testimony delivered in the presence of the prisoner on his trial would be totally inadmissible, neither can it be considered as a foundation for a commitment. Although in making a commitment the magistrate does not decide on the guilt of the prisoner, yet he does decide on the probable cause, and a long and painful imprisonment may be the consequence of his decision. This probable cause, therefore, ought to be proved by testimony in itself legal, and which, though from the nature of the case it must be *ex parte*, ought in many other respects to be such as a court and jury might hear. Two judges are of opinion that in this incipient stage of the prosecution an affidavit stating the general purport of a letter may be read, particularly where the person in possession of it is at too great a distance to admit of its being obtained, and that a commitment may be founded on it."

Trial of Colonel Aaron Burr. — Shortly after the decision in the above case the same question was presented to the circuit court of the United States, sitting at the city of Richmond, on the trial of Colonel Burr. The affidavit of Jacob Dunbaugh was offered, which was "taken on the fifteenth of April, 1807, before B. Cenas, a justice of the peace," and to which was subjoined a certificate of Governor William C. C. Claiborne, dated "at New Orleans, the sixteenth of April, 1807," and stating "that B. Cenas was a justice of the peace for the county of New Orleans." This was objected to, for the following reasons: "1. That an affidavit could, under no circumstances, be read, unless it were shown that the witness could not be produced and that the government had not had sufficient time to procure the attendance of Jacob Dunbaugh. 2. That though the governor of New Orleans had certified that B. Cenas was a justice of the peace, yet he had not said that it was the same B. Cenas before whom that affidavit was taken. 3. That B. Cenas had not stated in the caption of his certificate, or elsewhere, that the affidavit was taken 'at New Orleans,' so as to show that he was acting within his jurisdiction." On the motion to exclude the evidence of Jacob Dunbaugh, the chief justice, Marshall, delivered the opinion of the court, as follows:

"On the part of the United States, a paper, purporting to be an affidavit, has been offered in evidence, to the reading of which two exceptions are taken: 1. That an affidavit ought not to be admitted where the personal attendance of the witness could have been obtained. 2. That this paper is not so authenticated as to entitle itself to be considered as an affidavit. That a magistrate may commit upon affidavits has been decided in the suhim," applies only to the trial itself, and not to the preliminary examination. We have met with no decisions of the state courts on this point of constitutional construction. Yet, while the constitutional guaranty of the right of the accused to be

preme court of the United States, though not without hesitation. The presence of the witness, to be examined by the committing justice, confronted with the accused, is certainly to be desired; and ought to be obtained, unless considerable inconvenience and difficulty exist in procuring his attendance. An *ex parte* affidavit, shaped, perhaps, by the person pressing the prosecution, will always be viewed with some suspicion, and acted upon with some caution; but the court thought it would be going too far to reject it altogether. If it was obvious that the attendance of the witness was easily attainable, but that he was intentionally kept out of the way, the question might be otherwise decided.

"But the particular case before the court does not appear to be of this description. The witness resides a great distance away; and there is no evidence that the materiality of his testimony was known to the prosecutors or to the executive in time to have directed his attendance. It is true that general instructions which would apply to any individual might have been sent, and the attendance of this or any other material witness obtained under those instructions; but it would be requiring too much to say that the omission to do this ought to exclude an affidavit. This exception, therefore, will not prevail. The second is, that the paper is not so authenticated as to be introduced as testimony on a question which concerns the liberty of a citizen. This objection is founded on two omissions in the certificate. The first is, that the place at which the affidavit was taken does not appear. The second is, that the certificate of the governor does not state the person who administered the oath to be a magistrate; but goes no further than to say that a person of that name was a magistrate. That for aught appearing to the court, this oath may or may not, in point of fact, have been legally administered must be conceded. The place where the oath was administered not having been stated, it may have been administered where the magistrate had no jurisdiction, and yet the certificate be perfectly true. Of consequence, there is no evidence before the court that the magistrate had power to administer the oath, and was acting in his judicial capacity. The effect of testimony may often be doubtful, and courts must exercise their best judgment in the case; but of the verity of the paper there ought never to be a doubt. No paper writing ought to gain admittance into a court of justice as testimony unless it possesses those solemnities which the law requires. Its authentication must not rest upon probability, but must be as complete as the nature of the case admits of; this is believed to be a clear legal principle. In conformity with it is, as the court conceives, the practice of England and of this country, as is attested by the books of forms; and no case is recollected in which a contrary principle has been recognized. This principle is in some degree illustrated by the doctrine with respect to all courts of limited jurisdiction. Their proceedings are erroneous, if their jurisdiction be not conclusively shown. They derive no validity from the strongest probability that they had jurisdiction in the case; none certainly from the presumption that, being a court, a usurpation of jurisdiction will not be presumed. The reasoning applies, in full force, to the actings of a magistrate whose jurisdiction is local. Thus in the case of a warrant, it is expressly declared that the place where it was made ought to appear. The attempt to remedy this defect by comparing the date of the certificate given by the magistrate with that given by the governor can not succeed. The answer given at bar to this argument is conclusive; the certificate wants those circumstances which would make it testimony; and without them no part of it can be regarded.

"The second objection is equally fatal. The governor has certified that a man of the same name with the person who has administered the oath is a magistrate; but not that the person

§ 217. THE EVIDENCE. 265

"confronted with the witnesses against him" extends only to the trial, in many of the states, as in California, there are statutory provisions requiring the preliminary examination to be conducted in the presence of the accused and of his counsel.

who has administered it is a magistrate. It is too obvious to be controverted that there may be two or more persons of the same name, and consequently, to produce that certainty which the case readily admits of, the certificate of the governor ought to have applied to the individual who administered the oath. The propriety of this certainty and precision in a certificate, which is to authenticate any affidavit to be introduced into a court of justice, is so generally admitted that I do not recollect a single instance in which the principle has been departed from. It has been said that it ought to appear that there are two persons of the same name, or the court will not presume such to be the fact. The court presumes nothing. It may or may not be the fact, and the court can not presume that it is not. The argument proceeds upon the idea that an instrument is to be disproved by him who objects to it, and not that it is to be proved by him who offers it. Nothing can be more repugnant to the established usage of courts. How is it to be proved that there are two persons of the name of Cenas in the territory of Orleans? If, with a knowledge of several weeks, perhaps months, that this prosecution was to be carried on, the executive ought not to be required to produce this witness, ought the prisoner to be required, with the notice of a few hours, to prove that two persons of the same name reside in New Orleans? It has been repeatedly urged that a difference exists between the strictness of law which would be applicable to a trial in chief, and that which is applicable to a motion to commit for trial. Of the reality of this distinction the present controversy affords conclusive proof. At a trial in chief the accused possesses the valuable privilege of being confronted with his accuser. But there must be some limit to this relaxation, and it appears not to have extended so far as to the admission of a paper not purporting to be an affidavit, and not shown to be one. When it is asked whether every man does not believe that this affidavit was really taken before a magistrate, it is at once answered that this can not affect the case. Should a man of probity declare a certain fact within his own knowledge, he would be credited by all who knew him; but his declaration could not be received as testimony by the judge who firmly believed him. So a man might be believed to be guilty of a crime, but a jury could not convict him unless the testimony proved him to be guilty of it. This judicial disbelief of a probable circumstance does not establish a wide interval between common law and common sense. It is believed in this respect to show their intimate union.

"The argument goes to this, that the paper shall be received and acted upon as an affidavit, not because the oath appears to have been administered according to law, but because it is probable that it was so administered. This point seems to have been decided by the constitution. 'The right of the people,' says that instrument, 'to be secure in their persons, houses, papers, and effects, against unreasonable searches and seizures, shall not be violated; and no warrants shall issue but upon probable cause, supported by oath or affirmation, and particularly describing the places to be searched, and the persons or things to be seized.' The cause of seizure is not to be supported by a probable oath, or an oath that was probably taken, but by an oath absolutely taken. This oath must be a legal oath, and if it must be a legal oath, it must legally appear to the court to be so. This provision is not made for a final trial; it is made for the very case now under consideration. In the cool and temperate moments of reflection, undisturbed by that whirlwind of passion with which, in those party conflicts which most generally produce acts or accusations of treason, the human judgment is sometimes overthrown, the people of America have believed the power even of commitment to be capable of too much oppression in its execution to be placed, without restriction, even in the hands of the national legislature. Shall a judge disregard those barriers

And in Connecticut the accused is even admitted to the grand-jury room, and permitted to cross-examine the witnesses against him. This, however, is by sufferance of the grand jury, as the accused has no constitutional or statutory right to be present.[1]

§ 218. **Arrest on State Process.**—Where an officer of the United States has been arrested on state process for an alleged abuse of his powers or authority, the federal courts will not only hear the evidence which the officer wishes to offer to dispel or disprove the truth of the affidavits upon which the state authorities proceeded, but will consider those affidavits independently of such proof; and if, in the opinion of the court, those affidavits do not contain a *prima facie* ground for arrest, will discharge the officer without hearing any counter-evidence. The general

which the nation has deemed it proper to erect? The interest which the people have in this prosecution has been stated; but it is firmly believed that the best and true interest of the people is to be found in a rigid adherence to those rules which preserve the fairness of criminal prosecutions in every stage. If this was a case to be decided by principle alone, the court would certainly not receive this paper; but if the point is settled by decision, it must be conformed to.

"It has been said to be settled in the supreme court of the United States by admitting the affidavit of Wilkinson (*vide supra*, Bollman and Swartwout), to which an exception was taken, because it did not appear that the magistrate had taken the oaths prescribed by law. It was said that as by law he could not act until he had taken the oaths, and he was found acting, it must be presumed that this prerequisite was complied with; that is, that his acting as a magistrate under his commission was evidence that he was authorized so to act. It will not be denied that there is much strength in the argument; but the cases do not appear to be precisely parallel. The certificate that he is a magistrate, and that full faith is due to his acts, implies that he has qualified, if his qualification is necessary to his being a complete magistrate, whose acts are entitled to full faith and credit. It is not usual for a particular certificate that a magistrate has qualified to accompany his official acts. There is no secret of his qualification, and no particular testimonial of it could be obtained.

"These observations do not apply to the objections which exist. But it is said that the certificate is the same with that in Wilkinson's affidavit. If this objection had been taken and overruled, it would have ended the question; but it was not taken, so far as is now recollected, and does not appear to have been noticed by the court. It is not recollected by the judge who sat on that occasion, to have been noticed. A defect, if it be one, which was not observed, can not be cured by being passed over in silence.

"The case in Washington was a civil case, and turned upon the point that no form of the commission was prescribed; and consequently, that it was not necessary to appear on the face of it that it was directed to magistrates; that it was the duty of the clerk to direct it to magistrates, and he should not be presumed to have neglected his duty in a case in which his performance of it need not appear on the face of the instrument; and that the person, intending to take this exception, ought to have taken it sooner, and not surprise the opposite party when it was too late to correct it.

"But the great difference is, that the privy examination was a mere ministerial act; the administering an oath is a judicial act. The court is of opinion that the paper purporting to be an affidavit made by Dunbaugh can not be read, because it does not appear to be on oath:" 1 Burr's Trials, 97. For opinion in same case, see Marshall on the Federal Constitution, 53.

[1] State v. Wolcott, 21 Conn. 272.

rule is to discharge such officers, unless there be a positive oath of merits from the plaintiff, or a sworn detail of circumstances from others to supply its place. Mr. Justice Kane, in Ex parte Jenkins,[1] used language very apt to the above observations: "Because the judge of a state court, in a proceeding necessarily *ex parte*, may have been imposed on by misstatements or suppressions of fact, am I therefore constrained in another cause, under another law, within a different constitutional jurisdiction, to make my hearing *ex parte* also, to hearken only to him who has abused, it is said, the process of the law by falsehood or fraud, and refuse my ear to him whom the law specially enjoins me to relieve, if he has been wronged? What is to be the consequence? A man swears to an assault and battery; the entire truth told, he was arrested for robbing the mail or the mint. Another swears to a trespass in breaking his close and carrying away his goods; the goods were stolen, and have been recovered under a search warrant. Both affidavits are the truth, unless that means the whole truth; they make out the *prima facie* case of the plaintiff. What then? Is the officer to go to prison in default of bail, and to stay there because the rogue swore to only half the story? Or would the argument change if the plaintiff should substitute another man's oath for his own, keeping himself aloof the while, not caring to proclaim his whereabouts?"

§ 219. **Affidavit Should State Facts.**—In 1878 a plaintiff commenced an action against a defendant before a justice of the peace of the state of New York. He applied for a warrant of arrest, and alleged in his affidavit that the defendant was a non-resident of the county, and that he, the plaintiff, "has, as he verily believes, a good cause of action against Samuel Sisson for wrongful and fraudulent representations in the exchange of horses, by which this deponent was damaged to a large amount," etc. The court held that this affidavit did not state the facts required by statute; and that plaintiff's belief that he had a good cause of action was not sufficient to authorize the justice to issue his warrant. "The facts and circumstances," it said, "must be set forth: Clark v. Wellington, 5 Hun. 640; Whitney v. Shufelt, 1 Denio 592; Loder v. Phelps, 13 Wend. 46. He should have stated the facts from which the justice could judge whether or not there was a cause of action on tort, and hence whether it was necessary or proper that the warrant should be issued. Some positive averment should have been made which,

[1] 2 Wall. jun. 521.

if untrue, would expose the plaintiff to indictment for perjury. That he had a good cause of action was but a conclusion of law."[1] So, where one was arrested on a *capias ad respondendum*, it was said that the affidavit constituted an essential part of the writ on which an arrest was made, and was not intended to be a mere formal matter; that the debt must have been positively stated to be justly due—not that it was due in the opinion or belief of the witness from an examination of the account or the written instrument on which the action was founded—and that if something more than this evidence of indebtedness was not required, a *capias* would have been given without an affidavit.[2]

The supreme court of Indiana have also held, "in action on contract, the affidavit, whether made by the plaintiff himself or by a third person, must show that there is, at the time of suing out the writ, an existing debt actually due, for which an arrest may lawfully be made. It must be positive as to the sum due, and not as the deponent believes, nor as appears by an account stated," etc.[3] A similar decision was made by the circuit court in the district of Illinois.[4] But in allegations of fraud, though they be generally stated, and defectively and imperfectly, in the plaintiff's preliminary affidavit, if he substantiates them to the satisfaction of the judge, and they are not denied on oath or otherwise controverted by the defendant, he may be committed to abide the event of the suit. The affidavit may allege the fraud in general terms, and it is sufficient if the general allegation show probable cause; for the defendant may on oath deny all the allegations and demand proof of all the facts. If he refuses to be examined, there will be a presumption against him.[5] The above principles apply to the construction of statutes on arrest and imprisonment in actions on contracts. The proceedings are collateral to the action for a breach of contract, and in aid of it and dependent upon it, and not in the nature of a summary conviction, because evidence sufficient to support them will not sustain such a conviction. The affidavit should specify the nature and amount of the claim, to show that it is on contract, and that the amount of bail, if offered, may be fixed.

§ 220. **Where No Objection is Offered to Irregular Evidence.**—Upon the hearing on the return to a writ of ha-

---

[1] Wells v. Sisson, 14 Hun, 267.
[2] Nelson & Graydon v. Cutler & Tyrrell, 3 McLean, 326.
[3] Lewis v. Brackenridge, 1 Blackf. 112.
[4] Wright et al. v. Cogswell, 1 McLean, 471.
[5] Gosline v. Place, 32 Pa. St. 520.

beas corpus, which shows that the prisoner is detained by virtue of the judgment of a court, the district attorney must, if the minutes of the court furnished to the keeper imperfectly describe the crime of which the relator was convicted, produce or prove the records of the court by a certified copy thereof, if insisted upon by the relator; but if this form of proof is not required by the relator, he may show by his affidavit that the relator was actually convicted and sentenced under statute made and provided for the case. The court will hold the affidavit sufficient to act upon unless the objection is interposed.[1]

[1] People ex rel. Trainor v. Baker, 89 N. Y. 460.

CHAPTER XIV.

WHAT MAY BE INQUIRED INTO ON THE RETURN.

PART I.—ORDINARY EXTENT OF INQUIRY IN THE FEDERAL COURTS.

§ 221. Recollections of Chapter on "The Return."
§ 222. General Review of the Subject.
§ 223. Distinction between Jurisdiction and its Exercise Pointed out.
§ 224. Appearance of Jurisdiction upon Face of Proceedings.
§ 225. Distinction between Void and Voidable Jurisdictional Proceedings.
§ 226. A Leading Principle.
§ 227. General Rules and their Application.
§ 228. Conflict of Jurisdiction.
§ 229. Inquiry where there is No Formal or Technical Commitment.
§ 230. Inquiry into and behind Commitment.
§ 231. Inquiry into and behind Commitment made by a United States Commissioner.
§ 232. When Order for Discharge may be Entered.

PART II.—EXTENT OF INQUIRY IN THE STATE COURTS BEFORE INDICTMENT.

§ 233. General Inquiries.
§ 234. Inquiry Extending Only to Jurisdiction into and behind Warrant of Committing Magistrate.
§ 235. Examination of Depositions, Evidence, and the Entire Proceedings before the Committing Magistrate.
§ 236. Effect of Statutes on These Two Rules.
§ 237. Guilt or Innocence of the Prisoner.
§ 238. Commitment by Court of General Jurisdiction.
§ 239. Cause for Detention after Failure to Indict.
§ 240. Convictions by Inferior Courts.
§ 241. Vacating Orders of Court.
§ 242. Habeas Corpus Pending Examination on Criminal Charge.
§ 243. Waiving Examination.

PART III.—INQUIRIES AFTER INDICTMENT AND BEFORE JUDGMENT OF CONVICTION.

§ 244. Reasons why the Courts Decline to Make Inquiry into a Commitment after Indictment Found.
§ 245. Inquiry may Go to whether Indictment Charges Any Offense.
§ 246. Defective Indictment.
§ 247. "Guilty or not Guilty."
§ 248. Continuing Indictment.

§ 249. Two Bills of Indictment—Death Penalty on One, No Trial on the Other.
§ 250. Existence of Indictment—Its Legality—Bench Warrant.
§ 251. Judgment on Sufficiency of the Indictment.
§ 252. Process without Warrant of Law.
§ 253. Effect of Order Arresting Judgment.
§ 254. New Trial—Delay in Bringing to Trial.
§ 255. Discharge of Jury in Absence of Defendant.

PART I.—ORDINARY EXTENT OF INQUIRY IN THE FEDERAL COURTS.

§ 221. **Recollections of Chapter on "The Return."**—We have seen in the preceding pages that, under the common law as well as under the statute of 31 Car. II., the better rule seemed to be that the return was conclusive, and that none of the facts in it could be controverted. The return, if regular upon its face, imported absolute verity; and if the party in whose favor the writ was issued, suffered damage from the falsity of the return, his remedy was by action. We have also seen that if a false return retarded the administration of justice, the party making it was subject to be indicted. Notwithstanding this exposure to an action for false imprisonment, and to a bill of indictment being found, for making a false return, it was still left in the power of the officer, jailer, or other person upon whom the writ was served to make a conclusive declaration, so far as the proceedings on habeas corpus were concerned, in his own favor, and this was deemed an evil. This was in some measure remedied, as we have seen, by the passage of the English statute of 56 Geo. III., c. 100, which contained provisions for relief against imprisonment in civil cases.

The discussion before the house of lords, before referred to, left its impress upon American jurisprudence, and after the passage of the statute of 56 Geo. III., the mode of hearing by summary proof may be said to have been thoroughly ingrained into our whole system of criminal law relating to proceedings under habeas corpus, both in the federal and state courts, and in cases of imprisonment for "criminal or supposed criminal matters," as well as for imprisonment in civil cases. Under the common law and statute of 31 Car. II., if the return were regular and legal, the party was without remedy, and had to submit; but if the return itself showed that there was no lawful cause to commit the prisoner, the judge or court would discharge him, and in doubtful cases would either bail or remand until it could be determined whether there were sufficient cause or not for the detention. The validity of the warrant of commitment and return were tried upon their faces.[1] The question of jurisdiction in civil cases seems not always to have been open to inquiry upon the collateral proceeding by habeas corpus.[2]

[1] Fazakerly v. Baldoe, 6 Mod. 177, 178; 2 Lilly's Reg. 1 (c); Rex v. Fenwick, 3 Smith, 369; Queen v. Baines, 12 Ad. & El. 210. For returns, however, in civil cases, see Ex parte Dakins, 29 Eng. L. & Eq. 331, where affidavits were received to explain the return, showing privilege, etc.; Ex parte Lampon, 3 Deac. & Ch. 751, where an affidavit was allowed to be read, stating circumstances which were not set forth in the warrant of commissioners in bankruptcy. In the Matter of Dimes, 14 Ad. & El., Q. B., 554, the court would not grant time to file affidavits for the purpose of disclosing matters not apparent on the return to a writ of habeas corpus, unless the nature of the facts to be sworn to was suggested, and it was shown that such affidavits might be available. This writ was issued under the statute of 56 Geo. III., but Justice Coleridge said: "Whether a writ of habeas corpus be at common law or within the provisions of the statute of 56 Geo. III., c. 100, it is not every affidavit that can be received on the return to the writ. Counsel, therefore, who apply for time to file affidavits must suggest to the court the nature of the affidavits they propose to use, that the court may see whether they could be used."

[2] In a civil case, on an action for debt, instituted in the court of the chancellor of the university of Oxford, the defendant's residence was not properly shown, either by the warrant or other proceedings in the chancellor's court, or by the affidavits and sheriff's return to the habeas corpus, and it was held that the defendant was entitled to his discharge, for want of proof of residence, and this independently of the question whether or not the process of the chancellor's court could be executed at the place in question. After the arrest the defendant had appeared in the chancellor's court, waived objection to the jurisdiction, and entered into the merits. Upon these it was decreed that he should pay the debt and remain in custody till he did so. After this the habeas corpus issued; and it was held not too late, and that the defendant might still insist before the court of king's bench on the want of jurisdiction: Perrin v. West, 3 Ad. & El. 405.

So in another civil case, In the Matter of Bailey, 3 El. & Bl. 607, where the warrant of commitment failed to set forth the evidence, affidavits were used showing the evidence before the justice, and it was held open to the prisoner to show, by affidavit, that there was no evidence from which the justice might reasonably draw an inference that the relation of master and servant existed between the prisoner and his employer, for that would show that the justice had no jurisdiction.

But in Dimes' Case, 14 Ad. & El., Q. B., 554, a civil case, the return showed a commitment by a court of competent jurisdiction acting within its jurisdiction; and the court would not allow affidavits to be introduced to show that the court of first instance, the court of chancery, should not have adjudicated as it did. The proposition was, not to contradict the return, but to bring before the court facts showing a want of jurisdiction, not in the vice-chancellor who made the order of commitment, but in the lord chancellor, who issued the injunction for the breach of which the committal took place. It was said that the affidavits could only go to show that the vice-chancellor came to a wrong decision, in order to lead the court of queen's bench to review his decision, and which they had no power to do. Where the judgment complained of is in an inferior court, the case is different. There the judgment in which the vice is alleged to be is before the court, and they have power to quash it. In this case, however, the injunction, for the violation of which Dimes was committed, was not before the court. The proceedings of an inferior court, such as the court of quarter sessions, are brought before the superior court by *certiorari*, and there the queen's bench has a controlling power. But in this respect such a court differs from the court of chancery, whose committals neither the court of common pleas, court of exchequer, nor queen's bench will review. These two instances were, in reality, attacks on judgments by habeas corpus, but it has been thought not entirely inappropriate to mention them here.

And where the commitment was under process in a civil matter, as under the statute of 56 Geo. III., issued by a court of competent jurisdiction, although it was unfounded in fact and in law, and that known to the queen's bench, they would refuse to inquire into the merits, with a view to the discharge of the prisoner on habeas corpus.[1] It will thus be seen that the judges and courts in England confine themselves very closely to what appears upon the face of the return, where it appears to be legal and regular, and the process has been issued by a court of competent jurisdiction. The writ of habeas corpus seems to have a more extended use in the United States than it has in England, and inquiries under it are more varied and far-reaching here than in that country.

§ 222. **General Review of the Subject.**—The object of this chapter will be, further on, to show the ordinary extent of inquiry on the return to the writ of habeas corpus in the courts of the United States. The use of the writ as a collateral attack on judgments will be considered in a subsequent chapter. So will the extent of inquiry on the return to the writ in extradition cases, sentences of courts-martial, contempts, bail, questions of comity, detentions by private authority, and in appealed cases be hereafter considered.

Under sections 753 and 760 of the revised statutes of the United States,[2] it is perfectly obvious that the question of jurisdiction, in the commitment of persons for either civil or criminal matters, is always open and may be inquired into upon proceedings by habeas corpus. This may be prior to indictment, subsequent to it, or even after a regular prosecution, trial, and conviction. Under the judiciary act of 1789,[3] a return to a habeas corpus issued by a judge of the United States, showing an imprisonment under process, legal and valid on its face, was conceded to be conclusive, and that it precluded further inquiry into the cause of imprisonment; but under the act of congress of 1833,[4] and other subsequent acts, this conclusiveness vanished, and inquiry may now go on swift wings to the remotest nook of every material fact connected with the case, where error, irregularity, fraud, or mistake may lurk.

§ 223. **Distinction between Jurisdiction and its Exercise Pointed out.**—Jurisdiction has been defined by the supreme court of the United States to be "the power to hear

---

[1] Case of the Sheriff of Middlesex, 11 Ad. & El. 273.
[2] See habeas corpus act of the United States, ante, sec. 59.
[3] 1 Stat. at Large, 81.
[4] 4 Stat. at Large, 634; act of 1842, 5 Id. 539; act of 1867, 14 Id. 385; habeas corpus act of the United States, ante, sec. 59.

and determine a cause. It is *coram judice* whenever a case is presented which brings this power into action; if the petitioner states such a case in his petition, that on a demurrer the court would render judgment in his favor, it is an undoubted case of jurisdiction. Whether on an answer denying and putting in issue the allegations of the petition, the petitioner makes out his case, is the exercise of jurisdiction conferred by the filing of a petition containing all the requisites and in the manner prescribed by law."[1] So, too, where a circuit court has general jurisdiction over criminal matters, an offense cognizable in any court is cognizable in that court. "If the offense be punishable by law, that court is competent to inflict the punishment. The judgment of such a tribunal has all the obligation which the judgment of any tribunal can have. To determine whether the offense charged in the indictment be legally punishable or not, is among the most unquestionable of its powers and duties. The decision of this question is the exercise of jurisdiction, whether the judgment be for or against the prisoner."[2] Thus it will be seen that where a state of facts is shown or proved which confers jurisdiction, all else refers to the exercise of that jurisdiction, and which will not be inquired into by a superior or appellate court.

§ 224. **Appearance of Jurisdiction upon Face of Proceedings.**—The jurisdiction of all the federal courts should appear upon the face of the proceedings. The courts of the United States are all of limited jurisdiction, and their proceedings are erroneous if the jurisdiction be not shown upon them. Judgments rendered in such cases may certainly be reversed, but the supreme court of the United States will not hold such judgments rendered in the inferior courts to be absolute nullities which may be totally disregarded. Such proceedings are reversible on error or appeal. This holds good in civil causes as well as criminal.[3]

§ 225. **Distinction between Void and Voidable Jurisdictional Proceedings.**—To determine the question of jurisdiction, much may be learned from the words of Mr. Justice Baldwin of the supreme court of the United States. "The true line of distinction between courts whose decisions are conclusive if not removed to an appellate court, and those whose proceedings are nullities if their jurisdiction does not appear on their face, is

---

[1] United States v. Arredondo et al., 6 Pet. 709, and approved in Grignon's Lessee v. Astor et al., 2 How. 338; and in In re Bogart, 2 Saw. 401.

[2] Ex parte Tobias Watkins, 3 Pet. 203.

[3] Id. 204, 205.

this: a court which is competent by its constitution to decide on its own jurisdiction, and to exercise it to a final judgment, without setting forth in their proceedings the facts and evidence on which it is rendered, whose record is absolute verity, not to be impugned by averment or proof to the contrary, is of the first description; there can be no judicial inspection behind the judgment save by appellate power. A court which is so constituted that its judgment can be looked through for the facts and evidence which are necessary to sustain it, whose decision is not evidence of itself to show jurisdiction and its lawful exercise, is of the latter description; every requisite for either must appear on the face of their proceedings, or they are nullities."[1]

§ 226. **A Leading Principle.**—Finally, in the words of the same learned justice. "it is a universal principle, that where power or jurisdiction is delegated to any public officer or tribunal over a subject-matter, and its exercise is confided to his or their discretion, the acts so done are binding and valid as to the subject-matter; and individual rights will not be disturbed collaterally for anything done in the exercise of that discretion within the authority and power conferred. The only questions which can arise between an individual claiming a right under the acts done and the public, or any person denying its validity, are, power in the officer, and fraud in the party. All other questions are settled by the decision made or the act done by the tribunal or officer, whether executive: 1 Cranch, 170, 171; legislative: 4 Wheat. 423; 2 Pet. 412; 4 Id. 563; judicial: 11 Mass. 227; 11 Serg. & R. 429; adopted in 2 Pet. 167, 168; or special: 20 Johns. 739, 740; 2 Dow. 521, etc.; unless an appeal is provided for, or other revision, by some appellate or supervising tribunal, is prescribed by law."[2] To enable a court or judge to determine the question of jurisdiction, the power to determine it must be given by written law.[3]

§ 227. **General Rules and their Application.**—A circuit court may issue the writ of habeas corpus to review the proceedings in case of a conviction in a district court and imprisonment for a crime; and the supreme court will likewise issue the writ to review the proceedings of either of these courts. But it will not revise the same for error where the court below had jurisdiction of the cause and of the person, and where it would not be reviewable on a writ of error or appeal. In other

---

[1] Grignon's Lessee v. Astor et al., 2 How. 341.
[2] United States v. Arredondo et al., 6 Pet. 729.
[3] Ex parte Bollman & Swartwout, 4 Cranch, 94.

words, where the proceedings in the inferior court are entirely void the party may be discharged. The jurisdiction or power to hear and determine may at all times be inquired into, either before or after a judgment of final conviction, but where the power or jurisdiction exists, its exercise will not be inquired into.[1] Consequently, where the question is whether an act charged is a crime against the laws of the United States, an error in the decision will not affect the jurisdiction of the court nor warrant a discharge on habeas corpus.[2] So where an inferior court has committed a party for a contempt, having jurisdiction of the matter, the supreme court will not grant the writ of habeas corpus for his relief; but if either a state court or a federal court exceeds its jurisdiction or powers in making a commitment for a contempt, where the acts of alleged contempt are in the performance of a duty created by the constitution or a law or a treaty of the United States, the party will be discharged.[3]

§ 228. **Conflict of Jurisdiction.**—The federal courts determine the question of their own jurisdiction, and no state court can make any inquiry into it. After the return to a writ of habeas corpus is made, and the state court or judge is judicially apprised that the party is in custody under the authority of the United States, they can go no further. But the federal courts will inquire into the jurisdiction or power of a state court to sentence a party, or to commit him to prison, under an act of the legislature creating or attempting to create the offense for which the prisoner is convicted, and for which he is held in custody, and which is in violation of any provision of the constitution of the United States, a law thereof, or the provisions of a valid treaty.[4] In such cases the defect is not mere error or irregularity; it is not a mere wrongful exercise of jurisdiction; but it is defective in substance. The state court has no power or jurisdiction in the premises, for the prisoner is in custody in violation of a treaty of the United States, or a law or the constitution thereof.[5]

Where a party is in a state prison for an act done in pursuance of a law of the United States, the federal tribunals will extend

---

[1] Ex parte Watkins, 7 Pet. 568; In re Bogart, 2 Saw. 401; Ex parte Lange, 18 Wall. 178; Ex parte Yerger, 8 Id. 85; Ex parte Parks, 93 U. S. 18; Ex parte Curtis, 1 Supreme Court Rep. 381; Ex parte Carll, Id. 535; Ex parte Kenyon, 5 Dill. 385; Ex parte Shaffenburg, 4 Id. 271; Ex parte Dock Bridges, 2 Wood, 428.

[2] Ex parte Siebold, 100 U. S. 371.

[3] Ex parte Kearney, 7 Wheat. 38; The Case of the Electoral College of South Carolina, 1 Hughes, 571.

[4] Ableman v. Booth, 21 How. 506; Tarble's Case, 13 Wall. 397.

[5] In re Wong Yung Qui, 9 Rep. 366.

to him the hand of relief. The federal courts and judges have great respect for state authority, and it is with great reluctance, although acting within the undoubted scope of their jurisdiction, that they will take from a state officer a person committed to him by a state court, and charged with an offense against state laws. The federal courts have no general supervisory jurisdiction over the state courts, or any general power to interfere with persons or property in their custody, except in a few cases where the constitution and acts of congress have given such jurisdiction and power to the courts of the United States.

In the language of Mr. Justice Ballard of the sixth circuit for the state of Kentucky: "Ordinarily, the federal courts have no more authority to interfere with persons or property in custody under a process from a state court than the state courts have to interfere with persons or property in custody under a process from a federal court. The federal and state courts have in many instances a concurrent jurisdiction over the same persons and things, and the rule is almost universal, that the officer who first gets possession under process from his court has the preference. Therefore the general rule is, that if a person be imprisoned under a criminal or civil process of one, the other can not take him from such custody for any purpose whatever."[1] The federal courts, however, have no power to issue a writ of habeas corpus to bring up a party serving out a life sentence passed by a state court on a conviction of treason against the state, for any other purpose than to be used as a witness. This fact appearing in the return, the inquiry ceases.[2] They will only interfere where the party is in custody in violation of some provision of the laws of the United States, the constitution, or a treaty thereof. This does not imply any invasion of the sovereignty of the state whose process is thus treated. Neither is it based in any assumption or claim that a federal judge has any jurisdiction to revise or set aside the judgments of the courts or magistrates of the state. It is merely the exercise of power to inquire into the cause of imprisonment, and if such cause be within the contemplation of the acts of congress, to grant an order for the discharge of the imprisoned party. Furthermore, it does not import that a federal court or judge can protect an officer of the United States from punishment for a crime committed against the laws of the state, under pretense that he was doing his duty. The provisions of the acts of congress are

---

[1] U. S. ex rel. Roberts v. Jailer of Fayette Co., 2 Abb. U. S. 267, 282.
[2] Ex parte Dorr, 3 How. 103.

plain, and neither government must invade the jurisdictional dominion of the other. In one sense, they are two separate and distinct governments, and entirely foreign to each other; the laws of the United States, however, giving to the federal government power to revise the action of the state governments on proceedings by habeas corpus, when the effect of that action is the detention, imprisonment, or restraint of one in violation of any law of the United States, the constitution, or a treaty thereof.

§ 229. **Inquiry where there is No Formal or Technical Commitment.**—Mr. Justice Treat, of the United States district court for Missouri, said: "The question of jurisdiction does not depend in the slightest degree upon the fact whether there has been a formal commitment or not, or whether the prisoner is in jail; but the sole inquiry is, whether he is held in unlawful restraint of his liberty ' under or by color of the authority of the United States.'"[1] This is to be understood as applying to the federal courts of original jurisdiction, for he said also: "In no case known and accessible to this court has it ever been held that the United States courts of original jurisdiction can not issue the writ where a person is held in illegal restraint under or by color of the authority of the United States, whether there has been a technical ' commmitment ' or not."[2] With the exceptions made by the constitutional provision giving the supreme court of the United States original jurisdiction in all cases affecting ambassadors, other public ministers, and consuls, etc.,[3] that court has authority to issue the writ only in the exercise of its appellate jurisdiction, and a decision that the individual shall be imprisoned must always precede the application for a writ of habeas corpus, and this writ must always be issued for the purpose of revising that decision,[4] except where the supreme court has original jurisdiction under the constitution, and is therefore appellate in its nature. It will thus be seen that, except in the exercise of its original jurisdiction, the supreme court can not issue the writ, and therefore make no inquiry where there has been no commitment by any magistrate, court, or judge, for there would then be no action of a court over which it has appellate or revisory power, and which could come before it for revision. Outside of its original jurisdiction, the supreme court

---

[1] In the Matter of Emmett McDonald, 9 Am. Law Reg. 692.
[2] Id. 682.
[3] Const. U. S., art. 3 (judicial power).
[4] Ex parte Bollman and Swartwout, 4 Cranch, 75; Ex parte Burford, 3 Id. 448; Ex parte Watkins, 7 Pet. 568; Ex parte Hamilton, 3 Dall. 17; Marbury v. Madison, 1 Cranch, 137; Ex parte Kearney, 7 Wheat. 38; Ex parte McCardle, 7 Wall. 506; Ex parte McCardle, 6 Id. 318; Ex parte Yerger, 8 Id. 85.

limits itself to cases pending in or decided by those courts over which it has appellate or revisory power, over tribunals inferior to itself, or from whose decisions an appeal might ultimately be taken to the supreme court.[1]

We do not always find the doctrine thus laid down in all the books, but the caution of Mr. Justice Treat[2] will lead one right. In speaking of the decision rendered by Chief Justice Marshall in Bollman v. Swartwout,[3] he said: "To understand distinctly the views expressed by Chief Justice Marshall, it is necessary to keep constantly before the mind the fact that the supreme court was considering in what cases that tribunal, as an appellate tribunal and not a court of original jurisdiction, could issue the writ." And to conclude, where one is held by mere arbitrary will, and without any process, warrant, or any other legal authority, it is not necessary to the jurisdiction of any United States judge, or a United States court of original jurisdiction, that there shall have been a technical commitment; and the cause of detention, restraint, or imprisonment will be examined into as well without it as where it exists.

§ 230. **Inquiry into and behind Commitment.**—The federal courts will give an open and free investigation into the warrant of commitment by which a party is imprisoned, or go behind it and inquire into the facts upon which it is based, before a final judgment given by a court of competent jurisdiction. Where one has been committed by justices of the peace, without the statement of "some good cause certain, supported by oath," and has been improperly remanded to prison by a circuit court upon proceedings by habeas corpus, the supreme court will, on *certiorari*, pronounce the warrant of commitment made by the circuit court illegal and discharge the prisoner.[4] The judiciary act itself authorizes all the courts of the United States, and the judges thereof, to issue the writ "for the purpose of inquiring into the cause of commitment."[5] In the words of the renowned Marshall: "The writ of habeas corpus is a high prerogative writ known to the common law, the great object of which is the liberation of those who may be imprisoned without sufficient cause. It is in the nature of a writ of error, to ex-

---

[1] Ex parte Barry, 2 How. 65; Ex parte Dorr, 3 Id. 104; Barry v. Mercein et al., 5 Id. 103; In the Matter of Metzger, Id. 184; In re Kaine, 14 Id. 119, and authorities there cited; Ex parte Bollman and Swartwout, 4 Cranch, 75; Ex parte Tobias Watkins, 3 Pet. 193.

[2] In the Matter of Emmett McDonald, 9 Am. Law Reg. 675.

[3] Ex parte Bollman & Swartwout, 4 Cranch, 75.

[4] Ex parte Burford, 3 Cranch, 448

[5] 1 Stat. at Large, 81.

amine the legality of the commitment; it brings the body of the prisoner up, together with the cause of his commitment. The court can undoubtedly inquire into the sufficiency of that cause."[1] The supreme court discharged the prisoners Bollman and Swartwout, who had been committed by order of the circuit court on the charge of treason, but not confined under the judgment of a court, because the charge of treason did not appear to have been committed.[2]

Mr. Justice Grier, in Ex parte Jenkins, well lays down the rule: "A warrant of arrest issued by a justice of the peace has none of the characteristics of a judgment of a court of record, and is therefore not conclusive evidence that the prisoner is rightly deprived of his liberty. It is every day's practice to inquire into its regularity, and whether it has been issued on sufficient grounds to justify the arrest and imprisonment. If this could not be done, the writ of habeas corpus would little deserve the eulogies which it has received as a protection to the liberty of the citizen. Warrants of arrest issued on the application of private informers may show on their face a *prima facie* charge sufficient to give jurisdiction to the justice; but it may be founded on mistake, ignorance, malice, or perjury. To put a case very similar to the present, A. tells B. that he has seen C. kill D. B. runs off to a justice, swears to the murder boldly, without any knowledge of the fact, and takes out a warrant for C., who is arrested and imprisoned in consequence thereof. C. prays a habeas corpus, and shows that he was the sheriff of the county, and hanged D. in pursuance of a legal warrant. If a court could not discharge a prisoner in such a case, because the warrant was regular on its face, the writ of habeas corpus is of little use."[3]

According to the reporter's note in Bennett's Case,[4] Chief Justice Cranch and J. Morsell were disposed to lay down the rule of proceedings upon habeas corpus as follows—but Justice Thruston wishing for further time for consideration, they did not give the opinion in public—viz.: "Upon the return of the habeas corpus, if the commitment be in all respects regular and formal, and for an offense for which the committing magistrate had authority to commit, the court will, upon the request of the prisoner, issue a *certiorari* to certify the informations, examinations, and depositions taken by and remaining with the commit-

---

[1] Ex parte Tobias Watkins, 3 Pet. 201.
[2] Ex parte Bollman and Swartwout, 4 Cranch, 75.
[3] Ex parte Jenkins, 2 Wall. jun. 528.
[4] 2 Cranch C. Ct. 612.

§ 231. WHAT MAY BE INQUIRED INTO. 281

ting magistrate, in relation to such commitment; and if none such shall have been taken, will summon him to appear and state upon oath the evidence upon which he granted the warrant of commitment; and upon ascertaining such evidence, will consider the same, and thereupon proceed to bail, discharge, or remand the prisoner, as the magistrate ought to have done, unless the prisoner shall require that the witnesses shall be re-examined by the court; in which case they will order the witnesses to be summoned, and remand the prisoner until such witnesses can be had.

"If the commitment be so bad upon its face that the court must discharge the prisoner from that commitment, the court will, if they have sufficient evidence before them, commit the prisoner *de novo*, and order the witnesses to recognize for their appearance at the proper time and place to testify on behalf of the United States. If the witnesses upon whose testimony the prisoner was committed by the magistrate can not be had immediately, and the prisoner will not consent that their testimony shall be stated by the magistrate, and that the court shall proceed to act upon such statement as if the witnesses were present and had testified before the court, or if the committing magistrate be dead, the court will remand the prisoner for further examination until the testimony of the witnesses can be had."

While the court did not wish to consider themselves bound by the case as a precedent, out of which the above principles were evolved, we believe they set down a good rule, and one which has been generally followed since its birth in 1825.

§ 231. **Inquiry into and behind Commitment Made by a United States Commissioner.**—Where a prisoner has been committed by a United States commissioner to await the action of a grand jury of a circuit court of the United States, that court, in connection with a habeas corpus to inquire into the cause of his commitment, has power to issue a *certiorari* to the commissioner to bring up the proceedings which took place before him. Mr. Justice Shipman, in rendering a decision in such a case, said, in In re Martin, 5 Blatch. 303: "The next question is, What proceedings of the committing magistrate is the *certiorari* to operate upon and remove into this court? In determining this question, it is proper to notice, in the outset, the functions exercised by the commissioner in committing a prisoner to await the action of the grand jury. In this respect he exercises the powers common to all ordinary committing magistrates. If he finds probable cause to hold the party for trial, he commits him; if not, he discharges him. In neither case is his action final, nor a bar to further proceedings. If the prisoner is discharged, he may be again arrested, and, on sufficient evidence, may be committed. If he is committed, he may apply to the court to reduce his bail, or the prosecuting officer may apply to have it increased or to discharge him altogether. In none of these proceedings of the commissioner are his orders in the nature of a final judgment of a court of record; and it is a common practice for courts in England and in this country, to which a party has been committed for trial, to revise just such orders as the commissioner has made in the present case. This court has repeatedly increased and diminished bail fixed by commissioners, and its authority has never been questioned. Now, in order that this court may exercise intelligently its undoubted authority over such matters, it must be able to go behind the mere formal order of commitment. In order to fix the amount of bail, it must be possessed of sufficient evidence as to what are the peculiarities of the offense committed—whether it is a merely technical breach of law, or one attended by circumstances of peculiar aggravation or atrocity. This court had occasion not long since, on the application of a former district attorney, to inquire extensively into evidence for the purpose of fixing the bail of a swindler whose depredations on the treasury had been enormous. Indeed, the thirty-third section of the judiciary act expressly requires the court in fixing bail, in certain cases, to regard 'the nature and circumstances of the offense, and of the evidence, and the usages of law.'

"Now, in order to pass upon the evidence, the court must have the same before it. If it is not brought voluntarily into court, the court must have some power to compel its production. The witnesses are not always within its immediate reach, having given their testimony before the commissioner and gone to distant homes. In some cases they are abroad or on the high seas, and the prisoner stands committed on depositions sent home by consuls residing in foreign ports. It is a common practice for courts, in most places where the common law exists, to bring before them the evidence produced before the committing magistrate, and upon which his commitment is founded; and where the evidence is reduced to writing in the form of depositions, whether by the committing magistrate or by other competent authority, this is frequently done by a *certiorari* in aid of a habeas corpus. But in whatever manner the evidence is brought before the court, the court is not concluded by the finding of the committing magistrate: 2 Stra. 911, note; King v. Marks, 3 East, 157; Van Boven's Case, 9 Ad. & El., N. S., 676; Ex parte Tayloe, 5 Cow. 39; The People v. Martin, 1 Park. Cr. 187.[1] In the case of Ex parte Bollman, 4 Cranch, 114, Chief Justice Marshall remarked: 'I understand the clear opinion of the court to be (if I mistake it, my brethren will correct me), that it is unimportant whether the commitment be regular in point of form or not; for this court, having gone into an examination of the evidence upon which the commitment was grounded, will proceed to do that which the court below ought to have done.'"

§ 232. **When Order for Discharge may be Entered.**—Mr. Justice Blatchford, of the United States circuit court for the southern district of New York, has lately said, in the case of In re Esselborn: "In this case a writ of habeas corpus, returnable before this court forthwith, was issued on April 5, 1881, to the marshal of the United States for this district, to produce the body of George Esselborn, with the cause of his imprisonment. At the same time a writ of *certiorari* was issued to a United States commissioner to certify the cause of the detention of said Esselborn; the commissioner certified the proceedings before him, consisting of a complaint alleging a criminal offense and the testimony taken upon the examination on the surrender of the defendant on the complaint. The return of the marshal to the writ showed that a warrant of arrest on the complaint was

---

[1] To show that the English authorities cited by his honor are not inconsistent with the general rule which we have heretofore laid down, that the commitment made by a committing magistrate, if good and valid upon its face, could not, at common law or under the statute of 31 Car. II., be inquired into, it may be well enough to remark concerning them that we find no such inconsistency in 2 Stra. 911. In King v. Marks, 3 East, 157, the decision of the court seems to relate more particularly to the examination of the evidence before the committing magistrate with a view to bailing or recommitting the prisoner than with a view to an absolute discharge, but if not, the case may be regarded rather as an exception to the general rule; and Van Boven's Case was a commitment under the statute of 8 & 9 Vict., c. 87, sec. 50, or the smuggling act of 1845, and which enacted, in section 103, "that every conviction or warrant of commitment, 'for any offense committed against this or any act or acts relating to the customs,' shall be deemed valid and sufficient, in which the offense for which such punishment or penalty shall have been inflicted, or the cause of such forfeiture is set forth in the words of the act or acts by which such punishment or penalty has been inflicted, or under which such forfeiture has been incurred; and that no warrant of commitment for any such offense shall be held void by reason of any defect in such warrant, nor shall any party be entitled to be discharged out of custody on account of any such defect, provided it be alleged in such warrant that the said party has been convicted of such an offense; and provided it shall appear to the court or judge before whom such warrant is returned that such conviction proceeded upon good and valid grounds."

issued by the commissioner to the marshal; that the defendant appeared before the commissioner, and an examination was had, and the defendant was held to await the action of the grand jury; that the commissioner ordered that the defendant be discharged upon his own recognizance; that the defendant refused to give such recognizance, and that the commissioner then committed the defendant to the marshal in default of having given such recognizance. The case came before the court on the foregoing papers, and on April 5, 1881, the court made an order 'that the defendant may depart without giving any recognizance, subject to the issuing of a new warrant, if ordered by this court.' Nothing has since been done in the matter, and the counsel who appears for the defendant now, in September, 1881, asks the court to pass on the question as to whether the evidence before the commissioner constituted probable cause for holding the defendant to await the action of the grand jury, and to hold that it did not, and to discharge the defendant. The district attorney states that since the said order of April 5, 1881, was made, a grand jury has met and been discharged without indicting the defendant; that no information has been filed against him; that he is not in actual or constructive custody; that there is nothing to discharge him from; and that it would be a waste of time to pursue the habeas corpus proceedings any further. Under section 752 of the revised statutes,[1] the writ of habeas corpus is granted 'for the purpose of an inquiry into the cause of restraint of liberty.' There is not now in this case any such restraint of liberty or any such state of facts as requires that this court should pass on the question as to whether the defendant ought originally to have been held or committed to await the action of the grand jury, even if it would at any time have passed on that question. The defendant was held and committed only to await the action of the grand jury; and as no indictment or information has been filed against him, he is entitled to be discharged on that ground, and an order to that effect and for that cause may be entered, if desired."[2]

PART II.—EXTENT OF INQUIRY IN STATE COURTS BEFORE INDICTMENT.

§ 233. **General Inquiries.**—When it appears on the return that the prisoner is detained by virtue of any process, civil or criminal, from any court of competent jurisdiction, or issued

---

[1] See habeas corpus act of the United States, *ante*, sec. 59.
[2] 12 Rep. 454.

by any officer in the course of judicial proceedings before him, authorized by law, and the process is regular and valid upon its face, the presumption will be in favor of the legality of such imprisonment; and the burden of impeaching its legality will be thrown upon the prisoner. But this he may do in various ways. He may show that the jurisdiction of such court or officer has been exceeded; that there has been some act, omission, or event which has taken place since the issuing of such process, which entitles him to be discharged therefrom; that the process is defective in some matter of substance required by law; that though proper in form, it has been issued in a case not allowed by law; that the person having his custody is not the person allowed by law to detain him; that the process is not, in reality, authorized by any order, judgment, or decree of any court, or by any provision of law; or that he has been committed without reasonable or probable cause, etc. As a general rule, no mere defect of form in the warrant of commitment made by a committing magistrate, in committing one to prison, or to the custody of an officer, on any criminal charge, will authorize the discharge of an individual; and if it be shown that the prisoner is detained by virtue of process issued by any court or judge of the United States, in a case where such court or judge has exclusive jurisdiction, or by virtue of the final judgment or decree of any competent court of civil or criminal jurisdiction, or of any process issued upon such judgment or decree, or for any contempt specially and plainly charged in the commitment, by some court, officer, or body having authority to commit for the contempt so charged, he should be remanded, if the time during which such party may be legally detained in custody has not expired.

§ 234. **Inquiry, Extending Only to Jurisdiction, into and behind Warrant of Committing Magistrate.**—The decisions of the various courts of the Union, on the question as to whether anything more than the jurisdiction of a committing magistrate may be inquired into after a committment made by him and before indictment, have not been uniform. The decisions on this point may be divided into two classes, the last of which we shall consider in a subsequent section: 1. Those which hold that, upon a commitment regular and valid upon its face, the only open question before a court on the hearing of a return to a writ of habeas corpus is the jurisdiction of the committing magistrate; and, 2. Those which hold that not only the proceedings but the evidence taken before the committing magistrate may be examined, and the committment revised if necessary, or a commitment made *de novo* by the court hearing the matter. In some of the states each of these rules has been followed; one of the most notable instances being that of New York. Statutory enactments have, in many states, prescribed a limitation to inquiry;[1] but in dealing with the subject, want of room will compel us to speak principally of the law as found in the decisions of the courts. This diversity of practice is found, no doubt, in the fact that large discretion is allowed to judges on proceedings by habeas corpus. The practice set down in the first rule seems to have been followed in many of the states, and is probably supported by a preponderance of authorities; but we consider the second to be the soundest, most in accord with the spirit which gave birth to the writ of habeas corpus, and one from which will flow the greatest and best results of this beneficent writ. Congress, by its enactments, has sanctioned the second rule, and the learned and able federal judges and courts have sustained it in practice, and enforced its operation in a manner which ought to command the respect of all.

In order that the law as embodied in these two rules may be understood, by knowing the reasons thereof, we shall consider the arguments and doctrines advanced pro and con, and shall now begin with the first one stated.

In an early Georgia case, the prisoner was arrested and committed on a charge of felony. The affidavit and commitment were strong, positive, and unequivocal in terms. Written and parol evidence were offered to show that no felony had been committed, and that the prosecution was merely a dispute about the right of property. Judge Charlton, in rendering his opinion, said: " I will now state the reasons which induce the necessity for the adoption of the principles and doctrines advanced. The first reason is, that if the court undertakes to decide from evidence *dehors* that which is certified by the magistrate, it consequently goes into a plenary hearing of the merits of the case, and *per obliquum* decides on the innocency or guilt of the accused. It consolidates the facts with the law, against the maxim *de facto juratores, de lege judices respondent*, and against the law and the constitution, which place an ultimate condemnation and acquittal in the hands of a jury. Is there a greater hardship in refusing a full statement of the evidence on both sides before

---

[1] See construction of Missouri habeas corpus act, in Snowden et al. v. The State, 8 Mo. 483.

the court, at this incipient stage of the prosecution, than in that other stage of it, when the accusation is delivered to the grand inquest in the solemn form of an indictment, in which the whole republic complains of an injury to its peace, its government, and dignity? And yet the investigation before the grand jury is *ex parte*

"Another reason is, that if evidence on both sides is admitted at this stage of the prosecution, the court must weigh the credibility of the witnesses, which is the peculiar province of the jury. Cases may occur in which honest men may be temporarily the victims of perjury and malice; but virtue and integrity can not long suffer under the benignant reign of our laws. Is the citizen or the man illegally arrested? The indictment and the action for false imprisonment afford an ample redress. Is the citizen prosecuted without cause, with fraud and malice? He finds a reparation in the action of malicious prosecution. Is he falsely charged? The degradation and everlasting punishment of perjury atones for the outrage on his reputation and honor. * * * Though I can not receive this evidence in a motion to discharge the prisoner, yet I am not precluded by any principle of law from permitting it to regulate the bail which I conceive it proper to require." The prisoner was bailed.[1]

In Wisconsin this rule seems to be well sustained. In The State v. Bloom,[2] Mr. Justice Cole said: "We deem it necessary and proper on this occasion to call the attention of officers authorized to inquire on habeas corpus into the cause of detention or imprisonment of a party, to section 21, chapter 158, revised statutes. It will be seen that this section requires the officer, whenever the testimony shows that the person applying to be discharged has committed an offense, not to discharge him absolutely, but to hold him to bail. The general practice is to discharge the party absolutely whenever the commitment is irregular, although the evidence may be clear that he has committed a crime for which he should be tried and punished. Under such circumstances the statute requires the officer to proceed to let such party to bail, if the case be bailable, 'and good bail be offered,' and not to discharge absolutely. In this case, of course, the return showed that the imprisonment was lawful. But cases frequently arise where the evidence clearly shows that the party has committed a criminal offense, and yet

---

[1] State v. Asselin, Charlt. 184; see also Merriman v. Morgan, 7 Or. 68.
[2] 17 Wis. 521.

the officer releases him on account of some irregularity or defect in the warrant of commitment. This is all wrong, and in direct violation of the plain and wholesome provisions of the statute." The order of the county judge discharging defendant from imprisonment was reversed.

This rule was fully confirmed by the decision of the court, in 1879, in the cases of In re F. S. Eldred, and In re Oliver B. Ford.[1] Chief Justice Ryan, of the supreme court, expressed himself in this wise: "Upon the return of the sheriff to the writs of habeas corpus the prisoners, who are relators here, put in traverses of the recitals of the complaint in the warrant issued by the justice of the peace, going to the merits. To these the state demurred. And the learned counsel for the relators now insist that this court must pass upon the merits as raised by the demurrers to the traverses. The learned circuit judge before whom the writs of habeas corpus were heard is understood to have declined consideration of the merits, and to have passed upon the question of jurisdiction only. In this he was undoubtedly right. When a prisoner is held by legal process, the writ of habeas corpus does not operate, so to speak, by way of change of venue from the court or officer issuing the process of arrest, to the court or officer issuing the habeas corpus. The latter writ, in such a case, raises only the question of jurisdiction of the court or officer to issue the process of arrest. If anything can be settled by a long and uniform series of decisions in this court, this is: Re Booth, 3 Wis. 1; Re Booth and Rycraft, Id. 157; Re Blair, 4 Id. 522; Re O'Conner, 6 Id. 288; Re Falvey, 7 Id. 630; Re Boyle, 9 Id. 264; Re Tarble, 25 Id. 390; Re Perry, 30 Id. 268; Re Crandall, 34 Id. 177; Re Semler, 41 Id. 517. This rule is not disturbed, but is understood to be recognized in effect, in the late case of Re Pierce, 44 Id. 411. This rule excludes from the consideration of this court all the questions discussed at the bar, except the jurisdiction of the justice of the peace of Jefferson county, as an examining magistrate, to entertain a complaint against the owners of the dam in Rock county as a nuisance, involving the jurisdiction of the circuit court of Jefferson county, of an information or indictment against the dam in Rock county."

In Pennsylvania, at a *nisi prius* court in Philadelphia, it was said that unless it clearly appeared that a prisoner brought up on habeas corpus was entirely innocent the judge was bound to bail or remand him.[2] And, in 1875, where a warrant was issued

---
[1] 46 Wis. 530.
[2] Com. ex rel. Chew v. Carlisle, Bright. 36.

§ 234.   WHAT MAY BE INQUIRED INTO.   289

by a judge of the court of common pleas requiring the sheriff to take a person back to the county where a felony was alleged to have been committed, it was held, in an application for a habeas corpus before the same judge, that he had no power to inquire into the merits or facts of the charge alleged; and that he was to be satisfied only that the prisoner was the identical person, and that the process by which the return was sought was regular.[1]

In 1878 a very interesting question was also decided by the court of common pleas, and involving the subject under consideration. It was an action to recover of the defendant the penalty of five hundred pounds imposed by the eleventh section of the habeas corpus act of 1785, for causing a second arrest of the plaintiff upon a charge of larceny as bailee, after he had been previously discharged upon habeas corpus from commitment for the same offense. The plaintiff proved that in July, 1875, he was arrested on the oath of defendant, taken before a magistrate, and charged with larceny as bailee of a cart—when he was bound over and gave bail, no commitment being made out. He then applied to the presiding judge of the quarter sessions for a writ of habeas corpus, going through the usual form of having his bail surrender him to the sheriff, upon whom the writ was then served, and new bail immediately taken for his appearance. Return was made, and thereupon the testimony of the prosecutor (defendant in this suit) was heard, and Judge Pratt, deeming the evidence insufficient to make out a *prima facie* case, discharged the relator (the plaintiff). Defendant immediately applied for another magistrate's warrant against the plaintiff; and after hearing the prosecutor and some argument as to the identity of the offense with the one previously charged, the magistrate made out a commitment, but bail being offered, he revoked the commitment, and held the plaintiff to bail. At the trial the foregoing facts were testified to on the part of the plaintiff. The defendant offered no evidence. The case was left to the jury, with formal directions to find for the plaintiff if satisfied that the second arrest was for the same offense, and that the defendant knew it. By agreement, however, leave was reserved to the court in bank to enter a nonsuit or a judgment for defendant if they should be of opinion that the evidence did not bring the plaintiff's case within the statute.

Justice Mitchell: "There is a fundamental objection to the plaintiff's recovery, which is decisive of the whole case. Our

[1] Commonwealth v. Taylor et al., 11 Phila. 386.

habeas corpus act of 1785 is modeled upon the famous act of 31 Car. II. The history of the law demonstrates clearly that that act did not originate the writ of habeas corpus, but enlarged its scope and efficiency for the special purpose of speedy relief against arbitrary and illegal commitments to prison. There was an older writ of *habeas corpus ad subjiciendum* at common law, which is still in use for the purpose of rehearing the testimony taken before magistrates or courts of inferior jurisdiction, with a view to the reduction of bail or the discharge of the petitioner should the evidence fail to disclose a *prima facie* case against him.

"The act of 1785 is a highly penal statute, which makes no allowance for mistakes or mitigating circumstances, but imposes a specified and heavy penalty for any violation of the act, technical or substantial, as a matter of public policy, and without reference to the actual damages suffered. Such a statute, of course, is to be strictly construed. Its object, as already stated, was to provide a speedy and efficient remedy against commitments not under due authority of law. It does not contemplate an examination by the court or judge issuing it of the merits of the case, or of anything beyond the legal regularity of the commitment upon its face. Especially is this the case where the charge, as in the present instance, was a felony, and therefore within the express exception made by the statute.

"The facts in the present case show that the writ was applied for and issued by Judge Pratt for the purpose of a rehearing of the evidence, and to view the judgment of the committing magistrate upon its sufficiency to establish a *prima facie* case. This is the office, not of a writ of habeas corpus under the statute, but of the common-law writ *ad subjiciendum*: Williamson v. Lewis, 39 Pa. St. 27–30. We are therefore of opinion, upon the uncontradicted facts of this case, that the writ under which plaintiff was discharged from the first commitment by Judge Pratt was not a writ under the act of 1785, and that therefore the defendant in causing a second arrest after such discharge, did not incur the penalties of that act, and the plaintiff should have been nonsuited, or the jury decided to find a verdict for the defendant, and under the leave reserved at the trial by agreement of parties, we now enter judgment for the defendant."[1]

This rule is also well settled by judicial decisions in Vermont, and the court will not upon habeas corpus re-examine the pro-

---

[1] Schofield v. Root, 12 Phila. 333.

§ 234. WHAT MAY BE INQUIRED INTO. 291

ceedings of the magistrate.[1] And in Missouri the supreme court refused to inquire into the constitutionality of a law for the violation of which the prisoner was arrested and detained on legal process by a court having jurisdiction of the person and the offense, and was in custody of the proper officer and by virtue of a provision of the law. The court held that the prisoner, to be entitled to discharge, must come under one of the specifications of the statute which entitled him to discharge, and which is almost in the same words as the similar statutes of California and New York; and remarked: "The law to prevent the introduction of Texas cattle into the state during certain periods of the year was intended as a police and sanitary regulation, and whether the legislature exceeded its powers in the passage of that law, we will not inquire in this proceeding. The petitioner can have his trial, and if he is dissatisfied with the verdict and judgment, and desires to test the validity of the law, the courts are open to him, as they are to all other persons charged with the violation of the laws of the land."

"Admit this proceeding, and then every person charged with committing an offense of every kind and description whatsoever, instead of standing his trial and litigating the matter as the law directs, can come here and ask our advice as to the validity of the law under which he is arraigned. Such a precedent can not be established, and the legislature clearly saw the impolicy of the proceeding when it placed a prohibition upon it."[2]

In Maine, it is sufficient if the *mittimus* shows the offense to be one of which the justice of the peace had jurisdiction.[3] And in Iowa, the commitment for a contempt, made by a justice of the peace, will not be examined into any sooner than contempts of the processes of courts of general jurisdiction. Under their code, a justice of the peace has power, upon the application of a person desirous of obtaining the affidavit of another, to require the appearance of the latter before him by a subpœna issued for that purpose; and a refusal to obey a subpœna of the justice thus issued, or to answer when brought before him, is a contempt of his rightful authority, for which the person refusing may be committed by the justice. It will not excuse the witness, nor will it furnish ground for release from such commitment on habeas corpus, that the desired affi-

---

[1] Hathaway v. Holmes, 1 Vt. 417; Ex parte Kellogg, 6 Id. 509; In re Powers, 25 Id. 261; In re Tracy, Id. 96; In re Hosley, 22 Id. 363; In re Hackett, 53 Id. 354.

[2] In the Matter of Harris, 47 Mo. 164.

[3] Phinney, Petitioner, 32 Maine, 440.

davit would not be legally admissible in the proceeding pending in another forum, and in which it is desired to be used. The witness or person subpœnaed can not make himself judge of this matter; neither will a court or judge determine it in advance for him.[1]

This rule appears to prevail in Nebraska. Parker & Sawyer were merchants residing in and doing business in Saline county; and the traveling salesman of merchants in Douglas county sold them a bill of goods upon a verbal order of purchase. Parker & Sawyer signed no written contract. Evidence was introduced showing a delivery of the goods to a railroad for conveyance to Parker & Sawyer, but there was none to show that they accepted or received the same, or paid any portion of the purchase money. They were arrested upon a warrant issued by a police court in Douglas county, under a complaint of obtaining goods under "false pretenses." A writ of habeas corpus was sued out, and the contract was pronounced void under the statute of frauds; as a delivery of the goods to the railroad was not a delivery to Parker & Sawyer. And the evidence showing that the police court of Douglas county had no jurisdiction of the alleged offense.[2] In the case of Balcom,[3] the supreme court, only last year, said: "A writ of habeas corpus is not a proceeding to correct errors, and where it appears that the court whose action is sought to be reviewed has jurisdiction, that an offense has been committed, and there is testimony tending to show that the accused committed the offense, this court, in this proceeding, will not weigh evidence to see whether it is sufficient to hold the accused or not. Should it do so, the administration of justice would be obstructed, and the court would be usurping the duties of the grand jury."

In New Jersey, also, does the first rule find enforcement. There the chief justice of the supreme court, Joseph C. Hornblower, at chambers refused to discharge a defendant out of custody on a writ of habeas corpus, when the writ upon which he was detained was in itself a legal and proper one, and issued out of a court of competent jurisdiction, and where the only matter in dispute was the regularity of the process and the validity of the arrest.[4]

In California, defective commitments may be set aside on motion under statutory provisions, but under proceedings by

---

[1] Robb v. McDonald, 29 Iowa, 330.
[2] Ex parte Parker & Sawyer, 11 Neb. 309.
[3] 11 N. W. Rep. 312.
[4] Peltier v. Pennington et al., 2 Green, 312.

§ 234. WHAT MAY BE INQUIRED INTO. 293

habeas corpus, if the commitment be regular, legal, and valid upon its face, the courts will inquire only into the jurisdiction of the committing magistrate. But in determining this question, the supreme court in such proceedings have inquired whether an indictment charged any offense known to the law, where it appeared that the prisoner was by virtue of a commitment in due form detained to answer an indictment pending in the court of sessions of San Francisco county; as it involved the question of the jurisdiction of the committing officer, because the court derived its jurisdiction from the law, and its jurisdiction extended to such matters as the law declared to be criminal, and to no others, and when it undertook to imprison for an offense to which no criminality attached, it acted beyond its jurisdiction—a question which it was never doubted was a proper subject of inquiry in habeas corpus proceedings.[1] The judge or court may also inquire, in habeas corpus proceedings, whether the committing magistrate had jurisdiction, notwithstanding the necessary jurisdictional facts are recited in the commitment.[2] And in Ex parte McCullough,[3] Justice Sanderson, at chambers, declared that the functions of the writ of habeas corpus, where a party was in custody under process, extended no further than an inquiry into the jurisdiction of the court by which it was issued, and the validity of process upon its face.

The New York authority frequently cited to sustain this rule is found in the notes of 3 Hill, 659, note 30, where it was broadly laid down that, under the New York habeas corpus act of 1818, and under section 50 of the habeas corpus law in force in 1851,[4] if the object was to impeach the warrant as irregular, or as founded on an irregular or erroneous judgment, decree, or conviction, you can no more inquire of such things collaterally by habeas corpus than by action or indictment, and that the statute was not intended as an authority to inquire into the validity of writs, warrants, or other process, further than to ascertain whether they will protect the party suing them out, or the officer serving or executing them. But Mr. Justice Edmonds, of New York, said: "So far as this relates to 'judgments, decrees, and convictions,' it is unquestionably correct, for they can not be inquired into collaterally; but so far as it relates to writs, warrants, or other process before final judgment, it is far from

---

[1] In the Matter of John R. Corryell, 22 Cal. 178.
[2] The People v. Cassels, 5 Hill (N. Y.), 165.
[3] 35 Cal. 101.
[4] 2 R. S. (of 1836), 471.

being correct, and it is unsupported by any authority, except a dissenting opinion of one of the judges In the Matter of Prime," etc. This learned judge then closely scrutinized the authorities, and showed clearly that the ones cited to support this much of the note in 3 Hill, do not support the principle contended for.[1]

In the Matter of Prime, mentioned by Judge Edmonds, one of the dissenting judges, McCoun, agreed with his brethren, that upon a habeas corpus, where the officer returned the warrant upon which he held the party, if the warrant was good upon its face, that was all that could be inquired into; provided it was issued from a court of general jurisdiction; but he considered that where the writ was issued by a court of special and limited jurisdiction, conferred by statute, they could, under a habeas corpus, inquire whether the officer had the case properly within his jurisdiction, so as to exercise rightfully the power vested in him by statute. The dissenting judge referred to by Justice Edmonds was probably Presiding Justice Hurlbut, who said: "I doubt whether anything is properly before the court, upon this proceeding, except the warrant itself. If that is regular upon its face, and if the sheriff would be protected in an action of trespass, it is sufficient; and we can not discharge the prisoners. * * * Our simple object is to determine what are the functions of a writ of habeas corpus. I find here that certain facts were adduced before the officer, from which he inferred an unjust refusal (to pay certain judgments). If he erred, it was a judicial error, and can not be reviewed on a writ of habeas corpus. Whether he erred or not, is not for us now to say. We can not entertain a writ of habeas corpus to review errors of judgment, where there is colorable proof to authorize the process. That can only be done by *certiorari*."[2]

On a writ of habeas corpus in the same state, in 1870, to inquire into the detention of a person committed to the house of refuge, the supreme court refused to go behind the statement as to age contained in the warrant of commitment, and receive evidence that the individual was older than that specified in the statutory limit, and said the question must be raised by *certiorari*. They said they would not go behind the commitment to try that question, any more than the question of guilt on the charge of petit larceny.[3] In another instance was it adjudged

---

[1] The People v. Tompkins, 1 Park. Cr. 224.
[2] Id.
[3] People ex rel. McCabe v. The Superintendent of the House of Refuge, 8 Abb. Pr., N. S., 112.

§ 235. WHAT MAY BE INQUIRED INTO. 295

that it was not the province of a writ of habeas corpus to review errors or irregularities in an adjudication of an inferior tribunal, nor the sufficiency of evidence before it. It was only to ascertain whether there was jurisdiction to pronounce the sentence of commitment, and whether the commitment was in due form.[1]

§ 235. **Examination of Depositions, Evidence, and the Entire Proceedings before the Committing Magistrate.**— As before intimated, we rather lend our approval to this rule, which seems to have prevailed quite extensively, and to have stood side by side, in some of the states, with the more rigid one akin to that of the common law. In this rule, as well as in the other one, the question of jurisdiction is always open. In fact, one of the first and necessary elements of a valid commitment is the existence of jurisdiction to pass the sentence of commitment. If this jurisdiction does not exist, the prisoner should be discharged. We believe that inquiry should always be open as to the merits of a commitment made by a court or magistrate of special or limited jurisdiction, and before indictment or information filed. The jurisdiction of courts of special or limited jurisdiction should always affirmatively appear, which, however, is not the case with courts of general jurisdiction.[2]

In a commitment made by an inferior court of special and limited jurisdiction, or a justice thereof, it should state some act constituting a crime. Unless such an act is charged, there is a failure of jurisdiction.[3] So should it appear on the face of the process that there was no jurisdiction of the person, the process is void; or if the arrest was made without the territorial jurisdiction of the court; or if the prisoner was carried before a remote justice when there was one nearer before whom he ought to have been carried.[4] In fact, it seems necessary for the court to look beyond the warrants and into the affidavits to see whether the committing magistrate had colorable jurisdiction. In all cases in habeas corpus proceedings previous to indictment, the court will look into the depositions before the magistrate or before the coroner's inquest; and though the commitment be full, and in due form, yet if the testimony proves no crime, the court will discharge or bail. This practice prevails, of course, where no statute exists allowing a commitment to be set aside on motion for any specific cause. But where the statute is delinquent, the

---

[1] People v. John McCormack, 4 Park, Cr. 9.
[2] Ex parte Kearney, 55 Cal. 212.
[3] Ex parte Kearney, 55 Cal. 212.
[4] People v. Tompkins, 1 Park. Cr. 235.

prisoner may look for relief to the writ of habeas corpus. Courts and judges should have, and do have to a great extent where this rule prevails, authority to revise the cause of commitment, and to examine into the truth of the facts alleged in the return, and the officer may examine into the merits of the commitment, and hear the allegations and proofs arising thereon in a summary way, and dispose of the party as justice may require.

This is neither an impartial rule nor one which imposes onerous duties upon habeas corpus courts. The rule works well both ways. If the warrant alone is to be examined on its face, one innocent of any crime whatever might be compelled to stand his trial if the warrant was regular and valid; and on the other hand, one guilty of even the basest felony would be entitled to discharge if the warrant happened to be void or invalid even on its face. The doctrine of looking behind the commitment of the magistrate protects alike the interests of the accused and of the commonwealth. Where one has been committed for a felony, the court of original jurisdiction will look into the depositions, or otherwise inquire whether an offense has been committed, and bail or remand according to the exigencies of the case. In such a case it is never a matter of course to let the prisoner to bail, much less to discharge him; but he may, if brought up before indictment, insist that the depositions taken before the committing magistrate be looked into, as a part of the documentary authority on which the commitment was founded. For this purpose copies may be brought up by *certiorari*. But even here, if the court ascertain that there is no pretense for imputing any indictable offense to the prisoner, the court will discharge him. Notwithstanding the opinion entertained by some judges that it is beyond the domain of their duties to sit as an appellate court to review the sentences of committing magistrates, it is undoubtedly the intention of the law, as found in the statutory provisions, to give an individual committed for a crime by an examining magistrate an appeal from his commitment to the higher judges by virtue of the writ of habeas corpus; and where this second rule prevails, it seems to be in harmony with every principle of law and justice. It is true that the jurisdiction of the higher court over the process of the primary court is only collaterally appellate; this being the very reason why the writ of habeas corpus, in itself, can not have the effect of a writ of error or *certiorari*. For the verification of most of these propositions, laid down as law by Mr.

§ 235.   WHAT MAY BE INQUIRED INTO.   297

Justice Edmonds of New York, consult the following authorities.[1]

In New York, upon habeas corpus to inquire into the detention of a defendant arrested on civil process, the judge was held empowered to examine into the legality of the warrant in question, and the arrest or detention under it; and could discharge the prisoner if the case was one in which the process issued would not be allowed by law.[2] So in another instance, it was held that additional proof might be offered and received to the return on the hearing of a habeas corpus, and before indictment, of the facts stated in the affidavit alleging the crime upon which the defendant was committed before the magistrate.[3] And again, upon application by habeas corpus and *certiorari* for the discharge of a defendant from arrest, it was held that the court must determine the case upon the testimony taken before the committing magistrate, and that if, upon such testimony, there was a want of probable cause, it became the duty of the court to discharge the defendant.[4] Recorder Riker, at the city hall of the city of New York, also decided in an early case that the commitment of the committing magistrate was not conclusive, and on the return to a habeas corpus that one was held as a slave, inquired into the fact as to whether the person was a slave or not.[5]

In Pennsylvania the court of quarter sessions followed this rule in 1875, three years prior to rendering a decision[6] according to the first rule mentioned, and examined, in a hearing on an application for a writ of habeas corpus, not only the proceedings, but the evidence; and held that the commonwealth was not required to show the offense beyond a reasonable doubt, it being enough if the evidence was sufficient to warrant the court in saying that a verdict thereon would not be without evidence to sustain it.[7]

The supreme court of Iowa have held in a very recent case that the waiver of a preliminary examination before the committing magistrate will not deprive the defendant of the right, in a proceeding by habeas corpus, to introduce testimony for the purpose of showing that he is not detained upon sufficient evidence to sustain the charge made against him. The court also

---

[1] People v. Martin, 1 Park. Cr. 187; People v. Tompkins, Id. 225.
[2] Squires' Case, 12 Abb. Pr. 38.
[3] People v. Richardson, 18 How. Pr. 92; S. C., 4 Park. Cr. 656.
[4] People v. Stanley & Stewart, 18 How. Pr. 179.
[5] In the Matter of Stephen, 1 Wheel. Cr. Cas. 323.
[6] See sec. 234; Schofield v. Root, 12 Phila. 333.
[7] Gerdemann v. Commonwealth, 11 Phila. 374.

determined that a warrant of commitment issued to the sheriff of the county in which the examination is held will authorize the detention and custody of the prisoner by the sheriff of the next most convenient county having a jail.[1]

§ 236. **Effect of Statutes on These Two Rules.**—The fifty-eighth section of the habeas corpus act of New York[2] provides, "that if the prisoner appear to have been legally committed for the offense, or if he appear, by the testimony offered with the return or on the hearing, to be guilty, the court shall remand him," etc. This has been held to contemplate an examination of the evidence returned by the magistrate, or of evidence offered on the hearing, and allow such evidence then to be received. And where the court on the hearing sees fit to discharge the prisoner, if the district attorney has the necessary evidence, he can apply for a new commitment on such proof, and the court will commit the prisoner anew thereon. Where the district attorney offers to supply defects in the evidence, and produces sufficient testimony to fully establish the guilt of a prisoner, the court will not countenance a discreditable administration of justice by discharging him from custody.[3]

In 1877, it was held, under section 672 of the code of Kansas, Gen. Stat. 1868, p. 763,[4] that the judge or court issuing a writ of habeas corpus, on a petition alleging that the individual in whose behalf the writ is sued out is imprisoned without probable cause, might subpœna the prosecuting witness, investigate the criminal charge, and either discharge, let to bail, or recommit the prisoner, as law and justice required, although there was no defect in the charge or process. The case of The People v. Tompkins,[5] cited above, was approved by Chief Justice Horton of the supreme court, who said: "This section gives a party committed for a crime by an examining magistrate an appeal from his commitment by virtue of the writ of habeas corpus.[6]

So in Florida, a man threatened to do bodily harm to

---

[1] Cowell v. Patterson, 49 Iowa, 514.
[2] See 2 Fay's Dig., Habeas Corpus and Certiorari, sec. 43, 23.
[3] People v. Richardson, 18 How. Pr. 93; S. C., 4 Park. Cr. 656.
[4] The words running thus: "No person shall be discharged from an order of commitment issued by any judicial or peace officer for want of bail, or in cases not bailable on account of any defect in the charge or process, or for alleged want of probable cause; but in all such cases the court or judge shall summon the prosecuting witnesses, investigate the criminal charge, and discharge, let to bail, or recommit the prisoner, as may be just and legal, and recognize witnesses when proper."
[5] 1 Park. Cr. 224.
[6] In re Snyder, 17 Kan. 542. See Ex parte Mahone, 30 Ala. 49; Ex parte Champion, 52 Id. 311.

plaintiff and to do damage or injury to personal property, but not that mentioned in the statute, as threatening to burn a dwelling-house; on a complaint setting forth his threats he was sentenced to imprisonment by a committing magistrate, for want of sureties against doing damage to the property, and to keep the peace toward the complainant. On writ of error this was held erroneous. With the exception mentioned in the statute, sureties of the peace against doing damage to property were not authorized, either at common law or by statute, and imprisonment for want of giving such sureties was not allowed by law. And the commitment having been made for want of bail for an act not criminal, and also for one criminal, was adjudged irregular; and it was said by the supreme court that the security should have been fixed according to the degree of the criminal act charged, and that the primary court on habeas corpus, if required by the accused, should have heard and examined into the evidence for the purpose of determining what criminal act had been committed, and what probable cause was shown against the accused, whether the warrant of commitment was regular or irregular; because in that state the circuit judges are invested with the authority of committing magistrates, and the statutes relating to habeas corpus give ample power to examine into the cause of the imprisonment, and to discharge, admit to bail, or remand to custody, "as the law and the evidence shall require."[1]

Generally, no doubt, where statutes similar to the above are in force, and where no provision is made by statute to set aside commitments or informations for specified causes on motion, the second rule we have mentioned above is given full scope; and where the above-mentioned similar statutes do not exist, and none to authorize the setting aside of commitments or informations on motion, we believe, as before stated, that the better practice and the better reasoning sustain the doctrine of allowing a full inquiry into the proceedings and evidence before the committing magistrate.

§ 237. **Guilt or Innocence of the Prisoner.**—Following up the doctrines laid down in the preceding sections of this chapter, and under the statutory limitations there mentioned, we propose to show in this section that the better rule is that before indictment the whole question of the prisoner's guilt or innocence may be examined by the habeas corpus court. It is frequently said that this subject is not open to inquiry, and Mc-

[1] Ex parte Harfourd, 16 Fla. 283.

Leod's Case, 1 Hill, 394, is cited as an eminent authority, but Mr. Justice Edmonds, of the supreme court of New York, shows that the language of Mr. Justice Cowen in that case is entitled to no such binding force, as that point was not before the court, and the *dictum* was *obiter*. Said he: "The question raised there was, whether, after indictment, the court on habeas corpus would entertain the question of guilt or innocence, and on that question the authorities had been very uniform that it would not; and for very plain and simple reasons, that as the testimony before the grand jury would not be written and could not be looked into, the court or officer on the habeas corpus could not ascertain on what evidence the grand jury had acted, and could not entertain the question without receiving precisely the same testimony which the jury would be obliged to receive on the trial, and thus, in fact, usurp the province of the jury. Hence, it had been the practice of the English courts and our own, which was followed in the McLeod case, not to look into this question of guilt or innocence on habeas corpus, after indictment. But not so where the party was committed by the magistrate, nor even where he was committed on the coroner's inquest, because there were depositions which could be looked into." His honor, after citing several instances which were exceptions even to the rule that the commitment may be inquired into after indictment, said he did not understand this rule, whether it had few or many exceptions, to deny the power after indictment to look beyond the commitment. "It merely says that the court will not, not that it can not do so, and for very good reasons, as I have already mentioned. For equally good reasons it may and does do so, as is shown by the many cases where, after delay to bring on the trial of an indictment, the party has been discharged or bailed."[1]

---

[1] People v. Martin, 1 Park. Cr. 191. The reflections of Justice Edmonds on the subject of habeas corpus are worthy of great consideration, for he gave the law of the subject serious and careful attention. In this case will be found language showing this, for the first lines of his opinion read: "It is claimed in this case, in behalf of the prosecution, that the commitment of the magistrate is conclusive, and that I have no right on this return to look beyond the question of its regularity, or that if I do look beyond it, I can look only at the depositions taken before the magistrate. I had understood the law otherwise, and have always supposed that by means of this writ the officers who were authorized to allow it were by its very nature clothed with a certain revisory power over those by whose mandate any person might be restrained of his liberty. The earnest manner, however, in which the contrary doctrine was pressed upon my attention, the construction which has been put upon the decision of this court in the McLeod case, and the fact that the legislature has, once at least (by depriving the judges of the superior tribunals of the power of re-

§ 237. WHAT MAY BE INQUIRED INTO. 301

In Alabama is this doctrine the practice under their code. In the words of Justice Stone,¹ "we think a prisoner who is in custody simply on a warrant of commitment, issued after preliminary examination and before any indictment has been found, can, when brought on habeas corpus before a proper officer, claim as a matter of right that such officer shall hear and pass on all legal evidence which he offers touching the question of his guilt. If, on such examination, 'it appear that no offense has been committed, or that there is no probable cause for charging the defendant therewith,' the prisoner must be discharged. 'If it appear that an offense has been committed and there is probable cause to believe the defendant is guilty thereof,' the defendant must be bailed or committed, as the law directs.² In determining, as stated above, that prisoners can claim as a matter of right to have their witnesses heard, we think we are giving effect to the following provisions of the code (1852).³ We do not, in thus laying down the rule, intend to declare that there are not other cases in which witnesses should be heard. They are always heard, if offered, on applications for bail; and there are doubtless other cases of controverted fact where such practice would be proper."

This case was cited and approved by the supreme court of Alabama in 1875. The prisoner, by petition to a probate judge, showed that he was restrained of his liberty in the jail of Pike county by the keeper thereof, upon a commitment of a justice of the peace, charging him with having committed rape, and sued out a writ of habeas corpus to be brought before said judge to vising the action of the committing magistrate in fixing the amount of bail), departed from the great principles of the habeas corpus law, have caused me to hesitate in yielding to my first impressions, which I confess were rather the fruits of the reading of my early boyhood than of riper years, and have induced me, at some labor, to review the law on this subject at large. I by no means regret this, though it has been somewhat difficult to find among the pressing nature of my other avocations, time enough to devote to a task involving so extended an examination as I have given the subject, for an accurate and intimate knowledge of the properties of this great instrument of personal liberty, the writ of habeas corpus, can not but be valuable to every citizen." Mr. Edmonds also thought that the statutory enactment giving to the imprisoned party the power to deny any material fact set forth in the return, or to allege any fact to show the detention illegal, or that the party is entitled to his discharge, and whereupon the officer may hear such allegations and proofs as may be produced in support of the detention or against the same, and dispose of the party as the justice of the case may require, is broad enough to confer upon the officer the most ample power on habeas corpus to inquire into the guilt or innocence of the party as to the offense charged, for in that, if his detention be not illegal, he may be entitled to his discharge.

¹ Ex parte Mahone, 50 Ala. 49.
² Code (1852), secs. 3405, 3406.
³ Secs. 3740, par. 3; 3744, par. 4; 3722, 3723, 3732, 3733, 3734, 3746.

have the matter determined. The petition was demurred to, principally on the ground that it did not appear from the petition that the prisoner was illegally restrained of his liberty, but rather the contrary. The judge sustained the demurrer, dismissed the petition and writ of habeas corpus, "and refused to hear any witnesses touching the guilt or innocence of the prisoner, or to inquire in any way into the cause of said imprisonment or restraint; to all of which the prisoner excepted." On *mandamus* to compel said judge to hear and determine evidence in regard to the matter, the supreme court said that section 4262 of the revised code did not require that the petition should set forth that the prisoner is illegally restrained of his liberty, in addition to the averments made in it, which were exactly the ones prescribed by the code. The petition was verified. "Of course," says Mr. Justice Manning, "though this must be shown by the evidence, before the magistrate that issued the writ of habeas corpus would be justified in discharging the prisoner unconditionally. But is the petition demurrable because it does not assert the innocence of the prisoner or declare that he is illegally held in custody? * * * By section 4261 of the code the petition in such a case must be sworn to. And the humanity of our law is such that not only is a person held to be innocent until by some judicial proceeding he has been ascertained to be guilty, but the constitution further provides 'that he shall not be compelled to give evidence against himself, or be deprived of life, liberty, or property but by due process of law.' To require of a prisoner, therefore, in the petition in which he sets forth that he is restrained of his liberty—and by whom, and where, and on what pretense he is so restrained—to say in addition that he is illegally restrained, and make oath thereto, might be an infringement of his constitutional right to stand unquestioned and presumably innocent in the presence of his accusers. The petition, therefore, was not subject to the demurrer interposed by the solicitor; and the judge of probate erred in sustaining it and in thereupon dismissing it and the writ of habeas corpus." After showing that the evidence should have been received and passed upon, he continued: "Of course on such an examination, the judge making it should be careful to see that the proper legal steps be taken to get all the evidence on the question of the prisoner's guilt. And if the latter had been committed, after a prior investigation by an officer authorized by law to make it, the prisoner ought not to be discharged, without all the witnesses that

§ 238. WHAT MAY BE INQUIRED INTO. 303

had been previously examined against him, if still living and attainable, being produced and examined. In the absence of any material witness who previously testified in the examination against him, the question for consideration should relate only to the amount of bail, if the case be bailable; and if it be not, the prisoner should be remanded by the judge into custody, to be kept safely until discharged by due course of law. Great strictness in the forms of proceedings are not required in cases of habeas corpus." A rule *nisi* why the writ of mandate should not issue was granted.[1]

§ 238. **Commitment by Court of General Jurisdiction.**—Where a defendant has been arrested and imprisoned in a civil case, by virtue of a warrant issued by the judge of a court of general jurisdiction, another court or judge will not disturb the commitment if the judge making it had colorable jurisdiction. In such a New York case it was said in the decision of Mr. Justice Mason, on proceedings by habeas corpus before the supreme court, that "the court, or a majority of the judges, are decidedly of the opinion that in this case we can not review the regularity of the proceedings had before his honor, Judge Edmonds (one of the justices of the first judicial district and of the supreme court, who had issued two of the warrants, the other three being issued by a justice of a superior court); and that upon the writ of habeas corpus we can not look beyond the colorable authority of the judge to issue the warrants. We can not inquire into the technicalities or the strict regularity of the proceedings. This writ is not intended to review the regularity of the proceedings in any case, but rather to restore to his liberty the citizen who is imprisoned without color of law. In these cases we can merely look into the sheriff's return, which contains the several warrants by virtue of which he detains the relators; and also into the affidavits contained in the traverse, and upon which the judge issued the warrants, so far as to see

---

[1] Ex parte Champion, 52 Ala. 311. The statutes of New York, California, and Texas are similar to those of Alabama with respect to the allegation of an illegal restraint of liberty in the petition. None of them require that this allegation, which seems to be purely a conclusion of law, should be set up in the petition. The statutes of California and Texas will permit the allegation to be made, but do not make it mandatory. Perhaps some of the other states have statutes like these; and it seems consistent with what we have heretofore said in treating of the application for the writ that it should not contain conclusions of law, but only a statement of facts. The books swarm with authority on this point as one of pleading. There is little doubt that were a demurrer to be interposed to the petition, in states having like statutes to that of Alabama, and in a similar case, it would be overruled, as it was there: See 1 Paschal's Dig., art. 2597; 2 Fay's Dig., Habeas Corpus and Certiorari, p. 121, sec. 5; Penal Code of California, sec. 1474.

that the judge had colorable jurisdiction. Or in other words, if we find that the judge had jurisdiction of the process, and assumed to take proof upon the issuing of the same, and which proof he adjudged to be sufficient, we will not, upon the writ of habeas corpus, review his adjudication upon that question; nor undertake to say whether he erred in adjudging the proof to be sufficient. In looking into the warrants under which the present relators are imprisoned, we find them regular upon their face, and *prima facie* sufficient to justify the imprisonment; and when we come to look beyond the warrants, and examine the affidavits upon which they were issued, we are satisfied that at least there was colorable proof, in these cases, before the judge, upon which he might exercise his judgment in awarding the process. And this is as far as we intend to go in these cases."[1]

But in ordinary criminal proceedings commitments are seldom made, comparatively speaking, by courts of general jurisdiction. By statute, however, in some of the states the judges of the courts of general jurisdiction are made magistrates and are vested with authority to hold accused persons to answer. Commitments made by these magistrates are undoubtedly entitled to more consideration than a commitment made by an ordinary justice of the peace. These magistrates being vested with authority to hold accused persons to answer does not divest them of the power of passing upon the sufficiency of their own commitments as courts of superior jurisdiction. The one judge exercises the functions of two separate and distinct officers. The commitment is made by the judge as a magistrate and approved by himself as the judge of a superior court; consequently these commitments should not be reviewed by other superior courts of co-ordinate jurisdiction, or even by the supreme court, except for want of jurisdiction. And even proceedings for a review by the supreme court, to investigate that question, ought not to be entertained because the commitment was made by a court of general jurisdiction, and the jurisdiction of those courts will always be presumed. In some of the states the supreme court, the superior or district courts, and other courts of general jurisdiction, are all on the same base, so far as their authority, power, or jurisdiction is concerned, relative to proceedings on habeas corpus. They have the same powers, the same authority, the same jurisdiction. The statute has invested them all with the same panoply of power, and neither sustains to the other the relation of a superior or an inferior court, in the same sense

---

[1] In the Matter of Prime et al., 1 Barb. 340.

that a district, superior, or supreme court is superior to a court of the justice of the peace or other court of special and limited jurisdiction. The word "superior" or "inferior" can with no propriety be applied to the jurisdiction exercised by either. It is in each the same, one and identical. Therefore, to ask one of these tribunals to review the commitment made by another would be in reality a sort of collateral appeal from a jurisdiction to itself. And where the officer returns such a commitment, or the warrant upon which he holds the party, if the warrant is good upon its face, the inquiry should extend no further, because the commitment has been made by a court of general jurisdiction, and one court of general jurisdiction should not review the proceedings of another on the writ of habeas corpus. The principles of comity should prevail.

In a late California case, the petitioner for a writ of habeas corpus had been convicted for killing one Madden. On appeal a second trial was ordered, and after both the prosecution and defense had introduced their evidence, the district attorney moved the court that the jury be discharged from the further consideration of the case, on the ground that it appeared from the evidence that an offense of a higher nature than that charged in the indictment had been committed. The indictment, as it then stood, was for manslaughter. The court granted the motion, and made an order that the defendant be committed to answer any indictment which might be found against him for murder. On habeas corpus, the chief justice of the supreme court said: "The order was made by the district court, the judge of which court is a magistrate vested with authority to hold accused persons to answer (Penal Code, secs. 808–874), and was entered after hearing the evidence touching the alleged killing of Madden by the prisoner. Whether the order was irregularly entered, was erroneous, or what defense or advantage it may possibly afford the prisoner, should he be again put upon his trial for the killing of Madden, are questions which it is not the office of a writ of habeas corpus to present for our consideration." His honor referred to and approved of the observations in Ex parte McCullough, 35 Cal. 100.[1]

---

[1] Ex parte Granice, 51 Cal. 375. In the Pennsylvania case of Com. v. Taylor et al., 11 Phila. 386, a warrant was issued by a judge of the court of common pleas requiring a sheriff to take an individual back to the county where a felony was alleged to have been committed by him. On habeas corpus before the same judge, he held that he had no power to inquire into the merits or facts of the charge alleged, and was to be satisfied if the prisoner was the identical person, and the process by which the return was sought was regular.

§ 239. **Cause for Detention after Failure to Indict.—** Where a statute provided that, "when a person has been held to answer for a public offense, if an indictment be not found against him at the next term of the court at which he is held to answer, the court shall order the prosecution to be dismissed, unless good cause to the contrary be shown," Mr. Justice Wallace, of the supreme court of California, in discharging a prisoner under it, presented the law in the following manner: "The case in which a dismissal of the prosecution is not to follow upon the non-presentment of an indictment against the accused is exceptional; the accused has a right to depart, 'unless good cause to the contrary be shown.' This general provision of the statute, that the prisoner is not to be held indefinitely, is designed to secure to him a speedy trial; and this right is absolute, except some good cause be shown which may be supposed to take the case out of the operation of the general rule. What is 'good cause,' may be difficult to define with precision, since it must in a great measure be determined by reference to the particular circumstances appearing in each case. There should, undoubtedly, be some fact or circumstance disclosed to the court upon which its authority in this respect, somewhat discretional, could be brought into exercise. Its discretion is not to be arbitrary, but should proceed upon such knowledge or information as would enable it to determine for itself whether or not public justice requires the further detention of the prisoner, notwithstanding the delay upon the part of the prosecution. It must be admitted, too, I think, that ordinarily this discretion, when exercised by the court to which the law has intrusted it, is not subject to review, and that when exercised, the sufficiency or insufficiency of the grounds upon which it proceeded could not be examined here through the instrumentality of a writ of habeas corpus. The presumption that the discretion had been correctly exercised would ordinarily arise, if the record should state in terms that good cause appeared; so, too, if the record should recite a particular fact, or several facts, as being the facts upon which the court had proceeded in ordering the detention of the prisoner, the import of such fact or facts as being sufficient or insufficient to amount to 'good cause' would not be accurately weighed in this proceeding; it would rather be presumed that there were other existing facts not affirmatively disclosed upon the record which would support the action of the court in making the order.

"But in the case before me there can be no doubt that the cir-

§ 239   WHAT MAY BE INQUIRED INTO.   307

cumstance upon which the court acted in detaining the prisoner was in itself wholly and absolutely insufficient to support the order. The grand jury just discharged had recommended that the prisoner be detained; therefore he was detained. The record, too, states that the detention was 'without further or other cause than said recommendation being shown by the district attorney;' so that there is no room there for the indulgence of a presumption of the existence of some other and sufficient ground upon which the order might be supported.

"The grand jury seem in this instance to have assumed the exercise of the discretion which belonged alone to the court, and the court seems to have made the order in mere deference to the expressed opinion of the grand jury, and without any investigation or information concerning the circumstances of the case before it. The statement that the order was made for no other cause than the mere presentation of this recommendation is equivalent to the recital upon the record that no good cause—no cause at all—was shown, and where that condition appears, there is no power to detain the prisoner."[1]

This case was cited, followed, and approved in Nevada in 1876, on an application for a writ of habeas corpus before Chief Justice Hawley, at chambers. The petitioner had been committed to answer a charge of murder. The grand jury found no bill against him. The judge of the district court ordered that he, with others, be held to appear before the next grand jury of Nye county, Nevada, "upon sufficient cause having been shown the court why the case of the state of Nevada against said parties should be resubmitted to another grand jury." The prisoner, on the next day, applied to the judge of the district court to be admitted to bail, which application was denied. He then sued out a writ of habeas corpus, alleging that the above facts showed his restraint and confinement to be illegal, and asked to be discharged on his own recognizance or admitted to bail. The statute in that state was identical with the one above mentioned in California. His honor presumed that "sufficient cause" was shown, and in the absence of any showing to the contrary, was also bound to presume that the district court did not act arbitrarily in the premises; and having been charged with murder and committed for that offense, petitioner was not entitled to

---

[1] Ex parte Bull, 42 Cal. 197. Chief Justice Rhodes and Mr. Justice Crockett concurred in these views. The party had been held by a justice of the peace to appear before a grand jury to answer upon a charge of murder.

bail where the "proof was evident or the presumption great." "Ordinarily," said he, "the fact that a grand jury has investigated the charge and refused to find a bill ought to be sufficient to satisfy a court that the proof is not evident nor the presumption great; but notwithstanding such action upon the part of the grand jury, the court, in a case like this, would have the right, and it would be its duty upon the application of petitioner, to hear the testimony and decide for itself whether the proof of the defendant's guilt was evident or the presumption great. This is a question upon which courts and judges are invested with a legal discretion, which is at all times to be exercised with sound judgment upon a full consideration of all the facts and circumstances of each particular case, and when it appears that the presiding judge has acted, no other judge would be warranted in discharging the petitioner or admitting him to bail, unless it clearly appeared that the presiding judge had acted arbitrarily in the premises, and thereby abused his discretion." The writ was denied.[1]

§ 240. **Convictions by Inferior Courts.**—The rule permitting a liberal inquiry into commitments made by courts of special or limited jurisdiction is much stricter after final convictions by those courts, where, by statute, they have power to try and convict for certain offenses. After trial and conviction, these courts, of course, make a commitment, but it is of higher dignity than an ordinary commitment holding to answer. It has some of the elements of a final commitment to prison by a court of general jurisdiction. And the judgment or sentence of an inferior court, after trial and conviction, is entitled to more consideration than its sentence of commitment simply holding to answer. Its judgment is placed, to a great extent, beyond the reach of collateral attack by the writ of habeas corpus, as judgments of higher courts are. Where an inferior court has jurisdiction to try and pronounce sentence, its judgment, generally, should be regularly and directly attacked, when the object is to avoid its effect. Another reason why the convictions of inferior courts are entitled to more consideration than their mere commitment holding to answer is, that the power to try and convict is conferred upon them by statute, and which it is presumed they will follow in the exercise of a wise discretion; while, in ordinary examinations, although the power to hold them is also conferred by statute, the magistrate is only to be satisfied that there is reasonable or probable cause

[1] Ex parte Isbell, 11 Nev. 295.

to believe that a crime has been committed, and that the prisoner is the one who did it; and having no further power over the defendant than to put him upon his defense to an information or indictment which is tried in a higher court.

To illustrate by some New York cases—which may more properly belong to the chapter on impeaching judgments by habeas corpus; yet, as that chapter will be very full, they may be spared here to elucidate the subject under consideration: John B. Bennac was convicted by a justice of the peace of being a disorderly person, and was committed to jail in default of giving bail for his good behavior. On habeas corpus the circuit judge refused to discharge him from custody. On *certiorari* to the circuit judge from the supreme court, to review his decision, the supreme court, by Justice Willard, said, among other things: "The counsel for Bennac did not traverse the return of Crossett, the constable, to the habeas corpus, or allege any fact *aliunde* the return to show either that the imprisonment was illegal or that he was entitled to his discharge. Conceding that the prisoner was restrained of his liberty by a public officer, by virtue of process issued by a magistrate of competent jurisdiction, his counsel contended that he was entitled to his discharge, for the reason that the warrant, on its face, showed that no offense had been committed for which he was liable to be imprisoned. If this be true, no doubt the circuit judge erred in remanding him. It was for the prisoner to make out the jurisdictional defects, either by testimony *aliunde* the return or by the process itself. He took the latter course alone. If, then, there is enough on the face of the process to protect the party who issued it or the officer who served it from an action of trespass or false imprisonment—in short, if it is not absolutely void—the decision of the circuit judge should be affirmed. A warrant issued upon the conviction of a party as a disorderly person is not required to recite any fact but such conviction. It was insisted, however, that the recital in the warrant of commitment afforded evidence of the testimony before the justice upon which the conviction was founded, and that that testimony did not authorize the conviction.

"In answer to this, it may be said that the warrant was complete without reference to the facts recited. It described the offense, conviction, and sentence, and this is all that was necessary to its validity. It thus appears that the magistrate had jurisdiction both of the person and the crime. The recital of the facts proved before the justice was not required, nor can they be regarded on a habeas corpus. It does not appear that the facts recited were all the facts proved or admitted. To discharge the accused because the recited facts would not warrant a conviction would be to retry the cause on the merits in this collateral way. And it would be a retrial without any assurance that the whole facts were spread out in the warrant. This can not be done.

"If the justice convicts upon insufficient evidence, the remedy of the party injured, if any, is not by habeas corpus. If, then, we are to regard the facts recited as affording the evidence on which the magistrate acted, still they present no ground for a discharge. While the conviction remains in force and is not absolutely void, the warrant will authorize the arrest and imprisonment of the accused. And the conviction can not be attacked but by a direct proceeding, such as a writ of error, *certiorari*, motion to quash, etc., according to the nature of the case." The proceedings of the circuit judge were affirmed.[1]

Several convictions as vagrants were also examined on habeas corpus, the above principles being applied. One was before Hon. Josiah Sutherland, of the supreme court, at chambers. Catherine Forbes had been convicted as a common vagrant by a police justice, on proof that she was a common prostitute and an idle person, but without proof of any other fact or circumstance. Under the statute,[2] the judge considered that it was only a certain class of prostitutes, those without employment, who were declared to be vagrants; and said: "I have come to the conclusion that the warrant of commitment on its face is absolutely void, and that the prisoner must be discharged, on the ground that it does not appear on the face of the commitment that the prisoner has been duly convicted of being a vagrant, or indeed, that she has been convicted or committed for any offense or crime whatever," as no statute of that state had declared common prostitution or idleness to be a crime.[3] In connection with this, a perusal of Kearney's Case[4] will be instructive. It will be observed in these cases that there is a want of jurisdiction—a fatal defect—because no offense is charged which is known to the law; and a prisoner always has a right on habeas corpus, even by proof *aliunde*, to show that the court or magistrate acting as a court, who tried and sentenced him, has no jurisdiction.[5]

Another case came before Justice Ingraham, of the supreme

[1] Bennac v. The People, 4 Barb. 31.
[2] 1 R. S. 641, *633; Laws of 1833 tit. 2, c. 20.
[3] Forbes' Case, 11 Abb. Pr. 52.
[4] Ex parte Kearney, 55 Cal. 212.
[5] In the Matter of Divine, 21 How. Pr. 80.

court, at chambers. The prisoner had been committed as a vagrant by a police justice. His honor thought the practice of reviewing such convictions on habeas corpus was not to be commended, as the statute provided another mode for correcting errors of the justice which should be resorted to; and that if the commitment was regular, and the justice had jurisdiction of the matter, no relief should be afforded in such proceedings. It was enough if the offense of being a vagrant was charged, and that the prisoner was convicted on competent proof. It was sufficient if the commitment followed the record. It did not require that the justice should insert in the record the particular grounds on which the charge of vagrancy was based, and it could not be necessary to recite them in the commitment. He concurred with the views of Mr. Justice Sutherland, in the case of Catherine Forbes,[1] so far as they were expressed as to what was necessary to be proved in order to make out the offense; "and," said he, "unless on a review of the case it should appear that all the facts necessary to constitute the offense are proved, the conviction should be reversed; but as I do not consider that all such facts should necessarily be recited in the commitment, I feel bound to remand the prisoner, on the ground that the commitment is regular on its face, and the decision of the justice can not be reviewed in this proceeding." The prisoner was remanded.[2]

So was it determined in the New York court of common pleas, at chambers, that proceedings prior to a commitment for vagrancy could not be reviewed on habeas corpus, if the commitment was regular, and the record of conviction was properly made and filed. In this case before Justice Ingraham, he said: "If the allegations contained in the petition are true, injustice may have been done to the prisoner. It is there alleged that she was prohibited from producing witnesses on her own behalf, and from cross-examining witnesses produced against her, and that she is innocent of the charge made against her. But the guilt or innocence of the prisoner can not be inquired into upon habeas corpus after conviction. If there is any remedy—and that there should be one no one can doubt—it is by the supreme court on *certiorari*. I have no power in this proceeding to review the correctness of the decision of the magistrate."[3] The prisoner was remanded and the writ discharged.

[1] See *supra*.
[2] Gray's Case, 11 Abb. Pr. 56; S. C., 4 Park. Cr. 616; see also People v. Moore et al., 3 Park. Cr. 465.
[3] Stewart's Case, 1 Abb. Pr. 210.

§ 241. **Vacating Orders of Court.**—Where a court making an order in a cause has jurisdiction of the whole subject-matter and of the parties which it concerns, it is not competent for another court, under proceedings by habeas corpus, where the process upon which the petitioner is held is valid upon its face, to inquire into and determine whether or not the order of the court upon which the process is founded is erroneous. The power of the court of inquiry extends no further than to declare whether the order is void for the want of jurisdiction, or the process invalid upon its face. This may be shown thus: A lawful judgment had been recovered against petitioner, and an execution issued against his property. He held a paid-up life insurance policy, which he refused to deliver to the sheriff in satisfaction of the execution, on the ground that it was exempt under a statute[1] concerning life insurance policies. On proceedings supplementary to execution, taken and pursued in a regular manner, the court in which the judgment had been rendered made a final order requiring the petitioner to deliver the policy in satisfaction of the execution; and on his refusal to obey the order, committed him to the county jail until it should be obeyed. Chief Justice Sanderson of the supreme court of California, at chambers, said: "In my judgment, his order is not void, nor his process invalid." The prisoner was remanded. "Habeas corpus," said he, "is undoubtedly the proper remedy for every unlawful imprisonment, both in civil and criminal cases; but an imprisonment is not unlawful in the sense of this rule merely because the process or order under which the party is held has been irregularly issued or is erroneous. Process which has been irregularly issued may be set aside by the court or officer by whom it was issued, and erroneous judgments and orders may be reversed on appeal or writ of error. The writ of habeas corpus has not been given for the purpose of reviewing judgments or orders made by a court or judge or officer acting within their jurisdiction. To put it to such a use would be to convert it into a writ of error, and confer upon every officer who has authority to issue the writ appellate jurisdiction over the orders and judgments of the highest judicial tribunals in the land. County judges, though occupying an inferior position, and exercising an inferior jurisdiction, would be, by such a rule, empowered to review and practically reverse the judgments and orders of the district courts, and of the supreme court itself, and also of the federal courts exercising jurisdiction within the

[1] Stat. 1867–8, p. 500.

§ 242.   WHAT MAY BE INQUIRED INTO.   313

state. Establish the doctrine that the judgments and orders of courts may be reviewed on habeas corpus, upon the ground of error, and appeals for the corrections of errors may be dispensed with in all cases in which the arrest or imprisonment of persons is allowed. Every criminal action, every civil action in which an arrest is given, and every proceeding for a contempt could be brought to the supreme court by writ of habeas corpus. Not only that, but, as already suggested, inferior tribunals would be called upon to review the judgments of superior tribunals, and tribunals of equal grade to interfere and review each other's proceedings. Such a rule would render all judicial proceedings amorphous, and lead to the utmost confusion and disorder. It is well settled that habeas corpus can be put to no such use, and that its functions, where the party who has appealed to its aid is in custody under process, do not extend beyond an inquiry into the jurisdiction of the court by which it was issued, and the validity of the process upon its face." [1]

In deciding upon a question of false imprisonment, raised under a writ of habeas corpus, the judge may investigate the validity of any order of court relied upon. Thus where apprentices apply for a writ of habeas corpus, and the respondent sets out an order of court binding the petitioners to him, the order of the court should be produced and shown as authority, but the petitioners have the right to reply that the order is void. This they may do either by showing that they were not such persons as the court had the power to bind out at all, or that they had no notice of the proceedings against them, and therefore no opportunity of being heard. This resolves itself into a question of jurisdiction, and if judgment be rendered by a court having no jurisdiction, or against a person who has no notice to defend his rights, it is no judgment at all. "In all proceedings," said Justice Reade of the supreme court of North Carolina, "it is necessary that the person whose rights are to be affected should, in some way, be a party to the proceedings. It is not sufficient that the court should have jurisdiction of the subject-matter; it must also have jurisdiction of the person. It is a clear dictate of justice that no man shall be deprived of his rights of person or property without the privilege of being heard. And it is well settled, that judgment without service of process is void."[2]

§ 242. **Habeas Corpus Pending Examination on Criminal Charge.**—Where there is good reason to believe that a

[1] Ex parte McCullough, 35 Cal. 97.
[2] In the Matter of Ambrose, Phill. 91.

felony has been committed by a person who is detained on reasonable grounds of suspicion therefor to await examination before a committing magistrate upon the charge of having been concerned therein, a higher court will not interfere, pending the examination, to release him upon habeas corpus. The preliminary examination of a person charged with a crime, especially a non-bailable offense, must be made promptly, and should not be delayed to suit the mere convenience or personal accommodation of the officers of the law. The prisoner's rights are to be considered and respected; and he is not presumed to be guilty because he is under arrest. The presumption is the other way.[1]

§ 243. **Waiving Examination.**—In the state of Nevada it has been decided that in all cases where a party has been arrested, charged with a crime, and brought before a committing magistrate, an examination should take place; and that the practice of allowing persons so charged to waive an examination is irregular, and should be discontinued. The supreme court of that state has also decided that the issuance of a commitment by a justice of the peace, when examination is waived, without the introduction of any testimony, is erroneous, but furnishes no ground for petitioner's discharge upon habeas corpus.[2]

Part III.—Inquiries after Indictment and before Judgment of Conviction.

§ 244. **Reasons why the Courts Decline to Make Inquiry into a Commitment after Indictment Found.**— There is a vast difference between inquiring into a commitment before indictment found and one instituted afterwards. The former we have considered. Let us take a view of the latter. The testimony taken before the grand jury is not written, and they are not to disclose the evidence on which they act. The grand jury find an indictment, and when a court or judge attempts to go beyond the indictment, to the facts on which it was found, how are they to be ascertained? The court can not entertain the question without receiving precisely the same testimony which the jury would be obliged to receive on the trial. It would thus usurp the province of the jury. In what mode

---

[1] Matter of Peoples, 47 Mich. 626. But while one is presumed to be innocent before a commitment for a crime, and even during his trial for any offense however grave, he will not be presumed innocent after an indictment or information filed against him on proceedings by habeas corpus: See People v. Rulloff, 5 Park. Cr. 81.

[2] Ex parte Ah Bau & Ah You, 10 Nev. 264.

are the courts to be informed of the secrets of the jury-room, so as to determine whether the case presented there is or is not a criminal offense?

Again, establish the principle that inquiry may extend beyond the indictment, and where will the range of inquiry cease? The commitment may be regular and the detention legal, but the prisoner be innocent. Inquiry after indictment, however, would bring up the question of guilt or innocence to be determined, and that under summary proceedings by habeas corpus. Here the province of the jury is ignored, and every criminal, no matter how complicated the circumstances of his case might be, could, by a plea of not guilty, thus demand a summary trial by the court without jury. There is little difference between inquiring whether a party is innocent and trying his plea of not guilty. The question of guilt or innocence, therefore, should not be tried by the court or judge after indictment and upon habeas corpus; even should not the prisoner be discharged by proving his innocence, however clear the proof may be; but he ought to abide his trial by jury.[1]

[1] People v. Martin, 1 Park. Cr. 187; and People v. McLeod, 1 Hill (N. Y.), 377. This is a leading and valuable authority, and Mr. Justice Cowen of the supreme court of the state of New York gave the case great attention, and no doubt elaborated his opinion with unnecessary matter. The case was, however, one of great importance and attracted the attention of both the British government and that of the United States, because McLeod was an English subject, and had shot and killed on board the steamboat Caroline, which he was assisting to destroy, a subject of the queen of England, one Amos Durfee. He was indicted by a grand jury of Niagara county, in the state of New York, for the crime of murder, and the crime was alleged to have been committed at a certain time within the county of Niagara. After pleading not guilty, McLeod was in due form committed for trial. The British government formally demanded the release of McLeod by the United States government, on the ground "that the transaction on account of which McLeod has been arrested, and is to be put upon his trial, was a transaction of a public character, planned and executed by persons duly empowered by her majesty's colonial authorities to take any steps and to do any acts which might be necessary for the defense of her majesty's territories, and for the protection of her majesty's subjects; and that consequently those subjects of her majesty who engaged in that transaction were performing an act of public duty, for which they can not be made personally and individually answerable to the laws and tribunals of any foreign country." The act of which McLeod was accused of having committed was done under the direction and by the authority of an officer of the British government, and it was afterwards assumed, approved, and ratified by that government. Daniel Webster, the American secretary of state, was of opinion that after such avowal, approval, and ratification the "individuals concerned ought not, by the principles of public law and the general usage of civilized states, to be holden personally responsible in the ordinary tribunals of law for their participation in it." For further information concerning this case, the reader is referred to Congressional Globe and Appendix, 1st Sess. 27th Cong., vol. 10, 1841, p. 10, Appendix, where will be found a vast amount of learning concerning the case of McLeod. In conclusion, Justice Cowen doubtless did right in remanding the prisoner for trial, and

§ 245. **Inquiry may Go to whether Indictment Charges Any Offense.**—While inquiry can not extend beyond an indictment into fields of unknown facts, the indictment itself may be examined upon habeas corpus, although it appears that the defendant has been detained to answer it under a commitment in due form. The court, or judge of the court wherein such indictment is pending, may proceed to inquire whether it charges any offense known to the law, for this goes to the jurisdiction, which is always a proper subject of inquiry in a proceeding of this character. If such were not the case, the simple warrant of a court, however arbitrary it might be, would constitute a complete answer to the writ. An indictment must contain the statement of an offense known to the law, and, under the rules well settled by judicial decision that this may be inquired into, if the court or judge determines that it does not, the prisoner must be discharged as a matter of right, particularly in those states where a statute provides that he shall be discharged "when the process, though proper in form, has been issued in a case not allowed by law."[1]

§ 246. **Defective Indictment.**—Where the court renders such a judgment on the record as the law demands, and, on taking the whole record together, in investigating a proceeding on habeas corpus, and where a defective indictment is the point in controversy, is satisfied that enough appears, although the indictment is clearly defective, and so much so that a demurrer to it would be sustained, to retain the accused in custody until another term of court, it will not discharge the prisoner. A defect in an indictment for an assault with intent to commit murder, consisting in leaving out the name of the person assaulted, and without any averment that the person's name was "to the grand jury unknown," is not a sufficient ground upon which to discharge an accused party on habeas corpus in vaca-

in refusing the discharge of him upon habeas corpus. However, any further conflict between state and national authorities on this question was settled by an act of congress passed in 1842, by which the writ of habeas corpus was extended to prisoners being subjects or citizens of foreign states in custody under national or state authority for acts done or omitted by or under color of foreign authority, and alleged to be valid under the law of nations: See 5 Stat. at Large, 539. The act also provides for the discharge of such prisoners from custody if "it shall appear that the prisoner or prisoners is or are entitled to be discharged from such confinement, commitment, custody, or arrest, for or by reason of such alleged right, title, authority, privileges, protection, or exemption, so set up and claimed, and the laws of nations applicable thereto, and that the same exists in fact," etc.: Id. McLeod's Case is also found in 37 Am. Dec. 328–306, and 25 Wend. 483.

[1] In the Matter of Corryell, 22 Cal. 178.

tion;[1] and it is doubtful whether it would be sufficient in term time. The next court where the indictment is found, after the hearing, can either discharge the party or permit the defective indictment to be *nol prossed*, and order another one to be preferred, or the first indictment may be amended by consent of the accused. The indictment should, however, at first contain the name of the person assaulted.

§ 247. "**Guilty or Not Guilty.**"—It is a fundamental error to suppose or assume that an officer granting the writ of habeas corpus has a right to try the question whether a prisoner indicted is "guilty or not guilty" of the crime of which he is charged. The law of habeas corpus, both common and statutory, never contemplated that such a trial was to be had. As we have said above, the only way in which this question can be tried is by the intervention of a jury before a proper court, and in a capital case a man can not be tried, even by his own consent, except by a jury of twelve men.[2] The commitment made by an examining magistrate of inferior jurisdiction, such as a justice of the peace or police judge, may not only be reviewed, but the court may hear new proof, and bail or remand the prisoner, as justice may require. While this is true, the court will not discharge one duly committed on a regular indictment, upon proceedings by habeas corpus, as we have said before, although the prisoner may be able to clearly prove his innocence.[3] The rule in this respect seems to be as stringent as where one has been convicted and sentenced to a penitentiary upon perjured testimony. In a hearing before Justice Knox, of the New York supreme court,[4] it was asked: "Suppose a person is indicted for the murder of A. B., and committed, and subsequently A. B. is produced alive, may not that person, on habeas corpus, on producing A. B. alive before the officer, be acquitted and discharged of the offense as on a trial?" His honor answered, "No." "A trial in court," said he, "and an acquittal by a jury, or the entering of a *nolle prosequi* by the district attorney, by order of the court in which the indictment is pending, are the only methods by which the prisoner can be fully discharged."

"It is not necessary to say whether in the case supposed the officer might not properly be let to bail. If, in a given case, it appeared by the indictment that no offense was charged, that is to

---

[1] Ex parte Whitaker, 43 Ala. 323.
[2] Cancemi v. The People, 18 N. Y. 129.
[3] People v. Richardson, 18 How. Pr. 93; S. C., 4 Park. Cr. 656.
[4] People v. Rulloff, 5 Park. Cr. 77.

say, if the act charged as having been committed by the prisoner constituted no offense, as if, for instance, the prisoner was held on an indictment which charged 'that he had absented himself from the state, and he was guilty of a misdemeanor,' there would be nothing to try, and the prisoner might be discharged. But when there is an offense charged, a jury must come. If the officer issuing the writ can try the question which the prisoner asks him to try, and decide it in his favor and acquit, why may not the officer decide it against him and punish? If he can say he is not guilty, why may he not say he is guilty? This inevitably follows from the right to try, and then how would the officer execute his judgment? It would be a novel proceeding were an officer authorized to try and acquit, but not to convict. Such an officer would soon, I apprehend, monopolize all the criminal business of the country, especially when the persons tried were really guilty."

Suppose, then, that a prisoner, who is held to answer several indictments from which he thinks he ought to be discharged, asks: "How, then, am I ever to be discharged, if the district attorney will not move my trial; and the courts will not discharge me as the statute provides, or on a writ of habeas corpus?" Justice Knox, above mentioned, said to such a question in a New York case:[1] "To this it may be said that it is not to be supposed that courts, judges, or other officers will not do their duty, but the contrary. The statute provides that, previously to every court, the district attorney shall issue his precept, commanding the sheriff to bring all his prisoners before the court, with all papers and process relating to each, which precept the sheriff must obey: 2 R. S., 4th ed., 309, sec. 23; and then, unless satisfactory cause be shown for detaining him, he may be discharged. I hold, therefore, that the prisoner must be remanded, and be discharged after trial and acquittal, or by the entering of a *nolle prosequi* by the district attorney, or by order of the court under the sections of the statute already quoted."

§ 248. **Continuing Indictment.**—When an order of court is made continuing an indictment to a future term of court, it is the prisoner's right to be present, and he ought to be present. But an order of court continuing an indictment without the prisoner's presence is a mere irregularity, and it is a well-established rule, found all through the books, that irregularity and error can not be reached by habeas corpus, where the jurisdic-

[1] People v. Rulloff, 5 Park. Cr. 77.

§ 250. WHAT MAY BE INQUIRED INTO. 319

tion is unquestioned. Wherever a court has complete jurisdiction over the subject-matter of the indictment, and the sole and exclusive right and authority to try the same, any rulings or orders of the court stand as the lawful rulings of a court of competent jurisdiction, and should be respected as such by all other courts in collateral proceedings—as on habeas corpus. However erroneous or irregular they may be, they can not be overruled on habeas corpus, which in such cases takes cognizance only of such radical defects of a jurisdictional character as to render the proceedings not merely voidable, but void. Continuing an indictment does not divest the court of its jurisdiction.[1]

§ 249. **Two Bills of Indictment—Death Penalty on One—No Trial on the Other.**—Two bills of indictment were found in South Carolina against a prisoner for passing counterfeit bank bills. He demanded his trial on both, but was tried only on one, convicted, and sentenced to be hanged. He was not prosecuted on the second indictment, under the expectation that he would suffer death in consequence of his conviction on the first. He was pardoned, after his conviction, by the governor, and set at liberty. Afterwards he was arrested on the second indictment, and sought relief by habeas corpus. Three of the judges, a majority of the constitutional court of Columbia, were of opinion that the prisoner was entitled to his discharge. "The conviction on one indictment did not prevent the state from proceeding on the other. The prisoner demanded his trial in both cases, and he ought to have been tried at the second court, after demanding his trial on both indictments, or discharged as to the indictment not proceeded on. The solicitor and the court should not have calculated on his suffering death on the conviction in the case tried. A new trial might have been granted and the prisoner admitted to bail, or judgment might have been arrested, or (as it happened) there might be a prospect of his being pardoned." The other two judges, however, thought "it was unnecesary after conviction on one indictment to proceed on the other. The prisoner was pardoned at his own instance; the same as if he had escaped," etc. Motion granted effecting prisoner's discharge.[2]

§ 250. **Existence of Indictment—Its Legality—Bench Warrant.**—Upon proceedings by habeas corpus a court is not authorized to, nor will it, inquire into the question of fact as to

---

[1] People v. Ruloff, 5 Park. Cr. 84.
[2] State v. Stalnaker, 2 Brev. 44.

whether or not an indictment, regular upon its face, was ever found by the grand jury. This is an informality or irregularity merely which may be corrected by other processes known to the law.[1] Neither will the illegality of a grand jury that found the indictment be considered upon such proceedings.[2] Where the prisoner surrenders himself into the custody of a sheriff on a charge of murder, and is admitted to bail by a county judge, and is thereafter indicted for murder by the grand jury of the proper county, and is arrested and held in custody by the sheriff, under a bench warrant therefor, issued by the county court, he can not procure his release on habeas corpus. Where the county court has jurisdiction of the person of the defendant and of the indictment, the court is not restrained in the exercise of its jurisdiction, after an indictment has been found against the prisoner, by reason of any proceedings previously had in the matter. If the bail already given is considered to be sufficient security, the court may allow it to stand unchanged, but if not, it has power to order him to give additional bail or go into custody.

If the court consider it to be a case in which bail ought not to be taken, it may order him into custody notwithstanding any bail which may have been given before the indictment was found. In the words of Mr. Justice Sanderson: "It would be anomalous to hold that the court can, as it undoubtedly may, compel the defendant to come into court by its warrant for the purpose of giving additional bail or going into custody on a bailable offense, and yet can not compel him to come into court and go into custody on a charge which may not be bailable at all." The court does not exceed its jurisdiction in issuing the bench warrant, and the detention under it is lawful.[3] So again, where the judge of a district court sits as a committing magistrate, and has admitted a prisoner to bail to appear before the district court, and who has been ordered by that officer, sitting as a district judge, to be confined upon his refusal to furnish a new bond after a true bill of indictment found against him for manslaughter. No proceeding is required to authorize the judge to issue such an order, which is in the nature of a bench warrant.[4]

§ 251. **Judgment on Sufficiency of the Indictment.**— The habeas corpus act of Mississippi provided, that "it shall

[1] Ex parte Twohig & Fitzgerald, 13 Nev. 302.
[2] Ex parte Springer, 1 Utah, 214.
[3] Ex parte Cook, 35 Cal. 107.
[4] State ex rel. Thomas v. Bruslé, 14 Rep. 114.

not authorize the discharge out of prison of slaves, after commitment of indictment for any felony." Several slaves were committed upon an indictment charging an offense, or at least, what purported to be one, that of advising and conspiring to make insurrection. They were taken before a circuit judge on a writ of habeas corpus sued out by their owner, and remanded. The case was taken up to the high court of errors and appeals by writ of error to the decision of the circuit judge. Upon the hearing of the writ the evidence introduced was the record of the indictment referred to, and the proceedings thereupon in the circuit court, by which it appeared that the indictment contained three counts; that a demurrer was filed to the whole indictment and sustained, as to the first two counts, but overruled as to the third; in which condition the indictment was pending in the circuit court, when the writ was dismissed and the prisoners remanded. Under the statute quoted above, the state insisted that the writ was improperly granted, and should have been dismissed on that ground. On the other hand, it was said that the indictment charged no offense for which the slaves were punishable by indictment, and that, in consequence thereof, the indictment must be regarded as a nullity.

Mr. Justice Handy, of the court of errors, in delivering the opinion of the court, disposed of the case in this way: "It appears that, on demurrer, the indictment had been adjudged good and sufficient by the court in which it is pending, and that the case stood upon that judgment in that court when the writ of habeas corpus was sued out. Until that judgment was set aside or reversed it was the law of the case; and it was not competent to call it in question upon the writ of habeas corpus, and upon an adverse decision being made thereupon, to bring the question to this court by writ of error to that judgment. For that would be virtually to make the writ of habeas corpus a writ of error to the judgment of the circuit court, and call upon the judge to reverse the judgment upon the demurrer and declare the indictment, then duly pending in the circuit court, insufficient. So the court, upon writ of error to the judgment on the habeas corpus, is required virtually to reverse the judgment on the demurrer, when that judgment is not before us. All this is manifestly irregular, and not to be tolerated. The judgment of the circuit court, holding the indictment sufficient in law, must be taken as correct, until it be reversed; and that can only be done by this court, when it shall be brought before us on writ of error. The evil consequences arising from the course of proceeding, in resorting to the writ of habeas corpus in cases like this, are most obvious.

"1. The judgment of the circuit court upon the demurrer, if the writ be sustained, would be reversed without writ of error extending to it. In law it remains in force. What, then, is to be the course of proceeding of the court upon the indictment? It would be to proceed with the cause, treating the indictment as sufficient under the judgment previously pronounced. But the court would find that the prisoners had been taken from the custody of the law, and were not in the power of the court, having been discharged from prison under the writ of habeas corpus. Such a state of case would present a great anomaly.

"2. But to determine the indictment to be insufficient, and to discharge the prisoners on habeas corpus on that ground, and without hearing the evidence upon which the charge was founded, would be attended with another serious mischief.

"In such a case the only question presented would be the sufficiency of the indictment. It might be that the indictment in its form is insufficient, and on that ground that it would be liable to be quashed; and yet there might be sufficient cause upon the facts of the case to keep the prisoners in custody, to be proceeded against upon another indictment, which might be properly framed to meet the offense of which the prisoners were really guilty. And yet, in such a case, and as this case is here presented, the prisoners would be discharged, and might be placed beyond the reach of punishment, simply because the indictment was not technically sufficient to charge them with the offense intended to be charged. If such a course be justifiable upon sound principle, not only the sufficiency of all indictments for capital offenses, but the correctness of the decisions of the courts where they are pending, adjudging them to be sufficient, are subject to the determination of a judge at chambers, with power to overrule, in this informal mode of proceeding, the judgment of the proper court duly pronounced; and the same principle would give to a judge sitting on habeas corpus the power to annul the judgment of the circuit court upon final conviction, and this on the ground that the indictment was insufficient, in charging no offense. It is clear that such questions were not intended to be embraced and determined in the proceeding by habeas corpus.[1]

---

[1] The doctrine that the sufficiency of the indictment can not be inquired into in any case, we do not understand to be maintained by the court in this case. Its meaning is greatly qualified by the judge's words concerning the evidence to be adduced, showing whether the prisoner should

"We are therefore of opinion, that when there has been an indictment which has been held by the proper court to be good, and which judgment stands in full force, or when the prisoner, without such judgment, claims his discharge on habeas corpus, merely on the ground of the insufficiency of the indictment, without the adduction of the evidence on which the indictment is founded, showing that he should not be held in custody in the matter; in either of such cases, the writ of habeas corpus should not be entertained. It follows from this view, that the writ of habeas corpus was properly dismissed, and the judgment is affirmed."[1]

§ 252. **Process without Warrant of Law.**—A petitioner for a writ of habeas corpus alleged that the relator had, after conviction on the ninth of July, 1881, been sentenced to an imprisonment in the Alleghany county workhouse, in Pennsylvania, for a term of three months, and to pay a fine of five hundred dollars and the costs of prosecution; that he had served the term, and was discharged on the tenth of October; that on the same day he was arrested under alleged legal process issued by the clerk of the quarter sessions, and was committed to the common jail, where he remained. The writ was allowed and answer made, alleging that the discharge from the workhouse was illegal. On the hearing it appeared that the process under which the relator was arrested commanded his arrest to answer the same indictment upon which he had been tried and convicted.

Said Chief Justice Sharswood: "It may be that if the prisoner was illegally discharged from the county workhouse, the court of quarter sessions could have caused him to be rearrested on a bench warrant, and have returned him to the county work-

be held in custody or not. If no offense were really charged in an indictment, and the evidence was brought before the court showing such to be the fact, we apprehend that the court sitting on habeas corpus would discharge the prisoner. This is the course of the current of the later decisions on this point: See Kearney's Case, 55 Cal. 212; In the Matter of Corryel, 22 Id. 178. It goes to the point of jurisdiction so frequently mentioned heretofore. A court can punish for no act except what is made criminal by law; it has no power to punish for something unknown to the law It has jurisdiction to try and punish only for certain offenses, and those must be made criminal by law. If an indictment shows no offense, there is no criminality shown, and there is nothing of which a court can take jurisdiction; and if a court have no jurisdiction its action is void—a condition which it is the very object of habeas corpus to cure. Voidable informalities or irregularities are not reached by it, but fatal jurisdictional defects are ever within its range: See Ex parte Boland, 11 Tex. App. 159. This matter, however, will hereafter be more properly considered in the treatment of "Assailing judgments by habeas corpus."

[1] Emanuel & Giles v. The State, 36 Miss. 627.

house in pursuance of the original sentence and of the act of assembly cited. But it is very clear that the process by which he was arrested, after his discharge from the workhouse, and imprisoned in the county jail, was without warrant of law. The prisoner must therefore be discharged, without prejudice, however, to the right of the quarter sessions to issue a bench warrant, as above indicated."[1]

§ 253. **Effect of Order Arresting Judgment, etc.**—When a defendant has been indicted, tried, and found guilty of a felony, it has been held in California that the effect of an order arresting the judgment is to place the defendant, as nearly as other and controlling rules of law will permit, in the same situation in which he was before the indictment was found; and that upon its entry he must be discharged unless he is detained in custody by virtue of some other legal process or order which it is in the power of the court to make. The court may, of its own motion or upon the application of an interested party during the term, in any criminal case, modify or set aside an erroneous order; or, under section 443 of the practice act, arrest the judgment without motion, upon its own view of fatal defects in the indictment upon which such judgment may be rendered. But upon habeas corpus, any errors committed by the court in setting aside or modifying such order or judgment can not be considered, where the order upon which the party is held in custody is regular upon its face, and one which the court had power to make. Neither will once in jeopardy be reviewed or inquired into on habeas corpus. If pleaded and disregarded, it is an error to be corrected by appeal. An order erroneously granted is not necessarily void. If it were, it would be considered, for the question of jurisdiction would then be open, and the prisoner would be discharged for want of power in the court to act at all. Where the court has jurisdiction of the process and of the subject-matter, the inquiry ceases.[2]

§ 254. **New Trial—Delay in Bringing to Trial.**—The fact that a former conviction on an indictment has been reversed and a new trial ordered by a court of review, and on the prisoner's application, leaves matters to stand as if there never had been any trial on the indictment. In the eye of the law, he has not been tried at all, and it is not a violation of the constitutional provision, which declares that "no person shall be subject to be twice put in jeopardy for the same offense." And this

---

[1] Commonwealth ex rel. Herring v. Smith, 13 Rep. 124.
[2] Ex parte E. C. Hartman, 44 Cal. 32.

fact can not be made a tenable ground for the prisoner's discharge on habeas corpus.¹ Statutory provisions, under which a prisoner is declared to be entitled to his discharge if not brought to trial before "the end of the next term of the court, unless satisfactory cause be shown by the district attorney," have been decided not to be a "statute of limitations," and that a failure to comply with them is a mere irregularity, and one which forms no sufficient ground for a prisoner's discharge on habeas corpus.²

§ 255. **Discharge of Jury in Absence of Defendant.**—In a case on proceedings by the writ of habeas corpus, where the existence of the facts stated in the return is not denied, where the validity of the indictment is unquestioned, and where the fact is not disputed that the primary court regularly and lawfully acquired jurisdiction over the person of the accused, who was properly arraigned and put upon trial under the indictment, no inquiry can be had as to whether the relator was in fact present or absent when the jury was discharged from further consideration of the indictment, or whether the decision of the court in discharging them was correct or incorrect. And conceding that the court erred in discharging the jury, and that the alleged error was cognizable in a court of review, it could not be reviewed without the record in the cause was properly before the court of review in such a way as to give it a revisory power under its appellate jurisdiction. But such an error is a mere irregularity, and should not be reviewed under this writ. It does not affect the question of jurisdiction, and where a court has jurisdiction, it is within its power and authority, and is clearly its duty, to entertain, hear, and determine every question that may possibly or legitimately arise during the progress of the trial to final judgment of conviction or acquittal. The fact, therefore, if it be one that the court has improperly discharged the jury in the enforced absence of the prisoner, does not dispossess the court of its jurisdiction over the cause. If so, any further step or proceeding in the action is wholly nugatory, and the only judgment that can be rendered is one of dismissal for

---

¹ People v. Rulloff, 5 Park. Cr. 77.
² People v. Rulloff, 5 Park. Cr. 77. See also Clark v. Commonwealth, 29 Pa. St. 129, where it is said that under the third section of the habeas corpus act of Pennsylvania a prisoner can only claim his discharge on the last day of the second term after his arrest, when there has been a competent and regularly constituted court, before which he could have been indicted and tried. The act, it is said, was designed to prevent wrongful restraint of liberty growing out of the malice and procrastination of the prosecutor, but not to shield a prisoner in any case from the consequences of any delay made necessary by the law itself.

want of jurisdiction, instead of a judgment upon the merits, which alone can furnish any protection to the defendant against another prosecution for the same offense.

In 1877 Mr. Justice Cornell, of the supreme court of Michigan, in a case involving the above principles, quoted the language of the court in Tweed v. Liscomb,[1] "whether the determinations of the court upon any or all of the questions were right or wrong did not affect its jurisdiction. In other words, the court had jurisdiction to make wrong as well as right decisions in all the stages of the prosecution, and whether those made were right or wrong can not be raised on habeas corpus;" and said: "No final judgment upon the indictment herein has yet been reached, and therefore the district court has never yet been dispossessed of its jurisdiction over it, nor of the person of the accused. In the lawful exercise of this jurisdiction, it has the undoubted authority, under certain circumstances and for certain specified causes (Gen. Stat., c. 116, secs. 16, 17), to discharge the jury prior to a verdict, and to cause a retrial of the indictment before another jury. It necessarily had the right of determining upon the existence of these circumstances and causes, and whether it erred or not, its decision thereon was lawful and valid, until reversed on error. This conclusion is fully supported by the case of Wright v. The State, 5 Ind. 290, which is directly in point on the question under consideration, and we are confident no authority can be found in any way countenancing a contrary doctrine. In that case the jury, having failed to agree upon a verdict prior to the time designated for closing the term, was brought into court and discharged, against the defendant's objection. This was held an improper discharge of the jury, and that, under the laws of that state, it precluded a retrial of the indictment before another jury, yet the court refused to discharge the prisoner on habeas corpus, saying that he must apply for relief to the trial court wherein the indictment was pending.

"Fully agreeing with the doctrine of that case upon this point, it follows that no inquiry can be had in this proceeding whether the relator was in fact present or absent when the jury was discharged from the further consideration of the indictment, nor whether the decision of the trial court in discharging them was correct or incorrect, and the prisoner must be remanded.'"

[1] 60 N. Y. 559.   [2] State v. Sheriff of Hennepin Co., 24 Minn. 87.

CHAPTER XV.

HABEAS CORPUS AS A QUO WARRANTO.

§ 256. Title to Office.
§ 257. Sentences by Officers *de Facto*.
§ 258. Mere Usurpers, etc.

§ 256. **Title to Office** can not be inquired into on proceedings by habeas corpus, as we have elsewhere said. The writ may sometimes with propriety be used in the nature of a writ of error, yet it will not be converted into a *quo warranto* to determine a question of usurpation of office. The usual mode of trying such a question is by an information in the nature of a *quo warranto;* and when the incumbent of an office is exercising its functions, his title to it can not be tested in a collateral proceeding, but only in a direct proceeding to which he is a party.[1] So it has been held in Pennsylvania that the right of a president judge to exercise his functions within a county attached by the legislature to his district subsequent to his election, can not be questioned collaterally; that the court will take judicial notice of the legislation by which he claims to exercise his office, so far as to hold him a judge *de facto*, and as against all but the commonwealth, a judge *de jure;* and that the right and powers of a judge *de facto*, with color of title, can only be inquired into by *quo warranto*.[2] So a person acting as a police justice *de facto*, under color of an election in pursuance of an act of the legislature, may rightfully issue his warrant for the arrest of a person, and if the process is regular and legal, the prisoner will be remanded on habeas corpus without an inquiry by the court as to whether the magistrate was a police justice *de jure*.[3]

§ 257. **Sentences by Officers de Facto.**—Even where a sentence is passed by a *de facto* judge exercising the judicial

---

[1] Ex parte Call, jun., 2 Tex. App. 497; People v. Stephens, 5 Hill (N. Y.), 616; Russell v. Whiting, 1 Winst. 465; Ex parte Strahl, 16 Iowa, 369; In the Matter of Whiting, 2 Barb. 513; but more particularly the citations to the following sections.

[2] Clark v. Comm., 29 Pa. St. 129; Comm. v. Burrell, 7 Id. 34.

[3] In the Matter of Wakker, 3 Barb. 162.

office without any real right to do so, it can not properly be examined on habeas corpus, particularly if he acts under color of office.[1] As, for instance, where sentence was passed by a judge regularly appointed, and who continued to publicly act as such, no other person having been appointed in his stead, and the prisoner sought discharge by habeas corpus, upon the ground that the judge was disqualified under the constitution, by reason of having taken a seat in the legislature.[2] So the sentence of one by a circuit judge, who exercised his office under an appointment by the governor made without authority of law, was held valid and binding, though another person was entitled to exercise such office.[3]

§ 258. **Mere Usurpers, etc.**—But while the right of an incumbent to office, acting under color of right, will not be questioned on habeas corpus, though he is not an officer *de jure*, the act of a mere usurper, in imprisoning one, or doing anything prohibited or forbidden by law, may be inquired into. For there is a clear distinction between a bold, unwarranted assumption of right to exercise the duties of an officer and their exercise under color of right. An arrest by an officer, acting without any pretense of an election or appointment to office, or without any claim of right, would be illegal, and a court would immediately discharge the prisoner on habeas corpus.[4]

So, where one attempts to usurp or retain an office to which he has no right, he commits a wrongful act, and if he is imprisoned for it, he can not be released on habeas corpus. Thus, in New York it has been held that the statutes providing that officers refusing to pass over books, papers, etc., to their successors, or in default thereof to be committed, were obviously intended to be applicable, as against officers *de facto*, only to cases where the title of the relator to the office is clear, and that if the title is not clear, the remedy is by action in the nature of *quo warranto*. In that state Daniel S. Baker was illegally appointed supervisor, and an election afterwards had at which one Peck was elected his successor. Baker refused to pass over the books and papers to Peck, and was committed therefor. Baker then sued out a habeas corpus. But the court held that Peck's *prima facie* title was good and sufficient until overcome; that Baker had not even a colorable title; and that he was supervisor *de facto*, of itself formed no objection to the proceeding against him.[5]

---

[1] Griffin's Case, Chase, 364.
[2] Sheehan's Case, 122 Mass. 445.
[3] State v. Bloom, 17 Wis. 521.
[4] Ex parte Strahl, 16 Iowa, 369.
[5] In the Matter of Baker, 11 How. Pr. 418.

§ 258.   HABEAS CORPUS AS A QUO WARRANTO.

However, where one has been committed to prison for default in delivering up books, papers, etc., under such statutes, if the title of the applicant to the office is doubtful, or if it appears that it is contested with color of right, the officer has no jurisdiction to grant such order, and the prisoner may be discharged upon habeas corpus.[1]

[1] Devlin's Case, 5 Abb. Pr. 281.

CHAPTER XVI.

USE OF CERTIORARI.

PART I.—As Ancillary to the Habeas Corpus.
  § 259. In the English Law.
  § 260. Doctrine in the Federal Courts.
  § 261. In the State Courts.

PART II.—With Habeas Corpus as a Writ of Error.
  § 262. At Common Law.
  § 263. In the Federal Courts.
  § 264. In the State Courts.

PART I.—As Ancillary to the Habeas Corpus.

§ 259. **English Law.**—In England it may be laid down broadly that the writ of *certiorari* lies for the removal of all causes from inferior courts.[1] The court of king's bench exercises a general superintendency over all the courts of inferior criminal jurisdiction, and unless they are invested by statute with absolute judicature, it may remove the proceedings from any of them. This may be done at any stage of the proceeding, but is generally refused after issue joined.[2] This supervisory jurisdiction is exercised under the writ of *certiorari*, and not that of *habeas corpus cum causa;* because the habeas corpus only removes the plaint, whereas the *certiorari* would bring up all the proceedings from the inferior court, and then the superior court is enabled to do that which might be done in the inferior court.[3] A habeas corpus removed the body *cum causa*, and proceedings were begun anew in the superior court, and plaintiff declared *de novo*, but on *certiorari* he proceeds on the record as it stands when removed.[4] The record itself is never removed by habeas corpus as it is by *certiorari*;[5] besides, a *certiorari* goes to the judge, but a habeas corpus to the officer.[6] Again, where

---

[1] 1 Tidd's Pr., Am. notes, 397.
[2] Bac. Abr., Certiorari, A.
[3] Goodright v. Dring, 2 Dow. & Ry. 407.
[4] Woodcroft v. Kinaston, 2 Atk. 316; Hetherington v. Reynolds, Fortes. 269; Fazacharly v. Baldo, 1 Salk. 352.
[5] 2 Lilly's Reg. 8; Hetherington v. Reynolds, Fortes. 269.
[6] Hetherington v. Reynolds, Fortes. 269.

§ 259. USE OF CERTIORARI. 331

a *certiorari* issues, in order to use the record as evidence, then the tenor, if returned, is sufficient, and countervails the plea of *nul tiel record;* but when the record itself is to be proceeded upon, the record must be returned. And there is no difference when the proceeding upon the record is to be removed, whether it be before judgment or after; in both cases the record itself must be removed.[1] The effect of a habeas corpus in removal of causes is only to suspend the proceedings of the inferior court, but a *certiorari* removes the cause.[2]

The practice is to issue the writ of *certiorari* in connection with the writ of habeas corpus, the former to bring up the record, the latter to bring up the body. But while a superior court in the exercise of its revisory jurisdiction may discharge a prisoner held under criminal process, where the commitment is voidable only, or where the grounds of commitment are insufficient, it must have appellate jurisdiction in the given case. It is not sufficient that it has a more extensive jurisdiction, or is of higher dignity. It must have the power of revision in the particular case—the power to correct or reverse the action of the inferior court. Where no such power exists, a court will refuse to act.[3] The errors complained of, or the grounds of commitment, must be brought under review by means of appropriate process, and this is, as we have said, the writ of *certiorari* used in connection with the writ of habeas corpus.

The evidence given before the committing magistrate, in England, upon a criminal charge, is required to be reduced to writing and certified to the court to which the party accused may be recognized or required to appear, and in case of commitment, these depositions or examinations do not accompany the warrant of commitment. The command of the habeas corpus does not extend to them. That only requires a production of the body of the prisoner and a return of the warrant of commitment under which he is held. But courts have been willing to examine the depositions,[4] and to obtain them the writ of *certiorari* is resorted to, and which is usually issued at the same time with the habeas corpus, directed to the committing magistrate, and requiring him to bring up the examinations or depositions, not for the purpose of being acted upon separately under the

---

[1] Woodcroft v. Kinaston, 2 Atk. 316.
[2] Jameson v. Schonswar, 1 Dowl. 177; Fazacherly v. Baldo, 1 Salk. 352.
[3] Ex parte Cobbett, 53 Eng. Com. L. 185; Ex parte Partington, 51 Id. 648; S. C., 13 Mee. & W. 679; In the Matter of Dimes, 68 Eng. Com. L. 554; and numerous cases cited by court and counsel.
[4] 1 Ch. Crim. L. 128.

certiorari, but in order that the court may be furnished with the means of judging in what way they should dispose of the prisoner.[1] And upon the habeas corpus and the depositions brought up by the *certiorari* the case is heard.[2] It is always proper to have the depositions brought up by *certiorari*, yet where they have been verified by affidavit the court has sometimes allowed them to be read.[3]

§ 260. **Doctrine in the Federal Courts.**—As in England, the writ of *certiorari* has here always been considered, in appropriate cases, as ancillary to that of habeas corpus, and has long been issued by the courts of this country, as a means of rendering their jurisdiction under the latter writ effective.[4] The power of the federal courts to issue this writ is implied in the fourteenth section of the judiciary act of 1789,[5] and section 716 of the United States revised statutes. The writ of *certiorari* has been issued by the United States supreme court to a United States circuit court to have brought before the first-named court the proceedings of the last-named court under which the petitioner was restrained of his liberty; together with a writ of habeas corpus to produce the body of the petitioner.[6] These two writs may also be issued by the United States supreme court to a district court.[7] They may be issued by the circuit court to a district court[8] and by both the last-named courts to review the action of a United States commissioner or other committing magistrate, who acts under the laws of the United States.[9] The rule as to committing magistrates seems to be that the informations, depositions, examinations, etc., taken by and remaining with them in relation to commitments, are brought up on *certiorari*,[10] the evidence is examined on which the commitment was grounded, and the reviewing court will do that which the magistrate ought to have done.[11] In other words, the proper inquiry

---

[1] 1 Ch. Crim. L. 128.
[2] King v. Marks, 3 East, 157.
[3] Van Boven's Case, 9 Ad. & El., Q. B., 669.
[4] Ex parte Hamilton, 3 Dall. 17; Ex parte Burford, 3 Cranch, 448; Ex parte Jackson, 96 U. S. 727; Ex parte Bennett, 2 Cranch C. Ct. 612; In re Martin, 5 Blatchf. 303; Ex parte Siebold, 100 U. S. 371; Ableman v. Booth, 21 How. 506; Ex parte Bollman and Swartwout, 4 Cranch, 100.
[5] 1 Stat. at Large, 81, 82.
[6] Ex parte Lange, 18 Wall. 163; Ex parte Yerger, 8 Id. 85; Ex parte Wells, 18 How. 307; Ex parte Siebold, 100 U. S. 371.
[7] Ex parte Virginia, 100 U. S. 339; Ex parte Parks, 93 U. S. 18.
[8] Patterson v. United States, 2 Wheat. 221.
[9] In re Martin, 5 Blatchf. 303; Ex parte Bennett, 2 Cranch C. Ct. 612; In the Matter of Van Campen, 2 Ben. 419; In re Stupp, 12 Blatchf. 501; *contra:* Ex parte Van Orden, 3 Blatchf. 167.
[10] Ex parte Bennett, 2 Cranch C. Ct. 612.
[11] In re Martin, 5 Blatchf. 303; Ex parte Bollman and Swartwout, 4 Cranch, 75, 114; In the Matter of Van Campen, 2 Ben. 421.

is to be limited to ascertaining whether the magistrate had jurisdiction, and did not exceed his jurisdiction, and had before him legal and competent evidence of facts whereon to pass judgment as to the fact of criminality, and did not arbitrarily commit the accused without any legal evidence.[1] It will be noted in this connection that committing magistrates, as such, make no final judgments such as those of a court of record; for we shall have occasion in the next few pages to show how far *certiorari* and habeas corpus may be used as a writ of error, which, of course, lies to final judgments only.

A cause can be removed from a state court without the aid of the *certiorari* or the habeas corpus. Neither of them is required to remove the cause. They are issued by the clerk, and are intended to bring up the record and other proceedings from the state court, and to notify the state court that the cause has been removed, so that no further proceedings may be had in the state court. The cause is first removed, and then, after it has been removed, the *certiorari* or the habeas corpus issues for the above-named purposes.[2]

§ 261. **In the State Courts.**—The writs of habeas corpus and *certiorari* are often used as ancillary to each other, when necessary to give effect to the supervisory power of the higher judicatures. And this procedure has the express sanction of the statute in many of the states.[3] But where the *certiorari* is not a creature of the legislature, but is given by the constitution itself, the supervising courts may, under such a grant of power, issue writs of *certiorari*, though no act of the legislature concerning them has ever been passed.[4] The ordinary use of the *certiorari* is to review questions of law only,[5] but its scope may be extended by statute so that the facts may be reviewed under it.[6] The power of the superior tribunals to issue the writ of *certiorari* exists unless the jurisdiction is taken away by express words.[7] It is a discretionary writ, and is

[1] In re Stupp, 12 Blatchf. 501; Ex parte Lange, 18 Wall. 163; In re Herrich, 5 Blatchf. 414; In re Kaine, 14 How. 147; S. C., 3 Blatchf. 6, 16; In re Farez, 7 Id. 345; In re MacDonnell, 11 Id. 79; In re Stupp, 11 Blatchf. 124. That facts can not be reviewed see In re Vermaitre, 9 N. Y. Leg. Obs. 137; In re Kaine, 10 Id. 257; In re Heilbronn, 12 Id. 65; Ex parte Van Aernem, 3 Blatchf. 160, in which last case it was said that the merits of the magistrate's decision could not be reviewed on either the facts or the law.

[2] Abranches v. Schell, 4 Blatchf. 260.
[3] 3 N. Y. R. S., 6th ed., p. 874, art. 2; Gosline v. Place, 32 Pa. St. 520; Chapman v. Woodruff, 34 Ga. 91; McLaren v. Brown, Id. 588.
[4] Livingston v. Livingston, 24 Ga. 379.
[5] Corrie v. Corrie, 42 Mich. 509; S. C., 4 N. W. Rep. 213; Phillips v. Welch, 12 Nev. 158; People v. Humphreys, 24 Barb. 521.
[6] 3 N. Y. R. S., 6th ed., p. 874, art. 2.
[7] People v. Bradley, 60 Ill. 390.

often denied where the power to issue it is unquestionable, and where there is apparent error in the proceedings below.[1] It should not be granted where the party has another adequate remedy,[2] nor until the case is finally adjudicated below.[3]

It is provided by statute[4] in New York that if it appear from the facts set forth in the petition for a habeas corpus, that the cause, matter, or other offense for which the person is confined or detained is not bailable, the officer to whom such application is made, instead of awarding a habeas corpus, may grant a writ of *certiorari*, as if the latter writ had been directly applied for by the prisoner. The proceedings upon this writ are then the same as upon a habeas corpus, and the prisoner may be either bailed or discharged, as the court shall determine. But under this statute a superior court can not, under the ordinary *certiorari*, command an inferior tribunal before whom a proceeding is pending " to fully commit the petitioner for trial with or without bail, or to fully discharge him."[5] Proceedings in a state court by *certiorari*, to review a decision on a writ of habeas corpus in that court, do not prevent a court of the United States from proceeding on a writ of habeas corpus subsequently issued from the latter court.[6]

PART II.—WITH HABEAS CORPUS AS A WRIT OF ERROR.

§ 262. **At Common Law.**—It was said that "the court of king's bench hath a superintendency over all courts of an inferior criminal jurisdiction, and may, by the plenitude of its power, award a *certiorari* to have any indictment removed and brought before itself," to determine the validity of it, and to quash or affirm it.[7] And the use of *certiorari* in connection with the writ of habeas corpus, in examining, affirming, or reversing the proceedings and judgments given by inferior judges has been explained in this way: "As the *certiorari* alone removes not the body, so the habeas corpus alone removes not the record itself, but only the prisoner, with the cause of his commitment; and therefore, although upon the habeas corpus, and the return thereof, the court can judge of the sufficiency or insufficiency of the return and commitment, and bail and discharge, or remand the prisoner, as the case appears upon the return; yet they can not, upon the bare return of the habeas

---

[1] People v. Stilwell, 19 N. Y. 531; Rowe v. Rowe, 28 Mich. 353; People v. Mayer, 16 Barb. 362.
[2] People v. Supervisors of Queens, 1 Hill (N. Y.), 195.
[3] Lynde v. Noble, 20 Johns. 80.
[4] 3 N. Y. R. S., 6th ed., p. 874, sec. 66.
[5] People v. Donohue, 14 Hun, 133.
[6] Leary's Case, 6 Abb. N. C. 43.
[7] Bac. Abr., Certiorari, A.

corpus, give any judgment, or proceed upon the record of indictment, order, or judgment, without the record itself be removed by *certiorari*, but the same stands in the same force it did, though the return should be adjudged insufficient, and the party discharged thereupon of his imprisonment; and the court below may issue new process upon the indictment."[1]

The courts generally required the conviction itself to be brought before them before they would look at the defects of a commitment in execution.[2] Where both were defective, the defendants would be discharged.[3] But they would sometimes discharge for a defect in the commitment, as where the *certiorari* was withdrawn from the defendant in certain cases, but still remained in the crown, and where the conviction was not produced by the regular method,[4] on the part of the crown.[5] So the following rule resulted: "If the warrant of commitment be bad, and the justices or informer prefer to rely on a good conviction, it is for them to bring up such conviction by *certiorari*, and that it is not the duty of the defendant to remove a conviction of which he is not supposed to know anything, and which may not exist. If the conviction be not brought before the court, the court will not presume that there is a good one, or any, but will decide on the document actually before them."[6] All the courts, however, could not issue a *certiorari*. This was so of the court of exchequer. So, while their power to issue this writ was not co-extensive with their power to issue the writ of habeas corpus, they would, on the hearing of a habeas corpus, admit the record of conviction, although they had no power to compel its production by *certiorari*. The conviction was produced, verified by affidavit.[7] They have also discharged the prisoner for a defect properly cognizable only on *certiorari*.[8] The attorney general's fiat is a prerequisite to the writ of *certiorari*, and the court, without such fiat, will not direct a *certiorari* to issue for the purpose of bringing up the record on which to found a writ of error, and the general rule is that a writ of habeas corpus will not be granted where the party is in execution on a criminal charge,

---

[1] Bac. Abr., Habeas Corpus, B, 3.
[2] King v. Taylor et al., 7 Dow. & Ry. 622.
[3] Reg. v. Chaney, 6 Dowl. P. C. 281; Wickes v. Clutterbuck, 2 Bing. 483.
[4] King v. Rogers, 1 Dow. & Ry. 156; In re Allison, 28 Eng. L. & Eq. 281.
[5] Reg. v. Chaney, 6 Dowl. P. C. 281; Wickes v. Clutterbuck, 2 Bing. 483; In re Fletcher, 1 Dow. & L. 726; Reg. v. Martin, 2 Ad. & El., Q. B., 1037; In re Boothroyd, 15 Mee. & W. 1.

Reporter's note to Hammond's Case, 9 Ad. & El., Q. B., 99; In re Reynolds et al., 1 Dow. & L. 846.
[7] In re Allison, 29 Eng. L. & Eq. 406.
[8] In re Freestone, 36 Eng. L. & Eq. 532.

after judgment, on an indictment according to the course of the common law.[1]

§ 263. **In the Federal Courts.**—The writs of habeas corpus and *certiorari* seem to be used in the nature of a writ of error to review questions of jurisdiction only. The United States supreme court disclaims any general power of review over the judgments of the inferior courts in criminal cases, by the use of habeas corpus or otherwise. "While, therefore, it is true," says Mr. Justice Strong, "that a writ of habeas corpus can not generally be made to subserve the purposes of a writ of error, yet when a prisoner is held without any lawful authority, and by an order beyond the jurisdiction of an inferior federal court to make, this court will, in favor of liberty, grant the writ, not to review the whole case, but to examine the authority of the court below to act at all."[2]

§ 264. **In the State Courts.**—The power of all courts under the writ of *certiorari* is not co-extensive with their power under the writ of habeas corpus.[3] And a very important difference exists between the powers of courts having jurisdiction over both writs and those having power only over the writ of habeas corpus. The former, where both writs have been issued, may, for errors which render the conviction only voidable, reverse or quash the conviction, and discharge or remand the prisoner. The latter can only remand him, and leave him to his remedy by writ of error or *certiorari*.[4]

The action of a committing magistrate or court, on the question of admitting to bail, is the subject of review by an appellate jurisdiction, upon habeas corpus aided by the writ of *certiorari*.[5] But such action is final as to other magistrates or courts of co-ordinate or concurrent jurisdiction.[6] Where habeas corpus proceedings are had before a judge as an officer, and not as a court, a writ of *certiorari* to review the proceedings is properly directed to him.[7] A court will not review upon *certiorari*

---

[1] Ex parte Lees, El. B. & E. 828.
[2] Ex parte Virginia, 100 U. S. 339; Ex parte Yerger, 8 Wall. 85; Ex parte Lange, 18 Id. 163; Ex parte Burford, 3 Cranch, 448; Ex parte Bollman, 4 Id. 75; Patterson v. The United States, 2 Wheat. 221; see numerous cases cited in Ex parte Lange, 18 Wall. 166; Ex parte Siebold, 100 U. S. 371.
[3] State v. Glenn, 54 Md. 572.
[4] Stewart's Case, 1 Abb. Pr. 210; In the Matter of Baker, 11 How. Pr. 418; Case of the Twelve Commitments, 19 Abb. Pr. 394; People v. Kling, 6 Barb. 366; People v. Fullerton, 10 Hun, 63; People v. McCormack, 4 Park. Cr. 9; People v. Cavanagh, 2 Id. 650; People v. Mayer, 16 Barb. 362; and see Mercein v. The People, 25 Wend. 63; Tomlin v. Fisher, 27 Mich. 524.
[5] People v. Cunningham, 3 Park. Cr. 531.
[6] Id.
[7] People v. Kelly, 35 Barb. 444.

§ 264.   USE OF CERTIORARI.   337

the judgment of a court committing for a contempt.[1] Where the power to issue the writ of habeas corpus, in certain cases, is denied to designated courts and officers by legislation, the prisoner, upon a refusal of his application, must, in default of appeal, be left to his remedy by *certiorari*.[2] In Ohio it is held that a proceeding on *certiorari* to reverse an order made by a state judge discharging a prisoner on habeas corpus is in its nature a civil proceeding, and by the code must be by petition in error and not by *certiorari*.[3] In Alabama, on original applications for a habeas corpus, sued out under their statutes before a single magistrate, and for the purpose of drawing the validity of a judgment in question, the proceeding is regarded as of an original nature, and that it brings the judgment in question collaterally. Therefore, only illegality will be inquired into, and not errors or irregularities, however gross they may be.[4] But their statutes are not regarded as taking away from the courts the common-law power to award a *certiorari* to remove the record and a habeas corpus to remove the body. So where the validity of a judgment is assailed in this way, the proceeding is considered appellate in its nature, and a full inquiry may be made.[5]

[1] People v. Mitchell, Sheriff of N. Y., 29 Barb. 622.
[2] Childs v. Martin 69 N. C. 126; In re Schenck, 74 Id. 607.
[3] Ex parte Collier, 6 Ohio St. 55.
[4] Kirby v. The State, 62 Ala. 51; Ex parte Hubbard, 65 Ala. 473.
[5] Kirby v. The State, 62 Ala. 51.

HAB. COR.—29

CHAPTER XVII.

COMITY OF COURTS.

§ 265. **General Rules.**—Where a court of general jurisdiction, and legally competent to determine its own jurisdiction, has acquired prior jurisdiction *de facto*, over person or subject-matter, no other court will interfere with or seek to arrest its action, while the case is still pending and undetermined. This rule is sustained and supported by all the analogies of the law. It is right in principle, and preventive of unpleasant collision between different tribunals. A court should extend to other tribunals the same comity and the same confidence which it claims for itself.[1] This rule was clearly recognized in the celebrated Wisconsin cases, where it was decided that courts had a right to determine their own jurisdiction, and that no court was authorized to take matter out of another whose process had first attached and assume the right of adjudication before the former has had an opportunity to determine the matter for itself.[2] It is improper and unauthorized for one department of the government to deny to the others their appropriate powers and attempt to assume them itself.[3] So where one court has obtained jurisdiction of a case no other court of concurrent jurisdiction will interfere therewith; and when the jurisdiction of a court is exclusive, the law applies with still greater force; for then no other court will take jurisdiction at all to interfere with or interrupt its proceedings preliminarily.[4]

This is peculiarly true of the adjudications of the federal and state courts, and the tribunal to which the jurisdiction first at-

---

[1] Ex parte Bushnell and Ex parte Langston, 8 Ohio St. 599; Ex parte Booth, 3 Wis. 145; In re Bird, 2 Saw. 33; Brenan's Case, 10 Ad. & El., Q. B., 492; Com. v. Keeper etc., 1 Ashm. 10; Angel v. Smith, 9 Ves. 335; Ex parte Robinson, 6 McLean, 355.

[2] Ex parte Booth, 3 Wis. 145; Ex parte Robinson, 6 McLean, 355; Hagan v. Lucas, 10 Pet. 400; In re Tarble, 25 Wis. 390; S. C., 13 Wall. 397; Ableman v. Booth, 21 How. 506.

[3] In re Kemp, 16 Wis. 359; Ex parte Robinson, 6 McLean, 355; Hagan v. Lucas, 10 Pet. 400.

[4] Ex parte Booth, 3 Wis. 145; U. S. v. Morris, 2 Am. Law Reg. 351; Ex parte Robinson, 6 McLean, 355.

§ 265. COMITY OF COURTS.

taches retains it.¹ And it makes no difference whether that tribunal be federal or state, because the attempt to take a case from its jurisdiction would not only be resisted to the uttermost, but would be a subversion of the judicial power, before its final decision is given.² Nothing can be more scandalous or barbarous than a contest between two courts for the jurisdiction of a criminal prosecution involving the character, liberty, and property of an accused person. "Any court of proper sentiments," says Mr. Justice Hughes, "so far from seeking to secure such jurisdiction, would rather avoid it if that could legally be done."³ Where the federal courts have concurrent jurisdiction with the state courts, they will generally send the case to the latter authorities for prosecution, as the courts of the United States prefer to take that course in all cases of concurrent jurisdiction.⁴ Federal courts of co-ordinate jurisdiction will not interfere with each other,⁵ and state tribunals of concurrent jurisdiction follow the same rule; as, for instance, for one court to issue a habeas corpus to admit the prisoner to bail, where the application for bail is pending in another court.⁶

---

¹ Ex parte Sifford, 5 Am. Law Reg. 674; Ex parte Jenkins, 2 Wall. jun. 521; United States v. Morris, 2 Am. Law Reg. 351; Keating v. Spink, 3 Ohio St. 105.

² 1 Blatchf. 635, app.; Ex parte Bushnell, 8 Ohio St. 599.

³ Ex parte Tatem, 1 Hughes, 588.

⁴ Ex parte Tatem, 1 Hughes, 588; Smith v. McIver, 9 Wheat. 532.

⁵ Ex parte Alexander, 14 Fed. Rep. 680.

⁶ Ex parte Kittrel, 20 Ark. 499.

CHAPTER XVIII.

PRESUMPTIONS.

§ 266. Distinction between Superior and Inferior Courts.
§ 267. Presumptions of Jurisdiction Relating to Superior Courts.
§ 268. Presumptions of Jurisdiction Relating to Inferior Courts.

§ 266. **Distinction between Superior and Inferior Courts.**—Before stating the rules relating to presumptions, it will probably be well to advert to a distinction usually drawn between courts. In England the king's bench, under the old system, was a superior court; and the common pleas and exchequer were inferior courts as to the king's bench. In 1874, however, the courts of England were absorbed in the supreme court of judicature, and the reader must be referred to the judicature act of 1873 for further information concerning the relative dignity of the English courts. "All courts," in the language of Chief Justice Marshall, "from which an appeal lies are inferior courts in relation to the appellate court before which their judgment may be carried; but they are not therefore inferior courts in the technical sense of those words. They apply to courts of a special and limited jurisdiction, which are erected on such principles that their judgments, taken alone, are entirely disregarded, and the proceedings must show their jurisdiction."[1] The circuit, district, and territorial courts of the United States, though of limited jurisdiction, are not inferior courts;[2] neither are the state courts, in any sense of the word, inferior courts, except in the particular cases in which an appeal lies from their judgment to the supreme court of the United States; and in these cases the mode of proceeding is particularly prescribed, and is not by habeas corpus. "They are not inferior courts, because they emanate from a different authority, and are the creatures of a distinct government."[3]

Another definition, by Mr. Justice Baldwin of the United States supreme court in a later case, runs thus: "The true line of dis-

---
[1] Kempe's Lessee v. Kennedy et al., 5 Cranch, 173.
[2] Id. 185.
[3] Ex parte Bollman and Swartwout, 4 Cranch, 97.

tinction between courts whose decisions are conclusive if not removed to an appellate court, and those whose proceedings are nullities, if their jurisdiction does not appear on their face, is this: a court which is competent by its constitution to decide on its own jurisdiction, and to exercise it to a final judgment, without setting forth in its proceedings the facts and evidence on which it is rendered, whose record is absolute verity, not to be impugned by averment or proof to the contrary, is of the first description; there can be no judicial inspection behind the judgment save by appellate power. A court which is so constituted that its judgment can be looked through for the facts and evidence which are necessary to sustain it, whose decision is not evidence of itself to show jurisdiction and its lawful exercise, is of the latter description; every requisite for either must appear on the face of their proceedings, or they are nullities."[1] It must be observed that a court may have a limited and subordinate jurisdiction, and still not be an inferior court in the sense that it ought to certify everything precisely.[2]

§ 267. **Presumptions Relating to Jurisdiction of Superior Courts.**—"Superior courts are presumed to act by right, and not by wrong, and their acts and judgments are consequently self-sustaining and conclusive, unless plainly beyond the jurisdiction of the tribunals from whence they emanate. The presumption, however, in favor of the jurisdiction of superior courts necessarily ceases when the proceedings themselves negative the existence of jurisdiction. This is well settled as it regards the jurisdiction over the cause, and would seem to be equally true of their authority over the parties. When, therefore, the record shows expressly or by necessary implication that the court has proceeded without notice to the parties, the judgment will be void, and may be disregarded as such in any collateral proceeding in which it is called in question. The judgments of all courts are void in the absence of jurisdiction, but the jurisdiction of superior courts will be presumed, unless manifestly wanting."[3] One of the leading cases on this subject is that of Peacock v. Bell and Kendal,[4] where the rule is laid down that "nothing shall be intended to be out of the jurisdiction of a superior court but that which specially appears to be so; and on the contrary, nothing shall be intended to be within

---

[1] Grignon's Lessee v. Astor et al., 2 How. 341.
[2] Peacock v. Bell & Kendal, 1 Saund. 73.
[3] Crepps v. Durden et al., 1 Sm. L. C., part 2, 7th Am. ed., 1095, 1128, 1144, notes, and the numerous cases cited.
[4] 1 Saund. 74.

the jurisdiction of an inferior court but that which is so expressly alleged."

This is laid down by Mr. Hurd as a well-established and leading rule, but in habeas corpus proceedings in this country it is not applied with uniformity. In Vermont, a justice's court is inferior, but the presumption is in favor of its jurisdiction. "We are aware," said the court in Wright v. Hazen,[1] "that the decisions in New York, and probably in some of the other states, have required the justice to know the facts, limiting the extent of his jurisdiction, at his peril. But no such rule has ever been applied to courts of general jurisdiction, either in Westminster Hall or in this country, and the jurisdiction of justices of the peace has become so important and extensive, that we incline to believe sound policy requires us to extend the same rule of construction in favor of their jurisdiction, which is done in favor of courts of general jurisdiction." In 1881 this case was cited and approved by the Texas court of appeals, in Ex parte Boland.[2] The presumptions of law are there extended in favor of the jurisdiction of justices of the peace—the same as are accorded to courts of general jurisdiction—and the same rules, so far as applicable under their statutory provisions, apply in that state to mayors' and recorders' courts. They modify Mr. Hurd's rule, as laid down in Peacock v. Bell and Kendal,[3] to read as follows: "Nothing shall be intended to be out of the jurisdiction of a superior court or a justice's court, except that which specially appears to be so."[4]

In Connecticut a justice's court is a court of record, and its decisions stand upon the same grounds and are subject to the same rules as those of the superior courts, or those of general jurisdiction.[5] In Pennsylvania the tendency is to the same effect. In Clark v. McComman[6] the court say: "It is true that the proceedings of a justice are not technically a record, for the court is not a court of record; but they are in the nature of a record, and being judicial proceedings, they can not be controverted collaterally, or in a suit grounded on the judgment of the justice. Taking a recognizance is a judicial act, which can not be questioned except by the authority which takes it; and

---

[1] 24 Vt. 143; see Ex parte Kellogg, 6 Id. 509; Ex parte Tracy, 25 Id. 93; In re Dougherty, 27 Id. 325.
[2] 11 Tex. App. 168.
[3] Cited *supra*, sec. 266.
[4] See also Prince v. The State, 37 Tex. 477, where a mayor's court is called under the law a justice's court:
Darrah v. Westerlage, 44 Id. 388; Ex parte Scwartz, 2 Tex. App. 79; Yarbrough v. The State of Texas, 2 Tex. 519; Ex parte Call, jun., 2 Tex. App. 497.
[5] Holcomb v. Cornish, 8 Conn. 380.
[6] 7 Watts & S. 470.

this principle is necessary to preserve uniformity and certainty in judicial proceedings. In Hazelett v. Ford, 10 Watts, 101, it is ruled that the validity of a judgment of a justice of the peace can not be controverted in a collateral proceeding by a stranger to it. In the opinion it is said: 'The justice is a judge of a court which, deriving its jurisdiction from statutory grants, proceeds in most things according to the substance contained in the forms of the common law; and his docket, as to things adjudicated by him, has the conclusiveness of a record.' So in Coffman v. Hampton, 2 Watts & S. 377, the docket of a justice of the peace is the best evidence to show the cause of action before him, and parol evidence is inadmissible to contradict or vary it. The proceedings of a justice, as to their conclusiveness, are placed on the same platform as the adjudications of a common-law court; and it would be difficult to assign a reason for any distinction between them. The rule is founded in convenience, and is as applicable to one tribunal as the other."

The presumption is in favor of the proceedings of the orphans' court in the same state, but, like those of all tribunals, they are mere nullities when manifestly beyond the scope of the powers under which they take place.[1] In New York, the court of oyer and terminer has been called one of superior criminal jurisdiction,[2] and the common pleas pronounced one of general jurisdiction.[3] The court of sessions in the same state seems to be one of superior jurisdiction.[4] The county court of Bennington, Vermont, was, in an action brought in the state of New York, treated as one of general jurisdiction, and the settled rule of presumption was applied in favor of its powers.[5] So of the common pleas of the county of Hampshire.[6] The determination of mayors' courts in Alabama has lately been held, on habeas corpus, to be conclusive, until a superior tribunal, in a direct proceeding, pronounces the determination erroneous.[7] In Iowa, the judgment of the police magistrate, after conviction for an offense within his jurisdiction, has been held to be final and conclusive, until reversed on appeal or writ of error; "as final and conclusive as that of a court of general jurisdic-

---

[1] McPherson v. Cunliff, 11 Serg. & R. 422; Pres. of Orphans' Court v. Groff, 14 Id. 181; Herr v. Herr, 5 Pa St. 428; Painter v. Henderson, 7 Id. 48; Lockhart v. John, Id. 137.
[2] People v. Cavanagh, 2 Park. Cr. 650.
[3] Hart v. Seixas, 21 Wend. 45; Foot & Beebe v. Stevens, 17 Id. 483.
[4] People ex rel. Trainor v. Baker, 89 N. Y. 460.
[5] Wheeler v. Raymond, 8 Cow. 311.
[6] Smith v. Rhoades, 1 Day, 168.
[7] Ex parte Hubbard, 65 Ala. 473. As to mayors' courts, see also Stoner v. State, 4 Mo. 614.

tion, and it is no more allowable to revise the one than the other by a proceeding on habeas corpus."[1]

In his work on constitutional limitations,[2] Mr. Cooley says on this matter: "When the question is raised whether the proceedings of a court may not be void for want of jurisdiction, it will sometimes be important to note the grade of the court and the extent of its authority. Some courts are of general jurisdiction, by which is meant that their authority extends to a great variety of matters; while others are only of special and limited jurisdiction, by which it is understood that they have authority extending only to certain specified cases. The want of jurisdiction is equally fatal in the proceedings of each, but different rules prevail in showing it. It is not to be assumed that a court of general jurisdiction has in any case proceeded to adjudge upon matters over which it has no authority; and its jurisdiction is to be presumed, whether there are recitals in its records to show it or not. A record is not commonly suffered to be contradicted by parol evidence; but whenever a fact showing want of jurisdiction in a court of general jurisdiction can be proved without contradicting its recitals, it is allowable to do so, and thus defeat its effect."[3] It will thus be seen that the presumption in favor of the jurisdiction of the court of general jurisdiction is one of fact, and not conclusive. It may be rebutted. If it depends upon the existence of certain facts, and the court has passed upon those facts, the determination is conclusive until its judgment has been reversed or set aside, and this rule is as applicable to the judgments of inferior as of superior courts.[4] And the learned judge remarked: "There is nothing startling in the application of these well-recognized principles to proceedings by the habeas corpus, in favor of the citizen restrained of his liberty under color of judicial proceedings absolutely void."

§ 268. **Presumptions of Jurisdiction Relating to Inferior Courts.**—To show in full the two differences between courts of superior and those of inferior jurisdiction, made by Mr. Cooley, and adverted to in the preceding section, we will state his rules regarding inferior courts. After referring to the presumptions in favor of courts of general jurisdiction, whether there are recitals in its record to show it or not, he says: "On the other hand, no such intendment is made in favor of the

---

[1] Platt v. Harrison, 6 Iowa, 79.
[2] 5th ed., 502, 503.
[3] Cooley's Constitutional Limitations, 5th ed., 503, and authorities cited.
[4] Mr. Justice Allen, in People ex rel. Tweed v. Liscomb, 60 N. Y. 568, citing Staples v. Fairchilds, 3 Comst. 41; Chemung Canal Bank v. Judson, 8 Seld. 254.

§ 268.   PRESUMPTIONS.   345

judgment of a court of limited jurisdiction, but the recitals contained in the minutes of proceedings must be sufficient to show that the case was one of which the law permitted the court to take cognizance, and that the parties were subjected to its jurisdiction by proper process."[1] And in speaking of disproving jurisdiction by contradicting the record, he says: "But ,in the case of a court of special and limited authority, it is permitted to go still further, and to show a want of jurisdiction even in opposition to the recitals contained in the record.[2] As the jurisdiction of limited and inferior tribunals will not be presumed, and must be shown affirmatively to confer validity on their acts, when the facts necessary to give such a tribunal jurisdiction do not appear on the face of its proceedings, and are not proved *aliunde*, the whole will be invalid, and may be set aside as a nullity when called in question in the course of a collateral controversy.[3] If, however, jurisdiction depends upon a certain state of facts, which must be passed upon by the inferior courts themselves, and in respect to which the decision of the inferior court has been rendered, it must be held final and conclusive in all collateral inquiries, if there was any evidence whatever on which to base it, notwithstanding it may have erred in its conclusions."[4]

These principles have been applied by various state courts in habeas corpus proceedings.[5] A notable and striking instance of this may be found in Kearney's Case,[6] where the police court of the city and county of San Francisco was declared to be an inferior court of limited jurisdiction, "whose powers are conferred, and whose duties and mode of procedure are prescribed, by statute, and to which the rule applies that the evidence of its proceedings must affirmatively show jurisdiction of the person of the defendant, and over the subject-matter." A reasonable, sensible, and liberal construction of this rule is given by the supreme court of Kansas, on original proceedings in habeas corpus. "The jurisdiction of a justice of the peace is inferior and limited, and while it must affirmatively appear upon the whole record from the recitals therein that the justice has juris-

---

[1] Cooley's Constitutional Limitations, 5th ed., 502.
[2] Id., 503. But see 1 Sm. L. C., 7th ed., 1130.
[3] Notes to Crepps v. Durden et al., 1 Sm. L. C., 7th ed., 1095, and numerous authorities cited.
[4] Cooley's Constitutional Limitations, 5th ed., 503. For the California rule regarding presumptions as to matters in the court below, see Hahn v. Kelly, 34 Cal. 391. See also People v. Liscomb, 60 N. Y. 559; Levy v. Shurman, 6 Ark. 182.
[5] Byrd v. The State, 1 How. (Miss.) 163; Ex parte Murray, 43 Cal. 455, overruled in Kearney's Case, 55 Id. 212.
[6] 55 Cal. 212.

diction to hear and determine the case at issue, as jurisdiction will not be presumed, yet this rule does not apply to each process or order or entry issued or made by him. In brief, it is not necessary in issuing each process to recite all the facts conferring jurisdiction." [1]

Another general rule is that the proceedings of courts of general jurisdiction not acting within the scope of their general powers, but in the exercise of a special and statutory authority, stand on the same footing with courts of limited and inferior jurisdiction, and will be invalid, unless the authority on which they are founded has been strictly pursued.[2] But in Maryland it is said that the doctrine that where a special limited jurisdiction, distinct from its general jurisdiction, is conferred by statute on any tribunal, its power to act must appear on the face of the proceedings, does not apply to proceedings in cases of habeas corpus.[3] When, however, the existence of jurisdiction is once shown or admitted, the judgments of superior and inferior tribunals stand on the same footing, and are equally and absolutely conclusive.[4]

[1] Goldsmith's Petition, 24 Kan. 757.
[2] Notes to Crepps v. Durden et al., 1 Sm. L. C., 7th ed., 1095, and many authorities cited.
[3] Deckard v. State of Maryland, 38 Md. 186.
[4] Crepps v. Durden et al., 1 Sm. L. C., 7th ed., 1144, notes, and authorities cited.

CHAPTER XIX.

FALSE IMPRISONMENT.

§ 269. What is an Imprisonment.
§ 270. Acts of Indemnity during the Suspension of the Habeas Corpus Act.
§ 271. Arrest. What Constitutes.
§ 272. Restraint and Detention.
§ 273. Matters concerning Bail.

§ 269. **What is an Imprisonment.**—If it be necessary for a person to show that he is imprisoned without just cause, or that he is imprisoned at all, in order to obtain a writ of habeas corpus for his release from custody, it is very essential to know what constitutes an imprisonment, and it is the object and purpose of this chapter to give a brief outline of a few principles of law applicable to the subject. It is not always necessary that a person be actually confined within the silent walls of a jail or prison to be under duress, restraint, or imprisonment; neither is it necessary for a party to be actually confined to entitle him to a writ of habeas corpus, if he can show that the restraint or detention is without probable cause. Any confinement of the person is an imprisonment.[1] An imprisonment is lawful if it be by process from a court of jurisdiction, or by warrant from a legal officer having authority to commit to prison. The warrant must be in writing, under the hand and seal of a magistrate, and express the causes of the commitment. This should be done, both for the reason that it is unreasonable to send a prisoner to jail without alleging a crime against him, and that the commitment may be inquired into upon habeas corpus.[2]

§ 270. **During the Suspension of the Habeas Corpus Act** in England the crown was not authorized to "imprison suspected persons without giving any reasons therefor," and a magistrate so granting a warrant of commitment was liable for the consequences, if the detention was illegal. To protect those who could not defend themselves in an action for false impris-

[1] 1 Kerr's Ela. Com. 107. [2] Id.

onment, under these circumstances, acts of indemnity were passed during such suspensions.¹

§ 271. **Arrests.**—"Mere words will not constitute an arrest." If an officer says, "I arrest you," the party is not under restraint, and if he runs away it is no escape.² If an officer touches a party to be arrested, however, and the person instantly runs away, he is under arrest.³ An arrest made by an officer beyond the limits of his authority is void.⁴ Every arrest of a man for a civil cause, not warranted by legal process, is unlawful.⁵ It appears there are many authorities to show that "if a person be arrested under a process which was irregularly issued, it is a false imprisonment in the party at whose suit it was issued, for it was incumbent on him to take care that the process was regularly issued;" but the authorities are generally uniform, "that it is not a false imprisonment in an officer to arrest a person under the process of superior courts, although the process were irregularly issued." The arrest of a person under erroneous process is not false imprisonment, for the error is not attributable to mistake in an officer of the court, and not to the party at whose suit it was issued.⁶ If an officer, in consequence of a charge, takes a person for one moment in his possession, it is, in point of law, an imprisonment. A tapping on the shoulder, with the words, "You are my prisoner," or a submission into custody on account of a charge, even without an actual touching on the part of the officer, would be an imprisonment.⁷ But when nothing more passes than merely the charge—where the officer does not take possession of the person—it is not by law a false imprisonment.⁸

§ 272. **Restraint and Detention.**—Any forcible detention of a man's person or control over his movements is an imprisonment.⁹ Justice Baldwin defines imprisonment to be "the detention of another against his will, depriving him of the power of locomotion."¹⁰ In ordinary practice, words are sufficient to constitute an imprisonment if they impose a restraint upon the person, and the plaintiff is accordingly restrained; for he is not obliged to incur the risk of personal violence and insult by resisting until actual violence be used."¹¹ Keeping a

---

¹ 58 Geo. III., c. 6.
² Simpson v. Hill, 1 Esp. 431.
³ Russen v. Lucas, 1 Car. & P. 153, citing Gener v. Sparks, 1 Salk. 79; and Lawson v. Buzines, 3 Harr. (Del.) 416.
⁴ Lawson v. Buzines, 3 Harr. (Del.) 418.
⁵ Bac. Abr., Trespass, D, 3.
⁶ Id.
⁷ Russen v. Lucas, 1 Car. & P. 153.
⁸ Id.
⁹ Lawson v. Buzines, 3 Harr. (Del.) 418.
¹⁰ U. S. v. Benner, 1 Baldw. 239; Johnson v. Tompkins et al., Id. 600.
¹¹ Pike v. Hanson, 9 N. H. 493, citing 3 Stark. Ev. 1448.

§ 272. FALSE IMPRISONMENT. 349

person in a house against his will, or his forcible arrest and detention in the street, is an imprisonment.¹ The term "false" as used in connection with "imprisonment" means "illegal;" that is, without regard to the question whether any crime has been committed or a debt due. It is a term often carelessly and inaccurately used, and the exact determination of which is imperfectly understood.² It seems that in Wisconsin the state may discharge the parental duty which a parent owes to his child, but which he fails to perform, and that the commitment of the child to an industrial school is not an imprisonment as against parental right in the child. Under their statute, which goes to the total failure of the parent to provide for the child, and which was pronounced not to be invalid on the ground that it invaded any natural rights of parent and child, there was no provision made for service of process upon the parent or guardian. It was held in the supreme court of Wisconsin that where the commitment of the child was not made upon a conviction for crime, but simply for misfortune, the parent or guardian was not precluded under the statute from asserting any right to the custody and care of the child, which he might afterward be able and willing to resume and establish. By clearing his disability, on which the child's commitment was made, and showing that he is otherwise a proper custodian for the child, he would be entitled thereto, notwithstanding the commitment. We apprehend that a refusal of the school officers to deliver up the child under such circumstances would find its remedy in a writ of habeas corpus.³

Chief Justice Lord Campbell, of the court of queen's bench, considered that "a child under guardianship for nurture is supposed to be unlawfully imprisoned, when unlawfully detained from the custody of the guardian, and when delivered to him the child is supposed to be set at liberty."⁴

Judge Robert M. Charlton, of Georgia, gave it as his opinion, that "to confine the writ of habeas corpus at common law exclusively to cases of illegal confinement would be destructive of the ends of justice. It would enable a kidnaper to maintain possession of a child of tender years (taken by him by fraud or force from the bosom of its family), merely because its want of legal discretion would preclude the idea of its being

¹ 1 Kerr's Bla. Com. 107.
² 1 Chit. G. P. 48.
³ The Milwaukee Industrial School v. The Supervisors of Milwaukee Co., 40 Wis. 328.
⁴ Regina v. Clark, 40 Eng. L. & Eq. 114.

confined against its will. I apprehend that it is not going too far to say that the interests and welfare of society require, that under peculiar circumstances the fact that the child of tender years is detained improperly from the custody of the person entitled to its possession, is sufficient to ground and maintain the writ of habeas corpus."[1]

§ 273. **Bail.**—Required in actions of trover for the recovery of personal property, under the provisions of a statute of Georgia authorizing the owner of personal property to bring such suits, can not in any legal sense be considered an imprisonment for debt, even where the constitution of the state prohibited imprisonment for debt.[2] A defendant who has been brought into court and discharged from arrest on a criminal charge, and given bail, is not privileged from arrest on civil process immediately afterwards during the sitting of the court, and before he leaves the court-room. In the supreme court of Georgia it was said, in the language of Lord Chief Justice Campbell, "that the cases showed that an acquitted prisoner had no privilege *redeundo*, and that while remaining as a spectator he had no more privilege than any one else." This rule, it was said, also applied to a prisoner not acquitted but discharged on bail.[3]

A person discharged on bail is not imprisoned or restrained of his liberty in such a way as to entitle him to a writ of habeas corpus, directed to his bail. Justice Yeates, of the supreme court of Pennsylvania, upon a motion made that a habeas corpus issue to bail, that they might be discharged from their recognizances, because the defendants were in a legal sense under actual confinement and restrained of their liberty, and that their bail might surrender them, said that "the legislature, by certain acts, did not contemplate a party admitted to bail as a prisoner under commitment, besides confining the authority and requisition so to act solely to the court before whom the prisoner is to receive his trial. Would not a habeas corpus, directed to the bail of a supposed offender, be perfectly novel? Could we, or either of us, do an act which would amount to a legal discharge of the recognizances in the court of oyer and terminer?" Justice Smith inclined to the same view, but would give no decided opinion. The motion was denied.[4]

"In cases where the committing magistrate has no authority

[1] In the Matter of Mitchell, R. M. Charlt. 489.
[2] Harris v. Bridges, 57 Ga. 407.
[3] In the Matter of Mitchell, R. M. Charlt. 489.
[4] Respublica v. Arnold et al., 3 Yeates, 263.

§ 273.

to take bail, a habeas corpus may issue to the constable or other officer having the defendant in charge. * * * The object of the habeas corpus act was to prevent any wrongful or illegal restraint of personal liberty; and whenever a person is deprived of the privilege of going when and where he pleases, he is restrained of his liberty, and has a right to inquire if that restraint be illegal and wrongful, whether it be by a jailer, constable, or private individual. It is not necessary that the degradation of being incarcerated in a prison should be undergone to entitle any citizen who may consider himself unjustly charged with a breach of the laws to a hearing. The whole spirit of the law is in favor of liberty; and if the words were doubtful, they should be construed liberally in favor of that blessing."[1]

[2] Commonwealth v. Ridgway, 2 Ashm. 248.

CHAPTER XX.

WARRANTS.

PART I.—WARRANTS OF ARREST.

§ 274. General Warrants.
§ 275. The Direction.
§ 276. Name of the Offender.
§ 277. Statement of Offense in Magistrate's Warrant.
§ 278. Statement of Offense in Warrant of Superior Judge.
§ 279. Oath, Jurat, and Seal.

PART II.—WARRANTS TO ANSWER.

§ 280. Commitments for Treason.
§ 281. Cause and Certainty.
§ 282. Orders and Commitments by Superior Court.
§ 283. The Direction and Conclusion.
§ 284. Signature and Seal.
§ 285. What Face of Warrant should Show.

PART III.—REVIEW BY HABEAS CORPUS.

§ 286. The Warrant of Arrest.
§ 287. The Warrant of Commitment.

PART I.—WARRANTS OF ARREST.

§ 274. **General Warrants,** in England, have been pronounced illegal,[1] and in the United States are subject to the following constitutional restraint: The right of the people to be secure in their persons, houses, papers, and effects against unreasonable searches and seizures shall not be violated; and no warrants shall issue but upon probable cause, supported by oath or affirmation, and particularly describing the place to be searched and the persons or things to be seized.[2] Special warrants, however, such as warrants of arrest, warrants of commitment, to answer, etc., deserve special mention of their requisites, as they involve the validity or invalidity of legal process, so far as the warrants themselves may affect it. The validity of such process is often assailed on habeas corpus proceedings; and while the reader must be referred to the authorities con-

---

[1] Money v. Leach, 3 Burr. 1742; S. C., 1 W. Black. 555, 563.
[2] Constitution of the United States, Amendment IV.

tained in works on criminal law, and especially to local statutes, for exact and detailed information, a few general rules will be examined and illustrated.

§ 275. **The Direction.**—The word "warrant," in its primary sense, simply means an authority.[1] It is a written mandate, issued by a proper magistrate, and directed to a proper officer or indifferent person, commanding him to arrest the alleged offender, and bring him before the proper authority to answer for the crime.[2] The warrant ought to be directed to an officer authorized to execute it, and that officer should be the constable of the precinct or county where it is to be executed, because no other constable, and *a fortiori* no private person, is compelled to execute it.[3] It may also be directed to a particular person by name. In this case, the person mentioned has an authority coextensive with that of him who confers it.[4] It may be directed to a person, not by his name as an individual, but by the description of his official character.[5] It may also be directed to officers, either by their particular names, or by the description of their office, and, in the first case, the officer may execute the warrant anywhere within the jurisdiction of the magistrate who issued it; and in the latter case, not beyond the precincts of his office. Magistrates should be careful to direct their warrants in such a manner that the parties to be affected by them may know that the persons bearing the warrants are authorized to execute them, because, "according to the extent of the officer's authority," says Mr. Justice Bayley, "his death may be murder, manslaughter, or perhaps justifiable homicide."[6]

Though the warrant may be addressed to another, no one but the constable of the place where it is to be executed can be compelled to execute it.[7] A misnomer of the person in the process on which an arrest is made subjects the actors to an action for false imprisonment.[8] The warrant must contain a command to whom it is directed to make the arrest; a mere authority, license, or permission is not a warrant in law. The direction is an essential part of every warrant, and unless it is directed to the persons above named, it is not a sufficient or proper warrant. The practice of directing warrants to other than officers is not to be encouraged. Where the direction in

---

[1] 2 Rap. & Law. Law Dict. 1345.
[2] Rob. Elem. Law, sec. 480.
[3] 2 Chitty's Bla. Com., b. 4, p. 236.
[4] Id., citing Case of the Village of Chorley, 1 Salk. 176; 1 Ch. Crim. L. 38.
[5] 1 Ch. Crim. R. 38.
[6] Id.

[7] Commonwealth v. Keeper, etc., 1 Ashm. 183.
[8] Scott v. Ely, 4 Wend. 556; Griswold v. Sedgwick, 6 Cow. 456; S. C., 1 Wend. 126; Gurnsey & Knight v. Lovell, 9 Id. 319; Melvin v. Fisher, 8 N. H. 406.

the body of the warrant runs "to the sheriff or any constable of the county" in which the magistrate resides, an authority to execute the warrant can not be conferred upon one not an officer, by an indorsement on the back thereof, signed by the justice, "authorizing and empowering" such person to arrest the defendant and bring him before the justice. The indorsement is not a direction, and the warrant will not protect the one making an arrest under it.[1] It has been held that a warrant issued by order of the senate of the United States for the arrest of a witness for contempt in refusing to appear before a committee of the senate, and addressed only to the sergeant-at-arms of the senate, can not be served by deputy in the commonwealth of Massachusetts; and one so arrested was released on habeas corpus.[2]

§ 276. **Name of the Offender.**—The warrant must name or otherwise describe the person against whom it is issued.[3] The name must not be left in blanks to be filled up afterwards, though it may be inserted before the warrant's delivery to the officer. If the offender's name be unknown, the warrant may be issued against him by the best description the nature of the case will permit of; as, "as the body of a man whose name is unknown, but whose person is well known, and who is employed as the driver of cattle, and wears a badge, No. 573."[4] A warrant, however, leaving a blank for the Christian name of the person to be apprehended, and giving no reason for omitting it, but describing him only as the son of J. S. L., and stating the charge of assault without particularizing the time, place, or any other circumstances of the crime, has been held to be

---

[1] Abbott v. Booth, 51 Barb. 546.

[2] Sanborn v. Carleton, 15 Gray, 399. See generally, on this section, 1 Bish. Crim. Proc., 3d ed., sec. 187; 1 East P. C. 320; 1 Hale P. C. 581; 2 Id. 110; Kelsey v. Parmelee, 15 Conn. 260; Paul v. Vankirk, 6 Binn. 123; and Holley v. Mix & Clute, 3 Wend. 350; Regina v. Nesbitt, 2 Dow. & L. 529; Leverick v. Mercer, 14 Ad. & El., Q. B., 759; and King v. Weir et al., 1 Barn. & Cress. 288. Here a warrant was directed to "A. B., to the constables of W., and to all other his majesty's officers:" held, that the constables of W. (their names not being inserted in the warrant) could not execute it out of that district. See also Ex parte Branigan, 19 Cal. 133, that in case of the absence or inability to act of the justice issuing the warrant of arrest to bring before him for examination a party charged with crime, the officer making the arrest may take the party before another justice of the peace of the same county, who may make the examination and commit the party; that it is not necessary, to enable the officer to take the party arrested before another magistrate for examination in case of such absence or inability to act, that the warrant of arrest should contain a direction to that effect; and that a commitment by a justice of the peace of a city and county, if directed to the sheriff of said city and county, authorizes the warden of the county jail thereof to receive and retain the prisoner in his custody.

[3] 1 Ch. Crim. L. 38; Rob. Elem. Law, sec. 480.

[4] 1 Hale P. C. 577; 1 Ch. Crim. L. 39.

§ 276. WARRANTS. 355

too general and unspecific.¹ A warrant to arrest "John Doe or Richard Roe, whose other or true name is unknown," without any further description or means of identification of the offender's name, is void.² The arrest of a person by a wrong name can not be justified, though he was the person intended, unless it be shown that he was known as well by one name as the other.³ The warrant must be for the apprehension of some particular person, else it will be void; because the magistrate, and not the officer, is to judge of the ground of suspicion.⁴ The arrest of one person can not be justified under a writ sued out against another.⁵ The process on its face must authorize an arrest, or it will be void.⁶ For a mere inaccuracy in spelling the name, it still being *idem sonans*, the court will not interfere.⁷

An arrest of a felon may be justified by any person without warrant, whether there be time to obtain one or not, if a felony has in fact been committed by the person arrested.⁸ And even when there is only probable cause of suspicion, a private person may, without warrant, at his peril make an arrest. It is perilous, for nothing short of proving the felony will justify the arrest.⁹ It is thus seen that, in certain cases, private persons, as well as officers, may arrest felons. The following distinction shows the difference between the powers of peace-officers and private persons to arrest offenders: "If an innocent person is arrested upon suspicion by a private individual, such individual is excused if a felony was in fact committed and there was reasonable ground to suspect the person arrested. But if no felony was committed by any one, and a private individual arrest without warrant, such arrest is illegal, though an officer would be justified if he acted upon information from another which he had reason to rely on."¹⁰ Bishop says: "For a past offense lower than felony none of these officers [sheriffs, constables, police officers, and the like] can make an arrest without warrant; unless, for example, it is such a dangerous assault as may end

---

¹ Rex v. Hood, 1 Moo. C. C. 281.
² Commonwealth v. Crotty et al., 10 Allen, 403.
³ Mead v. Haws, 7 Cow. 332; Scott v. Ely, 4 Wend. 555; Gurnsey v. Lovell, 9 Id. 319.
⁴ Money v. Leach, 1 W. Black. 561; 1 Hale P. C. 580; 2 Chitty's Bla. Com., b. 2, p. 236.
⁵ Shadgett v. Clipson, 8 East. 329.
⁶ Griswold v. Sedgwick, 6 Cow. 456.
⁷ Ahitbol v. Beniditto, 2 Taunt. 401. See, generally, 1 Ch. Crim. L. 39; King v. Inhabitants of Winwick,

8 T. R. 454; 1 East P. C. 324; Hoye v. Bush, 1 Man. & G. 775; 1 Russ. on Crimes, 619; Casey's Justices' Manual, 177, an Australian work.
⁸ Holley v. Mix, 3 Wend. 350.
⁹ Wakely v. Hart et al., 6 Binn. 316; People ex rel. Johnson v. Nevins, 1 Hill (N. Y.), 154; Rohan v. Sawin, 5 Cush. 281; Mayo v. Wilson, 1 N. H. 53.
¹⁰ Chief Justice Savage, in Holley v. Mix, 3 Wend. 353; see 1 Bish. Crim. Proc., 3d ed., "The Arrest," secs. 155-224.

in felony by the death of the injured person. Where it is felony or treason, and is past, the distinction between the powers of the officer and the private person is this: should the one arrested be found not to be guilty, the private person will not be justified unless an offense had been committed by some one; while the officer is justified though no offense had been committed; yet both must have had reasonable cause to suspect the one apprehended."[1] The official proclamation by the governor, of the commission of a felony, published as the law directs, is sufficient evidence of the commission of it to justify an arrest of the supposed felon by a peace-officer without warrant.[2] If a writ of habeas corpus be obtained where the arrest is upon suspicion, and without a special warrant, proof must be given to show the suspicion to be well founded, or the prisoner will be discharged.[3] Where an officer arrests one for felony on a telegram, without warrant, his duty is the same as if he had made the arrest by warrant. He must take the prisoner, without unnecessary delay, before a proper officer, for the hearing of proof, or to be held, if the circumstances justify it, for further examination. If this is not done with reasonable diligence, the arrested party is entitled to a habeas corpus, to have his detention inquired into.[4]

§ 277. **Statement of Offense in Magistrate's Warrant.** It is a general rule that the offense must be stated with reasonable certainty. This applies to the warrant of arrest issued by the magistrate as well as to the commitment. The legal presumptions of which we have heretofore spoken do not apply to these processes of inferior courts any more than they do to their judgments, which will be treated in subsequent chapters. The South Carolina court of appeals have laid down the law very clearly concerning the form and effect of the common magistrate's criminal warrant. "It is a great mistake," said Mr. Justice Earle, "to suppose that a warrant for apprehension, or a warrant of commitment, need contain any statement at all of the evidence on which it is founded, or need enumerate any of the facts and circumstances accompanying the offense. There are several high authorities that it need not even contain a specification of the particular offense. But the better opinion, as

---

[1] 1 Bish. Crim. Proc., 3d ed., sec. 181, and authorities cited. See Boyleston v. Kerr, 2 Daly, 220; Burns v. Erben, 40 N. Y. 463.
[2] Eanes v. The State, 6 Humph. 53.
[3] Hurd on Habeas Corpus, 2d ed.,
397, citing 2 Inst. 52; see also In the Matter of Arthur Henry, 29 How. Pr. 187.
[4] In the Matter of Henry, 29 How. Pr. 185.

§ 277. WARRANTS. 357

well as the general and approved practice, is, that it should state the offense with convenient certainty—that it should not be for felony generally, but should contain the special nature of the felony; as, for felony of the death of J. S.; or burglary, in breaking the house of J. S." In the two cases, heard together, and giving rise to this opinion, the prisoners had been discharged on habeas corpus; and while no decision that could be made by the court would recapture the defendants, and bring them to justice, the attorney general urged the court to express an opinion which might prevent their former discharge from being urged on their behalf in case they should be retaken, and which might serve to guide magistrates in similar cases.[1] Just precisely how minute a warrant of arrest must be, is a question partly of local usage, and upon which the authorities are not quite harmonious, but it must state for what offense the arrest is to be made; though it need not descend into the particulars of the charge as the indictment does.[2]

Before a magistrate can issue his warrant for the apprehension of an offender, probable cause must be shown. This is "a reasonable ground of suspicion, supported by circumstances sufficiently strong in themselves to warrant a cautious man in the belief that the person accused is guilty of the offense with which he is charged."[3] But this need not all be detailed in the warrant. The cause named in the warrant must be a good cause, and be stated with certainty.[4] Little weight will be given in legal proceedings to an affidavit made upon information merely.[5] A warrant by a justice to apprehend J. S. to answer such matters as shall be objected against him, *ex parte domini regis*, without expressing the certainty of the crime, is not regular.[6] The substance of the complaint should be inserted in the body of the

---

[1] Dudley (S. C.), 295. These cases are given at length as a note to the celebrated and leading case of The People v. McLeod, 1 Hill (N. Y.), 377, heard on habeas corpus. The first was The State v. Everett. The prisoner was "charged before A. H. Brown, on the oath of A. Gibson, from circumstances, with larceny of bank bills of the Union Bank of Florida, valued at about seventy dollars; there being other bills lost, and one fifty-dollar and one twenty-dollar bill being found on the person of said James E. Everett." This was held to be an explicit charge of a distinct and specified offense—"felony plainly and specially expressed." The second was State v. Potter. Here the charge was that the prisoner had committed larceny, without any facts or circumstances to show whether it was grand or petit larceny. In such case the court, in favor of liberty, without more appearing from the depositions or examinations, would regard it as a charge of petit larceny, and admit to bail.

[2] 1 Bish. Crim. Proc., 3d ed., sec. 228, and authorities.
[3] Munns v. Dupont de Nemours, 3 Wash. 31.
[4] Ex parte Burford, 3 Cranch, 448.
[5] People v. Smith et al., 1 Cal. 1.
[6] 1 Hale P. C. 577.

warrant; yet if the warrant definitely refers to the complaint on the same paper—" to the offense described in the annexed complaint"—it has been held good.¹ But a warrant issued in North Carolina charging a person with having committed murder " somewhere between this place and the state of Texas" is void, as being too vague and indefinite.² Where statute requires the facts and circumstances to be set forth in the complaint, this must be done, whether the complainant can substantiate them by his oath or not. If he can not, a subpœna may be issued to compel the attendance of witnesses to testify concerning such facts and circumstances as are thus set forth.³

§ 278. **Statement of Offense in Warrant of Superior Judge.**—The warrant of an inferior magistrate does not differ materially from that of a superior one, except that the presumptions of law in favor of the latter will be more favorable than towards the former. The strictness, however, with which the proceedings of inferior tribunals are scrutinized only applies to the question of jurisdiction, and when the existence of jurisdiction is proved or conceded, the maxim *omnia rite acta* applies to them as well as to courts of general jurisdiction.⁴ The mandate or writ of a superior court or superior magistrate, as one of the judges of those courts acting according to the course of the common law, is not to be regarded or examined with the same strictness as the warrant of an ordinary magistrate, or other person acting by special statutory authority and out of the course of the common law. In the case of officers of special or limited jurisdiction, all instruments by which they act, such as warrants to arrest, commitments, orders, convictions, or inquisitions; ought, according to the course of the decisions, to show their authority on the face of them by direct averment or reasonable intendment; but not so with the process of superior courts acting by the authority of the common law. It will be presumed that writs issued by superior courts are duly issued and in a case in which they have jurisdiction, unless the contrary appears on the face of them. A failure to set forth the cause of arrest would be fatal in a warrant issued by an inferior court, but this omission will not invalidate the warrant issued by a superior court. In such a case, Lord Coke says, if it express no cause at all, it will be legal.⁵

¹ Commonwealth v. Dean, 9 Gray, 283; Commonwealth v. Hoye, Id. 283.
² Price v. Graham et al., 3 Jones, 545.
³ In the Matter of Morton, 10 Mich. 208.
⁴ Crepps v. Durden et al., 1 Sm. L. C., 7th ed., part 2, p. 1096, and numerous authorities there cited.
⁵ Gosset v. Howard, 10 Ad. & El. Q. B., 411; cited in Crepps v. Durden et al., 1 Sm. L. C., 7th ed., part 2,

§ 279. **Oath, Jurat, and Seal.**—At the earlier common law a justice of the peace could issue his warrant and commit without oath, though Lord Holt said "he is not wise if he doth so, for then he must make out the cause of commitment at his peril; but if oath be made, he is safe."[1] The recent doctrine of the king's bench, however, is that a magistrate has no power to issue a warrant of arrest without oath.[2] And most of the constitutions and statutes of this country have settled the question, that warrants for arrest shall issue only on probable cause supported by oath.[3] The usual and only proper evidence of the oath is the magistrate's certificate, and this, to the complaint as "taken and sworn before me," is sufficient.[4] Or any other like form from which this idea can be collected is sufficient.[5] If the jurat be inadequate in form, while the facts are sufficient, it may be amended.[6] The warrant must, of course, be signed by the officer issuing it, or it will be void upon its face. But whether it should be sealed or not is an unsettled question. Chitty says:[7] "It is generally laid down, that the warrant ought to be under the hand and seal of the justice who makes it;[8] but it seems sufficient if it be in writing and signed by him, unless a seal is expressly required by particular act of parliament."[9] In this country where statute prescribes a seal, it must be followed; but where no such requisite is prescribed, it is unnecessary.[10] But there are several respectable authorities to the effect that a seal is essential to a warrant issued by a magistate to arrest a person for a criminal offense, and that if there be no seal the warrant is void.[11] The term "warrant" implies a seal in cases where a

[1] p. 1101; and Peacock v. Bell, 1 Saund. 74; Parsons v. Loyd, 3 Wils. 341; Turner v. Felgate, 1 Lev. 95; Cotes v. Michill, 3 Id. 20; The Brewers' Case, Roll. 134. Ex parte Van Sandau, 1 Ph. 445, 605, cited by Parke, B., in delivering the judgment of the exchequer chamber in the main case in error from the queen's bench.

[1] 2 Hawk. P. C., c. 16, sec 17; 2 Hale P. C., c. 13, p. 105; Rex v. Pain, Holt, 294; S. C., Comberbach, 359; King v. Wilkes, 2 Wils. 151; Rex v. Wyndham, 1 Stra. 3; see Elsee v. Smith, 1 Dow. & Ry. 97; S. C., 2 Chit., Q. B., 304; State v. Lamos, 26 Me. 258; 1 Bish. Crim. Proc., 3d ed., sec 718, and authorities cited.

[2] Caudle v. Seymour, 41 Eng. Com. L. 825; S. C., 1 Gale & Dav. 454.

[3] Walker v. Cruikshank, 2 Hill (N. Y.), 296; Conner v. Commonwealth, 3 Binn. 38.

[4] State v. J. H., 1 Tyler, 444.

[5] See authorities cited in 1 Bish. Crim. Proc., 3d ed., sec. 231.

[6] State v. Smith, 54 Me. 33; see generally Ex parte Burford, 3 Cranch, 448; Sandford v. Nichols, 13 Mass. 286; State v. Killet, 2 Bailey, 289.

[7] 1 Ch. Crim. L. 38.

[8] Citing 1 Hale P. C. 577; 2 Id. 111; Com. Dig., Imprisonment, H. 7; Hawk. P. C., b. 2, c. 13, sec. 21; 4 Bla. Com. 290.

[9] Citing Redfield v. Cabell et al., Willes, 411; Burn's Justice, Warrant, iv.

[10] State v. Vaughn, Harp. 313; Davis v. Clements, 2 N. H. 390; Thompson v. Fellows, 1 Fost. 425; Millett v. Baker, 42 Barb. 215; State v. McNally, 34 Me. 210.

[11] State v. Worley, 11 Ired. 242; Welch v. Scott, 5 Id. 72; Tackett v. The State, 3 Yerg. 393.

seal has not been dispensed with by statute.[1] Whether there be a seal or not is a mixed question of law and fact, to be decided by the court and not by the jury.[2]

PART II.—WARRANTS TO ANSWER.

§ 280. **Commitment for Treason.**—At common law it was held that a commitment for treason ought to express the species of treason, else the commitment would be so ill as to entitle the prisoner to bail.[3] Yet a commitment generally for high treason was pronounced good though the commitment failed to express the overt act. Lord Coke put the case of treason *contra personam regis*, and admitted that to be sufficient.[4] So in the case of a commitment for treasonable practices it is not necessary to express in the warrant of commitment the particular species of treasonable practices.[5]

§ 281. **Cause and Certainty.**—The *mittimus* must state for what offense the commitment is made. The minuteness of this, however, is not well determined, and depends somewhat upon local usage.[6] It ought to be stated with certainty, in order that the court may determine whether it be lawful or not.[7] Thus a commitment by the mayor of London, "for divers causes well known to the mayor," was held not good for want of cause.[8] The warrant of commitment is sufficient if the *corpus delicti* be shown. It need not have the precision of an indictment, nor is it necessary to state in it that the act was feloniously committed.[9] But it ought to specify the species of felony: "as for felony of the death of J. S., or for burglary in breaking the house of J. S."[10] The charge that the prisoner "passed a counterfeit note, knowing it to be such," sufficiently sets forth an offense.[11] In California a commitment by a justice of the

---

[1] Beekman v. Traver, 20 Wend. 67; Smith v. Randall, 3 Hill (N.Y.), 495.
[2] State v. Worley, 11 Ired. 242.
[3] King v. Kendal & Roe, 1 Salk. 346.
[4] Rex v. Wyndham, 1 Stra. 3. This case was distinguished from King v. Kendal, 1 Salk. 346; see 3 Vin. Abr. 513.
[5] King v. Despard, 7 T. R. 736. A collection of many precedents will be found in this case. See generally, on this section, 2 Hawk. P. C., c. 16, sec. 16; Ex parte Bollman and Swartwout, 4 Cranch. 75; United States v. Aaron Burr, 4 Cranch, App., 470-507; S. C., Marshall on the Federal Constitution, 53.
[6] 1 Bish. Crim. Proc., 3d ed., sec. 228.
[7] Bac. Abr., Com., E; 2 Hale P. C. 122; 2 Hawk. P. C., c. 16, sec. 16; Ex parte Burford, 3 Cranch, 448.
[8] Boucher's Case, Cro. Jac. 81.
[9] 1 Ch. Crim. L. 113; Rex v. Croker, 2 Chit., Q. B., 138; State v. Everett and State v. Potter, 1 Dudley (S. C.), 295; State v. Killet, 2 Bailey, 289.
[10] King v. Wilkes, 2 Wils. 158; 1 Ch. Crim. L. 111; 2 Hale P. C. 122; State v. Everett and State v. Potter, 1 Dudley (S. C.), 295; State v. Killet, 2 Bailey, 289.
[11] State v. Killet, 2 Bailey, 289; see, in connection with this, State v. Munson, Hurd on Habeas Corpus, 2d ed., 385, citing 2 Hall's Jour. Jur. 257.

peace holding a party to appear before a grand jury to answer upon a charge of murder must state the name of the person alleged to have been murdered. But the omission of such name will not entitle the prisoner to his discharge on habeas corpus.[1] If a statement of facts constituting the offense be made, though it is not a statement of the offense as described in the legislative act, habeas corpus can not relieve.[2] A debtor was committed in Pennsylvania for fraud in making a contract. The commitment was held sufficient on habeas corpus that recited the allegations of the affidavit, the arrest and hearing of the parties; and set forth that, after hearing, the judge was satisfied that the demand of the plaintiff was on contract, and that the allegations were substantiated, "in that the said defendant had assigned and disposed of his property with the intent to defraud his creditors, and that he fraudulently contracted the debt respecting which the suit was brought."[3]

A warrant setting out the character in which the prisoner is committed in the disjunctive is not good.[4] A warrant need not set forth the authority under which it is granted.[5] A commitment for embezzlement is sufficient if it shows a sufficient offense to warrant the commitment, though it does not state the act to have been done feloniously, or with the precision of an indictment.[6] A warrant of commitment without any date is bad.[7] A warrant of commitment is not evidence of the facts which it recites.[8] A warrant of commitment stated that "H. B., in a certain affidavit, made and sworn to by him before C. C., a competent authority by law to administer the same, did falsely, wickedly, willfully, and corruptly commit willful and corrupt perjury." This was held bad, because it did not state that the perjury was committed in the course of a judicial proceeding.[9] In California a notary public has jurisdiction to administer an oath to the party acknowledging the execution of a deed for the purpose of identifying him. This is a judicial act; and as the testimony of the petitioner given on oath was material to the proceeding and shown to be false, there was, the supreme court said, probable cause for holding him to answer upon the charge of perjury, and they dismissed the habeas corpus.[10]

---

[1] Ex parte Bull, 42 Cal. 196.
[2] In re Perham, 5 Hurl. & N. 30.
[3] Gosline v. Place, 32 Pa. St. 520.
[4] Rex v. Evered, Cald. 26.
[5] Rex v. Goodall, 1 Ld. Ken. 122.
[6] Rex v. Croker, 2 Chit., Q. B., 138. As to the last phrase, see Rex v. Remnant, 2 Leach, 583; S. C., 5 T. R. 169, Nolan, 205; 1 East P. C. 420.
[7] Ex parte Fletcher, 1 Dow. & L. 726; S. C., 8 Jur. 146, 13 L. J., N. S., M. C., 16—Patteson.
[8] Stevens v. Clark, 2 Mbo. & R. 435; S. C., 1 Car. & M. 509—Cresswell.
[9] Reg. v. Bartlett, 7 Jur. 649; S. C., 12 L. J., N. S., M. C., 127—Wightman.
[10] Ex parte Carpenter, 12 Pac. C. L. J. 274.

A commitment issued without any previous examination is erroneous, but the prisoner can not take advantage of it on habeas corpus.[1] While it is not necessary, unless statutory provisions require it, to recite in a warrant of commitment the facts on which the charge is predicated,[2] we apprehend the better practice to be to state the time when the offense was committed, or the place of its commission, and also the name of the person injured. At least, enough particulars should be given to enable a court on the return to a writ of habeas corpus to determine what particular crime is charged against the prisoner.[3] If the commitment be good in substance, it will be sustained on habeas corpus, though it contain more than is necessary to be stated therein. The unnecessary matter will be regarded as surplusage.[4]

§ 282. **Orders and Commitments by Superior Court.**— Chief Justice Holt said: "When a prisoner is in court he may be committed by the court without any process; but if not, process must go."[5] When the prisoner is committed in court to the proper officer there present, there is no warrant of commitment; but the sheriff or other officer is nevertheless obliged to take notice of all commitments in court, and the order in court is his authority.[6] The principle that a court of record may commit without a formal warrant is recognized and followed in this country.[7] A bench warrant and a warrant of commitment, after indictment found, are sufficient, if they recite the fact of indictment and describe the offense generally, though more particularity may be required even by statute before indictment found.[8]

---

[1] Ex parte Ah Bau & Ah You, 10 Nev. 264.

[2] State v. Everett and State v. Potter, Dudley (S. C.), 295; S. C., note to People v. McLeod, 1 Hill (N. Y.), 377.

[3] State v. Bandy, 2 Ga. Dec. 40; In re Beebe, 3 Prac. Rep. (U. C.) 270-273, where it is held that a warrant of commitment which omitted to state the place where the alleged crime was committed was defective. As to cause, see also Ex parte Isbell, 11 Nev. 295; Ex parte Willoughby, 14 Id. 451. As to certainty, see also In the Matter of Martin, 3 Prac. Rep. (U. C.) 298. In California it is said that a commitment for larceny must state what property was stolen, to whom it belonged, its value, and the time when and the place where the offense was committed. And that a commitment for rape must state upon whom the alleged rape was committed, the use of violence—an essential ingredient of the offense—and the time and place where the alleged offense was committed: Ex parte Branigan, 19 Cal. 133.

[4] People v. Smith, 1 Cal. 1.

[5] Anon., Fortes, 242.

[6] Bethell's Case, 1 Salk. 348; Bac. Abr., Habeas Corpus, B, sec. 9.

[7] People ex rel. Johnson v. Nevins, 1 Hill (N. Y.), 154; State v. Heathman, Wright (Ohio), 690.

[8] Brady v. Davis, 9 Ga. 73. In the following language of Justice Nisbet will be found a distinction between a warrant to answer and process: "But these warrants are after presentment or indictment; they stand upon dif-

§ 283. **The Direction and Conclusion.**—The commitment must be directed both to a proper officer and to the keeper of a lawful place of imprisonment, commanding the officer to carry and deliver, and the keeper to receive and safely keep, the body of the accused during the time specified therein, or until he is released by due course of law.[1] But one will not be released on habeas corpus because he was committed to the jailer instead of the sheriff, to whom, in strictness, it ought to be made, for the jailer is an officer known to the law, and his custody is the sheriff's to many purposes.[2] The commitment, however, is not good if not directed to the sheriff, unless the person to whom it is directed is in some way the servant of the sheriff.[3] In a habeas corpus proceeding in Iowa it has been decided that the warrant of commitment, if issued to the sheriff of the county in which the examination is held, will authorize his detention and custody by the sheriff of the next most convenient county having a jail.[4]

§ 284. **Signature and Seal.**—The justice ought to sign the commitment or *mittimus* in his official character. This is ordinarily done, but it is not now absolutely essential to subscribe himself as "justice of the peace,"[5] though at common law the *mittimus* had to be in writing, under the hand and seal of the person by whom it was made, and expressing his office or authority, and the time and place at which it was made.[6] The

---

ferent ground. If the accused, after indictment, is in court or in custody, as soon as convenience admits, he is arraigned and put upon his trial; if not, process must issue to bring him into court. It is so called because it proceeds or issues forth, in order to bring the defendant into court to answer, and signifies the writs or judicial means by which he is brought in; and that proceeding which, before indictment, is called a warrant, is, after the indictment found, called process. Its object is simply to bring the accused into court; and when so brought in, he is retained by bail or commitment. Every court which by law can hear and determine offenses can issue process to bring the accused in to answer."

[1] Rob. Elem. Law, sec. 486, citing 4 Bla. Com. 300; 2 Hale P. C. 122-124; 1 Ch. Crim. L. 107-132; 1 Arch. Crim. Pr. & Pl., Pomeroy's notes, 147 –165; 1 Bish. Crim. Proc., 3d ed., secs. 234-236. The usual conclusion at common law was: "There to remain until he shall be discharged by due course of law:" See 2 Hawk. P. C. 174. But the commitment was not void on account of any irregularity in the conclusion. That would be regarded as mere surplusage, and the remainder would be sustained: 1 Hale P. C. 584. If there be in any case no "due course of law' whereby the accused may have his rights determined, this conclusion would now, no doubt, be irregular, if not void—following the rule in commitments on execution.

[2] Bethell's Case, 1 Salk. 348.
[3] Anon., Fortes. 242.
[4] Cowell v. Patterson, 49 Iowa, 514.
[5] Rex v. Goodall, Sayer, 129; S. C., 1 Ken. 122; 2 Hale P. C. 122, 123; Elderton's Case, 2 Ld. Raym. 978; S. C., 6 Mod. 73; State v. Manley, 1 Overt. 428; Jones v. Timberlake, 6 Rand. 678; see State v. Green, 3 Green (15 N. J.), 88; Ladow v. Groom, 1 Denio, 429.
[6] 2 Hawk. P. C., c. 16, sec. 13; 1 Burns' Justice, 677; 1 Hale P. C. 577; 4 Bla. Com. 290.

official character of the person issuing the warrant may be proved *aliunde*.¹

Where the distinction between sealed and unsealed instruments has been abolished by statute, the warrant of commitment need have no seal; but in the absence of any statutory provision on the subject, the omission of a seal will render the warrant void, and the prisoner detained by virtue of it may be discharged on habeas corpus.² In Canada it was held that a warrant of commitment under the statute of 31 Vic., c. 16, signed by one qualified justice of the peace and by an alderman who had not taken the necessary oath, was invalid to uphold the detention of a prisoner confined under it, though it might be a justification to a person acting under it on an action against him.³

§ 285. **What Face of Warrant should Show.**—Whether the authority to commit should appear in a warrant of commitment is not definitely settled. We have seen that our constitutions and statutes generally⁴ require the charge to be supported by an oath or affirmation before a warrant of arrest can issue. This oath or affirmation would then become essential to the jurisdiction of the magistrate; and where the examining tribunal of the magistrate is deemed inferior, the rule will doubtless require all facts essential to jurisdiction to expressly appear in the proceedings of these courts of inferior jurisdiction. Consequently, where these tribunals are so regarded, the warrant of commitment ought to show on its face that the charge is supported by oath or affirmation.⁵ But in those states where this jurisdiction is not deemed inferior, the warrant of commitment, perhaps, need not show an authority to commit, as the courts will not intend a want of authority in the person who issued the warrant, but, until the contrary appear, will presume that he had an authority. And while it is usual and best to state the authority, if it is not done the justice's authority may be supplied by parol evidence.⁶

---

¹ See cases cited in note 5, p. 363.
² Ex parte Bennett, 2 Cranch C. Ct. 612; Somervell v. Hunt, 3 Har. & McH. 113; State v. Buzine, 4 Harr. (Del.) 572; Lough v. Millard, 2 R. I. 436; State of Maine v. Drake, 36 Me. 366. *Contra:* State v. Vaughn, Harp. 313; Gano v. Hall, 42 N. Y. 67; S. C., 5 Park. Cr. 651.
³ Queen v. Boyle, 4 Prac. Rep. (U. C.) 256.
⁴ *Supra*, sec. 279.
⁵ Ex parte Burford, 3 Cranch, 448; Ex parte Bennett, 2 Cranch C. Ct. 612; Caudle v. Seymour, 41 Eng. Com. L. 825. See Conner v. Commonwealth, 3 Binn. 38; State v. J. H., 1 Tyler, 444.

⁶ Rex v. Goodall, Sayer, 129; Burns' Justice, tit. Com., iv; State v. Manley, 1 Overt. 428, 429; Gurney v. Tufts, 37 Me. 130; Commonwealth v. Murray, 2 Va. Cas. 504; Wyndham's Case, 1 Stra. 3; State v. Staples, 37 Me. 228; 2 Cowen & Hill's Notes to Phill. Ev., notes 292, 293; Crepps v. Durden et al., 1 Sm. L. C., 7th ed., 1095.

PART III.—REVIEW BY HABEAS CORPUS.

§ 286. **The Warrant of Arrest** may be impeached, for any radical defect contained in it, by habeas corpus. But its legality should be thus tested before final judgment; because, conceding the arrest to be illegal, the court obtains full jurisdiction of the person of the defendant after he has pleaded to the merits, and this first process then becomes immaterial.[1] In California it has been held on habeas corpus that it is too late to raise an objection to an affidavit or warrant of arrest, after examination and commitment, particularly where there is probable cause to suppose that a felony has been committed.[2] If the officer issuing the warrant had jurisdiction of the process, and received evidence deemed by him sufficient, this evidence will not be weighed on habeas corpus to determine its sufficiency. If the warrant of commitment is *prima facie* sufficient to justify the imprisonment, and the court finds, on looking beyond the warrant to the affidavit upon which it was issued, that there was at least colorable proof before the officer issuing the warrant of arrest, upon which his discretion might be exercised, it will go no further on habeas corpus; and if this appears the prisoner can not be discharged.[3] Where it is competent for the legislature to provide by law that on a charge of a crime or misdemeanor the process may be by summons instead of arrest, it is necessary that the summons contain a full and direct statement of the offense charged, and specify a time when, a place where, and the tribunal before which he is to appear and answer.[4]

§ 287. **The Warrant of Commitment** may also be examined into on this writ for irregularities. Indeed, it has been said that there is nothing properly before the court upon the return of a habeas corpus, except the warrant on which the relator is imprisoned.[5] On the return to a writ of habeas corpus, issued to inquire into the cause of detention, after commitment by a magistrate, and before indictment, additional proof may be received by the judge for the purpose of enabling him to decide upon the legality of the detention.[6] In California it is held that whether or not the order holding the prisoner to answer on a criminal charge is erroneous, or irregularly entered, can not be considered on habeas corpus proceedings.[7] Defects mentioned in the two preceding parts of this chapter can no

---

[1] Miller v. Rosier, 31 Mich. 475.
[2] People v. Smith, 1 Cal. 1.
[3] In the Matter of Prime, 1 Barb. 340.
[4] Herrick v. Smith, 1 Gray, 50.
[5] In the Matter of Prime, 1 Barb. 340.
[6] People v. Richardson, 4 Park. Cr. 656.
[7] Ex parte Granice, 51 Cal. 375.

doubt be inquired into on this writ; and if they are found to be so defective as to render the process void, the accused will be entitled to his discharge. But as we have elsewhere treated of what may be inquired into on habeas corpus, the reader is referred to other portions of this work for further, more detailed, and specific information on this question.[1]

[1] See chap. 14. See People v. Tompkins, 1 Park. Cr. 224; Wade v. Judge, 5 Ala. 130; Nelson & Graydon v. Cutler & Tyrrell, 3 McLean, 326; Commonwealth v. Murray, 2 Va. Cas. 504; Welch v. Scott, 5 Ired. 72; Geyger v. Stoy, 1 Dall. 146; Com. v. Ward, 4 Mass. 496; State v. Randolph, 26 Mo. 213, where it is said that the committing justice can not approve a recognizance taken by another justice; nor can a justice who does not sit at nor assist in the examination take a recognizance for the appearance of the prisoner.

CHAPTER XXI.
POWER OF COURTS AT THE HEARING.

PART I.—MAY RECOMMIT IF WARRANT IS DEFECTIVE.
- § 288. Practice in the English Courts.
- § 289. Illustrations.
- § 290. Practice in our Courts.
- § 291. Illustrations.

PART II.—MAY DISCHARGE OR LET TO BAIL THOUGH WARRANT IS PERFECT.
- § 292. Practice at Common Law.
- § 293. Practice in the United States.

PART I.—MAY RECOMMIT IF WARRANT IS DEFECTIVE.

§ 288. **Practice in the English Courts.**—The prisoner will not always be absolutely discharged, though the warrant of commitment under which he is held be defective, or even void—if the court is satisfied from the depositions that an offense has been committed. If the warrant is materially defective, the practice is to discharge from the defective commitment, and commit the prisoner *de novo*.[1] The writ of *certiorari* may be awarded to remove the examination and depositions upon which the commitment was founded in the inferior court, to the superior or revisory court, in order that this court may take into consideration the proofs, and either bail, remand, or discharge the prisoner as justice may require.[2] The writ of habeas corpus accompanied by the writ of *certiorari* seems to be in the nature of a writ of error to enable the court of king's bench to determine whether the imprisonment be illegal or not.[3] This court had general, original, and appellate jurisdiction in all criminal matters, and it was through these two writs that they acquired possession of the examination and depositions upon which the commitment was founded.[4] It was often conceded that if the

---

[1] Rex v. Marks, 3 East, 157; Bethell's Case, 1 Salk. 347; Ex parte Krans et al., 1 Barn. & Cress. 258; S. C., 2 Dow. & Ry. 411; 1 Ch. Crim. L. 132.

[2] Ex parte Krans, 2 Dow. & Ry. 411.

[3] Hammond v. Howell, 2 Mod. 219.

[4] Goodright v. Dring, 2 Dow. & Ry. 407; 1 Tidd's Pr., 3d Am. ed. from 9th Eng. ed., 405; King v. Massey, 6 Mau. & Sel. 108; King v. Jones, 1 Barn. & Ald. 209; Mitchell v. Mitcheson, 1 Barn. & Cress. 513; Ex parte Lees, El. Bl. & El. 828; Regina v. The

case stood upon the commitment alone, the prisoner would be entitled to his discharge, but this procedure, by habeas corpus and *certiorari*, was intended to help out a defective commitment, and, however irregular it might be, if the court discovered in the depositions sufficient evidence of any offense to justify the detention of the prisoner and put him upon his trial, he would not be discharged, but remanded in general terms.[1]

But it will be perceived that this left the prisoner free to sue out another writ of habeas corpus upon the same original defective commitment; and in 1802, at the time of the decision in King v. Marks, it occurred to the officers of the crown office to suggest an alteration of the practice in this respect, founded upon the consideration that prisoners thus remanded might renew the same application to another court or judge. So the rule in that case was changed to a discharge from the prisoner's confinement by virtue of the warrant mentioned in the return, and to a recommitment for the offense shown in the informations, etc.[2] But it must be distinctly understood, that if the court granting the habeas corpus does not have the power of a committing magistrate over the offense shown in the depositions, it must discharge the prisoner if the commitment can not be sustained. Thus where the convention act of 6 & 7 Vic., c. 75, vested in certain officers the power to arrest and deliver up fugitives from justice from France, the court of queen's bench refused to look into the depositions referred to by the warrant, and remand the prisoner on their own authority, for they had none of the kind in such a case, although they pronounced the warrant insufficient for the prisoner's detention; so they discharged him.[3]

The warrant by virtue of which a dangerous lunatic is held in custody may be insufficient, but the court will not discharge him as a matter of course, because the order of confinement does not fulfil the requirements of the statute under which the detention is claimed. In such a case, in answer to an argument that the court must necessarily, however inconvenient, allow the lunatic his common-law liberty, Lord Denman replied: "If the court thought that a party unlawfully received or detained was a lunatic, we should be betraying the common duties of mem-

---

Inhabitants of Cartworth, 1 Dow. & L. 837; Regina v. Chaney, 6 Dowl. P. C. 281; Woodcraft v. Kinaston, 2 Atk. 316; In re Boothroyd, 15 Mee. & W. 15; Askew v. Hayton, 1 Dowl. 510; Rex v. Justices etc., Id. 484.

[1] Ex parte Krans, 2 Dow. & Ry. 411; Bethell's Case, 1 Salk. 347; Regina v. Chaney, 6 Dowl. P. C. 281.

[2] King v. Marks et al., 3 East, 157.

[3] Ex parte Bessett, 51 Eng. Com. L. 480. This was an application at common law; the statute of 31 Car. II., c. 2, not being necessary to the right of making it.

bers of society if we directed a discharge. But we have no power to set aside the order, only to discharge. And should we, as judges or individuals, be justified in setting such a party at large? It is answered that there may be a fresh custody. But why so? Is it not better, if she be dangerous, that she should remain in custody till the great seal or the commissioners act? Therefore being satisfied, in my own mind, that there would be danger in setting her at large, I am bound by the most general principles to abstain from so doing; and I should be abusing the name of liberty if I were to take off a restraint for which those who are most interested in the party ought to be most thankful."[1]

The statute of 31 Car. II. prohibited the king's bench from letting to bail when the commitment was for felony or treason plainly expressed in the warrant of commitment; while at common law they could let to bail in such cases; and also examine the grounds of commitment and discharge the prisoner altogether, if it was evident that he had committed no crime; or if the depositions disclosed the fact that he had committed a different crime from the one mentioned in the warrant of commitment, they had the power to remand him for that, or commit him *de novo* for it. The king's bench had unlimited power to bail at common law, and to issue the habeas corpus in all proper cases, and to absolutely discharge. And this was independent of the statute of 31 Car. II. But on a habeas corpus sued out under this statute the prisoner could procure his liberty absolutely where he had not been indicted and tried the second term after his commitment, or where he had been tried and acquitted. In all other cases, he was required to be remanded or let to bail. That the king's bench, in the exercise of its common-law jurisdiction, as the court of supreme criminal judicature, had more comprehensive powers under the writ of habeas corpus than were conferred by the act of 31 Car. II. on the officers named in it, is apparent.[2]

§ 289. **Illustrations** of the general rule will be found in the case of The King v. Judd,[3] where it did not sufficiently appear to the court, from the commitment, that a felony had been committed. The court, however, were satisfied from the depositions that some offense had been committed by the prisoner, and they refused to discharge him, but admitted him to bail. In Rex v.

---

[1] In the Matter of Shuttleworth, 9 Ad. & El., Q. B., 651.
[2] See *ante*, sec. 58; Rex v. Marks, 3
East, 157; King v. Judd, 2 T. R. 255; Bethell's Case, 1 Salk. 347.
[3] 2 T. R. 255.

Hab. Cor.—24

Marks[1] will be found another where the prisoner was recommitted for an offense disclosed by the depositions, having been discharged from the defective commitment. In this case two of the justices expressed themselves as follows:

Grose, J.: "There is no doubt of the power of this court [king's bench] to bail, if they see occasion, in all cases of felony, even in case of murder, though there should be no doubt as to the validity of the warrant of commitment. On the other hand, there is as little doubt as to their power of remanding, notwithstanding the warrant of commitment be defective; and it is the constant practice of this court to remand prisoners in such cases, if it appear on reading the depositions that there is a fair ground to authorize them."

Le Blanc, J.: "This court have clearly a right to bail the parties accused in all cases of felony, if they see occasion, wherever there is any doubt either on the law or the fact of the case. And it is equally clear that though the warrant of commitment be informal, yet if upon the depositions returned the court see that a felony has been committed, and that there is a reasonable ground of charge against the prisoners, they will not bail but remand them. The same rule applies with respect both to the law and the fact: unless we see reason to doubt the truth of the fact charged, the prisoners must be remanded; and the same consequence follows, unless we see reason to doubt whether the fact charged constitutes any offense within the law."[2]

§ 290. **The Practice in our Courts** has conformed to that in Rex v. Marks, cited in the two preceding sections. In some

---

[1] 3 East, 157.

[2] In the Matter of Parker et al., the English court of exchequer said they were bound to look at the substance of the return; and if it contained sufficient matter in substance to show that the prisoners were lawfully detained they could not discharge them upon habeas corpus, though the return should in some respects be informal, or should go into matter not essential to the question. They declined to decide the questions involving the validity of the commitment, and remanded the prisoners for the reasons given below. The prisoners had been indicted in Lower Canada for treason, and under a statute of that province had applied for and received pardon upon the condition of transportation to Van Dieman's Land for fourteen years. In the execution of this condition the officers were proceeding to the point of destination with the prisoners, and had stopped with them in Liverpool. While means were there being prepared to transport the prisoners to Van Dieman's Land, they were delivered to the jailer of that city for safe keeping.

"This," said the court, "is the substance of the return, against which many ingenious objections have been urged, the principal of which seem to be, that the legislature of Upper Canada had no authority to make any such law; that if they had, it could be binding only within the precincts of that province; that it could communicate no authority to any person out of that province, and therefore could give none to the jailer of Liverpool; that even if it could have that effect, the pardon granted under that law being conditional, it was not competent to the prisoner to accept a pardon whereby he submitted himself to

§ 290.   POWER OF COURTS AT THE HEARING.   371

of the states the testimony of witnesses in criminal examinations is not reduced to writing; and when a superior court is passing upon the validity of a warrant of commitment upon a proceeding by habeas corpus the prisoner must be either remanded or discharged, as the court shall determine the sufficiency or insufficiency of the warrant upon its face. But even here the helping hand of the statute may intervene and give the court power to proceed and hear the case *de novo* when the warrant of commitment is fatally defective. In these states there are strong reasons why the commitment should show the facts constituting the offense, as there are no depositions to show upon what evidence the commitment is founded; because everything conducive to a full and fair hearing should be before the court, in order that it may determine whether the imprisonment is unlawful or not. Otherwise the powers of the court may be seriously restrained. The general rule is, that an invalid warrant will jus-

imprisonment or transportation; or that if it were competent for him to accept a pardon with such a condition, he has still a right to retract his consent, and to be set free from the obligation imposed upon him by the condition.

"All these topics have been elaborately argued on both sides, and have received due attention from the court; but in the view which we take of the case, we do not think it necessary to pronounce any opinion upon them. If the condition upon which alone the pardon was granted be void, the pardon must also be void. If the condition were lawful, but the prisoner did not assent to it nor submit to be transported, he can not have the benefit of the pardon; or if, having assented to it, his assent be revocable, we must consider him to have retracted it by this application to be set at liberty, in which case he is equally unable to avail himself of the pardon. Looking then at the return, the position of the prisoner appears to be this: that he has been indicted for high treason committed in Canada against her majesty; that he has confessed himself guilty of that treason; that he is liable to be tried for it in England; that he can not plead the pardon which he has renounced; and that he is now in the custody of the jailer of Liverpool, under such circumstances as would justify any subject of the crown of England in taking and detaining him in custody until he be dealt with according to law. Any subject who held him in custody, with a knowledge of the circumstances, would be guilty of a crime in aiding and assisting his escape, if he be permitted to go at large without lawful authority. How, then, can we order the jailer of Liverpool, or any other person who has him in custody, with knowledge of these circumstances, to let him go at large?

"If the prisoner can not be lawfully transported under his present circumstances, it is to be presumed that the government, upon being so certified, will take proper measures for prosecuting him, for the crime of treason, in England. For these reasons we are of opinion that the prisoner must be remanded:" See Case of the Canadian Prisoners, 5 Mee. & W. 31.

The queen's bench had previously remanded some of the prisoners, because while the warrant of commitment, as set forth in the return, was not minutely correct, it was substantially good: See Case of Leonard Watson et al., 9 Ad. & El. 731; S. C., Queen v. Batcheldor, 1 Per. & Dav. 516; S. C., Watson et al., 36 Eng. Com. L. 254. It will be seen, on inspection of these cases, that nothing turned on the point of a defective warrant of commitment. Had the warrant been adjudged materially defective, we have no right to presume that the practice in Rex v. Marks, cited *supra*, would not have been followed: See Queen v. Mount, 12 Eng. Rep., Moak's notes, 181.

tify the discharge of the prisoner, but this rule is not inflexible, even where there is no statute to direct the action of the court or judge under the writ of habeas corpus.

It is believed, however, that in a majority of the states some provision is made to have the evidence upon which the committing magistrate acted certified up, or otherwise properly presented to the court or officer hearing the habeas corpus.

Under this state of law, then, the rule is that if the commitment is found to be informal or insufficient, upon the hearing of the writ, the court will discharge the prisoner from that commitment, and recommit him in proper form, if there be sufficient cause.[1] The prisoner may be guilty of a different crime from that specified in the warrant. If so, it is the duty of the court to commit him for trial for the offense of which he appears to be guilty.[2] In California, upon a hearing on habeas corpus, if the offense be so defectively set forth in the warrant of commitment that the party can not be held under it, and it appears from the papers that he should not be discharged, the court will hold him for examination, and cause the witnesses to be subpœnaed for such purpose.[3] Same rule in Indiana.[4] With reference to a second commitment by a justice of the peace, Mr. Justice Field, when on the supreme bench of California, said: "There is no doubt that where an examination has been had by a magistrate, and a commitment has been issued by him which is defective in form or substance, a second commitment, omitting or correcting the defects of the first, may be issued, provided there be any order, or judgment, or entry of the magistrate, made at the conclusion of the examination, to which reference can be had to guide him in the matter. He can not resort merely to his own recollection for the facts of the case. The statute contemplates that his order, either of discharge or com-

---

[1] Ex parte Bennett, 2 Cranch C. Ct. 612; In the Matter of Percy, 2 Daly, 530; People v. Smith, 1 Cal. 1; Ex parte Branigan, 19 Id. 133; State v. Best et al., 7 Blackf. 611; Ex parte Ricord, 11 Nev. 287; Ex parte Burford, 3 Cranch, 448; Ex parte Harfourd, 16 Fla. 283; S. C., 13 Am. Law Rev. 543; In re Smith, 4 Col. 532; In re Balcom, 12 Neb. 316; Commonwealth ex rel. Chew v. Carlisle, Bright. 36; United States v. Johns, 4 Dall. 382; S. C., 1 Wash. 363; Commonwealth v. Crans, 2 Penn. L. J. 75; Ex parte Mason, 8 Mich. 70; Ex parte Tayloe, 5 Cow. 39; Ex parte Smith, Id. 273, where one was committed by a state magistrate for further examination touching a crime against the United States; Rust v. Van Vacter, 9 W. Va. 600; State v. Bloom, 17 Wis. 521; People v. Rhoner, 4 Park. Cr. 166; Wyeth v. Richardson, 10 Gray, 240, where it was decided that exceptions do not lie to the discharge of a prisoner on habeas corpus by a single judge; and see Kelley v. Thomas, 15 Gray, 192; Nicholls v. The State, 5 N. J. L. 539; Peter v. The State, 3 How. (Miss.) 433; 1 Bish. Crim. Proc. 3d ed., sec. 229.

[2] People v. Smith, 1 Cal. 1.

[3] Ex parte Branigan, 19 Cal. 133.

[4] State v. Best et al., 7 Blackf. 611.

§ 291.   POWER OF COURTS AT THE HEARING.   373

mittal, made upon the completion of the examination, shall be reduced to writing."¹

The court, sitting as a court, possesses the power to commit one charged with an offense. On this point we have the following opinion of Chief Justice Marshall: "It is believed to be a correct position that the power to commit for offenses of which it has cognizance is exercised by every court of criminal jurisdiction, and that courts as well as individual magistrates are conservators of the peace. Were it otherwise, the consequence would only be that it would become the duty of the judge to descend from the bench, and in his character as an individual magistrate to do that which the court is asked to do."² This principle was acted upon in a late case in the state of Nevada, where the supreme court were clearly of opinion that if they found the prisoner guilty of another offense than that stated in the warrant of commitment, they had, under the habeas corpus act, power to issue a new commitment.³ If the court or judge does not order a recommitment on his own motion, after the warrant of commitment has been adjudged void on habeas corpus, the prosecutor should make a motion for a new commitment, if one is sought, because the papers on which the first warrant is founded are *functus officio*.⁴

§ 291. **Illustrations.**—In Colorado, where an indictment contained two counts, and a *nolle prosequi* was entered as to one, and the other quashed, the indictment, as such, was held to be *functus officio*, and although the petitioner could no longer be called upon to plead to it as an indictment, it nevertheless remained as a sworn accusation against the petitioner, affording *prima facie* evidence of probable guilt, upon which the district court was warranted in remanding him to answer a new indictment formally drawn and more specifically describing the particular crimes charged. "Even where the prisoner is acquitted," said the court, "for a flaw in the indictment, he may be remanded to be tried at the next term on a new indictment.⁵ In the case of Gorden v. The State, 35 Ala. 432, the court says: 'Independent of statute, the circuit courts possess the undoubted power, where the judgment in a criminal case is arrested, and a *nolle prosequi* is entered by the state, to bind the defendant over to appear at the circuit court of the proper county to answer a new indictment for the same

¹ Ex parte Branigan, 19 Cal. 133.   ² 1 Burr's Trial, 79.
³ Ex parte Ricord, 11 Nev. 287.
⁴ People ex rel. Walters v. Conner, 15 Abb. Pr., N. S., 430.
⁵ Citing United States v. Smith, 2 Cranch C. Ct. 111.

offense.'[1] Bishop, in the first volume of his Criminal Procedure,[2] says: 'If an indictment is pronounced bad, the judge is not necessarily obliged to let the defendant go; but he may commit him, or hold him to bail to answer to a fresh indictment, or he may order the officer to take the prisoner before a justice of the peace to be proceeded against on fresh complaint.'"[3]

In California, where the defendant was committed on fatally defective warrants of commitment for rape and grand larceny, and it being evident that he should not be absolutely discharged, he was held for examination.[4] Where the prisoner is held under a warrant for embezzlement, and upon further testimony heard on habeas corpus, a district judge commits him for obtaining money under false pretenses, the order of the judge does not, *ipso facto*, discharge the petitioner from further custody under the warrant for embezzlement; and he may be discharged on habeas corpus by another from the warrant for obtaining money on false pretenses, and remanded upon the warrant for embezzlement.[5] If a party is brought before a circuit court of one county on habeas corpus to be discharged from illegal arrest, and it appears the imputed offense was committed in another county, he may be recognized to appear before the court having jurisdiction of the offense.[6]

A warrant of commitment is irregular in not stating or showing on its face that the justice issuing it had determined that there was probable cause to believe the prisoner guilty of the offense with which he stood charged.[7] This is all that another court examining the depositions or evidence before the committing magistrate will inquire into on habeas corpus, for the purpose of determining whether an offense has been committed.[8] In a Pennsylvania *nisi prius* court it has been ruled that unless it clearly appears that a prisoner brought up on habeas corpus is entirely innocent, the judge is bound to bail or remand. "But," in the language of Justice Gibson, "difficulty or hesitation as to the law, arising upon facts indisputably established, is not that kind of doubt of guilt which justifies in refusing to discharge, where the mind inclines, after full consideration, to pronounce in favor of innocence. It holds only as to doubt of the truth of the facts in evidence, with respect to which the

---

[1] Citing Nicholls v. The State, 5 N. J. L. 539; Peter v. The State, 3 How. (Miss.) 433.
[2] Sec. 229, 3d ed.
[3] In re Smith, 1 Cal. 1.
[4] Ex parte Branigan, 19 Cal. 133.
[5] Ex parte Ricord, 11 Nev. 287.
[6] Parrish v. The State, 14 Md. 238.
[7] People v. Rhoner, 4 Park. Cr. 166.
[8] United States v. Johns, 4 Dall. 382; S. C., 1 Wash. 363.

commonwealth as well as the prisoner has a right to go before a grand jury, who are the constitutional judges in that particular; but as to refusing to decide necessary questions of law, I have no discretion."[1]

PART II.—MAY DISCHARGE OR LET TO BAIL THOUGH WARRANT BE PERFECT.

§ 292. **Practice at Common Law.**—We have already treated of the incontrovertibility of the return at common law, and shown that the general rule was that neither at common law nor under the habeas corpus act of 31 Car. II. could it be controverted with a view to the absolute discharge of the prisoner.[2] With a view to bail, however, extrinsic evidence was sometimes received; sometimes rejected.[3] So when the courts were looking at a warrant of commitment to see what disposition they would make of the prisoner, they examined only the depositions taken before the committing magistrate. In one instance, where a felony was positively charged, they refused to bail, although eight affidavits of credible persons, proving the relator to be at another place at the time of the robbery, were read.[4] This, it will be seen, would have been controverting the truth of the return, which was not allowable. In another instance the court refused to examine a man brought before them, by admitting extrinsic evidence, to see whether he had been previously acquitted of a charge precisely similar.[5] Again, the defendant was charged with receiving stolen goods, knowing that they were stolen. His affidavit that he did not know they were stolen was rejected.[6] In the two latter cases the reason for rejecting the extrinsic evidence must have been the same as in the case of Rex v. Greenwood.

But the court may act upon the evidence before them, as shown by the depositions and proceedings before the committing magistrate; and even though the commitment be regular, the court will examine the proceedings, and if the evidence appear altogether insufficient, will admit to bail; for the court will rather look to the depositions which contain the evidence than to the commitment, in which the justice may have come to a false conclusion.[7]

[1] Commonwealth v. Carlisle, Bright. 36. Other cases: Commonwealth v. Hickey, 2 Pars. Sel. Cas. 317; Com. v. Crans, 3 Penn. L. J. 459; State v. Buzine, 4 Harr. (Del.) 575, cited by Hurd, 2d ed., on pp. 418–420.
[2] See "Return," sec. 166.
[3] 2 Hawk. P. C., c. 15, sec. 79; 1 Ch. Crim. L. 130.
[4] Rex v. Greenwood, 2 Stra. 1138.
[5] 1 Ch. Crim. L. 129.
[6] Id.
[7] 1 Ch. Crim. L. 129; King v. Marks, 3 East, 163.

§ 293. **The Practice in the United States** is to absolutely discharge the prisoner in those states where the inquiry is not limited to the commitment, and where a full hearing is had upon the facts of the case, if the evidence is insufficient to sustain any charge against the prisoner. When the court or judge thus summarily determines the facts of the case, by hearing testimony, arguments, etc., it is, said Chief Justice Marshall, "unimportant whether the commitment is regular or irregular in point of form; and the court having gone into an examination of the evidence on which the commitment is grounded, they will proceed to do that which the court below ought to have done."[1] But of course in those states where the return can not be controverted, no evidence extraneous to the depositions and informations taken by the magistrate ought to be admitted to controvert the facts contained in those depositions, or the charge exhibited in the warrant of commitment; because to allow this to be done would be to allow the return to be controverted in opposition to the doctrine of the common law.[2] In California, if a party who has been held to answer upon a criminal charge is not indicted by the grand jury at the term of court next after his commitment, he is entitled to be discharged, unless good cause be shown for his further detention.[3] In New York, if a judge, upon a habeas corpus, decides that the prisoner committed to jail under any process is not entitled to a discharge, he must remand him to the custody whence he was taken; he has no power to declare the prisoner entitled to the liberties of the jail, and has no power to remand him conditionally; as, "that he be remanded, etc., unless he give good and sufficient bail, to be approved by the sheriff, for the liberties of the jail."[4]

---

[1] Ex parte Bollman & Swartwout, 4 Cranch, 75; Ex parte Bennett, 2 Cranch C. Ct. 612; U. S. R. S., sec. 761; Cal. Penal Code, sec. 1489; 2 Fay's Dig., tit. Habeas Corpus and Certiorari, sec. 19 (2 R. S., sec. 39, p. 469); Code of Ala. 1876, sec. 4957; 1 Paschal's Dig., art. 2624, p. 488.

[2] State v. Asselin, T. U. P. Charlt. 184, citing King v. Horner, Leach, 270; Rex v. Greenwood, 2 Stra. 1138.

[3] Ex parte Bull, 42 Cal. 196.

[4] People v. Cowles, 4 Keyes, 38.

CHAPTER XXII.

ASSAILING JUDGMENTS OF SUMMARY CONVICTIONS BY HABEAS CORPUS.

§ 294. Definition and History.
§ 295. Constitutionality of These Statutes.
§ 296. How These Statutes are to be Construed.
§ 297. Errors, Irregularity, and Jurisdiction.
§ 298. Statement of Proceedings on Face of Commitment.
§ 299. Conviction without Authority of Law.
§ 300. Security to Keep the Peace.
§ 301. Commitment of Seaman.
§ 302. Commitment of Sheriff.
§ 303. Cumulative and Erroneous Sentences.
§ 304. Custody of Children.
§ 305. Commitment of Witness.

§ 294. **Definition and History.**—The judgments of justices of the peace upon offenders for minor and statutory police offenses are called summary convictions. There is no intervention of a jury, and as Mr. Justice Blackstone says, "the party is acquitted or condemned by the suffrage of such person only as the statute has appointed for his judge." Such offenses as common swearing, drunkenness, vagrancy, idleness, and a vast number of others that will be found enumerated in various statutes, come within this summary jurisdiction conferred upon these officers. In England the various offenses falling under the heads of idle, vagrant, and disorderly persons, and made subject to this summary jurisdiction, are defined and classified, and the punishments prescribed by the following statutes.[1] The punishment prescribed in those acts is imprison-

[1] 5 Geo. IV., c. 83, as amended by the statutes of 1 & 2 Vict., c. 38, 31 & 32 Vict., c. 52, and 32 & 33 Vict., 99—analyzed in 2 Broom & Hadley's Com. 467; an act to facilitate the performance of the duties of justices of the peace of sessions within England and Wales with respect to summary convictions and orders, enacted in 1848: 11 & 12 Vict. 241, c. 43—containing various schedules of forms of summonses, warrants, recognizances, commitments, convictions, etc.; and an act to amend the law relating to the summary jurisdiction of magistrates, enacted in 1879; 42 & 43 Vict. 236, c. 49, cited as the summary jurisdiction act of 1879, containing schedules of indictable offenses which can be dealt with summarily under this act, and of the extent of repeal.

ment and hard labor. This is not a new innovation on the jurisprudence of England. Notwithstanding the provision in the magna charta of King John,[1] and in that of 9 Hen. III., c. 29, which declares that no freeman shall be taken, imprisoned, or condemned, "but by lawful judgment of his peers, or by the law of the land," it has been the constant course of legislation in that kingdom for centuries past to confer summary jurisdiction upon justices of the peace for the trial and conviction of parties for minor and statutory police offenses; and this jurisdiction has been largely increased and extended in modern times, as will be seen by referring to the following works.[2] Workhouses and houses of correction, principally occupied by parties convicted by justices of the peace, have been maintained, certainly from the days of Queen Elizabeth to the present, as parts of the police system of that country; and both the jurisdiction and the means of punishment are deemed essential to the good government and well-being of society there; and it is not less so here. Such establishments have been maintained for the same purpose in some states of the American Union. This summary jurisdiction, however, is a creature of statutory birth entirely, and is unknown to the common law of England.[3]

§ 295. **Constitutionality of These Statutes.**—It appears that in England these statutes under which powers of summary conviction were given to justices of the peace, have never been supposed to be in violation of any right of the subject; at least, we have found no cases intimating such a doctrine. In this country the question has been raised, and so far as we have examined the matter, they have been expressly held to be constitutional. The declaration in the various constitutions, and declarations of rights that a party is entitled to a speedy trial by an impartial jury, is understood to refer to such crimes and accusations as have, by the regular course of the law and the established modes of procedure, been the subject of jury trial,

---

[1] Art. 35.
[2] Burns' Justice, title Conviction; Bac. Abr., title Justice of Peace; English summary jurisdiction act of 1879, and the other English statutes cited *supra;* and various statutory enactments of the states of the American Union.
[3] For citation of authorities showing in what states justices of the peace have summary jurisdiction to try persons for assaults and batteries, where they have power to try persons charged with petit larcenies, and where they may commit vagabonds, disorderly persons, tramps, vagrants, disorderly persons for default of sureties, professional thieves, etc., the reader is referred to the full and elaborate brief filed by Charles J. M. Gwinn, attorney general for the state of Maryland, in the case of State v. Glenn, 54 Md. 572.

§ 296.   JUDGMENTS OF SUMMARY CONVICTIONS.   379

and does not embrace every species of accusation involving either criminal or penal consequences.[1] "If the state has no power to provide by law for the summary trial and conviction of vagrant and disorderly persons by justices of the peace, it would clearly follow that no such power could be granted to be exercised under charters or ordinances of municipal corporations; and the consequence would be that, for the violation of all mere police ordinances, prescribing penalties for their infraction, it would be the right of the party accused to insist upon indictment and trial by a jury. Such a mode of proceeding, if it were practicable, has never been contended for, nor could such contention be maintained for a moment."[2] It is regarded as but a part of the police, as contradistinguished from the regular judiciary, powers of the state—a distinction which has from time immemorial been observed between the two, both in England and in the United States.[3] In New York it is said they are rather of the nature of public regulations to prevent crime and public charges and burdens, than of the nature of ordinary criminal laws prohibiting and punishing an act or acts as a crime or crimes.[4]

§ 296. **How These Statutes are to be Construed.**—One would naturally suppose, from reading the language concerning the general nature and requisites of summary convictions as stated by Burns in his "Burns' Justice,"[5] and by the circuit judge of New York in the case of The People v. Phillips,[6] with fifty or more authorities, that it would be next to impossible for an unlettered or unlearned justice of the peace to make a valid commitment. In fact, both in England and America these statutes authorizing summary conviction were looked upon as be-

---

[1] It is provided by the seventeenth section of chapter 49 of the English summary jurisdiction act of 1879, that a person when charged before a court of summary jurisdiction with an offense, in respect of the commission of which an offender is liable on summary conviction to be imprisoned for a term exceeding three months, and which is not an assault, may, on appearing before the court, and before the charge is gone into but not afterwards, claim to be tried by a jury. If the prisoner does not make this claim, the offense will be tried summarily: See 42 & 43 Vict. 242.

[2] Justice Alvey, of the court of appeals, in State v. Glenn, 54 Md. 572; see also People v. McCarthy, 45 How. Pr. 97; People v. Warner, Id.

97; Duffy v. People, 6 Hill (N. Y.), 75; People v. Phillips, 1 Park. Cr. 95; State v. Maxcy, 1 McMull. 501; Byers and Davis v. Commonwealth, 42 Pa. St. 89; Beers v. Beers, 4 Conn. 535; Murphy v. The People, 2 Cow. 815, where they are held not to be contrary to any provision in the constitution of the United States or of the state of New York; Tims v. The State, 26 Ala. 165; State v. Conlin, 27 Vt. 318; McGear v. Woodruff, 33 N. J. L. 213; Wharton's Cr. Pl. & Pr., 8th ed., 1880, sec. 80.

[3] Shafer and Wife v. Mumma, 17 Md. 331.

[4] People v. Forbes, 4 Park. Cr. 611.

[5] Title, Conviction, vol. 1, p. 729.

[6] 1 Park. Cr. 95.

ing in derogation of the common law, and formerly great strictness was exercised, not only in construing the law, but in canvassing the proceedings. In speaking of the former and present rules of the construction of summary proceedings before justices of the peace, and how the superior courts were formerly inclined to be astute in discovering defects in convictions by justices of the peace, in the exercise of this summary jurisdiction, Mr. Chitty says: "But these absurdities, the indulgence of which might induce a suspicion that the superior courts were formerly jealous of those inferior jurisdictions, have for some time been abandoned; and now the doctrine is, that whether it was expedient that those jurisdictions should have been erected, was a matter for the consideration of the legislature; but that as long as they exist, the courts ought to go all reasonable lengths to support the decisions of the justices, especially as in whatever light they were formerly seen, the country are now convinced that in general they derive considerable advantage from the exercise of the powers delegated to justices, and therefore in modern times they have received proper support from the courts of law;[1] and for the same reason the courts hold that although in drawing up convictions magistrates can not set all forms at naught;[2] yet, on the other hand, they ought not to be entangled in greater forms or ceremonies than the superior courts;[3] and in one of the latest decisions upon the subject it was established that the same, and not a stricter, rule of evidence is to be observed before justices as in the superior courts."[4] While these statutes are in themselves strictly construed,[5] whatever may have been the former doctrine of construction as applied to commitments in execution by magistrates or tribunals of special and limited jurisdiction, the doctrine seems now to be perfectly well established that the construction of such commitments must be liberal in support of

---

[1] Citing Justice Ashhurst in Rex v. Thompson, 2 T. R. 18.

[2] This summary jurisdiction was regarded with such disfavor by the courts, and the body of rules established by judicial decision became so cumbersome and severe, that the legislature, both of England and America, deemed it expedient to prescribe forms of conviction that the duties of magistrates in such proceedings should be clearly defined by positive enactment. The later English statutes on this subject are 11 & 12 Vict., c. 43; 31 & 32 Vict., c. 52; 32 & 33 Vict., c. 99; and 42 & 43 Vict., c. 49. And since the decision in People v. Phillips, cited *supra*, the legislature of New York have authorized a more general form of record by the act of April 12, 1853: Sess. Laws of 1853, p. 353.

[3] Citing Lord Kenyon in Rex v. Swallow, 8 T. R. 284.

[4] Citing Rex v. Turner, 5 Mau. & Sel. 206. See 2 Chit. G. P. 130, 131; Rex v. Thompson, 2 T. R. 18.

[5] People v. Forbes, 4 Park. Cr. 611; People v. Phillips, 1 Id. 95.

the lawfulness of the exercise of the jurisdiction, when considered on returns to the writ of habeas corpus.[1]

§ 297. **Errors, Irregularity, and Jurisdiction.** — Mere error or irregularity in these judgments can not be reviewed, any more than in other judgments. The writ of habeas corpus is not for such a purpose. Any objections in error, it has been said in England, appearing upon the face of the return will not be reviewed on habeas corpus if it is found that a sentence has been pronounced by a court of competent jurisdiction to inquire into the offense and with power to inflict such a punishment. All else will be presumed *omnia rite acta*.[2] In the United States, where it is generally competent for the prisoner to controvert the facts stated in the return to the writ of habeas corpus, "he may," says Mr. Justice Alvey, of the court of appeals of Maryland, "if he can, show that there has been no conviction in fact, or that it is simply void for the want of jurisdiction in the magistrate to make it; but if he desires to go behind the conviction recited in the warrant of commitment to question the regularity of the proceedings upon which the conviction is founded, or to impeach the conviction itself for errors therein, other than the want of jurisdiction in the premises, he should bring up the record of conviction by *certiorari* for examination on the return of the habeas corpus.[3] But where the justice has jurisdiction of the offense, with the power to try, convict, and commit therefor, and the commitment recites the conviction, the conviction will be presumed lawful until the contrary is shown. Upon no other principle could proceedings of this character be made effectual. As a general proposition, therefore, in such cases, mere errors or irregularities, if there be any, committed by the justice within the sphere of his jurisdiction, can not be inquired into collaterally on habeas corpus.[4] The writ of habeas corpus can not be made, unless it be by express statute, to perform the functions of a writ of error, in bringing under review a judgment or sentence of a competent tribunal, simply for errors or irregularities in the proceedings or in the rendition of the judgment or sentence; that must be done by some more direct and appropriate proceeding.[5] An imprisonment under a sentence by a court or magistrate of competent jurisdiction is not unlawful, unless the sentence, for some cause to be made apparent, be not merely

---

[1] State v. Glenn, 54 Md. 572 (1880).
[2] King v. Suddis, 1 East, 306.
[3] Justice Alvey, in State v. Glenn, 54 Md. 572.
[4] See People v. Gray, 4 Park. Cr. 616.
[5] Bell v. The State, 4 Gill, 301, 305; Rex v. Suddis, 1 East, 306; Ex parte Watkins, 3 Pet. 193; Ex parte Reed, 100 U. S. 13, 23.

erroneous, but an absolute nullity; though if it be shown to be such nullity, the party is entitled to his immediate discharge."[1]

§ 298. **Statement of Proceedings on Face of Commitment.**—Where a prisoner was committed by a justice of the peace under a warrant of execution, which recited that he had been convicted, etc., upon return to a writ of habeas corpus, it was objected that the warrant of commitment did not state on its face all the proceedings prescribed by the statute; to which Chief Justice Abbott, speaking for the court, replied: "We are bound to presume, until the contrary is shown, that there has been a good conviction, and that the magistrate has done everything required of him by law;" and in the conclusion of the opinion he said: "As we are bound to presume that there was a good conviction before commitment, I think we ought not to discharge the defendant." The distinction was made in this case between the record of conviction and the warrant of commitment, and the chief justice acknowledged his difficulty in subjecting the warrant of commitment to the same rules of construction applicable to convictions. "This," said he, "is a commitment in execution, and recites that the party has been convicted, and there is no distinction in the cases cited which authorizes us to look at the warrant of commitment with the same strictness of a conviction. The commitment is for two months unless the money shall be sooner paid. I think it is not necessary that the commitment should state to whom it should be paid. If the defendant pays the money over to the jailer, he will be discharged forthwith. It is not suggested that the magistrate did not direct to whom the money was to be paid before the conviction took place."[2] The commitment will be considered a true recital of the conviction, although the commitment may be defective, unless the conviction be removed either by appeal or *certiorari* for the inspection of the court exercising a supervisory revision.[3]

---

[1] Bell v. The State, 4 Gill, 305; Ex parte Watkins, 3 Pet. 193; Ex parte Reed, 100 U. S. 23; Com. v. Leckey, 1 Watts, 66, found cited in State v. Glenn, 54 Md. 572.

[2] Rex v. Rogers, 1 Dow. & Ry. 156; Rex v. Taylor, 7 Id. 622; Brenan and Galen's Case, 10 Ad. & El., Q. B., 492. But this distinction is probably of no consequence under the summary jurisdiction act of 1879.

[3] Regina v. Chaney, 6 Dowl. P. C. 281. But the summary jurisdiction act of 1879 provides, in section 33, that "any person aggrieved who desires to question a conviction, order, determination, or other proceeding of a court of summary jurisdiction, on the ground that it is erroneous in point of law, or is in excess of jurisdiction, may apply to the court to state a special case, setting forth the facts of the case and the grounds on which the proceeding is questioned, and if the court decline to state the case, may apply to the high court of justice for an order requiring the case to be stated;" and in section 40, that "a

§ 298.   JUDGMENTS OF SUMMARY CONVICTIONS.   383

In New York it is held that the commitment is sufficient if it follows the record, and when it is not required that the justice should insert in the record the particular grounds on which the charge of vagrancy is based, it can not be necessary to recite them in the commitment. The words defining the particular cause of vagrancy may therefore be regarded as surplusage, and the charge of being a vagrant and being committed therefor is sufficient. All the facts necessary to constitute the offense in summary convictions should be proved, but it is not necessary to recite them all in the commitment.[1] In Maine, complaints need not contain a recital of city by-laws on which they are founded.[2]

writ of *certiorari* or other writ shall not be required for the removal of any conviction, order, or other determination, in relation to which a special case is stated by a court of general or quarter sessions for obtaining the judgment or determination of a superior court:" 42 & 43 Vict. 251, 255. The following decision is purposely omitted from the text and inserted here to illustrate the English statutes just quoted: In the court of queen's bench, in 1875, it was held that section 26 of the prevention of cruelty to animals act—12 & 13 Vict., c. 92—reading, "No conviction under the authority of this act, nor any order, judgment, or proceeding relative thereto, shall be quashed for want of form, or be removed by *certiorari* or otherwise into any of her majesty's superior courts of record," precluded the issuing of a *certiorari* for the purpose of bringing up a case stated by justices in quarter sessions for the opinion of the court. But in speaking of stating the case, Justice Field, for the court, said: "The question whether a case was one of difficulty or not, fit to be reserved for the court, was to be determined by the sessions and not by the parties. But if they found it one of difficulty and stated a case for the opinion of the court, then it became necessary that a *certiorari* should issue to bring that case before the court, that being the only mode by which the order could be brought into the court having jurisdiction to quash or confirm it. But there can be no doubt that a great many orders good and valid, and worthy to have been upheld on the merits, were often quashed for some technical defect in an age in which technical and formal objections prevailed more than they happily do now; and hence it became common to insert in statutes a proviso that orders or convictions under these acts should not be quashed for errors in form or removed by *certiorari*. We think it could hardly be the intention of the legislature that a provision so directed, and properly directed, against objections of a technical and formal character, should extend to include the jurisdiction of the court to entertain any substantial question of law which the justices themselves being desirous of raising, this result being arrived at solely in consequence of an enactment prohibiting the putting in force of the formal machinery necessary for the purpose of bringing up the order from the court below. And if it were *res integra*, we should be much inclined to hold that writs of *certiorari*, issued for the purpose of bringing up a case stated by the sessions, were impliedly excepted from such enactments." The court, however, considered themselves bound by the long-standing judicial construction of the provision in question to hold that they had no power to issue the writ, and made the rule to quash it absolute: See Queen v. Chantrell, 10 L. R., Q. B., 38 Vict. 587.

[1] People v. Gray, 4 Park. Cr. 616; citing People v. Moore, 3 Id. 465; People v. Cavanagh, 2 Id. 660; Byers & Davis v. The Commonwealth, 42 Pa. St. 89; Bennae v. The People, 4 Barb. 31. *Contra:* People v. Forbes, 4 Park. Cr. 611, citing People v. Phillips, 1 Id. 95.

[2] O'Malia v. Wentworth, 65 Me. 130.

§ 299. **Conviction without Authority of Law.**—But the magistrate can not travel out of the statute and declare that to be a crime which is no crime, or disregard the description contained in the statute and classify persons according to his own judgment. Thus in New York it is held, that satisfactory evidence that a female is a common prostitute and idle person will not authorize her conviction as a vagrant under the statute. The statute does not declare common prostitutes as a class, or by name, to be vagrants, nor does it declare all idle persons to be vagrants, but only such idle persons as live without employment and yet have no means to maintain themselves. There was no such common-law offense or crime as vagrancy and idleness, and to commit one for such an offense who does not come within the description of the statute is without authority of law, and void, and the prisoner will be discharged.[1]

§ 300. **Security to Keep the Peace.**—Except as otherwise and further provided by statute, the common-law rule should at least be followed. This provided that a warrant of commitment for an offense must upon its face show the cause of commitment and the nature of the offense charged; so far at least as to show that the same was within the jurisdiction of the committing officer. And where the commitment is not for an actual offense, but merely to obtain security against an apprehended offense, the warrant must upon its face show the cause of committal; that is, the direction of the magistrate that the party shall find surety, and the neglect of the party to do so.[2] The complaint, where the object of the prosecutor is to obtain surety of the peace to prevent the commission of a crime, must be in writing and upon oath. It is intended to be a separate and distinct proceeding from the examination of the complainant, for the purpose of ascertaining whether that written complaint is well founded. Before such a complaint in writing has been made the magistrate has no jurisdiction to administer an oath to the complainant, or to his witnesses, for the purpose of ascertaining whether there was reason to fear the commission of the anticipated offense, and the complaint and the subsequent examination of the complainant can not properly be contained in the same paper. If, however, the warrant to arrest recite that there was a complaint in writing and upon oath, it will be

---

[1] People v. Forbes, 4 Park. Cr. 611; People v. Phillips, 1 Id. 95; Geter v. Commissioners of Tobacco Inspection, 1 Bay, 354. See also the well-considered case of Gurney v. Tufts, 37 Me. 130.

[2] Chancellor Walworth in Bradstreet v. Furgeson, 23 Wend. 637, citing Atkinson v. Carty, 1 Jebb & S. 369.

§ 300.   JUDGMENTS OF SUMMARY CONVICTIONS.   385

prima facie evidence that such proceedings were had. This will protect the magistrate in an action against him until the party denying the jurisdiction which depends on that fact shows the recital to be false. It is not necessary, however, to state in the *mittimus* the crime for the prevention of which the application for sureties of the peace is made. It is sufficient to state the refusal to find sureties against future anticipated breaches of the peace.[1]

Upon a conviction for disorderly conduct, the making and filing of a record is not necessary; but if it were, it seems that the omission to file one would not be ground for discharging the prisoner upon habeas corpus.[2] It is also held in New York that it is not necessary, in a commitment for disorderly conduct, to set forth the particular act complained of; and that a commitment for such offense, until the party shall find security for his good behavior, without qualification, is void. This was the common-law rule; but here the time of imprisonment should be limited to the term specified in the statute.[3] In that state error, irregularity, and judgments founded upon insufficient evidence may be assailed by *certiorari*, but not by habeas corpus.[4]

In Florida, sureties of the peace against doing damage to property, except as to threats to burn a dwelling-house, are not authorized by the common law or by statute, and imprisonment for want of such sureties is not allowed by law; so where one was held in custody on the warrant of a committing magistrate, for want of sureties against doing damage to the property, and to keep the peace toward the complainant, where it was stated in the complaint that the accused had threatened to do damage to a schooner, the proceeding was regarded as without authority of law, and the cause remanded that proceedings be had according to law.[5]

---

[1] Bradstreet v. Furgeson, 23 Wend. 637.

[2] Case of The Twelve Commitments, 19 Abb. Pr. 394; Williamson's Case, Id. 413. *Contra:* De La Montange's Case, cited in note, Id., where Recorder Hoffman remarked: "Without a commitment there can be no lawful imprisonment, and without a record there can be no lawful commitment:" See also Ann Doyle's Case, 19 Id. 269.

[3] Case of The Twelve Commitments, 19 Abb. Pr. 394; *contra:* Ann Doyle's Case, Id. 269, holds that exceptions of cases, provided for by statute, left this common-law power in full force. As to when an officer, person, or body will be deemed a court, and that an authentication by the signature of one of the commissioners of the board of public charities and correction is sufficient to authorize the transfer of prisoners from the city prison to the workhouse, if the act in terms purports to be their act, at least when questioned on habeas corpus, see Case of The Twelve Commitments, Id.

[4] See case last cited.

[5] Ex parte Harfourd, 16 Fla. 283; S. C., 13 Am. Law Rev. 543. A county judge issued the warrant; the circuit judge, the habeas corpus; and the supreme court the writ of error.

§ 301. **Commitment of Seaman.**—In Pennsylvania, a seaman shipped in a British port, but who had deserted in a port of the United States, and who was committed to prison by an alderman of the city of Philadelphia for safe keeping until he should find security to proceed on the voyage, or be delivered by due course of law—notwithstanding he had contracted to submit to certain statutes in England which authorized such imprisonment—was discharged on habeas corpus, on the ground that there was no law of the commonwealth or general government authorizing a justice of the peace or alderman to make such a summary commitment.[1]

§ 302. **Commitment of Sheriff.**—It has been held in Massachusetts that if a sheriff sells on execution spirituous and intoxicating liquors belonging to a judgment debtor, and is sentenced therefor by a justice of the peace, as for an unlawful sale,[2] and refuses to pay a fine or give a bond, as required by that statute, the one just cited, his imprisonment is lawful, and the judgment of the justice can not be successfully assailed by habeas corpus. But a simple mandate from a justice of the peace to a coroner to commit the sheriff to the county jail, the law having intrusted the jail and the prisoners therein to the rule, charge, and custody of the sheriff, until he shall comply with the order of the justice, is void, and the sheriff, if held by a coroner under such a warrant, will be discharged on habeas corpus.[3]

§ 303. **Cumulative and Erroneous Sentences.**—By section 18 of the English summary jurisdiction act of 1879, it is provided that "a court of summary jurisdiction shall not, by cumulative sentences of imprisonment (other than for default of finding sureties), to take effect in succession in respect of several assaults committed on the same occasion, impose on any person imprisonment for the whole exceeding six months."[4] In Maine it has been held that if the *mittimus* of a justice of the peace shows an offense to be one for which that officer has jurisdiction to impose a fine, as for unlawfully selling spirituous liquors, the failure to state the name of the purchaser, the quantity sold, or the time and place of the sale, and that there was a prosecutor, will not be sufficient to invalidate the judgment; neither will the fact that the justice erroneously ordered the fine to be paid to the state. It was thought that, were the case before the court on *certiorari*, the erroneous part could be re-

[1] Commonwealth v. Holloway, 1 Serg. & R. 390.
[2] Under Stat. 1852, c. 322, sec. 7.
[3] Adams v. Vose, 1 Gray, 51.
[4] 42 & 43 Vict., c. 49, p. 243.

versed, leaving the penalty unappropriated.¹ In a later case in the same state, the same doctrine prevailed. The court said: "As a rule, we will not look beyond the precept on which the prisoner is detained. The writ [of habeas corpus] will not be granted for defects in matters of form only; nor can it be used as a substitute for an appeal, a plea in abatement, a motion to quash, or a writ of error." ² It was also held that as sentences there to the reform school are during minority, the execution of the sentence may be delayed for such reasonable time as the court thinks proper, as the delay can not operate to the prejudice of the petitioner, is only making his imprisonment so much the shorter.³

§ 304. **Custody of Children.**—It was held in the first district of the supreme court, in 1872, in the Matter of Mary Miller,⁴ on *certiorari* to review a conviction and commitment of a child as a vagrant, that such commitment is a final judgment, and that the court should not inquire into the legality or justice of such a final judgment, or of an execution issued on such judgment. The same principle was announced in the first department of the supreme court, in 1876,⁵ in the case of a commitment of a child found in an employment contrary to the act of 1876, for the protection of children.⁶ In fact, it was here said in specific terms that the constitutionality of the statute under which the commitment was made could not be impeached, as that must involve the legality of the judgment. These two decisions, by so high an authority, would seem to be good law, at least on this question of summary commitments in such cases. But why should one be granted the constitutional privilege of assailing judgments in other cases for want of jurisdiction, and yet be deprived of it in these? The principles of law, so far as the question of jurisdiction is concerned, are the same in all cases; because a judgment under an unconstitutional law is as no judgment at all, and void.⁷ Indeed, three years after the first decision, and one year prior to the last one, the highest judicial tribunal in New York, the court of appeals, announced, in Tweed's Case, what we conceive to be the correct rule. It was there decided that the words "legality and justice," as

---

¹ Phinney, Petitioner, etc., 32 Me. 440, citing State v. Stinson, 17 Id. 154.
² O'Malia v. Wentworth, 65 Me. 129.
³ O'Malia v. Wentworth, 65 Me. 129. See generally, on this section, State v. Shattuck, 45 N. H. 205.
⁴ Note, in the Matter of Donohue, 1 Abb. N. C. 1; S. C., 52 How. Pr. 251.

⁵ See Matter of Donohue, 1 Abb. N. C. 1; S. C., 52 How Pr. 251.
⁶ Laws of 1876, p. 95, c. 122; see also Laws of 1874, p. 132, c. 116.
⁷ Ex parte Siebold, 100 U. S. 371; see also People ex rel. Tweed v. Liscomb, 60 N. Y. 591.

used in the statute prohibiting an inquiry, upon the return of the writ, into "the legality and justice of any process, judgment, decree, or execution" specified, etc., were not intended to include questions of jurisdiction or power. The writ of habeas corpus is not the creation of any statute, either here or in England, but it exists as a part of the common law, and legislative action can not abrogate it or impair its efficiency. Neither can state constitutions place cases, within the relief afforded by the writ at common law, beyond its reach. Statutory enactments are intended to add to the efficiency of the writ, and not to detract from its force.[1] And the broad current of numerous decisions, with few exceptions, all go to show that jurisdiction, at all times, may be inquired into on habeas corpus, though mere informality, error, and irregularity can not be.

§ 305. **Commitment of Witness.**—A court is not authorized to exact from a witness, who was not examined before the committing magistrate, an undertaking that he will appear and testify at the court to which the deposition and statements are sent. The power to require undertakings in such cases appears to be confined to witnesses who were examined before the committing magistrate. And where one is committed to prison for not complying with an order, even of a court of general jurisdiction, requiring him to give such an undertaking with sureties, he will be released on habeas corpus. "It is only in case of a failure to give an undertaking, when legally required to do so, that the court can commit a witness to prison."[2]

---

[1] People ex rel. Tweed v. Liscomb, 60 N. Y. 559; see also 2 R. S. 563, sec. 22, subd. 2; 2 R. S. 568, sec. 42.

[2] Ex parte Shaw, 61 Cal. 58. See Cal. P. C., secs. 878, 879, 881. As to who may be a competent witness in proceedings instituted to have one declared a disorderly person, and as to the finality and conclusiveness of such a judgment, see People of the State of New York ex rel. Smith v. The Commissioners of Public Charities, 9 Hun, 212.

CHAPTER XXIII.

ASSAILING JUDGMENTS FOR CONTEMPT BY HABEAS CORPUS.

§ 306. Definitions.
§ 307. Power of Courts to Punish for Contempt.
§ 308. Punishment for Contempt.
§ 309. Punishment for Contempt, Continued.
§ 310. Attachment for Contempt.
§ 311. Attachment, Continued.
§ 312. Commitments by Notary Public.
§ 313. Modifying Judgments.
§ 314. Assailing Judgment of Court of Competent Jurisdiction.
§ 315. In the Supreme Court of the United States.
§ 316. Conflict of Federal and State Authority in the United States Circuit and in the State Courts.
§ 317. Jurisdiction—Two Questions Involved in a Commitment for Contempt.
§ 318. The General Rule.
§ 319. Answering Questions.
§ 320. Orders of Court to Pay over Money.
§ 321. Conditions Impossible of Performance.
§ 322. Neglect to Pay Tax.
§ 323. Disobedience of Orders, Judgments, and Decrees of Court.
§ 324. Disobedience of Orders, Judgments, and Decrees of Court, Continued.
§ 325. Notice and Service of Orders, etc.—Ability to Pay—Demand, etc.
§ 326. Suspending Attorney.
§ 327. Malpractice of Sheriff.
§ 328. Judgment for Contempt under Unconstitutional Law.
§ 329. Irony.
§ 330. Disobedience of Subpœna.
§ 331. Jurisdiction to Commit—*Mandamus*.
§ 332. Jurisdiction—No Offense.
§ 333. Jurisdiction—Refusal to Give Evidence.
§ 334. "Until Discharged by Due Course of Law"—Time Certain—English Courts.
§ 335. "Until Further Order of the Court," Continued—Time Certain in the United States.
§ 336. Commitments for Contempt in Parliamentary Bodies.
§ 337. Definite Time Fixed by Statute.
§ 338. Exemption from Jury Service.
§ 339. Publication during Trial.

§ 340. Statement of Facts Need not be Made unless Statute Requires It.
§ 341. Where the Warrant of Commitment Omits to State Facts, the Cause can not be Inquired into.
§ 342. Judgments of "Superior" and "Inferior" Courts.
§ 343. Jury Trial—Change of Venue.
§ 344. Error and Irregularities must be Cured by Motion.
§ 345. Pardon.
§ 346. Evidence.

§ 306. **Definitions.**—Any disobedience to the rules, orders, process, or offense to the dignity of a court or judge;[1] any act calculated to impede, embarrass, or instruct the court in the administration of justice;[2] or any contumacious behavior, insulting language, or acts of violence which interrupt the regular proceedings in courts, are contempts of courts. Contempts are by the authorities divided into two classes: 1. Criminal contempts, which are committed in the immediate view and presence of the court. 2. Constructive or consequential contempts, which arise from matters not transpiring in court, but relating to a failure to comply with the orders and decrees issued by the court and to be performed elsewhere.[3] What constitutes a direct or criminal contempt is generally defined by statute, and its punishment prescribed. But indirect, constructive, or consequential contempts are a part of the common law. "Into this vortex of constructive contempts have been drawn, by the British courts, many acts which have no tendency to obstruct the administration of justice, but rather to wound the feelings or offend the personal dignity of the judge."[4] This branch of the law of contempts, however, has been much modified in the United States, by the constitutional guaranties for civil liberty and personal rights, the prevalence of free principles, and the general improvement of society. Any violation of the privileges of either house of parliament,[5] or of either house of congress,[6] or of either house of a state legislature, is also a contempt.[7] Contempts are treated by elementary writers as public wrongs, and the whole doctrine of contempts goes to the point that the offense is a wrong to the public, and not to the person of the functionary to whom it is offered, considered merely as an individual.[8]

[1] Whart. Law Lex., 7th ed., 190.
[2] Stuart v. The People, 3 Scam. 405.
[3] Androscoggin & Ken. R. R. v. And. R. R. Co., 49 Me. 400.
[4] Justice Breese, in Stuart v. The People, 3 Scam. 404.
[5] Burdett v. Abbott, 14 East, 158; Stockdale v. Hansard et al., 9 Ad. & El. 1; S. C., 11 Id. 253.
[6] In the Matter of Irwin, 9 Cong. Rec. 615.
[7] Burnham v. Morrissey, 14 Gray, 226.
[8] Ex parte Hickey, 4 Smed. & M. 783; State of Louisiana v. Sauvinet, 24 La. Ann. 119. Said Mr. Justice Thatcher, of Mississippi: "What is a contempt of court? Besides the vari-

§ 306.   ASSAILING JUDGMENTS FOR CONTEMPT.   391

It is readily understood, from the note just given, why many jurisdictions of the American Union punish only direct or criminal contempts—those committed in the presence of the court, or in violation of its orders. This is the rule in the federal courts.[1] Contempt of court has been defined by the supreme court of the United States, in the case of New Orleans v. Steamship Company,[2] to be "a specific criminal offense," and the fine

ous classes of contempts which were known to the common law of England and particularly described, besides these relating to officers and others connected with the courts, concerning which the law is plain and explicit, there are many which are claimed to lie exclusively within the discretion of courts. The belief in the existence of such is alone in the breast of the court. They may be construed to spring from a gesture, a word, or a look. Thus the court is constituted the judge of his own privileges and the vindicator of his own wrongs, whether real or supposed, and his jurisdiction in this particular is without measure. The offense is without specification and without definition; and though legally viewed, it is said to refer solely to the functionary, it necessarily touches and stimulates the individual, who finds it hard to separate himself from the office and station. It may thus become an offense of opinion, of feeling, or of prejudice—an offense which has no other legislation than the imperfections of human nature, blinded and misled by the circumstances of the moment, notions of caprice, and the improper bias of passion, or by those powerful but imperceptible influences from which the most upright and enlightened minds can not be considered or trusted to be wholly exempt. * * * It is a maxim of law that where a discretion is allowed courts in the punishment of defined offenses, that discretion must be regulated by law. But in this instance the law, as claimed, sets to itself no bounds, and under the influence of strong passions, punishment may be inflicted to a cruel, an unusual, and excessive degree. The records of the English courts are not without glaring examples, under this authority, which might be hence quoted as precedents for imitation. There are no guards there against a resort to the most tyrannical licentiousness, and it is not an unreasonable jealousy to distrust men clothed with arbitrary power. It is certainly better that the freedom of the citizen should be controlled by fixed and plain laws than to be left dependent upon the uncertain moderation of those in power. The authority to punish at pleasure and during pleasure is indeed more consonant and agreeable to a throne, without responsibility, than to tribunals of justice erected upon free and equal laws. The tenth [section] of the declaration of rights declares that no citizen shall be deprived of his life, liberty, or property but by due course of law. Yet by the doctrine of contempts as insisted upon there exists an offense not only undescribed and undefined in its nature and character, and one whose very existence is dependent upon the opinion and discretion of a judge, but a punishment, to use the words of Senator Clinton, in Yates v. The People, 6 Johns. 467, 'unlimited, uncontrolled, indefinite, arbitrary, and omnipotent.' 'It is to be remembered,' he adds, 'that summary convictions are against the genius and spirit of our institutions, and in derogation of civil liberty. The judge is without check, and the accused without the usual guards of freedom. There is no grand jury to accuse, no petty jury to try, but his property and liberty depend upon the fiat of the court. Here, then, is a case where an unjust and tyrannical judge may at pleasure imprison an innocent man for life, and being a judicial act for which he can not be questioned, thus place punishment at defiance. A doctrine pregnant with such horrible results can never be in unison with the letter or the spirit of a free and enlightened system of jurisprudence:'" Ex parte Hickey, 4 Smed. & M. 778.

[1] U. S. R. S., sec. 725.
[2] 20 Wall. 392, cited in Ex parte Crittenden, 7 Pac. C. L. J. 483, and in Fischer v. Hayes, 6 Fed. Rep. 63.

imposed to be a judgment in a criminal case.¹ The adjudication is a conviction, and the commitment in consequence thereof is execution.² "The conduct charged as constituting the contempt must be such that some degree of delinquency or misbehavior can be predicated of it; for if the act be plainly indifferent or meritorious, or if it be only the assertion of the undoubted right of the party, it will not become a criminal contempt by being adjudged to be so. The question whether the alleged offender really committed the act charged will be conclusively determined by the order or judgment of the court; and so with equivocal acts, which may be culpable or innocent according to the circumstances; but where the act is necessarily innocent or justifiable, it would be preposterous to hold it a cause of imprisonment." ³

§ 307. **Power of Courts to Punish for Contempt.**—Courts have an undoubted power to punish direct or criminal contempts,⁴ and this power to punish direct or criminal contempts also necessarily includes the power to punish indirect, consequential, or constructive contempts—such acts as are calculated to impede, embarrass, or obstruct the court in the ad-

---

¹ Burnham v. Morrissey, 14 Gray, 226.
² Ex parte Kearney, 7 Wheat. 39. See Crosby's Case, 3 Wils. 188; S. C., 2 W. Black. 756.
³ People v. Hackley, 24 N. Y. 78.
⁴ Watson v. Williams, 36 Miss. 331; U. S. R. S., sec. 725; Ex parte Lange, 18 Wall. 163, 167; Fischer v. Hayes, 6 Fed. Rep. 63; And. & Ken. R. R. Co. v. And. R. R. Co., 49 Me. 392; Stuart v. People, 3 Scam. 405; State v. Matthews, 37 N. H. 451; King v. Hobhouse, 2 Ch., Q. B., 207; State of Louisiana v. Sauvinet, 24 La. Ann. 119; Clark v. People, etc., 1 Breese, 340; and for numerous other authorities, see 13 Md. 634, app. In the case first cited, Mr. Justice Harris, of the high court of errors and appeals of Mississippi, used these words: "The power to fine and imprison for contempt, from the earliest history of jurisprudence, has been regarded as a necessary incident and attribute of a court, without which it could no more exist than without a judge. It is a power inherent in all courts of record, and co-existing with them by the wise provisions of the common law. A court without the power effectually to protect itself against the assaults of the lawless, or to enforce its orders, judgments, or decrees against the recusant parties before it, would be a disgrace to the legislation, and a stigma upon the age, which invented it. In this country all courts derive their authority from the people, and hold it in trust for their security and benefit. In this state [Mississippi] all judges are elected by the people, and hold their authority, in a double sense, directly from them; the power they exercise is but the authority of the people themselves, exercised through courts as their agents. It is the authority and laws emanating from the people which the judges sit to exercise and enforce. Contempts against these courts, in the administration of their laws, are insults offered to the authority of the people themselves, and not to the humble agents of the law, whom they employ in the conduct of their government. The power to compel the lawless offender against decency and propriety to respect the laws of his country, and submit to their authority (a duty to which the good citizen yields hearty obedience without compulsion) must exist, or courts and laws operate at last as a restraint upon the upright, who need no restraint, and a license to the offenders, whom they are made to subdue."

§ 307.   ASSAILING JUDGMENTS FOR CONTEMPT.   393

ministration of justice. These acts will be considered as done in the presence of the court. So of rules entered by the court prohibiting the publication of the evidence or other matters while a case is pending and undecided. The limitation of the power to such cases only is better calculated to strengthen the judiciary, and fasten it in the affections and esteem of the people, who have so large a stake in its purity and efficiency, than the enlarging of the power to embrace constructive contempts which do not materially impede, embarrass, or obstruct the court in administering the law;[1] and we believe this is as far as the American courts have generally gone. It has been decided that the house of commons has power to commit for a contempt of its privileges;[2] that the house of representatives of the United States may punish even persons not members thereof for contempt;[3] and that the house of representatives of Massachusetts have power to punish for contemptuous behavior in its presence or disobedience to its commands.[4] This authority, in fact, is incident to all legislative bodies.[5]

By statute in many of the states, courts, not those of record, have power to commit for contempts, as, for example, those of justices of the peace.[6] A notary public may commit for the same offense, for refusal to answer questions in the taking of depositions, which he is by law authorized to take, and where a statute authorizes the commitment to prison, by the court or other person authorized to take depositions or testimony, until such evidence be given.[7] But a sheriff can not restrain an individual of his liberty and imprison him in jail for disobeying an order of court—as requiring him to pay certain sums of money. It is the province of the court, and not of the sheriff, to adjudge a party guilty of a contempt and punish him therefor.[8] Every judge of a court of record has power to immediately commit for a contempt committed in his presence, and in the case of a contempt committed out of court, the contemner is called upon to show cause why he should not be committed, and he may file affidavits in the matter.[9] But while an inferior court may peremptorily punish a contempt committed in its

---

[1] Justice Breese, in Stuart v. The People, 3 Scam. 405.
[2] King v. Hobhouse, 2 Ch., Q. B., 207; Burdett v. Abbott, 14 East, 1.
[3] Anderson v. Dunn, 6 Wheat. 204.
[4] Burnham v. Morrissey, 14 Gray, 226.
[5] Anderson v. Dunn, 6 Wheat. 204.
[6] State v. Towle, 42 N. H. 540.
[7] Ex parte McKee, 18 Mo. 599; Ex parte Krieger, 7 Mo. App. 367; In the Matter of Abeles, 12 Kan. 451.
[8] Ex parte Lawler, 28 Ind. 241.
[9] Queen v. Lefroy, 8 L. R., Q. B., 134.

presence, its power does not extend to commit for a contempt committed out of court."¹

§ 308. **Punishment for Contempt.**—Contempts are sometimes punished by a fine;² sometimes by a commitment for an indefinite time, as until the fine is paid;³ sometimes by a commitment for a definite time;⁴ and sometimes by fine and imprisonment.⁵ The judgment of imprisonment is only pronounced in order to insure the payment of the fine; and if the payment of the fine may be enforced without having recourse to imprisonment; as where the contemner occupies a high position in society and is clearly able to pay the fine, there is no necessity to add the usual words in connection with the imposition of a fine, "and to be imprisoned till the fine be paid." Where means exist of enforcing the payment of the fine, the judgment of imprisonment may be remitted in the discretion of the court.⁶ This question has recently undergone a thorough examination in the case of Fischer v. Hayes.⁷ On the seventeenth of February, 1880, an order was made adjudging the contempt, and that defendant pay as a fine certain costs, etc., to be ascertained subsequently. No order that the defendant stand committed, etc., was then made. On March 13th another order was made, that the amount, which had in the mean time been determined, should be paid by the defendant as a fine for the contempt within thirty days from the order, and that if not paid, the defendant stand committed till it be paid, and that when paid it be turned over to the plaintiff, in reimbursement. It was contended by the defendant that the order of March 13th was void, because it ordered the defendant to stand committed, etc.; and also that the court exhausted its power in making the order of February 17th, and that even if it did not, it had no power to order the defendant to be committed until the fine should be paid; but the court, by Blatchford, C. J., held that the court had power to order the defendant to be committed until the fine should be paid, and that the court did not exhaust its power by the order of February 17th. That order adjudged the contempt, and set on foot a proceeding for ascertaining what amount of

---

¹ Queen v. Lefroy, 8 L. R., Q. B., 134; and on this section generally, see Ex parte Alexander, 2 Am. Law Reg. 44; Ex parte Summers, 5 Ired. 149; State v. Woodfin, Id. 199; Clark v. The People, 1 Breese, 340; Ex parte Adams, 25 Miss. 883; State v. Galloway and Rhea, 5 Coldw. 326.

² Ex parte Fernandez, 7 Jur., N. S., 529.

³ Ex parte Fernandez, 7 Jur., N. S., 529.

⁴ Id.

⁵ Id.

⁶ Onslow's and Whalley's Case, 9 L. R., Q. B., 229.

⁷ 6 Fed. Rep. 63, Jan. 26, 1881—Circuit Court S. D. New York. Proceedings for Contempt, in Equity.

§ 308.   ASSAILING JUDGMENTS FOR CONTEMPT.   395

pecuniary fine should be imposed therefor, directing on what principle and by what means it should be fixed. The subsequent order of March 13th fixed the amount, imposed it as a fine for the contempt, to be paid within a fixed time, and ordered commitment till payment. This was proper and regular.

"It is suggested," he said, "that section 725 [of the United States revised statutes] provides for the punishment of a contempt by fine or imprisonment, and that therefore a commitment for non-payment of the fine is unlawful, because such commitment is imprisonment. There is, however, no commitment or imprisonment if the fine be paid. There is not commitment and fine. The punishment by a fine is fully inflicted, under the terms of the order, if the fine be paid as the order directs, and in such case there can be no commitment. So, if there be a commitment for non-payment of the fine, there must be a discharge as soon as the fine is paid. The payment of the fine is the punishment. The awarding or infliction of the fine is no punishment. The commitment is an incident of the fine. It is not, in any manner, the 'imprisonment' allowed by the statute. The payment of the fine and a commitment for not paying it can not co-exist. The commitment is not a separate punishment or imprisonment added to the payment of a fine. It is in this view that it has always been held that where a statute authorizes or prescribes the infliction of a fine as a punishment either for a contempt of court or for a defined offense, it is lawful for the court inflicting the fine to direct that the party stand committed until the fine be paid, although there be no specific affirmative grant of power in the statute to make such direction." The supreme court of California has very fully and explicitly committed itself to this doctrine.[1]

---

[1] Ex parte Crittenden on Habeas Corpus, 7 Pac. C. L. J. 483, opinion filed May 2, 1881. "The power of courts," said Mr. Justice Smith, of the supreme court of Tennessee, "to punish for contempts without supervision by appeal or writ of error, though absolutely essential to the protection, efficacy, and existence of the courts, is nevertheless capable of being exercised unwisely and corruptly. Absolute and complete protection and redress against such injudicious or improper exercise of the power is, in its nature, as to many cases, impossible to be given. But in the matter of correcting the improper use of the power of courts to punish for contempts, the law furnishes a remedy, where the punishment is imprisonment, to a very large extent efficacious and speedy, though not always fully adequate to the purpose; and this remedy is by means of the writ of habeas corpus. If the judgment for the contempt be for cause for which the court has not jurisdiction, and it so appears upon the record, the judgment is void, and is no justification for the imprisonment. It stands on the law of universal application to the judgment of courts, that if the court has no jurisdiction, the judgment is void. If, therefore, it appears upon the face of the judgment or the record of the proceedings

§ 309. **Punishment for Contempt, Continued.**—Some interesting statutory constructions have lately been made in the supreme court of Wisconsin on proceedings for contempts and to protect the rights of parties in civil actions. Sections 21, 23, and 25 of the revised statutes of 1858, chapter 149, of that state, read respectively as follows.[1] It is said that section 23 upon which the judgment is rendered that the judgment is upon a cause of contempt for which the court has no statutory power to punish, or if it so appears that the punishment inflicted is not within the power prescribed by statute for such cause (see Matter of Smethurst, 2 Sandf. 724, and Ex parte Hickey, 4 Smed. & M. 751), the judgment will be void for want of jurisdiction of the court, and will be no justification for the imprisonment or sentence, and no sufficient answer to the writ of habeas corpus.

"It is not, however, to be understood, of what is here said, that it will be competent upon habeas corpus in cases of the kind on hand [writs of error from judgments on habeas corpus] for the judge or court hearing the habeas corpus to inspect and revise the evidence upon which the committing court acted, and to consider whether the evidence be enough to sustain the judgment of commitment or not. The committing court may err as to the force and effect of the evidence on which it founds its judgment. Error of that kind is not subject to revision upon proceedings by habeas corpus: See Smith v. McLendon, 59 Ga. 528.

"At common law, a general judgment for contempt, that is, a judgment which does not specify the particular cause of contempt on which the judgment is founded, is held to suffice and be valid: See Summers' Case, 5 Ired. 149, and authorities there cited. From this rule of the common law, we think proper to depart to the extent to require that in the courts of this state it shall be essential to the validity of a judgment for contempt of the kind under review here, that it shall state upon its face the cause of contempt alleged as the ground of jurisdiction on which the judgment is rendered. The ruling here made, in this respect, is the proper result from the legislative abridgment of the indefinite power at common law vested in the courts to punish for contempts. The jurisdiction at common law was indefinite and general. By statute here it is confined to specific causes. (This is so in many of the states, and of course the principles apply.) It is therefore pursuant to the policy indicated by the legislature, and warranted, in our judgment, by sound principle, to hold that the alleged cause of contempt upon which the judgment is rendered shall be set out upon the face of the judgment as the ground of jurisdiction upon which the judgment must rest for its validity. In this way the proper power of the courts to vindicate their dignity and maintain their safety, efficiency, and existence, may be to a large extent brought into harmony with the protection and safety of the citizen, against the inadvertent or unauthorized exercise of the power of the courts to punish contempts."

The court held, however, that instead of giving a strict construction to the legislative clauses concerning contempts, the proper construction is to give them a liberal application to the cases which may arise in the exigencies of the courts. It was also held that a judgment in the inferior courts of the state was not subject or liable to appeal in error or writ of error to the supreme court; and that contempts at common law, not falling within the five clauses prescribed by their code or other statutory enactments, were not punishable by the inferior courts of Tennessee; also that the sixth subsection of section 4106 of the code, reading, "Any other act or omission declared a contempt by law," was not intended to embrace, and did not embrace, the vast and undefined scope of contempts at common law, outside of the classes prescribed by statutory enactment: The State v. Galloway & Rhea, 5 Coldw. 326.

[1] Sec. 21. If an actual loss or injury has been produced to any party by the misconduct alleged, the court shall order a sufficient sum to be paid by the defendant to such party to in-

§ 309.   ASSAILING JUDGMENTS FOR CONTEMPT.   397

applies only to cases arising under section 21 of the same chapter, which, it will be seen, provides a civil remedy by indemnity to the injured party, and not to cases of punishment, as for a criminal contempt, mentioned in other provisions of said chapter. An appeal lies to the supreme court of that state from the order requiring payment of the indemnity, but not from the order imposing a fine or punishment. "Because," said Justice Lyon, "a conviction for contempt which results in the enforcement of a civil remedy by indemnity under section 21 is so essentially different from one which results in criminal punishment, the two proceedings can not be blended in one. Were this otherwise—were it competent for the court in the same order to punish a contempt criminally and also to award indemnity to the injured party—the portion of the order awarding indemnity could be brought to this court for review by appeal, while that portion which punishes the misconduct criminally could only be brought here by *certiorari* or writ of error. Civil and criminal proceedings can never thus be united and blended, at least, not without the sanction of some positive statute. Hence, the final order in contempt proceedings must be one thing or the other; it must impose criminal punishment for the misconduct, or enforce the civil remedy by awarding indemnity. It can not do both."

In the case giving rise to these opinions, a judgment of divorce awarded the exclusive care and custody of an infant child of the parties to the father. The mother, and petitioner for a habeas corpus, afterwards kidnaped and abducted the child, and removed it to Chicago. The mother was attached and brought before the court, ordered to restore the child, pay a fine of one dollar, and stand committed until she complied with such order. Held, that the "loss or injury" for which indemnity could be required under section 21 was a pecuniary loss or injury; that the father could not recover damages for such abduc-

demnify him, and to satisfy his costs and expenses, instead of imposing a fine upon such defendant; and in such case the payment and acceptance of such sum shall be an absolute bar to any action by such aggrieved party, to recover damages for such injury or loss.

Sec. 23. When the misconduct complained of consists in the omission to perform some act or duty which is yet in the power of the defendant to perform, he shall be imprisoned only until he shall have performed such act or duty, and paid such fine as shall be imposed, and the costs and expenses of the proceedings.

Sec. 25. In all other cases where no special provision is otherwise made by law, if imprisonment be ordered, it shall be for some reasonable time, not exceeding six months, and until the expenses of the proceedings are paid, and also, if a fine be imposed, until such fine be paid; and in the order and process of commitment the duration of such imprisonment shall be expressed.

tion and detention, and therefore, because of these two facts, the mother could not be lawfully committed for a continuing contempt under section 23; and that criminal punishment alone could lawfully be inflicted. Held further, that the order was in excess of the jurisdiction of the court; that the warrant of commitment " issued in a case not allowed by law "—contrary to the statute; that habeas corpus was properly brought; and that the prisoner should be discharged. The demurrer to the return was sustained.[1]

In Illinois, Justice Scates recognizes the general rule, but qualifies it in this way: " It is, indeed, denied that any appeal or writ of error lies from its judgment for contempt by any court. I will not undertake to decide the general question, but the power has its limits. The court may not treat any and every act as a contempt, and I have no doubt that the appellate court may revise and reverse its judgment when it exceeds its jurisdiction, by treating that as a contempt which, in law, is no contempt, and can not be. The supervision will be to ascertain that fact. We are not without precedent for this. One article in the impeachment of Judge Smith before the senate was for an illegal power; and in the case of Stuart v. The People, 3 Scam. 395, this court [the supreme court of Illinois] reversed a judgment of fine for a contempt imposed by the Cook circuit court."[2]

A justice of the peace who has imposed a fine upon a person for a contempt of his court can imprison him until the fine and costs are paid,[3] but the law abhors perpetual imprisonment, and when one is committed for contempt, a definite time should be stated; and when fined, a specific sum should be named. These questions are now generally settled, it is believed, by statutory enactments in most of the states, in such a way that the term of imprisonment can not exceed a stated time, and the amount of the fine be over a given sum. It may be added here that a fine for contempt may be followed by indictment for another offense, and that even a contempt itself is sometimes punished by indict-

---

[1] In re Ida Louisa Pierce, 44 Wis. 411. Chief Justice Ryan dissented from the judgment of the court in an elaborate and able opinion. The court also remarked: "It should have been said earlier in this opinion, that we think the order respecting the care and custody of the child Lottie Alice Alter 'is a matter depending in the court,' within the meaning of chapter 149, and hence a violation of that order may be punished as a contempt under the statute. This results from the fact that the court has continuing power over the matter, and may, at any time during the minority of the child, make any order in respect to her care and custody which her welfare may require."

[2] Ex parte Thatcher, 2 Gilm. 167.
[3] Brown v. The People, 19 Ill. 613.

§ 309.   ASSAILING JUDGMENTS FOR CONTEMPT.   399

ment. Also that the proceeding against a party for contempt is a distinct and separate offense from the cause pending when the contempt was committed—as distinct as an indictment for perjury is from the proceeding in which the false oath was taken.[1] It is no defense, on a trial for a contempt, to show that it merely obstructed the progress of an investigation which the court would have been obliged ultimately to dismiss for want of jurisdiction. But even if such were a good and legal defense, the party must make it on his trial for the contempt, and not interpose it after conviction on habeas corpus, and before a different tribunal.[2]

---

[1] See Com. v. Newton, 1 Grant Cas. 454; Ex parte Hardy, 68 Ala. 303; Fischer v. Hayes, 6 Fed. Rep. 63.

[2] Passmore Williamson's Case, 26 Pa. St. 9. One of the finest expositions of this subject will be found in the decision of Mr. Justice Fowler, of the supreme court of New Hampshire, in State v. Matthews, 37 N. H. 450, where he says, among other things: "In the service of an attachment for contempt, the officer may generally take bail or a bond for the appearance of the respondent at the return day, and to abide the order of court. Where the attachment is issued to enforce an appearance or answer, or for not paying costs or not obeying an order or decree, the respondent is to be brought into court by the officer: Citing People v. Tefft, 3 Cow. 340; Morris v. Marcy, 4 Ohio, 84; Daniell's Ch. Pl. & Pr. 527.

"Where an attachment is issued to enforce an appearance or an answer, it should specify the suit in which it is issued, and the object of the process; or if the body of the writ be general, the name of the suit and the cause of attachment should be indorsed upon it, so that the respondent may at once comply without application to the court; but when it is issued for contempt in disobeying an injunction, no specification or indorsement setting forth the cause of the proceeding is necessary: Citing Matter of Vanderbilt, 4 Johns. Ch. 57.

"After the respondent appears upon a rule to show cause, or is brought upon an attachment, he may submit his contempt to the court upon his own answer in the form of an affidavit, or he may demand of the prosecutor to file interrogatories for him to answer. The usual course when the alleged misconduct is denied is for the court to allow the prosecutor to file interrogatories intended to elicit a full statement of all the facts and circumstances of the alleged contempt. These may be filed in court, and the respondent's answers thereto taken by the clerk and reported by him to the court, who may proceed in a summary manner to decide the question of the guilt of the accused; or a master or commissioner may be appointed, before whom the interrogatories may be filed, and who will take down and report to the court the respondent's answers thereto, with such other testimony as either the respondent or the prosecutor may desire to have taken: Citing Herring v. Tylee, 1 Johns. Cas. 32; People v. Brown, 6 Cow. 41; People v. Ball, 5 Id. 415; Hollingsworth v. Duane, Wall. 78.

"Interrogatories may be amended for the purpose of explaining an ambiguity or calling out a fuller answer, and additional ones may be filed: Citing 1 Johns. Ch. 131, and 6 Cow. 41. The respondent is not confined to his own answers to the interrogatories exhibited to him, but may examine witnesses to exculpate himself: Citing Magennis v. Parkhurst, 3 Green's Ch. 433. The charge of contempt must be made out to the satisfaction of the court, and if it be not done by the answers of the respondent, the prosecutor may bring witnesses to support it, in addition to the testimony on which the attachment or order to show cause issued. The master or commissioner reports the proofs, and not his opinion of them: Citing Albany City Bank v. Schermerhorn, 9 Paige, 372.

"The sworn answers of the respondent are evidence in his favor, and to be considered and weighed with the other evidence in the case: Citing

§ 310. **Attachment for Contempt.**—The process of attachment for the punishment of contempts is as old as the law itself, and either direct or consequential contempts, both of which we have already defined,[1] are punished in this way.[2] "If the contempt be committed in the presence of the court, the offender may be instantly apprehended and imprisoned, at the discretion of the judges, without any further proof or examination. But in matters that arise at a distance, and of which the court can not have so perfect a knowledge, unless by the confession of the party or the testimony of others, if the judges upon affidavit see sufficient ground to suspect that a contempt has been committed, they either make a rule on the suspected party to show cause why an attachment should not issue against him;[3] or, in very flagrant cases of contempt, the attachment issues in the first instance; as it also does if no sufficient cause be shown to discharge, and thereupon the court confirms and makes absolute the original rule.[4] This process of attachment is merely intended to bring the party into court;[5] and when there, he must either stand committed or put in bail, in order to answer upon oath to such interrogatories as shall be administered to him, for the better information of the court with respect to the circumstances of the contempt.[6] These interrogatories are in the nature of a charge or accusation;[7] and if any one of the interrogatories is improper, the defendant may refuse to answer it, and move the court to have it struck out.[8] If the party can clear himself upon oath, he is discharged; but if perjured, may be prosecuted for the perjury.[9] If he confesses the contempt, the court will proceed to correct him by fine or imprisonment, or both. If the contempt be of such a nature that, when the fact is once acknowledged, the court can receive no further information by interrogatories than it is already possessed of, as in the case of a *rescuos*,[10] the defendant may be admitted to make such simple acknowledgment, and receive his judgment without answering to any interrogatories; but if he willfully and obsti-

---

Matter of Pitman, 1 Curt. 186; and proofs on both sides, including the answers of the respondent himself, are taken, and the court thereupon determine, from a consideration of the whole evidence, the guilt or innocence of the accused:" See also In the Matter of Watson, 5 Lans. 466, and Ex parte Field, 5 Blatchf. 63.

[1] See sec. 306.
[2] Watson v. Williams, 36 Miss. 331.
[3] Ex parte Cottrell, 59 Cal. 420.
[4] In the Matter of Smethurst, 2 Sandf. 724.
[5] Smith v. McLendon, 59 Ga. 523.
[6] People v. Nevins, 1 Hill (N.Y.), 154. *Contra:* Yates v. The People, 6 Johns. 337; see also Yates v. Lansing, 9 Id. 395; State v. Matthews, 37 N. H. 451.
[7] Citing Elderton's Case, 6 Mod. 73.
[8] Citing Rex v. Barber, 1 Stra. 444.
[9] Citing Elderton's Case, 6 Mod. 73.
[10] Citing Rex v. Elkins, 4 Burr. 2129.

§ 310.   ASSAILING JUDGMENTS FOR CONTEMPT.   401

nately refuses to answer, or answers in an evasive manner, he is then clearly guilty of a high and repeated contempt to be punished at the discretion of the court."[1]

The motives of one applying for the issuance of the process of attachment for disobedience of an order of court may be inquired into, and if an improper motive manifest itself, the attachment will be refused. This was done in the following case: A soldier of a regiment was held in custody as a prisoner by defendant. A habeas corpus was issued and directed to defendant, commanding him to bring the prisoner before the court. He failed, and a rule to show cause why he should not be punished for contempt of court was obtained against him. Upon service of the habeas corpus the defendant had referred the matter to the horse-guards, and received directions to discharge the plaintiff, which he obeyed. The affidavit of the defendant, Major Gavin, stated he had no intention of showing disrespect to the court, but that he supposed that after the discharge of the party he could not make any return to the writ. The court held that, while defendant ought to have made a return that he had discharged the party, there appeared to be no sufficient cause shown on the part of the applicant to induce them to issue the attachment.[2]

Where a writ of habeas corpus had been served on a party in France, and which had been disobeyed, the court of king's bench would not grant a rule absolute in the first instance for an attachment on the ground of his disobedience, although the English habeas corpus had been recognized and declared proper to be executed by the French tribunals; neither would they grant their warrant to apprehend the defendant for his contempt, under the statute of 56 Geo. III., c. 100, sec. 2, it appearing that the individual in question was confined in France. Patteson, J., remarked: "Before granting an attachment there must have been a good service of the writ, and I do not see how I can say this was a good service, having been effected out of the jurisdiction of the court. Even if I recognize the French laws, and grant that the service was properly effected according to these laws, still it remains a question whether that service is good by the English laws, so as to make a contempt of the

---

[1] 4 Kerr's Bla. Com. 297. For case where one can not be punished for continuing contempt under statutory law, see In re Pierce, 44 Wis. 411. For authority to punish disobedience of writ of habeas corpus, see People v. Bradley, 60 Ill. 390; Ex parte Bosen and Brandt or King v. Barber, 2 Keny. 289. See, generally, State v. Matthews, 37 N. H. 450; Gist et al. v. Bowman, 2 Bay, 182.

[2] Reg. v. Gavin, 15 Jur. 329, note.

English court. The place where the service was effected is material." J. Bayley, applicant for the attachment here, observed: "This court will recognize the French laws in cases where, under those laws, an arrest has been made in France on a *capias* in an action commenced in this country." His honor replied: "In that case the party is arrested under the authority of the French courts, and is brought here; when here, he is in custody under the writ of this court, and the court will not inquire by what means he is brought here." The court, however, consented to grant a rule *nisi* for an attachment, or allow a new writ of habeas corpus. Applicant elected to take a new writ, which was granted.[1]

§ 311. **Attachment, Continued.**—It has lately been held in Georgia—where an attorney at law was attached for contempt of court, in not paying over moneys belonging to his client, and after a verdict declaring that he had collected them—that when an attachment for contempt is made on a rule absolute under section 3956 of their code, declaring that "the plaintiff may have either an attachment or an execution issued from said rule absolute, and may have either of said processes returned, and the other issued at pleasure," after return into the clerk's office of a prior execution levied on land, the execution and the levy are both *functus officio*. In the language of Judge Bleckley, of the supreme court of Georgia, in reviewing on error the decision of Judge Clark, sitting at chambers, and on the hearing of a writ of habeas corpus sued out on the attorney's behalf: "The word 'returned,' as here used, certainly includes manual delivery into the clerk's office, and the question is, whether it necessarily means anything more. The statute does not expressly require that the sheriff shall make any entry, or that he shall do anything to prepare the execution to be returned. On looking to 11 Ga. 460, we find that returning an execution is held to be a separate and distinct thing from making an entry upon it, and that it is an act *in pais*, and may be proved by parol. It was there ruled that the sheriff's entry of *nulla bona* was not, in its date, even *prima facie* evidence of the time of the actual return of the *fi. fa.* It would seem to follow that an execution may be returned in a way to exchange it for another process, by simply

---

[1] Ex parte Wyatt, Will. Woll. & Dav. 76; S. C., 5 Dowl. P. C. 389. The reason of the application being made for a rule absolute in the first instance was, that the defendant was a prisoner for debt in the Marshalsea of the court of king's bench, and was making extraordinary efforts to arrange his debts with his creditors, and obtain his liberation and return to France, thereby removing himself out of the jurisdiction before he could be arrested, unless the application was granted in the form prayed.

bringing it back to the clerk's office and restoring it to the clerk who issued it. This was done in the present case before the attachment issued. For perfect regularity, the sheriff ought to have dismissed the levy and stated the reason therefor in an appropriate entry. But his failure to do so was but an irregularity, and was an omission that might be supplied by an entry *nunc pro tunc*. Instead of the levy operating to defeat the attachment, we think the attachment, when issued, operated to defeat the levy. When the plaintiff had the *fi. fa.* returned and the attachment issued, he abandoned the levy. The *fi. fa.* itself expired by operation of law, and of course the levy expired with it. Both of them became *functus officio*." This answered the allegation in his petition for a habeas corpus, that the levy had not been disposed of.

Another allegation in the petition, that the attachment issued without a rule *nisi* to show cause against it, and that the prisoner had had no opportunity to show cause why attachment should not issue; was answered by the fact that the original rule *nisi* called upon the attorney to show cause, not only why the rule should not be made absolute, but why he should not be attached for contempt of court. "This," said the judge, "was sufficient:" 57 Ga. 161. After the levy of the *fi. fa.*, and before the issuance of the attachment on the rule absolute, the delinquent attorney in this case was adjudged a bankrupt, and in his petition for a habeas corpus, it was further alleged that "the imprisonment was illegal because of the adjudication of bankruptcy, on his own petition, and the assignment thereunder of all his estate, real and personal, the proceedings being still pending, and no discharge from his debts having been granted." To this it was substantially replied, that the attorney's voluntary bankruptcy, and the usual assignment of his effects, after rule absolute and before attachment, would not prevent the attachment from issuing. Neither would the pendency of the proceedings in bankruptcy protect him from arrest and imprisonment by virtue of the attachment; nor could a judge at chambers discharge him on habeas corpus, because he testified that he was utterly unable to pay the amount of the rule, or any part thereof; as that would not render his imprisonment illegal, and that was the sole question for trial on the return of the habeas corpus. "Absolute inability," said Judge Clark, "to pay, when made manifest to the reasonable satisfaction of the court whose dignity and authority are concerned, will, it is to be presumed, have its due influence on that tribunal in expediting his restoration to liberty. Perpetual imprisonment, except of the contumacious, whose will refuses to second their ability, is not to be contemplated as likely to occur in a remedial proceeding by a court of justice."

The attorney also alleged illegal imprisonment, because, under the constitution and laws there could be no imprisonment for debt. "Imprisonment under an attachment for contempt," said his honor, "to compel obedience by an officer of court to a lawful order to pay over money which he has collected in the course of his official or professional duty, is not imprisonment for debt. It is sound disciplinary dealing with an unruly member of the forensic household. One who lives and moves within the precincts of the court misbehaves, to the injury of a person who has trusted him, and whose confidence he has abused, and the court orders him to make redress. He refuses, and the court, as the minister of the law, chastens him by imprisonment, and endeavors to coerce obedience. It is true, he is a debtor; but he is more than a debtor: he is an assistant in the affairs of justice, and as such bears a peculiar and special relation to the law. Through that relation the court acts upon him, treating him, not as a mere debtor who will not pay, but as a domestic of the law who refuses to obey his master." A fifth allegation of illegality was made in the petition, viz., "because no attachment for contempt has been issued, or ordered to be issued, by the judge of the superior court." But it was held that, as there was an express order by the court, as a part of the rule absolute, that an attachment should issue unless the money was paid in five days, no further order was necessary, and that the clerk was the proper officer to issue the attachment.

On the hearing of the first habeas corpus, which was before Judge Clark, sitting at chambers in Americus, Sumter county, and which was brought to release the petitioner from his imprisonment in the Webster county jail, the discharge of the prisoner under the writ was denied, and error assigned. He had offered to prove that he had not, in fact, collected the money for which the attachment issued; which offer was rejected, and its rejection complained of as error. But the supreme court of Georgia decided that the exclusion of evidence to controvert the finding of the jury on the issue of the attorney's original default was certainly not error. "It can not be," they said, "that such a question was open to inquiry on the hearing of a habeas corpus. The rule absolute rested on the verdict, and we can not see how it was possible to go behind the rule absolute, to say nothing of going behind the verdict." The judgment of Judge Clark was affirmed.[1]

§ 312. **Commitments by Notaries Public.**—The power to punish for contempts is an incident to all courts of justice independent of statutory provisions, and the power to enforce the observance of order, or punish for contumacy by fine or imprisonment, are powers which may not be dispensed with, because they are necessary to the exercise of all others. Statutes, however, in many of the states, confer upon justices of the peace and notaries public the power to punish for contempts when they are acting in their official capacity and exercising judicial functions. A justice of the peace has no authority to issue a warrant for the arrest of witnesses, to answer for alleged contempts in not appearing before him when subpœnaed, if the case in which they were to testify has been finally determined or ended; and witnesses so committed may be released upon habeas corpus. They, as well as the superior courts, must confine themselves to jurisdiction of the person and of the subject-matter, and act within the exercise of that jurisdiction.[2] In Kansas it is held that a witness may be subpœnaed to testify in a cause before a notary public by giving his deposition, and that if he refuses to testify, the notary may commit him for contempt in such refusal; and under their statutes if the contemner apply for a writ of habeas corpus, his petition will be denied, and he will be remanded to custody.[3] In a late case before the St. Louis court of appeals for the state of Missouri this matter of commitments for contempts by notaries public has been well considered, and that tribunal holds that in the refusal of a witness to answer questions in the taking of depositions before a notary, there is no presumption in favor of that officer's jurisdiction, that the jurisdictional facts found by him are not conclusive; and that it is in their province to see that such a commitment conforms to law. They say "that a notary, as a notary, has no power to commit for contempt; that contempt of court is a recognized offense, but there is no such thing known to the law as contempt of a notary public;" that the law has not invested such officers with arbitrary and omnipotent power to compel a witness to answer all questions, however incompetent, irrelevant, immaterial, inadmissible, and not perti-

[1] Smith v. McLendon, 59 Ga. 523.
[2] Clarke's Case, 12 Cush. 320.
[3] In the Matter of Abeles, 12 Kan. 451.

nent to any of the issues involved which may be asked; and that a refusal to answer such questions is not necessarily a contempt. They cite and approve the language of Justice Denio in People v. Hackley, 24 N. Y. 78,[1] and hold that if questions, which may be proper under certain contingencies in the case, are asked for the evident purpose of ascertaining facts to be used against the witness in another proceeding, a refusal to answer is not a contempt; and that where a notary commits for a refusal to answer a question, where the courts will not compel an answer, the courts will review the judgment. The court also held that to have power to commit for contempt, the notary must exercise formal functions substantially in the manner and under the circumstances prescribed and contemplated by law, and that he is amenable to the courts for any violation of his duties in the abuse of process, and that attorneys engaged in promoting such a proceeding are subject to punishment, on proper presentation, by disbarment or otherwise. In the case giving rise to the expression of these opinions the petitioner was discharged on habeas corpus.[2]

§ 313. Modifying Judgments.—The general power of the court over its own judgments, orders, and decrees, in both civil and criminal cases, during the existence of the term at which they are first made, is undeniable; but after final judgment has been rendered in a matter, the court can not vacate one sentence after the expiration of the term and substitute another, and cause it to be carried into execution. Neither can the judgment of the court, rendered and carried into execution before the expiration of the term, be vacated and another substituted for it, even before the close of the term. "No man can be twice lawfully punished for the same offense."[3] In Bank of the U. S. v. Moss it was held to be too late after final judgment and at the next term, and by motion only, to set aside a judgment on account of supposed want of jurisdiction; but this question of jurisdiction may be considered on habeas corpus.[4] In proceedings for contempt in a court of equity, that court has no power to vary a judgment rendered in such proceedings, after the expiration of the term in which it was imposed.[5] W. G. Shanks, city editor of the Tribune in New York, was committed to jail for contempt in refusing to answer questions put to him before the grand jury, as to the authorship of an article in that paper. He was brought before Judge Fancher on a writ of habeas corpus. A commit-

[1] See *supra*.
[2] Ex parte Krieger, 7 Mo. App. 367.
[3] Ex parte Lange, 18 Wall. 163; Bank of United States v. Moss, 6 How. 31; The Bank v. Labitut, 1 Woods', 11.
[4] Ex parte Lange, 18 Wall. 163.
[5] Fischer v. Hayes, 6 Fed. Rep. 63.

§ 314.   ASSAILING JUDGMENTS FOR CONTEMPT.   407

ment, called "Exhibit A," was produced. Court adjourned until the next day. During this time a new commitment—the first one being illegal—was made out by the district attorney, called "Exhibit B," and relied on in the return to the writ. The first commitment committed Shanks till he should answer the question he had refused to answer, and thereby made the sentence for an indefinite period, which was not in conformity with the statute which limited the time in such cases to thirty days. The second commitment had the additional words, "not exceeding thirty days." His honor discharged the editor.[1]

§ 314. **Assailing Judgment of Court of Competent Jurisdiction.**—The English doctrine seems to be that a commitment for a contempt generally, by a superior court, is sufficient, and is not examinable by any other court of co-ordinate jurisdiction;[2] but if the grounds from which the contempt was deduced be stated, in accordance with the general modern practice,[3] and they appear on the face of the return to a writ of habeas corpus to be clearly contrary to law, the prisoner will be entitled to his discharge, although the commitment be made by the house of commons.[4] In Brass Crosby's Case,[5] Lord

---

[1] "This [Exhibit A] was," his honor said, "the sheriff's only warrant for such detention when the habeas corpus was issued and served. The commitment states that the court had adjudged the petitioner guilty of a criminal contempt. The proof shows conclusively that the subsequent paper was not delivered to the sheriff until after the hearing on the habeas corpus case had commenced. Nor was it according to the order of the court. I can not regard this *ex post facto* paper as of any validity in this case, for two sufficient reasons. It is proved that the relator was not imprisoned or detained under it; and a man can not be first imprisoned and afterward adjudged in contempt. The judgment must precede the imprisonment. It appears from the evidence of the district attorney, that the Exhibit B was not signed by the side justices until October 23d, whereas the imprisonment took place on October 22d, and the sheriff held him in custody under Exhibit A, which is, in my opinion, an illegal commitment. The second commitment was not executed until the twenty-third, and could not legalize an existing imprisonment:" Shanks' Case, 15 Abb. Pr., N. S., 38. He also said: "A commitment for an indefinite time is not authorized by law, and the court has no jurisdiction to make it. There is a wide difference between an informal commitment and an illegal commitment. The former, if it be one which a court could make for a contempt, plainly charged, is sufficient, though in some form or part it be defective; for example, where it is not directed to any officer. But the latter, which, on its face, is shown to be illegal, is insufficient; for example, where it is directed by a civil court to a military officer, or enjoins a perpetual or indefinite imprisonment:" Id. 46.

[2] Bushell's Case. Freeman's K. B. & C. P. 1, note a; Burdett v. Abbott, 14 East, 150; Rex v. Davison, 4 Barn. & Ald. 336, 340. See also Brass Crosby's Case, 3 Wils. 188; S. C., 2 W. Black., 754; Rex v. Flower, 8 T. R. 325; Earl of Shaftsbury's Case, 5 Howell's State Trials, 1269; S. C , 1 Mod. 144.

[3] Stockdale v. Hansard, 9 Ad. & El. 228.

[4] Burdett v. Abbott, 14 East, 1; Bushell's Case, Vaugh. 156, 157; Stockdale v. Hansard, 9 Ad. & El. 1; Case of the Sheriff of Middlesex, 11 Id. 273. See also Regina v. Paty, 2 Ld. Raym. 1105; S. C., 2 Salk. 504. *Contra*: see Rex v. Eobhouse, 2 Ch., Q. B., 210.

[5] Brass Crosby's Case, 3 Wils. 188.

Chief Justice De Grey pronounced this principle: "When the house of commons adjudge anything to be a contempt or a breach of privilege, their adjudication is a conviction, and their commitment in consequence is execution; and the court can [not] discharge or bail a person that is in execution by the judgment of any other court. The house of commons, therefore, having an authority to commit, and that commitment being an execution, the question is, What can this court [the king's bench] do? It can do nothing when a person is in execution, by the judgment of a court having a competent jurisdiction; in such case, this court is not a court of appeal."

§ 315. **In the Supreme Court of the United States** was this case commented on, and its authority, as it stood at that time, confirmed in the case of Ex parte Kearney.[1] The circuit court of the District of Columbia had committed Kearney for an alleged contempt in refusing to answer a question on the trial of an indictment, because he conceived it tended materially to implicate him and to criminate him as a *particeps criminis*. There was no question but what the commitment was made by a court of competent jurisdiction, and in the exercise of an unquestionable authority. The only objection was, not that the primary court acted beyond its jurisdiction, but that it erred in its judgment of the law applicable to the case. The court refused to grant a writ of habeas corpus to inquire into the sufficiency of the cause of commitment, both because it had no appellate jurisdiction in criminal cases, and because, in the words of Mr. Justice Blackstone,[2] "the sole adjudication of contempt and the punishment thereof belongs exclusively, and without interfering, to each respective court, as infinite confusion and disorder would follow if courts could, by writs of habeas corpus, examine and determine the contempts of others."

An action of trespass was brought in the circuit court of the District of Columbia, against the sergeant-at-arms of the house of representatives of the United States, for an assault and battery and false imprisonment of the plaintiff on a warrant for a contempt of which he was adjudged guilty by the house. On error from the United States supreme court to this court, Mr. Justice Nelson delivered the opinion of the court, and resolved the question to the simple inquiry whether the house of representatives could take cognizance of contempts committed against themselves under any circumstances. The court decided that they could, because there was jurisdiction to justify

[1] 7 Wheat. 39 (1822).   [2] Brass Crosby's Case, 3 Wils. 204.

§ 316.   ASSAILING JUDGMENTS FOR CONTEMPT.   409

it. The judgment of the lower court was affirmed, the determination being that the action could not be maintained against the officer of the house.[1]

§ 316. **Conflict of Federal and State Authority.**—In the circuit courts of the United States and in the state courts this subject has received some attention. We quote from the Central Law Journal:[2] "In the case of Ex parte Hayne et al., recently before the United States circuit court of South Carolina, the petitioners, the board of canvassers for that state, had been committed for contempt, in not complying with the order of the state court directing them to canvass the vote of the state. They thereupon applied to the federal court for a habeas corpus, and on the return of the writ were discharged from custody. The court, Bond, J., held that the proceeding of the supreme court of the state was beyond its jurisdiction; that the board of canvassers were clothed, under the law, with discretionary powers, which required them to discriminate the votes, to determine and certify the candidates elected, after scrutiny, and that they were a part of the executive department of the government, and were in no wise subject to control as to what they should do after they had commenced to perform that duty to the judicial department; and that, as this was a general election, at which members of congress were to be elected, and electors of president and vice-president of the United States to be chosen, they were acting in a federal capacity, or in other words, in pursuance of the laws of the United States, and therefore, if disturbed in the exercise of their functions, they were entitled to the protection of the courts of the United States."[3]

An election was held in Dallas county, Alabama, in November, 1878, for a representative in congress. This county was within the middle district of Alabama, and within the territorial jurisdiction of the circuit court of the United States for that district. There seems to have been fraud in the election. By the ordinary process of the circuit court certain ballot-boxes, ballots, poll-lists, returns, etc., pertaining to the election, were brought before the grand jury of that court at the November term, 1878. The circuit court acquired jurisdiction of the subject-matter, and the papers in question were used in evidence, and true bills were found by the grand jury against several parties for alleged offenses concerning the election. Subsequently, and while these cases

---

[1] Anderson v. Dunn, 6 Wheat. 204.
[2] Vol. 4, p. 72.
[3] This is known as The Case of the Electoral College of South Carolina: See 1 Hughes, 571 (1876.)

were still pending and undetermined in said court, the city court of Selma, in said county and state, on application of the grand jury of that court, ordered subpœnas *duces tecum* to issue to Turner, Dimmick, Mayer, and Bibb, to appear *instanter* and bring with them the said ballot-boxes, poll-lists, ballots, etc. This they failed to do because the documents were, as said, in the custody of the United States circuit court. The city court then committed Turner and Mayer for contempt. Turner was marshal of the United States for the southern and middle districts of Alabama, and Mayer was United States district attorney for the northern and middle districts of Alabama. These two gentlemen brought habeas corpus, and district judge Bruce for the district of Alabama passed upon the matter at chambers and discharged the prisoners.[1]

---

[1] "This," his honor said, "is a case where the state courts and the federal courts have concurrent jurisdiction over the same subject, and it is a principle of law well settled that when the jurisdiction of a court, and the right of a plaintiff to prosecute his suit therein have once attached, that right can not be arrested or taken away by proceedings in another court, unless it be some court which may have a direct supremacy or control over the court where process has first taken possession, or some superior jurisdiction in the premises." The question on the hearing was whether these cases fell within section 753 of the United States revised statutes. "And," said his honor, "the question is not by what authority these petitioners are restrained of their liberty and detained in custody, but whether they were restrained of their liberty by any authority whatever, for an act done or omitted in pursuance of a law of the United States, or by an order, process, or decree of a court or judge thereof. Nor is the question which I am to consider on this hearing whether the proceedings in the city court of Selma against the petitioners, for an alleged contempt of the order and process of the court, were regular or irregular, or whether they were free from error, but the question is, Are these petitioners restrained of their liberty and detained in custody for an act done or omitted in pursuance of a law of the United States, or an order, process, or decree of a court or judge thereof? If it be true that they are so restrained, no matter by what authority, or by what formality or solemnity of judgment, they must be discharged. These gentlemen, like other citizens of the state of Alabama, owe duties of obedience to her laws and the process of her courts, and the fact that they are officers of the United States will not, and does not, absolve them from the duties which they owe as citizens of the state of Alabama. It can not be maintained, however, that the duties which they owe of obedience to the process of the state courts overbear and override their duties as officers of the United States, required, as they are by law, to attend upon the sessions of the courts of the United States, held in the district of their appointment." It did not clearly appear from the record whether the judgment of contempt was based solely upon the failure of the petitioners to produce the papers, matters, and things in question. The facts set forth in the affidavit of Turner, however, tended to show that the judgment of contempt was based solely upon the failure to produce the papers, matters, and things in question, and not upon the failure to appear *instanter* in person, in response to the subpœna. "The facts stated by the petitioners in their respective answers are not traversed, and it will hardly be contended that the duty of these officers to attend *instanter* and in person upon the session of the city court of Selma is of higher obligation than their duty under the laws of the United States to attend upon the sessions of the courts

§ 317. ASSAILING JUDGMENTS FOR CONTEMPT. 411

A soldier who is held to service in the army of the United States by an officer acting under the authority of the United States, and claiming to hold him as an enlisted soldier, can not be released on habeas corpus, when these facts *prima facie* appear, by a state court, judge, or officer, as they have no jurisdiction. There is no power to compel the production of the body of the soldier on the return of a writ issued in such a case, or to require the return to be verified by oath. If the state court attempt to do either of these things, and imprison a United States officer for contempt, in refusing to produce the body or make a verified return, a federal court will discharge him from confinement, because of a want of jurisdiction in the state court to render the judgment.[1]

So it has been held that a writ of habeas corpus can not issue out of a state court to inquire into the cause of a judgment for contempt, made by a federal court; although it is alleged that the federal court had no jurisdiction in the proceeding to adjudge the petitioner guilty of contempt.[2]

§ 317. **Jurisdiction — Two Questions Involved in a Commitment for Contempt.** — On a habeas corpus in a case of commitment for contempt only two questions can be examined, viz.: Had the court jurisdiction to commit? and, Is the commitment in legal form?[3] If these questions are affirmatively answered, the court issuing the writ can go no further. It can not inquire into the truth of the facts adjudicated in the lower court. But simple as these two pivotal questions appear to be, they give rise to other questions, in their determination, of a complicated character. What constitutes "jurisdiction," and what constitutes "legal form," have not been and can not be in all cases the subjects of well-settled judicial decision. The variety of forms in which these questions have been passed upon by the courts will necessarily compel a treatment of the subdivisions in subsequent sections. It may be observed here that judgment for contempts can not, any more than judgments after trial and conviction, be impeached for mere error or irregular-

of the United States, of which they are officers." Ex parte Turner, and Mayer, 3 Wood, 603. The following authorities were cited by Judge Bruce in his decision: Freeman v. Howe, 24 How. 450; Buck v. Colbath, 3 Wall. 334; Peck v. Jenness, 7 How. 612; New Orleans v. Steamship Co., 20 Wall. 387; Ex parte Jenkins, 2 Wall. jun. 521; Ex parte Robinson, U. S. Marshal, 6 McLean, 355.

[1] In re Neill, 8 Blatchf. 156. See Ex parte Robinson, U. S. Marshal, 4 Am. Law Reg. 617. *Contra:* supposed case by Chief Justice Lewis; Ex parte Passmore Williamson, 3 Am. Law Reg. 741.

[2] Ex parte Passmore Williamson, 3 Am. Law Reg. 741; Ex parte Hollman, 28 Iowa, 88.

[3] In the Matter of Percy, 2 Daly, 530.

ity. An attack on a judgment for contempt goes to the power of the court to act in the case. It assails proceedings which are void for want of jurisdiction.

§ 318. **The General Rule.**—Mr. Justice Yerger of the high court of errors and appeals for the state of Mississippi, said there was no instance in the English courts of a judge in vacation undertaking to decide upon the legality of a commitment in execution, by the judgment of any court of record.[1] But however this may be, in the United States, where the judges of courts have the same power in vacation under the habeas corpus acts which the courts themselves possess at common law, cases of treason and felony sometimes excepted, the judge of a court may investigate the question of jurisdiction in cases of contempt as well as the court itself, and a discharge by a judge in such cases for want of jurisdiction in the court rendering the judgment seems to be final and conclusive, and the party can not be again imprisoned for the same cause, unless by order of the court in which he is recognized to appear, or other court having jurisdiction of the matter. But a person who has been regularly committed and afterwards set at large can not be recommitted by an order grounded upon and reciting the original writ or attachment.[2]

Although the judgment or decision of a court or officer having competent jurisdiction can not be reviewed on habeas corpus, this general and well-recognized rule is sometimes materially modified by the meaning of the words " having competent jurisdiction." A court or officer can not commit for contempt without having competent jurisdiction, and wherever the want of jurisdiction can be shown, the stability of the general rule is shaken. There is no doubt that where the contempt has been committed in the face of and in the presence of the court, such as acts of misbehavior, rudeness, violence, or assailing the decisions of the court with sneers, sarcasms, or irony, etc., the question of jurisdiction can rarely be questioned; but in some other instances the question can be raised. Let us examine a few of them.

§ 319. **Answering Questions.**—In Texas, whose criminal bar and bench is one of the finest in the United States, it has been said: "The refusal of a witness to answer a legal and proper question is a decided contempt; and no matter in what

---

[1] Ex parte Adams, 25 Miss. 883.
[2] Yates v. The People, 6 Johns. 335, and various authorities cited in the next succeeding twenty sections. *Contra:* Yates v. Lansing, 9 Johns. 395.

respectful terms or deference of manner the refusal is made, he stands out against the authority of the court, and for that act he may be summarily dealt with by the court as for a contempt. The legality of the commitment, however, depends upon the power or jurisdiction of the court to ask the question. If the question be 'improper," if the court interrogate a witness about a matter over which it has no jurisdiction, and about which it has no right to inquire, the refusal of the witness to answer the interrogatory is no contempt of court, and any order or decision which punishes the refusal to answer as a contempt is void. The offense can not be made a contempt by merely adjudging it to be one; and to require a witness to submit to answer an illegal and improper question must be regarded as the personal command of the judge, rather than the judicial order of the court." The question here was: "What occurred between you and any one of the inmates of Fanny Kelly's house that was calculated to satisfy or convince you it was a house of prostitution?" The witness refused to answer this question propounded by the court, and was committed for contempt. The supreme court of that state said that he could not have returned an answer to the question "without branding himself with dishonor and committing a fresh offense against public morals and decency," and discharged him on habeas corpus.[1]

The same principle has been recognized in New York. The grand jury were investigating the acts of certain officials supposed to have received money to influence their actions. A. J. Hackley was summoned to appear and testify as to what he did "with the pile of bills received from Thomas Hope, and which he told you amounted to fifty thousand dollars." He refused to answer, as it would disgrace him, and have a tendency to accuse him of crime. He relied upon the maxim "that no man is held to accuse himself," and on the sixth section of article 1 of the constitution of New York. He was committed for contempt, and brought proceedings by habeas corpus and *certiorari* to determine the legality of the judgment. Justice Denio, of the New York court of appeals, said: "As a general rule, the propriety of a commitment for contempt is not examinable in any other court than the one by which it was awarded. This is especially true when the proceeding by which it is sought to be questioned is a writ of habeas corpus; as the question on the validity of the judgment then arises collaterally, and not by way of review. The habeas corpus act, moreover, declares that where

---

[1] Holman v. The Mayor of the City of Austin, 34 Tex. 668.

the detention of the party seeking to be discharged by habeas corpus appears to be for any contempt, plainly and specially charged in the commitment, ordered by a court of competent jurisdiction, he shall be remanded to the custody in which he was found. But this rule is, of course, subject to the qualification that the conduct charged as constituting the contempt must be such that some degree of delinquency or misbehavior can be predicated of it; for if the act be plainly indifferent or meritorious, or if it be only the assertion of the undoubted right of the party, it will not become a criminal contempt by being adjudged to be so. The question whether the alleged offender really committed the act charged will be conclusively determined by the order or judgment of the court; and so with equivocal acts, which may be culpable or innocent according to the circumstances; but where the act is necessarily innocent or justifiable, it would be preposterous to hold it a cause of imprisonment. Hence, if the refusal of Mr. Hackley, the relator, to answer the question propounded to him was only the assertion of a right secured to every person by the constitution, it was illegal to commit him for a contempt; and this error was certainly reached by the *certiorari* if not examinable on the return to the habeas corpus." But his honor held that Hackley was not protected by the constitution from answering before the grand jury, was not privileged, and that the judgment was valid.[1]

Several very interesting habeas corpus proceedings arose, in an early California case, out of the act of one Rowe, deputy state treasurer, in taking about three hundred thousand dollars out of the treasury to keep the vigilance committee at San Francisco from getting hold of it, as he said. The money was never returned, and an action was brought against the treasurer. Rowe was imprisoned by order of the sixth judicial district court for refusing to answer certain questions propounded to him in a proceeding against the state treasurer. During his imprisonment the treasurer resigned and the action against him abated. The questions then arose, Suppose the party should now signify his willingness to answer, how could he do so? What right has the court to pursue a cause abandoned by the parties, over which it has no jurisdiction? How can the party purge himself of the contempt by coming in and offering to answer questions which no one has any longer the right to ask? He was released on habeas corpus before the supreme court. Mr. Justice Burnett held in the case that

---

[1] People v. Hackley, 24 N. Y. 74; see also People v. Kelly, 21 How. Pr. 54.

§ 319. ASSAILING JUDGMENTS FOR CONTEMPT.

each court empowered to punish for contempt is not the sole and final judge in all cases of contempts; that neither by writ of habeas corpus, nor in any other form, can inferior courts or single judges set aside, review, or in any manner defeat the orders or judgments of superior courts; and that the disobedience of an order of court is only a contempt when it is a lawful order.[1]

[1] Ex parte Rowe, 7 Cal. 175. (2) Rowe was then committed by the court of sessions of Sacramento county for a contempt of court in refusing to answer certain questions propounded to him by the grand jury. On habeas corpus before the supreme court it was held that it was the right and duty of that court, by such a proceeding, to review the decisions of inferior courts in cases of contempts, as well as in others; that a commitment for contempt, "in refusing to answer certain questions propounded to him by the grand jury," was not in conformity with the statute requiring that "the act to be performed shall be specified in the warrant of commitment where the contempt consists in the omission to perform an act which is in the power of the person to perform;" because "what those questions were does not appear; whether they were legal or otherwise is not shown. No other court but the court of sessions can know the facts upon which the commitment was made. To say that a party must answer 'certain questions,' not stating them, is not 'specifying the act in the warrant of commitment,' which the court required the prisoner to perform. There is no limit set to the act to be performed; no specific duty pointed out. The questions may be two, or any greater number; all is indefinite and uncertain, and this court has no means of knowing what the prisoner is required to do. Now, in requiring that the act to be performed should be specified in the warrant of commitment, the statute must have had some object in view. What could that object be except to afford the means of judging of its correctness by other courts? If, then, we have the right to set aside the order of an inferior court in a case of contempt, it would seem clear that the warrant of commitment should state all the material facts upon which the action of the court is predicated. In the present case it should have been stated that the grand jury were inquiring into a certain question, stating it; that prisoner was sworn as a witness and certain questions propounded to him, stating them; that he refused to answer; that the facts were thereupon presented to the court by the grand jury, and the prisoner required by the court to answer, which, being refused, he was committed for contempt. The objection that such a course would defeat the ends of justice by making public the proceedings before the grand jury, though plausible, is not sound. The questions could be propounded in writing, and their character need not be made public. So, likewise, the proceedings under the writ, in a case of this kind, need not necessarily be known to any one but the officers of the court, the prisoner, and his counsel." Again was the prisoner discharged. (3) He was again committed for refusal to answer questions propounded to him by a grand jury, after having been ordered by the court to answer them. He refused on the ground that his answer would disgrace him, and would tend to subject him to punishment for a felony. He applied to the supreme court for a habeas corpus, and his petition was refused. He then applied for a rehearing, when the court pronounced their opinion as follows: "A witness is privileged from answering in two distinct cases, resting upon entirely different grounds: 1. When the answer tends to subject him to criminal punishment; and, 2. When the answer is not to any matter pertinent to the issue, and the answer would disgrace him, as, when upon cross-examination he is asked a question, the answer to which would tend to destroy his credibility as a witness. * * * The difference between the two classes of cases is further shown from the fact that when the answer would tend to disgrace a witness, and the question is not pertinent, the court will not even permit the question to be asked; while

In Indiana, an attorney at law refused to take the following oath before a grand jury: "You do solemnly swear that the evidence you shall give to the grand jury shall be the truth, the whole truth, and nothing but the truth, so help you God." This was too general for the disciple of Blackstone. The judge committed him for contempt, and the supreme court refused to review the judgment.[1]

Another attorney in New York got himself into a difficulty from which the court refused to extricate him on habeas corpus. In the court of common pleas, one Bettz was defending an action as landlord of the defendant. He was examined concerning some papers relative to the land in dispute. He said he had a few days before the trial delivered some papers to his attorney, the relator, who was also attorney for the defendant, and could not produce them. The attorney was then in court acting as attorney for defendant; was called as a witness, and questioned concerning the papers—whether they related to the land in dispute. He replied he could not state without examining a bundle of papers then in his possession in court; and on being directed by the court to look at such papers for the purpose of answering the question, refused to do so; and while the case was under consideration, the relator gave the bundle of papers to his client, with instructions to take them from the court. Subsequently he was examined in the same action, the trial having been adjourned to that time, and he then admitted that he had the papers in court; and he was then asked and

in the other case the question may be asked, and the witness must put himself upon his privilege. When the question is properly put, and the witness refuses to answer, his refusal is given under oath, and that refusal subjects him, practically and morally, to the same disgrace as if he had answered.

"It is not then upon the ground that the answer would disgrace the witness that he is privileged from answering in a case where his answer would tend to subject him to criminal punishment, but solely upon the ground that he shall not be compelled to give evidence against himself in a criminal case. The provision of our constitution was solely intended to protect the witness from being compelled to testify against himself in regard to a criminal offense, and when the answer would not involve criminal consequences, the constitution has no provision that will reach the case. The language of our constitution is that 'no person shall be compelled, in any criminal case, to be a witness against himself.' He can not, then, be a witness 'against himself,' unless his testimony can be used against him in his own case. The amendatory act of 1855 provides, that 'the testimony given by such witness shall in no instance be used against himself in any criminal prosecution.' We think the statute gives the witness that protection which was contemplated by the constitution, and that therefore the prisoner in this case was bound to answer." Application for rehearing denied: Ex parte Rowe, 7 Cal. 184; and see, in connection with Rowe's cases, People v. Hackley, 24 N. Y. 74; People v. Kelly, 21 How. Pr. 54; Ex parte Perkins, 18 Cal. 60.

[1] Lockwood v. State, 1 Ind. (Cart.) 161.

§ 319.   ASSAILING JUDGMENTS FOR CONTEMPT.   417

directed by the court to look at the papers, so far as to identify them, and to produce the papers, which he refused to do, giving as the reason that it would be a breach of privilege as the attorney for the defendant. Such question was stated to be pertinent to the issue, and the relator was adjudged guilty of contempt. Justice Ingraham of the supreme court decided that the attorney was not privileged from producing the papers as evidence in the case, and for the purposes of identification at least, whether he could have been required to have disclosed their contents or not—and which it was not necessary to decide; that the question of jurisdiction in the common pleas was not denied; and that the relator must be remanded.[1]

In New York, in 1843, where a witness was committed by a justice of the peace for refusing to answer questions put to him for the purpose of eliciting facts on which to found a criminal warrant of arrest, the party accused not being in the county where the justice resided, and the offense itself being committed elsewhere; it was held that the justice acted without jurisdiction, and that the prisoner was entitled to his discharge on habeas corpus, although in the case in question the supreme court on *certiorari* reversed the proceedings of the county court, discharging the prisoner, because the statutory notice required was not given to the district attorney. Justice Bronson said: "If the justice had authority to inquire into the alleged offense of Sally Grant, the commitment of Cassels could not be impeached upon habeas corpus for any supposed error of the justice in requiring the witness to answer an improper question." This, however, is qualified by the later New York decision,[2] because if an improper question is asked it affects the question of jurisdiction as much as any other question involving the want of power. The learned judge seemed to look upon the asking of an improper question as a mere error or irregularity; for, said he, "if there had been no such statute,[3] it is clear upon principle that the judgment or decision of any court of competent jurisdiction can not be reviewed on habeas corpus. If there has been error, the remedy is by *certiorari* or writ of error. When the return states the imprisonment to be by virtue of legal process, the officer may inquire whether in truth there be any process, and whether it appears upon its face to be valid; and he may also inquire whether any cause has arisen since

---

[1] People v. Sheriff, 7 Abb. Pr. 96; S. C., 29 Barb. 622.
[2] See People v. Hackley, 24 N. Y. 78 (1861); also Holman v. Mayor of Austin, 34 Tex. 673.
[3] 2 N. Y. R. S. 567, sec. 40, 42.

the commitment for putting an end to the imprisonment, as a pardon, reversal of judgment, payment of the fine, and the like. But he can not rejudge the judgment of the committing court or magistrate." With reference to the act of the justice he said: "But the prisoner had an undoubted right to show that the committing magistrate acted without authority; and this is so, notwithstanding the commitment recites the existence of the necessary facts to give jurisdiction. No court or officer can acquire jurisdiction by the mere assertion of it, or by falsely alleging the existence of facts on which jurisdiction depends. Now it turns out that, as the judge has found the facts, this supposed contempt did not happen, as the commitment states, ' on the trial of a cause ' before the justice, nor ' upon the examination of one Sally Grant on a criminal complaint.' Sally Grant was never brought before the justice. She was not in the county of Chenango, nor was it pretended that she had ever committed any offense in that county. The crime which they were attempting to fasten upon her was committed in the county of Rensselaer, where she lived. Here neither the crime nor the offender was in Chenango, and the justice was without the shadow of authority in attempting to inquire into the matter. The whole proceeding was *coram non judice*." [1]

In the state of New Hampshire the general rule of the conclusiveness of judgments for contempts was applied with some strictness where a justice of the peace had fined one for refusing to answer a question on the ground that it would disclose his case and the manner in which he proposed to prove it. Justice Bellows of the supreme court treated the matter at length, and cited many authorities, yet he recognized and examined the question, whether the magistrate had jurisdiction to punish the relator for contempt, and there being no suggestion of any want of authority to take the deposition of the relator, or to require him to answer proper questions, he was remanded.[2]

In Mississippi it was ordered by the circuit court of Hinds county "that George H. Adams be sent to jail, and remain there until he signifies his assent to the court to answer questions to the grand jury, or until the final adjournment of said grand jury at this term of the court." This was considered a good return, so far as showing that the prisoner was imprisoned by the judgment of a court of competent authority, and the high court of errors and appeals said it would not be proper to

---

[1] People v. Cassels, 5 Hill, 164.
[2] State ex rel. Welsh v. Towle, 42 N. H. 540.

§ 320.   ASSAILING JUDGMENTS FOR CONTEMPT.   419

examine into the proceedings, whether the questions asked the witness and refused by him to be answered were legal or not; and if that could be reviewed at all, it must be by an appellate tribunal. The prisoner was released, however, because it did not appear from the return that there had been any conviction or judgment of the circuit court for a contempt of the authority of that court, for it was held unlawful to imprison a person until convicted by a court of competent jurisdiction, and which conviction and judgment must appear by the record.[1]

§ 320. **Orders of Court to Pay over Money.**— In the supreme court of South Carolina, it has been said by A. J. Wright, J., that "a party committed for contempt, adjudged by a court of competent jurisdiction, will not be discharged under it. If, however, the alleged contempt is for disobedience of an order in which the court, in the matter before it, was without jurisdiction, the court having the right to grant the writ [of habeas corpus] may inquire into the legality of the caption and detention. Where a court in so important a matter as that which affects personal liberty oversteps the limits of its authority, and endeavors to enforce obedience to its unauthorized acts, it would be a reflection on the administration of public justice if there was no jurisdiction to which the imprisoned citizen could resort for enlargement." And this, whether the warrant issues in a civil or criminal proceeding. These principles were applied under the following circumstances: The surety of an administrator petitioned to the judge of probate to be relieved from his liability as surety. The judge cited the administrator to appear before him, took an account of his administration, found a balance to be due by him, and ordered him to pay it into court, and his letters to be revoked. The administrator failed to comply with the order, and he was ordered to be arrested and imprisoned, by the judge, until he did comply with the order. The sheriff made the arrest, and the administrator was discharged on habeas corpus by a circuit judge, on the ground that the imprisonment was without authority in law. The supreme court affirmed the judgment, and held that, in such a case, the probate judge had power to revoke the letters of administration, or to require a new bond, with additional sureties, but not to give a money decree against an administrator, or to imprison an administrator for failure to comply with the terms of a money decree, as that would be in violation of the constitutional provisions respecting imprisonment for debt.[2]

[1] Ex parte Adams, 25 Miss. 883.   [2] Gilliam v. McJunkin, 2 Rich. 442.

The failure to pay over the money was not called by the probate judge a contempt. But the supreme court seem to have so considered it.

In Wisconsin it has also been decided that, no matter how erroneous an order or judgment of a court may be, the party imprisoned can not be released upon habeas corpus; but if the court has no authority to make the order or judgment, it can be assailed. It was also held, that before one can be imprisoned for a contempt, he must be convicted of a contempt; as where he owes money which he has received as trustee and does not pay, and is imprisoned for this alone, without there being any proceedings taken to convict him of a contempt. Were a court, ordering one to be imprisoned for the non-payment of money, to determine that the trustee had the money then in his hands, and consequently had the ability to pay it, as well as the fact that he did not pay it, the constitutional question might arise, whether the refusal to pay the money would constitute a contempt for which he might be imprisoned. But when this is not done, and the trustee is imprisoned for not paying over the money, and without any adjudication of contempt, the imprisonment is unlawful, under a constitutional provision prohibiting imprisonment for debt arising out of or founded on a contract, and the prisoner will be discharged on habeas corpus.[1]

It has been held in California that the court has power to order the husband to pay money to the wife for her support during the pendency of divorce proceedings, and to order counsel fees and other legal expenses to be paid; and that such orders may be enforced by imprisonment for contempt for refusal to pay. It can not be argued that these sums ordered to be paid are debts within the meaning of the constitution, and that one can not be imprisoned for the refusal to pay such debts, except by proof of fraud. "It is well answered," say the supreme court, "that this is not a debt within the meaning of this article. The husband is bound to support the wife, yet this duty is an imperfect obligation which is not technically a debt. He does not owe her any specific amount of money, but he owes a duty to her which may be enforced by the order of a court, compelling him to pay her money. So alimony, temporary or permanent, may be decreed by the court; and this may be done, not in one gross sum or at any one time only, but in different sums at different times, at the discretion of the court. Nor does this power exhaust itself by a mere provision for the actual neces-

---

[1] In re Gaylord Blair, 4 Wis. 522.

sary support of the wife during the litigation; but it is equally within the power of the court to decree the payment of the legal expenses of the suit. Legal expenses may well be included in this provision, and this includes the fees to attorneys. This is not a debt, as has been decided by the supreme court of Connecticut in Lyon v. Lyon, 21 Conn. 185." In considering such a case on habeas corpus, the power of the original court to make the order is the only question. And where the court of first instance has jurisdiction, the prisoner will be remanded.[1]

In the same state disobedience of a decree of distribution by an executor or administrator has been held to be a contempt of court, and that an executor who was imprisoned for contempt by order of a superior court for refusing to pay over money under a decree of distribution could not be released upon habeas corpus, as the court had jurisdiction to make the order, and the process was valid upon its face. The inquiry could not extend beyond these two questions.[2]

§ 321. **Conditions Impossible of Performance.**—In Ex parte Maulsby's Case[3] the commitment was "until he purge the contempt, by appearing before the grand jury," etc.; "but," said Judge Bartol, "it appears that the grand jury has been discharged, so that it has become impossible for him to obey the court's process; and the question arises whether by reason of that fact he is entitled to be discharged, or in other words, whether the term of imprisonment as fixed by the warrant is ended. This point was not presented in the argument, but it seems to me upon the best reasons which I am able to apply to the subject, and by the analysis of the law, that on this ground it is my duty to discharge the petitioner. It is always competent to inquire whether anything has arisen since the commitment to put an end to the imprisonment, as a pardon, or an expiration of the term fixed by the commitment.[4] There is no doubt of the power of the court to commit until the party answer or testify, or produce papers before a grand jury. In such a case the commitment is a compulsory process to compel the party to obey the court's process; it must result from necessity that the term of imprisonment imposed is ended, and that the party is entitled to be discharged; otherwise the imprisonment would be perpetual. In this case, the duration of the imprisonment must be determined by the terms of the commitment and its legal operation and effect. It is until he purge the contempt by

[1] Ex parte Perkins, 18 Cal. 60.
[2] Ex parte Cohn, 55 Cal. 193.
[3] 13 Md. 641, app.
[4] People v. Cassels, 5 Hill, 164.

appearing before the grand jury and producing the papers to them. How can that be done after the grand jury has been discharged? It has become impossible, although the petitioner should be ready and willing to do so. If in an ordinary case a witness, failing to recognize, be committed to the custody of the sheriff, for the purpose of testifying to the grand jury, when the grand jury is finally discharged he is entitled to be released; and in my opinion the same principle applies to this case. The term of imprisonment fixed by the warrant is ended by operation of law: not because the court has not the power to commit for contempt for a period extending beyond the term of the court, but because in this case it has not done so. This point may not, perhaps, be free from doubt; but if that be conceded, it is my duty to cast whatever doubt may exist in favor of the liberty of the citizen, and I shall therefore order the discharge of the petitioner." So in New York a commitment for contempt in not delivering possession of property pursuant to an order of court must show on its face that the person committed had possession or control over the property, and on habeas corpus proceedings to release a prisoner from a commitment defective in this respect the court can not supply the defect by resorting to the papers on which the original order to give possession was made.[1]

§ 322. **Neglect to Pay Tax.**—Where a statute authorizes the receiver of taxes to make application to a court to enforce the payment of a tax which the person owing neglects or refuses to pay, and which has been imposed on him for personal property, the court may punish the delinquent as for a contempt, on account of his neglect to pay the tax, and if the jurisdiction of the court is sound, its adjudication is final and conclusive.

---

[1] People ex rel. Walters v. Conner, 15 Abb. Pr., N. S., 430. "When the time for doing an act or taking a proceeding is expressly fixed by act of parliament, the twelfth rule of order 32 of the consolidated general orders (providing for cases where the time for doing an act or taking a proceeding expires on a day on which the offices are closed) does not enable such act or proceeding to be done or taken after the expiration of the time so fixed. Accordingly, where the thirty days limited by the act of 11 Geo. IV., and 1 Wm. IV., c. 36, sec. 15, rule 5, as the period within which a defendant in custody under process of contempt ought to have been brought by habeas corpus to the bar of the court, expired on a day in term-time, but on which the courts were closed by special order of the lord chancellor: held, that the above-mentioned rule did not enable the plaintiff to bring the defendant to the bar of the court on the day on which the offices next opened; and upon motion on such last-named day that the defendant might be turned over to the custody of the keeper of the queen's prison, the court refused to make any order," and no attempt being made to detain the prisoner, he departed out of custody: Flower v. Bright, 2 John. & H. 590.

Whether right or wrong, the decision of the court upon the merits can not be inquired into on habeas corpus.[1]

§ 323. **Disobedience of Orders, Judgments, and Decrees of Court.**—In New York a petitioner applied to the supreme court on habeas corpus to be released from a commitment, by a justice of the supreme court presiding at special term, for a contempt in not complying with a judgment of the supreme court— to execute a conveyance of a house and lot. There was no doubt that the cause of commitment was one within the powers and authority of the court, so they remanded the prisoner.[2] Again, in the same state, one Kearney was convicted of contempt and committed to jail on attachment issued out of the New York common pleas, for disobedience of an order made by Judge Hilton, in proceedings supplementary to execution, directing Kearney to pay the plaintiff in such proceedings the amount of the judgment therein, with interest, and twenty-five dollars costs and disbursements, within ten days, or in default thereof that an attachment issue. Kearney sued out a habeas corpus from the supreme court. The order directing the attachment to issue appeared to be signed by Judge Daly as an order in a proceeding before him, but was entitled " at chambers of the court of common pleas of the city and county of New York," and was indorsed by the clerk of that court: " By special order of the court."

The point made in behalf of the prisoner was, that the proceedings not being before Judge Daly, he had not the authority nor jurisdiction, under section 302 of the code, to order the attachment to issue; and that the court of common pleas had not the jurisdiction to direct it to issue, but the judge alone before whom the proceeding was pending, and that the clerk marked the process " By special order of the court" in an unauthorized manner. But the court, after reviewing authorities,[3] held that the order of the judge directing the attachment to issue must be considered as the order of the court, and that the clerk regularly marked the writ. It was further objected that the process omitted to state that the prisoner was adjudged to be guilty of contempt; but the supreme court said that the attachment plainly charged one by clearly stating the facts constituting a contempt, and they so treated it. It was further objected that Kearney was imprisoned for non-payment of costs as well as of the judgment, and that imprisonment for costs had been abolished. But said the court: " Sections 297 and 301 [of

---

[1] Kahn's Case, 11 Abb Pr. 147.
[2] Davison's Case, 13 Abb. Pr. 129.
[3] Wicker v. Dresser, 13 How. Pr. 331; *contra:* Shepherd v. Dean, Id. 173.

the code], taken together, warrant the judge to order the payment of costs, if property be found in the hands of the debtor sufficient for that purpose. In such case the default of the prisoner in not paying the costs was a contempt, as well as in neglecting to pay the judgment. We are not at liberty to inquire whether the prisoner had the money or not. If the judge erred in adjudging that the prisoner had the money, his remedy exists in another way, but not by the writ of habeas corpus. Nor is the prisoner remediless. Section 302 authorizes the judge who committed him, or the court in which the judgment was rendered, to discharge him, if the prisoner is unable to pay the money directed to be paid or to endure his imprisonment."[1] Prisoner remanded.

So in proceedings under the New York statute for contempt,[2] where appellant was imprisoned under a commitment for a contempt of court in violating an order of injunction, and sought to be discharged on habeas corpus solely on the ground that in the amount of the fine imposed upon him there was included the sum of one hundred and fifty dollars for counsel fees in the proceedings to punish the appellant for contempt, it was held that the court had jurisdiction to determine the amount of costs and expenses to be imposed as a fine upon a conviction for contempt, and that if in determining this amount it included items which ought not properly to be allowed as costs and expenses, that would merely be an erroneous decision on a matter which the law had committed to its judgment, and would not constitute an excess of jurisdiction or power. "That such an error can not render the commitment void, or be reviewed on habeas corpus, is too plain a proposition to admit of argument."[3]

In Nevada, in the case of Phillips v. Welch et al.,[4] defendants had been perpetually enjoined from diverting any part of plaintiff's portion of water running in King's canyon, or otherwise depriving him of the use of the same for irrigation and for stock and domestic purposes. But E. D. Sweeney, one of the said defendants, did unlawfully and intentionally divert the waters of said stream in quantities largely in excess of the quantities authorized or permitted by the decree, and for uses and purposes not authorized but forbidden by it. On affidavit Sweeney was attached and fined heavily for contempt. He demurred to the

---

[1] Kearney's Case, 13 Abb. Pr. 459; S. C., 22 How. Pr. 309.
[2] 2 R. S. 1836, marg. p. 534.
[3] People exrel. Woolf v. Jacobs, 66 N. Y. 8.
[4] 11 Nev. 187.

sufficiency of the affidavit, in the district court of Ormsby county, but his demurrer was overruled.¹

In Mississippi, the strict rule is followed generally without qualification. There the court of probate has power to imprison by attachment, for a contempt, an administrator, guardian, or executor, for his failure or refusal to comply with any lawful order or decree of the court, and on the ground that each court is the sole and exclusive judge of contempts against its authority it has been held that there is no tribunal to review the judgment.²

§ 324. **Disobedience of Orders, Judgments, and Decrees of Court, Continued.**—Mr. Justice P. Davis of the supreme court of New York, has lately said: "There is no difficulty in officers clothed with the authority of judicial processes executing them in conformity to the dictates of good sense, as to time, place, and manner; and officers who do not do this have no right to demand that the laws shall be strained for their vindication or protection, especially when their acts may lead to the evils that attend a panic in a crowded theater."

John Smith was the doorkeeper of the private entrance to Niblo's theater, and through which actors and employees only were allowed to pass. Officers wished to enter that way for the purpose of arresting W. M. Devine, then upon the boards, and who was alleged to have the illegal custody of a child, the warrant being issued on application and petition of the Society for the Prevention of Cruelty to Children. The officers showed

---

¹ On an original application to the supreme court for a writ of *certiorari*, they said: "The essential fact to be determined by the court was whether or not the defendant Sweeney had, in disobedience of the decree and of the lawful process issued thereunder in the suit of Phillips v. Welch, deprived the said plaintiff, Phillips, of the quantity of water decreed to him in that case. There is an averment in the affidavit that Phillips was deprived of the water to which he was entitled, by the excessive and unlawful diversion and use of the water by Sweeney. It is also stated that Sweeney, in direct violation of said decree, unlawfully and intentionally diverted the waters of King's canyon creek in quantities largely in excess of the quantities authorized or permitted by the decree, to plaintiff's damage, etc. The affidavit shows the exact quantity to which Sweeney is entitled, and when it states that he used a greater quantity, it is as positive in its terms, in so far as the question of violating the decree and order is concerned, as if it stated the exact fractional part of the water of the stream which he had unlawfully diverted. But admitting that there is a defect in the manner of stating these facts, it does not, as did the omission in Batchelder v. Moore, 42 Cal. 414, reach the substance, so as to be 'obviously jurisdictional in its consequences.' The truth is, that in a case like the present, where the court acquired jurisdiction of the subject-matter and of the person of the petitioner, this court has no jurisdiction, either on appeal, writ of error, habeas corpus, or *certiorari*, and the writ must be dismissed:" Phillips v. Welch, Sweeney, Petitioner, 12 Nev. 158.

² Watson v. Williams, 36 Miss. 331.

their warrant to Smith, but he replied that he had peremptory orders to prevent the entrance of all other persons than those mentioned above, and he prevented the officers' entrance, but sent word to the manager, Gilmore, of the officers' presence. Gilmore was not found, and knew nothing of the actions at the door. Held, that the manager was not guilty of a contempt in resisting the mandate of a court where it appeared that the rule of exclusion above mentioned, and which had been a standing one for many years, was necessary for the proper management of the theater, and was made for that purpose, and when it did not appear that the appellant Gilmore had any notice of the action of the doorkeeper on the night in question, or intended in any way to shield the actor or prevent his arrest.[1]

There is a difference between the disobedience of an order of court and an adjudication of contempt. Where one was committed until he paid a fine of five thousand eight hundred and seventy-six dollars and fifty cents and interest, and there was no adjudication that it was in the defendant's power to pay, it

---

[1] "Of course," his honor said, "such a rule could not operate to prevent the entrance of officers armed with a lawful process, seeking persons charged with crime who might be upon the stage of the theater; but the act of the doorkeeper in excluding an officer can not be attributed as a criminal offense to the proprietor of the theater, on the simple ground that he had established such a general rule. The conduct of the officers in seeking to enter and serve the process at that time and during the performance in the theater, under the circumstances of this case, certainly deserves condemnation. They must have known that an entrance upon the stage of several officers for such a purpose, in the midst of a performance before a crowded house, would be likely to lead to excitement and commotion, probably alarming, if not dangerous, to the audience. Under such circumstances, a refusal to permit an entrance at that time for such purpose, although the strict legal right existed, can well be looked upon as less culpable than an actual criminal act, and certainly the law should not infer a criminal act from the mere existence of a reasonable general rule in respect of such admission, designed to preserve the theater from unreasonable invasion, and protect the audience from the possible consequences of such disturbance. Held, further, that to render a person guilty of contempt under sections 8 and 9 of the code of civil procedure, for resisting 'a lawful mandate of a court of record,' the mandate must have been issued by a court, and not by a justice thereof. We are unable to find anything in the evidence to uphold the conclusion that the appellant, by any act he is shown to have done, was amenable to the law for a criminal contempt. The order of the court below not only adjudges him guilty of such contempt, but imposes the heaviest penalty which the law permits therefor; to wit, an imprisonment in the county jail for the period of thirty days and a fine of two hundred and fifty dollars. We think the order was a mistaken exercise of the authority of the court given by the provisions of the code, and for that reason it is clearly our duty to reverse the same upon appeal, with ten dollars costs and disbursements against the respondent, the Society for the Prevention of Cruelty to Children:" The People of the State of N. Y. ex rel. The Society for the Prevention of Cruelty to Children v. Gilmore, 26 Hun, 1. When a mandate ought to be considered as issued by the court, was considered in this case; also, when by the justice signing the same.

§ 325. ASSAILING JUDGMENTS FOR CONTEMPT. 427

was held that the process was in the form of a commitment for contempt, and that the prisoner must be discharged; as he had a right to have an opportunity to answer on interrogatories as to his ability to pay.[1] In the same state it is held that a surrogate can not inflict a fine and then commit upon the fine. The statute[2] reads: "When any rule or order of court shall have been made for the payment of costs, or any other sum of money, and proof by affidavit shall have been made of the personal demand of such sum of money, and of a refusal to pay it, the court may issue a precept to commit the person so disobeying to prison until such sum and the costs and expenses of the proceeding be paid." The punishment here is simple imprisonment. The process is strictly and purely remedial. The nature of the imprisonment by fines is the most punitory in its character of any that can be inflicted, and it seems this was expressly intended to have been avoided by the above statute. But the other provisions of the statute are held to be punitive, in most instances purely so.[3] If, however, before a judgment debtor be committed, on an attachment issued for refusal to obey an order, made in supplementary proceedings, that she apply to the satisfaction of the judgment a sum of money belonging to her, and which has been adjudged to be in her possession, it is a commitment for contempt, and the debtor is not entitled to the liberties of jail as she would be where it was merely a disobedience of an order for the payment of money which it was not adjudged that she had. For want of such adjudication here the rule of contempt applies, although there has been no adjudication of contempt for refusal to pay over the money.[4]

§ 325. **Notice and Service of Orders, etc.—Ability to Obey—Demand, etc.**—Where a statute provides as follows,[5] the proceedings must be taken, or one will be released on habeas corpus from a commitment for contempt for disobeying an order of court to pay a stipulated attorney's fee for services in directing and managing an estate of which petitioner is executor.[6] It

---

[1] In the Matter of Watson, 3 Lans. 408.
[2] 2 N. Y. R. S. 1836, marg. p. 535, sec. 4.
[3] People v. Cowles, 4 Keyes, 38; In the Matter of Watson, 5 Lans. 466.
[4] People v. Cowles, 3 Abb. App. Dec. 507, reversing People v. Cowles, 34 How. Pr. 481.
[5] Sec. 1212, C. C. P. of Cal. Where the contempt is not committed in the immediate view and presence of the court or judge, a warrant of attachment may be issued to bring the person charged to answer, or, without a previous arrest, a warrant of commitment may upon notice or upon an order to show cause, be granted; and no warrant of commitment can be issued without such previous attachment to answer, or such notice or order to show cause.
[6] Ex parte Rush, 60 Cal. 5.

is also held in the supreme court of California that in a commitment for contempt of court in disobeying its order to pay alimony, "proof of a technical service of the order, and of a demand that it be complied with, would doubtless establish a case of disobedience, unless the person upon whom the demand was made was unable to comply with it. But it by no means follows that a disobedience of the order might not be shown without proof of such formal service or demand. The question whether the order had been disobeyed was one of fact, which the court making the order had to determine, and that determination can not be reviewed in this proceeding [by habeas corpus]: 'We do not sit as an appellate court upon matters of this sort, but as a court of original jurisdiction, invested with a special jurisdiction to discharge the petitioner when no legal cause of detention exists against him.'[1]

"Upon the same principle, we can not discharge the prisoner on the ground that he testified to his inability to comply with the order he is charged with having disobeyed. If he could not obey it, he should not be punished for not obeying it. But the question whether it was in his power to obey it was one of fact, which the court making the order had to determine, and we are not aware of any law which makes the statement of a party under oath that he is unable to comply with such an order absolutely conclusive. The court may, nevertheless, have good and sufficient reasons for disbelieving his statement. In this case we could not determine that question without reviewing all the evidence introduced upon the hearing before the superior court, and that we are not authorized to do in this proceeding. In Ex parte Cohen, 6 Cal. 318, the order of commitment did not contain a recital that it was in the power of Cohen to have complied with the order which he had disobeyed.[2] The order of commitment in this case does recite that it was in the power of the petitioner to have obeyed the order which he had disobeyed. Without reviewing the evidence, we could not determine whether that recital is true or not, and, as before stated, we can not review the evidence." This case was brought before the court by an attachment, and the court further said that the code[3] did not make a service of the judgment or order disobeyed, or a demand upon the person who was bound to obey it, a condition

---

[1] Citing Ex parte Perkins, 18 Cal. 60.

[2] "This being the case," said Mr. Justice Terry, in Cohen's case, "we are satisfied that the court exceeded its jurisdiction in making an order which, from the record alluded to, was equivalent to imprisonment for life."

[3] See Cal. C. C. P., sec. 1212, quoted *supra*.

§ 325. ASSAILING JUDGMENTS FOR CONTEMPT. 429

precedent to the issuing of an attachment against him for disobeying it; also that the writ of habeas corpus was not framed to retry issues of fact, or to review the proceedings of a legal trial.[1]

Prior to these proceedings Cottrell had made another application to the supreme court for discharge on habeas corpus, from a commitment for an alleged contempt of court in disobeying its order to pay alimony, and made the points that the court below exceeded its jurisdiction in increasing the amount over that decreed by the judgment entered in the action; and that no copy of the order was served upon him; but the court held that the code[2] authorized the court to modify its orders in this respect from time to time, and that the presence of petitioner in court when the order was made, and his subsequent refusal to obey it, was sufficient to authorize a proceeding against him for contempt.[3]

The supreme court of California have fully committed themselves to the doctrine, that to adjudge a party guilty of a contempt of court, for which he is fined and imprisoned, is to adjudge him guilty of a distinct criminal offense; that the imposition of the fine is a judgment in a criminal case; and that they have the power to review by habeas corpus, *certiorari*, or appeal the jurisdiction of the primary court to punish and imprison for such an offense. Hence it was held that a superior court had no authority on a rule to show cause, etc., to adjudge one guilty of contempt, and to fine and imprison him for not turning over to a receiver in insolvency moneys, property, and effects held in his possession, and under his control, and adversely to the insolvent debtor. Such a power, they say, can not be exercised over a party unless he has collected and holds the money, property, and effects as trustee for the estate of the insolvent debtor, and the court has jurisdiction over him as an officer of the court, or as a party to the proceedings. The petitioner claimed the property under title adverse to all the world; and the court said: "If his title is claimed to be invalid or fraudulent and void, he is entitled to be heard according to the forms of law. Proceedings to punish him for contempt for not delivering it up, without a trial according to law, to another who claims it, are not the appropriate proceedings for the trial of

---

[1] Citing Ex parte Bird, 19 Cal. 131; Ex parte Cottrell, 59 Id. 420; S. C., 8 Pac. C. L. J. 875; S. P., In the Matter of Bissell, 40 Mich. 63.
[2] Cal. C. C., sec. 139.
[3] Ex parte Cottrell, 59 Cal. 417. In this case the petitioner was cited to appear by an order to show cause: See Cal. C. C. P., sec. 1212, quoted *supra*.

issue of title. The issue as to such title should be tried in an appropriate action, in which the verdict of a jury or the findings of the court may be had upon issues properly framed for the purpose of definitely determining the question of title."[1]

In New York it has been held that where a party has been committed for contempt by the rule of a court of record, if it is such a rule as the court could legally make under any circumstances, all jurisdictional steps and matters of regularity are to be presumed; and it seems that even on *certiorari* to remove a summary conviction by an inferior court the superior court will intend the proper notice to acquire jurisdiction.[2] But in Vermont, while the supreme court thought they could not re-examine the adjudication of contempt of a court of competent jurisdiction, where a chancellor committed one for contempt—upon the showing of the adverse party, and without any notice to the person convicted—they regarded the judgment as "irregular," and discharged the party. Said Chief Justice Redfield: "I can find no precedent for any such proceeding, and in principle it is certainly a very irresponsible authority to extend to any tribunal. It is of the essence of all convictions or adjudications that the party accused should have an opportunity to be heard in his defense. Not always before a jury perhaps, but that he should at least, in contemplation of law, have some opportunity for defense. And in convictions for contempts, which are always a summary, an arbitrary, and offensive jurisdiction (unless the contempt be committed in view of the court or magistrate), the party accused is to have an opportunity to be heard before he is adjudged finally guilty of the contempt and punished. He may be and often is committed before the conviction for the contempt. But this is done to secure his presence before the court to answer for the contempt, when he may be convicted. It seems to be assumed, as the general rule of chancery law, that the parties being served with process for the general purposes of the suit may be proceeded against and adjudged guilty of contempt without notice or excuse therefor, and punished. But this is a distinct and independent matter as much as a new suit, and obviously requires a distinct notice as much as a new suit. Such is the uniform practice of courts of chancery, as far as we can learn, and for this irregularity we think the respondent is entitled to be discharged."[3]

[1] Ex parte Hollis, 59 Cal. 405, citing Larrabee v. Selby, 52 Id. 508.
[2] People v. Nevins, 1 Hill (N. Y), 154; In the Matter of Pércy, 2 Daly, 530.
[3] Ex parte Langdon, 25 Vt. 680.

§ 326. **Suspending Attorney.**—It has been held in Pennsylvania that the supreme court have jurisdiction to review a proceeding for contempt in the common pleas; that a failure on the part of a witness to appear and be examined, in obedience to the mandate of a subpœna, is not a contempt of court, but a contempt " of the process of the law;" that a contempt for not obeying a subpœna can only be punished by fine; and that a gentleman of the bar, in contempt of the process of the law, by neglecting to appear before an examiner to testify, can not be punished by suspending him from his profession. The supreme court, however, does not, they say, revise such cases upon their merits. " The courts having a limited jurisdiction in contempts, every fact found by them is to be taken as true, and every intendment is to be made in favor of their record, if it appears to us that they proceeded within and did not exceed their jurisdiction; but for the purpose of seeing that their jurisdiction has not been transcended, and that their proceedings, as they appear of record, have been according to law, we possess, and are bound to exercise, a supervisory power over the courts of the commonwealth." In such a case on *certiorari*, the supreme court restored a lawyer, who had been " stripped of his profession," to his rights and privileges as an attorney, on the ground of want of jurisdiction in the lower court to inflict such a punishment.[1]

§ 327. **Malpractice of Sheriff.**—In Indiana the strict rule was followed in such a case. The sheriff had been charged with fraud in not executing a *capias ad respondendum*. On rule, etc., attachment for contempt issued, and on its return interrogatories were answered by the defendant, the sheriff. Upon these the circuit court of Harrison county considered that the defendant had cleared himself of the alleged contempt, and ordered his discharge. On error to this court, Justice Blackford, of the supreme court, said: "It is contended on the part of the prosecutor, who is the judgment creditor, that the circuit court committed an error in setting aside the attachment and discharging the sheriff before he had satisfied the execution, which, without any justification, he had failed to execute. There can be no doubt that, had the circuit court, on the answer to interrogatories, been of opinion that the complaint of the prosecutor was well founded, they had authority to punish the sheriff for the contempt by way of fine or imprisonment. Had they considered their officer guilty of such gross malprac-

---

[1] Com. v. Newton, 1 Grant Cas. 453.

tice as to require his being compelled in this summary manner to satisfy the judgment, they might, for the contempt, have committed him to prison, or heavily amerced him, and have then refused to discharge him or remit the fine, until the judgment was satisfied.[1] In the present case, the court seem to have had no doubt of their authority on the subject, but to have been satisfied from the answer to interrogatories that the sheriff had, upon oath, purged the contempt; and they accordingly discharged him from the attachment. It must be borne in mind that this discharge of the sheriff by the circuit court does not at all determine the question of his liability to the judgment creditor for any neglect of duty in not serving the execution. By setting aside the attachment, the court below only determine that the sheriff has, upon oath, purged the contempt. With that determination we can have no concern. Whether the circuit court has been treated with contempt or not, is for that court alone to decide. Courts of record have exclusive control over charges for contempt; and their conviction or acquittal is final and conclusive." The writ of error was dismissed for want of jurisdiction.[2]

§ 328. **Judgment for Contempt under Unconstitutional Law.**—In Alabama the general rule is recognized that every court is the exclusive judge of a contempt committed in its presence or against its process; and that the exercise by a court of competent jurisdiction of the power to punish for such contempt can not be revised on error or assailed collaterally by writ of habeas corpus; but where there is either a total want of or an excess of jurisdiction in the court under the order or

---

[1] Rex v. The Sheriff of Middlesex, 1 H. Black. 544.

[2] The State on the Prosecution of Leavenworth v. Tipton, Late Sheriff of Harrison, 1 Blackf. 166. See also Johnston v. Commonwealth, 1 Bibb. 598, for strict rule; and also State v. White, T. U. P. Charlt. 136, where it is said: "In proceedings for contempts, if the return shows a good cause of commitment, it will be valid, though it may want form. This court will not, therefore, discharge persons committed for a contempt of the inferior courts; and especially this court will not discharge or admit to bail officers of such inferior courts committed for a contempt against them."

In Ex parte Cohen and Jones, 5 Cal. 495, it was said: "In the examination of this question, we should be careful to distinguish between the erroneous exercise of a power conferred by law and the usurpation of power. If the district court has jurisdiction, under any circumstances, to make an order requiring persons not parties to the record to deliver property to the officer of the court, the issuance of such an order in an improper case would be error certainly, which an appellate court would correct, but would not be a usurpation of power or an excess of jurisdiction. See also Ex parte Summers, 5 Ired. 149, for doctrine that if the court does not state the facts upon which it proceeds, a revising tribunal may, on a habeas corpus, discharge the party, if it plainly appear that the facts do not amount to a contempt. See State v. Woodfin, Id. 199.

§ 329.   ASSAILING JUDGMENTS FOR CONTEMPT.   433

judgment of which the process issued, an offender for an alleged contempt may be released upon habeas corpus. Thus, the constitutional provision of Alabama that "no person shall be imprisoned for debt" has reference only to obligations *ex contractu*, and no exception is made in cases of fraud. And under this state of constitutional law, a new and extensive jurisdiction is conferred by the general assembly upon courts of chancery not previously possessed, and having for its manifest object the coercion of the payment of an ordinary judgment debt by imprisonment under the guise of making a refusal to pay a contempt of court. As the legislature can not do indirectly what it is prohibited from doing directly, any law which it may pass seeking by evasion or indirect means to accomplish an unconstitutional end is void. John Hardy, of Alabama, was a judgment debtor of Ransom & Co. The city court of Selma ascertained and declared, under regular proceedings therefor, that Hardy had fifty-one thousand dollars' worth of United States bonds in his possession and under his control. Hardy was ordered to pay the judgment against him. He failed to do so, and was arrested and committed to jail for contempt. Hardy was discharged on habeas corpus, "retaining," as Chief Justice Brickell said in his elaborate and able dissenting opinion in this well-considered case, "the bonds; and his creditors are informed that the constitution forbids the enactment or execution of any law by which they can obtain from the large fund in the possession of their debtor the comparatively insignificant sums due them. I can not believe that is the law and justice of Alabama."[1]

§ 329. **Irony.**—The relator was acting as counsel for one Bergin, in the trial of a petty larceny case before a justice of the peace in Vermont. Some preliminary question was raised and discussed by the counsel, and decided by Justice Guild, who, after deciding the question, remarked to the complainant that "it might be convenient enough for Mr. Cooper [the relator] to have the supreme court sit here all the time." The complainant replied: "I don't think that is necessary, for I think this magistrate wiser than the supreme court." The justice instantly replied: "You are fined ten dollars for contempt." Cooper was arrested and imprisoned for the contempt. The case went on habeas corpus to the county court, and thence to the supreme court, but Mr. Cooper could not get the judgment against him reviewed. His plea of misapprehension as to the power of the

[1] Ex parte Hardy, 68 Ala. 303; S. C., 13 Cent. L. J. 50.

judge to fine him did not avail anything, or his mistake as to the justice's motives in asking him the question he did. In Vermont justices' courts are courts of record. Their jurisdiction is important and extensive, and in many matters final and exclusive. They have the power to fine and imprison, and their power to do so in this case was unquestioned, so they remanded Mr. Cooper.[1]

§ 330. **Disobedience of Subpœna.**—In Iowa the supreme court recognize the rule, and consider it well settled, that when one is being punished for contempt, unless the proceedings leading thereto are so grossly defective as to render them void, the judgment of commitment can not, in the absence of statute, be reviewed in any other tribunal, and certainly can not otherwise, or in other cases, be assailed under the writ of habeas corpus. Justices of the peace there[2] have power, when one person desires the affidavit of another, upon application of the former to require the appearance of the latter before him by subpœna; and a refusal to obey the justice's subpœna, or to answer when brought before him, is a contempt, and may be punished as such by that officer. The witness can not show a want of authority or jurisdiction in the justice by establishing the fact that the affidavit desired by the party at whose instance the subpœna was issued would not be legally admissible in the proceeding pending in another forum, for which it is sought or in which it is desired to be used. The witness can not make himself judge of this matter, and on habeas corpus in such a case he will not be released.[3]

§ 331. **Jurisdiction to Commit—Mandamus.**—A writ of *mandamus* can compel a public officer to do only what the law requires him to do, and it can not issue to one officer to compel another to do his duty. A board of county commissioners in Alabama were ordered by *mandamus* to levy and cause to be collected a tax. They held a meeting, levied the tax, and ordered the tax-collector to collect it. They performed all the duties which the law required them to do. But the tax-collector failed to do his duty—to collect the tax. His failure to do so was reported by the commissioners to the governor of the state. But the commissioners, notwithstanding this, were ordered by the circuit court of the United States for the middle district of Alabama to be committed for contempt for not causing the col-

---

[1] In re Cooper, 32 Vt. 253 265.
[2] Sec. 4038 of the Revision of 1860.
[3] Robb v. McDonald, 29 Iowa, 330; S. C., 6 Am. Law Rev. 320.

lection of the tax. This commitment was reviewed in the supreme court of the United States on habeas corpus, and Chief Justice Waite observed: "If the command of the peremptory writ of *mandamus* was in all respects such as the circuit court had jurisdiction to make, the proceedings for the contempt are not reviewable here; but if the command was in whole or in part beyond the power of the court, the writ, or so much as was in excess of jurisdiction, was void, and the court had no right in law to punish for any contempt of its unauthorized requirements. Such is the settled rule of decision in this court: Ex parte Lange, 18 Wall. 165; Ex parte Parks, 93 U. S. 22; Ex parte Siebold, 100 Id. 371; Ex parte Virginia, Id. 339. * * *

"As a necessary consequence, the writ must issue directly against him whose duty it is to do the thing which the parties seek to have done; for, as was said in Reg. v. Mayor of Derby, 2 Salk. 436, 'it is absurd that the writ should be directed to one person to command another.' The question here is, whether it was the duty of the tax-collector, under the law, to collect the special tax which the commissioners had levied. That question the creditor could have determined in a direct proceeding against the collector, without the help of the commissioners. It follows that if the command of the writ against the commissioners was what the circuit court has construed it to be, it was in excess of the jurisdiction of the court, and consequently void. If the command of the writ was in excess of jurisdiction, so necessarily were the proceedings for contempt in not obeying. We are led, therefore, to the conclusion that the order of the court under which the marshal holds the petitioners in custody was a nullity, and that a writ of habeas corpus should issue as prayed for, unless the parties are willing that an order of discharge shall be entered without further proceedings. It is consequently so ordered." [1]

§ 332. Jurisdiction—**No Offense.**—An order of commitment was in the following words: "Ordered that George H. Adams be sent to jail, and remain there until he signifies his assent to the court to answer questions to the grand jury, or until the final adjournment of said grand jury at this term of the court." On habeas corpus to be released from imprisonment under this judgment, Mr. Justice Yerger, of the high court of errors and appeals for the state of Mississippi, used the following words: "But it is clear that a general order to imprison a party unless he has been convicted either by a jury or

---

[1] Ex parte Rowland et al., 3 Mor. Trans. 608.

by the court is a mere nullity. The law requires that before a sentence of imprisonment shall be passed against a party, he should first be convicted of an offense. In ordinary cases, this conviction must be by the verdict of a jury. In the case of contempts, it may be by the judgment of the court. Still, in either case, the record must show a conviction. Now it will be seen from this return that there is no judgment of imprisonment for a contempt generally, or for a contempt in refusing to answer questions. There is not any conviction or adjudication by the court that Mr. Adams had been guilty of a contempt. Without such judgment the court had no right to commit him to prison, nor the sheriff to detain him. It is true, and was admitted on the argument, that Mr. Adams did refuse to answer questions asked by the grand jury, and it may be true that the court considered that a contempt for which he deserved imprisonment, but no such judgment has been rendered in the case; and however many contempts the prisoner may have committed, it is not lawful to imprison him until convicted thereof by the judgment of the court, which judgment and conviction must appear by the record. For this reason I direct that he be discharged from custody."[1]

§ 333. **Jurisdiction — Refusal to Give Evidence.** — A petitioner to the supreme court of Michigan for a habeas corpus was held by virtue of a commitment, apparently valid on its face, and charging him with contempt of court in refusing to give evidence. He was allowed to go behind the judgment and show that the court committing him had no jurisdiction of the proceeding in which he was called as a witness. He did this by reading a certified copy of the complaint in the action. The court held the complaint not sufficient to confer jurisdiction upon the justice of the peace before whom the action was pending, and discharged the prisoner.[2] In another case before the same court a petitioner was ordered to be discharged because the justice of the peace had obtained no jurisdiction, on account of the complaint not setting forth facts and circumstances, as required by statute. Justice Manning in this case concurred in discharging the prisoner, on the ground that the proceedings before the justice had become discontinued, and that the commitment would not authorize an imprisonment when the prisoner could not have an opportunity to purge his contempt by answering.[3]

---

[1] Ex parte Adams, 25 Miss. 892.
[2] In the Matter of John Morton, 10 Mich. 210.
[3] In the Matter of Hall, 10 Mich. 210.

§ 334. **"Until Discharged by Due Course of Law"—Time Certain—English Courts.**—A commitment for a contempt until the party is discharged by due course of law has been held in England to be uncertain and bad;[1] and the defendant, charged by justices of the peace with a contempt, was discharged from such a judgment. And where the words of the statute were, "He shall be committed till he submit himself to be examined by the commissioners"—in bankruptcy—the conclusion of a warrant of commitment running, "or otherwise discharged by due course of law," was held naught.[2] Lord Mansfield sustained an objection that one was not committed for any limited time where the commitment ran, "till he shall be discharged according to the laws and customs of this realm."[3] But where the commitment of two justices of the peace read, "That he [the relator] should be committed to the jail, there to remain without bail or mainprise until he should have made a fair and true account, and until such money, as upon the said account should appear to be remaining in his hands, should be paid by him or his sureties to W. S.," and it was ordered that he was to be kept in jail "until he should be discharged by due course of law," Lord Ellenborough, C. J., said: "Coupling the premises with the conclusion, is it not in effect the same as if the warrant had directed the jailer to detain the party until he had accounted? We must read the warrant as if the magistrates had in the conclusion recited over again the adjudication."[4]

The above were cases of commitments made by magistrates, and how far the same principles apply to the superior courts in England is left in some doubt by the decision of the court in Crawford's Case.[5] Said Pattison, justice of queen's bench: "There is no material question as to the form of the warrant till we come to the end. It there appears that the party is committed 'until further order.' Now I can not help thinking that this is in the nature of punishment, the offense being visited in this way by the court; and that it is not like a committal of a party till he answer, which is rather in the nature of process. Then, being a punishment, it ought to be as certain as a sentence. That was held in Rex v. James,[6] where magistrates committed a party for contempt of them in the execution of their office, till 'discharged by due course of law,' there being no course of law for discharging him; and this court said that the

---

[1] King v. James, 1 Dow. & Ry. 559; S. C., 5 Barn. & Ald. 894.
[2] Hollingshead's Case, 1 Salk. 351; Bracy's Case, 1 Ld. Raym. 100.
[3] Rex v. Hall, 3 Burr. 1636.
[4] Goffs' Case, 3 Mau. & Sel. 202.
[5] 13 Ad. & El. Q. B., 629 (1849).
[6] 5 Barn. & Ald. 894.

commitment should have been for a time certain. Mr. Peacock argues that this rule does not apply to superior courts; and he distinguishes the present case from cases where, as in the instance of magistrates, the proceedings might be brought up by *certiorari*. I do not know how far that distinction is good; but I think that no English court, if their attention were called to the point, would commit by way of punishment except for a time certain."

Much has been said in some of our American reports about the established usage of the English courts in directing the imprisonment "until the further order of the court," and that it is equivalent to saying, as in common warrants, "until he be delivered by due course of law." And that this usage can be distinctly traced back to the year-books. These assertions, however, seem to be unsupported by authority; and if the learned Justice Pattison, as late as 1849, was doubtful about the distinction referred to above, and thought that "no English court, if their attention were called to the point, would commit by way of punishment except for a time certain," such statements are to be received with caution. It is indeed true that commitments for contempts, made by the house of commons, were generally during the pleasure of the house.[1] But a commitment during the pleasure of the house of commons has, in the nature of the present condition of the law, undoubtedly been held by the courts, though we are unable at present to cite an authority, to be not indefinite, as the imprisonment must terminate with the adjournment of the house. And we have been unable to find any rule authorizing a commitment by the courts "until discharged by due course of law," or "until further order of the court." Precedents might frequently have been made by letting things pass without examination; but they would be unreliable as authority. The remarks made by Mr. Justice Powys, in Regina v. Paty,[2] are very suggestive: "If all commitments for contempts, even those by this court [the queen's bench] should come to be scanned, they would not hold water."

§ 335. **"Until Further Order of the Court," Continued—Time Certain—In the United States.**—Whatever may be the spirit of the English law on this subject, ours undoubtedly greatly favors the personal liberty of one who has been committed for a contempt. In other cases than those of contempts, relief will be granted against unjust imprisonment by means of

---

[1] King v. Hobhouse, 2 Ch., Q. B., 207; Case of The Sheriff of Middlesex, 11 Ad. & El. 273; Burdett v. Abbott, 14 East, 1.
[2] 2 Ld. Raym. 1108.

§ 335.   ASSAILING JUDGMENTS FOR CONTEMPT.   439

the writ of habeas corpus; and there is nothing sacred in commitments for contempts; there is nothing that forbids the hand of justice from extending relief; and there is nothing that invests the higher courts with unlimited and uncontrolled powers over personal liberty whenever they think fit to impute contempt.[1]

The doctrine in the note just given is indorsed in Illinois. There F. E. Hinckley was adjudged to be in contempt for refusing to surrender the books, papers, and money in his hands, as receiver of a railroad, to the receiver who succeeded him in

[1] In the case of Ex parte Alexander, 2 Am. Law Reg. 44, the petitioner applied for relief from imprisonment by means of a habeas corpus. He had been committed to jail "until the further order of the court for a contempt offered in violating the decree of sale." And in the opinion rendered by Chancellor Pirtle of the Louisville chancery court of Kentucky, there occurs this language, which we adopt and indorse and make our own for the purposes of illustrating our views on the subject of which this section treats: "Is it necessary that the courts in this country should have power to commit until further order of the court? I can not find it. I can see no call for it. I can see danger in it; and the law should not make danger where there is no necessity. A freeman should never, by the laws of freemen, be placed in such dreary uncertainty of imprisonment as that when he inquires of the 'law of the land' it can not tell him when it shall end. No absolute power lives in this country. It can not exist in a republic. Suppose the court should adjourn without having made any further order, the consideration of his case is cut off at once and entirely until the next term. So he must be left without any authority of the judiciary even to meditate his case. And a person committed for contempt, can not be bailed. The time should be fixed as to its maximum. Then the punishment is duly weighed at once. Then, too, the executive may see whether it may be proper to interpose his extraordinary power—a power scarcely ever exercised in America in cases of contempts, because of the leniency of our courts, and because the governors have deemed the pardoning of contempts an interference with the necessary power of the judiciary. When the time is fixed beyond which the court will not go, then the addition to the order 'or until the further order of the court' would keep the whole matter in charge of the court, so that on proper terms the party might be released before the time arrived. So when there is a commitment for the purpose of enforcing the payment of money or the delivery of property, the court should provide in the order that the party be discharged on giving surety for the money in some form when he has not got it; and on paying the price of the property, if it shall turn out that the party can not deliver it; and so of other cases, in order that nothing shall be inflicted but of necessity.

"I know it was decided in 1810 by the supreme court of New York, that a commitment until further order of the court was valid. This case was reversed by the senate, whether on this ground or not I do not know; nor do I regard the opinion of the senate, except for its argument: Case of Yates, 4 Johns. 318; S. C., 6 Id. 337. In the syllabus made by the reporter to the case of Yates v. Lansing, 9 Id. 395, it is said that what was decided by the supreme court in the first case was affirmed in this; but this is not authorized by what was decided in the case, and the syllabus is wrong. The judgment of the supreme court in New York is certainly a precedent that any of us at first thought might follow. But I do not think its doctrines can be derived from our institutions, nor do I think we can venture to transplant such from beyond the water; we can not even say it was the common law." The commitment of Alexander was pronounced invalid.

the management of the road. He was adjudged "to stand committed in the county jail until the further order of the court," and a *mittimus* was ordered to issue for the purpose of putting him there. On application of Hinckley for a writ of habeas corpus to be discharged from imprisonment, the supreme court said: "All judgments must be specific and certain. They must determine the rights recovered or the penalties imposed. They must be such as the defendant may readily understand and be capable of performing. If his committal had been for a definite period, or until he should perform a specified act, then the judgment would have been capable of being reviewed on error, but on such a judgment as this the appellate court can not know the duration of the imprisonment, and determine whether the confinement is reasonable, or is oppressive and wrong. Whether it is to extend to days, weeks, months, years, or for life, none can certainly know. That is still in the breast of the judge, and is, by its terms, to be determined in the future—not on a trial or on the performance of any act, but it depends alone on the will of the judge. Had this order been simply erroneous, we could have no power to discharge. In such a case error or appeal is the only remedy, but it is otherwise where the judgment and the process are void."[1]

So in the supreme court of Rhode Island was a *mittimus* pronounced illegal and void, because it directed the prisoner to be held in prison "until further order of the court"—thereby naming no definite term of imprisonment; and on habeas corpus the prisoner was discharged.[2] And in Vermont Mr. Justice Redfield held, that where an executor of a will was cited to show cause why he should not be committed for contempt for not obeying the order of a probate court to pay certain stipends to decedent's widow, and who was committed for contempt before he had a full hearing on the orders, which were, with one exception, continuous, and the duty accruing monthly, a commitment to jail to remain there "until he shall obey and perform said orders and decrees of said court, or otherwise be delivered by due course of law," was, as a punishment for contempt of the probate court, an irregular order, as being without limit; "and," said he, "if it be regarded as imprisonment until he purges himself by paying the stipends which he was adjuged in contempt for not paying, then he is held in contempt in matters in which he has had no hearing and no opportunity to be

---

[1] People ex rel. Hinckley v. Pirfenbrink, 96 Ill. 68 (1879).
[2] In the Matter of Hammel, 9 R. I. 248.

heard. He is imprisoned for contempt in matters that had not occurred at the time of the hearing, and in which there has been no adjudication of contempt." The relator was discharged.[1]

In Colorado, Sarah J. Brown was attached for contempt of an order of the third judicial district court to pay over to an administrator certain moneys belonging to an estate. After interrogation and examination by the court, "and thereupon, being fully advised in the premises," the court acted as follows: "It is ordered by the court that the defendant be discharged from the said writ of attachment, and that she go thereof without day." And included in this order was the further order that the petitioner be committed to jail till she should comply with the order of the court first made, to pay over certain moneys belonging to the administrator. On habeas corpus in the supreme court, that body decided that "the petitioner having appeared and purged the contempt, and been discharged by the court without day, the court was without jurisdiction to take any further action in or make any further order upon the attachment proceeding. It was closed; and the subsequent order committing the petitioner to prison was without any proceeding to support it. It was without authority of law, and is utterly void."[2]

§ 336. **Commitments for Contempts in Parliamentary Bodies.**—General parliamentary law in the United States limits the time of imprisonment of one committed for a contempt to the adjournment of the house in which it is committed.[3] Mr. Justice Johnson well remarks, in Anderson v. Dunn,[4] that "the American legislative bodies have never possessed or pretended to the omnipotence which constitutes the leading feature in the legislative assembly of Great Britain, and which may have led occasionally to the exercise of caprice under the specious appearance of merited resentment." The constitution of the United States gives power to each house of congress to punish its members for disorderly behavior,[5] and in Anderson v. Dunn,[6] it was held that this express grant of power " drew after it others, not expressed, but vital to their exercise; not substantive and independent indeed, but auxiliary and subordinate;" and that the express grant in one class of cases did not repel the assumption

---

[1] In re Leach, 51 Vt. 650, app.
[2] In re Brown, 4 Col. 438.
[3] Burnham v. Morrissey, 14 Gray, 226; Ex parte Maulsby, 13 Md. 642, app.; Ex parte Alexander, 2 Am. Law Reg. 44; Anderson v. Dunn, 6 Wheat. 230, 231.
[4] 6 Wheat. 231.
[5] Sec. 5, art. 1.
[6] Cited *supra*,

of the punishing power in any other. It short, it is there decided that the house of representatives of the United States may not only punish its own members for disorderly conduct, but it may punish others not members of the body for contempts committed in their presence; and the process is not confined to the district of Columbia. It has no bounds prescribed to its range but those of the United States.

In the application of George P. Burnham for a habeas corpus, it appeared that he was committed by the house of representatives of Massachusetts for twenty-five days unless he should sooner signify his willingness to produce books and papers called for by the special committee, and to satisfactorily answer the questions proposed to him by the house, for a contempt in refusing to comply with the order of a special committee of the house, and also of the house to produce certain books and papers required of him, on the ground that the papers were private—and yet expressly refusing to express or form an opinion whether the production of the books could in any way criminate him. Justice Hoar, in his decision of the case, said: "The house of representatives has the power, under the constitution, to imprison for contempt; but this power is limited to cases expressly provided for by the constitution, or to cases where the power is necessarily implied from those constitutional functions and duties to the proper performance of which it is essential. The power is directly conferred by the constitution: c. 1, sec. 3, arts. 10, 11; and the cases there enumerated are the only ones in which a sentence of imprisonment for a term extending beyond the session of the house can be imposed as a punishment. We consider the object of these provisions to have been twofold: 1. To extend the power beyond the limit which it had by common parliamentary law and custom, by authorizing the imposition of a sentence of imprisonment for a definite period, which should not be terminated by the ending of the session of the house; and, 2. To limit the power of punishing for constructive contempts, by expressly defining the cases in which it might be exercised. But we do not consider it as affecting the power of the house to secure, by proper means, the free and full performance of all its constitutional duties, and to exercise whatever powers are necessary to that end."

After showing that Burnham had been "guilty of disrespect to the house by contumacious behavior in its presence," within the meaning of the tenth article of chapter 1, section 3, of the constitution, and that he might be lawfully imprisoned for such

§ 336.   ASSAILING JUDGMENTS FOR CONTEMPT.

contemptuous behavior for a term not exceeding thirty days— the constitutional limit of the term of imprisonment—his honor continued: "The contempt thus committed in the presence of the house was a sufficient cause of imprisonment under the express provisions of the constitution, and justified a sentence of imprisonment for a fixed time. But to avoid misconstruction, the court wish to add that they do not intend to decide that refractory behavior of a witness before a committee would not authorize the house to arrest and imprison him, as a means of compelling his obedience. Such imprisonment would, however, be limited by the duration of the session. We think it no objection to the order and warrant that they made the imprisonment conditional upon the submission and obedience of the refractory witness, the whole term being within the constitutional limit."[1]

As the supreme court of Massachusetts in the above case exercised the power to consider whether the proceedings of the house of representatives were in conformity with the constitution and laws, so it was held in Wisconsin that where the supreme court issues a writ of habeas corpus, it has the further right to determine whether the committing body or magistrate had jurisdiction; that the state legislature has power to investigate charges of bribery against any of its members, or against the members of a previous legislature connected with the disposal of a trust committed to the legislature of the state, and continuing under its present and future guardianship and supervision; that witnesses may be compelled to attend before the legislature, or before a committee of either house, or a joint committee of both houses, and testify in such matters; and that witnesses refusing to so attend and testify may be punished as for a contempt. But the power, the constitutional right of the legislature to investigate these transactions, is the only question to be considered. The policy, the expediency of exercising the power, and the manner of conducting the investigation rest entirely in the sound discretion of the legislature. This investigation may be by a committee of one house, or by a committee of each house, acting separately or by committees acting jointly. The supreme court can not review the exercise of a constitutional jurisdiction by the legislature. It seems further that rules which in a court of law will excuse a witness from answering questions which will tend to criminate him or divulge the secrets of his clients have no application to investigations before the legislative body of a state. But where this

[1] Burnham v. Morrissey, 14 Gray, 239, 241.

is the case, we apprehend that a legislative provision will always be found in the statutes furnishing full protection to a witness claiming his constitutional right not to be compelled to be a witness against himself in any criminal case.[1]

§ 337. **Definite Time Fixed by Statute.**—William G. Shanks, city editor of the Tribune, was committed to the county jail of Kings county, New York, for contempt in refusing to answer questions put to him before the grand jury as to the authorship of an article in the Tribune. The commitment purported to direct "that the prisoner stand committed till he should answer the question he had refused to answer." This was the sheriff's only warrant for such detention when the habeas corpus was issued and served, and when the hearing on the habeas corpus case commenced.[2] Justice Fancher said: "Does it appear that 'the party has been legally committed'? The court had in this matter authority to commit for 'a term not exceeding thirty days.' It had no jurisdiction to order an unlawful commitment. Suppose the court had ordered the party to be imprisoned for thirty years: would it be contended that relief could not be had on habeas corpus from such an unlawful imprisonment? It comes back to the question of power. There are cases where, on habeas corpus, the inquiry into the practice or legality of the order or judgment directing imprisonment can not be made. Thus, where the legality of the order can be tested on an appeal, there an appeal must be the remedy. But the decisions which affect such cases are not applicable to this case, for the order of commitment is not an appealable order. It is not intended to deny that the court of oyer and terminer in Kings county had authority to inquire into the alleged contempt. The commitment can not be impeached for that cause. On habeas corpus, the court is deprived by statute of any power 'to inquire into the justice or propriety of any commitment for any contempt made by any court, officer, or body according to law, and charged in such commitment.'[3] The essential qualification of a valid commitment for contempt is that it be 'according to law.' The justice or propriety of the commitment can not be inquired into if it be 'according to law.' There is meaning in those words of the statute. The only limitation is against an inquiry into the justice or propriety

[1] In re Falvey and Kilbourn v. Massing, 7 Wis. 630.
[2] Particular attention is called to this because a different aspect of this case will be referred to in a subsequent section.
[3] 2 R. S. of 1836, marg. p. 568, sec. 42; same statute, 3 N. Y. R. S., 5th ed., 888, sec. 57.

§ 338.   ASSAILING JUDGMENTS FOR CONTEMPT.

of any commitment for contempt made 'according to law.' If the commitment be not according to law, its 'legality' may and should be inquired into. The statute[1] limits the period of imprisonment for contempt to thirty days, and is higher than the court which commits the petitioner for an unlimited period." The prisoner was discharged.[2]

§ 338. **Exemption from Jury Service.**—It has been held in the supreme court of Missouri, that a fire-warden who has been committed for a contempt in refusing to serve as a juror is not entitled to the writ of habeas corpus, notwithstanding the record shows upon its face that he is exempt by law from jury duty, and that he claimed his exemption.[3]

---

[1] 2 R. S. of 1836, marg. p. 278, sec. 11; same statute 3 N. Y. R. S., 5th ed., 470, sec. 9.

[2] Shanks' Case, 15 Abb. Pr., N. S., 38; and see Hackley's Case, 21 How. Pr. 103; S. C., 2 N. Y. 74; see also People ex rel. Hackley v. Kelly, 12 Abb. Pr. 150; People v. Sheriff, 29 Barb. 622; S. C., 7 Abb. Pr. 96.

[3] Ex parte Goodin, 67 Mo. 637. If this case is to be recognized as authority, it is simply because there was the unsupported opinion of three judges against the sound, logical, and correct conclusion, we think, of the two dissenting judges, one of whom was the learned Chief Justice Sherwood, who delivered an able and elaborate dissenting opinion, which was fully concurred in by Judge Henry. The opinions of Judges Napton, Hough, and Norton are not reported if they gave any. The chief justice reviewed Ex parte McKee, 18 Mo. 599; Ex parte Toney, 11 Id. 662; Ex parte Page, 49 Id. 291; Hurd on Habeas Corpus, 2d ed., 327, 328; Ex parte Perkins, 18 Cal. 60; Matter of Percy, 2 Daly, 530; Re Fernandez, 10 C. B., N. S., 3; Bushell's Case, Vaugh. 135; People v. Hackley, 24 N. Y. 75; Gilliam v. McJunkin, 2 S. C., N. S., 442; Holman v. Mayor, 34 Tex. 668; Ex parte Summers, 5 Ired. 149, as authorities sustaining his views, and said that many of the authorities opposed to the views he advanced would be found cited in State v. Towle, 42 N. H. 540. We have elsewhere (sec. 309) cited the authorities in State v. Towle to support only the language of the text concerning the subject there under consideration. His honor said: "I am fully aware there is a conflict of authority in reference to this matter. Were this case one not free from doubt as to whether the petitioner was exempt under the law—were it not patent of record, by reason of the facts there recited and admitted, that the criminal court had no more jurisdiction over his person than if he had been a woman or an infant—it would not be permitted to question collaterally the validity of the order of commitment in the present instance; but since it is plain that petitioner, upon the recorded facts, is exempt under the law from jury service, it must needs follow that he has not been guilty of a contempt, and that the jurisdiction of the court of criminal correction immediately ceased when those facts, constituting the exemption, were judicially ascertained and declared. Again, if we admit that petitioner is exempt under the law, it would seem clear that petitioner is entitled to his discharge under the very terms of the statute, because the act does not merely say that the petitioner shall be remanded if detained in custody for any contempt, specially and plainly charged in the commitment, by some court, officer, or body having authority to commit for a contempt [so charged]; but the significant words are added, 'so charged.' If the legislature had intended that every commitment for contempt should be conclusive against redress by habeas corpus, when the court, etc., had a general authority to commit for contempt, the words 'so charged' would possess not the slightest signification, and, therefore, I must think that unless that which is charged in the commitment amounts to a contempt when 'so charged,' a petitioner who seeks relief by habeas corpus should have such relief granted him."

§ 339. **Publication during Trial.**—The question of the power of the courts to control the publication of their proceedings while in progress has arisen several times in this country. Mr. Justice Smith, of the supreme court of Tennessee,[1] thus lays down the law: "Unquestionably the power exists, not, perhaps, by direct attachment of the publishing party after publication, but by the exclusion from the court of parties who are there for the purpose of reporting the testimony or proceedings of the court, except on condition of suspending publication till after the trial be completed, or such time before the completion as the court may judge proper.

In the case of The United States v. Holmes, 1 Wall. jun. 1–11, it was the opinion of the court there, under the act of congress of a general character,[2] and similar to the enactments of the code of Tennessee on this subject, that though the court has no power to punish, as for a contempt, the publication, during trial, of the testimony taken in a cause, yet it had the power to regulate the admission of persons within its own bar, and the proceedings there, and to exclude any person from coming or remaining in, for the purpose of taking testimony against the order of the court for publication during the trial. The power and the mode of preventing publication must rest largely in the discretion of the judge. It is, in its nature and the occasions and manner of its exercise, ordinarily without the possibility of control by a supervising court.[3] Any publication, pending a suit, reflecting upon the court, the jury, the parties, the officers of the court, the counsel, etc., with reference to the suit, or tending to influence the decision of the controversy, is a contempt of court, and may be punished by attachment.[4] But in Mississippi it is held that a newspaper article, published during the session of a court, pending the trial before that court of a prisoner indicted for murder, and charging the judge presiding over the court with being an aider and abettor of the murderer, is not a contempt of the court, but a mere libel upon the functionary.[5]

§ 340. **Statement of Facts Need not be Made unless Statute Requires It.**—Whether a proper case of contempt

---

[1] In the State v. Galloway & Rhea, 5 Coldw. 326.

[2] See act of March 2, 1831, c. 99, 4 Stats. at Large, 487; 2 U. S. R. S., sec. 725. See also Ex parte Robinson, 19 Wall. 505.

[3] The State v. Galloway & Rhea, 5 Coldw. 326.

[4] Hollingsworth v. Duane, Wall. 46. See also Clark v. The People, 1 Breese, 340, citing Stuart v. The People, 3 Scam. 395.

[5] Ex parte Hickey, 4 Smed. & M. 751, app. Read appendix to 1 Cal., containing proceedings in the House of Assembly in the matter of impeachment of Levi Parsons.

§ 340.   ASSAILING JUDGMENTS FOR CONTEMPT.   447

made out by a statement of facts constituting it should be expressed in the warrant of commitment, has undergone in England a very elaborate, anxious, and learned discussion, both in parliament and in the courts; and it seems now to be conceded that the facts constituting the alleged contempt need not be stated.[1] This being the law, it will readily be seen that an order of commitment for contempt can not be assailed or impeached, because it does not set out the facts on which the contempt arose—unless statute, as in some states of the American Union, requires them to be set forth. The facts constituting a contempt, however, should always be set out, whether required by statute or not. In the words of Lord Chief Justice Denman, in the case of the Sheriff of Middlesex:[2] "But the return, if it discloses a sufficient answer, puts an end to the case; and I think the production of a good warrant is a sufficient answer. Seeing that, we can not go into the question of contempt on affidavit, nor discuss the motives which may be alleged. Indeed (as the courts have said in some of the cases) it would be unseemly to suspect that a body, acting under such sanctions as a house of parliament, would, in making its warrant, suppress facts which, if discussed, might entitle the person committed to his liberty. If they ever did so act, I am persuaded that, on further consideration, they would repudiate such a course of proceeding. What injustice might not have been committed by the ordinary courts in past times, if such a course had been recognized!—as, for instance, if the recorder of London, in Bushell's Case, had, in the warrant of commitment, suppressed the fact that the jurymen were imprisoned for returning a verdict of acquittal. I am certain that such will never become the practice of any body of men amenable to public opinion."

So has it been said by a learned judge of the supreme court of North Carolina, Chief Justice Ruffin:[3] "Therefore, it befits every court which has a proper tenderness for the rights of the citizen and a due respect to its own character to state the facts explicitly, not suppressing those on which the person might be entitled to be discharged more than it would insert others which did not exist for the sake of justifying the commitment. A court which knows its duty, and is not conscious of violating it, will ever be desirous of putting upon the record or in its

[1] Lord Ellenborough and Bayley in Burdett v. Abbott, 14 East, 1; Hobhouse's Case, 3 Barn. & Ald. 420; Stockdale v. Hansard, 9 Ad. & El. 1; S. C., 3 Per. & Dav. 349; Case of Sheriff of Middlesex, 11 Ad. & El. 273; Bushell's Case, Freeman K. B. & C. P. 1.

[2] Case of Sheriff of Middlesex, 11 Ad. & El. 273.

[3] In Ex parte Summers, 5 Ired. 154.

process the truth of the case, especially as thereby a higher court may be able to enlarge a citizen illegally committed or fined."[1]

It seems that the intent of statutes which direct that the officer shall forthwith remand the prisoner, if it appear that he is detained in custody for any contempt, specially and plainly charged in the commitment, by some court having authority to commit for the contempt charged, and prohibiting an examination into the justice or propriety of any commitment for a contempt charged in such commitment is to prevent any officer out of court from reviewing the acts and judgment of the court in cases of contempts, and to leave to the court where the contempt has been committed the entire control of the case.[2] The commitment in charging the contempt need not detail the entire proceeding constituting it *in hæc verba*, so as fully to inform another court of the reasons why one is punished for a contempt. It is sufficient if the cause be substantially stated without entire precision.[3] All the preliminaries to warrant the imprisonment need not be set out.[4]

But these statutes can not vary the rule that one can not be committed without authority of law. The contempt charged must show a criminal offense known to the law, and for which the contemner may be punished. It goes to the question of jurisdiction; and "jurisdiction," said the court in People v. Liscomb,[5] "of the person of the prisoner and of the subject-matter are not alone conclusive, but the jurisdiction of the court to render a particular judgment is a proper subject of inquiry; and while the court can not, upon a return to the writ, go behind the judgment, and inquire into alleged error and irregularity preceding it, the question is presented and must be determined, whether upon the whole record the judgment was warranted by law, and was within the jurisdiction of the court."[6]

---

[1] See also Ex parte Maulsby, 13 Md. 625, app.; Davison's Case, 13 Abb. Pr. 129.

[2] Davison's Case, 13 Abb. Pr. 129.

[3] People v. Nevins, 1 Hill (N. Y.), 154.

[4] Davison's Case, 13 Abb. Pr. 129; Kahn's Case, 11 Id. 147; S. C., 19 How. Pr. 475; People v. Hicks, 15 Barb. 153; People v. Cassels, 5 Hill, 164; People v. Sheriff, 7 Abb. Pr. 96.

[5] 60 N. Y. 559.

[6] See generally, on this section, Queen v. Gossett, 3 Per. & Dav. 349; and case of the Sheriff of Middlesex, 11 Ad. & El. 273, where it is held that the merits of the commitment for contempt, even though the case be within the statute of 56 Geo. III., c. 100, can not be inquired into; also Matter of Cobbett, 7 Ad. & El., Q. B., 187, where it is held that a commitment by a court of equity for contempt need not adjudicate the contempt, it being enough to recite such adjudication; Ex parte Fernandez, 10 C. B., N. S., 3; Davison's Case, 13 Abb. Pr. 139; Fischer v. Hayes, 6 Fed. Rep. 63, where it is said that the order adjudging the contempt need not recite the offense, where the latter is set forth with sufficient particularity in the

§ 341. **Where the Warrant of Commitment Omits to State Facts, the Cause can not be Inquired into.**—Lord Chief Justice Denman, in the case of the Sheriff of Middlesex,[1] said on this point: "There is perhaps no case in the books entitled to so great weight as Burdett v. Abbott,[2] from the learning of the counsel who argued and the judges who decided it, the frequent discussions which the subject underwent, and the diligent endeavors made to obtain the fullest information upon it. The judgment of Lord Ellenborough there, as it bears on the point now before us, is remarkable. He says 'If a commitment appeared to be for a contempt of the house of commons generally, I would neither in the case of that court, or of any other of the superior courts, inquire further; but if it did not profess to commit for a contempt, but for some matter appearing on the return which could by no reasonable intendment be considered as a contempt of the court committing, but a ground of commitment palpably and evidently arbitrary, unjust, and contrary to every principle of positive law or national [natural] justice—I say that in the case of such a commitment (if it should ever occur, but which I can not possibly anticipate as ever likely to occur), we must look at it and act upon it as justice may require from whatever court it may profess to have proceeded.' Bayley, J., as well as Lord Ellenborough, appears to have been of opinion in that case that, if particular facts are stated in the warrant, and do not bear out the commitment, the court should act upon the principle recognized by Holt, C. J., in Regina v. Paty;[3] but that, if the warrant merely states a contempt in general terms, the court is bound by it. That rule was adopted by this court in Rex v. Hobhouse;[4] and in the late case of Stockdale v. Hansard,[5] there was not one of us who did not express himself conformably to it." The facts were stated in the celebrated Bushell's Case,[3] where he was committed "for giving a verdict against full and clear evidence."

The same doctrine appears to prevail in the United States. In the supreme court of North Carolina it has been said: "But if the commitment or fine be in a general form for a contempt,

affidavits and reports filed in the proceedings, and the order is connected therewith by sufficient reference, and further, that an order adjudging contempt for the violation of an injunction need not recite that such injunction was lawful: People v. Nevins, 1 Hill (N. Y.), 154.

[1] 11 Ad. & El. 235.
[2] 14 East, 1.
[3] 2 Ld. Raym. 1105.
[4] 2 Ch. Q. B. 207.
[5] 9 Ad. & El. 1.
[6] Vaugh. 135.

all other courts are bound by it, and the party can only free himself by urging the contempt before the court that has adjudged it."[1]

§ 342. **Judgments of "Superior" and "Inferior" Courts.** In the very excellent and *apropos* language of Mr. Justice Potter, of the supreme court of the state of New York: "The power of the judge on the hearing [of a habeas corpus] is judicial, not ministerial, and his judicial discretion must be exercised according to law. The duty, in all cases, is to grant release where the committing court or magistrate has acted without jurisdiction. Whether jurisdiction has been shown, in any given case, is often, as in the case before us, a question of legal intendment and construction. As presumptions are in favor of liberty, the court or magistrate whose process of commitment is brought under inquiry must have jurisdiction, not only of the subject-matter, but, especially in cases where personal liberty is restrained, must have jurisdiction of the person imprisoned. If want of jurisdiction appears on the face of the process, it is void as to everybody: not even the ministerial officer who executed it is protected. If the magistrate who issues the process to imprison had not the right to issue such process, the imprisonment is illegal, although he may have had jurisdiction of the subject-matter. Confusion is sometimes created in tracing the lines between courts of original jurisdiction, or courts of record, in which jurisdiction is always presumed, and inferior jurisdictions, where authority must be shown at every step, as well as the proper application of the statutes to the one case or the other. This is especially so in cases of commitments for contempt. In these cases there has been opened a still wider range for the examination of the question of jurisdiction than in other cases. But the rule, in one respect, is the same, whether the process issue from superior or inferior courts. In each, if there was no competent court to render the judgment or decree to be questioned, the judgment and process is equally void. The right to impeach jurisdiction extends to every court, both directly and collaterally; though in one case the jurisdiction is first to be intended, in the other not.[2] And though superior courts may imprison for contempt, committed in the presence of the court, without warrant, inferior courts or magistrates

---

[1] Ruffin, C. J., in Ex parte Summers, 5 Ired. 154; Ex parte Maulsby, 13 Md. 625, app.

[2] Citing People v. Nevins, 1 Hill (N. Y.), 154.

§ 342. ASSAILING JUDGMENTS FOR CONTEMPT.

can not commit without a formal warrant;[1] and, since the revised statutes,[2] contempts committed by the non-payment of money, in disobedience of a rule or order, require that the warrant of commitment must specially and plainly set forth the contempt charged in the commitment."[3] Where a witness refuses to answer a proper question before a grand jury, and this is reported to the court in the prisoner's presence, who not only does not deny the act but justifies it, and reiterates his refusal, the contempt is one "in the immediate view and presence of the court," an order of court is sufficient, without any affidavit or further evidence, to constitute a valid commitment.[4]

So has it lately been said in the St. Louis court of appeals for the state of Missouri, by Hayden, J.: "If, having jurisdiction of the subject-matter and of the person, a court, even of general jurisdiction, exceeds that jurisdiction by an excessive sentence, and this excess is patent on the face of the record, the judgment is considered as not merely erroneous or irregular, but void, and the petitioner entitled to his discharge.[5] The inquiry is as to the jurisdiction of the court to render the particular judgment, and not merely to render a judgment in the general matter. In the case of a court of general jurisdiction, however, every presumption is in its favor; and it must be assumed that such court has passed upon the jurisdictional facts, and thus its judgment can not be affected by matters *dehors* the record in a collateral proceeding like habeas corpus.[6] But in the case of a court of limited jurisdiction, and still more in the case of a mere notary, or other officer to whom the power to take depositions is given, there is no similar presumption. A contempt, indeed, is in itself a distinct and substantive offense, and in the case of a court of general jurisdiction there is no distinction in principle between a judgment pronounced after trial upon indictment and a summary committal for contempt, so far as concerns the question of collateral impeachment. In either case the court has pronounced on the jurisdictional facts, and the presumption

---

[1] See People v. Nevins, 1 Hill (N. Y.), 154; In the Matter of Percy, 2 Daly, 530.

[2] Citing 2 R. S. of 1829, 534, tit. XIII, sec. 4. This statutory enactment is found in many of the states.

[3] Citing In the Matter of Watson, 5 Lans. 466.

[4] People v. Kelly, 21 How. Pr. 54; Matter of Hackley, 24 N. Y. 74; In the Matter of Percy, 2 Daly, 530. See also People v. Nevins, 1 Hill (N. Y.), 154.

[5] Ex parte Page, 49 Mo. 291; The People v. Liscomb, 60 N. Y. 559.

[6] Ex parte Toney, 11 Mo. 661. See comments and explanation of this case by Chief Justice Sherwood in Ex parte Goodin, 67 Id. 641; that there were record recitals showing jurisdiction, and that they could not be collaterally attacked by a proceeding on habeas corpus, and that had the record shown a want of jurisdiction, the court would have granted the writ refused in that case.

is that it has decided correctly. But the presumption of jurisdiction which attaches to the higher court does not exist in reference to the inferior court or officers. The statute gives the power to the officer, under certain circumstances, to commit for contempt, but does not undertake to change the important rule in regard to courts of general and courts of limited jurisdiction."[1]

In Texas, it is said by P. Evans, justice of the supreme court, quoting the words of Justice Lawrence, in Welch v. Nash, 8 East, 403, that "justices can not, of course, give themselves jurisdiction by erroneously and capriciously deciding contrary to the truth upon the question upon which their jurisdiction depends. Justices can not give themselves jurisdiction by finding that as a fact which is not a fact."[2]

§ 343. **Jury Trial—Change of Venue.**—The "criminal prosecutions" and the "trials" spoken of in the constitution of the United States, and which it is declared shall be determined by jury, refer to those general and public offenses against the United States which, had they been committed against the separate states before the adoption of the constitution, would have required the presentment of a grand jury, and were triable by a petit jury. The constitution does not affect those proceedings in the tribunals of justice against officers and others, instituted at the instance of the party or the court, to coerce or punish them for contempts committed in the course of particular causes. These are not the "trials" which it is said shall be by jury, in the third article of the constitution, section 2; nor those "criminal prosecutions" intended by the eighth amendment, in which it is said: "It shall be the right of the party to have a speedy and public trial by an impartial jury."[3] Neither were contempts at common law cases for juries. A construction allowing a trial by jury would require the court to have the verdict of a jury every time an injunction is violated or an order disregarded to file books, deeds, or other papers, or to pay money into court by a receiver of the court or other officer, or even to file an answer, etc. Such a course would stop the wheels of justice, and render the necessary orders of the court merely nugatory.[4] It has been held in Illinois that informations

---

[1] Ex parte Krieger, 7 Mo. App. 367.
[2] Holman v. Mayor of Austin, 34 Tex. 668. As to whether a prisoner after being discharged can be again committed for the same cause, see conflicting cases of Yates, 4 Johns. 314; Yates v. Lansing, 9 Id. 395; Yates v. The People, 6 Id. 335; but see chapter on *Res Adjudicata*.
[3] Hollingsworth v. Duane, Wall. 96; State v. Woodfin, 5 Ired. 199.
[4] Ex parte Alexander, 2 Am. Law Reg. 44; see also State v. Matthews, 37 N. H. 450, citing Albany City Bank v. Schermerhorn, 9 Paige, 372; Neel v. State, 9 Ark. 259; also Ex parte Langdon, 25 Vt. 680.

against persons for contempts, in disturbing the order of the court in its presence or out of it, for breach of injunctions, and disobeying its orders and decrees, and such like, are not within the meaning nor of the character of informations in the fifth section of the act in relation to change of venue: R. S., c. 146.[1]

§ 344. **Errors and Irregularities must be Cured by Motion,** and should, in point of form, be finally judged of by the tribunal where they originate. Every court is the proper tribunal to judge of the regularity or abuse of its process; and the remedy for the alleged irregularity is an application to the court from which the process issued, and not an appeal to the writ of habeas corpus. The court has full power to relieve from error and irregularity on such application or motion, and the relief may be quite as speedy and effectual as by means of the writ of habeas corpus, unless the party by his own laches has lost his right to relief. In fact, as we have heretofore seen, mere error and irregularity are not curable at all upon habeas corpus unless they are so gross as to affect the question of jurisdiction.[2]

§ 345. **Pardon.**—It is said in England that the attachment for most species of contempts committed by parties to any suit or proceeding before a court, and especially for non-payment of costs and non performance of awards, is to be looked upon rather as a civil execution for the benefit of the injured party, though carried on in the shape of a criminal process for a contempt of the authority of the court. And therefore it has been held that such contempts and the process thereon, being properly the civil remedy of individuals for a private injury, are not released or affected by a general act of pardon.[3] But with this and a few other exceptions, the amiable prerogative of the crown, the power to pardon, is exercised as to all offenses merely against the crown or the public.[4]

In the United States this prerogative belongs to the president and to the governors of the states.[5] Contempts of court are public wrongs—distinct criminal offenses.[6] They are distinguished from ordinary crimes or misdemeanors, because in their punishment there is no intervention of a jury, the party being acquitted or condemned by the suffrage of such person only as the statute has appointed for his judge. The whole

---

[1] Crook et al. v. People, 16 Ill. 534.
[2] Davison's Case, 13 Abb. Pr. 129; Commonwealth v. Lecky, 1 Watts, 66; People v. Nevins, 1 Hill (N. Y), 154.
[3] 4 Kerr's Bla. Com. 296.
[4] 4 Ch. Bl. 314.
[5] See the constitutions.
[6] Commonwealth v. Newton, 1 Grant Cas. 454; Ex parte Hardy, 68 Ala. 315; Fischer v. Hayes, 6 Fed. Rep. 63; In the Matter of Percy, 2 Daly, 530; Ex parte Hickey, 4 Smed. & M. 751.

doctrine of contempts goes to the point that the offense is a wrong to the public, and not to the person of the functionary to whom it is offered, considered merely as an individual.[1] And in Mississippi, where the constitution of the state (art. 5, sec. 10) bestows upon the governor of the state "the power to grant reprieves and pardons, and to remit fines in all criminal and penal cases, except in those of treason and impeachment," it has been held that contempts of court are either crimes or misdemeanors in proportion to the aggravation of the offense, and as such are included within the pardoning power of the state.[2] This, too, is the doctrine in Louisiana.[3]

§ 346. **Evidence.**—We have seen that a statement of facts constituting a contempt need not be made unless the statute requires it, and that if a warrant merely state a contempt in general terms it is conclusive, and that another court can not go into the question of contempt on affidavit or otherwise, nor discuss the motives which may be alleged for suppressing the facts. But that if the court does state the facts upon which it proceeds, a revising tribunal may, on habeas corpus, discharge the party, if it appear that the facts do not amount to a contempt. The revisory tribunal, however, does not re-examine an order committing or fining a person for contempt, with the view of hearing the evidence, and trying the question *de novo*. A revisory tribunal will not rehear the evidence upon which the committing court acted to consider whether it be sufficient to sustain the judgment of commitment or not. The committing court may err as to the force and effect of the evidence on which it founds its judgment, but error of that kind is not subject to revision upon proceedings by habeas corpus. The defects must appear of record, and it alone must be relied upon. Where evidence touching a matter has been heard in the primary court, and the record can not be properly brought before a revisory tribunal by habeas corpus alone, the writ of *certiorari* may be used as ancillary to the habeas corpus to bring up a complete record. *Mandamus* may probably be used for the same purpose, but this use of it is unusual. When the evidence in the record is brought up on *certiorari*, it will of course be examined and acted upon as the revisory tribunal shall deem fit. The record should be set out in the return to the habeas corpus as well as in the return to the *certiorari*.[4]

---

[1] State of Louisiana v. Sauvinet, 24 La. Ann. 119; Ex parte Hickey, 4 Smed. & M. 751.
[2] Ex parte Hickey, 4 Smed. & M. 751.
[3] Id.
[4] See People v. Hackley, 24 N. Y. 75; People v. Bradley, 60 Ill. 390; Ex parte Krieger, 7 Mo. App. 367; State v. Galloway & Rhea, 5 Coldw. 337; Ex parte Summers, 5 Ired. 149; Smith v. McLendon, 59 Ga. 528; 1 Rap. & Law. Law Dict. 188.

CHAPTER XXIV.

ASSAILING JUDGMENTS OF COURTS OF SPECIAL OR LIMITED JURISDICTION IN CASES TRIABLE BY JURY.

PART I.—CRIMINAL CASES.

§ 347. Explanatory Remarks.
§ 348. Error and Irregularities not Reviewable.
§ 349. Defective Complaint.
§ 350. Retrial of Issue of Fact.
§ 351. Sentences Unauthorized by Law.
§ 352. Unauthorized Sentences, Continued—Ordinances Violated.
§ 353. Erroneous Sentences.
§ 354. When Sentence for Misdemeanor Begins to Run.
§ 355. Commitment or *Mittimus*.
§ 356. Remarks on Jurisdiction.

PART II.—CIVIL CASES.

§ 357. Void Summons, Judgment, and Execution.
§ 358. Process and Judgments Running by Wrong Name—*Ca. Sa.*
§ 359. *Capias ad Satisfaciendum*, Continued.
§ 360. Staying, and Failure to Issue, Execution.
§ 361. Defective Execution.

PART I.—CRIMINAL CASES.

§ 347. **Explanatory Remarks.**—We have seen, in the preceding pages, that summary convictions and the commitments in execution upon such judgments may be assailed for want of jurisdiction, and we have endeavored to make this plain by illustrations. In these purely summary proceedings the defendant can not claim a jury trial. We have seen, however, that the jurisdiction of inferior courts has been greatly extended in later times, and there is now a large class of cases triable before magistrates and inferior courts where the defendant has the right to claim a trial by jury; but if he waive a jury, these cases are tried summarily. It is our object now to show how judgments rendered in such cases may be assailed on habeas corpus. Subsequently attacks on judgments of courts of general jurisdiction will be treated. The object of treating the first class separately from the two latter is to show how these judgments of final criminal jurisdiction over some minor offenses are now regarded; and the second class separately from the third, to keep clear before the mind the only difference ordinarily recognized between superior and inferior courts—that there is a presumption in favor of the validity of the judgments of the former, none in favor of the latter. These presumptions will be found discussed in a previous chapter.

§ 348. **Errors and Irregularities not Reviewable.**—Irregularity has been defined by Tidd to be the want of adherence to some prescribed rule or mode of proceeding; and it consists either in omitting to do something that is necessary for the due and orderly conducting of a suit, or doing it in an unseasonable time or improper manner.[1] This has been quoted by many judges, both English and American, in laying down the general rule that the writ of habeas corpus can not reach such errors or irregularities as will render a judgment voidable only, but only such illegalities as render it void.[2] Void and voidable judgments may alike be reversed on appeal or writ of error; but the former only gives authority to discharge on habeas corpus,[3] which writ can not have the operation of an appeal, writ of error, or *certiorari*, or have the force or effect of those proceedings.[4] "Illegality can be affirmed only of radical defects, and signifies that which is contrary to the principles of law as distinguished from rules of procedure. Illegality denotes a complete defect in the proceedings."[5] Another distinction deserving notice between a mere irregularity and a complete defect in proceedings is, the former may be waived, but not the latter.[6] We shall devote a few succeeding sections to the illustration of these rules.

§ 349. **Defective Complaint.**—In Kansas a complaint filed under the dram-shop acts, and perhaps so defective that a motion in arrest of judgment ought to have been sustained, as it failed to charge in terms a sale without a license, but a general charge of unlawful selling, was held not to be such an absolute nullity as to entitle the defendant to discharge on habeas corpus, after he had pleaded not guilty, gone to trial, and had been convicted and sentenced.[7]

---

[1] 1 Tidd's Pr. 512.
[2] Ex parte Scwartz, 2 Tex. App. 74; Ex parte McGill, 6 Id. 498, and cases cited; Darrah v. Westerlage, 44 Tex. 388; Ex parte Sam, 51 Ala. 34; Ex parte Winston, 9 Nev. 71; Ex parte Hubbard, 65 Ala. 473; Ex parte Brown, 63 Id. 187.
[3] See preceding cases, and Justice Sanderson in Ex parte Gibson, 31 Cal. 619, citing Hurd on Habeas Corpus, 1st ed., 333.
[4] See preceding cases.
[5] Justice Sanderson in Ex parte Gibson, 31 Cal. 619, citing Hurd on Habeas Corpus, 1st ed., 333.
[6] 1 Tidd's Pr. 515.
[7] Prohibitory Amendment Cases, and cases cited, 24 Kan. 700.

§ 350.   JUDGMENTS IN CASES TRIABLE BY JURY.   457

§ 350. **Retrial of Issues of Fact.**—The writ of habeas corpus was not framed to retry issues of fact or to review the proceedings of a legal trial. As where a hotel-keeper was convicted on the sole charge of violating a "Sunday law," by keeping open a bar for the sale of liquors on Sunday contrary to statute, but made no defense on his trial that he kept a bar in the hotel as a part of the business of the hotel, he was not allowed to relitigate the matter on habeas corpus, the complaint not showing that the bar was kept as a part of the business of the hotel.[1] The recorder's court of the city of Galveston fined an individual for a violation of the fire ordinances of that city. He was arrested by the chief of police in default of payment, and sued out a writ of habeas corpus before Judge Dodge of the criminal district court of Galveston county, on the hearing of which he sought to disprove the charge on which he was found guilty by the recorder. On appeal it was held that the exclusion of such testimony was not error; that whether the proof warranted the judgment was not a matter that could be investigated by the judge on habeas corpus, it being reviewable only by an appellate court.[2] When a court has power to sentence, either to the state prison, penitentiary, or house of refuge for the crime of grand larceny, offenders over twenty-one to the state prison, those between twenty-one and sixteen either to the state prison or penitentiary at the discretion of the court, and those under sixteen to the state prison or house of refuge at the discretion of the court, and has, in the exercise of its discretion, determined the age of the offender, and designated the place of his imprisonment, and passed sentence upon him, it is a final adjudication of a court of competent jurisdiction, and can no more be inquired into on habeas corpus than can the guilt or innocence of a prisoner who has either pleaded or been found guilty of an offense by a jury, charged in an indictment. If such an error can be corrected at all, the same rule must be followed as for correcting errors in admitting or rejecting evidence, in charging or refusing to charge the jury, or rendering verdicts on insufficient evidence—and that is, by writ of error, motion for a new trial, etc., when the court has power to entertain such motion. The competency of the court rendering the judgment in this case was assailed, but unsuccessfully. Justice Jones, of the superior court of New York, intimated, however, that if the court had no authority to order imprisonment in the penitentiary

---

[1] Ex parte Bird, 19 Cal. 130; Stoner v. State of Missouri, 4 Mo. 614.
[2] Darrah v. Westerlage, 44 Tex. 388.

in any case, or if it appeared on the face of its record that the person so ordered to be imprisoned was not within the prescribed ages, the court might well be said to be not competent to render such judgment, and necessarily that the imprisonment would not be made under the judgment of a competent court.[1]

§ 351. **Sentences Unauthorized by Law.**—Where a primary court has sentenced an offender to pay a fine, it having power to punish only by fine or imprisonment, an appellate court, in doing that which the court below might have done and ought to have done, can not inflict a higher penalty for the offense than could by law be imposed by the primary court, although the appellate court may have a larger original jurisdiction, and have power in the exercise of such original jurisdiction to punish by fine and imprisonment. And where such a sentence has been imposed and the fine paid, a revisory court will, on habeas corpus, in the exercise of its discretionary powers, although a writ of error would be the ordinary remedy for the error in the judgment of the court below, discharge the prisoner, because the remainder of the punishment is not warranted by law. "It is somewhat analogous," said Chief Justice Shaw, "to the case of a jailer's holding a prisoner beyond the lawful time of his sentence;" and although the error is in the judgment, it consists in imposing any imprisonment after the fine has been imposed and paid. The only correction of the error is to reverse and annul that part of the judgment which imposes the imprisonment, and no judgment will then remain warranting the imprisonment. Hence the right of the prisoner to his discharge.[2] If a committing magistrate has sentenced and committed a prisoner to the reform school, as under sixteen years of age, he can not, on the ground of a mistake as to the prisoner's age, proceed to give a new sentence. The first sentence is not made void by such a mistake, and he has no right to take a prisoner from the reform school, to which he has been lawfully sentenced, unless to testify as a witness. The magistrate having, in the exercise of his jurisdiction, found and certified a fact, he will be presumed, so far as all collateral inquiries are concerned, to have done his duty, and a higher court, on the hearing of a habeas corpus, will not assume or inquire whether he allowed the statements of the accused or any other than legal evidence to guide him.[3] A prisoner can not be discharged, or have his

---

[1] People v. Keeper of the Penitentiary of the city of New York, 37 How. Pr. 494.

[2] James Feeley's Case, 12 Cush. 598.

[3] Ex parte Mason, 8 Mich. 70.

§ 351.   JUDGMENTS IN CASES TRIABLE BY JURY.   459

sentence remitted, because the keepers or inspectors of one prison have been remiss in not having removed him sooner to another prison as provided by law.¹ There is a difference between persons illegally restrained of their liberty and those legally confined under the sentence of the law. For improper treatment of the latter, some redress may be granted by the courts of law, but they can not be discharged on habeas corpus simply because they have been removed to one prison, when by law they should have been removed to another.²

Two separate and distinct punishments of the same offender need not necessarily stand or fall together; as where one was sentenced to imprisonment for thirty days, and a fine imposed of fifteen dollars, and it was also adjudged that unless the fine should be paid, he would be imprisoned for the term of four months, where statute prohibited the imprisonment for a longer term than thirty days for the non-payment of a fine, the sentence of thirty days' imprisonment was held valid, but the award of the four months' imprisonment was held to clearly exceed the jurisdiction of the committing justice, and consequently void, and was inoperative even for thirty days of the additional term.³

The effect of three consecutive terms of imprisonment is seen from the following language by the supreme court of the District of Columbia: "The relator appears to be imprisoned for three several terms of one hundred and eighty days each, without any specification as to the time of the beginning or ending of the last two terms of imprisonment. The sentences pronounced by the court do not provide that the period of imprisonment under these convictions are to commence at any future period, or after the expiration of the period mentioned in the former judgment. This omission is fatal to any imprisonment which exceeds that of a single sentence. The law is well settled that in a criminal case there is no error in a judgment making one term of imprisonment commence when another terminates, and when this forms part of the sentence, the judgment is then considered sufficiently certain as to the time when the successive sentences are to be carried into execution.⁴ It was contended at the argument that the commitment might be resorted to as a part of the record for the purpose of justifying the imprison-

¹ Pember's Case, 1 Whart. 439.
² Reddill's Case, 1 Whart. 445.
³ In the Matter of Sweatman, 1 Cow. 144; and see the English cases cited by counsel.
⁴ Citing Rex v. Wilkes, 4 Burr. 2577, 2578; Kite v. Commonwealth, 11 Met. 582; The Commonwealth v. Leath, 1 Va. Cas. 151.

ment beyond the first conviction, and it was sought to give effect to a memorandum on the commitments that they were to take effect after each other. In the first place, it is a rule that all process after judgment must strictly pursue the latter. A *mittimus* is merely to furnish the officer to whom it is directed a justification for the detention of the prisoner. It can not be used to control or vary the judgment, which is the only matter that can be carried into effect. So that even if this memorandum were embodied in the commitment, it could have no effect, for the reason that mere process can never be resorted to for the purpose of enlarging what the court has solemnly adjudged. The sentences in the second and third cases do not state that each imprisonment is to commence from and after the expiration of the imprisonment in those which preceded, and that important modification could not be added by a memorandum on the process." The prisoner having undergone confinement for the full period of a single sentence, was discharged from custody.[1]

§ 352. **Unauthorized Sentences, Continued—Ordinances Violated.**—Chief Justice Cope, of the supreme court of California, said of the court committing John R. Corryell:[2] "The court derives its jurisdiction from the law, and its jurisdiction extends to such matters as the law declares to be criminal, and none other; and when it undertakes to imprison for an offense to which no criminality is attached, it acts beyond its jurisdiction." This principle was afterwards applied in the well-considered case of Kearney.[3] He was tried, convicted, and sentenced in the police court of the city and county of San Francisco, under an ordinance thereof, which provides that "no person shall address to another, or utter in the presence of another, any words having a tendency to create a breach of the peace." This ordinance was construed to mean that the words must be uttered in the presence of the person whom they tend to provoke to such breach of the peace. The complaint failed to show that such person was pres-

---

[1] In re Jackson, 3 McArthur, 24.
[2] In the Matter of Corryell, 22 Cal. 178.
[3] Ex parte Kearney, 55 Cal. 212. In 5 Pac. C. L. J. 549, the reader will find an exhaustive review of this case under the head of "In re Denis Kearney —The Writ of Habeas Corpus—Its Uses and Abuses." It is well written, and shows exhaustive research and an able mind; but contrary to the author's prediction that the decision of the supreme court in the Kearney case would "go forth without authority, and come back without respect," it appears to be in perfect harmony with the advanced opinions of the highest judicial tribunals of the country. See also 14 Am. Law Rev. 675, for the same article. In the decision of the court, the case of Ex parte Tobias Watkins, 3 Pet. 193, was distinguished.

§ 352.   JUDGMENTS IN CASES TRIABLE BY JURY.   461

ent, or that he heard the words spoken, and consequently totally failed to charge an offense. The police court was decided to be an inferior one, as the rule that presumptions in favor of the judgments of courts of general jurisdiction have never been extended to courts of justices of the peace in California—the *dictum* in Ex parte Murray, 43 Cal. 455, to the contrary notwithstanding; and the police courts exercise a jurisdiction, so far as legislative enactments are concerned, substantially the same. And as no presumptions were to be indulged in favor of the judgments of inferior courts, it was held that the evidence of the proceedings of the police court must affirmatively show jurisdiction of the person of the defendant and of the subject-matter. On the contrary, "inasmuch as it affirmatively appears," said Mr. Justice McKinstry, in his elaborate and learned opinion, "from the record of the proceedings, that the petitioner was tried and sentenced to be punished for the commission of an act which is and under the existing laws can be no crime, the judgment of the police court is absolutely void. The petitioner must therefore be discharged."

Again, a petitioner was convicted in the police court of San Francisco, and adjudged to pay a fine of twenty dollars, and in default of payment thereof to be imprisoned in the county jail for ten days, of the offense of violating an ordinance of the city and county of San Francisco that each proprietor of a pool-table should, except where it was kept exclusively for family use, pay a license of six dollars a quarter. The act conferring upon the board of supervisors of San Francisco the power to enact this license ordinance provided that a violation of it should be punished by a fine of not less one hundred dollars. The board of supervisors provided by ordinance that violations of it should be punished by a fine of not less than one thousand dollars. On the hearing of the habeas corpus, it was decided that the judgment was absolutely void, as the court had no power under the act of the legislature to render a judgment in a less sum than one hundred dollars, and that the board of supervisors could not, in the ordinance, fix the penalty in a less sum than one hundred dollars; further, that petitioner was entitled to his discharge notwithstanding the punishment was more favorable than that authorized by law. The license ordinance was pronounced valid, and it was admitted that the police court had jurisdiction over the person of the petitioner and of the offense for which he was tried. But "it by no means follows that these two facts make valid, however erroneous it may be, any judgment the court may render in such a case," said Mr. Justice McKinstry, in delivering the opinion of the supreme court of California, and quoting Ex parte Lange, 18 Wall. 176. These two facts, he remarked, have been held by the supreme court of the United States not to be an infallible test of every judgment. His honor, in discharging the prisoner, concluded his opinion as follows: "We are strengthened in our conviction by the circumstance that never, so far as the reported cases are known to us, has it been held, where the return has shown the petitioner to be confined under a void judgment of a court which had jurisdiction to try him, that he was or could be legally restrained of his liberty under the warrant issued at the commencement of the proceedings against him."[1]

In Alabama, petitioner petitioned for a habeas corpus to procure his discharge from custody and imprisonment by the chief of police of the city of Montgomery, under a judgment and sentence pronounced by the mayor's court, convicting him of violating an ordinance of the city council by knowingly bringing stolen property into the city, and fining him one hundred dollars, etc. The validity of the ordinance was not impeached; "and the only inquiry," observed the court, "which can be made into the judgment and sentence of conviction of another court, returned as the cause of detention, and in justification of it, is into the legality of the judgment—the jurisdiction of the court rendering it. There can be no inquiry into its regularity; error in the proceedings it is not the function of the writ to correct. The judgment of the city court was right and proper—the only judgment it could render; and the application of the relator must be refused."[2] So in a late Illinois case, where a police magistrate had rendered judgment against one for violating an ordinance of the city of Polo, it was admitted by the supreme court that if the judgment was void, that question could be tried by habeas corpus or on error; but that question not being raised, the supreme court refused on writ of error to review the decision of a lower court, on habeas corpus, remanding the prisoner.[3]

We are aware that doctrines inconsistent with the above may be found occasionally in the books, but their authority is of little weight when compared with the numerous decisions on other points involving the same principles as a breach of city ordi-

---

[1] Ex parte Bernert, 7 Pac. C. L. J. 460.
[2] Ex parte Hubbard, 65 Ala. 473, citing Hurd on Habeas Corpus, 2d 324, 328; Ala. Code, 1876, secs. 4961, 4962; Ex parte Burnett, 30 Ala. 461; Ex parte Simmons, 62 Id. 416; Kirby v. The State, Id. 51.
[3] Ex parte Thompson, 93 Ill. 89.

nances—and which are adverse to such doctrines. Furthermore, care must be exercised in the examination of these seemingly adverse opinions, because they may have been determined upon appeal or writ of error, and there is sometimes a vast difference between the determination of a point upon an original application for a writ of habeas corpus, and the determination of the same point upon an appeal or writ of error from the original judgment or the judgment on the habeas corpus.[1]

§ 353. **Erroneous Sentences.**—In Ohio, where the statute required a sentence for a period of not less than three years for horse-stealing, and one was sentenced in such a case for only one year, the question arose on habeas corpus, Did this make the sentence void and the commitment unlawful? The question was considered one simply of jurisdiction; that the court had jurisdiction of the person of the defendant and of the subject-matter, and that therefore the judgment was not void, but erroneous. This will be seen to be in direct opposition to Ex parte Bernert, cited *supra*, and is not in harmony with the principle laid down in Ex parte Lange, 18 Wall. 163, that jurisdiction of the person and of the offense will not always make valid, however erroneous it may be, any judgment the court may render in such a case.[2] In the same state a sentence inflicted which is in excess of that authorized by law is also held to be simply erroneous, and not absolutely void. Writ of error to reverse the proceedings or sentence is the remedy, and redress will not be afforded on habeas corpus.[3]

But as that this view of the matter is not indorsed by the highest authority in the United States, we again call attention to Ex parte Lange, 18 Wall. 163.[4] Where statute limits the period of imprisonment in any given case, the judgment of a justice of the peace which fails to direct the time the defendant shall be imprisoned, where he is committed to prison until the payment of a fine imposed, is not void. This provision is simply directory, and not mandatory.[5] Neither can the judgment of a police court, sentencing one to imprisonment for the non-payment of a fine imposed for the violation of a city ordinance,

---

[1] Consult Ex parte Bernert, 7 Pac. C. L. J. 462; and the following cases cited: People v. Turley, 50 Cal. 469; People v. Ybarra, 17 Id. 171; Ooton v. The State, 5 Ala. 464; Barada v. The State, 13 Mo. 94; Logan's Case, 5 Gratt. 692. Also Ex parte Thompson, 93 Ill. 89, and cases cited; People v. Hessing, 28 Id. 410, overruled in Hammond v. The People, 32 Id. 446.
[2] Ex parte Shaw, 7 Ohio St. 81.
[3] Ex parte Van Hagan, 25 Ohio St. 432.
[4] See also People v. Liscomb, 60 N. Y. 559.
[5] Jackson v. Boyd, 53 Iowa, 536; S. C., 5 N. W. Rep. 734.

be collaterally impeached in a habeas corpus proceeding, conceding that, under an ordinance providing, "No summons or warrant shall be issued against any person lawfully arrested by any officer or member of the city police, but in every such case a trial shall be had upon the written report of the chief of police," etc., the chief of police is required to sign the written reports, where it appears from the record of the case, as incorporated in the return of respondent to the writ, that the report was signed by the chief of police; as the truth of such fact, for the purposes of the case, must be taken to be true, and the truth of it is not subject to collateral attack on habeas corpus—it appearing from the return of respondent that petitioner is held in custody by virtue of an execution issued upon a judgment of a competent court having jurisdiction of the subject-matter and petitioner.[1] In the supreme court of Michigan it has been held that the docket should be signed officially by a justice of the peace to make his judgment valid in a criminal case; and that where fine or imprisonment for a limited time or both are prescribed by law as the penalty for an offense, a judgment that the defendant pay a fine and stand committed until paid is void, as adjudging an indefinite term of imprisonment.[2]

§ 354. **When Sentence for Misdemeanor Begins to Run.**—It has lately been decided in New York that the sentence of imprisonment after conviction of a misdemeanor begins to run from the day it was pronounced, and that the sentence is being endured when in custody after the sentence has been pronounced.[3] The court, however, will not credit upon a sentence the period of imprisonment before trial and conviction and sentence,[4] nor give credit upon a sentence for felony commencing before the offender becomes an inmate of the state prison, except in the exercise of its discretion.[5]

---

[1] Ex parte Hollwedell, 74 Mo. 403, citing In re Truman, 44 Id. 181; In re Harris, 47 Id. 164; Ex parte Toney, 11 Id. 661; and distinguishing The City of Kansas v. Flanagan, 69 Id. 22.

[2] Howard v. People, 3 Mich. 207. As to sentence void in part and valid in part, see Ex parte Hunter, 16 Fla. 575. That where the judgment of the court does not specify the length of time of imprisonment the prisoner will be released after serving statutory time at rate fixed by law when a fine is imposed, but will be remanded until the expiration of that period, see People v. Markham, 7 Cal. 208. See Opinions of Attorney General, N. Y., 1796-1872, p. 518.

[3] People v. Lincoln, 25 Hun, 306.

[4] People ex rel. Stokes v. The Warden etc., 66 N. Y. 342.

[5] People ex rel. Stokes v. The Warden etc., 66 N. Y. 342; People v. Lincoln, 25 Hun, 306. See Ex parte Simmons, 62 Ala. 416. That a prisoner convicted and sentenced by a court of competent jurisdiction to perform hard labor for the county during a specified term can not be punished by a confinement in jail for such a period, see Ex parte

§ 355. **Commitment or Mittimus.**—"The jurisdiction of a justice of the peace is inferior and limited, and while it must affirmatively appear upon the whole record from the recitals therein that the justice has jurisdiction to hear and determine the case at issue, as jurisdiction will not be presumed, yet this rule does not apply to each process, or order, or entry issued or made by him. In brief, it is not necessary in issuing each process to recite all the facts conferring jurisdiction. It is not the practice, nor do we deem it necessary, to make an exemplification of all the proceedings in a conviction for a misdemeanor before a justice to constitute a valid *mittimus*."[1] When it appears that the justice had jurisdiction of the person and of the subject-matter, and had authority to imprison, and the sentence conforms to such authority, the recitals in the *mittimus* will be taken to be true, in the absence of all proof to the contrary. Errors committed by the justice on the trial can not be corrected by the court on the hearing of a habeas corpus.[2] When it appears that the imprisonment is under process valid on its face, and in no way impeached, the prisoner must be remanded. No insufficiency of the record, in point of form, and not going to the question of jurisdiction, will justify the discharge of the prisoner. It is not necessary that the commitment shall contain the names of the witnesses, or the testimony given by them. It is sufficient if it contain a brief statement of the offense charged and the conviction and judgment thereon.[3] The judgment need contain no recital of the particular offense, but only of the general offense, within which the particular one is included.[4]

§ 356. **Remarks on Jurisdiction.**—To show a want of competent authority in a court rendering a judgment, enough facts should appear in the application for a writ of habeas corpus to enable the court to form some judgment on the case.[5] Where the statute requires three justices to hold a court, the prisoner may impeach the judgment rendered by two of them, by show-

---

Pearson, 59 Ala. 654; and that the better practice is, where an alternative sentence is passed of fine and imprisonment, for the judge who sentences to fix some reasonable time within which the prisoner may pay the fine, see Broomhead v. Chisolm, 47 Ga. 390. If that is not done, the prisoner is entitled to a reasonable time within which to pay the fine; and if the fine be paid within a reasonable time, and is accepted by the officer authorized to receive it, the prisoner is entitled to his discharge: Id.

[1] In the Matter of Goldsmith, 24 Kan. 757; see Comp. Laws of Kansas, 1879, p. 775, sec. 19.
[2] In the Matter of O'Conner, 6 Wis. 288.
[3] People of the State of New York v. Neilson, 16 Hun, 214.
[4] Ex parte Murray, 43 Cal. 455.
[5] Ex parte Nye, 8 Kan. 99.

ing that one of the justices named was in fact absent—thereby showing that the court was not legally constituted.[1] Jurisdiction may always be impeached by showing the fact that it does not exist, but ordinarily neither error nor irregularity can be assailed. The want of power to hear and determine, and not error or irregularity in the exercise of that power, renders a judgment void. This principle runs through most of the authorities.[2] For the specified cases in which a party may be discharged on habeas corpus from custody under process of a legally constituted court, the reader is referred to the statutes of his own state.

PART II.—CIVIL CASES.

§ 357. **Void Summons, Judgment, and Execution.**— Where it is provided by statute that a summons accompanied by an order of arrest is returnable immediately, if it be not returned immediately the summons is void, and the judgment and execution rendered in the case are also void, particularly where the constable serves the process beyond the limits of his jurisdiction. Process issued on the tenth of January and returned on the twenty-first of the same month, and served upon one in Ogden by a constable of Salt Lake City, has been held utterly void. The judgment was reviewed on habeas corpus and prisoner discharged.[3]

§ 358. **Process and Judgments Running by Wrong Name—Capias ad Satisfaciendum.**—In Illinois it appears that where summonses were served upon the real parties intended to be sued; the proceedings, however, running against one of the defendants in a name which he did not bear at all, and by which he was never known, and against the other by his christian name alone, but by which he, too, was never known; and the judgments were entered by default against them, and run-

---

[1] Divine's Case, 11 Abb. Pr. 90; S. C., 5 Park. Cr. 62; and 21 How. Pr. 80.

[2] See Ex parte Sam, 51 Ala. 34, and Ex parte Winston, 9 Nev. 71, with preceding cases in this chapter.

[3] Ex parte Dixon, 1 Utah, 192. That an action on the custom, against an innkeeper or common carrier, is founded on tort or misfeasance, and not on contract, and that when the record of judgment in such a case fails to show all the facts necessary to authorize an arrest in the suit before judgment the prisoner will be released on habeas corpus from imprisonment on an execution against the body founded on such judgment, and which is issued without the order of the judge and on proof of the additional facts required to entitle the plaintiff to it, see People ex rel. Burroughs v. Willett, 26 Barb. 78. If a person while he is applying for the benefit of the insolvent laws, and previous to his liberation, has a judgment rendered against him for a debt contracted previous to his confinement, and after his discharge as an insolvent debtor is arrested by virtue of an execution issued upon that judgment, and committed to jail, such arrest and imprisonment are unlawful; State v. Ward, 8 N. J. L. 120.

ning in the same names, the parties may be lawfully arrested and imprisoned under writs of *capias ad satisfaciendum* sued out upon such judgments. And the prisoners can not have these judgments reviewed upon habeas corpus merely because they were not sued by their right names. This was held to be mere error or irregularity, if anything, and not reviewable in this way. An execution, it was said, can only be void when the judgment is void; and that is never the case where the court has jurisdiction of the subject-matter and the persons, particularly if the parties have had actual and timely notice.[1]

§ 359. **Capias ad Satisfaciendum, Continued.**—In Maryland, it has also been decided that a party in custody upon a writ of *capias satisfaciendum* issued upon a judgment rendered by a justice of the peace, upon a subject-matter within his jurisdiction, can not be discharged on habeas corpus. The same principle applies here as in criminal cases, that imprisonment under a judgment can not be unlawful unless the judgment be an absolute nullity, and where the judgment on which an execution has been issued is merely erroneous, it can not be successfully assailed by proceedings on habeas corpus.[2] When the habeas corpus act in South Carolina authorized justices of the peace and the quorum to grant the writ of habeas corpus in all cases where the judges could under that act, it was held by the court of appeals of that state that their authority was derived exclusively from the act, and confined to the very cases in which it was intended to afford a remedy; and that they had no such common-law power, as the habeas corpus act applied solely to cases where the prisoner was confined for "criminal or supposed criminal matters." In these cases alone, had the justices of the quorum and the peace the right to grant the writ, and in the exercise even of this limited jurisdiction, their judgments were not held conclusive. So where one was confined under process, the same in all legal consequences as the *capias ad satisfaciendum* of a court of law, and discharged by these officers on habeas corpus, the judgment was pronounced void, and no justification to the sheriff in discharging the prisoner in an action against him for an escape. It was said by the court that even though process be regarded as a compound of the properties of the *ne exeat*, injunction and attachment, it is still civil process, by whatever name it may be called, for all of them are of that character. Process can not be regarded as criminal

---

[1] Hammond v. The People, 32 Ill. 446.
[2] Bell v. State of Maryland, 4 Gill, 301.

process, whatever its form or title, unless it at least professes to subject the prisoner to a criminal charge or punishment.[1]

§ 360. **Staying, and Failure to Issue, Execution.**—In Missouri, in proceedings to enforce a municipal regulation through a fine, where defendant may at any time be discharged on paying the fine and costs, the same strictness is not applied, in considering the final process, as in case of commitments for purely criminal offenses. The ordinance which provides that the police justice of St. Louis must forthwith cause execution to issue for a fine not paid is construed to simply confer authority and prescribe a form, and does not compel the justice to proceed at once, regardless of circumstances; as every court having power to award execution has a discretionary power to grant a reprieve; and where there is good ground for staying execution, the police justice may exercise a discretion in the matter. In any case, the failure to issue execution in time is a mere irregularity which does not affect the judgment, and of which advantage can not be taken on habeas corpus. Where a legal cause of detention is shown, the prisoner will not be discharged under the habeas corpus act for a mere irregularity in respect to proceedings which do not render the proceedings void.[2]

§ 361. **Defective Execution.**—Statute sometimes provides that a writ or other process is not void or voidable by reason of any mistake or omission in the *teste* thereof; and where an execution recited that "the property execution was issued to the sheriff of the proper county, and was returned unsatisfied," when it should have named the county to which it was issued, and directed the return of the execution "as required by law," instead of requiring its return to be within sixty days from the time of the receipt by the sheriff, these two latter defects were held in a late case before the supreme court of New York to be mere defects in form only, and not in matter of substance required by law, rendering it void. The relator having been released on habeas corpus from imprisonment on such an execution issued on a prior judgment, an appeal was taken by the judgment creditor, and the supreme court, in remanding the relator to the custody of the sheriff, further added: "The execution may be amended upon motion as to these defects *nunc pro tunc*. The remedy of the relator is by motion to have the execu-

---

[1] Harvey v. Huggins, 2 Bailey, 252.
[2] As stated by Official Reporter, A. Moore Berry, in app. to 7 Mo. App. 564, containing a statement of points decided in cases not reported, and citing Ex parte Burns, No. 1455.

§ 361.   JUDGMENTS IN CASES TRIABLE BY JURY.   469

tion set aside. Such motion should be granted unless the court, upon the proper terms, allows the amendment. The writ of habeas corpus is the proper remedy only when the defects are matters of substance required by law, rendering the process void."[1]

[1] People ex rel. Utley v. Seaton & White, 25 Hun, 305, citing People ex rel. Thayer v. Bowe, 20 Id. 547; S. C., 21 Id. 614; Carpenter v. Simmons, 1 Robt. 360.

CHAPTER XXV.

ASSAILING JUDGMENTS OF COURTS OF GENERAL JURISDICTION BY HABEAS CORPUS.

PART I.—IN CRIMINAL CASES.

§ 362. General Principles.
§ 363. Errors can not be Reviewed.
§ 364. Place of Imprisonment—Error.
§ 365. Irregularities can not be Reviewed.
§ 366. Reviewing Evidence and Retrying Issues of Fact.
§ 367. Pleadings—Insufficiency of the Indictment or Information.
§ 368. Jurisdiction of Person and Subject-matter.
§ 369. Sentence by Court or Judge *de Facto.*
§ 370. Unauthorized Convictions.
§ 371. Power to Render the Particular Judgment.
§ 372. Erroneous Sentences.
§ 373. Excessive Sentences—In English and Federal Courts.
§ 374. Excessive Sentences, Continued—In the State Courts.
§ 375. The *Mittimus.*
§ 376. Cumulative Sentences.
§ 377. Power of Courts to Modify their Own Judgments.
§ 378. Miscellaneous Matters.
§ 379. Conflict of Jurisdiction.
§ 380. Power of United States Supreme Court to Review the Judgments of the Inferior Courts of the United States.
§ 381. Sentences in Violation of the Constitution or of United States Laws, and Acts Done or Omitted in Pursuance thereof.
§ 382. Courts-martial.

PART II.—IN CIVIL CASES.

§ 383. Mere Errors and Irregularities will not be Reviewed.
§ 384. *Capias ad Satisfaciendum.*
§ 385. Other Matters.

PART I.—IN CRIMINAL CASES.

§ 362. **General Principles.**—We come now to one of the most interesting branches of habeas corpus, the impeaching of judgments of courts of general jurisdiction by means of this writ. The extent to which this may be carried is the object of consideration in this chapter. We have previously seen that the attack on a judgment of conviction is collaterally appellate, and

§ 362. COURTS OF GENERAL JURISDICTION. 471

where the attack is collateral the judgment can not be impeached for error or irregularity, not extending so far as to affect the question of power or jurisdiction in the court to act in the case. This rule is well settled by numerous judicial decisions.[1] To determine, however, when the court rendering the judgment has jurisdiction of the person, of the subject-matter, and to render the particular judgment assailed, is a question difficult of solution. The decisions of the courts are not uniform or harmonious on this point, but the later decisions of very high authority go to show that jurisdiction of the person and of the subject-matter are not alone conclusive; but that the jurisdiction of the court to render the particular judgment in question is a proper subject of inquiry.[2] If any one of these three elements is lacking, the judgment is fatally defective, and the prisoner held under it may be released on habeas corpus.[3] Again, under section 753 of the revised statutes of the United States,[4] there is a class of cases where a writ of habeas corpus may issue from a federal court even after a defendant has been regularly indicted, tried, and convicted in a state court; and, in fact, to any prisoner anywhere "in custody for an act done or omitted in pursuance of a law of the United States or of an order, process, or decree of a court or judge thereof, or is in custody in violation of the constitution or of a law or treaty of the United States; or being a subject or citizen of a foreign state, and domiciled therein, is in custody for any act done or omitted under any alleged right, title, authority, privilege, protection, or exemption claimed under the commission, order, or sanction of any foreign state or under color thereof, the validity and effect whereof depend upon the law of nations." One indicted, tried, and convicted contrary to this statute may assail the judgment on habeas cor-

---

[1] People ex rel. Tweed v. Liscomb, 60 N. Y. 559; S. C., 11 Alb. L. J. 396; In the Matter of Petty, 22 Kan. 477; Ex parte Farnham, 3 Col. 545; Ex parte Virginia, 100 U. S. 339; Kirby v. The State, 62 Ala. 51; Ex parte Simmons, Id. 416; Ex parte Yerger, 8 Wall. 85; Ex parte Williams, 1 Wash. T. 240; Ex parte Gibson, 31 Cal. 619; Ex parte Smith, 2 Nev. 338; Ex parte Siebold, 100 U. S. 371; People ex rel. Davis v. Foster, 104 Ill. 156; People v. Cavanagh, 2 Park. Cr. 650; State of Louisiana v. Fenderson, 28 La. Ann. 82; Ex parte Hartman, 44 Cal. 32; Ex parte Parks, 93 U. S. 18; Petition of Semler, 41 Wis. 517; S. C., 16 Alb. L. J. 119; Ex parte Scwartz, 2 Tex. App. 74; Ex parte McGill, 6 Id. 498; Ex parte Boland, 11 Id. 159; In re Truman, 44 Mo. 181; Ex parte Mess, 12 Pac. C. L. J., 279.

[2] Ex parte Lange, 18 Wall. 163; People ex rel. Tweed v. Liscomb, 60 N. Y. 559; S. C., 11 Alb. L. J. 396; see Ex parte Kearney, 55 Cal. 212; In the Petition of Petty, 22 Kan. 477; S. C., 9 Cent. L. J. 135; Ex parte J. C. H., 17 Fla. 368; Ex parte Bulger, 60 Cal. 438; Miller v. Snyder, 6 Ind. 1; Petition of Crandall, 34 Wis. 177; Smith's Application, 2 Nev. 338.

[3] See cases cited in last note.

[4] See United States habeas corpus act, *ante*, sec. 59.

pus, and if the record on the hearing of the writ shows the act or omission mentioned in this section, or shows the imprisonment to be in violation of the constitution or a law or treaty of the United States, the prisoner will be discharged.[1]

And before proceeding to details, it may not be amiss to call attention to the statutes of many of the states which provide grounds of discharge for the prisoner in certain cases. In the foot-note will be found the provisions of the penal code of California, which closely resemble the laws of New York and Missouri, on this question; but for others the reader must be referred to the statutes of his own state.[2] The return to the writ or the record will often disclose many of the causes for which a judgment may be assailed on habeas corpus. The record is brought before the court by *certiorari*, error,[3] appeal,[4] or put in evidence to support some issue raised on the return. In the treatment of some of the following questions it will be observed that the issues raised on the return were sometimes heard on original applications for a habeas corpus, sometimes on *certiorari*, and frequently on appeal or error. The use of *certiorari* and appeals in assailing judgments will be viewed more fully in another chapter.[5] It may be remarked here, however, that it has a

---

[1] Ex parte Bridges, 2 Woods, 428; In re Wong Yung Qui, 9 Rep. 366; Ex parte McCready, 1 Hughes, 598; Ex parte Virginia, 100 U. S. 339; S. C., 14 Am. Law Reg. 320; Ex parte Clarke, 100 U. S. 399; In re Bull & Turtle, 4 Dill. 323.

[2] Sec. 1487. If it appears on the return of the writ that the prisoner is in custody by virtue of process from any court of this state, or judge or officer thereof, such prisoner may be discharged in any of the following cases, subject to the restrictions of the last section [which provides that the court or judge, if the time during which such party may be legally detained in custody has not expired, must remand such party, if it appears that he is detained in custody: 1. By virtue of process issued by any court or judge of the United States, in a case where such court or judge has exclusive jurisdiction; or, 2. By virtue of the final judgment or decree of any competent court of criminal jurisdiction, or of any process issued upon such judgment or decree]: 1. When the jurisdiction of such court or officer has been exceeded; 2. When the imprisonment was at first lawful, yet by some act, omission, or event which has taken place afterwards, the party has become entitled to a discharge; 3. When the process is defective in some matter of substance required by law, rendering such process void; 4. When the process, though proper in form, has been issued in a case not allowed by law; 5. When the person having the custody of the prisoner is not the person allowed by law to detain him; 6. Where the process is not authorized by any order, judgment, or decree of any court, nor by any provision of law; 7. Where a party has been committed on a criminal charge without reasonable or probable cause: See 2 Fay's Dig., Habeas Corpus and Certiorari, 123 (2 R. S. 568, sec. 41); 1 Mo. R. S. 1879, sec. 2650.

[3] See People ex rel. Tweed v. Liscomb, 60 N. Y. 559; S. C., 11 Alb. L. J. 396.

[4] Miller v. Snyder, 6 Ind. 1; Ex parte Boland, 11 Tex. App. 159; Petition of Crandall, 34 Wis. 177; Patterson v. Pressley, 70 Ind. 94; Ex parte Scwartz, 2 Tex. App. 74; Ex parte McGill, 6 Id. 498.

[5] See chaps. 5, 6, 16.

thousand times been said that the writ of habeas corpus does not operate as an appeal, writ of error, or *certiorari*, nor has it the force or effect of those proceedings.[1] We understand, however, that where an appeal is allowed from the judgment of a court or judge dismissing a case and remanding the prisoner, mere errors and irregularities will not be reviewed; but if the relator can show a want of power or jurisdiction in the lower court to render such a judgment, and that he is illegally restrained, he will be discharged even on the appeal from the judgment on the habeas corpus, the same as he would be where the hearing is on error, or where the record is brought up by *certiorari*, and shows fatal jurisdictional defects. In other words, whether the record be before the court by appeal, writ of error, or *certiorari*, jurisdiction is always a proper subject of inquiry; though to the extent of reviewing the subject of jurisdiction the writ of habeas corpus would seem to operate as an appeal.[2]

§ 363. **Errors can not be Reviewed.**—It has been said by a thousand courts and a thousand judges that alleged errors and irregularities behind the judgment can not be inquired into on habeas corpus; and that the writ of habeas corpus was never designed to be a writ of error, by which the errors or irregularities of final judgments could be revised. It deals with more radical defects, which go to the jurisdiction of the court or officer, and which render the proceeding or judgment void. No matter how flagrant the error, the party must prosecute his appeal, writ of error, or *certiorari;* his remedy is not by habeas corpus. On this writ nothing will be investigated except jurisdictional defects. Although by prosecuting his appeal, writ of error, or *certiorari*, the party may have errors reviewed, and the result of

---

[1] Ex parte McGill, 6 Tex. App. 498; Ex parte Scwartz, 2 Id. 74; Ex parte Boland, 11 Tex. App. 159; and probably like decisions in every other state of the Union.

[2] See Patterson v. Pressley, 70 Ind. 94; Ex parte Boland, 11 Tex. App. 159; Miller v. Snyder, 6 Ind. 1; Ex parte Scwartz, 2 Tex. App. 74; Ex parte McGill, 6 Id. 498; Ex parte Siebold, 100 U. S. 375, where Mr. Justice Bradley of the supreme court of the United States says: "The writ of habeas corpus can not be used as a mere writ of error. Mere error in the judgment or proceedings, under and by virtue of which a party is imprisoned, constitutes no ground for the issuance of the writ. Hence upon a return to a habeas corpus, that a prisoner is detained under a conviction and sentence by a court having jurisdiction of the cause, the general rule is that he will be instantly remanded. No inquiry will be instituted into the regularity of the proceedings, unless, perhaps, where the court has cognizance by writ of error or appeal to review the judgment. In such case, if the error be apparent and the imprisonment unjust, the appellate court may, perhaps, in its discretion, give immediate relief on habeas corpus, and thus save the party the delay and expense of a writ of error."

the review entitle him to an immediate discharge, it is no ground for his release on habeas corpus.[1]

The following examples will illustrate the general principle: If a verdict on a charge of felony is received and the jury discharged during the enforced absence of the relator in jail, it is held to be error for the court to thereafter pronounce judgment upon the verdict. The prisoner may avail himself of the error by writ of error, or other method prescribed by law, but not on habeas corpus.[2] A judgment entered on the minutes of the court, in a criminal case, is erroneous simply if it does not definitely state the offense of which the prisoner was convicted, or if it does not state it at all, but not void; provided it shows that he was indicted for some offense, and tried and convicted, and that the sentence passed on him was one which the court had jurisdiction to pronounce for an offense of which he might have been convicted under the indictment.[3] This question of non-adherence to a prescribed rule of procedure has lately been be-

---

[1] See, generally, People v. Liscomb, 60 N. Y. 559; S. C., 11 Alb. L. J. 396; In the Matter of Petty, 22 Kan. 477; S. C., 9 Cent. L. J. 135; Ex parte Farnham, 3 Col. 545; Ex parte Virginia, 100 U. S. 339; Kirby v. The State, 62 Ala. 51; Ex parte Simmons, Id. 416; Ex parte Yerger, 8 Wall. 85; Ex parte Siebold, 100 U. S. 371; Ex parte Williams, 1 Wash. T. 240; Ex parte Gibson, 31 Cal. 619; In re Schenck, 74 N. C. 607; Ex parte Smith, 2 Nev. 338; People ex rel Davis v. Foster, 104 Ill. 156; People v. Cavanagh, 2 Park. Cr. 650; State of Louisiana v. Fenderson, 28 La. Ann. 82; Ex parte Hartman, 44 Cal. 32; Petition of Semler, 41 Wis. 517; S. C., 16 Alb. L. J. 119; Ex parte Sewartz, 2 Tex. App. 74; Ex parte McGill, 6 Id. 498; Ex parte Boland, 11 Id. 159; In re Truman, 44 Mo. 181; Ex parte Mess, 12 Pac. C. L. J. 279; Ex parte Sam, 51 Ala. 34; Ex parte Winston, 9 Nev. 71; Herrick v. Smith, 1 Gray, 1; Matter of Eaton, 27 Mich. 1; Phinney, Petitioner, 32 Me. 440; In re Blair, 4 Wis. 522; Ex parte Granice, 51 Cal. 375; Commonwealth ex rel. Wilson v. Keeper etc., 26 Pa. St. 279; Williamson's Case, Id. 9; People v. McLeod, 1 Hill (N. Y.), 377; Ex parte McCullough, 35 Cal. 98; O'Malia v. Wentworth, 65 Me. 129; Rex v. Carlile, 4 Car. & P. 415; Ex parte Watkins, 3 Pet. 193; Baker's Case, 11 How. Pr. 418; Ex parte Reed, 100 U. S. 13; People v. Nevins, 1 Hill (N. Y.), 154; Ex parte Toney, 11 Mo. 661; Keen v. McDonough, 8 La. 185; Walbridge v. Hall, 3 Vert. 114; Olmsted v. Hoyt, 4 Day, 436; Ex parte Parks, 93 U. S. 18.

[2] Ex parte Farnham, 3 Col. 545; see Green v. The People, Id. 68.

[3] Ex parte Gibson, 31 Cal. 619. In this case Mr. Justice Sanderson made the distinction appear between void and voidable judgments. "An irregularity or error," said he, "which will render a judgment voidable, is 'the want of adherence to some prescribed rule or mode of proceeding; and it consists either in omitting to do something that is necessary for the due and orderly conducting of a suit or doing it in an unreasonable time or improper manner:' 1 Tidd's Pr. 512. 'It is the technical term for every defect in practical proceedings, or the mode of conducting an action or defense, as distinguished from defects in pleadings:' 3 Chit. G. P. 509. On the contrary, illegality can be affirmed only of radical defects, and signifies that which is contrary to the principles of law, as distinguished from rules of procedure. Illegality denotes a 'complete defect in the proceedings.'" See People v. Cavanagh, 2 Park. Cr. 650, that it is sufficient to state a conviction of misdemeanor without naming the offense. See also Ex parte McGill, 6 Tex. App. 498.

§ 363.   COURTS OF GENERAL JURISDICTION.   475

fore Justice Thornton of the same court, and the rule laid down in Ex parte Gibson followed. Irregularity, he said, in sentencing a prisoner convicted of a felony before the expiration of two days after verdict, section 1191 of the penal code of California providing in such cases that the judgment must be at least two days after the verdict, etc., is not ground for discharge on habeas corpus, because the judgment and process issued upon it are not void; though it may be an irregularity for which the judgment should be reversed on appeal.[1] Errors made by the court in the determination of questions arising on motions to quash the indictment, on demurrers, on motions to arrest judgment, etc., are not jurisdictional defects, though the question determined is, whether an act charged in an indictment is or is not a crime by the law which the court administers.[2] So one suffering a sentence of fine and period of imprisonment, until the costs of the prosecution are paid, can not on habeas corpus take advantage of the error of the court in refusing a discharge under a statute authorizing a discharge "after the expiration of the time for which he may be sentenced, and when it satisfactorily appears to the court that all legal means have been exhausted, and that the person has no estate wherewith to pay such fine and costs," etc. Neither will the error of the court in refusing to admit proper evidence on the application for such discharge avail the prisoner on habeas corpus.[3] It makes no difference whether the error occurred at the trial or is alleged to exist in the judgment, it can not be reviewed on habeas corpus;[4] nor can any error, irregularity, want of form, or defect which may be amended or remedied by further entry or motion.[5] So with any error committed by the court in setting aside or modifying an erroneous order in a criminal case; and also where one is imprisoned under an order regular upon its face, and which the court had power to make, no relief will be granted on habeas corpus because of error in granting the order. But the effect of an order arresting judgment in a criminal case is to place the defendant, as nearly as other and controlling rules of law will permit, in the same situation in which he was before

[1] Ex parte Mess, 12 Pac. C. L. J. 279; and see Ex parte Smith, 2 Nev. 338, to the same point, where it was held that if the record showed affirmatively that there was no interval of time between the plea of guilty and sentence, it was error simply, and the remedy was appeal, not habeas corpus.

[2] Ex parte Parks, 93 U. S. 18; Ex parte Shaffenburg, 4 Dill. 271.

[3] People ex rel. Davis v. Foster, 104 Ill. 156.

[4] People v. Cavanagh, 2 Park. Cr. 650.

[5] People v. Cavanagh, 2 Park. Cr. 650; People v. Nevins, 1 Hill (N.Y.), 154; People ex rel. Trainor v. Baker, 89 N. Y. 460, and the many cases cited by counsel for respondent to this point.

the indictment was found. Upon its entry he must be discharged unless he is detained in custody by virtue of some other legal process or order which it is in the power of the court to make.[1]

The relator and appellant had been convicted and fined in a mayor's court for an assault and battery. His attorney prepared an appeal bond, which, though defective, was approved by the mayor. Shortly afterwards the attorney discovered the defects in the bond already filed, prepared another, and presented it to the mayor, telling him that the first bond filed was defective; but the mayor declined to receive the second bond, on the ground that the case had been appealed to the county court, and that he had delivered the papers to the clerk. In the mean time the said appeal was dismissed for the want of a sufficient appeal bond, and a *procedendo* ordered to be issued to the mayor's court, which issued a *capias pro fine* for the appellant. Thereupon he sued out a habeas corpus before the county court, alleging that he had been denied the right of appeal. The county court dismissed the writ, and adjudged the prisoner to be remanded until payment of the fine and costs. Relator then appealed to the court of appeals from this judgment; but that court said: "If the mayor approved an insufficient appeal bond, and the county court dismissed the appeal because the appeal bond was not such as the law required, this matter can not be inquired into or corrected on habeas corpus. It has not been made to appear either that the mayor did not have jurisdiction to hear the case in the first instance, nor that the county court did not have jurisdiction over the appeal. We are unable to see, from anything in the record before us, that the relator has been illegally restrained of his liberty, or that the county judge erred in causing him to be remanded to the custody of the marshal until the fine and costs are paid. The judgment of the county court in dismissing the writ is affirmed."[2]

Where one was tried, convicted, fined, and arrested on a *capias pro fine*, for violating a city ordinance making it a penal offense to carry prohibited weapons within the corporate limits, but omitting to exempt travelers or persons fearing an attack upon their persons, in conformity with the penal code of the

---

[1] Ex parte Hartman, 44 Cal. 34.
[2] Ex parte Scwartz, 2 Tex. App. 74. It will be noted that in Texas the superior courts are inclined to hold that the presumptions of law in favor of the jurisdiction of justices of the peace, recorders' and mayors' courts, are the same as are accorded to courts of general jurisdiction: Ex parte Boland, 11 Id. 169.

§ 364. COURTS OF GENERAL JURISDICTION. 477

state, it was held, on habeas corpus, that the ordinance was not, therefore, void, but that it should be so construed that the provisions of the code and ordinance might stand together; and while the ordinance would not protect a person traveling or one who had reasonable ground for fearing an unlawful attack upon his person, the provisions of the code would protect him anywhere in the state, whether in or out of the said city limits. On appeal to the court of appeals from the judgment of the county court dismissing the trial of habeas corpus and remanding the prisoner, the judgment of the county court was affirmed.[1] In the language of the syllabus: "The defendant in a prosecution for bastardy escaped from the constable who had arrested him before the warrant had been returned; whereupon, the justice, without any appearance by the defendant, tried the cause and certified it up to the circuit court, where, without the issuance of any summons, warrant, or notice, and without any appearance by the defendant, except specially to move to dismiss the cause, the court defaulted the defendant, tried the cause, found the defendant guilty, assessed a recovery for the maintenance of the child, and ordered that on failure of the defendant to replevy the judgment, a warrant be issued by the clerk to the sheriff for his arrest and commitment: held, on a special finding of the foregoing facts, made in a petition by the defendant against the sheriff, for release from commitment on such warrant, that the judgment was unlawful and the commitment illegal."[2]

§ 364. **Place of Imprisonment—Error.**—If it be error to designate the county jail instead of the penitentiary as the place of confinement for one convicted of a misdemeanor, it can not be reviewed and corrected on habeas corpus.[3] The place of confinement should, however, be stated by the court,[4] and in federal practice a court does not exceed its power in fixing a part of the term of imprisonment in the county jail and the remainder in the penitentiary. The fact that the prisoner is retained for a time either before or after sentence in the county jail, and until he can be removed by the marshal, does not in either case authorize a writ of habeas corpus. Neither is it necessary, in order to clothe a federal court with authority to imprison in a state penitentiary, that a part of the punishment, by the terms of the sentence, should be hard labor, where

[1] Ex parte Boland, 11 Tex. App. 159.
[2] Patterson v. Pressley, 70 Ind. 94.
[3] People v. Cavanagh, 2 Park. Cr. 650.
[4] Ex parte Gibson, 31 Cal. 627; Ex parte Geary, 2 Biss. 485.

criminals are subjected by the laws of the state to hard labor, unless otherwise directed in their sentences, and as criminals sentenced by the federal courts shall be subject to the same discipline and treatment as convicts sentenced by the state courts. The conclusion of law is that federal convicts are subject to hard labor as a part of the imprisonment. Neither can the federal offender object that there is no express legislation by the state authorizing him to be there confined. The state only can make such objection.[1]

But in the following case the imprisonment was pronounced illegal, and the prisoner discharged: The prisoner was indicted for grand larceny. On the trial of the plea of not guilty, the jury by their verdict found him guilty of petit larceny, but assessed the value of the property stolen at more than twenty-five dollars, which, under section 4358 of the code of Alabama of 1876, amounted to grand larceny. The court, however, at its August term, 1878, sentenced the prisoner on the verdict to hard labor for the county. The court of county commissioners failed to establish any system of hard labor, and on the twenty-seventh of December, the sheriff still holding the defendant in custody, the prisoner applied to a circuit judge, in vacation, for a habeas corpus, but he was refused a discharge and remanded. On appeal to the supreme court, the questions as to whether the findings were consistent, or whether the circuit court should have passed sentence on the verdict, would not be inquired into; but it was held that the delay between the sentence of the prisoner and his delivery to the proper authorities, to be put to hard labor for the county, was unreasonable; and that the sheriff had no authority to detain him under the sentence. Further, that there was no authority to substitute imprisonment in jail for the sentence to hard labor, and that the commissioners' court having failed, for an unreasonable time after sentence, to establish a system of hard labor, the convict was entitled to his discharge.[2] So in cases of a breach of the peace or disorderly conduct in violation of municipal ordinances or by-laws, where statute authorizes the imprisonment of an offender, imprisonment is lawful. But when the statute in other cases requires the punishment to be a fine, or, in default of payment, that the offender may be sentenced to hard labor in the streets of the town, for a period not exceeding thirty days, the prisoner can not be sentenced to remain in custody until the fine and costs are fully paid, because it inflicts "imprisonment," when the charter provides "hard

---

[1] Ex parte Geary, 2 Biss. 485.   [2] Kirby v. The State, 62 Ala. 51.

labor." It is without warrant in law. It is also indefinite in duration, because the period of imprisonment is limited to thirty days. One imprisoned on a warrant or *mittimus* based on such sentence is entitled to his discharge on habeas corpus.[1]

§ 365. **Irregularities can not be Reviewed.**—What has been said of errors is equally true of irregularities. Mere irregularities, whether before or after judgment, can not avail a prisoner on habeas corpus, or justify the court in permitting a discharge for that reason alone. Irregularity has been defined above,[2] and the following illustrations will show the tendency of the courts on this point. Thus, in Petty's Case,[3] the prisoner was indicted, tried, and found guilty of murder in the first degree, in the district court of Greenwood county, Kansas. The murder was committed in 1866. He was tried in 1879, and sentenced pursuant to the laws of 1872. The penalty for his crime, the prisoner claimed, was prescribed by the law of 1866, and which was hanging, etc.; but he claimed that the law of 1872 so far changed the punishment as to render the same, as to him, *ex post facto* and unconstitutional, because it provided that he was to be taken to the penitentiary and hanged at any time after the expiration of one year, and in the mean time to be kept at hard labor, etc. He also claimed that by the act of 1872, all prior laws relating to the punishment of death were repealed, and that all of the act of 1872 relating to punishment for past offenses was void, because *ex post facto*. But the supreme court said on habeas corpus that the act of 1872 "did not release the petitioner from the penalty of his offense, and that the district court did not lose jurisdiction with the return of the verdict of the jury. Under the verdict, he was liable to be sentenced to the punishment of death. The sentence actually passed, omitted the appointment of a day on which the sentence should be executed, and provided that the governor should set the day of the execution at a time not less than one year from the day of sentence [as he was directed to do under the law of 1872]; but this was an irregularity, or rather an erroneous order, to carry out the sentence of death, and not a void judgment. The court had jurisdiction of the person of the prisoner and of the offense. The verdict was valid. The court had also the power to render a judgment of death, and therefore the pris-

---

[1] Ex parte Moore, 62 Ala. 471. As to construction of the ordinance, compare with Ex parte Boland, 11 Tex. App. 159, cited *supra*, sec. 363.

[2] See note to sec. 363.

[3] 22 Kan. 477; S. C., 9 Cent. L. J. 135.

oner can not be relieved on habeas corpus. An appeal is the remedy."[1]

Where the irregularity complained of is the selection of the grand jury by a judge acting under an appointment from the incumbent who is disabled by sickness, and before his commission by the governor, it can not be assailed by habeas corpus after conviction and sentence.[2] Nor can the question of fact as to whether or not an indictment regular upon its face, and upon which the relators were tried and convicted, was ever found by the grand jury be determined on this writ. Consequently the commitment of conviction can not be thus impeached.[3] Only one officer being present when the verdict was returned instead of two, as required by law, is an irregularity not vulnerable on habeas corpus.[4] So where one was tried upon his plea of guilty, and fined for unlawfully carrying arms, instead of rendering a judgment committing defendant to the custody of the sheriff until the fine and costs were paid, and awarding execution as provided by statute, the justice's judgment ordered a *capias pro fine* to issue, and upon this *capias* the defendant was arrested. He sued out habeas corpus, but the county judge refused his discharge, and on appeal this was considered a mere irregularity which could not be reviewed by means of this writ, and the judgment of the lower court was affirmed.[5] If a wife be convicted of furnishing intoxicating liquors contrary to law, when

[1] The court remarked: "This conclusion leads us to decide that as the murder with which the petitioner stands charged was committed in 1866, and as the law of 1872 was not passed until after the commission of the offense, the prisoner is not subject to the punishment of the act of 1872. If he is not exposed to the infliction of any penalty under the statutes in force prior to the act of 1872, then as that act can not apply in this case, the sentence and judgment are wholly void." The "lame logic" of the prisoner as analyzed by Justice Valentine is worthy of note. "He says that all of the act of 1872 relating to punishment for past offenses is void, because it is *ex post facto;* and yet he says that it is valid enough to drive all other acts inconsistent therewith out of existence. He says that his sentence is void because he was sentenced under the new law (that of 1872), which new law he says is void. He also says that he could not legally be sentenced under the old law, because it is inconsistent with the new law relating to punishments for past offenses, and is, therefore, by the new law, repealed. And he further says, that any saving clause continuing the old law in force for any purpose would be inconsistent with this new and void law; and therefore that this new and void law would repeal the saving clause, or at least prevent its operation in this particular case. Now, I do not think that any valid law can be repealed merely because it is inconsistent with some new law, unless this new law is itself valid. A void enactment certainly can not have the effect to repeal a valid law; and repeals by implication are never favored, even where the repealing law is itself valid."

[2] State of Louisiana v. Fenderson, 28 La. Ann. 82.

[3] Ex parte Twohig and Fitzgerald, 13 Nev. 302.

[4] Rex v. Carlile, 4 Car. & P. 415.

[5] Ex parte McGill, 6 Tex. App. 498.

§ 366. COURTS OF GENERAL JURISDICTION. 481

charged with the offense jointly with her husband, it is doubtless error and irregularity, and probably would be a ground for a new trial; but not a sufficient ground for the discharge of the wife on habeas corpus.[1]

§ 366. **Reviewing Evidence and Retrying Issues of Fact.**—The judgment of the court upon the facts, in cases of habeas corpus, has been said to be analogous to the verdict of a jury, and will not be disturbed by the reviewing court, provided there was enough evidence to support it, although there may have been other proof strongly in conflict with it.[2] Neither will the appellate court, for the purpose of discharging the applicant, consider the sufficiency of facts relied on as supporting a plea of former acquittal for the same offense for which he is in custody.[3] The novel proposition to introduce oral evidence to contradict the record, or to show error in the court rendering a judgment, will not be countenanced. It is, however, sometimes introduced in connection with the judgment record to show what was litigated by the parties; to show the facts more fully than they would be shown by the record.[4] Alleged former conviction and the bar of the statute of limitations are matters of defense, and are questions for the determination of the tribunal having jurisdiction to try the charge. The latter may involve an inquiry as to whether the petitioner has absented himself, or whether other legal impediment to the trial has existed. These are matters that will arise in the exercise of jurisdiction, as distinguished from the fact of the existence of jurisdiction, to hear and determine the charge. They are matters to be pleaded as a defense; and on habeas corpus, evidence tending to show an abuse of this exercise of jurisdiction will not be admitted before final judgment, much less after it.[5]

Indictments, not void upon their faces, and regularly returned to and pending in a court having jurisdiction thereof, can only be disposed of by some appropriate proceeding in such court, and the question as to whether they have all been found on the same evidence, and are for one and the same supposed offense, will not be considered on habeas corpus.[6] Sufficiency of the evidence upon which process is based, or the decision upon the regularity of proceedings upon which process is based,

---

[1] In re Dougherty, 27 Vt. 325. This was a conviction by a justice of the peace, but it will be remembered that the legal presumptions in Vermont are in favor of such officer's jurisdiction: See c. 18.

[2] Starr v. Barton, 34 Ga. 99; see State v. Bloom, 17 Wis. 521.

[3] Griffin v. The State, 5 Tex. App. 457; Perry v. The State, 41 Tex. 488.

[4] Ex parte Smith, 2 Nev. 338.

[5] In re Bogart, 2 Saw. 396.

[6] Perry v. The State, 41 Tex. 488.

not affecting the jurisdiction of the court or officer to issue the process, will not be considered under this writ; but parol evidence of a continuance may be received, if necessary, to supply the omission of a recital of such fact in the warrant.[1] After trial, conviction, and sentence to the penitentiary for the crime of larceny, the prisoner can not invoke the aid of a habeas corpus for his release simply on the ground that he was at the time of sentence under the age of imprisonment there; and particularly when this defense is first urged in the revisory court, and does not appear by the record of conviction. This question of age must be tried and determined by the trial court, and the fact will not be retried in another court.[2] Under the exceedingly liberal provisions of the late codes of Mississippi, when the record is silent, the courts apply the comprehensive maxim, *Omnia præsumuntur rite esse acta;* but notwithstanding the provision of the code,[3] which declares that the proceeding by habeas corpus shall not be held to authorize the discharge of any person "suffering imprisonment under lawful judgment," a convict in the penitentiary is entitled to be released under this proceeding if the record of his trial, as the same remains on file in the trial court, is so defective in its failure to show essential jurisdictional facts as to be a nullity; "because," say the courts, "the lawfulness of the judgments is the test of the efficacy of the writ, and the judgment itself must be tested by the record of the court which assumed to pronounce it."[4]

§ 367. **Pleadings—Insufficiency of the Indictment or Information.**—The sufficiency of the pleadings in a criminal case is always a question to be determined by the trial court; and when the court has jurisdiction of the person of the prisoner, of the subject-matter, and to render the particular judgment, the prisoner must abide by that determination, whether the decision be right or wrong. Again, says Mr. Justice Bradley, of the United States supreme court, "whether an act charged in an indictment is or is not a crime, is also a question to be met with at almost every stage of criminal proceedings, on motions to quash the indictment, on demurrers, on motions to arrest judgment, etc. The court may err, but it has jurisdiction of the question. If it errs, there is no remedy after final judgment, unless a writ of error lies to some superior court."[5] This is in accord with the views expressed by Chief Justice Marshall

---

[1] In the Matter of Baker, 11 How. Pr. 418.
[2] Ex parte Kaufman, 73 Mo. 588; S. C., 12 Cent. L. J. 574.
[3] Code of 1871, sec. 1397.
[4] Ex parte Phillips, 57 Miss. 357.
[5] Ex parte Parks, 93 U. S. 20.

§ 367. COURTS OF GENERAL JURISDICTION. 483

in rendering the decision of the supreme court of the United States in Ex parte Tobias Watkins.[1] The prisoner there claimed his right to discharge on habeas corpus, and after conviction and sentence in the circuit court of the District of Columbia, on the ground that the indictment charged no offense for which he was punishable in that court, or of which that court could take cognizance; and consequently, that the proceedings were *coram non judice* and totally void. His honor showed that the judgment of the circuit court could not be reviewed either on appeal or writ of error by the supreme court—that it was a judgment withdrawn by law from the revision of that court—and expressed himself as follows: "Can the court, upon this writ, look beyond the judgment, and re-examine the charges on which it was rendered? A judgment, in its nature, concludes the subject on which it is rendered and pronounces the law of the case. The judgment of a court of record whose jurisdiction is final is as conclusive on all the world as the judgment of this court would be. It is as conclusive on this court as it is on other courts. It puts an end to inquiry concerning the fact by deciding it.

"The counsel for the prisoner admit the application of these principles to a case in which the indictment alleges a crime cognizable in the court by which the judgment was pronounced; but they deny their application to a case in which the indictment charges an offense not punishable criminally according to the laws of the land. But with what propriety can this court look into the indictment? We have no power to examine the proceedings on a writ of error, and it would be strange if, under color of a writ to liberate an individual from unlawful imprisonment, we could substantially reverse a judgment which the law has placed beyond our control. An imprisonment under a judgment can not be unlawful, unless that judgment be an absolute nullity; and it is not a nullity if the court has general jurisdiction of the subject, although it should be erroneous. The circuit court for the District of Columbia is a court of record, having general jurisdiction over criminal cases. An offense cognizable in any court is cognizable in that court. If the offense be punishable by law, that court is competent to inflict the punishment. The judgment of such a tribunal has all the obligation which the judgment of any tribunal can have. To determine whether the offense charged in the indictment be legally punishable or not, is among the most unquestionable of its powers and duties. The decision of this question is the ex-

[1] 3 Pet. 192.

ercise of jurisdiction, whether the judgment be for or against the prisoner. The judgment is equally binding in the one case and in the other, and must remain in full force unless reversed regularly by a superior court capable of reversing it. If this judgment be obligatory, no court can look behind it. If it be a nullity, the officer who obeys it is guilty of false imprisonment. Would the counsel for the prisoner attempt to maintain this position? * * * Without looking into the indictments under which the prosecution against the petitioner was conducted, we are unanimously of opinion that the judgment of a court of general criminal jurisdiction justifies his imprisonment, and that the writ of habeas corpus ought not to be awarded."

The state courts, too, have generally declined, on habeas corpus, to look into the complaint, indictment, or information after judgment for the purpose of inquiring into its sufficiency. In Missouri the regularity of an indictment in a state court for passing, with intent to defraud, a United States treasury note, and the rightfulness of the judgment rendered thereon, can not be investigated in a collateral attack by habeas corpus. They hold that it must be done through proceedings operating directly upon the judgment itself.[1] In Michigan a petition for a writ of habeas corpus was presented to the superior court to test the sufficiency of the information on which a conviction was had; but the court denied the prayer of the petition, because to allow it "would be to make the writ of habeas corpus take the place of a writ of error."[2] In Texas this writ can not be used to impeach the sufficiency or validity of an indictment.[3] In Alabama "a party in custody under a defective indictment will not be discharged on habeas corpus, in vacation, because of the insufficiency of the indictment."[4] In Mississippi a judgment sustaining an indictment can not be assailed in this collateral way.[5] So in Nevada.[6] Outside of Chief Justice Marshall's opinion, a portion of which is quoted above, the most extended consideration of this question we have met with in the reports is that given to it by the learned Justice Cole of the supreme court of Wisconsin. The essential portion of his valuable opinion will be found in the foot-note.[7] The relator made an application to

---

[1] In re Truman, 44 Mo. 181.
[2] In the Matter of Eaton, 27 Mich. 1.
[3] Parker v. The State, 5 Tex. App. 579.
[4] Ex parte Whitaker, 43 Ala. 323.
[5] Emanuel and Giles v. The State, 36 Miss. 627.
[6] Ex parte Twohig and Fitzgerald, 13 Nev. 302.
[7] "Another question arising in the case is, Can the petitioner be relieved by means of this writ? or must he resort to some other appropriate process to correct and review the pro-

that court for a habeas corpus, and claimed his discharge on the ground that the first and second counts of the information did not charge him with any offense, and were void. But the court refused to inquire into the matter, and denied the writ.

This is one view of this important and difficult question, and it seems to be supported by the weight of authorities; but there ceedings of the circuit court? This leads to an inquiry as to the office of the writ, and what matters can be considered upon it. And at the outset it may be observed that the principle is well settled, that a writ of habeas corpus does not have the scope, nor is it intended to perform the office of a writ of error or appeal. This doctrine is almost elementary in the law. The writ, then, can not be resorted to for the purpose of reviewing and correcting orders and judgments which are erroneous merely. It deals with more radical defects, which go to the jurisdiction of the court or officer, and which render the proceeding or judgment void. A distinction between a proceeding or judgment which is void and one that is voidable only for error is recognized in the cases, and must be observed. Says Dixon, C. J., in Petition of Crandall, 34 Wis. 177: 'It is conceded that for mere error, no matter how flagrant, the remedy is not by writ of habeas corpus. For error the party imprisoned must prosecute his writ of error or certiorari. Nothing will be investigated on habeas corpus except jurisdictional defects, or illegality, as some courts and authors term it, by which is meant the want of any legal authority for the detention or imprisonment.' Page 179. To the same effect is the doctrine laid down in In re Blair, 4 Id. 522; In re O'Connor, 6 Id. 288; In re Perry, 30 Id. 268. Now the inquiry is, in the light of these adjudications, Did the circuit court act without jurisdiction, or in excess of its jurisdiction, in the matter complained of? or did it merely make a wrong decision? There can be no doubt that the circuit court had jurisdiction of the person of the petitioner, and of the offense charged in the information. But it is claimed that the first and second counts in the information charged no offense; in other words, that the information is insufficient, and that the motion to quash for that reason should be sustained. This may be at once conceded, but what follows? Manifestly this, that the circuit court gave a wrong decision where it clearly had jurisdiction, in holding a defective information good. The court committed an error, but there is no ground for saying it acted without jurisdiction in rendering its decision. If a demurrer had been filed to the information, and overruled by the court, precisely the same question would have been presented. It is a case of error for which the petitioner can only have relief on writ of error or some other appropriate process of review. He can not have relief on a writ of habeas corpus without making such writ perform all the office of a writ of error. This seems very obvious. Nor does the fact that this court, under the constitution, has appellate jurisdiction over the circuit courts in any way affect the question before us. For this court can only exert revisory or appellate jurisdiction on proper process proceeding according to the rules of law. It can not overlook and disregard the well-established distinction between the scope and operation of a writ of error and a writ of habeas corpus, and make the latter a substitute for the former. And the distinction has been clearly recognized in the above decisions. In the case of Hauser v. The State of Wisconsin, 33 Wis. 678, a strictly analogous question was considered. That was a *certiorari* to review the decision of the municipal court of Milwaukee refusing to quash a criminal information for a libel against a corporation. It was claimed that a corporation could not be the object of a criminal libel, and that the municipal court erred in holding the contrary. But this court held that even if that position was well taken, the real question presented to the municipal court for decision was, whether the information did or did not charge the accused with the commission of a criminal offense, and that this was in no sense a jurisdictional question.

is another taken by those learned in the law. Lord Hale said: "If it appear by the return of the writ that the party be wrongfully committed, or by one that hath no jurisdiction, or for a cause for which a man ought not to be imprisoned, he shall be discharged or bailed."[1] The same opinion was expressed by Chief Baron Gilbert, thus: "If the commitment be against law, as being made by one who had no jurisdiction of the cause, or for a matter for which by law no man ought to be punished, the court are to discharge."[2] And A. C. Freeman, the author of the standard work on judgments, writes: "If it be assumed that the court has jurisdiction and power to punish every conceivable act, then it is doubtless true that any deficiency in the indictment can not be a cause for release on habeas corpus. But no such power has ever been vested in any of our courts."[3] The following proposition was laid down in Corryell's Case[4] by the learned Chief Justice Cope of the supreme court of California: "The court derives its jurisdiction from the law, and its jurisdiction extends to such matters as the law declares criminal, and none other, and when it undertakes to imprison for an offense to which no criminality is attached, it acts beyond its jurisdiction." This principle was recognized and affirmed by Mr. Justice McKinstry in rendering the opinion of the same court in Kearney's Case,[5] and the language of Justice Cope was quoted approvingly by

---

It refused to review the decision on the motion to quash upon *certiorari*, and quashed the writ. The operation of the writ of *certiorari* is certainly as extensive as the writ of habeas corpus; still this court declined to examine upon that writ the correctness of the ruling of the municipal court in refusing to quash. The reason and principle of that decision are directly applicable to the case at bar. So in Ex parte Booth, 3 Id. 145, the petitioner applied to this court for a writ of habeas corpus to discharge him from imprisonment. It appeared that he was in confinement by force of a warrant of the district court of the United States, and that the object of the imprisonment was to compel him to answer an indictment for a violation of the fugitive-slave law. That law had been held to be unconstitutional by this court in a previous case. Whiton, C. J., says: 'These facts show that the district court of the United States has obtained jurisdiction of the case, and it is apparent that the indictment pending against the prisoner is for an offense of which the courts of the United States have exclusive jurisdiction. We do not see, therefore, how we can, consistently with the principles of our former decision, interfere:' Page 148. The writ was denied. The petition before us shows that the applicant is committed on an order of the circuit court for want of bail. He is held by the process of a court of competent jurisdiction, which had authority to make the order. For these reasons, neither the sufficiency of that order nor the correctness of the decision on the motion to quash will now be inquired into:" Petition of Semler, 41 Id. 523; S. C., 16 Alb. L. J. 119.

[1] Mr. Justice Bradley, citing 2 Hale P. C. 144.
[2] Mr. Justice Bradley, citing Bac. Abr., Habeas Corpus, B, 10.
[3] Freeman on Judgments, 678.
[4] 22 Cal. 178.
[5] 55 Cal. 212.

§ 368.   COURTS OF GENERAL JURISDICTION.   487

Mr. Justice Thornton. The court, however, was divided. Justices McKee, Sharpstein, and Ross concurred in the views of Justice McKinstry, but Chief Justice Morrison and Mr. Justice Myrick dissented from the opinions of their brethren.

But it may be said that the penal code of California has abolished common-law offenses,[1] and the decisions there are not generally applicable. Be that as it may, the position seems to be sound upon principle. That the state should hold the citizen responsible for something which is not a crime, can not be maintained under any law. That one imprisoned without having committed any crime is illegally restrained of his liberty, is unquestionably true. That the object of the writ of habeas corpus is to relieve from illegal imprisonment, is conceded. Therefore, if the prisoner can show, at any stage of the proceedings against him, that he has committed no offense, he annihilates the question of jurisdiction of the subject-matter— removes the foundation on which the charge against him rests, and should go free. It is true that such extreme cases seldom occur, but the mantle of the law should protect every citizen, and should guarantee the liberty of every subject, on habeas corpus, not guilty of a crime *mala in se* or *mala prohibita*. And why should one guilty of no crime be punished, while the violator of an unconstitutional law[2] receives the protection of the writ of habeas corpus? The reasoning in the latter case is simply this: only men who commit crimes are subject to punishment. The violation of an unconstitutional law constitutes no crime, for it is as no law, and void. Therefore such an offender shall not be punished, but will be released upon habeas corpus.

§ 368. **Jurisdiction of Person and Subject-matter** must exist in order to make a valid judgment, and if either is wanting, the judgment is void and the imprisonment without authority of law.[3] The question of jurisdiction over the subject-matter is one of fact, to be proved or admitted, as any other fact alleged in the indictment, in order to establish the conviction. Ordinarily, in criminal trials, the jurisdiction of the court over the place where the offense is alleged to have been committed is assumed. For instance, if the indictment charges the offense to have been committed within certain territorial limits, over which the court has jurisdiction, and the jurisdiction is admitted by pleading over, that ends the matter. But if that allegation is

[1] See sec. 6.
[2] Ex parte Siebold, 100 U. S. 376.
[3] Miller v. Snyder, 6 Ind. 1; Johnson v. United States, 3 McLean, 89; Cropper v. Commonwealth, 2 Rob. (Va.) 842; Ex parte Hayne, 4 Cent. L. J. 72; Ex parte Bridges, 2 Wood, 428.

traversed, and the jury find that the prisoner committed the offense within the jurisdiction of the court, as alleged, the defendant can not impeach that finding on habeas corpus by showing that the place where the offense was committed is without the said territorial limits.[1] Where there is a bar, under the statute of limitations, it should be pleaded. If not, it is waived, and the prisoner can not raise it on habeas corpus after sentence. The time laid in the indictment is not material, and the offense may be proved to have been committed at any other time.[2]

Whether the jurisdiction of a court be limited or not, if it entertains a cause without having gained jurisdiction of the person of the defendant, by having him before the court in the manner required by law, the proceedings are void; thus, where the statute requires that a certain person shall execute process, and it is executed by another, the proceeding is void. It gives no jurisdiction, and all the subsequent proceedings upon it are *coram non judice* and void.[3] The general principle is that the want of jurisdiction over the person or subject-matter appearing upon the record in a court of special or limited jurisdiction, except where the legal presumptions are in favor of such jurisdiction, is a good cause for discharge on habeas corpus. In courts of general jurisdiction, though the record fails to show jurisdiction of the person and subject-matter, their jurisdiction will be presumed where the imprisonment is under process valid on its face, and the prisoner must assume the burden of proving its invalidity by showing a want of jurisdiction;[4] but the court or officer having jurisdiction of the writ must necessarily in every case pass upon the question whether the process is void. If the record be challenged, the examination, of course, will be confined to it alone.[5]

The proceedings of a court having no jurisdiction to try felonies, but which proceeds to try, and sentences a prisoner to the penitentiary for such a crime, are an absolute nullity and void.[6] When the jury has been discharged from the further consideration of an indictment, and during the prisoner's absence, he can not avail himself on habeas corpus of this fact, or by this

---

[1] In re Newton, 16 Com. B. 97; S. C., 30 Eng. L. & Eq. 432; see Reg. v. Newton et al., 1 Jur., N. S., Q. B., 591; 3 Cent. L. J. 618, citing Ex parte Edgington, 10 Nev. 215; State of Louisiana v. Fenderson, 28 La. Ann. 82; People ex rel. Tweed v. Liscomb, 60 N. Y. 571; S. C., 11 Alb. L. J. 396; Deckard v. The State, 38 Md. 186.

[2] Johnson v. United States, 3 McLean, 89.

[3] Reynolds v. Orvis, 7 Cow. 269.

[4] People ex rel. Tweed v. Liscomb, 60 N. Y. 559, and numerous cases cited; see also People v. Cavanagh, 2 Park. Cr. 650; Deckard v. The State, 38 Md. 186; Brenan v. Gallan, 2 Cox C. C. 193.

[5] People v. Liscomb, 60 N. Y. 559.

[6] Miller v. Snyder, 6 Ind. 1.

means test the correctness of the decision of the court, if its jurisdiction is unimpaired.[1] A free colored person, tried and convicted by a court of oyer and terminer, when the statute provides that such an offense must be tried before a justice, is entitled to release on habeas corpus, as there is no jurisdiction existing in the trial court to try the prisoner for the offense.[2] Where the relator is in custody under a *capias pro fine*, the judgment imposing the fine can be revised on habeas corpus no further than to determine whether the court *a quo* had jurisdiction to render it.[3] Finally, if the court be found to have jurisdiction of the person, subject-matter, and to render the particular, final judgment rendered, no further inquiries can be made on habeas corpus.[4]

§ 369. **Sentence by Court or Judge de Facto.**—It is well settled that the writ of habeas corpus can not be used as a substitute for *quo warranto*. One convicted by a jury and sentenced in court by a judge *de facto*, acting *colore officii*, though not *de jure*, and detained in custody in pursuance of his sentence, can not properly be discharged on habeas corpus. As where one had been indicted, tried, convicted, and sentenced for a felony in a court presided over by a judge disqualified to hold office under the fourteenth amendment to the constitution of the United States, but who had been in office two years before the amendment was adopted.[5] Again, where the relator was convicted by a justice of the peace as a delinquent road-hand. He appealed to the county court and was again convicted. He then on habeas corpus to the court of appeals set up alleged ineligibility of the county judge in holding incompatible offices. But that court refused to revise the judgment, and gave as the result of the many authorities reviewed, " that in matters which concern the public the officer's title to his office (he being in the exercise of its duties) can not be questioned unless in a direct proceeding having for its object the contestation of his right to hold the office; and the appointment of one to an incompatible office with the one he holds at the time of appointment is not absolutely void; the first office becomes vacant on his accepting the second and qualifying for it."[6] For same

---

[1] State of Minnesota ex rel. Noonan v. Sheriff of Hennepin Co., 24 Minn. 87.
[2] Cropper v. Commonwealth, 2 Rob. (Va.) 842.
[3] Ex parte Boland, 11 Tex. App. 159.
[4] Ex parte Twohig, 13 Nev. 302; Ex parte Toney, 11 Mo. 661; Lumly Quarry, 7 Mod. 9; Anon., Id. 118.

[5] Griffin's Case, 1 Chase, 364.
[6] Ex parte Call, jun , 2 Tex. App. 497, citing to the first proposition: The People v. Stevens, 5 Hill, 630; Green v. Burke, 23 Wend. 490; The People v. White, 24 Id. 520; and to the second: People v. Carrique, 2 Hill (N. Y.), 93; Hoglan v. Carpenter, 4 Bush, 89. See as to presumptions

rule in Louisiana, see cases cited.[1] In Massachusetts the supreme judicial court holds "that when the court has jurisdiction of the case and of the party, and the warrant is sufficient to justify the officer, and the prisoner has no special privilege or exemption, his imprisonment is legal, and the law does not allow the authority of the judge by whom the court was held and the warrant issued to be disputed in a summary manner by the writ of habeas corpus."[2] In Wisconsin, where one was indicted, tried, convicted, and sentenced for a felony, at a term of court held by one who exercised the office of judge under an appointment by the governor, but which was made without authority of law, and against whom a judgment of ouster was afterwards rendered, the sentence was held valid and binding, and the supreme court said the discharge of the prisoner by a county judge on habeas corpus was wrong, and they reversed his judgment.[3]

§ 370. **Unauthorized Convictions.**—A conviction is sometimes void because unauthorized by law; and of course in such cases relief should be granted by habeas corpus. There may be a complete defect in the law under which a conviction is had, or there may be a "manifest want of criminality in the matter charged" sufficient to render the proceedings void. Take, for instance, Bushell's Case, decided in 1670, and which is usually cited under this head and is one of the leading authorities. "There twelve jurymen had been convited in the oyer and terminer for rendering a verdict (against the charge of the court) acquitting William Penn and others, who were charged with meeting in conventicle. Being imprisoned for refusing to pay their fines, they applied to the court of common pleas for a habeas corpus; and though the court, having no jurisdiction in criminal matters, hesitated to grant the writ, yet, having granted it, they discharged the prisoners, on the ground that their conviction was void, inasmuch as jurymen can not be indicted for rendering any verdict they choose. The opinion of Chief Justice Vaughan in the case has rarely been excelled for judicial eloquence."[4]

So, in the supreme court of the United States, a conviction

in favor of justices' courts in Texas, sec. 267; see also Clark v. Commonwealth, 29 Pa. St. 129, citing Commonwealth v. Burrell, 7 Barr, 34.

[1] State of Louisiana v. Fenderson, 28 La. Ann. 82; 13 Rep. 47, citing State of Louisiana ex rel. Williams v. Persdorf.

[2] 4 Cent. L. J. 524, citing Sheehan's Case, and contains citations of numerous cases.

[3] State v. Bloom, 17 Wis. 521.

[4] Mr. Justice Bradley, in Ex parte Siebold, 100 U. S. 371, citing T. Jones, 13; S. C., Vaugh. 135, and 6 Howell's State Trials, 999.

§ 370.   COURTS OF GENERAL JURISDICTION.   491

under an unconstitutional law is held to be unauthorized; or, as more fully expressed by Mr. Justice Bradley,[1] "the validity of the judgment is assailed on the ground that the acts of congress under which the indictments were found are unconstitutional. If this position is well taken, it affects the foundation of the whole proceedings. An unconstitutional law is void, and is as no law. An offense created by it is not a crime. A conviction under it is not merely erroneous, but is illegal and void, and can not be a legal cause of imprisonment. It is true, if no writ of error lies, the judgment may be final, in the sense that there may be no means of reversing it. But personal liberty is of so great moment in the eye of the law, that the judgment of an inferior court affecting it is not deemed so conclusive but that, as we have seen, the question of the court's authority to try and imprison the party may be reviewed on habeas corpus by a superior court or judge having authority to award the writ. We are satisfied the present is one of the cases in which the court is authorized to take such jurisdiction. We think so, because if the laws are unconstitutional and void, the circuit court acquired no jurisdiction of the causes."

In the state courts there has been some diversity of opinion on this matter—as to what relief should be granted on habeas corpus upon convictions made without authority of law. With respect to unconstitutional statutes, we believe the correct rule is laid down in Herrick v. Smith.[2] The following distinction was made on the authority of Riley's Case:[3] "When the proceedings are irregular or erroneous, if the court or magistrate has jurisdiction, the judgment is voidable only, and not void; and of course must stand good until reversed or annulled in a proper course of proceeding, by a court having authority to revise and annul it. But where it appears, on the face of the proceedings, that the magistrate had no jurisdiction, the proceedings are wholly void, the commitment is without authority, and the party committed is entitled to be discharged from his imprisonment without reversal of the judgment." There the court decided that the section of law under which the conviction was had was unconstitutional, that in consequence, the judgment was void, and that the prisoner must be released. In Kansas, where the plaintiff was charged, tried, convicted, and sentenced for wrongfully obtaining the signature of Lena McNeil to a certain deed of conveyance of real estate, the plaintiff,

[1] In Ex parte Siebold, 100 U. S. 376.
[2] 1 Gray, 49.   [3] 2 Pick. 172.

on habeas corpus, claimed that the sentence was void upon the sole ground that the acts for which he was sentenced were not punishable under the laws of that state. The supreme court understood the question to be before them in this way: "It is not whether the sentence is irregular only, or voidable; it is not whether the sentence might not be set aside or reversed for error, if the case were brought to this court on appeal; but it is whether such sentence is absolutely void, under all circumstances, if attacked collaterally as well as if attacked directly." The court proceeded to construe the statute under which the conviction was had, and the prisoner, of course, had the benefit of the court's passing upon the question, but they pronounced the statute constitutional, declared the sentence legal, and remanded the relator.[1]

In Alabama a municipal ordinance fixed the price of a license for retailing spirituous liquors within the corporate limits at one thousand dollars. Petitioner had violated this ordinance, and was sentenced to imprisonment. He applied to a probate judge for a habeas corpus, but the application was refused. On application to the supreme court they held that the town council had no authority to demand one thousand dollars as the price of a license, and that this invalidated the ordinance prescribing a penalty for retailing without such license, and that before the corporate authorities could complain that a supposed offender had retailed without a license, they must have provided some legal mode by which a retailer could obtain a license. To hold otherwise, they said, would be to authorize them to prohibit the traffic altogether. They directed the writ to issue.[2] So in New York it was decided before Justice Birdseye of the supreme court, that the board of health of the town of Castleton had no power to prohibit all persons from passing from within the quarantine, situate in that town, into any other part of the town, as such a regulation was in conflict with the powers conferred by the state on the officers of the quarantine establishment. The prisoner convicted and sentenced for a violation of such regulation was discharged on habeas corpus; the court

---

[1] In re Payson, 23 Kan. 757.
[2] Ex parte Burnett, 30 Ala. 461. The court construed the act to only authorize the granting of license, and not to confer the right to prohibit the sale of ardent spirits. They would not deny to the legislature the power to confer on corporations the right to prohibit the sale of ardent spirits by retail. Where the right was conferred, the corporation might enact a prohibitory ordinance; "but the price of a license demanded in this case—one thousand dollars—is in its nature prohibitory; such sum is so disproportionate to the cost of a license to retail under the general law that it can not be vindicated as one of the incidental powers of municipal corporations."

feeling no hesitation in declaring the regulation void, and that disobedience to it constituted no crime. "It can never be permitted," said his honor, "that even for the sake of the public health, any local, inferior board or tribunal shall repeal statutes, suspend the operation of the constitution, and infringe all the natural rights of the citizen."[1]

But in Michigan,[2] Missouri,[3] Nebraska,[4] Texas,[5] and Iowa[6] the courts will not, on habeas corpus, look beyond the judgment, and re-examine the charges on which it was rendered, or pronounce the judgment an absolute nullity on the ground that the constitutionality of the statute under which the conviction took place, or upon which the indictment was based, is controverted. That question, it is said, must be tested on appeal, writ of error, or trial in the appropriate court. In Platt v. Harrison,[7] it was held that the police magistrate before which the conviction took place had power to determine the constitutionality of the ordinance in question, and that his decision was final. But there the legal presumptions were in favor of the jurisdiction of courts of special or limited jurisdiction.

In Nevada[8] a justice of the peace was held to have original jurisdiction, and power to decide finally whether or not the law under which the prisoner was convicted and sentenced had been repealed by implication or otherwise; and substantially the same question was decided in the same way even by one of the inferior federal courts. The prisoner had been convicted on an indictment and sentenced by the second circuit court. On habeas corpus he then alleged that the statute under which the sentence was imposed upon him had been repealed before such sentence was passed; but Justice Woodruff of that court decided that he had no power on this writ, and in his capacity as judge, to review the judgment of conviction and sentence by the circuit court on such an allegation.[9]

The decisions of that high judicial tribunal, the supreme court of the United States, are everywhere respected; and since the judgment of that court in the late case of Ex parte Siebold[10] was rendered, the proposition there laid down, and as stated above, will hardly be questioned. And if the petitioner for a writ of habeas corpus can have the constitutionality of a law

[1] People v. Roff, 3 Park. Cr. 216.
[2] Matter of Underwood, 30 Mich. 502.
[3] In the Matter of Harris, 47 Mo. 164.
[4] Ex parte Fisher, 6 Neb. 309.
[5] Parker v. The State, 5 Tex. App. 579.
[6] Platt v. Harrison, 6 Iowa, 79.
[7] 6 Iowa, 79.
[8] Ex parte Winston, 9 Nev. 71.
[9] In re Callicott, 8 Blatchf. 89.
[10] 100 U. S. 371.

under which he is convicted and sentenced inquired into, there would seem to be a much stronger reason for inquiring into the reason of the prisoner's detention when he alleges that he has been convicted and sentenced under no law at all. It is impossible to reconcile the latter class of decisions with the first.[1] In the latter class of decisions the courts seem to proceed on the ground that the lower courts had jurisdiction to pass upon the questions involved, including the constitutionality of the statute under which conviction was had and judgment rendered, and that if they decided the law to be constitutional when it in reality was not, it was simply an error in the exercise of undoubted final jurisdiction. But we apprehend the true rule to be that when a prisoner alleges that the law under which he is convicted and sentenced is unconstitutional, or has been repealed before the trial and judgment, that he may have these matters passed upon by the highest judicial tribunals, whether the attack upon the judgment be collateral, as by habeas corpus, or direct, as by appeal or writ of error. The decision in Ex parte Siebold will probably tend to henceforth harmonize the decisions on this question.

§ 371. **Power to Render the Particular Judgment.**—In Ex parte Lange[2] we find this: "It is no answer to this to say that the court had jurisdiction of the person of the prisoner and of the offense under the statute. It by no means follows that these two facts make valid, however erroneous it may be, any judgment the court may render in such a case. If a justice of the peace, having jurisdiction to fine for a misdemeanor, and with the party properly charged before him, should render a judgment that he be hanged, it would simply be void. Why void? Because he had no power to render such a judgment. So, if a court of general jurisdiction should, on an indictment for libel, render a judgment of death, or confiscation of property, it would, for the same reason, be void."[3] The jurisdiction of the court to render the particular judgment is always a proper subject of inquiry; it is not enough to have simply jurisdiction

---

[1] Or with Ex parte Lange, 18 Wall. 163; Ex parte Kearney, 55 Cal. 212; Ex parte Bernert, 7 Pac. C. L. J. 460; People v. Liscomb, 60 N. Y. 559; S. C., 11 Alb. L. J. 396.

[2] 18 Wall. 163.

[3] But in Florida, where the prisoner was condemned to pay a certain sum under the bastardy act, and to remain imprisoned until he complied with an order to execute a bond, the court held the judgment good, on habeas corpus. The provision in the bill of rights that "no person shall be imprisoned for debt, except in case of fraud," the court said was a limitation upon the powers of each department of government, executive, legislative, and judicial, but it was clearly not a debt within the meaning of the constitution: Ex parte J. C. H., 17 Fla. 362, and numerous cases cited.

of the prisoner and the subject-matter to render any judgment valid. It matters not what the general powers and jurisdiction of a court may be; if it act without authority in the particular case, its judgments and orders are mere nullities, not voidable, but simply void, protecting no one acting under them, and constituting no hinderance to the prosecution of any right.[1] It may be here observed that statutes which prohibit the review of a court of competent jurisdiction apply only to such judgments as may be shown, by the record or otherwise, to be simply erroneous, and not to those judgments which could not, under any circumstances or upon any state of facts, have been pronounced.[2]

§ 372. **Erroneous Sentences.**—A judgment may be erroneous and not void, and it may be erroneous because it is void. The distinctions between void and merely voidable judgments are very nice, and they may fall under the one class or the other as they are regarded for different purposes.[3] The writ of habeas corpus can not be used as a writ of error. Mere error in the judgment or proceedings, under and by virtue of which a party is imprisoned, constitutes no ground for the issuance of the writ,[4] and it is well settled by both the state and federal courts that a judgment or sentence can not be assailed on habeas corpus, if it is merely erroneous, the court having given a wrong judgment when it had jurisdiction of the person and subject-matter.[5] Thus, where one was convicted of assault with intent to kill, and was sentenced to confinement in the penitentiary at hard labor, when such an offense was not punishable by confinement in the penitentiary, it was simply an error not relievable on habeas corpus, and the remedy was appeal.[6] Neither does it form any ground for discharge on habeas corpus that one convicted of a misdemeanor is erroneously sentenced to imprisonment in the county jail instead of the penitentiary.[7] So where the court made a manifest error and mistake in sentencing a convicted horse-thief for only one year to the penitentiary, when the law required the sentence for such an offense to be for a period of not less than three years, it was held not void, but erroneous.[8] A party convicted of an offense under a statute

---

[1] Elliott v. Piersol, 1 Pet. 340.
[2] People ex rel. Tweed v. Liscomb, 60 N. Y. 559; S. C., 11 Alb. L. J. 396.
[3] Justice Miller in Ex parte Lange, 18 Wall. 175.
[4] Ex parte Siebold, 100 U. S. 371.
[5] People ex rel. Tweed v. Liscomb, 60 N. Y. 559; S. C., 11 Alb. L. J. 396.
[6] Ex parte Bond, 30 Am. Rep. 20; S. C., 9 S. C. 80; also cited in 11 Cent. L. J. 59.
[7] People v. Cavanagh, 2 Park. Cr. 650; S. C., 2 Abb. Pr. 84.
[8] Ex parte Shaw, 7 Ohio St. 81; but see *contra*, Ex parte Bernert, 7 Pac. C. L. J. 460.

prescribing the amount of fine and period of imprisonment which may be imposed for it, and sentenced to pay a fine, may, in the court's discretion, be imprisoned until the fine is paid—no longer, however, we apprehend, than the period fixed by statute.[1] There is not even error in such a judgment. In Wisconsin, the petitioner was prosecuted upon an information against him for an assault with intent to kill. The jury found a verdict of "guilty of an assault as charged against him in the indictment," but the clerk had it in the return that the prisoner was convicted of and sentenced by the court for "an assault and battery." The petitioner was sentenced to imprisonment in the county jail for six months, to pay a fine of five hundred dollars, with costs of action, and to be imprisoned until payment thereof—a sentence authorized by law for an assault and battery, but not for a simple assault. Prisoner's counsel claimed that he had been sentenced for a crime which he had not committed, and that the fine exceeded, to the amount of the costs, the limit fixed by statute; but the court thought that the error, if any, did not go to the question of jurisdiction, and remanded petitioner. The court, however, stated that had a clear case of excess or want of jurisdiction been presented, the prisoner would have been entitled to his discharge.[2]

Error in deciding as to whether or not an ordinance was passed without authority of law will not, in Iowa, avail the prisoner convicted under it in assailing the judgment on habeas corpus.[3] Neither will the courts on this writ review alleged errors of law in the decision of such a question in Nebraska.[4] The same rule prevails in Alabama.[5] There it is erroneous to sentence a prisoner on a conviction for burglary to hard labor for the county for a period exceeding two years. The sentence should be imprisonment in the penitentiary when the term exceeds two years. But such a sentence, while it would be reversed on appeal or writ of error, is not void or a nullity, and is no cause for the prisoner's discharge on habeas corpus.[6] So in Wisconsin, the courts will not allow a resort to this writ for the purpose of reviewing orders or judgments which are merely erroneous, and made or rendered by a court having jurisdiction of the subject-matter and of the person.[7] In Georgia we find

---

[1] Ex parte Jackson, 96 U. S. 727.
[2] Petition of Crandall, 34 Wis. 177. See section on excessive sentences.
[3] Platt v. Harrison, 6 Iowa, 79.
[4] Ex parte Fisher, 6 Neb. 309.
[5] See Kirby v. The State, 62 Ala. 51; Ex parte Simmons, Id. 416.
[6] See Kirby v. The State, 62 Ala. 51; Ex parte Simmons, Id. 416. See section on excessive sentences.
[7] Petition of Semler, 41 Wis. 517; S. C., 16 Alb. L. J., 119.

the same doctrine. An industrious prisoner there complained on habeas corpus that he was sentenced to labor on only a part of the public works instead of all of them. The sentence was pronounced irregular, but not hurtful to any right of liberty, and not void. The court very pertinently asked, "Had he been sentenced to work three hours a day, would he be turned loose because he was not sentenced to work all day?" He waived his rights by not claiming a wider range when sentence was pronounced, and was remanded.[1]

§ 373. **Excessive Sentences—In English and Federal Courts.**—While two or three of the cases referred to in the preceding section seem to regard an excessive sentence as merely a voidable one, and not void, they are not in harmony with the weight of authorities concerning sentences imposed beyond the authority conferred by law. But the rule is not even uniform that a sentence beyond that authorized by law is void, yet this seems to be the better view and is doubtless the law as established by the authorities. Over one hundred years ago, in England, the defendants Collyer and Capon were brought on habeas corpus before the king's bench. It appeared that they had been convicted by a court of quarter sessions of an assault on Thomas Smith, and committed to New Prison, Clerkenwell, for the space of one month, "and to ask pardon upon their knees of the said Thomas Smith at the place where the offense was committed, and to cause an account of said sentence to be printed in the Daily Advertiser, and not to be discharged out of prison until they have undergone such imprisonment, asked such pardon, and caused such account to be published." The court disposed of the matter in this wise: "Every part of this judgment is illegal except the imprisonment. It has been said that the proper way for the defendants to be relieved against any part of this judgment is by writ of error; but it would be very hard that the defendants should continue in prison under the illegal parts of this judgment until they can obtain a reversal of those parts upon a writ of error." Though the fact is unreported, the prisoners were doubtless discharged.[2] This was an extraordinary

---

[1] Lark v. The State of Georgia, 55 Ga. 435. But see Ex parte Bernert, 7 Pac. C. L. J. 460.

[2] Rex v. Collyer and Capon, Say. 44. But while statutes in the United States often give the higher court, on writ of error, power to render such judgment as the court below ought to have rendered, it must be observed that this is not the English rule. The English courts will not touch an excessive judgment on habeas corpus, but on writ of error they go further than the courts of this country, and the settled practice there is "that where the inferior court on a valid indictment transcends its power in passing sentence, by giving one which

case, and not in accord with the later English rule requiring defective judgments to be directly attacked on writ of error, and not indirectly or collaterally by the summary means of habeas corpus; the courts holding that to allow the latter mode would be to virtually abrogate proceedings by writ of error.[1]

In the United States, in Ex parte Tobias Watkins,[2] Mr. Justice Story, in rendering the opinion of the supreme court, on a habeas corpus proceeding, disposed of the point regarding the eighth amendment to the constitution of the United States as follows: "It is addressed to courts of the United States exercising criminal jurisdiction, and is doubtless mandatory to them and a limitation upon their discretion. But this court has no appellate jurisdiction to revise the sentences of inferior courts in criminal cases; and can not, even if the excess of the fine were apparent on the record, reverse the sentence." But in later decisions this court has fully and clearly laid down the rule that a sentence or decree made even by a court of general jurisdiction over the person and subject-matter is, in either civil or criminal proceedings, as to any relief given or sentence imposed beyond that authorized by law, simply void. That is, void for the excess, but valid as to the remainder. For instance, as to a civil case, congress, by the confiscation act of July 17, 1862, authorized proceedings *in rem* to be instituted in the name of the United States, in any district court thereof, for the condemnation and sale of property seized by the United States, and belonging to persons engaged in the rebellion. Concurrently with the passage of this act, congress also adopted a joint resolution explanatory of it, whereby it was resolved that no punishment or proceedings under the act should be so construed as to work a forfeiture of the real estate of the offender beyond his natural life. A decree of confiscation against the property of French Forrest, alleged to be seised and possessed in fee, was claimed to affect all his estate, right, title, and interest in the property. Forrest's heir brought a suit against the purchaser of this property, but the latter defended his alleged right by insisting that the heir had no title in the property, because the decree and the sale under it necessarily trans-

---

the law does not authorize, the superior or appellate court will neither pass the proper sentence nor send back the record to the court below, in order that they may do so, but that they will reverse the judgment and discharge the prisoner:" See King v. Ellis, 5 Barn. & Cress. 395, and the well-considered case of King v. Bourne et al., 7 Ad. & El. 58.

[1] Ex parte Dunn, 5 Dow. & L. 345; S. C., 5 Com. B. 215, and 12 Jur. 99. See also Brenan and Galen's Case, 59 Eng. Com. L. 492; S. C., 10 Ad. & El., N. S., 492.

[2] 7 Pet. 568.

ferred the fee, and left nothing for the heir to inherit. But the court decided against the purchaser, and held "that the argument assumed what could not be admitted, that the district court established a confiscation reaching beyond the life of French Forrest, for whose offense the land was sold. Under the act of congress, the district court had no power to order a sale which should confer upon the purchaser rights outlasting the life of French Forrest. Had it done so, it would have transcended its jurisdiction. And it attempted no such thing. The decree has not that meaning."[1] This doctrine was reaffirmed in Day v. Micou,[2] where the court said that in Bigelow v. Forrest,[3] "we also determined that nothing more was within the jurisdiction or judicial power of the district court [than the life estate] and that consequently a decree condemning the fee could have no greater effect than to subject the life estate to sale."

"But why could it not?" asked Mr. Justice Miller, in delivering the opinion of the court in the case of Ex parte Lange,[4] brought directly before the court on petition for writs of habeas corpus and *certiorari*, and in which the above two cases were cited and approved. "Not because it wanted jurisdiction of the property or of the offense, or to render a judgment of confiscation, but because in the very act of rendering a judgment of confiscation it condemned more than it had authority to condemn. In other words, in a case where it had full jurisdiction to render one kind of judgment operative upon the same property, it rendered one which included that which it had a right to render and something more, and this excess was held simply void." Lange's case was this: He had been indicted in the circuit court of the United States for the southern district of New York for stealing, purloining, embezzling, and appropriating to his own use certain mail-bags belonging to the post-office department. The jury found him guilty of appropriating to his own use mail-bags, the value of which was less than twenty-five dollars. The statutory punishment for this offense was imprisonment for not more than one year or a fine of not less than ten dollars nor more than two hundred dollars. He was sentenced to one year's imprisonment and to pay a fine of two hundred dollars. He was committed in execution, but on the following day paid his fine. Five days after the original sentence was pronounced, and four days after the fine was paid,

---

[1] Bigelow v. Forrest, 9 Wall. 339.
[2] 18 Wall. 156.   [3] 9 Wall. 339.   [4] 18 Wall. 163.

Lange, still being in prison, was brought before the same court on habeas corpus. An order was entered vacating the former judgment, and the prisoner was again sentenced to one year's imprisonment from the date of the last sentence. On a second writ of habeas corpus the prisoner was remanded. The marshal claimed to hold under the last sentence. The whole record then went before the supreme court on *certiorari*, issued as auxiliary to the habeas corpus. On the inspection of the record it appeared upon its face that the last judgment by virtue of which Lange was imprisoned was rendered without any authority whatever, because the power of the court rendering such judgment in respect to that prosecution and indictment had become *functus officio* by reason of the prior judgment, valid in part, pronounced in the same cause and carried into execution, and the subsequent proceedings were void.[1]

§ 374. **Excessive Sentences, Continued—In the State Courts.**—The rule is the same in both the state and federal courts as regards the legal effect of an excessive sentence. It is good so far as the power of the court extends, but invalid as to the excess. An excessive sentence is not void *ab initio*. The whole sentence is not illegal and void because of the excess. As late as 1882 this was declared the settled law of New York.[2] Relator was sentenced to the penitentiary for one year and to pay a fine of five hundred dollars, and to stand committed until the fine was paid, at the rate of one dollar for each day's imprisonment. The prisoner claimed that the sentence was excessive because the minutes of the court showed that he was not convicted of the statutory crime for which he was sentenced, but of simple assault and battery, for which he might have been sentenced to the penitentiary for one year, and to pay a fine of only two hundred and fifty dollars. It was held by the court that the period of imprisonment was a separate portion of the sentence, complete in itself, and valid; and that the remainder of the sentence could be disregarded; and that the prisoner was not entitled to his discharge, on habeas corpus, until the expiration of the year.[3] As in Lange's Case, explained in the preced-

---

[1] Ex parte Lange, 18 Wall. 163. In this case the following was one of the illustrations used: "If on an indictment for treason the court should render a judgment of attaint, whereby the heirs of the criminal could not inherit his property, which should by the judgment of the court be confiscated to the state, it would be void as to the attainder, because in excess of the authority of the court, and forbidden by the constitution."

[2] People ex rel. Trainor v. Baker, 89 N. Y. 460, citing Matter of Sweatman, 1 Cow. 144; People ex rel. Tweed v. Liscomb, 60 N. Y. 559; S. C., 19 Am. Rep. 211; 11 Alb. L. J. 396; People ex rel. Woolf v. Jacobs, 66 N. Y. 8.

[3] People v. Baker, 89 N. Y. 460.

§ 374. COURTS OF GENERAL JURISDICTION. 501

ing section, it was decided by the court of appeals of New York in Tweed's Case, that but one sentence could be imposed on one judgment of conviction.[1] Where the statute makes battery punishable by fine or by imprisonment in the county jail not exceeding six months, or both, and the prisoner has been convicted of this crime and sentenced to three years' imprisonment in the house of correction, he will be released on habeas corpus at the expiration of the period of six months' imprisonment.[2] Of course there is no difficulty in impeaching a judgment on this writ where no jurisdiction to render it, or any part of it, exists at all. For example, where it is attempted, by a decree of divorce rendered in one state on service by publication, to fix the custody of minor children then in another state. Such a judgment is without jurisdiction and void.[3]

Opposed to these doctrines is the law in Ohio. A sentence

---

[1] Tweed had been tried, in the court of oyer and terminer, upon an indictment containing two hundred and twenty separate and distinct counts, each charging a separate and distinct misdemeanor, and identical in character. He was found guilty upon two hundred and four of the counts. Upon twelve of the counts the court sentenced him to twelve successive terms of imprisonment of one year each, and to fines of two hundred and fifty dollars each. Upon the other counts, to additional fines, amounting in all to twelve thousand five hundred dollars. The maximum punishment fixed by the statute under which he was indicted was one year's imprisonment and a fine of two hundred and fifty dollars; the prisoner, after serving one term of imprisonment, and paying the fine imposed by one sentence, applied upon habeas corpus to be discharged. The court of appeals held that, upon the trial of an indictment containing several counts, charging separate and distinct misdemeanors of the same grade, where a general verdict of guilty is rendered, or a verdict of guilty upon two or more specified counts they had no power to impose a sentence or cumulative sentences exceeding, in the aggregate, what was prescribed by statute as the maximum punishment for one offense of the character charged; that the provision of the revised statutes (2 R. S. 700, sec. 11), that upon a conviction of a person of two or more offenses, before sentence shall have been pronounced upon him for either, the imprisonment to which he shall be sentenced upon the second shall commence at the termination of the first term, and so on, applies only to separate convictions upon distinct trials, and not to convictions upon the same trial of several offenses joined in one indictment; and that the power of the court was exhausted by the first sentence, that the others were *coram non judice* and void; and that the relator should not be put to his writ of error to reverse or correct the judgment, but was entitled to be released on habeas corpus: See People ex rel. Tweed v. Liscomb, 60 N. Y. 559; S. C., 11 Alb. L. J. 396, and 19 Am. Rep. 211.

[2] Ex parte Bulger, 60 Cal. 438.

[3] Kline et al. v. Kline et al., 57 Iowa, 386. So, in Commonwealth v. Kirkbride, 7 Phila. 8; S. C., 2 Brews. 419, it was held in Pennsylvania that the judgment of every sister state was just as conclusive there as a judgment rendered in a Pennsylvania court; but that a foreign judgment could be attacked anywhere for fraud or absence of jurisdiction. Hence a finding of lunacy in another state was, on habeas corpus, held to be of no binding effect in Pennsylvania, where it appeared that no notice of the proceedings had been given. As to service of process, though it is not a habeas corpus case, it will not be unprofitable to read Pennoyer v. Neff, 95 U. S. 714, where some very important doctrines are enunciated.

in excess of that prescribed by law is there erroneous and voidable, but not absolutely void. The excessive punishment may be remitted on error or appeal, but not on habeas corpus.[1] And in Missouri [2] we find a complement to the reasoning of Mr. Justice McKinstry, in Ex parte Bernert.[3] In the Missouri case the prisoner was sentenced, on conviction of grand larceny, to ten years' imprisonment, when the statute allowed not more than seven years. On habeas corpus the whole sentence was, by the supreme court, pronounced void *ab initio*, on the ground that the lower court, in passing sentence, exceeded its jurisdiction, and did not act by authority of any provision of law, and that they had no power to reduce the term of imprisonment so as to bring it within the statutory limit. The prisoner was therefore discharged.

§ 375. **The Mittimus.**—The warrant of commitment is simply an authority and direction to the sheriff or other officer to convey the prisoner to the designated place of imprisonment, as to the penitentiary. This need not necessarily be left with

---

[1] Ex parte Van Hagan, 25 Ohio St. 426. See also In re Schenck, 74 N. C. 607, where the court refused to discharge a prisoner from the penitentiary on habeas corpus, even admitting that he was illegally confined, and left him to his *certiorari*.

[2] In Ex parte Page, 49 Mo. 291.

[3] 7 Pac. C. L. J. 460. In Judge Wagner's decision in the Missouri case occurs the following language: "It has been suggested that if the prisoner is not discharged, we should reduce the term so as to bring it within the limit prescribed by statute. But we know of no authority empowering us to act in proceedings of this kind. The statute makes it the duty of this court to examine the record and award a new trial, reverse or affirm the judgment or decision of the lower court, or give such judgment as that court ought to have given. But that provision in express terms is confined to appeals and writs of error, and can have no application in the present case. We are not aware of any authority by which we can undertake to modify a criminal sentence. In England the settled question is, that where the inferior court on a valid indictment transcends its power in passing sentence, by giving one which the law does not authorize, the superior or appellate court will neither pass the proper sentence nor send back the record to the court below, in order that they may do so, but that they will reverse the judgment and discharge the prisoner: King v. Ellis, 5 Barn. & Cress. 395; King v. Bourne, 7 Ad. & El. 58." These cases are directly in point, with the exception that they were both decided on writ of error, and not on habeas corpus. His honor further said that where the error complained of was one of fact, provable by evidence *dehors* the record, the court would not disturb the judgment on habeas corpus; but that where the error was one not arising out of a matter of fact, but patent on the face of the record, the record showing that the judgment of the court in passing sentence was illegal, and not simply erroneous or irregular, but absolutely void, as exceeding the jurisdiction of the court, and not being the exercise of an authority prescribed by law, the judgment could and should be revised in this collateral proceeding. If the proposition be true, as decided in Bernert's Case, cited *supra*, that a punishment inflicted less than that prescribed by law is void, because unauthorized by law, its natural complement would be that a sentence greater than that authorized by law should also be void *ab initio*. But neither of these cases is in harmony with either rule of law governing these two questions.

the keeper. If he has no other evidence of his authority to detain the prisoner, he should have that. But if the officer who brings a prisoner to the penitentiary furnished the keeper with a certified copy of the judgment of the court, then that is sufficient evidence of the keeper's authority, and he needs to have no other. A prisoner who has been properly and legally sentenced to prison can not be released simply because there is an imperfection in what is commonly called the *mittimus*. A proper *mittimus* can, if needed, be supplied at any time, and if the prisoner is safely in the proper custody, there is no office for a *mittimus* to perform.[1] It will thus be seen that the prisoner is detained by virtue of the judgment and not of the *mittimus*, and if the certified copy of the minutes of the court imperfectly describe the crime of which the prisoner was convicted, the keeper can, upon the return to a writ of habeas corpus, show, by the records of the court, what the precise crime was, and thereby that the sentence was valid and imprisonment authorized. But this must be proved by the records themselves, and not by parol evidence.[2] In case the *mittimus* appear to be absolutely void, the prisoner will be retained until a certified copy of the judgment has been obtained, or until a reasonable time has been allowed for that purpose; and if the judgment is good, the prisoner will be remanded; if it is void, he will be discharged.[3]

In respect to the commitment of prisoners by United States marshals to the custody of the jails of the states, the practice was for some time unsettled and not uniform in the different states; but the practice doubtless now is to commit by a regular *mittimus*, and to bring the prisoner up by a writ of habeas corpus, thereby furnishing the keeper of the jail and the marshal with the proper authority at all times to justify the execution of their duty.[4]

---

[1] People ex rel. Trainor v. Baker, 89 N. Y. 461.

[2] Id.

[3] Ex parte Gibson, 31 Cal. 619. Where, on habeas corpus, it becomes material to know of what particular misdemeanor the prisoner was convicted, in order to determine the legality of the commitment, resort may be had to the record, if one has been made up and filed, and if not, to the indictment upon which he was tried and convicted, and to which the entry in the minutes refers: See People v. Cavanagh, 2 Park. Cr. 650.

[4] Justice Nelson, in 1 Blatchf. 651, app. Sec. 1028 of the revised statutes of the United States provides what shall be the jailer's authority: "Whenever a prisoner is committed to a sheriff or jailer by virtue of a writ, warrant, or *mittimus*, a copy thereof shall be delivered to such sheriff or jailer as his authority to hold the prisoner, and the original writ, warrant, or *mittimus* shall be returned to the proper court or officer, with the officer's return thereon."

§ 376. **Cumulative Sentences.**—We have above adverted to the construction of the revised statutes of New York, showing how far cumulative judgments, aggregating a punishment in excess of that prescribed by law for the specific grade of offenses charged, are justified.[1] F. W. Peters had been indicted in one of the district courts of the United States. The indictment contained four counts, and set forth not less than two distinct offenses of a similar character. To this he pleaded guilty, and was sentenced to two years' imprisonment upon each count, each term commencing at the expiration of the preceding term. After two years, but before the expiration of four, the relator applied to be discharged on habeas corpus, upon the ground that the court had no authority to render cumulative judgments. The eighth circuit court for the western district of Missouri held that the judgment of the district court could not be pronounced void on this collateral assault, and was good at least for four years' imprisonment. Whether he could successfully apply to be discharged on habeas corpus at the end of four years, the court would not then determine, and remanded the prisoner.[2] But subsequently the two terms of two years each having expired, the petitioner renewed his application for discharge to the same court, and on the ground that the remaining distinct offenses were improperly joined; or in other words, the question was, whether it was competent for the district court to sentence the petitioner for both burglary and larceny charged in separate counts, but both appearing to be part of the same act. Under section 1024 of the United States revised statutes it was decided that separate offenses of the same class and growing out of the same transactions might be joined in one indictment in separate counts, provided they were such as could be "properly joined." The petitioner's prayer was denied.[3]

§ 377. **Power of Courts to Modify their Own Judgments.**—Courts of common law possessed the power to vacate their judgments during the term in which they were rendered, and the rule is still the same in all courts exercising jurisdiction in common-law cases, whether civil or criminal; and the remark is equally correct whether applied to a state or federal court. The power of a court over its judgments during the entire term in which they are rendered is unlimited. Every term continues until the call of the next succeeding term, unless previously

---

[1] See sec. 374.   [2] Ex parte Peters, 4 Dill. 169.
[3] Ex parte Peters, 12 Fed. Rep. 461.

§ 377.   COURTS OF GENERAL JURISDICTION.   505

adjourned *sine die;* and until that time the judgment may be modified or stricken out. During the same session or assize, or any adjournment thereof, says Mr. Archbold, the court may vacate the judgment passed upon the defendant, before it has become matter of record, and pass another less or even more severe.[1]

Judgments in criminal cases may be vacated before they become matter of record, but the rule seems to be that no court can make any alteration in the same when the judgment is once solemnly entered on the record, except as it may be reversed on appeal or writ of error for any material defect appearing on the face of it.[2] The final record, as defined by Justice Clifford of the supreme court of the United States, is as follows: "Minutes of the proceedings in a criminal trial are made on the docket by the clerk as they take place, but the record, except in capital cases, is not made until the end of the term or session of the court, when the whole proceedings are spread upon the record in a book or books kept for that purpose, which is, in the federal courts, the proper substitute for what is called the roll in the practice of the parent country. Such a record is never made up in ordinary criminal trials during the term, but the legal evidence of the proceedings rests in the minutes of the clerk, which, if need be, may be verified by his oath. Hence it is that even the strictest authorities admit that erroneous sentences may be corrected during the term in which they were imposed, as that could always be done in the parent country, although a writ of error would lie to correct the error if it was apparent on the face of the record. Accordingly it was held there that if the error was not corrected during the term, it could only be corrected by the appellate court; and inasmuch as the appellate court could only reverse or affirm the judgment of the court of original jurisdiction, it followed, in case the judgment was reversed, that the prisoner was discharged.[3]

But in the nature of this power there must be in criminal cases some limit to it.[4] No man can be twice lawfully punished

---

[1] Justice Clifford, in Ex parte Lange, 18 Wall. 192. See, generally, Freeman on Judgments, 3d ed., sec. 90; Noonan v. Bradley, 12 Wall. 129; King v. Justices, 1 Mau. & Sel. 442; 1 Arch. Crim. Pr. & Pl., Pomeroy's Notes, 593; Stickney v. Davis, 17 Pick. 169; State v. Harrison, 10 Yerg. (Tenn.) 541, where an indictment was lost; Ex parte Lange, 18 Wall. 167.

[2] Rex v. Justices, 1 Mau. & Sel. 442; Miller v. Finkle, 1 Park. Cr. 374.

[3] In Ex parte Lange, 18 Wall. 194, citing Commonwealth v. Weymouth, 2 Allen, 144.

[4] Ex parte Lange, 18 Wall. 168, where it is remarked that "the judgment of the courts in this class of cases extends to life, liberty, and property. The terms of many of them extend through considerable

for the same offense. This is clearly shown in Tweed's Case,[1] and in Lange's,[2] in each of which it was shown that there could be but one sentence imposed as the result of one judgment of conviction. In each of these cases, however, it will be remembered that the whole sentence was not absolutely void, but only a portion of it, and that the valid part had been suffered by the prisoner. Where no part of the sentence has been executed, the court can doubtless, during the same term, vacate its judgment and render another. But where a sentence has been passed, and which is not absolutely void, it may be a plausible, but it is an unsound, argument on habeas corpus to say that the judgment first rendered is erroneous, and must be treated as no judgment at all, and therefore presenting no bar to the rendition of a valid judgment; because the power of the court over the first judgment is just the same whether it is void or valid.[3] If by inadvertence in pronouncing a sentence a requirement of a statute has been overlooked, it may be corrected by the same tribunal before further action is taken.[4]

It will be noticed that these cases recognize the fact that the power of the court over its judgment stops at the point of execution, and clearly express or imply that after execution or warrant issued and executed, this power of summarily changing the record, or judgment, or sentence, by the rendition of another sentence, is at an end.

So it has been held on habeas corpus that the judge of a court has power to revise and increase a sentence imposed upon a convict during the same term of court, and before the original sentence had gone into effect or any action had upon it.[5] But where a convict had been committed to jail on a *mittimus* pursuant to a legal sentence, and the prisoner had suffered nineteen

periods of time, often many months, with adjournments and vacations in the same term, at the discretion of the judge. A criminal may be sentenced to a disgraceful punishment, as whipping, or, as in the old English law, to have his ears cut off, or to be branded in the hand or forehead. The judgment of the court to this effect being rendered and carried into execution before the expiration of the term, can the judge vacate that sentence and substitute fine or imprisonment, and cause the latter sentence also to be executed? Or if the judgment of the court is that the convict be imprisoned for four months, and he enters immediately upon the period of punishment, can the court, after it has been fully completed, because it is still in session of the same term, vacate that judgment and render another for three or six months' imprisonment, or for a fine? Not only the gross injustice of such a proceeding, but the inexpediency of placing such a power in the hands of any tribunal, is manifest."

[1] 60 N. Y. 559; S. C., 11 Alb. L. J. 396.
[2] 18 Wall. 163.
[3] Ex parte Lange, 18 Wall. 163.
[4] Miller v. Finkle, 1 Park. C. 374.
[5] Commonwealth v. Weymouth, 2 Allen, 144.

days of confinement, it was held that the judge could not recall and revoke the sentence, and impose a revised and greater one, although the punishment imposed by the new one was within the limit fixed by law. The first sentence was pronounced legal; the latter, null and void, and the prisoner remanded to serve out the first sentence.[1]

§ 378. **Miscellaneous Matters.**—A court has jurisdiction to inquire on habeas corpus into the legality of the imprisonment of a person held under its own sentence; as where one was legally convicted and sentenced, but claimed his discharge under the amnesty proclamation of December 3, 1863.[2] An individual in Nevada was sentenced to confinement in the prison of that state for the term of one year, to commence upon the expiration of another term. One year afterwards, upon appeal, the first judgment and sentence were adjudged void. On habeas corpus it was held that the last sentence commenced to run upon its rendition, and had expired by limitation, or it was void for uncertainty, as depending upon an impossible condition. In neither case was the warden entitled to the custody of the prisoner, and he was remanded to stand a new trial on the first case.[3] In Indiana, it is held that "the act of April 15, 1881, acts 1881, p. 560, providing for the collection of judgments for fines and forfeitures, by the issuance of an execution, and the imprisonment of the defendant upon the expiration of the stay secured to him by the entry of replevin bail, so far as it relates to judgments replevied before that date, is unconstitutional, and a writ of habeas corpus will lie to release a defendant so imprisoned."[4]

§ 379. **Conflict of Jurisdiction.**—Where the legality of the imprisonment has been inquired into on habeas corpus by a state court, and it is found that the prisoner is held by virtue of process issued by a court or judge of the United States having exclusive jurisdiction of the subject-matter of the process, the prisoner will be remanded—not alone because the provisions of the statute may require it, but also because of comity between courts.[5] And on petition for this writ, where it is shown on its face that an offense committed is exclusively cognizable by the laws of a state, and that the petitioner is not restrained of his liberty without due process of law, contrary to the constitution of the United States, the federal courts disclaim any jurisdiction

---

[1] Brown v. Rice, 57 Me. 55; see generally, on this section, Kirby v. State, 62 Ala. 51; Ex parte Page, 49 Mo. 291.
[2] In re Greathouse, 4 Saw. 487.
[3] Ex parte Roberts, 9 Nev. 44.
[4] Dinckerlocker v. Marsh, 75 Ind. 548.
[5] In re Booth, 3 Wis. 1.

to grant the prayer of the petition.¹ But where one has been sentenced by a state court for passing counterfeited national bank bills, the federal courts will discharge him from imprisonment, because a state court has no jurisdiction over such an offense.² So where one was convicted and undergoing a sentence of fine and imprisonment in the penitentiary, imposed by a state court, for the crime of perjury committed in the course of a judicial investigation conducted under authority of acts of congress, he was released by a federal court on habeas corpus, because this was an offense against the public justice of the United States, and exclusively cognizable in the courts of that government.³ In 1875 Kansas ceded exclusive jurisdiction over the military reservation of Fort Leavenworth to the United States. Subsequently a larceny was committed on the reservation, and the accused was committed for want of bail by a federal officer. He sought to be released by habeas corpus, on the ground that the state, and not the general government, had jurisdiction of the offense; but the circuit court for the district of Kansas held that the jurisdiction of the offense was in the courts of the United States, and not in those of Kansas, and denied the writ.⁴

A state statute creating an offense in violation of the federal constitution or a treaty of the United States is void. A judgment on conviction for such an offense is also void, and not merely erroneous or voidable; and on application to a federal court, the one against whom it is rendered may be relieved on habeas corpus.⁵ The supreme court of a territory, however, will not on this writ review the judgment of a territorial district court sentencing a murderer to imprisonment, on the alleged ground that the district court had no jurisdiction in the premises, and that the prisoner was tried under a territorial law, when in fact he should have been tried by a United States law.⁶ In Virginia, in a late case, 1878, where two colored persons were tried for murder by the state authorities, and by a jury exclusively white, in contravention of section 641 of the revised statutes of the United States, and article 14 of the late amendments to the constitution of the United States, the circuit court for the western district of Virginia, on habeas corpus, granted such relief as was permitted by the circumstances of the case,

---

¹ 1 Crim. L. Mag. 126, citing In re Taylor, 12 Chic. L. N., Oct. 4th, p. 17, 1880.
² Ex parte Houghton, 7 Fed Rep. 657.
³ Ex parte Dock Bridges, 2 Wood, 428; S. C., 2 Cent. L. J. 327.
⁴ Ex parte Hebard, 4 Dill. 380.
⁵ In re Wong Yung Qui, 9 Rep. 366; S. C., 4 Pac. C. L. J. 564.
⁶ Ex parte Williams, 1 Wash. T., N. S., 240.

§ 380.   COURTS OF GENERAL JURISDICTION.   509

and ordered the prisoners to be tried at the bar of that court by a mixed venire of both white and black, or at least summoned without distinction of race or color. This was not because the circuit court had any jurisdiction over state crimes or any authority to prosecute them, but merely to secure for the petitioners the equal protection of the laws of the state as guaranteed by the fourteenth amendment and the law in pursuance thereof—a sort of anomalous jurisdiction to enforce a fundamental part of the reconstruction policy of congress.[1] But a person who has been tried and convicted and sentenced to imprisonment by the courts of his state for violating a marriage law of the state can not assail the judgment in a federal court on habeas corpus upon the ground that such law violates the constitution or a law of the United States.[2]

§ 380. **Power of United States Supreme Court to Review the Judgments of the Inferior Courts of the United States.**—It is well established by judicial decision that the supreme court of the United States "has no general power to review the judgments of the inferior courts of the United States in criminal cases, by the use of the writ of habeas corpus or otherwise. Their jurisdiction is limited to the single question of the power of the court to commit the prisoner for the act of which he has been convicted. It is true that a writ of habeas corpus can not generally be made to subserve the purposes of a writ of error, yet where a prisoner is held without any lawful authority, and by an order beyond the jurisdiction of an inferior federal court to make, the supreme court will, in favor of liberty, grant the writ, not to review the whole case, but to examine the authority of the court below to act at all." The writ is usually issued in connection with the writ of *certiorari* to bring up the record of the inferior court.[3] A constitutional question may be examined when brought fairly before the court in this way. Thus a judge was indicted for excluding and failing to select

---

[1] Ex parte Reynolds, 3 Hughes, 559, cited in 1 Crim. L. Mag. 268. In one case there was, in the state trial, a "hung jury," and in the other a judgment of eighteen years' imprisonment in the state prison had been rendered. Justice Rives called attention to the fact that the law on which this application was founded was not familiar to the bar generally, and far less so to the public at large.

[2] Ex parte Kinney, 3 Hughes, 9, cited in 1 Crim. L. Mag. 268.

[3] Ex parte Lange, 18 Wall. 163, citing Hamilton's Case, 3 Dall. 17; Burford's Case, 3 Cranch, 448; Ex parte Bollman, 4 Id. 75; Ex parte Watkins, 3 Pet. 193; S. C., 7 Id. 568; Ex parte Metzger, 5 How. 176; Ex parte Kaine, 14 Id. 103; Ex parte Wells, 18 Id. 307; Ex parte Milligan, 4 Wall. 2; Ex parte McCardle, 6 Id. 318; S. C., 7 Id. 506; Ex parte Yerger, 8 Id. 85; see also Ex parte Virginia, 100 U. S. 339; Ex parte Siebold, Id. 371; Ex parte Curtis, 1 Sup. Ct. Rep. 381; Ex parte Carll, Id. 535.

as grand and petit jurors certain citizens of his county, of African race and black color. These persons possessed all other qualifications prescribed by law, but were excluded from the jury lists made out by him as such officer, on account of their race, color, and previous condition of servitude, and for no other reason. He attacked the constitutionality of the act of congress upon which the indictment was founded. But on the hearing of the petition the United States supreme court sustained the act, and denied the writ, as no object would be secured by issuing it.[1]

So where certain judges of election in the city of Baltimore, appointed under state laws, were tried, convicted, and sentenced[2] to fine and imprisonment for interfering with and resisting the supervisors of election and deputy marshals of the United States in the performance of their duty at an election of representatives to congress,[3] the supreme court refused the application for a habeas corpus because they thought the cause of the commitment to be lawful.[4] Ex parte Siebold was followed in Ex parte Clark,[5] where an officer of an election for a representative to congress, in the city of Cincinnati, was tried, convicted, and sentenced for a misdemeanor in a federal court[6] for violating a law of Ohio, in not conveying the ballot-box, after it had been sealed up and delivered to him for that purpose, to the county clerk, and for allowing it to be broken open. On the return to a habeas corpus issued by order of one of the justices of the court, it was decided that congress had constitutional power to enact the law, and ordered the prisoner to be remanded. Petitioner was tried, convicted, and sentenced in the circuit court for the southern district of New York, for a violation of section 3894 of the United States revised statutes, prohibiting letters or circulars concerning illegal lotteries, so-called gift concerts, or other similar enterprises offering prizes, or concerning schemes devised and intended to deceive and defraud the public, for the purpose of obtaining money under false pretenses, from being carried in the mail. On habeas corpus, he attacked the judgment by trying to impeach the constitutionality of the act of congress, but the supreme court had no doubt of its validity, and denied the writ.[7] So, on petition for this writ, was the prohibitory act,[8] providing

[1] Ex parte Virginia, 100 U. S. 339; S. C., 19 Am. Law Reg., N. S., 256; 14 Am. Law Rev. 320.
[2] Under secs. 5515 and 5522 of the U. S. R. S.
[3] Under secs. 2016, 2017, 2021, 2022, title 26, of the U. S. R. S.
[4] Ex parte Siebold, 100 U. S. 371.
[5] 100 U. S. 399.
[6] Under sec. 5515, U. S. R. S.
[7] Ex parte Jackson, 96 U. S. 727.
[8] Sec. 6 of the act of August 15, 1876, c. 287, 19 Stat. U. S.; 1 Sup. Rev. Stats. 245.

§ 381.   COURTS OF GENERAL JURISDICTION.   511

that all executive officers or employees of the United States not appointed by the president with the advice and consent of the senate are prohibited from requesting, giving to, or receiving from any other officer of employee of the government any money or property or other thing of value for political purposes, pronounced constitutional, and the relator remanded.[1]

But whether a matter for which one is indicted in an inferior court is or is not a crime against the laws of the United States is a question for that court alone, and will not be reviewed by the supreme court on habeas corpus.[2] Neither will it review questions arising on the evidence presented to sustain the charge.[3] The question of jurisdiction arose in Guiteau's Case.[4] He was in prison under sentence of death for the murder of President Garfield, and applied for a habeas corpus to be discharged from said imprisonment, on the grounds that the criminal court of the District of Columbia, by which he was tried and convicted, had no jurisdiction of his offense. The supposed want of jurisdiction was based on the fact that although the mortal wound was inflicted in the district, the death of the president took place in New Jersey, whereas the act under which the indictment was found[5] only declares that murder committed within any fort, arsenal, dockyard, magazine, or in any place or district of country under the exclusive jurisdiction of the United States shall suffer death, and jurisdiction is only given to the court to try "crimes and offenses committed within the District."[6] In conclusion, it may here be stated that an inferior federal court will not on habeas corpus look behind the record to review the sentence of a court of co-ordinate jurisdiction.[7]

§ 381. **Sentences in Violation of the Constitution or of United States Laws and Acts Done or Omitted in Pursuance thereof.**—This section is intimately connected with that on "conflict of jurisdiction," and should be read in connection with it. A person held in custody by virtue of the judgment of a court of another jurisdiction, and in violation of the constitution, laws, or treaties of the United States, may assail the judgment in a federal court, and the case will be there examined so

---

[1] Ex parte Curtis, 1 Sup. Ct. Rep. 381; S. C., 5 Mor. Trans. 469; and 106 U. S. 371.
[2] Ex parte Parks, 93 U. S. 18.
[3] Ex parte Carll, 106 U. S. 521; S. C., 1 Sup. Ct. Rep. 535.
[4] 14 Rep. 1.
[5] Sec. 5339 of the U. S. R. S.
[6] R. S., District of Columbia, sec. 763, as amended.
[7] Ex parte Alexander, 14 Fed. Rep. 680.

far as to ascertain that fact. For example, petitioner was convicted and sentenced in the circuit court for Cowees-cowee district, Cherokee nation, for larceny. He claimed to be held in custody in violation of the laws and constitution of the United States, and the treaty stipulations lawfully made between the United States and said nation, because the trial court had no jurisdiction of his offense. The circuit court for the western district of Arkansas found, on habeas corpus, that petitioner was a resident of Kansas at the time of his conviction, and that the place where the act was committed was beyond the territorial limits of the jurisdiction of the trial court. There being no jurisdiction of the person or of the subject-matter, the judgment was pronounced void, and the prisoner discharged.[1] In Virginia, McCready, a Marylander, was held to answer to an indictment for violating an act concerning the preservation of oysters. An inferior federal court ordered him to be discharged on habeas corpus, holding the act to be in violation of the fourth article of the constitution of the United States.[2] But McCready was convicted and fined five hundred dollars. On error to the supreme court of appeals of the state of Virginia the United States supreme court decided otherwise. "The precise question," said Chief Justice Waite, "to be determined in the case is, whether the state of Virginia can prohibit the citizens of other states from planting oysters in Ware river, a stream in that state where the tide ebbs and flows, when its own citizens have that privilege." It was decided that the state had the right, by reason of its ownership in the water-covered lands, to prohibit such planting; thus overruling the decision of the United States circuit court for the eastern district of Virginia on the habeas corpus.[3] For general law concerning acts done or omitted in pursuance of the constitution or a law of the United States, see U. S. R. S., sec. 753.[4]

§ 382. Courts-martial.—"The same constitution and the same legislative power which conferred civil jurisdiction on the national judiciary, also conferred jurisdiction over military and naval offenses upon courts-martial, appointed and supervised by the war and navy departments. Each is supreme while acting within the sphere of its own exclusive jurisdiction. In the terse and appropriate language of Attorney General Cushing:

---

[1] Ex parte Kenyon, 5 Dill. 385.
[2] Ex parte McCready, 1 Hughes, 598.
[3] McCready v. Virginia, 94 U. S. 391.
[4] *Ante*, sec. 59. See also, generally, the authorities cited in the two preceding sections.

§ 382. COURTS OF GENERAL JURISDICTION. 513

'A court-martial is a lawful tribunal, existing by the same authority that any other exists by, and the law, military, is a branch of law as valid as any other, and it differs from the general law of the land in authority only in this, that it applies to officers and soldiers of the army, but not to other members of the body politic, and that it is limited to breaches of military duty.'"[1] It is supposed that these courts were intended originally to be a partial substitute for the courts of chivalry of former times; such as were established in France and afterwards in England during mediæval times, for the trial of questions of honor.[2] Courts-martial are special tribunals with jurisdiction limited to a particular class of cases. If such a court exceeds its authority and undertakes to try and punish a person not within its jurisdiction, or to punish a person within its jurisdiction for an offense not within its jurisdiction, its judgment is void, and may be so declared by any court having jurisdiction of the proper parties and of the subject-matter. The decision of such a tribunal, in a case clearly without its jurisdiction, does not possess that apparent validity which will protect the officer who executes it. The court and the officers are all trespassers.[3]

If a court-martial has no jurisdiction over the subject-matter of the charge it has been convened to try, or shall inflict a punishment forbidden by the law, though its sentence shall be approved by the officers having a revisory power over it, civil courts may, on an action by a party aggrieved, inquire into the want of the court's jurisdiction and give him redress.[4] So while the judgment of a court of competent jurisdiction can not be successfully assailed on habeas corpus, jurisdiction to issue the writ for such purpose does exist where the inferior court has transcended its powers.[5] But where courts-martial have jurisdiction, their proceedings can be collaterally impeached for any mere error or irregularity committed within the sphere of their authority. Their judgments, when approved as required, rest on the same basis and are surrounded by the same considerations which give conclusiveness to the judgments of other legal tribunals, including as well the lowest as the highest, under like

---

[1] In re Bogart, 2 Saw. 396; 6 Opinions Att. Gen. 425.
[2] Ex parte Reed, 100 U. S. 13.
[3] Wise v. Withers, 3 Cranch, 331; Barrett v. Hopkins, 2 McCrary, 129; S. C., 7 Fed. Rep. 312.
[4] Dynes v. Hoover, 20 How. 82.
[5] Barrett v. Hopkins, 7 Fed. Rep. 312; S. C., 2 McCrary, 129.

circumstances. The exercise of discretion within authorized limits can not be assigned for error and made the subject of review by an appellate court. To warrant the discharge of a petitioner on habeas corpus, the sentence under which he is held must be not merely erroneous and voidable, but absolutely void.[1]

PART II.—IN CIVIL CASES.

§ 383. **Mere Errors and Irregularities will not be Reviewed.**—Habeas corpus in some of the states extends to persons imprisoned on final civil process.[2] But in civil cases, as in criminal, mere errors or irregularities will not be reviewed on habeas corpus. That is the proper remedy only where the judgment is void, and a judgment is not void because of mere error or irregularity in the previous proceedings. To obtain a discharge on habeas corpus from arrest under a body execution, the defects in the execution must be matters of substance required by law, rendering the process void and not

---

[1] Ex parte Reed, 100 U. S. 13. *Illustrations.*—A United States soldier is arrested for a crime, and his term of enlistment expires before his trial and conviction by court-martial. The jurisdiction, however, attaches by the arrest, and is retained by the court-martial for the purposes of trial, judgment, and execution, and the prisoner will not be released on habeas corpus: Barrett v. Hopkins, 7 Fed. Rep. 312; S. C., 2 McCrary, 129. A prisoner convicted by a military commission sitting in a state in which the operations of the civil courts were unobstructed was discharged on habeas corpus, because, he being neither a resident of a rebellious state, nor a prisoner of war, nor a person in the military or naval service, such commission had no jurisdiction to try, convict, or sentence him for any criminal offense: Ex parte Milligan, 4 Wall. 2. That congress has power under the constitution to provide for the trial and punishment of offenses committed in the naval service by courts-martial, without indictment or the intervention of a jury, see In re Bogart, 2 Saw. 396. In this case, it appearing that the naval court had jurisdiction of the crimes of embezzlement and desertion, with which the prisoner was charged, and also of his person, the federal court refused to interfere on habeas corpus. Same principle in Ex parte Mason's Case. Mason was sentenced by a court-martial for attempting to kill Charles J. Guiteau, the murderer of President Garfield. The court had jurisdiction, and the United States supreme court refused the petition for a habeas corpus and *certiorari:* 105 U. S. 696. So in Ex parte Reed. He objected to the adequacy of a sentence imposed upon him. The court revised it and imposed a severer one. On habeas corpus it was held that the court-martial had jurisdiction to pass the last sentence: 100 U. S. 13. Whether an enlistment be valid or not, one under arrest on a charge of desertion must abide the sentence of a court-martial before he can contest the validity of the enlistment, and pending the proceedings can not be discharged on habeas corpus: Commonwealth v. Gamble, 11 Serg. & R. 93. But there is no law authorizing courts-martial to proceed against any person without notice, consequently such proceeding is entitled unlawful; a sentence under such proceedings is nugatory, and one may successfully attack such a judgment in this collateral way: Meade v. The Deputy Marshal of the District of Virginia, 2 Wheel. Cr. Cas. 569.

[2] Ex parte Kellogg, 6 Vt. 509, and authorities cited in the succeeding notes of this section.

merely voidable, for in the latter case the remedy is by motion to set it aside.¹ But this is so only where the court out of which the process issues is one of competent jurisdiction.² Where this exists its judgment can not be assailed collaterally, and it is good until regularly reversed or annulled. To illustrate: a defendant has been properly served with process; he has suffered a judgment by default to be taken against himself, and has been arrested on a valid execution. He can not, on a writ of habeas corpus, show that he is not the true defendant, whose name he bears.² The prisoner is unlawfully detained if there be no judgment, or if it is one on which no execution against the person can lawfully issue. On habeas corpus the debtor may inquire into the regularity and propriety of the arrest so far as to determine whether the creditor had any right or authority to issue the process. Thus, on *certiorari* to review proceedings on habeas corpus, it was held in New York that where a defendant had disposed of his property *bona fide* at various times and for various purposes, by five separate and distinct instruments, three being valid, and two in law constructively fraudulent against creditors, he had not disposed of his property with intent to defraud within the meaning of the code.⁴ In cases where fraud is charged, said the court, proof of an actual intent should be required to justify an order of arrest; constructive guilt of a debtor, innocent in fact, should not be held a sufficient ground for his imprisonment.⁵

§ 384. **Capias ad Satisfaciendum.**—A habeas corpus is not the remedy for a *ca. sa.* which issued irregularly; the proper course being an application to the court from which it issued.⁶ This principle has been recognized in a similar case in Pennsylvania.⁷ So in New York, where the officer had acquired jurisdiction of the subject-matter and of the parties, but erroneously discharged one on habeas corpus from the custody of the sheriff on a *ca. sa.* Such discharge was held to be a protection to the sheriff in an action brought against him for the escape of the prisoner.⁸ However, if there is a want of jurisdiction to ren-

---

¹ Ex parte Kellogg, 6 Vt. 509; Gould's Ann. Dig. 181, citing People ex rel. Utley v. Seaton, 13 Week. Dig. 240; Commonwealth v. Lecky, 1 Watts, 66; Bank of United States v. Jenkins, 18 Johns. 305; Wiles v. Brown, 3 Barb. 37; In re Gorman, 6 Cent. L. J. 365.
² Peltier v. Pennington et al., 14 N. J. L. 312.
³ In re Gorman, 6 Cent. L. J. 365.
⁴ Sec. 179, subd. 5, Wait's Annotated Code of Civil Procedure.
⁵ Caldwell's Case, 13 Abb. Pr. 405; S. C., 35 Barb. 444.
⁶ Bank of United States v. Jenkins, 18 Johns. 305.
⁷ Commonwealth v. Lecky, 1 Watts, 66.
⁸ Wiles v. Brown, 3 Barb. 37.

der a particular judgment, habeas corpus is an efficient and available remedy. A defendant was in custody under a *capias ad satisfaciendum*, and gave a bond to take the benefit of the insolvent law. He was refused a discharge, and did not surrender himself to the sheriff, but remained at large. He was again arrested on an *alias ca. sa.* issued on the same judgment. His liberation on habeas corpus from the last arrest was refused. The supreme court of New Jersey held this to be without authority and illegal. The plaintiff's remedy, they said, was on the bond. The prisoner was discharged. That court also held that a person in jail under a *ca. sa.* issued on a judgment founded upon contract might be discharged on habeas corpus.[1]

§ 385. **Other Matters.**—An execution debtor is estopped from denying, on habeas corpus, the existence or corporate capacity of the plaintiff, in whose name the judgment against him was rendered.[2] In the absence of all testimony, the higher court will presume that an officer, as of a corporation, acted in his official capacity.[3] If the prisoner grounds his claim to be discharged upon certain papers, or documents prescribed by statute, and not upon matter *in pais*, upon which an issue to the jury might be expected to arise, he may enforce his right by writ of habeas corpus.[4] Where judgment and execution issue thereon before plaintiff's death, but where the commitment is made subsequent to this time, the prisoner can not impeach the process on habeas corpus.[5] As to effect of non-imprisonment act of New York (Laws of 1831, c. 300), see case cited.[6] In Alabama, it has been held that in a proceeding by habeas corpus brought by one arrested on a *capias ad respondendum*, the state and not the plaintiff in the action should be made the adverse party; and that an order in such a proceeding is not a final judgment or sentence which may be reviewed on error, but justice may be attained by *mandamus* or other appropriate writ.[7] When a habeas corpus has issued to one imprisoned on a *ca. sa.*, every one interested in continuing the imprisonment

---

[1] State v. Blundell, 39 N. J. L. 612.
[2] Ex parte Sargeant, 17 Vt. 425.
[3] Ex parte Sargeant, 17 Vt. 425. See Nelson & Graydon v. Cutter & Tyrrell, 3 McLean, 326.
[4] Ex parte Davis, 18 Vt. 401.
[5] Commonwealth v. Whitney, 10 Pick. 434. As to when *audita querela* will lie for a man taken in execution, see Lovejoy v. Webber, 10 Mass. 101.
[6] People ex rel. Eldridge et al. v. Fancher, 3 N. Y. Sup. Ct. 189.
[7] Wade v. Judge, 5 Ala., N. S., 130.

§ 385.   COURTS OF GENERAL JURISDICTION.   517

is entitled to notice of the time and place of the return of the writ.[1]

[1] Ex parte Beatty, 12 Wend. 229. Where relator's property was attached, and the service was irregular, though notice in fact was given him, and he committed in execution, Justice Collamer, of the supreme court of Vermont, on habeas corpus, said: "The irregularity of the service was matter for abatement, and as a general rule, matter in abatement not pleaded is waived, and can not be assigned for error. In this case it was pleaded in abatement, and adjudged upon by the justice, and is *res adjudicata*. His decision on a question within his jurisdiction is conclusive until appealed from and reversed. However this may be, the irregularity of the deputation and service could at most only vitiate the process on which it was [based]. It could not render the execution void. Habeas corpus is not a proceeding to set aside an irregular or an erroneous judgment. To discharge the prisoner would deprive the creditor of enforcing his judgment, and at the same time leave it in full force unreversed. What could then be done? The execution can only be treated as void when the judgment is void. This is never the case when the court has jurisdiction of the subject-matter and the parties, especially if the defendant has had actual and timely notice. Where judgment and execution are void, even the officer issuing the execution is a trespasser. To hold the judgment of a court void for informality, irregularity, or error in the previous proceedings would expose them to passing judgments even on pleas in abatement at the most imminent personal peril. This judgment is not void, nor has the same been appealed from, or in any way reversed. Prisoner remanded:" Ex parte Kellogg, 6 Vt. 509.

CHAPTER XXVI.

RES ADJUDICATA.

§ 386. Writ of Error, etc.
§ 387. Cases Affecting Custody of Children.
§ 388. Statutory Provisions, Writs of Error, Appeals, etc.
§ 389. Second Applications.

§ 386. **Writ of Error.**—At common law the legal incidents belonging to *res adjudicata* do not seem to have attached to a judgment on habeas corpus. A writ of error does not lie to a final order made in such a proceeding.[1] But this appears to be in perfect harmony with the well-recognized common-law rule that the defendant has a right to the opinion of every court as to the propriety of his imprisonment, and has the right to renew his application for a writ of habeas corpus as often as he desires.[2] This shows that the decision upon the habeas corpus is not understood to be of that conclusive character which is necessary to support a writ of error.

In the United States, where one unlawfully imprisoned is refused a discharge on habeas corpus by the highest tribunal in a state, he may, if his case comes within the jurisdiction of the federal courts, make a direct application to them for relief, but we know of no provision of law authorizing him to prosecute a writ of error to such judgment. But the judgment of a state court on habeas corpus may be made the subject of review by the supreme court of the United States on a writ of error, issued from that court to the state court, at the instance of the attorney general, whenever a right has been claimed under the constitution or laws of the United States, and the decision of the

---

[1] Wilson's Case, 7 Ad. & El., Q. B., 984; Bushell's Case, Freem. K. B. & C. P., 1; Burdett v. Abbott, 14 East, 91, note; City of London's Case, 4 Fraser, 8 Co. 121; King v. Bythell, 12 Mod. 75; King v. Dean and Chapter of Trinity Chapel in Dublin, 8 Id. 27; Pender v. Herle, 3 Bro. P. C. 505; King v. Suddis, 1 East, 306. *Contra:* Queen v. Paty et al., 2 Salk. 503; S. C., 2 Ld. Raym. 1105.

[2] Ex parte Partington, 2 Dow. & L. 650; S. C., 13 Mee. & W. 678; King v. Suddis, 1 East, 306.

state court is against it.[1] The federal courts themselves are governed by the principles of the common law,[2] except as modified by statute, and a writ of error to a final judgment on habeas corpus is, we believe, unknown to them, except to the territorial courts of the United States.[3] In the federal courts the doctrine of *res adjudicata* does not apply.[4]

The prevailing doctrine in the state courts, independent of statutory provisions, is that a decision upon a habeas corpus is not appealable or subject to review, and that the doctrine of *res adjudicata* has no application to such a case. The prisoner is entitled to the opinion of all the courts as to his freedom, and in his applications for the writ of habeas corpus may exhaust the entire judicial power of the state. Consequently, the decision is not a final one. Whether the decision is the simple order of a judge, or the determination of a court, the effect is the same. In neither case is there any such final judgment as will sustain a writ of error;[5] because a refusal to discharge the prisoner on habeas corpus is not a bar to another application for the same writ before another officer or court.[6]

---

[1] Ableman v. Booth and U. S. v. Booth, 21 How. 506; Tarble's Case, 13 Wall. 397.

[2] Ex parte Watkins, 3 Pet. 193; Ex parte Randolph, 2 Brock. 447.

[3] Potts et al. v. Chumasero, 92 U. S. 358.

[4] Ex parte Kaine, 3 Blatchf. 1. Read the remarks of Justice McLean, in Ex parte Robinson, 6 McLean, 360.

[5] In the Matter of Perkins, 2 Cal. 424; Ex parte Ellis, 11 Id. 222; In the Matter of Ring, 28 Id. 247; Yates v. The People, 6 Johns. 429; Hammond v. The People, 32 Ill. 446; Wade v. Judge, 5 Ala. 130; Bell v. The State, 4 Gill, 301; Ex parte Mitchell, 1 La. Ann. 413; Howe v. The State, 9 Mo. 690; Ex parte Thompson, 93 Ill. 89; Ex parte Alexander, Louisville Ch. Ct. (Ky.), 2 Am. Law Reg. 44; People v. Brady, 56 N. Y. 182; Ex parte Reynolds, 6 Park. Cr. 276; In the Matter of Stephen, 1 Wheel. Cr. Cas. 326. That exceptions do not lie to a discharge by a single judge: Wyeth v. Richardson, 10 Gray, 240.

[6] See authorities cited in last note. The prisoner ought certainly on a second application for a habeas corpus, not be estopped by the refusal of a discharge on his first application when he produces a new state of facts on the last hearing entitling him to a discharge, or obtains new and important evidence: People v. Fancher, 1 Hun, 27; In re Curley, 34 Iowa, 184; Hammond v. The People, 32 Ill. 446; McFarland v. Johnson, 27 Tex. 105; Ex parte Ring, 28 Cal. 247; Lea v. White, 4 Sneed, 73; Ex parte Robinson, 6 McLean, 360; In re Blair, 4 Wis. 522; In the Matter of Stephen, 1 Wheel. Cr. Cas. 326. But the cases have not all been uniform on this question. In Yates v. The People, 6 Johns. 337, it was decided that a writ of error did lie upon the award remanding the prisoner on a habeas corpus. In People v. Cunningham, 3 Park. Cr. 531, the decision by one court or magistrate on a question of admitting to bail was held to be final and conclusive as to co-ordinate jurisdictions. In Perry et al. v. McLendon, Sheriff, 62 Ga. 598, the judgment on a habeas corpus proceeding is said to be final until reversed, and though twice drawn in question, the judgment here was pronounced conclusive. It was also held that all matter as to points necessarily involved was *res adjudicata*, whether actually presented or not. And appeals have been allowed: Dodge's Case, on a *ca. sa.*, however, 6 Mart. (La.) 569; Ex parte La Fonta, 2 Rob. (La.) 495; Weddington v. Sloan, 15 B. Mon. 147; Com. v. Biddle, 6 Penn. Law Jour. 287, 4 Clark, 35.

The cases cited thus far in this section hold that the principle of *res adjudicata* does not apply to a particular class of judgments; viz., those remanding the prisoner. A distinction must be made between this class and those discharging the prisoner. In the latter class of cases the rule has almost uniformly been, independent of statutory provisions, that the judgment of discharge, whether erroneous or not, and being in favor of personal liberty, is final and conclusive, and not subject to appeal or writ of error. The law is thus laid down in the well-considered and valuable case of Ex parte Jilz.[1]

§ 387. **Custody of Children.**—The decisions affecting this class of cases must also be distinguished. In New York the principle of *res adjudicata* is deemed applicable to proceedings on habeas corpus, so far as they involve an inquiry into and a determination of the rights of husband and wife to the custody of one of their children. The decision on a former writ will there be conclusive in a subsequent application, unless some new fact has occurred which has "altered the state of the case, or the relative claims of the parents to the custody of the child in any material respect."[2] "The principles of public policy requiring the application of the doctrine of estoppel to judicial proceedings, in order to secure the repose of society," says Mr. Freeman, the Tribonian of the modern law, "are as imperatively demanded in the cases of private individuals contesting private rights under the form of proceedings on habeas corpus, as if the litigation were conducted in any other form."[3] Otherwise, as is well stated in the opinion of Senator Paige, "such unhappy controversies as these may endure until the entire impoverishment or the death of the parties renders further continuance impracticable. If a final adjudication upon a habeas corpus is not to be deemed *res adjudicata*, the consequences will be lamentable. This favored writ will become an engine of oppression, instead of a writ of liberty."[4]

[1] 64 Mo. 205; People v. Brady, 56 N. Y. 182; Com. v. McBride, 2 Brews. 545.
[2] Mercein v. The People, 25 Wend. 63. This case is distinguished from others in People v. Brady, 56 N. Y. 182.
[3] Freeman on Judgments, sec. 324.
[4] Mercein v. The People, 25 Wend. 99. See also In the Matter of Da Costa, 1 Park. Cr. 129; People ex rel. Barry v. Mercein, 3 Hill (N. Y.), 399; and Massachusetts case, in accord with the foregoing ones, McConologue, 107 Mass. 170, where it is said that "the judicial discharge of a prisoner upon habeas corpus conclusively settles that he was not liable to be held in custody upon the then existing state of facts. Nor is it material that the petition for the first writ was made by the prisoner's father, and that for the present writ by himself. Neither the form of the writ, nor the effect of the discharge, is varied by the name in which the petition is presented:" Ex parte Milburn, 9 Pet. 704; Spalding v. The

§ 388. **Statutory Provisions.**—The principle that a writ of error will lie upon the award remanding the prisoner on a habeas corpus is now embodied in the legislation of New York. The attorney general may also prosecute the writ.[1] The writ of error will also lie in Georgia,[2] Connecticut,[3] Florida,[4] Indiana,[5] and other states of the Union to a judgment on habeas corpus. Such a decision may also be reviewed, under statutory authority, by appeal in many of the states, as in Iowa,[6] Indiana,[7] Missouri,[8] Minnesota, and Texas. In some of the states the review may be had at the instance of the state when the prisoner is discharged,[9] as well as at the instance of the prisoner when he is remanded. Where the appeal suspends the order of discharge, the prisoner will be remanded if the order be reversed.[10] Where the appeal does not suspend the order of discharge, however, no decision will recapture the defendants.[11] When such is its effect, the appellate court can not effectually correct the error of the inferior tribunal. Thus it was said in Texas that the law in force in 1863 conferred no right of appeal upon the respondent, from a judgment of the district court, or of a judge in chambers; and that an appeal in such cases was restricted to the applicant.[12] It was also held in the same state that the statute made no provision for an appeal on the part of the prisoner where the writ was denied; but that from a decision refusing his application for it after trial he might appeal.[13] In Minnesota, an order discharging the prisoner may be reviewed by appeal, but not by *certiorari*.[14] In California, no appeal lies from the order of a judge admitting a party to bail under the

---

[1] People, 7 Hill, 301; and Betty's Case, 20 Law Rep. 455, were cited. In People v. Burtnett, 5 Park. Cr. 113, it was said that a prior decision on habeas corpus concerning the custody of a minor was *res adjudicata*, and that the only mode of correcting the decision, if wrong, was by *certiorari*: S., C., 13 Abb. Pr. 8. Decisions relating to the disposition of infant children, were also held conclusive in State v. Malone, 3 Sneed, 413, and People v. Cooper, 8 How. Pr. 288.
[1] 3 N. Y. R. S., Banks' ed., 5th, p. 883, sec. 86; People ex rel. Tweed v. Liscomb, 60 N. Y. 559; S. C., 11 Alb. L. J. 396.
[2] Lark v. The State, 55 Ga. 435.
[3] McCready v. Wilcox, 33 Conn. 321.
[4] Ex parte Finch, 15 Fla. 630.
[5] Lumm v. The State, 3 Port. 293.
[6] State v. Kirkpatrick, 54 Iowa, 373; Kline v. Kline, 57 Id. 386.
[7] Speer v. Davis, 38 Ind. 271; Miller v. Snyder, 6 Port. 1; Nichols v. Cornelius, 7 Id. 611; lies from order made either in term-time or vacation, and without the filing of a bond.
[8] Ferguson v. Ferguson et al., 36 Mo. 197.
[9] The State v. Everett, and State v. Porter, Dudley (S. C.), 295.
[10] People v. Cavanagh, 2 Park. Cr. 650.
[11] State v. Everett etc., Dudley (S. C.) 295.
[12] McFarland v. Johnson, 27 Tex. 105.
[13] Ex parte Ainsworth, 27 Tex. 731; see Ex parte Coupland, 26 Id. 386; Ex parte Foster, 5 Tex. App. 625; Ex parte McGill, 6 Id. 498; Ex parte Boland, 11 Id. 159.
[14] State v. Buckham. 29 Minn. 462.

provisions of the habeas corpus act.¹ In Utah, when the defendant is discharged, no appeal lies from the order either by the defendant named in the habeas corpus or by the people.² In Alabama³ and Maryland⁴ no appeal lies from a decision on habeas corpus. In Tennessee an appeal does not lie from a judge or court discharging or not, upon a habeas corpus.⁵ Appeals and writs of error lie to a decision on habeas corpus in Mississippi.⁶

§ 389. **Second Applications.**—While the decision on a writ of habeas corpus, independently of statutory provisions, is not a final judgment, and therefore not subject to review on a writ of error or appeal, it is entitled to some consideration on a second application, and may warrant the refusal of the second. This occurs where the case has already been heard upon the same evidence, where the facts and circumstances are the same. When this is so, the first judgment will be undisturbed.⁷ But even where statute makes the decision conclusive upon all matters which were or might have been investigated upon the hearing of the case, it does not preclude the issuance of a second writ, based upon subsequently occurring events. The new writ, however, must be based upon facts which have actually occurred since the hearing on the original writ, and not upon newly discovered evidence as to the old facts.⁸ A decision on a habeas corpus in one state will not be considered as *res adjudicata* in another.⁹

---

¹ The People v. Schuster, 40 Cal. 627.
² In re Clasby, 1 West Coast Rep. 524.
³ Guilford v. Hicks, 36 Ala. 95.
⁴ Roth & Boyle v. House of Refuge, 31 Md. 329.
⁵ State v. Galloway & Rhea, 5 Coldw. 326.
⁶ Ex parte Phillips, 57 Miss. 357; Hamilton v. Flowers, Id. 14; Emanuel v. State, 36 Id. 627.
⁷ Ex parte Lawrence, 5 Binn. 304; Ex parte Campbell, 20 Ala. 89; cases cited in Hill's note to People v. McLeod, 3 Hill (N. Y.), 676; In the Matter of Place, 34 How. Pr. 259.
⁸ Ex parte Pattison, 56 Miss. 161.
⁹ State v. Brearly, 2 South. 555; Maria v. Kirby, 12 B. Mon. 550.

CHAPTER XXVII.

THE RIGHT TO BAIL.

PART I.—POWER TO BAIL, BAILABLE OFFENSES, EVIDENCE, ETC.

§ 390. Doctrine of the Common Law.
§ 391. 31 Car. II. and Other English Statutes.
§ 392. The Power to Bail, and Bailable Offenses in the United States.
§ 393. Right to Bail, and for What Offenses.
§ 394. Legislative Powers.

PART II.—INQUIRY BEFORE INDICTMENT.

§ 395. Who may Bail.
§ 396. Application is Addressed to Sound Discretion of Court.
§ 397. Excessive Bail.
§ 398. To Reduce Bail.
§ 399. Examination and Reducing Offense to Bailable One.
§ 400. Examination of Evidence.

PART III.—INQUIRY AFTER INDICTMENT.

§ 401. Rules for Guidance of Court's Discretion.
§ 402. Meaning of "when Proof is Evident."
§ 403. Presumption Great.
§ 404. When Prisoner must Take Initiative.
§ 405. Evidence.
§ 406. Evidence, Continued.
§ 407. Special and Extraordinary Circumstances.
§ 408. Disagreement of Jury—New Trial, etc.
§ 409. Other Circumstances.
§ 410. Sickness of the Prisoner.
§ 411. Continuance—Term.
§ 412. Arrest on Bench-warrant.
§ 413. Excessive Bail.
§ 414. Insanity of Prisoner.
§ 415. Appeal from Judgment Refusing Bail.
§ 416. Appeal from Order Admitting to Bail.

PART IV.—INQUIRY AFTER CONVICTION.

§ 417. But before Final Judgment.
§ 418. Bail Pending Steps to Reverse Sentence.
§ 419. After Sentence or Commitment in Execution.

PART I.—POWER TO BAIL, BAILABLE OFFENSES, EVIDENCE, ETC.

§ 390. **Doctrine of the Common Law.**—The right to bail existed at the ancient common law,[1] and though the prisoner could not demand bail as a matter of right, he might, and still may, except where the matter is otherwise regulated by statute, be admitted to bail for any offense. He could be bailed for treason, murder, manslaughter, forgery, rape, libels—in short, as we have said, for all felonies and misdemeanors whatsoever.[2] This plenitude of power was exercised by the court of king's bench or any judge thereof in vacation,[3] but the general rule was, "Whosoever is judge of the offense may bail the offender." This power rested in the sound legal discretion of the judge awarding the writ of habeas corpus; but in the rules which the court and judges observed, they were guided by a series of decisions;[4] for the discretion to be exercised by a court of justice is not a wild but a sound discretion, and to be confined within those limits to which an honest man, competent to discharge the duties of his office, ought to confine himself.[5] There appears to have been but one exception to this discretionary power, and that was where one was committed in execution. This, of course, included commitments for contempt.[6]

Admission to bail was not allowed for a capital offense, and in fact, it was not usual to bail in any case of felony, unless when, in consequence of a defect in the commitment and in the examination and depositions, it appeared doubtful whether any offense had been committed.[7] On the other hand, the commitment might be perfect, yet the depositions which contained the evidence would be examined, and if the evidence appeared to be insufficient the courts would bail the prisoner.[8] The courts were inclined to look more to the depositions than to the commitment for their direction, because the justice may have come to a wrong conclusion.[9] If the court could collect from the depositions that a felony had been committed, they would not

---

[1] Bac. Abr., Bail in Criminal Cases, A; Hawk. P. C., b. 2, c. 15; 2 Hale P. C., c. 15; 3 Reeves Hist. Eng. Law, 195; Com. Dig., Bail.

[2] Bac. Abr., Bail in Criminal Cases, A; 2 Hale P. C., c. 15; Hawk. P. C., b. 2, c. 15; Rex v. Grieffenburgh, 4 Burr. 2179; Rex v. Rudd, 1 Cow. 331; Com. Dig., Bail.

[3] See cases collected in Bac. Abr., Bail in Criminal Cases; 2 Hale P. C., c. 15; Hawk. P. C., b. 2, c. 15.

[4] For cause, see Com. Dig., Bail, F, 1–10.

[5] Lord Kenyon in Wilson v. Rastall, 4 T. R. 757; Rex v. Wilkes, 4 Burr. 2539.

[6] Com. Dig., Bail, F, 2; see Earl of Shaftesbury's Case, 1 Mod. 158, note a; Ld. Mayor of London's Case, 3 Wils. 199; King v. Brooke, 2 T. R. 190; Rex v. Waddington, 1 East, 159.

[7] See cases cited in 1 Ch. Crim. L. 99, note k.

[8] See cases cited in 1 Ch. Crim. L. 129, note r.

[9] 1 Ch. Crim. L. 129, and cases cited.

bail the prisoner, however defective the *mittimus* might be, but remand him upon a special rule.¹ It was not always practicable, however, to examine the evidence. Thus in one case it was said: "If a man be found guilty of murder by the coroner's inquest, we sometimes bail him, because the coroner proceeds upon depositions taken in writing which we may look into. Otherwise, if a man be found guilty of murder by a grand jury, because the court can not take notice of their evidence, which they by their oath are bound to conceal."²

The rule laid down by Hawkins, when to bail, runs thus: "Bail is only proper where it stands indifferent whether the party be guilty or innocent of the accusation against him, as it often does before his trial; but where that indifference is removed, it would, generally speaking, be absurd to bail him."³ One charged with murder before bill found may be admitted to bail if it appear from the depositions that the offense amounts only to manslaughter;⁴ but it is otherwise after indictment.⁵ Bail will be refused where a felony is positively charged, though an *alibi* be supported by the strongest evidence.⁶ Neither will extrinsic evidence be admitted to determine whether a man brought before the court had been previously acquitted of a charge precisely similar.⁷ The court refused to bail a person for receiving stolen goods where the defendant's affidavit admitted the receipt of the goods, but denied that he knew them to be stolen; because this was a fact triable only by jury, and if they should allow such a proceeding in case of such a mistake, all the prisoners in England would lay their cases before them, and they, instead of the jury, would have to try the truth of the fact for which the prisoners were committed. Beside it might very much encourage the compounding of felonies between the prosecutor and prisoner.⁸ The court will refuse, at the request of an accused party, that a physician and surgeon of his own nominating be appointed to be present at the dressing of a person's wound, produced by a dangerous stab from the prisoner, so as to satisfy the court that he is out of danger, and in order that they may bail the prisoner.⁹ Where the prisoner has been charged with larceny, and the charge is sworn to, the court will not grant a habeas corpus to bail him.¹⁰

---

¹ King v. Marks, 3 East, 157.
² Lord Mohun's Case, 1 Salk. 104.
³ B. 2, c. 15, sec. 40.
⁴ Rex v. Dalton, 2 Stra. 911; Rex v. Magrath, Id. 1242.
⁵ Bac. Abr., Bail in Crim. Cas., cited in Regina v. Andrews, 2 Dow. & L. 10.
⁶ Rex v. Greenwood, 2 Stra. 1138.
⁷ Rex v. Acton, 2 Stra. 851; S. C., 1 Barn. K. B. 250; Anon., 2 Id. 83. But see King v. Crisp, 2 Id. 271.
⁸ Rex v. Parnam, Cunn. 96.
⁹ Rex v. Salisbury, 1 Stra. 547.
¹⁰ Queen v. Mickal, 11 Mod. 261.

In great misdemeanors the court will require very ample securities.[1] Where no cause of commitment is expressed in the *mittimus* or return, the prisoner will be bailed at least, if not discharged.[2] On satisfactory evidence that the habeas corpus and bail piece were lost, the court would allow a new habeas corpus and a new bail piece with the old bail.[3] The prisoner could be bailed upon a habeas corpus to appear *de die in diem* until the court determined the sufficiency of the return.[4] The bail are the legal guardians of the defendant, and they should look after their own prisoner.[5] The course formerly was to bring up the party into court in all cases, however great the distance; but of late, where the court thinks fit, upon having affidavits of poverty or inability to travel, they will grant a rule to show cause and decide upon motion whether the party shall be discharged or bailed, and if the latter, will direct the bail to be taken before a magistrate in the neighborhood.[6]

§ 391. **31 Car. II. and Other English Statutes.**—Bail, in England, has been greatly regulated by statutes, both early and late. But for these statutes, excepting that of Charles II., and the practice under them, we must refer the reader to the works of Hawkins,[7] Hale,[8] and Chitty,[9] where the whole subject of bail is fully treated. In Chitty [10] will be found the power of justices of the peace, as regulated by statute, to bail, showing when they can not bail, when they have a discretionary power, and when they must bail. It may here be remarked that the power to bail after indictment, after conviction, and for high crimes generally was rightfully lodged in the hands of the superior courts and of its judges. The statute of Charles enacted that if any person committed for felony, upon his petition in open court to be brought to trial, should not be indicted and tried the second term after commitment, or upon his trial should be acquitted, he should be discharged from imprisonment; but this has been held in this country, where this statute was once in force, not to authorize the discharge of the prisoner, as a matter of right, from a criminal prosecution, and that it evidently alluded to persons who were within the four walls of a prison, that they

---

[1] 1 Ch. Crim. L. 130.
[2] Barkham's Case, 3 Cro. Car. 507; Lawson's Case, Id. 507. But see Anon., Id. 579, and Chambers' Case, Id. 133.
[3] Pease v. Shrimpton, Styles, 261.
[4] Rex v. Davison, 1 Raym. 603; Armstrong v. Lisle, 1 Salk. 60.
[5] Lawes v. Hutchinson, 3 Dowl. P. C. 506.
[6] Rex v. Jones, 1 Barn. & Ald. 209; Rex v. Massey, 6 Mau. & Sel. 108; Ex parte Cross, 2 Hurl. & N. 354; 1 Ch. Crim. L. 130.
[7] B. 2, c. 15.
[8] 2 P. C., c. 15.
[9] 1 Crim. L. 93, 98, 128.
[10] Id. 95.

should be discharged from their confinement on bail or on their own recognizances, according to the nature and circumstances of every case, and that this clause did not relate to persons who were not actually in custody or imprisoned, or who were out on bail.¹ This statute prohibits one committed for felony or treason plainly expressed in the warrant, from being let to bail. But in all cases of felonies the courts maintain their power to bail the accused parties, whenever there is any doubt either in the law or the fact of the case. Again, where the warrant of commitment is informal, if the depositions show that a felony has been committed and that there is reasonable ground of charge against the prisoners, they will not bail, but remand them. The same rule applies both to the law and the fact. Unless the truth of the facts charged is doubted, the courts remand; and the same consequence follows, unless they see reason to doubt whether the fact charged constitutes an offense within the law.² Lord Mansfield said a man committed on suspicion only had a right to be bailed under this act.³ For views expressed in some of the courts of this country regarding the English law of bail, see authorities cited below.⁴

§ 392. **The Power to Bail and Bailable Offenses in the United States** are regulated by sections 1014, 1015, and 1016 of the revised statutes of the United States.⁵ They provide that bail may be admitted upon all arrests in criminal cases where the punishment may be death; but in such cases it shall be taken only by the supreme court or a circuit court, or by a justice of the supreme court, a circuit judge, or a judge of a district court, who shall exercise their discretion therein, having regard to the nature and circumstances of the offense, and of the evidence, and to the usages of law. And that bail shall be admitted upon all arrests in criminal cases where the offense is not punishable by death; and in such cases it may be taken by any justice or judge of the United States, or by any commissioner of a circuit court to take bail, or by any chancellor, judge of a supreme or superior court, chief or first judge of common pleas, mayor of a city, justice of the peace, or other magistrate, of any state where the offender may be found, and agreeably

---

¹ State v. Buyck, 2 Bay, 563.
² See habeas corpus act, *ante*, sec. 58; King v. Marks, 3 East, 157.
³ King v. Walker, 1 Leach Cas. in Crown Law, 98, note *a*.
⁴ Yarbrough v. The State, 2 Tex. 519; State v. Maurignos, T. U. P. Charlt. 24; State v. Everett & Potter, Dudley (S. C.), 295; People v. McLeod, 1 Hill (N. Y.), 377; In the Matter of Goodhue, 1 Wheel. Cr. Cas. 427; People v. Goodwin, Id. 434; Ex parte Tayloe, 5 Cow. 39; Street v. The State, 43 Miss. 1.
⁵ See ed. of 1873–4.

to the usual mode of process against offenders in such state, etc.[1]

§ 393. **The Right to Bail and for What Offenses** has been the subject of constitutional protection in all of the states, with the exception, we believe, of New York, Georgia, New Hampshire, Maryland, Massachusetts, Virginia, and West Virginia. In all of the constitutions of the various states, except-

---

[1] See United States v. Brawner, 7 Fed. Rep. 86; United States v. Hamilton, 3 Dall. 17. The Chinese exclusion act has lately received a construction from the United States district court of California. A reference to it here may not be entirely appropriate, but rather than omit reference to it altogether, we shall give it a brief notice. It has been held that, when a Chinese person is detained on board of a ship and refused the right to land, either by authority of the ship's master or by the collector of the port, he is restrained of his liberty under or by color of the authority of the United States, and is entitled, as of common right, to sue out a writ of habeas cerpus, that the legality of his detention and restraint may be passed upon by the court; and that when his body is produced in obedience to the writ, the control of his person remains with the court, which may commit him to the custody of the marshal, or hold him to bail to await the decision of the court. And as the court has no power to detain the ship bringing such Chinese passengers, and pending the investigation of their right to land the same disposition of the passenger may be had, awaiting the president's direction, after it has been determined that such Chinese passenger is not entitled to be or remain in the United States. Such Chinese passengers have no right to a trial by jury, but may have their personal privileges fully and adequately determined on habeas corpus. The order of the president may operate retrospectively as well as prospectively, but it can not revise the judgment of the justice, judge, or commissioner: Matter of Chow Goo Pooi, 1 West Coast Rep. 535. These applications for discharge on the writ of habeas corpus may be divided into three classes: 1. Applications on the ground of previous residence; 2. Applications founded on the production of Canton certificates; 3. Applications on the part of children brought to or sent for by their parents or guardians. And as to the first class, it has been held that a Chinese laborer who was a resident of the United States on November 17, 1880, the date of the treaty with China, and who left this country before the Chinese restriction act went into operation, has a right to return without producing a custom-house certificate, the burden of proof, however, being on him to show such facts by clear and satisfactory evidence. Further, that Chinese who were not in the United States at the date of such treaty are not within the provisions of the second article of such act. As to the second class, it has been held that Chinese laborers who were in the United States at the date of the treaty, but who left the same after the act went into practical operation, and neglected to procure a custom-house certificate, are not entitled to return. And concerning the third class, it has been held that Chinese children, whose parents are lawfully within the United States, are not excluded therefrom by any provision of the restriction act. In the horde of cases giving rise to the above rulings, Chinese persons were held to be competent witnesses; and it must be observed that Chinese persons thus seeking to land on our shores are not criminals. "No punishment," says Hoffman, D. J., "as such, is inflicted upon them. The consequence of their being unlawfully here is that they will be sent back to the country whence they came. The power conferred and exercised is essentially a police power. It is closely analogous to the power freely exercised in the east with regard to idiots, imbeciles, lunatics, paupers, and other classes whose presence is deemed incompatible with the safety or welfare of our own people. The Chinese laborer is met at the frontier, as it were, and not having the right to enter the country, is denied admission to it:" In the Matter of Tung Yeong, Id. 647; In the Matter of Chow Goo Pooi, Id. 535.

ing Illinois, it is declared that excessive bail shall not be required.[1] In all of the constitutions declaring when persons shall be bailable the excepted crimes are "capital offenses," except in Rhode Island where it is for "offenses punishable by death or imprisonment for life;" and in Louisiana, where, after conviction, the crime or offense "is punishable with death or imprisonment at hard labor;" and in Indiana, Michigan, Oregon, and Nebraska, where "treason and murder" are excepted. In all the states except Maine, Connecticut, New Jersey, Alabama, Mississippi, Louisiana, Michigan, Iowa, Wisconsin, Minnesota, and South Carolina, where provisions are made in their constitutions regulating bail, the right to bail in the unexcepted cases is limited by the "conviction;" in those the right to bail in the unexcepted cases is unlimited. But in the excepted cases all the constitutions, except that of Texas, have a limiting clause. It is "where the proof is evident or the presumption great." The Texas constitution of 1876 stops at "when the proof is evident."

In the states enumerated above, where the right to bail has not been secured by constitutional provisions, it is protected by the court in as ample a manner as by the court of king's bench in England.[2] "It may be doubted," says Hurd, "whether the right to the writ of habeas corpus, as it is regulated by the habeas corpus acts in several of the states, is co-extensive with the constitutional or common-law right to be let to bail. There are cases excepted in those acts, from the benefit of that writ, in which the prisoner may clearly be entitled to be bailed. If in those cases where the imprisonment is not and is not alleged to be illegal, the writ of habeas corpus may be granted for the sole purpose of admitting the prisoner to bail, as has sometimes been done, it must be by virtue of some special statute or of that "sovereign jurisdiction in criminal matters" which belongs only to the highest court."[3]

§ 394. **Legislative Powers.**—In Indiana, the excepted cases, as we have said, are murder or treason, and the right to bail in these cases is expressly prohibited by the constitution.

---

[1] The constitution of the United States provides that "excessive bail shall not be required," but this provision does not bind the states; yet we have seen that the same provision is incorporated in all of the state constitutions but one: Const. U. S., Amend., art. 8; Commonwealth v. Hitchings, 5 Gray, 482.

[2] See Ex parte Tayloe, 5 Cow. 39; Jones v. Kelly, 17 Mass. 116; Evans v. Foster, 1 N. H. 374; State v. Everett, decided in South Carolina before the adoption of their new constitution, Dudley (S. C.), 295; State v. McLeod, 1 Hill (N. Y.), 377.

[3] Habeas Corpus, 2d ed., 432.

In the remainder of the states, if bail in the excepted cases is prohibited, it is by implication only. In California, the admission to bail in capital cases, where the proof is evident or the presumption great, may be made a matter of discretion, and may be forbidden by legislation, but in no other cases. In all other cases the admission to bail is a right which the accused can claim, and which no judge or court can properly refuse.[1] And in Alabama it has been denied that there is an implied prohibition by the constitution respecting the excepted cases. Chilton, J., said: " It is believed that the history of the legislation of the state, both before and since the adoption of the constitution, and the numerous decisions of this court upon similar statutes, as well as the spirit of other portions of the constitution, very satisfactorily show that the above clause (except for capital offenses when the proof is evident or the presumption great) in the bill of rights was not designed to deny to the legislature the power to pass laws providing for bail in capital cases where the proof was evident or the presumption great. At the common law all cases were bailable; but it was competent for the legislature, in the absence of a constitutional inhibition, to deprive the citizen of this right, or so to modify it as to render it valueless. The clause was designed not to place a perpetual restriction upon the common-law right of the citizens of the state in the matter of bail, but on the contrary, to secure it by the fundamental law of the state, and to place this right, in the given cases, beyond the power of either legislative or judicial interposition; creating, however, no restriction upon the legislature as to the excepted cases, ' where the proof is evident or the presumption great.' "[2] Opposed to this view, however, is the doctrine in Pennsylvania, where it has been held that "where a crime is charged which is short of a capital felony, the judges are bound to admit the prisoner to bail; but where a capital felony is charged, and the proof of it is evident or the presumption great, no power exists anywhere to admit to bail."[3]

PART II.—INQUIRY BEFORE INDICTMENT.

§ 395. **Who may Bail.**—In ancient times, the sheriff possessed judicial powers as well as ministerial, and was the principal bailing officer.[4] In many states of the American Union

---

[1] C. J. Field, in People v. Tinder and Smith, 19 Cal. 539. Here a legislative provision is also mentioned which conflicted with the fundamental law.

[2] Ex parte Croom & May, 19 Ala. 561.

[3] Commonwealth ex rel. Chauncey v. Keeper of the Prison, 2 Ashm. 227.

[4] Bac. Abr., Bail in Criminal Cases.

he may take bail;[1] in others not.[2] Bishop evolves this rule from the authorities: "In general, all judges of the superior courts, and especially those who are authorized to issue the writ of habeas corpus, whether sitting as a court or in chambers, may grant bail in criminal cases. On narrower ground, the power to hear an accusation carries with it the authority to bail the accused person if bailable; and there are circumstances and localities in which a judge not having this jurisdiction can not take bail. A justice of the peace while exercising a jurisdiction over a particular cause not finally disposed of, can, as incident thereto, grant bail. And by the statutes in some of the states his authority extends somewhat further. But he has not the full power of the judges of the higher courts."[3]

§ 396. **Application is Addressed to Sound Discretion of Court.** And even while it has unlimited powers to bail, it will not do so in the absence of special reasons, except where it is a matter of right. In other words, all persons have the constitutional right to be bailed, except when the proof is positive or the presumption great that they have been guilty of a capital offense; and even when the proof against them is of this character, they may be admitted to bail, within the sound discretion of the presiding judge, if there be exceptional circumstances that seem to demand it. The admission to bail, however, where there is evident proof or great presumption of guilt of a capital offense, is not a constitutional right, but a matter resting in the sound judicial discretion of the trial judge, who should not grant it save under extraordinary circumstances.[4] The judge before whom a prisoner is brought by habeas corpus for the purpose of giving bail may exercise his own discretion as to the amount of the penalty of the recognizance, without regard to the amount fixed by the magistrate who committed

---

[1] 1 Bish. Cr. Proc., 3d ed., sec. 251, and cases collected.

[2] Id.

[3] 1 Bish. Cr. Proc., 3d ed., sec. 251, and cases collected. See, generally, State of Iowa v. Klngman, 14 Iowa, 404.

[4] Ex parte Bridewell, 57 Miss. 39, where the rule announced in Commonwealth v. Keeper of the Prison, 2 Ashm. 227, that bail would be denied in all cases where a court would refuse to set aside a verdict of conviction of a capital crime, was pronounced as extreme on the one hand, and as violative of the organic law as the rule of the high court of errors and appeals laid down in Moore's Case, 36 Miss. 142; and again in Beall's Case, 39 Id. 715, that the court might admit to bail even in cases where the jury might or perhaps ought on the same evidence to render a verdict of guilty for murder. Street's Case, 43 Id. 1, was also criticised. The court followed the principle of law laid down in Wray's Case, 30 Id. 673.

the prisoner.[1] In granting bail, each case must stand upon its intrinsic merits.[2]

§ 397. **Excessive Bail** shall not be required, and an action lies for demanding it, but not against a judicial officer. Here indictment or impeachment is the remedy. For a long discussion of the English doctrine on this subject, see Evans v. Foster.[3] To require larger bail than the prisoner can give is to require excessive bail, and to deny bail in a case clearly bailable by law. The discretion of the magistrate in taking bail is to be guided by the compound consideration of the ability of the prisoner to give bail and the atrocity of the offense.[4] Upon a charge of counterfeiting, five thousand dollars bail was held to be excessive, and the amount was reduced to two thousand five hundred dollars, the usual amount required in the United States district court for the western district of Tennessee, although it is frequently increased under special circumstances.[5] Where excessive bail is required in an action for a mere tort, the revisory court may discharge the defendant upon habeas corpus, if he give bail in a reasonable sum.[6]

§ 398. **To Reduce Bail.**—The judge of a federal court has, without any writ of habeas corpus, ample power, acting under the authority of section 1014 of the revised statutes of the United States, to reduce bail if he thinks it excessive, and to review the action of the commissioner, or other committing magistrate, on a proceeding under that section.[7] In California no appeal lies from the order of a judge of a lower court admitting a prisoner to bail on habeas corpus;[8] and in Texas no appeal lies from the order of a lower court dismissing a motion to reduce the amount of bail, as it is not a final judgment from which an appeal will lie. But this ruling on the part of the supreme court will not preclude the lower court from afterwards having jurisdiction to entertain a motion to reduce the

---

[1] State v. Best, 7 Blackf. 611.
[2] Ex parte Dyson, 25 Miss. 356. See generally, on this section, Ex parte Tayloe, 5 Cow. 39; Ex parte Finch, 15 Fla. 630; Finch v. State of Florida, Id. 633; Ex parte Banks, 28 Ala. 89; Ex parte Wray, 30 Miss. 673; People v. Hyler, 2 Park. Cr. 570; Commonwealth v. Rutherford, 5 Rand. 646; Ex parte Harfourd, 16 Fla. 283; People v. Tinder, 19 Cal. 539; People v. Van Horne, 8 Barb. 158; United States v. Lawrence, 4 Cranch C. Ct. 518; People ex rel. Cowley v. Bowe, 58 How. Pr. 393; Ex parte Jones, 20 Ark. 9; People v. Dixon, 4 Park. Cr. 651; People v. Cole, 6 Id. 695; McConnell v. The State, 13 Tex. App. 390.
[3] 1 N. H. 374.
[4] U. S. v. Lawrence, 4 Cranch C. Ct. 518, cited and approved in U. S. v. Brawner, 7 Fed. Rep. 86.
[5] U. S. v. Brawner, 7 Fed. Rep. 86.
[6] Jones v. Kelly, 17 Mass. 116; See Bethuram v. Black, 11 Bush, 628; McConnell v. The State, 13 Tex. App. 390.
[7] U. S. v. Brawner, 7 Fed. Rep. 86.
[8] People v. Schuster, 40 Cal. 627.

amount of bail.[1] A prisoner committed for a failure to procure bail which appears excessive possesses the right to be brought before a court on habeas corpus, and to have the sum reduced, if, under all the circumstances, it is thought too large.[2] But when, under all the circumstances of the case, it clearly appears from the evidence that the defendant is unable to give such bail as the court believes sufficient to insure his appearance, the court will not, merely for the sake of reduction, reduce the amount of bail.[3] The authority and discretion of a court having jurisdiction of an offense should be exercised in admitting to bail, increasing or reducing bail, etc., whenever substantial justice may thereby be promoted.[4]

§ 399. **Examination, and Reducing Offense to Bailable One.**—Upon the question of bail before indictment, the examinations before the justice of the peace or coroner may and should be looked into to ascertain whether a crime has been committed, and if so, the strength of the proofs in regard to it. If this brings the case within the established rule requiring bail to be taken, the prisoner must be admitted to bail.[5]

§ 400. **Examination of Evidence.**—On a question of bail before indictment, the magistrate may inquire as to the guilt of the prisoner; but bail in criminal cases, says Justice Hurlbut, is not based on the grace or favor of the court, but solely on the doubt which may exist as to the prisoner's guilt. When guilt is past dispute, he ought not to be bailed. The law then demands that his punishment shall be certain, and will not tolerate any facilities for his escape.[6] To make this inquiry witnesses may be called, and the prisoner disposed of as justice may require, on original applications for the habeas corpus.[7] The court is not concluded by the finding of a coroner's inquest, but will examine the depositions to see whether a crime has been committed, its nature and the strength of proof by which the accusation was supported.[8] Sometimes evidence which will not be received on a motion to discharge the prisoner will be considered to regulate the bail deemed necessary.[9]

Where a lower court of general jurisdiction has examined witnesses personally present in court, and refused to admit to bail, in prosecution for murder, a reviewing court will hold that

[1] Miller v. The State, 43 Tex. 579.
[2] Evans v. Foster, 1 N. H. 378.
[3] People v. Town, 3 Scam. 19.
[4] Ex parte Ryan, 44 Cal. 555. See Bethuram v. Black, 11 Bush 628.
[5] People v. Beigler, 3 Park. Cr. 316, and cases cited.
[6] People v. Lohman, 2 Barb. 450; cited and approved in People v. Bowe, 58 How. Pr. 393.
[7] State v. Best, 7 Blackf. 611.
[8] Ex parte Tayloe, 5 Cow. 39.
[9] State v. Asselin, T. U. P. Charlt. 190.

the one below was competent to judge of the credibilty of the witnesses; but where the application for bail is made and denied, upon the testimony taken before the committing magistrate, the reviewing court will give to the prisoner the benefit of all reasonable doubts arising from a conflict of testimony.[1] Where a petitioner has been committed by a magistrate to answer to a charge of murder, the court will not anticipate the action of the jury by discharging the prisoner from actual custody, with or without bail, upon evidence which they are not prepared to say is so insufficient as that a verdict requiring a capital sentence— based upon it—should not be permitted to stand.[2] In Troia's Case, just cited, the court quoted and relied upon the Pennsylvania rule,[3] that "it is a safe rule, where malicious homicide is charged, to refuse bail in all cases where a judge would sustain a capital conviction, if pronounced by a jury, on such evidence of guilt as was exhibited to him on the hearing of the application to admit to bail," and which is so often found in the books.

Mr. Justice Chalmers, of Mississippi, severely criticises the Pennsylvania rule, and says that the error of it " is in failing to give due effect to a verdict of conviction, or in overlooking the vast change it effects in the attitude of the party. By it the legal presumption of innocence is overthrown, all doubtful questions of fact are resolved in favor of the state, and the credibility or non-credibility of witnesses is conclusively established." "As before remarked," he continues, "where no error of law has been committed to the prejudice of the accused, the verdict [of conviction] will not be set aside unless the court can say that it is without evidence to support it, or that upon a review and inspection of all the evidence the finding is plainly erroneous. To apply such a test to a proceeding for bail, and to declare that it will be denied unless the relator has demonstrated that the evidence against him is of a like unsatisfactory character, is to reverse the constitutional requirement that it shall be granted unless the proof of guilt be evident or the presumption great."[4]

So the rule laid down by the supreme court of Mississippi is this: "Upon an application for bail by writ of habeas corpus, the burden is upon the relator to show that he is illegally deprived of his liberty; and the officer hearing the case should

---

[1] Ex parte Jones, 20 Ark. 9.
[2] In the Matter of Salvator Troia on habeas corpus, Sup. Ct. Cal. Opinion filed Sept. 17, 1883.
[3] Laid down by the court of common pleas of Philadelphia county, and found in Commonwealth v. Keeper of Prison, 2 Ashm. 227.
[4] Ex parte Bridewell, 57 Miss. 39.

require the production of all the available testimony for the prosecution, and should, if necessary, postpone the hearing until it can be obtained. If, upon the whole testimony adduced before him, he entertains a reasonable doubt whether the relator committed the act or whether in so doing he was guilty of a capital crime, he should admit him to bail in such sum and with such sureties as will, in his opinion, certainly insure his appearance. If bail is refused, and the matter comes before us for review, we shall apply the same rule, keeping in mind the *prima facie* legal presumption that the action of the judge below was correct."[1] A defendant charged with murder, and whose case has been resubmitted to another grand jury, may have testimony heard on an application, in the court in which his case is pending, and that court should determine whether the proof of defendant's guilt is evident or the presumption great. But when this judge has acted, no other court can discharge or admit to bail, unless it clearly appears that the presiding judge has acted arbitrarily in the matter.[2]

A commitment for want of bail for an act not criminal, and also for a criminal act, is irregular. The security should be fixed according to the degree of the criminal act charged, and the court on habeas corpus should, if required by the accused, hear and examine into the evidence for the purpose of determining what criminal act has been committed, and the probable cause shown against the accused, and this whether the warrant of commitment was regular or irregular.[3]

PART III.—INQUIRY AFTER INDICTMENT.

§ 401. **Rules for Guidance of Court's Discretion.**—1. The bail should be sufficiently high to give a reasonable assurance that the undertaking will be complied with. When there is so strong a probability of conviction as to warrant the belief that the accused person would seek to evade trial and punishment by flight and at the expense of any mere pecuniary forfeiture, he should not be bailed.[4] The object of arrest and impris-

---

[1] Ex parte Bridewell, 57 Miss. 39. It was said in Moore's Case, decided in the same state in 1858, that on application for bail the high court of errors and appeals could grant the application, even in cases where the jury might, and perhaps ought, on the same evidence, to render a verdict of guilty of murder. But this seems to have been an extreme doctrine: 36 Miss. 142.

[2] Ex parte Isbell, 11 Nev. 295.

[3] Ex parte Harford, 16 Fla. 283; see Hight v. United States, 1 Morr. 407; see also Ex parte Champion, 52 Ala. 311; People v. Smith, 1 Cal. 9; People v. Willett, 6 Abb. Pr. 37; S. C., 26 Barb. 78; People v. McLeod, 1 Hill (N. Y.), 377; People v. Lohman, 2 Barb. 454.

[4] People v. Dixon, 4 Park. Cr. 651; Ex parte Tayloe, 5 Cow. 54, and cases cited therein.

onment, prior to conviction, is not to punish the accused, but to insure his forthcoming to abide his trial, and the punishment which may be inflicted on him by the sentence of the law upon conviction.[1] 2. The power to require bail is not to be used in such a manner as to make it an instrument of oppression. Thus, in a case clearly bailable by law, to require larger bail than the prisoner can give is, in effect, to refuse bail.[2] 3. The nature of the offense and the circumstances under which it was committed are to be considered. After an indictment for murder, as in other cases, the question as to whether bail shall be taken is one resting entirely in the sound discretion of the court. Although, as a general proposition, in cases of murder, the temptation to flee from justice is supposed to outweigh all inducements to remain growing out of pecuniary obligation, yet circumstances, showing a conscious want of guilt, or probability of no conviction, may properly be shown as reasons for admitting to bail.[3] 4. The pecuniary circumstances of the accused are to be regarded, and proof may be taken upon this point. Thus, that the defendant is a man of fortune is a fact which may well be considered in fixing the amount of his bail.[4] These rules are incorporated in the code of criminal procedure of Texas, art. 296, and it is there held that the assessment of the amount of bail is a matter within the discretion of the court, judge, magistrate, or officer taking the same, and will not be revised by the court of appeals, unless it clearly appears that the discretion has been abused and the constitution violated.[5]

§ 402. **Meaning of "when Proof is Evident."** — In Texas the rule for determining whether or not bail should be granted is prescribed as follows: "To refuse bail in all cases where a judge would sustain a capital conviction, if pronounced by a jury, on such evidence of guilt as is exhibited on the hearing for bail. To admit to bail where the evidence would not sustain such conviction." It is also said: "If the evidence is clear and strong, leading a well-guarded and dispassionate judgment to the conclusion that the offense has been committed, that the accused is the guilty agent, and that he would probably be punished capitally if the law is administered, bail is not a matter of right."[6] These are the rules in Pennsylvania[7] and

---

[1] People v. Dixon, 4 Park. Cr. 651; Ex parte Tayloe, 5 Cow. 54, and cases cited therein.
[2] U. S. v. Lawrence, 4 Cranch C. Ct. 518.
[3] People v. Cole, 6 Park. Cr. 695.
[4] Ex parte Banks, 28 Ala. 89.
[5] McConnell v. The State, 13 Tex. App. 390.
[6] Ex parte Foster, 5 Tex. App. 625; cited and approved in Ex parte Beacom, 12 Id. 318.
[7] Com. v. Keeper etc., 2 Ashm. 227.

Ohio,[1] and were followed in Mississippi prior to the decision in Ex parte Bridewell, cited in the last section of part 2, above.[2]

§ 403. "**Presumption Great.**"—The term "proof is evident or presumption great" is intended to indicate the same degree of certainty, whether the evidence be direct or circumstantial. The design is to secure the right of bail in all cases, except where the facts show with reasonable certainty that the prisoner is guilty of a capital offense.[3] It will be observed that the Texas constitution of 1876 differs from that of 1845 in omitting the words " or presumption great." But the provision of the new constitution is not so construed as to prevent bail after indictment found, upon an examination of the evidence in such manner as is prescribed by law.[4] The prisoner should be bailed in all cases where the presumptions are decidedly in favor of his innocence, and the strength of the presumption of guilt is to be determined from an examination of the testimony under which the accused is held.[5]

The indictment creates a presumption of guilt.[6] In the words of that great jurist, Field, "the indictment is something more than a mere accusation based upon probable cause: it is an accusation based upon legal testimony of a direct and positive character, and is the concurring judgment of at least twelve of the grand jurors[7] selected to inquire into all public offenses committed or triable within their county, that upon the evidence presented to them the defendant is guilty. Such being the case, an indictment for a capital offense does, of itself, furnish a presumption of the guilt of the defendant too great to entitle him to bail as a matter of right under the constitution, or as a matter of discretion under the legislation of the state. It creates a presumption of guilt for all purposes except the trial before a petit jury. Indeed, if it did not create such presumption, the defendant held under it, or by virtue of the warrant based upon it, without other evidence of his guilt, would be entitled to his discharge absolutely. If it furnished no such presumption, it would not justify the exaction of bail or the detention of the defendant."[8]

---

[1] State v. Summons, 19 Ohio, 139.
[2] Street v. The State, 43 Miss. 1, where a number of cases are reviewed.
[3] McCoy v. The State, 25 Tex. 33.
[4] Ex parte McKinney, 5 Tex. App. 500.
[5] People v. Hyler et al., 2 Park. Cr. 570.
[6] People v. Van Horne, 8 Barb. 158; Hight v. United States, 1 Morr. 407; People v. Dixon, 4 Park. Cr. 651; People v. Hyler, 2 Id. 570.
[7] Cal. Crim. Prac. Act, sec. 229.
[8] In People v. Tinder, 19 Cal. 539. See State v. Mills, 2 Dev. 421; Territory v. Benoit, 1 Mart. (La.) 142; United States v. Aaron Burr, 1 Burr's Trial, 312; United States v. Jones et al., 3 Wash. 224; Ex parte Tayloe, 5 Cow. 56, reviewed by his honor, and sustaining the text. For departures

§ 404. **When Prisoner must Take Initiative.**—In Texas it is said that if a habeas corpus for allowance of bail be sued out, and it appears upon the hearing that the applicant is in legal custody to answer an indictment for a capital offense, this suffices to show *prima facie* that the offense is non-bailable. In other words, the applicant must show that, though held to answer a charge of a capital offense, the proof is not evident. In this the prisoner must take the initiative. The question to be determined by the court is, in such a case, whether, upon the whole evidence adduced (when the evidence is gone into), the guilt is apparent. Is it evident that he is guilty of a capital offense, *i. e.*, murder in the first degree, and therefore not bailable? And this question should be determined without reference to whether the evidence was introduced by the applicant or by the state, and without reference to the *prima facie* case which would, in the absence of proof, be made by the production of a *capias* and a valid indictment. The whole evidence must be sufficient to satisfy the court that the proof of the guilt of the accused is evident, or the applicant is entitled to bail.[1] In the same state, even after indictment found, the party charged is entitled to bail if the proof establishes the *corpus delicti* but fails to implicate him in its perpetration.[2]

In Alabama a prisoner under indictment for murder is presumed to be guilty of the charge in the highest degree, and he must overcome this presumption by proof,[3] and unless the court to which the application for bail is made is of opinion, on all the evidence adduced, that the proof is evident or the presumption great, the prisoner is entitled to bail as a matter of right.[4] In California one being prosecuted by information for the crime of murder may be bailed where the evidence does not show the proof to be evident or the presumption great.[5] When a party stands indicted for a capital offense, and the prosecution does not admit the offense to be less than capital, and no facts are produced to warrant any other conclusion, the prisoner will not be admitted to bail.[6]

---

from the rule, see Republic v. Wingate, referred to in 2 Tex. 523; Yarbrough v. The State, Id.; Lumm v. The State, 3 Port. 294; State v. Hill, 3 Brev. 89, which his honor also reviewed. Read Street v. The State, 43 Miss. 1, and cases reviewed, some of which are cited above in this note.

[1] Ex parte Randon, 12 Tex. App. 146, and where it is said that the doctrine in Ex parte Scoggin, 6 Id. 546, does not contravene these rules. Same principle in Zembrod v. The State, 25 Tex. 519. In Texas the courts are not authorized to discharge a defendant without bail after an indictment has been found: Parker v. The State, 5 Tex. App. 579.

[2] Ex parte Bomar, 9 Tex. App. 610.
[3] Ex parte Vaughan, 44 Ala. 417.
[4] Ex parte Bryant, 34 Ala. 270.
[5] Ex parte Strange, 59 Cal. 416.
[6] Ex parte Springer, 1 Utah, 214.

§ 405. THE RIGHT TO BAIL. 539

One imprisoned in default of bail by order of a court in which a criminal information is pending against him will not be discharged on habeas corpus, on the ground that the information is insufficient to charge him with any offense, or that the court in which it is pending refused to quash it for that reason. But where one has subsequently been held to bail before a magistrate, and has given the bail required, and for the same offense as stated in the pending information, the court which committed for default of bail should, on the prisoner's application for that purpose, inquire into the fact, and if true, grant the proper relief in respect to bail.[1]

§ 405. **Evidence.**—As in many of the states the indictment creates a great presumption of guilt against the defendant, the important question arises, whether the finding of the grand jury can be reviewed on the application for bail, or its effect in creating such presumption be repelled by affidavits or oral testimony as to the guilt or innocence of the prisoner. In California it is held that the finding of the grand jury can not be the subject of review upon the application for bail, and that affidavits or oral testimony as to the guilt or innocence of the defendant can not be received to repel the presumption arising from the indictment, unless special and extraordinary circumstances exist. And malice or mistake in the institution of the prosecution are not circumstances sufficient to justify the reception of evidence so as to rebut the presumption created by the indictment in capital cases, on the application for bail.[2] This seems to be the better rule, and prevails in the courts of many of the states.[3] It is also the rule of the federal courts.[4] The reason of this rule is that provision is not generally made for the preservation of the testimony taken before grand juries, and to permit the procedure mentioned above in ordinary cases, where no such circumstances exist, "would result," says Mr. Justice Field, "in rendering the application for bail in the majority of cases in effect a trial upon the merits. If such evidence were admissible on the part of the defendant, the public prosecutor could justly claim a right to controvert it; and thus counter-affidavits or conflicting oral testimony would be pre-

---

[1] Petition of Semler, 41 Wis. 517. See, generally, Street v. The State, 43 Miss. 1.

[2] People v. Tinder, 19 Cal. 539.

[3] Territory v. Benoit, 1 Mart. (La.) 142; Hight v. United States, 1 Morr. 407; State v. Mills, 2 Dev. 420; People v. McLeod, 1 Hill (N. Y.), 377;

Ex parte Tayloe, 5 Cow. 56; People v. Dixon, 4 Park. Cr. 651; People v. Cole, 6 Id. 695; Finch v. State of Florida, 15 Fla. 633; Ex parte Harfourd, 16 Id. 283.

[4] United States v. Jones, 3 Wash. 224; United States v. Aaron Burr, 1 Burr's Trial, 312.

sented, 'transforming,' as is justly observed by the supreme court of New York in The People v. Hyler, 'a motion to bail into an examination into the guilt or innocence of the prisoner.' 'The rule,' continues the court in that case, 'seems to be well settled to the contrary, and with reason, because to open the whole question of guilt or innocence to proof on a motion to admit to bail would be attended with most serious inconvenience.'"[1]

In some of the states, however, there is a departure from this rule. In Virginia the judgment of the examining court and finding of the grand jury are not so conclusive of the probable guilt of the prisoner as to exclude the examination of testimony by the judge with reference to the question of probable guilt or innocence, on the prisoner's motion to be let to bail. But if the court is satisfied that there is material evidence for the commonwealth that is not before the court, or before the examining court, or spread on the record, he should refuse the motion.[2] In South Carolina the indicted may be admitted to bail, and the court may hear and consider affidavits tending to show that the prosecution was instituted from malice or mistake.[3] In Indiana the case may be fully investigated after notice given to the party interested in resisting the application for bail, or his attorney, and after witnesses have been summoned to testify in the premises. So there one indicted for murder in the first degree may sue out a writ of habeas corpus to be let to bail, and upon proof that he is guilty of a bailable homicide, may be allowed to give bail.[4] In Mississippi the practice varied for many years prior to the decision in Ex parte Wray, 30 Miss. 673, but since then the practice has been to receive testimony *aliunde* the indictment to reduce the grade of the crime from murder to manslaughter.[5] Yet it is not claimed that the indictment is placed entirely out of the question on the hearing of the habeas corpus, because it would then simply become a question of guilty or not guilty on the evidence. But it is said that this is not the issue, for it were absurd to say that the judge could discharge, however clear the proof of innocence might be. Nor is it in any sense a review or revisal of the grounds of the action of the grand jury, for the judge can not revise their finding, or put the party on final trial for a less grade of crime. This is the

[1] 2 Park. Cr. 571; cited in People v. Tinder, 19 Cal. 546. See Cal. Pen. C., sec. 1270.
[2] Commonwealth v. Rutherford, 5 Rand. 646.
[3] State v. Hill, 3 Brev. 89.
[4] Lumm v. The State, 3 Port. 293; see Ex parte Halpine, 30 Ind. 254.
[5] Street v. The State, 43 Miss. 1.

§ 406. THE RIGHT TO BAIL. 541

issue: "Is the presumption great or the proof evident that the prisoner is guilty of a capital crime?"[1] Statutory provision may, of course, affect the rule. In Texas, if it appears by the return and the papers attached that the party stands indicted for a capital offense, the statute provides that the judge or court shall, nevertheless, proceed to hear such testimony as may be offered on the part of the applicant and the state, and may either remand the defendant or admit him to bail, as the law and the case may justify. It is incumbent on the indicted to show that he is entitled to bail, else it will be refused.[2] In Alabama, unless the court to which the application is made is of opinion upon the evidence adduced that the prisoner is guilty of murder in the first degree, he must be bailed, though after indictment.[3]

§ 406. **Evidence, Continued.**—In Texas, when the record in a habeas corpus trial fails to disclose the pecuniary circumstances of an applicant for bail, the court of appeals can not consider that question. This is on appeal from the court below. This question, however, may properly be considered if the record shows the prisoner's circumstances.[4] On an appeal from the judgment of the lower court refusing bail, the record should bring up evidence of the ability of the applicant to give or procure bail, so as to enable the appellate court, if bail be allowed, to determine the proper amount.[5] The practice on appeals on habeas corpus proceedings refusing bail is for the appellate court to determine the case exclusively on the facts and the law arising upon the record, but neither the facts nor the law, in affirming a judgment refusing bail, will ordinarily be discussed, lest it prejudice the rights of the applicant on his final trial.[6] Purely incidental questions which arose on the hearing will not be reviewed or revised.[7] In such cases, if the record shows conflicting testimony on the controlling questions of the case, the superior advantages of the court *a quo* to determine the comparative credibility of the conflicting witnesses will be regarded; and if no error is apparent in the action of the court below, its judgment refusing bail will be affirmed.[8] The court below granted a second habeas corpus, but ruled that the evidence upon which

---

[1] Street v. The State, 43 Miss. 1; see Ex parte Bridewell, 57 Id. 39.
[2] Ex parte Scoggin, 6 Tex. App. 546; see Ex parte Bomar, 9 Id. 610.
[3] Ex parte Banks, 28 Ala. 89.
[4] McConnell v. The State, 13 Tex. App. 390.
[5] Ex parte Walker and Black, 3 Tex. App. 668.
[6] Ex parte Rothschild, 2 Tex. App. 560, 587.
[7] Id.
[8] Ex parte Beacom, 12 Tex. App. 318. To the same point, Drury v. The State, 25 Tex. 45; see Ex parte Bomar, 9 Tex. App. 610.

it was based was not newly discovered, etc., as required by law. But while the Texas court of appeals concurred in that view, it would not for that reason, or because the applicant was not entitled to the writ, affirm the judgment refusing bail. The writ having been granted and the proofs heard by the court below, and the evidence having become part of the record, they said they were required to hear the facts and law arising thereon, and to enter such judgment and make such orders as the law and the nature of the case required.[1]

It seems that in New York, after the indictment has been found, the inquest of the coroner and the depositions before the magistrate can no longer be looked into; because the prisoner is then held under the indictment, and not on the warrants founded upon those depositions, and as the proof before the grand jury may be quite different from that before the committing magistrate.[2] But before indictment found, the finding of an inquisition of murder or manslaughter by a coroner's inquest will not conclude a court from looking into the depositions to ascertain the fact, and evidence supporting it.[3] In California, where there was evidence to show that death resulted from acts of petitioner, done with intent to procure an abortion, but none to show actual intent to kill, the prisoner was admitted to bail.[4] In Texas, when the return shows that an applicant is held by a warrant of commitment from an examining court, for a capital offense, or a *capias* issued on an indictment for such an offense, it presupposes an examination into the facts, and throws the burden of proof upon him to show that his restraint is illegal and that he is entitled to bail.[5] So where an appellant was in jail under a *capias* based upon an indictment charging him with murder in the first degree, he sued out a habeas corpus for bail. He procured process for all the witnesses named in the indictment, and he examined such of them as appeared. The evidence tended to show that the deceased had been killed, but neither identified him as the man for whose murder the appellant was indicted nor connected the appellant with the homicide. Bail was refused in the court below, but allowed, on appeal, in the one above.[6]

§ 407. **Under Special and Extraordinary Circumstances,** as we have said, bail may be allowed. But, says

[1] Ex parte Foster, 5 Tex. App. 625.
[2] People v. Dixon, 4 Park. Cr. 651; People v. McLeod, 1 Hill (N. Y.), 377; People v. Van Horne, 8 Barb. 163.
[3] Ex parte Tayloe, 5 Cow. 39.
[4] Ex parte Wolff, 57 Cal. 94.
[5] Ex parte Scoggin, 6 Tex. App. 546.
[6] Ex parte Randon, 12 Tex. App. 145.

Mr. Justice Field, what circumstances will be deemed of such a character as to justify, on the application for bail, the consideration of evidence offered against the presumption of guilt created by the indictment, it is difficult to state in general terms. His honor, however, enumerates the following: "The existence, at the time the indictment was found, of great popular excitement with reference to the prisoner, or the offense charged against him, likely to bias and warp the judgment of the grand jurors;[1] the existence of the party charged to have been murdered; or a clear confession by another of the commission of the offense for which the defendant is indicted."[2] In California, before the district courts had been organized, their terms fixed, or the judges appointed—and also on account of there being no secure place to confine the prisoners until the day of trial—they were admitted to bail on charges of felony. Had these reasons not existed, they would have been remanded.[3] Where the prisoner has been tried and acquitted of the same offense, or where the supposed murder was a homicide committed in a war between two nations, may also be mentioned.[4]

§ 408. **Disagreement of Jury—New Trial, etc.**—Bail may sometimes be taken after indictment found in capital cases where no special and extraordinary circumstances exist. As where the public prosecutor admits that the evidence which he can produce will not warrant a conviction for a capital offense, or where he admits facts from which it is evident that no such conviction can take place. So where upon trial the evidence for the prosecution and defense has been produced, and the jury have disagreed, or where, after verdict, a new trial has been granted for the insufficiency of the evidence to warrant a conviction. In such cases the court may allow bail, in its discretion, without hearing other evidence as to the guilt or innocence of the accused.[5] But the court will not as a matter of course admit to bail because the jury in a trial for murder have not agreed upon a verdict.[6] The jury's discharge, when they are unable to agree upon a verdict, without the prisoner's consent may also be considered, as it protracts what may have already been a long confinement before the prisoner was placed

---

[1] Citing Robinson's Case, indicted for murder alleged to have been committed during the riots of 1850 at Sacramento.
[2] People v. Tinder, 19 Cal. 539.
[3] People v. Smith, 1 Cal. 9.
[4] Finch v. State, 15 Fla. 633, citing Judge Tallmadge's review of the opinion of the court in McLeod's Case, published in appendix to 26 Wend. 697.
[5] People v. Tinder, 19 Cal. 539; People v. Cole, 6 Park. Cr. 695.
[6] State of Ohio v. Summons, 19 Ohio, 139; Ex parte Pattison, 56 Miss. 161.

upon his trial.¹ Where a jury have disagreed twice upon the question of guilt, a doubt may well be raised, and where it is satisfactorily shown that the attendance of the accused to stand his trial will certainly follow, in the exercise of a sound discretion, the court may admit to bail. The fact that the prisoner refused to escape when the jail was broken, and that he had an opportunity to do so, is one in his favor, and also that he had at first voluntarily surrendered himself. All these facts taken together are strong circumstances to show that the proof is not evident or the presumption great.² Where two grand juries out of three have adjudged that, upon the evidence by the state, the crime is only manslaughter, and the third that it was murder, the court, on a motion to bail, will give the prisoner the benefit of the presumption of law that his offense is only manslaughter; and particularly, if the public prosecutor consent, the prisoner will be admitted to bail, when the court possesses the power to bail him.³ In one case, however, on a trial for murder, where six of the jury were for acquittal and six for conviction of murder, the latter being willing to find a verdict of manslaughter in the third degree, the court, on all the facts of the case, refused to admit to bail; though a second could not soon be had, yet the prisoner's health was not suffering materially by imprisonment.⁴

On a habeas corpus for bail, the affidavits of jurors are competent evidence to show the disagreement of the jury on a former trial. The applicant is not confined to the record, and he may show extraneous facts, such as those relating to the presentation of the indictment, the payment or discharge of a fine, etc.⁵ Also when under indictment for murder or other capital offense, the prisoner is entitled on habeas corpus to produce such evidence as may operate to convince the court that the offense is of such grade, or that there are such strong doubts in the case that a jury should not, upon the case as presented, convict of a capital offense, for the purpose of being discharged on bail.⁶ After a first refusal to admit to bail, a subsequent mistrial before a jury will give jurisdiction on a second habeas corpus, and authorize the production of newly developed exculpatory evidence, which may warrant the enlargement of the petitioner on bail.⁷

---

¹ Ex parte McLaughlin, 41 Cal. 211.
² In the Matter of Alexander, 59 Mo. 598.
³ People v. Van Horne, 8 Barb. 158.
⁴ People v. Cole, 6 Park. Cr. 695.
⁵ People v. Cole, 6 Park. Cr. 695.
⁶ Finch v. State, 15 Fla. 633; Holley v. The State, Id. 688.
⁷ Ex parte Pattison, 56 Miss. 161; see, generally, People v. Perry, 8 Abb. Pr., N. S., 27.

§ 409. **Other Circumstances,** independent of any consideration of the merits of the prosecution, frequently arise, where bail, after indictment for a capital offense, may be properly asked and allowed. The following are of the most frequent occurrence: where the trial of the prisoner has been unreasonably delayed;[1] where the trial is postponed, even upon sufficient reasons, from term to term;[2] where any event has happened postponing indefinitely the further prosecution of the action, as the repeal of the statute giving the jurisdiction of the court to try the indictment (where such jurisdiction depends upon statute) without provision for its transfer to any other tribunal; and where the law creating the offense charged has been repealed without a reservation of the penalty for past offenses.[3] The courts and judges must do what is right between the prisoner and the state, and the prisoner ought not to be bailed on the ground that he can not have an immediate trial, when the court is ready and willing to afford him that remedy.[4] A prisoner under indictment for a capital offense can not be admitted to bail as a matter of right on account of the absence of witnesses for the state, even where the statutory affidavit is made. And where it is not made at the term of court at which the prisoner should be tried, and in the court in which the indictment is pending, the judge hearing the habeas corpus may allow it to be made even after the adjournment, and at any time before the prisoner is actually discharged on bail.[5] The application for bail by one under indictment for murder may be made upon motion in term time, or by habeas corpus in term time or vacation.[6] And where the prisoner has not been tried in accordance with the statute, it must be made to the court in which the indictment is pending.[7]

§ 410. **Sickness of the Prisoner** may also be another cause for being admitted to bail. At common law it was con-

---

[1] 15 Rep. 828; Street v. The State, 43 Miss. 20.

[2] Cal. Crim. Prac. Act, secs. 594, 595.

[3] Mr. Justice Field, in People v. Tinder, 19 Cal. 539, and there see statute and cases cited. For instance of bail being refused, where the trial had been postponed in consequence of the absence of witnesses for the prosecution, although it was alleged that on the face of the depositions, as taken before the coroner, the charge of murder could not be sustained, read Regina v. Andrews 2 Dow. & L. 10. After the bill of indictment was found, and given out after the prisoners had been admitted to bail, they demanded their trial. The state put it off generally, because it was not ready for trial. On motion for discharge it was refused: Logan v. The State, 3 Brev. 415. Where one was bailed for want of prosecution in olden times, see Rex v. Lord Delamere, Comb. 6.

[4] State v. Roger, 7 La. Ann. 382.

[5] Ex parte Chaney, 3 Ala. 424; Regina v. Andrews, 2 Dow. & L. 10.

[6] Lynch v. State, 38 Ill. 494.

[7] In the Matter of Spradlend, 38 Mo. 547.

sidered reasonable to bail him where he had lain a long time, and his health was in danger, and particularly when it did not appear on affidavit when one of the king's material witnesses would be present.[1] In the federal courts of the United States the prisoner is sometimes bailed for this cause after indictment. In United States v. Jones et al.,[2] Mr. Justice Washington said: "As to Jones, it is proved by the physician who has attended him since February in jail, that his health is bad, his complaint pulmonary, and that in his opinion confinement during the summer might so far increase his disorder as to render it ultimately dangerous. The humanity of our laws, not less than the feelings of the court, favors the liberation of a prisoner upon bail under such circumstances. It is not necessary, in our view of the subject, that the danger which may arise from his confinement should be either immediate or certain. If in the opinion of a skillful physician the nature of his disorder is such that confinement must be injurious, and may be fatal, we think he ought to be bailed." This was done.

This rule prevails in the state courts. A prisoner indicted for a felony will be let out on bail when continued confinement endangers his life.[3] But bail should not be granted on the ground of bad health, unless it appears by the evidence as probable that confinement has produced, or is likely to produce, fatal or serious results.[4] The defendant's suffering by imprisonment, and its effect upon his health, etc., may be shown like other extraneous facts.[5]

§ 411. **Continuance—Term.**—The officer hearing an application, in a capital case, for bail by writ of habeas corpus, should require the production of all the available testimony for the prosecution, and should, if necessary, postpone the hearing until it can be obtained.[6] And if the judge is prevented, by other business or indisposition, from disposing of the application during the term, it is his duty, if desired by the prisoner, to fix upon as early a day in vacation as may be convenient for hearing the application.[7] Where the venue of a murder case has been changed from one county to another, and has been twice continued in the latter on the application of the state, the defendants may apply to the latter court for the privilege of

---

[1] Rex v. Earl of Ailsbury, Comb. 422. See Rex v. Bishop, 1 Stra. 9, and cases cited pro and con by counsel in Captain Kirk's Case, 5 Mod. 455.

[2] 3 Wash. 224.

[3] Archer's Case, 6 Gratt. 705; Commonwealth v. Semmes, 11 Leigh, 665; Street v. The State, 43 Miss. 20.

[4] Ex parte Pattison, 56 Miss. 161; Ex parte Bridewell, 57 Id. 39.

[5] People v. Cole, 6 Park. Cr. 695.

[6] Ex parte Bridewell, 57 Miss. 44.

[7] Ex parte Kittrel, 20 Ark. 499.

bail without having made a formal demand for trial. And notwithstanding the continuance of the cause, they are authorized to make their application at the same term of the court in which the second continuance was granted to the state. While a habeas corpus for bail is a correct procedure in such a case, a motion in the court below would suffice.[1] The word "term" means the period of time prescribed by law during which the court is required to be held, unless the business is sooner disposed of, and not the time during which the court may actually be in session.[2]

§ 412. **While under Arrest on a Bench-warrant**, the defendant can not be let to bail before he has been taken to the county where he has been indicted.[3] Neither can a defendant admitted to bail, taken before indictment for a felony, be discharged by habeas corpus from arrest on a bench-warrant issued after an indictment for the same felony. The powers of the court in which the indictment is pending are unfettered. It may permit the original bail to stand, or order the defendant into custody for the purpose of procuring additional bail, if it be a bailable case.[4]

§ 413. **Excessive Bail.**—The court in which an indictment is pending is not in any way embarrassed, on an application to admit to bail, by any action theretofore taken by the committing magistrate. It has power to fix the amount, and should exercise its discretion in admitting to bail and increasing or reducing bail, etc., whenever substantial justice may thereby be promoted. In a proceeding to increase or diminish bail, the prisoner will be assumed to be guilty, after indictment.[5] To constitute excessive bail, it must be *per se* unreasonably great and clearly disproportionate to the offense involved, or the peculiar circumstances appearing must show it to be so in the particular case.[6] Bail fixed by the committing magistrate in the sum of fifteen thousand dollars, on a charge of attempting to murder an officer, has been held to be not excessive.[7] The sum of one hundred and twelve thousand dollars has been held not excessive bail for ten distinct felonies—such being the amount alleged to have been received by the prisoner by reason of the commission of such felonies.[8] A mere difference of opinion

---

[1] Ex parte Walker and Black, 3 Tex. App. 668.
[2] Ex parte Croom and May, 19 Ala. 561.
[3] In the Matter of Gorsline, 21 How. Pr. 85.
[4] Ex parte Cook, 35 Cal. 107.
[5] Ex parte Ryan, 44 Cal. 555; Ex parte Duncan, 53 Id. 410; Ex parte Duncan, 54 Id. 75.
[6] See cases cited in preceding note.
[7] Ex parte Ryan, 44 Cal. 555.
[8] Ex parte Duncan, 53 Cal. 410.

between the court or judge and the committing officer will not justify the former in interfering with the amount of bail fixed by the latter.[1] A showing of the prisoner's poverty may be considered in fixing the amount of bail.[2] The facts of a case will be looked into in determining the amount of bail, and for the guidance of an appellate court the records should furnish them with such information as an examining court would require before fixing the amount if bail be granted.[3] And if an appeal be prosecuted to secure a reduction of bail averred to be excessive, the judgment below will be affirmed, unless the record discloses the pecuniary circumstances of the defendant.[4]

§ 414. **Insanity of Prisoner.**—A prisoner should neither be absolutely discharged nor let to bail on habeas corpus, if it is dangerous to permit him to be at large while under mental delusion. And this though the prisoner has been acquitted by the verdict of the jury on the issue of insanity.[5] Where the guilt of a party charged with a capital crime depends upon the issue of his sanity or insanity at the time of the commission of the imputed crime, if the testimony upon the subject of his insanity is of a character to induce the belief that it is not a case in which the "proof is evident or presumption great," he is, after indictment found, entitled to bail.[6]

§ 415. **Appeal from Judgment Refusing Bail.**—In Texas, the judgment of a district court refusing bail has always been held the subject of appeal.[7] But in the case of conflict, or apparent contradiction of evidence, or where the credibility of witnesses is involved, great deference will be paid to the construction placed upon it by the court below.[8] The appeal may also be taken from a judgment in chambers.[9] The case in the appellate court must be determined exclusively on the facts and the law arising upon the record.[10] The appeal, however, does not lie from the refusal of the lower court to issue the habeas corpus;[11] nor from an order dismissing a motion to reduce the amount of bail, as this is not a final judgment from which an

---

[1] Ex parte Duncan, 54 Cal. 75.
[2] Ex parte Bridewell, 57 Miss. 54.
[3] Ex parte Walker, 3 Tex. App. 674.
[4] McConnell v. The State, 13 Tex. App. 401.
[5] U. S. v. Lawrence, 4 Cranch C. Ct. 518.
[6] Zembrod v. The State, 25 Tex. 519; see facts of this case touching the prisoner's insanity where the court held that bail should be allowed.

[7] Ex parte Walker, 3 Tex. App. 669; Ex parte Randon, 12 Id. 145; Ex parte Beacom, Id. 318; McConnell v. The State, 13 Id. 390. Compare Yarbrough v. State, 2 Tex. 519.
[8] Drury v. The State, 25 Tex. 45.
[9] Ex parte Rothschild, 2 Tex. App. 560.
[10] Ex parte Rothschild, 2 Tex. App. 560; Ex parte Scoggin, 6 Id. 546; Ex parte Jones, 7 Id. 365.
[11] Ex parte Foster, 5 Tex. App. 625.

§ 415.   THE RIGHT TO BAIL.   549

appeal will lie.¹ This right of appeal in Texas, in habeas corpus cases, is a creature of the statute; and it is explicitly laid down that the orders of the appellate court shall act directly upon the officers or other persons having the custody of the applicant, and not be transmitted through the medium of inferior tribunals, as in other cases of appeal.²

Formerly, in Mississippi, a prisoner was entitled, as a matter of right, to a writ of error to revise the judgment of a court or judge refusing his application for bail;³ but if the testimony was conflicting or the credibility of witnesses involved, the appellate court looked favorably upon the conclusion of the lower court.⁴ Now, an appeal is allowed, as in Texas.⁵ In Illinois, the writ of error has been used for the same purpose; and it has there been held that the refusal of the lower court to hear evidence upon an application for bail by a party indicted for murder is not such a final judgment as may be reviewed by the supreme court.⁶ Also, that the decision of the lower court will not be so reviewed unless all the evidence heard below is incorporated in the record.⁷ There, too, the presumptions are all in favor of the ruling of the lower court.⁸ In Florida, the granting of a writ of error to a judgment in a habeas corpus proceeding refusing bail is a matter of discretion with the supreme court. The proceeding is *ex parte*, and no notice is required unless directed by the court. A petition setting forth the nature of the case, and accompanied by a certified copy of the record, is the proper basis for such motion.⁹ In Alabama, the prisoner, on refusal of bail, may petition the supreme court for a habeas corpus and such other remedial process as may be necessary to render its control effectual and complete.¹⁰ In Indiana, the prisoner may prosecute his writ of error, on refusal of bail, to the supreme court;¹¹ or appeal.¹² In Arkansas, upon a sufficient showing of facts, a *certiorari* will be awarded to revise proceedings refusing bail.¹³ The presumptions are favorable to the court below in conflict of testimony, etc.¹⁴ The same proceedings are doubtless allowed in some of the other states.

¹ Miller v. The State, 43 Tex. 579.
² Ex parte Erwin, 7 Tex. App. 292. See, generally, Ex parte Rucker and Quisenberry, 6 Id. 81; Ex parte McKinney, 5 Id. 500.
³ Moore v. The State, 36 Miss. 137.
⁴ Street v. The State, 43 Miss. 1.
⁵ Ex parte Bridewell, 57 Miss. 39.
⁶ Lynch v. The State, 38 Ill. 494.
⁷ People v. Hessing, 28 Ill. 410.
⁸ Id.

⁹ Ex parte Finch, 15 Fla. 630; Ex parte Harfourd, 16 Id. 283; Finch v. The State, 15 Id. 633.
¹⁰ Ex parte Croom and May, 19 Ala. 561; Ex parte Chaney, 8 Id. 424.
¹¹ Lumm v. The State, 3 Port. 293.
¹² Ex parte Halpine, 30 Ind. 254.
¹³ Ex parte Good et al., 19 Ark. 410, and where the practice is stated.
¹⁴ Ex parte Jones, 20 Ark. 9.

§ 416. **Appeal from Order Admitting to Bail.**—In California it has been held that no appeal on the part of the state lies from the order of a judge admitting a party to bail under the provisions of the habeas corpus act.[1] Neither can one who has been admitted to bail, given bond, and been released, prosecute an appeal on the ground that he should have been discharged.[2]

PART IV.—INQUIRY AFTER CONVICTION.

§ 417. **But before Final Judgment.**—A conviction at common law did not deprive the judges of the power to bail,[3] and where the conviction appeared to be erroneous, this would be done.[4] But where a man was convicted of an infamous crime by a jury, and afterward moved for a new trial, or in arrest of judgment, he was considered no longer bailable; for, said the court, "nothing but the four walls of a prison is a sufficient security for the safe keeping of such a man till he receives his punishment, as an example to others—the great end of the criminal law. In minor offenses, however, bail pending steps to reverse the sentence may be taken to have the prisoner abide final judgment.[5] This seems to be the later English doctrine.[6]

In this country, except where the right of the prisoner to give bail after conviction for a capital offense has been regulated by constitution or statute, the rules and the practice of the common law have prevailed. This has notably been the case in Mississippi, where the courts exercise the power of bailing after conviction in all cases not capital, whenever sound discretion will warrant it.[7] This is done to secure the appearance of the prisoner to abide the sentence of the court.[8] Other American courts have accepted bail after sentence in cases not capital, though not with the same freedom as before conviction.[9] And this has sometimes been aided by express legislation in some of the states.[10]

§ 418. **Bail Pending Steps to Reverse Sentence.**—After a prisoner has been found guilty of a crime, and sentenced by the court of first instance, he may wish to prosecute an appeal or writ of error. And pending these proceedings, he may some-

---

[1] State v. Schuster, 40 Cal. 627.
[2] Ex parte Walker, 53 Miss. 306.
[3] Rex v. Bishop, 1 Stra. 9; King v. Mayor of Saltash, 2 Show. 96; Armstrong v. Lisle, 1 Salk. 60.
[4] 2 Hawk. P. C. 175; 1 Bac. Abr., Bail in Criminal Cases, 581.
[5] State v. Connor, 2 Bay, 34.
[6] Reg. v. Harris, 4 Cox C. C. 21.
[7] Ex parte Dyson, 25 Miss. 356; Davis v. The State, 6 How. (Miss.) 399.
[8] Ex parte Dyson, 25 Miss. 356.
[9] 1 Bish. Cr. Proc., 3d ed., sec. 253, and cases cited.
[10] Id.; see Longworth's Case, 7 La. Ann. 247, and cases cited.

times be let to bail in cases not capital.¹ "But," says Mr. Justice Hurlbut, "at each step of the proceedings, the grounds upon which the prisoner can be let to bail diminish as the evidences of his guilt increase, because bail is not based on the grace or favor of the court, but solely on the doubt which may exist as to his guilt. After conviction and sentence, his claims to be let to bail are further diminished; but as he may still be innocent, and as he may have something to urge against the legality of his sentence, he may apply to be bailed, and if it appear that his conviction was unjust, or there is a serious doubt of his guilt, his application may be granted. But at this stage of the proceedings, the legal doubts concerning the guilt of the prisoner ought to be considered as so well settled against him that the application for bail, if made to a judge at chambers, should be very cautiously entertained, and only granted in cases of great question and difficulty."²

In California, the constitution, declaring bail to be a matter of right, contemplates only those cases in which the party has not already been convicted, and the statute which makes bail a matter of discretion after conviction of manslaughter has been pronounced not unconstitutional.³ So admission to bail here, pending an appeal, after conviction of felony, is a matter of discretion merely; and in general should not be allowed, except where circumstances of an extraordinary character have intervened.⁴ And should not be allowed except by a judge of the court in which the conviction was had, or by a justice of the supreme court.⁵ The appeal must be *bona fide*, and not frivolous.⁶ Bail in criminal cases removed by writ of error from state to federal courts, if bailable, must be in a reasonable sum, as ordered and approved by the state court.⁷

§ 419. **After Sentence or Commitment in Execution.** The prisoner can not ordinarily be bailed; for then the punishment itself would fail.⁸ As in a case of commitment for con-

---

¹ Armstrong v. Lisle, 1 Salk. 60.
² In People v. Lohman, 2 Barb. 454, cited in People ex rel. Cowley v. Bowe, 58 How. Pr. 393.
³ Ex parte Voll, 41 Cal. 29.
⁴ Ex parte Smallman et al., 54 Cal. 35; Ex parte Marks, 49 Cal. 680. So in North Carolina: State v. Ward, 2 Hawk. 443; but in Louisiana it has been held the constitutional right of the prisoner to demand it: Longworth's Case, 7 La. Ann. 247 (1852). See Ex parte Scwartz, 2 Tex. App. 74.

⁵ Ex parte Marks, 49 Cal. 680; see Cal. Pen. C., sec. 1243.
⁶ Ex parte Hoge, 48 Cal. 3. See Ex parte Carty, Sup. Ct. Cal., Dec. 29, 1883. For case where appellants were twice convicted, and where the sufficiency of the evidence in the cases was not passed upon by the courts, but reversed each time for errors in matter of law with reference to the trials below, and yet admitted to bail, see Ex parte Walker, 3 Tex. App. 668.
⁷ U. S. R. S., sec. 1017.
⁸ Corbett v. The State, 24 Ga. 391.

tempt.[1] And the common-law doctrine seems to be that after the prisoner is committed in execution of the sentence he can not have bail, pending proceedings to have the sentence reversed.[2] But in cases not capital, prisoners may now be allowed bail in England, under recent statutes, when they are taking such proceedings as in justice demand the acceptance of bail in the mean time.[3] This is also the doctrine in many of our states.[4]

[1] In the Matter of Percy, 2 Daly, 530.
[2] Ex parte Lees, 1 El. B. & El. 828; Anon., 3 Cro. Car. 579; Anon., 11 Mod. 45; see Armstrong v. Lisle, 1 Salk. 60; King v. Mayor of Saltash, 2 Show. 96.
[3] 1 Bish. on Crim. Proc., 3d ed., sec. 253, and cases cited.
[4] Id.

CHAPTER XXVIII.
HUSBAND AND WIFE.

§ 420. Remarks.
§ 421. Husband for Wife.
§ 422. Wife for or against Husband.

§ 420. **Remarks.**—The object of this and the next four succeeding chapters will be to show the use of the writ of habeas corpus in claims for private custody founded upon the domestic relations. Its scope, both at common law and in the United States, extends to husband, parent, guardian, and master, for the purpose of inquiring into any alleged illegal restraint of wife, child, ward, or apprentice. In this use of the writ it must be observed that it is not to enforce a right of custody, but to remove unlawful restraint. It has been said in England that the party thus interested in the custody will be presumed to represent the wishes of the person restrained, so far as to enable him to set the remedial power of the court in motion, but that properly speaking, it extends no further than this. Further on it will be seen that the court makes no order in the case of adults in relation to the custody, except where circumstances require it, as in the case of idiots, lunatics, helpless persons, etc., but leaves them to their pleasure. If the application for the writ is made by the person restrained, and in which an illegal detention is set forth, the court will pass upon the question: remand if legal, discharge if illegal. And gross abuse, even of legal custody, may be inquired into, and relief given if it be so.

§ 421. **Husband for Wife.**—The husband has the right to the custody of his wife so long as she is willing to submit to it, and if he is deprived of that right by another, who holds the wife in custody against her will, his remedy to recover her person is by habeas corpus. But on a motion for this writ to a private person, on the husband's application to bring up the body of his wife, the affidavit must state that she is detained against her will. The seduction of the wife away from her husband is cause of action, but not ground for a habeas corpus. The wife must be under restraint for the husband to secure the writ.[1] If

---

[1] Ex parte Newton, 2 Smith, 617.

a wife is by her own desire living apart from her husband, and is under no restraint, the court will not grant a habeas corpus on the application of the husband, for the purpose of restoring her to his custody.[1] And where the husband has joined in articles of separation, and covenanted that his wife may live alone, and that he will never disturb her, or any person with whom she may live, he can have no habeas corpus; because, if for no other reason, his agreement is a renunciation of his marital right to seize her or force her back to live with him.[2] In such a case a court of chancery will enjoin the husband from infringing such a covenant.[3] The fact of restraint must appear upon the return, or the wife will be left at liberty by the court to go where she pleases.[4] The above cases are different from the case of an infant, because there the parent has the right to the custody of the child, and if the infant is of tender years, the court will order it to be delivered to its father. But a husband has no such right at common law to the custody of his wife.[5]

§ 422. **Wife for or against Husband.**—A wife may move for a habeas corpus on behalf of the husband.[6] It may also issue at the wife's instance, and against the husband, when she is improperly restrained by him; as where he forced her into a coach as she was coming from church one Sunday, and carried her into the mint, and kept her in strict confinement.[7] Until guilty of cruelty, or until judicial separation, the husband is entitled to the custody of his wife, and to detain her if she desires improperly to leave him; so a habeas corpus obtained on her behalf against him will be discharged in such a case. The wife is not in improper custody, because the proper residence of a wife is with her husband. No court would force her to return if cruelty were shown. The divorce and matrimonial court act provides her with a remedy. Here the husband has the custody, and no cruelty being shown, or conjugal rights affected, he is entitled to it.[8] Upon the same principle, if the wife be confined by reason of ill health, and her husband refuses to allow improper parties to see her, and to whom she wishes to dispose of her separate property, we apprehend the writ would be refused.

[1] Queen v. Leggatt, 18 Ad. & El., Q. B., 781; Ex parte Sandilands, 12 Eng. L. & Eq. 463; S.C., 21 L.J. Rep., N.S., Q. B., 342; Rex v. Clarkson, 1 Stra. 445; Schouler's Dom. Rel., 3d ed., 61.
[2] Rex v. Mead, 1 Burr. 542; Sanders v. Rodway, 13 Eng. L. & Eq. 463; S. C., 16 Jur. 1005.
[3] See cases cited in preceding note.
[4] See above cases.
[5] Ex parte Sandilands, 12 Eng. L. & Eq. 463; S. C., 21 L. J. Rep., N. S., Q. B., 342.
[6] Cobbett v. Hudson, 15 Ad. & El. Q. B. 988.
[7] Lister's Case, 8 Mod. 22; 2 Lilly's Reg. 8.
[8] In re Price, 2 F. & F. 263.

CHAPTER XXIX.

PARENT FOR HIS CHILD.

§ 423. Upon What Restraint the Writ is Based.
§ 424. Powers of Common-law Courts.
§ 425. Powers of Courts of Chancery.

§ 423. **Upon What Restraint the Writ is Based.**—The basis of the common law, as well as of the statutory writ of habeas corpus, is an illegal restraint, and this fact must be admitted or proved to exist to warrant any further proceedings on the writ.[1] But "illegal restraint" has a wider scope of meaning in this class of cases than it had in the original design of the use of the writ. "The term 'imprisonment,'" says Hurd, " usually imports a restraint contrary to the wishes of the prisoner; and the writ of habeas corpus was designed as a remedy for him, to be invoked at his instance, to set him at liberty, not to change his keeper. But in the case of infants an unauthorized absence from the legal custody has been treated, at least for the purpose of allowing the writ to issue, as equivalent to imprisonment; and the duty of returning to such custody as equivalent to a wish to be free."[2] The improper detention of a child, particularly one of tender years, from the person entitled to its possession, is sufficient ground to maintain the writ of habeas corpus.[3] It is not necessary that force or restraint be exerted upon the infant.[4] For all legal purposes the child is in the custody of those with whom it lives.[5] The writ may issue at the instance of either parent,[6] and not only without privity of the child, but against its express wishes.[7]

---

[1] People v. Porter, 1 Duer, 724.
[2] Hurd on Habeas Corpus, 2d ed., 453.
[3] In the Matter of Mitchell, R. M. Charlt. 489.
[4] Ex parte McClellan, 1 Dow. P. C. 81.
[5] Mercein v. The People, 25 Wend. 64.
[6] Ex parte Templer, 2 Saund. & C. 169; Ex parte Witte, 13 Com. B. 680; Ex parte Sandilands, 12 Eng. L. & Eq. 465; S. C., 21 L. J. Rep., N. S., Q. B., 342; King v. Greenhill, King v. Dobbin, and King v. Wilson, 4 Ad. & El. 644; United States v. Green, 3 Mason, 482.
[7] Com. v. Hamilton, 6 Mass. 273; In re Mitchell, R. M. Charlt. 480; State v. Baldwin, 5 N. J. Ec. 454; Com. v. Taylor, 3 Met. 72.

§ 424. **The Power of the Common-law Courts**, in cases relating to the custody of infants, extended chiefly to the protection of the child from violence, and to release it from improper custody.[1] The court of king's bench disclaimed any right to care for the person with respect to education.[2] This jurisdiction was exercised by the court of chancery; and when applications were made to the court of king's bench relative to care and protection for the purposes of education, they were generally referred to a master in chancery for final disposition.[3] In fact, on an application for a habeas corpus at the instance of the father in king's bench to have his children restored to him, that court would inquire whether they were wards of the court of chancery, and whether there were any proceedings in the court respecting them; and if there were, would decline to grant the writ.[4] Lord Mansfield's rule, where the writ of habeas corpus was applied for, was this: "The court is bound, *ex debito justitiæ*, to set the infants free from an improper restraint; but it is not bound to deliver them over to anybody, nor to give them any privilege. This must be left to their [the court's] discretion, according to the circumstances that shall appear before them."[5]

§ 425. **Powers of Courts of Chancery.**—It has sometimes been supposed that a chancellor or a court of equity possesses ampler powers under the writ of habeas corpus than a judge or court of law can exercise. But this is a mistake. The jurisdiction in such cases and the powers under the writ are exactly the same.[6] The mistake arises from a confusion of the chancellor's jurisdiction over wards with that on habeas corpus. The court of chancery has a general right delegated by the crown, as *parens patriæ*, to interfere in particular cases for the benefit of such as are incapable to protect themselves. But there must be a suit depending relative to the infant or his estate to entitle the court to this jurisdiction, and unless it is to care for the infant's property, chancery will not assume jurisdiction over him

---

[1] Forsyth's Custody of Infants, sec. 35, found in 52 Law Lib., N. S.
[2] Wellesley v. Wellesley, 2 Bligh, N. S., 136; Ex parte Skinner, 9 Moore, 278.
[3] See case last cited.
[4] Wellesley v. Wellesley, 2 Bligh, N. S., 142. See Rex v. Isley, 5 Ad. & El. 441.
[5] Rex v. Delaval, 3 Burr. 1436. See Com. v. Addicks, 5 Bin. 520; U. S. v. Green, 3 Mason, 483; Matter of Waldron, 13 Johns. 417; Matter of Wollstonecraft, 4 Johns. Ch. 79.
[6] Forsyth's Custody of Infants, 52 Law Lib., N. S., c. 3; Lyons v. Blenkin, Jac. 255; In re Fynn, 12 Jur. 713; Crowley's Case, 2 Swans. 79; Lyons v. Blenkin, Jac. 245, note; People v. Mercein, 8 Paige, 55; Matter of Wollstonecraft, 4 Johns. Ch. 80; Manneville v. Manneville, 10 Ves. 53.

§ 425.   PARENT FOR HIS CHILD.   557

as a ward, except for nurture only.¹ When the infant is a ward of the court of chancery, many circumstances can be given attention which will not be weighed on a habeas corpus alone, without any cause in court.² The powers of the courts of chancery in England have been enlarged by acts of parliament: Talfourd's act, 2 & 3 Vict., c. 54, and the infants custody act, 36 & 37 Id., c. 12, of 1873, which repealed the Talfourd act; and both of which will hereafter be referred to.

[1] Wellesley v. Duke of Beaufort, 2 Russ. 1; S. C., 3 Eng. Ch. R. 10; Johnstone v. Beattie, 10 Cl. & Fin. 42; 2 Story's Eq. Jur., sec. 1351; People v. Mercein, 8 Paige, 55; Wellesley v. Wellesley, 2 Bligh, N. S., 126; Butler v. Freeman, Amb. 302.

[2] Lyons v. Blenkin, Jac. 254.

CHAPTER XXX.

CUSTODY OF LEGITIMATE CHILDREN IN ENGLAND.

PART I.—DOCTRINES IN ENGLAND AT LAW.

§ 426. The Rights of the Father during his Life.
§ 427. Appointment of Testamentary Guardian.
§ 428. Surrender of Custody by Parent.
§ 429. How Far the Courts will Actively Interfere to Deliver the Custody of a Child.
§ 430. The Court's Discretion.
§ 431. Infant's Liberty of Choice.
§ 432. Infant's Age of Discretion.
§ 433. The Parent's Right of Access to Children, though not Entitled to their Custody.

PART II.—ENGLISH DOCTRINES IN EQUITY.

§ 434. Cause of the Talfourd Act.
§ 435. Provisions of the Talfourd Act, 2 & 3 Vict., c. 54.
§ 436. Effect of This Act.
§ 437. Modes of Procedure.

PART I.—DOCTRINES IN ENGLAND AT LAW.

§ 426. **The Rights of the Father during his Life.**—At common law the father had an unlimited right to the custody of his children, subject only to the control of the courts in gross breaches of duty.[1] When he abused that right to the detriment of the child, the courts would protect the child; but where no abuse of that right was shown, the father was entitled to have the child restored to him.[2] In conflicting claims between parents for the custody of their legitimate children, the right of the father was held paramount to that of the mother; but the first and cardinal rule by which the courts were governed in awarding the custody was the welfare of the child, and not the tech-

---

[1] Curtis v. Curtis, 5 Jur., N. S., 1147; In re Pulbrook, 11 Jur. 185; In the Matter of Hakewill, 22 Eng. L. & Eq. 395; Rex v. De Manneville, 1 Smith, 358; Rex v. Greenhill, 4 Ad. & El. 624; collection of cases in Moak's note to In the Matter of Andrews, 4 Eng. Rep. 261; Forsyth's Custody of Infants; 52 Law Lib., c. 3; 15 Cent. L. J. 281.

[2] King v. De Manneville, 5 East, 220; Forsyth's Custody of Infants, 52 Law Lib., c. 3; Ex parte Skinner, 9 Moore, 278; 15 Cent. J. L. 281; and cases above cited.

§ 426.   LEGITIMATE CHILDREN, IN ENGLAND.   559

nical legal right.[1] The courts were not quite so free to exercise their discretion in the father's favor, by giving him the custody of his child, when the child was not in the father's custody; but if he already had the custody, it would not take it from him, unless he was guilty of neglect or abuse, or his conduct was such that there was probability of moral contamination.[2] But the mere fact of illicit intercourse by the father was held insufficient, unless his conduct was so grossly immoral and his life so impure that the mind of the infant was likely to become poisoned by association with him; or unless the child was brought in contact with the woman with whom its father sustained immoral relations.[3] The courts had no jurisdiction to remove a child from the custody of the father or mother merely because it would be for the benefit of the child. Neither would the peculiar religious opinions or the poverty of the father form any ground for removing a child from his custody; nor mere acts of harshness or severity by the father, not such as would be injurious to the health of the children, or the fact of a somewhat passionate temper.[4]

In the words of Knight Bruce, V. C., "The acknowledged right of a father with respect to the custody and guardianship of his infant children is conferred by the law, it may be with a view to the performance by him of his duties towards such children, and in a sense upon the condition of his performing those duties; but there is great difficulty in closely defining them. It is substantially impossible to ascertain them and to watch over their full performance, nor could a court of justice usefully attempt it. A man may be in narrow circumstances, he may be negligent and injudicious, and faulty as the father of minors; he may be a person from whom the discreet, the intelligent, and the well-disposed, exercising a private judgment, would wish his children to be for their sakes and for his own removed. He may be all this without rendering himself liable to be interfered with. Before the court can act, it must be satisfied not only that it has the means of acting safely and effectually, but also that the father has so conducted himself, and has shown himself to be a

---

[1] Ex parte Fynn, 12 Jur. 713; Archer's Case, 1 Ld. Raym. 673; Forsyth's Custody of Infants, sec. 40; Rex v. Delaval et al., 3 Burr. 1434; Blisset's Case, Lofft. 748.

[2] Rex v. Greenhill, 4 Ad. & El. 624; Forsyth's Custody of Infants, sec. 44; Ex parte Skinner, 9 Moore, 278; 15 Cent. L. J. 281.

[3] Rex v. Greenhill, 4 Ad. & El. 624; Forsyth's Custody of Infants, sec. 20; In re Pulbrook, referring to Rex v. Greenhill, 11 Jur. 185; In re Fynn, 12 Id. 716; Rex v. Wilson, 4 Ad. & El. 645, note.

[4] Curtis v. Curtis, 5 Jur., N. S., 1147.

person of such a description, and is placed in such a position, as to render it not merely better for the children, but essential for their safety or to their welfare in some very serious and important respect, that his right should be treated as lost or suspended or interfered with. If the word 'essential' is too strong, it is not much too strong."[1] While this language was used by a vice-chancellor on the hearing of a habeas corpus sued out by the father at common law to recover possession of his children, infants under seven, and in the possession of their mother and grandmother, it must be remembered that, as we have said in the preceding chapter, courts of law and equity, under the writ of habeas corpus, possess exactly the same power and discretion.

In one case, a father in possession of an infant, even though but eight months old, was held to be entitled to retain it as against the mother, so long as no neglect could be imputed to him.[2] It may be said, then, that courts of common law, whenever they were satisfied that infants were subject to any illegal or improper restraint, or where cruelty or personal ill usage on the part of parents or guardians was shown, would interfere in behalf of the infants. They would, like the court of chancery, protect infants against moral contamination arising from a vicious connection formed by either parent, limiting themselves, however, to cases where that connection was kept up in the presence of the child. As to general misconduct on the part of the father, it had to be very gross before they would interfere.[3] It will be seen from the foregoing cases cited that when the father had not been guilty of conduct justifying the mother's separation from him, she had technically no right to the custody of their children. The above doctrines are still the common law; but acts of parliament have conferred additional powers upon courts of chancery which will be hereafter mentioned.

§ 427. **Appointment of Testamentary Guardian.**—The power of appointing such a guardian was first conferred on the father by the statute of 12 Car. II., c. 24. And it gave him power, notwithstanding the protests of the mother, to commit their child's custody to a stranger.[4] The mother has no such right,[5] and none to interfere with the guardian in respect to the custody or education of the child, however amiable or refined

---

[1] In the Matter of Fynn, 12 Jur. 713.
[2] Rex v. De Manneville, 5 East, 221. See also Ex parte Skinner, 9 Moore, 278; 15 Cent. L. J. 281.
[3] Forsyth's Custody of Infants, sec. 44.
[4] In re Andrews, Moak's Notes, 4 Eng. Rep. 278.
[5] Forsyth's Custody of Infants, 52 Law Lib., sec. 70.

§ 428.   LEGITIMATE CHILDREN, IN ENGLAND.   561

she may be,[1] although the court of chancery has power to control his action in a proper case.[2] A person who has been duly appointed under the above statute, by the will of a father, to be the guardian of his child, stands in *loco parentis;* and having, therefore, a legal right to the custody of the infant, may, in order to obtain possession of such ward, claim a writ of habeas corpus, which a common-law court has no discretion to refuse, if the applicant be a fit person and the child too young to choose for itself. Where, however, the validity of the testamentary appointment is disputed, the court will direct an issue to be tried by a jury in order to establish the same.[3]

§ 428. **Surrender of Custody by Parent.**—In the case of Reg. v. Smith, it was held by Earle, J., in the bail court, that a contract by the father of a child with a third person, that the latter should have the custody of the child, was in the nature of a mere consent, and might be revoked by the father, and that he was entitled on a habeas corpus to have the child delivered over to him.[4]

"Indeed," says Mr. Justice Archibald of the queen's bench, as late as 1873, "it appears to have been the invariable practice of the common-law courts, on an application for a habeas corpus, to bring up the body of a child detained from the father (and the case would be the same as to a testamentary guardian) to enforce the father's right to the custody, even against the mother, unless the child be of an age to judge for itself, or there be an apprehension of cruelty from the father, or of contamination in consequence of his immorality or gross profligacy."[5] There must be some other element than a mere contract to deprive the father of the custody of his children at common law, whether it be made with the mother, under articles of separation, or with third persons. The father could not, however, always claim the custody of his child in a court of chancery after having emancipated it by contract. But while a court of chancery would often hold that a parent had waived his parental right by consent, long-continued acquiescence, and other acts,

---

[1] Forsyth's Custody of Infants, 52 Law Lib., sec. 72.
[2] Id., sec. 74.
[3] In the Matter of Andrews, 4 Eng. Rep. 261; see also Queen v. Clarke, In the Matter of Race, 7 El. & Bl. 186; S. C., 26 L. J., N. S., Q. B., 169, where, no testamentary guardian having been appointed, the father being dead, the right of custody to a child between seven and fourteen was held on habeas corpus to be in the legal guardian for nurture—the mother in this case, when not affected by the wishes of the ward.
[4] Queen v. Smith, In re Boreham, 22 L. J., N. S., Q. B., 116; S. C., 17 Jur. 24, and 16 Eng. L. & Eq. 221; see Moak's Notes, In re Andrews, 4 Eng. Rep. 280; Queen v. Clarke, In the Matter of Race, 7 El. & Bl. 186.
[5] In the case of In re Andrews, 4 Eng. Rep. 265.

and determine the custody accordingly, this jurisdiction was the same as that employed in the matter of wards, or as *parens patriæ*, and with which we have no concern, as the powers of a judge or court of law are the same as those of a chancellor or court of equity under the writ of habeas corpus.[1] But it may be said that a contract between husband and wife is not binding, they being one in law, and the effect would be a contract with the husband himself.[2] It is contrary to public policy, and not legally binding. But if the contract is equitable and ought to be enforced, it will be.[3]

§ 429. **How Far the Courts will Actively Interfere to Deliver the Custody of a Child.**—Lord Mansfield thus laid down the law on this point: "In cases of writs of habeas corpus directed to private persons to bring up infants, the court is bound *ex debito justitiæ* to set the infant free from an improper restraint; but they are not bound to deliver them over to anybody, nor to give them any privilege. This must be left to their [the court's] discretion, according to the circumstances that shall appear before them."[4] As it will protect a man's wife from violence as she departs from the court, so it will also see that an infant does not depart in injurious custody. When an infant is brought before the court on habeas corpus, if he be of an age to exercise a choice, the court leaves him to elect where he will go. If he be not of that age, says Chief Justice Denman, and a want of direction would only expose him to dangers or seductions, the court must make an order for his being placed in the proper custody.[5]

§ 430. **The Court's Discretion,** after the infant's release upon habeas corpus, is governed in its exercise, to some extent, by the principles employed by chancery in the selection of guardians,[6] and is judicial in its nature. The father, and after him the mother, is the guardian by nurture of his infant children,[7] and the child, when delivered to its rightful custodian, is supposed to be set free.[8] But the right of the father is not ab-

[1] See American cases cited in Bantz's article, 15 Cent. L. J. 285; Lyons v. Blenkin, Jac. 245–270.
[2] 1 Bla. Com. 468.
[3] Hope v. Hope, 8 De Gex, M. & G. 731; Walrond v. Walrond, John. 18; Hamilton v. Hector, 2 Eng. Rep., Moak's Notes, 393; S. C., L. R., 13 Eq. Cas., 511; Moak's Notes to In re Andrews, 4 Eng. Rep. 280.
[4] Rex v. Delaval, et al., 3 Burr. 1434.
[5] King v. Greenhill, 4 Ad. & El. 640. See King v. Isley, 5 Id. 441; Forsyth's Custody of Infants, 52 Law Lib., secs. 44, 74; In re Pulbrook, 11 Jur. 185; In re Fynn, 12 Id. 713; Rex v. De Manneville, 5 East, 220; Rex v. Johnson, 1 Stra. 579; In re Lloyd, 3 Man. & Gr. 547; Matter of Doyle, Clarke Ch. 154; Matter of Lloyd, 4 Scott N. R. 200; Queen v. Clarke, In the Matter of Race, 7 El. & Bl. 186.
[6] Hurd on Habeas Corpus, 2d ed., 458.
[7] Forsyth's Custody of Infants, 52 Law Lib., sec. 67.
[8] Queen v. Clarke, In the Matter of Race, 7 El. & Bl. 194.

solute. His power over his child, however despotic the law may allow it to be in other respects as to the child itself, is still subordinate to the power and constitution of the state, and will not justify anything *contra rem publicam*. Society has an interest in the welfare and morals of the infant;[1] and as the present and future welfare of the infant is the leading consideration, the court will exercise its discretion in attaining that end by sometimes giving the custody to a third person other than the parents.[2] The words of a writer on this subject, Gideon D. Bantz,[3] meet our approval: "It is in respect to children of very tender age that the most latitude in discretion is usually exercised; in all other respects the only proper course is to adhere rigidly to the rule of law respecting parental rights, and as far as the nature of the proceedings will admit to those of equity in the appointment of guardians: a discretion thus exercised more definitely and satisfactorily protects the moral interests and safety of the infant."

§ 431. **Infant's Liberty of Choice.**—It is often said in the English reports that after the infant has arrived at an age when it has sufficient intelligence to determine for itself, the court will allow it to choose with whom it will go when released on habeas corpus. But in thus consulting the wishes of the infant as to its custody, it must not be supposed that the infant has a controlling right of choice. It has no controlling legal right of election as to its custody, and it was never intended to subject the legal right of custody to the infant's mere caprice, nor to emancipate it from proper custody. The welfare of the child being the object of solicitude, no consideration calculated to influence the decision of the question should be overlooked. "Hence," in the words of Hurd, "the wishes of the child are consulted, not because it has a legal right to demand it, but because it is material for the court to understand them, that it may be the better prepared to exercise its discretion wisely. It is not the whim or caprice of the child which the court respects, but its feelings, its attachments, its reasonable preference, and its probable contentment. It is a mere rule of procedure founded upon the duty of the court to exercise a wise circumspection, and not upon any legal right of the infant to decide for himself and the court the question of custody."[4]

---

[1] Blissett's Case, Lofft. 748.
[2] Blissett's Case, Lofft, 748; see Queen v. Clarke, In the Matter of Race, 7 El. & Bl. 186.
[3] 15 Cent. L. J. 284.

[4] Hurd on Habeas Corpus, 2d ed., 532, 533; see Rex v. Greenhill, 4 Ad. & El. 624; Matter of Lloyd, 4 Scott N. R. 200; Queen v. Clarke, In the Matter of Race, 7 El. & Bl. 186; Mat-

§ 432. **Infant's Age of Discretion.**—In England guardianship for or by nurture only occurs where the infant is without any other guardian, and none can have it except the father or mother. It extends no further than the custody and government of the infant's person, and determines at the age of fourteen in the case of both males and females.[1] Under seven has sometimes been called the age of nurture; but this is the peculiar nurture required by a child from its mother, and is entirely different from guardianship for nurture, which belongs to the father in his life-time, even from the birth of the child. The rights of neither guardian can be impaired during the period of guardianship, except by immorality or other conduct of a very gross nature. So in Queen v. Clarke,[2] a child of ten, the father being dead, was given on habeas corpus to the mother; and the rule laid down that within the age of nurture, fourteen, the child's wishes will not be consulted against the claim of the guardian by nurture, as until that age the child, in judgment of law, is not of sufficient discretion to choose for itself.[3] While age and not mental capacity is thus made the criterion in such cases, it ought probably to be regarded more as a rule of procedure than as an absolute and inflexible rule.

§ 433. **The Parent's Right of Access to Children, though not Entitled to their Custody,** while not an absolute right, was carefully guarded by the common-law courts, and they would usually permit such access at reasonable times and in a reasonable manner.[4] But if such access were detrimental to the child in any material way, they would refuse such access in their discretion. The spirit of the law may be found in this illustration: Lord Penzance refused the mother access to her child, on the ground that it would be injurious to its permanent health, she having been an inmate of a lunatic asylum, being a very excitable, violent woman, having no power to restrain herself, and constantly indulging in stimulants. His lordship, however, held that he would not refuse the mother access unless satisfied that it would cause real and serious injury to the child, adding: "I say real and serious injury, because in cases of this

---

ter of Doyle, Clarke Ch. 154; In re Lloyd, 3 Man. & Gr. 547; Rex v. Johnson, 1 Stra. 579.

[1] Forsyth's Custody of Infants, 52 Law Lib., sec. 67; Ratcliff's Case, 3 Co. Rep. 37, note 13; Co. Lit. 88 b.

[2] 7 El. & Bl. 186; S. C., 40 Eng. L. & Eq. 109, and cases cited.

[3] See In re Moore, 11 I. R. C. L. 1; In re Preston, 5 Dow. & L. 247; In re Lloyd, 3 Man. & G. 547; Rex v. Johnson, 1 Stra. 579; In re Connor, 16 I. R. C. L. 112; and cases collected in Rex v. Greenhill, 4 Ad. & El. 624.

[4] Suggate v. Suggate, 1 Sw. & Tr. 492; Barnes v. Barnes, L. R., 1 Prob. & Div., 463, 464.

kind it frequently happens that affidavits are put in to show that the child is a weakly child and in poor health, so that it had better not be excited, and that quiet and rest are the best things for it, and so forth; which affidavits the court is very often in the habit of disregarding in favor of the father or mother who wishes to see the child." So his lordship required the affidavit of two medical gentlemen to show that access to it by the mother would be likely to cause real and serious injury.[1]

PART II.—ENGLISH DOCTRINES IN EQUITY.

§ 434. **Cause of the Talfourd Act.**—The general rule of law, as stated by Sir George Jessel, master of the rolls, in the chancery division of the high court of justice, in a late case in England, 1876, was, "that you could not take away the custody of a child from its father, before the passing of the act commonly known as Sergeant Talfourd's act (1839), except you showed that either he was unfit to remain the custodian of the child, or that his so remaining would be an injury to the child. You had to show either the one case or the other. That was the result of the authorities."[2] But this act to amend the law relating to the custody of infants introduced some new features into chancery practice. Before stating them let us see what was the cause of this enactment of parliament.

It may be attributed to the common law as laid down in Rex v. Greenhill.[3] Here the mother had separated from her husband on account of the open, flagrant, and avowed adultery of the latter. The mother had taken the three female children, all under six years of age, to the house of their maternal grandmother. Greenhill had not brought the adulteress to his house, or into contact with his child, and it does not appear that he intended to do so. He was, however, on the habeas corpus brought by himself against his wife, allowed the custody of the children as against her. In this case Chief Justice Denman said: "The court has, it is true, intimated that the right of the father would not be acted upon where the enforcement of it would be attended with danger to the child; as where there was an apprehension of cruelty, or of contamination by some exhibition of gross profligacy. But here it is impossible to say that such danger exists. Although there is an illicit connection between Mr. Greenhill and Mrs. Graham, it is not pretended that she is keeping the house to which the children are

[1] Philip v. Philip, 27 L. T. 592.
[2] In re Taylor, 4 L. R., Ch. Div., 157.
[3] 4 Ad. & El. 624.

to be brought, or that there is anything in the conduct of the parties so offensive to decency as to render it improper that the children should be left under the control of their father. And he promises the same conduct with respect to them for the future."

The law as thus declared in this case was so shocking to the moral sense of the British public, "that Sergeant Talfourd, to his everlasting honor, although he had been counsel for the husband, immediately brought a bill into parliament to change the law and restore the mother to her natural rights, to be put upon an equality with her husband in relation to the care and custody of her children, within the age of nurture, and finally succeeded in carrying his bill through both houses of parliament by a large majority, though it was once defeated in the house of lords."[1]

---

[1] Per Chancellor Walworth, in Mercein v. The People, 25 Wend. 64. Having shown the interest that Sergeant Talfourd, counsel for the father, took in having such an objectionable common-law doctrine modified, it may not be uninteresting to give the words of one of the learned justices who decided the case, during the debate on the bill in the house of lords, July 18, 1839. In speaking of the case of Rex v. Greenhill, decided three years before in the king's bench, Denman, C. J., said: "He believed that there was not one judge who had not felt ashamed of the state of the law, and that it was such as to render it odious in the eyes of the country. The effect in that case was to enable the father to take his children from his young and blameless wife, and place them in charge of a woman with whom he cohabited:" 49 Parl. Debates, 494. See Mercein v. The People, 25 Wend. 104.

In the preceding year, 1838, Lord Lyndhurst said, in the house of lords, in relation to the same case and the same bill, that, "by the law of England, as it then stood, the father had an absolute right to the custody of his children, and to take them from the mother. However pure might be her conduct, however amiable, however correct in all the relations of life, the father might, if he thought proper, exclude her from all access to the children, and might do this from the most corrupt motives. He might be a man of the most profligate habits, for the purpose of extorting money, or in order to induce her to accede to his profligate conduct, he might exclude her from all access to their common children, and the course of the law would afford her no redress; that was the state of the law as it then existed: need we say that it was a cruel law, that it was unnatural, that it was tyrannous, and that it was unjust?" 44 Parl. Debates, 3d series, 744; Mercein v. The People, 25 Wend. 104; In re Andrews, 4 Eng. Rep., Moak's Notes, 268.

The accurate observations of Mr. Forsyth on this doctrine are worthy of note. "It must be admitted," he says, "that the application of this law, which enforces with such jealous care the rights of the father, has often been extremely harsh. He might be a man of the most immoral character, and his conduct towards the mother such as to render it impossible for her, without all sacrifice of dignity and self-respect, to live with him; and yet, provided only that he was cautious enough not to bring his children into actual contact with pollution, and did not physically ill treat them, he had the entire control over and disposition of them, and might imbitter the life of the mother by depriving her of the society of her offspring. And what untold suffering might she not be called upon to endure in the mental struggle between the affection which prompted her to submit to insult and injury for their sake, and the desire to escape from such usage by abandoning her home:" Forsyth's Custody of Infants, 52 Law Lib., sec. 7.

§ 435. **The Provisions of the Talfourd Act, 2 & 3 Vict., c. 54, are:** "1. That it shall be lawful for the lord chancellor and the master of the rolls in England and Ireland, respectively, upon hearing the petition of the mother of any infant or infants being in the sole custody or control of the father thereof, or of any person by his authority, or of any guardian after the death of the father, if he shall see fit to make order for the access of the petitioner to such infant or infants, at such times and subject to such regulations as he shall deem convenient and just; if such infant or infants shall be within the age of seven years, to make order that such infant or infants shall be delivered to and remain in the custody of the petitioner until attaining such age, subject to such regulations as he shall deem convenient and just. * * *

"4. Provided, always, that no order shall be made by virtue of this act whereby any mother against whom adultery shall be established by judgment in an action for criminal conversation at the suit of her husband, or by the sentence of an ecclesiastical court, shall have the custody of any infant or access to any infant, anything herein contained to the contrary notwithstanding."

§ 436. **Effect of the Talfourd Act.**—This act of the legislature, passed after much difficulty and opposition, enabled courts of equity, but not courts of law, to make regulations on the subject of the custody of infants, and to take into account the feelings of the mother, bringing them more in unison with the dictates of humanity. The act did not apply to the courts of common law, as will appear on its face, and their doctrines remain the same.

Hence, for the mother to take advantage of the privileges conferred upon her by law, she must resort to chancery. Jessel, M. R., says that "the act took away that right [mentioned in the first section of this part] of the father in the most express terms, for the act was confined to the cases where the child was in the sole custody of the father, and it gave to the then court of chancery the jurisdiction which is now transferred to the high court of justice, that is to say, in terms an absolute discretionary power as to the custody of the infant on the application of the mother, when the child was under seven years of age, and this power was by a recent act, passed in 1873,[1] extended to

---

[1] Called the "Infants Custody Act," and containing but three sections; the third repealed the statute of 2 & 3 Vict., above mentioned, and the first and second read as follows: "1. From and after the passage of this act, it shall be lawful for the high court of chancery in England or in Ireland, respectively, upon hearing the petition by her next friend of the mother of any

cases where the child was under sixteen years of age. Therefore the law was altered by Talfourd's act to this extent, that that which was formerly the absolute right of the father became and is now (1876) subject to the discretionary power of the judge. When I say the 'discretionary power of the judge,' I mean that, though the act of parliament gave the power in the most ample terms in which language could express it, 'if he should see fit'—or, as the recent act expresses it, 'as the court shall deem proper, or shall direct'—yet, of course, like every other power given to a judge, the discretion of the judge is to be exercised on judicial grounds—not capriciously, but for substantial reasons.

"Soon after the passing of Talfourd's act it became necessary to consider what should be the guiding rules as regards this discretion; and one ground was that put by Lord Cottenham in Warde v. Warde,[1] who said that one object of the act was to prevent the husband making use of the guardianship of the children, not for its legitimate object, namely, the proper maintenance and education of the children, but for the purpose of putting pressure on the wife, and compelling her to forego her legal rights and remedies against him in cases of misconduct, or in cases in which he wished to appropriate to himself property which by law was hers, or had been her separate property; or otherwise to control her in the disposition either of her person or her property. That was no doubt one motive, but that was not the only motive: there were others.

"Another motive was obvious enough, namely, that whereas the courts had refused to deprive the father of the custody of the child except in a very extreme case of misconduct in future, where the wife was innocent, the court was to exercise a wider

---

infant or infants under sixteen years of age, to order that the petitioner shall have access to such infant or infants at such times and subject to such regulations as the court shall deem proper, or to order that such infant or infants shall be delivered to the mother, and remain in or under her custody or control, or shall, if already in her custody or under her control, remain therein until such infant or infants shall attain such age, not exceeding sixteen, as the court shall direct; and further, to order that such custody or control shall be subject to such regulations as regards access by the father or guardian of such infant or infants, and otherwise, as said court shall deem proper. 2.

No agreement contained in any separation deed made between the father and mother of an infant or infants shall be held to be invalid by reason only of its providing that the father of such infant or infants shall give up the custody or control thereof to the mother; provided always, that no court shall enforce any such agreement if the court shall be of opinion that it will not be for the benefit of the infant or infants to give effect thereto:" 8 L. R., 36 & 37 Vict. c. 12. Read, with this last section, Regina v. Smith, In re Boreham, 16 Eng. L. Eq. 221; S. C., 22 L. J., N. S., Q. B. 116, and 17 Jur. 24.

[1] 2 Ph. 786.

§ 437.   LEGITIMATE CHILDREN, IN ENGLAND.   569

discretion, and consider other reasons besides; and Sir George Turner, in considering, In re Halliday's Estate,[1] the rule of the court applicable to that case, said there was to be kept in mind first of all the paternal right; secondly, the marital duty; and thirdly, the interests of the children.

"Now it is quite plain that the two latter considerations were the grounds which induced the legislature to interfere. The father had already sufficient protection by the common law. His rights were certainly large enough. Marital misconduct of a gross character, if it injured the children, was certainly provided for before, and therefore what the legislature intended to provide for was the protection of the wife and children, for the petition was to be the wife's; and the child, of course, must have its interests protected and cared for. In other words, the only alteration in the law was, that you could have the custody of the children given to the wife; that is to say, she was the only person who acquired new rights; but of course, in deciding who is to have the custody of the children, you must have a great regard to the interests of the children."[2]

§ 437. **Method of Proceeding.**—We will close our view of the English law on this subject by observing that the method of proceeding to obtain the custody of a child at law is by habeas corpus,[3] and in equity the proceeding is by petition.[4]

---

[1] 17 Jur. 56.

[2] In re Taylor, an Infant, L. R., 4 Ch. Div., 157. In this case the husband had abandoned his wife, and kidnaped the only child of the marriage, a boy three years old. He was also a co-respondent in a pending divorce suit charging him with adultery. The wife petitioned by her next friend, under the infant's custody act, 1873 (36 & 37 Vict., c. 12), praying for care, custody, etc., of her child. Opposing affidavits, stating defects of temper in the mother, etc., and her consequent unfitness to direct the child's training and education, were filed, but his lordship made an order for immediate delivery of the child to the mother, with liberty of access at reasonable times by the father, and the paternal grandfather and grandmother; and by analogy to Talfourd's act, gave the father liberty to apply for a scheme for the maintenance and education of the child on his attaining seven years of age; but he did not mean to intimate, he said, that he would necessarily take away the custody of the child from the mother at that period; that will depend on the circumstances when the application is made. See comments on the Talfourd act in In re Fynn, 12 Jur. 718; note cases cited by counsel in the same. Note cases cited by court and counsel (among whom was Forsyth) in Curtis v. Curtis, 5 Jur., N. S., 1147. See Talbot v. Shrewsbury, 4 Jur. 380; Shelley v. Westbrooke, Jac. 266; Wellesley v. Duke of Beaufort, 2 Russ. 1; Milford v. Milford, L. R., 1 Prob. & Div., 715; Cartlidge v. Cartlidge, 2 Sw. & Tr. 567; S. C., 31 L. J., N. S., P. M. & A., 85; Barnes v. Barnes, L. R., 1 Prob. & Div., 463; In re Andrews, 4 Eng. Rep., Moak's Notes, 269, 270.

[3] Forsyth's Custody of Infants, 52 Law Lib., sec. 34; In re Andrews, 4 Eng. Rep. 261.

[4] In re Taylor, an Infant, L. R., 4 Ch. Div., 157.

CHAPTER XXXI.

CUSTODY OF LEGITIMATE CHILDREN IN THE UNITED STATES.

§ 438. Application of English Cases.
§ 439. Scope of Habeas Corpus in Cases Affecting the Custody of Children.
§ 440. Authority to Apply for a Habeas Corpus.
§ 441. The Father's Rights to the Custody of his Children.
§ 442. The Same, Continued.
§ 443. The Mother's Rights.
§ 444. How Far a Parent may by Agreement Surrender the Custody of his Child.
§ 445. How Far the Courts will Actively Interfere to Deliver the Custody of a Child.
§ 446. Welfare of the Child to be Considered.
§ 447. Infants' Liberty of Choice.
§ 448. Test of Infant's Judgment.
§ 449. Parent's Right of Access, though not Entitled to Custody.
§ 450. *Supersedeas*, Appeal, Action, and Foreign Jurisdiction.
§ 451. In Divorce Matters.
§ 452. Doctrines in Chancery.

§ 438. **Application of English Cases.**—We must again call attention to the fact that courts of law and courts of equity, in the exercise of jurisdiction over the writ of habeas corpus, possess exactly the same power and discretion.[1] The adjudged cases in the English courts, it must be noticed, in matters concerning the custody of children, are, in this country, except where the courts exercise common-law powers, almost wholly inapplicable; because in all the English cases, without an exception, the habeas corpus was a common-law and not the statutory writ, and the powers exercised by the court those which the common law and not the statute confers. In this country the powers and duties of officers in such cases are now generally prescribed by statute, and the officers are confined in their actions by the provisions of the statute, except where the common law is administered; or has been, as in New

---

[1] Hurd on Habeas Corpus, 2d ed., 455; People v. Wilcox, 22 Barb. 178.

§ 439. LEGITIMATE CHILDREN, IN THE UNITED STATES. 571

York, New Jersey, South Carolina, Massachusetts, and other states, as shown by the earlier cases. The object of 31 Car. II., it will be remembered, was to relieve those committed and imprisoned upon a criminal charge, leaving all other cases of unjust imprisonment or detention to the habeas corpus at common law.[1]

§ 439. **Scope of Habeas Corpus in Cases Affecting the Custody of Children.**—The primary use of this writ is to remove an illegal imprisonment or restraint; and such imprisonment is the basis of the statutory as well as the common-law writ.[2] When this restraint is disproved the writ has performed its functions and the jurisdiction ceases.[3] The detention of a child, particularly one of tender years, from the one entitled to its custody amounts to legal restraint. This restraint may exist without the exercise of force or coercion; as where the individual having it in custody interferes by influence over the affections of the child, or studiously guards and keeps it beyond the reach of its proper custodian, or endeavors to maintain a determination in the child not to go to its proper custodian, and to repel all attempts on the part of such a one to obtain possession of the child—and particularly if this duress be against the child's will.[4] The proper office of the writ being to release from illegal restraint, nothing more is to be done than to discharge the infant when the party is of years of discretion and *sui juris*. But if he is not of an age to determine for himself, the court or judge must decide for him, and make an order for his being placed in the proper custody. In order to do this, the court must determine to whom the right of custody belongs, or to whom it shall be given.[5] The office of the writ is not to recover the possession of the persons detained, but simply to free them from all illegal restraints upon their liberty.[6] A child, however, in the custody of its general guardian, duly appointed by a court having jurisdiction of such matters, can not be deemed to be under illegal restraint or imprisonment merely from the guardian's refusal to deliver such child to its mother.[7] It is a

---

[1] People ex rel. Tappan v. Porter, 1 Duer, 709; People v. Wilcox, 22 Barb. 178.

[2] People ex rel. Tappan v. Porter, 1 Duer, 709; State v. Baird & Torrey, 18 N. J. Eq. 194.

[3] People ex rel. Tappan v. Porter, 1 Duer, 709.

[4] People ex rel. Trainer v. Cooper, 8 How. Pr. 288.

[5] Rust v. Van Vacter, 9 W. Va. 600; In the Matter of Wollstonecraft, 4 Johns. Ch. 79.

[6] State v. Baird & Torry, 18 N. J. Eq. 194; People ex rel. Davenport v. Kling, 6 Barb. 366; Foster et Ux. v. Alston, 6 How. (Miss.) 406; State ex rel. Sharpe v. Banks, 25 Ind. 495; Ex parte Schumpert, 3 Rich. 344; People ex rel. Wilcox v. Wilcox, 22 Barb. 178; Armstrong v. Stone and Wife, 9 Gratt. 102; Com. ex rel. Goerlitz v. Barney, 4 Brews. 408; In re Mitchell, R. M. Charlt. 489.

[7] People ex rel. Wilcox v. Wilcox, 22 Barb. 178.

quœre in New York whether a parent, guardian, or other person, in the lawful custody of an infant child, although using such child, or permitting it to be used, for purposes prohibited by the act to prevent and punish wrongs to children, can be properly regarded as holding the child in illegal confinement or custody, within the meaning of section 65 of their habeas corpus act.[1] The petition should state the locality of the confinement, so that the discretion of the court or judge, as to the place of the return of the writ, can be exercised.[2] Where it appeared on the return to a writ of habeas corpus for a child that the petitioner had left the child in the custody of the respondent, it was held that a demand for the child was necessary before legal proceedings could be instituted, and they could be commenced then only if the respondent, having the power to do so, had refused to restore the child.[3]

§ 440. **Authority to Apply for a Habeas Corpus.**—We have seen that the writ may be maintained by one who is entitled to custody without the consent or privity of the child, and even against its express wishes;[4] but the English rule that the application will be rejected unless it is authorized[5] has been followed in this country. The one promoting the application must either be entitled to custody, or have been duly authorized by the person detained. He must stand in the position of parent, guardian, or some one entitled to the infant's custody; and if he does not, and has not been invited by the minor to sue out a writ of habeas corpus, he has no right to do so.[6] But if it appear that the complaint is made by authority from the plaintiff and at his request, expressed either directly to the defendant, or indirectly through some other person, an action on the case for causing a writ of habeas corpus to be issued and served upon the person therein alleged to be restrained without his authority and against his consent can not be maintained.[7]

§ 441. **The Father's Rights to the Custody of his Children** are in this country not as absolute as they were in England. Our courts of law, while adopting the legal principle that the father is usually entitled to the custody of his children,

---

[1] See 2 R. S., Edm. ed., 593; People v. Gilmore, 26 Hun, 1.
[2] People ex rel. Rosenthal v. Cowles, 59 How. Pr. 287.
[3] Speer v. Davis, 38 Ind. 271; read Justice Brewer's decision on Bullen's Petition, 28 Kan. 781.
[4] People v. Mercein, 3 Hill (N. Y.), 399; and as is shown in In re Mitchell, R. M. Charlt. 489; State v. Baldwin, 5 N. J. Eq. 454; Commonwealth v. Taylor, 3 Met. 73.
[5] Ex parte Child, 29 Eng. L. & Eq. 259; Case of the Hottentot Venus, 13 East, 194; Rex v. Clarke, 3 Burr. 1362.
[6] In re Poole, 2 McArthur, 583.
[7] Linda v. Hudson, 1 Cush. 385.

§ 441. LEGITIMATE CHILDREN, IN THE UNITED STATES.

have been inclined to modify it by adopting the equitable principle that this right must yield to considerations affecting the welfare of the children, and by regarding more highly the rights of the mother. And this change from the doctrines of the common law has been brought about in some of the states by legislation.[1] A review of the adjudged cases will show this to be the tendency of the modern decisions. Upon this subject no inflexible rules can be given; but it is quite certain that our courts will generally hold that a husband false to his marital vows will probably prove an unfit guardian for his children. In the absence of statute, the stern rule of the common law unquestionably makes the rights of the father, under ordinary circumstances, paramount to the mother's. And it is apprehended that it is the duty of the court, in awarding the custody of an infant under the provisions of any statute, to make such order in relation thereto as is proper and right.[2] The adjudged cases in the United States, and cited in this section, nearly all make the father's right to his child paramount to the mother's where each is blameless. Under the statutes of Iowa the father has no right to the custody of a minor child paramount to that of the mother; the welfare of the child is the controlling consideration in determining to whom the custody shall be awarded where a controversy arises. In such a case an unweaned child, fifteen months old, was awarded the mother, she not being an improper person to have its custody.[3]

In the following cases, cited in the note,[4] the rule of the common law was laid down and followed: that the father is entitled to the custody of his children, and in the absence of good and sufficient cause shown to the judge, such as ill-usage, noto-

---

[1] Dumain et Ux. v. Gwynne, 10 Allen, 270.
[2] Cole v. Cole, 23 Iowa, 433.
[3] State v. Kirkpatrick, 54 Iowa, 373.
[4] Rust v. Van Vacter, 9 W. Va. 600; State v. Baird, 18 N. J. Eq. 194, and where it will be seen that infants in New Jersey under seven years of age have been excepted by statute; People ex rel. Nickerson v. ——, 19 Wend. 16; People v. Humphreys, 24 Barb. 521, where it is held, however, that the father's right may be forfeited by misconduct, lost by disqualification, or suspended by reason of the tender age of the child and its welfare requiring it to be with the mother; but a strong case must exist to warrant this deprivation of the father's right even for a limited period; People v. Olmstead, 27 Barb. 1, citing numerous English cases, and where it was said that this superior legal right of the father is subject to the control of equity; State v. Paine, 4 Humph. App., sec. 523. A distinction seems to be made in some of the cases just cited, viz., if the father has possession of the children, the courts are not so ready to exercise their discretion in depriving him of the custody, and to act upon the particular circumstances of the case in the interest and welfare of the children, as where he has lost possession of them. As to paramount authority, see also People v. Cooper, 8 How. Pr. 288; People v. Mercein, 3 Hill (N. Y.), 399; Ex parte Hewitt, 11 Rich. 326; Ex parte Williams, Id. 452.

rious and grossly immoral conduct, or great impurity of life, with which his children come in contact so as to be in danger of contamination, want of ability to support, etc., he would not be regarded as an improper person to whom the custody might be awarded, in the absence of the infant's choice.

The father is not entitled as a matter of right, or as a matter of course, to an order on the return to a writ of habeas corpus, that the mother, or other person in possession of his child, shall deliver it to him,[1] but the courts will exercise a sound discretion for the benefit of the children in disposing of their custody.[2] It has been said in Pennsylvania that the old common-law view of the absolute right of the father to the service of the child was never a part of the law of that state.[3] The father is *prima facie* entitled to the custody of his children, and where he is of good character and able and willing to maintain them, his right is paramount to that of all other persons, except probably in the single case of an infant of such tender years as to necessarily require for its own good the care of its mother.[4] In such a case, where the parents are separated, and where the infant is of a delicate and sickly habit, requiring the peculiar care and attention of a mother, a transfer of custody from the mother to the father will not be ordered, particularly where the qualifications of the father for the proper discharge of the parental office are not equal to the mother's.[5]

§ 442. **The Father's Rights to the Custody of his Children, Continued.**—The later cases in New York have gone far to qualify the old rule, as shown by the citations from that state in the preceding section, that the father had an absolute right to his children superior to that of the mother and all others. The question there is now placed upon the ground more generally recognized, that the interest of the child is the paramount consideration.[6] Other states have doubtless come around to this

---

[1] U. S. v. Green, 3 Mason, 482; Ex parte Schumpert, 6 Rich. 344; Ellis v. Jesup et Ux., 11 Bush, 403.

[2] U. S. v. Green, 3 Mason, 482; Ex parte Schumpert, 6 Rich. 344; Ellis v. Jesup et Ux., 11 Bush, 403; Bennet v. Bennet, 2 Beas. 114, and where the statute of New Jersey, mentioned above, was pronounced not unconstitutional; State v. Stigall, 2 Zab. 286; Johnson v. Terry, 34 Conn. 259; Ex parte Hewitt, 11 Rich. 326; Ex parte Williams, Id. 452; State v. Smith, 6 Greenl. 400, and cases cited, where it said that the father has no exclusive and vested right in any case to the custody of his children; In re Mitchell, R. M. Charlt. 489; Brinster v. Compton, 68 Ala. 299.

[3] Com. v. Gilkeson, 1 Phila. 194; S. C., 7 Leg. Int. 195.

[4] Com. v. Smith, 1 Brews. 547; State v. Bratton, 15 Am. Law Reg., N. S., 359; and see next note.

[5] Mercein v. The People, 25 Wend. 63; State v. Stigall, 2 Zab. 286; Clark v. Bayer, 32 Ohio St. 299; Hunt v. Hunt, 4 G. Greene, 216.

[6] People ex rel. Johnson v. Erbert, 17 Abb. Pr. 395, containing abstracts of several decisions at chambers, not reported, but which illustrate the gen-

more humane doctrine. Where there is no improper restraint shown upon the part of the father, the court on habeas corpus will ordinarily award the custody of his children to him, unless he is an unsuitable person, and clearly unfit for the trust which the law has confided to him, or has, by some legal act, parted with his parental rights.[1] But where a child has been committed to the house of refuge, the father, if an unsuitable person, is not entitled to the custody of his child on the hearing of a habeas corpus, on the ground that he had no notice of the proceeding under which the child was committed;[2] because, while the father has the first title to guardianship by nature, his claim may be disregarded by the court acting on a principle of natural justice, if his character and conduct render him unfit to be a guardian, and the child taken from him and given to another.[3] His children will not be delivered to him when it would manifestly be to their detriment and discomfort,[4] nor taken from the mother, living with her father, and given to the father of the children, when it appears that they are well provided for by the mother, and not likely to be by their father.[5]

Where a child has been committed to a public institution as prescribed by statute, the court will not, on proceedings by habeas corpus instituted by the parent to recover his child, inquire into the legality, regularity, or sufficiency of the proceedings before the magistrate which resulted in such commitment.[6] Where the mother of two female children had been divorced from her husband on account of her adultery, the court, on a habeas corpus, delivered them to the father; as the children no longer required those attentions which a mother alone can properly bestow, and having arrived at an age when their morals were likely to be injured by bad example.[7] If the father is dead, the mother is entitled to the custody as of right, subject, however, to the court's discretion; and she does not lose this right by a second marriage. The petition for a writ of habeas corpus to obtain possession of a child may be in the name of the infant by his *prochein ami*, or in the name of the person claiming the posses-

---

eral subject and the later views; In the Matter of Gregg, 5 N. Y. Leg. Obs. 265, where the question is ably discussed.

[1] State ex rel. Herrick v. Richardson, 40 N. H. 272; Ex parte Boaz, 31 Ala. 425; Com. v. Briggs et al., 16 Pick. 203.

[2] Cinn. House of Refuge v. Ryan, 37 Ohio St. 197.

[3] Com. v. Smith, 1 Brews. 547; State ex rel. Sharpe v. Banks, 25 Ind. 495; People v. Chegary, 18 Wend. 637.

[4] In the Matter of Cuneen, 17 How. Pr. 516.

[5] Nickols v. Giles, 2 Root, 461.

[6] People ex rel. Roddy v. N. Y. Juv. Asylum, 12 Abb. Pr. 92.

[7] Com. v. Addicks, 2 Serg. & R. 174; S. C., 5 Binn. 520.

sion, and where this person is the mother, and she is married, it may be in the names of her husband and herself.¹

"When an infant or minor is out of the possession and custody of the father," says Mr. Justice Stone, of the supreme court of Alabama, in a late case, and habeas corpus is resorted to by the latter to obtain such custody, it does not follow as necessary matter of right that the prayer of the petition will be •granted. The court is clothed with a sound discretion to grant or refuse relief, always to be exercised for the benefit of the infant primarily, but not arbitrarily in disregard of the father's natural right to be preferred. If the father be reasonably suitable, and able to maintain and rear his child, his prayer should ordinarily be granted. If, on the other hand, he be unsuitable or unable properly to care for his offspring, and especially if that offspring, having sufficient judgment, prefer not to return to him, the court should grant no relief in the premises, but leave the parties *in statu quo.*"²

---

¹ Armstrong v. Stone et Ux., 9 Gratt. 102; People v. Wilcox, 22 Barb. 178; see State v. Scott et Ux., 30 N. H. 274; Com. v. Hamilton, 6 Mass. 272, where the court refused to deliver an infant to her mother, who had married a second husband, not because she was married a second time, but because the infant desired to remain where she was.

² Brinster v. Compton, 68 Ala. 299; see Ex parte Boaz, 31 Id. 425. In the supreme judicial court of Massachusetts, Judge Hoar said, in considering the father's rights as affected by the condition of the child: "Suppose by a pure misfortune, as insanity, or being cast away and being compelled to live among savages, a father has left his child destitute and dependent upon charity; does that give the child the right to form such new relations as to take from the father the right to the custody of the child? Upon the best reflection, I am satisfied that it does. When the father by misfortune is compelled to leave the child utterly helpless, the child ought to be considered as emancipated by the father. If by misfortune the child has made new relations in life, so deep and strong as to change its whole nature and character, the father has no right to reclaim it. I am satisfied that this is a sound proposition. The child is not the father's property. It is a human being, and has rights of its own. The father has a right to the custody of the child, because, from general experience, the natural and trained affections of the child attach to the father and those of the father to the child. If the father has left the child at an age too early for it to remember him, and it is placed in circumstances so that it must perish unless cared for, and other persons have expended money and become attached to the child, and the child has formed such associations as can not be severed without injury to it [which was the main case under discussion], then the father has no legal right to sunder those ties. He is not to be separated from his child. His acquaintance is yet to be formed. It being proved that the father left the child, and by misfortune or accident failed to discover where the child was, and in the mean time that the child had been taken care of by the respondents until she has arrived to years of discretion, and that it is intended to remove her to a distant state, where the mode of life will be different from that to which she has been accustomed, the law will not allow the father to have the custody of the child. It is within the judicial duty of the court to determine that the assent of the father has been given to the arrangement, which can not be terminated without injury to the child. This principle would apply under the same circumstance if a

§ 443. **The Mother's Rights,** in this country, to the custody of her legitimate children, have to some extent been necessarily mentioned in the two preceding sections, in speaking of the rights of the father; but we shall in this section make a few additional observations. In cases where the infant child is of such tender years as to require the personal care of the mother, she is undoubtedly entitled to its custody when this question is in controversy.[1] Where there was sufficient evidence to sustain a finding that the child was five years old, but weighing only a little over thirty pounds, and not a hearty boy, the divorced mother was awarded its custody on habeas corpus, she being a suitable person.[2] The family, however, is the unit of government, and should be cherished and guarded. A wife without a husband and a husband without a wife are well said to be doubtful and dangerous conditions. So where a mother has not been blameless in occurrences preceding a separation, she should not be rewarded for her faults by the interposition of the court. "If she breaks up the household, and departs from her husband's house wrongfully, whether it be done of her own purpose, or from weakly yielding to the evil influences of others, she is not to be allowed to take with her the children of the union."[3] Where the general rule is that a wife can not be admitted as a witness for or against her husband, either in civil or criminal proceedings, an exception is made in habeas corpus proceedings where the wife has been the injured party. So she is a competent witness for the defendant to prove acts of cruelty committed by her husband on her,

---

father became insane. A human being can not be treated like a piece of property. So if a child, by a misfortune, were nurtured in a warm climate, if it appeared that by a sudden removal to another climate its health would be injured, this right of the father would not exist. The father, in this case, should be glad that his child had fallen among people who have been so good to her, and that she has been made a little girl that he may be proud of. It would be cruel in him to take her away, depriving her of the society of her sister, her only relation, and putting her among those who in all things are strangers to her, except that of blood." The court did not hold an absolute forfeiture of the father's rights, however. The legal proposition upon which the above decision rests was concurred in by all five members of the court: In the Matter of Jeremiah O'Neal, Petitioner for a writ of habeas corpus, 3 Am. Law Rev. 578.

[1] Clark v. Bayer, 32 Ohio St. 299; State v. Stigall, 2 Zab. 286; Com. v. Addicks, 2 Serg. & R. 174; S. C., 5 Binn. 520; State v Smith, 6 Greenl. 400; State ex rel. Lynch v. Bratton, 15 Am. Law Reg., N. S., 359; Waud v. Wand, 14 Cal. 512; Mercein v. The People, 25 Wend. 63; The D'Hautville's Case, Hurd on Habeas Corpus, 2d ed., 479; People v. Mercein, 8 Paige, 46, where the infant was twenty-one months old; In the Matter of Pray, 60 How. Pr. 194; State v. Kirkpatrick, 54 Iowa, 373.

[2] Reeves v. Reeves, 75 Ind. 342.

[3] People v. Olmstead, 27 Barb. 10; People ex rel. Nickerson v. ——, 19 Wend. 16.

and which justified her separation from him, and her refusal to return to his house; but she can not testify as to his general character, or as to any misconduct of his in other respects.[1] So an inquiry as to the father's ill treatment of his wife is pertinent as bearing upon the father's right to take the children from their mother.[2] If the statement of a witness is highly improbable, it should be corroborated.[3]

If the mother has at one period of her life been addicted to the excessive use of intoxicating liquors, the court will not award her the custody of her children, although she has abandoned the habit, until her complete reformation is established by time, and nine months have been allowed as a reasonable time in such a case for a renewal of her application.[4] In Mississippi, it is said that "he who harbors a child absconding from its home, and forbids the exercise of parental authority [in this case the mother's] to enforce a return, does, within the meaning of the act [section 1396 of the code of 1871], withhold the child from the custody of the person entitled to it."[5] In the same state, the father, as the head of the family, is regarded as being entitled to the custody of his children, yet that this right is modified by the circumstances of each case. So where the husband deserted his family, left them among strangers and without means, and the mother with her little girls found a pleasant and permanent home with her father, the father was not allowed to afterwards recover the children on habeas corpus, although he repented of having broken up the family, and made proposals to again cohabit with his wife, and which proposals she refused.[6]

[1] People ex rel. Barry v. Mercein, 8 Paige, 46; read People v. Brooks, 35 Barb. 85; People ex rel. Nickerson v. ——, 19 Wend. 16.

[2] In the Matter of Pray, 60 How. Pr. 194; read People v. Brooks, 35 Barb. 85; Garner v. Gordon, 41 Ind. 92; People ex rel. Nickerson v. ——, 19 Wend. 16.

[3] Commonwealth v. Smith, 1 Brews. 547.

[4] Id.

[5] Justice Chalmers, in Moore v. Christian, 56 Miss. 408. Such detention in this state is a criminal offense; and in this case, though the boy was thirteen years old, had permission to leave if he wished, and remained from inclination, the court went so far as to order him to be remanded to the custody of his mother; his honor saying: "While in doubtful cases the wishes of a child of this age will be sought, and to some extent be observed, we can not for a moment agree that a boy of thirteen can be allowed at pleasure to abandon his filial duties, and select elsewhere a home more agreeable either to his desires or his worldly interests. So to hold would simply be to offer a premium to the children of the poor to shirk the duties to which their station in life has called them, and to permit them, at the sacrifice of all the natural affections, to set about bettering their condition at a period of life when the law dedicates both their persons and their services to parental control." The boy's rendezvous was with a kind man of good character and means, to whom his father had contracted him, but his mother was a widow woman, poor, and dependent. This decision partly overruled: Maples v. Maples, 49 Miss. 393.

[6] McShan v. McShan, 56 Miss. 413.

§ 444. LEGITIMATE CHILDREN, IN THE UNITED STATES. 579

The custody and care of the younger children will be awarded to the mother, "where spiritualism, with its usual tendency to free-love on the part of the husband, works its legitimate results in the separation of his wife from him; and where the husband's means have so justified, the older children have in such a case been put to a boarding-school—and all this without any particular modification of the sentiment that he is a public fool."[1] Upon the return to a writ of habeas corpus sued out by the mother to recover her minor children, there may be a denial of material facts which it sets forth, and new allegations under oath in support of the application will be received; but the father, or other person detaining the infant, will be allowed to give further evidence on his part.[2] As between the mother and third persons, the mother's right is superior, where she is a suitable and respectable person.[3]

§ 444. **How Far a Parent may by Agreement Surrender the Custody of his Child.**—In some of the states this matter has been regulated by legislation, the power being expressly conferred upon the parent to relinquish the services and custody of his child, as in California.[4] We have seen in the preceding section that in Mississippi a father can not by contract with a stranger bargain away the rights of the mother after his death; yet there he may appoint a testamentary guardian of the person or estate of his children.[5] And although in New York and New Jersey, before 1847, it was held that a father had no right to dispose of his children, except for some specific and temporary purpose, such as apprenticeship during the father's life, or guardianship after his death—on the common-law ground that he was entitled to the custody of his minor children, as guardian by nature and guardian for nurture; that such guardianship was not assignable; that such care and custody was a personal trust in the father, and that he had no general power to dispose of them to another[6]—yet the later decisions in this country are undoubtedly against the repudiation of an agreement by a

[1] In re Holmes, 19 How. Pr. 329.
[2] People ex rel. Ordronaux v. Chegary, 18 Wend. 637.
[3] Armstrong v. Stone et Ux., 9 Gratt. 102. For statutory provisions in New York, see 2 Fay's Dig. 566.
[4] C. C., sec. 211.
[5] Moore v. Christian, 56 Miss. 408.
[6] People v. Mercein, 3 Hill (N. Y.), 399; see also Mercein v. People, 25 Wend. 63, a case especially valuable for its references; State ex rel. Mayne v. Baldwin, 5 N. J. Eq. 454; so in State ex rel. Hodgdon v. Libbey, 44 N. H. 321, but here the interests of the child were held to be paramount, and that if the relation between the child and respondent under the agreement had been of such duration and character that the happiness of the child would be endangered by severing it, the agreement would be enforced.

parent to surrender to another the right to the custody of his infant children, and unless a clear breach of the agreement or abuse of the child is shown, the courts will not assist him to recover it on habeas corpus.

Husband and wife, being in law one person, can not contract with each other, and the father can not divest himself of his right by an agreement with the mother.[1] A consent on his part that the mother might have the child for the time being can no more deprive him of his superior right than such consent would release him from his obligations to the child.[2] An agreement between husband and wife as to the custody of their children, made previous to a decree for divorce, will not have a controlling influence upon the decision of the court with respect to the care and custody of such children.[3] But in Maine, where a husband and wife had separated, pursuant to articles of agreement previously entered into, and in which the husband stipulated that in the event of such separation the children should remain with her, the court, on a habeas corpus by the father, ordered the children into the custody of the mother pursuant to the agreement, and on two grounds: because the statute authorized the father to transfer his power, and because the welfare of the children demanded it.[4]

Where the duties of maintenance and education have been properly performed by a third person to whom the father has surrendered his infant child, the authority of the father ceases, and passes to the person standing in *loco parentis;*[5] and he can not reassert that right on habeas corpus against such person, or against the wishes of the child;[6] and this though he is not bound by the contract.[7] Where the parental control over an infant child is released to another by voluntary contract, such contract is not revocable without sufficient legal reasons shown therefor, such as bad treatment, etc.[8] A deed by which the father parts with his parental control to his infant child may not be in the form required by the statute for indentures of apprenticeship; but it will bind the father, though not the child, and the father can not avail himself of habeas corpus in such case.[9] Such indentures are voidable only by the apprentice, and can not be avoided by any other person or party.[10] In Texas the power of

[1] Johnson v. Terry, 34 Conn. 259.
[2] Hunt v. Hunt, 4 G. Greene, 216.
[3] Cook v. Cook, 1 Barb. Ch. 639.
[4] State v. Smith, 6 Greenl. 400.
[5] Ellis v. Jesup et Ux., 11 Bush, 403.
[6] Com. v. Gilkeson, 1 Phila. 194; 7 Leg. Int. 195.
[7] Id.
[8] Janes v. Cleghorn, 54 Ga. 9; Bently v. Terry, 59 Id. 555.
[9] State ex rel. Jewett v. Barrett et Ux., 45 N. H. 15.
[10] Fowler v. Hollenbeck & Fillow, 9 Barb. 309.

§ 444. LEGITIMATE CHILDREN, IN THE UNITED STATES. 581

the father, as guardian by nature over the person and estate of his minor child, is, under statute, not assignable by deed without confirmation by the county court.[1]

While a parent may relinquish or forfeit his right of custody to his child by contract, he may also do so by desertion or abandonment, bad conduct, or being in a condition of total inability to afford his minor children necessary care and support;[2] and where the right has thus been lost or forfeited through the parent's fault or misfortune, the parent can not necessarily revive his right by reformation, or otherwise reinstating himself in a position to properly care for and maintain his child. A court will, on habeas corpus, in such a case, exercise a sound discretion in view of all the circumstances, with reference to the welfare of the child itself.[3] Where a child's father is dead, and the mother signs a contract to surrender it to the care and guardianship, etc., of an institution, without specifying any time during which the child should so remain, she may, it is held in Indiana, regain custody of the infant at any time, if she be a suitable person, etc.[4] In Massachusetts, it has been held that a contract made under the following circumstances is valid: The husband was intemperate, and confined for crime; thereby causing his wife to live away from him. She was unable to support her children, and voluntarily gave them to a charitable institution, established as a home for destitute children, under a written contract stipulating that the children were to be placed out or adopted in a good family, and that the mother was not to try to discover who had them, or to deprive those holding them of the children's custody. But on a habeas corpus afterwards brought by the parents to recover their children, the court, it was said, would act for the welfare of the children, but would not, in so doing, be restricted to the ordinary modes of trial, or require the children to be brought into open court, or

[1] Byrne v. Love et al., 14 Tex. 81.
[2] State v. Bratton, 15 Am. Law Reg., N. S., 359; Clarke v. Bayer, 32 Ohio St. 299; in the Matter of O'Neal, 3 Am. Law Rev. 578. Where a child has been left on respondent's doorsteps in a basket, and in a sick and almost dying condition, and has been cared for by him and his wife, they, being suitable persons, will be allowed to retain it on habeas corpus afterwards brought by a pretended parent, especially where he is unfit for the child's custody, and where the evidence of identity is conflicting: Young v. The State, 15 Ind. 480.
[3] In the Matter of O'Neal, 3 Am. Law Rev. 578; State v. Bratton, 15 Am. Law Reg., N. S., 359. But in Johnson v. Terry, 34 Conn. 259, it was held that the neglect of the father in allowing his children to remain away for several years from his home, and in their mother's charge, but without the father's consent, did not constitute an emancipation of them: See Ex rel. Shaw v. Nacthwey, 43 Iowa, 653.
[4] Wishard v. Medaris, 34 Ind. 168.

let their residence be disclosed to their parents.[1] Where the custody of a child has been transferred to another just before the issuing of a writ of habeas corpus, the return is bad unless it discloses the reason for such change, for the object of transfer may have been to avoid the process of the court.[2]

§ 445. **How Far the Courts will Actively Interfere to Deliver the Custody of a Child.**—It is unnecessary to multiply authorities under this section, because one rule generally prevails throughout the United States, and that is substantially the one laid down by Lord Mansfield in Rex v. Delaval:[3] "That in cases of writs of habeas corpus directed to private persons to bring up infants, the court is bound *ex debito justitiæ*, to set the infant free from an improper restraint. But they are not bound to deliver the infant over to any particular person. This must be left to their discretion, according to the circumstances that shall appear before them."[4] That the order of the court is discretionary will be found in nearly all of the cases. If the infant is of the age of choice, the court will often advise and instruct him as to the choice he should make; but if he be under that age, or be, from mental incapacity, incapable of choosing, it will substitute its discretion for his choice.[5] And the court, if it see any ill purpose in the proceedings, will not only discharge the infant from illegal restraint, but will protect the child in returning,[6] as the court will never allow a child to depart from the court in injurious custody.[7] In one case where it appeared that the father and mother were living separate, with mutual criminations and recriminations, on habeas corpus proceedings instituted by the father to remove their infant children from the custody of the mother, then residing with her father, the court ordered the oldest boy, five years of age, to be delivered to the father, and the others, a girl one year old and a boy three and a half, to remain with the mother.[8]

---

[1] Dumain et Ux. v. Gwynne, 10 Allen, 270.

[2] Sears v. Dessar, 28 Ind. 472.

[3] 3 Burr, 1434.

[4] In the Matter of Waldron, 13 Johns. 417; Com. v. Addicks, 5 Binn. 520; S. C., 2 Serg. & R. 174; In re Stephens, Dudley (Ga.), 42; State v. Paine, 4 Humph., sec. 523, a case especially valuable for its fine collection of common-law cases cited by counsel: Com. v. Nutt, 1 Browne, 143, and other cases in the various states.

[5] Ex parte Schumpert, 6 Rich. 344.

[6] In the Matter of Kottman, 2 Hill (S. C.), 363; In the Matter of McDowle, 8 Johns. 328; Com. v. Briggs et al., 16 Pick. 203; Ex parte Williams, 11 S. C. 452; Com. v. Smith, 1 Brews. 547; Brinster v. Compton, 68 Ala. 299.

[7] State ex rel. Lynch v. Bratton, 15 Am. Law Reg., N. S., 359; In the Matter of McDowle, 8 Johns. 328; Ex parte Williams, 11 S. C. 452; Boyd v. Glass, 34 Ga. 253; Com. v. Smith, 1 Brews. 547; In re Mitchell, R. M. Charlt. 489; Brinster v. Compton, 68 Ala. 299.

[8] State v. Stigall, 2 Zab. 286. For case showing where the mother was permitted to retain possession of a

§ 446. **The Welfare of the Child is to be Considered** in this exercise of discretion on the part of the courts in determining to whom the custody of the infant shall be awarded, and they will look both to the present and future interests and good of the infant in the application of this first and cardinal rule.[1] It is truly said that this rule is the "pole star" by which the courts are guided in such cases. But this welfare depends upon so many and ever-varying circumstances that it is not subject to any definite rules. This is expressive of the general doctrine, and it would be idle to attempt to cite authorities for each modification or limitation of it, or exception to it. The domestic relations and the relative rights of parent and child are of almost sacred and inestimable value, but they are under the control and regulation of municipal laws, which may and must declare how far the rights and control of the parent shall extend over the child, how they shall be exercised, and where they shall terminate.[2]

The duty of arbitrating between the claims of rival parents, in view of the best interests of the children, is, says Chief Justice Beasley of the court of errors and appeals of New Jersey, "felt to be one of painful responsibility." This discretion, he says, "is, as far as practicable, to be regulated by settled rules and admitted principles. In the exercise of such a function, the circumstances of each case must, of necessity, become impor-

---

child, and held responsible for its maintenance, and the father indemnified from all liability for its support and maintenance, see Ex parte Schumpert, 6 Rich. 344

[1] In re Mitchell, R. M. Charlt. 489; Brinster v. Compton, 68 Ala. 299; Corrie v. Corrie, 4 N. W. Rep. 213; Garner v. Gordon, 41 Ind. 92; In re Bort, 25 Kan. 308; S. C., 20 Am. Law Reg., N. S., 493; U. S. v. Green, 3 Mason, 482; Matter of Heather Children, 50 Mich. 261; State v. King, 1 & 2 Ga. Dec. 93; Nickols v. Giles, 2 Root, 461; Ellis v. Jesup et Ux., 11 Bush, 403; People v. Wilcox. 22 Barb. 178; Rowe v. Rowe, 28 Mich. 353; Com. v. Barney, 4 Brews. 408; Ex rel. Shaw v. Nacthwey, 43 Iowa, 653; In re Poole, 2 McArthur, 583; State v. Kirkpatrick, 54 Iowa, 373; Bustamento v. Analla, 1 N. M. 255; House of Refuge v. Ryan, 37 Ohio St. 197; Kline v. Kline, 57 Iowa, 383; Janes v. Cleghorn, 63 Ga. 335; Damain et Ux. v. Gwynne, 10 Allen, 270; In the Matter of Pray, 60 How. Pr. 194; the excellent opinion of Mr. Justice Brewer, in Bullen's Petition, 28 Kan. 781; State v. Stigall, 2 Zab. 286; State v. Paine, 4 Humph. 523, with many citations of cases; Com. v. Addicks et Ux., 5 Binn. 520; S. C., 2 Serg. & R. 174; Cole v. Cole, 23 Iowa, 433; Drumb v. Keen et Ux., 47 Id. 435; People v. Erbert, 17 Abb. Pr. 395, and abstracts of cases in reporter's notes; Clark v. Bayer, 32 Ohio St. 299; Wand v. Wand, 14 Cal. 512; McShan v. McShan, 56 Miss. 413; Ex parte Schumpert, 6 Rich. 344; Ex parte Williams, 11 Id. 452; State v. Baird, 18 N. J. Eq. 194; In re Cuneen, 17 How. Pr. 516; Gishwiler et al. v. Dodez, 4 Ohio St. 615; People v. Kling, 6 Barb. 366; In re Waldron, 13 Johns. 417 State v. Smith, 6 Greenl. 400; In re Hansen, 1 Edm. Sel. Cas. 9. These cases have not all been cited to support the text. They contain illustrations of the application of the court's discretion in these cases, and will be found convenient in looking up authority on many other points treated in this chapter.

[2] Bennet v. Bennet, 2 Beas. 114.

tant elements entering into the grounds of decision. The character of the respective parents, the age, health, sex, and number of the children, and the pecuniary resources liable to contribution for their maintenance and education, are all considerations which should and must exert more or less influence over the judicial result."[1]

The words of Mr. Justice Graves of the supreme court of Michigan are *apropos:* "In contests of this kind, the opinion is now nearly universal that neither of the parties has any rights that can be allowed to seriously militate against the welfare of the child. The paramount consideration is what is really demanded by its best interests. It is doing no violence to what is taught by judicial experience to assume that the disputing parties will be more alive to the satisfaction of their own feelings and interests than to the true end of the inquisition; while the innocent subject of the contention is utterly unable to speak or act for itself, and is in danger of being lost sight of in the strife for its possession. No other occasion can call more loudly for judicial vigilance in reaching for the exact truth, and in putting aside with an unsparing hand the mere technicalities of procedure. The fate or interest of the child is not to depend on what the parties may see proper to state or to evade in their formal altercations, nor on any artificial rule of pleading. There should be full inquiry and an exhaustive examination on oath in order that the tribunal may have all the light practicable."[2]

§ 447. **Infant's Liberty of Choice.**—The courts in cases of conflicting claims for the custody of a minor child nearly always consult the wishes of the infant; and where the child has reached the age of discretion, it will often be allowed to make its own choice, although the person chosen is not one whom the court would voluntarily appoint. But this is no controlling legal right of the infant. It is not entitled to its absolute freedom from all custody, but an adult is. It is not the whim or caprice of the child which the courts respect, but its feelings, its attachments, its preferences, and its probable contentment; and it is a well-settled rule of law that whether the court will regard the preference of an infant depends upon the reasonableness of his wish, and the intelligence which he manifests.[3]

---

[1] State v. Baird, 21 N. J. Eq. 384.
[2] Corrie v. Corrie, 42 Mich. 509; S. C., 4 N. W. Rep. 213.
[3] State ex rel. Lynch v. Bratton, 15 Am. Law Reg., N. S., 359; In re Poole, 2 McArthur, 583; Ex rel. Shaw v. Nacthwey, 43 Iowa, 653; Commonwealth v. Hammond, 10 Pick. 274; In the Matter of Wollstonecraft, 4 Johns. Ch. 79; State v. Stigall, 2 Zab. 286; Ex parte Ralston, R. M. Charlt. 119; In the Matter of Hansen, 1 Edm. Sel. Cas. 9; Ellis v. Jesup et Ux., 11 Bush, 403; Gishwiler et al.

§ 448. **Mental Capacity, and not Age,** is the criterion in the United States for determining whether an infant be of sufficient judgment and discretion to choose for himself. The period of discretion and judgment of the child begins when it can reason sensibly, though as a child, in regard to its condition, its feelings, and its future welfare. This period begins with some children very early in life, and with others very late. When the infant shows sufficient intelligence and capacity to declare an election when under illegal restraint, and there be no objection to the person chosen, the court will, as said before, permit it to follow its own inclinations, otherwise the court will direct its choice or make the award on its own discretion.[1] In Wisconsin it is said that an infant over fourteen will, in every case, be permitted to choose for himself.[2] In People v. Porter,[3] Duer, J., said that in the case of an infant of tender years "it can only be discharged from the restraint of one person by giving it into the custody of another," and that this exception at common law—of not only freeing from illegal restraint, but of delivering those incapable of making a choice into custody—was more apparent than real, since in such cases "the questions of right of custody and of illegal restraint are so inseparably connected that in pronouncing judgment both must be determined; and it is only when the infant is not before the court, but is still in the possession of the person whose restraint is held to be illegal, that a positive order for its delivery is made." And such an order amounts to a discharge for the reason first stated.

When an infant has been discharged on habeas corpus from illegal restraint, his conduct is not to be considered absolutely unrestrained; and a judge in telling a minor, even of the age of choice, that he is free to go where he pleases, is not to be understood as leaving room for the misconstruction that he is not bound to obey his parents. So judges have sometimes thought

v. Dodez, 4 Ohio St. 615; Bennet v. Bennet, 2 Beas. 114; Ex parte Schumpert, 6 Rich. 344; State v. Baird, 18 N. J. Eq. 194; Bustamento v. Analla, 1 N. M. 255; People ex rel. v. Wehle v. Weissenbach, 6 N. Y. 385; In re Goodenough, 19 Wis. 274; State v. Richardson, 40 N. H. 272; State v. Banks, 25 Ind. 495; People v. Porter, 1 Duer, 709; Commonwealth v. Hamilton, 6 Mass. 272; State v. Scott et Ux., 30 N. H. 274; People v. Mercein, 8 Paige, 46; Armstrong v. Stone et Ux., 9 Gratt. 102; People v. Wilcox, 22 Barb. 178; Moore v. Christian, 56 Miss. 408.

[1] State v. Lynch, 15 Am. Law Reg., N. S., 359; Armstrong v. Stone et Ux., 9 Gratt. 102; Ellis v. Jesup et Ux., 11 Bush, 403; Rust v. Van Vacter, 9 W. Va. 600; Commonwealth v. Taylor, 3 Met. 72; State v. Richardson, 40 N. H. 272; State v. Banks, 25 Ind. 495; Ex parte Schumpert, 6 Rich. 344; In re Poole, 2 McArthur, 583.

[2] In re Goodenough, 19 Wis. 274.

[3] 1 Duer, 709.

it wiser and more prudent to express what would be implied by a simple order of discharge, and declare the one entitled to custody to take it.[1]

§ 449. **Parents' Right of Access, though not Entitled to Custody.**—While a court will often declare one parent or the other, or both, not entitled to the custody of their infant children, it will rarely fail to order that the parents shall have access to their children at all reasonable times and places. This is one of the powers of a court of equity, but it is often exercised by either courts of law or equity having jurisdiction of the subject on habeas corpus.[2] The children will also be permitted to visit their parents occasionally.[3] But these visits by either parent are not to be used for depriving the other of the children, either by persuasion or force. These orders permitting such visits, and the limitations upon them, all rest in the sound discretion of the court.[4]

§ 450. **Supersedeas, Appeal, Action, and Foreign Jurisdiction.**—A party wishing a *supersedeas* should first file his bill of exceptions, because until then he is not entitled to it. But in cases where irreparable injury may result from immediate execution of the judgment, a correct practice is, upon notice being given to the court that a bill of exceptions will be filed, to allow a reasonable time for this to be done before the judgment is carried into effect.[5] And it has been held erroneous, after a finding in favor of the mother and against the guardian, after an appeal has been perfected, for the judge to change the custody of the children from the guardian to the mother pending the appeal.[6] No action can be maintained by a parent to recover damages for the removal of his infant child so as to prevent the production of its body upon a habeas corpus, unless such parent has the right to its custody, and the child is capable of rendering services of value.[7] In proceedings for the recovery of infant children on habeas corpus it may appear on the return that they are in a foreign jurisdiction, but the respondent must show that he has no power of control over the children, or the court will not be deprived of jurisdiction, or the respondent excused from producing the bodies of the children; because the important

---

[1] Ex parte Williams, 11 Rich. 452; Moore v. Christian, 56 Miss. 408. See Moore v. Christian, 56 Miss. 408, in note to sec. 443.

[2] In the Matter of O'Neal, 3 Am. Law Rev. 578; State v. Baird, 18 N. J. Eq. 194; State v. Baird, 21 N. Y. Eq. 384; People v. Chegary, 18 Wend. 637; Commonwealth v. Smith, 1 Brew. 547; and see Wand v. Wand, 14 Cal. 512; Moak's notes in In re Andrews, 4 Eng. Rep. 261.

[3] People v. Chegary, 18 Wend. 637.

[4] State v. Baird, 18 N. J. Eq. 194.

[5] Lindsey v. Lindsey, 14 Ga. 657.

[6] Garner v. Gordon, 41 Ind. 92.

[7] Rising v. Dodge, 2 Duer, 42.

question is, Where is the power of control exercised?[1] A valid order made by a court of competent jurisdiction can not be obstructed, revoked, or changed by another court, in a collateral proceeding by habeas corpus, by ordering a child to be taken from the custody of an officer to whom it has been intrusted with instructions to deliver it to its guardian, and given to another, though a bond has been given.[2]

§ 451. **In Divorce Matters.**—The children may be committed to the care and custody of either the father or mother, and a decree to this effect may bind the parties *inter esse*, but it does not conclude the court as to the best interests of the children. So though such a decree has been made, it is the duty of a court whenever the possession and custody of minor children is sought by habeas corpus, to make such order for their care and custody as the best interests and welfare of the children may require. And in doing this, in such a case, the children may be taken from the custody of either parent, and committed to that of a third person.[3] The jurisdiction of the court in such matters is a sort of continuing jurisdiction, and on proper application may be invoked to modify orders originally made in respect to the custody of children whenever the nature of the case requires it.[4] And where the custody of children, in a decree for divorce, has been awarded to either parent by a court of competent jurisdiction, another court, while such decree remains in force, can not, as between the parties to the decree, legally interfere with the custody as decreed, either by habeas corpus or letters of guardianship.[5] On habeas corpus by a parent to recover the custody of his infant child, when his legal right to such custody has before been declared by a decree in an action for divorce, a copy of the decree need not be filed with the petition.[6]

§ 452. **Doctrines in Chancery.**—The writ of habeas corpus is a common-law writ, and confers no jurisdiction to appoint guardians of infants, to superintend their education, and to instruct them in correct habits of life. A court of chancery is the appropriate tribunal for such a purpose.[7] Proceedings on

---

[1] Rivers v. Mitchell, 57 Iowa, 193; S. C., 13 Rep. 106; 10 N. W. Rep. 626; see In the Matter of Jackson, 15 Mich. 417.

[2] Justice MacArthur in In re Poole, 2 MacArthur, 583.

[3] Shaw v. McHenry, Judge, etc., 2 N. W. Rep. 1096.

[4] In the Matter of Bort, 25 Kan. 308; S. C., 20 Am. L. Reg., N. S. 493.

[5] Hoffman v. Hoffman, 15 Ohio St. 427.

[6] Id.

[7] Sears v. Dessar, 28 Ind. 472. Other cases relating to the custody of children and provisions for them: Burritt v. Burritt, 29 Barb. 124; Darnall v. Mullikin et al., 8 Tanner (Ind.), 152; Bush v. Bush, 37 Ind. 164.

habeas corpus to recover the custody of infants are regarded as actions at law,[1] but we have seen the plenitude of power which the courts of law have exercised in these cases respecting the custody of infants; an exercise of power, Hurd says, which it might be difficult to completely defend. It may, however, be explained by recognizing the fact that in such cases the courts have sometimes exercised a degree of equity jurisdiction; but it is far short of the power exercised by a court in equity sitting as the representative of the sovereign in the character of *parens patriæ*. We have more than once shown that the courts of law and the courts of equity, in the exercise of their respective jurisdictions under the writ of habeas corpus, possess exactly the same power and discretion. So, the jurisdiction of the courts of chancery, as *parens patriæ*, not being entirely germane to our general subject, we shall simply cite a few cases relating to that well-known power;[2] and observe that the authority of the state, as *parens patriæ*, to assume the guardianship and education of neglected homeless children as well as neglected orphans, is unquestioned,[3] and she will not permit the judgment of her tribunals in such cases to be disregarded or set aside without her consent.[4] But a court should not assume the wardship of a child with parents living unless it is clear that the parent labors under a moral or natural disability sufficient to disqualify him in the performance of his duties to his offspring.[5] Where a mother sues out a writ of habeas corpus to recover children in the custody of their father, he may bring them into court, and surrender them to the custody of the court as *parens patriæ*, pending the litigation. And where the habeas corpus proceedings, by mutual consent, have been abandoned, and an order entered to that effect, an additional clause, not contained in the written consent, further directing that the children named in the writ, shall be remanded to the custody of the father, the respondent, does not vitiate the order. The court, by this clause, simply surrenders its control as *parens patriæ*, and restores it to the father, whose right has been disturbed by the process.[6]

[1] Kline v. Kline, 57 Iowa, 386.
[2] People ex rel. Tappan v. Porter, 1 Duer, 709; People v. Mercein, 8 Paige, 46; State v. King, 1 and 2 Ga. 93; Striplin v. Ware, 36 Ala. 87; In the Matter of Wollstonecraft, 4 Johns. Ch. 80; People v. Olmstead, 27 Barb. 9; People v. Wilcox, 22 Id. 178; State v. Baird, 21 N. J. Eq. 384.
[3] House of Refuge v. Ryan, 37 Ohio St. 197.
[4] Com. v. Reed, 59 Pa. St. 425.
[5] Hunt v. Hunt, 4 Iowa, 216.
[6] Matter of Viele, 44 How. Pr. 14.

CHAPTER XXXII.

CUSTODY OF ILLEGITIMATE CHILDREN.

§ 453. Views of the English Courts.
§ 454. Doctrine in the United States.

§ 453. **In England,** the better opinion on this question seems to be that the putative father of a bastard child has no right to its custody,[1] and that the mother, as against every one else, has the right to its custody, where she is not unworthy of the trust.[2] And, in true accordance with the spirit of the writ of habeas corpus, the court will simply deliver the child from undue or illegal restraint, when such is imposed upon it.[3] If the child be under the age of discretion, the courts will deliver it to the proper custodian, the mother, when she is a proper and suitable person;[4] or, if she be not a worthy trustee, the infant may, in the court's discretion, be delivered to another person.[5] If the child be of the age of discretion, it will be allowed to choose for itself.[6] Although the courts have restored an illegitimate child to its mother on habeas corpus, where the child has been taken from the mother by force, the cases seem consistent enough when the fact is recognized that the child in such case was under the age of discretion. So it must have been restored under an exercise of discretion, which all courts have in such cases, and not simply by virtue of the writ of habeas corpus.

§ 454. **In the United States,** the doctrine that the putative father of an illegitimate child has no right to its custody as against the mother, but that the mother, when a proper person, does have the right to the child's custody, is well settled

---

[1] King v. Soper, 5 T. R. 278; King v. Nagapen, 2 Notes of Cases at Madras, 253; Ex parte Knee, 1 Bos. & Pul. 148; see Strangeways v. Robinson, 4 Taunt. 497.

[2] See cases just cited.

[3] In re Lloyd, 3 Man. & G. 547.

[4] King v. Nagapen, 2 Notes of Cases at Madras, 253; Ex parte Knee, 1 Bos. & Pul. 148.

[5] The same principles apply here as to the children born in lawful wedlock. See English doctrine in a preceding chapter.

[6] In re Lloyd, 3 Man. & G. 547; S. C., 4 Scott's N. R. 200; Rex v. Moseley, 5 East, 223; King v. Hopkins, 7 Id. 578; King v. Soper, 5 T. R. 278.

by judicial decision.¹ This is expressive of the general doctrine, but it is subject, of course, to certain limitations. The father is entitled to the custody of his illegitimate child over every other person except the mother.² But if the putative father wrongfully and fraudulently obtains possession of such a child, and retains such possession until obliged to relinquish it by the court, on habeas corpus, it has been held that an action for false imprisonment will lie, in the name of the child.³ The right of the mother to the custody of illegitimate infant children is not so absolute as to prevent a court from interfering to take the infant from the custody of its mother, under special circumstances of ill treatment. The humanity of courts is exercised in these cases to prevent ill usage, etc., as it is in the case of legitimate children.⁴ The infant's liberty of choice, maturity of judgment, welfare of the infant, etc., are governed by the same rules as are laid down in the chapter concerning legitimate children, when these matters arise. Except as otherwise provided by statute, the mother is bound to maintain her illegitimate child.⁵ An officer authorized to bind out minors whose parents are unable to support them, etc., can not apprentice an illegitimate child without the consent of the mother, unless it be shown that she is unable to support her child, or some other legal reason be shown.⁶

Nor can another guardian be appointed for such child by a probate court without notice to the mother of the application for such appointment.⁷ The mother may give her illegitimate child away to keep, etc., without forfeiting her right to reclaim its custody at her pleasure. She may even marry after the gift, yet she and her husband may then obtain the child's custody during its infancy.⁸ Although the mother, in her life-time, may intrust her illegitimate child to a certain person, there to remain until its majority, the guardian of such child, after the mother's death, is, it has been held in Indiana, entitled to the orphan's

---

¹ Bustamento v. Analla, 1 N. M. 255; People v. Mitchell et al., 44 Barb. 245; Robalina v. Armstrong, 15 Id. 247; In the Matter of Doyle, 1 Clarke Ch. 154; Dalton v. The State, 6 Blackf. 357; People v. Kling, 6 Barb. 366; People v. Landt, 2 Johns. 374; Alfred v. McKay, 36 Ga. 440; People v. Cooper, 8 How. Pr. 288.

² People v. Cooper, 8 How. Pr. 288; In the Matter of Doyle, 1 Clarke Ch. 154, citing 2 Kent's Com. 178.

³ Robalina v. Armstrong, 15 Barb. 247.

⁴ People v. Landt, 2 Johns. 374.
⁵ People v. Kling, 6 Barb. 366.
⁶ Alfred v. McKay, 36 Ga. 440; see Copeland v. The State, 60 Ind. 394.
⁷ Dalton v. The State, 6 Blackf. 357. See Bustamento v. Analla, 1 N. M. 255.
⁸ Bustamento v. Analla, 1 N. M. 255. As to compromise of putative father with the officers of a town having charge of the support of illegitimate children, see People v. Mitchell, 44 Barb. 245.

§ 454.   CUSTODY OF ILLEGITIMATE CHILDREN.   591

custody, and it will be awarded to him after a hearing on habeas corpus. This, however, is under a mandatory statute relating to guardians.[1] In Texas, after an illegitimate child reaches the age of seven years, the father has an equal claim with the mother to its guardianship.[2] A gift, in consideration of the release of a debt, made many years previous by a servant to her master of her illegitimate child, of which he was the father, that he might maintain and educate such child "as a legitimate father," gives him no right to treat the child as a peon; and in such case, where the mother sues out a writ of habeas corpus to obtain such minor child illegally held as a peon or servant by a stranger, the rejection of evidence of the plaintiff's unfitness to have the custody of such child has been held not error as against the defendant, for the reason that it is not material to the issue between the parties. It is also held that the testimony of the child in such a case, that she is willing to remain in the defendant's service, is not satisfactory evidence.[3]

[1] Johns v. Emmert, 62 Ind. 533.
[2] Byrne v. Love, 14 Tex. 81.
[3] Bustamento v. Analla, 1 N. M. 255.

CHAPTER XXXIII.

MASTER AND APPRENTICE.

§ 455. Which One may Obtain the Writ.
§ 456. Concerning the Indentures.

§ 455. **Which One may Obtain the Writ.**—We have seen that the writ of habeas corpus may issue without the privity of a minor child, on the application of one entitled to the custody, because there is an authority shown. This rule applies more particularly to the relations of parent and child and guardian and ward, the guardian standing, of course, in *loco parentis*. But it does not apply, in an unlimited sense, to the relation of master and apprentice. We believe the cases will support this view: Where the apprentice is under such a restraint as to prevent him from performing his duties to his master, the master may set the powers of a court in motion by means of habeas corpus, and without the consent of the apprentice, to have him brought before the court to ascertain this fact, which, if claimed to exist, should be set up in the petition. The court can then relieve the apprentice from his illegal restraint, and he can go with his master and perform his services, if he wishes. But where the evident purpose of the master is to recover the custody and services of his apprentice, and particularly where it appears that the apprentice does not wish to return to such service, the writ ought not to issue at all at the instance of the master. The relation of master and apprentice is a mere business relation between the parties, and for any bad faith on the part of the apprentice, the master has his action on the bond. For a court, therefore, to issue a writ of habeas corpus, at the instance of the master to recover his apprentice, except where the apprentice is willing to return to him, but is restrained from so doing, would be very much like enforcing a specific performance for personal services. Further, specific performance must be decreed in a court of equity, and as such a court will not enforce an obligation of this kind, there is no relief in this way, either in law or equity. In short, the writ of habeas corpus can not be converted into an action for the specific performance of a contract.

Again, in the few cases where the writ has been granted to enable the master to recover the custody of his apprentice, the writ has been converted into a species of "personal replevin." Neither can this use of the writ be defended upon principle, as the object of the writ of habeas corpus is simply to secure personal liberty. But the writ may always issue upon the application of the apprentice, or with his consent, if he be under illegal restraint; because in his case the true object of the writ, the security of personal liberty, is subserved. As to the effect of the issuance of the writ, however, upon the apprentice, it makes no difference whether it issues at the instance of the master or the apprentice, because on the hearing it will be determined whether or not the apprentice is under any illegal restraint. If so, he is set at liberty, and in either case he may go where he chooses, as a court will not go so far as to order him into the custody of his master.[1]

§ 456. **Concerning the Indentures.**—An infant can not be bound as an apprentice, unless he is a party to and executes the deed or indenture. And where the indentures are not conformable to the statute, they are voidable by the apprentice only, and not by any other person.[2] But the indentures of apprenticeship may be vacated by the consent of all the parties, on the ground "that contracts may be dissolved by the consent of the parties."[3] And an infant may be, by the writ of habeas corpus, discharged from his indentures, on account of any illegality or

---

[1] King v. Reynolds, 6 T. R. 497; King v. Edwards, 7 Id. 745; Lea v. White, 4 Sneed, 24; Ex parte Grocot, 2 App. from Mag. to K. B. 594; Rex v. Fenwick, 3 Smith, 369; State v. Brearly and Berryman, 2 South. 555; In the Matter of McDowles, 8 Johns. 328; Commonwealth v. Robinson, 1 Serg. & R. 352; Graham v. Graham, Id. 330; Fowler v. Hollenbeck, 9 Barb. 309; Musgrove v. Kornegay et al., 7 Jones, 71; People v. Gates, 39 How. Pr. 74; Commonwealth v. Hamilton, 6 Mass. 272; Commonwealth v. Harrison, 11 Id. 63; People v. Weissenbach et al., 60 N. Y. 385; Cannon v. Stuart, 3 Houst. 223; Ballenger v. McLain, 54 Ga. 159; People v. Hoster, 14 Abb. Pr., N. S., 414; Matter of Barre, Id. 426; People v. Pillow, 1 Sanc. 672. See Commonwealth v. Beck, 1 Browne, 277; In re Goodenough, 19 Wis. 274, where it seems to be held that the court will deliver a minor into the custody of his master, if the indentures are valid, on the ground that the law supposes the master to have the right to the custody of his apprentice, that so situated he is under no restraint, and that to deliver the apprentice into the master's custody is to restore him to that liberty which is established by law—and that where the indentures are void, the apprentice will be delivered to his parents' custody if under fourteen years of age and they are not unsuitable persons for the trust.

[2] In the Matter of McDowles, 8 Johns. 328; Fowler v. Hollenbeck, 9 Barb. 309; People v. Gates, 39 How. Pr. 74; People v. Weissenbach, 60 N. Y. 385.

[3] Graham v. Graham, 1 Serg. & R. 330.

invalidity in the binding.¹ Notwithstanding the early practice in Pennsylvania of leaving doubtful issues of fact, in indentures of apprenticeship, to be tried by a jury,² it has lately been decided in New York that the constitutional right of trial by jury and due process of law does not extend to conflicting claims for the custody of children in such cases.³

[1] Cannon v. Stuart, 3 Houst. 223; Musgrove v. Kornegay, 7 Jones, 71; In the Matter of Goodenough, 19 Wis. 274; Com. v. Hamilton, 6 Mass. 272; Ballenger v. McLain, 54 Ga. 159; Comas v. Reddish, 35 Id. 236; People v. Gates, 39 How. Pr. 74; People v. Weissenbach, 60 N. Y. 385. See People v. Hoster, 14 Abb. Pr., N. S., 414; In the Matter of Barre, Id. 426.

[2] Graham v. Graham, 1 Serg. & R. 330.

[3] Matter of Donohue, 1 Abb. N. C. 1.

CHAPTER XXXIV.
GUARDIAN AND WARD.

§ 457. Guardian may have the Writ of Habeas Corpus to Bring up his Ward.

§ 457. **Guardian may Have the Writ of Habeas Corpus to Bring up his Ward** where he is under restraint; but it is a well-settled proposition of law that the right of guardianship will not be tried on habeas corpus;[1] and the discretion of the court must be exercised in awarding the custody of the ward to his guardian. The guardian may have his ward released from illegal restraint on habeas corpus, but he can not, under this writ, claim his custody, or rather ask that the writ be used as a means for transferring the custody of the ward to himself. These cases, so far as their nature will permit, are disposed of just the same as the conflicting claims to the custody of legitimate children which has been disposed of in a preceding chapter; and what we said there relative to how far the courts would interfere to deliver the custody of a child, the consideration of the child's welfare, its liberty of choice, and the test of its mental caliber, etc., applies in these cases. The object of the writ of habeas corpus is to secure personal liberty, and not to enforce any of the domestic relations. So, when freed from illegal restraint, the court will permit an infant, if it have sufficient discretion to make a free and unbiased choice, to go where it pleases.[2] If not competent to judge for itself, the court will exercise its discretion, for the best welfare of the child, in fixing its custody, though the legal or natural rights of parents be set

---

[1] King v. Smith, 7 Mod. 234; S. C., Ld. Hardwicke's Rep. 149, and 2 Stra. 967; Villareal v. Mellish, 2 Swans. 538, and cases cited in reporter's note; late case of Andrews, L. R., 8 Q. B., 153, and cases cited; State v. Cheeseman, 2 South. 445; Commonwealth v. Smith, 1 Brews. 547; Matter of Wollstonecraft, 4 Johns. Ch. 79; State v. Glover, 1 Harr. (N. J.) 419; Commonwealth v. Barney, 4 Brews. 408; Mathews v. Wade et ux., 2 W. Va. 464; Commonwealth v. Addicks et ux., 5 Binn. 520; S. C., 2 Serg. & R. 174; Commonwealth v. Hammond, 10 Pick. 274; Ferguson v. Ferguson et al., 36 Mo. 197; The People v. Mercein, 8 Paige, 46; In re Poole, 2 MacArthur, 583; McConologue's Case, 107 Mass. 171.

[2] Ex parte Ralston, R. M. Charlt. 119.

aside or held in abeyance.[1] Where the grandmother, having a child under seven, was unable to properly maintain and educate her, the court, on habeas corpus, awarded its custody to its guardian, the child being too young to make a choice, for better care and education.[2] In contests between the mother of minor children and their guardian, it has been said that the wishes of the parties should be placed out of view and the best interests of the children considered.[3] In such a case the court will often favor the mother's right of custody until the period arrives when it is proper that the testamentary guardian take possession of the minors for the purpose of their education, etc.[4] A testamentary guardian has the legal right to the custody and possession of his wards, but this, without being impaired, may be controlled in the interests of the child.[5] In Connecticut it has been held that the right of the mother as natural guardian to the custody of her minor children after the father's death is inferior to the right of a guardian appointed by probate;[6] and in New York, that the appointment of a guardian, made by a surrogate, is to be deemed valid until reversed, and that it can not be assailed collaterally by habeas corpus.[7]

The custody of a guardian appointed by a surrogate constitutes no illegal restraint or imprisonment merely because the guardian refuses to deliver the child to its mother.[8] To give a court jurisdiction on a writ of habeas corpus the ward must be restrained of his liberty; and where the mother took her child away from its testamentary guardian by force, but where the child remained with its mother willingly, and the welfare of the child would be promoted by allowing it to remain, the court on a habeas corpus refused to restore the ward, although it appeared the guardian was in every way fitted for his trust.[9] It may be here remarked that a court of equity may take a minor child from a guardian appointed by the surrogate on the death of its father, and deliver it to the mother when the child's interests demand it; but this is not done on habeas corpus.[10] The courts of one state will recognize the foreign appointment of a guardian in another, as creating the relation of guardian and ward between the parties in the first-named state, subject, of course, to the laws of said first-named state, as to any exercise

---

[1] Com. v. Barney, 4 Brews. 408.
[2] Ex parte Ralston, R. M. Charlt. 119.
[3] Garner v. Gordon, 41 Ind. 92.
[4] Payne v. Payne, 39 Ga. 174.
[5] Ward v. Roper, 7 Humph. 80.
[6] Macready v. Wilcox, 33 Conn. 321.
[7] People v. Wilcox, 22 Barb. 178.
[8] Id.
[9] Foster et Ux. v. Alston, 6 How. (Miss.) 406.
[10] Wilcox v. Wilcox, 14 N. Y. 575.

§ 457.   GUARDIAN AND WARD.   597

of power by virtue of such relation, either as to the person or property of the ward. But when a foreign guardian in said first-named state, or any one else, attempts to exercise any restraint over the person of any one within the borders of such state, the writ of habeas corpus may be used to inquire into such restraint. And on the return, the whole subject of guardianship may be fully investigated and the ward disposed of according to the principles of law above set forth, in the discretion of the court. A guardian, however, holding a ward's person is not guilty of false imprisonment, and changes made in the ward's residence from one state to another are regarded with suspicion by courts of chancery, lest the ward be imposed upon.[1] A return setting up a will as authority for restraint is bad on demurrer, if it contain no copy of the will.[2] Private parties to a habeas corpus can not, by any private agreement, bargain away the rights of the infant or ward.[3] In Michigan, guardianship of a minor's estate gives no right to the custody of its person, and a guardian can not have a habeas corpus as a matter of right to recover the custody of his wards there under fourteen years of age, where it does not clearly appear that their change of custody would be for their interest and welfare.[4]

[1] Townsend v. Kendall, 4 Minn. 412; see In the Matter of Jackson, 15 Mich. 417.
[2] Shaw v. Smith, 8 Tanner (Ind.), 485.
[3] Com. v. Reed, 59 Pa. St. 425.
[4] Matter of the Heather Children, 50 Mich. 261.

CHAPTER XXXV.

PARDONS.

§ 458. Nature and Acceptance of Pardons.

§ 458. **Nature and Acceptance of Pardons.**—Questions involving the nature of pardons sometimes arise in habeas corpus proceedings. Lord Coke has said that a pardon is a work of mercy whereby the king forgives crimes.[1] It is frequently conditional, as he may extend his mercy upon what terms he pleases, and annex to his bounty a condition precedent or subsequent, on the performance of which the validity of the pardon will depend.[2] If the felon does not perform the condition of the pardon, it will be altogether void; and he may be brought to the bar and remanded to suffer the punishment to which he was originally sentenced.[3] If the condition upon which alone the pardon was granted be void, the pardon must also be void. If the condition were lawful, but the prisoner did not assent to it, he can not have the benefit of the pardon; or if, having assented to it, his assent be revocable, he must be considered to have retracted it by an application for habeas corpus to be set at liberty, in which case he is equally unable to avail himself of the pardon.[4] The convict can not accept the condition and then contend on habeas corpus proceedings that the pardon is absolute and the condition void.

---

[1] 3 Inst. 233.

[2] Co. Lit. b, 274, 276; 2 Hawk. P. C., c. 37, sec. 45; 4 Bla. Com. 401; Ex parte Wells, 18 How. 307, where sentence of death may be commuted into imprisonment for life; State v. Smith, 1 Bailey, 283; S. C., 19 Am. Dec. 679, that offender shall leave the state and never return; State v. Chancellor, 1 Strobh. 347; In re Greathouse, 4 Saw. 487, compliance with proclamation of the president of December 8, 1863; Ex parte Marks, Sup. Ct. Cal., opinion filed July 24, 1883.

[3] Bac. Abr., Pardon, E; Ex parte Wells, 18 How. 307; Ex parte Marks, Sup. Ct. Cal., opinion filed July 24, 1883; State v. Chancellor, 1 Strobh. 347; State v. Smith, 1 Bailey, 283; S. C., 19 Am. Dec. 679. And he may be remitted to his former sentence, though it extend to the taking of his life: See cases last cited; Flavell's Case, 8 Watts & S. 197; Addington's Case, 2 Bailey, 516; People v. Potter, 1 Park. Cr. 47; United States v. Wilson, 7 Pet. 150.

[4] Canadian Prisoners' Case, 5 Mee. & W. 32; S. C., 9 Ad. & El. 731, and 36 Eng. Com. L. 254; Ex parte Marks, Sup. Ct. Cal., opinion filed July 24, 1883.

§ 458. PARDONS.

In Ex parte Wells[1] it was said: "As to the suggestion that conditional pardons can not be considered as being voluntarily accepted by convicts so as to be binding upon them, because they are made whilst under *duress per minas* and duress of imprisonment, it is only necessary to remark that neither applies to this case, as the petitioner was legally in prison. 'If a man be legally imprisoned, and either to procure his discharge, or on any other fair account, seal a bond or deed, this is not duress or imprisonment, and he is not at liberty to avoid it. And a man condemned to be hanged can not be permitted to escape the punishment altogether by pleading that he had accepted his life by *duress per minas.*' And if it be further urged, as it was in the argument of this case, that no man can make himself a slave for life by convention, the answer is, that the petitioner had forfeited his life for crime, and had no liberty to part with." A prisoner confined under a legal sentence can voluntarily accept a conditional pardon,[2] but he can not be forced to accept it for his own benefit, as he may prefer the penalty of the offense. It has been held that one under sentence of a United States circuit court, and who has been pardoned conditionally for his offense, but who has refused to accept it, though the pardon remained unrevoked and ready for his acceptance at any moment he saw fit to avail himself of it, he having notice of it, is in no condition to invoke a United States circuit judge, on habeas corpus, to set aside the sentence of the court on the ground that the law under which such sentence was passed was repealed before judgment was pronounced upon him. The pardon, it was said, made him free, and he was under no restraint except that caused by his own voluntary act.[3] A pardon in one respect is unlike a commission; as under the constitution and laws of the United States it must be regarded as a deed, of which delivery is an essential element of validity, and until a pardon is delivered it may be revoked.[4] A pardoned convict can not be held in confinement to compel payment of costs adjudged against him, but when so held will be released on habeas corpus.[5]

[1] 18 How. 307.
[2] In re Greathouse, 4 Saw. 487.
[3] In re Callicot, 8 Blatchf. 89.
[4] In the Matter of Du Puy, 3 Ben. 307.
[5] Ex parte Gregory, 56 Miss. 164.

CHAPTER XXXVI.

FOREIGN EXTRADITION.

PART I.—EXTRADITION TO THE UNITED STATES.

§ 459. The Demand.
§ 460. Application for a Habeas Corpus.
§ 461. Illegal Extradition.
§ 462. Can the Surrendered Fugitive be Tried for an Offense other than the Extradition Crime?

PART II.—EXTRADITION FROM THE UNITED STATES.

§ 463. Executive Functions.
§ 464. Judicial Functions—Issuance of Habeas Corpus.
§ 465. Reviewing Decision of Commissioner on Habeas Corpus.
§ 466. Of the Complaint, Statement of Offense, Authentication of Documents, etc.
§ 467. Checks of Legal Functions upon Each Other.
§ 468. Conflict between State and Federal Authority.

PART I.—EXTRADITION TO THE UNITED STATES.

§ 459. **The Demand.**—The subject of extradition would fill a volume; and in fact Mr. Spear has written a volume upon it. The limits of this work will confine our treatment of it to those questions principally which have arisen under habeas-corpus proceedings. The direct object of an extradition treaty between two nations, says the learned author above mentioned, is to secure to each of the parties the right to demand the surrender of a fugitive criminal upon the terms and for the purpose specified in the treaty, and consequently to establish a corresponding obligation to make the surrender. Sovereign nations have the right to deliver up such fugitives to each other without any treaty stipulations to this effect; yet the right of positive demand, implying the obligation of delivery, results only from a treaty.[1]

Unless otherwise specially provided for by statute, the general principle in respect to all demands is that they must proceed from the supreme political authority of the demanding state.[2] As to all intercourse with foreign nations this authority

---

[1] Spear on Extradition, 194.   [2] 7 Opin. Att. Gen. 6.

in the United States is by the constitution vested in the president. Hence every requisition upon a foreign government for the delivery of a fugitive criminal must, in the absence of a stipulation otherwise, be made by him, usually through the secretary of state, or by a foreign minister, or other agent authorized by him to make it. Some of the treaties of the United States, however, contain special stipulations on this point.[1] The object to be gained in actually procuring extradition is to bring the case within the treaty and within the operation of the laws of the foreign government for its execution. Hence the procedure in every demand by the United States should be adapted to the laws of the country on which the demand is made.[2]

§ 460. **Application for a Habeas Corpus.**—When the case has been brought within the terms of the treaty, and the fugitive criminal is within the domain of his own government, he may, if he considers himself in custody in violation of a treaty of the United States, apply to the federal tribunals for a writ of habeas corpus. This the federal judges or federal courts can grant under sections 751 and 753 of the United States revised statutes, acting, of course, within their respective jurisdictions. There can hardly be any doubt that section 753 of the United States revised statutes covers the case of a person extradited to the United States under the provisions of a treaty, and thereafter held as a prisoner in violation of such treaty. Upon the hearing of the case the court or judge is to determine whether the prisoner's restraint violates any provision of a treaty, either express or implied, and if this is found to be true, he will be discharged. Where fugitive criminals have been surrendered to the United States charged with offenses against state authority, and delivered up to that authority, and are by the state dealt with in a way that violates the treaty, the federal tribunals will exercise their now unquestioned power to supply a corrective remedy by means of the writ of habeas corpus.

§ 461. **Illegal Extradition.**—An application for a writ of habeas corpus has been refused by a federal court to a person charged with forgery and larceny in Illinois, extradited from Peru, with which country the United States has an extradition treaty covering these crimes, and being in custody under legal warrants, although the prisoner alleged that he was removed from Peru under proceedings not in conformity with the treaty. The writ was refused, because if granted the prisoner could not

[1] Spear on Extradition, 196.   [2] Id., 199.

be discharged from custody. His remedy, it was said, was by plea to the indictments.[1]

An arrest procured by fraud or trick is illegal. Where a party has not in fact been guilty of a crime, a proceeding founded on the allegation that it was committed, and which is a mere device to enable an arrest, is an abuse of process, and the arrest can not be sustained. The relator was indicted in New York on a charge of burglary in the third degree, and forcibly seized in France and brought back to New York under the form of the extradition treaty. Immediately on his arrival he was arrested there in several civil actions, at the suit of a number of creditors, for fraud in the purchase of goods there prior to his going to France, and was also arrested on a bench warrant by the sheriff of New York on indictment for the crime of burglary in the third degree, and was imprisoned for want of bail. The relator's extradition had ostensibly been for the crime of burglary. Under the treaty of February 24, 1845, between the United States and France, the common-law offense of burglary is recognized as such by both governments; but the crime of burglary in the third degree, under the statutes of New York, is unknown to the common law. There is no provision in the treaty mentioned concerning it, and no power to demand the extradition of a fugitive from one government to the other for such a crime. On habeas corpus and *certiorari*, before Mr. Justice Fancher, of the New York supreme court of appeals, the whole proceeding was pronounced illegal and unauthorized, and it was held that the creditors who had procured and caused to be served the orders of arrest were responsible for the seizure of the relator on French soil and for his extradition to the United

---

[1] Ex parte Ker, 16 Rep. 580 (U. S. C. C., Northern Dist. Ill., Oct. 8, 1883.) Ker was forcibly kidnaped from Peru, without any regard to treaty stipulations, and forcibly brought back to Cook county, Ill., and delivered to the sheriff by whom the writs of *capias* from the criminal court were served on him, and on which he was held in custody. It was claimed that the criminal court never acquired jurisdiction of his person, and that the process, though regular, was not under the circumstances due process of law. Mr. Justice Drummond said he deprecated this act without authority of law, as an outrage upon personal rights and personal liberty, but could not consider that this private wrong done in taking possession of the person of the defendant, to be returned to Illinois, vitiated and destroyed the process issued from a competent court for the offenses charged against the defendant so as to prevent his arrest; because while in Peru the relator was not under the protection of the laws of the United States, but of the laws of Peru, and if he was taken contrary to the provisions of the treaty between the two countries, he was taken in violation of the laws of Peru, and if the act so done was against the laws of Peru, for that violation the party had his remedy under the laws of Peru, enforceable here or elsewhere, and not, properly speaking, under the laws of the United States.

States—an abuse of process which required the court to set aside the arrest. The fact, however, that the prisoner had been forcibly brought within the jurisdiction of the courts was held to be no ground for discharging him in a criminal matter, and for which he was not extradited. It was said that the extradition treaty does not apply in such a case. So the prisoner was remanded on the bench warrant served by the sheriff, charging him with burglary in the third degree.[1] But in England, where the applicant for a habeas corpus was accused of committing forgery in the United States, he was arrested on board of a steamer at Queenstown harbor by an Irish police officer without any warrant, brought before a magistrate there, and detained in prison under the magistrate's warrant. It was held that the arrest of the offender, who might be extradited, would be supported though no warrant for his arrest had been issued by a local magistrate.[2] The international extradition of fugitives from justice is a duty of comity, not of strict right, and it is the settled policy of the United States not to make such extradition except in virtue of express stipulations to that effect. Hence the United States ought not to ask for extradition in any case as an act of mere comity. Larceny is not included in the causes of extradition stipulated as between Great Britain and the United States, and for this crime, therefore, and others not enumerated in the treaty, neither government can claim the extradition of fugitives from justice taking refuge in the dominions of the other.[3]

§ 462. **Can the Surrendered Fugitive be Tried for an Offense Other than the Extradition Crime?**—The authorities on this question are in conflict, but the doctrine mostly favored is that the trial of the offender is impliedly prohibited for any other offense than that for which he has been surrendered without first affording him an opportunity to return. This is the view taken by the supreme court of appeals of Kentucky upon a review of the decision made in the lower court in the case of Hawes, who stood indicted in the Kenton criminal court of that state for uttering forged paper, for embezzlement, and also upon four separate and distinct charges of forgery. He was found to be a resident of Canada, and in February, 1877, was demanded by the president of the United States, and surrendered by the Canadian authorities to answer three of said

---

[1] In the Matter of Lagrave, 45 How. Pr. 301; S. C., 14 Abb. Pr., N. S., 333.

[2] Reg. v. Weil, 15 Rep. 412 (1883).

[3] 6 Opin. Att. Gen. Cushing, 85; Adriance et al. v. Lagrave, 59 N. Y. 110.

charges of forgery. Hawes was acquitted of all the charges, but the authorities of Kenton county attempted to have him tried upon the indictment for embezzlement. The court below refused to try Hawes for any of the offenses for which he stood indicted, except for the three charges of forgery mentioned in the warrant of extradition, and granted a motion to set aside the returns of the sheriff on the various bench warrants upon which the defendant had been arrested, and released him from custody. The order appealed from was approved and affirmed in the appellate court.[1] So it was held in the supreme court of New York, on appeals from orders denying motions to set aside orders of arrest, that when a fugitive from justice is surrendered under an extradition treaty, it is for the sole and single purpose of being tried for the crime mentioned in the proceedings taken against him, and for none other. As to all other matters, he is, it was said, entitled to the protection of the laws of the country surrendering, so far as his personal liberty would have been secured by them, in case no removal of his person had been made. The prisoner is entitled to return to the country from which he was taken after the purposes of justice are satisfied.[2] This is the view of Mr. Justice Hoffman, of the district court of California, who admits, however, that this prohibition, if rigorously applied, might often defeat justice. "If, for example, the surrender be for an attempt to commit murder, and after surrender the person assaulted should die. Or if, supposing larceny to be an extradition crime, the fugitive should be surrendered for robbery or burglary, and on examination of the proofs they should be found insufficient to show the force in the one case, and the effraction of the premises in the other, or if he should be surrendered for larceny and the offense should turn out to be embezzlement, or *vice versa*, in these and similar cases the application of the rule would work a failure of justice." But his honor suggests that it would not be difficult to provide

---

[1] Commonwealth v. Hawes, 13 Ky. (Bush), 697. Found, also, in 17 Alb. L. J. 325, and Spear on Extradition, 138. Lindsay, C. J., alluded to U. S. v. Caldwell, 8 Blatchf. 131, and U. S. v. Lawrence, 13 Id. 295, the doctrines of which have been sanctioned in England, but showed that the rule in the United States is different from that which prevails in England, because the governments are differently organized. The treaty, he said, under which the alleged immunity was asserted, being part of the supreme law, the court had the power, and it was its duty, if the claim was well founded, to secure to him its full benefit.

[2] Bacharach v. Lagrave, 1 Hun (N. Y.), 689. This case arose out of the circumstances and facts of Lagrave's Case, narrated in the preceding section. Here, Petrie v. Fitzgerald, 1 Daly, 401, was distinguished; Williams v. Bacon, 10 Wend. 636, doubted.

§ 463.   FOREIGN EXTRADITION.   605

for them by new treaty stipulations.[1] Mr. Spear, in his work on extradition, favors this rule.

On the other hand, as opposed to this view of the question, we have a contrary doctrine by the court of appeals of New York. Two of the seven judges dissented from the doctrine announced. Sanford E. Church, chief justice, in delivering the opinion of the court, said that he had examined the subject with some care, in respect to an implied treaty obligation binding upon and enforceable by the courts, not to detain the accused for any act, criminal or civil, committed prior to the extradition, except the crime specified in the proceedings, with a view, if possible, to arrive at the same result as the court below,[2] which he regarded eminently just as a principle, but that his examination had created doubts of the legal soundness of the position. This question, that distinguished jurist said, was one of good faith for the two governments, a political and not a judicial question, and was not one for the defendant to raise. He also remarked that the whole subject of extradition is confided to the federal government.[3]

PART II.—EXTRADITION FROM THE UNITED STATES.

§ 463. **Executive Functions.**—The law of the United States governing extradition matters is found in the revised statutes, title 66, and it will be seen that the functions to be performed are in part executive, belonging to the president and to executive officers of the United States subject to his control, and in part judicial, being assigned to specified magistrates of the law. When the government making the demand presents a case which comes within the provisions of the treaty, the obligation of delivery is imperative. The president's mandate is usually the commencement of proceedings in the case. But such

---

[1] United States v. Watts, 8 Saw. 370; and where the cases of Com. v. Hawes, 13 Ky. (Bush), 697; U. S. v. Caldwell, 8 Blatchf. 131; U. S. v. Lawrence, 13 Id. 295, and Bacharach v. Lagrave, 1 Hun (N. Y.), 689, are commented upon.

[2] Bacharach v. Lagrave, 1 Hun (N. Y.), 689.

[3] Adriance v. Lagrave, 59 N. Y. 110, and numerous authorities cited by counsel and court, and where the learned justice gives his views of the English extradition act of 1870, 33 & 34 Vict., c. 52. His honor, in alluding to the facts in Lagrave's Case, and given in the preceding section, said:

"It has been decided in other actions in favor of parties who were held to have been concerned in procuring the defendant to be brought within the jurisdiction of the court by extradition proceedings, in bad faith, for the purpose of arresting him on civil process, that he should be discharged from arrest, on the ground that such persons should not receive an advantage through their wrongful acts. But this rule does not apply to persons not concerned in the trick or device by which the party was brought within the jurisdiction of the court." See 14 Abb. Pr., N. S., 333, note, and cases cited.

evidence of criminality as would be required to justify an order of extradition is not necessary to justify him in issuing it. It is sufficient if the evidence creates a *prima facie* presumption of guilt. But the preponderance of authority goes to show that the president's mandate is not absolutely necessary to the commencement of extradition proceedings before judicial tribunals, and any foreign government entitled by treaty to the extradition of a fugitive from justice, may apply to the courts in the first instance for his arrest.[1] A direct and positive power seems to be conferred upon magistrates qualified to entertain extradition proceedings by the extradition law of the United States above referred to, and this law contains no provision making the exercise of the power dependent upon a previous mandate issued by the president. In no case does it appear that the authority conferred upon the president to issue a warrant for the arrest of the fugitive, supersedes the power given by law to these magistrates.

The delivery of a prisoner can not be made until the facts of the case are judicially ascertained and certified to the secretary of state, and until this preliminary has been supplied an extradition warrant can not be legally issued. But this preliminary does not exclude the president's discretion; and even after the evidence of criminality has been judicially deemed sufficient, and, as such, certified to him, he may, in the exercise of his executive discretion, refuse to deliver the party thus accused, because his power is not simply ministerial.[2] And this though the prisoner's discharge has been refused on a writ of habeas corpus.[3] But the executive warrant of extradition is not so absolutely final as to deprive the prisoner of the benefit of habeas corpus, if the writ is issued before the warrant is carried into effect and the prisoner placed beyond the jurisdiction of the court. To this remedy he is entitled, so long as he remains within the jurisdiction of the United States. The federal courts have asserted the power to look behind the warrant of extradition issued by the secretary of state, so far, at least, as to see whether it issued in a proper case, and upon an examination by a competent magistrate.[4]

---

[1] In re Kaine, 14 How. 103; In re Kaine, 10 N. Y. Leg. Obs. 257; In re Thomas, 12 Blatchf. 370; In re Kelley, 9 Am. Law Rev. 167; Ex parte Ross, 2 Bond, 252; In re Calder, 6 Opin. Att. Gen. 91. *Contra:* Ex parte Kaine, 3 Blatchf. 1; In re Henrich, 5 Id. 414; In re Farez, 7 Id. 34; In re McDonnell, 11 Id. 79.

[2] In re Stupp, 12 Blatchf. 501.

[3] In re Stupp, 11 Blatchf. 124; 14 Opinion Att. Gen. 281.

[4] In re Kaine, 3 Blatchf. 1; Matter of Metzger, 1 Barb. 248; British Prisoners, 1 Woodb. & M. 66, citing Ex parte Smith, 3 McLean, 121; S. C., 6 L. R. 57; Milburn's Case, 9 Pet. 704; In re McDonnell, 11 Blatchf. 170.

§ 464. **Judicial Functions—Issuance of Habeas Corpus.**
There never has been any question about the power of the circuit and district courts of the United States and the judges thereof to issue the writ of habeas corpus in extradition cases within the limits of their jurisdiction.[1] Sections 751 and 752 of the United States revised statutes prescribe the powers of these courts and officers to issue the writ of habeas corpus, but we have heretofore seen that the jurisdiction of the United States supreme court is established by the constitution, and with the exceptions therein mentioned is appellate only.[2] And we have shown it to be well settled that it will, outside of the exceptions mentioned, issue the writ of habeas corpus only in aid of its appellate jurisdiction. The case of a prisoner held in custody in extradition proceedings, it seems, does not come within this province of appellate jurisdiction, and the United States supreme court has refused to issue the writ in such cases.[3] This court has also, in like manner and on like grounds, disclaimed the power to hear and determine the grounds of detention of a prisoner under this writ where it has been issued by one of its justices at chambers, and by analogy to the practice of the king's bench has been made returnable to the whole court.[4]

§ 465. **Reviewing Decision of Commissioner on Habeas Corpus.**—If the magistrate, upon hearing the case, deems the evidence sufficient to sustain the charge, he is then directed by statute to certify the same, together with a copy of all the testimony taken before him, to the secretary of state, and also issue his warrant for the commitment of the person so charged to the proper jail, there to remain until the surrender shall be made. But if the commissioner deems the evidence insufficient, and hence discharges the accused, that is the end of the case, unless there be a new complaint and a new arrest. It is our purpose now to inquire to what extent these judicial proceedings before and by the commissioner are considered final. The rule expressive of the doctrine which now obtains is that such proceedings are not necessarily final, but are within proper limits subject to a review by habeas corpus, or by writs of habeas corpus and *certiorari*. There has, however, unfortunately

---

[1] Ex parte Van Aernam, 3 Blatchf. 160; Ex parte Van Hoven, 4 Dill. 411; S. C., Id. 415; In re McDonnell, 11 Blatchf. 79; S. C., 11 Id. 170; In re Farez, 7 Id. 34; S. C., Id. 345; Ex parte Kaine, 3 Id. 1; In re Henrich, 5 Id. 414.
[2] Const., art. III, sec. 2.
[3] Matter of Metzger, 5 How. 176; Ex parte Kaine, 14 Id. 103.
[4] Ex parte Kaine, 14 How. 103.

been a vigorous conflict of opinion on this question. The judges in the early cases limited their inquiries to the question of the jurisdiction of the commissioner to proceed in the premises. If they found that such jurisdiction existed, they refused to review the decision of such commissioner on the merits. Whether the evidence which he had admitted was competent or incompetent, or whether he had decided in favor of surrendering the person upon evidence which was sufficient or insufficient, was a question which was wholly for him to determine, subject, of course, to the final action of the executive, as above intimated.[1]

Another class of cases subsequently went to show that the courts would, on habeas corpus, examine the evidence upon which the commissioner had based his decision, and discharge the prisoner if there was no evidence to support the magistrate's decision, or if it were based upon incompetent evidence, or where there appeared to be a substantial defect of proof, or where error had been committed in rejecting evidence offered by the prisoner.[2] The recent cases, however, show that the courts and judges now follow the old rule. They will inquire whether the commissioner has acquired jurisdiction of the matter, by conforming to the treaty and statutes; whether he has exceeded his jurisdiction; and whether he has any legal or competent evidence of facts before him on which to exercise a judgment as to the criminality of the accused. But they will not inquire whether the legal evidence of facts before the commissioner was sufficient or insufficient to warrant his conclusion. Neither will the court, if there was legal and competent evidence of facts before the commissioner, for him to consider in making up his decision as to the criminality of the accused, hold the proceedings illegal, and discharge the prisoner on habeas corpus because some other evidence was introduced which was not legal or competent, but was held to be so by the commissioner, and was considered by him on the question of fact. Neither will they discharge him on this writ, because they, on weighing all the evidence which the commissioner considered, would have come to a different conclusion; or because they, on an exclusion of such of the evidence as they may think was not legal or competent, would come, on the remainder of the evidence, to a dif-

---

[1] Matter of Metzger, 5 How. 176; Matter of Veremaitré, 10 N. Y. Leg. Obs. 137; Matter of Kaine, Id. 257; Matter of Heilbronn, 12 Id. 165; Ex parte Van Aernam, 3 Blatchf. 160.
[2] Ex parte Kaine, 3 Blatchf. 1; In re Henrich, 5 Id. 414; In re Farez, 7 Id. 345; In the Matter of Van Campen, 2 Ben. 419. In Henrich's Case, 5 Blatchf. 414, rules are prescribed for proceeding under extradition treaties.

ferent conclusion of fact from that at which the commissioner arrived. The case will not be retried.[1]

§ 466. **Of the Complaint, Statement of Offense, Authentication of Documents, etc.**—The complaint upon which the warrant of arrest is asked should set forth clearly, but briefly, the substance of the offense charged, and the substantial, material features thereof.[2] If forgery of "obligations, papers, titles, or instruments of credit" be charged without specifying the kind of obligations forged, the character of the papers, or the nature of the titles or instruments of credit, the complaint is defective at common law, does not fairly inform the accused of the charge, does show probable cause for arrest, and the prisoner will be discharged on habeas corpus.[3] But the alleged fugitive may be arrested a second time on a new complaint, either with or without a new warrant of the president,[4] and it may be founded, if on oath, upon the strength of telegrams and depositions.[5] A complaint, however, made simply upon information and belief is fatally defective and gives the commissioner no jurisdiction. On such a complaint the prisoner will be discharged on habeas corpus and *certiorari*.[6] The complaint need not show that the warrant has been issued against the accused abroad, or is defective because it does not aver personal knowledge of the deponent, being a foreign consul, of the facts charged. An official statement of the charge by a consul, made with distinctness enough to enable the accused to understand what is charged, is a sufficient complaint.[7] The warrant need not show that the commissioner was appointed to issue the particular warrant. An averment of his authority to issue such warrants generally is sufficient.[8] But

---

[1] In re Stupp, 12 Blatchf. 501 (1875); In re Farez, 7 Id. 34; In re McDonnell, 11 Id. 170; In re Stupp, Id. 124; Ex parte Geissler, 4 Fed. Rep. 188; In re Doig, Id. 193; In re Fowler, Id. 303. See In re McDonnell, 11 Blatchf. 170, that the prisoner will not be discharged for an error committed by the commissioner in the reception of evidence: Matter of Wiegand, 14 Id. 370; In re Vandervelpen, Id. 137; In re Wahl, 15 Id. 334, that the commissioner's decision is not subject to review upon the weight of evidence, though the court will still look far enough to see that there was some competent evidence before the commissioner, on which to exercise his jurisdiction and to base his judgment: Ex parte Van Hoven, 4 Dill. 415, that the case will not be heard on the merits by a court, as that is the commissioner's province; In re Farez, 7 Blatchf. 345, that while in custody under a writ of habeas corpus, the prisoner can not be arrested on a second warrant; but, Ex parte Van Hoven, 4 Dill. 415, that he may be arrested on a new complaint after his discharge.

[2] Ex parte Joseph Smith, the Mormon prophet, 3 McLean, 121.

[3] Ex parte Van Hoven, 4 Dill. 411.

[4] 6 Opin. Att. Gen. 91; Ex parte Van Hoven, 4 Dill. 415.

[5] Ex parte Van Hoven, 4 Dill. 411.

[6] Ex parte Lane, 6 Fed. Rep. 34.

[7] Farez' Case, 2 Abb. U. S. 346.

[8] Id.

the complaint and warrant should show upon their face that the commissioner issuing the warrant is duly empowered to act in cases of that description;[1] and if the person making the complaint has no personal knowledge of the facts, it should appear that he is a representative of the foreign government, acting in an official capacity. Or he should produce an indictment against the party charged, or depositions tending to show his guilt, or, at least, set forth with particularity the sources and details of his information, in order that the arrest may appear to be sought upon something more than a mere rumor or suspicion of the fugitive's guilt.[2] The commissioner has no power to amend the complaint or warrant, or supply defects by his certificate, after the case is closed and a writ of *certiorari* is served upon him to produce the record of his proceedings.[3] The prisoner may be discharged from a final commitment if unlawful, but remanded for an examination *de novo*, if properly held under the warrant of arrest.[4]

In the first class of documentary evidence mentioned in the act of June 19, 1876,[5] the originals must be documents that may be received in the tribunals of the foreign country as evidence of the criminality of the accused person, in respect to the offense charged against him there, and as if the inquiry concerning the criminality of his offense were being had in such foreign tribunals. And such originals must be authenticated in a legal manner, such as would entitle them to be received as such evidence in the foreign tribunals. The second class must be copies of such original documents, and authenticated according to the law of such foreign country. The certificate of the United States diplomatic or consular officers is not the only competent proof that the originals or copies are properly authenticated. It may be done by oral proof, which may also be received to show what the law of the foreign country is as to such authentication, and that such authentication is according to the law of the foreign country.[6]

§ 467. **Checks of Legal Functions upon Each Other.—** "The law," says Mr. Spear, in his valuable work on extradition, "by thus distributing the legal functions to be performed between the executive and the judicial departments of the gov-

---

[1] Ex parte Lane, 6 Fed. Rep. 34.
[2] Id.
[3] Id.
[4] Farez' Case, 2 Abb. U. S. 346.
[5] 19 U. S. Stat. at Large, c. 133, amending sec. 5271, U. S. R. S.
[6] In re Fowler, 4 Fed. Rep. 303. The reader is referred to In re McDonnell, 11 Blatchf. 79, for full information as to what constitutes a good warrant.

ernment, secures to the party accused the highest certainty that he will be surrendered to a foreign government only when all the necessary conditions are present. The judiciary can not surrender him, and the president can not do it until the judiciary has decided that the case is a proper one for delivery, and even then he may revise and reject that decision. This furnishes an ample protection against any abuse of the extradition power, especially when we add that the writ of habeas corpus, as a means of testing the legality of the proceedings, is always available to the party if sought for before his actual surrender and removal from the country."[1]

§ 468. **Conflict between State and Federal Authority.** In one very interesting and important case, the judge of a state court on habeas corpus assumed jurisdiction to hear and determine the legality of the prisoner's detention, under the laws of the state, notwithstanding the prisoner was held in custody, in a proceeding for his extradition to England, by a marshal of the United States.[2] This was in 1853, and the prisoner was discharged. But since, the cases of Ableman v. Booth[3] and Tarble's Case[4] have settled beyond controversy that the state courts have no such jurisdiction. They have no such jurisdiction, because the whole subject of foreign intercourse is, by the constitution of the United States, committed to the federal government, and upon all questions relating thereto it alone can speak and act.[5] Such an act, therefore, on the part of a state court is an unwarrantable interference with federal process and federal power. Under the rule laid down by the United States supreme court in Tarble's Case,[6] as well as in Ableman v. Booth,[7] the marshal, where a state court attempts such an exercise of authority, need not produce the body of the prisoner before the state court, but may simply return the facts, and that he detains him under the authority and process of the United States, and he will not be in contempt for further disobeying the writ.[8]

---

[1] Spear on Extradition, 224.
[2] Matter of Heilbonn, 1 Park. Cr. 429; see also Matter of Lagrave, 45 How. Pr. 301; S. C., 14 Abb. Pr., N. S., 333.
[3] 21 How. 506.
[4] 13 Wall. 397; see Holmes v. Jennison, 14 Pet. 540, 598, that a state has no power to deliver up a foreign fugitive.
[5] People v. Curtis, 50 N. Y. 321, where Chief Justice Church held the statute of New York passed in 1822, and providing for the surrender of fugitives from justice from foreign countries to be unconstitutional, and a warrant issued by the governor in pursuance thereof void. See also Passmore Williamson's Case, 26 Pa. St. 9.
[6] 13 Wall. 397.
[7] 21 How. 506.
[8] Note to In re McDonnell, 11 Blatchf. 170–195.

CHAPTER XXXVII.

INTERSTATE EXTRADITION.

PART I.—CONSTITUTIONAL AND LEGISLATIVE PROVISIONS.

§ 469. Constitution of the United States.
§ 470. Statutory Enactment.
§ 471. State Authority.
§ 472. Authority in Absence of State Legislation.

PART II.—DUTY AND DISCRETION OF EXECUTIVE.

§ 473. The Demanding Discretion.
§ 474. The Delivering Discretion.

PART III.—JUDICIAL POWERS.

§ 475. Courts can not Control Discretion of Executive.
§ 476. The Affidavit.
§ 477. Concerning the Indictment.
§ 478. Person Charged must be Shown to be a Fugitive Criminal.
§ 479. Authentication of the Papers.
§ 480. Vacating Executive Warrant—Sufficiency of the Papers.
§ 481. Awaiting Requisition.
§ 482. Can Only be Tried for Extradition Crime.
§ 483. Illegal Extradition.
§ 484. Other Matters.

PART IV.—JURISDICTION OF THE FEDERAL COURTS.

§ 485. May Issue Habeas Corpus in Cases of Interstate Extradition.
§ 486. Scope of Inquiry.
§ 487. Conflict of Jurisdiction.

PART II.—CONSTITUTIONAL AND LEGISLATIVE PROVISIONS.

§ 469. **The United States Constitution** provides that "a person charged in any state with treason, felony, or other crime, who shall flee from justice and be found in another state, shall, on demand of the executive authority of the state from which he fled, be delivered up, to be removed to the state having jurisdiction of the crime."[1] Thus has the constitution prescribed a definite rule upon the subject of interstate extradition, and with this sort of extradition the usages of nations, or their treaties with each other in respect to the extradition of fugitives

[1] Sec. 2, art. 4.

from justice, have nothing to do. The states are governed by the constitutional rule, whether it corresponds or not with the rules adopted in international extradition. Each state, subject to constitutional limitations, has the right to determine what shall be a crime in that state, and it has nothing to do with the law of nations, or with treaties between nations, in interpreting and applying the constitutional rule. This provision is a part of the supreme law of the land, a part of the law of each state; and state officers whose duty it is to adjudicate or execute the laws are governed by it the same as by every other law in force. And had congress never made any provision for carrying this clause of the constitution into effect, it would clearly be the duty of the states to supply the requisite legislation.[1]

§ 470. **Statutory Enactment.**—But congress has passed an act covering this matter, the substance of which is found in section 5278 of the United States revised statutes.[2] The states can pass no laws inconsistent with the constitutional provision concerning the extradition of fugitive criminals, or with this legislation of congress for its enactment. Both are the supreme law of the land, and neither can be invaded or superseded by the legislative power of the states.

§ 471. **State Authority.**—This brings us to the question, Does the law of congress prohibit auxiliary legislation by the states concerning fugitive criminals? From the words of Mr. Justice Story,[3] it would seem "that the legislation of congress, if constitutional, must supersede all state legislation upon the same subject, and by necessary implication, prohibit it." "But," says Mr. Spear, "the principle thus laid down by the supreme

---

[1] Matter of Romaine, 23 Cal. 585; Spear on Extradition, pt. 2, c. 1.

[2] Which reads as follows: "Whenever the executive authority of any state or territory demands any person, as a fugitive from justice of the executive authority of any state or territory to which such person has fled, and produces a copy of an indictment found, or an affidavit made before a magistrate of any state or territory, charging the person demanded with having committed treason, felony, or other crime, certified as authentic by the governor or chief magistrate of the state or territory from whence the person so charged has fled, it shall be the duty of the executive authority of the state or territory to which such person has fled to cause him to be arrested and secured, and to cause notice of the arrest to be given to the executive authority making such demand, or to the agent of such authority appointed to receive the fugitive, and to cause the fugitive to be delivered to such agent when he shall appear. If no such agent appears within six months from the time of the arrest, the prisoner may be discharged. All costs or expenses incurred in the apprehending, securing, and transmitting such fugitive to the state or territory making such demand, shall be paid by such state or territory." The territories are treated as if they were states: Prigg v. Commonwealth of Pennsylvania, 16 Pet. 539; brought up in The State v. Loper, Ga. Dec., pt. 2, p. 33, but not decided.

[3] In Prigg v. The Commonwealth of Pennsylvania, 16 Pet. 539; Houston v. Moore, 5 Wheat. 1, 21, 22.

court of the United States, though strongly stated, and perhaps without the necessary qualification, has not by the states been practically understood to exclude legislation of this character. The demand is evidently the initial point at which the constitution and the law begin to operate; and prior to this, neither, by its own terms, has any application to the case. The states can not legislate against the constitution and the law of congress, nor do anything to impair the full operation and effect of their provisions, or substitute a different mode of attaining the end; yet it does not follow that the states can do nothing on the subject at that stage in which neither the constitution nor federal legislation acts upon it at all, provided that what they do is not inconsistent with the end named in the constitution or with what congress has done for its attainment." [1] As the constitutionality of the act of congress has never been questioned, and as every executive in the Union has constantly acted upon and admitted its validity,[2] the fact that statutes have been enacted in most or all of the states authorizing the arrest of persons on the charge of being fugitives from the justice of other states, or warrant issued by a magistrate in advance of the executive demand,[3] ought to settle the question that state legislation with reference to fugitive criminals, not inconsistent with the constitution or the law of congress, to carry the constitutional provision into effect, is not excluded by the regulation of congress. The states have at least assumed this proposition and acted upon it. Where the preliminaries to extradition are specified, authorized, and regulated by special statutes, they must be complied with, or the prisoner may be discharged upon habeas corpus.[4]

§ 472. **Authority in the Absence of State Legislation.** The paramount constitutional duty of the state to make the surrender of a fugitive criminal, upon proper executive demand, seems to be nowise in conflict with its reserved power to deal with the criminal fugitive in the absence of such demand.[5] And for various reasons assigned, this judicial power has been frequently exercised,[6] it having never, so far as we are aware, been questioned except in one instance.[7] The reason given in one

---

[1] Spear on Extradition, 245, 246.
[2] Mr. Justice Story, in Prigg. v. Com. of Pennsylvania, 16 Pet. 620. Spear on Extradition, 253, 259.
[4] And pronounced constitutional in California, in Ex parte White, 49 Cal. 433; see Prigg v. Com. of Penn., 16 Pet. 539.
[5] Ex parte Rosenblat, 51 Cal. 285.
[6] The People v. Schenck, 2 Johns. 479; State v. Howell, R. M. Charlt. 120; State v. Loper, Ga. Dec., pt. 2, p. 33; Matter of Fetter, 3 Zab. 311; State v. Buzine, 4 Harr. 572; Com. v. Deacon, 10 Serg. & R. 125; Matter of Romaine, 23 Cal. 585; People v. Goodhue, 2 Johns. Ch. 198.
[7] The People v. S. & J. Wright, 2 Cai. 212.

case for the detention in custody of a fugitive criminal for a reasonable time, in order to give the foreign executive an opportunity to make a regular demand for his delivery under the constitution of the United States, was that it was justified by "the law of nations and the law of this land."[1] In another it was "the more effectually to accomplish the intent of the government by preventing the escape of the criminal."[2] And in a third it was said that "to enable the executive to perform his duty, it is necessary that magistrates should have the power to arrest and commit the fugitive before as well as after a demand has been made. The exercise of the power is essential to carry into effect the provision of the constitution; otherwise an immunity may be offered to the most atrocious criminals. If a felon notoriously guilty of murder can, by escaping into another state, set the law at defiance until a demand is regularly made on the executive and a warrant is issued for his arrest, the object of the constitution may be defeated and the act of congress rendered nugatory."[3] The evidence, however, to justify such arrests and detentions should be sufficient to put the accused on trial before a court of competent jurisdiction. The value and weight of the evidence is of course determined in each case by the magistrate, but the accused, if committed to prison, may sue out a writ of habeas corpus or *certiorari*, or both, to have the legality of his detention examined.[4]

PART II.—DUTY AND DISCRETION OF EXECUTIVE.

§ 473. **The Demanding Discretion.**—The crime charged must be "treason, felony, or other crime," and which includes any offense against the laws of the state or territory making the demand.[5] But neither the constitutional provision nor the act of congress makes the demand a duty imposed by law upon any executive, and neither touches the question whether it shall be made or not. The question, so far as the constitution and the law of congress have any application to it, is thus left to the discretion of the executive authority of each state or territory. This is qualified only by a specification of the conditions upon which the demand, if made, shall involve the obligation of delivery. "The implication," says Mr. Spear, "is that each ex-

---

[1] The State v. Loper, Ga. Dec., pt. 2, p. 33.
[2] Com. v. Deacon, 10 Serg. & R. 125.
[3] State v. Buzine, 4 Harr. 572.
[4] Id.
[5] Kentucky v. Dennison, 24 How. 66; Taylor v. Taintor, 16 Wall. 366; Brown's Case, 112 Mass. 409; Commonwealth v. Green, 17 Id. 515; Matter of Fetter, 3 Zab. 311; Matter of Voorhees, 32 N. J. L. 141; Matter of Clark, 9 Wend. 212; People v. Brady, 56 N. Y. 182; Matter of Hughes, Phill. L. 57; Johnston v. Riley, 13 Ga. 97.

ecutive has the power, either with or without statutory law providing therefor, to make a demand; but whether he shall in any case exercise the power is a matter for him to determine."[1] But this executive discretion may be legally regulated by legislation in the states and territories, and has been in some of them.[2] Rules for the guidance of governors will be found in Mr. Spear's valuable work on extradition.

§ 474. **The Delivering Discretion,** however, is a subject of much importance. The duty imposed upon the executive by the act of congress is a moral one, and not mandatory. It is simply declaratory of the grave duty which every moral reason requires him to perform.[3] Congress may legislate as to the duties of the executive of a territory, but it has no power to thus legislate for the executive of a state. And if the governor of a state refuses to discharge the duty concerning the delivery of fugitive criminals, imposed upon him by the act of congress, there is no power delegated to the general government, either through the judicial department or any other department, to use any coercive means to compel him.[4] As the law of congress can not be enforced against a declining executive, it will at once be seen that there should be a law in every state imposing the duty of the executive under designated circumstances; and in such legislation the words "it shall be the duty," etc., would imply the operation of power to command and coerce obedience.[5] Massachusetts has a law relating to the duty of her executive in surrendering fugitive criminals as well as in demanding them[6]—a law which leaves him a large discretion, yet fixes the limits within which he must act, and beyond which he must not pass. This law is said to have been held constitutional in that state, but we have failed to find a decision to that effect. Ohio, also, has such a law, and when the case is shown to be within the provisions of the constitution of the United States and the act of congress on the subject, little discretion is vested in the governor of the state to which the fugitive criminal has fled, and it is ordinarily his imperative duty to issue his warrant of extradition. But if he happen to issue it inadvertently or

---

[1] Spear on Extradition, 318.

[2] Pub. Stat. Mass., 1882, c. 218. That a state has no authority to demand fugitives who have fled to foreign countries, and that a statute authorizing such demand is unconstitutional and void, see Holmes v. Jennison, 14 Pet. 540; People v. Curtis, 50 N. Y. 326.

[3] Kentucky v. Dennison, 24 How. 66; Prigg v. The Commonwealth of Pennsylvania, 16 Pet. 539; Matter of Briscoe, 51 How. Pr. 422; Hibler v. The State, 43 Tex. 197; Taylor v. Taintor, 16 Wall. 366.

[4] Kentucky v. Dennison, 24 How. 66.

[5] Id.

[6] Pub. Stat. Mass., 1882, c. 218.

improvidently, as upon a requisition which he afterwards finds to be forged or otherwise defective, he may revoke it, whether issued by himself or his predecessor, and when this is done, the grounds of such revocation can not be inquired into on habeas corpus, though at the time of such revocation the prisoner may have actually been in the custody of the agent of the demanding state.[1]

A fugitive criminal can only be delivered up upon the formal requisition of the governor of the state, in compliance with the constitutional provision. The fact that the alleged fugitive has been arrested, and is detained by the order of a court, does not of itself give any executive jurisdiction over the case. The court has no power to deliver up the prisoner, and no executive has this power until the executive of some other state or territory has, by a demand, furnished the necessary condition.[2] But the duty of making a surrender is not "absolute and unqualified," even when all the papers are in due form. It is dependent upon "the circumstances of the case." The requisition must be made in good faith according to the letter and intent of the constitution and the law, and not in violation of the spirit and design of both. And the governor, upon whom a demand is made, has the right, even when all the papers are technically correct, to inquire whether the requisition is made for a different purpose from the one named in the constitution. In such a case the executive will exercise his discretion in refusing to comply with the request.[3] But the responsibility of deciding delicate and embarrassing questions devolves not alone on the executive. The prisoner restrained of his liberty is always entitled to the privilege of habeas corpus, and the governor will always see that, before the fugitive is actually delivered to the agent of another state or territory, he has a reasonable opportunity to apply for a writ of habeas corpus to have the legality of his imprisonment tested by the judiciary. The summary manner of the prisoner's removal in extradition proceedings will never be allowed to cheat him out of this common-law privilege, for frauds and abuses are sometimes found in these proceedings, as well as in others.

PART III.—JUDICIAL POWERS.

§ 475. **Courts can not Control Discretion of Executive.**—We have seen that the discretion of the governor of a

[1] Work v. Corrington, 34 Ohio St. 64; S. C., 6 Cent. L. J. 377; In re Carroll, Chic. L. N., September 28, 1878. See People v. Brady, 56 N. Y. 182; In the Matter of Adams, 7 Law Rep. 386; 18 Alb. L. J. 166. See also Matter of Briscoe, where a sheriff resorted to habeas corpus to secure the custody of a prisoner to which he was entitled: 51 How. Pr. 422.
[2] Botts v. Williams, 17 B. Mon. 687.
[3] Spear on Extradition, 339, 340.

state can not be controlled by the federal judiciary,[1] and the same rule is well settled in the states. The judiciary will never thus attempt to invade the executive branch of the government.[2] But in deciding questions which arise under writs of habeas corpus, the judiciary may review and control the action of the governor in regard to points of law.[3]

§ 476. **The Affidavit.**—There must be a legal accusation, by indictment or affidavit, charging the party with the commission of crime, and that would have justified his arrest and commitment to prison, or holding him to bail, in the state or territory in which the crime is alleged to have been committed, had he not fled therefrom, to authorize his arrest in the state or territory where he has sought refuge, and his removal therefrom to the state or territory having jurisdiction of the crime. The executive of the demanding state is not authorized by the constitutional provision to make the demand unless the party has been charged in the regular course of judicial proceedings.[4] A prosecution must have been commenced against him and pending against him for the alleged crime in the state having jurisdiction of the offense. Unless this has been done, the alleged fugitive will be discharged on habeas corpus.[5] The evidence that such proceedings have been commenced is a copy of the indictment found, or an affidavit made before a magistrate in that state.[6] The papers must show a *prima facie* case, and the affidavit must be so explicit in the necessary allegations of fact as to justify a magistrate in committing the accused.[7]

The fugitive, on habeas corpus, can not impeach the validity of the affidavit upon which the requisition was founded, if it distinctly charge the commission of an offense, which is all that is necessary. It need not set forth the crime charged with all the legal exactness of an indictment. The affidavit, furthermore, need not state that the prisoner is a "fugitive from justice." An allegation that he committed the crime and then secretly fled is sufficient from which to deduce the conclusion.[8] But if it appears clearly from the affidavit that no crime is

---

[1] Kentucky v. Dennison, 24 How. 66; In re Jackson, 12 Am. Law Rev. 602.
[2] In re Manchester, 5 Cal. 237; Ex parte Sheldon, 34 Ohio St. 319.
[3] In re Hughes, Phill. 57; In re Manchester, 5 Cal. 237.
[4] Kentucky v. Dennison, 24 How. 66.
[5] Ex parte White, 49 Cal. 433.
[6] Ex parte White, 49 Cal. 433.
[7] Ex parte Smith, 3 McLean, 121; The People v. Brady, 56 N. Y. 182; Matter of Heyward, 1 Sandf. 701; Matter of Fetter, 3 Zab. 311; Matter of Leland, 7 Abb. Pr., N. S., 64; Matter of Rutter, Id. 67.
[8] In the Matter of Manchester, 5 Cal. 237.

charged in it, the prisoner will be released on habeas corpus.[1] The fact that an inferior magistrate of the state whence the criminal has fled has issued a warrant of arrest upon such a defective affidavit does not justify the inference that a legal crime is charged in the affidavit.[2] An affidavit merely embodying a hearsay statement that the prisoner is charged with crime in the state whence he has fled, and is a fugitive from justice, without presenting an authenticated copy of the charge or indictment in such state, is insufficient; and in such a case, the court will not, on habeas corpus and *certiorari*, ordinarily remand the prisoner for detention until the proper documents can be procured, but he will be discharged.[3] Neither is the affidavit of an attorney, communicating information, and received by telegraph, sufficient authority for the arrest and imprisonment of a fugitive criminal from such state, or to show that he is charged in such state with the commission of an offense against its laws. An authentic copy of the charge or indictment must be presented. In such a case the prisoner will be discharged on habeas corpus without waiting for the arrival of a proper warrant from the executive.[4]

§ 477. **Concerning the Indictment.**—If the charge of criminality be in the form of an indictment by a grand jury, it must have the usual features of a charge made in this way, and if it appear to have been returned in this form, certified by the governor of the state whence the fugitive criminal has fled, and substantially charges a crime, a court will not, on habeas corpus, discharge the prisoner because of formal defects in the indictment; because this is a question of technical pleading to be tried and determined in the state in which the indictment was found.[5] And it is incompetent upon habeas corpus to show that the indictment upon which the requisition was issued was procured improperly or upon insufficient evidence.[6]

§ 478. **Person Charged must be Shown to be a Fugitive Criminal.**—When a person infringes the criminal laws of

---

[1] In re Greenough, 31 Vt. 279; People v. Brady, 56 N. Y. 182; Matter of Leland, 7 Abb. Pr., N. S., 64.
[2] People v. Brady, 56 N. Y. 182.
[3] Matter of Leland, 7 Abb. Pr., N. S., 64.
[4] Matter of Rutter, 7 Abb. Pr., N. S., 67; Matter of Donahue, 1 Pac. C. L. Mag. 22.
[5] Davis' Case, 122 Mass. 324; S. C., 12 Am. Law Rev. 753, and 5 Cent. L. J. 273; In re Voorhees, 32 N. J. L. 141; In re Greenough, 31 Vt. 279; In re Clark, 9 Wend. 212; Matter of Manchester, 5 Cal. 237; Matter of Briscoe, 51 How. Pr. 422; People v. Brady, 56 N. Y. 182; Brown's Case, 112 Mass. 409; State v. Schlemn, 4 Harr. 577; Matter of Leland, 7 Abb. Pr., N. S., 64; and late case of Ex parte Sheldon, 34 Ohio St. 319.
[6] U. S. v. McClay, 4 Cent. L. J. 255; Matter of Donahue, 1 Pac. C. L. Mag. 22. See Hibler v. The State, 43 Tex. 197.

a state and departs therefrom without waiting to abide the consequences of such act, he is a fugitive from justice within the meaning of the provision of the constitution.[1] But it has been held that a citizen and resident of Iowa, charged with having been constructively guilty of an offense in another state, and upon which a requisition was based, but who never in fact fled therefrom, is not a fugitive from justice within the meaning of the constitution, and he was released on habeas corpus.[2] It is sufficient to find the person charged with crime in another state. He need not have fled there, and may even be there against his will, having been brought back on requisition from a third state; but this will not preclude his rendition from such state to the one whence he first fled. He can not under such circumstances be released on habeas corpus.[3] One can not be extradited between states of the Union except for offenses strictly criminal, and with which he has been legally charged as a fugitive from justice,[4] and it has been held, in the late and valuable Ohio case of Wilcox v. Nolze,[5] that the act of congress is confined to persons who are actually and not constructively present in the demanding state when they violate its laws. So, on habeas corpus for discharge from arrest on a warrant of extradition issued by the governor in compliance with the requisition of the governor of another state, it was held that parol evidence was admissible to show that there had been no such actual presence of the accused in the demanding state. But after an alleged fugitive from justice has been arrested on an extradition warrant, he will not on habeas corpus be discharged on the ground that there was no evidence before the executive issuing the warrant, showing that the fugitive had fled from the demanding state to avoid prosecution.[6]

§ 479. **Authentication of the Papers.**—The law provides that there must be presented a copy of the indictment or affidavit, "certified as authentic by the governor or chief magistrate of the state or territory from whence the person so charged fled," and its object is to enable the executive upon whom the demand is made to determine whether there is probable cause for believing that a crime has been committed. The governor of the state issuing the requisition for the fugitive is the only proper judge

---

[1] In the Matter of Voorhees, 32 N. J. L. 141; People v. Pinkerton, 17 Hun, 199; Matter of Donahue, 1 Pac. C. L. Mag. 22, a case valuable for the many American authorities collected concerning extradition.
[2] Jones v. Leonard, 50 Iowa, 106.
[3] People v. Sennott, 20 Alb. L. J. 230; S. C., 1 Crim. L. Mag. 265.
[4] In the Matter of Cannon, 47 Mich. 481.
[5] 34 Ohio St. 520.
[6] Ex parte Sheldon, 34 Ohio St. 319.

of the authenticity of the affidavit; and when the requisition certifies that the affidavit is "duly authenticated according to the laws" of said state, it is sufficient.[1] A complaint charging the fugitive with a crime may be made on oath in the demanding state to a person styled a trial justice; and the certificate of the governor of such state, in making a demand of the governor of another state for the surrender of the fugitive criminal, that a copy of such complaint produced with the demand is authentic, sufficiently authenticates the capacity of the person as a magistrate authorized to receive the complaint.[2]

§ 480. **Vacating Executive Warrant, and Sufficiency of the Papers.**—The law specifies the evidence upon which the arrest of an alleged fugitive criminal, for purposes of extradition, is lawful, and makes the governor of the state or territory to whom the requisition is addressed the judge of its existence, authenticity, and weight. If it is conformable to law, and the governor, in his discretion, acts upon it, his act should not be questioned by the courts, except in some rare and exceptional cases, an instance of which will be found in the Ohio case cited in section 478. The prisoner, however, on habeas corpus may ask the court to determine whether the evidence is such as the law prescribes. The requirements of the law must be exactly fulfilled: there must be a proper demand for the surrender of the fugitive; there must be a copy of a legal indictment or affidavit accompanying the demand and charging the fugitive with crime in the demanding state or territory; the copy must have been duly authenticated by the demanding executive; and the executive to whom the demand was addressed must have issued his warrant for the arrest of the accused party.[3] When these facts appear upon the return to a habeas corpus, a court will rarely attempt to afford relief under this remedy, except it be called for by some extrinsic or extraneous matter. The general rule, supported by a preponderance of authorities, is, that the warrant of the governor is *prima facie* evidence, at least, that all necessary legal prerequisites have been complied with, and if the previous proceedings appear to be regular, is, as a general rule, conclusive evidence of the right to remove the prisoner to the state from which he fled.[4] In California it has been held that, on habeas

---

[1] In the Matter of Manchester, 5 Cal. 237.
[2] Kingsbury's Case, 106 Mass. 223; State v. Hufford, 28 Iowa, 391. See Hibler v. The State, 43 Tex. 197.
[3] Matter of Heyward 1 Sandf. 701; Ex parte McKean, 3 Hughes, 23; Spear on Extradition, 304.
[4] Ex parte Sheldon, 34 Ohio St. 319; Ex parte Watson, 2 Cal. 59; In the

corpus, no inquiry can be made as to whether the affidavit for extradition is a forgery.[1]

The question of the identity of the party arrested with the party described as the alleged fugitive, in the mandate of the governor, is of course always open to inquiry on habeas corpus.[2] And it seems that the legislature of Pennsylvania has expressly limited the habeas corpus examination of the case to the question of identity. In Indiana, where the identity of the person arrested with the person named in the warrant is alleged in the return to a habeas corpus, it is held that the question whether that person committed the crime can only be tried in the demanding state.[3] The executive, in the exercise of official discretion and authority, may withhold the papers upon which his warrant is founded. And it is not necessary that they should accompany the warrant when it is returned to a habeas corpus.[4] Under these circumstances, the warrant itself can only be looked to for the evidence that the essential conditions of its issue have been complied with, and it is sufficient if it recites what the law requires.[5] Where a requisition recited that "the annexed papers duly authenticated show that by affidavit the prisoner stands charged with larceny," and there was no copy of the affidavit, it was held that the governor was not authorized to issue his warrant for the arrest of the fugitive.[6] In Indiana, the governor, upon the requisition of the governor of Kentucky, issued his warrant for the arrest of a fugitive from justice, and it was held, on habeas corpus, that the warrant was *prima facie* evidence that an indictment was pending against the prisoner as stated therein; and that it sufficiently showed the authority of the agent to make the arrest without producing any authority from the governor of Kentucky.[7] Where the return to a writ of habeas corpus, sued out by a prisoner held under requisition proceedings, shows a substantial compliance with the act of congress concerning fugitive criminals, the prisoner will be remanded.[8]

Matter of Clark, 9 Wend. 212; State v. Schlemn, 4 Harr. 577; Ex parte Manchester, 5 Cal. 237; Davis's Case, 122 Mass. 324; S. C., 12 Am. Law Rev. 753, and 5 Cent. L. J. 273; Com. v. Hall, 9 Gray, 262; Kingsbury's Case, 106 Mass. 223; Brown's Case, 112 Id. 409; Hibler v. The State, 43 Tex. 197; Taylor v. Taintor, 16 Wall. 366; Leary's Case, 6 Abb. N. C. 43; S. C., 10 Ben. 197, and 1 Crim. L. Mag. 265; People v. Pinkerton, 17 Hun, 199; S. C., 77 N. Y. 245. Contra: People v. Brady, 56 N. Y. 182; Jones v. Leonard, 50 Iowa, 106.
[1] Ex parte Manchester, 5 Cal. 237.
[2] Leary's Case, 10 Ben. 197; S. C., 6 Abb. N. C. 43, and 1 Crim. L. Mag. 265.
[3] Robinson v. Flanders, 29 Ind. 10.
[4] Id.
[5] People v. Donohue, 84 N. Y. 438.
[6] Ex parte Pfitzer, 28 Ind. 450.
[7] Nichols v. Cornelius, 7 Ind. 611; see Robinson v. Flanders, 29 Id. 10.
[8] Ex parte Bayley, 1 West Coast Rep. 485.

§ 481. **Awaiting Requisition.**—In order to hold a fugitive from justice to await the requisition of the governor of another state, it must affirmatively appear from the complaint on file before the committing magistrate of the state to which the fugitive has fled that a crime has been committed in the other state; that the accused has been charged in that state with such crime; and that he has fled from justice and is within such state. These are essential jurisdictional facts, and must be shown to authorize an arrest; they can not be inferred.[1] And the legality of the prisoner's detention may be inquired into on habeas corpus before his examination is closed. The prisoner, in proving his traverse to the return to the habeas corpus, may prove the documents on which his arrest was founded by the best evidence at hand, or which he can procure with reasonable diligence, without regard to the ordinary rules of evidence, and there is no impropriety in his calling the justice who issued the process, and the clerk of his court, who are competent witnesses, to prove on what papers the process issued. The evidence to remand a prisoner detained on an irregular commitment must be at latest presented on the hearing of the habeas corpus. It can not be presented when the judge is ready to announce his order for the prisoner's discharge.[2] After commitment by a magistrate, it must appear on the return to the habeas corpus that he had jurisdiction of the subject before him. A commitment in which the only reference to the crime is a statement that the prisoner is "charged with forgery on oath of ——," is not sufficient. It ought to state the facts charged or found to constitute the offense with sufficient certainty to enable the court, on habeas corpus, to determine what particular crime is charged.[3] Where property is taken into a state by a fugitive, as money obtained by robbery, and it is sought to hold him as a fugitive from justice on that ground, he must be specifically charged with that offense in the language of the statute of such state.[4] On proper evidence a fugitive criminal may be detained a reasonable time before demand made by the executive of the state or territory whence he has fled, in order that communication may be had with such executive.[5]

§ 482. **Can Only be Tried for Extradition Crime.**—A person who has been demanded for prosecution as a fugitive

[1] Matter of Heyward, 1 Sandf. 701; Ex parte Lorraine, 16 Nev. 63.
[2] Matter of Heyward, 1 Sandf. 701.
[3] Matter of Leland, 7 Abb. Pr., N. S., 64; Matter of Rutter, Id. 67; State v. Hufford, 28 Iowa, 391.
[4] Ex parte Lorraine, 16 Nev. 63. See Ex parte Cubreth, 49 Cal. 435.
[5] Ex parte Romanes, 1 Utah, 23.

criminal by a state, and who could not have been demanded on any other ground, can not have his original accusation dropped by the prosecuting authority, and be arrested and tried after arriving there, on a different complaint, without being given an opportunity to return. No department of the government can sanction such a use of the requisition without the plainest perversion of justice.[1]

§ 483. **Illegal Extradition.**—But where a fugitive criminal has been charged with an extraditable offense by indictment in the state whence he fled, and has been forcibly and illegally arrested in the state to which he has fled, and extradited on requisition, etc., he may nevertheless be held and tried in the first-named state unless the governor of the last-named state makes a demand for the fugitive's release on account of the illegal proceedings; in which case, however, he would be set at large.[2]

§ 484. **Other Matters.**—Bail is sometimes allowed a fugitive criminal by statute;[3] but in Texas it is held that if such a person has the right of appeal on habeas corpus proceedings, he is not entitled to go at large, on bail or otherwise, pending his appeal; and that the right of bail guaranteed by the bill of rights does not obtain in extradition cases originating under that clause of the constitution of the United States which requires the rendition of fugitives from justice.[4] Where the prisoner has already been delivered up by the governor for the extradition crime, and has been admitted to bail, forfeited his bond, and again become a fugitive, it is clearly within the power of the governor surrendering him to order a second arrest and surrender.[5] Where the governor revokes his warrant, while the fugitive is in the custody of the agent of the demanding state and within the jurisdiction where it was issued, and the revocation under seal was presented to a court on a hearing of habeas

---

[1] Cannon's Case, 47 Mich. 481; S. C., 11 N. W. Rep. 280.

[2] Dow's Case, 18 Pa. St. 37; S. P., In re Miles, 52 Vt. 609; see Cannon's Case, 47 Mich. 481; S. C., 11 N. W. Rep. 280.

[3] Cal. P. C., sec. 1552. The question may well arise whether such a statute is constitutional. In the language of Mr. Justice Clark, of the Texas court of appeals: "If upon arrest under a warrant of extradition bail is allowable, the federal constitution is set at naught, and delivery in the state having jurisdiction of the offense would have its price, regulated generally by the amount of the bail bond, where one could be given at all, and a fundamental provision which was intended to apply to all classes of citizens would be restricted to the poor and unfortunate who were not able to furnish bail. Such can not be the proper construction of the two constitutions: Ex parte Erwin, 7 Tex. App. 288; see Cannon's Case, 47 Mich. 481; S. C., 11 N. W. Rep. 280; also Bagnall v. Ableman, 4 Wis. 163.

[4] Ex parte Erwin, 7 Tex. App. 288.

[5] In the Matter of Hughes, Phill. 57.

§ 485.   INTERSTATE EXTRADITION.   625

corpus proceedings, the prisoner has been discharged.¹ The demand for the delivery of a fugitive from justice does not abrogate or postpone a lawful jurisdiction that has been put in force against him for an offense committed in the state or territory to which he has fled, and on which the demand is made. When the party is held under civil process, the same principle applies.²

PART IV.—JURISDICTION OF THE FEDERAL COURTS.

§ 485. **May Issue Habeas Corpus in Cases of Interstate Extradition.**—We have, in the preceding pages, seen that the state courts exercise jurisdiction in these cases under the writ of habeas corpus, and so long as their decisions do not come in conflict with federal authority they will no doubt remain undisturbed; but the federal courts are not only claiming jurisdiction to issue the writ of habeas corpus when parties are held in custody under state laws, for acts done by virtue of requisitions by the executive of one state upon the executive of a sister state,³ but that they have exclusive jurisdiction in such cases.⁴ And notwithstanding we have felt it our duty to show the decisions of the state courts and their application to the various questions raised, we are strongly inclined to think that the federal courts are right, particularly when we recollect that, federal stipulations excepted, the states of the Union are independent sovereignties, and that the only right which one of them has to claim the arrest of a fugitive from its justice in the territory of another is purely conventional, and that the right created by treaty stipulation in the federal constitution can be exercised only in the way therein pointed out. By the constitution of the United States the whole subject of interstate extradition is remitted to the cognizance of the general government,⁵ and the mode of proceeding and the evidence necessary to support the demand of a fugitive criminal is prescribed by the law of congress.⁶ These cases then would certainly seem to be such as arise under the constitution and laws of the United States; and

---

¹ In re Carroll, Chic. L. N., Sept. 28, 1878.
² Troutman's Case, 4 Zab. 634.
³ United States v. McClay, 4 Cent. L. J. 255; In the Matter of Titus, 8 Ben. 411; In re Jackson, 12 Am. Law Rev. 602; Ex parte McKean, 3 Hughes, 23; In the Matter of Leary, 10 Ben. 197; S. C., 6 Abb. N. C. 43, and 1 Crim. L. Mag. 265; Ex parte Smith, 3 McLean, 121; In re Doo Woon, 1 West Coast Rep. 333; In re Robb, Id. 439; 6 Opin. Att. Gen. 713. But see People v. Fiske, 45 How. Pr. 294, where it is claimed that state judges are clothed with concurrent jurisdiction in cases of extradition; See note to In re McDonnell, 11 Blatchf. 192.
⁴ In the matter of Titus, 8 Ben. 411. See Prigg v. Com. of Pennsylvania, 16 Pet. 622.
⁵ Sec. 2, art. 4.
⁶ Act of 1793, now sec. 5278, U. S. R. S.

if the prisoner be in custody, he " is in custody under order or by color of the authority of the United States," and creating a case, of course, in which the federal courts have jurisdiction; a case, too, according to the doctrines in Ableman v. Booth,[1] and and Tarble's Case,[2] in which it is for the courts or judicial officers of the United States, and those courts or officers alone, to grant the prisoner release on habeas corpus.

§ 486. **Scope of Inquiry.**—Upon the trial of a writ of habeas corpus, in a case involving an alleged kidnaping, it has been held proper to allow the relators to go behind the indictment, not only for the purpose of showing identity, a question always open on proceedings by habeas corpus,[3] but to show that they were indicted for acts alleged to have been done under a requisition of the executive of one of the states of the Union. It has been held improper, however, in such cases, to show that the indictment upon which the requisition issued was procured improperly or upon insufficient evidence.[4] When a fugitive criminal alleges, on petition for a habeas corpus, that he is unlawfully deprived of his liberty, the court, if it can act at all, may inquire whether the governor's warrant is *prima facie* sufficient to justify the arrest and removal. The right to hold the relator depends wholly upon the sufficiency of the warrant of extradition on its face, and nothing else, and ordinarily a court will not on habeas corpus look behind the warrant.[5] It is a common principle that a process of arrest must be legally sufficient upon its face, and if the warrant of extradition is not *prima facie* sufficient under the constitution and laws of congress, the prisoner may successfully invoke the aid of habeas corpus.[6] "The facility with which indictments are sometimes obtained," says Judge Withey, "affords sufficient justification, not only to the executive of a state on whom a demand for extradition is made, but to the courts, to see that the case falls

---

[1] 21 How. 506.
[2] 13 Wall. 397.
[3] In the Matter of Leary, 10 Ben. 197; S. C., 6 Abb. N. C. 43.
[4] U. S. v. McClay, 4 Cent. L. J. 255.
[5] Leary's Case, 10 Ben. 197; S. C., 6 Abb. N. C. 43.
[6] Where an individual charged with an offense committed in another state has been committed as a fugitive from justice by the committing magistrate of a state, it is competent for a federal court, on habeas corpus, to inquire into the validity of the *mittimus*, and if it does not set out in terms such facts as are required by law to give him authority to arrest and detain the prisoner, the relator will be discharged. 1. It must appear and be shown that the person has fled from the demanding state, and from justice; 2. The person must have been demanded by such other state; 3. He must be demanded as a fugitive from justice; 4. A copy of an indictment found or affidavit, etc., charging the person with crime, must be presented, and be certified as authentic: In re Jackson, 12 Am. Law Rev. 602; Ex parte McKean, 3 Hughes, 23.

§ 487. INTERSTATE EXTRADITION. 627

within the laws."[1] A warrant for the arrest and return of a fugitive criminal must recite or set forth the evidence necessary to authorize the state executive to issue it; and unless it does, it is illegal and void.[2] The detention of the prisoner must be legal at the time of the service of the habeas corpus, or he will be discharged. Valid subsequent process is insufficient.[3] A copy of the papers, or evidence thereof, however, need not accompany or be annexed to the governor's warrant, and though the defendant craves oyer of the same, the respondent need not produce them, nor can defendant compel their production by *certiorari* against the governor.[4]

§ 487. **Conflict of Jurisdiction** between state and federal courts sometimes arise in extradition proceedings. The old doctrine in the states was, that the state writ of habeas corpus, issued by the proper authority, had to be obeyed, to whomsoever it might have been directed and by what process soever he might have claimed to restrain the prisoner.[5] But now the rule is, that a state court can not compel obedience to its writ where it appears on the return that the prisoner is held under authority of the United States.[6] This is forcibly illustrated in a very recent California case. Charles H. Bayley, a fugitive from justice, had been arrested upon a warrant issued by the governor of California on a demand by the governor of Oregon, and delivered into the custody of W. L. Robb, who was duly commissioned and authorized by the governor of Oregon to receive him and convey him to Oregon. This duty Robb was performing, in accordance with the act of congress, when he was served with a writ of habeas corpus, sued out by Bayley from a superior court of the city and county of San Francisco. Robb made a return, stating that he held Bayley for the purpose of conveying him to Oregon, under and in pursuance of the laws of the United States, by virtue of the commission from the governor of Oregon, the warrant of arrest of the governor of California, and arrest under it, annexing thereto copies of said documents and exhibiting the originals; but respectfully declined to produce the body of Bayley, on the expressed ground that, as it appeared to the court that Bayley was in custody under the laws of the United States, it had no jurisdiction to proceed further

---

[1] In re Jackson, 12 Am. Law Rev. 602.
[2] In re Doo Woon, 1 West Coast Rep. 333.
[3] In re Doo Woon, 1 West Coast Rep. 333.
[4] Leary's Case, 10 Ben. 197; S. C., 6 Abb. N. C. 43.
[5] Bagnall v. Ableman, 4 Wis. 163.
[6] Ableman v. Booth, 21 How. 506; Tarble's Case, 13 Wall. 397; see Cannon's Case, 47 Mich. 481.

or to require him to produce the body of the prisoner. But the court took a different view on this point, adjudged Robb guilty of contempt in declining to produce the body of Bayley, and to be imprisoned until he should comply with the commands of the writ in this particular.

Robb then applied for and obtained a writ of habeas corpus from the supreme court of California, which on the return, and without alluding to the cases of Ableman v. Booth[1] or Tarble's Case,[2] decided that the court below had power to compel the production of the body of the prisoner, in order that the cause of his imprisonment and detention might be inquired into, that petitioner was guilty of contempt by his refusal, and remanded the prisoner.[3] Both were then in jail, and Robb, not liking this state of things, applied for and obtained a writ of habeas corpus from the circuit court for the district of California. Circuit Judge Sawyer, for the court, reviewed in a masterly manner the cases of Ableman v. Booth[4] and Tarble's Case,[5] showed their application to the case under consideration, and said: "When the governor of a state, acting under the provision of congress, upon the demand of the authorities of another state, issues his warrant for the arrest of a party charged with a crime, and that party is arrested by any proper officer and delivered over to the party empowered by the state where the offense was committed, to be carried to that state, and delivered to its proper authorities, we have no doubt that the governor issuing the warrant, the officer executing it, and the party to whom he is delivered are acting by virtue and under the authority of the act of congress,[6] and no other, and *pro hac vice* are officers or agents of the United States.[7] From the time of arrest till he is delivered to the authorities of the state demanding his surrender, the party is in the custody of the law—and that law a law of the United States, and the supreme law of the land."[8] His honor showed that Robb was not required to produce the body in court; in fact, that he would have been justified in resisting such production by force, because that would have given the court physical power to assume control, and would have been equivalent to a surrender of the prisoner. The relator was discharged.[9]

[1] 21 How. 507.
[2] 13 Wall. 397.
[3] In re Robb, 1 West Coast Rep. 255. See Ex parte Bayley, Id. 485.
[4] 21 How. 507.
[5] 13 Wall. 397.
[6] Secs. 5278, 5279, U. S. R. S.
[7] Ex parte Smith, 3 McLean, 129; Prigg's Case, 16 Pet. 539.
[8] In re Robb, 1 West Coast Rep. 439. The same principle indorsed in 6 Opin. Att. Gen. 713; People v. Fiske, 45 How. Pr. 294; and see note to In re McDonnell, 11 Blatchf. 192.
[9] If the very able counsel for the petitioner in this case, Mr. Alfred Clarke, believed that the federal courts have exclusive jurisdiction in that

Where a prisoner alleges that he is illegally restrained of his liberty under or by color of the authority of the United States, and files his petition for a writ of habeas corpus in a federal court, such court has jurisdiction of the petition, although a proceeding by *certiorari* is pending in a state court, at the prisoner's suit, for a review of the decision of an inferior court dismissing a writ of habeas corpus issued on his petition. And where a fugitive criminal is held under the warrant of a governor, it is not necessary on habeas corpus proceedings before a federal court, instituted at the suit of the prisoner, to give notice of the proceedings to the attorney general of the state.[1]

class of cases—a position which he seems to have conclusively established in his masterly yet peculiar brief—it s an amusing fact that he did not first apply for his client's relief to the circuit court.

[1] In the Matter of Leary, 10 Ben. 197; S. C., 6 Abb. N. C. 43.

NOTE.

Since the above section was written, Robb's case went, on writ of error, to the supreme court of the United States, and the judgment of the supreme court of California was affirmed. The jurisdiction of state tribunals and federal courts over fugitives from justice has thus been permanently settled. The supreme court of the United States decides that an agent, appointed by the demanding state to receive a fugitive from justice from the surrendering state, is not an officer of the United States, within the meaning of former adjudications of that court; and that a state court has power on habeas corpus, in inter-state extradition, to compel the production of the body of the prisoner before it, so that the cause of his imprisonment and detention can be inquired into. It is now understood that "congress has not undertaken to invest the judicial tribunals of the United States with exclusive jurisdiction of issuing writs of habeas corpus in proceedings for the arrest of fugitives from justice, and their delivery to the authorities of the state in which they stand charged with crime." It is said, too, that "subject, then, to the exclusive and paramount authority of the national government, by its own judicial tribunals, to determine whether persons held in custody by authority of the courts of the United States, or by the commissioners of such courts, or by officers of the general government, acting under its laws, are so held in conformity with law, the states have the right, by their own courts or by the judges thereof, to inquire into the grounds upon which any person within their respective territorial limits is restrained of his liberty, and to discharge him, if it be ascertained that such restraint is illegal; and this, notwithstanding such illegality may arise from a violation of the constitution or the laws of the United States:" Robb v. Connolly, 4 Sup. Ct. Rep. 544; 3 West Coast Rep. 265.

FORMS
USED IN
HABEAS CORPUS PROCEEDINGS.

PETITIONS.

FORM I.
Petition for a Habeas Corpus.

To the Supreme Court[1] of the United States:

The petitioner, ..., of the state of ...., complaining, shows that he is unjustly and unlawfully detained and imprisoned by ...., in the jail,[2] at ...., in the state of ......, by virtue of a warrant[3] of commitment issued under the following circumstances:

Your petitioner is a citizen of the United States, and has been a citizen of the state of .... for over twenty years, and at the time of the grievances herein complained of had never been in the military or naval service of the United States; that on the ...... day of ......, ..., while at home in said state, he was arrested by order of ...., then commanding the military district of ...., and has ever since been kept in close confinement; that on the .... day of ...., ..., he was brought before a military commission convened at ...., by order of said ...., upon the following charges:

---

[1] Or other court, or justice, or judge, as the case may be, properly designated by name.

[2] Or otherwise naming the place of confinement.

[3] Or otherwise describing the process by virtue of which the prisoner is held, or stating the cause of detention.

1. Conspiracy against the government of the United States. 2. Affording aid and comfort to rebels against the authority of the United States. 3. Inciting insurrection. 4. Disloyal practices; and 5. Violation of the laws of war.[1]

Your petitioner objected to the authority of the commission to try him on said charges, but his objections were overruled, and said commission proceeded to try him, and found him guilty of all the charges, and sentenced him to suffer death by hanging, and he was ordered to be hanged on Friday, the nineteenth day of May, 1865, which sentence was approved by the President of the United States.

Your petitioner further shows that while he was being detained and imprisoned as aforesaid, and more than twenty days after his said arrest, the circuit court of the United States for the district of ...... was convened at ......, where he was and is kept in confinement, and a grand jury was then and there convened and in attendance on said court, and duly impaneled, charged, and sworn, and held its sittings, and finally adjourned without having found any bill of indictment against him, etc., and your petitioner is held, detained, and imprisoned by virtue of said proceedings, and on an order of said commission, to await the execution of said sentence.

And your petitioner claims that said military commission had no jurisdiction or authority, legally, to try and sentence him in the manner and form above stated.

Wherefore, to be relieved of said unlawful detention and imprisonment, your petitioner prays that a writ of habeas corpus, to be directed to the said ...., may issue in this behalf, so that your petitioner may be forthwith brought before this court to do, submit to, and receive what the law may require. ....

VERIFICATION.

United States of America, District of ......, ss.

.... , being duly sworn, deposes and says that he is the petitioner-named in the foregoing petition subscribed by him; that he has read the same[2] and knows the contents thereof, and that the statements therein made are true as he verily believes. ....

Subscribed and sworn to this .... day of ......, ...

............,
United States Commissioner.

[1] Or statement of any other offense for which the prisoner is held.
[2] Or heard the foregoing petition read.

FORM II.

Another Form of Petition for a Habeas Corpus—Second Application.

In the matter of the application of ...., for a writ of habeas corpus. Petition for writ.

To the Supreme Court of the State of ......:[1]

The petition of .... respectfully shows that he is unlawfully imprisoned, detained, confined, and restrained of his liberty by ...., sheriff of the county of ......, in this state, at ......, in the said county of ......, in the state of ......

That the said imprisonment, detention, confinement, and restraint are illegal; and that the illegality thereof consists in this, to wit:

That the only pretext or cause of such arrest and detention is by virtue of a warrant of arrest issued out of a justice's court of said county, upon a complaint charging petitioner with a violation of an ordinance of the board of supervisors of said county;[2] the mode and particulars of the adoption of such ordinance, together with a copy of the same, as well as a copy of the complaint filed against petitioner for a violation of said ordinance, are hereinafter set out.

That therefore said justice issued out of said court a warrant requiring the arrest of this petitioner upon said charges. Such warrant was delivered to ...., sheriff of said county, and he, by virtue of the same, and not otherwise, arrested this petitioner and yet holds him in custody thereunder.

That since said arrest, and during the time that petitioner has been held in custody under said warrant, petitioner has petitioned the superior court of said county for the issuance of a writ of habeas corpus, which application was heard on its merits by said court and denied, and applicant was remanded into custody.

That such application made to the superior court for such writ was based on the same facts that this application is based on.

Wherefore your petitioner prays that a writ of habeas corpus may be granted, directed to the said ...., sheriff of ...... county, commanding him to have the body of petitioner before your honorable court,[3] at a time and place therein to be

---

[1] Or other court, justice, or judge designated by name.

[2] Here set out in what the invalidity of the ordinance consists, and a copy of the ordinance, complaint, etc.

[3] Or as the case may be.

specified, to do and receive what shall then and there be considered by your honors concerning him, together with the time and cause of his detention, and said writ; and that petitioner may be restored to his liberty.

Dated ....

State of ......, county of ......, ss.

............, being duly sworn, deposes and says that he is the petitioner named in the foregoing petition subscribed by him, that he has read the same,[1] and knows the contents thereof, and that the statements therein made he believes to be true.

....
Subscribed and sworn to before me this ...... day of ......,
....
Notary Public.

FORM III.
Usual Form of Petition.
Application for Writ by Party Confined.

To the Honorable, ..., Justice of the Supreme Court of the State of ......:[2]

The petition of .... respectfully shows to your honors that he is now a prisoner, confined in the custody of ...., sheriff of the county of ......, in the county jail, in the ...... of ......, in said county, for a supposed criminal offense, to wit.[3] Your petitioner also shows that such confinement is by virtue of a warrant, a copy of which is hereto annexed,[4] and your petitioner avers that to the best of his knowledge he is not committed or detained by virtue of any process issued by any court of the United States, or any judge thereof, in a case where such courts or judges have exclusive jurisdiction under the laws of the United States, or have acquired such jurisdiction by the commencement of any suit in such courts, or by virtue of any final judgment or decree of any competent court[5] of criminal[6] jurisdiction, or by virtue of any process issued upon such judgment or decree. And your petitioner further states that he is advised by counsel, ..., Esq., residing at ......, and so believes, that his said impris-

---

[1] Or heard the foregoing petition read.
[2] Or to the court, as the case may be.
[3] Here insert the alleged offense.
[4] If a copy can be obtained; if one can not be obtained, state the reason why, and the effort made to obtain such copy.
[5] Or tribunal.
[6] Or civil. Make these clauses conform to the statute providing for cases in which the party must be remanded.

onment is illegal, and that said illegality consists in this, to wit:[1] Wherefore, your petitioner prays a writ of habeas corpus, to the end that he may be discharged from custody.[2]

............, ...
His Attorney.
Dated, ...
Add verification.

FORM IV.

Application by a Third Party.

To the Honorable ...., Justice of the Supreme Court of the State of ......:

The petition of .... respectfully shows that .... is imprisoned and restrained of his liberty by,[3] and that the said .... is so confined and restrained at;[4] and that according to the best of your petitioner's knowledge and belief the cause or pretense of the aforesaid confinement or restraint of the said .... is as follows, etc.[5] And your petitioner further states that he is advised by counsel, ..., Esq., residing at the ...... of ......, ..., and so believes, that the said imprisonment of .... is illegal, and that said illegality consists in this, to wit.[6] Wherefore your petitioner prays a writ of habeas corpus, to the end that he may be discharged from custody.[7]

....
His Attorney. ....
Dated ......
Add verification.

FORM V.

Petition where there is Danger that the Party may be Carried out of the State, or that some Injury may Accrue before the Writ can Issue.

After setting out, in full, an application substantially that in Form IV. add: And your petitioner further states, that the said ...., in whose custody the said ... . is, threatens to carry the said .... out of the state, and has told several persons publicly that such was his intention; that your petitioner had a conversation with the said .... this morning, in which the said .... then stated

---

[1] State the alleged illegality.
[2] Or, to the end that he may be bailed, etc.
[3] State by whom, and how, etc.
[4] Naming the place.
[5] State the same.
[6] State the alleged illegality.
[7] Or, to the end that he may be bailed, etc.

to your petitioner that he should leave immediately with the said .... for the state of ......, and that neither your petitioner nor any other person had any power to prevent him from doing so.[1] Wherefore your petitioner asks that a warrant immediately issue to take the said ....

Dated ....

Add verification.

FORM VI.

Petition to Obtain a Habeas Corpus for the Purpose of being Bailed.

To the Honorable ...., Judge of the Superior Court of the County of ......, State of ......

The petition of ...., now a prisoner in the jail of the county of ......, and in the custody of the keeper thereof, respectfully represents that he is now in confinement, and detained in the said jail, upon a charge of having burglariously broken and entered the dwelling-house of one ...., on the night of, etc., by virtue of a commitment under the hand and seal of ...., one of the justices of the peace of said county, and the petitioner is able to give good and sufficient bail for his appearance, in whatever court it may be prosecuted, to answer the said charge and any other that may be brought against him; he therefore prays that a writ of habeas corpus may be granted to bring him before your honor, to be bailed accordingly.

VERIFICATION.

State of ......, County of ......, ss.

............, the above-named petitioner, being duly sworn, on his oath says, that the facts set forth in the above petition are true. ....

Subscribed and sworn to before me this ..... day of ......, A. D. ....,

Notary Public.

FORM VII.

Petition for Habeas Corpus in Case of Private Restraint; as That of Master or Other Person.

To the Honorable ...., Judge of the Superior Court of the County of ......, State of ......

The petition of .... respectfully shows: That he is

---

[1] Set forth the facts showing the illegal confinement of ...., and that he will be carried out of the state, or irreparably injured, before he can be relieved on habeas corpus or *certiorari*.

now restrained of his liberty by ...., at ......, in said county and state, illegally and wrongfully, and for no criminal or supposed criminal matter. He therefore prays your honor to grant a writ of habeas corpus, directed to the said ...., commanding him to bring before your honor the petitioner's body, to do as and abide such order as your honor may direct.[1]

FORM VIII.

Petition for Habeas Corpus by a Parent for a Child.

To the Honorable ...., one of the Associate Justices of the Supreme Court of ...... :

The petition of .... respectfully shows: That your petitioner's daughter, ..., aged ..... years, is illegally restrained of her liberty by ...., of ......, county of ......, state of ..... , and that she is not detained for any criminal or supposed criminal matter. The petitioner therefore prays your honor to grant a writ of habeas corpus, pursuant to the statute in such case made and provided, to bring up the body of the said .... to abide such order as your honor may direct.[1]   ....

FORM IX.

Habeas Corpus ad Testificandum—Affidavit and Application.

In the Circuit Court of .... County, State of ...., Plaintiff, v. ...., Defendant. State of ......, County of ......, ss.

............, plaintiff above named, being duly sworn, says: That this action is brought upon, etc.[2] That the defense to said action is as follows.[3] And deponent says that ...., who is now a prisoner in the custody of the sheriff of the county of ...... under an execution upon a final judgment, etc.,[4] is and will be a material witness for this deponent on the trial of said action, as he is advised by ...., Esq., his counsel in this action, residing at ...... in said county, and verily believes to be true; and that he can not safely proceed to the trial of said

---

[1] Append the ordinary verification: See forms 1, 2, 3.
[2] Describe the cause of action.   [3] Set up the defense.
[4] Set forth for what he is in custody.

cause without the testimony of the said ...., as he is also advised by his said counsel and believes.

And this deponent further states that his said action is noticed for trial at a circuit court to be held at the court-house in ......, in the county of ......, on the ...... day of ......, ...

Sworn, etc.

WRITS.

FORM X.

Writ of Habeas Corpus ad Subjiciendum.

In the Supreme Court[1] of the State of ......[1] In the Matter of ....[1] Writ of Habeas Corpus. The People of the State of ...... to ....,[2] greeting:

We command you, that you have the body of ...., by you imprisoned and detained, as it is said, together with the time and cause of such imprisonment and detention, by whatsoever name the said .... shall be called or charged, before the justices of our supreme court at the supreme court room, in the ...... building, in the city of ......,[3] immediately after the receipt of this writ,[4] to do and receive what shall then and there be considered and determined concerning the said ...., and have you then and there this writ.

Witness, the honorable ...., chief justice of your supreme court,[5] at ......, the ...... day of ......, ...

............, Clerk,[6]

By ...., Deputy Clerk.

............, Attorney.

[1] Change title of court, venue, and title of cause, to suit the case.
[2] Or to a sheriff, officer, or any other individual who unjustly detains another person.
[3] Or before ...., judge of the superior court of the county of ......, state of ......, at the court room of the said superior court, or other designated place.
[4] Or at a specified day and hour, as soon after the issuance of the writ as the same can be reasonably returned and heard.
[5] Or as the name and title may be.
[6] Where seals are required the writ should be sealed. This is noted in the indorsement by the word *allocutur*—let it be sealed. The fees, too, should be noted in states where they are allowed.

INDORSEMENT THEREON.

Allowed the ...... day of ......, ..., on the application of ....[1]   ....,
Justice of the Supreme Court.

FORM XI.
Another Writ of Habeas Corpus.

In the Supreme Court[2] of the United States.[2]
In the Matter of ..... [2] Writ of habeas corpus.
The President of the United States of America to ...., Marshal, etc.[3]

We command you that the body of ...., by you detained and imprisoned, it is said, you have forthwith[4] before our court,[5] etc., at the city of Washington,[6] together with the cause of the detention of the said ...., to undergo and receive what our said court shall consider concerning him in this behalf; and have you then and there this writ.

Witness the honorable ...., chief justice of the supreme court of the United States, this ...... day of ......, ...[7]   [L. S.]   ....
Clerk of the Supreme Court of the United States.[8]

FORM XII.
Writ of Habeas Corpus ad Testificandum.

...... county, ss.
The State of ...... to the Sheriff of the said county, Greeting:

We command you that you have the body of ...., detained in our prison under your costody, it is said, under safe and secure conduct, by whatsoever name the said .... may be charged, before the judges of our circuit court, at a court to be held at ......, on the ...... day of ...... next, to testify the truth according to his knowledge in a certain cause

---

[1] Stating the person's name. Where seals are required, add "Let it be sealed." And if the charges for bringing up the prisoner are required to be paid, add to the indorsement: "Fees for bringing up and returning the prisoner to be tendered in advance;" or, "And the charges for bringing up such prisoner, amounting to . .... dollars, are hereby required to be paid by petitioner on whose application this writ is issued."

[2] Adapt title of court, venue, and title of cause to case.
[3] Or sheriff or other person.
[4] Or at a designated time.
[5] Or a circuit or district court, or a judge thereof.
[6] Or other specified place.
[7] Or other justice, as the case may be.
[8] Or circuit or district court, if issued in such jurisdiction.

in our said court, before our said judges, depending, and then and there to be tried, wherein .... is plaintiff and .... is defendant; and that immediately after the said .... gives his testimony before our said judges, you return him to our said prison, etc., and have you then and there this writ.

Witness the Honorable ...., judge of our said circuit court, this ...... day of ......, A. D. one thousand eight hundred and ...., Clerk.[1]
............, Attorney.

INDORSEMENT.

Allowed this ...... day of ......, ...
....
Judge of the Circuit Court.

FORM XIII.

Another Form of Habeas Corpus ad Testificandum.

The President of the United States of America to the Marshal of the District of ......, Greeting:[2]

You are hereby commanded that you have the body of .... now in prison,[3] under your custody, it is said, under safe and secure conduct, before, etc.,[4] to testify the truth, according to his knowledge, in a certain case now depending, etc.,[5] and immediately after the said .... shall then and there have given his testimony, that you return him to the said prison,[6] under safe and secure conduct, and have you there then this writ.

Witness, etc.[7]

---

[1] Make changes to suit the case.
[2] Conforming to the English style, that process shall run in the name of the king or queen.
[3] Or as the case may be.
[4] As in the subpœna.
[5] Id.
[6] Or as the case may be.
[7] As in the *capias*.

RETURNS.

FORM XIV.

Return to a Writ of Habeas Corpus where Certain Facts Correspond with those Alleged in the Petition.

To the Supreme Court of the United States:[1]

............, to whom the within[2] writ is directed, has now here before the court[3] the body of .... therein named, as thereby commanded. And I certify that the cause of the detention of the said .... is a warrant of commitment,[4] directed to me, a copy of which is hereto annexed, marked "Exhibit A," and made a part hereof, issued in the manner and under the circumstances and for the purpose set forth in the petition of the said .... herein. ....

                                                  Marshal, etc.[5]

Dated this ...... day of ......, ...

N. B.—All returns to writs of habeas corpus should be verified. If the person making the return is not a sworn public officer, and acting as such in making such return, he should verify it in the usual form.

FORM XV.

Return Where Petitioner is not in Custody.

To the Honorable ...., Justice of the Supreme Court of ......:[6]

............, sheriff of the county of ....., the defendant in the within writ mentioned, for return thereto, respectfully submits to your honor that the said ...., therein named, is not now, nor was at the time of the issuing of the said writ, nor at any time since has he been, in the custody, power, or possession of or confined or restrained of his liberty by the said .... Therefore he can not have the body of the

---

[1] Or to a justice thereof. Or to the circuit or district court, as the case may be. Or to the Honorable ...., circuit judge of the United States circuit court for the ...... circuit; or to the Honorable ...., district judge of the United States district court for the district of ......

[2] Or annexed.
[3] Or your honor.
[4] Or order or other process.
[5] Or as the *descriptio personæ* may be.
[6] Or to the court before which the return is directed to be made.

said .... before your honor, as by the within writ he is commanded.

Dated ....,
Sheriff.[1]

FORM XVI.

Where the Prisoner has been Transferred to the Custody of Another.

State of ......, County of ......, ss.:

I hereby certify that at the time of the service of the within[2] writ upon me, the said .... therein named was not in my custody, or under my power or restraint; that on the ...... day of ......, ..., I had the said prisoner in my custody; that the authority and true cause of such imprisonment was as follows;[3] that on the ...... day of ......, ..., I delivered the body of the said .... to ...., for the following cause, and upon the following authority.[4]

............, Sheriff, etc.

FORM XVII.

Return where Petitioner is in Custody.

To the Honorable ...., Justice of the Supreme Court of ......:[5]

............, sheriff of the county of ......, the defendant in the within-mentioned writ, for return thereto, respectfully submits to your honor, that true it is that the said .... therein named, is confined and restrained of his liberty by the said ...., but the said .... alleges that the said .... is so restrained lawfully,[6] which is the true

---

[1] Make the necessary changes to suit the facts and circumstances of the case.

[2] Or annexed.

[3] Here set forth at large the cause of imprisonment. If held by written authority, add: That annexed hereto, and forming a part of this return, is a copy of the warrant of commitment —or other written authority, by virtue of which I so had and detained the said .... in my custody, the original of which is herewith produced; and if the original is no longer in his hands, state that fact and give the substance thereof.

[4] Here state at large the cause of transfer, and authority therefor, and if by warrant or other written authority, annex thereto a copy, and add: And I annex hereto, as a part of this return, a copy of the warrant— or other written authourity, by virtue of which such transfer was made. Or, if the prisoner has not been transferred, but is not in custody; recite as above except, instead of transfer, state the fact of his not being in custody, and the reason therefor; as, That on the ...... day of ......, ..., the said .... broke from the jail of the county of ......, and escaped from my custody, and has not since been retaken.

[5] Or as the case may be.

[6] Here set out the authority for detaining the petitioner; as, in some of the states, by virtue of a writ of *capias ad respondendum*, issued out of the circuit court of the county of ...... against him, at the suit of ...., the tenor of which is as follows [inserting copy], which is the true cause of his imprisonment.

cause of his imprisonment. Wherefore the said ....
has here before your honor the body of the said ....,
together with the said writ, as therein he is commanded.
Dated ....
                                         Sheriff, etc.[1]

FORM XVIII.
Return to Habeas Corpus or Certiorari.

State of ......, County of ...... ss.

I hereby certify that at the time of the service upon me of the within[2] writ, the said .... therein named was and still is in my custody; that the authority and true cause of such imprisonment is as follows.[3]

Dated ....
                                         Sheriff, etc.

FORM XIX.
Return to Habeas Corpus ad Testificandum.

State of ......, County of ......, ss.

I, ..., sheriff, etc., do certify that the prisoner within named is held by me pursuant to,[4] and I now have the said prisoner here before your honors pursuant to the within writ.

Dated ....
                                         Sheriff, etc.

FORM XX.
Where the Prisoner was Committed on Execution.

To, etc.[5]

I do certify that the body of the within-named .... is in execution, at the suit of ...., for the sum of one hundred dollars, returnable before, etc., on the ...... day of ......, ... Nevertheless, the body of the said ....
I have ready, etc. So answers

                                         ....

---

[1] Or as the case may be.
[2] Or annexed.
[3] Here set forth at length the cause of imprisonment. If held by written authority, add: That annexed hereto, and forming a part of this return, is a copy of the warrant of commitment, or other written authority, by virtue of which said .... is by me detained, the original of which is herewith produced. If the writ is a habeas corpus, add, after stating the cause of imprisonment: And in obedience to said writ, I have the body of the said .... now here before the court or officer, as the case may be.
[4] Here state authority and cause of detention; or, if practicable, annex copy of commitment, in which case add: "the commitment, a copy of which is hereto annexed, and forms a part of this return."
[5] Giving the proper direction.

FORM XXI.

Where the Prisoner was Committed for Contempt.

To the Honorable ...., Judge of the Superior Court of the County of ......, State of ......[1]

I, ..., sheriff of the county of ......, do certify that the body of the within-named .... is in execution for contempt of court under the order of ...., a justice of the peace of said county, and which reads as follows, viz.[2] Nevertheless, the body of the said .... I have ready, etc. So answers

....

Sheriff, etc.

FORM XXII.

Where the Prisoner was Committed on Warrant.

To, etc.[3]

I, ..., sheriff of the county of ......, state of ......, do certify that before the coming of this writ to me directed, to wit, on the ...... day of ......, ..., ..., in the said writ named, was committed to my custody by virtue of a certain warrant[4] under the hand and seal of ......, ..., a justice of the peace of the county aforesaid, the tenor of which said warrant follows in these words: "To the keeper of the jail," etc.,[5] and this is the cause of the taking and detaining of the aforesaid .... in my custody. Neverthless the body of the said .... I have ready, etc. So answers

............,

Sheriff, etc.

FORM XXIII.

Where the Prisoner was Committed on Suspicion.

To, etc.[6]

I do certify that before the coming of this writ, the within-named .... was committed to the prison of the city of ......, on suspicion of counterfeiting the moneys of the United States,[7] and for that cause and no other, in the same prison is detained. Nevertheless the body of the said .... I have ready, etc. So answers

............,

Keeper, etc.

---

[1] Or other appropriate direction.
[2] Here set forth the order of court, or warrant of commitment.
[3] Giving the proper direction.
[4] Or *mittimus*.
[5] As in the warrant.
[6] Giving proper direction.
[7] Or on suspicion of larceny, or as the case may be.

FORM XXIV.

Where the Prisoner was Committed on Indictment.

To the Judges, etc.

I do certify that before the coming of this writ, to wit, at a court of, etc., held, etc., before, etc., the within-named .... was indicted for, etc.,[1] ......, and by the same court was committed to the prison of ......, which said indictment remains before the said judges at, etc. Nevertheless the body of the said .... I have ready, etc. So answers

.............,
Respondent, etc.

FORM XXV.

Additional Clause to Return where the Prisoner is Held for Several Causes.

And also the said .... is detained in the prison of the said county by virtue of a certain writ of, etc.,[2] against him, at the suit of ...., of a plea of, etc.[3] And also of the bill of the said ...., against him, the said ...., for ...... dollars, returnable before the judges at ......, the ...... day of ...... last past. And these are the causes of the taking and obtaining of the aforesaid .... Nevertheless, the body of the said .... I have ready, etc. So answers

Dated ......

.............,
Keeper, etc.

FORM XXVI.

Return where Infants are in Custody.

In the Superior Court of the County of ......, State of ...., ..., plaintiffs, v. ...., ..., defendants. Return to writ of habeas corpus. To ...., Judge of said Superior Court:

The within-named .... and ......, his wife, do hereby certify to your honor, that the within-named plaintiffs, ... and ...., are detained by and are under the protection of the said ...., in the county of ......, for the purpose of being educated and maintained by her as

---
[1] Here set forth the cause of indictment.
[2] Here set forth the writ.
[3] Setting out the plea.

their guardian, under the will of their grandmother, ..., deceased, and according to the trusts and directions for those purposes contained in the said will.

Dated at ......, this ...... day of ......, ...

................,
...........¹

FORM XXVII.

Return where the Body Only is Brought.

The body of the within-named ...., by me before taken and detained, before the judges within named, at the day and place within contained, I have ready as within I am commanded. So answers

FORM XXVIII.

Where the Prisoner can not be Brought, Owing to his Infirmity.

Languidus in Prisona.

After stating that the prisoner is in custody, and giving the cause of his imprisonment as in form No. 17, add: That the said .... is now so sick,² that the production of him would endanger his life,³ and for that reason I do not produce his body here, in obedience to said writ.⁴

Dated, ...

FORM XXIX.

Where Prisoner is under Sentence of Death.

The same return is made as in form No. 17, down to the clause relating to the production of his body. This clause is omitted, as the body, under such circumstances, is not produced on habeas corpus.

---

¹ Make changes to suit the case.
² Or infirm.
³ Or health.

⁴ This return should accompanied by the affidavits of one or more reputable physicians.

MISCELLANEOUS FORMS

FORM XXX.
Order Granting Writ.

In the Superior Court of the County of ......, State of ......
In the Matter of the Application of .... for a Writ of Habeas Corpus. Order granting Writ.

On reading and filing the petition of ...., duly signed and verified by him, whereby it appears that he is illegally imprisoned and restrained of his liberty by ...., at the county jail in the said county of ......, in the state of ......, and stating wherein the illegality consists, from which it appears to me that a writ of habeas corpus ought to issue.

It is ordered that a writ of habeas corpus issue out of and under the seal of the superior court of the county of ......, state of ......, directed to the said ...., commanding him to have the body of the said .... before me, in the court room of the said court, on the ...... day of ......, ..., at two o'clock P. M. of that day, to do and receive what shall then and there be considered concerning the said ...., together with the time and cause of his detention, and that he have then and there the said writ.

Dated at ......, on the ...... day of ......, A. D. ......

....

Superior Judge.

FORM XXXI.
Form of Notice of Application to the District Attorney.

The People of the State of ...... v. ......   In the Superior Court of the County of ....

To ...., District Attorney.

Please take notice, that a writ of habeas corpus has been issued to the sheriff of ...... county, commanding said sheriff to bring up the body of the above-named defendant before the Honorable ...., judge of the superior court of said county, that he may be discharged. And you will please appear and show cause to the contrary.

Said writ is made returnable at ten o'clock in the forenoon of the ...... inst.

Dated at ......, this ...... day of ......, ...

....,
Attorney for Defendant.

FORM XXXII.

Notice of Application to other Interested Parties.

To ....:

You will please take notice that a writ of habeas corpus has been issued by the supreme court, to inquire into the cause of the imprisonment of ...., now confined in the jail of ...... county, under a process in which you have or claim some interest; and that said writ is made returnable before the said court, at the supreme court-room in ......, on the ...... day of ......, ..., at ten o'clock A. M. of that day.

Dated at ......, this ...... day of ......, ...

....,
Attorney for Relator.

FORM XXXIII.

Commitment for Disobedience of Writ.

To the Sheriff of the County of ......, State of ......:

Whereas, ... has been brought before me on a warrant issued by me, stating that he, the said ...., to whom, etc.;[1] and whereas, the said .... still refuses to obey the said writ of habeas corpus, by producing the body of the said ...., according to the command of the said writ, and by not making a full and explicit return to said writ of habeas corpus. These are therefore to command you, in the name of the people of the state of ......, forthwith to convey the said .... to the jail of said county, and there commit him to close custody in such jail, without being allowed the liberties thereof, there to remain until he shall make return to the writ in such warrant mentioned, and also comply with my order this day made, wherein the said ...... was ordered, etc.[2]

---

[1] Recite the warrant.
[2] Here state any further order made in the premises respecting the relief sought, etc.

FORM XXXIV.
Attachment for Disobedience of Writ.

To the Sheriff of ...... County, State of ....

It appearing satisfactorily to me, on the oath of ...., that ...., to whom a writ of habeas corpus was delivered commanding him to bring before me ...., in the said writ named, has neglected to obey the said writ, according to the command thereof, by not producing the said .... before me, and also by not making a return to such writ within the time limited by law, and no sufficient excuse having been shown for such neglect, these are therefore to command you, in the name of the people of the state of ......, forthwith to arrest the said .... and bring him immediately before me at my office in the court-house of ......, in said county.

Given under my hand and seal at the city of ......, aforesaid, on the ...... day of ......, ...

[L. S.] ....,

Superior Judge of ...... County, ...

............, Attorney.

FORM XXXV.
Certificate of Service of Writs of Habeas Corpus.

State of ......, County of ......, ss.

I certify that on the ...... day of ......, ..., I served the writ, of which the within [1] is a copy, on ...., the person to whom the same is directed, by delivering to and leaving with him, personally, the said writ at his office, in the city of ......[2].

Dated ....

---

[1] Or annexed.

[2] Where the person to be served can not with due diligence be found, add after the word "directed": By leaving the same at ......—the jail or other place where the prisoner is confined—with ...., keeper of said jail, or ...., a person of proper age, having charge, for the time, of the said prisoner; not having been able, with due diligence, to find the said ...., to whom said writ is directed; and at the same time paying or tendering to him the sum of ...... dollars, his fees or charges for bringing up the prisoner. Where the person upon whom the writ ought to be served keeps himself concealed, or refuses admittance, proceed as above to the word "directed" and add: By affixing the same in a conspicuous place on the outside of his dwelling-house, or other place where the prisoner is confined. When the prisoner is in custody of a sheriff, marshal, coroner, or constable, the following additional clause must be added where required by statute: And delivering to him an undertaking pursuant to—statutory section—a copy of which is hereto annexed.

Where the writ is allowed on the application of the attorney general or a district attorney, no fees need be tendered in states where they are allowed, and no undertaking given. The form of a certificate of service of *certiorari* to inquire into the cause of detention is substantially the same as the above form.

FORM XXXVI.
Bond on Serving the Writ.

Know all men by these presents that I, ..., of the town of ......, in the county of ......, am held and firmly bound unto ...., sheriff of said county, in the penal sum of ...... dollars,[1] to be paid to the said ...., or to his certain attorney, executors, administrators, or assigns, for the payment of which well and truly to be made, I bind myself, my heirs, executors, and administrators, firmly by these presents. Sealed with my seal, this ...... day of ......, ...

The condition of this bond is such, that whereas one .... is now confined as a prisoner in the custody of the said ...., sheriff aforesaid, and a writ of habeas corpus has been issued by the supreme court[2] to inquire into the cause of his detention, directed to the said sheriff; now, therefore, the condition of this obligation is such, that if the said ... . shall pay to the said sheriff the charges of carrying back the said ...., if he shall be remanded on the habeas corpus, and if the said .... shall not escape by the way, either in going to or returning from the court house in ......, then this obligation to be void; otherwise to remain in full force.   .... [SEAL.]

Sealed in the presence of ....

FORM XXXVII.
Precept to Bring Up the Party Illegally Restrained.

To the Sheriff of the County of ......, State of ......

Whereas, a writ of habeas corpus has heretofore been issued by me, directed to ...., in which he, the said ...., was commanded to have the body of ...., by him imprisoned and detained, as it was said, together with the time and cause of such imprisonment, and which writ has been duly served upon the said ....; and whereas the said .... has neglected to produce the body of the said ...., according to the command of said writ; and for which neglect an attachment has been issued against the said ....

---
[1] Double the amount for which the prisoner is detained. If detained for no amount, then in the amount provided for by statute.

[2] Or as the case may be.

These are, therefore, to command you, in the name of the people of the state of ......, forthwith to bring before me the said ...., at my office in the city of ......, in said county and state.

....
Superior Judge. [SEAL.]

....
Attorney.

FORM XXXVIII.
Warrant under Form V.

To ...., Sheriff of the County of ......:[1]

Whereas, ... has applied to me for a warrant to take ...., alleged to be illegally confined by[2] ....; and whereas, it appears from the proofs before me on such application;[3] from which facts it satisfactorily appears to me that the said .... is held in illegal confinement[4] by the said ...., and that there is good reason to believe that he will be carried out of the state[5] before he can be relieved by the issuing of a habeas corpus or *certiorari*.

These are, therefore, to command you, in the name of the people of the state of ......, that you forthwith take the said .... and bring him before me, to be dealt with according to law.

Given under my hand and seal, at ...... in said county, this ...... day of ......, ... [L. S.]
............, Attorney.

FORM XXXIX.
Certiorari from the United States Supreme Court to a United States Circuit Court.

The United States of America. The President of the United States of America to the judge of Circuit Court of the United States for the Southern District of ......, greeting:

You are hereby commanded that, searching the record and proceedings in the matter of ...., you certify forthwith to the supreme court of the United States, under your seal, a full, true, and complete transcript of said record and proceed-

---

[1] Or to any constable of the county of.
[2] Or in the custody of.
[3] Recite the facts upon which the warrant is issued.
[4] Or custody.
[5] Or will suffer irreparable injury.

ings, plainly and distinctly, and in as full and ample a manner as the same now remains before you, together with this writ, so that the said supreme court of the United States may be able thereon to proceed and do what shall appear to them of right ought to be done. Herein fail not.

Witness, the Honorable ...., chief justice of the said supreme court, this ...... day of ......, ...

............, Clerk of Supreme Court.

FORM XL.

Certiorari.

The People of the State of ......, to the Sheriff of ...... County.[1]

We command you, that you certify fully and at large to our justices of our supreme court,[2] at ......, on the ...... day of ...... next,[3] the day and cause of the imprisonment of ...., by you detained, as it is said, by whatsoever name the said .... is called or charged. And have you then and there this writ.

Witness ...., one of the justices[4] of the said court,[5] the ...... day of ......, ...

FORM XLI.

Traverse to Return.

Before the Honorable ...., Judge of the Superior Court of ......, State of ......

The said ...., in answer to the return of the said ...., sheriff, etc., of the county of ......, ..., to the writ of habeas corpus directed to him in the above matter, denies that,[6] etc. And the said ...., in further answering said return, shows that,[7] etc.

N. B. This answer should be verified unless made by an officer.

---

[1] Or to the person detaining the prisoner.

[2] At a special term or general term thereof, to be held, etc.; or to ...., justice of the supreme court, or otherwise, as the case may be.

[3] Or immediately after the receipt of this writ.

[4] Or judges.

[5] Or county judge, or otherwise, as the case may be.

[6] Here set forth the allegations in the return which the party wishes to traverse.

[7] Here allege any matter showing the party to be illegally imprisoned, or entitled to his discharge.

FORM XLII.
Recognizance on being Bailed.

In the Superior Court of the County of ......, State of ......:

The People of the State of ......, plaintiff, v. ...., defendant. Indicted for burglary.

Whereas, an order having been made on the ...... day of ......, A. D. eighteen hundred and ......, by ...., a justice of the peace of ...... county, that .... be held to answer[1] upon a charge of burglary in breaking into the house of ...., and upon which he has been admitted to bail in the sum of ...... dollars, by the said superior court of ..... county.

Now, therefore, we, ..., by occupation a ...., and ...., by occupation a ...., hereby undertake that the above-named .... will appear and answer the charge above mentioned, in whatever court it may be prosecuted, and will at all times hold himself amenable to the orders and process of the court, and if convicted, will appear for judgment and render himself in execution thereof; or if he fails to perform either of these conditions, that we will pay to the people of the state of ......, the sum of ...... dollars.

....
....

Witnessed and approved by me this ...... day of ......, A. D., ...[2]
............,
Superior Judge of the County of ......

State of ......, County of ......, ss.:

.... and ...., whose names are subscribed as the sureties to the above undertaking, being severally duly sworn, each for himself, says, that he is a resident and a freeholder[3] within the county of ......, state of ......, and that he is worth the amount specified in the said undertaking as the penalty thereof, over and above all his debts and liabilities, exclusive of property exempt from execution.   ....
............[4]

Subscribed and sworn to before me this ...... day of ......, A. D. ...., County Clerk.

---

[1] Or an indictment having been found, etc.

[2] Or acknowledged before me, etc., followed by the officer's signature.

[3] Or householder.

[4] The justification forms no part of the contract of the sureties, and in no manner affects their liability: People v. Penniman, 37 Cal. 271.

FORM XLIII.
Order of Discharge.

The body of ...., in the foregoing writ of habeas corpus mentioned, being brought before me, at the time and place in the said writ named, and the return thereto being read and considered, and it appearing to me that the facts and circumstances therein set forth are not sufficient to justify his imprisonment, and no sufficient cause for the detention of the said .... appearing, I, ..., justice of the supreme court, do hereby order that the said .... be by the said sheriff forthwith discharged from imprisonment and detention for the cause aforesaid.

Given under my hand and seal this ...... day of ......,
............,
Justice of the Supreme Court of ......

INDEX.

INDEX.

N. B.—The Figures Refer to the Sections.

A

AFFIDAVIT.
admissibility and value of, as evidence, 217, *note*.
allowed, to fortify return, 129.
allowed, to show conviction and sentence, when, 129, 220.
alleging facts upon information merely, value of, 136.
attachment for falsifying, 207.
authority must be shown by, or application will be refused, 91, 92, 93, 96, 99, 100, 116.
contained in traverse, looked into, 238.
charging crime in extradition proceedings, 476.
defects in, when advantage should be taken of them, 136.
defective, how viewed, 208.
entitled in several causes for *habeas corpus cum causa*, 99.
ex parte, viewed with suspicion, 217, *note*.
examination of, upon which warrant issued, 238.
for attachment, 124.
false, and issuance of writ thereon, 112.
in civil cases, 219.
must be made on oath, 217, *note*.
not essence of the writ, 90.
of juror, competent evidence to show disagreement of jury on former trial, 408.
of husband for recovery of wife must state that she is detained against her will, 421.
of facts shown without objection, effect of, 198.
proving truth of, 155.
requisites of, 217, *note*.
should state facts, 219.
time for filing allowed, when, 211.
time for filing not granted, when, 211.
truth of, may be rebutted, 218.
to show want of jurisdiction, 211.
to contradict return, 212.
to contradict return not expressly authorized by 31 Car. II., 212.
to questions of bail was permitted by 31 Car. II., 213.
to enlarge time for making return, 214.
to fortify return, 215.

AFFIDAVIT—*Continued.*
  to contradict statements in warrant, 216.
  use of in English practice, 209–216.
  value of evidence by, 207.
  verity of, must never be doubted, 217, *note.*
  verifying depositions, 259.
                              See EVIDENCE.
AMENDMENT.
  before final disposition of case, 128.
  of return, not always allowed, 128.
  of return, generally allowed, 126, 128.
  of records, 129.
APPRENTICE. See MASTER AND APPRENTICE.
APPLICATION.
  can not be denied where granting it is made an imperative duty by statute, 94.
  construction of statute requiring it to be made in the county, 89.
  costs of, when taxable to county, 119.
  can not be granted upon mere moral restraint, 87, 131.
  errors in warrant of arrest or warrant of commitment, effect of, 136.
  for *habeas corpus ad testificandum* is made to judge in chambers, not to court, 90.
  for attachment, 124.
  for second writ—what must be shown, 90.
  for discharge from indentures of apprenticeship, 136.
  for writ in extradition proceedings, 459.
  how made in federal courts, 59, 88.
  how made in the state courts, 88.
  judgment on first, is entitled to consideration on second, 389.
  may be made whether judgment is under civil or criminal process, 87.
  may be made by another in prisoner's behalf, 91.
  must be granted, when, 93.
  may be denied in excepted cases mentioned in statute, 94.
  must be grounded upon affidavit, 210.
  must show authority, 440.
  must state facts, 89, 126.
  requisites of the petition, 89.
  special bail may make, 93.
  should be made to local court or judge, 108.
  shows authority, when, 455.
  should be made to trial court, when, 90.
  should be made to court nearest applicant, and not one nearest residence of applicant, 89.
  should not be made for bail, pending application for bail in another court, 90.
  second application—not barred by refusal of discharge on first, 386.
  second application—newly discovered evidence, 108, 188, 189.
  second application—evidence upon subsequently occurring events, 189, 389.
  second application—when grounds of refusal should be shown, 90.

APPLICATION—*Continued.*
    to conduct defense in person—made to what court—and how, 93.
    under what circumstances it may be made, 87.
    when the application will be entertained, 88.
    when application ought to be denied, 94.
    who may make, 91.
    who is the applicant under certain circumstances, 89.
    when application will be refused, 90.
    when public prosecutor may make, 93.
    will not be allowed to review mere errors or irregularities, 94.
        See PETITION.

APPEALS.
    can not be taken from order admitting to bail, 41.
    conditions of, to United States circuit court and United States supreme court, 59.
    from United States district to United States circuit court, 59, 64, *note,* 66.
    from order fixing bail—appellate proceedings, 413.
    from judgment refusing bail, 415.
    from judgment in extradition proceedings, 484.
    may be brought to reverse proceedings not showing jurisdiction upon their face, 224.
    "once in jeopardy" taken advantage of on appeal, 253.
    pending, custody of child should not be changed, 450.
    pending, certain state proceedings to be deemed null and void, 59.
    practice on, in Texas, 188.
    statutory provisions relating to, 388.
    to supreme court of the United States, 59, 64.
    to reverse erroneous judgments or orders, 241, 263.
    writ of error or appeal to territorial courts, 68.

ARREST.
    defined, 271.
    on bail piece, 125.
    officers making, protected by valid warrant, 155.
    officers making, protected by judgment, 130.

ARREST OF JUDGMENT.
    effect of order in, 253.

ASSAILING JUDGMENTS OF COURTS OF SPECIAL OR LIMITED JURISDICTION IN CASES TRIABLE BY JURY.
    a general rule, 268.
    contempts, 234.
    capias ad satisfaciendum, 358, 359.
    convictions by inferior courts entitled to much consideration, 240.
    contents of *mittimus,* recitals, etc., 355.
    defective execution, 361.
    defective complaint, 349.
    errors and irregularities not reviewable, 348.
    erroneous sentences, 353.
    effect of evidence, 199 *a.*

660   INDEX.

ASSAILING JUDGMENTS OF COURTS, ETC.—*Continued.*
    how to show a want of competent authority, 356.
    in criminal cases, 347-356.
    in civil cases, 357-361.
    process and judgments running by wrong name, 358.
    retrial of issues of fact, 350.
    sentences unauthorized by law, 351, 352.
    sentences for violation of ordinances, 352.
    staying, and failure to issue, execution, 360.
    the only question presented, 185.
    void summons, judgment, and execution in civil cases, 357.
    want of jurisdiction, 211.
    when sentence for misdemeanor begins to run, 354.

ASSAILING JUDGMENTS OF SUMMARY CONVICTION.
    by direct proceedings, as writ of error, motion to quash, *certiorari*, etc., 240.
    constitutionality of statutes authorizing summary convictions, 295.
    conviction without authority of law, 299.
    cumulative and erroneous sentences, 303.
    commitment of seaman, 301.
    commitment of sheriff, 302.
    commitment of witness, 305.
    definition of summary convictions, 294.
    errors and irregularities not reviewable, 297.
    history of summary commitments, 294.
    how statutes authorizing summary convictions are construed, 296.
    in cases involving the custody of children, 304.
    jurisdiction of justices of the peace, 294, *note.*
    removal of conviction by *certiorari,* 297, 298.
    recitals in *mittimus,* 298.
    rules in such convictions, 240.
    statement of offense on face of commitment, 298.
    security to keep the peace, 300.

ASSAILING JUDGMENTS FOR CONTEMPT.
    attachment for contempt, 310, 311.
    ability to obey orders, etc., 325.
    commitment must be "according to law," 337.
    commitments for contempt in parliamentary bodies, 336.
    contempt in pleading exemption from jury service, 338.
    contempts are not pardonable in England, 345.
    contempts are pardonable in some American states, 345.
    conditions impossible of performance, 321.
    commitment for contempt in using ironical language, 329.
    commitments for contempt by notaries public, 312.
    commitment of witness for refusing to enter into undertaking to appear, 305.
    conflict of federal and state authority, 316.
    definite time fixed by statute, 337.
    disobedience of orders, judgments, and decrees of court, 323, 324.
    demand to comply with order, 325.

INDEX. 661

ASSAILING JUDGMENTS FOR CONTEMPT—*Continued*.
    disobedience of subpœna, 330.
    errors of law not assailable, 315.
    errors and irregularities must be cured by motion, 344.
    evidence not heard, or questions tried *de novo*, 346.
    for want of jurisdiction, 308, *note*.
    general rule as to sufficiency of commitment for contempt, 314.
    had the court jurisdiction to commit? 317.
    is the commitment in legal form? 317.
    jury trial not allowed in contempt cases, 343.
    jurisdiction. No offense, 332.
    jurisdiction. Refusal to give evidence, 332.
    jurisdiction can not be acquired by mere assertion of it, 319.
    jurisdiction to commit. *Mandamus*, 331.
    meaning of words "so charged," 338, *note*.
    modifying judgments, 313.
    malpractice of sheriff, 327.
    no inquiry where warrant omits to state facts, 341.
    no change of venue allowed, 343.
    neglect to pay tax, 322.
    notice and service of orders, etc., 325.
    of superior and inferior courts, 342.
    of court of competent jurisdiction, 314.
    orders of court to pay over money, 320.
    only two questions involved in a commitment for contempt, 317.
    publication of proceedings during trial, 339.
    proceedings void for want of jurisdiction, assailable, 317.
    punishment for contempt, 308, 309.
    punishing contempt criminally and awarding indemnity in same order, 309.
    record must be relied upon, 346.
    refusing to answer questions, no contempt, when, 319.
    return of commitment for contempt, 327, *note*.
    statement of facts need not be made in warrant of commitment, unless statute requires it, 340.
    suspending attorney for contempt, 326.
    the general rule, 318.
    time certain in the English courts, 334.
    time certain in the American courts, 335.
    under unconstitutional law, 328.
    "until discharged by due course of law," 334.
    "until further order of the court," 335.
        See CONTEMPT.

ASSAILING JUDGMENTS OF COURTS OF GENERAL JURISDICTION.
    by the federal courts, 362.
    conviction under unconstitutional law, 72, 304, 370.
    conviction without authority of law, 136, 252, 370.
    conviction in state court of offense cognizable only in federal court, 159.
    constitutionality of statute providing for credit system, 94.
    conviction under ordinance, error in, 372.

ASSAILING JUDGMENTS OF COURTS, ETC.—*Continued.*

conviction under void municipal ordinance, 370.
cumulative sentences, 376.
court inquiring into legality of its own sentence, 378.
conflict of jurisdiction—state and federal courts, 379.
capias ad satisfaciendum, 384.
distinction between void and voidable jurisdictional proceedings, 225, 226, 370.
definition of conclusive judgment, 225, 226.
erroneous sentences, 372.
excessive sentences—English and federal courts, 373.
excessive sentences—state courts, 374.
error in designating place of imprisonment not reviewable, 364.
errors and irregularities not reviewable, 94, 365.
errors and irregularities not reviewable in civil cases, 383.
effect of want of certified copy of judgment in commitment, 93.
execution for sum in excess of jurisdiction, void, 93.
elapse of day assigned for execution, 94.
for fatal jurisdictional defects, 251, *note*.
insufficiency of the indictment or information, 251, 367.
invalidity of judgment where one of the three essential elements is lacking, 362.
imperfections in *mittimus*, no ground for, 127.
in criminal cases, 362-382.
in civil cases, 383-385.
in insolvency proceedings, 93.
jurisdictional defects, only, examined, 363.
judgment is simply erroneous, when, 363.
judgment of state court for violation of marriage law not reviewable in federal court, 379.
judgment of state court sentencing a party in violation of United States laws will be inquired into by federal court, 228, 381.
judgment, of superior courts, generally, 267.
jurisdiction over person and subject-matter, effect of, 368.
order of court exceeding jurisdiction, 93.
power to render the particular judgment, 362, 368, 371.
power of the United States supreme court to review judgments of the inferior federal courts, 72, 380.
power of courts to modify their own judgments, 377.
power of courts to modify their own judgments ceases, when, 377.
process can not be impeached for error, irregularity, or want of form, 136, 141.
questions of evidence sustaining charge, not reviewable, 380.
review of proceedings in inferior federal courts, 227.
reviewing evidence and retrying issues of fact, 366.
replevying judgments, 378.
review in various civil matters, 385.
sustaining sufficiency of indictment, 251.
sentence without warrant in law, 364.
sentence by court or judge *de facto*, 257, 369.
sentence commences to run, when, 378.

INDEX. 663

ASSAILING JUDGMENTS OF COURTS, ETC.—*Continued.*
    sentences of courts-martial, 382.
    sentences in violation of the constitution, or of United States laws, and
        acts done or omitted in pursuance thereof, 381.
    sentences of co-ordinate jurisdictions, 380.
    sentence less than that sanctioned by law, 94.
    the *mittimus*, 375.
    three essential elements of a valid judgment, 362, 368, 371.
    unreversed sentence, 126.
    under void proceedings, 93.
    void judgment, 241.
    void civil process, 93.
    when judgment will not be reviewed in territorial courts, 379.
    when prisoner has not been removed according to law, 94.
    where *audita querela* is the remedy, 94, *note.*

ATTACHMENT.
    affidavit for, 124.
    for contempt, at common law, 137.
    for contempt, in the United States, 137.
    for falsifying affidavits, 207.
    for contempt, generally, 309, *note*, 310, 311.
    federal officer not liable to, when, 132.
    may issue to enforce return, 124.
    non-bailable, practice under, 125
    should issue, when, 124.
    writ of, need express no particulars, 124.

ATTORNEYS.
    are officers of court, 125.
    and subject to its jurisdiction, 125.
    commitment of, 125.

AUDITA QUERELA.
    is sometimes proper remedy, instead of habeas corpus, 173.

AUTHORITY OF THE UNITED STATES.
    defined, 85.
    return under, 163.

B

BAIL. See RIGHT TO BAIL.

BILL OF RIGHTS.
    prohibited excessive bail, 33.

BENCH WARRANT.
    authorizes detention, 250.
    sufficient, if it describes offense generally, 282.

C

CERTAINTY.
    required in return, 126.
    required in warrants to answer, 281.
    required in statement of offense in warrant of arrest, 277.

CERTIORARI.
    as ancillary to the habeas corpus, 259–261, 346.
    and habeas corpus, as a wit of error, are used in the federal courts to review questions of jurisdiction only, 263.
    goes to judge, habeas corpus to officer, 259, 264.
    in aid of habeas corpus, 64, 145, 156, *note*, 260, 288.
    not needed to remove cause from state courts, 260.
    pending in state court does not affect power of federal court to act, 487.
    power of courts under, not co-extensive with that under habeas corpus, 264.
    power of courts to issue, not co-extensive with that to issue habeas corpus, 262.
    power of, with habeas corpus, as a writ of error, at common law, 262.
    purposes of, 260, 299, 303, 319.
    to certify informations, examinations, depositions, etc., 230, 235.
    to bring up complete record, 380.
    to correct flagrant errors, 363, 367, *note*.
    to review errors in judgments, 234.
    to bring up conviction, 297, 298, 325.
    to restore attorney, stripped of his profession, 326.
    to United States commissioner, 231.
    to review judgment fixing custody of children, 387, *note*.
    use of, in English law, 259, 262.
    use of, in the federal courts, 260.
    use of, in the state courts, 261, 262, 264.
    what will not be reviewed under, 264.
    with habeas corpus, as a writ of error; as to review question admitting to bail, 262–264.
    will not compel production of extradition papers, when, 486.

COMITY OF COURTS.
    co-ordinate tribunals will not interfere with each others' process, 94, 238.
    general rules concerning, 265.
    in commitments for contempt, 327, *note*.
    in questions of exclusive jurisdiction, 379.
    in not reviewing sentences of co-ordinate jurisdictions, 380.
    state and federal jurisdictions, 131, 132.

COMMITMENT TO ANSWER. See WARRANT TO ANSWER.

CONCLUSIONS OF LAW.
    should be avoided in petition, 89, 237, *note*.

CONDONATION OF OFFENSE.
    condition of, prescribed by the king, 8, 9.
    parliament refusing, against its privileges, 10, *note*.

CONTEMPT.
    attachment for, 309, 310, 311.
    amendment of commitment for, 128.
    commitment for, by privy councilors, without cause shown, 8.
    commitment for, need express no particulars, 124, 125.
    commitment of attorney for, in refusing to pay over moneys, 125.
    definition of, 28, 137, 306.

CONTEMPT—*Continued.*
    evasive, false, or insufficient return is a contempt, 137.
    every court sole judge of its own contempts, 28.
    failure to make return, a contempt, 137.
    is not a pardonable offense in England, 345.
    is a pardonable offense in some American states, 345.
    is a subject of conviction, 125.
    is a distinct criminal offense, 309, 325, 345.
    in not delivering possession of property, 94.
    is not committed by refusal to serve writ, when, 132.
    in refusing to pay over moneys, etc., 137.
    may be punished by attachment, 124.
    none, in disobeying void writ, 124.
    not a bailable offense, 390.
    power of courts to punish for, 307.
    practice in proceedings for, 309.
    return of commitment for, not allowed to be controverted at common law, 8.
    specially and plainly charged in the commitment, 233.
    willful disobedience of writ, a contempt, 88.
    where prisoner can not be found, 114.
        See ASSAILING JUDGMENTS FOR CONTEMPT.

COSTS.
    convict pardoned can not be detained to pay, 119.
    distinction between, and expenses, 113.
    generally and under 31 Car. II., 113.
    in federal courts—legislation, decisions, and rules, 117.
    in the state courts, 118.
    in particular instances, 116.
    in civil cases, 113.
    in bankruptcy proceedings, 114.
    is a debt not affected by pardon, 119.
    judicial constructions, relative to, 119.
    must be paid by one making frivolous applications, 116.
    non-payment of, no excuse for not producing body, 124.
    on *habeas corpus ad satisfaciendum*, 113.
    on *habeas corpus ad testificandum*, 115.
    officer not liable for, after prisoner's discharge, 119.
    on several writs, 119.
    public prosecutor not required to enter security for, 119.
    reduction of, 119.
    statutory provisions of the states, 118, *note.*
    when apportioned, 115.
    when court will disclaim jurisdiction to award, 116.
    when officers are entitled to fees for each writ, 119.
    when taxable to county, 119.
    when *habeas corpus cum causa* can not issue to compe payment of, 114.

COURTS-MARTIAL.
    defined, 382.

COURTS. See JURISDICTION OF COURTS TO ISSUE THE WRIT.

666   INDEX.

CUSTODY OF LEGITIMATE CHILDREN IN ENGLAND.
    appointment of testamentary guardian, 427.
    cause of the Talfourd act, 434.
    doctrines at law, 426–433.
    doctrines in equity, 434–437.
    effect of the Talfourd act, 436.
    father's right to custody of children not absolute, 430.
    how far the courts will actively interfere to deliver the custody of a child, 429.
    how the court's discretion is governed, 430.
    infant's liberty of choice, 431.
    infant's age of discretion, 432.
    parent's right of access to children, though not entitled to their custody, 433.
    proceeding is by habeas corpus to recover child at law, 437.
    proceeding is by petition to recover child in equity, 437.
    rights of the father during his life, 426.
    surrender of custody by parent, 428.
    several provisions of the Talfourd act, 435.
    the mother acquired new rights under the Talfourd act, 436.
    the infants' custody act, 436, *note*.
        See FATHER, MOTHER, INFANT, PARENT FOR HIS CHILD, and PETITION FOR WRIT.

CUSTODY OF LEGITIMATE CHILDREN IN THE UNITED STATES.
    application of English cases, 438.
    authority to apply for a habeas corpus, 440.
    distinction between cases where child is in custody and where it is out of custody, 441, *note*.
    doctrines in chancery, 452.
    father's right to the custody of his children not so absolute in the United States as it was in England, 441, 442.
    father's right paramount to mother's where each is blameless, 441.
    father's right, how lost, 441, *note*.
    how far a parent may, by agreement, surrender the custody of his child, 444.
    how far the courts will actively interfere to deliver the custody of a child, 445.
    infant's liberty of choice, 447.
    interest of child the paramount consideration, 442, 442, *note*, 444, *note*, 446.
    in divorce matters, 451.
    Lord Mansfield's rule, substantially, prevails, 445.
    mental capacity, and not age, is test for determining infant's judgment and discretion, 448.
    neither parent has any rights that can be allowed to seriously militate against the welfare of the child, 447.
    parent's right of access, though not entitled to custody, 449.
    scope of habeas corpus in cases affecting the custody of children, 439.
    superiority of mother's right, as to third parties, where she is a suitable and respectable person, 443.

CUSTODY OF LEGITIMATE CHILDREN IN THE U. S.—*Continued.*
 supersedeas, appeal, action, and foreign jurisdiction, 450.
 the mother's right, 443.
  See FATHER, MOTHER, INFANT, PARENT FOR HIS CHILD, and PETITION FOR WRIT.

CUSTODY OF ILLEGITIMATE CHILDREN.
 doctrines in the United States, 454.
 views of the English courts, 453.

DEFINITION.
 of "authority of the United States," 85.
 of applicant for writ, 89.
 of arrest, 271.
 of contempt, generally, 28, 137, 309.
 of certainty, 126.
 of courts-martial, 382.
 of constructive or consequential contempts, 306
 of conclusive judgment, 225.
 of direct or criminal contempts, 306, 309.
 of doubt, 291.
 of imprisonment, 269, 272.
 of error, 348, 363, *note.*
 of excessive bail, 413.
 of full return, 126.
 of false imprisonment, 269, 272.
 of "good cause," 239.
 of issue, 169.
 of irregularity, 348, 363, *note.*
 of inferior court, 266.
 of judicial discretion, 96.
 of jurisdiction, 223, 317.
 of "legal form," 317.
 of legal commitment, 125.
 of *mittimus*, 375.
 of "presumption great," 403.
 of process, 160.
 of return, general, 120.
 of summary convictions, 294.
 of superior court, 266.
 of term, 411.
 of unlawful imprisonment, 241.
 of void judgment, 370.
 of voidable judgment, 370.
 of void proceedings, 158.
 of voidable proceedings, 158.
 of words, "so charged," 338, *note.*
 of warrant, 275.
 of "when proof is evident," 402.

DEMURRER.
 to indictment, 251.

668 INDEX.

DEMURRER—*Continued.*
    to justification, 172.
    to plea, 172.
    to petition, 169, 237.
    to return, 156, 309.
    to return, when good, 457.

DETENTION.
    cause of, how shown, 165.

DISCRETION.
    judicial, 96.
    judicial, how exercised, 239.
    judicial, must be regulated by law, 306, *note.*

DISTINCTION.
    as to strictness of law applicable to trial in chief, and that on motion to commit for trial, 217, *note.*
    between arresting officer and jailer, 130.
    between committing by rule, and by writ, 125.
    between costs and expenses, 113.
    between cases of merit, and those without merit, should be made at the trial, 89.
    between common-law and statutory writ, 87.
    between cases where child is in custody, and out of custody, 441, *note.*
    between contempts and ordinary crimes or misdemeanors, 345.
    between disobedience of order of court, and adjudication of contempt, 324.
    between erroneous exercise of power, and usurpation of power, 327, *note*
    between exercising general powers and a special or statutory jurisdiction, 268.
    between facts in return, and those upon record, 172.
    between inquiries before judgment and after, 240.
    between jurisdiction and its exercise pointed out, 223.
    between judgment of imprisonment and judgment for costs, 119.
    between judgment of court and *mittimus,* 129.
    between judgment of discharge and that remanding the prisoner, 386.
    between judgments fixing custody of children and other judgments, 386.
    between judgments made by legal court and those made by no court at all, 211.
    between mere irregularity and a complete defect in proceedings, 348.
    between officers acting as magistrates and as judges of courts of general jurisdiction, 238.
    between original applications and those in which a revisory or correctionary jurisdiction is exercised, 196.
    between power of courts under both habeas corpus and *certiorari,* and under habeas corpus only, 264.
    between power of peace officer and that of private person to arrest offender, 276.
    between rules prevailing in showing a want of jurisdiction, 267.
    between riot and rescue, 154.
    between superior and inferior courts, 238, 266.

INDEX. 669

DISTINCTION—*Continued*.
    between void and voidable jurisdictional proceedings, 158, 225, 370.
    between value of evidence *viva voce* and that by affidavit, 178.
    between warrant to answer and process, 282, *note*.
    in bankruptcy proceedings, 148.

DUE PROCESS OF LAW.
    denotes legality of process, 89.
    justifies imprisonment, 89.
    may exist in behalf of unjust suitor as well as of just one, 89.

DURATION OF IMPRISONMENT.
    confinement in remote islands, garrisons, and other places, 12.
    often excessive prior to 31 Car. II., 12.

E

ERROR.
    defined, 348, 363, *note*.
    in warrant of arrest may be examined, when, 286.
    in warrant of commitment may be examined, when, 278.
    in entry of order not considered, 238, 253.
    in designating place of imprisonment not reviewable, 364.
    in summary convictions not reviewable, 297, 304.
    in discharging jury in defendant's absence, 255.
    in exclusion of testimony, 350.
    in continuing indictment without prisoner's presence, 248.
    no ground for discharge, 94, 127, 136, 158, 170, 241, 251, *note*, 264.
    not rendering execution void, 385, *note*.
    not reviewable in assailing judgments of any kind on habeas corpus, 315,
        348, 355, 356, 362, 363, 383.
    reviewed by *certiorari* and habeas corpus, 259.

EVIDENCE.
    affidavit should state facts, 219.
    adducing, to impeach indictment, 251.
    arrest on state process, 218.
    additional proof, 190.
    aliunde, to prove what, 199 *a*, 240, 284.
    after indictment, in letting to bail, 405, 406.
    admission of, in federal courts, 59.
    by affidavit in civil cases, 219.
    by parol may be admitted to prove want of jurisdiction, in a court of
        general jurisdiction, if the recitals of the judgment are not contra-
        dicted, 267.
    commenting on testimony—not done in Texas and Mississippi, 206.
    correcting errors in, 196.
    contradicting return, 197.
    conversations, 195.
    competent testimony, 193.
    case once heard upon the same evidence, 187.
    commitment without testimony, 184.
    contempt in refusing to give, 333.
    conviction and sentence may be shown by affidavit, when, 220.

EVIDENCE—*Continued.*
    contradicting return by affidavit, 212.
    does it sustain the charge? 204.
    defective affidavits, 207.
    denying statement in warrant by affidavit, 216.
    defendant has a right to be confronted by witnesses, 199 *b*.
    enlarging for return by affidavit, 214.
    examination of indictment, 213.
    effect of failure to object to irregular evidence, 220.
    examination of, with a view to bail, before indictment, 400.
    falsifying affidavits, 207.
    fortifying return by affidavit, 215.
    federal courts may hear, as to imprisonment under state process, 132.
    fine against defaulting witness, 202.
    hearing evidence, *de novo*, 182.
    hearsay evidence, 194.
    impeaching witnesses, 200.
    in extradition proceedings, 476–479.
    if insufficient to support charge, bail is allowed, 390.
    officers may be examined as witnesses, 203.
    of service, 205.
    of precise crime may be shown by records of court, 375.
    nature of, where bail is not allowed, 393.
    not heard anew in reviewing judgments of contempt, 346.
    oral evidence, as well as written, will be received, 178, 198, 208.
    oral evidence never admitted to contradict record, 178, 198, 366.
    prisoner can not introduce his defense by witnesses, 204.
    prisoner may produce himself as witness, 93.
    postponement of trial for further testimony, 191.
    proper evidence, 192.
    record evidence, 198.
    return may be traversed orally, 178.
    reviewed by *certiorari*, 259, 260.
    rule concerning inquiry into commitments made by magistrates not uniform, 179.
    subpœna for witness, 201.
    statement of evidence in judgment, 185.
    sufficient evidence to authorize commitment, 179.
    second application—newly discovered evidence, 188.
    several indictments found on the same evidence, 186.
    taken before committing magistrate must be set forth in petition, 183.
    to prove jurisdiction over subject-matter, 368.
    to sustain charge, not reviewable, 380.
    to show disagreement of jury on former trial, 408.
    to impeach commitment, 93.
    to impeach judgment of inferior court, 268.
    testing verity of affidavits in conflict of jurisdiction, 218.
    use of affidavits in English practice, 209.
    upon subsequently occurring events, 189.
    value of evidence by affidavit, 207.
    when burden of proof rests upon prisoner, 136.

INDEX. 671

EVIDENCE—*Continued.*
whole explanation brought out on cross-examination, 204.
waiving examination without introduction of, is error, 243.
where return can not be controverted, 293.
weighing evidence taken before committing magistrate, 180, 181.
See AFFIDAVIT.

EXTRADITION. See FOREIGN AND INTERSTATE EXTRADITION.

F

FALSE IMPRISONMENT.
arrests, legal and illegal, 271.
action of, under 31 Car. II., 58.
acts of indemnity for, 270.
defined, 269, 270, 272.
guardian holding ward's person not guilty of, 457.
is not created by being out on bail, 273.
of child, 272.
questions of, how investigated, 241.
restraint and detention, 272.

FATHER.
may have writ to recover custody of his child, 91, 112.
See CUSTODY OF CHILDREN, INFANT, PARENT FOR HIS CHILD, AND PETITION FOR WRIT.

FOREIGN EXTRADITION.
application for a habeas corpus, 460.
authentication of documents, 466.
can the surrendered fugitive be tried for an offense other than the extradition crime? 462.
commissioners have no power to amend complaint, when, 466.
commitment for examination *de novo*, 466.
conflict of jurisdiction between state and federal authority, 468
checks of legal functions upon each other, 467.
discharge from final commitment if unlawful, 466.
extradition to the United States, 459–463.
extradition from the United States, 463–468.
executive functions, 463.
executive warrant not absolutely final, 463.
federal courts will look behind warrant of extradition, 463.
illegal extradition, 461.
issuance of habeas corpus, 464.
judicial functions, 464.
jurisdiction of commissioner subject to inquiry, 465.
offense should be clearly stated, 466.
president's mandate not necessary to the commencement of judicial proceedings, 463.
reviewing decision of commissioner on habeas corpus, 465.
requisites of complaint, 466.
sufficiency or insufficiency of legal evidence of facts not a subject of inquiry, 465.

FOREIGN EXTRADITION—*Continued.*
    the demand, 459.
    weighing excluded evidence, 465.
    when delivery of prisoner can be made, 463.
    whole subject of extradition confided to the federal government, 462.

FORMS. See INDEX TO FORMS.

G

GEO. III., 56.
    allowed inquiry into truth of return, 34, 221.
    extended power of issuing writ in vacation, 34.
    fortifying return under, by affidavit, 215.
    return could be controverted under, 170, 212, 221.
    simplified proceedings under the writ very much, 88.

GUARDIAN AND WARD.
    best interest of ward should be considered, 457.
    changes of ward from one state to another regarded with suspicion, 457.
    writ may issue at instance of guardian to bring up his ward, 457.

GUARDIANSHIP.
    investigation into questions of, 170, 457.

H

HABEAS CORPUS ACT, 31 CAR. II.
    auspicious times of the bill's passage, 21.
    adopted in South Carolina, 41.
    adopted in New York (1787), 48.
    adopted in New Jersey (1795), 48.
    basis of similar acts in the United States, 48.
    brief review of, 25 *a*–37.
    controverting return under, 166, 167, 221.
    copy of the act, 58.
    did not provide for cases of imprisonment without warrant, 34.
    difficulties concerning returns under, 34.
    did not authorize use of affidavits to contradict return, 212.
    denial of writ to province of Quebec, 46.
    enumeration of abuses under, 25 *b*.
    eulogies upon the act, 37.
    extended to Virginia in 1710, 45.
    exceptions to application of act, 28–31.
    issuance of writ under, 99.
    its relation to other acts, 23.
    it introduced no new principle, 25 *a*, 92, 100.
    it altered not the practice, 25 *a*, 92, 100.
    operation of the act, 32.
    opinion of James II., concerning, 35.
    opinion of Chalmers concerning its extension to the colonies, 39.
    passage of the act, 19.
    permitted affidavits to questions of bail, 213.
    prohibited the sending of prisoners beyond the seas, 31.

INDEX. 673

HABEAS CORPUS ACT, 31 CAR. II.—*Continued.*
    resolution for, credited to Sir Edward Coke, 25 *a*, *note*.
    recognized and practically adopted in Maryland, 42.
    removal of prisoners, 30.
    recommitment of prisoners, 30.
    requirements to take advantage of, 36.
    right to bail under, 391.
    service of writ under, 109.
    speculations concerning the king's assent to it, 22.
    treason and felony, 29, 288.
    to what the act may be assigned, 24.
    why the act is famous, 20.
    was applicable only to criminal offenses, 34, 87, 88.
    was practically adopted in the colonies, 38, 39, 45.

HABEAS CORPUS ACT OF THE UNITED STATES.
    copy of the act, 59.

HABEAS CORPUS BILL.
    auspicious times of the bill's passage, 21.
    bill of 1674, 13.
    passage of the bill, 19.

HABEAS CORPUS AD SATISFACIENDUM.
    costs on, 113.
    objections to, 111.

HABEAS CORPUS AD TESTIFICANDUM.
    costs on, 115, 116.
    how obtained, 90.
    prisoner may have, 93.

HABEAS CORPUS CUM CAUSA.
    effect of habeas corpus in removal of causes, 259.
    how allowed at common law, 109.
    insufficient return to, 128.
    may be had by bail to render prisoner in their own discharge, 91.
    not needed to remove cause from state court, 260.
    objections to, 111.
    prisoner may be rendered on civil process, 91.
    rule upon process, 142.
    service of writ in the United States, 109.
    upon affidavit entitled in several causes, 99.
    when it will issue, 76.

HISTORY OF THE WRIT IN ENGLAND.
    ancient writs devised to secure personal liberty, 3 *a*.
    arguments by Noy, Selden, and others, in the Knights Case, 4.
    Bushell's Case settled the immunity of juries for their verdicts, 11.
    commitment of the five Knights, 3 *b*–6.
    compensation for unjust imprisonment, 9.
    cases of Streater, and Fox the Quaker, 10.
    contempt by members of the house of commons, 8.
    condition of prisoners during the reign of Car. II., 14.

HISTORY OF THE WRIT IN ENGLAND—*Continued.*
had become an admitted constitutional remedy prior to 31 Car. II., 3 *a.*
history of star-chamber and other arbitrary proceedings, 8, 9.
habeas corpus bill of 1674, 13.
issuance of the writ in vacation time, 17.
imperfections of the writ, 18.
iniquity and destructiveness of the judgment in the Knights Case, 6.
long duration of imprisonment, 12.
may be traced to the Roman interdict, 1.
no cause certified in return led to Petition of Right, 7.
removal of prisoners in cases of sickness, 15.
signing of Magna Charta, 2.
the celebrated Jenkes Case, 16, 100.
the celebrated Bushell and Shaftesbury cases, 11.
this writ was used throughout the reign of Charles II., 10.
See HABEAS CORPUS ACT, 31 Car. II.

HISTORY OF THE WRIT IN THE UNITED STATES.
articles of confederation contained no provision relating to, 47.
cases of the Presbyterian ministers, New York, 44.
colonies claimed to inherit birthright to English laws, 38.
conflict between state and federal governments regarding it, 48.
conclusiveness of return under judiciary act of 1789, 222.
change effected by act of 1833, and subsequent acts, 222.
discussion of return before house of lords left its impress upon American jurisprudence, 221.
federal jurisdiction, given by act of September 24, 1789, 48.
its history in South Carolina, 41.
its history in Maryland, 42.
its history in New Jersey and Pennsylvania, 43.
its history in Virginia, 45.
opinion of Chalmers concerning extension of habeas corpus act to the colonies, 39.
provision of the constitution of the United States, 47.
use of the writ in Massachusetts, 40.
was not only known, but used, in the colonies, 38, 39.
See SUSPENSION OF THE WRIT.

HUSBAND.
can not have writ for wife where he has, by agreement, renunciated his marital right, 421.
can not have writ for wife, unless she is under restraint, 421.
has right to custody of wife, 421.
may have writ to recover custody of wife, 91, 93.
writ issues in favor of, when wife is in custody of another against her will, 421.

I

IDENTITY.
always an open question on habeas corpus, 93, 170, 238.
and includes that of fugitives from justice, 480, 486.

INDICTMENT.
    after, guilt or innocence can not be examined into, 244.
    before, guilt or innocence may be examined into, 237.
    cause for detention after failure to indict, 239.
    continuing, 248.
    can not be retried after discharge of jury, 255.
    charging, or not charging, crime, matter not reviewable in federal courts, 380.
    charging, or not charging, crime, is a matter reviewable in some of the state courts, 245, 251.
    defective indictment, 246.
    existence of, inquiry concerning, 250.
    flaw in, no ground for discharge, 291.
    federal courts will go behind, in extradition cases, 486.
    "guilty or not guilty," 247.
    insufficiency of, or of information, 367.
    inquiry as to bail, before, 395–400.
    inquiry as to bail, after, 401–416.
    in extradition cases, must show authenticity, 466.
    judgment on sufficiency of, 251.
    legality of, inquiry concerning, 250.
    must have usual features of, in extradition cases, 477.
    reversal of former conviction on—effect of, 254.
    schedule of indictable offenses, 294, *note*.
    trial on new indictment, 291.
    two bills of indictment—death penalty on one—no trial on the other, 249.

INFANT.
    changing custody of, 176.
    contempt in not complying with order of court concerning, 309.
    costs, in case relating to, when not awarded, 116.
    costs, when taxable to county, 119.
    custody of, should not be changed pending appeal, 450.
    evidence in case relating to, 195.
    false imprisonment of child, 272.
    husband's right to, 421.
    in foreign jurisdiction, 450.
    judgment fixing custody of, conclusive, 387.
    Michigan decision respecting child in foreign jurisdiction, 108, *note*.
    parents may have writ for restoration of child, 112.
    production of the body, 163.
    return, concerning, must be full and complete, 161, 161, *note*.
    reviewing summary conviction of child as vagrant, 304.
    when demand should be made for child, 157.
        See CUSTODY OF CHILDREN, FATHER, MOTHER, PARENT FOR HIS CHILD, and PETITION FOR WRIT.

INJUNCTION.
    to restrain issuance of writ, 93.

INQUIRY, EXTENT OF.
    a leading principle regarding void and voidable jurisdictional proceedings, 226.

INQUIRY, EXTENT OF—*Continued.*
    after indictment and before judgment of conviction, 244–255.
    as to delay in bringing to trial, 254.
    as to subsequently occurring events, 319.
    as to legality of indictment, 250.
    by federal courts where there is no formal or technical commitment, 229.
    by federal courts into and behind commitment, 230.
    by federal courts into and behind commitment made by a United States commissioner, 231.
    continuing indictment, 248.
    concerning existence of indictment, 250.
    ceases, generally, where court has jurisdiction of process and subject-matter, 253.
    can not extend to title to office, 256.
    conflict of jurisdiction between federal and state courts, 228.
    class of cases where jurisdiction of committing magistrate is the only open question, 234.
    class of cases holding that the entire proceedings before the committing magistrate may be examined and reviewed, if necessary, 234, 235.
    can not extend to questions of evidence presented to sustain the charge, when, 380.
    does not extend into warrant of commitment for contempt, where it omits to state facts, 341.
    distinction between void and voidable jurisdictional proceedings, 225, 241.
    discharge of jury in defendant's absence, 255.
    distinction between jurisdiction and its exercise pointed out, 223.
    defective indictment, 246.
    effect of statutes on rules allowing only jurisdiction to be inquired into, and those allowing a full and free investigation, 236.
    extending only to jurisdiction, into and behind warrant of committing magistrate, 234.
    extends into warrant of commitment for contempt where statute requires statement of facts to be made, 342.
    federal courts will inquire into jurisdiction of state court to sentence a party in violation of federal laws, 228.
    "guilty or not guilty," 247.
    general inquiries, 233.
    habeas corpus pending examination on criminal charge, 242.
    into guilt or innocence may be made before indictment, 237.
    into commitment by court of general jurisdiction, 238.
    into matters concerning new trial, 254.
    into validity of civil process, 238.
    into cause for detention after failure to indict, 239.
    into convictions by inferior courts, 240.
    into guilt or innocence can not be made after indictment found, 244.
    into validity of bench warrant, 250.
    into validity of judgment sustaining an indictment, 251.
    into process without warrant of law, 252.
    into effect of order arresting judgment, 253.
    jurisdiction must appear upon face of proceedings, and this in civil causes as well as criminal, 224.

INQUIRY, EXTENT OF—*Continued.*
    jurisdiction in civil cases not always open to inquiry at common law, 222, 222, *note.*
    jurisdiction in either civil or criminal cases always open to inquiry in the United States, and at any time, 222.
    may go to whether indictment charges any offense, 245.
    ordinary extent of in the federal courts, 221, 232.
    of court may extend into legality of its own sentence, 378.
    review of proceedings in inferior federal courts, 227.
    regular and legal return was conclusive at common law, and under 31 Car. II., 221.
    range of, on *mesne* process, 136.
    range of, by federal courts into state process, 132.
    reasons why the courts decline to make inquiry into a commitment after indictment found, 244.
    two bills of indictment, death penalty on one—no trial on the other, 249.
    vacating orders of court, 241.
    waiving examination, 243.
    will not extend to "once in jeopardy," 253.
    when order of discharge may be entered, 232.

INTERSTATE EXTRADITION.
    authority of state in absence of state legislation to deal with criminal fugitives, 472.
    awaiting requisition, 481.
    authentication of the papers, 479, 486.
    bail sometimes allowed by statute, 484.
    constitutionality of statute permitting bail, 484, *note.*
    constitutional and legislative provisions, 469–472.
    congressional enactments, 470.
    courts can not control executive discretion, 475.
    concerning the indictment, 477.
    case illustrating conflict of jurisdiction between state and federal courts, and showing the supremacy of the federal law, 487.
    does the law of congress prohibit auxiliary legislation by the states concerning fugitive criminals? 471.
    duty and discretion of executive, 473, 474.
    demanding discretion, 473.
    delivering discretion, 474.
    detention under civil process, 484.
    evidence to commence proceedings, 476–481.
    evidence necessary to support demand prescribed by the law of congress, 485.
    federal courts will look behind indictment, 486.
    illegal extradition, 483.
    jurisdiction of the federal courts, 485–487.
    judicial powers, 475–484.
    legal accusation by indictment or information, 476.
    provisions of the constitution of the United States, 469.
    person charged must be shown to be a fugitive criminal, 478.
    prisoner can only be tried for extradition crime, 482.

INTERSTATE EXTRADITION—*Continued*.
    rules for guidance of governors, 473.
    revocation of governor's warrant, 484.
    scope of inquiry in the federal courts, 486.
    sufficiency of the papers, 480.
    vacating executive warrant, 480.
    validity of governor's warrant will not be determined in anticipation of arrest, 89.
    what must be shown to authorize detention, 486.
    when production of papers can not be enforced, 486.
    what warrant for arrest must show, 486.
    whole subject of extradition is remitted, by the constitution of the United States, to the general government, 485.

IRREGULARITY.
    defined, 348, 363, *note*.
    in discharging jury in defendant's absence, 255.
    in entry of order not considered, 238, 253.
    in continuing indictment without prisoner's presence, 248.
    in warrant of arrest may be examined, when, 286.
    in warrant of commitment may be examined, when, 287.
    in failure to issue execution in time, not reviewable, 360.
    no ground for discharge, 94, 127, 136, 158, 170, 241, 251, *note*, 264.
    not assailable in attacking judgments of any kind, 297, 304, 348, 355, 356, 362, 363, 365, 383.
    not rendering execution void, 385, *note*.
    some irregularities not reviewable, 365.

ISSUANCE OF WRIT IN VACATION TIME.
    before 31 Car. II., when difficulties were experienced in obtaining it then, 17.
    by justices of the supreme court of the United States, 73.
    issued upon what principle, 92.
    may be issued in England in vacation, 17, 88.
    may be issued in the United States in vacation, 17, 88.
    nature of allowance, 96.
    probable effect of stereotyping common law concerning, 18.
    under 31 Car. II., 58, 99, 100, 101.
    was refused in Jenkes Case, 16, 100.
    what Coke says in his Institutes, 16.

ISSUES.
    custody of prisoner during the trial, 175, 176.
    change of custody of prisoner, 176.
    change of venue, 174.
    generally tried before a court or judge, 173.
    how tried, 169–174.
    jury trial, 172, 173.
    mode of trial at common law, 171.
    of law, 169.
    of law defined, 169.
    of law and fact, 170.

INDEX. 679

ISSUES—*Continued*.
 of law and fact, how raised, 169, 170.
 of "guilty or not guilty," before indictment, 237.
 of "guilty or not guilty" after indictment, 247.
 of guardianship not tried, 170.
 what facts are put in issue, 170.
    See TRIAL OF ISSUES.

J

JAILER.
 may substitute return prepared by counsel for his own, 135.

JUDICIAL ACT.
 administering oath is a judicial act, 217, *note*.
 true of oath administered by a notary public, 281.

JUDICIAL NOTICE.
 subjects of, 154.

JUDGMENT.
 commitment or *mittimus* of justice of the peace, 355.
 court may inquire into legality of its own sentence, 378.
 certified copy of—effect of production of, 375.
 cumulative sentences, 376.
 definition of conclusive judgment, 225, 226.
 erroneous sentences, 353, 363, 372.
 erroneous, may be reversed on appeal or writ of error, 241.
 excessive sentences in English courts, 372.
 excessive sentences in federal courts, 372.
 excessive sentences in the state courts, 374.
 fatally defective, if one of the three essential elements be lacking, 362.
 fixing custody of children, conclusive, 387.
 how proved, 126.
 is what authorizes detention, 129, 375.
 irregular, is not reviewable, 365.
 is simply erroneous, when, 363.
 jurisdiction must exist to render particular judgment, 340, 342.
 legal court, and no court at all—distinctions, 211.
 may be modified, when, 313, 377.
 of court of general jurisdiction, how assailed, 362-385.
 of inferior federal courts not reviewable by United States supreme court, except for want of jurisdiction, 380.
 of superior and inferior courts in contempt cases, 342.
 of summary conviction—see assailing judgments of summary conviction, 294-305.
 of court of special or limited jurisdiction in cases triable by jury—how assailed, 347-361.
 of contempts—how assailed, 306-346.
 of superior and inferior courts stand upon the same footing when jurisdiction is once shown, 268.
 of inferior court, entitled to much consideration, 240.
 of superior court how impeached, 267.

JUDGMENT—*Continued.*
    of inferior court, how impeached, 268.
    of discharge, conclusive, 386.
    of courts-martial, 382.
    of committing magistrate is not so final as that of a court of record, 260.
    on sufficiency of the indictment, 251.
    protects arresting officer, 130.
    power to modify, ceases when, 377.
    replevy of, 378.
    remanding prisoner, not conclusive, 386.
    refusing bail, how reviewed, 415.
    recitals in, and contradiction of, 185, 267.
    reversal of former conviction on indictment, 254.
    sentence by court or judge *de facto*, 255, 369.
    sentence commences to run, when, 354, 378.
    sentences of co-ordinate jurisdictions, 380.
    sentences in violation of federal laws, 381.
    sentences unauthorized by law, 351, 352.
    three essential elements of validity, 362, 368.
    void, defined, 370.
    voidable, defined, 370.
    void, and void execution under void summons, 357.
    valid, when there is jurisdiction to render it, and jurisdiction over the person and subject-matter, 362, 368, 371.
    without service of process, is void, 241.

JURISDICTION.
    always an open question, 222, 240, 251, *note*, 342.
    all instruments by which limited jurisdictions act should show authority on their face, 278, 285.
    can not be acquired by mere assertion of it, 319.
    colorable, effect of, 136.
    conflict of, respecting child in foreign jurisdiction, 108.
    conflict of, respecting service of writ of habeas corpus—federal and state courts, 132.
    defined, 223, 317.
    distinction between jurisdiction and its exercise pointed out, 223.
    excess of, may be shown, 233.
    for execution in excess of, prisoner may be discharged, 93.
    for order of court, in excess of, prisoner may be discharged, 93.
    in summary convictions, 297.
    in summary convictions may be questioned, 304.
    judgment under void proceedings entitles prisoner to discharge, 93.
    must exist to render particular judgment, 340, 342.
    need not be affirmatively shown in each order, process, or entry of inferior courts, 268, 285.
    of process and subject-matter ends inquiry, when, 252.
    of inferior courts must affirmatively appear from the record, 268, 285.
    of inferior courts may be impeached by denying recitals in their judgments, 268, 285.

JURISDICTION—*Continued.*
    of courts of general jurisdiction exercising a special or statutory authority, 268, 285.
    of person and subject-matter, effect of, 240, 241, 342, 362, 368.
    of state court to sentence a party in violation of federal law inquired into by federal court, 228.
    of three essential elements must exist to render a judgment valid, 362, 368, 371.
    of the supreme court of the United States to review the judgments of the inferior federal courts, 380.
    of court to modify its own judgment, 377.
    of court to modify its own judgment ceases, when, 377.
    of court to inquire into legality of its own sentence, 378.
    of state court to render judgment for violation of state marriage law not reviewable in federal courts, 379.
    over subject-matter is one of fact to be proved as any other, 368.
    one committed on civil process, void for want of jurisdiction, may be discharged on habeas corpus, 93.
    one committed on void proceedings will be discharged, 93.
    process of superior court need not show authority on its face, 278, 285.
    questioning, on defective warrant, 149.
    rules to show want of, in superior courts, 267, 285.
    rules to show want of, in inferior courts, 267, 285.
    reviewed by habeas corpus and *certiorari*, 263.
    showing want of, 199 *a.*
    to detain under bench warrant, 250, 282.
    to render wrong, as well as right, decisions, 255.
    want of, in a court of general jurisdiction, may be shown by parol evidence, if its recitals are not contradicted, 267, 285.
    want of, shown by affidavit, 211.
    wide range in contempt cases for examination of questions of, 342.

JURISDICTION OF COURTS AND OFFICERS TO COMMIT FOR CONTEMPT.
    by order, and without warrant, in criminal cases, 125.
    by order, and without warrant, in civil cases, 125.
    See CONTEMPT and ASSAILING JUDGMENTS FOR CONTEMPT.

JURISDICTION, CONCURRENT, OF THE WRIT BY STATE AND FEDERAL COURTS.
    definition of "authority of the United States," 85.
    state courts have no concurrent jurisdiction when party is in custody under "authority of the United States," 83, 84, 85, 86.
    Tarble's Case, 13 Wall. 397, and its effect, 86.
    views of state courts prior to Ableman v. Booth, 82.
    views of inferior federal courts prior to Ableman v. Booth, 82.

JURISDICTION, CONFLICT OF, BETWEEN STATE AND FEDERAL COURTS.
    arrest on state process, evidence, 218.
    causes of various provisions of section 753 of the revised statutes of the United States, 78.

682 INDEX.

JURISDICTION, CONFLICT OF, ETC.—*Continued.*
    classes of cases when writ may issue under section 753 of the revised statutes of the United States, 78.
    case illustrating the supremacy of federal laws in extradition proceedings, 486.
    effect of conviction in state court of offense cognizable only in federal court, 159.
    federal courts will inquire into the jurisdiction of a state court to sentence a party in violation of federal laws, 228.
    instances in which federal courts have granted the writ, as well as refused a discharge under it, in cases conflicting with state authority, 78, *note.*
    in case of commitment for contempt, 316.
    in production of body held under federal authority, 316.
    in cases of foreign extradition, 468.
    in cases of interstate extradition, 485, 487.
    in awarding attachment for contempt, 124.
    judgment of state court for violation of marriage law not reviewable in federal court, 379.
    paramount authority of federal courts in cases involving questions of international law, 81.
    pending appeal, certain state proceedings to be deemed null and void, 59.
    proceedings on state *certiorari* may be interfered with by federal habeas corpus, 261.
    range of inquiry by federal courts into state process, 132.
    should not unnecessarily interfere with each other's process, 131.
    when one is fully protected, if held under state authority, 79.
    when federal courts will protect one held in custody under a law or treaty of the United States, 80.
    where federal courts have exclusive jurisdiction, 379.

JURISDICTION OF COURTS TO ISSUE THE WRIT.
    at common law, 60, 88.
    appellate jurisdiction of the United States supreme court, 63, 64, 69, 73.
    application within the county—construction of statute, 89.
    before statute of 31 Car. II., 100.
    compared with, to issue *certiorari*, 262.
    circuit courts of the United States, 66, 69.
    district courts of the United States, 65, 69.
    enumeration of courts whence it issued in England, 30, 60, 61.
    federal courts have exclusive jurisdiction to issue when party is held under authority of the United States, 83, 84, 85, 86.
    habeas corpus cum causa, 76.
    instances in which the writ has been granted by the supreme court of the United States, 69, *note.*
    instances in which a discharge on the writ has been refused by the supreme court of the United States, 69, *note.*
    instances in which the district and circuit courts of the United States have granted the writ, 66, *note, a.*
    instances in which a discharge on the writ has been refused by the district and circuit courts of the United States, 66, *note, b.*

JURISDICTION OF COURTS TO ISSUE THE WRIT—*Continued.*
   in the territories, 67.
   in enlistment cases, 86, *note.*
   limitations and benefits of the writ, 69.
   must be shown as writ issues not as matter of course, 75.
   ought to appear on face of writ, or petition, 90.
   original jurisdiction of the supreme court of the United States, 62.
   of the federal courts generally, 59, 108, 227, 228, 229, 230.
   of federal courts, prescribed by act of September 24, 1789, 48.
   state courts—essentially the same as federal courts, 77.
   statutory jurisdiction, 61.
   territorial extension of jurisdiction, 73, 108, 108, *note.*
   the supreme court of the United States has no appellate jurisdiction to issue in a civil suit unless there has been a final judgment, 70.
   that of the United States supreme court is limited to the single question of the power of the court below to commit the prisoner for the act of which he has been convicted, 72.
   United States supreme court will issue to review conviction under unconstitutional law, 72.
   writ was once refused by Lord Chancellor Nottingham in vacation time, 16.
   was afterwards issued out of chancery in vacation time, 17.
   was regularly issued of king's bench in term time only, 17.
   writ of error or appeal to territorial courts, 68.

JURISDICTION OF OFFICERS TO ISSUE THE WRIT.
   at common law, 88.
   application within the county—construction of statute, 89.
   issued by justice of the peace—when void, 89.
   of justices of the supreme court of the United States in vacation time, 73.
   of state officers—none to interfere with authority of the United States, 86.
   ought to appear on face of writ or petition, 90.
   United States judges and justices, generally, 108.

L

LEGISLATIVE POWER.
   to deprive the prisoner of the right to bail, 394.

M

MAGISTRATES, COMMITTING.
   findings of, not conclusive, 231.
   judges of superior courts, acting as, 238.
   make no such final judgments as a court of record, 260.
   powers of United States commissioners common to all, 231.

MAGNA CHARTA.
   provided immunity from arbitrary imprisonment, 25 *a.*

MANDAMUS.
   refused to compel admission to bail, when, 97.
   to compel judge to hear and determine evidence, 237.
   to compel the bringing up of a complete record, 346.

MANDAMUS—*Continued.*
    will compel habeas corpus to issue when properly applied for, 97.
    will not control discretionary matters in court below, 97.

MASTER AND APPRENTICE.
    application for discharge from letters of apprenticeship, 136.
    apprentice convicted without authority of law may be discharged on habeas corpus, 136.
    concerning the indentures, 456.
    doctrine evolved from the cases, 455.
    indenture of apprenticeship is voidable at election of infant, 136.
    issue of fact may be raised by apprentice in replying that the indentures of apprenticeship are void, 170.
    master may file petition to recover custody of apprentice, 93, 94.
    writ may always issue upon application of apprentice, 455.

MINISTERIAL ACT.
    the privy examination is a, 217, *note*.

MITTIMUS.
    at common law, 284.
    certified copy of minutes of court, 198.
    defined, 375.
    does not authorize detention, 375.
    for contempt, 335.
    inquiry into validity of, by federal courts in extradition proceedings, 486.
    if based on sentence unauthorized by law, 364.
    of justice of the peace, recitals in, etc., 355.
    office of, 127.
    proper, can be supplied at any time, 375.
    recitals in, of summary conviction, 298.
    signature to, 284.
    to answer, minuteness of, 281.
    though ever so defective, bail would not be allowed at common law, if felony had been committed, 390.

MOTION TO DISCHARGE.
    what it raises, 169.
    what is examined on, 169.

MOTHER.
    may have habeas corpus for child, 112.
        See CUSTODY OF CHILDREN, INFANT, PARENT FOR HIS CHILD, and PETITION FOR WRIT.

N

NATURE OF HABEAS CORPUS.
    can not be used as a writ of review or *certiorari*, 196.
    can not be used to try rights of guardianship, 170.
    can not be used to try rights of property, 170.
    can not be used as a writ of *quo warranto*, 170.
    is a high prerogative writ, 230.
    is summary in its character, 177.

NATURE OF HABEAS CORPUS—*Continued*.
    is the *cause* or *suit* of the party making the application, 92.
    is a civil proceeding, 70, 174.
    issues in civil cases as matter of course, 93.
    may issue in civil as well as criminal cases, 93.
    not a mere ministerial act, 92, 96, 107.
    to free from illegal restraint; not to punish, 131, 164, 169.
    when a ministerial act, 96.
        See WRIT OF HABEAS CORPUS.

NOTARIES PUBLIC.
    may administer oath for purposes of identification, 281.
    may commit for contempt, 312.

NOTICE.
    avails nothing, when, 125.
    effect of want of, 105.
    intendment of, to acquire jurisdiction, 325.
    must be given by courts-martial of their proceedings, 332, *note*.
    must be given that rights may be defended, 241.
    none required in Florida, in granting writ of error to judgment refusing bail, 415.
    of allowance of habeas corpus, 105.
    of service of orders of court, etc., 325.
    of attachment in civil case, 385, *note*.
    of proceedings in federal court not necessary to be given to attorney general of state in extradition matters, when, 487.
    to those interested in continuing imprisonment, 385.
    when to be given, 105.

O

OBJECTIONS.
    to return, 136.
    to evidence by affidavit, 208.
    to irregular evidence, 220.

OFFICERS.
    making arrest are protected by valid warrant, 155.
    making arrest are protected by valid judgment, 130.

ORIGIN OF THE WRIT
    may be traced to the Roman law, 1.

P

PARDON.
    convict pardoned can not be held to compel payment of costs, 119, 458.
    does not extend to contempts in England, 345.
    extends to contempt in some American states, 345.
    nature and acceptance of, 458.
    remits punishment, but not costs, which is a debt, 119.
    regarded as a deed, 458.
    unlike a commission, 458.
    void, when condition is void, 458.
    void, when felon does not perform its conditions, 458.

PARENT FOR HIS CHILD.
enlargement of chancery powers in England as to wife's right, 425.
Lord Mansfield's rule on application for habeas corpus in such cases, 424.
power of common-law courts in cases relating to the custody of infants, 424.
powers of courts of chancery under the writ of habeas corpus, 425.
upon what restraint the writ is issued, 423.

PENALTY FOR REFUSING THE WRIT.
as well as delay in issuing it, 58, 92, 96.
when officers are subject to, 96.

PETITION OF RIGHT.
some of its provisions, 7.
what lead to it, 7.

PETITION FOR WRIT.
allegations of illegal restraint in, 237, *note*.
effect of omitting prisoner's name, 90.
must state facts, 89, 112.
must show wherein illegality of imprisonment consists, 89.
must show for what offense prisoner was arrested, 89.
must set forth evidence given before committing magistrate, 89.
must aver locality of confinement, 89.
must affirmatively negative exceptions of statute, 89.
must ordinarily be verified, 90, 91, 95, 101.
may sometimes issue without affidavit, 90.
must show probable cause, 92.
must be accompanied by sworn copy of warrant, or other process of detention, or affidavit that such copy has been asked for and refused, 89, 90, 92.
requisites of, 89.
should state evidence taken before committing examining officer or magistrate, 183.
to reduce bail, should allege that it is excessive, 90.
to transfer custody of children, should disclose a full statement of facts, 90, 112.
to recover custody of children, should state locality of confinement, 439.
upon subsequently occurring events, 189.
when made by guardian, must contain letters of guardianship, 90.
when not demurrable, 89.
See APPLICATION.

PRACTICE.
after commitment on regular indictment, 247.
as to custody of prisoner during the trial, 175.
as to prisoner conducting defense in person, 93.
concerning the trial of issues, 173.
concerning the *mittimus*, 375.
concerning production of the body, 163.
examination into cause on rule *nisi*, 150.
examination of the facts on a habeas corpus, 71.
form of writ in such proceedings, 93.
in allowing return to be controverted or impeached, 147, 212.

INDEX. 687

PRACTICE—*Continued.*
    in hearing arguments on the return, 141.
    in making full answer to return, 134.
    in allowing amendments before case is finally disposed of, 128.
    in not always allowing amendments to return, 128.
    in enforcing return prior to 31 Car. II., 124.
    in enforcing return since 31 Car. II., 124.
    in awarding costs, 113-119.
    in serving the writ, 109.
    in issuing writ either at common law or under statute, 99. 100, 101.
    in federal courts of making answer to return of writ, 90.
    in admitting to bail at common law, 390.
    in admitting to bail under 31 Car. II. and other English statutes, 391.
    in admitting to bail in federal courts, 392.
    in admitting to bail generally, 395-419.
    in reviewing judgments of contempt, 346.
    in view of the difference between superior and inferior court, 342.
    in proceedings for contempt, 309, *note*, 310, 311.
    in discharging or letting to bail, though warrant is perfect, 292, 293.
    in recommitting where warrant is defective, 288-291.
    in examination of depositions, evidence, and the entire proceedings before the committing magistrate, 234, 235.
    in extending inquiry only to jurisdiction into and behind warrant of committing magistrate, 234.
    in not requiring great strictness in habeas corpus cases, 237.
    in conflict of jurisdiction in considering verity of affidavits, 218.
    in England, concerning use of affidavits, 209-216.
    in examining cases upon affidavit, 208.
    in reception of evidence, 204.
    in receiving evidence *aliunde* to impeach return, 199.
    in allowing crime to be shown by records of court, 198.
    in postponing trial for further evidence, 191.
    in granting more than one writ, 189.
    in not issuing habeas corpus, as matter of course; jurisdiction must be shown, 75, 88, 92, 107.
    not to disclose full case in petition, 90.
    of keeping return in court, 146.
    of courts discharging from one commitment and committing *de novo*, 126.
    of officers under non-bailable attachment, 125.
    of courts in committing for disobedience of order, 125.
    of federal court, where writ issues to custodian of foreign subject, 59.
    of federal courts as to hearing, 59.
    of courts of chancery in contempt cases, 325.
    of English courts in the use of *certiorari*, rule, 259-262.
    of federal courts in the use of *certiorari*, rule, 260.
    of state courts in the use of *certiorari*, rule, 261.
    on appeal in Texas, 188.
    origin of rule allowing recommitment, though warrant is defective, 288.
    practice at common law of issuing writ, 88, 92.
    proceedings are governed by the common law, 74, 92.
    rule upon process, 142.

PRACTICE—*Continued.*
    same principles prevail in United States, 101.
    time when errors should be corrected, 158.
    where case has been once heard upon same evidence, 187.
    when there is delay in making return, 128.
    will not interfere with each other's process, 94.
    writ does not issue where party is not entitled thereto by his own showing, 92.
    when it is clear that prisoner would be remanded, writ will be refused, 75.
    what is determined upon an examination of the facts on a habeas corpus, 71.

PRELIMINARY EXAMINATION.
    is a ministerial act, 217, *note.*
    must be made promptly, 242.
    waiving examination, 243.

PLACES TO WHICH THE WRIT WILL RUN.
    at common law, and under English statutes, 58, 107.
    referred to, 30, 61, 73, *note.*
    rule of locality in the United States, 108.

POWER OF COURT.
    becomes *functus officio,* when, 373.
    origin of rule allowing recommitment when warrant is defective, 288.
    of chancery and court of law, exactly the same under habeas corpus, 425.
    state courts can not compel production of body, when, 316.
    to compel production of body, 137.
    to compel obedience to writ, 137.
    to recommit if warrant is defective, 288–291.
    to discharge or let to bail though warrant is perfect, 292–293.
    to punish for contempts, 307.
    to relieve from error or irregularity on motion, 344.
    to modify their own judgments, 377.
    to modify judgment ceases, when, 377.
    to inquire into its own sentence, 378.
    under *certiorari* not co-extensive with that under habeas corpus, 264.
    United States supreme court has no general power to review the judgments of the inferior federal courts, 380.

PRESUMPTIONS.
    are in favor of liberty, 342.
    favoring legality of imprisonment, 233.
    in favor of rulings of judge in lower court on questions of evidence, 177.
    in favor of sanity, where that is in issue, 181.
    in favor of rulings of lower court, generally, 198.
    in favor of ruling of lower court in refusing or admitting to bail, 415.
    may be rebutted, 267.
    of guilt, before indictment, 242.
    of guilt, after indictment, 242, *note.*
    of guilt, raised by indictment, 403, 405.
    of jurisdiction relating to inferior courts, 268, 278, 285, 368.

PRESUMPTIONS—*Continued*.
    rules concerning, 267, 278, 285.
    relating to jurisdiction of superior courts, 267, 278, 285, 368.
    relating to courts acting within the sphere of their jurisdiction, 196.
    repelled from lapse of time, 199 *a*.
    that discretion has been correctly exercised, 239.
    when they will be extended in favor of committing officer, 89.

PROCESS.
    civil, validity of, 357–361, 383, 384.
    defined, 160.
    defective execution, 361.
    defects in, may be amended by further entry or motion, 136.
    existence of, may be questioned, 319.
    imprisonment under, valid on its face, deemed *prima facie* legal, 136.
    in civil case, void summons, judgment, and execution, 357.
    irregular, may be set aside, when, 241.
    judgments running by wrong name, 358.
    must authorize commitment for contempt, or it is invalid, 342.
    must show authority, when, 267, 268, 278, 285.
    must authorize arrest, or it will be void, 276.
    must be impeached by prisoner, 136.
    need not show authority, when, 267, 268, 278, 285.
    of arrest must be legally sufficient upon its face, 486.
    regular and valid, detention under, 233.
    service of, must be made, or judgment is void, 241.
    served by wrong person—proceeding void, 368.
    validity of, upon its face, may be questioned, 319.
    valid subsequent process, insufficient in extradition matters, 486.
    validity or invalidity of, as affected by special warrants, 274.
    without authority of law, 252.
        See WARRANTS OF ARREST, WARRANT OF COMMITMENT, WARRANT TO ANSWER, JURISDICTION OF COURTS TO ISSUE THE WRIT, JUDGMENT, INQUIRY, and ASSAILING JUDGMENTS—of all kinds.

PRODUCTION OF THE BODY.
    direction of federal courts, 59.
    penalties for not producing, 124.
    sufficient reasons for not producing, 163.
    requirements of 31 Car. II., 58.
    when prisoner may be brought into court, 112.

PRISONS.
    condition of, during the reign of Charles II., 14.

PRISONER.
    can not introduce his defense by witnesses, 204.
    can have guilt or innocence examined into before indictment, 237.
    can not have guilt or innocence examined into after indictment, 244.
    can not take advantage of discharge of jury in his absence, 255.
    custody of, during the trial, 175, 176.
    changing custody of, 176.
    has a right to be present when indictment is continued, 248.

PRISONER—*Continued.*
    may show right to bail by affidavit, even under 31 Car. II., 213.
    may be discharged from first commitment and be committed *de novo,*
        126, 229, 230, 231.
    may be lawfully detained under bench warrant, 250.
    may be committed without process, where, 282.
    may be recommitted *de novo*, though warrant is defective, 288–291.
    may be discharged or let to bail though warrant be perfect, 292–293.
    may be bailed where evidence is insufficient to support charge, 390.
    must be discharged when illegally detained, 120.
    must assume burden of impeaching process, when, 136.
    must be discharged when statute does not warrant his imprisonment, 120.
    not entitled to bail where "proof was evident or presumption great," 239.
    not entitled to habeas corpus when out on bail, 94.
    pardoned convict can not be held to compel payment of costs, 119.
    right to bail generally, 390–419.
    removal of, in cases of sickness, 15.
    right to press for trial, 18.
    removal of, provisions of 31 Car. II., 30.
    recommitment of, provisions of 31 Car. II., 30.
    speedy trial of, sometimes evaded by colorably assigning treasonable or
        felonious causes for their commitment, 18.
    sending, beyond the seas prohibited, 31, 58.
    to answer interrogatories on attachment, when, 124.

PRIVILEGED FROM ARREST.
    governor of state, 94.
    under civil process, when, 93.

Q

QUO WARRANTO.
    habeas corpus can not be used as a writ of, 170.
    inquiry on habeas corpus can not be made into title to office, 256.
    mere usurpers of office, etc., 258.
    sentences by officers *de facto,* 257, 369.

R

RECOGNIZANCE.
    approval of, can not be made by magistrate, when, 287, *note.*

RECOMMITMENT.
    after discharge, can not be made upon original warrant or writ, 140.
    de novo, when first warrant is defective, origin of rule, 288.
    not allowed except by order of court, 58.
    penalty for, 58.

REMOVAL OF CAUSES.
    when *habeas corpus cum causa* will issue, 76.
            See HABEAS CORPUS CUM CAUSA.

REPLEVY.
    of judgments, 378.

INDEX.   691

RES ADJUDICATA—HOW THE DECISION ON HABEAS CORPUS IS
    REGARDED.
   conclusiveness of plea in abatement, 385, *note*.
   decision on habeas corpus not of that conclusive character sufficient to
       support a writ of error, 386.
   distinction between judgment remanding prisoner and that discharging
       him, 386.
   decision in one state not considered as *res adjudicata* in another, 389.
   has no application to, in state courts, 386.
   has no application in federal courts, 386.
   issuance and maintenance of second writ not concluded by first applica-
       tion, 189, 386.
   judgment of discharge, conclusive, 386.
   judgments fixing custody of children regarded as conclusive, 387.
   judgment remanding prisoner not conclusive, 386.
   refusal of discharge on one writ no bar to another application, 74.
   statutory provisions, 388.
   second applications, 389.

RETURN.
   amendment of, 126, 128.
   action of false return, 138.
   arguments that it must express notice of the charge, 4, 6.
   at common law, could be made returnable before justice who issued it, 88.
   a few instances of a good return, 162.
   a few instances of a bad return, 161.
   by special command of the king—sufficiency of, 3 *b*, 4-6.
   by whom to be made, 120, 123.
   contradicting by affidavit, 212.
   conclusiveness of return by United States officer, 131, 132.
   cases illustrative of certainty in, 126, *note*.
   controverting return, 129, 147.
   could not be controverted at common law, 137, 166, 166, *note*.
   can be controverted now, 137, 147.
   certainty required, 123.
   defined, 120.
   direction of, 121.
   difficulties concerning, under 31 Car. II., not controvertible, 34.
   disposition of, at common law, showing no cause of commitment, 8.
   discussing validity of warrant upon rule to show cause, 150, 151.
   evidence to contradict return, 197.
   evidence *aliunde* for the same purpose, 199 *a*.
   evidence and matter of law to be returned, 126.
   evasive, false, or insufficient, a contempt of court, 121, 124, 126, 126, *note*,
       137.
   form of, and effect of want of, 121, 126, 137.
   fortifying by affidavit, 215.
   facts of, are open to investigation, 137.
   full return in the United States, 126.
   failure to make, is a contempt of court, 137.
   how made under federal statutes, 50.

RETURN—*Continued.*
    impeaching return, 199 *a.*
    in contempt cases, should set out record, 346.
    is watched with jealous scrutiny, especially when it concerns the custody of infants, 126, 137.
    imports verity, 122, 147.
    in times of war, 120.
    jailer may substitute return prepared by counsel for his own, 135.
    judicial notice, subjects of, 154.
    might be controverted under 56 Geo. III., 34, 172.
    may be controverted in the United States, 168, 168, *note*, 170.
    may be traversed orally, 178.
    may be fully controverted under federal statutes, 59.
    may be fortified by affidavit, 129.
    may be amended before final disposition of case, 128.
    may not, however, always be amended, 128.
    may be enforced by attachment, 124.
    may be heard in respondent's absence, 123.
    may be confessed and avoided, 167.
    must be signed, 121, 122.
    may be made returnable before whole court when writ is issued by a single justice of the supreme court of the United States, 73.
    making bad return on good judgment, 153.
    must show that evidence was given in prisoner's presence, when, 144.
    must show that respondent has no power of control where child is in foreign jurisdiction, 450.
    must remain in court, 146.
    need not specially set out documents referred to, 147.
    new habeas corpus, when not required, 139.
    negativing exceptions of statute, 121.
    of warrant of commitment, 90.
    of denial of a copy of the warrant of commitment, 90.
    of certified minutes of court showing judgment and sentence, 90.
    of corrected copy of execution, 94, *note.*
    of execution against the person, 156.
    order of argument on the return, 141.
    of immaterial averments, 126.
    of substituted warrant, 143.
    of warrant need not always be made, 127.
    of certified minutes of court, 127.
    of certified judgment of the court, 127.
    of warrant issued at commencement of proceedings, effect of under void judgment, 130.
    of final judgment or decree, effect of, 131.
    objections to the return, 136.
    objection to return in bankruptcy proceedings, 136.
    of commitment for contempt, 11.
    of officers, 122.
    practice in making full answer to, 134.
    prisoner discharged where return is too general, 10.
    questioning jurisdiction on defective warrant, 149.

RETURN—*Continued.*
    quashing return, 152.
    recommitment, 140.
    rule upon process, 142.
    relying upon a conviction where commitment is bad, 145.
    reply to return, denying truth of the matters contained in affidavit on which *capias* issued, 155.
    setting up will as authority for detention of child, 457.
    should be liberally construed, 125.
    sufficient return of conviction of felony and treason, 126.
    state court can not determine what is a crime against the United States, 159.
    sufficient reasons for not producing the body, 163.
    statement of the cause of arrest, 164.
    statement of the cause of detention, how shown, 165.
    should be made without delay, 120.
    should be accompanied by what, 120.
    truth of whole matter must be returned where there is no warrant, 121.
    time when errors should be corrected, 158.
    true return could not be enforced at common law, 138.
    truthfulness of, 137.
    time may be enlarged for return of writ, 133.
    time fixed for, under 31 Car. II., 58.
    verification of, 122, 147.
    when it will be received, 123.
    which satisfies the writ, 107, 147.
    when writ will not be made returnable before court or justice issuing it in first instance, 83.
    when demand should be made for child, 157.
    when warrant must contain certain words, 148.
    when prisoner will at once be discharged, 132.
    when writ will be dismissed, 131.
    written authority always to be returned, 126.

RIGHT TO BAIL.
    affidavits to show, under 31 Car. II., 213.
    after conviction, 417.
    after sentence or commitment in execution, 419.
    appeal from judgment refusing bail, 415.
    and for what offenses, the subject of constitutional protection in all of the states, 393.
    application is addressed to sound discretion of court, 396.
    admission to bail by United States commissioner, 231.
    attorney to pay costs of notices of bail, when, 116.
    bailable offenses at common law, 38.
    burden of proof rests upon prisoner, when, 404.
    bail could render prisoners in their own discharge on *habeas corpus cum causa*, and on either civil or criminal process, 91.
    costs on justification of bail, 116.
    continuance, term, 412.
    doctrines of the common law respecting, 390.

694 INDEX.

RIGHT TO BAIL—*Continued.*
    excessive bail, 93, 94.
    excessive bail, what is, 413.
    excessive bail, and how regulated on appeal, 413.
    excessive bail prohibited by bill of rights, 33.
    excessive bail not to be required, 397.
    examination, and reducing offense to bailable one, 399.
    examination of evidence with a view to bail, 400.
    evidence respecting the charge, 390.
    evidence after indictment, 405, 406.
    habeas corpus can not issue to bail of a supposed offender, 273.
    inquiry before indictment, 395–400.
    in circumstances independent of merits of prosecution, 409.
    instance of admission to bail *sub silentio*, 16.
    increase of bail on application of prosecuting officer, 231.
    in extradition proceedings, 484.
    in case of insanity of prisoner, 414.
    inquiry after indictment, 401–416.
    inquiry after conviction but before final judgment, 417–419.
    legislative powers concerning, 394.
    meaning of "when proof is evident," 402.
    not allowed at common law, if felony had been committed, though *mittimus* were ever so defective, 390.
    no appeal from order admitting to bail, 416.
    of Chinese traders coming to our shores, when, 392.
    one out on bail not privileged from arrest on civil process, 273.
    one in execution for contempt not entitled to, 327, *note*.
    order admitting to bail not appealable, 388.
    pending steps to reverse sentence, 418.
    prisoner not entitled to bail where the "proof was evident," or the "presumption great," 239.
    prisoners out on bail are not restrained of their liberty, 94.
    power of special bail over principal, 93.
    prisoner may be allowed bail when guilty of bailable homicide, where indictment is not conclusive of grade of offense, 93.
    petition for reduction of, should allege that the bail is excessive, 90.
    provisions of 16 Car. I., c. 10, concerning, 9.
    provisions of 31 Car. II., concerning, 27, 29, 32, 33, 288.
    prisoners sometimes bailed when no cause for commitment was shown, 8.
    prisoner may sometimes be bailed on account of sickness, 410.
    "presumption great," 403.
    power to bail, and bailable offenses as regulated by the United States revised statutes, 392.
    power to bail, bailable offenses, evidence, etc., 390–394.
    reduction of bail, 231, 398.
    rules for guidance of court's discretion, 401.
    right of prisoner to bail generally, 199 *b*, 390–419.
    sureties on bail bond, when discharged, 130.
    special and extraordinary circumstances under which bail may be allowed, 407.

RIGHT TO BAIL—*Continued*.
    to be allowed in bailable cases, 125.
    under 31 Car. II. and other English statutes, 391.
    when allowed for treason or felony, if not tried, etc., 58.
    when bail are discharged—not having rendered principal, 93.
    when a suit in equity has been instituted against a party, 93.
    while application for bail is pending in one court, application for it should not be made to another, 90.
    when committed by special command of the king, 4, 6.
    who may bail, 395.
    when jury has disagreed—new trial, etc., 408.
    while under arrest on bench warrant, 412.

S

SECURITY AGAINST ESCAPE.
    case illustrating, 126, *note*.
    generally, 113–119.
    regulated by statute, 118.

SECURITY FOR GOOD BEHAVIOR.
    early requirements of, at common law, 8, 9.

SERVICE.
    acknowledgment of, 126, *note*.
    evidence of, 124, 205.
    of attachment, irregular, in civil case, 385, *note*.
    of orders of court, etc., 325.
    of process must be made or judgment is void, 141.
    refusal to serve is not a contempt, when, 132.
    of writ at common law, 109.
    of writ under 31 Car. II., 109.
    of writ in state courts, 109.

STAR-CHAMBER.
    abolition of it, and other arbitrary courts, 9.
    one imprisoned by arbitrary order entitled to habeas corpus, 9.
    proceedings in, 8, 9.

STATUTES.
    abolishment of arbitrary proceedings by, 16 Car. I., c. 10, 9.
    of Charles II.—see HABEAS CORPUS ACT, 31 Car. II.
    of George III.—see 56 Geo. III.
    United States habeas corpus act—see HABEAS CORPUS ACT OF THE UNITED STATES.

SUMMONS.
    when void, 357.

SURETIES.
    on bail bond, when discharged, 130.

SUSPENSION OF THE WRIT.
    acts of indemnity for false imprisonment during, 270.
    act itself is suspended in England, 50.
    argument that president may suspend it in the United States, 52, *note*.

SUSPENSION OF THE WRIT—*Continued.*
  act of congress authorizing its suspension by the president, 52.
  congress only possesses the power in the United States, 51.
  expiration of authority conferred by act of congress on the president, 55.
  in the United States it is the *privilege* which is suspended, 50.
  neither congress nor president can suspend privilege of state writ, 56.
  once a debatable question in the United States, 51.
  president has no power to suspend it, 51.
  power in England rests in parliament alone, 51.
  remarks of Jeremy Bentham concerning, 50.
  suspension of privilege does not suspend writ itself, 50.
  suspension of the writ ordered in the United States, 53.
  to whom the suspension applied in the act of congress, 54.
  validity of the act of congress suspending it questioned, 54.
  was suspended in the Confederate States, 57.
        See HISTORY OF THE WRIT.

T

TERRITORIAL COURTS.
  when judgment of, will not be reviewed, 378.

TERMS.
  abolished in England by judicature act of 1873, 88.
  defined, 411.

TRIAL OF ISSUES.
  change of venue, 174.
  custody of prisoner during the trial, 175, 176.
  jury trial, 172.
  mode of trial at common law, 171.
  no jury allowed in contempt cases, 343.
  no change of venue allowed in contempt cases, 343.
  postponement for further testimony, 191.
  time fixed for hearing by federal statute, 59.
        See ISSUES.

U

UNDERTAKING.
  can not be exacted from witness, when, 305.

V

VACATION. See ISSUANCE OF WRIT IN VACATION TIME.

VENUE.
  no change of, allowed in contempt cases, 343.

VOID AND VOIDABLE PROCEEDINGS.
  defined, 158.
  proceeding is void if process is served by wrong person, 368.
  voidable proceedings are reversible on appeal, or writ of error, or *certiorari*, 348, 363.
  void proceedings are reversible on habeas corpus, 348, 363.
        See ASSAILING JUDGMENTS—of all kinds, JUDGMENTS, and JURISDICTION OF COURTS TO ISSUE THE WRIT.

W

WARD. See GUARDIAN AND WARD.

WARRANTS OF ARREST.
    direction of, 275.
    execution of, 275.
    invalidity of general warrants, 274.
    may be impeached for what, 286.
    name of the offender, 276.
    oath, jurat, and seal, 279.
    probable cause must be shown before warrant of arrest can issue, 277.
    requisites of warrants of arrest, 275–279.
    statement of offense in magistrate's warrant, 277.
    statement of offense in warrant of superior judge, 278.

WARRANTS TO ANSWER.
    by superior courts, 282.
    commitment for treason, 280.
    cause and certainty, 281.
    distinction between warrant to answer and process, 282, *note*.
    direction and conclusion of, 283.
    erroneous, if issued without previous examination, 281.
    may be impeached for what, 287.
    requisites of warrants to answer, 280–285.
    signature and seal of, 284, *note*.
    second commitment to supply defects of first, 290.
    though perfect, prisoner may sometimes be admitted to bail, 292, 293.
    what face of warrant should show, 285, 291.
    when defective, prisoner may sometimes be recommitted, 288–291.
    when papers upon which first warrant issued become *functus officio*, 290.
        See WARRANT OF COMMITMENT.

WARRANT OF COMMITMENT.
    arbitrary commitments abolished by 16 Car. I., c. 10, 9.
    arguments that it ought to express nature of the charge, 4, 6.
    as for being a disorderly person, must recite what, 240.
    bail denied, when committed by special command of the king, 4, 6, *note*.
    commitment without stating cause led to petition of right, 7.
    commitment in violation of petition of right, 8.
    copy of, to accompany application or petition, either at common law or under statute, 90, 92, 99, 100, 101.
    denial of copy of, under 31 Car. II., 27.
    detention by special command of the king, 7.
    detention by privy councilors without cause shown, 8.
    defined, 127.
    defective, 121.
    defective, questioning jurisdiction on, 149.
    for contempt, need not contain statement of facts, unless statute requires it, 340.
    finding of committing magistrate not conclusive, 231.
    how impeached, 93.
    how it must recite a conviction, 145, 240.

WARRANT OF COMMITMENT—*Continued.*
    investigation into, 230.
    in summary convictions, 240.
    in bankruptcy proceedings, 126, 148.
    if insufficient, prisoner discharged, 120.
    issued without authority of law, 93.
    must contain certified copy of judgment as entered in minutes of court; or prisoner, even after judgment, will be discharged, unless a certified copy of a valid judgment can be obtained, 93.
    must contain definite and certain statement of offense, 93.
    must show what, 121.
    not entitled to as much consideration as a commitment after conviction, 240.
    need not always be returned, 127.
    need not disclose all facts showing existence of jurisdiction, 198, 240.
    of no effect, under void judgment, 130.
    object of, 130.
    omitting to state facts of contempt, can not be inquired into unless statute requires it, 341.
    prisoner may be discharged from first commitment and be committed *de novo*, 126, 229, 230, 231.
    provisions of 31 Car. II. did not provide for cases of imprisonment without warrant, 34.
    provisions of 31 Car. II., relating to statement of cause of commitment, 26.
    prisoner will be discharged where want of jurisdiction appears upon face of warrant, 93.
    recommitment can not be made upon original warrant, 140.
    regular, or valid upon its face, 140, 164.
    return of substituted warrant, 143.
    recitals in, 240.
    setting aside, defective, 234, 235.
    statements in, not controvertible by affidavit, 216.
    successive warrants of commitment, 143, *note.*
    uncertainty in, 126.
    unimportant whether it be regular in point of form, 231, 233.
    when it has discharged its function, 130.
    which operates as a conviction, 144.
    when void, 126.
    when prisoner will be released, 93.
        See WARRANTS TO ANSWER.

WIFE.
    may have writ for husband, 126, *note*, 422.
    may have writ against husband, 422.

WITNESS.
    may be brought up on habeas corpus, 94.

WRIT OF ERROR.
    certiorari with habeas corpus as, 262.
    does not lie from final order in proceedings by habeas corpus, 386.
    is allowed upon final decision on proceedings by habeas corpus in Georgia, 89.

INDEX. 699

WRIT OF ERROR—*Continued*.
  lies to state court from the supreme court of the United States, 386.
  may be brought to reverse proceedings not showing jurisdiction upon their face, 224.
  prosecution of, on refusal of bail, 445.
  statutory provisions relative to, 388.
  to reverse erroneous orders or judgments, 241, 263.
  will not be dismissed, where, 94.
  wife may bring, in Georgia, upon final judgment on habeas corpus, refusing the discharge of her husband, 126, *note*.

WRIT OF HABEAS CORPUS.
  amendment of, 110.
  can not issue upon false affidavit, 207.
  can not be used to try rights of guardianship, 170.
  can not be used as a writ of review or *certiorari*, 196, 348.
  can not be used to try rights of property, 170.
  can not be used as a writ of *quo warranto*, 170.
  disobedience of writ, 58.
  goes only to complete defect in proceedings, 348.
  how and to whom directed, 106, 273.
  how marked under 31 Car. II., 58, 103.
  how granted at common law, 88, 100.
  how issued under statutes, 101.
  is a civil proceeding, 70, 174.
  issues to relieve from gross abuse of custody in the domestic relations, 420, 440, 455.
  issues not as matter of course, 92, 96, 99, 107.
  must issue upon probable cause, 92.
  may issue in behalf of prisoner, when, 91, 93, 94.
  must be answered, 120.
  motion to quash, 169.
  noting allowance of, 104.
  notice of allowance, 105.
  not affected by question of residence, 105.
  new writ, when not required, 138.
  not to extend to prisoners in jail unless, etc., 59.
  need not be served, when, 132.
  objections to, 111.
  objects of, 59, 131, 164, 169, 170, 230, 238, 241, 273, 439, 457.
  proceedings under, are summary in their character, 177.
  power under, compared with that under *certiorari*, 262, 264.
  proceedings thereon in vacation time, 58.
  rule of locality in the United States, 108.
  service of, at common law, 109.
  service of, in state courts, 109.
  should not be granted without inquiry, 92.
  signature and seal, 102.
  time of return, under 31 Car. II., 58.
  when void, 273, 439, 457.
  when prisoner may be brought into court, 112.

WRIT OF HABEAS CORPUS—*Continued.*
    where it runs at common law and under English statutes, 107.
    will relieve where force is used to enforce performance of contract, 93.
    will not issue to bail of supposed offender, 273.
    will not issue where party is not entitled thereto on his own showing, 92, 99.
        See NATURE OF HABEAS CORPUS; INQUIRY, EXTENT OF; JURISDICTION OF COURTS TO ISSUE THE WRIT, and ASSAILING JUDGMENTS—of all kinds.

INDEX TO FORMS.

N. B.—The First Figures Refer to Pages; the Second, to the Form Number.

A

ATTACHMENT.
   for disobedience of writ, 649—34.

B

BOND.
   on serving the writ, 650—36.

C

CERTIFICATE.
   of service of writs of habeas corpus, 649—35.

CERTIORARI.
   federal writ of, 651—39.
   state writ of, 652—40.

COMMITMENT.
   for disobedience of writ, 648—33.

N

NOTICE.
   of application for writ to district attorney, 647—31.
   of application for writ to other interested parties, 648—32.

O

ORDER.
   granting writ, 647—30.
   of discharge, 654—43.

P

PETITION.
   by a third party for habeas corpus, 635—4.
   by a parent for a child, 637—8.
   in case of private restraint, as that of master or other person, 636—7.
   for the purpose of being bailed, 636—6.
   for a habeas corpus, 631—1.
   for a habeas corpus, another form, 632—1.
   second application, 633—2.
   to testify, affidavit and application, 637—9.
   under extraordinary circumstances, 635—5.
   usual form of, by party confined, 634—3.

PRECEPT.
   to bring up party illegally restrained, 650—37.

R

RECOGNIZANCE.
    on being bailed, 653—42.

RETURN.
    for several causes of detention, additional clauses, 645—25.
    to habeas corpus, or *certiorari*, 643—18.
    to *habeas corpus ad testificandum*, 643—19.
    where facts correspond with those in petition, 641—14.
    where petitioner is not in custody, 641—15.
    where custody of prisoner has been transferred, 642—16.
    where petitioner is in custody, 642—17.
    where prisoner was committed on execution, 643—20.
    where prisoner was committed for contempt, 644—21.
    where prisoner was committed on warrant, 644—22.
    where prisoner was committed on suspicion, 644—23.
    where prisoner was committed on indictment, 645—24.
    where infants are in custody, 645—26.
    where the body only is brought, 646—27.
    where body of prisoner is too infirm to be brought, 646—
    where prisoner is under sentence of death, 646—29.

T

TRAVERSE.
    to return, 652—41.

W

WARRANT.
    under extraordinary circumstances, 651—38.

WRIT.
    of *habeas corpus ad subjiciendum*, 638—10.
    of same kind, another form, 639—11.
    of *habeas corpus ad testificandum*, 639—12.
    of same kind, another form, 640—13.

www.ingramcontent.com/pod-product-compliance
Lightning Source LLC
Chambersburg PA
CBHW031152020526
44117CB00042B/229